Algebra for Colleges and Schools

Henry Sinclair Hall, Samuel Ratcliffe Knight, Frank Louis Sevenoak

Nabu Public Domain Reprints:

You are holding a reproduction of an original work published before 1923 that is in the public domain in the United States of America, and possibly other countries. You may freely copy and distribute this work as no entity (individual or corporate) has a copyright on the body of the work. This book may contain prior copyright references, and library stamps (as most of these works were scanned from library copies). These have been scanned and retained as part of the historical artifact.

This book may have occasional imperfections such as missing or blurred pages, poor pictures, errant marks, etc. that were either part of the original artifact, or were introduced by the scanning process. We believe this work is culturally important, and despite the imperfections, have elected to bring it back into print as part of our continuing commitment to the preservation of printed works worldwide. We appreciate your understanding of the imperfections in the preservation process, and hope you enjoy this valuable book.

DEPARTMENT OF EDUCATION
LELAND STANFORD JUNIOR UNIVERSITY

ALGEBRA

THE MACMILLAN COMPANY
NEW YORK · BOSTON · CHICAGO · DALLAS
ATLANTA · SAN FRANCISCO

MACMILLAN & CO., Limited
LONDON · BOMBAY · CALCUTTA
MELBOURNE

THE MACMILLAN CO. OF CANADA, Ltd.
TORONTO

ALGEBRA

FOR COLLEGES AND SCHOOLS

BY

H. S. HALL, M.A., AND S. R. KNIGHT, B.A.

REVISED AND ENLARGED
FOR THE USE OF AMERICAN SCHOOLS

BY

F. L. SEVENOAK, A.M.

PRINCIPAL OF THE ACADEMIC DEPARTMENT
STEVENS INSTITUTE OF TECHNOLOGY

New York
THE MACMILLAN COMPANY
1913

All rights reserved

629209

COPYRIGHT, 1896, 1897, 1913,
BY THE MACMILLAN COMPANY.

First edition, 1895. Second edition, revised and enlarged, 1896. Reprinted with corrections, January, 1897; August, October, 1897; August, 1898; October, 1898; July, August, 1899; September, 1899; January, July, 1900; July, 1901; April, August, October, 1902; March, September, December, 1903; February, July, 1904; May, 1905; January, July, 1906; March, 1907; January, October, 1908; March, August, 1909; July, 1910; January, 1911; March, 1912; February, 1913. Third edition, September, 1913.

Norwood Press
J. S. Cushing Co. — Berwick & Smith Co.
Norwood, Mass., U.S.A.

PREFACE.

WITHIN a comparatively short time, the algebra requirement for admission to many of our Colleges and Schools of Science has been much increased in both thoroughness of preparation and amount of subject-matter. This increase has made necessary the rearrangement and extension of elementary algebra, and it is for this reason that the present revision of Hall and Knight's *Elementary Algebra* has been undertaken.

The marked success of the work, and the hearty endorsement by many of our ablest educators of the treatment of the subject as therein presented, warrant the belief that the present edition, with its additional subject-matter, will be found a desirable arrangement and satisfactory treatment of every part of the subject required for admission to any of our Colleges or Schools of Technology.

Many changes in the original chapters have been made, among which we would call attention to the following: A proof, by mathematical induction, of the binomial theorem for positive integral index has been added to Chapter XXXIX.; a method of finding a factor that will rationalize any binomial surd follows the treatment of binomial quadratic surds; Chapter XLII. has been re-written in part, and appears as a chapter on equations in quadratic form; and the chapter on logarithms has been enlarged by the addition of a four-place table of logarithms with explanation of its use.

Chapters XXI., XXV., XXX., XXXIII., XXXVIII., XLII., XLIII., XLIV., XLV., XLVI., XLVII., and XLVIII. treat of portions of the subject that have not appeared in former editions. A chapter on General Theory of Equations is not usually found in an Elementary Algebra, but properly finds here a place in accordance with the purpose of the present revision; and its introduction makes the work available for use in college classes. Carefully selected exercises are given with each chapter, and at the end of the work a large miscellaneous collection will be found.

The *Higher Algebra* of Messrs. Hall and Knight has been drawn upon, and the works of Todhunter, Chrystal, and DeMorgan consulted in preparing the new chapters.

I gratefully acknowledge my indebtedness to Prof. J. Burkitt Webb of the Stevens Institute of Technology both for contributions of subject-matter, and valuable suggestions as to methods of treatment. My thanks are also due to Prof. W. H. Bristol, of the same institution, for suggestions as to the arrangement of the chapter on General Theory of Equations.

FRANK L. SEVENOAK.

JUNE, 1895.

PREFACE TO SECOND EDITION.

THE printing of the present edition from entirely new plates has enabled us to correct a few typographical errors found in the first edition, and give, at the suggestion of friends, a somewhat fuller explanation of the more difficult parts of the subject. We hope that the addition of new material to Chapters III., IV., V., X., XX., XXI., XLII., XLVIII., and of several sets of Miscellaneous Examples, will render the book still more acceptable to those whose commendation of the former edition has given us much pleasure.

JUNE, 1896.

PREFACE TO THIRD EDITION.

The present edition contains additional material on Graphs. The subject has been treated in a single chapter (Chapter XLIX.) with the idea that the majority of teachers prefer such an arrangement.

Class-room experience has shown that Arts. 632–645 may be used with profit in connection with a first reading of Chapter XVII., and Arts. 646–649, 657–660 in connection with Chapter XXVI.

August, 1913.

CONTENTS.

CHAPTER		PAGE
I.	Definitions. Substitutions	1
II.	Negative Quantities. Addition of Like Terms	9
III.	Simple Brackets. Addition. Subtraction	13
	Commutative Law for Addition and Subtraction	15
	Associative Law for Addition and Subtraction	15
	Dimension, Degree, Ascending and Descending Powers	17
	Miscellaneous Examples I.	23
IV.	Multiplication	24
	Commutative Law for Multiplication	25
	Associative Law for Multiplication	25
	Index Law for Multiplication	25
	Distributive Law for Multiplication	26
	Multiplication of Compound Expressions	27
	Rule of Signs	28
	Note on Arithmetical and Symbolical Algebra	29
	Distributing the Product	31
	Products written by Inspection	35
	Multiplication by Detached Coefficients	37
V.	Division	38
	Index Law for Division	39
	Division of Compound Expressions	40
	Important Cases in Division	44
	Horner's Method of Synthetic Division	46
VI.	Removal and Insertion of Brackets	48
	Miscellaneous Examples II.	53
VII.	Simple Equations	55

CONTENTS.

CHAPTER		PAGE
VIII.	Symbolical Expression	60
IX.	Problems Leading to Simple Equations	65
X.	Resolution into Factors	70
	Trinomial Expressions	72
	Difference of Two Squares	78
	Important Cases	82
	Sum or Difference of Two Cubes	82
	Miscellaneous Cases	83
	Converse Use of Factors	85
	The Factor Theorem	87
XI.	Highest Common Factor	92
	Factor Theorem Employed	98
XII.	Lowest Common Multiple	102
XIII.	Fractions	107
	Reduction to Lowest Terms	108
	Multiplication and Division	110
	Addition and Subtraction	114
	Rules for Change of Sign	121
	Cyclic Order	124
XIV.	Complex Fractions. Mixed Expressions	126
	Miscellaneous Exercise on Fractions	132
XV.	Fractional and Literal Equations	136
XVI.	Problems	141
	Miscellaneous Examples III.	144
XVII.	Simultaneous Equations	147
	Elimination by Addition or Subtraction	148
	Elimination by Substitution	149
	Elimination by Comparison	150
	Equations involving Three Unknown Quantities	152
	Reciprocal	154
	Literal Simultaneous Equations	157
XVIII.	Problems	160
XIX.	Indeterminate and Impossible Problems. Negative Results	165
	Meaning of $\frac{a}{0}$, $\frac{a}{\infty}$, $\frac{0}{0}$, $\frac{\infty}{\infty}$	167

CONTENTS.

CHAPTER		PAGE
XX.	Involution	169
	To square a Multinomial	171
	To cube a Multinomial	173
	Application of Binomial Theorem	173
XXI.	Evolution	176
	Square Root of a Multinomial	177
	Cube Root of a Multinomial	181
	Some Higher Roots	185
	The nth Root of a Multinomial	186
	Square and Cube Root of Numbers	187
XXII.	The Theory of Indices	191
	Meaning of Fractional Exponent	193
	Meaning of Zero Exponent	193
	Meaning of Negative Exponent	194
XXIII.	Surds (Radicals)	203
	Reduction of Surds	205
	Addition and Subtraction of Surds	207
	Multiplication of Surds	208
	Division of Surds	209
	Compound Surds	211
	Factor which will rationalize any Binomial Surd	214
	Properties of Quadratic Surds	216
	Square Root of a Binomial Surd	217
	Square Root of a Binomial Surd by Inspection	218
	Equations involving Surds	220
XXIV.	Imaginary Quantities	222
	Imaginary Unit	223
	Fundamental Algebraic Operations	225
XXV.	Problems	227
	Miscellaneous Examples IV.	232
XXVI.	Quadratic Equations	235
	Pure Quadratic Equations	236
	Affected Quadratic Equations	237
	Solution by Formula	239
	Solution by Factoring	241
	Formation of Equations with Given Roots	242
	Values found for the Unknown Quantity which do not satisfy the Original Equation	243

CHAPTER		PAGE
XXVII.	Equations in Quadratic Form	245
XXVIII.	Simultaneous Equations involving Quadratics	249
	Homogeneous Equations of the Same Degree	253
	Symmetrical Equations	254
	Miscellaneous Cases	255
XXIX.	Problems	258
XXX.	Theory of Quadratic Equations	264
	Number of the Roots	264
	Character of the Roots	265
	Relation of Roots and Coefficients	266
	Formation of Equations with Given Roots	267
	Miscellaneous Theorems	272
	Remainder Theorem	272
	Symmetry	273
XXXI.	Indeterminate Equations of the First Degree	276
XXXII.	Inequalities	279
	Miscellaneous Examples V.	283
XXXIII.	Ratio	286
	Proportion	291
	Transformations that may be made in a Proportion	293
	Variation	296
XXXIV.	Arithmetical Progression	301
	Geometrical Progression	308
	Harmonical Progression	313
XXXV.	Permutations and Combinations	319
XXXVI.	Probability (Chance)	331
	Miscellaneous Examples VI.	334
XXXVII.	Binomial Theorem: Proof for Positive Integral Index	338
	The General Term	341
	Simplest Form of the Binomial Theorem	342
	Proof by Mathematical Induction	343
	Equal Coefficients	345
	Greatest Coefficient	345

CONTENTS.

CHAPTER		PAGE
	Greatest Term	345
	Sum of the Coefficients	347
	Expansion of Multinomials	347
	Application when Index is Negative or Fractional	347
XXXVIII.	Logarithms	352
	Properties of Logarithms	353
	Characteristic and Mantissa	354
	Advantages of Common Logarithms	355
	Logarithms transformed from Base a to Base b	357
	Logarithms in Arithmetical Calculation	358
	Four-place Table of Logarithms	360
	Use of the Table	362
	Cologarithms	365
	Exponential Equations	366
XXXIX.	Interest and Annuities	367
XL.	Limiting Values and Vanishing Fractions	370
XLI.	Convergency and Divergency of Series	377
	Tests for Convergency	377
	Auxiliary Series	383
XLII.	Undetermined Coefficients	386
	Functions of Finite Dimensions	386
	Functions of Infinite Dimensions	390
	Expansion of Fractions into Series	391
	Expansion of Surds into Series	392
	Reversion of Series	393
	Partial Fractions	394
	The General Term	397
XLIII.	Continued Fractions	400
	Formation of Successive Convergents	403
	Limits to Error	407
	Recurring Continued Fractions	409
XLIV.	Summation of Series	413
	Scale of Relation	413
	The Sum of n Terms	415

CONTENTS.

CHAPTER		PAGE
	The General Term	417
	The Method of Differences	418
	Any Required Term	419
	The Sum of n Terms	420
	Piles of Shot and Shells	422
	Interpolation	425
XLV.	Binomial Theorem: Proof for Any Index	426
XLVI.	Exponential and Logarithmic Series	430
XLVII.	Determinants	435
	Minors	437
	Vanishing of a Determinant	438
	Multiplication of a Determinant	438
	A Determinant expressed as the Sum of Two Other Determinants	439
	Simplification of Determinants	440
	Solution of Simultaneous Equations of the First Degree	444
	Signs of the Terms	447
	Determinant of Lower Order	448
XLVIII.	Theory of Equations	450
	Horner's Method of Synthetic Division	451
	Number of the Roots	453
	Depression of Equations	453
	Formation of Equations	454
	Relations between the Roots and the Coefficients	454
	Fractional Roots	458
	Imaginary Roots	458
	Transformation of Equations	460
	Standard Form of Reciprocal Equations	466
	Descartes' Rule of Signs	469
	Derived Functions	472
	Equal Roots	472
	Location of the Roots	474
	Sturm's Theorem and Method	476
	Graphical Representation of Functions	480
	Solution of Higher Numerical Equations	483
	Newton's Method	483

CHAPTER		PAGE
	The Cube Roots of Unity	486
	Cardan's Method	487
	Biquadratic Equations	488
	Incommensurable Roots	491
	Horner's Method of Approximation	492
	Any Root of Any Number	495
	Miscellaneous Examples VII.	496
XLIX.	Graphical Representation of Functions	517
	Application to Simultaneous Equations	524
	Measurement on Different Scales	536
	Practical Applications	545
	Miscellaneous Applications of Linear Graphs	559

ALGEBRA.

CHAPTER I.

DEFINITIONS. SUBSTITUTIONS.

1. Algebra treats of quantities as in Arithmetic, but with greater generality; for while the quantities used in arithmetical processes are denoted by *figures*, which have a single definite value, algebraic quantities are denoted by *symbols*, which may have any value we choose to assign to them.

The symbols of quantity employed are usually the letters of our own alphabet; and, though there is no restriction as to the numerical values a symbol may represent, it is understood that in the same piece of work it keeps the same value throughout. Thus, when we say "let a equal 1," we do not mean that a must have the value 1 always, but only in the particular example we are considering. Moreover, we may operate with symbols without assigning to them any particular numerical value; indeed it is with such operations that Algebra is chiefly concerned.

We begin with the definitions of Algebra, premising that the symbols $+$, $-$, $\times$, $\div$, $(\ )$, $=$ will have the same meanings as in Arithmetic. Also, for the present, it will be assumed that all the algebraic symbols employed represent integral numbers.

2. An algebraic expression is a collection of symbols; it may consist of one or more **terms**, which are the parts separated from each other by the signs $+$ and $-$. Thus, $7a + 5b - 3c - x + 2y$ is an expression consisting of five terms.

NOTE. When no sign precedes a term the sign $+$ is understood.

3. Expressions are either **simple** or **compound**. A *simple expression* consists of *one* term, as $5a$. A *compound expression* consists of *two or more* terms. Compound expressions may be further distinguished. Thus an expression of *two* terms, as $3a - 2b$, is often called a **binomial**, and one of *three* terms, as $2a + 3b + c$, a **trinomial**. Simple expressions are frequently spoken of as **monomials**, and compound expressions as **multinomials** or **polynomials**.

4. When two or more quantities are multiplied together the result is called the **product**. One important difference between the notation of Arithmetic and Algebra should be here remarked. In Arithmetic the product of 2 and 3 is written 2×3, whereas in Algebra the product of a and b may be written in any of the forms $a \times b$, $a \cdot b$, or ab. The form ab is the most usual. Thus, if $a = 2$, $b = 3$, the product $ab = a \times b = 2 \times 3 = 6$; but in Arithmetic 23 means "twenty-three," or $2 \times 10 + 3$.

5. Each of the quantities multiplied together to form a product is called a **factor** of the product. Thus 5, a, b are the factors of the product $5ab$.

NOTE. The beginner should carefully notice the difference between **term** and **factor**.

6. When one of the factors of an expression is a numerical quantity, it is called the **coefficient** of the remaining factors. Thus, in the expression $5ab$, 5 is the coefficient. But the word coefficient is also used in a wider sense, and it is sometimes convenient to consider any factor, or factors, of a product as the coefficient of the remaining factors. Thus, in the product $6abc$, $6a$ may be appropriately called the coefficient of *bc*. A coefficient which is not merely numerical is sometimes called a **literal coefficient**.

NOTE. When the coefficient is unity it is usually omitted, and we write simply a, instead of $1\,a$.

7. A **power** of a quantity is the product obtained by repeating that quantity any number of times as a factor, and is expressed by writing the number of factors to the right of the quantity and above it. Thus,

$a \times a$ is called the *second power* of a, and is written a^2;

$a \times a \times a$ is called the *third power* of a, and is written a^3;

and so on.

The **index** or **exponent** is the number which expresses the power of any quantity. Thus 2, 5, 7 are respectively the indices of a^2, a^5, a^7.

NOTE. a^2 is usually read "a squared"; a^3 is read "a cubed"; a^4 is read "a to the fourth"; and so on.

When the index is unity it is omitted, and we write simply a, instead of a^1. Thus a, $1\,a$, a^1, and $1\,a^1$ all have the same meaning.

8. The beginner must be careful to distinguish between *coefficient* and *index*.

Ex. 1. What is the difference in meaning between $3\,a$ and a^3?
By $3\,a$ we mean the product of the quantities 3 and a.
By a^3 we mean the product of the quantities a, a, a.
Thus, if $a = 4$,
$$3\,a = 3 \times a = 3 \times 4 = 12;$$
$$a^3 = a \times a \times a = 4 \times 4 \times 4 = 64.$$

Ex. 2. If $b = 5$, distinguish between $4\,b^2$ and $2\,b^4$.

Here $4\,b^2 = 4 \times b \times b = 4 \times 5 \times 5 = 100$;

whereas $2\,b^4 = 2 \times b \times b \times b \times b = 2 \times 5 \times 5 \times 5 \times 5 = 1250.$

Ex. 3. If $x = 1$, find the value of $5\,x^4$.

Here $5\,x^4 = 5 \times x \times x \times x \times x = 5 \times 1 \times 1 \times 1 \times 1 = 5.$

NOTE. The beginner should observe that every power of 1 is 1.

Ex. 4. If $a = 4$, $x = 1$, find the value of $5\,x^a$.
$$5\,x^a = 5 \times x^a = 5 \times 1^4 = 5 \times 1 = 5.$$

4　ALGEBRA.

9. The Sign of Continuation, ···, is read "**and so on.**"

10. The Sign of Deduction, ∴, is read "**therefore**" or "**hence.**"

11. In arithmetical multiplication the order in which the factors of a product are written is immaterial. Thus

$$3 \times 4 = 4 \times 3.$$

In like manner in Algebra *ab* and *ba* each denote the product of the two quantities represented by the letters *a* and *b*, and have therefore the same value. Although it is immaterial in what order the factors of a product are written, it is usual to arrange them alphabetically. Fractional coefficients which are greater than unity are usually kept in the form of improper fractions.

Ex. If $a = 6$, $x = 7$, $z = 5$, find the value of $\frac{13}{8} axz$.

Here $\frac{13}{8} axz = \frac{13}{8} \times 6 \times 7 \times 5 = 273$.

EXAMPLES I. a.

If $a = 7$, $b = 2$, $c = 1$, $x = 5$, $y = 3$, find the value of

1. $14x$.
2. x^3.
3. $3ax$.
4. a^3.
5. $5by$.
6. b^5.
7. $3b^2$.
8. $2ax$.
9. $6c^4$.
10. $4y^3$.

If $a = 8$, $b = 5$, $c = 4$, $x = 1$, $y = 3$, find the value of

11. $3c^2$.
12. $7y^3$.
13. $5ab$.
14. $9xy$.
15. $8b^3$.
16. $3x^5$.
17. x^3.
18. $7y^4$.
19. c^x.
20. b^y.
21. y^c.
22. x^b.
23. y^b.
24. a^y.
25. b^x.

If $a = 5$, $b = 1$, $c = 6$, $x = 4$, find the value of

26. $\frac{1}{4} x^4$.
27. $\frac{5}{12} c^3$.
28. $\frac{3}{8} x^3$.
29. $\frac{1}{10} ax$.
30. 3^x.
31. 2^c.
32. 8^b.
33. 7^x.
34. $\frac{7}{15} acx$.
35. $\frac{1}{4} bcx$.

12. When several different quantities are multiplied together a notation similar to that of Art. 7 is adopted. Thus *aabbbbcddd* is written $a^2b^4cd^3$. And conversely $7a^3cd^2$ has the same meaning as $7 \times a \times a \times a \times c \times d \times d$.

Ex. 1. If $x = 5$, $y = 3$, find the value of $4x^2y^3$.

$$4x^2y^3 = 4 \times 5^2 \times 3^3 = 4 \times 25 \times 27 = 2700.$$

DEFINITIONS. SUBSTITUTIONS.

Ex. 2. If $a = 4$, $b = 9$, $x = 6$, find the value of $\dfrac{8\,bx^2}{27\,a^3}$.

$$\dfrac{8\,bx^2}{27\,a^3} = \dfrac{8 \times 9 \times 6^2}{27 \times 4^3} = \dfrac{8 \times 9 \times 36}{27 \times 64} = \tfrac{3}{2} = 1\tfrac{1}{2}.$$

13. If one factor of a product is equal to 0, the product must be equal to 0, *whatever values the other factors may have.* A factor 0 is usually called a *zero factor*.

For instance, if $x = 0$, then ab^3xy^2 contains a zero factor. Therefore $ab^3xy^2 = 0$ when $x = 0$, whatever be the values of a, b, y.

Again, if $c = 0$, then $c^3 = 0$; therefore $ab^2c^3 = 0$, whatever values a and b may have.

NOTE. Every power of 0 is 0.

EXAMPLES I. b.

If $a = 7$, $b = 2$, $c = 0$, $x = 5$, $y = 3$, find the value of

1. $4\,ax^2$.
2. a^3b.
3. $8\,b^2y$.
4. $3\,xy^2$.
5. $\tfrac{3}{4}b^2x$.
6. $\tfrac{2}{3}b^3y^2$.
7. $\tfrac{2}{3}xy^4$.
8. a^3c.
9. a^2cy.
10. $8\,x^3y$.

If $a = 2$, $b = 3$, $c = 1$, $p = 0$, $q = 4$, $r = 6$, find the value of

11. $\dfrac{3\,a^2r}{8\,b}$.
12. $\dfrac{8\,ab^2}{9\,q^2}$.
13. $\dfrac{6\,a^3c}{b^2}$.
14. $\dfrac{4\,cr^2}{9\,a^3}$.
15. $3\,a^2b^c$.
16. $\tfrac{1}{2}ba^r$.
17. $\dfrac{8\,b}{9\,a^r}$.
18. $5\,a^bc^r$.
19. $\dfrac{2\,a^2p}{7\,r}$.
20. $3^a 2^b$.
21. $2^r a^b$.
22. $c^b b^q$.
23. $\dfrac{5\,a^r b^q}{64\,r^a}$.
24. $\dfrac{27\,a^q}{32}$.
25. $\dfrac{64}{q^r}$.

14. DEFINITION. The **square root** of any proposed expression is that quantity whose square, or second power, is equal to the given expression. Thus the square root of 81 is 9, because $9^2 = 81$.

The square root of a is denoted by $\sqrt[2]{a}$, or more simply $\sqrt{a}$.

Similarly the **cube, fourth, fifth,** etc., **root** of any expression is that quantity whose third, fourth, fifth, etc., power is equal to the given expression.

The roots are denoted by the symbols $\sqrt[3]{\,}$, $\sqrt[4]{\,}$, $\sqrt[5]{\,}$, etc.

EXAMPLES: $\sqrt[3]{27} = 3$; because $3^3 = 27$.

$\sqrt[5]{32} = 2$; because $2^5 = 32$.

ALGEBRA.

The symbol $\sqrt{}$ is sometimes called the **radical sign**.

Ex. 1. Find the value of $5\sqrt{(6\,a^3b^4c)}$, when $a = 3$, $b = 1$, $c = 8$.

$$5\sqrt{(6\,a^3b^4c)} = 5 \times \sqrt{(6 \times 3^3 \times 1^4 \times 8)}$$
$$= 5 \times \sqrt{(6 \times 27 \times 8)} = 5 \times \sqrt{1296}$$
$$= 5 \times 36 = 180.$$

Ex. 2. Find the value of $\sqrt[3]{\left(\dfrac{ab^4}{8\,x^3}\right)}$, when $a = 9$, $b = 3$, $x = 5$.

$$\sqrt[3]{\left(\frac{ab^4}{8\,x^3}\right)} = \sqrt[3]{\left(\frac{9 \times 3^4}{8 \times 5^3}\right)} = \sqrt[3]{\left(\frac{9 \times 81}{8 \times 125}\right)} = \sqrt[3]{\left(\frac{9 \times 9 \times 9}{1000}\right)} = \frac{9}{10}.$$

EXAMPLES I. c.

If $a = 8$, $c = 0$, $k = 9$, $x = 4$, $y = 1$, find the value of

1. $\sqrt{(2\,a)}$.
2. $\sqrt{(kx)}$.
3. $\sqrt{(2\,ax)}$.
4. $\sqrt{(2\,ak^2)}$.
5. $\sqrt[3]{(3\,k)}$.
6. $\sqrt[3]{(ax^3)}$.
7. $\sqrt[3]{(8\,x^3y^3)}$.
8. $\sqrt[3]{(cy^5)}$.
9. $2\,x\sqrt{(2\,ay)}$.
10. $5\,y\sqrt{(4\,kx)}$.
11. $3\,c\sqrt{(kx)}$.
12. $2\,xy\sqrt{(4\,y^5)}$.
13. $\sqrt{\left(\dfrac{8\,x^3}{ak}\right)}$.
14. $\sqrt{\left(\dfrac{25\,a}{2\,k}\right)}$.
15. $\sqrt{\left(\dfrac{16\,x}{49\,y^3}\right)}$.
16. $\sqrt{\left(\dfrac{ca^2}{16\,k}\right)}$.
17. $\sqrt[3]{\left(\dfrac{3\,a}{k^2}\right)}$.
18. $\sqrt[3]{\left(\dfrac{ax^3}{27\,y^3}\right)}$.

If $a = 4$, $b = 1$, $c = 2$, $d = 9$, $x = 5$, $y = 8$, find the value of

19. $\sqrt{(8\,ac)}$.
20. $6\sqrt{(4\,b^3)}$.
21. $7\sqrt{(5\,dx)}$.
22. $\sqrt{(c^5y)}$.
23. $\sqrt{\left(\dfrac{1}{5\,xy^2}\right)}$.
24. $\sqrt{\left(\dfrac{1}{8\,acd}\right)}$.
25. $\dfrac{1}{\sqrt{(9\,a^3c^2)}}$.
26. $\dfrac{1}{\sqrt{(5\,c^4x)}}$.
27. $\sqrt[3]{\left(\dfrac{1}{4\,cx^3}\right)}$.
28. $\dfrac{1}{\sqrt[3]{(8\,ab^2c)}}$.
29. $\sqrt[3]{\left(\dfrac{3\,x^3}{d^2y}\right)}$.
30. $\sqrt[3]{\left(\dfrac{5\,b^3}{x^4y}\right)}$.
31. $\sqrt{d^c}$.
32. $\sqrt{y^a}$.
33. $\sqrt{b^d}$.
34. $\sqrt{d^b}$.

15. We now proceed to find the numerical value of expressions which contain more than one term. In these, each term can be dealt with singly by the rules already

DEFINITIONS. SUBSTITUTIONS.

given, and by combining the terms the numerical value of the whole expression is obtained.

16. We have already, in Art. 8, called attention to the importance of carefully distinguishing between *coefficient* and *index*; confusion between these is such a fruitful source of error with beginners that it may not be unnecessary once more to dwell on the distinction.

Ex. 1. When $c = 5$, find the value of $c^4 - 4c + 2c^3 - 3c^2$.

Here
$$c^4 = 5^4 = 5 \times 5 \times 5 \times 5 = 625;$$
$$4c = 4 \times 5 = 20;$$
$$2c^3 = 2 \times 5^3 = 2 \times 5 \times 5 \times 5 = 250;$$
$$3c^2 = 3 \times 5^2 = 3 \times 5 \times 5 = 75.$$

Hence the value of the expression $= 625 - 20 + 250 - 75 = 780$.

Ex. 2. When $p = 9$, $r = 6$, $k = 4$, find the value of
$$\frac{1}{3}\sqrt[3]{\left(\frac{pr}{k^2}\right)} + \sqrt{(3k + k^3 + 5)} - \frac{2r^2}{9k}.$$

$$\frac{1}{3}\sqrt[3]{\left(\frac{pr}{k^2}\right)} + \sqrt{(3k + k^3 + 5)} - \frac{2r^2}{9k} = \frac{1}{3}\sqrt[3]{\left(\frac{54}{16}\right)} + \sqrt{(12 + 64 + 5)} - \frac{2 \times 36}{9 \times 4}$$
$$= \tfrac{1}{3}\sqrt[3]{\tfrac{27}{8}} + \sqrt{81} - 2$$
$$= \tfrac{1}{3} \times \tfrac{3}{2} + 9 - 2 = 7\tfrac{1}{2}.$$

17. By Art. 13 any term which contains a *zero factor* is itself zero, and may be called a *zero term*.

Ex. 1. If $a = 2$, $b = 0$, $x = 3$, $y = 1$, find the value of
$$4a^3 - ab^3 + 2xy^2 + 3abx.$$
The expression $= (4 \times 2^3) - 0 + (2 \times 3 \times 1) + 0$
$= 32 - 0 + 6 + 0 = 38.$

NOTE. The two *zero terms* do not affect the result.

Ex. 2. Find the value of $\tfrac{3}{5}x^2 - a^2y + 7abx - \tfrac{5}{2}y^3$, when $a = 5$, $b = 0$, $x = 7$, $y = 1$.
$\tfrac{3}{5}x^2 - a^2y + 7abx - \tfrac{5}{2}y^3 = \tfrac{3}{5} \times 7^2 - 5^2 \times 1 + 0 - \tfrac{5}{2} \times 1^3$
$= 29\tfrac{2}{5} - 25 - 2\tfrac{1}{2} = 1\tfrac{9}{10}.$

NOTE. The *zero term* does not affect the result.

18. In working examples the student should pay attention to the following hints:

1. Too much importance cannot be attached to neatness of style and arrangement. The beginner should remember that neatness is in itself conducive to accuracy.

ALGEBRA.

2. The sign $=$ should never be used except to connect quantities which are equal. Beginners should be particularly careful not to employ the sign of equality in any vague and inexact sense.

3. Unless the expressions are very short the signs of equality in the steps of the work should be placed one under the other.

4. It should be clearly brought out how each step follows from the one before it; for this purpose it will sometimes be advisable to add short verbal explanations; the importance of this will be seen later.

EXAMPLES I. d.

If $a = 2, b = 3, c = 1, d = 0$, find the numerical value of

1. $6a + 5b - 8c + 9d$.
2. $3a - 4b + 6c + 5d$.
3. $6ab - 3cd + 2da - 5cb + 2db$.
4. $abc + bcd + cda + dab$.
5. $3abc - 2bcd + 2cda - 4dab$.
6. $2bc + 3cd - 4da + 5ab$.
7. $3bcd + 5cda - 7dab + abc$.
8. $a^2 + b^2 + c^2 + d^2$.
9. $2a^2 + 3b^3 - 4c^4$.
10. $a^4 + b^4 - c^4$.

If $a = 1, b = 2, c = 3, d = 0$, find the numerical value of

11. $a^3 + b^3 + c^3 + d^3$.
12. $\frac{1}{2}bc^3 - a^3 - b^3 - \frac{3}{4}ab^2c$.
13. $3abc - b^2c - 6a^3$.
14. $2a^2 + 2b^2 + 2c^2 + 2d^2 - 2bc - 2cd - 2da - 2ab$.
15. $a^2 + 2b^2 + 2c^2 + d^2 + 2ab + 2bc + \frac{2}{3}cd$.
16. $2c^2 + 2a^2 + 2b^2 - 4cb + 6abcd$.
17. $13a^2 + \frac{11}{9}c^4 + 20ab - 16ac - 16bc$.
18. $6ab - \frac{1}{3}ac^2 - 2a + \frac{1}{8}b^4 - 3d + \frac{2}{3}c^3$.
19. $125b^4c - 9d^5 + 3abc^2d$.

If $a = 8, b = 6, c = 1, x = 9, y = 4$, find the value of

20. $\frac{5}{3}a - \frac{1}{6}b^3 + \frac{1}{8}y^2$.
21. $\frac{5}{27}ax - \frac{32}{y^2} - \frac{6a}{cxy}$.
22. $\frac{3a^2b}{cxy^2} - \frac{5y}{a}$.
23. $\sqrt[3]{\left(\frac{6cy^4}{x^2}\right)} + 2\sqrt{\left(\frac{3a^3}{4b^3}\right)}$.
24. $\sqrt[3]{(bxy)} - \frac{1}{6}b^2 + \frac{8x^2}{b^2y}$.
25. $\frac{1}{4}ac - \sqrt{\left(\frac{b^2}{9y}\right)} - \sqrt[3]{\left(\frac{by}{x^2}\right)}$.
26. $\frac{5b^2y^3}{12a^2x} - \sqrt[3]{\left(\frac{ax^4}{b^2y^2}\right)} + \sqrt{\left(\frac{ab^5}{3x}\right)}$.

CHAPTER II.

NEGATIVE QUANTITIES. ADDITION OF LIKE TERMS.

19. In his arithmetical work the student has been accustomed to deal with numerical quantities connected by the signs $+$ and $-$; and in finding the value of an expression such as $1\frac{3}{4} + 7\frac{2}{3} - 3\frac{1}{5} + 6 - 4\frac{1}{5}$ he understands that the quantities to which the sign $+$ is prefixed are *additive*, and those to which the sign $-$ is prefixed are *subtractive*, while the first quantity, $1\frac{3}{4}$, to which no sign is prefixed, is counted among the additive terms. The same notions prevail in Algebra; thus in using the expression $7a + 3b - 4c - 2d$ we understand the symbols $7a$ and $3b$ to be additive, while $4c$ and $2d$ are subtractive.

20. But in Arithmetic the sum of the additive terms is always greater than the sum of the subtractive terms; and if the reverse were the case, the result would have no arithmetical meaning. In Algebra, however, not only may the sum of the subtractive terms exceed that of the additive, but a subtractive term may stand alone, and yet have a meaning quite intelligible.

Hence all algebraic quantities may be divided into **positive quantities** and **negative quantities**, according as they are expressed with the sign $+$ or the sign $-$; and this is quite irrespective of any actual process of addition and subtraction.

This idea may be made clearer by one or two simple illustrations.

(i) Suppose a man were to gain \$100 and then lose \$70, his total *gain* would be \$30. But if he first gains \$70 and then loses \$100 the result of his trading is a *loss* of \$30.

The corresponding algebraic statements would be

$$\$100 - \$70 = +\$30,$$
$$\$70 - \$100 = -\$30,$$

and the negative quantity in the second case is interpreted as a *debt*, that is, a sum of money opposite in character to the positive quantity, or *gain*, in the first case; in fact it may be said to possess a subtractive quality which would produce its effect on other transactions, or perhaps wholly counterbalance a sum gained.

(ii) Suppose a man starting from a given point were to walk along a straight road 100 yards forwards and then 70 yards backwards, his distance from the starting-point would be 30 yards. But if he first walks 70 yards forwards and then 100 yards backwards his distance from the starting-point would be 30 yards, but *on the opposite side of it*. As before we have

$$100 \text{ yards} - 70 \text{ yards} = +30 \text{ yards},$$
$$70 \text{ yards} - 100 \text{ yards} = -30 \text{ yards}.$$

In each of these cases the man's *absolute distance* from the starting-point is the same; but by taking the positive and negative signs into account, we see that -30 is a distance from the starting-point *equal in magnitude but opposite in direction* to the distance represented by $+30$. Thus the negative sign may here be taken as indicating *a reversal of direction*.

Many other illustrations might be chosen; but it will be sufficient here to remind the student that a subtractive quantity is always opposite in character to an additive quantity of equal *absolute value*.

NOTE. Absolute value is the value taken independently of the signs $+$ and $-$.

21. DEFINITION. When any number of quantities are connected by the signs $+$ and $-$, the resulting expression is called their **algebraic sum**. Thus $11a - 27a + 13b - 5b$ is an algebraic sum. This expression, however, is not, as will be shown, in its simplest form.

ADDITION OF LIKE TERMS.

22. Addition is the process of finding in *simplest form* the algebraic sum of any number of quantities.

23. Like terms, or **similar terms**, do not differ, or differ only in their numerical coefficients. Other terms are called **unlike**, or **dissimilar**. Thus $3a$, $7a$; $5a^2b$, $2a^2b$; $3a^3b^2$, $-4a^3b^2$ are pairs of like terms; and $4a$, $3b$; $7a^2$, $9a^2b$ are pairs of unlike terms.

ADDITION OF LIKE TERMS.

Rule I. *The sum of a number of like terms is a like term.*

Rule II. *If all the terms are positive, add the coefficients.*

Ex. Find the value of $8a + 5a$.

Here we have to increase 8 like things by 5 like things of the same kind, and the aggregate is 13 of such things;

for instance, $\qquad$ 8 lbs. $+ 5$ lbs. $= 13$ lbs.

Hence also, $\qquad 8a + 5a = 13a$.

Similarly, $\qquad 8a + 5a + a + 2a + 6a = 22a$.

Rule III. *If all the terms are negative, add the coefficients numerically and prefix the minus sign to the sum.*

Ex. To find the sum of $-3x$, $-5x$, $-7x$, $-x$.

Here the word *sum* indicates the aggregate of 4 subtractive quantities of like character. In other words, we have to *take away* successively 3, 5, 7, 1 like things, and the result is the same as taking away $3 + 5 + 7 + 1$ such things in the aggregate.

Thus the sum of $-3x$, $-5x$, $-7x$, $-x$, is $-16x$.

Rule IV. *If the terms are not all of the same sign, add together separately the coefficients of all the positive terms and the coefficients of all the negative terms; the difference of these two results, preceded by the sign of the greater, will give the coefficient of the sum required.*

Ex. 1. The sum of $17x$ and $-8x$ is $9x$, for the difference of 17 and 8 is 9, and the greater is positive.

Ex. 2. To find the sum of $8a$, $-9a$, $-a$, $3a$, $4a$, $-11a$, a.

The sum of the coefficients of the positive terms is 16.
The sum of the coefficients of the negative terms is 21.

The difference of these is 5, and the sign of the greater is negative: hence the required sum is $-5a$.

ALGEBRA.

We need not, however, adhere strictly to this rule, for the terms may be added or subtracted in the order we find most convenient.

This process is called **collecting terms**.

Ex. 3. Find the sum of $\frac{2}{3}a$, $3a$, $-\frac{1}{4}a$, $-2a$.

The sum $= 3\frac{2}{3}a - 2\frac{1}{4}a = 1\frac{5}{12}a = \frac{17}{12}a$.

NOTE. The sum of two quantities numerically equal but with opposite signs is zero. The sum of $5a$ and $-5a$ is 0.

EXAMPLES II.

Find the sum of

1. $5a, 7a, 11a, a, 23a$.
2. $4x, x, 3x, 7x, 9x$.
3. $7b, 10b, 11b, 9b, 2b$.
4. $6c, 8c, 2c, 15c, 19c, 100c, c$.
5. $-3x, -5x, -11x, -7x$.
6. $-5b, -6b, -11b, -18b$.
7. $-3y, -7y, -y, -2y, -4y$.
8. $-c, -2c, -50c, -13c$.
9. $-11b, -5b, -3b, -b$.
10. $5x, -x, -3x, 2x, -x$.
11. $26y, -11y, -15y, y, -3y, 2y$.
12. $5f, -9f, -3f, 21f, -30f$.
13. $2s, -3s, s, -s, -5s, 5s$.
14. $7y, -11y, 16y, -3y, -2y$.
15. $5x, -7x, -2x, 7x, 2x, -5x$.
16. $7ab, -3ab, -5ab, 2ab, ab$.

Find the value of

17. $-9x^2 + 11x^2 + 3x^2 - 4x^2$.
18. $3a^2x - 18a^2x + a^2x$.
19. $3a^3 - 7a^3 - 8a^3 + 2a^3 - 11a^3$.
20. $4x^3 - 5x^3 - 8x^3 - 7x^3$.
21. $4a^2b^2 - a^2b^2 - 7a^2b^2 + 5a^2b^2 - a^2b^2$.
22. $-9x^4 - 4x^4 - 12x^4 + 13x^4 - 7x^4$.
23. $7abcd - 11abcd - 41abcd + 2abcd$.
24. $\frac{1}{2}x - \frac{1}{3}x + x + \frac{2}{3}x$.
25. $\frac{2}{3}a + \frac{1}{5}a - \frac{1}{2}a$.
26. $-5b + \frac{1}{4}b - \frac{3}{2}b + 2b - \frac{1}{2}b + \frac{7}{4}b$.
27. $-\frac{1}{2}x^2 - 2x^2 - \frac{2}{3}x^2 + x^2 + \frac{1}{2}x^2 + 1\frac{1}{6}x^2$.
28. $-ab - \frac{1}{2}ab - \frac{1}{3}ab - \frac{1}{4}ab - \frac{1}{3}ab + ab + \frac{5}{12}ab$.
29. $\frac{2}{3}x - \frac{1}{4}x + \frac{5}{8}x - 2x + 1\frac{1}{6}x - \frac{1}{3}x + x$.
30. $-\frac{2}{3}x^2 - \frac{1}{4}x^2 - \frac{1}{3}x^2 - \frac{1}{4}x^2 - x^2$.

CHAPTER III.

SIMPLE BRACKETS. ADDITION. SUBTRACTION.

24. When a number of arithmetical quantities are connected by the signs $+$ and $-$, the value of the result is the same in whatever order the terms are taken. This also holds in the case of algebraic quantities.

Thus $a - b + c$ is equivalent to $a + c - b$, for in the first of the two expressions b is taken from a, and c added to the result; in the second c is added to a, and b taken from the result. Similar reasoning applies to all algebraic expressions. Hence we may write the terms of an expression in any order we please.

Thus it appears that the expression $a - b$ may be written in the equivalent form $-b + a$.

To illustrate this we may suppose, as in Art. 20, that a represents a gain of a dollars, and $-b$ a loss of b dollars: it is clearly immaterial whether the gain precedes the loss, or the loss precedes the gain.

25. Brackets ( ) are used, as in Arithmetic, to indicate that the terms enclosed within them are to be considered as one quantity. The full use of brackets will be considered in Chap. VI.; here we shall deal only with the simpler cases.

$8 + (13 + 5)$ means that 13 and 5 are to be added and their sum added to 8. It is clear that 13 and 5 may be added separately or together without altering the result.

Thus $\qquad 8 + (13 + 5) = 8 + 13 + 5 = 26.$

Similarly $a + (b + c)$ means that the sum of b and c is to be added to a.

Thus $\qquad a + (b + c) = a + b + c.$

$8 + (13 - 5)$ means that to 8 we are to add the excess of 13 over 5; now if we add 13 to 8 we have added 5 too much, and must therefore take 5 from the result.

Thus $\qquad 8 + (13 - 5) = 8 + 13 - 5 = 16.$

Similarly $a + (b - c)$ means that to a we are to add b, diminished by c.

Thus $\qquad a + (b - c) = a + b - c \quad \ldots \quad (1).$

In like manner,

$$a + b - c + (d - e - f) = a + b - c + d - e - f. \quad (2)$$

Conversely,

$$a + b - c + d - e - f = a + b - c + (d - e - f). \quad (3)$$

Again, $a - b + c = a + c - b,$ [Art. 24.]
$\qquad\qquad\quad = $ the sum of a and $c - b$,
$\qquad\qquad\quad = $ the sum of a and $-b + c$, [Art. 24.]
therefore $\qquad a - b + c = a + (-b + c) \quad \ldots \quad (4).$

By considering the results (1), (2), (3), (4), we are led to the following rule:

Rule. *When an expression within brackets is preceded by the sign $+$, the brackets can be removed without making any change in the expression.*

Conversely: *Any part of an expression may be enclosed within brackets and the sign $+$ prefixed, the sign of every term within the brackets remaining unaltered.*

Thus the expression $a - b + c - d + e$ may be written in any of the following ways,

$$a + (-b + c - d + e).$$
$$a - b + (c - d + e),$$
$$a - b + c + (-d + e).$$

26. The expression $a - (b + c)$ means that from a we are to take the sum of b and c. The result will be the same whether b and c are subtracted separately or in one sum.

Thus $\qquad a - (b + c) = a - b - c.$

SIMPLE BRACKETS.

Again, $a - (b - c)$ means that from a we are to subtract the excess of b over c. If from a we take b we get $a - b$; but by so doing we shall have taken away c too much, and must therefore add c to $a - b$. Thus
$$a - (b - c) = a - b + c.$$
In like manner, $a - b - (c - d - e) = a - b - c + d + e.$

Accordingly the following rule may be enunciated:

Rule. *When an expression within brackets is preceded by the sign* $-$, *the brackets may be removed if the sign of every term within the brackets be changed.*

Conversely: *Any part of an expression may be enclosed within brackets and the sign* $-$ *prefixed, provided the sign of every term within the brackets be changed.*

Thus the expression $a - b + c + d - e$ may be written in any of the following ways,
$$a - (+b - c - d + e),$$
$$a - b - (-c - d + e),$$
$$a - b + c - (-d + e).$$

We have now established the following results:

I. *Additions and subtractions may be made in any order.*
Thus $a + b - c + d - e - f = a - c + b + d - f - e$
$$= a - c - f + d + b - e.$$

This is known as the **Commutative Law for Addition and Subtraction.**

II. *The terms of an expression may be grouped in any manner.*
Thus $a + b - c + d - e - f = (a + b) - c + (d - e) - f$
$$= a + (b - c) + (d - e) - f = a + b - (c - d) - (e + f).$$

This is known as the **Associative Law for Addition and Subtraction.**

ADDITION OF UNLIKE TERMS.

27. When two or more *like* terms are to be added together we have seen that they may be collected and the result expressed as a single like term. If, however, the terms are *unlike*, they cannot be collected. Thus in finding the sum of two unlike quantities a and b, all that can be done is to connect them by the sign of addition and leave the result in the form $a + b$.

Also, by the rules for removing brackets, $a+(-b)=a-b$; that is, the algebraic sum of a and $-b$ is written in the form $a - b$.

28. It will be observed that in Algebra the word *sum* is used in a wider sense than in Arithmetic. Thus, in the language of Arithmetic, $a - b$ signifies that b is to be subtracted from a, and bears that meaning only; but in Algebra it also means the sum of the two quantities a and $-b$ without any regard to the relative magnitudes of a and b.

Ex. 1. Find the sum of $3a - 5b + 2c$; $2a + 3b - d$; $-4a + 2b$.

$$\begin{aligned}
\text{The sum} &= (3a - 5b + 2c) + (2a + 3b - d) + (-4a + 2b) \\
&= 3a - 5b + 2c + 2a + 3b - d - 4a + 2b \\
&= 3a + 2a - 4a - 5b + 3b + 2b + 2c - d \\
&= a + 2c - d,
\end{aligned}$$

by collecting like terms.

The addition is more conveniently effected by the following rule:

Rule. *Arrange the expressions in lines so that the like terms may be in the same vertical columns: then add each column, beginning with that on the left.*

$$\begin{array}{l}
3a - 5b + 2c \\
2a + 3b \quad\quad - d \\
-4a + 2b \\
\hline
a \quad\quad\quad + 2c - d
\end{array}$$

The algebraic sum of the terms in the first column is a, that of the terms in the second column is zero. The single terms in the third and fourth columns are brought down without change.

Ex. 2. Add together $-5ab + 6bc - 7ac$; $8ab + 3ac - 2ad$; $-2ab + 4ac + 5ad$; $bc - 3ab + 4ad$.

$$\begin{array}{l}
-5ab + 6bc - 7ac \\
\quad 8ab \quad\quad + 3ac - 2ad \\
-2ab \quad\quad + 4ac + 5ad \\
-3ab + bc \quad\quad\quad + 4ad \\
\hline
-2ab + 7bc \quad\quad\quad + 7ad
\end{array}$$

Here we first rearrange the expressions so that like terms are in the same vertical columns, and then add up each column separately.

ADDITION.

EXAMPLES III. a.

Find the sum of

1. $a + 2b - 3c$; $-3a + b + 2c$; $2a - 3b + c$.
2. $3a + 2b - c$; $-a + 3b + 2c$; $2a - b + 3c$.
3. $-3x + 2y + z$; $x - 3y + 2z$; $2x + y - 3z$.
4. $-x + 2y + 3z$; $3x - y + 2z$; $2x + 3y - z$.
5. $4a + 3b + 5c$; $-2a + 3b - 8c$; $a - b + c$.
6. $-15a - 19b - 18c$; $14a + 15b + 8c$; $a + 5b + 9c$.
7. $25a - 15b + c$; $13a - 10b + 4c$; $a + 20b - c$.
8. $-16a - 10b + 5c$; $10a + 5b + c$; $6a + 5b - c$.
9. $5ax - 7by + cz$; $ax + 2by - cz$; $-3ax + 2by + 3cz$.
10. $20p + q - r$; $p - 20q + r$; $p + q - 20r$.

Add together the following expressions

11. $-5ab + 6bc - 7ca$; $8ab - 4bc + 3ca$; $-2ab - 2bc + 4ca$.
12. $15ab - 27bc - 6ca$; $14ab - 18bc + 10ca$; $-49ab + 45bc - 3ca$.
13. $5ab + bc - 3ca$; $ab - bc + ca$; $-ab + bc + 2ca$.
14. $pq + qr - rp$; $-pq + qr + rp$; $pq - qr + rp$.
15. $x + y + z$; $2x + 3y - 2z$; $3x - 4y + z$.
16. $2a - 3b + c$; $15a - 21b - 8c$; $3a + 24b + 7c$.
17. $4xy - 9yz + 2zx$; $-25xy + 24yz - zx$; $23xy - 15yz + zx$.
18. $17ab - 13bc + 8ca$; $-5ab + 9bc - 7ca$; $2ab - 7bc - ca$.
19. $47x - 63y + z$; $-25x + 15y - 3z$; $-22x + 48y + 15z$.
20. $23a - 17b - 2c$; $-9a + 15b + 7c$; $-13a + 3b - 4c$.

DIMENSION, DEGREE, ASCENDING AND DESCENDING POWERS.

29. Each of the letters composing a term is called a **dimension** of the term, and the number of letters involved is called the **degree** of the term. Thus the product abc is said to be *of three dimensions*, or *of the third degree;* and ax^4 is said to be *of five dimensions*, or *of the fifth degree.*

A numerical coefficient is not counted. Thus $8a^2b^5$ and a^2b^5 are each *of seven dimensions*, or *of the seventh degree.*

But it is sometimes useful to speak of the dimensions of an expression with regard to any one of the letters it involves. For instance, the expression $8\,a^3b^4c$, which is of eight dimensions, may be said to be of three dimensions in a, of four dimensions in b, and of one dimension in c.

30. A compound expression is said to be **homogeneous** when all its terms are of the same degree. Thus $8\,a^6 - a^4b^2 + 9\,ab^5$ is a *homogeneous expression of six dimensions*, or *of the sixth degree*.

31. Different powers of the same letter are **unlike terms**; thus the result of adding together $2\,x^3$ and $3\,x^2$ cannot be expressed by a single term, but must be left in the form $2\,x^3 + 3\,x^2$.

Similarly, the algebraic sum of $5\,a^2b^2 - 3\,ab^3$ and $-b^4$ is $5\,a^2b^2 - 3\,ab^3 - b^4$. This expression is in its simplest form and cannot be abridged.

32. In adding together several algebraic expressions containing terms with different powers of the same letter, it will be found convenient to arrange all the expressions in **descending** or **ascending powers** of that letter. This will be made clear by the following examples.

Ex. 1. Add together $3\,x^3 + 7 + 6\,x - 5\,x^2$; $2\,x^2 - 8 - 9\,x$; $4\,x - 2\,x^3 + 3\,x^2$; $3\,x^3 - 9\,x - x^2$; $x - x^2 - x^3 + 4$.

$$
\begin{array}{r}
3\,x^3 - 5\,x^2 + 6\,x + 7 \\
2\,x^2 - 9\,x - 8 \\
-2\,x^3 + 3\,x^2 + 4\,x \\
3\,x^3 - x^2 - 9\,x \\
-x^3 - x^2 + x + 4 \\
\hline
3\,x^3 - 2\,x^2 - 7\,x + 3
\end{array}
$$

In writing the first expression we put in the first term the highest power of x, in the second term the next highest power, and so on till the last term, in which x does not appear. The other expressions are arranged in the same way, so that in each column we have *like powers of the same letter*. The result is in *descending* powers of x.

Ex. 2. Add together
$3\,ab^2 - 2\,b^3 + a^3$; $5\,a^2b - ab^2 - 3\,a^3$; $8\,a^3 + 5\,b^3$; $9\,a^2b - 2\,a^3 + ab^2$.

$$
\begin{array}{r}
-2\,b^3 + 3\,ab^2 \qquad\quad + a^3 \\
- ab^2 + 5\,a^2b - 3\,a^3 \\
5\,b^3 \qquad\qquad\quad + 8\,a^3 \\
ab^2 + 9\,a^2b - 2\,a^3 \\
\hline
3\,b^3 + 3\,ab^2 + 14\,a^2b + 4\,a^3
\end{array}
$$

Here each expression is arranged according to *descending* powers of b, and *ascending* powers of a.

ADDITION.

EXAMPLES III. b.

Find the sum of the following expressions:

1. $2ab + 3ac + 6abc$; $-5ab + 2bc - 5abc$; $3ab - 2bc - 3ac$
2. $2x^2 - 2xy + 3y^2$; $4y^2 + 5xy - 2x^2$; $x^2 - 2xy - 6y^2$.
3. $3a^2 - 7ab - 4b^2$; $-6a^2 + 9ab - 3b^2$; $4a^2 + ab + 5b^2$.
4. $x^2 + xy - y^2$; $-z^2 + yz + y^2$; $-x^2 + xz + z^2$.
5. $-x^2 - 3xy + 3y^2$; $3x^2 + 4xy - 5y^2$; $x^2 + xy + y^2$.
6. $x^3 - x^2 + x - 1$; $2x^3 - 2x + 2$; $-5x^3 + 5x + 1$.
7. $2x^3 - x^2 - x$; $4x^3 + 8x^2 + 7x$; $-6x^3 - 6x^2 + x$.
8. $9x^2 - 7x + 5$; $-14x^2 + 15x - 6$; $20x^2 - 40x - 17$.
9. $10x^3 + 5x + 8$; $3x^3 - 4x^2 - 6$; $2x^3 - 2x - 3$.
10. $a^3 - ab + bc$; $ab + b^3 - ac$; $ac - bc + c^3$.
11. $5a^3 - 3c^3 + d^3$; $b^3 - 2a^3 + 3d^3$; $4c^3 - 2a^3 - 3d^3$.
12. $6x^3 - 2x + 1$; $2x^3 + x + 6$; $x^2 - 7x^3 + 2x - 4$.
13. $a^3 - a^2 + 3a$; $3a^3 + 4a^2 + 8a$; $5a^3 - 6a^2 - 11a$.
14. $x^2 + y^2 - 2xy$; $2z^2 - 3y^2 - 4yz$; $2x^2 - 2z^2 - 3xz$.
15. $x^3 - 2y^3 + x$; $y^3 - 2x^3 + y$; $x^3 + 2y^3 - x + y^3$.
16. $x^3 + 3x^2y + 3xy^2$; $-3x^2y - 6xy^2 - x^3$; $3x^2y + 4xy^2$.
17. $a^3 + 5ab^2 + b^3$; $b^3 - 10ab^2 - a^3$; $5ab^2 - 2b^3 + 2a^2b$.
18. $x^5 - 4x^4y - 5x^3y^3$; $3x^4y + 2x^3y^3 - 6xy^4$; $3x^3y^3 + 6xy^4 - y^5$
19. $a^3 - 4a^2b + 6abc$; $a^2b - 10abc + c^3$; $b^3 + 3a^2b + abc$.
20. $x^3 - 4x^2y + 6xy^2$; $2x^2y - 3xy^2 + 2y^3$; $y^3 + 3x^2y + 4xy^2$.

Add together the following expressions:

21. $\frac{1}{2}a - \frac{1}{3}b$; $-a + \frac{2}{3}b$; $\frac{1}{4}a - b$.
22. $-\frac{1}{3}a - \frac{1}{2}b$; $-\frac{2}{3}a + \frac{1}{4}b$; $-2a - b$.
23. $-2a + \frac{1}{2}c$; $-\frac{1}{3}a - 2b$; $\frac{4}{5}b - 3c$.
24. $-\frac{13}{8}a - \frac{11}{4}c$; $2a - 3b$; $\frac{11}{5}b - c$.
25. $\frac{1}{4}x^2 + \frac{1}{2}xy - \frac{1}{4}y^2$; $-x^2 - \frac{2}{3}xy + 2y^2$; $\frac{2}{3}x^2 - xy - \frac{5}{4}y^2$.
26. $3a^2 - \frac{2}{3}ab - \frac{1}{2}b^2$; $-\frac{3}{5}a^2 + 2ab - \frac{2}{5}b^2$; $-\frac{2}{7}a^2 - ab + b^2$.
27. $\frac{5}{6}x^2 - \frac{1}{4}xy + \frac{3}{10}y^2$; $-\frac{3}{4}x^2 + 1\frac{1}{5}xy - y^2$; $\frac{1}{2}x^2 - xy + \frac{1}{3}y^2$.
28. $-\frac{3}{4}x^3 + 5ax^2 - \frac{2}{5}a^2x$; $x^3 - \frac{37}{8}ax^2 + \frac{1}{2}a^2x$; $-\frac{1}{2}x^3 + \frac{3}{4}a^2x$.
29. $\frac{2}{3}x^2 - \frac{1}{4}xy - 7y^2$; $\frac{2}{5}xy + \frac{13}{5}y^2$; $-\frac{5}{6}x^2 + 4y^2$.
30. $\frac{1}{2}a^3 - 2a^2b - \frac{3}{5}b^3$; $\frac{1}{3}a^2b - \frac{3}{4}ab^2 + 2b^3$; $-\frac{1}{4}a^3 + ab^2 + \frac{1}{2}b^3$.

SUBTRACTION.

33. Subtraction is the inverse of Addition. The simplest cases have been considered under the head of addition of *like* terms, of which some are negative. [Art. 23.]

Thus
$$5a - 3a = 2a,$$
$$3a - 7a = -4a,$$
$$-3a - 6a = -9a.$$

Also, by the rule for removing brackets [Art. 26],
$$3a - (-8a) = 3a + 8a$$
$$= 11a,$$
and
$$-3a - (-8a) = -3a + 8a$$
$$= 5a.$$

SUBTRACTION OF UNLIKE TERMS.

34. The method is shown in the following example:

Ex. Subtract $3a - 2b - c$ from $4a - 3b + 5c$.

The result of subtraction $= 4a - 3b + 5c - (3a - 2b - c)$
$$= 4a - 3b + 5c - 3a + 2b + c$$
$$= 4a - 3a - 3b + 2b + 5c + c$$
$$= a - b + 6c.$$

It is, however, more convenient to arrange the work as follows, *the signs of all the terms in the lower line being changed.*

$$\begin{array}{r} 4a - 3b + 5c \\ -3a + 2b + c \\ \hline a - b + 6c \end{array}$$

by addition

Rule. *Change the sign of every term in the expression to be subtracted, and add it to the other expression.*

NOTE. It is not necessary that in the expression to be subtracted the signs should be *actually* changed; the operation of changing signs ought to be performed mentally.

SUBTRACTION.

Ex. 1. From $5x^2 + xy - 3y^2$ take $2x^2 + 8xy - 7y^2$.

$$5x^2 + xy - 3y^2$$
$$2x^2 + 8xy - 7y^2$$
$$\overline{3x^2 - 7xy + 4y^2}.$$

Ex. 2. Subtract $3x^2 - 2x$ from $1 - x^3$.

Terms containing different powers of the same letter being *unlike* must stand in different columns.

$$-x^3 \qquad\qquad +1$$
$$\qquad 3x^2 - 2x$$
$$\overline{-x^3 - 3x^2 + 2x + 1}.$$

The rearrangement of terms in the first line is not *necessary*, but it is convenient, because it gives the result of subtraction in descending powers of x.

EXAMPLES III. c.

Subtract

1. $4a - 3b + c$ from $2a - 3b - c$.
2. $a - 3b + 5c$ from $4a - 8b + c$.
3. $2x - 8y + z$ from $15x + 10y - 18z$.
4. $15a - 27b + 8c$ from $10a + 3b + 4c$.
5. $-10x - 14y + 15z$ from $x - y - z$.
6. $-11ab + 6cd$ from $-10bc + ab - 4cd$.
7. $4a - 3b + 15c$ from $25a - 16b - 18c$.
8. $-16x - 18y - 15z$ from $-5x + 8y + 7z$.
9. $ab + cd - ac - bd$ from $ab + cd + ac + bd$.
10. $-ab + cd - ac + bd$ from $ab - cd + ac - bd$.

From

11. $3ab + 5cd - 4ac - 6bd$ take $3ab + 6cd - 8ac - 5bd$.
12. $yz - xz + xy$ take $-xy + yz - xz$.
13. $-2x^3 - x^2 - 3x + 2$ take $x^3 - x + 1$.
14. $-8x^2y + 15xy^2 + 10xyz$ take $4x^2y - 6xy^2 - 5xyz$.
15. $\frac{1}{2}a - b + \frac{1}{4}c$ take $\frac{1}{3}a + \frac{1}{2}b - \frac{1}{2}c$.
16. $\frac{3}{4}x + y - z$ take $\frac{1}{2}x - \frac{1}{2}y - \frac{1}{3}z$.
17. $-a - 3b$ take $\frac{2}{3}a + \frac{1}{3}b - \frac{1}{2}c$.
18. $\frac{1}{2}x - \frac{3}{5}y + \frac{1}{10}z$ take $-\frac{1}{2}x + \frac{4}{5}y - \frac{1}{10}z$.
19. $-\frac{3}{4}x - \frac{3}{5}y - 5z$ take $\frac{2}{3}x - \frac{3}{5}y - 1\frac{1}{3}z$.
20. $-\frac{1}{2}x + \frac{2}{3}y - \frac{1}{6}$ take $\frac{1}{3}x - \frac{3}{2}y - \frac{1}{8}$.

EXAMPLES III. d.

From

1. $3xy - 5yz + 8xz$ take $-4xy + 2yz - 10xz$.
2. $-8x^2y^2 + 15x^3y + 13xy^3$ take $4x^2y^2 + 7x^3y - 8xy^3$.
3. $-8 + 6ab + a^2b^2$ take $4 - 3ab - 5a^2b^2$.
4. $a^2bc + b^2ca + c^2ab$ take $3a^2bc - 5b^2ca - 4c^2ab$.
5. $-7a^2b + 8ab^2 + cd$ take $5a^2b - 7ab^2 + 6cd$.
6. $-8x^2y + 5xy^2 - x^2y^2$ take $8x^2y - 5xy^2 + x^2y^2$.
7. $10a^2b^2 + 15ab^2 + 8a^2b$ take $-10a^2b^2 + 15ab^2 - 8a^2b$.
8. $4x^2 - 3x + 2$ take $-5x^2 + 6x - 7$.
9. $x^3 + 11x^2 + 4$ take $8x^2 - 5x - 3$.
10. $-8a^2x^2 + 5x^2 + 15$ take $9a^2x^2 - 8x^2 - 5$.

Subtract

11. $x^3 - x^2 + x + 1$ from $x^3 + x^2 - x + 1$.
12. $3xy^2 - 3x^2y + x^3 - y^3$ from $x^3 + 3x^2y + 3xy^2 + y^3$.
13. $b^3 + c^3 - 2abc$ from $a^3 + b^3 - 3abc$.
14. $7xy^2 - y^3 - 3x^2y + 5x^3$ from $8x^3 + 7x^2y - 3xy^2 - y^3$.
15. $x^4 + 5 + x - 3x^3$ from $5x^4 - 8x^3 - 2x^2 + 7$.
16. $a^3 + b^3 + c^3 - 3abc$ from $7abc - 3a^3 + 5b^3 - c^3$.
17. $1 - x + x^5 - x^4 - x^3$ from $x^4 - 1 + x - x^3$.
18. $7a^4 - 8a^2 + 3a^5 + a$ from $a^2 - 5a^3 - 7 + 7a^5$.
19. $10a^2b + 8ab^2 - 8a^3b^3 - b^4$ from $5a^2b - 6ab^2 - 7a^3b^3$.
20. $a^3 - b^3 + 8ab^2 - 7a^2b$ from $-8ab^2 + 15a^2b + b^3$.

From

21. $\frac{1}{2}x^2 - \frac{1}{3}xy - \frac{1}{2}y^2$ take $-\frac{3}{8}x^2 + xy - y^2$.
22. $\frac{2}{3}a^2 - \frac{1}{2}a - 1$ take $-\frac{2}{3}a^2 + a - \frac{1}{2}$.
23. $\frac{1}{3}x^2 - \frac{1}{2}x + \frac{1}{4}$ take $\frac{1}{3}x - 1 + \frac{1}{2}x^2$.
24. $\frac{3}{8}x^2 - \frac{2}{3}ax$ take $\frac{1}{3} - \frac{1}{4}x^2 - \frac{1}{8}ax$.
25. $\frac{3}{4}x^3 - \frac{1}{3}xy^2 - y^3$ take $\frac{1}{2}x^2y - \frac{1}{3}y^3 - \frac{1}{4}xy^2$.
26. $\frac{1}{4}a^3 - 2ax^2 - \frac{1}{3}a^2x$ take $\frac{1}{3}a^2x + \frac{1}{4}a^3 - \frac{1}{2}ax^2$.

35. We shall close this chapter with an exercise containing miscellaneous examples of Addition and Subtraction.

SUBTRACTION.

MISCELLANEOUS EXAMPLES I.

1. To the sum of $2a - 3b - 2c$ and $2b - a + 7c$ add the sum of $a - 4c + 7b$ and $c - 6b$.

2. From $5x^3 + 3x - 1$ take the sum of $2x - 5 + 7x^2$ and $3x^2 + 4 - 2x^3 + x$.

3. Subtract $3a - 7a^3 + 5a^2$ from the sum of $2 + 8a^2 - a^3$ and $2a^3 - 3a^2 + a - 2$.

4. Subtract $5x^2 + 3x - 1$ from $2x^3$, and add the result to $3x^2 + 3x - 1$.

5. Add the sum of $2y - 3y^2$ and $1 - 5y^3$ to the remainder when $1 - 2y^2 + y$ is subtracted from $5y^3$.

6. Take $x^2 - y^2$ from $3xy - 4y^2$, and add the remainder to the sum of $4xy - x^2 - 3y^2$ and $2x^2 + 6y^2$.

7. Find the sum of $5a - 7b + c$ and $3b - 9a$, and subtract the result from $c - 4b$.

8. Add together $3x^2 - 7x + 5$ and $2x^3 + 5x - 3$, and diminish the result by $3x^2 + 2$.

9. What expression must be added to $5x^2 - 7x + 2$ to produce $7x^2 - 1$?

10. What expression must be added to $4x^3 - 3x^2 + 2$ to produce $4x^3 + 7x - 6$?

11. What expression must be subtracted from $3a - 5b + c$ so as to leave $2a - 4b + c$?

12. What expression must be subtracted from $9x^2 + 11x - 5$ so as to leave $6x^2 - 17x + 3$?

13. From what expression must $11a^2 - 5ab - 7bc$ be subtracted so as to give for remainder $5a^2 + 7ab + 7bc$?

14. From what expression must $3ab + 5bc - 6ca$ be subtracted so as to leave a remainder $6ca - 5bc$?

15. To what expression must $7x^3 - 6x^2 - 5x$ be added so as to make $9x^3 - 6x - 7x^2$?

16. To what expression must $5ab - 11bc - 7ca$ be added so as to produce zero?

17. If $3x^2 - 7x + 2$ be subtracted from zero, what will be the result?

18. Subtract $3x^3 - 7x + 1$ from $2x^2 - 5x - 3$, then subtract the difference from zero, and add this last result to $2x^2 - 2x^3 - 4$.

19. Subtract $3x^2 - 5x + 1$ from unity, and add $5x^2 - 6x$ to the result.

CHAPTER IV.

MULTIPLICATION.

36. Multiplication in its primary sense signifies repeated addition.

Thus $\quad 3 \times 4 = 3$ taken 4 times
$$= 3 + 3 + 3 + 3.$$

Here the multiplier contains 4 units, and the number of times we take 3 is the same as the number of units in 4.

Again $\quad a \times b = a$ taken b times
$$= a + a + a + \cdots, \text{ the number of terms being } b.$$

Also $3 \times 4 = 4 \times 3$; and so long as a and b denote positive whole numbers, it is easy to show that $a \times b = b \times a$.

37. When the two quantities to be multiplied together are not positive whole numbers, we may define multiplication as *an operation performed on one quantity which when performed on unity produces the other*. For example, to multiply $\frac{4}{5}$ by $\frac{3}{7}$, we perform on $\frac{4}{5}$ that operation which when performed on unity gives $\frac{3}{7}$; that is, we must divide $\frac{4}{5}$ into 7 equal parts and take 3 of them. Now each part will be equal to $\dfrac{4}{5 \times 7}$, and the result of taking 3 of such parts is expressed by $\dfrac{4 \times 3}{5 \times 7}$.

Hence $\quad \dfrac{4}{5} \times \dfrac{3}{7} = \dfrac{4 \times 3}{5 \times 7}.$

MULTIPLICATION.

Also, by the last article,

$$\frac{4 \times 3}{5 \times 7} = \frac{3 \times 4}{7 \times 5} = \frac{3}{7} \times \frac{4}{5}.$$

$$\therefore \frac{4}{5} \times \frac{3}{7} = \frac{3}{7} \times \frac{4}{5}.$$

The reasoning is clearly general, and we may now say that $a \times b = b \times a$, where a and b are any positive quantities, integral or fractional.

The same is true for any number of quantities, hence *the factors of a product may be taken in any order.* This is the **Commutative Law for Multiplication.**

38. Again, *the factors of a product may be grouped in any way we please.*

Thus $\quad abcd = a \times b \times c \times d$
$$= (ab) \times (cd) = a \times (bc) \times d = a \times (bcd).$$

This is the **Associative Law for Multiplication.**

39. Since, by definition, $a^3 = aaa$, and $a^5 = aaaaa$,

$$\therefore a^3 \times a^5 = aaa \times aaaaa = aaaaaaaa = a^8 = a^{3+5};$$

that is, *the index of a letter in the product is the sum of its indices in the factors of the product.* This is the **Index Law for Multiplication.**

Again, $\quad 5a^2 = 5aa$, and $7a^3 = 7aaa$.

$$\therefore 5a^2 \times 7a^3 = 5 \times 7 \times aaaaa = 35a^5.$$

When the expressions to be multiplied together contain powers of different letters, a similar method is used.

Ex. $5a^3b^2 \times 8a^2bx^3 = 5aaabb \times 8aabxxx = 40a^5b^3x^3$.

NOTE. The beginner must be careful to observe that in this process of multiplication *the indices of one letter cannot combine in any way with those of another.* Thus the expression $40a^5b^3x^3$ admits of no further simplification.

40. Rule. *To multiply two simple expressions together, multiply the coefficients together and prefix their product to the product of the different letters, giving to each letter an index equal to the sum of the indices that letter has in the separate factors.*

The rule may be extended to cases where more than two expressions are to be multiplied together.

Ex. 1. Find the product of x^2, x^3, and x^8.

The product $= x^2 \times x^3 \times x^8 = x^{2+3} \times x^8 = x^{2+3+8} = x^{13}$.

The product of three or more expressions is called **the continued product**.

Ex. 2. Find the continued product of $5x^2y^3$, $8y^2z^5$, and $3zx^4$.

The product $= 5x^2y^3 \times 8y^2z^5 \times 3zx^4 = 120\, x^6 y^5 z^6$.

MULTIPLICATION OF A COMPOUND EXPRESSION BY A SIMPLE EXPRESSION.

41. By definition,

$$(a+b)m = m+m+m+\cdots \text{ taken } a+b \text{ times}$$
$$= (m+m+m+\cdots \text{ taken } a \text{ times}),$$

together with $(m+m+m+\cdots \text{ taken } b \text{ times})$

$$= am + bm \quad \ldots \ldots \ldots \quad (1).$$

Also $(a-b)m = m+m+m+\cdots$ taken $a-b$ times
$$= (m+m+m+\cdots \text{ taken } a \text{ times}),$$

diminished by $(m+m+m+\cdots \text{ taken } b \text{ times})$

$$= am - bm \quad \ldots \ldots \ldots \quad (2).$$

Similarly, $(a-b+c)m$
$$= am - bm + cm.$$

Hence *the product of a compound expression by a single factor is the algebraic sum of the partial products of each term of the compound expression by that factor.* This is known as the **Distributive Law for Multiplication**.

MULTIPLICATION.

Ex. $3(2a + 3b - 4c) = 6a + 9b - 12c.$

$(4x^2 - 7y - 8z^3) \times 3xy^2 = 12x^3y^2 - 21xy^3 - 24xy^2z^3.$

NOTE. It should be observed that for the present a, b, c, m denote positive whole numbers, and that a is supposed to be greater than b.

EXAMPLES IV. a.

Find value of

1. $5x^2 \times 7x^5.$
2. $4a^3 \times 5a^8.$
3. $7ab \times 8a^3b^2.$
4. $6xy^2 \times 5x^3.$
5. $8a^3b \times b^5.$
6. $2abc \times 3ac^3.$
7. $2a^3b^3 \times 2a^3b^3.$
8. $5a^2b \times 2a.$
9. $4a^2b^3 \times 7a^5.$
10. $5a^4b^3 \times x^2y^2.$
11. $x^3y^3 \times 6a^2x^4.$
12. $abc \times xyz.$
13. $3a^4b^7x^3 \times 5a^3bx.$
14. $4a^3bx \times 7b^2x^4.$
15. $5a^2x \times 8cx.$

Multiply

16. $5x^3y^3$ by $6a^3x^3.$
17. $2x^2y$ by $x^5y^7.$
18. $3a^3x^4y^7$ by $a^2x^5y^9.$
19. $ab + bc$ by $a^3b.$
20. $5ab - 7bx$ by $4a^2bx^3.$
21. $5x + 3y$ by $2x^2.$
22. $a^2 + b^2 - c^2$ by $a^3b.$
23. $bc + ca - ab$ by $abc.$
24. $5a^2 + 3b^2 - 2c^2$ by $4a^2bc^3.$
25. $5x^2y + xy^2 - 7x^2y^2$ by $3x^3.$

MULTIPLICATION OF COMPOUND EXPRESSIONS.

42. If in Art. 41 we write $c + d$ for m in (1), we have

$$(a+b)(c+d) = a(c+d) + b(c+d)$$
$$= (c+d)a + (c+d)b \quad \text{[Art. 37.]}$$
$$= ac + ad + bc + bd.$$

Again, from (2)

$$(a-b)(c+d) = a(c+d) - b(c+d)$$
$$= (c+d)a - (c+d)b$$
$$= ac + ad - (bc + bd)$$
$$= ac + ad - bc - bd.$$

Similarly, by writing $c - d$ for m in (1)

$$(a+b)(c-d) = a(c-d) + b(c-d)$$
$$= (c-d)a + (c-d)b$$
$$= ac - ad + bc - bd.$$

Also, from (2)
$$(a-b)(c-d) = a(c-d) - b(c-d)$$
$$= (c-d)a - (c-d)b$$
$$= ac - ad - (bc - bd)$$
$$= ac - ad - bc + bd.$$

If we consider each term on the right-hand side of this last result, and the way in which it arises, we find that

$$(+a) \times (+c) = +ac,$$
$$(-b) \times (-d) = +bd,$$
$$(-b) \times (+c) = -bc,$$
$$(+a) \times (-d) = -ad.$$

These results enable us to state what is known as the **Rule of Signs** in multiplication.

Rule of Signs. *The product of two terms with like signs is positive; the product of two terms with unlike signs is negative.*

43. The rule of signs, and especially the use of the negative multiplier, will probably present some difficulty to the beginner. Perhaps the following numerical instances may be useful in illustrating the interpretation that may be given to multiplication by a negative quantity.

To multiply 3 by -4 we must do to 3 what is done to unity to obtain -4. Now -4 means that unity is taken 4 times and the result made negative; therefore $3 \times (-4)$ implies that 3 is to be taken 4 times and the product made negative.

But 3 taken 4 times gives $+12$.
$$\therefore 3 \times (-4) = -12.$$

Similarly, -3×-4 indicates that -3 is to be taken 4 times, and the sign changed; the first operation gives -12, and the second $+12$.

Thus $\qquad (-3) \times (-4) = +12.$

MULTIPLICATION.

Hence, *multiplication by a negative quantity indicates that we are to proceed just as if the multiplier were positive, and then change the sign of the product.*

44. NOTE ON ARITHMETICAL AND SYMBOLICAL ALGEBRA.

Arithmetical Algebra is that part of the science which deals solely with symbols and operations arithmetically intelligible. Starting from purely arithmetical definitions, we are enabled to prove certain fundamental laws.

Symbolical Algebra assumes these laws to be true in every case, and thence finds what meaning must be attached to symbols and operations which under unrestricted conditions no longer bear an arithmetical meaning. Thus the results of Arts. 41 and 42 were proved from arithmetical definitions which require the symbols to be positive whole numbers, such that a is greater than b and c is greater than d. By the principles of Symbolical Algebra we assume these results to be universally true when all restrictions are removed, and accept the interpretation to which we are led thereby.

Henceforth we are able to apply the Law of Distribution and the Rule of Signs without any restriction as to the symbols used.

45. To familiarize the beginner with the principles we have just explained we add a few examples in substitutions where some of the symbols denote negative quantities.

Ex. 1. If $a = -4$, find the value of a^3.
Here $a^3 = (-4)^3 = (-4) \times (-4) \times (-4) = -64$.
Ex. 2. If $a = -1$, $b = 3$, $c = -2$, find the value of $-3 a^4 bc^3$.
Here $\qquad -3 a^4 bc^3 = -3 \times (-1)^4 \times 3 \times (-2)^3$
$\qquad\qquad = -3 \times 1 \times 3 \times (-8) = 72$.

EXAMPLES IV. b.

If $a = -2$, $b = 3$, $c = -1$, $x = -5$, $y = 4$, find the value of

1. $3 a^2 b$.
2. $8 abc^2$.
3. $-5 c^3$.
4. $6 a^2 c^2$.
5. $4 c^3 y$.
6. $3 a^2 c$.
7. $-b^2 c^2$.
8. $3 a^3 c^2$.
9. $-7 a^3 bc$.
10. $-2 a^4 bx$.
11. $-4 a^2 c^4$.
12. $3 c^3 x^3$.
13. $5 a^2 x^2$.
14. $-7 c^4 xy$.
15. $-8 ax^3$.
16. $4 c^5 x^3$.
17. $-5 a^2 b^2 c^2$.
18. $-7 a^3 c^3$.
19. $8 c^4 x^3$.
20. $7 a^5 c^4$.

80 ALGEBRA.

If $a = -4$, $b = -3$, $c = -1$, $f = 0$, $x = 4$, $y = 1$, find the value of

21. $3a^2 + bx - 4cy$.
22. $2ab^2 - 3bc^2 + 2fx$.
23. $fa^2 - 2b^3 - cx^3$.
24. $3a^2y^3 - 5b^2x - 2c^3$.
25. $2a^3 - 3b^3 + 7cy^4$.
26. $3b^2y^4 - 4b^2f - 6c^4x$.
27. $2\sqrt{(ac)} - 3\sqrt{(xy)} + \sqrt{(b^2c^4)}$.
28. $3\sqrt{(acx)} - 2\sqrt{(b^2y)} - 6\sqrt{(c^2y)}$.
29. $7\sqrt{(a^2x)} - 3\sqrt{(b^4c^2)} + 5\sqrt{(f^2x)}$.
30. $3c\sqrt{(3bc)} - 5\sqrt{(4c^2y^3)} - 2cy\sqrt{(3bc^5)}$.

46. The following examples further illustrate the rule of signs and the law of indices.

Ex. 1. Multiply $4a$ by $-3b$.

By the rule of signs the product is negative; also $4a \times 3b = 12ab$.

$$\therefore 4a \times (-3b) = -12ab.$$

Ex. 2. Multiply $-5ab^3x$ by $-ab^3x$.

Here the absolute value of the product is $5a^2b^6x^2$, and by the rule of signs the product is positive.

$$\therefore (-5ab^3x) \times (-ab^3x) = 5a^2b^6x^2.$$

Ex. 3. Find the continued product of $3a^2b$, $-2a^3b^2$, $-ab^4$.

$3a^2b \times (-2a^3b^2) = -6a^5b^3$;
$(-6a^5b^3) \times (-ab^4) = +6a^6b^7$.

Thus the complete product is $6a^6b^7$.

This result, however, may be written down at once; for

$$3a^2b \times 2a^3b^2 \times ab^4 = 6a^6b^7,$$

and by the rule of signs the required product is positive.

Ex. 4. Multiply $6a^3 - 5a^2b - 4ab^2$ by $-3ab^2$.

The product is the algebraic sum of the partial products formed according to the rule enunciated in Art. 40;

thus $(6a^3 - 5a^2b - 4ab^2) \times (-3ab^2) = -18a^4b^2 + 15a^3b^3 + 12a^2b^4$.

EXAMPLES IV. c.

Multiply together

1. ax and $-3ax$.
2. $-2abx$ and $-7abx$.
3. a^2b and $-ab^2$.
4. $6x^2y$ and $-10xy$.
5. $-abcd$ and $-3a^2b^3c^4d^5$.
6. xyz and $-5x^2y^3z$.
7. $3xy + 4yz$ and $-12xyz$.
8. $ab - bc$ and a^2bc^3.

MULTIPLICATION. 31

9. $-x-y-z$ and $-3x$.
10. $a^2-b^2+c^2$ and abc.
11. $-ab+bc-ca$ and $-abc$.
12. $-2a^2b-4ab^2$ and $-7a^2b^2$.
13. $5x^2y-6xy^2+8x^2y^2$ and $3xy$.
14. $-7x^3y-5xy^3$ and $-8x^3y^3$.
15. $-5xy^2z+3xyz^2-8x^2yz$ and xyz.
16. $4x^2y^2z^2-8xyz$ and $-12x^3yz^3$.
17. $-13xy^2-15x^2y$ and $-7x^3y^3$.
18. $8xyz-10x^3yz^3$ and $-xyz$.
19. $abc-a^2bc-ab^2c$ and $-abc$.
20. $-a^2bc+b^2ca-c^2ab$ and $-ab$.

Find the product of

21. $2a-3b+4c$ and $-\tfrac{1}{2}a$.
22. $3x-2y-4$ and $-\tfrac{3}{8}x$.
23. $\tfrac{1}{2}a-\tfrac{1}{3}b-c$ and $\tfrac{1}{4}ax$.
24. $\tfrac{5}{7}a^2x^2-\tfrac{1}{3}ax^3$ and $-\tfrac{7}{4}a^2x$.
25. $-\tfrac{1}{2}a^2x^2$ and $-\tfrac{1}{3}a^2+ax-\tfrac{1}{4}x^2$.
26. $-\tfrac{1}{4}xy$ and $-3x^2+\tfrac{1}{4}xy$.
27. $-\tfrac{1}{2}x^3y^2$ and $-\tfrac{1}{3}x^2+2y^3$.

47. The results of Art. 41 may be extended to the case where one or both of the expressions to be multiplied together contain more than two terms. For instance
$$(a-b+c)m = am - bm + cm;$$
replacing m by $x-y$, we have
$$(a-b+c)(x-y) = a(x-y) - b(x-y) + c(x-y)$$
$$= (ax-ay) - (bx-by) + (cx-cy)$$
$$= ax - ay - bx + by + cx - cy.$$

48. These results enable us to state the general rule for multiplying together any two compound expressions.

Rule. *Multiply each term of the first expression by each term of the second. When the terms multiplied together have like signs, prefix to the product the sign +, when unlike prefix —; the algebraic sum of the partial products so formed gives the complete product.*

This process is called **Distributing the Product.**

Ex. 1. Multiply $x+8$ by $x+7$.

$$\begin{array}{r} x+8 \\ x+7 \\ \hline x^2+8x \\ +7x+56 \\ \hline x^2+15x+56 \end{array}$$

by addition

NOTE. We begin on the left and work to the right, placing the second result one place to the right, so that like terms may stand in the same vertical column.

Ex. 2. Multiply $2x - 3y$ by $4x - 7y$.

$$
\begin{array}{r}
2x - 3y \\
4x - 7y \\
\hline
8x^2 - 12xy \\
-14xy + 21y^2 \\
\hline
\end{array}
$$

by addition $\quad 8x^2 - 26xy + 21y^2$

EXAMPLES IV. a.

Find the product of

1. $x + 5$ and $x + 10$.
2. $x + 5$ and $x - 5$.
3. $x - 7$ and $x - 10$.
4. $x - 7$ and $x + 10$.
5. $x + 7$ and $x - 10$.
6. $x + 7$ and $x + 10$.
7. $x + 6$ and $x - 6$.
8. $x + 8$ and $x - 4$.
9. $x - 12$ and $x - 1$.
10. $x + 12$ and $x - 1$.
11. $x - 15$ and $x + 15$.
12. $x - 15$ and $-x + 3$.
13. $-x - 2$ and $-x - 3$.
14. $-x + 7$ and $x - 7$.
15. $-x + 5$ and $-x - 5$.
16. $x - 13$ and $x + 14$.
17. $x - 17$ and $x + 18$.
18. $x + 19$ and $x - 20$.
19. $-x - 16$ and $-x + 16$.
20. $-x + 21$ and $x - 21$.
21. $2x - 3$ and $x + 8$.
22. $2x + 3$ and $x - 8$.
23. $x - 5$ and $2x - 1$.
24. $2x - 5$ and $x - 1$.
25. $3x - 5$ and $2x + 7$.
26. $3x + 5$ and $2x - 7$.
27. $5x - 6$ and $2x + 3$.
28. $5x + 6$ and $2x - 3$.
29. $3x - 5y$ and $3x + 5y$.
30. $3x - 5y$ and $3x - 5y$.
31. $a - 2b$ and $a + 3b$.
32. $a - 7b$ and $a + 8b$.
33. $3a - 6b$ and $a - 8b$.
34. $a - 9b$ and $a + 5b$.
35. $x + a$ and $x - b$.
36. $x - a$ and $x + b$.
37. $x - 2a$ and $x + 3b$.
38. $ax - by$ and $ax + by$.
39. $xy - ab$ and $xy + ab$.
40. $2pq - 3r$ and $2pq + 3r$.

MULTIPLICATION.

49. We shall now give a few examples of greater difficulty.

Ex. 1. Find the product of $3x^2 - 2x - 5$ and $2x - 5$.

$$\begin{array}{l} 3x^2 - 2x - 5 \\ 2x - 5 \\ \hline 6x^3 - 4x^2 - 10x \\ - 15x^2 + 10x + 25 \\ \hline 6x^3 - 19x^2 + 25 \end{array}$$

Each term of the first expression is multiplied by $2x$, the first term of the second expression; then each term of the first expression is multiplied by -5; like terms are placed in the same columns and the results added.

Ex. 2. Multiply $a - b + 3c$ by $a + 2b$

$$\begin{array}{l} a - b + 3c \\ a + 2b \\ \hline a^2 - ab + 3ac \\ + 2ab - 2b^2 + 6bc \\ \hline a^2 + ab + 3ac - 2b^2 + 6bc \end{array}$$

When the coefficients are fractional, we use the ordinary process of Multiplication, combining the fractional coefficients by the rules of Arithmetic.

Ex. 3. Multiply $\frac{1}{3}a^2 - \frac{1}{2}ab + \frac{2}{3}b^2$ by $\frac{1}{2}a + \frac{1}{3}b$.

$$\begin{array}{l} \frac{1}{3}a^2 - \frac{1}{2}ab + \frac{2}{3}b^2 \\ \frac{1}{2}a + \frac{1}{3}b \\ \hline \frac{1}{6}a^3 - \frac{1}{4}a^2b + \frac{1}{3}ab^2 \\ \phantom{\frac{1}{6}a^3} + \frac{1}{9}a^2b - \frac{1}{6}ab^2 + \frac{2}{9}b^3 \\ \hline \frac{1}{6}a^3 - \frac{5}{36}a^2b + \frac{1}{6}ab^2 + \frac{2}{9}b^3 \end{array}$$

50. If the expressions are not arranged according to powers ascending or descending of some common letter, a rearrangement will be found convenient.

Ex. Multiply $2xz - z^2 + 2x^2 - 3yz + xy$ by $x - y + 2z$.

$$\begin{array}{l} 2x^2 + xy + 2xz - 3yz - z^2 \\ x - y + 2z \\ \hline 2x^3 + x^2y + 2x^2z - 3xyz - xz^2 \\ - 2x^2y - 2xyz - xy^2 + 3y^2z + yz^2 \\ + 4x^2z + 2xyz + 4xz^2 - 6yz^2 - 2z^3 \\ \hline 2x^3 - x^2y + 6x^2z - 3xyz + 3xz^2 - xy^2 + 3y^2z - 5yz^2 - 2z^3 \end{array}$$

EXAMPLES IV. e

Multiply together

1. $a + b + c$ and $a + b - c$.
2. $a - 2b + c$ and $a + 2b - c$.
3. $a^2 - ab + b^2$ and $a^2 + ab + b^2$.
4. $x^2 + 3y^2$ and $x + 4y$.
5. $x^3 - 2x^2 + 8$ and $x + 2$.
6. $x^4 - x^2 y^2 + y^4$ and $x^2 + y^2$.
7. $x^2 + xy + y^2$ and $x - y$.
8. $a^2 - 2ax + 4x^2$ and $a^2 + 2ax + 4x^2$.
9. $16a^2 + 12ab + 9b^2$ and $4a - 3b$.
10. $a^2 x - ax^2 + x^3 - a^3$ and $x + a$.
11. $x^2 + x - 2$ and $x^2 + x - 6$.
12. $2x^3 - 3x^2 + 2x$ and $2x^2 + 3x + 2$.
13. $- a^5 + a^4 b - a^3 b^2$ and $- a - b$.
14. $x^3 - 7x + 5$ and $x^2 - 2x + 3$.
15. $a^3 + 2a^2 b + 2ab^2$ and $a^2 - 2ab + 2b^2$.
16. $4x^2 + 6xy + 9y^2$ and $2x - 3y$.
17. $x^2 - 3xy - y^2$ and $-x^2 + xy + y^2$.
18. $b^3 - a^2 b^2 + a^3$ and $a^3 + a^2 b^2 + b^3$.
19. $x^2 - 2xy + y^2$ and $x^2 + 2xy + y^2$.
20. $ab + cd + ac + bd$ and $ab + cd - ac - bd$.
21. $-3a^2 b^2 + 4ab^3 + 15a^3 b$ and $5a^2 b^2 + ab^3 - 3b^4$.
22. $27x^3 - 36ax^2 + 48a^2 x - 64a^3$ and $3x + 4a$.
23. $a^2 - 5ab - b^2$ and $a^2 + 5ab + b^2$.
24. $x^2 - xy + x + y^2 + y + 1$ and $x + y - 1$.
25. $a^2 + b^2 + c^2 - bc - ca - ab$ and $a + b + c$.
26. $-x^3 y + y^4 + x^2 y^2 + x^4 - xy^3$ and $x + y$.
27. $x^{12} - x^9 y^2 + x^6 y^4 - x^3 y^6 + y^8$ and $x^3 + y^2$.
28. $3a^2 + 2a + 2a^3 + 1 + a^4$ and $a^2 - 2a + 1$.
29. $- ax^2 + 3axy^2 - 9ay^4$ and $- ax - 3ay^2$.
30. $-2x^3 y + y^4 + 3x^2 y^2 + x^4 - 2xy^3$ and $x^2 + 2xy + y^2$.
31. $\frac{1}{2} a^2 + \frac{1}{3} a + \frac{1}{4}$ and $\frac{1}{2} a - \frac{1}{3}$.
32. $\frac{1}{2} x^2 - 2x + \frac{2}{3}$ and $\frac{1}{2} x + \frac{1}{3}$.

MULTIPLICATION. 35

33. $\frac{2}{3}x^2 + xy + \frac{3}{8}y^2$ and $\frac{1}{3}x - \frac{1}{2}y$.
34. $\frac{1}{2}x^2 - ax - \frac{3}{4}a^2$ and $\frac{3}{4}x^2 - \frac{1}{2}ax + \frac{1}{3}a^2$.
35. $\frac{1}{2}x^2 - \frac{3}{4}x - \frac{1}{4}$ and $\frac{1}{2}x^2 + \frac{3}{4}x - \frac{1}{4}$.
36. $\frac{3}{4}ax + \frac{1}{3}x^2 + \frac{1}{4}a^2$ and $\frac{1}{4}a^2 + \frac{3}{4}x^2 - \frac{3}{4}ax$.

NOTE. Examples involving literal, fractional, and negative exponents will be found in the chapter on the Theory of Indices.

51. Products Written by Inspection. Although the result of multiplying together two binomial factors, such as $x + 8$ and $x - 7$, can always be obtained by the methods already explained, it is of the utmost importance that the student should learn to write the product rapidly *by inspection*.

This is done by observing in what way the coefficients of the terms in the product arise, and noticing that they result from the combination of the numerical coefficients in the two binomials which are multiplied together; thus

$$(x + 8)(x + 7) = x^2 + 8x + 7x + 56$$
$$= x^2 + 15x + 56.$$

$$(x - 8)(x - 7) = x^2 - 8x - 7x + 56$$
$$= x^2 - 15x + 56.$$

$$(x + 8)(x - 7) = x^2 + 8x - 7x - 56$$
$$= x^2 + x - 56.$$

$$(x - 8)(x + 7) = x^2 - 8x + 7x - 56$$
$$= x^2 - x - 56.$$

In each of these results we notice that:

1. The product consists of three terms.
2. The first term is the product of the first terms of the two binomial expressions.
3. The third term is the product of the second terms of the two binomial expressions.
4. The middle term has for its coefficient the sum of the numerical quantities (taken with their proper signs) in the second terms of the two binomial expressions.

ALGEBRA.

The intermediate step in the work may be omitted, and the products written at once, as in the following examples:

$$(x+2)(x+3) = x^2 + 5x + 6.$$
$$(x-3)(x+4) = x^2 + x - 12.$$
$$(x+6)(x-9) = x^2 - 3x - 54.$$
$$(x-4y)(x-10y) = x^2 - 14xy + 40y^2.$$
$$(x-6y)(x+4y) = x^2 - 2xy - 24y^2.$$

By an easy extension of these principles we may write the product of *any* two binomials.

Thus
$$(2x + 3y)(x - y) = 2x^2 + 3xy - 2xy - 3y^2$$
$$= 2x^2 + xy - 3y^2.$$
$$(3x - 4y)(2x + y) = 6x^2 - 8xy + 3xy - 4y^2$$
$$= 6x^2 - 5xy - 4y^2.$$

EXAMPLES IV. f.

Write the values of the following products:

1. $(x+8)(x-5)$.
2. $(x+6)(x-1)$.
3. $(x-3)(x+10)$.
4. $(x-1)(x+5)$.
5. $(x+7)(x-9)$.
6. $(x-10)(x-8)$.
7. $(x-4)(x+11)$.
8. $(x-2)(x+4)$.
9. $(x+2)(x-2)$.
10. $(a-1)(a+1)$.
11. $(a+9)(a-5)$.
12. $(a-3)(a+12)$.
13. $(a-8)(a+4)$.
14. $(a-8)(a+8)$.
15. $(a-6)(a+13)$.
16. $(a+3)(a+3)$.
17. $(a-11)(a+11)$.
18. $(a-8)(a-8)$.
19. $(x-3a)(x+2a)$.
20. $(x+6a)(x-5a)$.
21. $(x+3a)(x-3a)$.
22. $(x+4y)(x-2y)$.
23. $(x+7y)(x-7y)$.
24. $(x-3y)(x-3y)$.
25. $(3x-1)(x+1)$.
26. $(2x+5)(2x-1)$.
27. $(3x+7)(2x-3)$.
28. $(4x-3)(2x+3)$.

MULTIPLICATION.

29. $(3x+8)(3x-8)$.
30. $(2x-5)(2x-5)$.
31. $(3x-2y)(3x+y)$.
32. $(3x+2y)(3x+2y)$.
33. $(2x+7y)(2x-5y)$.
34. $(5x+3a)(5x-3a)$.
35. $(2x-5a)(x+5a)$.
36. $(2x+a)(2x+a)$.

MULTIPLICATION BY DETACHED COEFFICIENTS.

52. In the following cases we lessen the labor of multiplication by using the **Method of Detached Coefficients**:

(i.) When two compound expressions contain but one letter.

(ii.) When two compound expressions are homogeneous and contain but two letters.

Ex. 1. Multiply $2x^3 - 4x^2 + 5x - 5$ by $3x^2 + 4x - 2$.

Writing coefficients only,
$$\begin{array}{r} 2 - 4 + 5 - 5 \\ 3 + 4 - 2 \\ \hline 6 - 12 + 15 - 15 \\ + 8 - 16 + 20 - 20 \\ - 4 + 8 - 10 + 10 \\ \hline 6 - 4 - 5 + 13 - 30 + 10 \end{array}$$

Inserting the literal factors according to the law of their formation, which is readily seen, we have for the complete product,

$$6x^5 - 4x^4 - 5x^3 + 13x^2 - 30x + 10.$$

Ex. 2. Multiply $3a^4 + 2a^3b + 4ab^3 + 2b^4$ by $2a^2 - b^2$.

$$\begin{array}{r} 3 + 2 + 0 + 4 + 2 \\ 2 + 0 - 1 \\ \hline 6 + 4 + 0 + 8 + 4 \\ -3 - 2 - 0 - 4 - 2 \\ \hline 6 + 4 - 3 + 6 + 4 - 4 - 2 \end{array}$$

In the first expression the term containing a^2b^2 is missing, so we write a zero in the corresponding term in the line of coefficients. In the second expression we write a zero for the coefficient of the missing term ab.

The law of formation of literal factors is readily seen, and we have for the complete product,

$$6a^6 + 4a^5b - 3a^4b^2 + 6a^3b^3 + 4a^2b^4 - 4ab^5 - 2b^6.$$

EXAMPLES IV. g.

1. Multiply $x^5 + x^4 + x^2 + 2x + 1$ by $x^3 + x - 2$.
2. Multiply $a^3 + 6a^2b + 12ab^2 + 8b^3$ by $3a^3 + 2b^3$.
3. Multiply $2a^4 - 3a^2 + 4a + 4$ by $2a^2 - 3a - 2$.
4. Multiply $3x^5 + 2x^4y - x^3y^2 + xy^4$ by $x^2 + 4xy - 5y^2$.

CHAPTER V.

DIVISION.

53. When a quantity a is divided by the quantity b, the **quotient** is defined to be that which when multiplied by b produces a. The operation is denoted by $a \div b$, $\frac{a}{b}$, or a/b; in each of these modes of expression a is called the **dividend**, and b the **divisor**.

Division is thus the inverse of multiplication, and
$$(a \div b) \times b = a.$$

54. *The* **Rule of Signs** *holds for division.*

Thus
$$ab \div a = \frac{ab}{a} = \frac{a \times b}{a} = b.$$
$$-ab \div a = \frac{-ab}{a} = \frac{a \times (-b)}{a} = -b.$$
$$ab \div (-a) = \frac{ab}{-a} = \frac{(-a) \times (-b)}{-a} = -b.$$
$$-ab \div (-a) = \frac{-ab}{-a} = \frac{(-a) \times b}{-a} = b.$$

Hence in division as well as multiplication
like signs produce $+$,
unlike signs produce $-$.

55. Since Division is the inverse of Multiplication, it follows that the Laws of Commutation, Association, and Distribution, which have been established for Multiplication, hold for Division.

DIVISION OF SIMPLE EXPRESSIONS.

56. The method is shown in the following examples:

Ex. 1. Since the product of 4 and x is $4x$, it follows that when $4x$ is divided by x the quotient is 4,
or otherwise, $\qquad 4x \div x = 4.$

Ex. 2. Divide $27\, a^5$ by $9\, a^3$.
The quotient $= \dfrac{27\, a^5}{9\, a^3} = \dfrac{27\, aaaaa}{9\, aaa}$ We remove from the divisor and dividend the factors common to both, as in Arithmetic.
$\qquad\qquad = 3\, aa = 3\, a^2.$
Therefore $\qquad\qquad 27\, a^5 \div 9\, a^3 = 3\, a^2.$

Ex. 3. Divide $35\, a^3 b^2 c^3$ by $7\, ab^2 c^2$.
The quotient $\qquad = \dfrac{35\, aaa \cdot bb \cdot ccc}{7\, a \cdot bb \cdot cc} = 5\, aa \cdot c = 5\, a^2 c.$

We see, in each case, that *the index of any letter in the quotient is the difference of the indices of that letter in the dividend and divisor.* This is called the **Index Law for Division**.

We can now state the complete rule:

Rule. *The index of each letter in the quotient is obtained by subtracting the index of that letter in the divisor from that in the dividend.*

To the result so obtained prefix with its proper sign the quotient of the coefficient of the dividend by that of the divisor.

Ex. 4. Divide $45\, a^6 b^2 x^4$ by $-9\, a^5 b x^2$.
$\qquad$ The quotient $= (-5) \times a^{6-5} b^{2-1} x^{4-2}$
$\qquad\qquad\qquad\quad = -5\, a^3 b x^2.$

Ex. 5. $\quad -21\, a^2 b^3 \div (-7\, a^2 b^2) = 3\, b.$

Note. If we apply the rule to divide any power of a letter by the same power of the letter, we are led to a curious conclusion.

Thus, by the rule $\qquad a^3 \div a^3 = a^{3-3} = a^0;$
but also $\qquad\qquad\quad a^3 \div a^3 = \dfrac{a^3}{a^3} = 1.$
$\qquad\qquad\qquad\quad \therefore\; a^0 = 1.$

This result will appear somewhat strange to the beginner, but its full significance will be explained in the chapter on the Theory of Indices.

DIVISION OF A COMPOUND EXPRESSION BY A SIMPLE EXPRESSION.

57. Rule. *To divide a compound expression by a single factor, divide each term separately by that factor, and take the algebraic sum of the partial quotients so obtained.*

This follows at once from Art. 40.

Ex. 1. $(9x - 12y + 3z) \div -3 = -3x + 4y - z$.

Ex. 2. $(36 a^3b^2 - 24 a^2b^5 - 20 a^4b^2) \div 4 a^2b = 9 ab - 6 b^4 - 5 a^2b$.

Ex. 3. $(2 x^2 - 5 xy + \frac{3}{2} x^2y^3) \div -\frac{1}{2} x = -4 x + 10 y - 3 xy^3$.

EXAMPLES V. a.

Divide

1. $3 x^3$ by x^2.
2. $27 x^4$ by $-9 x^3$.
3. $-35 x^6$ by $7 x^3$.
4. x^3y^3 by x^2y.
5. a^4x^3 by $-a^2x^3$.
6. $12 a^5b^6c^6$ by $-3 a^4b^2c$.
7. $-a^5c^9$ by $-ac^8$.
8. $15 x^5y^7z^4$ by $5 x^2y^2z^2$.
9. $-16 x^3y^2$ by $-4 xy^2$.
10. $-48 a^9$ by $-8 a^8$.
11. $63 a^7b^8c^3$ by $9 a^5b^5c^3$.
12. $7 a^2bc$ by $-7 a^2bc$.
13. $28 a^4b^3$ by $-4 a^3b$.
14. $16 b^2yx^2$ by $-2 xy$.
15. $-50 y^3x^3$ by $-5 x^3y$.
16. $x^3 - 3 x^2 + x$ by x.
17. $x^6 - 7 x^5 + 4 x^4$ by x^2.
18. $10 x^7 - 8 x^6 + 3 x^4$ by x^3.
19. $15 x^5 - 25 x^4$ by $-5 x^3$.
20. $-24 x^6 - 32 x^4$ by $-8 x^3$.
21. $34 x^3y^2 - 51 x^2y^3$ by $17 xy$.
22. $a^2 - ab - ac$ by $-a$.
23. $a^3 - a^2b - a^2b^2$ by a^2.
24. $3 x^3 - 9 x^2y - 12 xy^2$ by $-3 x$.
25. $4 x^4y^4 - 8 x^3y^2 + 6 xy^3$ by $-2 xy$.
26. $\frac{1}{2} x^5y^2 - 3 x^3y^4$ by $-\frac{1}{2} x^3y^2$.
27. $-\frac{1}{2} x^2 + \frac{2}{3} xy + \frac{10}{3} x$ by $-\frac{1}{6} x$.
28. $-2 a^5x^3 + \frac{1}{4} a^4x^4$ by $\frac{1}{7} a^3x$.

DIVISION OF COMPOUND EXPRESSIONS.

58. We employ the following rule:

Rule. 1. *Arrange divisor and dividend according to ascending or descending powers of some common letter.*

2. *Divide the term on the left of the dividend by the term on the left of the divisor, and put the result in the quotient.*

DIVISION. 41

3. *Multiply the* WHOLE *divisor by this quotient, and put the product under the dividend.*

4. *Subtract and bring down from the dividend as many terms as may be necessary.*

Repeat these operations till all the terms from the dividend are brought down.

Ex. 1. Divide $x^2 + 11x + 30$ by $x + 6$.

Arrange the work thus:

$$x + 6 \,)\, x^2 + 11x + 30 \,($$

divide x^2, the first term of the dividend, by x, the first term of the divisor; the quotient is x. Multiply the *whole* divisor by x, and put the product $x^2 + 6x$ under the dividend. We then have

$$\begin{array}{r} x + 6\,)\,x^2 + 11x + 30\,(x \\ x^2 + 6x \\ \hline 5x + 30 \end{array}$$

by subtraction

On repeating the process above explained we find that the next term in the quotient is $+5$.

The entire operation is more compactly written as follows:

$$\begin{array}{r} x + 6\,)\,x^2 + 11x + 30\,(x + 5 \\ x^2 + 6x \\ \hline 5x + 30 \\ 5x + 30 \\ \hline \end{array}$$

The reason for the rule is this: the dividend may be divided into as many parts as may be convenient, and the complete quotient is found by taking the sum of all the partial quotients. Thus $x^2 + 11x + 30$ is divided by the above process into two parts, namely, $x^2 + 6x$, and $5x + 30$, and each of these is divided by $x + 6$; thus we obtain the complete quotient $x + 5$.

Ex. 2. Divide $24x^2 - 65xy + 21y^2$ by $8x - 3y$.

$$\begin{array}{r} 8x - 3y\,)\,24x^2 - 65xy + 21y^2\,(3x - 7y \\ 24x^2 - 9xy \\ \hline -56xy + 21y^2 \\ -56xy + 21y^2 \\ \hline \end{array}$$

EXAMPLES V. b.

Divide

1. $x^2 + 3x + 2$ by $x + 1$.
2. $x^2 - 7x + 12$ by $x - 3$.
3. $a^2 - 11a + 30$ by $a - 5$.
4. $a^2 - 49a + 600$ by $a - 25$.
5. $3x^2 + 10x + 3$ by $x + 3$.
6. $2x^2 + 11x + 5$ by $2x + 1$.
7. $5x^2 + 11x + 2$ by $x + 2$.
8. $2x^2 + 17x + 21$ by $2x + 3$.
9. $4x^2 + 23x + 15$ by $4x + 3$.
10. $6x^2 - 7x - 3$ by $2x - 3$.
11. $3x^2 + x - 14$ by $x - 2$.
12. $3x^2 - x - 14$ by $x + 2$.
13. $6x^2 - 31x + 35$ by $2x - 7$.
14. $12a^2 - 7ax - 12x^2$ by $3a - 4x$.
15. $15a^2 + 17ax - 4x^2$ by $3a + 4x$.
16. $12a^2 - 11ac - 36c^2$ by $4a - 9c$.
17. $-4xy - 15y^2 + 96x^2$ by $12x - 5y$.
18. $7x^3 + 96x^2 - 28x$ by $7x - 2$.
19. $100x^3 - 3x - 13x^2$ by $3 + 25x$.
20. $27x^3 + 9x^2 - 3x - 10$ by $3x - 2$.
21. $16a^3 - 46a^2 + 39a - 9$ by $8a - 3$.

59. The process of Art. 58 is applicable to cases in which the divisor consists of more than two terms.

Ex. 1. Divide $6x^5 - x^4 + 4x^3 - 5x^2 - x - 15$ by $2x^2 - x + 3$.

$$2x^2 - x + 3 \overline{\smash{)}\, 6x^5 - x^4 + 4x^3 - 5x^2 - x - 15} \,(\, 3x^3 + x^2 - 2x - 5$$

$$\underline{6x^5 - 3x^4 + 9x^3}$$
$$2x^4 - 5x^3 - 5x^2$$
$$\underline{2x^4 - x^3 + 3x^2}$$
$$-4x^3 - 8x^2 - x$$
$$\underline{-4x^3 + 2x^2 - 6x}$$
$$-10x^2 + 5x - 15$$
$$\underline{-10x^2 + 5x - 15}$$

Ex. 2. Divide $a^3 + b^3 + c^3 - 3abc$ by $a + b + c$.

$$a + b + c \,\overline{\smash{)}\, a^3 - 3abc + b^3 + c^3} \,(\, a^2 - ab - ac + b^2 - bc + c^2$$

$$\underline{a^3 + a^2b + a^2c}$$
$$-\ a^2b - a^2c - 3abc$$
$$\underline{-\ a^2b - ab^2 - abc}$$
$$-a^2c + ab^2 - 2abc$$
$$\underline{-a^2c \qquad - abc - ac^2}$$
$$ab^2 - abc + ac^2 + b^3$$
$$\underline{ab^2 \qquad\qquad + b^3 + b^2c}$$
$$-\ abc + ac^2 - b^2c$$
$$\underline{-\ abc \qquad - b^2c - bc^2}$$
$$ac^2 + bc^2 + c^3$$
$$\underline{ac^2 + bc^2 + c^3}$$

NOTE. The result of this division will be referred to later.

DIVISION.

60. Sometimes it will be found convenient to arrange the expressions in *ascending* powers of some common letter.

Ex. Divide $2a^3 + 10 - 16a - 39a^2 + 15a^4$ by $2 - 4a - 5a^2$.

$$2 - 4a - 5a^2 \overline{)10 - 16a - 39a^2 + 2a^3 + 15a^4} (5 + 2a - 3a^2$$
$$\underline{10 - 20a - 25a^2}$$
$$4a - 14a^2 + 2a^3$$
$$\underline{4a - 8a^2 - 10a^3}$$
$$- 6a^2 + 12a^3 + 15a^4$$
$$\underline{- 6a^2 + 12a^3 + 15a^4}$$

61. When the coefficients are fractional, the ordinary process may still be employed.

Ex. Divide $\frac{1}{4}x^3 + \frac{7}{12}xy^2 + \frac{1}{12}y^3$ by $\frac{1}{2}x + \frac{1}{3}y$.

$$\frac{1}{2}x + \frac{1}{3}y \overline{)\frac{1}{4}x^3 + \frac{7}{12}xy^2 + \frac{1}{12}y^3} (\frac{1}{2}x^2 - \frac{1}{3}xy + \frac{1}{4}y^2$$
$$\underline{\frac{1}{4}x^3 + \frac{1}{6}x^2y}$$
$$- \frac{1}{6}x^2y + \frac{7}{12}xy^2$$
$$\underline{- \frac{1}{6}x^2y - \frac{1}{9}xy^2}$$
$$\frac{1}{4}xy^2 + \frac{1}{12}y^3$$
$$\underline{\frac{1}{4}xy^2 + \frac{1}{12}y^3}$$

In the examples given hitherto the divisor has been exactly contained in the dividend. When the division is not exact, the work should be carried on until the remainder is of lower dimensions [Art. 29] than the divisor.

EXAMPLES V. a.

Divide

1. $x^3 - x^2 - 9x - 12$ by $x^2 + 3x + 3$.
2. $2y^3 - 3y^2 - 6y - 1$ by $2y^2 - 5y - 1$.
3. $6m^3 - m^2 - 14m + 3$ by $3m^2 + 4m - 1$.
4. $6a^5 - 13a^4 + 4a^3 + 8a^2$ by $3a^3 - 2a^2 - a$.
5. $x^4 + x^3 + 7x^2 - 6x + 8$ by $x^2 + 2x + 8$.
6. $a^4 - a^3 - 8a^2 + 12a - 9$ by $a^2 + 2a - 3$.
7. $a^4 + 6a^3 + 13a^2 + 12a + 4$ by $a^2 + 3a + 2$.
8. $2x^4 - x^3 + 4x^2 + 7x + 1$ by $x^2 - x + 3$.
9. $x^5 - 5x^4 + 9x^3 - 6x^2 - x + 2$ by $x^2 - 3x + 2$.
10. $x^5 - 4x^4 + 3x^3 + 3x^2 - 3x + 2$ by $x^2 - x - 2$.

ALGEBRA.

11. $30x^4 + 11x^3 - 82x^2 - 5x + 3$ by $2x - 4 + 3x^3$.
12. $30y + 9 - 71y^3 + 28y^4 - 35y^2$ by $4y^2 - 13y + 6$.
13. $6k^5 - 15k^4 + 4k^3 + 7k^2 - 7k + 2$ by $3k^3 - k + 1$.
14. $15 + 2m^4 - 31m + 9m^2 + 4m^3 + m^5$ by $3 - 2m - m^2$.
15. $2x^3 - 8x + x^4 + 12 - 7x^2$ by $x^2 + 2 - 3x$.
16. $x^5 - 2x^4 - 4x^3 + 19x^2$ by $x^3 - 7x + 5$.
17. $192 - x^4 + 128x + 4x^2 - 8x^3$ by $16 - x^2$.
18. $14x^4 + 45x^3y + 78x^2y^2 + 45xy^3 + 14y^4$ by $2x^2 + 5xy + 7y^2$.
19. $x^5 - x^4y + x^3y^2 - x^3 + x^2 - y^3$ by $x^3 - x - y$.
20. $x^5 + x^4y - x^3y^2 + x^3 - 2xy^2 + y^3$ by $x^2 + xy - y^2$.
21. $a^9 - b^9$ by $a^3 - b^3$. 22. $x^9 - y^9$ by $x^2 + xy + y^2$.
23. $x^7 - 2y^{14} - 7x^5y^4 - 7xy^{12} + 14x^3y^8$ by $x - 2y^2$.
24. $a^3 + 3a^2b + b^3 - 1 + 3ab^2$ by $a + b - 1$.
25. $x^8 - y^8$ by $x^3 + x^2y + xy^2 + y^3$. 26. $a^{12} - b^{12}$ by $a^2 - b^2$.
27. $a^{12} + 2a^6b^6 + b^{12}$ by $a^4 + 2a^2b^2 + b^4$.
28. $1 - a^3 - 8x^3 - 6ax$ by $1 - a - 2x$.

Find the quotient of

29. $\frac{1}{8}a^3 - \frac{9}{4}a^2x + \frac{27}{2}ax^2 - 27x^3$ by $\frac{1}{2}a - 3x$.
30. $\frac{1}{27}a^3 - \frac{1}{12}a^2 + \frac{1}{16}a - \frac{1}{64}$ by $\frac{1}{3}a - \frac{1}{4}$.
31. $\frac{3}{4}a^2c^3 + \frac{8}{125}a^5$ by $\frac{1}{5}a^2 + \frac{1}{2}ac$.
32. $\frac{8}{27}x^5 - \frac{243}{512}ax^4$ by $\frac{2}{3}a - \frac{3}{4}x$.
33. $\frac{9}{16}a^4 - \frac{3}{4}a^3 - \frac{7}{4}a^2 + \frac{4}{3}a + \frac{16}{9}$ by $\frac{3}{2}a^2 - \frac{4}{3} - a$.
34. $36x^2 + \frac{1}{9}y^2 + \frac{1}{4} - 4xy - 6x + \frac{1}{3}y$ by $6x - \frac{1}{3}y - \frac{1}{2}$.

62. Important Cases in Division. The following examples in division may be easily verified; they are of great importance and should be carefully noticed.

$$\text{I.} \begin{cases} \dfrac{x^2 - y^2}{x - y} = x + y, \\[6pt] \dfrac{x^3 - y^3}{x - y} = x^2 + xy + y^2, \\[6pt] \dfrac{x^4 - y^4}{x - y} = x^3 + x^2y + xy^2 + y^3, \end{cases}$$

and so on; the divisor being $x - y$, the terms in the quotient *all positive*, and the index in the dividend *either odd or even*.

II. $\begin{cases} \dfrac{x^3 + y^3}{x + y} = x^2 - xy + y^2, \\ \dfrac{x^5 + y^5}{x + y} = x^4 - x^3y + x^2y^2 - xy^3 + y^4, \\ \dfrac{x^7 + y^7}{x + y} = x^6 - x^5y + x^4y^2 - x^3y^3 + x^2y^4 - xy^5 + y^6, \end{cases}$

and so on; the divisor being $x + y$, the terms in the quotient *alternately positive and negative*, and the index in the dividend *always odd*.

III. $\begin{cases} \dfrac{x^2 - y^2}{x + y} = x - y, \\ \dfrac{x^4 - y^4}{x + y} = x^3 - x^2y + xy^2 - y^3, \\ \dfrac{x^6 - y^6}{x + y} = x^5 - x^4y + x^3y^2 - x^2y^3 + xy^4 - y^5, \end{cases}$

and so on; the divisor being $x + y$, the terms in the quotient *alternately positive and negative*, and the index in the dividend *always even*.

IV. The expressions $x^2 + y^2$, $x^4 + y^4$, $x^6 + y^6$ ... (where the index is *even*, and the terms *both positive*), are *never* divisible by $x + y$ or $x - y$.

All these different cases may be more concisely stated as follows:

(1) $x^n - y^n$ is divisible by $x - y$ if n be *any* whole number.

(2) $x^n + y^n$ is divisible by $x + y$ if n be any *odd* whole number.

(3) $x^n - y^n$ is divisible by $x + y$ if n be any *even* whole number.

(4) $x^n + y^n$ is never divisible by $x + y$ or $x - y$ when n is an *even* whole number.

NOTE. General proofs of these statements will be found in Art. 106.

DIVISION BY DETACHED COEFFICIENTS.

63. In Art. 52 we considered certain cases of compound expressions in which the work of multiplication could be shortened by using the *Method of Detached Coefficients*. In the same cases the labor of division can be considerably abridged by using detached coefficients, and employing an arrangement of terms known as **Horner's Method of Synthetic Division.** The following examples illustrate the method:

Ex. 1. Divide $3x^5 - 8x^4 - 5x^3 + 26x^2 - 28x + 24$ by $x^3 - 2x^2 - 4x + 8$.

$$\begin{array}{r|rrrrrrl}
 & 1 & 3 - 8 - 5 + 26 - 28 + 24 & \text{Dividend} \\
\text{Divisor} & 2 & 6 + 12 - 24 \\
 & 4 & - 4 - 8 + 16 \\
 & -8 & + 6 + 12 - 24 \\
\hline
\text{Quotient} & & 3 - 2 + 3 + 0 + 0 + 0
\end{array}$$

Inserting the literal factors in the quotient according to the law of their formation, which is readily seen, we have for a complete quotient, $3x^2 - 2x + 3$.

EXPLANATION. The column of figures to the left of the vertical line consists of the coefficients of the divisor, *the sign of each after the first being changed*, which enables us *to replace the process of subtraction by that of addition* at each successive stage of the work. Dividing the first term of the dividend by the first term of the divisor, we obtain 3, the first term of the quotient. Multiplying 2, 4, and − 8, the remaining terms of the divisor, by this first term of the quotient gives the *second horizontal line*. We then *add* the terms in the second column to the right of the vertical line and obtain − 2, which is the coefficient of the second term of the quotient. With this coefficient as a multiplier, and using 2, 4, and − 8 again as a multiplicand, we form the *third horizontal line*. Adding the terms in the third column gives 3, which is the third term of the quotient. With this coefficient as a multiplier and the same multiplicand as before, we form the *fourth horizontal line*. As only zeros now appear in the quotient, the division is exact.

Ex. 2. Divide $2a^7 + 7a^6b + 12a^5b^2 + 10a^4b^3 - 4a^3b^4$ by $2a^3 + 3a^2b - b^3$ to *four terms* in the quotient.

$$\begin{array}{r|rrrr}
2 & 2 + 7 + 12 + 10 & -4a^3b^4 + 0\,a^2b^5 + 0\,ab^6 \\
-3 & -3 + 0 + 1 \\
0 & - 6 + 0 & +2 \\
1 & - 9 & +0 & +3 \\
 & & -3 & +0 & +1 \\
\hline
\text{Quotient} & 1 + 2 + 3 + 1 & -5 & +3 & +1
\end{array}$$

Inserting literal factors, $a^4 + 2a^3b + 3a^2b^2 + ab^3$ is the complete quotient, and $-5a^3b^4 + 3a^2b^5 + ab^5$ is the remainder.

EXPLANATION. The term ab^2 in the divisor is missing, so we write 0 for the coefficient of this term in the column of figures on the left of the vertical line. We add the columns as in Ex. 1, but as the first term of the divisor is 2, *we divide each sum by 2 before placing the result in the line of quotients*. We then use these quotients as multipliers, the multiplicand being in each case -3, 0, and 1, and form the horizontal lines as in Ex. 1. Having obtained the required number of terms in the *quotient*, the remainder is found by adding the rest of the columns and setting down the results *without dividing by* 2. By continuing the first horizontal line (dividend), as shown in this example, we at once see what literal factors the remainder must contain.

EXAMPLES V. d.

Divide:

1. $a^4 - 4a^3 + 2a^2 + 4a + 1$ by $a^2 - 2a - 1$.

2. $a^4 - 4a^3b + 6a^2b^2 + b^4 - 4ab^3$ by $a^2 + b^2 - 2ab$.

3. $a^5 - 10a^4b + 16a^3b^2 - 12a^2b^3 + ab^4 + 2b^5$ by $(a-b)^2$.

4. $x^8 - 2b^4x^4 + b^8$ by $x^3 + bx^2 + b^2x + b^3$.

5. $x^5 - 3x^2y^3 + 8xy^4 - 5y^5$ by $x^2 - 4xy + y^2$ to four terms in the quotient.

CHAPTER VI.

REMOVAL AND INSERTION OF BRACKETS.

64. We frequently find it necessary to enclose within brackets part of an expression already enclosed within brackets. For this purpose it is usual to employ brackets of different forms. The brackets in common use are ( ), { }, [ ]. Sometimes a line called a **vinculum** is drawn over the symbols to be connected; thus $a - \overline{b + c}$ is used with the same meaning as $a - (b + c)$, and hence

$$a - \overline{b + c} = a - b - c.$$

65. To **remove brackets** it is usually best to begin with the inside pair, and in dealing with each pair in succession we apply the rules already given in Arts. 25, 26.

Ex. 1. Simplify, by removing brackets, the expression
$$a - 2b - [4a - 6b - \{3a - c + (5a - 2b - \overline{3a - c + 2b})\}].$$

Removing the brackets one by one, we have
$$a - 2b - [4a - 6b - \{3a - c + (5a - 2b - 3a + c - 2b)\}]$$
$$= a - 2b - [4a - 6b - \{3a - c + 5a - 2b - 3a + c - 2b\}]$$
$$= a - 2b - [4a - 6b - 3a + c - 5a + 2b + 3a - c + 2b]$$
$$= a - 2b - 4a + 6b + 3a - c + 5a - 2b - 3a + c - 2b$$
$$= 2a, \text{ by collecting like terms.}$$

Ex. 2. Simplify the expression
$$-[-2x - \{3y - (2x - 3y) + (3x - 2y)\} + 2x].$$

The expression $= -[-2x - \{3y - 2x + 3y + 3x - 2y\} + 2x]$
$$= -[-2x - 3y + 2x - 3y - 3x + 2y + 2x]$$
$$= 2x + 3y - 2x + 3y + 3x - 2y - 2x$$
$$= x + 4y.$$

REMOVAL AND INSERTION OF BRACKETS.

EXAMPLES VI. a.

Simplify by removing brackets:

1. $a - (b - c) + a + (b - c) + b - (c + a)$.
2. $a - [b + \{a - (b + a)\}]$.
3. $a - [2a - \{3b - (4c - 2a)\}]$
4. $\{a - (b - c)\} + \{b - (c - a)\} - \{c - (a - b)\}$.
5. $2a - (5b + [3c - a]) - (5a - [b + c])$.
6. $-\{-[-(a - \overline{b - c})]\}$.
7. $-(-(-(-x))) - (-(-y))$.
8. $-[a - \{b - (c - a)\}] - [b - \{c - (a - b)\}]$.
9. $-[-\{-(b + c - a)\}] + [-\{-(c + a - b)\}]$.
10. $-5x - [3y - \{2x - (2y - x)\}]$.
11. $-(-(-a)) - (-(-(-x)))$.
12. $3a - [a + b - \{a + b + c - (a + b + c + d)\}]$.
13. $-2a - [3x + \{3c - (4y + 3x + 2a)\}]$.
14. $3x - [5y - \{6z - (4x - 7y)\}]$.
15. $-[5x - (11y - 3x)] - [5y - (3x - 6y)]$.
16. $-[15x - \{14y - (15z + 12y) - (10x - 15z)\}]$.
17. $8x - \{16y - [3x - (12y - x) - 8y] + x\}$.
18. $-[x - \{z + (x - z) - (z - x) - z\} - x]$.
19. $-[a + \{a - (a - x) - (a + x) - a\} - a]$.
20. $-[a - \{a + (x - a) - (x - a) - a\} - 2a]$.

66. A coefficient placed before any bracket indicates that every term of the expression within the bracket is to be multiplied by that coefficient.

NOTE. The line between the numerator and denominator of a fraction is a kind of vinculum. Thus $\dfrac{x - 5}{3}$ is equivalent to $\tfrac{1}{3}(x - 5)$.

Again, an expression of the form $\sqrt{(x + y)}$ is often written $\sqrt{x + y}$, the line above being regarded as a vinculum indicating the square root of the compound expression $x + y$ *taken as a whole*.

Thus $\sqrt{25 + 144} = \sqrt{169} = 13$,
whereas $\sqrt{25} + \sqrt{144} = 5 + 12 = 17$.

67. Sometimes it is advisable to simplify in the course of the work.

Ex. Find the value of
$$84 - 7[-11x - 4\{-17x + 3(8 - \overline{9 - 5x})\}].$$

The expression $= 84 - 7[-11x - 4\{-17x + 3(8 - 9 + 5x)\}]$
$= 84 - 7[-11x - 4\{-17x + 3(5x - 1)\}]$
$= 84 - 7[-11x - 4\{-17x + 15x - 3\}]$
$= 84 - 7[-11x - 4\{-2x - 3\}]$
$= 84 - 7[-11x + 8x + 12]$
$= 84 - 7[-3x + 12]$
$= 84 + 21x - 84$
$= 21x.$

When the beginner has had a little practice, the number of steps may be considerably diminished.

EXAMPLES VI. b.

Simplify by removing brackets:

1. $a - [2b + \{3c - 3a - (a + b)\} + 2a - (b + 3c)]$.
2. $a + b - (c + a - [b + c - (a + b - \{c + a - (b + c - a)\})])$.
3. $a - (b - c) - [a - b - c - 2\{b + c - 3(c - a) - d\}]$.
4. $2x - (3y - 4z) - \{2x - (3y + 4z)\} - \{3y - (4z + 2x)\}$.
5. $b + c - (a + b - [c + a - (b + c - \{a + b - (c + a - b)\})])$.
6. $a - (b - c) - [a - b - c - 2\{b + c\}]$.
7. $3a^2 - [6a^2 - \{8b^2 - (9c^2 - 2a^2)\}]$.
8. $b - (c - a) - [b - a - c - 2\{c + a - 3(a - b) - d\}]$.
9. $-20(a - d) + 3(b - c) - 2[b + c + d - 3\{c + d - 4(d - a)\}]$.
10. $-4(a + d) + 24(b - c) - 2[c + d + a - 3\{d + a - 4(b + c)\}]$
11. $-10(a + b) - [c + a + b - 3\{a + 2b - (c + a - b)\}] + 4c.$
12. $a - 2(b - c) - [-\{-(4a - b - c - 2\{a + b + c\})\}]$.
13. $2(3b - 5a) - 7[a - 6\{2 - 5(a - b)\}]$.
14. $6\{a - 2[b - 3(c + d)]\} - 4\{a - 3[b - 4(c - d)]\}$.
15. $5\{a - 2[a - 2(a + x)]\} - 4\{a - 2[a - 2(a + x)]\}$.
16. $-10\{a - 6[a - (b - c)]\} + 60\{b - (c + a)\}$.
17. $-3\{-2[-4(-a)]\} + 5\{-2[-2(-a)]\}$.
18. $-2\{-[-(x - y)]\} + \{-2[-(x - y)]\}$.

REMOVAL AND INSERTION OF BRACKETS. 51

19. $\frac{1}{4}\{a - 5(b - a)\} - \frac{3}{2}\{\frac{1}{3}(b - \frac{a}{3}) - \frac{2}{9}[a - \frac{3}{4}(b - \frac{4a}{5})]\}$.

20. $35\left[\frac{3x - 4y}{5} - \frac{1}{10}\{3x - \frac{1}{2}(7x - 4y)\}\right] + 8(y - 2x)$.

21. $\frac{2}{3}\{\frac{1}{2}(a - b) - 3(b - c)\} - \{\frac{b - c}{2} - \frac{c - a}{3}\} - \frac{1}{2}\{c - a - \frac{2}{3}(a - b)\}$

22. $\frac{1}{2}x - \frac{1}{2}(\frac{2}{3}y - \frac{1}{4}z) - [x - \{\frac{1}{2}x - (\frac{2}{3}y - \frac{1}{4}z)\} - (\frac{2}{3}y - \frac{1}{4}z)]$.

INSERTION OF BRACKETS.

68. The converse operation of inserting brackets is important. The rules for doing this have been enunciated in Arts. 25, 26; for convenience we repeat them.

Rule I. *Any part of an expression may be enclosed within brackets and the sign + prefixed, the sign of every term within the brackets remaining unaltered.*

Ex. $\quad a - b + c - d - e = a - b + (c - d - e)$.

Rule II. *Any part of an expression may be enclosed within brackets and the sign − prefixed, provided the sign of every term within the brackets be changed.*

Ex. $\quad a - b + c - d - e = a - (b - c) - (d + e)$.

69. The terms of an expression can be bracketed in various ways.

Ex. The expression $ax - bx + cx - ay + by - cy$
may be written $\quad (ax - bx) + (cx - ay) + (by - cy)$,
or $\quad (ax - bx + cx) - (ay - by + cy)$,
or $\quad (ax - ay) - (bx - by) + (cx - cy)$.

70. A factor, common to every term within a bracket, may be removed and placed outside as a multiplier of the expression within the bracket.

Ex. 1. In the expression
$$ax^3 - cx + 7 - dx^2 + bx - c - dx^3 + bx^2 - 2x$$
bracket together the powers of x so as to have the sign + before each bracket.

The expression $= (ax^3 - dx^3) + (bx^2 - dx^2) + (bx - cx - 2x) + (7 - c)$,
$= x^3(a - d) + x^2(b - d) + x(b - c - 2) + (7 - c)$
$= (a - d)x^3 + (b - d)x^2 + (b - c - 2)x + 7 - c.$

In this last result the compound expressions $a - d$, $b - d$, $b - c - 2$ are regarded as the coefficients of x^3, x^2, and x respectively.

Ex. 2. In the expression $-a^2x - 7a + a^2y + 3 - 2x - ab$ bracket together the powers of a so as to have the sign $-$ before each bracket.

The expression $= -(a^2x - a^2y) - (7a + ab) - (2x - 3)$
$= -a^2(x - y) - a(7 + b) - (2x - 3)$
$= -(x - y)a^2 - (7 + b)a - (2x - 3).$

EXAMPLES VI. c.

In the following expressions bracket the powers of x so that the signs before all the brackets shall be positive:

1. $ax^4 + bx^2 + 5 + 2bx - 5x^2 + 2x^4 - 3x.$
2. $3bx^2 - 7 - 2x + ab + 5ax^3 + cx - 4x^3 - bx^2.$
3. $2 - 7x^3 + 5ax^2 - 2cx + 9ax^3 + 7x - 3x^2.$

In the following expressions bracket the powers of x so that the signs before all the brackets shall be negative:

4. $ax^2 + 5x^3 - a^2x^4 - 2bx^3 - 3x^2 - bx^4.$
5. $7x^3 - 3c^2x - bx^5 + 5ax + 7x^5 - abcx^3.$
6. $3b^2x^4 - bx - ax^4 - cx^4 - 5c^2x - 7x^4.$

Simplify the following expressions, and in each result regroup the terms according to powers of x:

7. $ax^3 - 2cx - [bx^2 - \{cx - dx - (bx^3 + 3cx^2)\} - (cx^2 - bx)].$
8. $5ax^3 - 7(bx - cx^2) - \{6bx^2 - (3ax^2 + 2ax) - 4cx^3\}.$
9. $ax^2 - 3\{-ax^3 + 3bx - 4[\tfrac{1}{6}cx^3 - \tfrac{2}{3}(ax - bx^2)]\}.$
10. $x^5 - 4bx^4 - \tfrac{1}{6}\left[12ax - 4\left\{3bx^4 - 9\left(\dfrac{cx}{2} - bx^5\right) - \tfrac{3}{4}ax^4\right\}\right].$

71. In certain cases of addition, multiplication, etc., of expressions which involve literal coefficients, the results may be more conveniently written by grouping the terms according to powers of some common letter.

Ex. 1. Add together $ax^3 - 2bx^2 + 3$, $bx - cx^3 - x^2$, and $x^3 - ax^2 + cx$.

The sum $= ax^3 - 2bx^2 + 3 + bx - cx^3 - x^2 + x^3 - ax^2 + cx$
$= ax^3 - cx^3 + x^3 - ax^2 - 2bx^2 - x^2 + bx + cx + 3$
$= (a - c + 1)x^3 - (a + 2b + 1)x^2 + (b + c)x + 3.$

Ex. 2. Multiply $ax^2 - 2bx + 3c$ by $px - q$.
The product $= (ax^2 - 2bx + 3c)(px - q)$
$= apx^3 - 2bpx^2 + 3cpx - aqx^2 + 2bqx - 3cq$
$= apx^3 - (2bp + aq)x^2 + (3cp + 2bq)x - 3cq.$

EXAMPLES VI. d.

Add together the following expressions, and in each case arrange the result according to powers of x:

1. $ax^3 - 2cx$, $bx^2 - cx^3$, and $cx^2 - x$.
2. $x^2 - x - 1$, $ax^2 - bx^3$, $bx + x^3$.
3. $a^2x^3 - 5x$, $2ax^2 - 5ax^3$, $2x^3 - bx^2 - ax$.
4. $ax^2 + bx - c$, $qx - r - px^2$, $x^2 + 2x + 3$.
5. $px^3 - qx$, $qx^2 - px$, $q - x^3$, $px^2 + qx^3$.

Multiply together the following expressions, and in each case arrange the result according to powers of x:

6. $ax^2 + bx + 1$ and $cx + 2$.
7. $cx^2 - 2x + 3$ and $ax - b$.
8. $ax^2 - bx - c$ and $px + q$.
9. $2x^2 - 3x - 1$ and $bx + c$.
10. $ax^2 - 2bx + 3c$ and $x - 1$.
11. $px^2 - 2x - q$ and $ax - 3$.
12. $x^3 + ax^2 - bx - c$ and $x^3 - ax^2 - bx + c$.
13. $ax^3 - x^2 + 3x - b$ and $ax^3 + x^2 + 3x + b$.
14. $x^4 - ax^3 - bx^2 + cx + d$ and $x^4 + ax^3 - bx^2 - cx + d$.

MISCELLANEOUS EXAMPLES II.

1. Find value of $(a - b)^2 + (b - c)^2 + (a - b) + 2c^2$ when $a = 1$, $b = 2$, $c = -3$.

2. Find the sum of $2x$, $3x^2$, 5, $-3x^3$, -4, x, $-6x^2$, $8x^3$, arranging result in descending powers.

3. Diminish the sum of $b^3 + 7b^2 - 5$ and $4b^2 - 3b + 7$ by $11b^2 + 2$.

4. Show that $(1+x)^2(1+y^2) - (1+x^2)(1+y)^2 = 2(x-y)(1-xy)$.

5. Simplify $(a + b)(a + c) - (a - b)(a - c)$.

6. Subtract the sum of $3m^3 - 4m + 1$ and $m^2 - 3m$ from $4m^3 + 2m^2 - 7m$.

7. What expression must be taken from the sum of $a + 3b$, $4a^2 - 5a$, $b^2 + 2a$, $2a - 3b^2$ in order to produce $a^2 - b^2$?

8. Find value of $a^2 + (c+d)\left(\sqrt{\left(\dfrac{ad}{c}\right)} + d\right)$ when $a=2$, $c=9$, $d=8$.

9. Multiply $a^2 + (b-c)^2$ by $b + c + 1$.

10. Divide $343 x^3 + 512 y^3$ by $7x + 8y$.

11. If $a = 1$, $b = 2$, $c = 3$, $d = 4$, find the value of
$$a + [(b-c)(2d-b)] - \left(\frac{\sqrt{(2ad-b^2)}}{d} - 4c\right).$$

12. What number must be added to $2x^2 - 3xy^2 + 6$ to produce $7x^2 + \frac{1}{3}xy^2 - x^2y + 5$?

13. Simplify $(x-y) - \{3x - (x+y)\} + \{(2x - 3y) - (x - 2y)\}$.

14. Show that $a(a-1)(a-2)(a-3) = (a^2 - 3a + 1)^2 - 1$.

15. $x^4 - 10x^2 + 9 \div x^2 - 2x - 3$.

16. Simplify $9a - (2b - c) + 2d - (5a + 3b) + 4c - 2d$, and find its value when $a = 7$, $b = -3$, $c = -4$.

17. Multiply $3a^2b - 4ab^3c + 2a^3b^2c^3$ by $-6a^2b^2c^3$, and divide the result by $3ab^2c^2$.

18. If $a = -1$, $b = 2$, $c = 0$, $d = 1$, find the value of
$$ad + ac - a^2 - cd + c^2 - a + 2c + a^2b + 2a^3.$$

19. Find the sum of $3a + 2b$, $-5c - 2d$, $3e + 5f$, $b - a + 2d$, $-2a - 3b + 5c - 2f$.

20. Subtract $ax^2 - 4$ from zero, and add the difference to the sum of $2x^3 - 5x$ and unity.

21. Multiply $\frac{1}{8}x^2 + \frac{1}{3}xy - \frac{1}{2}y^2$ by $\frac{1}{10}x^2 - \frac{1}{2}xy + \frac{2}{3}y^2$.

22. Divide $6a^4 - a^3b + 2a^2b^2 + 13ab^3 + 4b^4$ by $2a^2 - 3ab + 4b^2$.

23. Simplify $5x^4 - 8x^3 - (2x^2 - 7) - (x^4 + 5) + (3x^3 - x)$, and subtract the result from $4x^4 - x + 2$.

24. Simplify by removing brackets $5[x - 4\{x - 3(2x - \overline{3x+2})\}]$.

25. If $a = 1$, $b = 2$, $c = 3$, and $d = 4$, find value of
$$(c+d)(a-cd) + \sqrt{\frac{ab(cd+bcd)+c^2}{bd(b+c+d-a)}}.$$

26. Express by means of symbols
   (1) b's excess over c is greater than a by 7.
   (2) Three times the sum of a and $2b$ is less by 5 than the product of b and c.

27. Simplify
$$3a^2 - (4a - b^2) - \{2a^2 - (3b - a^2) - \overline{2b - 3a}\} - \{5b - 7a - (c^2 - b^2)\}.$$

28. Find the continued product of
$$x^2 + xy + y^2,\ x^2 - xy + y^2,\ x^4 - x^2y^2 + y^4.$$

CHAPTER VII.

SIMPLE EQUATIONS.

72. An **equation** asserts that two expressions are equal, but we do not usually employ the word equation in so wide a sense.

Thus the statement $x + 3 + x = 2x + 3$, which is *always* true whatever value x may have, is called an **identical equation**, or an **identity**. The **sign of identity** frequently used is $\equiv$.

The parts of an equation to the right and left of the sign of equality are called **members** or **sides** of the equation, and are distinguished as the *right side* and *left side*.

73. Certain equations are only true for particular values of the symbols employed. Thus $3x = 6$ is only true when $x = 2$, and is called an **equation of condition**, or more usually an **equation**. Consequently an **identity** is an equation which is *always* true whatever be the values of the symbols involved; whereas an **equation**, in the ordinary use of the word, is only true for *particular* values of the symbols. In the above example $3x = 6$, the value 2 is said to **satisfy** the equation. The object of the present chapter is to explain how to treat an equation of the simplest kind in order to discover the value which satisfies it.

74. The letter whose value it is required to find is called the **unknown quantity**. The process of finding its value is called **solving the equation**. The value so found is called the **root** or the **solution** of the equation.

75. The solution of equations, and the operations subsidiary to it, form an extremely important part of Mathematics. All sorts of mathematical problems consist in the indirect determination of some quantity by means of its relations to other quantities which are known, and these relations are all expressed by means of equations. The operation in general of solving a problem in Mathematics, other than a transformation, is first, to express the conditions of the problem by means of one or more equations, and secondly, to solve these equations. For example, the problem which is expressed by the equation above given is the very simple question, "What is the number such that if multiplied by 3, the product is 6?" In the present chapter, it is the second of these two operations, the solution of an equation, that is considered.

76. An equation which involves the unknown quantity in the **first degree** is called a **simple equation**.

The process of solving a simple equation depends upon the following **axioms**:

1. If to equals we add equals, the sums are equal.
2. If from equals we take equals, the remainders are equal.
3. If equals are multiplied by equals, the products are equal.
4. If equals are divided by equals, the quotients are equal.

77. Consider the equation $7x = 14$.

It is required to find what numerical value x must have consistent with this statement.

Dividing both sides by 7, we get
$$x = 2 \quad \ldots \ldots \quad \text{(Axiom 4)}.$$

Similarly, if $\dfrac{x}{2} = -6$,

multiplying both sides by 2, we get
$$x = -12 \quad \ldots \ldots \quad \text{(Axiom 3)}.$$

Again, in the equation $7x - 2x - x = 23 + 15 - 10$, by collecting terms, we have $4x = 28$.
$$\therefore x = 7.$$

SIMPLE EQUATIONS.

TRANSPOSITION OF TERMS.

78. To solve $3x - 8 = x + 12$.

Here the unknown quantity occurs on both sides of the equation. We can, however, **transpose** any term from one side to the other by simply *changing its sign*. This we proceed to show.

Subtract x from both sides of the equation, and we get
$$3x - x - 8 = 12 \quad \ldots \quad \text{(Axiom 2)}.$$
Adding 8 to both sides, we have
$$3x - x = 12 + 8 \quad \ldots \quad \text{(Axiom 1)}.$$

Thus we see that $+x$ has been removed from one side, and appears as $-x$ on the other; and -8 has been removed from one side and appears as $+8$ on the other.

It is evident that similar steps may be employed in all cases. Hence we may enunciate the following rule:

Rule. *Any term may be transposed from one side of the equation to the other by changing its sign.*

79. We may **change the sign of every term** in an equation; for this is equivalent to multiplying both sides by -1, which does not destroy the equality (Axiom 3).

Ex. Take the equation $\quad -3x - 12 = x - 24$.
Multiplying both sides by -1, $3x + 12 = -x + 24$,
which is the original equation with the sign of every term changed.

80. We can now give a general rule for solving a simple equation with one unknown quantity.

Rule. *Transpose all the terms containing the unknown quantity to one side of the equation, and the known quantities to the other. Collect the terms on each side; divide both sides by the coefficient of the unknown quantity, and the value required is obtained.*

Ex. 1. Solve $5(x - 3) - 7(6 - x) + 3 = 24 - 3(8 - x)$.
Removing brackets, $5x - 15 - 42 + 7x + 3 = 24 - 24 + 3x$;
transposing, $\quad 5x + 7x - 3x = 24 - 24 + 15 + 42 - 3$;
collecting terms, $\quad 9x = 54$.
$\therefore x = 6$.

Ex. 2. Solve $5x - (4x-7)(3x-5) = 6 - 3(4x-9)(x-1)$.

Simplifying, we have
$$5x - (12x^2 - 41x + 35) = 6 - 3(4x^2 - 13x + 9),$$
and by removing brackets,
$$5x - 12x^2 + 41x - 35 = 6 - 12x^2 + 39x - 27.$$

Erase the term $-12x^2$ on each side and transpose;

thus $\qquad 5x + 41x - 39x = 6 - 27 + 35;$

collecting terms, $\qquad 7x = 14.$

$\qquad\qquad\qquad \therefore x = 2.$

NOTE. Since the $-$ sign before a bracket affects every term within it, in the first line of work of Ex. 2, we do not remove the brackets until we have formed the products.

Ex. 3. Solve $7x - 5[x - \{7 - 6(x-3)\}] = 3x + 1$.

Removing brackets, we have
$$7x - 5[x - \{7 - 6x + 18\}] = 3x + 1,$$
$$7x - 5[x - 25 + 6x] = 3x + 1,$$
$$7x - 5x + 125 - 30x = 3x + 1;$$

transposing, $\qquad 7x - 5x - 30x - 3x = 1 - 125;$

collecting terms, $\qquad -31x = -124;$

$\qquad\qquad\qquad \therefore x = 4.$

81. It is extremely useful for the beginner to acquire the habit of occasionally **verifying**, that is, proving the truth of his results. Proofs of this kind are interesting and convincing; and the habit of applying such tests tends to make the student self-reliant and confident in his own accuracy.

In the case of simple equations we have only to show that when we substitute the value of x in the two sides of the equation we obtain the same result.

Ex. To show that $x = 2$ *satisfies* the equation
$5x - (4x-7)(3x-5) = 6 - 3(4x-9)(x-1).$ Ex. 2, Art. 80.

When $x=2$, the left side $5x-(4x-7)(3x-5) = 10 - (8-7)(6-5)$
$$= 10 - 1 = 9.$$

The right side $6 - 3(4x-9)(x-1) = 6 - 3(8-9)(2-1)$
$$= 6 - 3(-1) = 9.$$

Thus, since these two results are the same, $x = 2$ satisfies the equation.

SIMPLE EQUATIONS.

EXAMPLES VII.

Solve the following equations:

1. $3x + 15 = x + 25$.
2. $2x - 3 = 3x - 7$.
3. $3x + 4 = 5(x - 2)$.
4. $2x + 3 = 16 - (2x - 3)$
5. $8(x - 1) + 17(x - 3) = 4(4x - 9) + 4$.
6. $15(x - 1) + 4(x + 3) = 2(7 + x)$.
7. $5x - 6(x - 5) = 2(x + 5) + 5(x - 4)$.
8. $8(x - 3) - (6 - 2x) = 2(x + 2) - 5(5 - x)$.
9. $7(25 - x) - 2x = 2(3x - 25)$.
10. $3(169 - x) - (78 + x) = 29x$.
11. $5x - 17 + 3x - 5 = 6x - 7 - 8x + 115$.
12. $7x - 39 - 10x + 15 = 100 - 33x + 26$.
13. $118 - 65x - 123 = 15x + 35 - 120x$.
14. $157 - 21(x + 3) = 163 - 15(2x - 5)$.
15. $179 - 18(x - 10) = 158 - 3(x - 17)$.
16. $97 - 5(x + 20) = 111 - 8(x + 3)$.
17. $x - [3 + \{x - (3 + x)\}] = 5$.
18. $5x - (3x - 7) - \{4 - 2x - (6x - 3)\} = 10$.
19. $14x - (5x - 9) - \{4 - 3x - (2x - 3)\} = 30$.
20. $25x - 19 - [3 - \{4x - 5\}] = 3x - (6x - 5)$.
21. $(x + 1)(2x + 1) = (x + 3)(2x + 3) - 14$.
22. $(x + 1)^2 - (x^2 - 1) = x(2x + 1) - 2(x + 2)(x + 1) + 20$.
23. $2(x + 1)(x + 3) + 8 = (2x + 1)(x + 5)$.
24. $6(x^2 - 3x + 2) - 2(x^2 - 1) = 4(x + 1)(x + 2) - 24$.
25. $2(x - 4) - (x^2 + x - 20) = 4x^2 - (5x + 3)(x - 4) - 64$.
26. $(x + 15)(x - 3) - (x^2 - 6x + 9) = 30 - 15(x - 1)$.
27. $2x - 5\{3x - 7(4x - 9)\} = 66$.
28. $20(2 - x) + 3(x - 7) - 2[x + 9 - 3\{9 - 4(2 - x)\}] = 22$.
29. $x + 2 - [x - 8 - 2\{8 - 3(5 - x) - x\}] = 0$.
30. $3(5 - 6x) - 5[x - 5\{1 - 3(x - 5)\}] = 23$.
31. $(x + 1)(2x + 3) = 2(x + 1)^2 + 8$.
32. $3(x - 1)^2 - 3(x^2 - 1) = x - 15$.
33. $(3x + 1)(2x - 7) = 6(x - 3)^2 + 7$.
34. $x^2 - 8x + 25 = x(x - 4) - 25(x - 5) - 16$.
35. $x(x + 1) + (x + 1)(x + 2) = (x + 2)(x + 3) + x(x + 4) - 2$.
36. $2(x + 2)(x - 4) = x(2x + 1) - 21$.
37. $(x + 1)^2 + 2(x + 3)^2 = 3x(x + 2) + 35$.
38. $4(x + 5)^2 - (2x + 1)^2 = 3(x - 5) + 180$.
39. $84 + (x + 4)(x - 3)(x + 5) = (x + 1)(x + 2)(x + 3)$.
40. $(x + 1)(x + 2)(x + 6) = x^3 + 9x^2 + 4(7x - 1)$.

CHAPTER VIII.

Symbolical Expression.

82. In solving algebraic problems the chief difficulty of the beginner is to express the conditions of the question by means of symbols. A question proposed in algebraic symbols will frequently be found puzzling, when a similar arithmetical question would present no difficulty. Thus, the answer to the question "find a number greater than x by a" may not be self-evident to the beginner, who would of course readily answer an analogous arithmetical question, "find a number greater than 50 by 6." The process of addition which gives the answer in the second case supplies the necessary hint; and, just as the number which is greater than 50 by 6 is $50 + 6$, so the number which is greater than x by a is $x + a$.

83. The following examples will perhaps be the best introduction to the subject of this chapter. After the first we leave to the student the choice of arithmetical instances, should he find them necessary.

Ex. 1. By how much does x exceed 17 ?
Take a numerical instance; "by how much does 27 exceed 17 ?"
The answer obviously is 10, which is equal to $27 - 17$.
Hence the excess of x over 17 is $x - 17$.
Similarly the defect of x from 17 is $17 - x$.

Ex. 2. If x is one *part* of 45 the other part is $45 - x$.

Ex. 3. How far can a man walk in a hours at the rate of 4 miles an hour?
In 1 hour he walks 4 miles.
In a hours he walks a times as far, that is, $4a$ miles.

Ex. 4. A and B are playing for money; A begins with \$$p$ and B with q dimes: after B has won \$$x$, how many dimes has each?

What B has won A has lost,

$\therefore$ A has $10(p - x)$ dimes,

B has $q + 10x$ dimes.

EXAMPLES VIII. a.

1. What must be added to x to make y?

2. By what must 3 be multiplied to make a?

3. What dividend gives b as the quotient when 5 is the divisor?

4. What is the defect of $2c$ from $3d$.

5. By how much does $3k$ exceed k?

6. If 100 be divided into two parts, and one part be x, what is the other?

7. What number is less than 20 by c?

8. What is the price in cents of a oranges at ten cents a dozen?

9. If the difference of two numbers be 11, and if the smaller be x, what is the greater?

10. If the sum of two numbers be c, and one of them is 20, what is the other?

11. What is the excess of 90 over x?

12. By how much does x exceed 30?

13. If 100 contains x 5 times, what is the value of x.

14. What is the cost in dollars of 40 books at x dimes each?

15. In x years a man will be 36 years old, what is his present age?

16. How old will a man be in a years if his present age is x years?

17. If x men take 5 days to reap a field, how long will one man take?

18. What value of x will make $5x$ equal to 20?

19. What is the price in dimes of 120 apples, when the cost of two dozen is x cents?

20. How many hours will it take to walk x miles at 4 miles an hour?

21. How far can I walk in x hours at the rate of y miles an hour?

22. How many miles is it between two places, if a train travelling p miles an hour takes 5 hours to perform the journey?

23. A man has a dollars and b dimes, how many cents has he?

24. If I spend x half-dollars out of a sum of $20, how many half-dollars have I left?

25. Out of a purse containing a and b dimes a man spends c cents; express in cents the sum left.

26. By how much does $2x - 5$ exceed $x + 1$?

27. What number must be taken from $a - 2b$ to leave $a - 3b$?

28. If a bill is shared equally amongst x persons, and each pays four dimes, how many cents does the bill amount to?

29. If I give away c dimes out of a purse containing a dollars and b half-dollars, how many dimes have I left?

30. If I spend x quarters a week, how many dollars do I save out of a yearly income of $$y$?

31. A bookshelf contains x Latin, y Greek, and z English books; if there are 100 books, how many are there in other languages?

32. I have x dollars in my purse, y dimes in one pocket, and z cents in another; if I give away a half-dollar, how many cents have I left?

33. In a class of x boys, y work at Classics, z at Mathematics, and the rest are idle; what is the excess of workers over idlers?

84. We add a few harder examples worked out in full.

Ex. 1. What is the present age of a man who x years hence will be m times as old as his son now aged y years?

In x years the son's age will be $y + x$ years; hence the father's age will be $m(y + x)$ years; therefore *now* the father's age is $m(y + x) - x$ years.

Ex. 2. Find the simple interest on $$k$ in n years at f per cent.

Interest on $100 for 1 year is $$f$,

∴ . . . . $1 . . . . $$\dfrac{f}{100}$,

∴ . . . . $$k$ . . . . $$\dfrac{kf}{100}$,

∴ Interest on $$k$ for n years is $$\dfrac{nkf}{100}$.

Ex. 3. A room is x yards long, y feet broad, and a feet high; find how many square yards of carpet will be required for the floor, and how many square yards of paper for the walls.

SYMBOLICAL EXPRESSION.

(1) The area of the floor is $3xy$ square feet;

∴ the number of square yards of carpet required is $\dfrac{3xy}{9} = \dfrac{xy}{3}$.

(2) The perimeter of the room is $2(3x + y)$ feet;

∴ the area of the walls is $2a(3x + y)$ square feet;

∴ number of square yards of paper required is $\dfrac{2a(3x + y)}{9}$.

Ex. 4. The digits of a number beginning from the left are a, b, c; what is the number?

Here c is the digit in the units' place; b standing in the tens' place represents b tens; similarly a represents a hundreds.

The number is therefore equal to a hundreds $+ b$ tens $+ c$ units
$$= 100a + 10b + c.$$

If the digits of the number are inverted, a new number is formed which is symbolically expressed by
$$100c + 10b + a.$$

Ex. 5. What is (1) the sum, (2) the product of three consecutive numbers of which the least is n?

The numbers consecutive to n are $n+1, n+2$.

∴ the sum $= n + (n+1) + (n+2)$
$$= 3n + 3.$$

And the product $= n(n+1)(n+2)$.

We may remark here that any *even* number may be denoted by $2n$, where n is *any* positive whole number; for this expression is exactly divisible by 2.

Similarly, any odd number may be denoted by $2n + 1$; for this expression when divided by 2 leaves remainder 1.

EXAMPLES VIII. b.

1. Write four consecutive numbers of which x is the least.
2. Write three consecutive numbers of which y is the greatest.
3. Write five consecutive numbers of which x is the middle one.
4. What is the next even number after $2n$?
5. What is the odd number next before $2x + 1$?
6. Find the sum of three consecutive odd numbers of which the middle one is $2n + 1$.

7. A man makes a journey of x miles. He travels a miles by coach, b by train, and finishes the journey by boat. How far does the boat carry him?

8. A horse eats a bushels and a donkey b bushels of corn in a week; how many bushels will they together consume in n weeks?

9. If a man was x years old 5 years ago, how old will he be y years hence?

10. A boy is x years old, and five years hence his age will be half that of his father. How old is the father now?

11. What is the age of a man who y years ago was m times as old as a child then aged x years?

12. A's age is double B's, B's is three times C's, and C is x years old : find A's age.

13. What is the interest on $1000 in b years at c per cent. ?

14. What is the interest on $$x$ in a years at 5 per cent. ?

15. What is the interest on 50a$ in a years at a per cent. ?

16. What is the interest on 24xy$ in x months at y per cent. per annum?

17. A room is x yards in length, and y feet in breadth; how many square feet are there in the area of the floor?

18. A square room measures x feet each way; how many square yards of carpet will be required to cover it?

19. A room is p feet long and x yards in width; how many yards of carpet two feet wide will be required for the floor?

20. What is cost in dollars of carpeting a room a yards long, b feet broad, with carpet costing c dimes a square yard?

21. A room is a yards long and b yards broad; in the middle there is a carpet c feet square; how many square yards of oil-cloth will be required to cover the rest of the floor?

22. How long will it take a person to walk b miles if he walks 20 miles in c hours?

23. A train is running with a velocity of x feet per second; how many miles will it travel in y hours?

24. How many men will be required to do in x hours what y men do in xz hours?

CHAPTER IX.

Problems Leading to Simple Equations.

85. The principles of the last chapter may now be employed to solve various problems.

The method of procedure is as follows:

Represent the unknown quantity by a symbol, as x, and express in symbolical language the conditions of the question; we thus obtain a simple equation which can be solved by the methods already given in Chapter VII.

NOTE. Unknown quantities are usually represented by the last letters of the alphabet.

Ex. 1. Find two numbers whose sum is 28, and whose difference is 4.

Let x represent the smaller number, then $x + 4$ represents the greater.

Their sum is $x + (x + 4)$, which is to be equal to 28.

Hence $$x + x + 4 = 28;$$
$$2x = 24;$$
$$\therefore x = 12,$$
and $$x + 4 = 16,$$
so that the numbers are 12 and 16.

The beginner is advised to test his solution by proving that it *satisfies* the conditions of the question.

Ex. 2. Divide 60 into two parts, so that three times the greater may exceed 100 by as much as 8 times the less falls short of 200.

Let x represent the greater part, then $60 - x$ represents the less

Three times the greater part is $3x$, and its excess over 100 is
$$3x - 100.$$

Eight times the less is $8(60 - x)$, and its defect from 200 is
$$200 - 8(60 - x).$$

Whence the symbolical statement of the question is
$$3x - 100 = 200 - 8(60 - x);$$
$$3x - 100 = 200 - 480 + 8x,$$
$$480 - 100 - 200 = 8x - 3x,$$
$$5x = 180;$$
$$\therefore x = 36, \text{ the greater part,}$$
and $60 - x = 24$, the less.

Ex. 3. Divide \$47 between A, B, C, so that A may have \$10 more than B, and B \$8 more than C.

Suppose that C has x dollars; then B has $x + 8$ dollars, and A has $x + 8 + 10$ dollars.

Hence
$$x + (x + 8) + (x + 8 + 10) = 47;$$
$$x + x + 8 + x + 8 + 10 = 47,$$
$$3x = 21;$$
$$\therefore x = 7,$$

so that C has \$7, B \$15, A \$25.

Ex. 4. A person spent \$112.80 in buying geese and ducks; if each goose cost 14 dimes, and each duck 6 dimes, and if the total number of birds bought was 108, how many of each did he buy?

In questions of this kind it is of essential importance to have all quantities expressed in the same denomination; in the present instance it will be convenient to express the money in dimes.

Let x represent the number of geese, then $108 - x$ represents the number of ducks.

Since each goose cost 14 dimes, x geese cost $14x$ dimes.

And since each duck cost 6 dimes, $108 - x$ ducks cost $6(108 - x)$ dimes.

Therefore the amount spent is
$$14x + 6(108 - x) \text{ dimes};$$
but the question states that the amount is also \$112.80, that is, 1128 dimes.

Hence
$$14x + 6(108 - x) = 1128;$$
dividing by 2,
$$7x + 324 - 3x = 564,$$
$$4x = 240;$$
$$\therefore x = 60, \text{ the number of geese};$$
and $108 - x = 48$, the number of ducks.

PROBLEMS LEADING TO SIMPLE EQUATIONS.

Ex. 5. A is twice as old as B; ten years ago he was four times as old; what are their present ages?

Let x represent B's age in years, then $2x$ represents A's age.

Ten years ago their ages were respectively, $x-10$ and $2x-10$ years; thus we have
$$2x - 10 = 4(x-10);$$
$$2x - 10 = 4x - 40,$$
$$2x = 30;$$
$$\therefore x = 15,$$

so that B is 15 years old, A 30 years.

NOTE. In the above examples the unknown quantity x represents a *number* of dollars, ducks, years, etc.; and the student must be careful to avoid beginning a solution with a supposition of the kind, "let x = A's share," or "let x = the ducks," or any statement so vague and inexact.

EXAMPLES IX.

1. One number exceeds another by 5, and their sum is 29; find them.

2. The difference between two numbers is 8; if 2 be added to the greater the result will be three times the smaller; find the numbers.

3. Find a number such that its excess over 50 may be greater by 11 than its defect from 89.

4. What number is that which exceeds 8 by as much as its double exceeds 20?

5. Find the number which multiplied by 4 exceeds 40 as much as 40 exceeds the original number.

6. A man walks 10 miles, then travels a certain distance by train, and then twice as far by coach. If the whole journey is 70 miles, how far does he travel by train?

7. What two numbers are those whose sum is 58, and difference 28?

8. If 288 be added to a certain number, the result will be equal to three times the excess of the number over 12; find the number.

9. Twenty-three times a certain number is as much above 14 as 16 is above seven times the number; find it.

10. Divide 105 into two parts, one of which diminished by 20 shall be equal to the other diminished by 15.

11. Divide 128 into two parts, one of which is three times as large as the other.

12. Find three consecutive numbers whose sum shall equal 84.

13. The difference of the squares of two consecutive numbers is 35; find them.

14. The sum of two numbers is 8, and one of them with 22 added to it is five times the other; find the numbers.

15. Find two numbers differing by 10 whose sum is equal to twice their difference.

16. A and B begin to play each with $60. If they play till A's money is double B's, what does A win?

17. Find a number such that if 5, 15, and 35 are added to it, the product of the first and third results may be equal to the square of the second.

18. The difference between the squares of two consecutive numbers is 121; find the numbers.

19. The difference of two numbers is 3, and the difference of their squares is 27; find the numbers.

20. Divide $380 between A, B, and C, so that B may have $30 more than A, and C may have $20 more than B.

21. A sum of $7 is made up of 46 coins which are either quarters or dimes; how many are there of each?

22. If silk costs five times as much as linen, and I spend $48 in buying 22 yards of silk and 50 yards of linen, find the cost of each per yard.

23. A father is four times as old as his son; in 24 years he will only be twice as old; find their ages.

24. A is 25 years older than B, and A's age is as much above 20 as B's is below 85; find their ages.

25. A's age is three times B's, and in 18 years A will be twice as old as B; find their ages.

26. A is four times as old as B, and in 20 years will be twice as old as C, who is 5 years older than B; find their ages.

27. A's age is six times B's, and fifteen years hence A will be three times as old as B; find their ages.

28. A sum of $16 was paid in dollars, half-dollars, and dimes. The number of half-dollars used was four times the number of dollars and twice the number of dimes; how many were there of each?

29. The sum of the ages of A and B is 30 years, and five years hence A will be three times as old as B; find their present ages.

30. I spend $69.30 in buying 20 yards of calico and 30 yards of silk; the silk costs as many quarters per yard as the calico costs cents per yard; find the price of each.

PROBLEMS LEADING TO SIMPLE EQUATIONS.

31. I purchase 127 bushels of grain. If the number of bushels of wheat be double that of the corn, and seven more than five times the number of bushels of corn equals the number of bushels of oats, find the number of bushels of each.

32. The length of a room exceeds its breadth by 3 feet; if the length had been increased by 3 feet, and the breadth diminished by 2 feet, the area would not have been altered; find the dimensions.

33. The length of a room exceeds its breadth by 8 feet; if each had been increased by 2 feet, the area would have been increased by 60 feet; find the original dimensions of the room.

34. A and B start from the same place walking at different rates; when A has walked 15 miles B doubles his pace, and 6 hours later passes A; if A walks at the rate of 5 miles an hour, what is B's rate at first?

35. A sum of money is divided among A, B, and C, so that A and B have together $20, A and C $30, and B and C $40; find the share of each.

36. A man sold two pieces of cloth, losing $6 more on the one than on the other. If his entire loss was $4 less than four times the smaller loss, find the amount lost on each piece.

37. Two men received the same sum for their labor; but if one had received $10 more, and the other $8 less, then one would have had three times as much as the other. What did each receive?

38. In a certain examination the number of successful candidates was four times the number of those who failed. If there had been 14 more candidates and 6 less had failed, the number of those who passed would have been five times the number of those who failed. Find the number of candidates.

39. A purse contains 14 coins, some of which are quarters and the rest dimes. If the coins are worth $2 altogether, how many are there of each kind?

40. An estate was divided among three persons in such a way that the share of the first was three times that of the second, and the share of the second twice that of the third. The first received $900 more than the third. How much did each receive?

CHAPTER X.

Resolution into Factors.

86. Definition. When an algebraic expression is the product of two or more expressions, each of these latter quantities is called **a factor** of it, and the determination of these quantities is called the **resolution** of the expression into its factors.

87. Rational expressions do not contain square or other roots (Art. 14) in any term.

88. Integral expressions do not contain a *letter* in the denominator of any term. Thus, $x^2 + 3xy + 2y^2$, and $\frac{1}{3}x^2 + \frac{1}{2}xy - \frac{1}{2}y^2$ are integral expressions.

89. In this chapter we shall explain the principal rules by which the resolution of rational and integral expressions into their component factors, which are rational and integral expressions, may be effected.

WHEN EACH OF THE TERMS IS DIVISIBLE BY A COMMON FACTOR.

90. The expression may be simplified by dividing each term separately by this factor, and enclosing the quotient within brackets; the common factor being placed outside as a coefficient.

Ex. 1. The terms of the expression $3a^2 - 6ab$ have a common factor $3a$.
$$\therefore 3a^2 - 6ab = 3a(a - 2b).$$
Ex. 2. $5a^2bx^3 - 15abx^2 - 20b^3x^2 = 5bx^2(a^2x - 3a - 4b^2)$.

RESOLUTION INTO FACTORS.

EXAMPLES X. a.

Resolve into factors:

1. $a^3 - ax$.
2. $x^3 - x^2$.
3. $2a - 2a^2$.
4. $7p^2 + p$.
5. $8x - 2x^2$.
6. $5ax - 5a^3x^2$.
7. $15 + 25x^2$.
8. $16x + 64x^2y$.
9. $15a^2 - 225a^4$.
10. $54 - 81x$.
11. $10x^3 - 25x^4y$.
12. $3x^3 - x^2 + x$.
13. $3a^4 - 3a^3b + 6a^2b^2$.
14. $2x^2y^3 - 6x^2y^2 + 2xy^3$.
15. $6x^3 - 9x^2y + 12xy^2$.
16. $5x^5 - 10a^2x^3 - 15a^3x^3$.
17. $7a - 7a^3 + 14a^4$.
18. $38a^3x^5 + 57a^4x^2$.

WHEN THE TERMS CAN BE GROUPED SO AS TO CONTAIN A COMMON FACTOR.

91. Ex. 1. Resolve into factors $x^2 - ax + bx - ab$.

Noticing that the first two terms contain a factor x, and the last two terms a factor b, we enclose the first two terms in one bracket, and the last two in another. Thus,

$$x^2 - ax + bx - ab = (x^2 - ax) + (bx - ab)$$
$$= x(x - a) + b(x - a) \quad . \quad . \quad . \quad (1)$$
$$= (x - a)(x + b),$$

since each bracket of (1) contains the same factor $x - a$.

Ex. 2. Resolve into factors $6x^2 - 9ax + 4bx - 6ab$.

$$6x^2 - 9ax + 4bx - 6ab = (6x^2 - 9ax) + (4bx - 6ab)$$
$$= 3x(2x - 3a) + 2b(2x - 3a)$$
$$= (2x - 3a)(3x + 2b).$$

Ex. 3. Resolve into factors $12a^2 - 4ab - 3ax^2 + bx^2$.

$$12a^2 - 4ab - 3ax^2 + bx^2 = (12a^2 - 4ab) - (3ax^2 - bx^2)$$
$$= 4a(3a - b) - x^2(3a - b)$$
$$= (3a - b)(4a - x^2).$$

NOTE. In the first line of work it is usually sufficient to see that each pair contains some common factor. Any suitably chosen pairs will bring out the same result. Thus, in the last example, by a different arrangement, we have

$$12a^2 - 4ab - 3ax^2 + bx^2 = (12a^2 - 3ax^2) - (4ab - bx^2)$$
$$= 3a(4a - x^2) - b(4a - x^2)$$
$$= (4a - x^2)(3a - b).$$

The same result as before, for the order in which the factors of a product are written is of course immaterial.

EXAMPLES X. b.

Resolve into factors:

1. $a^2 + ab + ac + bc$.
2. $a^2 - ac + ab - bc$.
3. $a^2c^2 + acd + abc + bd$.
4. $a^2 + 3a + ac + 3c$.
5. $2x + cx + 2c + c^2$.
6. $x^2 - ax + 5x - 5a$.
7. $5a + ab + 5b + b^2$.
8. $ab - by - ay + y^2$.
9. $mx - my - nx + ny$.
10. $mx - ma + nx - na$.
11. $2ax + ay + 2bx + by$.
12. $3ax - bx - 3ay + by$.
13. $6x^2 + 3xy - 2ax - ay$.
14. $mx - 2my - nx + 2ny$.
15. $ax^2 - 3bxy - axy + 3by^2$.
16. $x^2 + mxy - 4xy - 4my^2$.
17. $2x^4 - x^3 + 4x - 2$.
18. $3x^3 + 5x^2 + 3x + 5$.
19. $x^4 + x^3 + 2x + 2$.
20. $y^3 - y^2 + y - 1$.
21. $axy + bcxy - az - bcz$.
22. $f^2x^2 + g^2x^2 - ag^2 - af^2$.

TRINOMIAL EXPRESSIONS.

92. When the Coefficient of the Highest Power is Unity. Before proceeding to the next case of resolution into factors the student is advised to refer to Chap. IV. Art. 51. Attention has there been drawn to the way in which, in forming the product of two binomials, the coefficients of the different terms combine so as to give a trinomial result. Thus, by Art. 51,

$$(x+5)(x+3) = x^2 + 8x + 15 \quad \ldots \quad (1),$$
$$(x-5)(x-3) = x^2 - 8x + 15 \quad \ldots \quad (2),$$
$$(x+5)(x-3) = x^2 + 2x - 15 \quad \ldots \quad (3),$$
$$(x-5)(x+3) = x^2 - 2x - 15 \quad \ldots \quad (4).$$

We now propose to consider the converse problem: namely, the resolution of a trinomial expression, similar to those which occur on the right-hand side of the above identities, into its component binomial factors.

By examining the above results, we notice that:

1. The first term of both the factors is x.
2. The *product* of the second terms of the two factors is equal to the *third term* of the trinomial; thus in (2) above we see that 15 is the product of -5 and -3; while in (3) -15 is the product of $+5$ and -3.

RESOLUTION INTO FACTORS.

3. The *algebraic sum* of the second terms of the two factors is equal to the *coefficient of x* in the trinomial; thus in (4) the sum of -5 and $+3$ gives -2, the coefficient of x in the trinomial.

In showing the application of these laws we will first consider a case where the *third term of the trinomial is positive.*

Ex. 1. Resolve into factors $x^2 + 11x + 24$.
The second terms of the factors must be such that their product is $+24$, and their sum $+11$. It is clear that they must be $+8$ and $+3$.
$$\therefore x^2 + 11x + 24 = (x+8)(x+3).$$

Ex. 2. Resolve into factors $x^2 - 10x + 24$.
The second terms of the factors must be such that their product is $+24$, and their sum -10. Hence they must *both* be *negative*, and it is easy to see that they must be -6 and -4.
$$\therefore x^2 - 10x + 24 = (x-6)(x-4).$$

Ex. 3. $x^2 - 18x + 81 = (x-9)(x-9) = (x-9)^2.$

Ex. 4. $x^4 + 10x^2 + 25 = (x^2+5)(x^2+5) = (x^2+5)^2.$

Ex. 5. Resolve into factors $x^2 - 11ax + 10a^2$.
The second terms of the factors must be such that their product is $+10a^2$, and their sum $-11a$. Hence they must be $-10a$ and $-a$.
$$\therefore x^2 - 11ax + 10a^2 = (x-10a)(x-a).$$

NOTE. In examples of this kind the student should always verify his results, by forming the product (*mentally*, as explained in Chapter IV.) of the factors he has chosen.

EXAMPLES X. c.

Resolve into factors:

1. $a^2 + 3a + 2$.
2. $a^2 + 2a + 1$.
3. $a^2 + 7a + 12$.
4. $a^2 - 7a + 12$.
5. $x^2 - 11x + 30$.
6. $x^2 - 15x + 56$.
7. $x^2 - 21x + 108$.
8. $x^2 - 21x + 80$.
9. $x^2 + 21x + 90$.
10. $x^2 - 19x + 84$.
11. $x^2 - 19x + 78$.
12. $x^2 - 18x + 45$.
13. $x^2 + 20x + 96$.
14. $x^2 - 26x + 165$.
15. $x^2 - 21x + 104$.
16. $a^2 + 30a + 225$.
17. $a^2 + 54a + 729$.
18. $a^2 - 38a + 361$.
19. $a^2 - 14ab + 49b^2$.
20. $a^2 + 5ab + 6b^2$.
21. $m^2 - 13mn + 40n^2$.
22. $m^2 - 22mn + 105n^2$.
23. $x^2 - 23xy + 132y^2$.
24. $x^2 - 26xy + 169y^2$.
25. $x^4 + 8x^2 + 7$.
26. $x^4 + 9x^2y^2 + 14y^4$.

27. $x^2 + 49xy + 600y^2$.
28. $x^2y^2 + 34xy + 289$.
29. $a^4b^4 + 37a^2b^2 + 300$.
30. $a^2 - 29ab + 54b^2$.
31. $x^4 + 162x^2 + 6561$.
32. $12 - 7x + x^2$.
33. $20 + 9x + x^2$.
34. $132 - 23x + x^2$.
35. $88 + 19x + x^2$.
36. $130 + 31xy + x^2y^2$.
37. $204 - 29x^2 + x^4$.
38. $216 + 35x + x^2$.

93. Next consider a case where *the third term of the trinomial is negative*.

Ex. 1. Resolve into factors $x^2 + 2x - 35$.

The second terms of the factors must be such that their product is -35, and their *algebraic sum* $+2$. Hence they must have *opposite* signs, and the greater of them must be *positive* in order to give its sign to their sum.

The required terms are therefore $+7$ and -5.
$$\therefore x^2 + 2x - 35 = (x + 7)(x - 5).$$

Ex. 2. Resolve into factors $x^2 - 3x - 54$.

The second terms of the factors must be such that their product is -54, and their *algebraic sum* -3. Hence they must have *opposite* signs, and the greater of them must be *negative* in order to give its sign to their sum.

The required terms are therefore -9 and $+6$.
$$\therefore x^2 - 3x - 54 = (x - 9)(x + 6).$$

Remembering that in these cases the numerical quantities *must have opposite signs*, if preferred, the following method may be adopted.

Ex. 3. Resolve into factors $x^2y^2 + 23xy - 420$.

Find two numbers whose product is 420, and whose *difference* is 23. These are 35 and 12; hence inserting the signs so that the positive may predominate, we have
$$x^2y^2 + 23xy - 420 = (xy + 35)(xy - 12).$$

EXAMPLES X. d.

Resolve into factors:

1. $x^2 - x - 2$.
2. $x^2 + x - 2$.
3. $x^2 - x - 6$.
4. $x^2 - 2x - 3$.
5. $x^2 + 2x - 3$.
6. $x^2 + x - 56$.
7. $x^2 - 4x - 12$.
8. $a^2 - a - 20$.
9. $a^2 + a - 20$.
10. $a^2 - 4a - 117$.
11. $x^2 + 9x - 36$.
12. $x^2 + x - 156$.

RESOLUTION INTO FACTORS. 75

13. $x^2 + x - 110$.
14. $x^2 - 9x - 90$.
15. $x^2 - x - 240$.
16. $a^2 - 12a - 85$.
17. $a^2 - 11a - 152$.

18. $x^2y^2 - 5xy - 24$.
19. $x^2 + ax - 42a^2$.
20. $x^2 - 32xy - 105y^2$.
21. $x^2 + 18x - 115$.
22. $x^2 + 16x - 260$.

23. $a^2 - 11a - 26$.
24. $a^2y^2 + 14ay - 240$.
25. $a^4 - a^2b^2 - 56b^4$.
26. $x^4 - 14x^2 - 51$.
27. $y^4 + 6x^2y^2 - 27x^4$.

28. $a^2 + 12abx - 28b^2x^2$.
29. $a^2 - 18axy - 243x^2y^2$.
30. $x^4 + 13a^2x^2 - 300a^4$.

31. $x^4 - a^2x^2 - 132a^4$.
32. $x^4 - a^2x^2 - 462a^4$.
33. $x^6 + x^3 - 870$.

34. $2 + x - x^2$.
35. $6 + x - x^2$.

36. $110 - x - x^2$.
37. $380 - x - x^2$.

38. $120 - 7ax - a^2x^2$.

94. When the Coefficient of the Highest Power is not Unity.

Again, referring to Chap. IV. Art. 51, we may write the following results:

$$(3x + 2)(x + 4) = 3x^2 + 14x + 8 \quad . \quad . \quad . \quad (1),$$
$$(3x - 2)(x - 4) = 3x^2 - 14x + 8 \quad . \quad . \quad . \quad (2),$$
$$(3x + 2)(x - 4) = 3x^2 - 10x - 8 \quad . \quad . \quad . \quad (3),$$
$$(3x - 2)(x + 4) = 3x^2 + 10x - 8 \quad . \quad . \quad . \quad (4).$$

The converse problem presents more difficulty than the cases we have yet considered.

Consider the result $3x^2 - 14x + 8 = (3x - 2)(x - 4)$.

The first term $3x^2$ is the product of $3x$ and x.

The third term $+8$ is the product of -2 and -4.

The middle term $-14x$ is the result of adding together the two products $3x \times -4$ and $x \times -2$.

Again, consider the result $3x^2 - 10x - 8 = (3x + 2)(x - 4)$.

The first term $3x^2$ is the product of $3x$ and x.

The third term -8 is the product of $+2$ and -4.

The middle term $-10x$ is the result of adding together the two products $3x \times -4$ and $x \times 2$; and its sign is negative because the greater of these two products is negative.

Considering in a similar manner results (1) and (4), we see that:

1. If the *third term* of the trinomial is *positive*, then the *second terms* of its factors have both the *same sign*, and this sign is the same as that of the *middle term* of the trinomial.

76 ALGEBRA.

2. If the *third term* of the trinomial is *negative*, then the *second terms* of its factors have *opposite signs*.

95. The beginner will frequently find that it is not easy to select the proper factors at the first trial. Practice alone will enable him to detect at a glance whether any pair he has chosen will combine so as to give the correct coefficients of the expression to be resolved.

Ex. Resolve into factors $7x^2 - 19x - 6$.

Write $(7x\ \ 3)(x\ \ 2)$ for a first trial, noticing that 3 and 2 must have opposite signs. These factors give $7x^2$ and -6 for the first and third terms. But since $7 \times 2 - 3 \times 1 = 11$, the combination fails to give the correct coefficient of the middle term.

Next try $(7x\ \ 2)(x\ \ 3)$.

Since $7 \times 3 - 2 \times 1 = 19$, these factors will be correct if we insert the signs so that the negative shall predominate.

Thus $\qquad 7x^2 - 19x - 6 = (7x + 2)(x - 3)$.

[Verify by mental multiplication.]

96. In actual work it will not be necessary to put down all these steps at length. The student will soon find that the different cases may be rapidly reviewed, and the unsuitable combinations rejected at once.

Ex. 1. Resolve into factors $14x^2 + 29x - 15$ . . . . . . (1),
$\qquad\qquad\qquad\qquad\qquad 14x^2 - 29x - 15$ . . . . . . (2).

In each case we may write $(7x\ \ 3)(2x\ \ 5)$ as a first trial, noticing that 3 and 5 must have opposite signs.

And since $7 \times 5 - 3 \times 2 = 29$, we have only now to insert the proper signs in each factor.

In (1) the positive sign must predominate.
In (2) the negative sign must predominate.

Therefore $\quad 14x^2 + 29x - 15 = (7x - 3)(2x + 5)$.
$\qquad\qquad\ \ 14x^2 - 29x - 15 = (7x + 3)(2x - 5)$.

Ex. 2. Resolve into factors $5x^2 + 17x + 6$ . . . . . . (1),
$\qquad\qquad\qquad\qquad\qquad 5x^2 - 17x + 6$ . . . . . . (2).

In (1) we notice that the factors which give 6 are both positive.
In (2) we notice that the factors which give 6 are both negative.

RESOLUTION INTO FACTORS.

And therefore for (1) we may write $(5x+\ )(x+\ )$.
(2) we may write $(5x-\ )(x-\ )$.
And, since $5 \times 3 + 1 \times 2 = 17$, we see that
$$5x^2 + 17x + 6 = (5x+2)(x+3).$$
$$5x^2 - 17x + 6 = (5x-2)(x-3).$$

In each expression the third term 6 also admits of factors 6 and 1, but this is one of the cases referred to above which the student would reject at once as unsuitable.

Ex. 3. $9x^2 - 48xy + 64y^2 = (3x - 8y)(3x - 8y)$
$= (3x - 8y)^2.$

Ex. 4. $6 + 7x - 5x^2 = (3 + 5x)(2 - x).$

NOTE. In Chapter XXVI. a method of obtaining the factors of *any* trinomial in the form $ax^2 + bx + c$ is given.

EXAMPLES X. e.

Resolve into factors:

1. $2x^2 + 3x + 1.$
2. $3x^2 + 5x + 2.$
3. $2x^2 + 5x + 2.$
4. $3x^2 + 10x + 3.$
5. $2x^2 + 9x + 4.$
6. $3x^2 + 8x + 4.$
7. $2x^2 + 11x + 5.$
8. $3x^2 + 11x + 6.$
9. $5x^2 + 11x + 2.$
10. $3x^2 + x - 2.$
11. $4x^2 + 11x - 3.$
12. $3x^2 + 14x - 5.$
13. $2x^2 + 15x - 8.$
14. $2x^2 - x - 1.$
15. $3x^2 + 7x - 6.$
16. $2x^2 + x - 28.$
17. $3x^2 + 13x - 30.$
18. $6x^2 + 7x - 3.$
19. $2x^2 - x - 15.$
20. $3x^2 + 19x - 14.$
21. $6x^2 - 31x + 35.$
22. $4x^2 + x - 14.$
23. $3x^2 - 13x + 14.$
24. $4x^2 + 23x + 15.$
25. $2x^2 - 5xy - 3y^2.$
26. $8x^2 - 38x + 35.$
27. $15x^2 - 77x + 10.$
28. $12x^2 - 31x - 15.$
29. $24x^2 + 22x - 21.$
30. $72x^2 - 145x + 72.$
31. $24x^2 - 29xy - 4y^2.$
32. $2 - 3x - 2x^2.$
33. $6 + 5x - 6x^2.$
34. $4 - 5x - 6x^2.$
35. $5 + 32x - 21x^2.$
36. $18 - 33x + 5x^2.$
37. $8 + 6x - 5x^2.$
38. $20 - 9x - 20x^2.$
39. $10 - 5x - 15x^2.$

97. We add an exercise containing miscellaneous examples on the preceding cases.

EXAMPLES X. f.

Resolve into factors:

1. $x^2 + 13x + 42.$
2. $143 - 24ax + a^2x^2.$
3. $2x^2 + 7x + 6.$
4. $a^2b^2 - 3abc - 10c^2.$

5. $x^2 + x - 6$.
6. $2ax^2 + 3axy - 2bxy - 3by^2$.
7. $x^2 + 7xy - 60y^2$.
8. $a^2 - ay - 210y^2$.
9. $x^2 - 21x + 110$.
10. $24 + 37x - 72x^2$.
11. $98 - 7x - x^2$.
12. $3x^2 + 23x + 14$.
13. $2x^2 + 3x - 2$.
14. $x^2 - 20xy - 96y^2$.
15. $a^2 - 20abx + 75b^2x^2$.
16. $a^2 - 24a + 95$.
17. $7 + 10x + 3x^2$.
18. $a^2 - 4a - 21$.
19. $x^2 + 43xy + 390y^2$.
20. $x^2 + 23x + 102$.
21. $amx^2 + bmxy - anxy - bny^2$.
22. $6x^2 - 7x - 3$.
23. $3 + 11x - 4x^2$.
24. $12x^2 - 23xy + 10y^2$.
25. $3x^2 + 7x + 4$.
26. $a^2 - 32a + 256$.
27. $3x^2 - 19x - 14$.
28. $x^2 - 19x + 90$.
29. $x^2 + 3x - 40$.
30. $x^2y^2 - 16xy + 39$.
31. $204 - 5x - x^2$.
32. $15x^2 + 224x - 15$.
33. $3x^2 + 41x + 26$.
34. $65 + 8xy - x^2y^2$.

WHEN AN EXPRESSION IS THE DIFFERENCE OF TWO SQUARES.

98. By multiplying $a + b$ by $a - b$ we obtain the identity
$$(a+b)(a-b) = a^2 - b^2,$$
a result which may be verbally expressed as follows:

The product of the sum and the difference of any two quantities is equal to the difference of their squares.

Conversely, *the difference of the squares of any two quantities is equal to the product of the sum and the difference of the two quantities.*

Ex. 1. Resolve into factors $25x^2 - 16y^2$.
$$25x^2 - 16y^2 = (5x)^2 - (4y)^2.$$

Therefore the first factor is the sum of $5x$ and $4y$, and the second factor is the difference of $5x$ and $4y$.
$$\therefore 25x^2 - 16y^2 = (5x + 4y)(5x - 4y).$$

The intermediate steps may usually be omitted.

Ex. 2. $\quad 1 - 49c^6 = (1 + 7c^3)(1 - 7c^3).$

RESOLUTION INTO FACTORS.

The difference of the squares of two numerical quantities is sometimes conveniently found by the aid of the formula

$$a^2 - b^2 = (a+b)(a-b).$$

Ex. 3. $(329)^2 - (171)^2 = (329 + 171)(329 - 171)$
$= 500 \times 158 = 79000.$

EXAMPLES X. g.

Resolve into factors:

1. $x^2 - 4$.
2. $a^2 - 81$.
3. $y^2 - 100$.
4. $c^2 - 144$.
5. $49 - c^2$.
6. $121 - x^2$.
7. $400 - a^2$.
8. $x^2 - 9a^2$.
9. $y^2 - 25x^2$.
10. $36x^2 - 25b^2$.
11. $9x^2 - 1$.
12. $36p^2 - 49q^2$.
13. $4k^2 - 1$.
14. $49 - 100k^2$.
15. $1 - 25x^2$.
16. $9x^2 - y^2$.
17. $p^2q^2 - 36$.
18. $a^2b^2 - 4c^2d^2$.
19. $x^4 - 9$.
20. $9a^4 - 121$.
21. $25x^2 - 64$.
22. $81a^4 - 49x^4$.
23. $x^6 - 25$.
24. $1 - 36a^6$.
25. $9x^4 - a^2$.
26. $81x^6 - 25a^2$.
27. $x^4a^2 - 49$.
28. $a^2 - 64x^6$.
29. $a^2b^2 - 9x^6$.
30. $x^6y^6 - 4$.
31. $1 - a^2b^2$.
32. $9 - 4a^2$.
33. $9a^4 - 25b^4$.
34. $x^4 - 16b^2$.
35. $x^2 - 25y^2$.
36. $25 - 64x^2$.
37. $121a^2 - 81x^2$.
38. $p^2q^2 - 64a^4$.
39. $64x^2 - 25z^6$.
40. $49x^4 - 16y^4$.
41. $81p^4z^6 - 25b^2$.
42. $16x^{16} - 9y^6$.
43. $36x^{36} - 49a^{14}$.
44. $1 - 100a^6b^4c^2$.
45. $25x^{10} - 16a^8$.

Find, by resolving into factors, the value of:

46. $(575)^2 - (425)^2$.
47. $(121)^2 - (120)^2$.
48. $(750)^2 - (250)^2$.
49. $(339)^2 - (319)^2$.
50. $(753)^2 - (253)^2$.
51. $(101)^2 - (99)^2$.
52. $(1723)^2 - (277)^2$.
53. $(1639)^2 - (739)^2$.
54. $(1811)^2 - (689)^2$.

99. When One or Both of the Squares is a Compound Expression. We employ the method of the preceding articles, as is shown in the following examples:

Ex. 1. Resolve into factors $(a + 2b)^2 - 16x^2$.

The sum of $a + 2b$ and $4x$ is $a + 2b + 4x$, and their difference is $a + 2b - 4x$.

$$\therefore (a + 2b)^2 - 16x^2 = (a + 2b + 4x)(a + 2b - 4x).$$

Ex. 2. Resolve into factors $x^2 - (2b - 3c)^2$.

The sum of x and $2b - 3c$ is $x + 2b - 3c$, and their difference is
$$x - (2b - 3c) = x - 2b + 3c.$$
$$\therefore x^2 - (2b - 3c)^2 = (x + 2b - 3c)(x - 2b + 3c).$$

If the factors contain like terms, they should be collected so as to give the result in its simplest form.

Ex. 3.
$$(3x + 7y)^2 - (2x - 3y)^2$$
$$= \{(3x + 7y) + (2x - 3y)\}\{(3x + 7y) - (2x - 3y)\}$$
$$= (3x + 7y + 2x - 3y)(3x + 7y - 2x + 3y)$$
$$= (5x + 4y)(x + 10y).$$

EXAMPLES X. h.

Resolve into factors:

1. $(a + b)^2 - c^2$.
2. $(a - b)^2 - c^2$.
3. $(x + y)^2 - 4z^2$.
4. $(x + 2y)^2 - a^2$.
5. $(a + 3b)^2 - 16x^2$.
6. $(x + 5a)^2 - 9y^2$.
7. $(x + 5c)^2 - 1$.
8. $(a - 2x)^2 - b^2$.
9. $(2x - 3a)^2 - 9c^2$.
10. $9x^2 - (2a - 3b)^2$.
11. $1 - (a - b)^2$.
12. $c^2 - (5a - 3b)^2$.
13. $(a + b)^2 - (c + d)^2$.
14. $(a - b)^2 - (x + y)^2$.
15. $(7x + y)^2 - 1$.
16. $(a + b)^2 - (m - n)^2$.
17. $(a - n)^2 - (b + m)^2$.
18. $(b - c)^2 - (a - x)^2$.
19. $(4a + x)^2 - (b + y)^2$.
20. $(a + 2b)^2 - (3x + 4y)^2$.
21. $1 - (7a - 3b)^2$.
22. $(a - b)^2 - (x - y)^2$.
23. $(a - 3x)^2 - 16y^2$.
24. $(2a - 5x)^2 - 1$.
25. $(a + b - c)^2 - (x - y + z)^2$.

Resolve into factors and simplify:

26. $(x + y)^2 - x^2$.
27. $x^2 - (y - x)^2$.
28. $(x + 3y)^2 - 4y^2$.
29. $(24x + y)^2 - (23x - y)^2$.
30. $(5x + 2y)^2 - (3x - y)^2$.
31. $9x^2 - (3x - 5y)^2$.
32. $(7x + 3)^2 - (5x - 4)^2$.
33. $(3a + 1)^2 - (2a - 1)^2$.
34. $16a^2 - (3a + 1)^2$.
35. $(2a + b - c)^2 - (a - b + c)^2$.
36. $(x - 7y + z)^2 - (7y - z)^2$.
37. $(x + y - 8)^2 - (x - 8)^2$.
38. $(2x + a - 3)^2 - (3 - 2x)^2$.

100. Compound Expressions Arranged as the Difference of two Squares. By suitably grouping the terms, compound expressions can often be expressed as the difference of two squares, and so be resolved into factors.

RESOLUTION INTO FACTORS.

Ex. 1. Resolve into factors $a^2 - 2ax + x^2 - 4b^2$.
$$a^2 - 2ax + x^2 - 4b^2 = (a^2 - 2ax + x^2) - 4b^2$$
$$= (a-x)^2 - (2b)^2$$
$$= (a-x+2b)(a-x-2b).$$

Ex. 2. Resolve into factors $9a^2 - c^2 + 4cx - 4x^2$.
$$9a^2 - c^2 + 4cx - 4x^2 = 9a^2 - (c^2 - 4cx + 4x^2)$$
$$= (3a)^2 - (c-2x)^2$$
$$= (3a + c - 2x)(3a - c + 2x).$$

Ex. 3. Resolve into factors $12xy + 25 - 4x^2 - 9y^2$.
$$12xy + 25 - 4x^2 - 9y^2 = 25 - (4x^2 - 12xy + 9y^2)$$
$$= (5)^2 - (2x - 3y)^2$$
$$= (5 + 2x - 3y)(5 - 2x + 3y).$$

Ex. 4. Resolve into factors $2bd - a^2 - c^2 + b^2 + d^2 + 2ac$.

Here the terms $2bd$ and $2ac$ suggest the proper preliminary arrangement of the expression. Thus
$$2bd - a^2 - c^2 + b^2 + d^2 + 2ac = b^2 + 2bd + d^2 - a^2 + 2ac - c^2$$
$$= b^2 + 2bd + d^2 - (a^2 - 2ac + c^2)$$
$$= (b+d)^2 - (a-c)^2$$
$$= (b+d+a-c)(b+d-a+c).$$

EXAMPLES X. k.

Resolve into factors:

1. $x^2 + 2xy + y^2 - a^2$.
2. $a^2 - 2ab + b^2 - x^2$.
3. $x^2 - 6ax + 9a^2 - 16b^2$.
4. $4a^2 + 4ab + b^2 - 9c^2$.
5. $x^2 + a^2 + 2ax - y^2$.
6. $2ay + a^2 + y^2 - x^2$.
7. $x^2 - a^2 - 2ab - b^2$.
8. $y^2 - c^2 + 2cx - x^2$.
9. $1 - x^2 - 2xy - y^2$.
10. $c^2 - x^2 - y^2 + 2xy$.
11. $x^2 + y^2 + 2xy - 4x^2y^2$.
12. $a^2 - 4ab + 4b^2 - 9a^2c^2$.
13. $x^2 + 2xy + y^2 - a^2 - 2ab - b^2$.
14. $a^2 - 2ab + b^2 - c^2 - 2cd - d^2$.
15. $x^2 - 4ax + 4a^2 - b^2 + 2by - y^2$.
16. $y^2 + 2by + b^2 - a^2 - 6ax - 9x^2$.
17. $x^2 - 2x + 1 - a^2 - 4ab - 4b^2$.
18. $9a^2 - 6a + 1 - x^2 - 8dx - 16d^2$.
19. $x^2 - a^2 + y^2 - b^2 - 2xy + 2ab$.
20. $a^2 + b^2 - 2ab - c^2 - d^2 - 2cd$.
21. $4x^2 - 12ax - c^2 - k^2 - 2ck + 9a^2$.
22. $a^2 + 6bx - 9b^2x^2 - 10ab - 1 + 25b^2$.
23. $a^4 - 25x^6 + 8a^2x^2 - 9 + 30x^3 + 16x^4$.

82 ALGEBRA.

101. Important Cases. By a slight modification some expressions admit of being written in the form of the difference of two squares, and may then be resolved into factors by the method of Art. 98.

Ex. 1. Resolve into factors $x^4 + x^2y^2 + y^4$.

$$x^4 + x^2y^2 + y^4 = (x^4 + 2x^2y^2 + y^4) - x^2y^2$$
$$= (x^2 + y^2)^2 - (xy)^2$$
$$= (x^2 + y^2 + xy)(x^2 + y^2 - xy)$$
$$= (x^2 + xy + y^2)(x^2 - xy + y^2)$$

Ex. 2. Resolve into factors $x^4 - 15x^2y^2 + 9y^4$.

$$x^4 - 15x^2y^2 + 9y^4 = (x^4 - 6x^2y^2 + 9y^4) - 9x^2y^2$$
$$= (x^2 - 3y^2)^2 - (3xy)^2$$
$$= (x^2 - 3y^2 + 3xy)(x^2 - 3y^2 - 3xy).$$

EXAMPLES X. 1.

Resolve into factors :

1. $x^4 + 16x^2 + 256$.
2. $81a^4 + 9a^2b^2 + b^4$.
3. $x^4 + y^4 - 7x^2y^2$.
4. $m^4 + n^4 - 18m^2n^2$.
5. $x^4 - 6x^2y^2 + y^4$.
6. $4x^4 + 9y^4 - 93x^2y^2$.
7. $4m^4 + 9n^4 - 24m^2n^2$.
8. $9x^4 + 4y^4 + 11x^2y^2$.
9. $x^4 - 19x^2y^2 + 25y^4$.
10. $16a^4 + b^4 - 28a^2b^2$.

WHEN AN EXPRESSION IS THE SUM OR DIFFERENCE OF TWO CUBES.

102. If we divide $a^3 + b^3$ by $a + b$ the quotient is $a^2 - ab + b^2$; and if we divide $a^3 - b^3$ by $a - b$ the quotient is $a^2 + ab + b^2$.

We have therefore the following identities:

$$a^3 + b^3 = (a + b)(a^2 - ab + b^2);$$
$$a^3 - b^3 = (a - b)(a^2 + ab + b^2).$$

These results are very important, and enable us to resolve into factors any expression which can be written as the sum or the difference of two cubes.

Ex. 1. $\quad 8x^3 - 27y^3 = (2x)^3 - (3y)^3$
$$= (2x - 3y)(4x^2 + 6xy + 9y^2).$$

NOTE. The middle term $6xy$ is the *product* of $2x$ and $3y$.

Ex. 2. $64a^3 + 1 = (4a)^3 + (1)^3$
$= (4a + 1)(16a^2 - 4a + 1)$.

We may usually omit the intermediate step and write the factors at once.

Ex. 3. $343a^6 - 27x^3 = (7a^2 - 3x)(49a^4 + 21a^2x + 9x^2)$.

Ex. 4. $8x^9 + 729 = (2x^3 + 9)(4x^6 - 18x^3 + 81)$.

EXAMPLES X. m.

Resolve into factors:

1. $x^3 - y^3$.
2. $x^3 + y^3$.
3. $x^3 - 1$.
4. $1 + a^3$.
5. $8x^3 - y^3$.
6. $x^3 + 8y^3$.
7. $27x^3 + 1$.
8. $1 - 8y^3$.
9. $a^3b^3 - c^3$.
10. $8x^3 + 27y^3$.
11. $1 - 343x^3$.
12. $64 + y^3$.
13. $125 + a^3$.
14. $216 - a^3$.
15. $a^3b^3 + 512$.
16. $1000y^3 - 1$.
17. $x^3 + 64y^3$.
18. $27 - 1000x^3$.
19. $a^3b^3 + 216c^3$.
20. $343 - 8x^3$.
21. $a^3 + 27b^3$.
22. $27x^3 - 64y^3$.
23. $125x^3 - 1$.
24. $216p^3 - 343$.
25. $x^3y^3 + z^3$.
26. $a^3b^3c^3 - 1$.
27. $343x^3 + 1000y^3$.
28. $729a^3 - 64b^3$.
29. $8a^3b^3 + 125x^3$.
30. $x^3y^3 - 216z^3$.
31. $x^6 - 27y^3$.
32. $64x^6 + 125y^3$.
33. $8x^3 - z^6$.
34. $216x^6 - b^3$.
35. $a^3 + 343b^3$.
36. $a^6 + 729b^3$.
37. $8x^3 - 729y^6$.
38. $p^3q^3 - 27x^3$.
39. $z^3 - 64y^6$.
40. $x^3y^3 - 512$.

103. Miscellaneous Cases of Resolution into Factors.

Ex. 1. Resolve into factors $16a^4 - 81b^4$.
$$16a^4 - 81b^4 = (4a^2 + 9b^2)(4a^2 - 9b^2)$$
$$= (4a^2 + 9b^2)(2a + 3b)(2a - 3b).$$

Ex. 2. Resolve into factors $x^6 - y^6$.
$$x^6 - y^6 = (x^3 + y^3)(x^3 - y^3)$$
$$= (x + y)(x^2 - xy + y^2)(x - y)(x^2 + xy + y^2).$$

NOTE. When an expression can be arranged either as the difference of two squares, or as the difference of two cubes, each of the methods explained in Arts. 98, 102 will be applicable. It will, however, be found simplest to first use the rule for resolving into factors the difference of two squares.

In all cases where an expression to be resolved contains a simple factor common to each of its terms, this should be first taken outside a bracket as explained in Art. 90.

Ex. 3. Resolve into factors $28x^4y + 64x^3y - 60x^2y$.

$$28x^4y + 64x^3y - 60x^2y = 4x^2y(7x^2 + 16x - 15)$$
$$= 4x^2y(7x - 5)(x + 3).$$

Ex. 4. Resolve into factors $x^3p^2 - 8y^3p^2 - 4x^3q^2 + 32y^3q^2$.

The expression $= p^2(x^3 - 8y^3) - 4q^2(x^3 - 8y^3)$
$= (x^3 - 8y^3)(p^2 - 4q^2)$
$= (x - 2y)(x^2 + 2xy + 4y^2)(p + 2q)(p - 2q)$.

Ex. 5. Resolve into factors $4x^2 - 25y^2 + 2x + 5y$.

$$4x^2 - 25y^2 + 2x + 5y = (2x + 5y)(2x - 5y) + 2x + 5y$$
$$= (2x + 5y)(2x - 5y + 1).$$

EXAMPLES X. o.

Resolve into two or more factors:

1. $a^2 - y^2 - 2yz - z^2$.
2. $x^6 - y^6z^6$.
3. $6x^2 - x - 77$.
4. $729y^6 - 64x^6$.
5. $x^6 - 4096$.
6. $2mn + 2xy + m^2 + n^2 - x^2 - y^2$.
7. $33x^2 - 16x - 65$.
8. $a^4 + b^4 - c^4 - d^4 + 2a^2b^2 - 2c^2d^2$.
9. $m^3x + m^3y - n^3x - n^3y$.
10. $(a + b + c)^2 - (a - b - c)^2$.
11. $4 + 4x + 2ay + x^2 - a^2 - y^2$.
12. $x^2 - 10x - 119$.
13. $a^2 - b^2 - c^2 + d^2 - 2(ad - bc)$.
14. $x^2 - a^2 + y^2 - 2xy$.
15. $a^2 + x^2 - (y^2 + z^2) - 2(yz - ax)$.
16. $21x^2 + 82x - 39$.
17. $1 - a^2x^2 - b^2y^2 + 2abxy$.
18. $c^5d^3 - c^2 - a^2c^3d^3 + a^2$.
19. $a^2x^6 - a^2y^6 - b^2x^6 + b^2y^6$.
20. $x^2 - 6x - 247$.
21. $a^3x^2 - c^3x^2 - a^3y^2 + c^3y^2$.
22. $acx^2 - bcx + adx - bd$.
23. $a^2x - b^2x + a^2y - b^2y$.
24. $x^4 + 4x^2y^2z^2 + 4y^4z^4$.
25. $a^3b^3 + 512$.
26. $2x^2 + 17x + 35$.
27. $500x^2y - 20y^3$.
28. $a^5 - 8a^2b^3$.
29. $a^2x^3 - 16x^3y^2$.
30. $b^2 + c^2 - a^2 - 2bc$.
31. $5x^4 - 15x^3 - 90x^2$.
32. $14a^2x^3 - 35a^3x^2 + 14a^4x$.
33. $x^8 - 1$.
34. $1 - (m^2 + n^2) + 2mn$.
35. $75x^4 - 48a^4$. 36. $5a^4b^4 - 5ab$.
37. $8x^2y + 52xy + 60y$.
38. $3x^2y^2 + 26axy + 35a^2$.
39. $729a^7b - ab^7$.
40. $a^8x^6 - 64a^2y^6$.
41. $a^{12} - b^{12}$.
42. $24x^2y^2 - 30xy^3 - 36y^4$.
43. $(a + b)^4 - 1$.
44. $a^4 - (b + c)^4$.
45. $(c + d)^3 - 1$.

RESOLUTION INTO FACTORS. 85

46. $1-(x-y)^3$.
47. $250(a-b)^3+2$.
48. $(c+d)^3+(c-d)^3$.
49. $8(x+y)^3-(2x-y)^3$.
50. x^2-4y^2+x-2y.
51. a^2-b^2+a-b.
52. $(a+b)^2+a+b$.
53. a^3+b^3+a+b.
54. a^2-9b^2+a+3b.
55. $4(x-y)^3-(x-y)$.
56. $x^4y-x^2y^3-x^3y^2+xy^4$.
57. $4a^2-9b^2+2a-3b$.

58. Resolve $x^{16}-y^{16}$ into five factors.

CONVERSE USE OF FACTORS.

104. The actual processes of multiplication and division can often be partially or wholly avoided by a skilful use of factors.

It should be observed that the formulæ which the student has seen exemplified in the preceding pages are just as useful in their converse as in their direct application. Thus the formula for resolving into factors the difference of two squares is equally useful as enabling us to write at once the product of the sum and the difference of two quantities.

Ex. 1. Multiply $2a+3b-c$ by $2a-3b+c$.

These expressions may be arranged thus:

$$2a+(3b-c) \text{ and } 2a-(3b-c).$$

Hence the product $= \{2a+(3b-c)\}\{2a-(3b-c)\}$
$= (2a)^2-(3b-c)^2$ [Art. 98.]
$= 4a^2-(9b^2-6bc+c^2)$
$= 4a^2-9b^2+6bc-c^2$.

Ex. 2. Divide the product of $2x^2+x-6$, and $6x^2-5x+1$ by $3x^2+5x-2$.

Denoting the division by writing the divisor under the dividend (Art. 53), with a horizontal line between them, the required quotient

$$= \frac{(2x^2+x-6)(6x^2-5x+1)}{3x^2+5x-2}$$

$$= \frac{(2x-3)(x+2)(3x-1)(2x-1)}{(3x-1)(x+2)}$$

$$= (2x-3)(2x-1).$$

Ex. 3. Prove the identity
$$17(5x+3a)^2 - 2(40x+27a)(5x+3a) = 25x^2 - 9a^2.$$

Since each term of the first expression contains the factor $5x+3a$, the first side

$$= (5x+3a)\{17(5x+3a) - 2(40x+27a)\}$$
$$= (5x+3a)(85x+51a-80x-54a)$$
$$= (5x+3a)(5x-3a)$$
$$= 25x^2 - 9a^2.$$

Ex. 4. Show that $(2x+3y-z)^3 + (3x+7y+z)^3$ is divisible by $5(x+2y)$.

The given expression is of the form $A^3 + B^3$, and therefore has a divisor of the form $A+B$.

Therefore $(2x+3y-z)^3 + (3x+7y+z)^3$
is divisible by $(2x+3y-z) + (3x+7y+z)$,
that is, by $5x+10y$,
or by $5(x+2y)$.

EXAMPLES X. p.

Find the product of

1. $2x - 7y + 3z$ and $2x + 7y - 3z$.
2. $3x^2 - 4xy + 7y^2$ and $3x^2 + 4xy + 7y^2$.
3. $5x^2 + 5xy - 9y^2$ and $5x^2 - 5xy - 9y^2$.
4. $7x^2 - 8xy + 3y^2$ and $7x^2 + 8xy - 3y^2$.
5. $x^3 + 2x^2y + 2xy^2 + y^3$ and $x^3 - 2x^2y + 2xy^2 - y^3$.
6. $(x+y)^2 + 2(x+y) + 4$ and $(x+y)^2 - 2(x+y) + 4$.
7. Multiply the square of $a+3b$ by $a^2 - 6ab + 9b^2$.
8. Divide $(4x+3y-2z)^2 - (3x-2y+3z)^2$ by $x+5y-5z$.
9. Divide $x^8 + 16a^4x^4 + 256a^8$ by $x^2 + 2ax + 4a^2$.
10. Divide $(x^2+7x+10)(x+3)$ by x^2+5x+6.
11. Divide $(3x+4y-2z)^2 - (2x+3y-4z)^2$ by $x+y+2z$.

Prove the following identities:

12. $(a+b)^3 - (a-b)^2(a+b) = 4ab(a+b)$.
13. $c^4 - d^4 - (c-d)^3(c+d) = 2cd(c^2-d^2)$.
14. $(x+y)^4 - 3xy(x+y)^2 = (x+y)(x^3+y^3)$.

15. Show that the square of $x + 1$ exactly divides
$$(x^3 + x^2 + 4)^3 - (x^3 - 2x + 3)^3.$$

16. Show that $(3x^2 - 7x + 2)^3 - (x^2 - 8x + 8)^3$ is divisible by $2x - 3$, and by $x + 2$.

105. The Factor Theorem. *If any rational and integral expression containing x becomes equal to 0 when a is written for x, it is exactly divisible by $x - a$.*

Let P stand for the expression. Divide P by $x - a$ until the remainder no longer contains x. Let R denote this remainder, and Q the quotient obtained. Then
$$P = Q(x - a) + R.$$

Since this equation is true for all values of x, we will assume that x equals a. By hypothesis, the substitution of a for x makes P equal to 0; thus,
$$0 = Q(0) + R.$$
$$\therefore R = 0.$$

As the remainder is 0, the expression is exactly divisible by $x - a$.

The following examples illustrate the application of this principle:

Ex. 1. Resolve into factors $x^3 + 3x^2 - 13x - 15$.

By trial we find that this expression becomes 0 when $x = 3$; hence, $x - 3$ is a factor. Dividing by $x - 3$, we obtain the quotient
$$x^2 + 6x + 5.$$
The factors of this expression are easily seen to be $x + 1$ and $x + 5$; hence,
$$x^3 + 3x^2 - 13x - 15 = (x - 3)(x + 1)(x + 5).$$

Ex. 2. Resolve into factors $x^3 + 6x^2 + 11x + 6$.

It is evident that substituting a positive number for x will not make the expression equal to 0. By substituting -1, however, for x, the expression becomes $-1 + 6 - 11 + 6$, or 0; hence,
$$x^3 + 6x^2 + 11x + 6$$
is divisible by $x + 1$. Dividing by $x + 1$, we obtain the quotient $x^2 + 5x + 6$, and factoring this expression we have
$$x^3 + 6x^2 + 11x + 6 = (x + 1)(x + 2)(x + 3).$$

NOTE. The student should notice that the only numerical values that need be substituted for x are the *factors* of the *last term* of the expression, and that we *change the sign* of the factor substituted before connecting it with x. Thus, in Ex. 1, the factor 3 gives a divisor $x - 3$, and in Ex. 2, the factor $- 1$ gives a divisor $x + 1$.

Ex. 3. Without actual division, show that $5x^5 - 6x^3 + 1$ is divisible by $x - 1$.

If the expression is divisible by $x-1$, it will become 0, or "vanish," when 1 is substituted for x. Making this substitution, we obtain 0; hence the division is possible.

EXAMPLES X. r.

Without actual division, show that $x - 2$ is a factor of each of the following expressions:

1. $x^3 - 5x + 2$.
2. $x^3 + x^2 - 4x - 4$.
3. $x^3 - 7x^2 + 16x - 12$.
4. $x^3 - 8x^2 + 17x - 10$.

Determine by inspection whether $x + 3$ is a factor of any of the following expressions:

5. $x^3 - 7x + 6$.
6. $x^3 + 6x^2 + 11x + 6$.
7. $x^3 + 6x + 6$.
8. $x^3 + 3x^2 + x + 3$.
9. Show that $32x^{10} - 33x^5 + 1$ is divisible by $x - 1$.

Resolve into factors.

10. $2x^3 + 4x^2 - 2x - 4$.
11. $3x^3 - 6x^2 - 3x + 6$.

106. We shall employ the **Factor Theorem** in giving general proofs of the statements made in Art. 62.

We suppose n to be a positive integer.

(I.) $x^n - y^n$ is always *divisible by* $x - y$.

By Art. 105, $x^n - y^n$ is exactly divisible by $x - y$ if the substitution of y for x in the expression $x^n - y^n$ gives zero as a result. Making this substitution we have

$$x^n - y^n = y^n - y^n = 0.$$

Therefore $x^n - y^n$ is *always* divisible by $x - y$.

(II.) $x^n - y^n$ *is divisible by* $x + y$ *when n is even.*

If this be true, the substitution of $-y$ for x in the expression $x^n - y^n$ gives zero as a result. Making this substitution we have

$$x^n - y^n = (-y)^n - y^n.$$

When n is even, this expression becomes $y^n - y^n$, or zero. Therefore $x^n - y^n$ is divisible by $x + y$ when n is even.

(III.) $x^n + y^n$ is **never** *divisible by* $x - y$.

Here the substitution of y for x in the expression $x^n + y^n$ gives
$$x^n + y^n = y^n + y^n = 2y^n.$$

As this expression is not zero, $x^n + y^n$ is *never* divisible by $x - y$.

(IV.) $x^n + y^n$ is divisible by $x + y$ when n **is odd**.

Here the substitution of $-y$ for x in the expression $x^n + y^n$ gives
$$x^n + y^n = (-y)^n + y^n.$$

When n *is odd*, this expression becomes $-y^n + y^n$, or zero. Therefore $x^n + y^n$ is divisible by $x + y$ when n *is odd*.

The results of the present article may be conveniently stated as follows:

(i.) For all positive integral values of n,
$$x^n - y^n = (x - y)(x^{n-1} + x^{n-2}y + x^{n-3}y^2 + \cdots + y^{n-1}).$$

(ii.) When n is odd,
$$x^n + y^n = (x + y)(x^{n-1} - x^{n-2}y + x^{n-3}y^2 - \cdots + y^{n-1}).$$

(iii.) When n is even,
$$x^n - y^n = (x + y)(x^{n-1} - x^{n-2}y + x^{n-3}y^2 - \cdots - y^{n-1}).$$

107. We shall now discuss some cases of greater difficulty, and also show how certain expressions of frequent occurrence, which are not integral, may be separated into factors. The student may omit this portion of the chapter until reading the subject a second time.

Ex. 1. Resolve $a^9 - 64 a^3 - a^6 + 64$ into **six factors.**

The expression
$= a^3(a^6 - 64) - (a^6 - 64)$
$= (a^3 - 64)(a^6 - 1)$
$= (a^3 + 8)(a^3 - 8)(a^3 - 1)$
$= (a + 2)(a^2 - 2a + 4)(a - 2)(a^2 + 2a + 4)(a - 1)(a^2 + a + 1).$

Ex. 2. $\quad a(a-1)x^2 - (a-b-1)xy - b(b+1)y^2$
$= \{ax - (b+1)y\}\{(a-1)x + by\}.$

108. From Ex. 2, Art. 59, we see that the quotient of $a^3 + b^3 + c^3 - 3abc$ by $a+b+c$ is $a^2 + b^2 + c^2 - bc - ca - ab$. Thus
$$a^3 + b^3 + c^3 - 3abc$$
$$= (a+b+c)(a^2 + b^2 + c^2 - bc - ca - ab) \quad . \quad . \quad (1).$$

This result is important and should be carefully remembered. We may note that the expression on the left consists of the sum of the cubes of three quantities a, b, c, diminished by three times the product abc. Whenever an expression admits of a similar arrangement, the above formula will enable us to resolve it into factors.

Ex. 1. Resolve into factors $a^3 - b^3 + c^3 + 3abc$.
$$a^3 - b^3 + c^3 + 3abc = a^3 + (-b)^3 + c^3 - 3a(-b)c$$
$$= (a - b + c)(a^2 + b^2 + c^2 + bc - ca + ab),$$
$-b$ taking the place of b in formula (1).

Ex. 2.
$$x^3 - 8y^3 - 27 - 18xy = x^3 + (-2y)^3 + (-3)^3 - 3x(-2y)(-3)$$
$$= (x - 2y - 3)(x^2 + 4y^2 + 9 - 6y + 3x + 2xy).$$

109. Expressions which can be put into the form $x^3 \pm \dfrac{1}{y^3}$ may be separated into factors by the rules for resolving the sum or the difference of two cubes. [Art. 102.]

Ex. 1. $\dfrac{8}{a^3} - 27 b^6 = \left(\dfrac{2}{a}\right)^3 - (3 b^2)^3$
$$= \left(\dfrac{2}{a} - 3 b^2\right)\left(\dfrac{4}{a^2} + \dfrac{6 b^2}{a} + 9 b^4\right).$$

Ex. 2. Resolve $a^2 x^3 - \dfrac{8 a^2}{y^3} - x^3 + \dfrac{8}{y^3}$ into four factors.

$a^2 x^3 - \dfrac{8 a^2}{y^3} - x^3 + \dfrac{8}{y^3} = x^3(a^2 - 1) - \dfrac{8}{y^3}(a^2 - 1)$
$$= (a^2 - 1)\left(x^3 - \dfrac{8}{y^3}\right)$$
$$= (a+1)(a-1)\left(x - \dfrac{2}{y}\right)\left(x^2 + \dfrac{2x}{y} + \dfrac{4}{y^2}\right).$$

EXAMPLES X. s.

Resolve into two or more factors:

1. $x^2y + 3xy^2 - 3x^3 - y^3$.
2. $4mn^2 - 20n^3 + 45nm^2 - 9m^3$.
3. $ab(x^2 + 1) + x(a^2 + b^2)$.
4. $y^2z^2(x^4 - 1) + x^2(y^4 - z^4)$.
5. $a^3 + (a + b)ax + bx^2$.
6. $pn(m^2 + 1) - m(p^2 + n^2)$.
7. $6bx(a^2 + 1) - a(4x^2 + 9b^2)$.
8. $(2a^2 + 3y^2)x + (2x^2 + 3a^2)y$.
9. $(2x^2 - 3a^2)y + (2a^2 - 3y^2)x$.
10. $a(a - 1)x^2 + (2a^2 - 1)x + a(a + 1)$.
11. $3x^2 - (4a + 2b)x + a^2 + 2ab$.
12. $2a^2x^2 - 2(3b - 4c)(b - c)y^2 + abxy$.
13. $(a^2 - 3a + 2)x^2 + (2a^2 - 4a + 1)x + a(a - 1)$.
14. $a(a + 1)x^2 + (a + b)xy - b(b - 1)y^2$.
15. $b^3 + c^3 - 1 + 3bc$.
16. $a^3 + 8c^3 + 1 - 6ac$.
17. $a^3 + b^3 + 8c^3 - 6abc$.
18. $a^3 - 27b^3 + c^3 + 9abc$.
19. $a^3 - b^3 - c^3 - 3abc$.
20. $8a^3 + 27b^3 + c^3 - 18abc$.
21. $\dfrac{27}{a^3b^3} - 1$.
22. $216a^3 - \dfrac{b^3}{8}$.
23. $\dfrac{x^3}{125} + y^3$.
24. $\dfrac{m^3n^3}{729} - 1$.
25. $\dfrac{a^3b^3}{125} + 1000$.
26. $\dfrac{x^3}{512} - \dfrac{64}{x^3}$.

27. Resolve $x^8 + 81x^4 + 6561$ into three factors.
28. Resolve $(a^4 - 2a^2b^2 - b^4)^2 - 4a^4b^4$ into four factors.
29. Resolve $4(ab + cd)^2 - (a^2 + b^2 - c^2 - d^2)^2$ into four factors.
30. Resolve $x^8 - \dfrac{1}{256}$ into four factors.
31. Resolve $x^{18} - y^{18}$ into six factors.

Resolve into four factors:

32. $\dfrac{a^3}{x^2} - 8x - a^3 + 8x^3$.
33. $x^9 + x^3y^6 - 8x^6y^3 - 8y^9$.
34. $x^9 + x^6 + 64x^3 + 64$.
35. $4a - 9b + \dfrac{4b^3}{a^2} - \dfrac{9a^3}{b^2}$.
36. $\dfrac{xy^3}{72} - \dfrac{x^3y^5}{32} - \dfrac{1}{9x^2} + \dfrac{y^2}{4}$.
37. $x^6 - 25x^2 + 6\tfrac{1}{4} - \dfrac{1}{4}x^4$.

Resolve into five factors:

38. $x^7 + x^4 - 16x^3 - 16$.
39. $16x^7 - 81x^5 - 16x^4 + 81$.

CHAPTER XI.

HIGHEST COMMON FACTOR.

110. DEFINITION. The **Highest Common Factor** of two or more algebraic expressions is the expression of *highest dimensions* (Art. 29) which divides each of them without remainder.

The abbreviation H.C.F. is sometimes used instead of the words *highest common factor*.

SIMPLE EXPRESSIONS.

111. The H.C.F. can be written by inspection.

Ex. 1. The highest common factor of a^4, a^3, a^2, a^6 is a^2.

Ex. 2. The highest common factor of a^3b^4, ab^5c^2, a^2b^7c is ab^4; for a is the highest power of a that will divide a^3, a, a^2; b^4 is the highest power of b that will divide b^4, b^5, b^7; and c is not a *common* factor.

112. If the expressions have numerical coefficients, find by Arithmetic their greatest common measure, and prefix it as a coefficient to the algebraic highest common factor.

Ex. The highest common factor of $21 a^4x^3y$, $35 a^2x^4y$, $28 a^3xy^4$ is $7 a^2xy$; for it consists of the product of
 (1) the numerical greatest common measure of the coefficients;
 (2) the highest power of each letter which divides every one of the given expressions.

EXAMPLES XI. a.

Find the highest common factor of

1. $4 ab^2$, $2 a^2b$.
2. $3 x^2y^2$, x^3y^2.
3. $6 xy^2z$, $8 x^2y^3z^2$.
4. abc, $2 ab^2c$.
5. $5 a^3b^3$, $15 abc^2$.
6. $9 x^2y^2z^2$, $12 xy^3z$.

7. $4 a^2 b^3 c^2$, $6 a^3 b^2 c^3$.
8. $7 a^2 b^4 c^5$, $14 ab^2 c^3$.
9. $49 ax^2$, $63 ay^2$, $56 az^2$.
10. $17 ab^2 c$, $34 a^2 bc$, $51 abc^2$.
11. $a^3 x^2 y^2$, $b^3 xy^2$, $c^3 x^2 y$.

12. $25 xy^2 z$, $100 x^2 yz$, $125 xy$.
13. $a^2 bpxy$, $b^2 qxy$, $a^3 bxr^2$.
14. $15 a^5 b^3 c^7$, $60 a^3 b^7 c^5$, $25 a^4 b^5 c^2$.
15. $35 a^2 c^3 b$, $42 a^3 cb^2$, $30 ac^2 b^3$.
16. $24 a^3 b^2 c^3$, $16 a^5 b^4 c^2$, $40 a^3 b^3 c^5$.

COMPOUND EXPRESSIONS.

113. H. C. F. of Compound Expressions which can be factored by Inspection. The method employed is similar to that of the preceding article.

Ex. 1. Find the highest common factor of

$$4 cx^3 \text{ and } 2 cx^3 + 4 c^2 x^2.$$

It will be easy to pick out the common factors if the expressions are arranged as follows:

$$4 cx^3 = 4 cx^3,$$
$$2 cx^3 + 4 c^2 x^2 = 2 cx^2 (x + 2 c);$$

therefore the H. C. F. is $2 cx^2$.

Ex. 2. Find the highest common factor of

$$3 a^2 + 9 ab, \ a^3 - 9 ab^2, \ a^3 + 6 a^2 b + 9 ab^2.$$

Resolving each expression into its factors, we have

$$3 a^2 + 9 ab = 3 a(a + 3 b),$$
$$a^3 - 9 ab^2 = a(a + 3 b)(a - 3 b),$$
$$a^3 + 6 a^2 b + 9 ab^2 = a(a + 3 b)(a + 3 b);$$

therefore the H. C. F. is $a(a + 3 b)$.

114. When there are two or more expressions containing different powers of the same *compound* factor, the student should be careful to notice that the highest common factor must contain the highest power of the compound factor which is common to all the given expressions.

Ex. 1. The highest common factor of

$$x(a - x)^2, \ a(a - x)^3, \text{ and } 2 ax(a - x)^5 \text{ is } (a - x)^2.$$

Ex. 2. Find the highest common factor of

$$ax^2 + 2 a^2 x + a^3, \ 2 ax^2 - 4 a^2 x - 6 a^3, \ 3 (ax + a^2)^2.$$

Resolving the expressions into factors, we have
$$ax^2 + 2a^2x + a^3 = a(x^2 + 2ax + a^2)$$
$$= a(x+a)^2 \quad \ldots \quad (1),$$
$$2ax^2 - 4a^2x - 6a^3 = 2a(x^2 - 2ax - 3a^2)$$
$$= 2a(x+a)(x-3a) \quad \ldots \quad (2),$$
$$3(ax + a^2)^2 = 3a^2(x+a)^2 \quad \ldots \quad (3).$$

Therefore from (1), (2), (3), by inspection, the highest common factor is $a(x+a)$.

EXAMPLES XI. b.

Find the highest common factor of

1. $a^2 + ab,\ a^2 - b^2$.
2. $(x+y)^2,\ x^2 - y^2$.
3. $2x^2 - 2xy,\ x^3 - x^2y$.
4. $6x^2 - 9xy,\ 4x^2 - 9y^2$.
5. $x^3 + x^2y,\ x^3 + y^3$.
6. $a^3b - ab^3,\ a^5b^2 - a^2b^5$.
7. $a^3 - a^2x,\ a^3 - ax^2,\ a^4 - ax^3$.
8. $a^2 - 4x^2,\ a^2 + 2ax$.
9. $a^2 - x^2,\ a^2 - ax,\ a^2x - ax^2$.
10. $4x^2 + 2xy,\ 12x^2y - 3y^3$.
11. $20x - 4,\ 50x^2 - 2$.
12. $6bx + 4by,\ 9cx + 6cy$.
13. $x^2 + x,\ (x+1)^2,\ x^3 + 1$.
14. $xy - y,\ x^4y - xy$.
15. $x^2 - 2xy + y^2,\ (x-y)^3$.
16. $x^3 + a^2x,\ x^4 - a^4$.
17. $x^3 + 8y^3,\ x^2 + xy - 2y^2$.
18. $x^4 - 27a^3x,\ (x-3a)^2$.
19. $x^2 + 3x + 2,\ x^2 - 4$.
20. $x^2 - x - 20,\ x^2 - 9x + 20$.
21. $x^2 - 18x + 45,\ x^2 - 9$.
22. $2x^2 - 7x + 3,\ 3x^2 - 7x - 6$.
23. $x^5 - xy^2,\ x^3 + x^2y + xy + y^2$.
24. $a^3x - a^2bx - 6ab^2x,\ a^2bx^2 - 4ab^2x^2 + 3b^3x^2$.
25. $2x^2 + 9x + 4,\ 2x^2 + 11x + 5,\ 2x^2 - 3x - 2$.
26. $3x^4 + 8x^3 + 4x^2,\ 3x^5 + 11x^4 + 6x^3,\ 3x^4 - 16x^3 - 12x^2$.
27. $2x^4 + 5x^3 + 3x^2,\ 6x^4 + 13x^3 + 6x^2,\ 2x^4 - 7x^3 - 15x^2$.
28. $12x + 6x^2 + 6,\ 6x + 3x^2 + 3,\ 18x + 3x^2 + 15$.
29. $x^4 + 4x^2 + 3,\ x^4 + 5x^2 + 6,\ 3x^4 + 11x^2 + 6$.
30. $2a^2 + 7ad + 6d^2,\ 2a^2 + 9ad + 9d^2,\ 6a^2 + 11ad + 3d^2$.
31. $2x^2 + 8xy + 6y^2,\ 4x^2 + 14xy + 6y^2,\ 2x^2 + 10xy + 12y^2$.

115. H. C. F. of Compound Expressions which cannot be factored by Inspection. To find the highest common factor in such cases, we adopt a method analogous to that used in Arithmetic for finding the greatest common measure of two or more numbers.

NOTE. The term *greatest common measure* is sometimes used instead of *highest common factor;* but, strictly speaking, the term *greatest common measure* ought to be confined to arithmetical quantities; for the highest common factor is not necessarily the greatest common measure in all cases, as will appear later. (Art. 121.)

116. We begin by working out examples illustrative of the algebraic process of finding the highest common factor, postponing for the present the complete proof of the rules we use. But we may conveniently enunciate two principles, which the student should bear in mind in reading the examples which follow.

I. *If an expression contains a certain factor, any multiple of the expression is divisible by that factor.*

II. *If two expressions have a common factor, it will divide their sum and their difference; and also the sum and the difference of any multiples of them.*

Ex. Find the highest common factor of
$$4x^3 - 3x^2 - 24x - 9 \text{ and } 8x^3 - 2x^2 - 53x - 39.$$

$$
\begin{array}{r|l|l|l}
x & 4x^3 - 3x^2 - 24x - 9 & 8x^3 - 2x^2 - 53x - 39 & 2 \\
  & 4x^3 - 5x^2 - 21x   & 8x^3 - 6x^2 - 48x - 18 & \\
2x & 2x^2 - 3x - 9   & 4x^2 - 5x - 21 & 2 \\
   & 2x^2 - 6x   & 4x^2 - 6x - 18 & \\
3 & 3x - 9   & x - 3 & \\
   & 3x - 9   & & \\
\end{array}
$$

Therefore the H. C. F. is $x - 3$.

EXPLANATION. First arrange the given expressions according to descending or ascending powers of x. The expressions so arranged having their first terms of the same order, we take for divisor that whose highest power has the smaller coefficient. Arrange the work in parallel columns as above. When the first remainder $4x^2 - 5x - 21$ is made the divisor we put the quotient x to the *left* of the dividend. Again, when the second remainder $2x^2 - 3x - 9$ is in turn made the divisor, the quotient 2 is placed to the *right*; and so on. As in Arithmetic, the last divisor $x - 3$ is the highest common factor required.

117. This method is only useful to determine the *compound* factor of the highest common factor. *Simple* factors of the given expressions must be first removed from them.

and the highest common factor of these, if any, must be observed and multiplied into the *compound* factor given by the rule.

Ex. Find the highest common factor of

$$24x^4 - 2x^3 - 60x^2 - 32x \text{ and } 18x^4 - 6x^3 - 39x^2 - 18x.$$

We have $24x^4 - 2x^3 - 60x^2 - 32x = 2x(12x^3 - x^2 - 30x - 16)$,

and $18x^4 - 6x^3 - 39x^2 - 18x = 3x(6x^3 - 2x^2 - 13x - 6)$.

Also $2x$ and $3x$ have the common factor x. Removing the simple factors $2x$ and $3x$, and *reserving* their common factor x, we continue as in Art. 116.

$$
\begin{array}{r|l|l|r}
2x & 6x^3 - 2x^2 - 13x - 6 & 12x^3 - x^2 - 30x - 16 & 2 \\
 & 6x^3 - 8x^2 - 8x & 12x^3 - 4x^2 - 26x - 12 & \\ \cline{2-3}
2 & 6x^2 - 5x - 6 & 3x^2 - 4x - 4 & x \\
 & 6x^2 - 8x - 8 & 3x^2 + 2x & \\ \cline{2-3}
 & 3x + 2 & -6x - 4 & -2 \\
 & & -6x - 4 &
\end{array}
$$

Therefore the H. C. F. is $x(3x+2)$.

118. So far the process of Arithmetic has been found exactly applicable to the algebraic expressions we have considered. But in many cases certain modifications of the arithmetical method will be found necessary. These will be more clearly understood if it is remembered that, at every stage of the work, the remainder must contain as a factor of itself the highest common factor we are seeking. [See Art. 116, I & II.]

Ex. 1. Find the highest common factor of

$$3x^3 - 13x^2 + 23x - 21 \text{ and } 6x^3 + x^2 - 44x + 21.$$

$$
\begin{array}{r|l|r}
3x^3 - 13x^2 + 23x - 21 & 6x^3 + x^2 - 44x + 21 & 2 \\
 & 6x^3 - 26x^2 + 46x - 42 & \\ \cline{2-2}
 & 27x^2 - 90x + 63 &
\end{array}
$$

Here on making $27x^2 - 90x + 63$ a divisor, we find that it is not contained in $3x^3 - 13x^2 + 23x - 21$ with an *integral* quotient. But noticing that $27x^2 - 90x + 63$ may be written in the form $9(3x^2 - 10x + 7)$, and also bearing in mind that every remainder in the course of the work contains the H.C.F., we conclude that the H. C. F. we are seeking is contained in $9(3x^2 - 10x + 7)$. But the two original ex-

HIGHEST COMMON FACTOR.

pressions have no *simple* factors, therefore their H. C. F. can have none. We may therefore *reject* the factor 9 and go on with divisor $3x^2 - 10x + 7$. Resuming the work, we have

$$\begin{array}{r|l|l}
x & 3x^3 - 13x^2 + 23x - 21 & 3x^2 - 10x + 7 \; \big| \; x \\
 & 3x^3 - 10x^2 + 7x & 3x^2 - 7x \\ \cline{2-3}
-1 & -3x^2 + 16x - 21 & -3x + 7 \; \big| \; -1 \\
 & -3x^2 + 10x - 7 & -3x + 7 \\ \cline{2-2}
 & 2)\,6x - 14 & \\
 & \overline{\;3x - 7\;} &
\end{array}$$

Therefore the highest common factor is $3x - 7$.

The factor 2 has been removed on the same grounds as the factor 9 above.

Ex. 2. Find the highest common factor of

$$2x^3 + x^2 - x - 2 \quad \ldots \ldots \ldots (1),$$
and
$$3x^3 - 2x^2 + x - 2 \quad \ldots \ldots \ldots (2).$$

As the expressions stand we cannot begin to divide one by the other without using a fractional quotient. The difficulty may be obviated by *introducing* a suitable factor, just as in the last case we found it useful to remove a factor when we could no longer proceed with the division in the ordinary way. The given expressions have no common *simple* factor, hence their H. C. F. cannot be affected if we multiply either of them by any simple factor.

Multiply (2) by 2, and use (1) as a divisor:

$$\begin{array}{r|l|l}
 & 2x^3 + x^2 - x - 2 & 6x^3 - 4x^2 + 2x - 4 \; \big| \; 3 \\
 & 7 & 6x^3 + 3x^2 - 3x - 6 \\ \cline{2-3}
-2x & 14x^3 + 7x^2 - 7x - 14 & -7x^2 + 5x + 2 \\
 & 14x^3 - 10x^2 - 4x & 17 \\ \cline{2-3}
17x & 17x^2 - 3x - 14 & -119x^2 + 85x + 34 \; \big| \; -7 \\
 & 17x^2 - 17x & -119x^2 + 21x + 98 \\ \cline{2-3}
14 & 14x - 14 & 64)\,64x - 64 \\
 & 14x - 14 & x - 1
\end{array}$$

Therefore the H. C. F. is $x - 1$.

After the first division the factor 7 is introduced because the first remainder $-7x^2 + 5x + 2$ will not divide $2x^3 + x^2 - x - 2$.

At the next stage the factor 17 is introduced for a similar reason, and finally the factor 64 is removed as explained in Ex. 1.

From these examples it appears that we may multiply or divide either of the given expressions, or any of the remainders which occur in the course of the work, by any factor which does not divide both of the given expressions.

NOTE. If, in Ex. 2, the expressions had been arranged in *ascending* powers of x, it would have been found unnecessary to introduce a numerical factor in the course of the work.

119. The use of the **Factor Theorem** (Art. 105) often lessens, in a very marked degree, the work of finding the highest common factor. Thus in Ex. 2 of the preceding article it is easily seen that both expressions become equal to 0 when 1 is substituted for x, hence $x-1$ is a factor. Dividing the first of the given expressions by $x-1$, we obtain a quotient $2x^2 + 3x + 2$. It is evident that this will not divide the second expression, hence $x-1$ is the H. C. F.

120. When the **Method of Division by Detached Coefficients** (Art. 63) is employed in finding the H. C. F., the following is a convenient arrangement.

Ex. Find the H. C. F. of
$$x^4 + 3x^3 + 12x - 16 \text{ and } x^3 - 13x + 12.$$

We write the literal factors of the dividend until we reach a term of the same degree as the first term of the divisor.

$$\begin{array}{r|rrrr}
x^3 & x^4 + 3x^3 + & 0 + 12 - 16 \\
0 & & 0 & + 13 - 12 \\
+13 & & & 0 + 39 - 36 \\
-12 & & & \\
\hline
& x + 3 \; ; & & 13 + 39 - 52
\end{array}$$

The addition of the terms in the third column gives $13x^2$, which is of lower *degree* than the first term of the divisor, hence we can proceed no further with the division and have for a remainder $13x^2 + 39x - 52$. Removing from this remainder the factor 13, as it is not a factor of the given expressions, we have for a second divisor $x^2 + 3x - 4$. The first divisor, as written *before the signs were changed*, forms the second dividend:

$$\begin{array}{r|rrrr}
x^2 & x^3 + 0\,x^2 - 13 + 12 \\
-3 & & -3 & + 4 \\
+4 & & & + 9 - 12 \\
\hline
& x - 3 \; ; & 0 & \cdot 0
\end{array}$$

since there is no remainder, the last divisor, as written *before the signs were changed*, is the H. C. F. Thus $x^2 + 3x - 4$ is the H. C. F.

HIGHEST COMMON FACTOR.

121. Let the two expressions in Ex. 2, Art. 118, be written in the form

$$2x^3 + x^2 - x - 2 = (x-1)(2x^2 + 3x + 2),$$
$$3x^3 - 2x^2 + x - 2 = (x-1)(3x^2 + x + 2).$$

Then their highest common factor is $x-1$, and therefore $2x^2 + 3x + 2$ and $3x^2 + x + 2$ *have no algebraic common divisor*. If, however, we put $x=6$, then

$$2x^3 + x^2 - x - 2 = 460,$$
and $$3x^3 - 2x^2 + x - 2 = 580;$$

and the greatest common measure of 460 and 580 is 20; whereas 5 is the numerical value $x-1$, the algebraic highest common factor. Thus the numerical values of the algebraic highest common factor and of the arithmetical greatest common measure do not in this case agree.

The reason may be explained as follows: when $x=6$, the expressions $2x^2 + 3x + 2$ and $3x^2 + x + 2$ become equal to 92 and 116 respectively, and have a common arithmetical factor 4; whereas the expressions have no algebraic common factor.

It will thus often happen that the highest common factor of two expressions and their numerical greatest common measure, when the letters have particular values, are not the same; for this reason the term greatest common measure is inappropriate when applied to algebraic quantities.

EXAMPLES XI. c.

Find the highest common factor of the following expressions:

1. $x^3 + 2x^2 - 13x + 10,\ x^3 + x^2 - 10x + 8.$
2. $x^3 - 5x^2 - 99x + 40,\ x^3 - 6x^2 - 86x + 35.$
3. $x^3 + 2x^2 - 8x - 16,\ x^3 + 3x^2 - 8x - 24.$
4. $x^3 - x^2 - 5x - 3,\ x^3 - 4x^2 - 11x - 6.$
5. $x^3 + 3x^2 - 8x - 24,\ x^3 + 3x^2 - 3x - 9.$
6. $a^3 - 5a^2x + 7ax^2 - 3x^3,\ a^3 - 3ax^2 + 2x^3.$
7. $2x^3 - 5x^2 + 11x + 7,\ 4x^3 - 11x^2 + 25x + 7.$
8. $2x^3 + 4x^2 - 7x - 14,\ 6x^3 - 10x^2 - 21x + 35.$

9. $3x^4 - 3x^3 - 2x^2 - x - 1,\ 9x^4 - 3x^3 - x - 1$.
10. $3x^3 - 3ax^2 + 2a^2x - 2a^3,\ 3x^3 + 12ax^2 + 2a^2x + 8a^3$.
11. $2x^3 - 9ax^2 + 9a^2x - 7a^3,\ 4x^3 - 20ax^2 + 20a^2x - 16a^3$.
12. $10x^3 + 25ax^2 - 5a^3,\ 4x^3 + 9ax^2 - 2a^2x - a^3$.
13. $24x^4y + 72x^3y^2 - 6x^2y^3 - 90xy^4,\ 6x^4y^2 + 13x^3y^3 - 4x^2y^4 - 15xy^5$.
14. $4x^5a^2 + 10x^4a^3 - 60x^3a^4 + 54x^2a^5,\ 24x^5a^3 + 30x^3a^5 - 126x^2a^6$.
15. $4x^5 + 14x^4 + 20x^3 + 70x^2,\ 8x^7 + 28x^6 - 8x^5 - 12x^4 + 56x^3$.
16. $72x^3 - 12ax^2 + 72a^2x - 420a^3,\ 18x^3 + 42ax^2 - 282a^2x + 270a^3$.
17. $x^5 - x^3 - x + 1,\ x^7 + x^6 + x^4 - 1$.
18. $1 + x + x^3 - x^5,\ 1 - x^4 - x^6 + x^7$.

122. The statements of Art. 116 may be proved as follows:

I. If F divides A it will also divide mA.
For suppose $A = aF$, then $mA = maF$.
Thus F is a factor of mA.

II. If F divides A and B, then it will divide $mA \pm nB$.
For suppose $A = aF$, $B = bF$,
then $\quad mA \pm nB = maF \pm nbF$
$\quad\quad\quad\quad\quad\quad = F(ma \pm nb)$.
Thus F divides $mA \pm nB$.

123 We may now enunciate and prove the rule for finding the highest common factor of any two compound algebraic expressions.

We suppose that any simple factors are first removed. (See Example, Art. 117.)

Let A and B be the two expressions after the simple factors have been removed. Let them be arranged in descending or ascending powers of some common letter; also let the highest power of that letter in B be not less than the highest power in A.

Divide B by A; let p be the quotient, and C the remainder. Suppose C to have a *simple* factor m. Remove this factor, and so obtain a new divisor D. Further, suppose that in order to make A divisible by D it is **necessary to** multiply A by a *simple* factor n. Let q be the next quotient and E the remainder. Finally, divide D by E; let r be the quotient, and suppose that there is no remainder. Then E will be the H. C. F. required.

The work will stand thus:

$$
\begin{array}{r}
A)B(p \\
\underline{pA} \\
m)C \\
\overline{D)nA}(q \\
\underline{qD} \\
\overline{E)D}(r \\
\underline{rE}
\end{array}
$$

First, to show that E is *a* common factor of A and B.

By examining the steps of the work, it is clear that E divides D, therefore also qD; therefore $qD + E$, therefore nA; therefore A, since n is a *simple* factor.

Again E divides D, therefore mD, that is, C. And since E divides A and C, it also divides $pA + C$, that is, B. Hence E divides both A and B.

Secondly, to show that E is the *highest* common factor.

If not, let there be a factor X of higher dimensions than E.

Then X divides A and B, therefore $B - pA$, that is, C; therefore D (since m is a *simple* factor); therefore $nA - qD$, that is, E.

Thus X divides E; which is impossible, since by hypothesis, X is of higher dimensions than E.

Therefore E is the highest common factor.

124. The highest common factor of three expressions A, B, C may be obtained as follows:

First determine F the highest common factor of A and B; next find G the highest common factor of F and C; then G will be the required highest common factor of A, B, C.

For F contains *every* factor which is common to A and B, and G is the highest common factor of F and C. Therefore G is the highest common factor of A, B, C.

CHAPTER XII.

Lowest Common Multiple.

125. DEFINITION. The **Lowest Common Multiple** of two or more algebraic expressions is the expression of *lowest dimensions* which is divisible by each of them without remainder.

The abbreviation L. C. M. is sometimes used instead of the words *lowest common multiple*.

SIMPLE EXPRESSIONS.

126. The L. C. M. can be written by inspection.

Ex. 1. The lowest common multiple of a^4, a^3, a^2, a^6 is a^6.

Ex. 2. The lowest common multiple of a^3b^4, ab^5, a^2b^7 is a^3b^7; for a^3 is the lowest power of a that is divisible by each of the quantities a^3, a, a^2; and b^7 is the lowest power of b that is divisible by each of the quantities b^4, b^5, b^7.

127. If the expressions have numerical coefficients, find by Arithmetic their least common multiple, and prefix it as a coefficient to the algebraic lowest common multiple.

Ex. The lowest common multiple of $21\,a^4x^3y$, $35\,a^2x^4y$, $28\,a^3xy^4$ is $420\,a^4x^4y^4$; for it consists of the product of

(1) the numerical least common multiple of the coefficients;

(2) the lowest power of each letter which is divisible by every power of that letter occurring in the given expressions.

EXAMPLES XII. a.

Find the lowest common multiple of

1. x^3y^2, xyz.
2. $3x^2yz$, $4x^3y^3$.
3. $5a^2bc^3$, $4ab^2c$.
4. $12\,ab$, $8\,xy$.
5. ac, bc, ab.
6. a^2c, bc^2, cb^2.
7. $2x$, $3y$, $4z$.
8. $3x^2$, $4y^2$, $3z^2$.
9. $7a^2$, $2ab$, $3b^3$.

LOWEST COMMON MULTIPLE.

10. a^2bc, b^2ca, c^2ab.
11. $5a^2c, 6cb^2, 3bc^2$.
12. $2x^2y^3, 3xy, 4x^3y^4$.
13. $35a^2c^3b, 42a^3cb^2, 30ac^2b^3$.
14. $66a^4b^2c^3, 44a^3b^4c^2, 24a^2b^3c^4$.
15. $7a^2b, 4ac^2, 6ac^3, 21bc$.

COMPOUND EXPRESSIONS.

128. L.C.M. of Compound Expressions which can be factored by Inspection. The method employed is similar to that of the preceding article.

Ex. 1. The lowest common multiple of $6x^2(a-x)^2$, $8a^3(a-x)^3$ and $12ax(a-x)^5$ is $24a^3x^2(a-x)^5$.

For it consists of the product of

(1) the numerical L.C.M. of the coefficients;

(2) the lowest power of each factor which is divisible by every power of that factor occurring in the given expressions.

Ex. 2. Find the lowest common multiple of
$$3a^2 + 9ab, \ 2a^3 - 18ab^2, \ a^3 + 6a^2b + 9ab^2.$$
$$3a^2 + 9ab = 3a(a + 3b),$$
$$2a^3 - 18ab^2 = 2a(a + 3b)(a - 3b),$$
$$a^3 + 6a^2b + 9ab^2 = a(a + 3b)(a + 3b)$$
$$= a(a + 3b)^2.$$

Therefore the L.C.M. is $6a(a + 3b)^2(a - 3b)$.

EXAMPLES XII. b.

Find the lowest common multiple of

1. $x^2, x^2 - 3x$.
2. $21x^3, 7x^2(x+1)$.
3. $a^2 + ab, ab + b^2$.
4. $4x^2y - y, 2x^2 + x$.
5. $6x^2 - 2x, 9x^2 - 3x$.
6. $x^2 + 2x, x^2 + 3x + 2$.
7. $x^2 - 3x + 2, x^2 - 1$.
8. $(a + x)^3, a^3 + x^3$.
9. $a^2 + x^2, (a + x)^2$.
10. $(a - x)^2, a^2 - x^2$.
11. $(1 + x)^3, 1 + x^3$.
12. $x^2 + 4x + 4, x^2 + 5x + 6$.
13. $x^2 - 5x + 4, x^2 - 6x + 8$.
14. $1 - x^3, (1 - x)^3$.
15. $(a - x)^3, a^3 - x^3$.
16. $x^2 + x - 20, x^2 - 10x + 24, x^2 - x - 30$.
17. $x^2 + x - 42, x^2 - 11x + 30, x^2 + 2x - 35$.
18. $2x^2 + 3x + 1, 2x^2 + 5x + 2, x^2 + 3x + 2$.
19. $a^2 - x^2, (a - x)^2, a^3 - x^3$.

20. $3x^2 + 11x + 6,\ 3x^2 + 8x + 4,\ x^2 + 5x + 6$.
21. $5x^2 + 11x + 2,\ 5x^2 + 16x + 3,\ x^2 + 5x + 6$.
22. $1 + x^2,\ (1 + x)^2,\ 1 + x^3$.
23. $2x^2 + 3x - 2,\ 2x^2 + 15x - 8,\ x^2 + 10x + 16$.
24. $3x^2 - x - 14,\ 3x^2 - 13x + 14,\ x^2 - 4$.
25. $12x^2 + 3x - 42,\ 12x^3 + 30x^2 + 12x,\ 32x^2 - 40x - 28$.
26. $3x^4 + 26x^3 + 35x^2,\ 6x^2 + 38x - 28,\ 27x^3 + 27x^2 - 30x$.
27. $60x^4 + 5x^3 - 5x^2,\ 60x^2y + 32xy + 4y,\ 40x^3y - 2x^2y - 2xy$.
28. $8x^2 - 38xy + 35y^2,\ 4x^2 - xy - 5y^2,\ 2x^2 - 5xy - 7y^2$.
29. $12x^2 - 23xy + 10y^2,\ 4x^2 - 9xy + 5y^2,\ 3x^2 - 5xy + 2y^2$.
30. $6ax^3 + 7a^2x^2 - 3a^3x,\ 3a^2x^2 + 14a^3x - 5a^4,\ 6x^2 + 39ax + 45a^2$.
31. $4ax^2y^2 + 11axy^2 - 3ay^2,\ 3x^3y^3 + 7x^2y^3 - 6xy^3,\ 24ax^2 - 22ax + 4a$.

129. L. C. M. of Compound Expressions which cannot be factored by Inspection. When the given expressions are such that their factors cannot be determined by inspection, they must be resolved by finding the highest common factor.

Ex. Find the lowest common multiple of

$2x^4 + x^3 - 20x^2 - 7x + 24$ and $2x^4 + 3x^3 - 13x^2 - 7x + 15$.

The highest common factor is $x^2 + 2x - 3$.

By division, we obtain

$2x^4 + x^3 - 20x^2 - 7x + 24 = (x^2 + 2x - 3)(2x^2 - 3x - 8)$.

$2x^4 + 3x^3 - 13x^2 - 7x + 15 = (x^2 + 2x - 3)(2x^2 - x - 5)$.

Therefore the L. C. M. is $(x^2 + 2x - 3)(2x^2 - 3x - 8)(2x^2 - x - 5)$.

130. We may now give the proof of the rule for finding the lowest common multiple of two compound algebraic expressions.

Let A and B be the two expressions, and F their highest common factor. Also suppose that a and b are the respective quotients when A and B are divided by F; then $A = aF$, $B = bF$. Therefore, since a and b have no common factor, the lowest common multiple of A and B is abF, by inspection.

LOWEST COMMON MULTIPLE.

131. There is an important relation between the highest common factor and the lowest common multiple of two expressions which it is desirable to notice.

Let F be the highest common factor, and X the lowest common multiple of A and B. Then, as in the preceding article,
$$A = aF, \ B = bF,$$
and
$$X = abF.$$
Therefore the product
$$\begin{aligned}AB &= aF \times bF \\ &= F \times abF \\ &= FX \ \ldots \ \ldots \ \ldots \ (1).\end{aligned}$$

Hence *the product of two expressions is equal to the product of their highest common factor and lowest common multiple.*

Again, from (1) $X = \dfrac{AB}{F} = \dfrac{A}{F} \times B = \dfrac{B}{F} \times A;$

hence *the lowest common multiple of two expressions may be found by dividing their product by their highest common factor; or by dividing either of them by their highest common factor, and multiplying the quotient by the other.*

132. The lowest common multiple of three expressions A, B, C may be obtained as follows:

First find X, the L. C. M. of A and B. Next find Y, the L. C. M. of X and C; then Y will be the required L. C. M. of A, B, C.

For Y is the expression of lowest dimensions which is divisible by X and C, and X is the expression of lowest dimensions divisible by A and B. Therefore Y is the expression of lowest dimensions divisible by all three.

EXAMPLES XII. c.

1. Find the highest common factor and the lowest common multiple of $x^2 - 5x + 6$, $x^2 - 4$, $x^3 - 3x - 2$.

2. Find the lowest common multiple of
$$ab(x^2 + 1) + x(a^2 + b^2) \text{ and } ab(x^2 - 1) + x(a^2 - b^2).$$

3. Find the lowest common multiple of $xy - bx$, $xy - ay$, $y^2 - 3by + 2b^2$, $xy - 2bx - ay + 2ab$, $xy - bx - ay + ab$.

4. Find the highest common factor and the lowest common multiple of $x^3 + 2x^2 - 3x$, $2x^3 + 5x^2 - 3x$.

5. Find the lowest common multiple of
$$1 - x, \ (1 - x^2)^2, \ (1 + x)^3.$$

6. Find the lowest common multiple of
$$x^2 - 10x + 24, \ x^2 - 8x + 12, \ x^2 - 6x + 8.$$

7. Find the highest common factor and the lowest common multiple of $6x^3 + x^2 - 5x - 2$, $6x^3 + 5x^2 - 3x - 2$.

8. Find the lowest common multiple of
$$(bc^2 - abc)^2, \ b^2(ac^2 - a^3), \ a^2c^2 + 2ac^3 + c^4.$$

9. Find the lowest common multiple of
$$x^3 - y^3, \ x^3y - y^4, \ y^2(x - y)^2, \ x^2 + xy + y^2.$$
Also find the highest common factor of the first three expressions.

10. Find the highest common factor of
$$6x^2 - 13x + 6, \ 2x^2 + 5x - 12, \ 6x^2 - x - 12.$$
Also show that the lowest common multiple is the product of the three quantities divided by the square of the highest common factor.

11. Find the lowest common multiple of
$$x^4 + ax^3 + a^3x + a^4, \ x^4 + a^2x^2 + a^4.$$

12. Find the highest common factor and the lowest common multiple of $3x^3 - 7x^2y + 5xy^2 - y^3$, $x^2y + 3xy^2 - 3x^3 - y^3$,
$$3x^3 + 5x^2y + xy^2 - y^3.$$

13. Find the highest common factor of
$$4x^3 - 10x^2 + 4x + 2, \ 3x^4 - 2x^3 - 3x + 2.$$

14. Find the lowest common multiple of
$$a^2 - b^2, \ a^3 - b^3, \ a^3 - a^2b - ab^2 - 2b^3.$$

15. Find the highest common factor and the lowest common multiple of $(2x^2 - 3a^2)y + (2a^2 - 3y^2)x$, $(2a^2 + 3y^2)x + (2x^2 + 3a^2)y$.

16. Find the highest common factor and the lowest common multiple of $x^3 - 9x^2 + 26x - 24$, $x^3 - 12x^2 + 47x - 60$.

17. Find the highest common factor of
$$x^3 - 15ax^2 + 48a^2x + 64a^3, \ x^2 - 10ax + 16a^2.$$

18. Find the lowest common multiple of
$$21x(xy - y^2)^2, \ 35(x^4y^2 - x^2y^4), \ 15y(x^2 + xy)^2.$$

CHAPTER XIII.

FRACTIONS.

133. DEFINITION. If a quantity x be divided into b equal parts, and a of these parts be taken, the result is called *the fraction $\frac{a}{b}$ of x.*

If x be the unit, the fraction $\frac{a}{b}$ of x is called simply "the fraction $\frac{a}{b}$"; so that *the fraction $\frac{a}{b}$ represents a equal parts, b of which make up the unit.*

The quantity above the horizontal line is spoken of as the numerator, and that below the line as the denominator of the fraction.

134. A **Simple Fraction** is one of which the numerator and denominator are whole numbers.

REDUCTION OF FRACTIONS.

135. *To reduce a fraction* is to change its form without changing its value.

136. To prove that $\frac{a}{b} = \frac{ma}{mb}$, where a, b, m are positive integers.

By $\frac{a}{b}$ we mean a equal parts, b of which make up the unit, (1);

by $\frac{ma}{mb}$ we mean ma equal parts, mb of which make up the unit, (2).

But
$$b \text{ parts in } (1) = mb \text{ parts in } (2);$$
$$\therefore 1 \text{ part in } (1) = m \text{ parts in } (2);$$
$$\therefore a \text{ parts in } (1) = ma \text{ parts in } (2);$$

that is,
$$\frac{a}{b} = \frac{ma}{mb}.$$

Conversely,
$$\frac{ma}{mb} = \frac{a}{b}.$$

Hence, *The value of a fraction is not altered if we multiply or divide the numerator and denominator by the same quantity.*

137. Reduction of a Fraction to its Lowest Terms. As shown in the preceding article an algebraic fraction may be changed into an equivalent fraction by dividing numerator and denominator by any common factor; if this factor be the *highest common factor*, the resulting fraction is said to be **reduced to its lowest terms**.

Ex. 1. Reduce to lowest terms $\dfrac{24\, a^3 c^2 x^3}{36\, a^5 x^2}$.

$$\frac{24\, a^3 c^2 x^3}{36\, a^5 x^2} = \frac{2^3 \times 3\, a^3 c^2 x^3}{2^2 \times 3^2\, a^5 x^2} = \frac{2\, c^2 x}{3\, a^2}.$$

Ex. 2. Reduce to lowest terms $\dfrac{24\, a^3 c^2 x^2}{18\, a^3 x^2 - 12\, a^2 x^3}$.

$$\frac{24\, a^3 c^2 x^2}{18 a^3 x^2 - 12\, a^2 x^3} = \frac{24\, a^3 c^2 x^2}{6\, a^2 x^2 (3a - 2x)} = \frac{4\, ac^2}{3a - 2x}$$

Ex. 3. Reduce to lowest terms $\dfrac{6 x^2 - 8 xy}{9\, xy - 12\, y^2}$.

$$\frac{6 x^2 - 8 xy}{9\, xy - 12\, y^2} = \frac{2\, x(3x - 4y)}{3\, y(3x - 4y)} = \frac{2\, x}{3\, y}.$$

NOTE. The beginner should be careful not to begin cancelling until he has expressed both numerator and denominator in the most convenient form, by resolution into factors where necessary.

EXAMPLES XIII. a.

Reduce to lowest terms:

1. $\dfrac{12\, mn^2 p}{15\, m^2 n p^2}$.
2. $\dfrac{46\, x^3 y^4 z^5}{69\, x^2 y^3 z^4}$.
3. $\dfrac{ax}{a^2 x^2 - ax}$.
4. $\dfrac{3\, a^2 - 6\, ab}{2\, a^2 b - 4\, ab^2}$.
5. $\dfrac{abx + bx^2}{acx + cx^2}$.
6. $\dfrac{15\, a^2 b^2 c}{100(a^3 - a^2 b)}$.

FRACTIONS.

7. $\dfrac{4x^2 - 9y^2}{4x^2 + 6xy}.$

8. $\dfrac{20(x^3 - y^3)}{5x^2 + 5xy + 5y^2}.$

9. $\dfrac{x(2a^2 - 3ax)}{a(4a^2x - 9x^3)}.$

10. $\dfrac{x^3 - 2xy^2}{x^4 - 4x^2y^2 + 4y^4}.$

11. $\dfrac{(xy - 3y^2)^2}{x^3y^2 - 27y^5}.$

12. $\dfrac{x^2 - 5x}{x^2 - 4x - 5}.$

13. $\dfrac{3x^2 + 6x}{x^2 + 4x + 4}.$

14. $\dfrac{5a^3b + 10a^2b^2}{3a^2b^2 + 6ab^3}.$

15. $\dfrac{x^3y + 2x^2y + 4xy}{x^3 - 8}.$

16. $\dfrac{3a^4 + 9a^3b + 6a^2b^2}{a^4 + a^3b - 2a^2b^2}.$

17. $\dfrac{x^4 - 14x^2 - 51}{x^4 - 2x^2 - 15}.$

18. $\dfrac{x^2 + xy - 2y^2}{x^3 - y^3}.$

19. $\dfrac{2x^2 + 17x + 21}{3x^2 + 26x + 35}.$

20. $\dfrac{a^2x^2 - 16a^2}{ax^2 + 9ax + 20a}.$

21. $\dfrac{3x^2 + 23x + 14}{3x^2 + 41x + 26}.$

22. $\dfrac{27a + a^4}{18a - 6a^2 + 2a^3}.$

138. When the factors of the numerator and denominator cannot be determined by inspection, we find the highest common factor, by the rules given in Chapter XI.

Ex. Reduce to lowest terms $\dfrac{3x^3 - 13x^2 + 23x - 21}{15x^3 - 38x^2 - 2x + 21}.$

First Method. The H.C.F. of numerator and denominator is $3x - 7$.

Dividing numerator and denominator by $3x - 7$, we obtain as respective quotients $x^2 - 2x + 3$ and $5x^2 - x - 3$.

Thus $\dfrac{3x^3 - 13x^2 + 23x - 21}{15x^3 - 38x^2 - 2x + 21} = \dfrac{(3x-7)(x^2 - 2x + 3)}{(3x-7)(5x^2 - x - 3)} = \dfrac{x^2 - 2x + 3}{5x^2 - x - 3}.$

This is the simplest solution for the beginner; but in this and similar cases we may often effect the reduction without actually going through the process of finding the highest common factor.

Second Method. By Art. 116, the H.C.F. of numerator and denominator must be a factor of their sum $18x^3 - 51x^2 + 21x$, that is, of $3x(3x - 7)(2x - 1)$. If there be a common divisor it must clearly be $3x - 7$; hence arranging numerator and denominator so as to show $3x - 7$ as a factor,

the fraction $= \dfrac{x^2(3x-7) - 2x(3x-7) + 3(3x-7)}{5x^2(3x-7) - x(3x-7) - 3(3x-7)}$

$= \dfrac{(3x-7)(x^2 - 2x + 3)}{(3x-7)(5x^2 - x - 3)} = \dfrac{x^2 - 2x + 3}{5x^2 - x - 3}.$

139. If either numerator or denominator can readily be resolved into factors we may use the following method.

Ex. Reduce to lowest terms $\dfrac{x^3 + 3x^2 - 4x}{7x^3 - 18x^2 + 6x + 5}$.

The numerator $= x(x^2 + 3x - 4) = x(x + 4)(x - 1)$.

Of these factors the only one which can be a common divisor is $x - 1$. Hence, arranging the denominator,

the fraction $= \dfrac{x(x + 4)(x - 1)}{7x^2(x - 1) - 11x(x - 1) - 5(x - 1)}$

$= \dfrac{x(x + 4)(x - 1)}{(x - 1)(7x^2 - 11x - 5)} = \dfrac{x(x + 4)}{7x^2 - 11x - 5}$.

EXAMPLES XIII. b.

Reduce to lowest terms:

1. $\dfrac{a^3 - a^2b - ab^2 - 2b^3}{a^3 + 3a^2b + 3ab^2 + 2b^3}$.

2. $\dfrac{x^3 - 5x^2 + 7x - 3}{x^3 - 3x + 2}$.

3. $\dfrac{a^3 + 2a^2 - 13a + 10}{a^3 + a^2 - 10a + 8}$.

4. $\dfrac{2x^3 + 5x^2y - 30xy^2 + 27y^3}{4x^3 + 5xy^2 - 21y^3}$.

5. $\dfrac{4a^3 + 12a^2b - ab^2 - 15b^3}{6a^3 + 13a^2b - 4ab^2 - 15b^3}$.

6. $\dfrac{1 + 2x^2 + x^3 + 2x^4}{1 + 3x^2 + 2x^3 + 3x^4}$.

7. $\dfrac{x^2 - 2x + 1}{3x^3 + 7x - 10}$.

8. $\dfrac{3a^3 - 3a^2b + ab^2 - b^3}{4a^2 - 5ab + b^2}$.

9. $\dfrac{4x^3 + 3ax^2 + a^3}{x^4 + ax^3 + a^3x + a^4}$.

10. $\dfrac{4x^3 - 10x^2 + 4x + 2}{3x^4 - 2x^3 - 3x + 2}$.

11. $\dfrac{16x^4 - 72x^2a^2 + 81a^4}{4x^2 + 12ax + 9a^2}$.

12. $\dfrac{6x^3 + x^2 - 5x - 2}{6x^3 + 5x^2 - 3x - 2}$.

13. $\dfrac{5x^3 + 2x^2 - 15x - 6}{7x^3 - 4x^2 - 21x + 12}$.

14. $\dfrac{4x^4 + 11x^2 + 25}{4x^4 - 9x^2 + 30x - 25}$.

15. $\dfrac{3x^3 - 27ax^2 + 78a^2x - 72a^3}{2x^3 + 10ax^2 - 4a^2x - 48a^3}$.

16. $\dfrac{ax^3 - 5a^2x^2 - 99a^3x + 40a^4}{x^4 - 6ax^3 - 86a^2x^2 + 35a^3x}$.

MULTIPLICATION AND DIVISION OF FRACTIONS.

140. Rule I. To multiply a fraction by an integer. *Multiply the numerator by that integer; or, if the denominator be divisible by the integer, divide the denominator by it.*

FRACTIONS. 111

The proof is as follows:

(1) $\frac{a}{b}$ represents a equal parts, b of which make up the unit; $\frac{ac}{b}$ represents ac equal parts, b of which make up the unit; and the number of parts taken in the second fraction is c times the number taken in the first;

that is, $$\frac{a}{b} \times c = \frac{ac}{b}.$$

(2) $$\frac{a}{bd} \times d = \frac{ad}{bd} = \frac{a}{b}.$$ [Art. 136.]

Hence $\frac{a}{b} \times b = \frac{ab}{b} = a$; that is, the fraction $\frac{a}{b}$ is the quantity which must be multiplied by b in order to obtain a. Now the quantity which must be multiplied by b in order to obtain a is the quotient resulting from the division of a by b [Art. 53]; therefore we may define a fraction thus: *the fraction $\frac{a}{b}$ is the quotient of a divided by b.*

141. Rule II. To divide a fraction by an integer. *Divide the numerator, if it be divisible, by the integer; or, if the numerator be not divisible, multiply the denominator by that integer.*

The proof is as follows:

(1) $\frac{ac}{b}$ represents ac equal parts, b of which make up the unit; $\frac{a}{b}$ represents a equal parts, b of which make up the unit.

The number of parts taken in the first fraction is c times the number taken in the second. Therefore the second fraction is the quotient of the first fraction divided by c;

that is, $$\frac{ac}{b} \div c = \frac{a}{b}.$$

(2) But if the numerator be not divisible by c, we have
$$\frac{a}{b} = \frac{ac}{bc};$$
$$\therefore \frac{a}{b} \div c = \frac{ac}{bc} \div c = \frac{a}{bc}, \text{ by the preceding case.}$$

142. Rule III. To multiply together two or more fractions. *Multiply the numerators for a new numerator, and the denominators for a new denominator.*

To find the value of $\frac{a}{b} \times \frac{c}{d}$.

Let $$x = \frac{a}{b} \times \frac{c}{d}.$$

Multiplying each side by $b \times d$, we have
$$x \times b \times d = \frac{a}{b} \times \frac{c}{d} \times b \times d$$
$$= \frac{a}{b} \times b \times \frac{c}{d} \times d \qquad \text{[Art. 37.]}$$
$$= a \times c. \qquad \text{[Art. 140.]}$$
$$\therefore xbd = ac.$$

Dividing each side by bd, we have
$$x = \frac{ac}{bd};$$
$$\therefore \frac{a}{b} \times \frac{c}{d} = \frac{ac}{bd}.$$

Similarly, $\frac{a}{b} \times \frac{c}{d} \times \frac{e}{f} = \frac{ace}{bdf}$; and so for any number of fractions.

143. Rule IV. To divide one fraction by another. *Invert the divisor, and proceed as in multiplication.*

Since division is the inverse of multiplication, we may define the quotient x, when $\frac{a}{b}$ is divided by $\frac{c}{d}$, to be such that
$$x \times \frac{c}{d} = \frac{a}{b}.$$

FRACTIONS. 113

Multiplying by $\dfrac{d}{c}$, we have $x \times \dfrac{c}{d} \times \dfrac{d}{c} = \dfrac{a}{b} \times \dfrac{d}{c}$;

$$\therefore x = \dfrac{ad}{bc}.$$

Hence $\qquad \dfrac{a}{b} \div \dfrac{c}{d} = \dfrac{ad}{bc} = \dfrac{a}{b} \times \dfrac{d}{c}.$ [Art. 142.]

Ex. 1. Simplify $\dfrac{2a}{3b} \times \dfrac{3c^2}{4a^3} \times \dfrac{5bc}{6abc}.$

The expression $= \dfrac{2 \times 3 \times 5 \times abc^3}{3 \times 4 \times 6 \times a^4 b^2 c} = \dfrac{5 c^2}{12 a^3 b}.$

Ex. 2. Simplify $\dfrac{2a^2 + 3a}{4a^3} \times \dfrac{4a^2 - 6a}{12a + 18}.$

$\dfrac{2a^2 + 3a}{4a^3} \times \dfrac{4a^2 - 6a}{12a + 18} = \dfrac{a(2a+3)}{4a^3} \times \dfrac{2a(2a-3)}{6(2a+3)} = \dfrac{2a-3}{12a},$

by cancelling those factors which are common to both numerator and denominator.

Ex. 3. Simplify $\dfrac{6x^2 - ax - 2a^2}{ax - a^2} \times \dfrac{x-a}{9x^2 - 4a^2} \div \dfrac{2x+a}{3ax + 2a^2}.$

The expression
$= \dfrac{6x^2 - ax - 2a^2}{ax - a^2} \times \dfrac{x-a}{9x^2 - 4a^2} \times \dfrac{3ax + 2a^2}{2x+a}$
$= \dfrac{(3x-2a)(2x+a)}{a(x-a)} \times \dfrac{x-a}{(3x+2a)(3x-2a)} \times \dfrac{a(3x+2a)}{2x+a} = 1,$

since all the factors cancel each other.

EXAMPLES XIII. c.

Simplify

1. $\dfrac{7a^2b^3}{9ax^2y} \times \dfrac{18 x^2 c}{15 ac^4}.$

2. $\dfrac{21 k^2 p^3}{13 mn^2} \div \dfrac{28 p^2 k^3}{39 m^2 n^3}.$

3. $\dfrac{2x^2y}{3yz} \times \dfrac{5z^2x}{7xy^2} \div \dfrac{21 x^2 y^3 z^2}{40 xy^2 z}.$

4. $\dfrac{m^2}{8n} \times \dfrac{36 p^3 q^2}{81 mn} \div \dfrac{15 mpx^5}{27 n^2 x^3 y}.$

5. $\dfrac{14x^2 - 7x}{12x^3 + 24x^2} \div \dfrac{2x-1}{x^2 + 2x}.$

6. $\dfrac{a^2 b^2 + 3ab}{4a^2 - 1} \div \dfrac{ab+3}{2a+1}.$

7. $\dfrac{x^2 - 4a^2}{ax + 2a^2} \times \dfrac{2a}{x - 2a}.$

8. $\dfrac{a^2 - 121}{a^2 - 4} \div \dfrac{a+11}{a+2}.$

9. $\dfrac{16x^2 - 9a^2}{x^2 - 4} \times \dfrac{x-2}{4x-3a}$.

10. $\dfrac{25a^2 - b^2}{9a^2x^2 - 4x^2} \times \dfrac{x(3a+2)}{5a+b}$.

11. $\dfrac{x^2 + 5x + 6}{x^2 - 1} \times \dfrac{x^2 - 2x - 3}{x^2 - 9}$.

12. $\dfrac{x^2 + 3x + 2}{x^2 + 9x + 20} \times \dfrac{x^2 + 7x + 12}{x^2 + 5x + 6}$.

13. $\dfrac{2x^2 + 5x + 2}{x^2 - 4} \times \dfrac{x^2 + 4x}{2x^2 + 9x + 4}$.

14. $\dfrac{b^4 - 27b}{2b^2 + 5b} \times \dfrac{4b^2 - 25}{2b^2 - 11b + 15}$.

15. $\dfrac{2x^2 + 13x + 15}{4x^2 - 9} \div \dfrac{2x^2 + 11x + 5}{4x^2 - 1}$.

16. $\dfrac{3a^2 + 3ax}{(a-x)^2} \times \dfrac{2a^2 + ax - 3x^2}{a^2 - x^2}$.

17. $\dfrac{x^2 - 14x - 15}{x^2 - 4x - 45} \div \dfrac{x^2 - 12x - 45}{x^2 - 6x - 27}$.

18. $\dfrac{2 + 5x + 3x^2}{(1+x)^3} \div \dfrac{4x^2}{1 + x^3}$.

19. $\dfrac{2x^2 - x - 1}{2x^2 + 5x + 2} \times \dfrac{4x^2 + x - 14}{16x^2 - 49}$.

20. $\dfrac{a^2 - 2ab - 3b^2}{(a+b)^3} \div \dfrac{a^2 - 4ab + 3b^2}{a^3 + b^3}$.

21. $\dfrac{x^3 - 6x^2 + 36x}{x^2 - 49} \div \dfrac{x^4 + 216x}{x^2 - x - 42}$.

22. $\dfrac{64p^2q^2 - z^4}{x^2 - 4} \times \dfrac{(x-2)^2}{8pq + z^2} \div \dfrac{x^2 - 4}{(x+2)^3}$.

23. $\dfrac{a^2 - 2a - 3}{(a+3)^2} \times \dfrac{a^2 - a - 12}{a^2 + 9}$.

24. $\dfrac{x^2 - x - 20}{x^2 - 25} \times \dfrac{x^2 - x - 2}{x^2 + 2x - 8} \div \dfrac{x+1}{x^2 + 5x}$.

25. $\dfrac{x^2 - 18x + 80}{x^2 - 5x - 50} \times \dfrac{x^2 - 6x - 7}{x^2 - 15x + 56} \times \dfrac{x+5}{x-1}$.

26. $\dfrac{1 - x^2}{1 - x^3} \times \dfrac{1 - 3x^2 + 2x^3}{(1-x)^3}$.

27. $\dfrac{x^2 - 5x - 14}{(x-2)^2} \times \dfrac{x^2 - 11x + 18}{x^2 - 4} \div \dfrac{x^2 - 16x + 63}{ax^3 - 4ax^2 + 4ax}$.

ADDITION AND SUBTRACTION OF FRACTIONS

144. To prove $\quad \dfrac{a}{b} + \dfrac{c}{d} = \dfrac{ad + bc}{bd}$.

We have $\quad \dfrac{a}{b} = \dfrac{ad}{bd}$, and $\dfrac{c}{d} = \dfrac{bc}{bd}$. $\qquad$ [Art. 136.]

FRACTIONS.

Thus in each case we divide the unit into bd equal parts, and we take first ad of these parts, and then bc of them; that is, we take $ad + bc$ of the bd parts of the unit; and this is expressed by the fraction $\dfrac{ad + bc}{bd}$.

$$\therefore \quad \frac{a}{b} + \frac{c}{d} = \frac{ad + bc}{bd}.$$

Similarly, $\qquad \dfrac{a}{b} - \dfrac{c}{d} = \dfrac{ad - bc}{bd}.$

145. Here the fractions have been both expressed with a common denominator bd. But if b and d have a common factor, the product bd is not the lowest common denominator, and the fraction $\dfrac{ad + bc}{bd}$ *will not be in its lowest terms.* To avoid working with fractions which are not in their lowest terms, we take the *lowest* common denominator, which is the lowest common multiple of the denominators of the given fractions.

Rule I. To reduce fractions to their lowest common denominator. *Find the L. C. M. of the given denominators, and take it for the common denominator; divide it by the denominator of the first fraction, and multiply the numerator of this fraction by the quotient so obtained; and do the same with all the other given fractions.*

Ex. 1. Express with lowest common denominator

$$\frac{a}{3xy}, \quad \frac{b}{6xyz}, \quad \frac{c}{2yz}.$$

The lowest common multiple of the denominators is $6xyz$. Dividing this by each of the denominators in turn, and multiplying the corresponding numerators by the respective quotients, we have the equivalent fractions

$$\frac{2az}{6xyz}, \quad \frac{b}{6xyz}, \quad \frac{3cx}{6xyz}.$$

Ex. 2. Express with lowest common denominator

$$\frac{5x}{2a(x-a)} \quad \text{and} \quad \frac{4a}{3x(x^2 - a^2)}.$$

The lowest common denominator is $6\,ax(x-a)(x+a)$.

We must, therefore, multiply the numerators by $3\,x(x+a)$ and $2\,a$ respectively.

Hence the equivalent fractions are

$$\frac{15\,x^2(x+a)}{6\,ax(x-a)(x+a)} \text{ and } \frac{8\,a^2}{6\,ax(x-a)(x+a)}.$$

146. We may now enunciate the rule for the addition or subtraction of fractions.

Rule II.   To add or subtract fractions. *Reduce them to the lowest common denominator; add or subtract the numerators, and retain the common denominator.*

Ex. 1. Find the value of $\dfrac{2\,x+a}{3\,a}+\dfrac{5\,x-4\,a}{9\,a}$.

The lowest common denominator is $9\,a$.

Therefore the expression $=\dfrac{3(2\,x+a)+5\,x-4\,a}{9\,a}$

$$=\frac{6\,x+3\,a+5\,x-4\,a}{9\,a}=\frac{11\,x-a}{9\,a}.$$

Ex. 2. Find the value of $\dfrac{x-2\,y}{xy}+\dfrac{3\,y-a}{ay}-\dfrac{3\,x-2\,a}{ax}$.

The lowest common denominator is axy.

Thus the expression $=\dfrac{a(x-2\,y)+x(3\,y-a)-y(3\,x-2\,a)}{axy}$

$$=\frac{ax-2\,ay+3\,xy-ax-3\,xy+2\,ay}{axy}=0,$$

since the terms in the numerator destroy each other.

EXAMPLES XIII. d.

Find the value of

1. $\dfrac{2\,x-1}{3}+\dfrac{x-5}{6}+\dfrac{x-4}{4}$.

2. $\dfrac{2\,x-3}{9}-\dfrac{x+2}{6}+\dfrac{5\,x+8}{12}$.

3. $\dfrac{x-7}{15}+\dfrac{x-9}{25}-\dfrac{x+8}{45}$.

4. $\dfrac{2\,x+5}{x}-\dfrac{x+3}{2\,x}-\dfrac{27}{8\,x^2}$.

5. $\dfrac{a-b}{ab}+\dfrac{b-c}{bc}+\dfrac{c-a}{ca}$.

6. $\dfrac{a-2\,b}{2\,a}-\dfrac{a-5\,b}{4\,a}+\dfrac{a+7\,b}{8\,a}$.

7. $\dfrac{a-x}{x} + \dfrac{a+x}{a} - \dfrac{a^2-x^2}{2ax}$.

8. $\dfrac{2a^2-b^2}{a^2} - \dfrac{b^2-c^2}{b^2} - \dfrac{c^2-a^2}{c^2}$.

9. $\dfrac{x-3}{5x} + \dfrac{x^2-9}{10x^2} - \dfrac{8-x^3}{15x^3}$.

10. $\dfrac{2}{xy} - \dfrac{3y^2-x^2}{xy^3} + \dfrac{xy+y^2}{x^2y^2}$.

11. $\dfrac{2x-3y}{xy} + \dfrac{3x-2z}{xz} + \dfrac{5}{x}$.

12. $\dfrac{a^2-bc}{bc} - \dfrac{ac-b^2}{ac} - \dfrac{ab-c^2}{ab}$.

Ex. 3. Simplify $\dfrac{2x-3a}{x-2a} - \dfrac{2x-a}{x-a}$.

The lowest common denominator is $(x-2a)(x-a)$.

Therefore the expression $= \dfrac{(2x-3a)(x-a)-(2x-a)(x-2a)}{(x-2a)(x-a)}$

$= \dfrac{2x^2-5ax+3a^2-(2x^2-5ax+2a^2)}{(x-2a)(x-a)}$

$= \dfrac{2x^2-5ax+3a^2-2x^2+5ax-2a^2}{(x-2a)(x-a)}$

$= \dfrac{a^2}{(x-2a)(x-a)}$.

NOTE. In finding the value of such an expression as

$$-(2x-a)(x-2a),$$

the beginner should first express the product in brackets, and then remove the brackets, as we have done. After a little practice he will be able to take both steps together.

The work will sometimes be shortened by first reducing the fractions to their lowest terms.

Ex. 4. Simplify $\dfrac{x^2+5xy-4y^2}{x^2-16y^2} - \dfrac{2xy}{2x^2+8xy}$.

The expression $= \dfrac{x^2+5xy-4y^2}{x^2-16y^2} - \dfrac{y}{x+4y}$

$= \dfrac{x^2+5xy-4y^2-y(x-4y)}{x^2-16y^2}$

$= \dfrac{x^2+5xy-4y^2-xy+4y^2}{x^2-16y^2}$

$= \dfrac{x^2+4xy}{x^2-16y^2} = \dfrac{x}{x-4y}$.

EXAMPLES XIII. e.

Find the value of

1. $\dfrac{1}{x+2} + \dfrac{1}{x+3}$.

2. $\dfrac{2}{x+3} - \dfrac{1}{x+4}$.

3. $\dfrac{3}{x-6} - \dfrac{1}{x+2}$.

4. $\dfrac{a}{x+a} - \dfrac{b}{x+b}$.

5. $\dfrac{a}{x-a} + \dfrac{b}{x-b}$.

6. $\dfrac{a+x}{a-x} - \dfrac{a-x}{a+x}$.

7. $\dfrac{x+2}{x-2} - \dfrac{x-2}{x+2}$.

8. $\dfrac{x-4}{x-2} - \dfrac{x-7}{x-5}$.

9. $\dfrac{a}{x-a} - \dfrac{a^2}{x^2-a^2}$.

10. $\dfrac{a}{x^2-4} + \dfrac{b}{(x-2)^2}$.

11. $\dfrac{3}{x-3} + \dfrac{2x}{x^2-9}$.

12. $\dfrac{1}{2x-3y} - \dfrac{x+y}{4x^2-9y^2}$.

13. $\dfrac{1}{1-x^3} - \dfrac{1}{(1-x)^3}$.

14. $\dfrac{x+a}{x-2a} - \dfrac{x^2+2a^2}{x^2-4a^2}$.

15. $\dfrac{4a^2+b^2}{4a^2-b^2} - \dfrac{2a-b}{2a+b}$.

16. $\dfrac{2x^2}{x^2-y^2} - \dfrac{2x}{x+y}$.

17. $\dfrac{x}{1-x^2} - \dfrac{x}{1+x^2}$.

18. $\dfrac{1}{x(x-y)} + \dfrac{1}{y(x+y)}$.

19. $\dfrac{2}{a(x^2-a^2)} - \dfrac{2}{x(x+a)^2}$.

20. $\dfrac{xy}{25x^2-y^2} + \dfrac{x}{5x+y}$.

21. $\dfrac{y}{x(x^2-y^2)} + \dfrac{x}{y(x^2+y^2)}$.

22. $\dfrac{x+a}{(x^2+a^2)} - \dfrac{x-a}{(x+a)^2}$.

23. $\dfrac{x^2-4a^2}{x^2-2ax} - \dfrac{x+4a}{x+2a}$.

24. $\dfrac{x^2+xy+y^2}{x+y} + \dfrac{x^2-xy+y^2}{x-y}$.

25. $\dfrac{1}{a-2x} - \dfrac{(a+2x)^2}{a^3-8x^3}$.

26. $\dfrac{a^3+b^3}{a^2-ab+b^2} - \dfrac{a^3-b^3}{a^2+ab+b^2}$.

147. Some modification of the foregoing general methods may sometimes be used with advantage. The most useful artifices are explained in the examples which follow, but no general rules can be given which will apply to all cases.

Ex. 1. Simplify $\quad \dfrac{a+3}{a-4} - \dfrac{a+4}{a-3} - \dfrac{8}{a^2-16}$.

Taking the first two fractions together, we have the expression

$$= \dfrac{a^2-9-(a^2-16)}{(a-4)(a-3)} - \dfrac{8}{a^2-16} = \dfrac{7}{(a-4)(a-3)} - \dfrac{8}{(a+4)(a-4)}$$

$$= \dfrac{7(a+4)-8(a-3)}{(a+4)(a-4)(a-3)} = \dfrac{52-a}{(a+4)(a-4)(a-3)}.$$

FRACTIONS.

Ex. 2. Simplify $\dfrac{1}{2x^2+x-1}+\dfrac{1}{3x^2+4x+1}$.

The expression $=\dfrac{1}{(2x-1)(x+1)}+\dfrac{1}{(3x+1)(x+1)}$

$=\dfrac{3x+1+2x-1}{(2x-1)(x+1)(3x+1)}$

$=\dfrac{5x}{(2x-1)(x+1)(3x+1)}$.

Ex. 3. Simplify $\dfrac{1}{a-x}-\dfrac{1}{a+x}-\dfrac{2x}{a^2+x^2}-\dfrac{4x^3}{a^4+x^4}$.

Here it should be evident that the first two denominators give L. C. M. a^2-x^2, which readily combines with a^2+x^2 to give L. C. M. a^4-x^4, which again combines with a^4+x^4 to give L. C. M. a^8-x^8. Hence it will be convenient to proceed as follows:

The expression $=\dfrac{a+x-(a-x)}{a^2-x^2}-\cdots-\cdots$

$=\dfrac{2x}{a^2-x^2}-\dfrac{2x}{a^2+x^2}-\cdots$

$=\dfrac{4x^3}{a^4-x^4}-\dfrac{4x^3}{a^4+x^4}=\dfrac{8x^7}{a^8-x^8}$.

EXAMPLES XIII. 1.

Find the value of

1. $\dfrac{1}{x+y}-\dfrac{1}{x-y}+\dfrac{2x}{x^2-y^2}$.

2. $\dfrac{1}{2x+y}+\dfrac{1}{2x-y}-\dfrac{3x}{4x^2-y^2}$.

3. $\dfrac{5}{1+2x}-\dfrac{3x}{1-2x}-\dfrac{4-13x}{1-4x^2}$.

4. $\dfrac{2a}{2a+3b}+\dfrac{3b}{2a-3b}-\dfrac{8b^2}{4a^2-9b^2}$.

5. $\dfrac{1}{a+x}+\dfrac{1}{(a+x)^2}-\dfrac{1}{a^2-x^2}$.

6. $\dfrac{10}{9-a^2}-\dfrac{2}{3+a}-\dfrac{1}{3-a}$.

7. $\dfrac{5x}{6(x^2-1)}-\dfrac{1}{2(x-1)}+\dfrac{1}{3(x+1)}$.

8. $\dfrac{1}{2(a-b)}-\dfrac{1}{2(a+b)}-\dfrac{b}{a^2-b^2}$.

9. $\dfrac{1}{1+x}-\dfrac{2}{(1+x)^2}+\dfrac{3}{(1+x)^2}$.

10. $\dfrac{2a}{2a-3}-\dfrac{5}{6a+9}-\dfrac{4(3a+2)}{3(4a^2-9)}$.

11. $\dfrac{3}{x-2}+\dfrac{2}{3x+6}+\dfrac{5x}{x^2-4}$.

12. $\dfrac{x}{x^3+y^3}-\dfrac{y}{x^3-y^3}+\dfrac{x^3y+xy^3}{x^6-y^6}$.

13. $\dfrac{1}{x^2-9x+20}+\dfrac{1}{x^2-11x+30}$.

14. $\dfrac{1}{x^2-7x+12}-\dfrac{1}{x^2-5x+6}$.

15. $\dfrac{1}{2x^2-x-1}-\dfrac{1}{2x^2+x-3}$ 17. $\dfrac{4}{4-7a-2a^2}-\dfrac{3}{3-a-10a^2}$

16. $\dfrac{1}{2x^2-x-1}-\dfrac{3}{6x^2-x-2}$. 18. $\dfrac{5}{5+x-18x^2}-\dfrac{2}{2+5x+2x^2}$.

19. $\dfrac{1}{x+1}-\dfrac{1}{(x+1)(x+2)}+\dfrac{1}{(x+1)(x+2)(x+3)}$.

20. $\dfrac{5x}{2(x+1)(x-3)}-\dfrac{15(x-1)}{16(x-3)(x-2)}-\dfrac{9(x+3)}{16(x+1)(x-2)}$.

21. $\dfrac{a+3b}{4(a+b)(a+2b)}+\dfrac{a+2b}{(a+b)(a+3b)}-\dfrac{a+b}{4(a+2b)(a+3b)}$.

22. $\dfrac{2}{x^2-3x+2}+\dfrac{2}{x^2-x-2}-\dfrac{1}{x^2-1}$.

23. $\dfrac{x}{x^2+5x+6}+\dfrac{15}{x^2+9x+14}-\dfrac{12}{x^2+10x+21}$.

24. $\dfrac{3}{x^2-1}+\dfrac{4}{2x+1}+\dfrac{4x+2}{2x^2+3x+1}$.

25. $\dfrac{5(2x-3)}{11(6x^2+x-1)}+\dfrac{7x}{6x^2+7x-3}-\dfrac{12(3x+1)}{11(4x^2+8x+3)}$.

26. $\dfrac{x-3}{x+2}-\dfrac{x-2}{x+3}+\dfrac{1}{x-1}$. 28. $\dfrac{1+2a}{1-2a}-\dfrac{1-2a}{1+2a}-\dfrac{8a}{(1-2a)^2}$.

27. $\dfrac{x-3}{x-4}-\dfrac{x+4}{x+3}-\dfrac{5}{x^2-16}$. 29. $\dfrac{1}{1+x}-\dfrac{x}{1+x^3}-\dfrac{x^2}{(1-x)^3}$.

30. $\dfrac{24x}{9-12x+4x^2}-\dfrac{3+2x}{3-2x}+\dfrac{3-2x}{3+2x}$.

31. $\dfrac{1}{3-x}-\dfrac{1}{3+x}-\dfrac{2x}{9+x^2}$. 32. $\dfrac{1}{2a+3}+\dfrac{1}{2a-3}-\dfrac{4a}{4a^2+9}$.

33. $\dfrac{1}{4(1+x)}+\dfrac{1}{4(1-x)}+\dfrac{1}{2(1+x^2)}$.

34. $\dfrac{3}{8(a-x)}+\dfrac{1}{8(a+x)}-\dfrac{a-x}{4(a^2+x^2)}$.

35. $\dfrac{2x}{4+x^2}+\dfrac{1}{2-x}-\dfrac{1}{2+x}$. 36. $\dfrac{5}{3-6x}-\dfrac{5}{3+6x}-\dfrac{x}{2+8x^2}$.

37. $\dfrac{1}{2a-8x}-\dfrac{a}{3a^2+48x^2}+\dfrac{1}{2a+8x}$.

38. $\dfrac{1}{6a^2+54}+\dfrac{1}{3a-9}-\dfrac{a}{3a^2-27}$. 39. $\dfrac{2x}{2+x}-\dfrac{4x}{(2+x)^2}-\dfrac{2x^2}{4-x^2}$.

40. $\dfrac{1}{8-8x}-\dfrac{1}{8+8x}+\dfrac{x}{4+4x^2}-\dfrac{x}{2+2x^4}$.

148. We have thus far assumed both numerator and denominator to be positive integers, and have shown in Art. 140 that a fraction itself is the quotient resulting from the division of numerator by denominator. But in algebra division is a process not restricted to positive integers, and we shall now extend this definition as follows: *The algebraic fraction $\dfrac{a}{b}$ is the quotient resulting from the division of a by b, where a and b may have any values whatever.*

149. By the preceding article $\dfrac{-a}{-b}$ is the quotient resulting from the division of $-a$ by $-b$; and this is obtained by dividing a by b, and, by the rule of signs, prefixing $+$.

Therefore $\qquad \dfrac{-a}{-b} = +\dfrac{a}{b} = \dfrac{a}{b}$ . . . . (1).

Again, $\dfrac{-a}{b}$ is the quotient resulting from the division of $-a$ by b; and this is obtained by dividing a by b, and, by the rule of signs, prefixing $-$.

Therefore $\qquad \dfrac{-a}{b} = -\dfrac{a}{b}$ . . . . (2).

Similarly, $\qquad \dfrac{a}{-b} = -\dfrac{a}{b}$ . . . . (3).

These results may be enunciated as follows:

(1) *If the signs of* BOTH *numerator and denominator of a fraction be changed, the sign of the whole fraction will be unchanged.*

(2) *If the sign of* EITHER *numerator or denominator alone be changed, the sign of the whole fraction will be changed.*

The principles here involved are so useful in certain cases of reduction of fractions that we quote them in another form, which will sometimes be found more easy of application.

1. *We may change the sign of every term in the numerator and denominator of a fraction without altering its value.*

2. *We may change the sign of a fraction by simply changing the sign of every term in* EITHER *the numerator or denominator*

NOTE. The student should keep clearly in his mind the distinction between *term* and *factor*. The rule governing change of sign for factors will be given in Art. 150.

Ex. 1. $$\frac{b-a}{y-x} = \frac{-b+a}{-y+x} = \frac{a-b}{x-y}$$

Ex. 2. $$\frac{x-x^2}{2y} = -\frac{-x+x^2}{2y} = -\frac{x^2-x}{2y}.$$

Ex. 3. $$\frac{3x}{4-x^2} = -\frac{3x}{-4+x^2} = -\frac{3x}{x^2-4}.$$

The intermediate step may usually be omitted.

Ex. 4. Simplify $\dfrac{a}{x+a} + \dfrac{2x}{x-a} + \dfrac{a(3x-a)}{a^2-x^2}.$

Here it is evident that the lowest common denominator of the first two fractions is $x^2 - a^2$, therefore it will be convenient to alter the sign of the denominator in the third fraction.

Thus the expression $= \dfrac{a}{x+a} + \dfrac{2x}{x-a} - \dfrac{a(3x-a)}{x^2-a^2}$

$$= \frac{a(x-a) + 2x(x+a) - a(3x-a)}{x^2-a^2}$$

$$= \frac{ax - a^2 + 2x^2 + 2ax - 3ax + a^2}{x^2 - a^2} = \frac{2x^2}{x^2 - a^2}.$$

Ex. 5. Simplify $\dfrac{5}{3x-3} + \dfrac{3x-1}{1-x^2} + \dfrac{1}{2x+2}.$

The expression $= \dfrac{5}{3(x-1)} - \dfrac{3x-1}{x^2-1} + \dfrac{1}{2(x+1)}$

$$= \frac{10(x+1) - 6(3x-1) + 3(x-1)}{6(x^2-1)}$$

$$= \frac{10x + 10 - 18x + 6 + 3x - 3}{6(x^2-1)} = \frac{13 - 5x}{6(x^2-1)}.$$

EXAMPLES XIII. g.

Simplify

1. $\dfrac{1}{4x-4} - \dfrac{1}{5x+5} + \dfrac{1}{1-x^2}.$

2. $\dfrac{3}{1+a} - \dfrac{2}{1-a} - \dfrac{5a}{a^2-1}.$

3. $\dfrac{x+2a}{x+a} + \dfrac{2(a^2-4ax)}{a^2-x^2} - \dfrac{3a}{x-a}.$

4. $\dfrac{x-a}{x+a} + \dfrac{a^2+3ax}{a^2-x^2} + \dfrac{x+a}{x-a}.$

FRACTIONS.

5. $\dfrac{1}{2x+1} + \dfrac{1}{2x-1} + \dfrac{4x}{1-4x^2}$

6. $\dfrac{3x}{1-x^2} - \dfrac{2}{x-1} - \dfrac{2}{x+1}$.

7. $\dfrac{2-5x}{x+3} - \dfrac{3+x}{3-x} + \dfrac{2x(2x-11)}{x^2-9}$.

8. $\dfrac{3-2x}{2x+3} - \dfrac{2x+3}{3-2x} + \dfrac{12}{4x^2-9}$.

9. $\dfrac{5}{2b+2} - \dfrac{3}{4b-4} + \dfrac{11}{6-6b^2}$.

10. $\dfrac{1}{6a+6} + \dfrac{1}{6-6a} - \dfrac{1}{3a^2-3}$.

11. $\dfrac{y^2}{x^3-y^3} + \dfrac{x^3y^2}{y^6-x^6}$.

12. $\dfrac{x^2-y^2}{xy} - \dfrac{xy-y^2}{xy-x^2}$.

13. $\dfrac{x^2+y^2}{x^2-y^2} + \dfrac{x}{x+y} + \dfrac{y}{y-x}$.

14. $\dfrac{x^2+2x+4}{x+2} - \dfrac{x^2-2x+4}{2-x}$.

15. $\dfrac{1}{2a+5b} + \dfrac{3a}{25b^2-4a^2} + \dfrac{1}{2a-5b}$.

16. $\dfrac{2b-a}{x-b} - \dfrac{3x(a-b)}{b^2-x^2} + \dfrac{b-2a}{b+x}$.

17. $\dfrac{ax^2+b}{2x-1} + \dfrac{2(bx+ax^2)}{1-4x^2} - \dfrac{ax^2-b}{2x+1}$.

18. $\dfrac{a+c}{(a-b)(x-a)} + \dfrac{b+c}{(b-a)(x-b)}$.

19. $\dfrac{a-c}{(a-b)(x-a)} - \dfrac{b-c}{(b-a)(b-x)}$.

20. $\dfrac{2a+y}{(x-a)(a-b)} + \dfrac{a+b+y}{(x-b)(b-a)} - \dfrac{x+y-a}{(x-a)(x-b)}$.

21. $\dfrac{1}{(a^2-b^2)(x^2+b^2)} + \dfrac{1}{(b^2-a^2)(x^2+a^2)} - \dfrac{1}{(x^2+a^2)(x^2+b^2)}$.

22. $\dfrac{1}{x+a} + \dfrac{4a}{x^2-a^2} + \dfrac{1}{a-x} - \dfrac{2a}{x^2+a^2}$.

23. $\dfrac{3}{x+a} - \dfrac{1}{x+3a} + \dfrac{3}{a-x} + \dfrac{1}{x-3a}$.

24. $\dfrac{1}{4a^3(a+x)} - \dfrac{1}{4a^3(x-a)} + \dfrac{1}{2a^2(a^2+x^2)} - \dfrac{a^4}{a^8-x^8}$.

25. $\dfrac{x}{x^2-y^2} - \dfrac{y}{x^2+y^2} + \dfrac{x^3+y^3}{y^4-x^4} + \dfrac{xy}{(x+y)(x^2+y^2)}$.

26. $\dfrac{b}{a(a^2-b^2)} + \dfrac{a}{b(a^2+b^2)} + \dfrac{a^4+b^4}{ab(b^4-a^4)} - \dfrac{a^6}{b^8-a^8}$.

150. From Art. 149 it follows that:

(1) Changing the signs of **an odd number of factors** of numerator or denominator changes the sign before the fraction.

(2) Changing the signs of an **even number of factors** of numerator or denominator does not change the sign before the fraction.

Consider the expression

$$\frac{1}{(a-b)(a-c)} + \frac{1}{(b-c)(b-a)} + \frac{1}{(c-a)(c-b)}.$$

By changing the sign of the second factor of each denominator, we obtain

$$-\frac{1}{(a-b)(c-a)} - \frac{1}{(b-c)(a-b)} - \frac{1}{(c-a)(b-c)} \quad . \quad (1).$$

Now it is readily seen that the L.C.M. of the denominators is $(a-b)(b-c)(c-a)$, and the expression

$$= \frac{-(b-c)-(c-a)-(a-b)}{(a-b)(b-c)(c-a)}$$

$$= \frac{-b+c-c+a-a+b}{(a-b)(b-c)(c-a)} = 0.$$

151. There is a peculiarity in the arrangement of this example which it is desirable to notice. In the expression (1) the letters occur in what is known as **Cyclic Order**; that is, b follows a, a follows c, c follows b. Thus, if a, b, c are arranged round the circumference of a circle, as in the annexed diagram, if we start from any letter and move round in the direction of the arrows, the other letters follow in cyclic order, namely abc, bca, cab.

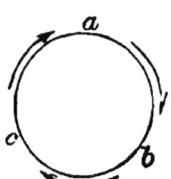

The observance of this principle is especially important in a large class of examples in which the differences of three letters are involved. Thus we are observing cyclic order when we write $b-c$, $c-a$, $a-b$; whereas we are violating cyclic order by the use of arrangements such as $b-c$, $a-c$, $a-b$, or $a-c$, $b-a$, $b-c$. It will always be found that the work is rendered shorter and easier by following cyclic order from the beginning, and adhering to it throughout the question.

EXAMPLES XIII. h.

Find the value of

1. $\dfrac{a}{(a-b)(a-c)} + \dfrac{b}{(b-c)(b-a)} + \dfrac{c}{(c-a)(c-b)}.$

2. $\dfrac{b}{(a-b)(a-c)} + \dfrac{c}{(b-c)(b-a)} + \dfrac{a}{(c-a)(c-b)}.$

3. $\dfrac{z}{(x-y)(x-z)} + \dfrac{x}{(y-z)(y-x)} + \dfrac{y}{(z-x)(z-y)}.$

4. $\dfrac{y+z}{(x-y)(x-z)} + \dfrac{z+x}{(y-z)(y-x)} + \dfrac{x+y}{(z-x)(z-y)}.$

5. $\dfrac{b-c}{(a-b)(a-c)} + \dfrac{c-a}{(b-c)(b-a)} + \dfrac{a-b}{(c-a)(c-b)}.$

6. $\dfrac{x^2yz}{(x-y)(x-z)} + \dfrac{y^2zx}{(y-z)(y-x)} + \dfrac{z^2xy}{(z-x)(z-y)}.$

7. $\dfrac{1+a}{(a-b)(a-c)} + \dfrac{1+b}{(b-c)(b-a)} + \dfrac{1+c}{(c-a)(c-b)}.$

8. $\dfrac{p-a}{(p-q)(p-r)} + \dfrac{q-a}{(q-r)(q-p)} + \dfrac{r-a}{(r-p)(r-q)}.$

9. $\dfrac{p+q-r}{(p-q)(p-r)} + \dfrac{q+r-p}{(q-r)(q-p)} + \dfrac{r+p-q}{(r-p)(r-q)}.$

10. $\dfrac{a^2}{(a^2-b^2)(a^2-c^2)} + \dfrac{b^2}{(b^2-c^2)(b^2-a^2)} + \dfrac{c^2}{(c^2-a^2)(c^2-b^2)}.$

11. $\dfrac{x+y}{(p-q)(p-r)} + \dfrac{x+y}{(q-r)(q-p)} + \dfrac{x+y}{(r-p)(r-q)}.$

12. $\dfrac{q+r}{(x-y)(x-z)} + \dfrac{r+p}{(y-z)(y-x)} + \dfrac{p+q}{(z-x)(z-y)}.$

CHAPTER XIV.

Complex Fractions. Mixed Expressions.

152. We now propose to consider some miscellaneous questions involving fractions of a more complicated kind than those already discussed.

In the previous chapter, the numerator and denominator have been regarded as integers; but cases frequently occur in which the numerator or denominator of a fraction is itself fractional.

153. A Complex Fraction is one that has a fraction in the numerator, or in the denominator, or in both.

Thus $\dfrac{a}{\frac{b}{c}}, \dfrac{\frac{a}{b}}{x}, \dfrac{\frac{a}{b}}{\frac{c}{d}}$ are Complex Fractions.

In the last of these types, the outside quantities, a and d, are sometimes referred to as the *extremes*, while the two middle quantities, b and c, are called the *means*.

154. By definition (Art. 148) $\dfrac{\frac{a}{b}}{\frac{c}{d}}$ is the quotient resulting from the division of $\dfrac{a}{b}$ by $\dfrac{c}{d}$; and this by Art. 143 is $\dfrac{ad}{bc}$.

$$\therefore \dfrac{\frac{a}{b}}{\frac{c}{d}} = \dfrac{ad}{bc}.$$

COMPLEX FRACTIONS.

155. From the preceding article we deduce an easy method of writing down the simplified form of a complex fraction.

Multiply the extremes for a new numerator, and the means for a new denominator.

Ex. $$\frac{\dfrac{a+x}{b}}{\dfrac{a^2-x^2}{ab}} = \frac{ab(a+x)}{b(a^2-x^2)} = \frac{a}{a-x},$$

by cancelling common factors in numerator and denominator.

156. The student should especially notice the following cases, and should be able to write off the results readily.

$$\frac{1}{\dfrac{a}{b}} = 1 \div \frac{a}{b} = 1 \times \frac{b}{a} = \frac{b}{a},$$

$$\frac{a}{\dfrac{1}{b}} = a \div \frac{1}{b} = a \times b = ab.$$

$$\frac{\dfrac{1}{a}}{\dfrac{1}{b}} = \frac{1}{a} \div \frac{1}{b} = \frac{1}{a} \times \frac{b}{1} = \frac{b}{a}.$$

157. We now proceed to show how complex fractions can be reduced by the rules already given.

Ex. 1. $$\frac{\dfrac{a}{b}+\dfrac{c}{d}}{\dfrac{a}{b}-\dfrac{c}{d}} = \left(\frac{a}{b}+\frac{c}{d}\right) \div \left(\frac{a}{b}-\frac{c}{d}\right) = \frac{ad+bc}{bd} \div \frac{ad-bc}{bd}$$

$$= \frac{ad+bc}{bd} \times \frac{bd}{ad-bc} = \frac{ad+bc}{ad-bc}.$$

Ex. 2. $$\frac{x+\dfrac{a^2}{x}}{x-\dfrac{a^4}{x^3}} = \left(x+\frac{a^2}{x}\right) \div \left(x-\frac{a^4}{x^3}\right) = \frac{x^2+a^2}{x} \div \frac{x^4-a^4}{x^3}$$

$$= \frac{x^2+a^2}{x} \times \frac{x^3}{x^4-a^4} = \frac{x^2}{x^2-a^2}.$$

Ex. 3. Simplify $\dfrac{\dfrac{a^2+b^2}{a^2-b^2}-\dfrac{a^2-b^2}{a^2+b^2}}{\dfrac{a+b}{a-b}-\dfrac{a-b}{a+b}}.$

The numerator $=\dfrac{(a^2+b^2)^2-(a^2-b^2)^2}{(a^2+b^2)(a^2-b^2)}=\dfrac{4a^2b^2}{(a^2+b^2)(a^2-b^2)}.$

Similarly, the denominator $=\dfrac{4ab}{(a+b)(a-b)}.$

Hence the fraction $=\dfrac{4a^2b^2}{(a^2+b^2)(a^2-b^2)} \div \dfrac{4ab}{(a+b)(a-b)}$

$=\dfrac{4a^2b^2}{(a^2+b^2)(a^2-b^2)} \times \dfrac{(a+b)(a-b)}{4ab}=\dfrac{ab}{a^2+b^2}.$

Note. To ensure accuracy and neatness, when the numerator and denominator are somewhat complicated, the beginner is advised to simplify each separately as in the above example.

In the case of complex fractions like the following, called **Continued Fractions**, we begin from the lowest fraction, and simplify step by step.

Ex. 4. Simplify $\dfrac{9x^2-64}{x-1-\dfrac{1}{1-\dfrac{x}{4+x}}}.$

The expression $=\dfrac{9x^2-64}{x-1-\dfrac{1}{\dfrac{4+x-x}{4+x}}}=\dfrac{9x^2-64}{x-1-\dfrac{4+x}{4}}$

$=\dfrac{9x^2-64}{\dfrac{4x-4-(4+x)}{4}}=\dfrac{9x^2-64}{\dfrac{3x-8}{4}}$

$=\dfrac{4(9x^2-64)}{3x-8}=4(3x+8).$

EXAMPLES XIV. a.

Find the value of

1. $\dfrac{\dfrac{m}{n}-\dfrac{l}{m}}{\dfrac{a}{m}-\dfrac{b}{n}}.$

2. $\dfrac{\dfrac{1}{x}+\dfrac{1}{y}}{\dfrac{1}{x}-\dfrac{1}{y}}.$

3. $\dfrac{a+\dfrac{b}{d}}{x-\dfrac{y}{d}}.$

4. $\dfrac{1+\dfrac{c}{x}}{\dfrac{b}{x}-1}.$

COMPLEX FRACTIONS.

5. $\dfrac{2+\dfrac{3a}{4b}}{a+\dfrac{8b}{3}}.$

7. $\dfrac{1-\dfrac{y^2}{x^2}}{1+\dfrac{y^2}{x^2}}.$

9. $\dfrac{a}{b+\dfrac{c}{d}}.$

11. $\dfrac{\dfrac{a}{b}+\dfrac{c}{d}}{\dfrac{m}{n}+\dfrac{k}{p}}.$

6. $\dfrac{3a+\dfrac{7b}{8c}}{3c+\dfrac{7b}{8a}}.$

8. $\dfrac{1}{a+\dfrac{b}{c}}.$

10. $\dfrac{x}{x-\dfrac{m}{n}}.$

12. $\dfrac{x-\dfrac{1}{x}}{1+\dfrac{1}{x}}.$

13. $\dfrac{x+5+\dfrac{6}{x}}{1+\dfrac{6}{x}+\dfrac{8}{x^2}}.$

14. $\dfrac{\dfrac{1}{x}-\dfrac{2}{x^2}-\dfrac{3}{x^3}}{\dfrac{9}{x}-x}.$

15. $\dfrac{2x^2-x-6}{\dfrac{4}{x^2}-1}.$

16. $\dfrac{2}{1-x^2}\div\left(\dfrac{1}{1-x}-\dfrac{1}{1+x}\right).$

17. $\left(\dfrac{a^3-b^3}{a-b}-\dfrac{a^3+b^3}{a+b}\right)\div\dfrac{4ab}{a^2-b^2}.$

18. $\left(\dfrac{a^2-ax+x^2}{a-x}-\dfrac{a^2+ax+x^2}{a+x}\right)\div\dfrac{x^3}{a^2-x^2}.$

19. $\left(y+\dfrac{xy}{y-x}\right)\left(y-\dfrac{xy}{x+y}\right)\times\dfrac{y^2-x^2}{y^2+x^2}.$

20. $\left(\dfrac{x}{1+x}+\dfrac{1-x}{x}\right)\div\left(\dfrac{x}{1+x}-\dfrac{1-x}{x}\right).$

21. $\dfrac{\dfrac{a+b}{a-b}-\dfrac{a-b}{a+b}}{1-\dfrac{a^2+b^2}{(a+b)^2}}.$

26. $\dfrac{1}{4x+\dfrac{4x}{1+\dfrac{2(x+y)}{6-x}}}.$

22. $\dfrac{\dfrac{a}{x^2}+\dfrac{x}{a^2}}{\dfrac{1}{a^2}-\dfrac{1}{ax}+\dfrac{1}{x^2}}.$

27. $\dfrac{a}{x+\dfrac{m}{y+\dfrac{n}{z}}}.$

23. $\dfrac{\dfrac{1}{3x-2}-\dfrac{1}{3x+2}}{9-\dfrac{4}{x^2}}.$

28. $\dfrac{1}{1-\dfrac{1+x}{x-\dfrac{1}{x}}}.$

24. $1+\dfrac{x}{1+x+\dfrac{2x^2}{1-x}}.$

29. $\dfrac{x-2}{x-2-\dfrac{x}{x-\dfrac{x-1}{x-2}}}.$

25. $\dfrac{1}{a-\dfrac{a^2-1}{a+\dfrac{1}{a-1}}}.$

30. $\dfrac{1}{x-\dfrac{1}{x+\dfrac{1}{x}}}-\dfrac{1}{x+\dfrac{1}{x-\dfrac{1}{x}}}.$

158. Sometimes it is convenient to express a single fraction as a group of fractions.

Ex. $\dfrac{5x^2y - 10xy^2 + 15y^3}{10x^2y^2} = \dfrac{5x^2y}{10x^2y^2} - \dfrac{10xy^2}{10x^2y^2} + \dfrac{15y^3}{10x^2y^2}$

$\qquad\qquad\qquad = \dfrac{1}{2y} - \dfrac{1}{x} + \dfrac{3y}{2x^2}$

MIXED EXPRESSIONS.

159. We may often express a fraction in an equivalent form, partly integral and partly fractional. It is then called a **Mixed Expression**.

Ex. 1. $\dfrac{x+7}{x+2} = \dfrac{(x+2)+5}{x+2} = 1 + \dfrac{5}{x+2}.$

Ex. 2. $\dfrac{3x-2}{x+5} = \dfrac{3(x+5)-15-2}{x+5} = \dfrac{3(x+5)-17}{x+5} = 3 - \dfrac{17}{x+5}.$

In some cases actual division may be advisable.

Ex. 3. Show that $\dfrac{2x^2 - 7x - 1}{x - 3} = 2x - 1 - \dfrac{4}{x-3}.$

Performing the indicated division, we obtain a quotient $2x - 1$, and a remainder -4.

Therefore $\dfrac{2x^2 - 7x - 1}{x - 3} = 2x - 1 - \dfrac{4}{x-3}.$

160. If the numerator be of lower dimensions (Art. 29) than the denominator, we may still perform the division, and express the result in a form which is partly integral and partly fractional.

Ex. Prove that $\dfrac{2x}{1+3x^2} = 2x - 6x^3 + 18x^5 - \dfrac{54x^7}{1+3x^2}.$

By division $\quad 1+3x^2)\,2x \qquad (2x - 6x^3 + 18x^5$

$\qquad\qquad\qquad \underline{2x + 6x^3}$

$\qquad\qquad\qquad\quad -6x^3$

$\qquad\qquad\qquad\quad \underline{-6x^3 - 18x^5}$

$\qquad\qquad\qquad\qquad\qquad 18x^5$

$\qquad\qquad\qquad\qquad\qquad \underline{18x^5 + 54x^7}$

$\qquad\qquad\qquad\qquad\qquad\qquad -54x^7$

whence the result follows.

MIXED EXPRESSIONS.

Here the division may be carried on to any number of terms in the quotient, and we can stop at any term we please by taking for our remainder the fraction whose numerator is the remainder last found, and whose denominator is the divisor.

Thus, if we carried on the quotient to four terms, we should have

$$\frac{2x}{1+3x^2} = 2x - 6x^3 + 18x^5 - 54x^7 + \frac{162x^9}{1+3x^2}.$$

The terms in the quotient may be fractional; thus if x^2 is divided by $x^3 - a^3$, the first four terms of the quotient are $\frac{1}{x} + \frac{a^3}{x^4} + \frac{a^6}{x^7} + \frac{a^9}{x^{10}}$, and the remainder is $\frac{a^{12}}{x^{10}}$.

161. Miscellaneous examples in multiplication and division occur which can be dealt with by the preceding rules for the reduction of fractions.

Ex. Multiply $x + 2a - \dfrac{a^2}{2x+3a}$ by $2x - a - \dfrac{2a^2}{x+a}$.

The product $= \left(x + 2a - \dfrac{a^2}{2x+3a}\right) \times \left(2x - a - \dfrac{2a^2}{x+a}\right)$

$= \dfrac{2x^2 + 7ax + 6a^2 - a^2}{2x+3a} \times \dfrac{2x^2 + ax - a^2 - 2a^2}{x+a}$

$= \dfrac{2x^2 + 7ax + 5a^2}{2x+3a} \times \dfrac{2x^2 + ax - 3a^2}{x+a}$

$= \dfrac{(2x+5a)(x+a)}{2x+3a} \times \dfrac{(2x+3a)(x-a)}{x+a}$

$= (2x + 5a)(x - a)$.

EXAMPLES XIV. b.

Express each of the following fractions as a group of simple fractions in lowest terms:

1. $\dfrac{3x^2y + xy^2 - y^3}{9xy}$.

2. $\dfrac{3a^3x - 4a^2x^2 + 6ax^3}{12ax}$.

3. $\dfrac{a^3 - 3a^2b + 3ab^2 + b^3}{2ab}$.

4. $\dfrac{a+b+c}{abc}$.

5. $\dfrac{bc + ca + ab}{abc}$.

6. $\dfrac{a^3bc - 3ab^3c + 2abc}{6abc}$.

Perform the following divisions, giving the remainder after four terms in the quotient:

7. $x \div (1 + x)$.
8. $a \div (a - b)$.
9. $(1 + x) \div (1 - x)$.
10. $1 \div (1 - x + x^2)$.
11. $x^2 \div (x + 3)$.
12. $1 \div (1 - x)^2$.

13. Show that $\dfrac{a^3 - b^3}{(a-b)^2} = a + 2b + \dfrac{3b^2}{a-b}$.

14. Show that $x^2 - xy + y^2 - \dfrac{2y^3}{x+y} = \dfrac{x^3 - y^3}{x+y}$.

15. Show that $\dfrac{60 x^3 - 17 x^2 - 4x + 1}{5x^2 + 9x - 2} = 12x - 25 + \dfrac{49}{x+2}$.

16. Show that $1 + \dfrac{a^2 + b^2 - c^2}{2ab} = \dfrac{(a+b+c)(a+b-c)}{2ab}$.

17. Divide $x + \dfrac{16x - 27}{x^2 - 16}$ by $x - 1 + \dfrac{13}{x+4}$.

18. Multiply $a^2 - 2ax + 4x^2 - \dfrac{16x^3}{a+2x}$ by $3 - \dfrac{6x(a+4x)}{a^2 + 2ax + 4x^2}$.

19. Divide $b^2 + 3b - 2 - \dfrac{12}{b-3}$ by $3b + 6 - \dfrac{2b^2}{b-3}$.

20. Divide $a^2 + 9b^2 + \dfrac{65 b^4}{a^2 - 9b^2}$ by $a + 3b + \dfrac{13b^2}{a-3b}$.

21. Multiply $4x^2 + 14x + \dfrac{98x - 27}{2x - 7}$ by $\dfrac{1}{6} - \dfrac{3x + 29}{12x^2 + 18x + 27}$.

162. We add an exercise in which most of the processes connected with fractions will be illustrated.

EXAMPLES XIV. c.

Simplify the following fractions:

1. $\dfrac{4a(a^2 - x^2)}{3b(c^2 - x^2)} \div \left[\dfrac{a^2 - ax}{bc + bx} \times \dfrac{a^2 + 2ax + x^2}{c^2 - 2cx + x^2} \right]$.

2. $\dfrac{x(x+a)(x+2a)}{3a} - \dfrac{x(x+a)(2x+a)}{6a}$.

3. $\dfrac{1}{b}\left(\dfrac{1}{a-b} - \dfrac{1}{a+2b}\right) - \dfrac{2}{a^2 + ab - 2b^2}$.

4. $\left(\dfrac{x+y}{x-y}\right)^2 - \left(\dfrac{x-y}{x+y}\right)^2$.

5. $\dfrac{2}{x-1} + \dfrac{2}{x+1} - \dfrac{4x}{x^2 - x + 1}$.

6. $\left(\dfrac{x^2}{1-x^4} + \dfrac{2x^4}{1-x^8}\right) \div \left(\dfrac{x^2 + 1}{x}\right)^2$.

FRACTIONS.

7. $\dfrac{1}{x} - \dfrac{1}{(x+1)^2} - \dfrac{2}{x+1} + \dfrac{x}{1+x+x^2}$

8. $\dfrac{1+x^3}{1+2x+2x^2+x^3}.$

9. $\dfrac{2x^3 - 9x^2 + 27}{3x^3 - 81x + 162}.$

10. $\dfrac{a}{b} - \dfrac{(a^2-b^2)x}{b^2} + \dfrac{a(a^2-b^2)x^2}{b^2(b+ax)}.$

11. $\left\{\dfrac{x^4-a^4}{x^2-2ax+a^2} + \dfrac{x^2+ax}{x-a}\right\} \times \dfrac{x^5-a^2x^3}{x^3+a^3} \div \left(\dfrac{x}{a}-\dfrac{a}{x}\right).$

12. $\dfrac{a^2-x^2}{a^2+ax+x^2} \div \dfrac{\left(1-\dfrac{x}{a}\right)^3\left(1+\dfrac{x}{a}\right)^3}{a^3-x^3}.$

13. $\dfrac{x^4-2x^2+1}{3x^5-10x^3+15x-8}.$

14. $\dfrac{a^3+a(1+a)y+y^2}{a^4-y^2}.$

15. $\dfrac{1}{a} + \dfrac{2}{a+1} + \dfrac{3}{a+2} - \dfrac{\dfrac{4}{a}}{1+\dfrac{1}{a}}.$

16. $\dfrac{x+3}{2x^2+9x+9} + \dfrac{1}{2} \times \dfrac{1}{2x-3} - \dfrac{1}{x-\dfrac{9}{4x}}.$

17. $\dfrac{2}{x^3+x^2+x+1} - \dfrac{2}{x^3-x^2+x-1}.$

18. $\dfrac{1-a^2}{(1+ax)^2-(a+x)^2} + \dfrac{1}{2}\left(\dfrac{1}{1-x}+\dfrac{1}{1+x}\right).$

19. $\dfrac{2x^3-x^2-2x+1}{x^3-3x+2}.$

20. $\dfrac{x^2-6x+8}{4x^3-21x^2+15x+20}.$

21. $\dfrac{2a}{(x-2a)^2} - \dfrac{x-a}{x^2-5ax+6a^2} + \dfrac{2}{x-3a}.$

22. $\dfrac{1}{2}\left(\dfrac{a^2+x^2}{a^2-x^2}\right) - \dfrac{1}{2} \times \dfrac{a+x}{a-x} - \left(\dfrac{a}{a+x}\right)^2.$

23. $\dfrac{x}{2}\left(\dfrac{1}{x-y}-\dfrac{1}{x+y}\right) \times \dfrac{x^2-y^2}{x^2y+xy^2} \div \dfrac{1}{x+y}.$

24. $\dfrac{1}{x+y} \div \left[\dfrac{y}{2}\left(\dfrac{1}{x+y}+\dfrac{1}{x-y}\right) \times \dfrac{x^2-y^2}{x^2y+xy^2}\right].$

25. $\left(3x-5-\dfrac{2}{x}\right)\left(3x+5-\dfrac{2}{x}\right) \div \left(x-\dfrac{4}{x}\right).$

26. $\left\{\dfrac{2}{x}-\dfrac{1}{a+x}+\dfrac{1}{a-x}\right\} \div \left(\dfrac{a+x}{a-x}-\dfrac{a-x}{a+x}\right).$

27. $\dfrac{1}{2x-1} - \dfrac{2x - \dfrac{1}{2x}}{4x^2 - 1}.$

28. $\left(b + \dfrac{ab}{b-a}\right)\left(b - \dfrac{ab}{a+b}\right)\left(\dfrac{b^2 - a^2}{b^2 + a^2}\right).$

29. $\left\{ \dfrac{b + \dfrac{a-b}{1+ab}}{1 - \dfrac{(a-b)b}{1+ab}} - \dfrac{a - \dfrac{a-b}{1-ab}}{1 - \dfrac{a(a-b)}{1-ab}} \right\} \div \left(\dfrac{a}{b} - \dfrac{b}{a}\right).$

30. $\dfrac{\dfrac{x^2 + y^2}{y} - x}{\dfrac{1}{y} - \dfrac{1}{x}} \times \dfrac{x^2 - y^2}{x^3 + y^3}.$

31. $\dfrac{2(x^2 - \frac{1}{4})}{2x+1} + \tfrac{1}{2}.$

32. $\dfrac{a + \dfrac{b-a}{1+ab}}{1 - \dfrac{a(b-a)}{1+ab}} \times \dfrac{\dfrac{x+y}{1-xy} - y}{1 + \dfrac{y(x+y)}{1-xy}}.$

33. $\dfrac{\dfrac{a+b}{a-b} + \dfrac{a-b}{a+b}}{\dfrac{a-b}{a+b} - \dfrac{a+b}{a-b}} \times \dfrac{ab^3 - a^3 b}{a^2 + b^2}.$

34. $\dfrac{(1-x^2)(1-x^3)}{x(1+x)(1-x)^2} - \dfrac{x^3 + \dfrac{1}{x^3}}{x^2 + \dfrac{1}{x^2} - 1}.$

35. $\left\{ x^3 - \dfrac{1}{x^3} - 3\left(x - \dfrac{1}{x}\right) \right\} \div \left(x - \dfrac{1}{x}\right).$

36. $\dfrac{1 + \dfrac{1}{m}}{\dfrac{1}{m}} \times \dfrac{\dfrac{1}{m}}{m^2 + \dfrac{1}{m}} + \dfrac{\dfrac{1}{m}}{m - 1 + \dfrac{1}{m}}.$

37. $\dfrac{\dfrac{x}{y} + \dfrac{y}{x} - 1}{\dfrac{x^2}{y^2} + \dfrac{x}{y} + 1} \times \dfrac{1 + \dfrac{y}{x}}{x - y} \div \dfrac{1 + \dfrac{y^3}{x^3}}{\dfrac{x^2}{y} - \dfrac{y^2}{x}}.$

38. $\dfrac{1}{a^2 - 2} - \dfrac{2}{a^2 - 1} + \dfrac{2}{a^2 + 1} - \dfrac{1}{a^2 + 2}.$

39. $\dfrac{1}{6m - 2n} + \dfrac{1}{3m + 2n} - \dfrac{3}{6m + 2n}.$

40. $\dfrac{3}{4(1-x)^2} + \dfrac{3}{8(1-x)} + \dfrac{1}{8(1+x)} + \dfrac{x-1}{4(1+x^2)}.$

41. $\dfrac{4}{9(x-2)} + \dfrac{5}{9(x+1)} - \dfrac{1}{3(x+1)^2} - \dfrac{1}{x + 2 + \dfrac{1}{x}}.$

42. $\left(\dfrac{x^2}{y} + \dfrac{y^2}{x}\right)\left(\dfrac{1}{y^2 - x^2}\right) - \dfrac{y}{x^2 + xy} + \dfrac{x}{xy - y^2}.$

43. $\dfrac{x^2 - (y-z)^2}{(x+z)^2 - y^2} + \dfrac{y^2 - (z-x)^2}{(x+y)^2 - z^2} + \dfrac{z^2 - (x-y)^2}{(y+z)^2 - x^2}.$

44. $\dfrac{x^2 - (y - 2z)^2}{(2z+x)^2 - y^2} + \dfrac{y^2 - (2z-x)^2}{(x+y)^2 - 4z^2} + \dfrac{4z^2 - (x-y)^2}{(y+2z)^2 - x^2}.$

45. $\dfrac{(x-y)(y-z) + (y-z)(z-x) + (z-x)(x-y)}{x(z-x) + y(x-y) + z(y-z)}.$

46. $\dfrac{a-b-c}{(a-b)(a-c)} + \dfrac{b-c-a}{(b-c)(b-a)} + \dfrac{c-a-b}{(c-a)(c-b)}.$

47. $\dfrac{c+a}{(a-b)(a-c)} + \dfrac{a+b}{(b-c)(b-a)} + \dfrac{b+c}{(c-a)(c-b)}.$

48. $\dfrac{x^2 - (2y - 3z)^2}{(3z+x)^2 - 4y^2} + \dfrac{4y^2 - (3z-x)^2}{(x+2y)^2 - 9z^2} + \dfrac{9z^2 - (x-2y)^2}{(2y+3z)^2 - x^2}.$

49. $\dfrac{9y^2 - (4z - 2x)^2}{(2x+3y)^2 - 16z^2} + \dfrac{16z^2 - (2x-3y)^2}{(3y+4z)^2 - 4x^2} + \dfrac{4x^2 - (3y-4z)^2}{(4z+2x)^2 - 9y^2}.$

50. $\dfrac{\dfrac{1}{x} - \dfrac{x+a}{x^2+a^2}}{\dfrac{1}{a} - \dfrac{a+x}{a^2+x^2}} + \dfrac{\dfrac{1}{x} - \dfrac{x-a}{x^2+a^2}}{\dfrac{1}{a} - \dfrac{a-x}{a^2+x^2}}.$

51. $\dfrac{(x+a)(x+b) - (y+a)(y+b)}{x - y} - \dfrac{(x-a)(y-b) - (x-b)(y-a)}{(a-b)}.$

52. $\left(\dfrac{a+x}{a^2 - ax + x^2} - \dfrac{a-x}{a^2 + ax + x^2}\right) + \left(\dfrac{a^2 + x^2}{a^3 - x^3} - \dfrac{a^2 - x^2}{a^3 + x^3}\right).$

53. $\dfrac{\dfrac{x-1}{3} + \dfrac{x-1}{x-2}}{\dfrac{x+2}{4} + \dfrac{x+2}{x-3}} + \dfrac{\dfrac{x+3}{7} - \dfrac{x+3}{x+4}}{\dfrac{x-2}{3} + \dfrac{x-2}{x-1}}.$

54. $\dfrac{\left(\dfrac{3x + x^3}{1 + 3x^2}\right)^2 - 1}{\dfrac{3x^2 - 1}{x^3 - 3x} + 1} + \dfrac{\dfrac{9}{x^2} - \dfrac{33 - x^2}{3x^2 + 1}}{\dfrac{3}{x^2} - \dfrac{2(x^2+3)}{(x^3 - x)^2}}.$

CHAPTER XV.

FRACTIONAL AND LITERAL EQUATIONS.

163. In this chapter we propose to give a miscellaneous collection of equations. Some of these will serve as a useful exercise for revision of the methods already explained in previous chapters; but we also add others presenting more difficulty, the solution of which will often be facilitated by some special artifice.

The following examples worked in full will sufficiently illustrate the most useful methods.

Ex. 1. Solve $4 - \dfrac{x-9}{8} = \dfrac{x}{22} - \dfrac{1}{2}$.

Multiply by 88, which is the least common multiple of the denominators, and we get
$$352 - 11(x-9) = 4x - 44;$$
removing brackets, $\quad 352 - 11x + 99 = 4x - 44;$
transposing, $\quad -11x - 4x = -44 - 352 - 99;$
collecting terms and changing signs, $15x = 495;$
$$\therefore x = 33.$$

NOTE. In this equation $-\dfrac{x-9}{8}$ is regarded as a single term with the minus sign before it. In fact it is equivalent to $-\frac{1}{8}(x-9)$, the line between the numerator and denominator having the same effect as a bracket.

Ex. 2. Solve $\dfrac{8x+23}{20} - \dfrac{5x+2}{3x+4} = \dfrac{2x+3}{5} - 1$.

Multiply by 20, and we have
$$8x + 23 - \frac{20(5x+2)}{3x+4} = 8x + 12 - 20.$$

By transposition, $\quad 31 = \dfrac{20(5x+2)}{3x+4}.$

FRACTIONAL AND LITERAL EQUATIONS. 137

Multiplying across, $93x + 124 = 20(5x + 2)$,
$$84 = 7x;$$
$$\therefore x = 12.$$

Ex. 3. Solve $\dfrac{x-8}{x-10} + \dfrac{x-4}{x-6} = \dfrac{x-5}{x-7} + \dfrac{x-7}{x-9}.$

This equation might be solved by clearing of fractions, but the work would be very laborious. The solution will be much simplified by proceeding as follows:

Transposing, $\dfrac{x-8}{x-10} - \dfrac{x-5}{x-7} = \dfrac{x-7}{x-9} - \dfrac{x-4}{x-6}.$

Simplifying each side *separately*, we have
$$\frac{(x-8)(x-7)-(x-5)(x-10)}{(x-10)(x-7)} = \frac{(x-7)(x-6)-(x-4)(x-9)}{(x-9)(x-6)};$$
$$\therefore \frac{x^2-15x+56-(x^2-15x+50)}{(x-10)(x-7)} = \frac{x^2-13x+42-(x^2-13x+36)}{(x-9)(x-6)};$$
$$\therefore \frac{6}{(x-10)(x-7)} = \frac{6}{(x-9)(x-6)}.$$

Hence, since the numerators are equal, the denominators must be equal; that is,
$$(x-10)(x-7) = (x-9)(x-6),$$
$$x^2 - 17x + 70 = x^2 - 15x + 54,$$
$$16 = 2x;$$
$$\therefore x = 8.$$

Ex. 4. Solve $\dfrac{5x-64}{x-13} - \dfrac{2x-11}{x-6} = \dfrac{4x-55}{x-14} - \dfrac{x-6}{x-7}.$

We have $5 + \dfrac{1}{x-13} - \left(2 + \dfrac{1}{x-6}\right) = 4 + \dfrac{1}{x-14} - \left(1 + \dfrac{1}{x-7}\right);$
$$\therefore \frac{1}{x-13} - \frac{1}{x-6} = \frac{1}{x-14} - \frac{1}{x-7}.$$

Simplifying each side *separately*, we have
$$\frac{7}{(x-13)(x-6)} = \frac{7}{(x-14)(x-7)},$$
$$(x-13)(x-6) = (x-14)(x-7),$$
$$x^2 - 19x + 78 = x^2 - 21x + 98,$$
$$2x = 20;$$
$$\therefore x = 10.$$

164. To solve equations whose coefficients are decimals, we may express the decimals as common fractions, and proceed as before; but it is often found more simple to work entirely in decimals.

Ex. 1. Solve $\quad .375x - 1.875 = .12x + 1.185.$

Transposing, $\quad .375x - .12x = 1.185 + 1.875;$

collecting terms, $\quad (.375 - .12)x = 3.06,$

that is, $\quad .255x = 3.06;$

$$\therefore x = \frac{3.06}{.255} = 12.$$

Ex. 2. Solve $\quad .\dot{6}x + .25 - \frac{1}{3}x = 1.\dot{8} - .75x - \frac{1}{3}.$

Expressing the decimals as common fractions, we have

$$\tfrac{2}{3}x + \tfrac{1}{4} - \tfrac{1}{3}x = 1\tfrac{8}{9} - \tfrac{3}{4}x - \tfrac{1}{3};$$

clearing of fractions, $24x + 9 - 4x = 68 - 27x - 12;$

transposing, $\quad 24x - 4x + 27x = 68 - 12 - 9,$

$$47x = 47;$$

$$\therefore x = 1.$$

EXAMPLES XV. a.

1. $\dfrac{4(x+2)}{5} = 7 + \dfrac{5x}{13}.$

2. $\dfrac{x+4}{14} + \dfrac{x-4}{6} = 2.$

3. $\dfrac{x+20}{9} + \dfrac{3x}{7} = 6.$

4. $\dfrac{x-8}{7} + \dfrac{x-3}{3} + \dfrac{5}{21} = 0.$

5. $\dfrac{5(x+5)}{8} - \dfrac{2(x-3)}{7} = 5\tfrac{10}{11}.$

6. $\dfrac{x}{2} + \dfrac{x}{3} - \dfrac{x}{4} + \dfrac{x}{5} = 7\tfrac{1}{6}.$

7. $\dfrac{3x}{4} - \dfrac{6}{17}(x+10) - (x-3) = \dfrac{x-7}{51} - 4\tfrac{3}{4}.$

8. $3 + \dfrac{x}{4} = \dfrac{1}{2}\left(4 - \dfrac{x}{3}\right) - \dfrac{5}{6} + \dfrac{1}{3}\left(11 - \dfrac{x}{2}\right).$

9. $\dfrac{1}{5}(x-8) + \dfrac{x+4}{4} + \dfrac{x-1}{7} = 7 - \dfrac{23-x}{5}.$

10. $x - \left(3x - \dfrac{2x-5}{10}\right) = \dfrac{1}{6}(2x - 57) - \dfrac{5}{3}.$

11. $\dfrac{2x-5}{5} + \dfrac{x-3}{2x-15} = \dfrac{4x-3}{10} - 1\tfrac{1}{10}.$

12. $\dfrac{4(x+3)}{9} = \dfrac{8x+37}{18} - \dfrac{7x-29}{5x-12}.$

FRACTIONAL AND LITERAL EQUATIONS.

13. $\dfrac{(2x-1)(3x+8)}{6x(x+4)} - 1 = 0.$

14. $\dfrac{4x+5}{5x+3} - \dfrac{2x+1}{5x+2} = 0.$

15. $\dfrac{4}{x+3} - \dfrac{2}{x+1} = \dfrac{5}{2x+6} - \dfrac{2\frac{1}{2}}{2x+2}.$

16. $\dfrac{7}{x-4} - \dfrac{60}{5x-30} = \dfrac{10\frac{1}{2}}{3x-12} - \dfrac{8}{x-6}.$

17. $\dfrac{3}{4-2x} + \dfrac{30}{8(1-x)} = \dfrac{3}{2-x} + \dfrac{5}{2-2x}.$

18. $\dfrac{25 - \frac{x}{3}}{x+1} + \dfrac{16x+4\frac{1}{2}}{3x+2} = 5 + \dfrac{23}{x+1}.$

19. $\dfrac{30+6x}{x+1} + \dfrac{60+8x}{x+3} = 14 + \dfrac{48}{x+1}.$

20. $\dfrac{x}{x-2} - \dfrac{x+1}{x-1} = \dfrac{x-8}{x-6} - \dfrac{x-9}{x-7}.$

21. $\dfrac{x+5}{x+4} - \dfrac{x-6}{x-7} = \dfrac{x-4}{x-5} - \dfrac{x-15}{x-16}.$

22. $\dfrac{x-7}{x-9} - \dfrac{x-9}{x-11} = \dfrac{x-13}{x-15} - \dfrac{x-15}{x-17}.$

23. $\dfrac{x+3}{x+6} - \dfrac{x+6}{x+9} = \dfrac{x+2}{x+5} - \dfrac{x+5}{x+8}.$

24. $\dfrac{x+2}{x} + \dfrac{x-7}{x-5} - \dfrac{x+3}{x+1} = \dfrac{x-6}{x-4}.$

25. $\dfrac{4x-17}{x-4} + \dfrac{10x-18}{2x-3} = \dfrac{8x-30}{2x-7} + \dfrac{5x-4}{x-1}.$

26. $\dfrac{5x-8}{x-2} + \dfrac{6x-44}{x-7} - \dfrac{10x-8}{x-1} = \dfrac{x-8}{x-6}.$

27. $\dfrac{2x-3}{.3x-.4} = \dfrac{.4x-.6}{.06x-.07}.$

28. $\dfrac{x-2}{.05} - \dfrac{x-4}{.0625} = 56.$

29. $.08\dot{3}(x - .625) = .0\dot{9}(x - .59375).$

30. $(2x + 1.5)(3x - 2.25) = (2x - 1.125)(3x + 1.25).$

31. $\dfrac{.3x-1}{.5x-.4} = \dfrac{.5+1.2x}{2x-.1}.$

32. $\dfrac{1-1.4x}{.2+x} = \dfrac{.7(x-1)}{.1-.5x}.$

33. $\dfrac{(.3x-2)(.3x-1)}{.2x-1} - \dfrac{1}{6}(.3x-2) = .4x - 2.$

LITERAL EQUATIONS.

165. In the equations we have discussed hitherto the coefficients have been numerical quantities, but equations often involve *literal* coefficients. [Art. 6.] These are supposed to be known, and will appear in the solution.

Ex. 1. Solve $(x+a)(x+b) - c(a+c) = (x-c)(x+c) + ab.$

Multiplying out, we have

$$x^2 + ax + bx + ab - ac - c^2 = x^2 - c^2 + ab;$$

whence $\qquad ax + bx = ac,$

$\qquad\qquad (a+b)x = ac;$

$$\therefore x = \dfrac{ac}{a+b}.$$

Ex. 2. Solve $\dfrac{a}{x-a} - \dfrac{b}{x-b} = \dfrac{a-b}{x-c}$.

Simplifying the left side, we have

$$\dfrac{a(x-b) - b(x-a)}{(x-a)(x-b)} = \dfrac{a-b}{x-c},$$

$$\dfrac{(a-b)x}{(x-a)(x-b)} = \dfrac{a-b}{x-c};$$

$$\therefore \dfrac{x}{(x-a)(x-b)} = \dfrac{1}{x-c}.$$

Multiplying across, $x^2 - cx = x^2 - ax - bx + ab$,

$$ax + bx - cx = ab,$$
$$(a + b - c)x = ab;$$

$$\therefore x = \dfrac{ab}{a+b-c}.$$

EXAMPLES XV. b.

1. $ax - 2b = 5bx - 3a$.
2. $a^2(x-a) + b^2(x-b) = abx$.
3. $x^2 + a^2 = (b-x)^2$.
4. $(x-a)(x+b) = (x-a+b)^2$.
5. $a(x-2) + 2x = 6 + a$.
6. $m^2(m-x) - mnx = n^2(n+x)$.
7. $(a+x)(b+x) = x(x-c)$.
8. $(a-b)(x-a) = (a-c)(x-b)$.
9. $\dfrac{2x+3a}{x+a} = \dfrac{2(3x+2a)}{3x+a}$.
10. $\dfrac{2(x-b)}{3x-c} = \dfrac{2x+b}{3(x-c)}$.
11. $\dfrac{1}{a} - \dfrac{1}{x} = \dfrac{1}{x} - \dfrac{1}{b}$.
12. $\dfrac{2}{3}\left(\dfrac{x}{a}+1\right) = \dfrac{3}{4}\left(\dfrac{x}{a}-1\right)$.
13. $\dfrac{a}{x} = c(a-b) + \dfrac{b}{x}$.
14. $\dfrac{9a}{b} - \dfrac{3x}{b} = \dfrac{4b}{a} - \dfrac{2x}{a}$.
15. $\dfrac{x-a}{b-x} = \dfrac{x-b}{a-x}$.
16. $\dfrac{x-a}{2} = \dfrac{(x-b)^2}{2x-a}$.
17. $\dfrac{1}{4}x(x-a) - \left(\dfrac{x+a}{2}\right)^2 = \dfrac{2a}{8}\left(x - \dfrac{a}{2}\right)$.
18. $(a+b)x^2 - a(bx + a^2) = bx(x-a) + ax(x-b)$.
19. $b(a+x) - (a+x)(b-x) = x^2 + \dfrac{bc^2}{a}$.
20. $b(a-x) - \dfrac{a}{b}(b+x)^2 + ab\left(\dfrac{x}{b}+1\right)^2 = 0$.
21. $x^2 + a(2a-x) - \dfrac{3b^2}{4} = \left(x - \dfrac{b}{2}\right)^2 + a^2$.
22. $(2x-a)\left(x + \dfrac{2a}{3}\right) = 4x\left(\dfrac{a}{3} - x\right) - \dfrac{1}{2}(a-4x)(2a+3x)$.

CHAPTER XVI.

Problems leading to Fractional and Literal Equations.

166. We here give some problems which lead to equations with fractional and literal coefficients.

Ex. 1. Find two numbers which differ by 4, and such that one-half of the greater exceeds one-sixth of the less by 8.

Let x represent the smaller number, then $x + 4$ represents the greater.

One-half of the greater is represented by $\frac{1}{2}(x + 4)$, and one-sixth of the less by $\frac{1}{6}x$.

Hence $\qquad \frac{1}{2}(x + 4) - \frac{1}{6}x = 8;$
multiplying by 6, $\qquad 3x + 12 - x = 48;$
$\qquad\qquad\qquad 2x = 36;$
$\qquad\qquad\therefore x = 18,$ the less number,
and $\qquad\qquad x + 4 = 22,$ the greater.

Ex. 2. A has $180, and B has $84; after B has won from A a certain sum, A has then five-sixths of what B has; how much did B win?

Suppose that B wins x dollars, A has then $180 - x$ dollars, and B has $84 + x$ dollars.

Hence $\qquad 180 - x = \frac{5}{6}(84 + x);$
$\qquad 1080 - 6x = 420 + 5x,$
$\qquad\qquad 11x = 660;$
$\qquad\qquad\therefore x = 60.$

Therefore B wins $60.

EXAMPLES XVI.

1. Find a number such that the sum of its sixth and ninth parts may be equal to 15.

2. What is the number whose eighth, sixth, and fourth parts together make up 13?

3. There is a number whose fifth part is less than its fourth part by 3: find it.

4. Find a number such that six-sevenths of it shall exceed four-fifths of it by 2.

5. The fifth, fifteenth, and twenty-fifth parts of a number together make up 23: find the number.

6. Two consecutive numbers are such that one-fourth of the less exceeds one-fifth of the greater by 1: find the numbers.

7. Two numbers differ by 28, and one is eight-ninths of the other: find them.

8. There are two consecutive numbers such that one-fifth of the greater exceeds one-seventh of the less by 3: find them.

9. Find three consecutive numbers such that if they be divided by 10, 17, and 26, respectively, the sum of the quotients will be 10.

10. A and B begin to play with equal sums, and when B has lost five-elevenths of what he had to begin with, A has gained $6 more than half of what B has left: what had they at first?

11. From a certain number 3 is taken, and the remainder is divided by 4; the quotient is then increased by 4 and divided by 5, and the result is 2: find the number.

12. In a cellar one-fifth of the wine is port and one-third claret: besides this it contains 15 dozen of sherry and 30 bottles of hock: how much port and claret does it contain?

13. Two-fifths of A's money is equal to B's, and seven-ninths of B's is equal to C's, in all they have $770: what have they each?

14. A, B, and C have $1285 among them: A's share is greater than five-sixths of B's by $25, and C's is four-fifteenths of B's: find the share of each.

15. A man sold a horse for $35 and half as much as he gave for it, and gained thereby $10: what did he pay for the horse?

16. The width of a room is two-thirds of its length. If the width had been 3 feet more, and the length 3 feet less, the room would have been square: find its dimensions.

17. What is the property of a person whose income is $430, when he has two-thirds of it invested at 4 per cent, one-fourth at 3 per cent, and the remainder at 2 per cent?

18. I bought a certain number of apples at three for a cent, and five-sixths of that number at four for a cent: by selling them at sixteen for six cents I gain $3\frac{1}{2}$ cents: how many apples did I buy?

19. Find two numbers such that the one may be n times as great as the other, and their sum equal to b.

PROBLEMS. 143

20. A man agreed to work a days on these conditions: for each day he worked he was to receive c cents, and for each day he was idle he was to forfeit d cents. At the end of a days he received m cents. How many days was he idle?

21. A sum of money is divided among three persons: the first receives a dollars more than a third of the whole sum; the second receives b dollars more than a half of what remains; and the third receives c dollars, the amount which is left. Find the original sum.

22. Out of a certain sum a man paid $96; he loaned half of the remainder, and then spent one-fifth of what he had left. After these deductions he still had one-tenth of the original sum. How much had he at first?

23. A man moves 12 miles in an hour and a half, rowing with the tide, and requires 4 hours to return, rowing against a tide one-quarter as strong: find the velocity of the stronger tide.

24. A man moves a miles in b hours, rowing with the tide, but requires c hours to return, rowing against a tide d times as strong as the first: find the velocity of the stronger tide.

25. A has a certain sum of money from which he gives to B $4 and one-sixth of what remains; he then gives to C $5 and one-fifth of what remains, and finds that he has given away half of his money. How many dollars had A, and how many dollars did B receive?

26. The fore-wheel of a carriage is a feet, and the hind-wheel is b feet in circumference. What is the distance passed over when the fore-wheel has made c revolutions more than the hind-wheel?

27. In a certain weight of gunpowder the nitre composed 10 pounds more than two-thirds of the weight, the sulphur $4\frac{1}{2}$ pounds less than one-sixth, and the charcoal $5\frac{1}{2}$ pounds less than one-fifth of the nitre. What was the weight of the gunpowder?

28. Two-thirds of A's money is equal to B's, and three-fourths of B's is equal to C's; together they have $650. What amount has each?

29. A dealer spends $1450 in buying horses at $100 each and cows at $30 each; through disease he loses 10 per cent of the horses and 20 per cent of the cows. By selling the remainder at the price he gave for them he receives $1260: find how many of each kind he bought.

30. A, B, C start from the same place at the rates of c, $c + d$, $c + 2d$ miles an hour respectively: B starts k hours after A; how long after B must C start in order that they may overtake A at the same instant, and how far will they then have walked?

MISCELLANEOUS EXAMPLES III.

1. Subtract $p^3 - 4p^2 + 8$ from unity, and $3p^2 - p - 7$ from zero, and add the results.

2. Simplify $(x-y)^2 + (x-z)^2 + 2\{(x-y)(z-x) + yz\}$.

3. Solve $5\{x - 2[x - 3(x-1)]\} = 70$.

4. Divide $x^4 + x^3 - 24x^2 - 35x + 67$ by $x^2 + 2x - 3$.

5. Find the factors of

   (i.) $(a+b)^2 - 121$; (ii.) $a^4 - b^4$; (iii.) $x^2 - 5x - 14$.

6. Find the H. C. F. of $a^3 - 2a^2 + 1$ and $2a^3 + a^2 + 4a - 7$.

7. A man being asked his age said: "Ten years ago I was five times as old as my son, but 20 years hence, I shall be only twice as old as he." How old was he?

8. Solve (i.) $6 - \dfrac{x-1}{2} - \dfrac{x-2}{3} = \dfrac{3-x}{4}$;

   (ii.) $\dfrac{4x-9}{27} - \dfrac{x-3}{4} = \dfrac{5x-8}{6} - \dfrac{x+6}{2}$.

9. By how much does $y^3 - 3y^2 + 8y + 9$ exceed $y - 4y^2 + 6 - y^3$?

10. Show that
    $(ax + by)^2 + (ay - bx)^2 + c^2x^2 + c^2y^2 = (x^2 + y^2)(a^2 + b^2 + c^2)$.

11. Solve (i.) $\dfrac{2x-1}{3} - \dfrac{3x-2}{4} = \dfrac{5x-4}{6} - \dfrac{7x+6}{12}$;

    (ii.) $(3x-1)^2 + (4x-2)^2 = (5x-3)^2$.

12. If $x = 1$, $y = 2$, $z = 3$, find the value of
    $(x-y)[(x+z) + (y-z)] - x^2 + y(y+z) - zy$.

13. Find the factors of (i.) $a^2 + 17ab + 60b^2$; (ii.) $10a^2 + 79a - 8$.

14. Simplify (i.) $\dfrac{ac}{a^2 - 4y^2} + \dfrac{bd}{ac + 2cy}$;

    (ii.) $\dfrac{a}{ab + b^2} + \dfrac{b}{a^2 - ab} + \dfrac{a}{a^2 - b^2}$.

15. Find the L. C. M. of $x^3 + 6x^2 + 11x + 6$ and $x^3 - 7x + 6$.

16. The difference between the numerator and the denominator of a proper fraction is 8, and if each be increased by 17, the fraction becomes equal to $\frac{3}{4}$: find it.

17. Solve (i.) $20(7x+4) - 18(3x+4) - 5 = 25(x+5)$;

    (ii.) $\frac{1}{3}(x+1) + \frac{1}{4}(x+3) = \frac{1}{5}(x+4) + 16$.

18. Divide (i.) $2x(x^2 - 1)(x+2)$ by $x^2 + x - 2$;

    (ii.) $5x(x-11)(x^2 - x - 156)$ by $x^3 + x^2 - 132x$.

MISCELLANEOUS EXAMPLES III.

19. A boy is one-sixth the age of his father, and five years older than his sister; the united ages of all three being 51, how old is each?

20. Find the continued product of $x^2 + ax + a^2$, $x^2 - ax + a^2$, $x^4 - a^2x^2 + a^4$.

21. Show without actual division that $x - 3$ is a factor of the expression $x^3 - 2x^2 - 5x + 6$.

22. Simplify (i.) $\dfrac{x}{9} + \dfrac{2}{3} + \dfrac{4}{x-6} - \dfrac{2x}{3(x-6)}$;

(ii.) $\dfrac{2}{a-x} - \dfrac{1}{2a-x} + \dfrac{1}{x}$.

23. Find the H. C. F. of $2a^3 + a^2 - a - 2$ and $a^5 - a^3 - 2a^2 + 2a$ by the usual method. Is the work shortened by proceeding as in Art. 119? Show that the square of the H. C. F. is contained in the second expression.

24. Divide $x^6 + 19x^3 - 216$ by $(x^2 - 3x + 9)(x - 2)$.

25. Simplify (i.) $\dfrac{p+2}{2} - \dfrac{p}{p+2} - \dfrac{p^3 - 2p^2}{2p^2 - 8}$; (ii.) $\dfrac{3}{x^2 - 4} + \dfrac{1}{(x-2)^2}$.

26. Find the factors of (i.) $14a^2 - 11a - 15$; (ii.) $a^4 + 5a^2b^2 + 9b^4$.

27. Of a party 5 more than one-third are Americans, 7 less than one-half are Englishmen, and the remainder, 8 in number, are Germans: find the number in the party.

28. Solve (i.) $2(5x - 2) - 3(5x - 8) = 5(x + 1) - (2x - 11)$;

(ii.) $\dfrac{2x - 9}{27} + \dfrac{x}{18} - \dfrac{x - 3}{4} = 8\tfrac{1}{4} - x$.

29. Simplify (i.) $\dfrac{1}{a(x^2 + a^2)} - \dfrac{1}{x(x+a)^2}$; (ii) $\dfrac{1 + x + x^2}{1 - x^3} + \dfrac{x - x^2}{(1-x)^3}$.

30. Find three numbers whose sum is 21, and of which the greatest exceeds the least by 4, and the middle one is half the sum of the other two.

31. Employ the Factor Theorem in finding the H. C. F. of
$a^3 - 2a^2 + 1$ and $2a^3 + a^2 + 4a - 7$.

32. Show that $\dfrac{3(x^2 + x - 2)}{x^2 - x - 2} - \dfrac{3(x^2 - x - 2)}{x^2 + x - 2} - \dfrac{8x}{x^2 - 4} = \dfrac{4x}{x^2 - 1}$.

33. Two trains go from P to Q by different routes, one of which is 15 miles longer than the other. A train on the shorter route takes 6 hours, and a train on the longer, travelling 10 miles less per hour, takes $8\tfrac{1}{2}$ hours. Find length of each route.

34. Find the factors of

(i.) $4x^2 - 4xy - 15y^2$; (ii.) $9x^4 - 82x^2y^2 + 9y^4$.

35. Solve $\dfrac{17 - 3x}{5} - \dfrac{2 + 4x}{3} = \dfrac{14 + 7x}{3} + 5 - 6x$.

36. The number of months in the age of a man on his birthday in 1875 was exactly half of the number denoting the year in which he was born. In what year was he born?

37. Simplify (i.) $\dfrac{2x - 7}{(x - 3)^2} - \dfrac{2(x + 2)}{x^2 - 9}$; (ii.) $\dfrac{1}{2x^2 - \frac{1}{2}} + \dfrac{1}{(2x + 1)^2}$.

38. Divide $x^8 + x^6y^2 + x^4y^4 + x^2y^6 + y^8$ by $x^4 - x^3y + x^2y^2 - xy^3 + y^4$ and find the value of the quotient when $x = 0$ and $y = 1$.

39. Simplify (i.) $\dfrac{1 - x}{1 - x + x^2} - \dfrac{\frac{1}{x}\left(\frac{1}{x} - 2\right)}{\frac{1}{x^3} + 1}$;

(ii.) $\dfrac{x}{1 + \dfrac{x}{1 - x + \dfrac{x}{1 + x}}} + \dfrac{1 + x + x^2}{1 + 3x + 3x^2 + 2x^3}$.

40. A regiment has sufficient food for m days; but if it were reinforced by p men, would have food enough for n days only. Find the number of men in the regiment.

41. Solve (i.) $\dfrac{x - \frac{1}{b}}{d} + \dfrac{x - \frac{1}{c}}{b} + \dfrac{x - \frac{1}{d}}{c} = 0$;

(ii.) $\dfrac{x - a}{b} + \dfrac{x + b}{a} = \dfrac{a + b}{a}$.

42. Simplify $(1 + a)^2 \div \left\{1 + \dfrac{a}{1 - a + \dfrac{a}{1 + a + a^2}}\right\}$.

CHAPTER XVII.

SIMULTANEOUS EQUATIONS.

167. Consider the equation $2x + 5y = 23$, which contains *two* unknown quantities.

From this we get $\quad y = \dfrac{23 - 2x}{5} \quad \cdot \cdot \cdot \cdot \cdot \cdot \cdot$ (1).

Now for every value we give to x there will be one corresponding value of y. Thus we shall be able to find as many pairs of values as we please which satisfy the given equation. Such an equation is called *indeterminate*.

For instance, if $x = 1$, then from (1) $y = \frac{21}{5}$.

Again, if $x = -2$, then $y = \frac{27}{5}$; and so on.

But if also we have a second equation of the same kind expressing a different relation between x and y, such as

$$3x + 4y = 24,$$

we have from this $\quad y = \dfrac{24 - 3x}{4} \cdot \quad \cdot \cdot \cdot \cdot \cdot \cdot$ (2).

If now we seek values of x and y which satisfy *both* equations, the values of y in (1) and (2) must be identical.

Therefore $\quad \dfrac{23 - 2x}{5} = \dfrac{24 - 3x}{4}.$

Multiplying across, $92 - 8x = 120 - 15x;$
$$7x = 28;$$
$$\therefore x = 4.$$

Substituting this value in equation (1), we have

$$y = \dfrac{23 - 2x}{5} = \dfrac{23 - 8}{5} = 3.$$

Thus, if both equations are to be satisfied by the *same* values of x and y, there is only one solution possible.

148   ALGEBRA.

168. DEFINITION. When two or more equations are satisfied by the same values of the unknown quantities, they are called **simultaneous equations**.

169. In the example already worked, we have used the method of solution which best illustrates the meaning of the term *simultaneous equations;* but in practice it will be found that this is rarely the readiest mode of solution. It must be borne in mind that since the two equations are simultaneously true, *any* equation formed by combining them will be satisfied by the values of x and y which satisfy the original equations. Our object will always be to obtain an equation which involves *one only* of the unknown quantities.

170. The process by which we cause either of the unknown quantities to disappear is called **elimination**. It may be effected in different ways, but three methods are in general use: (1) by **Addition** or **Subtraction**; (2) by **Substitution**; and (3) by **Comparison**.

ELIMINATION BY ADDITION OR SUBTRACTION.

171. Ex. 1. Solve $\quad 7x + 2y = 47 \ldots \ldots \ldots$ (1),
$\quad\quad\quad\quad\quad\quad\quad\quad\quad 5x - 4y = 1 \ldots \ldots \ldots$ (2).

Here it will be more convenient to eliminate y.

Multiplying (1) by 2, $\quad 14x + 4y = 94,$
and from (2) $\quad\quad\quad\quad 5x - 4y = 1;$
adding, $\quad\quad\quad\quad\quad\quad 19x = 95;$
$\quad\quad\quad\quad\quad\quad\quad\quad \therefore x = 5.$

To find y, substitute this value of x in *either* of the given equations.

Thus from (1) $\quad\quad\quad 35 + 2y = 47;$
$\quad\quad\quad\quad\quad\quad\quad\quad \therefore y = 6,\ \}$
and $\quad\quad\quad\quad\quad\quad\quad x = 5.\ \}$

In this solution we eliminated y by *addition*.

Ex. 2. Solve $\quad 3x + 7y = 27 \ldots \ldots \ldots$ (1),
$\quad\quad\quad\quad\quad\quad 5x + 2y = 16 \ldots \ldots \ldots$ (2).

SIMULTANEOUS EQUATIONS.

To eliminate x we multiply (1) by 5 and (2) by 3, so as to make the coefficients of x in both equations equal. This gives

$$15x + 35y = 135,$$
$$15x + 6y = 48;$$

subtracting, $\quad 29y = 87;$

$$\therefore y = 3.$$

To find x, substitute this value of y in *either* of the given equations.

Thus from (1) $\quad 3x + 21 = 27;$

$$\therefore x = 2,$$
and $\quad y = 3.$

In this solution we eliminated x by *subtraction*.

Rule. *Multiply, when necessary, in such a manner as to make the coefficients of the unknown quantity to be eliminated equal in both equations. Add the resulting equations if these coefficients are unlike in sign; subtract if like in sign.*

ELIMINATION BY SUBSTITUTION.

172. Ex. Solve $\quad 2x - 5y = 1 \ldots \ldots \ldots (1),$
$\quad\quad\quad\quad\quad\quad 7x + 3y = 24 \ldots \ldots \ldots (2).$

Transposing $-5y$ in (1), and dividing by 2, we obtain

$$x = \frac{5y + 1}{2}.$$

Substituting this value of x in (2) gives

$$7\left(\frac{5y+1}{2}\right) + 3y = 24.$$

Whence $\quad 35y + 7 + 6y = 48,$
and $\quad 41y = 41;$
$\quad\quad \therefore y = 1.$

This value substituted in *either* (1) or (2) gives

$$x = 3.$$

Rule. *From one of the equations, find the value of the unknown quantity to be eliminated in terms of the other and known quantities; then substitute this value for that quantity in the other equation, and reduce.*

ELIMINATION BY COMPARISON.

173. Ex. Solve $\quad x + 15y = 53 \ldots \ldots \ldots$ (1).
$\qquad\qquad\qquad y + 3x = 27 \ldots \ldots \ldots$ (2).

From (1) $\qquad x = 53 - 15y,$

and from (2) $\qquad x = \dfrac{27 - y}{3}.$

Placing these values of x equal to each other, we have

$$53 - 15y = \dfrac{27 - y}{3}.$$

Whence $\qquad 159 - 45y = 27 - y,$
and $\qquad\qquad 44y = 132;$
$\qquad\qquad\quad \therefore y = 3.$

Substituting this value in *either* (1) or (2) gives

$$x = 8.$$

Rule. *From each equation find the value of the unknown quantity to be eliminated in terms of the other and known quantities; then form an equation with these values, and reduce.*

EXAMPLES XVII. a.

Solve the equations:

1. $3x + 4y = 10,$
   $4x + y = 9.$
2. $x + 2y = 13,$
   $3x + y = 14.$
3. $4x + 7y = 29,$
   $x + 3y = 11.$
4. $2x - y = 9,$
   $3x - 7y = 19.$
5. $5x + 6y = 17,$
   $6x + 5y = 16.$
6. $2x + y = 10,$
   $7x + 8y = 53.$
7. $8x - y = 34,$
   $x + 8y = 53.$
8. $15x + 7y = 29,$
   $9x + 15y = 39.$
9. $14x - 3y = 39,$
   $6x + 17y = 35.$
10. $28x - 23y = 33,$
    $63x - 25y = 101.$
11. $35x + 17y = 86,$
    $66x - 13y = 17.$
12. $15x + 77y = 92,$
    $55x - 33y = 22.$
13. $5x - 7y = 0,$
    $7x + 5y = 74.$
14. $21x - 50y = 60,$
    $28x - 27y = 199.$
15. $39x - 8y = 99,$
    $52x - 15y = 80.$
16. $5x = 7y - 21,$
    $21x - 9y = 75.$
17. $6y - 5x = 18,$
    $12x - 9y = 0.$
18. $8x = 5y,$
    $13x = 8y + 1.$
19. $3x = 7y,$
    $12y = 6x - 1.$
20. $19x + 17y = 0,$
    $2x - y = 53.$
21. $93x + 15y = 123,$
    $15x + 93y = 201$

SIMULTANEOUS EQUATIONS.

174. We add a few cases in which, before proceeding to solve, it will be necessary to simplify the equations.

Ex. 1. Solve $\quad 5(x+2y)-(3x+11y)=14 \quad \ldots \ldots$ (1),

$\qquad\qquad\qquad 7x-9y-3(x-4y)=38 \quad \ldots \ldots$ (2).

From (1) $\quad 5x+10y-3x-11y=14$;

$\qquad\qquad\therefore\ 2x-y=14 \quad \ldots \ldots$ (3).

From (2) $\quad 7x-9y-3x+12y=38$;

$\qquad\qquad\therefore\ 4x+3y=38 \quad \ldots \ldots$ (4).

From (3) $\qquad 6x-3y=42$;

and hence we may find $x=8$, and $y=2$.

Ex. 2. Solve $3x-\dfrac{y-5}{7}=\dfrac{4x-3}{2} \quad \ldots \ldots \ldots$ (1),

$\qquad\dfrac{3y+4}{5}-\tfrac{1}{3}(2x-5)=y \quad \ldots \ldots \ldots$ (2).

Clear of fractions. Thus

from (1) $\qquad 42x-2y+10=28x-21$;

$\qquad\qquad\therefore\ 14x-2y=-31 \quad \ldots \ldots \ldots$ (3).

From (2) $\quad 9y+12-10x+25=15y$;

$\qquad\qquad\therefore\ 10x+6y=37 \quad \ldots \ldots \ldots$ (4).

Eliminating y from (3) and (4), we find that

$$x=-\tfrac{11}{13}.$$

Eliminating x from (3) and (4), we find that

$$y=\tfrac{207}{26}.$$

NOTE. Sometimes, as in the present instance, the value of the second unknown is more easily found by elimination than by substituting the value of the unknown already found.

EXAMPLES XVII. b.

1. $\dfrac{2x}{3}+y=16,$

   $x+\dfrac{y}{4}=14.$

2. $\dfrac{x}{5}+\dfrac{y}{2}=5,$

   $x-y=4.$

3. $\dfrac{5x}{6}-y=3,$

   $x-\dfrac{5y}{6}=8.$

4. $x-y=5,$

   $\dfrac{x}{4}-\dfrac{y}{5}=2.$

5. $\dfrac{x}{9}+\dfrac{y}{7}=10,$

   $\dfrac{x}{3}+y=50.$

6. $x=3y,$

   $\dfrac{x}{3}+y=34.$

7. $\frac{2}{3}x - \frac{1}{12}y = 3,$
$4x - y = 20.$

8. $\frac{1}{2}x - \frac{1}{3}y = 4,$
$\frac{1}{7}x + \frac{1}{15}y = 3.$

9. $2x + y = 0,$
$\frac{1}{3}y - 3x = 8.$

10. $\frac{x}{7} + \frac{y}{5} = 1\frac{3}{7},$
$x + \frac{y}{3} = 4\frac{2}{3}.$

11. $3x - 7y = 0,$
$\frac{2}{3}x + \frac{1}{3}y = 7.$

12. $\frac{x}{5} - \frac{y}{4} = 0,$
$3x + \frac{1}{3}y = 17.$

13. $\frac{3x-1}{2} - \frac{y}{4} = \frac{7}{2},$
$x + 3y = 9.$

14. $\frac{x}{3} + \frac{y}{4} = 3x - 7y - 37 = 0.$

15. $\frac{x+1}{10} = \frac{3y-5}{2} = \frac{x-y}{8}.$

SIMULTANEOUS EQUATIONS INVOLVING THREE UNKNOWN QUANTITIES.

175. In order to solve simultaneous equations which contain two unknown quantities we have seen that we must have two equations. Similarly, we find that in order to solve simultaneous equations which contain three unknown quantities we must have three equations.

Rule. *Eliminate one of the unknowns from any pair of the equations, and then eliminate the same unknown from another pair. Two equations involving two unknowns are thus obtained, which may be solved by the rules already given. The remaining unknown is then found by substituting in any one of the given equations.*

Ex. 1. Solve
$6x + 2y - 5z = 13$ . . . . . . (1),
$3x + 3y - 2z = 13$ . . . . . . (2),
$7x + 5y - 3z = 26$ . . . . . . (3).

Choose y as the unknown to be eliminated.

Multiply (1) by 3 and (2) by 2,
$18x + 6y - 15z = 39,$
$6x + 6y - 4z = 26;$

subtracting, $12x - 11z = 13$ . . . . . . (4).

Again, multiply (1) by 5 and (3) by 2,
$30x + 10y - 25z = 65,$
$14x + 10y - 6z = 52;$

subtracting, $16x - 19z = 13$ . . . . . . (5).

SIMULTANEOUS EQUATIONS.

Multiply (4) by 4 and (5) by 3,
$$48x - 44z = 52,$$
$$48x - 57z = 39;$$
subtracting, $\quad 13z = 13;$
$$\therefore z = 1,$$
and from (4) $\quad x = 2,$
from (1) $\quad y = 3.$

NOTE. After a little practice the student will find that the solution may often be considerably shortened by a suitable combination of the proposed equations. Thus, in the present instance, by adding (1) and (2) and subtracting (3) we obtain $2x - 4z = 0$, or $x = 2z$. Substituting in (1) and (2), we have two easy equations in y and z.

Ex. 2. Solve
$$\frac{x}{2} - 1 = \frac{y}{6} + 1 = \frac{z}{7} + 2,$$
$$\frac{y}{3} + \frac{z}{2} = 13.$$

From the equation $\quad \frac{x}{2} - 1 = \frac{y}{6} + 1,$

we have $\quad 3x - y = 12 \ldots \ldots (1).$

Also, from the equation $\quad \frac{x}{2} - 1 = \frac{z}{7} + 2,$

we have $\quad 7x - 2z = 42 \ldots \ldots (2).$

And, from the equation $\quad \frac{y}{3} + \frac{z}{2} = 13,$

we have $\quad 2y + 3z = 78 \ldots \ldots (3).$

Eliminating z from (2) and (3), we have
$$21x + 4y = 282;$$
and from (1) $\quad 12x - 4y = 48;$
whence $x = 10$, $y = 18$. Also by substitution in (2) we obtain $z = 14$.

Ex. 3. Consider the equations
$$5x - 3y - z = 6 \ldots \ldots (1),$$
$$13x - 7y + 3z = 14 \ldots \ldots (2),$$
$$7x - 4y = 8 \ldots \ldots (3).$$

Multiplying (1) by 3 and adding to (2), we have
$$28x - 16y = 32,$$
or $\quad 7x - 4y = 8.$

Thus the combination of equations (1) and (2) leads us to an equation which is identical with (3), and so to find x and y we have but a single equation $7x - 4y = 8$, the solution of which is indeterminate. [Art. 167.]

In this and similar cases the anomaly arises from the fact that the equations are not *independent;* in other words, one equation is deducible from the others, and therefore contains no *relation* between the unknown quantities which is not already implied in the other equations.

EXAMPLES XVII. c.

1. $x + 2y + 2z = 11$,
   $2x + y + z = 7$,
   $3x + 4y + z = 14$.

2. $x + 3y + 4z = 14$,
   $x + 2y + z = 7$,
   $2x + y + 2z = 2$.

3. $x + 4y + 3z = 17$,
   $3x + 3y + z = 16$,
   $2x + 2y + z = 11$.

4. $3x - 2y + z = 2$,
   $2x + 3y - z = 5$,
   $x + y + z = 6$.

5. $2x + y + z = 16$,
   $x + 2y + z = 9$,
   $x + y + 2z = 8$.

6. $x - 2y + 3z = 2$,
   $2x - 3y + z = 1$,
   $3x - y + 2z = 9$.

7. $3x + 2y - z = 20$,
   $2x + 3y + 6z = 70$,
   $x - y + 6z = 41$.

8. $2x + 3y + 4z = 20$,
   $3x + 4y + 5z = 26$,
   $3x + 5y + 6z = 31$.

9. $3x - 4y = 6z - 16$,
   $4x - y - z = 5$,
   $x = 3y + 2(z - 1)$.

10. $5x + 2y = 14$,
    $y - 6z = -15$,
    $x + 2y + z = 0$.

11. $x - \dfrac{y}{5} = 6$,
    $y - \dfrac{z}{7} = 8$,
    $z - \dfrac{x}{2} = 10$.

12. $\dfrac{y + z}{4} = \dfrac{z + x}{3} = \dfrac{x + y}{2}$,
    $x + y + z = 27$.

13. $\dfrac{y - z}{3} = \dfrac{y - x}{2} = 5z - 4x$,
    $y + z = 2x + 1$.

14. $2x + 3y = 5$,
    $2z - y = 1$,
    $7x - 9z = 3$.

15. $\tfrac{1}{2}(x + z - 5) = y - z$
    $= 2x - 11 = 9 - (x + 2z)$.

16. $x + 20 = \dfrac{3y}{2} + 10$
    $= 2z + 5 = 110 - (y + z)$.

176. DEFINITION. If the product of two quantities be equal to unity, each is said to be the **reciprocal** of the other. Thus if $ab = 1$, a and b are reciprocals. They are so called

SIMULTANEOUS EQUATIONS.

because $a = \dfrac{1}{b}$, and $b = \dfrac{1}{a}$; and consequently a is related to b exactly as b is related to a.

The reciprocals of x and y are $\dfrac{1}{x}$ and $\dfrac{1}{y}$ respectively, and in solving the following equations we consider $\dfrac{1}{x}$ and $\dfrac{1}{y}$ as the unknown quantities.

Ex. 1. Solve
$$\dfrac{8}{x} - \dfrac{9}{y} = 1 \quad \ldots \ldots \ldots (1),$$
$$\dfrac{10}{x} + \dfrac{6}{y} = 7 \quad \ldots \ldots \ldots (2).$$

Multiply (1) by 2 and (2) by 3; thus
$$\dfrac{16}{x} - \dfrac{18}{y} = 2,$$
$$\dfrac{30}{x} + \dfrac{18}{y} = 21;$$

adding, $\qquad \dfrac{46}{x} = 23;$

multiplying across, $\qquad 46 = 23x,$

$$\therefore x = 2;$$

and by substituting in (1), $\quad y = 3.$

Ex. 2. Solve $\dfrac{1}{2x} + \dfrac{1}{4y} - \dfrac{1}{3z} = \dfrac{1}{4} \quad \ldots \ldots (1),$

$$\dfrac{1}{x} = \dfrac{1}{3y} \quad \ldots \ldots \ldots (2),$$

$$\dfrac{1}{x} - \dfrac{1}{5y} + \dfrac{4}{z} = 2\tfrac{2}{15} \quad \ldots \ldots (3);$$

clearing of fractional coefficients, we obtain

from (1) $\qquad \dfrac{6}{x} + \dfrac{3}{y} - \dfrac{4}{z} = 3 \quad \ldots \ldots (4),$

from (2) $\qquad \dfrac{3}{x} - \dfrac{1}{y} = 0 \quad \ldots \ldots \ldots (5),$

from (3) $\qquad \dfrac{15}{x} - \dfrac{3}{y} + \dfrac{60}{z} = 32 \quad \ldots \ldots (6).$

Multiply (4) by 15 and add the result to (6); we have

$$\frac{105}{x}+\frac{42}{y}=77;$$

dividing by 7, $\quad \dfrac{15}{x}+\dfrac{6}{y}=11 \quad \ldots \ldots \quad (7);$

from (5), $\quad \dfrac{18}{x}-\dfrac{6}{y}=0;$

adding, $\quad \dfrac{33}{x}=11;$

$$\therefore \left.\begin{array}{r}x=3,\\y=1,\\z=2.\end{array}\right\}$$

from (5),
from (4)

EXAMPLES XVII. d.

1. $\dfrac{5}{x}+\dfrac{6}{y}=3,$
$\dfrac{15}{x}+\dfrac{3}{y}=4.$

2. $\dfrac{6}{x}-\dfrac{7}{y}=2,$
$\dfrac{2}{x}+\dfrac{14}{y}=3.$

3. $\dfrac{12}{x}-\dfrac{4}{y}=2,$
$\dfrac{3}{x}-\dfrac{2}{y}=0.$

4. $\dfrac{5}{x}+\dfrac{16}{y}=79,$
$\dfrac{16}{x}-\dfrac{1}{y}=44.$

5. $\dfrac{21}{x}+\dfrac{12}{y}=5,$
$\dfrac{1}{y}-\dfrac{1}{x}=\dfrac{1}{42}.$

6. $\dfrac{5}{x}+\dfrac{3}{y}=30,$
$\dfrac{9}{x}-\dfrac{5}{y}=2.$

7. $\dfrac{8}{x}-\dfrac{9}{y}=7,$
$6\left(\dfrac{1}{x}+\dfrac{1}{y}\right)=1.$

8. $\dfrac{25}{x}+\dfrac{24}{y}=1,$
$20\left(\dfrac{2}{x}+\dfrac{3}{y}\right)=7.$

9. $\dfrac{4}{x}+\dfrac{27}{y}=42,$
$\dfrac{14}{x}-\dfrac{15}{y}=1.$

10. $\dfrac{3}{x}+\dfrac{5}{y}=\dfrac{8}{15},$
$9y-22x=\dfrac{3xy}{25}.$

11. $\dfrac{1}{4x}+\dfrac{1}{3y}=2,$
$\dfrac{1}{y}-\dfrac{1}{2x}=1.$

12. $2y-x=4xy,$
$\dfrac{4}{y}-\dfrac{3}{x}=9.$

13. $\dfrac{1}{x}-\dfrac{2}{y}+4=0,$
$\dfrac{1}{y}-\dfrac{1}{z}+1=0,$
$\dfrac{2}{z}+\dfrac{3}{x}=14.$

14. $\dfrac{1}{x}+\dfrac{1}{y}+\dfrac{1}{z}=36,$
$\dfrac{1}{x}+\dfrac{3}{y}-\dfrac{1}{z}=28,$
$\dfrac{1}{x}+\dfrac{1}{3y}+\dfrac{1}{2z}=20.$

LITERAL SIMULTANEOUS EQUATIONS.

177. Ex. 1. Solve
$$ax + by = c \quad \ldots \ldots \ldots (1),$$
$$a'x + b'y = c' \quad \ldots \ldots \ldots (2).$$

The notation here first used is one that the student will frequently meet with in the course of his reading. In the first equation we choose certain letters as the coefficients of x and y, and we choose *corresponding letters with accents* to denote corresponding quantities in the second equation. There is no necessary connection between the values of a and a', read "a and a prime," and they are as different as a and b; but it is often convenient to use the same letter thus slightly varied to mark some common meaning of such letters, and thereby assist the memory. Thus a and a' have a common property as being coefficients of x; b, b' as being coefficients of y.

Sometimes instead of accents letters are used with a *suffix*, such as a_1, a_2, a_3; b_1, b_2, b_3, etc., read "a sub one, a sub two," etc.

To return to the equation
$$ax + by = c \quad \ldots \ldots \ldots (1),$$
$$a'x + b'y = c' \quad \ldots \ldots \ldots (2).$$

Multiply (1) by b' and (2) by b. Thus
$$ab'x + bb'y = b'c,$$
$$a'bx + bb'y = bc';$$
by subtraction, $(ab' - a'b)x = b'c - bc'$;
$$\therefore x = \frac{b'c - bc'}{ab' - a'b} \quad \ldots \ldots (3).$$

As previously explained in Art. 171, we might obtain y by substituting this value of x in *either* of the equations (1) or (2); but y is more conveniently found by eliminating x, as follows:

Multiplying (1) by a' and (2) by a, we have
$$aa'x + a'by = a'c,$$
$$aa'x + ab'y = ac';$$
by subtraction, $(a'b - ab')y = a'c - ac'$;
$$\therefore y = \frac{a'c - ac'}{a'b - ab'}.$$

or, changing signs in the terms of the numerator and denominator so as to have the same denominator as in (3),

$$y = \frac{ac' - a'c}{ab' - a'b}, \text{ and } x = \frac{b'c - bc'}{ab' - a'b}.$$

Ex. 2. Solve
$$\frac{x-a}{c-a} + \frac{y-b}{c-b} = 1 \quad \ldots \ldots \quad (1),$$

$$\frac{x+a}{c} + \frac{y-a}{a-b} = \frac{a}{c} \quad \ldots \ldots \quad (2).$$

From (1) by clearing of fractions, we have
$$x(c-b) - a(c-b) + y(c-a) - b(c-a) = (c-a)(c-b),$$
$$x(c-b) + y(c-a) = ac - ab + bc - ab + c^2 - ac - bc + ab,$$
$$x(c-b) + y(c-a) = c^2 - ab \quad \ldots \ldots \quad (3).$$

Again, from (2), we have
$$x(a-b) + a(a-b) + cy - ca = a(a-b),$$
$$x(a-b) + cy = ac \quad \ldots \ldots \quad (4).$$

Multiply (3) by c and (4) by $c-a$ and subtract,
$$x\{c(c-b) - (c-a)(a-b)\} = c^3 - abc - ac(c-a),$$
$$x(c^2 - ac + a^2 - ab) = c(c^2 - ab - ac + a^2);$$
$$\therefore x = c;$$

and therefore from (4) $\quad y = b.$

EXAMPLES XVII. e.

1. $ax + by = l,$
   $bx + ay = m.$

2. $lx + my = n,$
   $px + qy = r.$

3. $ax = by,$
   $bx + ay = c.$

4. $ax + by = a^2,$
   $bx + ay = b^2.$

5. $x + ay = a',$
   $ax + a'y = 1.$

6. $px - qy = r,$
   $rx - py = q.$

7. $\dfrac{x}{a} + \dfrac{y}{b} = \dfrac{1}{ab},$
   $\dfrac{x}{a'} - \dfrac{y}{b'} = \dfrac{1}{a'b'}.$

8. $\dfrac{x}{a} - \dfrac{y}{b} = 0,$
   $bx + ay = 4ab.$

9. $\dfrac{3x}{a} + \dfrac{2y}{b} = 3,$
   $\dfrac{9x}{a} - \dfrac{6y}{b} = 3.$

10. $qx - rb = p(a-y),$
    $\dfrac{qx}{a} + r = p\left(1 + \dfrac{y}{b}\right).$

11. $\dfrac{x}{m} + \dfrac{y}{m'} = 1,$
    $\dfrac{x}{m'} - \dfrac{y}{m} = 1.$

12. $px + qy = 0,$
    $lx + my = n.$

13. $(a-b)x = (a+b)y,$
    $x + y = c.$

14. $(a-b)x+(a+b)y=2a^2-2b^2$,
    $(a+b)x-(a-b)y=4ab$.

15. $\dfrac{x}{a}+\dfrac{y}{b}=1$, $\dfrac{x}{3a}+\dfrac{y}{6b}=\dfrac{2}{3}$.

16. $\dfrac{x}{a}+\dfrac{y}{b}=2$, $\dfrac{x}{a'}=\dfrac{y}{b'}$.

17. $\dfrac{x}{a}-\dfrac{y}{b}=1$, $\dfrac{x}{b}+\dfrac{y}{a}=\dfrac{a}{b}$.

18. $\dfrac{x}{c+d}+\dfrac{y}{c-d}=2$,
    $cx-dy=c^2+d^2$.

19. $\dfrac{a}{bx}+\dfrac{b}{ay}=a+b$,
    $\dfrac{b}{x}+\dfrac{a}{y}=a^2+b^2$.

20. $ay+bx=2xy$,
    $cy+dx=3xy$.

21. $\dfrac{x+y}{x-y}=\dfrac{l}{m-n}$,
    $\dfrac{x+m}{y+m}=\dfrac{l+m}{l+n}$.

22. $\dfrac{m}{l}x+\dfrac{l}{m}y=\left(\dfrac{1}{l}+\dfrac{1}{m}\right)(m^2+l^2)$,
    $(x+y)(m^2+l^2)=2(m^3+l^3)+ml(x+y)$.

23. $bx+cy=a+b$, $ax\left(\dfrac{1}{a-b}-\dfrac{1}{a+b}\right)+cy\left(\dfrac{1}{b-a}-\dfrac{1}{b+a}\right)=\dfrac{2a}{a+b}$.

24. $(a-b)x+(a+b)y=2(a^2-b^2)$, $ax-by=a^2+b^2$.

CHAPTER XVIII.

Problems leading to Simultaneous Equations.

178. In the Examples discussed in the last chapter we have seen that it is essential to have as many equations as there are unknown quantities to determine. Consequently in the solution of problems which give rise to simultaneous equations, it will always be necessary that the statement of the question should contain as many *independent conditions* as there are quantities to be determined.

Ex. 1. Find two numbers whose difference is 11, and one-fifth of whose sum is 9.

Let x represent the greater number, y the less.

Then $\qquad x - y = 11 \qquad \ldots \ldots \ldots$ (1).

Also, $\qquad \dfrac{x+y}{5} = 9,$

or $\qquad x + y = 45 \qquad \ldots \ldots \ldots$ (2).

By addition, $2x = 56$; and by subtraction, $2y = 34$.
The numbers are therefore 28 and 17.

Ex. 2. If 15 lbs. of tea and 10 lbs. of coffee together cost $15.50, and 25 lbs. of tea and 13 lbs. of coffee together cost $24.55, find the price of each per pound.

Suppose a pound of tea to cost x cents and a pound of coffee to cost y cents.

Then from the question, we have

$\qquad\qquad 15x + 10y = 1550 \qquad \ldots \ldots \ldots$ (1),
$\qquad\qquad 25x + 13y = 2455 \qquad \ldots \ldots \ldots$ (2)

Multiplying (1) by 5 and (2) by 3, we have

$\qquad\qquad 75x + 50y = 7750,$
$\qquad\qquad 75x + 39y = 7365.$

Subtracting, $\qquad 11y = 385,$
$\qquad\qquad\qquad y = 35.$

PROBLEMS LEADING TO SIMULTANEOUS EQUATIONS.

And from (1) $\qquad 15x + 350 = 1550.$
Whence $\qquad 15x = 1200;$
$$\therefore x = 80.$$

Therefore the cost of a pound of tea is 80 cents, and the cost of a pound of coffee is 35 cents.

Ex. 3. A person spent $6.80 in buying oranges at the rate of 3 for 10 cents, and apples at 15 cents a dozen; if he had bought five times as many oranges and a quarter of the number of apples, he would have spent $25.45. How many of each did he buy?

Let x represent the number of oranges and y the number of apples.

$$x \text{ oranges cost } \frac{10x}{3} \text{ cents,}$$
$$y \text{ apples cost } \frac{15y}{12} \text{ cents;}$$
$$\therefore \frac{10x}{3} + \frac{15y}{12} = 680 \quad \ldots \ldots \quad (1).$$

Again, $5x$ oranges cost $5x \times \frac{10}{3}$, or $\frac{50x}{3}$ cents, and $\frac{y}{4}$ apples cost $\frac{y}{4} \times \frac{15}{12}$, or $\frac{15y}{48}$ cents;

$$\therefore \frac{50x}{3} + \frac{15y}{48} = 2545 \quad \ldots \ldots \quad (2).$$

Multiply (1) by 5 and subtract (2) from the result;
then $\qquad \left(\frac{75}{12} - \frac{15}{48}\right)y = 855;$
or $\qquad \frac{285y}{48} = 855;$
$$\therefore y = 144;$$
and from (1) $\qquad x = 150.$

Thus there were 150 oranges and 144 apples.

Ex. 4. If the numerator of a fraction is increased by 2 and the denominator by 1, it equals $\frac{5}{8}$; and if the numerator and denominator are each diminished by 1, it equals $\frac{1}{2}$: find the fraction.

Let x represent the numerator of the fraction, y the denominator; then the fraction is $\frac{x}{y}$.

From the first supposition, $\qquad \frac{x+2}{y+1} = \frac{5}{8} \quad \ldots \ldots \quad (1),$

from the second, $\qquad \frac{x-1}{y-1} = \frac{1}{2} \quad \ldots \ldots \quad (2).$

These equations give $x = 8$, $\qquad y = 15.$
Thus the fraction is $\frac{8}{15}$.

Ex. 5. The middle digit of a number between 100 and 1000 is zero, and the sum of the other digits is 11. If the digits be reversed, the number so formed exceeds the original number by 495. Find it.

Let x represent the digit in the units' place;

y represent the digit in the hundreds' place;

then, since the digit in the tens' place is 0, the number will be represented by $100y + x$. [Art. 84, Ex. 4.]

And if the digits are reversed, the number so formed will be represented by $100x + y$.

$$\therefore 100x + y - (100y + x) = 495,$$

or

$$100x + y - 100y - x = 495;$$

$$\therefore 99x - 99y = 495,$$

that is,

$$x - y = 5 \quad \ldots \ldots \quad (1).$$

Again, since the sum of the digits is 11, and the middle one is 0, we have

$$x + y = 11 \quad \ldots \ldots \quad (2).$$

From (1) and (2) we find $x = 8$, $y = 3$.

Hence the number is 308.

EXAMPLES XVIII.

1. Find two numbers whose sum is 34, and whose difference is 10.

2. The sum of two numbers is 73, and their difference is 37: find the numbers.

3. One-third of the sum of two numbers is 14, and one-half of their difference is 4: find the numbers.

4. One-nineteenth of the sum of two numbers is 4, and their difference is 30: find the numbers.

5. Half the sum of two numbers is 20, and three times their difference is 18: find the numbers.

6. Six pounds of tea and eleven pounds of sugar cost $5.65, and eleven pounds of tea and six pounds of sugar cost $9.65. Find the cost of tea and sugar per pound.

7. Six horses and seven cows can be bought for $250, and thirteen cows and eleven horses can be bought for $461. What is the value of each animal?

8. A, B, C, D have $290 between them; A has twice as much as C, and B has three times as much as D; also C and D together have $50 less than A. Find how much each has.

9. A, B, C, D have $270 between them; A has three times as much as C, and B five times as much as D; also A and B together have $50 less than eight times what C has. Find how much each has.

PROBLEMS LEADING TO SIMULTANEOUS EQUATIONS.

10. Four times B's age exceeds A's age by twenty years, and one-third of A's age is less than B's age by two years: find their ages.

11. One-eleventh of A's age is greater by two years than one-seventh of B's, and twice B's age is equal to what A's age was thirteen years ago: find their ages.

12. In eight hours A walks twelve miles more than B does in seven hours; and in thirteen hours B walks seven miles more than A does in nine hours. How many miles does each walk per hour?

13. In eleven hours C walks $12\frac{1}{2}$ miles less than D does in twelve hours; and in five hours D walks $3\frac{1}{4}$ miles less than C does in seven hours. How many miles does each walk per hour?

14. Find a fraction such that if 1 be added to its denominator it reduces to $\frac{1}{2}$, and reduces to $\frac{2}{3}$ on adding 2 to its numerator.

15. Find a fraction which becomes $\frac{1}{2}$ on subtracting 1 from the numerator and adding 2 to the denominator, and reduces to $\frac{1}{4}$ on subtracting 7 from the numerator and 2 from the denominator.

16. If 1 be added to the numerator of a fraction it reduces to $\frac{1}{3}$; if 1 be taken from the denominator it reduces to $\frac{1}{4}$. Required the fraction.

17. If $\frac{3}{4}$ be added to the numerator of a certain fraction the fraction will be increased by $\frac{1}{21}$, and if $\frac{1}{4}$ be taken from its denominator the fraction becomes $\frac{2}{3}$: find it.

18. The sum of a number of two digits and of the number formed by reversing the digits is 110, and the difference of the digits is 6: find the numbers.

19. The sum of the digits of a number is 13, and the difference between the number and that formed by reversing the digits is 27: find the numbers.

20. A certain number of two digits is three times the sum of its digits, and if 45 be added to it the digits will be reversed: find the number.

21. A certain number between 10 and 100 is eight times the sum of its digits, and if 45 be subtracted from it the digits will be reversed: find the number.

22. A man has a number of silver dollars and dimes, and he observes that if the dollars were turned into dimes and the dimes into dollars he would gain $2.70; but if the dollars were turned into half-dollars and the dimes into quarters he would lose $1.30. How many of each had he?

23. In a bag containing black and white balls, half the number of white is equal to a third of the number of black; and twice the whole number of balls exceeds three times the number of black balls by four. How many balls did the bag contain?

24. A number consists of three digits, the right hand one being zero. If the left hand and middle digits be interchanged, the number is diminished by 180; if the left hand digit be halved and the middle and right hand digits be interchanged, the number is diminished by 454: find the number.

25. The wages of 10 men and 8 boys amount to $22.30; if 4 men together receive $3.40 more than 6 boys, what are the wages of each man and boy?

26. A grocer wishes to mix sugar at 8 cents a pound with another sort at 5 cents a pound to make 60 pounds to be sold at 6 cents a pound. What quantity of each must he take?

27. A traveller walks a certain distance; had he gone half a mile an hour faster, he would have walked it in four-fifths of the time; had he gone half a mile an hour slower, he would have been $2\frac{1}{2}$ hours longer on the road: find the distance.

28. A man walks 35 miles partly at the rate of 4 miles an hour, and partly at 5; if he had walked at 5 miles an hour when he walked at 4, and *vice versâ*, he would have covered 2 miles more in the same time: find the time he was walking.

29. Two persons, 27 miles apart, setting out at the same time are together in 9 hours if they walk in the same direction, but in 3 hours if they walk in opposite directions: find their rates of walking.

30. When a certain number of two digits is doubled, and increased by 10, the result is the same as if the number had been reversed, and doubled, and then diminished by 8; also the number itself exceeds 3 times the sum of its digits by 18: find the number.

31. If I lend a sum of money at 6 per cent, the interest for a certain time exceeds the loan by $100; but if I lend it at 3 per cent, for a fourth of the time, the loan exceeds its interest by $425. How much do I lend?

32. A takes 3 hours longer than B to walk 30 miles; but if he doubles his pace he takes 2 hours less time than B: find their rates of walking.

CHAPTER XIX.

Indeterminate and Impossible Problems. Negative Results. Meaning of $\dfrac{a}{0}, \dfrac{a}{\infty}, \dfrac{0}{0}, \dfrac{\infty}{\infty}$.

INDETERMINATE AND IMPOSSIBLE PROBLEMS.

179. By reference to Art. 167, it will be seen that a single equation involving two unknown quantities is satisfied by an indefinitely great number of sets of values of the unknowns involved, and that it is essential to have as many equations expressing different, or independent conditions, as there are unknown quantities to be determined. If the conditions of a problem furnish a *less* number of independent equations than quantities to be determined, the problem is said to be **indeterminate**. If, however, the conditions give us a *greater* number of independent equations than there are unknown quantities involved, the problem is **impossible**.

Suppose the problem furnishes

$$3x + y = 10,$$
$$2x + y = 5,$$
$$x + y = 3.$$

From (1) and (2) we obtain $x = 5$ and $y = -5$. From (2) and (3) we obtain $x = 2$ and $y = 1$. These values cannot all be true at the same time, hence the problem is *impossible*.

NEGATIVE RESULTS.

180. A *is* 40 years old, and B's age *is* three-fifths of A's. When *will* A be five times as old as B?

Let x represent the number of years that *will* elapse.

Then
$$40 + x = 5(24 + x);$$
$$\therefore 40 + x = 120 + 5x,$$
or
$$x = -20.$$

According to this analysis, A will be five times as old as B in -20 years. The meaning of this result ought to be at once evident to a thoughtful student. Were the result any positive number of years, we would simply count that number forward from the present time (represented by the word "is" in the problem); manifestly then the -20 years refers to past time. Hence the problem should read, "A is 40 years old, and B's age is three-fifths of A's. When *was* A five times as old as B?"

Suppose the problem read

A is 40 years old, and B's age is three-fifths of A's: find the time at which A's age is five times that of B.

Let us assume that x years *will* elapse.

Then
$$40 + x = 5(24 + x);$$
$$\therefore x = -20.$$

Interpreting this result, we see that we should have assumed that x years *had* elapsed.

The student will notice that the word "will" in the first statement *suggested* that we should assume x as the number of years that *would* elapse, and that the negative result showed a fault in the enunciation of the problem; but that the problem, as given in the next discussion, *permitted* us to make one of two possible suppositions as to the nature of the unknown quantity, so that the negative result indicates simply a wrong choice.

Hence in the solution of problems involving equations of the first degree, *negative results* indicate

(1) *A fault in the enunciation of the problem*, or

(2) *A wrong choice between two possible suppositions, as to the nature of the unknown quantity, allowed by the problem.*

Generally it will be easy for the student to make such changes as will give an analogous possible problem.

INDETERMINATE AND IMPOSSIBLE PROBLEMS.

EXAMPLES XIX.

Make such necessary changes in the statements of the following problems as will render them possible arithmetically.

1. A is 27 years old and B 15; in how many years will A be twice as old as B?
2. What are the two numbers whose difference is 50, and sum 40?
3. If to the sum of twice a certain number and ⅕ of the same number 10 be added, the result is equal to twice the number.
4. A man loses $400, and then finds that 6 times what he had at first is equal to 5 times what he has left.
5. What fraction is that which becomes ⅘ when 1 is subtracted from its numerator, and ½ when 1 is subtracted from its denominator?
6. A is to-day 25 years old, and B's age is ⅖ of A's: find the date when A's age is twice that of B.

MEANING OF $\frac{a}{0}$, $\frac{a}{\infty}$, $\frac{0}{0}$, $\frac{\infty}{\infty}$.

181. Meaning of $\frac{a}{0}$. Consider the fraction $\frac{a}{x}$ in which the numerator a has a *certain fixed value*, and the denominator x is a *quantity subject to change;* then it is clear that the smaller x becomes, the larger does the value of the fraction $\frac{a}{x}$ become. For instance,

$$\frac{a}{\frac{1}{10}} = 10\,a, \quad \frac{a}{\frac{1}{1000}} = 1000\,a, \quad \frac{a}{\frac{1}{100000}} = 100000\,a.$$

By making the denominator x sufficiently small, the value of the fraction $\frac{a}{x}$ can be made as large as we please; that is, as the denominator x approaches to the value 0, the fraction becomes infinitely great. The symbol ∞ is used to express a quantity infinitely great, or more shortly *infinity*. The full verbal statement, given above, is sometimes written

$$\frac{a}{0} = \infty.$$

182. Meaning of $\frac{a}{\infty}$. If, in the fraction $\frac{a}{x}$, the denominator x gradually increases and finally becomes infinitely large, the fraction $\frac{a}{x}$ becomes infinitely small; that is, as the denominator of a fraction approaches to the value *infinity*, the fraction itself approaches to the value 0. This full verbal statement is sometimes written

$$\frac{a}{\infty} = 0.$$

183. Meaning of $\frac{0}{0}$. The symbol $\frac{0}{0}$ may be indeterminate in *form* or in *fact*. Thus the value of $\frac{x^2-4}{x-2}$ when $x=2$ is $\frac{0}{0}$, but by putting the fraction in the form $\frac{(x+2)(x-2)}{x-2}$ we see that the expression is equivalent to $x+2$, which becomes 4 when $x=2$. Again, $\frac{x^3-a^3}{x-a} = \frac{0}{0}$ when $x=a$, but by putting the fraction in the form $\frac{(x-a)(x^2+xa+a^2)}{x-a}$ we see that the expression is equivalent to x^2+xa+a^2, or $3a^2$, when $x=a$. These fractions assumed the form $\frac{0}{0}$ under particular conditions, but it is evident that they do not necessarily have the same value.

On the other hand, the symbol $\frac{0}{0}$ may show that a value is really indeterminate. Thus, solving in the regular way the equations

$$x + y + 2 = 0,$$
$$2x + 2y + 4 = 0,$$

we get $x = \frac{4-4}{2-2} = \frac{0}{0}$, and we can easily see that x can have any value whatever if we give y a value to suit, so that the value of x is indeterminate.

184. Meaning of $\frac{\infty}{\infty}$. Inasmuch as $\frac{1}{\infty} = 0$, what is true of $\frac{0}{0}$ is equally so of $\frac{\infty}{\infty}$.

CHAPTER XX.

INVOLUTION.

185. Definition. Involution is the general name for repeating an expression as a factor, so as to find its second, third, fourth, or any other power.

Involution may always be effected by actual multiplication. Here, however, we shall give some rules for writing at once

(1) any power of a monomial;
(2) the square and cube of any binomial;
(3) the square and cube of any multinomial;
(4) any power of a binomial expressed by a positive integer.

186. It is evident from the **Rule of Signs** that

(1) no **even power** of *any* quantity can be *negative;*
(2) any **odd power** of a quantity will have *the same sign* as the quantity itself.

Note. It is especially worthy of notice that the *square* of every expression, whether positive or negative, is *positive.*

INVOLUTION OF MONOMIALS.

187. From definition we have, by the rules of multiplication,

$$(a^2)^3 = a^2 \cdot a^2 \cdot a^2 = a^{2+2+2} = a^6.$$
$$(-x^3)^2 = (-x^3)(-x^3) = x^{3+3} = x^6.$$
$$(-a^5)^3 = (-a^5)(-a^5)(-a^5) = -a^{5+5+5} = -a^{15}.$$
$$(-3a^3)^4 = (-3)^4(a^3)^4 = 81\,a^{12}.$$

Hence we obtain the following rule for raising a simple expression to any proposed power:

Rule. (1) *Raise the coefficient to the required power by Arithmetic, and prefix the proper sign found by Art. 42.*

(2) *Multiply the index of every factor of the expression by the exponent of the power required.*

EXAMPLES.
(1) $(-2x^2)^5 = -32x^{10}$.
(2) $(-3ab^3)^6 = 729 a^6 b^{18}$.
(3) $\left(\dfrac{2 ab^3}{3 x^2 y}\right)^4 = \dfrac{16 a^4 b^{12}}{81 x^8 y^4}$.

It will be seen that in the last case the numerator and the denominator are operated upon separately.

EXAMPLES XX. a.

Write the square of each of the following expressions:

1. $3 ab^3$.
2. $5 x^2 y^5$.
3. $-2 abc^2$.
4. $11 b^2 c^3$.
5. $4 xyz^3$.
6. $-\tfrac{2}{3} a^2 b^3$.
7. $\dfrac{2 x^2}{3 y^3}$.
8. $-\dfrac{4}{3 x^2 y}$.
9. $-\dfrac{7 ab}{3}$.
10. $\dfrac{3 a^2 b^3}{4 c^5 x^4}$.
11. $-2 xy^2$.
12. $-\dfrac{3 a^5}{5 x^3}$.

Write the cube of each of the following expressions:

13. $2 ab^2$.
14. $3 x^3$.
15. $-2 a^7 c^2$.
16. $-3 a^3 b$.
17. $\dfrac{1}{3 y^2}$.
18. $-\dfrac{3 x^5}{5 a^3}$.
19. $7 x^2 y^4$.
20. $-\tfrac{2}{3} a^5$.

Write the value of each of the following expressions:

21. $(3 a^2 b^3)^4$.
22. $(-a^2 x)^6$.
23. $(-2 x^3 y)^5$.
24. $\left(\dfrac{1}{2 a^2}\right)^7$.
25. $\left(\dfrac{3 x^4}{2 y^3}\right)^5$.
26. $\left(\dfrac{2 x^3}{3 y}\right)^3$.
27. $\left(-\dfrac{x^3}{3}\right)^7$.
28. $\left(-\dfrac{2 x^5}{3 a^4}\right)^6$.
29. $\left(-\dfrac{2 a^2 x^3}{5 bc^2}\right)^4$.

TO SQUARE A BINOMIAL.

188. By multiplication we have
$$(a+b)^2 = (a+b)(a+b) = a^2 + 2ab + b^2 \quad . \quad . \quad (1),$$
$$(a-b)^2 = (a-b)(a-b) = a^2 - 2ab + b^2 \quad . \quad . \quad (2).$$

Rule I. *The square of the sum of two quantities is equal to the sum of their squares increased by twice their product.*

INVOLUTION. 171

Rule II. *The square of the difference of two quantities is equal to the sum of their squares diminished by twice their product.*

Ex. 1. $(x + 2y)^2 = x^2 + 2 \cdot x \cdot 2y + (2y)^2$
$= x^2 + 4xy + 4y^2.$

Ex. 2. $(2a^3 - 3b^2)^2 = (2a^3)^2 - 2 \cdot 2a^3 \cdot 3b^2 + (3b^2)^2$
$= 4a^6 - 12a^3b^2 + 9b^4.$

189. These rules may sometimes be conveniently applied to find the squares of numerical quantities.

Ex. 1. The square of $1012 = (1000 + 12)^2$
$= (1000)^2 + 2 \cdot 1000 \cdot 12 + (12)^2$
$= 1000000 + 24000 + 144$
$= 1024144.$

Ex. 2. The square of $98 = (100 - 2)^2$
$= (100)^2 - 2 \cdot 100 \cdot 2 + (2)^2$
$= 10000 - 400 + 4$
$= 9604.$

TO SQUARE A MULTINOMIAL.

190. We may now extend the rules of Art. 188 thus:
$(a + b + c)^2 = \{(a + b) + c\}^2$
$= (a + b)^2 + 2(a + b)c + c^2$ [Art. 188, Rule 1.]
$= a^2 + b^2 + c^2 + 2ab + 2ac + 2bc.$

In the same way we may prove
$(a - b + c)^2 = a^2 + b^2 + c^2 - 2ab + 2ac - 2bc$
$(a + b + c + d)^2 = a^2 + b^2 + c^2 + d^2 + 2ab + 2ac$
$+ 2ad + 2bc + 2bd + 2cd.$

In each instance we observe that the square consists of
(1) the sum of the squares of the several terms of the given expression;
(2) twice the sum of the products two and two of the several terms, taken with their proper signs; that is, in each

product the sign is + or − according as the quantities composing it have like or unlike signs.

NOTE. The *square terms* are always positive.

The same laws hold whatever be the number of terms in the expression to be squared.

Rule. *To find the square of any multinomial: to the sum of the squares of the several terms add twice the product (with the proper sign) of each term into each of the terms that follow it.*

Ex. 1. $(x-2y-3z)^2 = x^2 + 4y^2 + 9z^2 - 2 \cdot x \cdot 2y - 2 \cdot x \cdot 3z + 2 \cdot 2y \cdot 3z$
$= x^2 + 4y^2 + 9z^2 - 4xy - 6xz + 12yz.$

Ex. 2. $(1+2x-3x^2)^2 = 1 + 4x^2 + 9x^4 + 2 \cdot 1 \cdot 2x - 2 \cdot 1 \cdot 3x^2 - 2 \cdot 2x \cdot 3x^2$
$= 1 + 4x^2 + 9x^4 + 4x - 6x^2 - 12x^3$
$= 1 + 4x - 2x^2 - 12x^3 + 9x^4.$

EXAMPLES XX. b.

Write the square of each of the following expressions:

1. $a + 3b.$
2. $a - 3b.$
3. $x - 5y.$
4. $2x + 3y.$
5. $3x - y.$
6. $3x + 5y.$
7. $9x - 2y.$
8. $5ab - c.$
9. $a - b - c.$
10. $a + b - c.$
11. $a + 2b + c.$
12. $2a - 3b + 4c.$
13. $x^2 - y^2 - z^2.$
14. $xy + yz + zx.$
15. $x - y + a - b.$
16. $2x + 3y + a - 2b.$
17. $m - n - p - q.$
18. $\dfrac{a}{2} - 2b + \dfrac{c}{4}.$
19. $\dfrac{a}{3} - 3b - \dfrac{3}{2}.$
20. $\tfrac{1}{2}x^2 - x + \tfrac{1}{2}.$

TO CUBE A BINOMIAL.

191. By actual multiplication, we have
$(a+b)^3 = (a+b)(a+b)(a+b)$
$= a^3 + 3a^2b + 3ab^2 + b^3 \quad \ldots \quad (1),$
$(a-b)^3 = a^3 - 3a^2b + 3ab^2 - b^3 \quad \ldots \quad (2).$

From these results we obtain the following rule:—

Rule. *To find the cube of any binomial: take the cube of the first term, three times the square of the first by the second, three times the first by the square of the second, and the cube of the last.*

INVOLUTION.

If the binomial be the sum of the quantities, all signs will be $+$; if the difference of two quantities, the signs will be alternately $+$ and $-$, commencing with the first.

EXAMPLES XX. c.

Write the cube of each of the following expressions:

1. $x + a$.
2. $x - a$.
3. $x - 2y$.
4. $2ab - 3c$.
5. $x^2 + 4y^2$.
6. $4x^2 - 5y^2$.
7. $2a^3 - 3b^2$.
8. $5x^5 - 4y^4$.
9. $a - \dfrac{2b}{3}$.
10. $\dfrac{a}{3} + 2$.
11. $\dfrac{x^2}{3} - 3x$.
12. $\dfrac{a}{6} + 2x$.

TO CUBE ANY MULTINOMIAL.

192. Consider a trinomial:

$$(a+b+c)^3 = [a+(b+c)]^3$$
$$= a^3 + 3a^2(b+c) + 3a(b+c)^2 + (b+c)^3$$
$$= a^3 + b^3 + c^3 + 3a^2(b+c) + 3b^2(a+c)$$
$$+ 3c^2(a+b) + 6abc.$$

Rule. *To cube a multinomial: take the cube of each term, three times the square of each term by every other term, and six times the product of every three different terms. The signs are determined by the law of signs for multiplication.*

EXAMPLES XX. d.

Write the cube of each of the following expressions:

1. $1 + x + x^2$.
2. $1 + x - x^2$.
3. $1 - 2x + 3x^2$.
4. $a + bx + x^2$.
5. $2a + bx - cx^2$.
6. $3x + 2x^2 - x^3$.
7. $\dfrac{x}{2} + \dfrac{x^2}{3} - x^3$.
8. $1 + x + x^2 + x^3$.
9. $2 - 3x + x^2 + 2x^3$.

TO RAISE A BINOMIAL TO ANY POWER EXPRESSED BY A POSITIVE INTEGER [BINOMIAL THEOREM].

193. By actual multiplication, we obtain the following identities:

$$(a+b)^3 = a^3 + 3a^2b + 3ab^2 + b^3;$$
$$(a+b)^4 = a^4 + 4a^3b + 6a^2b^2 + 4ab^3 + b^4.$$

In these results, spoken of as expansions, we notice that:

(1) *The number of terms equals the index of the binomial plus one.*

(2) *The exponent of a in the first term is the same as the index of the binomial, and decreases by one in each succeeding term.*

(3) *The quantity b appears for the first time in the second term of the expansion with an exponent 1, and its exponent increases by one in each succeeding term.*

(4) *The coefficient of the first term is 1.*

(5) *The coefficient of the second term is the same as the index of the binomial.*

(6) *The coefficient of any term may be found by multiplying the coefficient of the preceding term by the exponent of a in that term, and dividing the result by the exponent of b plus 1.*

Ex. 1. Expand $(a+b)^6$.

$$(a+b)^6 = a^6 + a^5 + a^4 + a^3 + a^2 + a$$
$$+ b\ \ + b^2\ \ + b^3\ \ + b^4\ \ + b^5\ \ + b^6$$

Coefficients, $\quad 1 + 6 \quad + 15 \quad + 20 \quad + 15 \quad + 6 \quad + 1$

Multiplying, $\quad a^6 + 6a^5b + 15a^4b^2 + 20a^3b^3 + 15a^2b^4 + 6ab^5 + b^6$

Ex. 2. Expand $(a - 2b^2)^4$.

$$(a - 2b^2)^4 = [a + (-2b^2)]^4$$
$$= a^4 + a^3 + a^2 + a$$
$$+ (-2b^2) + (-2b^2)^2 + (-2b^2)^3 + (-2b^2)^4$$

Coefficients, $\quad 1 + 4 \quad + 6 \quad + 4 \quad + 1$

Multiplying, $\quad a^4 - 8a^3b^2 + 24a^2b^4 - 32ab^6 + 16b^8$

NOTE. The student will observe that in the line of coefficients, terms at equal distances from the beginning and the end are equal.

194. The same method may be used in expanding any multinomial.

Ex. Expand $(a + 2b - c)^3$.

$$(a + 2b - c)^3 = [(a + 2b) + (-c)]^3$$
$$= (a + 2b)^3 + (a + 2b)^2 + (a + 2b)$$
$$+ (-c) \quad + (-c)^2 \quad + (-c)^3$$

Coefficients, $\quad 1 \quad\quad + 3 \quad\quad + 3 \quad\quad + 1$

Multiplying, $\quad (a+2b)^3 - 3(a+2b)^2c + 3(a+2b)c^2 - c^3$

INVOLUTION. 175

Performing the operations indicated, we have
$a^3 + 6a^2b - 3a^2c + 12ab^2 - 12abc + 3ac^2 + 8b^3 - 12b^2c$
$\qquad\qquad\qquad\qquad\qquad\qquad\qquad\qquad + 6bc^2 - c^3.$

NOTE. A full discussion of the Binomial Theorem for Positive Integral Index is given in Chapter XXXVII.

EXAMPLES XX. e.

Expand the following expressions:

1. $(x+y)^5$.
2. $(a-b)^5$.
3. $(2a+b)^6$.
4. $(3x+2y)^5$.
5. $(2x-3b)^5$.
6. $(c^2+d^3)^6$.
7. $(2ab-c^2)^5$.
8. $(3a^2b^2-2cd^3)^5$.
9. $(\frac{1}{2}x^3+z^3)^5$.
10. $\left(\dfrac{a^2b}{3}-\dfrac{c^2}{4}\right)^5$.
11. $\left(\dfrac{2abc}{3}-\dfrac{2d^2}{5}\right)^4$.
12. $\left(\dfrac{2a}{x}-\dfrac{b^2}{z}\right)^5$.
13. $(a+2b+3c)^3$.
14. $(a-b+c)^3$.
15. $(2a-\dfrac{b}{2}-c^2)^3$.
16. $(a+b-2c)^4$.
17. $(a+b+c-d)^3$.
18. $(a+2b+c-2d)^3$.
19. $(a-2b+c-d)^4$.

20. Find the middle term of $(a+1)^{10}$.
21. Find the two middle terms of $(x-y)^{11}$.
22. Find the term independent of a in $\left(\dfrac{a^4}{2}-\dfrac{2}{a^3}\right)^7$.

CHAPTER XXI.

EVOLUTION.

195. The root of any proposed expression is that quantity which being repeated as a factor the requisite number of times produces the given expression. (Art. 14.)

The operation of finding the root is called **Evolution**: it is the inverse of Involution.

196. By the **Rule of Signs** we see that

(1) any **even root** of a *positive* quantity may be either *positive* or *negative*;

(2) no **negative** quantity can have an *even* root;

(3) every **odd root** of a quantity has the same sign as the quantity itself.

NOTE. It is especially worthy of notice that every positive quantity has two square roots equal in magnitude, but opposite in sign.

Ex. $\sqrt{(9 a^2 x^6)} = \pm 3 a x^3.$

In the present chapter, however, we shall confine our attention to the positive root.

EVOLUTION OF MONOMIALS.

197. From a consideration of the following examples we will be able to deduce a general rule for extracting any proposed root of a monomial.

EXAMPLES. (1) $\sqrt{(a^6 b^4)} = a^3 b^2$ because $(a^3 b^2)^2 = a^6 b^4.$

(2) $\sqrt[3]{(-x^9)} = -x^3$ because $(-x^3)^3 = -x^9.$

(3) $\sqrt[5]{(c^{20})} = c^4$ because $(c^4)^5 = c^{20}.$

(4) $\sqrt[4]{(81 x^{12})} = 3 x^3$ because $(3 x^3)^4 = 81 x^{12}.$

EVOLUTION.

Rule. (1) *Find the root of the coefficient by Arithmetic, and prefix the proper sign found by Art. 42.*

(2) *Divide the exponent of every factor of the expression by the index of the proposed root.*

EXAMPLES.
(1) $\sqrt[3]{(-64 x^6)} = -4 x^2$.
(2) $\sqrt[4]{(16 a^8)} = 2 a^2$.
(3) $\sqrt{\left(\dfrac{81 x^{10}}{25 c^4}\right)} = \dfrac{9 x^5}{5 c^2}$.

It will be seen that in the last case we operate separately upon the numerator and the denominator.

EXAMPLES XXI. a.

Write the square root of each of the following expressions:

1. $4 a^2 b^4$.
2. $9 x^6 y^2$.
3. $25 x^4 y^6$.
4. $16 a^4 b^2 c^6$.
5. $81 a^6 b^8$.
6. $100 x^8$.
7. $a^{20} b^{16} c^4$.
8. $a^8 b^2 c^{12}$.
9. $\dfrac{324 x^{12}}{169 y^6}$.
10. $\dfrac{81 a^{18}}{36 b^{12}}$.
11. $\dfrac{256 x^2 y^4}{289 p^{14}}$.
12. $\dfrac{400 a^{40} b^{20}}{81 x^{10} y^{18}}$.

Write the cube root of each of the following expressions:

13. $27 a^6 b^8 c^3$.
14. $-8 a^{12} b^9$.
15. $64 x^6 y^8 z^{12}$.
16. $-343 a^{12} b^{18}$.
17. $-\dfrac{x^{12} y^9}{125}$.
18. $\dfrac{8 x^9}{729 y^{15}}$.
19. $\dfrac{125 a^3 b^6}{216 x^6 y^9}$.
20. $-\dfrac{27 x^{27}}{64 y^{63}}$.
21. $-\dfrac{343 x^{15}}{512 z^{21}}$.

Write the value of each of the following expressions:

22. $\sqrt[6]{(729 a^{18} b^6)}$.
23. $\sqrt[5]{(256 a^8 x^{64})}$.
24. $\sqrt[5]{(-x^{10} y^{15})}$.
25. $\sqrt[7]{\dfrac{128}{a^{63} b^{56}}}$.
26. $\sqrt[10]{\dfrac{a^{80} x^{50}}{b^{100}}}$.
27. $\sqrt[9]{\dfrac{a^{18}}{b^{27} c^{36}}}$.
28. $\sqrt[11]{\dfrac{x^{11} y^{44}}{z^{121}}}$.

EVOLUTION OF MULTINOMIALS.

198. The Square Root of Any Multinomial. Since the square of $a + b$ is $a^2 + 2ab + b^2$, we have to discover a process by which a and b, the terms of the root, can be found when $a^2 + 2ab + b^2$ is given.

The first term, a, is the square root of a^2.

Arrange the terms according to powers of one letter a. The first term is a^2, and its square root is a. Set this down as the first term of the required root. Subtract a^2 from the given expression and the remainder is $2ab + b^2$ or $(2a + b) \times b$.

Thus, b, the second term of the root, will be the quotient when the remainder is divided by $2a + b$.

This divisor consists of two terms:
1. The double of a, the term of the root already found.
2. b, the new term itself.

The work may be arranged as follows:

$$a^2 + 2ab + b^2 \, (a + b$$
$$\underline{a^2}$$
$$2a + b \quad | \underline{2ab + b^2}$$
$$ \, 2ab + b^2$$

Ex. 1. Find the square root of $9x^2 - 42xy + 49y^2$.

$$9x^2 - 42xy + 49y^2 \, (3x - 7y$$
$$\underline{9x^2}$$
$$6x - 7y \quad | \underline{-42xy + 49y^2}$$
$$ \, -42xy + 49y^2$$

EXPLANATION. The square root of $9x^2$ is $3x$, and this is the first term of the root.

By doubling this we obtain $6x$, which is the first term of the divisor. Divide $-42xy$, the first term of the remainder, by $6x$ and we get $-7y$, the new term in the root, which has to be annexed both to the root and divisor. Next multiply the complete divisor by $-7y$ and subtract the result from the first remainder. There is now no remainder and the root has been found.

The process can be extended so as to find the square root of any multinomial. The first two terms of the root will be obtained as before. When we have brought down *the second remainder*, the first part of the new divisor is obtained by doubling the terms of the root already found. We then divide the first term of the remainder by the first term of the new divisor, and set down the result as the next term in the root and in the divisor. We next multiply the complete divisor by the last term of the root and subtract the product from the last remainder. If there is now no remainder the root has been found; if there is a remainder we continue the process.

Ex. 2. Find the square root of

$$25x^2a^2 - 12xa^3 + 16x^4 + 4a^4 - 24x^3a.$$

EVOLUTION.

Rearrange in descending powers of x.

$$16x^4 - 24x^3a + 25x^2a^2 - 12xa^3 + 4a^4\ (4x^2 - 3xa + 2a^2$$
$$\underline{16x^4}$$

$8x^2 - 3xa$ | $-24x^3a + 25x^2a^2$
 | $\underline{-24x^3a + 9x^2a^2}$

$8x^2 - 6xa + 2a^2$ | | $16x^2a^2 - 12xa^3 + 4a^4$
 | | $\underline{16x^2a^2 - 12xa^3 + 4a^4}$

EXPLANATION. When we have obtained two terms in the root, $4x^2 - 3xa$, we have a remainder

$$16x^2a^2 - 12xa^3 + 4a^4.$$

Double the terms of the root already found and place the result, $8x^2 - 6xa$, as the first part of the divisor. Divide $16x^2a^2$, the first term of the remainder, by $8x^2$, the first term of the divisor; we get $+2a^2$ which we annex both to the root and divisor. Now multiply the complete divisor by $2a^2$ and subtract. There is no remainder and the root is found.

EXAMPLES XXI. b.

Find the square root of each of the following expressions:

1. $x^2 - 10xy + 25y^2$.
2. $4x^2 - 12xy + 9y^2$.
3. $81x^2 + 18xy + y^2$.
4. $25x^2 - 30xy + 9y^2$.
5. $a^4 - 2a^3 + 3a^2 - 2a + 1$.
6. $4x^4 - 12x^3 + 29x^2 - 30x + 25$.
7. $9x^4 - 12x^3 - 2x^2 + 4x + 1$.
8. $x^4 - 4x^3 + 6x^2 - 4x + 1$.
9. $4a^4 + 4a^3 - 7a^2 - 4a + 4$.
10. $1 - 10x + 27x^2 - 10x^3 + x^4$.
11. $4x^2 + 9y^2 + 25z^2 + 12xy - 30yz - 20xz$.
12. $16x^6 + 16x^7 - 4x^8 - 4x^9 + x^{10}$.
13. $x^6 - 22x^4 + 34x^3 + 121x^2 - 374x + 289$.
14. $25x^4 - 30ax^3 + 49a^2x^2 - 24a^3x + 16a^4$.
15. $4x^4 + 4x^2y^2 - 12x^2z^2 + y^4 - 6y^2z^2 + 9z^4$.
16. $6ab^2c - 4a^2bc + a^2b^2 + 4a^2c^2 + 9b^2c^2 - 12abc^2$.
17. $-6b^2c^2 + 9c^4 + b^4 - 12c^2a^2 + 4a^4 + 4a^2b^2$.
18. $4x^4 + 9y^4 + 13x^2y^2 - 6xy^3 - 4x^3y$.
19. $1 - 4x + 10x^2 - 20x^3 + 25x^4 - 24x^5 + 16x^6$.
20. $6acx^5 + 4b^2x^4 + a^2x^{10} + 9c^2 - 12bcx^2 - 4abx^7$.

199. When the expression whose root is required contains fractional terms, we may proceed as before, the fractional part of the work being performed by the rules explained in Chapter XIII.

200. There is one important point to be observed when an expression contains powers of a certain letter and also powers of its reciprocal. Thus in the expression

$$2x + \frac{1}{x^2} + 4 + x^3 + \frac{5}{x} + 7x^2 + \frac{8}{x^3},$$

the order of *descending* powers is

$$x^3 + 7x^2 + 2x + 4 + \frac{5}{x} + \frac{1}{x^2} + \frac{8}{x^3};$$

and the numerical quantity 4 stands between x and $\frac{1}{x}$.

The reason for this arrangement will appear in Chapter XXII.

Ex. Find the square root of $24 + \frac{16y^2}{x^2} - \frac{8x}{y} + \frac{x^2}{y^2} - \frac{32y}{x}$.

Arrange the expression in descending powers of y.

$$\frac{16y^2}{x^2} - \frac{32y}{x} + 24 - \frac{8x}{y} + \frac{x^2}{y^2} \left(\frac{4y}{x} - 4 + \frac{x}{y} \right.$$

$$\frac{16y^2}{x^2}$$

$$\frac{8y}{x} - 4 \quad \bigg| -\frac{32y}{x} + 24$$

$$\quad\quad\quad\quad\ -\frac{32y}{x} + 16$$

$$\frac{8y}{x} - 8 + \frac{x}{y} \quad \bigg| 8 - \frac{8x}{y} + \frac{x^2}{y^2}$$

$$\quad\quad\quad\quad\quad\quad 8 - \frac{8x}{y} + \frac{x^2}{y^2}$$

Here the second term in the root, -4, arises from division of $-\frac{32y}{x}$ by $\frac{8y}{x}$, and the third term, $\frac{x}{y}$, arises from division of 8 by $\frac{8y}{x}$; thus $8 \div \frac{8y}{x} = 8 \times \frac{x}{8y} = \frac{x}{y}$.

EVOLUTION.

EXAMPLES XXI. c.

Find the square root of each of the following expressions

1. $\dfrac{x^2}{25} + \dfrac{2xy}{5} + y^2$.

2. $\dfrac{x^2}{y^2} + \dfrac{10x}{y} + 25$.

3. $\dfrac{x^2}{4y^2} - \dfrac{2x}{y} + 4$.

4. $\dfrac{x^2}{y^2} - \dfrac{2ax}{by} + \dfrac{a^2}{b^2}$.

5. $\dfrac{64x^2}{9y^2} + \dfrac{32x}{3y} + 4$.

6. $\dfrac{9x^2}{25} - 2 + \dfrac{25}{9x^2}$.

7. $\dfrac{a^4}{64} + \dfrac{a^3}{8} - a + 1$.

8. $x^4 + 2x^3 - x + \tfrac{1}{4}$.

9. $-3a^3 + \tfrac{25}{9} + a^4 - 5a + \tfrac{17}{12}a^2$.

10. $x^4 - 2x + \tfrac{1}{9} + 2\tfrac{1}{3}x^2 - 6x^3$.

11. $\dfrac{a^4}{4} + \dfrac{a^3}{x} + \dfrac{a^2}{x^2} - ax - 2 + \dfrac{x^2}{a^2}$.

12. $x^4 - 2x^3 + \dfrac{3x^2}{2} - \dfrac{x}{2} + \dfrac{1}{16}$.

13. $\dfrac{x^4}{4} + 4x^2 + \dfrac{ax^2}{3} + \dfrac{a^2}{9} - 2x^3 - \dfrac{4ax}{3}$.

14. $\dfrac{9a^2}{x^2} - \dfrac{6a}{5x} + \dfrac{101}{25} - \dfrac{4x}{15a} + \dfrac{4x^2}{9a^2}$.

15. $16m^4 + \tfrac{16}{3}m^2n + 8m^2 + \tfrac{1}{3}n^2 + \tfrac{4}{3}n + 1$.

16. $4x^4 + 32x^2 + 96 + \dfrac{64}{x^4} + \dfrac{128}{x^2}$.

201. The Cube Root of Any Multinomial. Since the cube of $a+b$ is $a^3 + 3a^2b + 3ab^2 + b^3$, we have to discover a process by which a and b, the terms of the root, can be found when $a^3 + 3a^2b + 3ab^2 + b^3$ is given.

The first term a is the cube root of a^3.

Arrange the terms according to powers of one letter a; then the first term is a^3, and its cube root a. Set this down as the first term of the required root. Subtract a^3 from the given expression, and the remainder is

$$3a^2b + 3ab^2 + b^3 \text{ or } (3a^2 + 3ab + b^2) \times b.$$

Now the first term of the remainder is the product of $3a^2$ and b. Thus to obtain b we divide the first term of the remainder by three times the square of the term already found.

Having found b we can complete the divisor, which consists of the following three terms:

1. Three times the square of a, the term of the root already found.

2. Three times the product of this first term a and the new term b.

3. The square of b.

The work may be arranged as follows:

$$a^3 + 3a^2b + 3ab^2 + b^3 \, | \, \underline{a + b}$$

$$\underline{a^3}$$

$3(a)^2 = 3a^2$ $| \, 3a^2b + 3ab^2 + b^3$

$3 \times a \times b = +3ab$

$(b)^2 = \underline{ +b^2}$

$3a^2 + 3ab + b^2$ $| \, 3a^2b + 3ab^2 + b^3$

Ex. 1. Find the cube root of $8x^3 - 36x^2y + 54xy^2 - 27y^3$.

$$8x^3 - 36x^2y + 54xy^2 - 27y^3 \, | \, \underline{2x - 3y}$$

$$\underline{8x^3}$$

$3(2x)^2 = 12x^2$ $| \, -36x^2y + 54xy^2 - 27y^3$

$3 \times 2x \times (-3y) = -18xy$

$(-3y)^2 = \underline{ +9y^2}$

$12x^2 - 18xy + 9y^2$ $| \, -36x^2y + 54xy^2 - 27y^3$

EXPLANATION. The cube root of $8x^3$ is $2x$, and this is the first term of the root.

By taking three times the square of this first term we obtain $12x^2$, which is the first term of the divisor, and is called the "trial divisor." Divide $-36x^2y$, the first term of the remainder, by $12x^2$ and we get $-3y$, the new term in the root. To complete the divisor, we first annex to the trial divisor three times the product of $2x$, the part of the root already found, and $-3y$, the new term of the root: this is $-18xy$. We then annex the square of $-3y$, the new term, and the divisor is complete. We next multiply this divisor by the new term, and subtract the result from the first remainder. There is now no remainder and the root has been found.

The process can be extended so as to find the cube root of any multinomial. The first two terms of the root will be obtained as before. When we have brought down *the second remainder*, we form the trial divisor by taking three times the square of the two terms of the root already found, and proceed as is shown in the following example.

EVOLUTION. 183

Ex. 2. Find the cube root of $27 + 108x + 90x^2 - 80x^3 - 60x^4 + 48x^5 - 8x^6$.

$$27 + 108x + 90x^2 - 80x^3 - 60x^4 + 48x^5 - 8x^6 \,(3 + 4x - 2x^2$$
$$\underline{27}$$

$$3 \times (3)^2 = 27 \qquad | \,108x + 90x^2 - 80x^3$$
$$3 \times 3 \times 4x = +36x$$
$$(4x)^2 = \underline{+16x^2}$$
$$27 + 36x + 16x^2 \,| \,108x + 144x^2 + 64x^3$$

$$3 \times (3 + 4x)^2 = 27 + 72x + 48x^2 \qquad |\; -54x^2 - 144x^3 - 60x^4 + 48x^5 - 8x^6$$
$$3 \times (3 + 4x) \times (-2x^2) = -18x^2 - 24x^3$$
$$(-2x^2)^2 = \underline{+4x^4}$$
$$27 + 72x + 30x^2 - 24x^3 + 4x^4 \;|\; -54x^2 - 144x^3 - 60x^4 + 48x^5 - 8x^6$$

$$-54x^2 - 144x^3 - 60x^4 + 48x^5 - 8x^6$$

EXPLANATION. When we have obtained two terms in the root, $3 + 4x$, we have a remainder

Take 3 times the square of the root already found and place the result, $27 + 72x + 48x^2$, as the first part of the new divisor. Divide $-54x^2$, the first term of the remainder, by 27, the first term of the divisor; this gives a new term of the root $-2x^2$. To complete the divisor we take 3 times the product of $(3 + 4x)$ and $-2x^2$, and also the square of $-2x^2$. Now multiply the complete divisor by $-2x^2$ and subtract; there is no remainder, and the root is found.

EXAMPLES XXI. d.

Find the cube root of each of the following expressions:

1. $a^3 + 3a^2 + 3a + 1$.
2. $a^3x^3 - 3a^2x^2y^2 + 3axy^4 - y^6$.
3. $64a^3 - 144a^2b + 108ab^2 - 27b^3$.
4. $1 + 3x + 6x^2 + 7x^3 + 6x^4 + 3x^5 + x^6$.
5. $1 - 6x + 21x^2 - 44x^3 + 63x^4 - 54x^5 + 27x^6$.
6. $a^3 + 6a^2b - 3a^2c + 12ab^2 - 12abc + 3ac^2 + 8b^3 - 12b^2c + 6bc^2 - c^3$
7. $8a^6 - 36a^5 + 66a^4 - 63a^3 + 33a^2 - 9a + 1$.
8. $8x^6 + 12x^5 - 30x^4 - 35x^3 + 45x^2 + 27x - 27$.
9. $27x^6 - 54x^5a + 117x^4a^2 - 116x^3a^3 + 117x^2a^4 - 54xa^5 + 27a^6$.
10. $27x^6 - 27x^5 - 18x^4 + 17x^3 + 6x^2 - 3x - 1$.
11. $24x^4y^2 + 96x^2y^4 - 6x^5y + x^6 - 96xy^5 + 64y^6 - 56x^3y^3$.
12. $216 + 342x^2 + 171x^4 + 27x^6 - 27x^5 - 109x^3 - 108x$.

202. We add some examples of cube root where fractional terms occur in the given expressions.

Ex. Find the cube root of $54 - 27x^3 + \dfrac{8}{x^6} - \dfrac{36}{x^3}$.

Arrange the expression in *ascending* powers of x.

$$\dfrac{8}{x^6} - \dfrac{36}{x^3} + 54 - 27x^3 \left(\dfrac{2}{x^2} - 3x \right.$$

$$\dfrac{8}{x^6}$$

$$3 \times \left(\dfrac{2}{x^2}\right)^2 \qquad = \dfrac{12}{x^4} \qquad \qquad -\dfrac{36}{x^3} + 54 - 27x^3$$

$$3 \times \dfrac{2}{x^2} \times (-3x) = \qquad -\dfrac{18}{x}$$

$$(-3x)^2 \qquad \qquad = \qquad \qquad + 9x^2$$

$$\overline{\dfrac{12}{x^4} - \dfrac{18}{x} + 9x^2} \quad \Big| \; -\dfrac{36}{x^3} + 54 - 27x^3$$

EXAMPLES XXI. e.

Find the cube root of each of the following expressions:

1. $\dfrac{x^3}{8} - \dfrac{3x^2}{4} + \dfrac{3x}{2} - 1$.
2. $8x^3 - 4x^2y^2 + \dfrac{2}{3}xy^4 - \dfrac{y^6}{27}$.
3. $\dfrac{27x^3}{64y^3} - \dfrac{27x^2}{8y^2} + \dfrac{9x}{y} - 8$.
4. $\dfrac{x^6}{y^3} - 6x^4 + 12x^2y^3 - 8y^6$.

EVOLUTION.

5. $\dfrac{x^3}{y^3} + \dfrac{6x^2}{y^2} + \dfrac{9x}{y} - 4 - \dfrac{9y}{x} + \dfrac{6y^2}{x^2} - \dfrac{y^3}{x^3}$.

6. $\dfrac{x^3}{27} - \dfrac{x^2}{3} + 2x - 7 + \dfrac{18}{x} - \dfrac{27}{x^2} + \dfrac{27}{x^3}$.

7. $\dfrac{x^3}{a^3} - \dfrac{12x^2}{a^2} + \dfrac{54x}{a} - 112 + \dfrac{108a}{x} - \dfrac{48a^2}{x^2} + \dfrac{8a^3}{x^3}$.

8. $\dfrac{64a^3}{x^3} - \dfrac{192a^2}{x^2} + \dfrac{240a}{x} - 160 + \dfrac{60x}{a} - \dfrac{12x^2}{a^2} + \dfrac{x^3}{a^3}$.

9. $\dfrac{6b}{a} + \dfrac{6a}{b} - 7 + \dfrac{a^3}{b^3} - \dfrac{3a^2}{b^2} - \dfrac{3b^2}{a^2} + \dfrac{b^3}{a^3}$.

10. $\dfrac{60x^4}{y^4} - \dfrac{80x^3}{y^3} - \dfrac{90x^2}{y^2} + \dfrac{8x^6}{y^6} + \dfrac{108x}{y} - 27 + \dfrac{48x^5}{y^5}$.

203. Some Higher Roots. The *fourth* root of an expression is obtained by extracting the square root of the square root of the expression.

Similarly by successive applications of the rule for finding the square root, we may find the *eighth, sixteenth* ⋯ root. The *sixth* root of an expression is found by taking the cube root of the square root, or the square root of the cube root.

Similarly by combining the two processes for extraction of cube and square roots, other higher roots may be obtained.

Ex. 1. Find the fourth root of
$$81x^4 - 216x^3y + 216x^2y^2 - 96xy^3 + 16y^4.$$
Extracting the square root by the rule we obtain $9x^2 - 12xy + 4y^2$; and *by inspection*, the square root of this is $3x - 2y$, which is the required fourth root.

Ex. 2. Find the sixth root of
$$\left(x^3 - \dfrac{1}{x^3}\right)^2 - 6\left(x - \dfrac{1}{x}\right)\left(x^3 - \dfrac{1}{x^3}\right) + 9\left(x - \dfrac{1}{x}\right)^2.$$
By inspection, the square root of this is
$$\left(x^3 - \dfrac{1}{x^3}\right) - 3\left(x - \dfrac{1}{x}\right),$$
which may be written $\quad x^3 - 3x + \dfrac{3}{x} - \dfrac{1}{x^3};$

and the cube root of this is $\quad x - \dfrac{1}{x},$

which is the required sixth root.

We conclude the subject of higher roots by giving a rule, which depends upon the Binomial Theorem, for finding the *n*th root of any multinomial.

(1) *Arrange the terms according to the descending powers of some letter.*

(2) *Take the nth root of the first term, and this will be the first term of the root.*

(3) *When* ANY NUMBER OF TERMS *of the root have been found, subtract from the given multinomial the nth power of the part of the root already found, and divide the first term of the remainder by n times the $(n-1)$th power of the* FIRST TERM *of the root, and this will be the next term of the root.*

204. When an expression is not an exact square or cube, we may perform the process of evolution, and obtain as many terms of the root as we please.

Ex. To find four terms of the square root of $1 + 2x - 2x^2$.

$$1 + 2x - 2x^2 (1 + x - \tfrac{1}{2}x^2 + \tfrac{1}{2}x^3$$

$$\begin{array}{r|l}
 & 1 \\
2 + x & \overline{2x - 2x^2} \\
 & 2x + x^2 \\
2 + 2x - \tfrac{1}{2}x^2 & \overline{-3x^2} \\
 & -3x^2 - 3x^3 + \tfrac{9}{4}x^4 \\
2 + 2x - 3x^2 + \tfrac{1}{2}x^3 & \overline{3x^3 - \tfrac{9}{4}x^4} \\
 & 3x^3 + 3x^4 - \tfrac{3}{2}x^5 + \tfrac{1}{4}x^6 \\
 & \overline{-\tfrac{21}{4}x^4 + \tfrac{3}{2}x^5 - \tfrac{1}{4}x^6.}
\end{array}$$

Thus the required result is $1 + x - \tfrac{1}{2}x^2 + \tfrac{1}{2}x^3$.

EXAMPLES XXI. 1.

Find the fourth roots of the following expressions:

1. $x^4 - 28x^3 + 294x^2 - 1372x + 2401$.
2. $16 - \dfrac{32}{m} + \dfrac{24}{m^2} - \dfrac{8}{m^3} + \dfrac{1}{m^4}$.
3. $a^4 + 8a^3x + 16x^4 + 32ax^3 + 24a^2x^2$.
4. $1 + 4x + 2x^2 - 8x^3 - 5x^4 + 8x^5 + 2x^6 - 4x^7 + x^8$.
5. $1 + 8x + 20x^2 + 8x^3 - 26x^4 - 8x^5 + 20x^6 - 8x^7 + x^8$.

EVOLUTION.

Find the sixth roots of the following expressions:

6. $1 + 6x + 15x^2 + 20x^3 + 15x^4 + 6x^5 + x^6$.
7. $x^6 - 12ax^5 + 240a^4x^2 - 192a^5x + 60a^2x^4 - 160a^3x^3 + 64a^6$.
8. $a^6 - 18a^5x + 135a^4x^2 - 540a^3x^3 + 1215a^2x^4 - 1458ax^5 + 729x^6$

Find the eighth roots of the following expressions:

9. $x^8 - 8x^7y + 28x^6y^2 - 56x^5y^3 + 70x^4y^4 - 56x^3y^5 + 28x^2y^6 - 8xy^7 + y^8$.
10. $\{x^4 + 2(p-1)x^3 + (p^2 - 2p - 1)x^2 - 2(p-1)x + 1\}^4$.

Find to four terms the square root of

11. $a^2 - x$. 12. $x^2 + a^2$. 13. $a^4 - 3x^2$. 14. $9a^2 + 12ax$.

Find to three terms the cube root of

15. $1 - 6x + 21x^2$. 16. $27x^6 - 27x^5 - 18x^4$. 17. $64 - 48x + 9x^2$.

18. Find the fifth root of

$$a^{10} - 10a^9 + 50a^8 - 160a^7 + 360a^6 - 592a^5 + 720a^4$$
$$- 640a^3 + 400a^2 - 160a + 32.$$

19. $a^{10} - 5a^9 + 20a^8 - 50a^7 + 105a^6 - 161a^5 + 210a^4 - 200a^3$
$$+ 160a^2 - 80a + 32.$$

20. $a^{10} + 5a^9 + 5a^8 - 10a^7 - 15a^6 + 11a^5 + 15a^4 - 10a^3$
$$- 5a^2 + 5a - 1.$$

205. Square and Cube Root of Numbers. Before leaving the subject of Evolution it may be useful to remark that the ordinary rules for extracting square and cube roots in Arithmetic are based upon the algebraic methods we have explained in the present chapter.

Ex. 1. Find the square root of 5329.

Since 5329 lies between 4900 and 6400, that is between $(70)^2$ and $(80)^2$, its square root consists of two figures and lies between 70 and 80. Hence, corresponding to a, the first term of the root in the algebraic process of Art. 198, we here have 70.

The analogy between the algebraic and arithmetical methods will be seen by comparing the cases we give below.

$$\begin{array}{r|l} & a^2 + 2ab + b^2(a+b \\ & a^2 \\ \hline 2a+b & 2ab + b^2 \\ & 2ab + b^2 \end{array} \qquad \begin{array}{r|l} & 5329(70+3=73. \\ & 4900 \\ \hline 140+3=143 & 429 \\ & 429 \end{array}$$

Ex. 2. Find the square root of 53824.

Here 53824 lies between 40000 and 90000, that is between $(200)^2$ and $(300)^2$.

$$\begin{array}{r}a\ b\ c\\ 53824(200+30+2=232\\ 40000\end{array}$$

$2a+b\ldots 400+30=430\,|\,13824$
12900
$2(a+b)+c\ldots 460+2=462|924$
$\phantom{2(a+b)+c\ldots 460+2=462|}924$

Ex. 3. Find the cube root of 614125.

Since 614125 lies between 512000 and 729000, that is between $(80)^3$ and $(90)^3$, therefore its cube root consists of two figures and lies between 80 and 90.

$$\begin{array}{r}a+b\\ 614125(80+5=85.\\ 512000\end{array}$$

$3a^2 = 3 \times (80)^2 = 19200\,|\,102125$
$3 \times a \times b = 3 \times 80 \times 5 = 1200$
$b^2 = 5 \times 5 = 25$
$20425\,|\,102125$

206. We shall now show that in extracting either the square or the cube root of any number, when a certain number of figures have been obtained by the common rule, that number may be nearly doubled by ordinary division.

207. If the square root of a number consists of $2n+1$ figures, when the first $n+1$ of these have been obtained by the ordinary method, the remaining n may be obtained by division.

Let N denote the given number; a the part of the square root already found, that is the first $n+1$ figures found by the common rule, with n ciphers annexed; x the remaining part of the root.

Then
$$\sqrt{N} = a + x;$$
$$\therefore N = a^2 + 2ax + x^2;$$
$$\therefore \frac{N-a^2}{2a} = x + \frac{x^2}{2a} \quad \ldots \ldots \ldots \quad (1).$$

EVOLUTION.

Now $N - a^2$ is the remainder after $n + 1$ figures of the root, represented by a, have been found; and $2a$ is the divisor at the same stage of the work. We see from (1) that $N - a^2$ divided by $2a$ gives x, the rest of the quotient required, increased by $\frac{x^2}{2a}$. We shall show that $\frac{x^2}{2a}$ is a *proper fraction*, so that by neglecting the remainder arising from the division, we obtain x, the rest of the root.

For x contains n figures, and therefore x^2 contains $2n$ figures at most; also a is a number of $2n + 1$ figures (the last n of which are ciphers) and thus $2a$ contains $2n + 1$ figures at least; and therefore $\frac{x^2}{2a}$ is a proper fraction.

From the above investigation, by putting $n = 1$, we see that *two* at least of the figures of a square root must have been obtained in order that the method of division, used to obtain the next figure of the square root, may give that figure correctly.

Ex. Find the square root of 290 to five places of decimals.

```
        290(17.02
         1
    27 |190
       |189
  3402   |10000
         | 6804
           3196
```

Here we have obtained four figures in the square root by the ordinary method. Three more may be obtained by division only, using 2×1702, that is 3404, for divisor, and 3196 as remainder. Thus

```
3404)31960(938
     30636
     13240
     10212
      30280
      27232
       3048
```

And therefore to five places of decimals $\sqrt{290} = 17.02938$.

It will be noticed that in obtaining the second figure of the root, the division of 190 by 20 gives 9 for the next figure; this is too great, and the figure 7 has to be obtained tentatively.

208. If the cube root of a number consists of $2n+2$ figures, when the first $n+2$ of these have been obtained by the ordinary method, the remaining n may be obtained by division.

Let N denote the given number; a the part of the cube root already found, that is, the first $n+2$ figures found by the common rule, with n ciphers annexed; x the remaining part of the root.

Then
$$\sqrt[3]{N} = a + x;$$
$$N = a^3 + 3a^2x + 3ax^2 + x^3;$$
$$\therefore \frac{N-a^3}{3a^2} = x + \frac{x^2}{a} + \frac{x^3}{3a^2} \quad \ldots \ldots \quad (1).$$

Now $N - a^3$ is the remainder after $n+2$ figures of the root, represented by a, have been found; and $3a^2$ is the divisor at the same stage of the work. We see from (1) that $N - a^3$ divided by $3a^2$ gives x, the rest of the quotient required, increased by $\frac{x^2}{a} + \frac{x^3}{3a^2}$. We shall show that this expression is a *proper fraction*, so that by neglecting the remainder arising from the division, we obtain x, the rest of the root.

By supposition, x is less than 10^n, and a is greater than 10^{2n+1}; therefore $\frac{x^2}{a}$ is less than $\frac{10^{2n}}{10^{2n+1}}$; that is, less than $\frac{1}{10}$; and $\frac{x^3}{3a^2}$ is less than $\frac{10^{3n}}{3 \times 10^{4n+2}}$; that is, less than $\frac{1}{3 \times 10^{n+1}}$; hence $\frac{x^2}{a} + \frac{x^3}{3a^2}$ is less than $\frac{1}{10} + \frac{1}{3 \times 10^{n+1}}$, and is therefore a proper fraction.

CHAPTER XXII.

The Theory of Indices.

209. Hitherto all the definitions and rules with regard to indices have been based upon the supposition that they were positive integers; for instance,

(1) $\quad a^{14} = a \cdot a \cdot a \cdots$ to fourteen factors.

(2) $\quad a^{14} \times a^{3} = a^{14+3} = a^{17}$.

(3) $\quad a^{14} \div a^{3} = a^{14-3} = a^{11}$.

(4) $\quad (a^{14})^{3} = a^{14 \times 3} = a^{42}$.

The object of this chapter is twofold; first, to give *general* proofs which shall establish the laws of combination in the case of positive integral indices; secondly, to explain how, in strict accordance with these laws, intelligible meanings may be given to symbols whose indices are fractional, zero, or negative.

We shall begin by proving, directly from the definition of a positive integral index, three important propositions.

210. Definition. When m is a *positive integer*, a^m stands for the product of m factors each equal to a.

211. Prop. I. *To prove that* $a^m \times a^n = a^{m+n}$, *when* m *and* n *are positive integers.*

By definition, $\quad a^m = a \cdot a \cdot a \cdots$ to m factors;

$\qquad\qquad\qquad a^n = a \cdot a \cdot a \cdots$ to n factors;

$\therefore a^m \times a^n = (a \cdot a \cdot a \cdots$ to m factors$) \times (a \cdot a \cdot a \cdots$ to n factors$)$

$\qquad\qquad = a \cdot a \cdot a \cdots$ to $m + n$ factors

$\qquad\qquad = a^{m+n}$, by definition.

Cor. If p is also a positive integer, then
$$a^m \times a^n \times a^p = a^{m+n+p};$$
and so for any number of factors.

212. Prop. II. To prove that $a^m \div a^n = a^{m-n}$, when m and n are positive integers, and m is greater than n.

$$a^m \div a^n = \frac{a^m}{a^n} = \frac{a \cdot a \cdot a \cdots \text{ to } m \text{ factors}}{a \cdot a \cdot a \cdots \text{ to } n \text{ factors}}$$
$$= a \cdot a \cdot a \cdots \text{ to } m-n \text{ factors}$$
$$= a^{m-n}.$$

213. Prop. III. To prove that $(a^m)^n = a^{mn}$, when m and n are positive integers.

$(a^m)^n = a^m \cdot a^m \cdot a^m \cdots$ to n factors
$= (a \cdot a \cdot a \cdots \text{ to } m \text{ factors})(a \cdot a \cdot a \cdots \text{ to } m \text{ factors}) \cdots$
the bracket being repeated n times,
$$= a \cdot a \cdot a \cdots \text{ to } mn \text{ factors}$$
$$= a^{mn}.$$

214. These are the fundamental laws of combination of indices, and they are proved directly from a definition which is intelligible only on the supposition that the indices are *positive* and *integral*.

But it is found convenient to use fractional and negative indices, such as $a^{\frac{4}{5}}$, a^{-7}; or, more generally, $a^{\frac{p}{q}}$, a^{-n}; and these have at present no intelligible meaning. For the definition of a^m [Art. 210], upon which we based the three propositions just proved, is no longer applicable when m is *fractional* or *negative*.

Now it is important that all indices, whether positive or negative, integral or fractional, should be governed by the same laws. We therefore determine meanings for symbols such as $a^{\frac{p}{q}}$, a^{-n}, in the following way: we assume that they conform to the fundamental law, $a^m \times a^n = a^{m+n}$, and accept

THE THEORY OF INDICES.

the meaning to which this assumption leads us. It will be found that the symbols so interpreted will also obey the other laws enunciated in Props. II. and III.

215. To find a meaning for $a^{\frac{p}{q}}$, p and q being positive integers.

Since $a^m \times a^n = a^{m+n}$ is to be true for *all* values of m and n, by replacing each of the indices m and n by $\frac{p}{q}$, we have

$$a^{\frac{p}{q}} \times a^{\frac{p}{q}} = a^{\frac{p}{q}+\frac{p}{q}} = a^{\frac{2p}{q}}.$$

Similarly, $a^{\frac{p}{q}} \times a^{\frac{p}{q}} \times a^{\frac{p}{q}} = a^{\frac{2p}{q}} \times a^{\frac{p}{q}} = a^{\frac{2p}{q}+\frac{p}{q}} = a^{\frac{3p}{q}}.$

Proceeding in this way for 4, 5, $\cdots q$ factors, we have

$$a^{\frac{p}{q}} \times a^{\frac{p}{q}} \times a^{\frac{p}{q}} \cdots \text{ to } q \text{ factors} = a^{\frac{qp}{q}};$$

that is, $\qquad (a^{\frac{p}{q}})^q = a^p.$

Therefore, by taking the qth root,

$$a^{\frac{p}{q}} = \sqrt[q]{a^p},$$

or, in words, $a^{\frac{p}{q}}$ is equal to "*the qth root of a^p.*"

EXAMPLES. (1) $x^{\frac{5}{7}} = \sqrt[7]{x^5}.$

(2) $a^{\frac{1}{3}} = \sqrt[3]{a}.$

(3) $4^{\frac{3}{2}} = \sqrt{4^3} = \sqrt{64} = 8.$

(4) $a^{\frac{2}{3}} \times a^{\frac{5}{6}} = a^{\frac{2}{3}+\frac{5}{6}} = a^{\frac{3}{2}}.$

(5) $k^{\frac{a}{2}} \times k^{\frac{2}{3}} = k^{\frac{a}{2}+\frac{2}{3}} = k^{\frac{3a+4}{6}}.$

(6) $3 a^{\frac{2}{3}} b^{\frac{1}{2}} \times 4 a^{\frac{1}{6}} b^{\frac{5}{6}} = 12 a^{\frac{2}{3}+\frac{1}{6}} b^{\frac{1}{2}+\frac{5}{6}} = 12 a^{\frac{5}{6}} b^{\frac{4}{3}}.$

216. To find a meaning for a^0.

Since $a^m \times a^n = a^{m+n}$ is to be true for *all* values of m and n, by replacing the index m by 0, we have

$$a^0 \times a^n = a^{0+n} = a^n;$$

$$\therefore a^0 = \frac{a^n}{a^n} = 1.$$

Hence any quantity with zero index is equivalent to 1.

Ex. $x^{b-c} \times x^{c-b} = x^{b-c+c-b} = x^0 = 1.$

217. To find a meaning for a^{-n}.

Since $a^m \times a^n = a^{m+n}$ is to be true for *all* values of m and n, by replacing the index m by $-n$, we have

$$a^{-n} \times a^n = a^{-n+n} = a^0.$$

But $\qquad a^0 = 1.$

Hence $\qquad a^{-n} = \dfrac{1}{a^n},$

and $\qquad a^n = \dfrac{1}{a^{-n}}.$

From this it follows that *any factor may be transferred from the numerator to the denominator of an expression, or vice-versa, by merely changing the sign of the index.*

EXAMPLES. (1) $x^{-3} = \dfrac{1}{x^3}.$

(2) $\dfrac{1}{y^{-\frac{1}{2}}} = y^{\frac{1}{2}} = \sqrt{y}.$

(3) $27^{-\frac{2}{3}} = \dfrac{1}{27^{\frac{2}{3}}} = \dfrac{1}{\sqrt[3]{(27)^2}} = \dfrac{1}{\sqrt[3]{3^6}} = \dfrac{1}{3^2} = \dfrac{1}{9}.$

218. To prove that $a^m \div a^n = a^{m-n}$ for all values of m and n.

$$a^m \div a^n = a^m \times \dfrac{1}{a^n} = a^m \times a^{-n}$$
$$= a^{m-n}, \text{ by the fundamental law.}$$

EXAMPLES. (1) $a^3 \div a^5 = a^{3-5} = a^{-2} = \dfrac{1}{a^2}.$

(2) $c \div c^{-\frac{3}{5}} = c^{1+\frac{3}{5}} = c^{1\frac{3}{5}}.$

(3) $x^{a-b} \div x^{a-c} = x^{a-b-(a-c)} = x^{c-b}.$

219. The method of finding a meaning for a symbol, as explained in the preceding articles, deserves careful attention. The usual algebraic process is to make choice of symbols, give them meanings, and then prove the rules for their combination. Here the process is reversed; the symbols are given, and the law to which they are to conform, and from this the meanings of the symbols are determined.

THE THEORY OF INDICES.

220. The following examples will illustrate the different principles we have established.

EXAMPLES. (1) $\dfrac{3 a^{-2}}{5 x^{-1} y} = \dfrac{3 x}{5 a^2 y}$.

(2) $\dfrac{2 a^{\frac{1}{2}} \times a^{\frac{2}{3}} \times 6 a^{-\frac{7}{3}}}{9 a^{-\frac{5}{3}} \times a^{\frac{3}{2}}} = \dfrac{4}{3} a^{\frac{1}{2}+\frac{2}{3}-\frac{7}{3}+\frac{5}{3}-\frac{3}{2}} = \dfrac{4}{3} a^{-1} = \dfrac{4}{3a}$.

(3) $\dfrac{\sqrt{x^3} \times \sqrt[3]{y^2}}{\sqrt[6]{y^{-2}} \times \sqrt[4]{x^6}} = \dfrac{x^{\frac{3}{2}} \times y^{\frac{2}{3}}}{y^{-\frac{1}{3}} \times x^{\frac{3}{2}}} = x^{\frac{3}{2}-\frac{3}{2}} y^{\frac{2}{3}+\frac{1}{3}} = x^0 y = y$.

(4) $2\sqrt{a} + \dfrac{3}{a^{-\frac{1}{2}}} + a^{\frac{5}{2}} = 2 a^{\frac{1}{2}} + 3 a^{\frac{1}{2}} + a^{\frac{5}{2}}$

$\qquad = 5 a^{\frac{1}{2}} + a^{\frac{5}{2}} = a^{\frac{1}{2}}(5 + a^2)$.

EXAMPLES XXII. a.

Express with positive indices:

1. $2 x^{-\frac{1}{4}}$.
2. $3 a^{-\frac{2}{3}}$.
3. $4 x^{-2} a^3$.
4. $3 \div a^{-2}$.
5. $\dfrac{1}{4 a^{-2}}$.
6. $\dfrac{1}{5 x^{-\frac{1}{2}}}$.
7. $\dfrac{3 a^{-3} x^2}{5 y^2 c^{-4}}$.
8. $\dfrac{x^a y^{-b}}{b^{-a}}$.
9. $2 x^{\frac{1}{2}} \times 3 x^{-1}$.
10. $1 \div 2 a^{-\frac{1}{2}}$.
11. $x y^2 \times x^{-1}$.
12. $a^{-2} x^{-1} \div 3 x$.
13. $\dfrac{1}{\sqrt{x^3}}$.
14. $\dfrac{1}{4 \sqrt[5]{x^{-3}}}$.
15. $\dfrac{2}{\sqrt{y^{-3}}}$.
16. $\dfrac{\sqrt[4]{x^3}}{\sqrt{x^{-1}}}$.

17. $a^{-2} x^{-\frac{1}{2}} \div a^{-3}$.
18. $\sqrt[3]{a^{-1}} \div \sqrt[3]{a}$.
19. $\sqrt[5]{a^{-3}} \div \sqrt[5]{a^7}$.

Express with radical signs and positive indices:

20. $x^{\frac{3}{5}}$.
21. $a^{-\frac{1}{2}}$.
22. $5 x^{-\frac{1}{2}}$.
23. $2 a^{-\frac{1}{x}}$.
24. $\dfrac{1}{2 a^{\frac{1}{3}}}$.
25. $\dfrac{2}{b^{-\frac{3}{4}}}$.
26. $\dfrac{c^{-\frac{1}{3}}}{2}$.
27. $\dfrac{1}{x^{-\frac{1}{z}}}$.
28. $a^{-\frac{1}{3}} \times 2 a^{-\frac{1}{2}}$.
29. $x^{-\frac{2}{3}} \div 2 a^{-\frac{1}{2}}$.
30. $7 a^{-\frac{1}{2}} \times 3 a^{-1}$.
31. $\dfrac{2 a^{-2}}{a^{-\frac{3}{2}}}$.
32. $\dfrac{a^{-\frac{1}{2}}}{3 a}$.
33. $\dfrac{4 x^{-1}}{x^{-\frac{1}{3}}}$.
34. $\dfrac{\sqrt[3]{x^{-a}}}{\sqrt[5]{x^2}}$.

35. $\sqrt[3]{a^2} \times \sqrt[3]{a^3}$.
36. $\sqrt[5]{a^{-x}} \div \sqrt[5]{a^{-2x}}$.
37. $\sqrt[2a]{x} \times \sqrt[a]{x^2}$.
38. $\sqrt[a]{x} \div \sqrt[2a]{x^3}$.
39. $\sqrt[3x]{a^3} \div \sqrt[x]{a^2}$.
40. $\sqrt[4]{a^n} \times \sqrt[3]{a^n} \div \sqrt[12]{a^{5n}}$.

ALGEBRA.

Find the value of

41. $16^{\frac{3}{4}}$. 43. $125^{\frac{2}{3}}$. 45. $36^{-\frac{3}{2}}$. 47. $243^{\frac{2}{5}}$. 49. $(\frac{81}{16})^{\frac{3}{4}}$.

42. $4^{-\frac{3}{2}}$. 44. $8^{-\frac{2}{3}}$. 46. $\dfrac{1}{25^{-2}}$. 48. $(\frac{8}{27})^{-\frac{1}{3}}$. 50. $(\frac{32}{243})^{-\frac{7}{5}}$.

221. To prove that $(a^m)^n = a^{mn}$ is true for all values of m and n.

Case I. Let n be a *positive integer*.

Now, *whatever be the value of* m

$$(a^m)^n = a^m \cdot a^m \cdot a^m \cdots \text{to } n \text{ factors}$$
$$= a^{m+m+m+\cdots \text{to } n \text{ terms}} = a^{mn}.$$

Case II. Let m be unrestricted as before, and let n be a *positive fraction*. Replacing n by $\dfrac{p}{q}$, where p and q are positive integers, we have $(a^m)^n = (a^m)^{\frac{p}{q}}$.

Now the qth power of $(a^m)^{\frac{p}{q}} = \{(a^m)^{\frac{p}{q}}\}^q = (a^m)^{\frac{p}{q} \cdot q}$, [Case I.]
$$= (a^m)^p = a^{mp}. \quad \text{[Case I.]}$$

Hence by taking the qth root of these equals,

$$(a^m)^{\frac{p}{q}} = \sqrt[q]{a^{mp}} = a^{\frac{mp}{q}}. \qquad \text{[Art. 215.]}$$

Case III. Let m be unrestricted as before, and let n be any *negative quantity*. Replacing n by $-r$, where r is *positive*, we have

$$(a^m)^n = (a^m)^{-r} = \dfrac{1}{(a^m)^r}, \qquad \text{[Art. 217.]}$$
$$= \dfrac{1}{a^{mr}}, \qquad \text{[Case II.]}$$
$$= a^{-mr} = a^{mn}.$$

Hence Prop. III., Art. 213, $(a^m)^n = a^{mn}$ has been shown to be universally true.

EXAMPLES.   (1) $(b^{\frac{2}{3}})^{\frac{6}{7}} = b^{\frac{2}{3} \times \frac{6}{7}} = b^{\frac{4}{7}}$.

(2) $\{(x^{-2})^3\}^{-4} = (x^{-6})^{-4} = x^{24}$.

(3) $(x^{\frac{1}{a-c}})^{a^2-c^2} = x^{\frac{1}{a-c} \times (a^2-c^2)} = x^{a+c}$.

THE THEORY OF INDICES.

222. To prove that $(ab)^n = a^n b^n$, whatever be the value of n; a and b being any quantities whatever.

Case I. Let n be a *positive integer*.

Now $(ab)^n = ab \cdot ab \cdot ab \cdots$ to n factors
$= (a \cdot a \cdot a \cdots \text{to } n \text{ factors})(b \cdot b \cdot b \cdots \text{to } n \text{ factors}) = a^n b^n$.

Case II. Let n be a *positive fraction*. Replacing n by $\frac{p}{q}$, where p and q are *positive integers*, we have $(ab)^n = (ab)^{\frac{p}{q}}$.

Now the qth power of $(ab)^{\frac{p}{q}} = \{(ab)^{\frac{p}{q}}\}^q = (ab)^p$, [Art. 221.]
$$= a^p b^p = \left(a^{\frac{p}{q}} b^{\frac{p}{q}}\right)^q. \quad \text{[Case I.]}$$

Taking the qth root, $(ab)^{\frac{p}{q}} = a^{\frac{p}{q}} b^{\frac{p}{q}}$.

Case III. Let n have *any negative value*. Replacing n by $-r$, where r is positive,
$$(ab)^n = (ab)^{-r} = \frac{1}{(ab)^r} = \frac{1}{a^r b^r} = a^{-r} b^{-r} = a^n b^n.$$

Hence the proposition is proved universally.

This result may be expressed in a verbal form by saying that *the index of a product may be distributed over its factors*.

NOTE. An index is not distributive over the **terms** of an expression. Thus $(a^{\frac{1}{2}} + b^{\frac{1}{2}})^2$ is not equal to $a + b$. Again $(a^2 + b^2)^{\frac{1}{2}}$ is equal to $\sqrt{a^2 + b^2}$, and cannot be further simplified.

EXAMPLES. (1) $(yz)^{a-c}(zx)^c(xy)^{-c} = y^{a-c} z^{a-c} z^c x^c x^{-c} y^{-c} = y^{a-2c} z^a$.

(2) $\{(a-b)^k\}^{-l} \times \{(a+b)^{-k}\}^l = (a-b)^{-kl} \times (a+b)^{-kl}$
$= \{(a-b)(a+b)\}^{-kl} = (a^2 - b^2)^{-kl}$.

223. Since in the proof of Art. 222 the quantities a and b are *wholly unrestricted*, they may themselves involve indices.

EXAMPLES. (1) $(x^{\frac{1}{2}} y^{-\frac{1}{2}})^{\frac{4}{3}} \div (x^2 y^{-1})^{-\frac{1}{3}} = x^{\frac{2}{3}} y^{-\frac{2}{3}} \div x^{-\frac{2}{3}} y^{\frac{1}{3}} = x^{\frac{4}{3}} y^{-1}$.

(2) $\left(\dfrac{a^{\frac{2}{3}} \sqrt{b^{-1}}}{b \sqrt[3]{a^{-2}}} \div \sqrt{\dfrac{a \sqrt{b^{-4}}}{b \sqrt{a^{-2}}}}\right)^6 = \left(\dfrac{a^{\frac{2}{3}} b^{-\frac{1}{2}}}{b a^{-\frac{2}{3}}} \div \sqrt{\dfrac{ab^{-2}}{ba^{-1}}}\right)^6$

$= (a^4 b^{-\frac{3}{2}} \div \sqrt{a^2 b^{-3}})^6 = (a^{\frac{4}{3}} b^{-\frac{3}{2}} + ab^{-\frac{3}{2}})^6 = (a^{\frac{1}{3}})^6 = a^2$.

EXAMPLES XXII. b.

Simplify and express with positive indices:

1. $(\sqrt{a^2 b^3})^6$.
2. $(\sqrt[9]{x^{-4}y^3})^{-3}$.
3. $(x^a y^{-b})^3 \times (x^3 y^2)^{-a}$.
4. $\left(\dfrac{16 x^2}{y^{-2}}\right)^{-\frac{1}{4}}$.
5. $\left(\dfrac{27 x^3}{8 a^{-3}}\right)^{-\frac{2}{3}}$.
6. $\left(\dfrac{a^{-\frac{1}{2}}}{4 c^2}\right)^{-2}$.
7. $\left\{\sqrt[4]{(x^{-\frac{2}{3}} y^{\frac{1}{2}})^3}\right\}^{-\frac{2}{3}}$.
8. $\sqrt[4]{x \sqrt[3]{x^{-1}}}$.
9. $(4 a^{-2} \div 9 x^2)^{-\frac{1}{2}}$.
10. $(x \div \sqrt[n]{x})^n$.
11. $(x \times \sqrt[n]{x^{-\frac{1}{n}}})^{\frac{n^2}{1-n}}$.
12. $(\sqrt[5]{x^b} \div \sqrt[a]{x})^{\frac{1}{1-a}}$.

13. $\sqrt{a^{-2}b} \times \sqrt[3]{ab^{-3}}$.
14. $\sqrt[3]{ab^{-1}c^{-2}} \times (a^{-1}b^{-2}c^{-4})^{-\frac{1}{3}}$.
15. $\sqrt[5]{a^{4b}x^6} \times (a^{\frac{2}{3}}x^{-1})^{-b}$.
16. $\sqrt[3]{x^{-1}\sqrt{y^3}} \div \sqrt{y\sqrt[3]{x}}$.
17. $(a^{-\frac{1}{2}}\sqrt[3]{x})^{-3} \times \sqrt{x^{-2}\sqrt{a^{-6}}}$.
18. $\sqrt[n]{a^{n+k}b^{2n-k}} \div (a^{\frac{1}{n}}b^{-\frac{1}{n}})^k$.
19. $\sqrt[3]{(a+b)^5} \times (a+b)^{-\frac{2}{3}}$.
20. $\{(x-y)^{-3}\}^n \div \{(x+y)^n\}^3$.
21. $\left(\dfrac{a^{-2}b}{a^3 b^{-4}}\right)^{-3} \div \left(\dfrac{ab^{-1}}{a^{-3}b^2}\right)^5$.
22. $\left\{\dfrac{\sqrt[3]{a}}{\sqrt[4]{b^{-1}}} \cdot \left(\dfrac{b^{\frac{1}{4}}}{a^{\frac{1}{3}}}\right)^2 \div \dfrac{a^{-\frac{1}{3}}}{b^{-\frac{1}{2}}}\right\}^6$.
23. $(a^{-\frac{1}{2}}x^{\frac{1}{3}}\sqrt{ax^{-\frac{1}{3}}\sqrt[4]{x^{\frac{1}{3}}}})^{\frac{1}{3}}$.
24. $\sqrt[4]{(a+b)^6} \times (a^2 - b^2)^{-\frac{1}{2}}$.
25. $\left(\dfrac{a^{-3}}{b^{-\frac{2}{3}}c}\right)^{-\frac{3}{2}} \div \left(\dfrac{\sqrt{a^{-\frac{1}{2}}} \cdot \sqrt[5]{b^3}}{a^2 c^{-1}}\right)^{-2}$.
26. $\left(\dfrac{a^{-\frac{2}{3}}x^{\frac{1}{2}}}{x^{-1}a}\right)^2 \div \sqrt[3]{\dfrac{a^{-1}}{x^{-3}}}$.
27. $\left(\sqrt[5]{\dfrac{a^{\frac{1}{2}}x^{-2}}{x^{\frac{1}{2}}a^{-2}}} \times \sqrt[3]{\dfrac{a\sqrt{x}}{x^{-1}\sqrt{a}}}\right)^{-4}$.
28. $\dfrac{\sqrt[3]{(a^3 b^3 + a^6)}}{\sqrt[3]{(b^6 - a^3 b^3)^{-1}}}$.
29. $(a^{n^2-1})^{\frac{n}{n+1}} + \dfrac{\sqrt[n]{a^{2n}}}{a}$.
30. $(x^{\frac{n}{n+1}})^{n^2-1} + \dfrac{\sqrt{x^{2n}}}{x}$.
31. $\left\{\dfrac{a^{p-q}}{\sqrt[q]{a^{q^2-pq}}} \times a^{2(p-q)}\right\}^n$.
32. $(x^{\frac{a}{b}}y^{-1})^b \div \left(\dfrac{x^{a^2-b^2}}{y^{ab+b^2}}\right)^{\frac{1}{a+b}}$.
33. $\left(\dfrac{x^{-2}y^3}{x^3 y^{-2}}\right)^{-\frac{1}{5}} \times \left(\dfrac{y^5 x^{-3}}{x^3 y^{-3}}\right)^{-1}$.
34. $\left(\dfrac{y^{-3}}{x^{\frac{2}{7}}z^{-1}}\right)^{-\frac{3}{2}} \times \left(\dfrac{y^{\frac{14}{3}}x^{-1}}{z^{-\frac{21}{4}}}\right)^{\frac{3}{7}}$.
35. $\dfrac{2^n \times (2^{n-1})^n}{2^{n+1} \times 2^{n-1}} \times \dfrac{1}{4^{-n}}$.
36. $\dfrac{2^{n+1}}{(2^n)^{n-1}} \div \dfrac{4^{n+1}}{(2^{n-1})^{n+1}}$.

224. Since the index-laws are universally true, all the ordinary operations of multiplication, division, involution, and evolution are applicable to expressions which contain fractional and negative indices.

THE THEORY OF INDICES.

225. In Art. 200, we pointed out that the descending powers of x are

$$\cdots x^3,\ x^2,\ x,\ 1,\ \frac{1}{x},\ \frac{1}{x^2},\ \frac{1}{x^3},\ \cdots.$$

A reason is seen if we write these terms in the form

$$\cdots x^3,\ x^2,\ x^1,\ x^0,\ x^{-1},\ x^{-2},\ x^{-3},\ \cdots.$$

Ex. 1. Multiply $3x^{-\frac{1}{3}} + x + 2x^{\frac{2}{3}}$ by $x^{\frac{1}{3}} - 2$.

Arrange in descending powers of x.

$$\begin{array}{l}
x\ \ + 2x^{\frac{2}{3}} + 3x^{-\frac{1}{3}} \\
\underline{x^{\frac{1}{3}} - 2} \\
x^{\frac{4}{3}} + 2x\ \ + 3 \\
\underline{\quad\quad - 2x\ \ - 4x^{\frac{2}{3}} - 6x^{-\frac{1}{3}}} \\
x^{\frac{4}{3}} - 4x^{\frac{2}{3}} + 3\ \ - 6x^{-\frac{1}{3}}
\end{array}$$

Ex. 2. Divide $16a^{-3} - 6a^{-2} + 5a^{-1} + 6$ by $1 + 2a^{-1}$.

$$\begin{array}{l}
2a^{-1} + 1)\,16a^{-3} - \ \ 6a^{-2} + \ \ 5a^{-1} + 6\,(8a^{-2} - 7a^{-1} + 6 \\
\quad\quad\quad\ \ \underline{16a^{-3} + \ \ 8a^{-2}} \\
\quad\quad\quad\quad\quad\ \ -14a^{-2} + \ \ 5a^{-1} \\
\quad\quad\quad\quad\quad\ \ \underline{-14a^{-2} - \ \ 7a^{-1}} \\
\quad\quad\quad\quad\quad\quad\quad\quad\quad\ \ 12a^{-1} + 6 \\
\quad\quad\quad\quad\quad\quad\quad\quad\quad\ \ \underline{12a^{-1} + 6}
\end{array}$$

Ex. 3. Find the square root of

$$\frac{4x^2}{y} + \frac{\sqrt{x^3}}{y^{-\frac{1}{2}}} - 2x + \frac{y}{4} + x^3 - 4\sqrt{(x^5 y^{-1})}.$$

Use fractional indices, and arrange in descending powers of x.

$$x^3 - 4x^{\frac{5}{2}}y^{-\frac{1}{2}} + 4x^2 y^{-1} + x^{\frac{3}{2}}y^{\frac{1}{2}} - 2x + \frac{y}{4}\ \Big(x^{\frac{3}{2}} - 2xy^{-\frac{1}{2}} + \frac{y^{\frac{1}{2}}}{2}\Big)$$

$$\begin{array}{l}
\phantom{2x^{\frac{3}{2}} - 4xy^{-\frac{1}{2}} + \frac{y^{\frac{1}{2}}}{2}\ \Big|}\underline{x^3} \\
2x^{\frac{3}{2}} - 2xy^{-\frac{1}{2}}\ \Big|\,-4x^{\frac{5}{2}}y^{-\frac{1}{2}} + 4x^2 y^{-1} \\
\phantom{2x^{\frac{3}{2}} - 2xy^{-\frac{1}{2}}\ \Big|}\,\underline{-4x^{\frac{5}{2}}y^{-\frac{1}{2}} + 4x^2 y^{-1}} \\
2x^{\frac{3}{2}} - 4xy^{-\frac{1}{2}} + \frac{y^{\frac{1}{2}}}{2}\ \Big|\ x^{\frac{3}{2}}y^{\frac{1}{2}} - 2x + \frac{y}{4} \\
\phantom{2x^{\frac{3}{2}} - 4xy^{-\frac{1}{2}} + \frac{y^{\frac{1}{2}}}{2}\ \Big|}\,\underline{x^{\frac{3}{2}}y^{\frac{1}{2}} - 2x + \frac{y}{4}}
\end{array}$$

Note. In this example it should be observed that the introduction of negative indices enables us to avoid the use of algebraic fractions.

EXAMPLES XXII. c.

1. Multiply $3x^{\frac{1}{3}} - 5 + 8x^{-\frac{1}{3}}$ by $4x^{\frac{1}{3}} + 3x^{-\frac{1}{3}}$.
2. Multiply $3a^{\frac{2}{3}} - 4a^{\frac{1}{3}} - a^{-\frac{1}{3}}$ by $3a^{\frac{1}{3}} + a^{-\frac{1}{3}} - 6a^{-\frac{2}{3}}$.
3. Find the product of $c^x + 2c^{-x} - 7$ and $5 - 3c^{-x} + 2c^x$.
4. Find the product of $5 + 2x^{2a} + 3x^{-2a}$ and $4x^a - 3x^{-a}$.
5. Divide $21x + x^{\frac{2}{3}} + x^{\frac{1}{3}} + 1$ by $3x^{\frac{1}{3}} + 1$.
6. Divide $15a - 3a^{\frac{1}{3}} - 2a^{-\frac{1}{3}} + 8a^{-1}$ by $5a^{\frac{2}{3}} + 4$.
7. Divide $16a^{-3} + 6a^{-2} + 5a^{-1} - 6$ by $2a^{-1} - 1$.
8. Divide $5b^{\frac{2}{3}} - 6b^{\frac{1}{3}} - 4b^{-\frac{2}{3}} - 4b^{-\frac{1}{3}} - 5$ by $b^{\frac{1}{3}} - 2b^{-\frac{1}{3}}$.
9. Divide $21a^{3x} + 20 - 27a^x - 26a^{2x}$ by $3a^x - 5$.
10. Divide $8c^{-n} - 8c^n + 5c^{3n} - 3c^{-3n}$ by $5c^n - 3c^{-n}$.

Find the square root of

11. $9x - 12x^{\frac{1}{2}} + 10 - 4x^{-\frac{1}{2}} + x^{-1}$.
12. $25a^{\frac{2}{3}} + 16 - 30a - 24a^{\frac{1}{3}} + 49a^{\frac{4}{3}}$.
13. $4x^n + 9x^{-n} + 28 - 24x^{-\frac{n}{2}} - 16x^{\frac{n}{2}}$
14. $12a^x + 4 - 6a^{3x} + a^{4x} + 5a^{2x}$.
15. Multiply $a^{\frac{3}{2}} - 8a^{-\frac{3}{2}} + 4a^{-\frac{1}{2}} - 2a^{\frac{1}{2}}$ by $4a^{-\frac{3}{2}} + a^{\frac{3}{2}} + 4a^{-\frac{1}{2}}$.
16. Multiply $1 - 2\sqrt[3]{x} - 2x^{\frac{1}{2}}$ by $1 - \sqrt[6]{x}$.
17. Multiply $2\sqrt[3]{a^5} - a^{\frac{1}{3}} - \dfrac{3}{a}$ by $2a - 3\sqrt[3]{\dfrac{1}{a}} - a^{-\frac{5}{3}}$.
18. Divide $\sqrt[3]{x^2} + 2x^{\frac{1}{3}} - 16x^{-\frac{2}{3}} - \dfrac{32}{x}$ by $x^{\frac{1}{6}} + 4x^{-\frac{1}{3}} + \dfrac{4}{\sqrt{x}}$.
19. Divide $1 - \sqrt{a} - \dfrac{2}{a^{-1}} + 2a^2$ by $1 - a^{\frac{1}{2}}$.
20. Divide $4\sqrt[3]{x^2} - 8x^{\frac{1}{3}} - 5 + \dfrac{10}{\sqrt[3]{x}} + 3x^{-\frac{2}{3}}$ by $2x^{\frac{5}{12}} - \dfrac{12}{\sqrt{x}} - \dfrac{3}{\sqrt[4]{x}}$.

Find the square root of

21. $9x^{-4} - 18x^{-3}\sqrt{y} + \dfrac{15y}{x^2} - 6\sqrt{\left(\dfrac{y^3}{x^2}\right)} + y^2$.
22. $4\sqrt{x^3} - 12\sqrt[4]{(x^3 y)} + 25\sqrt{y} - 24\sqrt[4]{\left(\dfrac{y^3}{x^3}\right)} + 16x^{-\frac{3}{2}}y$
23. $81\left(\dfrac{\sqrt[3]{x^4}}{y^2} + 1\right) + 36\dfrac{x^{\frac{1}{3}}}{\sqrt{y}}(x^{\frac{2}{3}}y^{-1} - 1) - 158\dfrac{\sqrt[3]{x^2}}{y}$.
24. $\dfrac{x^{-2}}{16} + 1 + \dfrac{9}{\sqrt[3]{y^{-2}}} + \dfrac{1 - 3\sqrt[3]{y}}{2x} - 6\sqrt[3]{y}$.

226. The following examples will illustrate the formulæ of earlier chapters when applied to expressions involving fractional and negative indices.

Ex. 1. $(a^{\frac{h}{k}} - b^{\frac{p}{q}})(a^{-\frac{h}{k}} + b^{-\frac{p}{q}}) = a^{\frac{h}{k}-\frac{h}{k}} - a^{-\frac{h}{k}}b^{\frac{p}{q}} + a^{\frac{h}{k}}b^{-\frac{p}{q}} - b^{\frac{p}{q}-\frac{p}{q}}$

$$= 1 - a^{-\frac{h}{k}}b^{\frac{p}{q}} + a^{\frac{h}{k}}b^{-\frac{p}{q}} - 1$$

$$= a^{\frac{h}{k}}b^{-\frac{p}{q}} - a^{-\frac{h}{k}}b^{\frac{p}{q}}.$$

Ex. 2. Multiply $2x^{2p} - x^p + 3$ by $2x^{2p} + x^p - 3$.

The product $= \{2x^{2p} - (x^p - 3)\}\{2x^{2p} + (x^p - 3)\}$

$$= (2x^{2p})^2 - (x^p - 3)^2 = 4x^{4p} - x^{2p} + 6x^p - 9.$$

Ex. 3. The square of $3x^{\frac{1}{2}} - 2 - x^{-\frac{1}{2}}$

$$= 9x + 4 + x^{-1} - 2 \cdot 3x^{\frac{1}{2}} \cdot 2 - 2 \cdot 3x^{\frac{1}{2}} \cdot x^{-\frac{1}{2}} + 2 \cdot 2 \cdot x^{-\frac{1}{2}}$$

$$= 9x + 4 + x^{-1} - 12x^{\frac{1}{2}} - 6 + 4x^{-\frac{1}{2}}$$

$$= 9x - 12x^{\frac{1}{2}} - 2 + 4x^{-\frac{1}{2}} + x^{-1}.$$

Ex. 4. Divide $a^{\frac{3n}{2}} + a^{-\frac{3n}{2}}$ by $a^{\frac{n}{2}} + a^{-\frac{n}{2}}$.

The quotient $= (a^{\frac{3n}{2}} + a^{-\frac{3n}{2}}) \div (a^{\frac{n}{2}} + a^{-\frac{n}{2}})$

$$= \{(a^{\frac{n}{2}})^3 + (a^{-\frac{n}{2}})^3\} \div (a^{\frac{n}{2}} + a^{-\frac{n}{2}})$$

$$= (a^{\frac{n}{2}})^2 - a^{\frac{n}{2}} \cdot a^{-\frac{n}{2}} + (a^{-\frac{n}{2}})^2 = a^n - 1 + a^{-n}.$$

EXAMPLES XXII. d.

Write the value of

1. $(x^{\frac{1}{2}} - 7)(x^{\frac{1}{2}} + 3)$.
2. $(4x - 5x^{-1})(4x + 3x^{-1})$.
3. $(7x - 9y^{-1})(7x + 9y^{-1})$.
4. $(x^m - y^n)(x^{-m} + y^{-n})$.
5. $(a^x - 2a^{-x})^2$.
6. $(a^x + a^{\frac{1}{x}})^2$.
7. $(x^2 - \frac{1}{2}x^{-a})^2$.
8. $(5x^ay^b - 3x^{-a}y^{-b})(4x^ay^b + 5x^{-a}y^{-b})$.
9. $(\frac{1}{2}a^{\frac{1}{3}} - a^{-\frac{1}{3}})^2$.
10. $(3x^ay^{-b} + 5x^{-a}y^b)(3x^ay^b - 5x^{-a}y^{-b})$.

11. $(a^x - \frac{1}{2} - a^{-x})^2$.

12. $(x^{\frac{1}{a}} - x^{-\frac{1}{a}} + x)^2$.

13. $\{(a+b)^{\frac{1}{2}} + (a-b)^{\frac{1}{2}}\}^2$.

14. $\{(a+b)^{\frac{1}{2}} - (a-b)^{-\frac{1}{2}}\}^2$.

Write the quotient of

15. $x - 9a$ by $x^{\frac{1}{2}} + 3a^{\frac{1}{2}}$.

16. $x^{\frac{3}{2}} - 27$ by $x^{\frac{1}{2}} - 3$.

17. $a^{2x} - 16$ by $a^x - 4$.

18. $x^{3a} + 8$ by $x^a + 2$.

19. $c^{2x} - c^{-x}$ by $c^a - c^{-\frac{x}{2}}$.

20. $1 - 8a^{-3}$ by $1 - 2a^{-1}$.

21. $a^{4x} - x^6$ by $a^{2x} + x^3$.

22. $x^{-4} - 1$ by $x^{-1} + 1$.

23. $x^{\frac{5}{3}} - 1$ by $x^{\frac{1}{3}} - 1$.

24. $x^{5n} + 32$ by $x^n + 2$.

Find the value of

25. $(x + x^{\frac{1}{2}} - 4)(x + x^{\frac{1}{2}} + 4)$.

26. $(2x^{\frac{1}{3}} + 4 + 3x^{-\frac{1}{3}})(2x^{\frac{1}{3}} + 4 - 3x^{-\frac{1}{3}})$.

27. $(2 - x^{\frac{1}{3}} + x)(2 + x^{\frac{1}{3}} + x)$.

28. $(a^x + 7 + 3a^{-x})(a^x - 7 - 3a^{-x})$.

29. $\dfrac{a^{\frac{4}{3}} - 8a^{\frac{1}{3}}b}{a^{\frac{2}{3}} + 2\sqrt[3]{ab} + 4b^{\frac{2}{3}}}$.

30. $\dfrac{x - 7x^{\frac{1}{2}}}{x - 5\sqrt{x} - 14} \div \left(1 + \dfrac{2}{\sqrt{x}}\right)^{-1}$.

31. $\dfrac{x^{\frac{2}{3}} - 4\sqrt[3]{x^{-2}}}{\sqrt[3]{x^2} + 4 + 4x^{-\frac{2}{3}}}$.

32. $\dfrac{a^{\frac{3}{2}} + ab}{ab - b^3} - \dfrac{\sqrt{a}}{\sqrt{a} - b}$.

CHAPTER XXIII.

Surds (Radicals).

227. A **surd** is an indicated root which cannot be exactly obtained.

Thus $\sqrt{2}$, $\sqrt[3]{5}$, $\sqrt[5]{a^3}$, $\sqrt{a^2+b^2}$ are surds.

By reference to the preceding chapter it will be seen that these are only cases of fractional indices; for the above quantities might be written

$$2^{\frac{1}{2}},\ 5^{\frac{1}{3}},\ a^{\frac{3}{5}},\ (a^2+b^2)^{\frac{1}{2}}.$$

Since surds may always be expressed as quantities with fractional indices they are subject to the same laws of combination as other algebraic symbols.

228. A surd is sometimes called an **irrational quantity**; and quantities which are not surds are, for the sake of distinction, termed **rational quantities.**

229. Surds are sometimes spoken of as **radicals.** This term is also applied to quantities such as $\sqrt{a^2}$, $\sqrt{9}$, $\sqrt[3]{27}$, etc., which are, however, *rational quantities in surd form.*

230. The **order** of a surd is indicated by the root symbol, or surd index. Thus $\sqrt[3]{x}$, $\sqrt[n]{a}$ are respectively surds of the third and nth orders.

The surds of the most frequent occurrence are those of the second order; they are sometimes called **quadratic surds.** Thus $\sqrt{3}$, $\sqrt{a}$, $\sqrt{x+y}$ are quadratic surds.

231. A **mixed surd** is one containing a factor whose root can be extracted.

This factor can evidently be removed and its root placed before the radical as a **coefficient**. It is called the **rational factor**, and the factor whose root cannot be extracted is called the **irrational factor**.

232. When the coefficient of the surd is unity, it is said to be **entire**.

233. When the irrational factor is integral, and all rational factors have been removed, the surd is in its **simplest form**.

234. When surds of the *same order* contain the same *irrational factor*, they are said to be **similar** or **like**.

Thus $5\sqrt{3}, 2\sqrt{3}, \frac{1}{5}\sqrt{3}$ are *like* surds.

But $3\sqrt{2}$ and $2\sqrt{3}$ are *unlike* surds.

235. In the case of numerical surds such as $\sqrt{2}, \sqrt[3]{5}, \cdots$, although the *exact* value can never be found, it can be determined to any degree of accuracy by carrying the process of evolution far enough.

Thus $\sqrt{5} = 2.236068\cdots$;

that is $\sqrt{5}$ lies between 2.23606 and 2.23607; and therefore the error in using either of these quantities instead of $\sqrt{5}$ is less than .00001. By taking the root to a greater number of decimal places we can approximate still nearer to the true value.

It thus appears that it will never be *absolutely necessary* to introduce surds into numerical work, which can always be carried on to a certain degree of accuracy; but we shall in the present chapter prove laws for combination of surd quantities which will enable us to work with symbols such as $\sqrt{2}, \sqrt[3]{5}, \sqrt[4]{a}, \cdots$ with absolute accuracy so long as the symbols are kept in their surd form. Moreover it will be found that even where approximate numerical results are required, the work is considerably simplified and shortened by operating with surd symbols, and afterwards substituting numerical values, if necessary.

SURDS. 205

REDUCTION OF SURDS.

236. Transformation of Surds of Any Order into Surds of a Different Order having the Same Value. A surd of any order may be transformed into a surd of a different order having the same value. Such surds are said to be **equivalent**.

EXAMPLES. (1) $\sqrt[3]{2} = 2^{\frac{1}{3}} = 2^{\frac{4}{12}} = \sqrt[12]{2^4}$.

(2) $\sqrt[p]{a} = a^{\frac{1}{p}} = a^{\frac{q}{pq}} = \sqrt[pq]{a^q}$.

237. Surds of different orders may therefore be transformed into surds of the same order. This order may be *any* common multiple of each of the given orders, but it is usually most convenient to choose the *least* common multiple.

Ex. Express $\sqrt[4]{a^3}$, $\sqrt[3]{b^2}$, $\sqrt[6]{a^5}$ as surds of the same lowest order.

The least common multiple of 4, 3, 6 is 12; and expressing the given surds as surds of the twelfth order they become $\sqrt[12]{a^9}$, $\sqrt[12]{b^8}$, $\sqrt[12]{a^{10}}$.

238. Surds of different orders may be arranged according to magnitude by transforming them into surds of the same order.

Ex. Arrange $\sqrt{3}$, $\sqrt[3]{6}$, $\sqrt[4]{10}$ according to magnitude.

The least common multiple of 2, 3, 4 is 12; and, expressing the given surds as surds of the twelfth order, we have

$\sqrt{3} = \sqrt[12]{3^6} = \sqrt[12]{729}$,
$\sqrt[3]{6} = \sqrt[12]{6^4} = \sqrt[12]{1296}$,
$\sqrt[4]{10} = \sqrt[12]{10^3} = \sqrt[12]{1000}$.

Hence arranged in ascending order of magnitude the surds are

$\sqrt{3}$, $\sqrt[4]{10}$, $\sqrt[3]{6}$.

EXAMPLES XXIII. a.

Express as surds of the twelfth order with positive indices:

1. $x^{\frac{1}{3}}$.
2. $a^{-1} \div a^{-\frac{1}{2}}$.
3. $\sqrt[4]{ax^3} \times \sqrt[3]{a^{-1}x^{-2}}$.
4. $\dfrac{1}{a^{-\frac{2}{4}}}$.
5. $\dfrac{1}{\sqrt[8]{a^{-14}}}$.
6. $\sqrt[6]{\dfrac{1}{a^{-2}}}$.

Express as surds of the nth order with positive indices:

7. $\sqrt[3]{x^2}$. 9. $a^{\frac{1}{2}}$. 11. $\sqrt[3]{\dfrac{1}{x^n y^n}}$. 13. $\dfrac{x^{-\frac{1}{2}}}{y^2}$.

8. x^a. 10. $\sqrt{a^{-\frac{1}{n}}}$. 12. $\dfrac{1}{a^{-1}}$. 14. $\dfrac{a^{\frac{1}{2}}}{x^{-n}}$.

Express as surds of the same lowest order:

15. $\sqrt{a}$, $\sqrt[9]{a^5}$.   18. $\sqrt[16]{x^4}$, $\sqrt[12]{x^{10}}$.   21. $\sqrt{5}$, $\sqrt[3]{11}$, $\sqrt[4]{13}$.

16. $\sqrt[3]{a^8}$, $\sqrt{a}$.   19. $\sqrt[21]{a^8 b^4}$, $\sqrt[7]{ab}$.   22. $\sqrt[4]{8}$, $\sqrt{3}$, $\sqrt[8]{6}$.

17. $\sqrt[6]{x^3}$, $\sqrt[9]{x^6}$, $\sqrt[20]{x^5}$.   20. $\sqrt{ax^2}$, $\sqrt[10]{a^9 x^6}$.   23. $\sqrt[4]{2}$, $\sqrt[9]{8}$, $\sqrt[6]{4}$.

239. Reduction of a Surd to its Simplest Form. The root of any expression is equal to the product of the roots of the separate factors of the expression.

For $\qquad \sqrt[n]{ab} = (ab)^{\frac{1}{n}} = a^{\frac{1}{n}} b^{\frac{1}{n}},$ [Art. 222.]

$\qquad\qquad\qquad = \sqrt[n]{a} \cdot \sqrt[n]{b}.$

Similarly, $\qquad \sqrt[n]{abc} = \sqrt[n]{a} \cdot \sqrt[n]{b} \cdot \sqrt[n]{c};$

and so for any number of factors.

EXAMPLES.   (1) $\sqrt[3]{15} = \sqrt[3]{3} \cdot \sqrt[3]{5}.$

(2) $\sqrt[3]{a^6 b} = \sqrt[3]{a^6} \cdot \sqrt[3]{b} = a^2 \sqrt[3]{b}.$

(3) $\sqrt{50} = \sqrt{25} \cdot \sqrt{2} = 5\sqrt{2}.$

Hence it appears that a surd may sometimes be expressed as the product of a rational quantity and a surd; when the surd factor is integral and as small as possible, the surd is in its *simplest form* [Art. 233].

Thus the simplest form of $\sqrt{128}$ is $8\sqrt{2}$.

Conversely, the coefficient of a surd may be brought under the radical sign by first raising it to the power whose root the surd expresses, and then placing the product of this power and the surd factor under the radical sign.

EXAMPLES.   (1) $7\sqrt{5} = \sqrt{49} \cdot \sqrt{5} = \sqrt{245}.$

(2) $a \sqrt[8]{b} = \sqrt[8]{a^8} \cdot \sqrt[8]{b} = \sqrt[8]{a^8 b}.$

In this form a surd is said to be an *entire surd* [Art. 232].

By the same method any rational quantity may be expressed in the form of a surd. Thus 2 may be written as $\sqrt{4}$, and 3 as $\sqrt[3]{27}$.

SURDS.

240. When the surd has the form of a fraction, we multiply both numerator and denominator by such a quantity as will make the denominator a perfect power of the same degree as the surd, and then take out the rational factor as a coefficient.

EXAMPLES. (1) $\sqrt{\frac{1}{2}} = \sqrt{\frac{2}{4}} = \sqrt{2 \times \frac{1}{4}} = \frac{1}{2}\sqrt{2}$.

(2) $\sqrt{\frac{mx}{ab}} = \sqrt{\frac{abmx}{a^2b^2}} = \frac{1}{ab}\sqrt{abmx}$.

EXAMPLES XXIII. b.

Express in the simplest form:

1. $\sqrt{288}$.
2. $\sqrt{147}$.
3. $\sqrt[3]{256}$.
4. $\sqrt[3]{432}$.
5. $3\sqrt{150}$.
6. $2\sqrt{720}$.
7. $5\sqrt{245}$.
8. $\sqrt[3]{1029}$.
9. $\sqrt[4]{3125}$.
10. $\sqrt[3]{-2187}$.
11. $\sqrt{36a^3}$.
12. $\sqrt{27a^3b^5}$.
13. $\sqrt{\frac{2}{7}}$.
14. $\sqrt[3]{\frac{1}{4}}$.
15. $\sqrt{\frac{2a}{b}}$.
16. $\sqrt[3]{1\frac{1}{2}}$.
17. $\sqrt[3]{-108\,x^4y^3}$.
18. $\sqrt[n]{x^{3n}y^{2n+5}}$.
19. $\sqrt[p]{x^a+py^{2p}}$.
20. $\sqrt{a^3 + 2a^2b + ab^2}$.
21. $\sqrt[3]{8x^4y - 24x^3y^2 + 24x^2y^3 - 8xy^4}$.

Express (1) as entire surds, (2) in simplest form:

22. $11\sqrt{2}$.
23. $14\sqrt{5}$.
24. $6\sqrt[3]{4}$.
25. $5\sqrt[3]{6}$.
26. $\frac{4}{11}\sqrt[4]{7\frac{1}{8}}$.
27. $\frac{3ab}{2c}\sqrt{\frac{20\,c^2}{9\,a^2b}}$.
28. $\frac{3x}{y}\sqrt{\frac{a^2y^3}{x^2}}$.
29. $\frac{a}{x^2}\sqrt{\frac{3\,x^3}{a}}$.
30. $\frac{2a}{3x}\sqrt[3]{\frac{27\,x^4}{a^2}}$.
31. $\frac{2a}{b}\sqrt[4]{\frac{b^4}{8\,a^3}}$.
32. $a\sqrt[n]{\frac{b^2}{a^{n-2}}}$.
33. $\frac{a}{b}\sqrt[p]{\frac{b^{p+1}}{a^{p-1}}}$.
34. $\frac{y}{x^n}\sqrt{\frac{x^{2n+1}}{y^3}}$.
35. $(x+y)\sqrt{\frac{x-y}{x+y}}$.
36. $\frac{ax}{a-x}\sqrt{\frac{a^2-x^2}{a^2x^2}}$.

ADDITION AND SUBTRACTION OF SURDS.

241. To add and subtract like **surds**: *Reduce them to their simplest form, and prefix to their common irrational part the sum of the coefficients.*

Ex. 1. The sum of $3\sqrt{20}$, $4\sqrt{5}$, $\dfrac{\sqrt{5}}{5}$

$$= 6\sqrt{5} + 4\sqrt{5} + \frac{1}{5}\sqrt{5} = \frac{51}{5}\sqrt{5}.$$

Ex. 2. The sum of $x\sqrt[3]{8x^3a} + y\sqrt[3]{-y^3a} - z\sqrt[3]{z^3a}$

$$= x \cdot 2x\sqrt[3]{a} + y(-y)\sqrt[3]{a} - z \cdot z\sqrt[3]{a}$$
$$= (2x^2 - y^2 - z^2)\sqrt[3]{a}.$$

242. Unlike surds *cannot be collected.*

Thus the sum of $5\sqrt{2}$, $-2\sqrt{3}$, and $\sqrt{6}$ is $5\sqrt{2} - 2\sqrt{3} + \sqrt{6}$, and cannot be further simplified.

EXAMPLES XXIII. c.

Find the value of

1. $3\sqrt{45} - \sqrt{20} + 7\sqrt{5}$.
2. $4\sqrt{63} + 5\sqrt{7} - 8\sqrt{28}$.
3. $\sqrt{44} - 5\sqrt{176} + 2\sqrt{99}$.
4. $2\sqrt{363} - 5\sqrt{243} + \sqrt{192}$.
5. $2\sqrt[3]{189} + 3\sqrt[3]{875} - 7\sqrt[3]{56}$.
6. $5\sqrt[3]{81} - 7\sqrt[3]{192} + 4\sqrt[3]{648}$.
7. $3\sqrt[4]{162} - 7\sqrt[4]{32} + \sqrt[4]{1250}$.
8. $5\sqrt[3]{-54} - 2\sqrt[3]{-16} + 4\sqrt[3]{686}$.
9. $4\sqrt{128} + 4\sqrt{75} - 5\sqrt{162}$.
10. $5\sqrt{24} - 2\sqrt{54} - \sqrt{6}$.
11. $\sqrt{252} - \sqrt{294} - 48\sqrt{\tfrac{1}{8}}$.
12. $3\sqrt{147} - \tfrac{7}{3}\sqrt{\tfrac{1}{3}} - \sqrt{\tfrac{1}{27}}$.

MULTIPLICATION OF SURDS.

243. To multiply two surds of the same order: *Multiply separately the rational factors and the irrational factors.*

For $\quad a\sqrt[n]{x} \times b\sqrt[n]{y} = ax^{\frac{1}{n}} \times by^{\frac{1}{n}} = abx^{\frac{1}{n}}y^{\frac{1}{n}}$

$$= ab(xy)^{\frac{1}{n}} = ab\sqrt[n]{xy}.$$

EXAMPLES. (1) $5\sqrt{3} \times 3\sqrt{7} = 15\sqrt{21}$.

(2) $2\sqrt{x} \times 3\sqrt{x} = 6x$.

(3) $\sqrt[4]{a+b} \times \sqrt[4]{a-b} = \sqrt[4]{(a+b)(a-b)} = \sqrt[4]{a^2 - b^2}$.

If the surds are not in their simplest form, it will save labor to reduce them to this form before multiplication.

Ex. The product of $5\sqrt{32}$, $\sqrt{48}$, $2\sqrt{54}$
$= 5 \cdot 4\sqrt{2} \times 4\sqrt{3} \times 2 \cdot 3\sqrt{6} = 480 \cdot \sqrt{2} \cdot \sqrt{3} \cdot \sqrt{6} = 480 \times 6 = 2880$

SURDS.   209

244. To multiply surds of different orders: *Reduce them to equivalent surds of the same order, and proceed as before.*

Ex. Multiply $5 \sqrt[3]{2}$ by $2 \sqrt{5}$.

The product $= 5 \sqrt[6]{2^2} \times 2 \sqrt[6]{5^3} = 10 \sqrt[6]{2^2} \times \sqrt[6]{5^3} = 10 \sqrt[6]{500}$.

EXAMPLES XXIII. d.

Find the value of

1. $2\sqrt{14} \times \sqrt{21}$.
2. $3\sqrt{8} \times \sqrt{6}$.
3. $5\sqrt{a} \times 2\sqrt{3}$.
4. $2\sqrt{15} \times 3\sqrt{5}$.
5. $8\sqrt{12} \times 3\sqrt{24}$.
6. $\sqrt[3]{x+2} \times \sqrt[3]{x-2}$.
7. $\sqrt[3]{168} \times \sqrt[3]{147}$.
8. $5\sqrt[3]{128} \times 2\sqrt[3]{432}$.
9. $a\sqrt{b^3} \times b^2\sqrt{a}$.
10. $\frac{2}{3}\sqrt[4]{6} \times \sqrt[4]{3}$.
11. $\frac{3}{x}\sqrt{\frac{a^2}{x}} \times \frac{4}{3}\sqrt{\frac{x^3}{2\,a^4}}$.
12. $\frac{1}{2}\sqrt{\frac{a}{b}} \times \frac{1}{3}\sqrt[5]{\frac{b^2}{a^2}}$.

DIVISION OF SURDS.

245. Suppose it is required to find the numerical value of the quotient when $\sqrt{5}$ is divided by $\sqrt{7}$.

At first sight it would seem that we must find the square root of 5, which is 2.236···, and then the square root of 7, which is 2.645···, and finally divide 2.236··· by 2.645···; three troublesome operations.

But we may avoid much of this labor by multiplying both numerator and denominator by $\sqrt{7}$, so as to make the denominator a rational quantity. Thus

$$\frac{\sqrt{5}}{\sqrt{7}} = \frac{\sqrt{5}}{\sqrt{7}} \times \frac{\sqrt{7}}{\sqrt{7}} = \frac{\sqrt{5 \times 7}}{7} = \frac{\sqrt{35}}{7}.$$

Now $\sqrt{35} = 5.916\cdots$

$$\therefore \frac{\sqrt{5}}{\sqrt{7}} = \frac{5.916\cdots}{7} = .845\cdots$$

246. The great utility of this artifice in calculating the numerical value of surd fractions suggests its convenience in the case of *all* surd fractions, even where numerical

P

values are not required. Thus it is usual to simplify $\dfrac{a\sqrt{b}}{\sqrt{c}}$ as follows:

$$\frac{a\sqrt{b}}{\sqrt{c}} = \frac{a\sqrt{b} \times \sqrt{c}}{\sqrt{c} \times \sqrt{c}} = \frac{a\sqrt{bc}}{c}.$$

The process by which surds are removed from the denominator of any fraction is known as **rationalizing the denominator**. It is effected by multiplying both numerator and denominator by any factor which renders the denominator rational. We shall return to this point in Art. 250.

247. To divide surds: *Express the result as a fraction and rationalize the denominator.*

Ex. 1. Divide $4\sqrt{75}$ by $25\sqrt{56}$.

The quotient
$$= \frac{4\sqrt{75}}{25\sqrt{56}} = \frac{4 \times 5\sqrt{3}}{25 \times 2\sqrt{14}} = \frac{2\sqrt{3}}{5\sqrt{14}}$$
$$= \frac{2\sqrt{3} \times \sqrt{14}}{5\sqrt{14} \times \sqrt{14}} = \frac{2\sqrt{42}}{5 \times 14} = \frac{\sqrt{42}}{35}.$$

Ex. 2. $\quad \dfrac{\sqrt[3]{b}}{\sqrt[3]{c^2}} = \dfrac{\sqrt[3]{b} \times \sqrt[3]{c}}{\sqrt[3]{c^2} \times \sqrt[3]{c}} = \dfrac{\sqrt[3]{bc}}{\sqrt[3]{c^3}} = \dfrac{\sqrt[3]{bc}}{c}.$

EXAMPLES XXIII. e.

Find the value of

1. $\sqrt{10} \div \sqrt{2}$.
2. $3\sqrt{7} \div 2\sqrt{8}$.
3. $2\sqrt{120} \div \sqrt{3}$.
4. $21\sqrt{384} \div 8\sqrt{98}$.
5. $5\sqrt{27} \div 3\sqrt{24}$.
6. $-13\sqrt{125} \div 5\sqrt{65}$.
7. $6\sqrt{14} \div 2\sqrt{21}$.
8. $\dfrac{3\sqrt{11}}{2\sqrt{98}} \div \dfrac{5}{7\sqrt{22}}$.
9. $\dfrac{3\sqrt{48}}{5\sqrt{112}} \div \dfrac{6\sqrt{84}}{\sqrt{392}}$.
10. $\dfrac{3}{a-b}\sqrt{\dfrac{2x}{a-b}} \div \sqrt{\dfrac{18x^3}{(a-b)^5}}$.

Given $\sqrt{2} = 1.41421$, $\sqrt{3} = 1.73205$, $\sqrt{5} = 2.23607$, $\sqrt{6} = 2.44949$, $\sqrt{7} = 2.64575$: find to four decimal places the numerical value of

11. $\dfrac{14}{\sqrt{2}}$.
12. $\dfrac{25}{\sqrt{5}}$.
13. $\dfrac{10}{\sqrt{7}}$.
14. $\dfrac{48}{\sqrt{6}}$.
15. $\dfrac{60}{\sqrt{5}}$.
16. $144 \div \sqrt{6}$.
17. $\sqrt{2} \div \sqrt{3}$.
18. $\dfrac{1}{2\sqrt{3}}$.
19. $\dfrac{1}{\sqrt{500}}$.
20. $\dfrac{4}{\sqrt{243}}$.
21. $\dfrac{25}{\sqrt{252}}$.
22. $\sqrt{\dfrac{256}{1575}}$.
23. $\dfrac{3}{2\sqrt{96}}$.

COMPOUND SURDS.

248. Hitherto we have confined our attention to **simple surds**, such as $\sqrt[4]{5}$, $\sqrt[3]{a}$, $\sqrt{x+y}$. An expression involving two or more simple surds is called a **compound surd**; thus $2\sqrt{a} - 3\sqrt{b}$; $\sqrt[3]{a} + \sqrt[4]{b}$ are compound surds. A binomial, which has a surd in one or both of the terms, is called a **binomial surd**.

249. Multiplication of Compound Surds. We proceed as in the multiplication of compound algebraic expressions.

Ex. 1. Multiply $2\sqrt{x} - 5$ by $3\sqrt{x}$.
The product $= 3\sqrt{x}(2\sqrt{x} - 5) = 6x - 15\sqrt{x}$.

Ex. 2. Multiply $2\sqrt{5} + 3\sqrt{x}$ by $\sqrt{5} - \sqrt{x}$.
The product $= (2\sqrt{5} + 3\sqrt{x})(\sqrt{5} - \sqrt{x})$
$= 2\sqrt{5} \cdot \sqrt{5} + 3\sqrt{5} \cdot \sqrt{x} - 2\sqrt{5} \cdot \sqrt{x} - 3\sqrt{x} \cdot \sqrt{x}$
$= 10 - 3x + \sqrt{5x}$.

Ex. 3. Find the square of $2\sqrt{x} + \sqrt{7 - 4x}$.
$(2\sqrt{x} + \sqrt{7-4x})^2 = (2\sqrt{x})^2 + (\sqrt{7-4x})^2 + 4\sqrt{x} \cdot \sqrt{7-4x}$
$= 4x + 7 - 4x + 4\sqrt{7x - 4x^2}$
$= 7 + 4\sqrt{7x - 4x^2}$.

EXAMPLES XXIII. f.

Find the value of

1. $(3\sqrt{x} - 5) \times 2\sqrt{x}$.
2. $(\sqrt{x} - \sqrt{a}) \times 2\sqrt{x}$.
3. $(\sqrt{a} + \sqrt{b}) \times \sqrt{ab}$.
4. $(\sqrt{x+y} - 1) \times \sqrt{x+y}$.
5. $(2\sqrt{3} + 3\sqrt{2})^2$.
6. $(\sqrt{7} + 5\sqrt{3})(2\sqrt{7} - 4\sqrt{3})$.
7. $(3\sqrt{5} - 4\sqrt{2})(2\sqrt{5} + 3\sqrt{2})$.
8. $(3\sqrt{a} - 2\sqrt{x})(2\sqrt{a} + 3\sqrt{x})$.
9. $(\sqrt{x} + \sqrt{x-1}) \times \sqrt{x-1}$.
10. $(\sqrt{x+a} - \sqrt{x-a}) \times \sqrt{x+a}$.
11. $(\sqrt{a+x} - 2\sqrt{a})^2$.
12. $(2\sqrt{a} - \sqrt{1+4a})^2$.
13. $(\sqrt{a+x} - \sqrt{a-x})^2$.
14. $(\sqrt{a+x} - 2)(\sqrt{a+x} - 1)$.
15. $(\sqrt{2} + \sqrt{3} - \sqrt{5})(\sqrt{2} + \sqrt{3} + \sqrt{5})$.
16. $(\sqrt{5} + 3\sqrt{2} + \sqrt{7})(\sqrt{5} + 3\sqrt{2} - \sqrt{7})$.

Write the square of

17. $\sqrt{2x+a} - \sqrt{2x-a}$.
18. $\sqrt{x^2 - 2y^2} + \sqrt{x^2 + 2y^2}$.
19. $\sqrt{m+n} + \sqrt{m-n}$.
20. $3\sqrt{a^2+b^2} - 2\sqrt{a^2-b^2}$.
21. $3x\sqrt{2} - 3\sqrt{7-2x^2}$.
22. $\sqrt{4x^2+1} - \sqrt{4x^2-1}$.

250. If we multiply together the sum and the difference of any two quadratic surds, we obtain a *rational product*. This result should be carefully noted.

EXAMPLES. (1) $(\sqrt{a}+\sqrt{b})(\sqrt{a}-\sqrt{b}) = (\sqrt{a})^2 - (\sqrt{b})^2 = a - b$.
(2) $(3\sqrt{5}+4\sqrt{3})(3\sqrt{5}-4\sqrt{3}) = (3\sqrt{5})^2 - (4\sqrt{3})^2 = 45 - 48 = -3$.
Similarly, $(4-\sqrt{a+b})(4+\sqrt{a+b}) = (4)^2 - (\sqrt{a+b})^2 = 16-a-b$.

251. DEFINITION. When two binomial quadratic surds differ only in the sign which connects their terms, they are said to be **conjugate**.

Thus $3\sqrt{7} + 5\sqrt{11}$ is conjugate to $3\sqrt{7} - 5\sqrt{11}$.
Similarly, $a - \sqrt{a^2 - x^2}$ is conjugate to $a + \sqrt{a^2 - x^2}$.

The product of two conjugate surds is rational. [Art. 250.]

Ex. $(3\sqrt{a} + \sqrt{x-9a})(3\sqrt{a} - \sqrt{x-9a})$
$= (3\sqrt{a})^2 - (\sqrt{x-9a})^2 = 9a - (x-9a) = 18a - x$.

252. Division of Compound Surds. If the divisor is a binomial quadratic surd, express the division by means of a fraction, and rationalize the denominator by multiplying numerator and denominator by the surd which is conjugate to the divisor.

Ex. 1. Divide $4 + 3\sqrt{2}$ by $5 - 3\sqrt{2}$.

The quotient $= \dfrac{4+3\sqrt{2}}{5-3\sqrt{2}} = \dfrac{4+3\sqrt{2}}{5-3\sqrt{2}} \times \dfrac{5+3\sqrt{2}}{5+3\sqrt{2}}$
$= \dfrac{20 + 18 + 12\sqrt{2} + 15\sqrt{2}}{25 - 18} = \dfrac{38 + 27\sqrt{2}}{7}$.

Ex. 2. Rationalize the denominator of $\dfrac{b^2}{\sqrt{a^2+b^2}+a}$.

The expression $= \dfrac{b^2}{\sqrt{a^2+b^2}+a} \times \dfrac{\sqrt{a^2+b^2}-a}{\sqrt{a^2+b^2}-a}$
$= \dfrac{b^2\{\sqrt{a^2+b^2}-a\}}{(a^2+b^2)-a^2} = \sqrt{a^2+b^2}-a$.

SURDS.

Ex. 3. Divide $\dfrac{\sqrt{3}+\sqrt{2}}{2-\sqrt{3}}$ by $\dfrac{7+4\sqrt{3}}{\sqrt{3}-\sqrt{2}}$.

The quotient $= \dfrac{\sqrt{3}+\sqrt{2}}{2-\sqrt{3}} \times \dfrac{\sqrt{3}-\sqrt{2}}{7+4\sqrt{3}}$

$= \dfrac{(\sqrt{3})^2 - (\sqrt{2})^2}{14 - 12 + 8\sqrt{3} - 7\sqrt{3}}$

$= \dfrac{1}{2+\sqrt{3}} = 2 - \sqrt{3}$, on rationalizing.

Ex. 4. Given $\sqrt{5} = 2.236068$, find the value of $\dfrac{87}{7-2\sqrt{5}}$.

Rationalizing the denominator,

$\dfrac{87}{7-2\sqrt{5}} = \dfrac{87(7+2\sqrt{5})}{49-20}$

$= 3(7+2\sqrt{5})$

$= 34.416408$.

It will be seen that by rationalizing the denominator we have avoided the use of a divisor consisting of 7 figures.

253. In a similar manner, where the denominator involves three quadratic surds, we may by two operations render that denominator rational.

Ex. $\dfrac{\sqrt{2}}{\sqrt{2}+\sqrt{3}-\sqrt{5}}$.

The expression $= \dfrac{\sqrt{2}(\sqrt{2}+\sqrt{3}+\sqrt{5})}{(\sqrt{2}+\sqrt{3}-\sqrt{5})(\sqrt{2}+\sqrt{3}+\sqrt{5})}$

$= \dfrac{2+\sqrt{6}+\sqrt{10}}{2\sqrt{6}} = \dfrac{(2+\sqrt{6}+\sqrt{10})\sqrt{6}}{(2\sqrt{6})\sqrt{6}}$

$= \dfrac{3+\sqrt{6}+\sqrt{15}}{6}$

EXAMPLES XXIII. g.

Find the value of

1. $(9\sqrt{2}-7)(9\sqrt{2}+7)$.
2. $(3+5\sqrt{7})(3-5\sqrt{7})$.
3. $(5\sqrt{8}-2\sqrt{7})(5\sqrt{8}+2\sqrt{7})$.
4. $(2\sqrt{11}+5\sqrt{2})(2\sqrt{11}-5\sqrt{2})$.
5. $(\sqrt{a}+2\sqrt{b})(\sqrt{a}-2\sqrt{b})$.
6. $(3c-2\sqrt{x})(3c+2\sqrt{x})$.
7. $(\sqrt{a+x}-\sqrt{a})(\sqrt{a+x}+\sqrt{a})$.
8. $(\sqrt{2p+3q}-2\sqrt{q})(\sqrt{2p+3q}+2\sqrt{q})$.
9. $(\sqrt{a+x}+\sqrt{a-x})(\sqrt{a+x}-\sqrt{a-x})$.
10. $(5\sqrt{x^2-3y^2}+7a)(5\sqrt{x^2-3y^2}-7a)$.

11. $29 \div (11 + 3\sqrt{7})$.
12. $17 \div (3\sqrt{7} + 2\sqrt{3})$.
13. $(3\sqrt{2} - 1) \div (3\sqrt{2} + 1)$.
14. $(2\sqrt{3} + 7\sqrt{2}) \div (5\sqrt{3} - 4\sqrt{2})$.
15. $(2x - \sqrt{xy}) \div (2\sqrt{xy} - y)$.
16. $(3 + \sqrt{5})(\sqrt{5} - 2) \div (5 - \sqrt{5})$.
17. $\dfrac{\sqrt{a}}{\sqrt{a} - \sqrt{x}} \div \dfrac{\sqrt{a} + \sqrt{x}}{\sqrt{x}}$.
18. $\dfrac{2\sqrt{15} + 8}{5 + \sqrt{15}} \div \dfrac{8\sqrt{3} - 6\sqrt{5}}{5\sqrt{3} - 3\sqrt{5}}$.

Rationalize the denominator of

19. $\dfrac{25\sqrt{3} - 4\sqrt{2}}{7\sqrt{3} - 5\sqrt{2}}$.
20. $\dfrac{10\sqrt{6} - 2\sqrt{7}}{3\sqrt{6} + 2\sqrt{7}}$.
21. $\dfrac{\sqrt{7} + \sqrt{2}}{9 + 2\sqrt{14}}$.
22. $\dfrac{2\sqrt{3} + 3\sqrt{2}}{5 + 2\sqrt{6}}$.
23. $\dfrac{y^2}{x + \sqrt{x^2 - y^2}}$.
24. $\dfrac{x^2}{\sqrt{x^2 + a^2} + a}$.
25. $\dfrac{\sqrt{1 + x^2} - \sqrt{1 - x^2}}{\sqrt{1 + x^2} + \sqrt{1 - x^2}}$.
26. $\dfrac{2\sqrt{a + b} + 3\sqrt{a - b}}{2\sqrt{a + b} - \sqrt{a - b}}$.
27. $\dfrac{\sqrt{9 + x^2} - 3}{\sqrt{9 + x^2} + 3}$.
28. $\dfrac{3 + \sqrt{6}}{5\sqrt{3} - 2\sqrt{12} - \sqrt{32} + \sqrt{50}}$.
29. $\dfrac{\sqrt{10} + \sqrt{5} + \sqrt{3}}{\sqrt{3} + \sqrt{10} - \sqrt{5}}$.
30. $\dfrac{(\sqrt{3} + \sqrt{5})(\sqrt{5} + \sqrt{2})}{\sqrt{2} + \sqrt{3} + \sqrt{5}}$.

Given $\sqrt{2} = 1.41421$, $\sqrt{3} = 1.73205$, $\sqrt{5} = 2.23607$: find to four places of decimals the value of

31. $\dfrac{1}{2 + \sqrt{3}}$.
32. $\dfrac{3 + \sqrt{5}}{\sqrt{5} - 2}$.
33. $\dfrac{\sqrt{5} + \sqrt{3}}{4 + \sqrt{15}}$.
34. $\dfrac{\sqrt{5} - 2}{9 - 4\sqrt{5}}$.
35. $\dfrac{7\sqrt{5} + 15}{\sqrt{5} - 1} \times \dfrac{\sqrt{5} - 2}{3 + \sqrt{5}}$.
36. $(2 - \sqrt{3})(7 - 4\sqrt{3}) \div (3\sqrt{3} - 5)$.

254. To find a factor which will rationalize any binomial surd.

CASE I. Suppose the given surd is $\sqrt[p]{a} - \sqrt[q]{b}$.

Let $\sqrt[p]{a} = x$, $\sqrt[q]{b} = y$, and let n be the L.C.M. of p and q; then x^n and y^n are both rational.

Now $x^n - y^n$ is divisible by $x - y$ for all values of n, and
$$x^n - y^n = (x - y)(x^{n-1} + x^{n-2}y + x^{n-3}y^2 + \cdots + y^{n-1}).$$

Thus the rationalizing factor is
$$x^{n-1} + x^{n-2}y + x^{n-3}y^2 + \cdots + y^{n-1};$$
and the rational product is $x^n - y^n$.

SURDS.

CASE II. Suppose the given surd is $\sqrt[n]{a} + \sqrt[n]{b}$.
Let x, y, n have the same meanings as before; then

(1) If n is even, $x^n - y^n$ is divisible by $x + y$, and
$$x^n - y^n = (x + y)(x^{n-1} - x^{n-2}y + \cdots + xy^{n-2} - y^{n-1}).$$
Thus the rationalizing factor is
$$x^{n-1} - x^{n-2}y + \cdots + xy^{n-2} - y^{n-1};$$
and the rational product is $x^n - y^n$.

(2) If n is odd, $x^n + y^n$ is divisible by $x + y$, and
$$x^n + y^n = (x + y)(x^{n-1} - x^{n-2}y + \cdots - xy^{n-2} + y^{n-1}).$$
Thus the rationalizing factor is
$$x^{n-1} - x^{n-2}y + \cdots - xy^{n-2} + y^{n-1};$$
and the rational product is $x^n + y^n$.

Ex. 1. Find the factor which will rationalize $\sqrt{3} + \sqrt[3]{5}$.

Let $x = 3^{\frac{1}{2}}$, $y = 5^{\frac{1}{3}}$; then x^6 and y^6 are both rational, and
$$x^6 - y^6 = (x + y)(x^5 - x^4y + x^3y^2 - x^2y^3 + xy^4 - y^5);$$
thus, substituting for x and y, the required factor is
$$3^{\frac{5}{2}} - 3^{\frac{4}{2}} \cdot 5^{\frac{1}{3}} + 3^{\frac{3}{2}} \cdot 5^{\frac{2}{3}} - 3^{\frac{2}{2}} \cdot 5^{\frac{3}{3}} + 3^{\frac{1}{2}} \cdot 5^{\frac{4}{3}} - 5^{\frac{5}{3}},$$
or $\qquad 3^{\frac{5}{2}} - 9 \cdot 5^{\frac{1}{3}} + 3^{\frac{3}{2}} \cdot 5^{\frac{2}{3}} - 15 + 3^{\frac{1}{2}} \cdot 5^{\frac{4}{3}} - 5^{\frac{5}{3}};$

and the rational product is $3^{\frac{6}{2}} - 5^{\frac{6}{3}} = 3^3 - 5^2 = 2$.

Ex. 2. Express $\qquad (5^{\frac{1}{2}} + 9^{\frac{1}{4}}) \div (5^{\frac{1}{2}} - 9^{\frac{1}{8}})$

as an equivalent fraction with a rational denominator.

To rationalize the denominator, which is equal to $5^{\frac{1}{2}} - 3^{\frac{1}{4}}$, put $5^{\frac{1}{2}} = x$, $3^{\frac{1}{4}} = y$; then since
$$x^4 - y^4 = (x - y)(x^3 + x^2y + xy^2 + y^3),$$
the required factor is $5^{\frac{3}{2}} + 5^{\frac{2}{2}} \cdot 3^{\frac{1}{4}} + 5^{\frac{1}{2}} \cdot 3^{\frac{2}{4}} + 3^{\frac{3}{4}}$;
and the rational denominator is $5^{\frac{4}{2}} - 3^{\frac{4}{4}} = 5^2 - 3 = 22$.

$\therefore$ the expression $= \dfrac{(5^{\frac{1}{2}} + 3^{\frac{1}{4}})(5^{\frac{3}{2}} + 5^{\frac{2}{2}} \cdot 3^{\frac{1}{4}} + 5^{\frac{1}{2}} \cdot 3^{\frac{2}{4}} + 3^{\frac{3}{4}})}{22}$

$= \dfrac{5^{\frac{4}{2}} + 2 \cdot 5^{\frac{3}{2}} \cdot 3^{\frac{1}{4}} + 2 \cdot 5^{\frac{2}{2}} \cdot 3^{\frac{2}{4}} + 2 \cdot 5^{\frac{1}{2}} \cdot 3^{\frac{3}{4}} + 3^{\frac{4}{4}}}{22}$

$= \dfrac{14 + 5^{\frac{3}{2}} \cdot 3^{\frac{1}{4}} + 5 \cdot 3^{\frac{1}{2}} + 5^{\frac{1}{2}} \cdot 3^{\frac{3}{4}}}{11}$

PROPERTIES OF QUADRATIC SURDS.

255. *The square root of a rational quantity cannot be partly rational and partly a quadratic surd.*

If possible let $\sqrt{n} = a + \sqrt{m}$;
then by squaring, $n = a^2 + m + 2a\sqrt{m}$;
$$\therefore \sqrt{m} = \frac{n - a^2 - m}{2a},$$
that is, a surd is equal to a rational quantity, which is impossible.

256. *If $x + \sqrt{y} = a + \sqrt{b}$, then will $x = a$ and $y = b$.*

For if x is not equal to a, let $x = a + m$; then
$$a + m + \sqrt{y} = a + \sqrt{b};$$
that is, $\sqrt{b} = m + \sqrt{y}$;
which is impossible. [Art. 255.]

Therefore $x = a$,
and consequently, $y = b$.

If therefore $x + \sqrt{y} = a + \sqrt{b}$,
we must also have $x - \sqrt{y} = a - \sqrt{b}$.

257. It appears from the preceding article that in any equation of the form
$$x + \sqrt{y} = a + \sqrt{b} \quad \ldots \ldots \quad (1),$$
we may equate the rational parts on each side, and also the irrational parts; so that the equation (1) is really equivalent to *two* independent equations, $x = a$ and $y = b$.

258. *If $\sqrt{a + \sqrt{b}} = \sqrt{x} + \sqrt{y}$, then will $\sqrt{a - \sqrt{b}} = \sqrt{x} - \sqrt{y}$.*

For by squaring, we obtain
$$a + \sqrt{b} = x + 2\sqrt{xy} + y;$$
$$\therefore a = x + y, \quad \sqrt{b} = 2\sqrt{xy}. \quad [\text{Art. 257.}]$$
Hence $a - \sqrt{b} = x - 2\sqrt{xy} + y,$
and $\sqrt{a - \sqrt{b}} = \sqrt{x} - \sqrt{y}.$

SURDS. 217

259. To find the square root of a binomial surd.

Suppose $\sqrt{a + \sqrt{b}} = \sqrt{x} + \sqrt{y}$;
then as in Art. 258,

$$x + y = a \quad \ldots \ldots \ldots (1);$$
$$2\sqrt{xy} = \sqrt{b} \quad \ldots \ldots \ldots (2).$$

Since
$$(x - y)^2 = (x + y)^2 - 4xy$$
$$= a^2 - b \quad \ldots \text{ from (1) and (2)};$$
$$\therefore x - y = \sqrt{a^2 - b}.$$

Combining this with (1), we find

$$x = \frac{a + \sqrt{a^2 - b}}{2}, \text{ and } y = \frac{a - \sqrt{a^2 - b}}{2}.$$

$$\therefore \sqrt{a + \sqrt{b}} = \sqrt{\frac{a + \sqrt{(a^2 - b)}}{2}} + \sqrt{\frac{a - \sqrt{(a^2 - b)}}{2}}.$$

260. The values just found for x and y are compound surds unless $a^2 - b$ is a perfect square. Hence the method of Art. 259 for finding the square root of $a + \sqrt{b}$ is of no practical utility except when $a^2 - b$ is a perfect square.

Ex. Find the square root of $16 + 2\sqrt{55}$.
Assume $\sqrt{16 + 2\sqrt{55}} = \sqrt{x} + \sqrt{y}$.
Then $16 + 2\sqrt{55} = x + 2\sqrt{xy} + y$;

$$\therefore x + y = 16 \quad \ldots \ldots \ldots (1),$$
$$2\sqrt{xy} = 2\sqrt{55} \quad \ldots \ldots \ldots (2).$$

Since
$$(x - y)^2 = (x + y)^2 - 4xy$$
$$= 16^2 - 4 \times 55 \quad \ldots \text{ by (1) and (2)},$$
$$= 4 \times 9.$$
$$\therefore x - y = \pm 6 \quad \ldots \ldots \ldots (3).$$

From (1) and (3) we obtain
$$x = 11, \text{ or } 5, \text{ and } y = 5, \text{ or } 11.$$

That is, the required square root is $\sqrt{11} + \sqrt{5}$.
In the same way we may show that
$$\sqrt{16 - 2\sqrt{55}} = \sqrt{11} - \sqrt{5}.$$

NOTE. Since every quantity has two square roots equal in magnitude but opposite in sign, strictly speaking we should have

the square root of $16 + 2\sqrt{55} = \pm(\sqrt{11} + \sqrt{5})$,

the square root of $16 - 2\sqrt{55} = \pm(\sqrt{11} - \sqrt{5})$.

However, it is usually sufficient to take the positive value of the square root, so that in assuming $\sqrt{a - \sqrt{b}} = \sqrt{x} - \sqrt{y}$ it is understood that x is greater than y. With this proviso it will be unnecessary in any numerical example to use the double sign at the stage of work corresponding to equation (3) of the last example.

261. When the binomial whose square root we are seeking consists of *two* quadratic surds, we proceed as explained in the following example.

Ex. Find the square root of $\sqrt{175} - \sqrt{147}$.

Since $\sqrt{175} - \sqrt{147} = \sqrt{7}(\sqrt{25} - \sqrt{21}) = \sqrt{7}(5 - \sqrt{21})$,

$\therefore \sqrt{\sqrt{175} - \sqrt{147}} = \sqrt[4]{7} \cdot \sqrt{5 - \sqrt{21}}$.

But $\sqrt{5 - \sqrt{21}} = \sqrt{\tfrac{7}{2}} - \sqrt{\tfrac{3}{2}}$;

$\therefore \sqrt{\sqrt{175} - \sqrt{147}} = \sqrt[4]{7}(\sqrt{\tfrac{7}{2}} - \sqrt{\tfrac{3}{2}})$.

262. To find the square root of a binomial surd by inspection.

Ex. 1. Find the square root of $11 + 2\sqrt{30}$.

We have only to find two quantities whose sum is 11, and whose product is 30, thus

$$11 + 2\sqrt{30} = 6 + 5 + 2\sqrt{6 \times 5} = (\sqrt{6} + \sqrt{5})^2.$$

$\therefore \sqrt{11 + 2\sqrt{30}} = \sqrt{6} + \sqrt{5}$.

Ex. 2. Find the square root of $53 - 12\sqrt{10}$.

First write the binomial so that the surd part has a coefficient 2;

thus $53 - 12\sqrt{10} = 53 - 2\sqrt{360}$.

We have now to find two quantities whose sum is 53 and whose product is 360; these are 45 and 8;

hence $53 - 12\sqrt{10} = 45 + 8 - 2\sqrt{45 \times 8}$

$= (\sqrt{45} - \sqrt{8})^2$;

$\therefore \sqrt{53 - 12\sqrt{10}} = \sqrt{45} - \sqrt{8}$

$= 3\sqrt{5} - 2\sqrt{2}$.

SURDS.

Ex. 3. Find the square root of $a + b + \sqrt{2ab + b^2}$.

Rewrite the binomial so that the surd part has a coefficient 2; thus

$$a + b + \sqrt{2ab + b^2} = a + b + 2\sqrt{\frac{2ab + b^2}{4}}$$

We have now to find *two quantities whose sum is* $(a + b)$ and whose product is $\dfrac{2ab + b^2}{4}$; these are $\dfrac{2a + b}{2}$, and $\dfrac{b}{2}$; hence

$$a + b + \sqrt{2ab + b^2} = \frac{2a + b}{2} + \frac{b}{2} + 2\sqrt{\frac{2a+b}{2} \times \frac{b}{2}}$$

$$= \left(\sqrt{\frac{2a+b}{2}} + \sqrt{\frac{b}{2}}\right)^2;$$

$$\therefore \sqrt{a + b + \sqrt{2ab + b^2}} = \sqrt{a + \frac{b}{2}} + \sqrt{\frac{b}{2}}.$$

NOTE. The student should observe that when the coefficient of the surd part of the binomial is unity, he can make this coefficient 2 if he will also *multiply the quantity under the radical by* ¼.

263. Assuming $\sqrt[3]{a + \sqrt{b}} = x + \sqrt{y}$, the method of Art. 258 gives us $\sqrt[3]{a - \sqrt{b}} = x - \sqrt{y}$.

EXAMPLES XXIII. h.

Find the square roots of the following binomial surds:

1. $7 - 2\sqrt{10}$.
2. $13 + 2\sqrt{30}$.
3. $8 - 2\sqrt{7}$.
4. $5 + 2\sqrt{6}$.
5. $75 + 12\sqrt{21}$.
6. $18 - 8\sqrt{5}$.
7. $41 - 24\sqrt{2}$.
8. $83 + 12\sqrt{35}$.
9. $47 - 4\sqrt{33}$.
10. $2\frac{1}{4} + \sqrt{5}$.
11. $4\frac{1}{3} - \frac{4}{3}\sqrt{3}$.
12. $16 + 5\sqrt{7}$.
13. $\sqrt{27} + 2\sqrt{6}$.
14. $\sqrt{32} - \sqrt{24}$.
15. $3\sqrt{5} + \sqrt{40}$.
16. $2a + 2\sqrt{a^2 - b^2}$.
17. $ax - 2a\sqrt{ax - a^2}$.
18. $a + x + \sqrt{2ax + x^2}$.
19. $2a - \sqrt{3a^2 - 2ab - b^2}$.
20. $1 + a^2 + (1 + a^2 + a^4)^{\frac{1}{2}}$.

Find the fourth roots of the following binomial surds:

21. $17 + 12\sqrt{2}$.
22. $56 + 24\sqrt{5}$.
23. $\frac{3}{2}\sqrt{5} + 3\frac{1}{2}$.
24. $14 + 8\sqrt{3}$.
25. $49 - 20\sqrt{6}$.
26. $248 + 32\sqrt{60}$.

Find, by inspection, the value of

27. $\sqrt{3 - 2\sqrt{2}}$.
28. $\sqrt{4 + 2\sqrt{3}}$.
29. $\sqrt{6 - 2\sqrt{5}}$.
30. $\sqrt{19 + 8\sqrt{3}}$.
31. $\sqrt{8 + 2\sqrt{15}}$.
32. $\sqrt{9 - 2\sqrt{14}}$.
33. $\sqrt{11 + 4\sqrt{6}}$.
34. $\sqrt{15 - 4\sqrt{14}}$.
35. $\sqrt{29 + 6\sqrt{22}}$.

Express with rational denominator

36. $\dfrac{1}{\sqrt[3]{3} - \sqrt{2}}$.

37. $\dfrac{1}{\sqrt[3]{3} - 1}$.

38. $\dfrac{\sqrt{2} \cdot \sqrt[3]{3}}{\sqrt[3]{3} + \sqrt{2}}$.

39. $\dfrac{\sqrt{8} + \sqrt[3]{4}}{\sqrt{8} - \sqrt[3]{4}}$.

40. $\dfrac{1}{\sqrt[5]{5} - \sqrt[3]{3}}$.

41. $\dfrac{\sqrt[3]{3}}{\sqrt{3} + \sqrt[6]{9}}$.

42. $\dfrac{1}{2 + \sqrt[4]{7}}$.

43. Find value of $\sqrt{\dfrac{6 + 2\sqrt{3}}{33 - 19\sqrt{3}}}$.

EQUATIONS INVOLVING SURDS.

264. Sometimes equations are proposed in which the unknown quantity appears under the radical sign. Such equations are varied in character and often require special artifices for their solution. We shall consider a few of the simpler cases, which can generally be solved by the following method:

Bring to one side of the equation a single radical term by itself: on squaring both sides this radical will disappear. By repeating this process any remaining radicals can in turn be removed.

Ex. 1. Solve $\quad 2\sqrt{x} - \sqrt{4x - 11} = 1.$
Transposing, $\quad 2\sqrt{x} - 1 = \sqrt{4x - 11}.$
Square both sides; then $4x - 4\sqrt{x} + 1 = 4x - 11,$
$$4\sqrt{x} = 12,$$
$$\sqrt{x} = 3;$$
$$\therefore x = 9.$$

Ex. 2. Solve $\quad 2 + \sqrt[3]{x - 5} = 13.$
Transposing, $\quad \sqrt[3]{x - 5} = 11.$
Here we must *cube* both sides; thus $x - 5 = 1331;$
whence $\quad x = 1336.$

EXAMPLES XXIII. k.

1. $\sqrt{x - 5} = 3.$
2. $\sqrt[3]{4x - 7} = 5.$
3. $7 - \sqrt{x - 4} = 3.$
4. $13 - \sqrt[3]{5x - 4} = 7.$
5. $\sqrt{5x - 1} = 2\sqrt{x + 3}.$
6. $2\sqrt{3 - 7x} - 3\sqrt{8x - 12} = 0.$
7. $2\sqrt[3]{5x - 35} = 5\sqrt[3]{2x - 7}.$
8. $\sqrt{9x^2 - 11x - 5} = 3x - 2.$

SURDS. 221

9. $\sqrt[4]{2x+11} = \sqrt{5}$.

10. $\sqrt{4x^2 - 7x + 1} = 2x - 1\frac{1}{3}$.

11. $\sqrt{x + 25} = 1 + \sqrt{x}$.

12. $\sqrt{8x + 33} - 3 = 2\sqrt{2x}$.

13. $\sqrt{x+3} + \sqrt{x} = 5$.

14. $10 - \sqrt{25 + 9x} = 3\sqrt{x}$.

15. $\sqrt{x-4} + 3 = \sqrt{x+11}$.

16. $\sqrt{9x-8} = 3\sqrt{x+4} - 2$.

17. $\sqrt{4x+5} - \sqrt{x} = \sqrt{x+3}$.

18. $\sqrt{25x-29} - \sqrt{4x-11} = 3\sqrt{x}$.

19. $\sqrt{x + 4ab} = 2a + \sqrt{x}$.

20. $\sqrt{x} + \sqrt{4a+x} = 2\sqrt{b+x}$.

265. When radicals appear in a fractional form in an equation, we must clear of fractions in the ordinary way, combining the irrational factors by the rules already explained in this chapter.

Ex. Solve $\quad \sqrt{9+2x} - \sqrt{2x} = \dfrac{5}{\sqrt{9+2x}}$.

Clearing of fractions,
$$9 + 2x - \sqrt{2x(9+2x)} = 5,$$
$$4 + 2x = \sqrt{2x(9+2x)}.$$
Squaring, $\quad 16 + 16x + 4x^2 = 18x + 4x^2$,
$$16 = 2x,$$
$$x = 8.$$

EXAMPLES XXIII. L

1. $\dfrac{6\sqrt{x} - 21}{3\sqrt{x} - 14} = \dfrac{8\sqrt{x} - 11}{4\sqrt{x} - 13}$.

2. $\dfrac{9\sqrt{x} - 23}{3\sqrt{x} - 8} = \dfrac{6\sqrt{x} - 17}{2\sqrt{x} - 6}$.

3. $\dfrac{\sqrt{x} + 3}{\sqrt{x} - 2} = \dfrac{3\sqrt{x} - 5}{3\sqrt{x} - 13}$.

4. $2 - \dfrac{\sqrt{x} + 3}{\sqrt{x} + 2} = \dfrac{\sqrt{x} + 9}{\sqrt{x} + 7}$.

5. $\dfrac{2\sqrt{x} - 1}{2\sqrt{x} + \frac{1}{3}} = \dfrac{\sqrt{x} - 2}{\sqrt{x} - \frac{1}{3}}$.

6. $\dfrac{6\sqrt{x} - 7}{\sqrt{x} - 1} - 5 = \dfrac{7\sqrt{x} - 26}{7\sqrt{x} - 21}$.

7. $\dfrac{12\sqrt{x} - 11}{4\sqrt{x} - 4\frac{2}{3}} = \dfrac{6\sqrt{x} + 5}{2\sqrt{x} + \frac{2}{3}}$.

8. $\sqrt{1+x} + \sqrt{x} = \dfrac{2}{\sqrt{1+x}}$.

9. $\sqrt{x-1} + \sqrt{x} = \dfrac{2}{\sqrt{x}}$.

10. $\sqrt{x} - \sqrt{x-8} = \dfrac{2}{\sqrt{x-8}}$.

11. $\sqrt{x+5} + \sqrt{x} = \dfrac{10}{\sqrt{x}}$.

12. $2\sqrt{x} - \sqrt{4x-3} = \dfrac{1}{\sqrt{4x-3}}$.

13. $3\sqrt{x} = \dfrac{8}{\sqrt{9x-32}} + \sqrt{9x-32}$.

14. $\sqrt{x} - 7 = \dfrac{1}{\sqrt{x}+7}$.

15. $(\sqrt{x}+11)(\sqrt{x}-11) + 110 = 0$.

16. $2\sqrt{x} = \dfrac{12 - 6\sqrt{x}}{2\sqrt{x} - 3}$.

CHAPTER XXIV.

IMAGINARY QUANTITIES.

266. An **imaginary quantity** is an indicated even root of a negative quantity. In distinction from imaginary quantities all other quantities are spoken of as **real quantities**. Although from the rule of signs it is evident that a negative quantity cannot have a real square root, yet quantities represented by symbols of the form $\sqrt{-a}$, $\sqrt{-1}$, are of frequent occurrence in mathematical investigations, and their use leads to valuable results. We therefore proceed to explain in what sense such roots are to be regarded.

When the quantity under the radical sign is negative, we can no longer consider the symbol $\sqrt{\ }$ as indicating a possible arithmetical operation; but just as $\sqrt{a}$ may be defined as a symbol which obeys the relation $\sqrt{a} \times \sqrt{a} = a$, *so we shall define $\sqrt{-a}$ to be such that* $\sqrt{-a} \times \sqrt{-a} = -a$, and we shall accept the meaning to which this assumption leads us.

It will be found that this definition will enable us to bring imaginary quantities under the dominion of ordinary algebraic rules, and that through their use results may be obtained which can be relied on with as much certainty as others which depend solely on the use of real quantities.

267. Any imaginary expression not involving the operation of raising to a power indicated by an exponent that is an irrational or imaginary expression, can be reduced to the form $a + b\sqrt{-1}$, which may be taken as the *general type* of all imaginary expressions. Here a and b are real quantities, but not necessarily rational. An imaginary expression in

IMAGINARY QUANTITIES.

this form is called a **complex number**. If $a=0$, the form becomes $b\sqrt{-1}$, which is called a **pure imaginary expression**.

268. By definition, $\sqrt{-1} \times \sqrt{-1} = -1$.

$$\therefore \sqrt{a} \cdot \sqrt{-1} \times \sqrt{a} \cdot \sqrt{-1} = a(-1);$$

that is, $(\sqrt{a} \cdot \sqrt{-1})^2 = -a$.

Thus the product $\sqrt{a} \cdot \sqrt{-1}$ may be regarded as equivalent to the imaginary quantity $\sqrt{-a}$.

269. It will generally be found convenient to indicate the imaginary character of an expression by the presence of the symbol $\sqrt{-1}$ which is called the **imaginary unit**; thus

$$\sqrt{-4} = \sqrt{4 \times (-1)} = 2\sqrt{-1}.$$
$$\sqrt{-7a^2} = \sqrt{7a^2 \times (-1)} = a\sqrt{7}\sqrt{-1}.$$

270. We shall always consider that, in the absence of any statement to the contrary, of the signs which may be prefixed before a radical the positive sign is to be taken. But in the use of imaginary quantities the following point deserves notice.

Since $(-a) \times (-b) = ab$,

by taking the square root, we have

$$\sqrt{-a} \times \sqrt{-b} = \pm \sqrt{ab}.$$

Thus in forming the product of $\sqrt{-a}$ and $\sqrt{-b}$ it would appear that either of the signs $+$ or $-$ might be placed before $\sqrt{ab}$. This is not the case, for

$$\sqrt{-a} \times \sqrt{-b} = \sqrt{a} \cdot \sqrt{-1} \times \sqrt{b} \cdot \sqrt{-1}$$
$$= \sqrt{ab}(\sqrt{-1})^2 = -\sqrt{ab}.$$

271. In dealing with imaginary quantities we apply the laws of combination which have been proved in the case of other surd quantities.

Ex. 1. $a + b\sqrt{-1} \pm (c + d\sqrt{-1}) = a \pm c + (b \pm d)\sqrt{-1}$.

Ex. 2. The product of $a + b\sqrt{-1}$ and $c + d\sqrt{-1}$
$$= (a + b\sqrt{-1})(c + d\sqrt{-1})$$
$$= ac - bd + (bc + ad)\sqrt{-1}.$$

272. The symbol $\sqrt{-1}$ is often represented by the letter i; but until the student has had a little practice in the use of imaginary quantities he will find it easier to retain the symbol $\sqrt{-1}$. The successive powers of $\sqrt{-1}$, or i, are as follows:

$$(\sqrt{-1})^1 = \sqrt{-1}, \quad i = i;$$
$$(\sqrt{-1})^2 = -1, \quad i^2 = -1;$$
$$(\sqrt{-1})^3 = -\sqrt{-1}, \quad i^3 = -i;$$
$$(\sqrt{-1})^4 = 1, \quad i^4 = 1;$$

and since each power is obtained by multiplying the one before it by $\sqrt{-1}$, or i, we see that the results must now recur.

273. If $a + b\sqrt{-1} = 0$, then $a = 0$, and $b = 0$.

For, if $\quad a + b\sqrt{-1} = 0,$
then $\quad b\sqrt{-1} = -a;$
$$\therefore -b^2 = a^2;$$
$$\therefore a^2 + b^2 = 0.$$

Now a^2 and b^2 are both positive, hence their sum cannot be zero unless each is separately zero; that is, $a = 0$, and $b = 0$.

274. If $a + b\sqrt{-1} = c + d\sqrt{-1}$, then $a = c$, and $b = d$.

For, by transposition, $a - c + (b-d)\sqrt{-1} = 0$; therefore, by the last article, $a - c = 0$, and $b - d = 0$; that is, $\quad a = c$ and $b = d$.

Thus in order that two imaginary expressions may be equal it is necessary and sufficient *that the real parts should be equal, and the imaginary parts should be equal.*

The student should carefully note this article and make use of it as opportunity may offer in the solution of equations involving imaginary expressions.

275. When two imaginary expressions differ only in the sign of the imaginary part, they are said to be **conjugate**.

Thus $a - b\sqrt{-1}$ is conjugate to $a + b\sqrt{-1}$.

Similarly $\sqrt{2} + 3\sqrt{-1}$ is conjugate to $\sqrt{2} - 3\sqrt{-1}$.

276. The sum and the product of two conjugate imaginary expressions are both real.

For $\quad a + b\sqrt{-1} + a - b\sqrt{-1} = 2a$.

Again $(a + b\sqrt{-1})(a - b\sqrt{-1}) = a^2 - (-b^2) = a^2 + b^2$.

277. If the denominator of a fraction is of the form $a + b\sqrt{-1}$, it may be rationalized by multiplying the numerator and the denominator by the conjugate expression $a - b\sqrt{-1}$. For instance,

$$\frac{c + d\sqrt{-1}}{a + b\sqrt{-1}} = \frac{(c + d\sqrt{-1})(a - b\sqrt{-1})}{(a + b\sqrt{-1})(a - b\sqrt{-1})}$$

$$= \frac{ac + bd + (ad - bc)\sqrt{-1}}{a^2 + b^2}$$

$$= \frac{ac + bd}{a^2 + b^2} + \frac{ad - bc}{a^2 + b^2}\sqrt{-1}.$$

Thus, by reference to Art. 271, we see that *the sum, difference, product, and quotient of two imaginary expressions is in each case an imaginary expression of the same form.*

278. Fundamental Algebraic Operations upon Imaginary Quantities.

Ex. 1. Find value of $\sqrt{-a^4} + 5\sqrt{-9a^4} - 2\sqrt{-4a^4}$.

$$\sqrt{-a^4} = \sqrt{a^4(-1)} \quad = \quad a^2\sqrt{-1}$$
$$5\sqrt{-9a^4} = 5\sqrt{9a^4(-1)} \quad = \quad 15a^2\sqrt{-1}$$
$$-2\sqrt{-4a^4} = -2\sqrt{4a^4(-1)} = - \quad 4a^2\sqrt{-1}$$
$$= \quad 12a^2\sqrt{-1}$$

Ex. 2. Multiply $2\sqrt{-3}$ by $3\sqrt{-2}$.

$$2\sqrt{-3} = 2\sqrt{3}\sqrt{-1};$$
$$3\sqrt{-2} = 3\sqrt{2}\sqrt{-1};$$
$$(2\sqrt{3}\sqrt{-1})(3\sqrt{2}\sqrt{-1}) = 6\sqrt{6}(\sqrt{-1})^2 = -6\sqrt{6}.$$

Q

Ex. 3. Divide $2 + 3\sqrt{-1}$ by $2 + \sqrt{-1}$.

$$\frac{2 + 3\sqrt{-1}}{2 + \sqrt{-1}} = \frac{(2 + 3\sqrt{-1})(2 - \sqrt{-1})}{(2 + \sqrt{-1})(2 - \sqrt{-1})} = \frac{7 + 4\sqrt{-1}}{4 - (-1)} = \frac{7 + 4\sqrt{-1}}{5}.$$

279. The method of Art. 262 may be used in finding the square root of $a + b\sqrt{-1}$.

Ex. Find the square root of $-7 - 24\sqrt{-1}$.

$$-7 - 24\sqrt{-1} = -7 - 2\sqrt{-144}.$$

We have now to find two quantities whose sum is -7 and whose product is -144; these are 9 and -16;

hence $\quad -7 - 24\sqrt{-1} = 9 + (-16) - 2\sqrt{9 \times (-16)}$

$$= (\sqrt{9} - \sqrt{-16})^2;$$

$$\therefore \sqrt{-7 - 24\sqrt{-1}} = \pm(3 - 4\sqrt{-1}).$$

EXAMPLES XXIV.

Simplify:

1. $\sqrt{-8} + \sqrt{-18}$.
2. $4\sqrt{-27} + 3\sqrt{-12}$.
3. $5\sqrt{-16} - 2\sqrt{-9}$.
4. $2\sqrt{-20} + 3\sqrt{-45} - \sqrt{-80}$.
5. $2\sqrt{-a^2x^2} + 7\sqrt{-4a^2x^2} + 12\sqrt{-36a^2x^2}$.
6. $\sqrt{-\frac{1}{2}} - \sqrt{-\frac{2}{4}} + \sqrt{-\frac{27}{16}} + \sqrt{-\frac{1}{8}}$.
9. $(2\sqrt{-2} + \sqrt{-3})(\sqrt{-3} - \sqrt{-5})$.
7. $(\sqrt{-3})(\sqrt{-12})$.
10. $(2 + \sqrt{-a})(3 - \sqrt{-a})$.
8. $(2 + \sqrt{-2})(1 - \sqrt{-3})$.
11. $(4 + \sqrt{-2})(2 - 3\sqrt{-5})$.
12. $(2\sqrt{-3} + 3\sqrt{-2})(4\sqrt{-3} - 5\sqrt{-2})$.
13. $\sqrt{27} + \sqrt{-3}$.
14. $-\sqrt{-4} + (\sqrt{-2} + \sqrt{-8})$.
15. $(-\sqrt{-a^2} + \sqrt{-2}) + (2\sqrt{-1} - \sqrt{-2})$.

Express with rational denominator:

16. $\dfrac{1}{3 - \sqrt{-2}}$.
17. $\dfrac{3\sqrt{-2} + 2\sqrt{-5}}{3\sqrt{-2} - 2\sqrt{-5}}$.
18. $\dfrac{3 + 2\sqrt{-1}}{2 - 5\sqrt{-1}} + \dfrac{3 - 2\sqrt{-1}}{2 + 5\sqrt{-1}}$.
19. $\dfrac{a + x\sqrt{-1}}{a - x\sqrt{-1}} - \dfrac{a - x\sqrt{-1}}{a + x\sqrt{-1}}$.

Find the square root of

20. $-5 + 12\sqrt{-1}$.
21. $-11 - 60\sqrt{-1}$.
22. $-47 + 8\sqrt{-3}$.

Express in the form $a + ib$:

23. $\dfrac{3 + 5i}{2 - 3i}$.
24. $\dfrac{\sqrt{3} - i\sqrt{2}}{2\sqrt{3} - i\sqrt{2}}$.
25. $\dfrac{1 + i}{1 - i}$.

CHAPTER XXV.

PROBLEMS.

280. In previous chapters we have given collections of problems which lead to simple equations. We add here a few examples of somewhat greater difficulty.

Ex. 1. A grocer buys 15 lbs. of figs and 28 lbs. of currants for $2.60; by selling the figs at a loss of 10 per cent, and the currants at a gain of 30 per cent, he clears 30 cents on his outlay: how much per pound did he pay for each?

Let x, y denote the number of cents in the price of a pound of figs and currants respectively; then the outlay is

$$15x + 28y \text{ cents.}$$
$$\therefore 15x + 28y = 260 \ldots \ldots \ldots (1).$$

The loss upon the figs is $\frac{1}{10} \times 15x$ cents, and the gain upon the currants is $\frac{3}{10} \times 28y$ cents; therefore the total gain is

$$\frac{42y}{5} - \frac{3x}{2} \text{ cents;}$$
$$\therefore \frac{42y}{5} - \frac{3x}{2} = 30 \ldots \ldots \ldots (2).$$

From (1) and (2) we find that $x = 8$, and $y = 5$; that is, the figs cost 8 cents a pound, and the currants cost 5 cents a pound.

Ex. 2. At what time between 4 and 5 o'clock will the minute-hand of a watch be 13 minutes in advance of the hour-hand?

Let x denote the required number of minutes after 4 o'clock; then, as the minute-hand travels twelve times as fast as the hour-hand, the hour-hand will move over $\frac{x}{12}$ minute divisions in x minutes. At 4 o'clock the minute-hand is 20 divisions behind the hour-hand, and finally is 13 divisions in advance; therefore the minute-hand moves over $20 + 13$, or 33 divisions more than the hour-hand.

228   ALGEBRA.

Hence $\qquad x = \dfrac{x}{12} + 33,$

$\qquad\qquad \tfrac{11}{12} x = 33;$

$\qquad\qquad \therefore x = 36.$

Thus the time is 36 minutes past 4.

If the question be asked as follows: "At what *times* between 4 and 5 o'clock will there be 13 minutes between the two hands?" we must also take into consideration the case when the minute-hand is 13 divisions *behind* the hour-hand. In this case the minute-hand gains 20 − 13, or 7 divisions.

Hence $\qquad x = \dfrac{x}{12} + 7,$

which gives $\qquad x = 7\tfrac{7}{11}.$

Therefore the *times* are $7\dfrac{7'}{11}$ past 4, and 36' past 4.

Ex. 3. Two persons A and B start simultaneously from two places, c miles apart, and walk in the same direction. A travels at the rate of p miles an hour, and B at the rate of q miles; how far will A have walked before he overtakes B?

Suppose A has walked x miles, then B has walked $x - c$ miles.

A, walking at the rate of p miles an hour, will travel x miles in $\dfrac{x}{p}$ hours; and B will travel $x - c$ miles in $\dfrac{x-c}{q}$ hours: these two times being equal, we have

$$\dfrac{x}{p} = \dfrac{x-c}{q},$$

$$qx = px - pc;$$

whence $\qquad x = \dfrac{pc}{p-q}.$

Therefore A has travelled $\dfrac{pc}{p-q}$ miles.

Ex. 4. A train travelled a certain distance at a uniform rate. Had the speed been 6 miles an hour more, the journey would have occupied 4 hours less; and had the speed been 6 miles an hour less, the journey would have occupied 6 hours more. Find the distance.

Let the speed of the train be x miles per hour, and let the time occupied be y hours; then the distance traversed will be represented by xy miles.

PROBLEMS. 229

On the first supposition the speed per hour is $x+6$ miles, and the time taken is $y-4$ hours. In this case the distance traversed will be represented by $(x+6)(y-4)$ miles.

On the second supposition the distance traversed will be represented by $(x-6)(y+6)$ miles.

All these expressions for the distance must be equal;

$$\therefore xy = (x+6)(y-4) = (x-6)(y+6).$$

From these equations we have

$$xy = xy + 6y - 4x - 24,$$

or $\qquad 6y - 4x = 24 \ \ldots\ \ldots\ \ldots$ (1);

and $\qquad xy = xy - 6y + 6x - 36,$

or $\qquad 6x - 6y = 36 \ \ldots\ \ldots\ \ldots$ (2).

From (1) and (2) we obtain $x = 30$, $y = 24$.

Hence the distance is 720 miles.

Ex. 5. A person invests $\$3770$, partly in 3 per cent Bonds at $\$102$, and partly in Railway Stock at $\$84$ which pays a dividend of $4\frac{1}{2}$ per cent; if his income from these investments is $\$136.25$ per annum, what sum does he invest in each?

Let x denote the number of dollars invested in Bonds, y the number of dollars invested in Railway Stock; then

$$x + y = 3770 \ \ldots\ \ldots\ \ldots\ (1).$$

The income from Bonds is $\$\dfrac{3x}{102}$, or $\$\dfrac{x}{34}$; and that from Railway Stock is $\$\dfrac{4\frac{1}{2}y}{84}$, or $\$\dfrac{3y}{56}$.

Therefore $\qquad \dfrac{x}{34} + \dfrac{3y}{56} = 136\frac{1}{4} \ \ldots\ \ldots\ $ (2).

From (2) $\qquad x + \tfrac{51}{28}y = 4632\frac{1}{2},$

and by subtracting (1) $\qquad \tfrac{23}{28}y = 862\frac{1}{2};$

whence $\qquad y = 28 \times 37\frac{1}{2} = 1050;$

and from (1) $\qquad x = 2720.$

Therefore he invests $\$2720$ in Bonds and $\$1050$ in Railway Stock.

EXAMPLES XXV.

1. A sum of $\$100$ is divided among a number of persons; if the number had been increased by one-fourth each would have received a half-dollar less: find the number of persons.

2. I bought a certain number of marbles at four for a cent; I kept one-fifth of them, and sold the rest at three for a cent, and gained a cent: how many did I buy?

3. I bought a certain number of articles at five for six cents; if they had been eleven for twelve cents, I should have spent six cents less: how many did I buy?

4. A man at whist wins twice as much as he had to begin with, and then loses $16; he then loses four-fifths of what remained, and afterwards wins as much as he had at first: how much had he originally, if he leaves off with $80?

5. A number of two digits exceeds five times the sum of its digits by 9, and its ten-digit exceeds its unit-digit by 1: find it.

6. The sum of the digits of a number less than 100 is 6; if the digits be reversed the resulting number will be less by 18 than the original number: find it.

7. A man being asked his age replied, "If you take 2 years from my present age the result will be double my wife's age, and 3 years ago her age was one-third of what mine will be in 12 years." What were their ages?

8. At what time between one and two o'clock are the hands of a watch first at right angles?

9. At what time between 3 and 4 o'clock is the minute-hand one minute ahead of the hour-hand?

10. When are the hands of a clock together between the hours of 6 and 7?

11. It is between 2 and 3 o'clock, and in 10 minutes the minute-hand will be as much before the hour-hand as it is now behind it: what is the time?

12. At an election a majority of 162 was three-elevenths of the whole number of voters: find the number of votes on each side.

13. A certain number of persons paid a bill; if there had been 10 more each would have paid $2 less; if there had been 5 less each would have paid $2.50 more: find the number of persons, and what each had to pay.

14. A man spends $100 in buying two kinds of silk at $4.50 and $4 a yard; by selling it at $4.25 per yard he gains 2 per cent: how much of each did he buy?

15. Ten years ago the sum of the ages of two sons was one-third of their father's age: one is two years older than the other, and the present sum of their ages is fourteen years less than their father's age: how old are they?

16. A basket of oranges is emptied by one person taking half of them and one more, a second person taking half of the remainder and one more, and a third person taking half of the remainder and six more. How many did the basket contain at first?

17. A person swimming in a stream which runs $1\frac{1}{2}$ miles per hour, finds that it takes him four times as long to swim a mile up the stream as it does to swim the same distance down: at what rate does he swim?

18. At what *times* between 7 and 8 o'clock will the hands of a watch be at right angles to each other? When will they be in the same straight line?

19. The denominator of a fraction exceeds the numerator by 4; and if 5 is taken from each, the sum of the reciprocal of the new fraction and four times the original fraction is 5: find the original fraction.

20. Two persons start at noon from towns 60 miles apart. One walks at the rate of four miles an hour, but stops $2\frac{1}{2}$ hours on the way; the other walks at the rate of 3 miles an hour without stopping: when and where will they meet?

21. A, B, and C travel from the same place at the rates of 4, 5, and 6 miles an hour respectively; and B starts 2 hours after A. How long after B must C start in order that they may overtake A at the same instant?

22. A dealer bought a horse, expecting to sell it again at a price that would have given him 10 per cent profit on his purchase; but he had to sell it for $50 less than he expected, and he then found that he had lost 15 per cent on what it cost him: what did he pay for the horse?

23. A man walking from a town, A, to another, B, at the rate of 4 miles an hour, starts one hour before a coach travelling 12 miles an hour, and is picked up by the coach. On arriving at B, he finds that his coach journey has lasted 2 hours: find the distance between A and B.

24. What is the property of a person whose income is $1140, when one-twelfth of it is invested at 2 per cent, one-half at 3 per cent, one-third at $4\frac{1}{2}$ per cent, and the remainder pays him no dividend?

25. A person spends one-third of his income, saves one-fourth, and pays away 5 per cent on the whole as interest at $7\frac{1}{2}$ per cent on debts previously incurred, and then has $110 remaining: what was the amount of his debts?

26. Two vessels contain mixtures of wine and water; in one there is three times as much wine as water, in the other five times as much water as wine. Find how much must be drawn off from each to fill a third vessel which holds seven gallons, in order that its contents may be half wine and half water.

27. There are two mixtures of wine and water, one of which contains twice as much water as wine, and the other three times as much wine as water. How much must there be taken from each to fill a pint cup, in which the water and wine shall be equally mixed?

28. Two men set out at the same time to walk, one from A to B, and the other from B to A, a distance of a miles. The former walks at the rate of p miles, and the latter at the rate of q miles an hour: at what distance from A will they meet?

29. A train runs from A to B in 3 hours; a second train runs from A to C, a point 15 miles beyond B, in $3\frac{1}{4}$ hours, travelling at a speed which is less by 1 mile per hour. Find distance from A to B.

30. Coffee is bought at 36 cents and chicory at 9 cents per lb.: in what proportion must they be mixed that 10 per cent may be gained by selling the mixture at 33 cents per lb.?

31. A man has one kind of coffee at a cents per pound, and another at b cents per pound. How much of each must he take to form a mixture of $a-b$ lbs., which he can sell at c cents a pound without loss?

32. A man spends c half-dollars in buying two kinds of silk at a dimes and b dimes a yard respectively; he could have bought 3 times as much of the first and half as much of the second for the same money. How many yards of each did he buy?

33. A man rides one-third of the distance from A to B at the rate of a miles an hour, and the remainder at the rate of $2b$ miles an hour. If he had travelled at a uniform rate of $3c$ miles an hour, he could have ridden from A to B and back again in the same time. Prove that
$$\frac{2}{c} = \frac{1}{a} + \frac{1}{b}.$$

34. A, B, C are three towns forming a triangle. A man has to walk from one to the next, ride thence to the next, and drive thence to his starting-point. He can walk, ride, and drive a mile in a, b, c minutes respectively. If he starts from B he takes $a+c-b$ hours, if he starts from C he takes $b+a-c$ hours, and if he starts from A he takes $c+b-a$ hours. Find the length of the circuit.

MISCELLANEOUS EXAMPLES IV.

1. Distinguish between *like* and *unlike* terms. Pick out the like terms in the expression $a^3 - 3ab + b^2 - 2a^3 + 3b^2 + 5ab + 7a^3$.

2. Subtract $-2a^3 + 3a^2b + 5b^3 - 4ab^2$ from $-1 - 2ab^2 + 3b^3$ and multiply the result by $-1 + 2a - b$.

3. Divide $8x^3 - 8x^2y + 4xy^2 - y^3$ by $2x - y$.

MISCELLANEOUS EXAMPLES IV.

4. If the number of dollars I possess is represented by $+a$, what will $-a$ denote?

5. Factor the following expressions:
(i.) $a^2 - 64$,
(ii.) $a^3 - 27$.

6. Find the value of $\dfrac{1}{6x-2} - \dfrac{1}{2x - \frac{2}{3}} + \dfrac{1}{3x-1}$.

7. Solve $\dfrac{17-3x}{5} - \dfrac{2+4x}{3} = \dfrac{14+7x}{3} + 5 - 6x$.

8. There is a number of two digits which when divided by the unit digit gives a quotient 6; but if the digits be inverted the number is increased by 36: find the number.

9. Find the H. C. F. of $4x^3 - 16x^2 + 13x - 3$
and $3x^3 - 13x^2 + 13x - 3$.

10. Simplify $(\sqrt[3]{a^8}) \times (\sqrt[5]{a^7}) \times a^{-\frac{2}{3}} \div a^{\frac{3}{5}}$.

11. Find the value of $20\sqrt{\frac{1}{4}} + 14\sqrt{\frac{3}{7}} + 2\sqrt{21} - 7\sqrt{8} + \sqrt[3]{\frac{1}{2}} + \sqrt[3]{\frac{1}{16}}$.

12. Simplify $\dfrac{1}{x - \dfrac{2}{x+\frac{1}{2}}} \times \dfrac{1}{2 + \dfrac{1}{x}} \div \dfrac{x}{2x - \dfrac{x+4}{x+1}}$

13. Find the value of $\left[a^2 - \left\{ (3b - c) + b^2 - \dfrac{2a}{b} \right\} - c^2 \right]$ when $a=2, b=3, c=4$.

14. Solve $\dfrac{a}{x-a} + \dfrac{b}{x+b} = \dfrac{c}{x-a}$.

15. Find the L. C. M. of $1-x$, $1-x^2$, $1-x^3$, and $(1-x)^3$.

16. Solve
$\dfrac{3x}{5} + \dfrac{2y}{3} = 3\frac{2}{3}$,
$\dfrac{2x}{3} - \dfrac{2y}{5} = 1\frac{3}{5}$.

17. Simplify $\dfrac{3x}{2} - y - \left\{ 2x - \dfrac{y}{2} - 7 - \left(\dfrac{x}{2} - 4 \right) + 2 - \dfrac{x}{2} \right\}$.

18. Find the square root of $x^6 + 8x^4 - 2x^3 + 16x^2 - 8x + 1$.

19. Solve the equations
(i.) $\dfrac{3x}{2} - \dfrac{5}{7} = 21x - \left(\dfrac{2x}{3} + \dfrac{143}{42} \right)$.
(ii.) $2\left(\dfrac{5x}{3} - 1 \right) + \dfrac{11}{5} + \dfrac{14x}{15} = \dfrac{2x+7}{5} - 7$.

20. Expand the following binomials:
(i.) $(x+3a)^4$,
(ii.) $\left(2x - \dfrac{a}{2} \right)^5$.

21. The sum of the two digits of a number is 8 times their difference; if the digits be inverted, the number is diminished by 18: find the number.

22. Find the factors of (i.) $x^2 - 9x - 36$, (ii.) $2x^2 - 3x - 14$, and (iii.) $a^4b^4 - 7a^2b^2x^2 + x^4$.

23. Rationalize the denominator of $\dfrac{3 + 3\sqrt{5}}{5 - 2\sqrt{3}}$, and simplify $\sqrt{13 + 4\sqrt{3}}$.

24. Simplify $\dfrac{x^4 + 3x^3 - 11x^2 - 3x + 10}{x^3 + 3x^2 - 6x - 8}$.

For what values of x will both numerator and denominator vanish?

25. Solve the equations

(i.) $\quad 2x + 3y + 4z = 31$,
$\quad\quad\; x + 4y + \;\; z = 18$,
$\quad\quad 3x + \;\; y + 2z = 16$.

(ii.) $\dfrac{x-y}{2} + \dfrac{x+y}{3} = \dfrac{25}{6}$, $x + y - 5 = \tfrac{2}{3}(y - x)$.

26. Simplify $\sqrt{-8} + \sqrt{-\tfrac{1}{2}} - \sqrt{-18} + \sqrt{-2 + 2\sqrt{-3}}$.

27. Simplify $\left(2x - \dfrac{x^2 - y^2}{x}\right)\left(3y + \dfrac{x^2 + y^2}{y}\right) \div \left(\dfrac{x^2}{y^2} + 5 + \dfrac{4y^2}{x^2}\right)$.

28. Find the middle term of the expansion of $\left(\dfrac{a}{x} + \dfrac{x}{a}\right)^{10}$.

29. Simplify $\dfrac{\dfrac{a^3}{b^3} - \dfrac{b^3}{a^3}}{\left(\dfrac{a}{b} - \dfrac{b}{a}\right)\left(\dfrac{a}{b} + \dfrac{b}{a} - 1\right)} \times \dfrac{\dfrac{1}{b} - \dfrac{1}{a}}{\dfrac{1}{a^2} + \dfrac{1}{b^2} + \dfrac{1}{ab}}$.

30. Solve the equations

(i.) $a(x - a) - b(x - b) = (a + b)(x - a - b)$.
(ii.) $(a + b)x - ay = a^2$, $(a^2 + b^2)x - aby = a^3$.

31. A sum of $10.10 is divided among 7 women and 10 men; the same sum could have been divided among 23 women and 4 men. Find how much each woman and man receives.

32. Find the cube root of $8x^6 + 12x^5 + 18x^4 + 13x^3 + 9x^2 + 3x + 1$, and the square root of $y^2 + 4y + 10 + \dfrac{12}{y} + \dfrac{9}{y^2}$.

33. Simplify $\sqrt[a+b]{\left(\dfrac{x^a}{x^b}\right)^{ab} \div \left\{\dfrac{(x^{a-b})^a}{(x^{a+b})^b}\right\}^b}$.

34. Simplify $\sqrt{59 - 24\sqrt{6}} + [(\sqrt{-6} + \sqrt{-3})(\sqrt{-3} + 2\sqrt{-1})]$.

CHAPTER XXVI.

Quadratic Equations.

281. Suppose the following problem were proposed for solution:

A dealer bought a number of horses for $280. If he had bought four less, each would have cost $8 more; how many did he buy?

We should proceed thus:

Let $x =$ the number of horses; then $\dfrac{280}{x} =$ the number of dollars each cost.

If he had bought 4 less, he would have had $x - 4$ horses, and each would have cost $\dfrac{280}{x-4}$ dollars.

$$\therefore 8 + \frac{280}{x} = \frac{280}{x-4};$$

whence $\quad x(x-4) + 35(x-4) = 35x;$

$\therefore x^2 - 4x + 35x - 140 = 35x;$

$\therefore x^2 - 4x = 140.$

This equation involves the *square* of the unknown quantity; and in order to complete the solution of the problem we must discover a method of solving such equations.

282. DEFINITION. An equation which contains the square of the unknown quantity, *but no higher power*, is called a **quadratic equation**, or an **equation of the second degree**.

If the equation contains both the square and the first power of the unknown, it is called an **affected quadratic**; if it contains only the square of the unknown it is said to be a **pure quadratic.**

Thus $2x^2 - 5x = 3$ is an affected quadratic,
and $5x^2 = 20$ is a pure quadratic.

PURE QUADRATIC EQUATIONS.

283. A *pure quadratic* may be considered as a simple equation in which the *square* of the unknown quantity is to be found.

Ex. Solve $\dfrac{9}{x^2 - 27} = \dfrac{25}{x^2 - 11}$.

Multiplying across, $9x^2 - 99 = 25x^2 - 675$;
transposing, $16x^2 = 576$;
$\therefore x^2 = 36$;
and taking the square root of these equals, we have
$$x = \pm 6.$$

NOTE. We prefix the double sign to the number on the right-hand side for the reason given in Art. 196.

284. In extracting the square root of the two sides of the equation $x^2 = 36$, it might seem that we ought to prefix the double sign to the quantities on both sides, and write $\pm x = \pm 6$. But an examination of the various cases shows this to be unnecessary. For $\pm x = \pm 6$ gives the four cases:
$$+x = +6, \ +x = -6, \ -x = +6, \ -x = -6,$$
and these are all included in the two already given, namely, $x = +6, x = -6$. Hence when we extract the square root of the two sides of an equation, it is sufficient to put the double sign before the square root of *one* side.

EXAMPLES XXVI. a.

Solve the following equations:

1. $4x^2 + 5 = x^2 + 17$.
2. $3x^2 + 3 = \dfrac{2x^2}{3} + 24$.
3. $(x+1)(x-1) = 2x^2 - 4$.
4. $\dfrac{2x^2 - 6}{2} - \dfrac{x^2 - 4}{4} - \dfrac{5x^2 - 10}{7} = 0$.
5. $x^2 + 2 = \dfrac{(x-1)^3 - x + 24}{x + 2}$

6. $\dfrac{x-a}{x+a} + \dfrac{x+a}{x-a} = 5.$

7. $\dfrac{3(x^2-1)}{x^2-1} + \dfrac{4(x^2-4)}{x^2+3} - \dfrac{3(9x^2-1)}{(x^2-1)(x^2+3)} = 7.$

8. $(2x-c)(x+d) + (2x+c)(x-d) = 2cd(2cd-1).$

AFFECTED QUADRATIC EQUATIONS.

285. The equation $x^2 = 36$ is an instance of the simplest form of quadratic equations. The equation $(x-3)^2 = 25$ may be solved in a similar way; for taking the square root of both sides, we have two *simple* equations,

$$x - 3 = \pm 5.$$

Taking the upper sign, $x - 3 = +5$, whence $x = 8$;
taking the lower sign, $x - 3 = -5$, whence $x = -2.$
∴ the solution is $x = 8$, or -2.

Now the given equation $(x-3)^2 = 25$
may be written $x^2 - 6x + (3)^2 = 25,$
or $x^2 - 6x = 16.$

Hence, by retracing our steps, we learn that the equation

$$x^2 - 6x = 16$$

can be solved by first adding $(3)^2$ to each side, and then extracting the square root; and we add 9 to each side because this quantity added to the left side makes it a *perfect square*.

Now whatever the quantity a may be,

$$x^2 + 2ax + a^2 = (x+a)^2,$$
and $$x^2 - 2ax + a^2 = (x-a)^2;$$

so that, if a trinomial is a perfect square, and *its highest power*, x^2, *has unity for a coefficient*, the term without x must be equal to the *square of half the coefficient of x*.

Ex. 1. Solve $7x = x^2 - 8.$

Transpose so as to have the terms involving x on one side, and the square term positive.

Thus $x^2 - 7x = 8.$

238   ALGEBRA.

Completing the square, $x^2 - 7x + (\frac{7}{2})^2 = 8 + \frac{49}{4}$;
that is, $(x - \frac{7}{2})^2 = \frac{81}{4}$;
                       $\therefore x - \frac{7}{2} = \pm \frac{9}{2}$;
                       $\therefore x = \frac{7}{2} \pm \frac{9}{2} = 8$, or -1.

NOTE. We do not work out $(\frac{7}{2})^2$ on the left-hand side.

Ex. 2. Solve $32 - 3x^2 = 10x$.
Transposing, $3x^2 + 10x = 32$.
Divide throughout by 3, so as to make the coefficient of x^2 unity.
Thus $x^2 + \frac{10}{3}x = \frac{32}{3}$;
completing the square, $x^2 + \frac{10}{3}x + (\frac{5}{3})^2 = \frac{32}{3} + \frac{25}{9}$;
that is $(x + \frac{5}{3})^2 = 12\frac{1}{9}$;
                       $\therefore x + \frac{5}{3} = \pm 1\frac{1}{3}$;
                       $\therefore x = -\frac{5}{3} \pm 1\frac{1}{3} = 2$, or $-5\frac{1}{3}$.

Ex. 3. Solve $7(x + 2a)^2 + 3a^2 = 5a(7x + 23a)$.
Simplifying, $7x^2 + 28ax + 28a^2 + 3a^2 = 35ax + 115a^2$,
that is, $7x^2 - 7ax = 84a^2$.
Whence $x^2 - ax = 12a^2$;
completing the square, $x^2 - ax + \left(\dfrac{a}{2}\right)^2 = 12a^2 + \dfrac{a^2}{4}$;
that is, $\left(x - \dfrac{a}{2}\right)^2 = \dfrac{49a^2}{4}$;
                       $\therefore x - \dfrac{a}{2} = \pm \dfrac{7a}{2}$;
                       $\therefore x = 4a$, or $-3a$.

286. We see then that the following are the steps required for solving an affected quadratic equation.

(1) *If necessary, simplify the equation so that the terms in x^2 and x are on one side of the equation, and the term without x on the other.*

(2) *Make the coefficient of x^2 unity and positive by dividing throughout by the coefficient of x^2.*

(3) *Add to each side of the equation the square of half the coefficient of x.*

(4) *Take the square root of each side.*
(5) *Solve the resulting simple equations.*

287. The quadratic equations considered hitherto have had two roots. Sometimes, however, there is only *one solu-*

QUADRATIC EQUATIONS.

tion. Thus if $x^2 - 2x + 1 = 0$, then $(x-1)^2 = 0$, whence $x = 1$ is the only solution. Nevertheless, in this and similar cases we find it convenient to say that the quadratic has *two equal roots*.

EXAMPLES XXVI. b.

1. $5x^2 + 14x = 55$.
2. $3x^2 + 121 = 44x$.
3. $25x = 6x^2 + 21$.
4. $8x^2 + x = 30$.
5. $3x^2 + 35 = 22x$.
6. $x + 22 - 6x^2 = 0$.
7. $15 = 17x + 4x^2$.
8. $21 + x = 2x^2$.
9. $9x^2 - 143 - 6x = 0$.
10. $12x^2 = 29x - 14$.
11. $20x^2 = 12 - x$.
12. $19x = 15 - 8x^2$.
13. $21x^2 + 22x + 5 = 0$.
14. $50x^2 - 15x = 27$.
15. $18x^2 - 27x - 26 = 0$.
16. $5x^2 = 8x + 21$.
17. $15x^2 - 2ax = a^2$.
18. $21x^2 = 2ax + 3a^2$.
19. $6x^2 = 11kx + 7k^2$.
20. $12x^2 + 23kx + 10k^2 = 0$.
21. $12x^2 - cx - 20c^2 = 0$.
22. $2(x-3) = 3(x+2)(x-3)$.
23. $(x+1)(2x+3) = 4x^2 - 22$.
24. $(3x-5)(2x-5) = x^2 + 2x - 3$.
25. $a^2x^2 - 2ax + a^2 = b$.
26. $cdx^2 = c^2x + d^2x - cd$.
27. $\dfrac{5x-1}{x+1} = \dfrac{3x}{2}$.
28. $\dfrac{3x-8}{x-2} = \dfrac{5x-2}{x+5}$.
29. $\dfrac{5x-7}{7x-5} = \dfrac{x-5}{2x-13}$.
30. $\dfrac{x+3}{2x-7} - \dfrac{2x-1}{x-3} = 0$.
31. $\dfrac{x+4}{x-4} + \dfrac{x-2}{x-3} = 6\tfrac{1}{3}$.
32. $\dfrac{1}{3-x} - \dfrac{4}{5} = \dfrac{1}{9-2x}$.
33. $\dfrac{x}{x+3} + \dfrac{2}{x+6} = \dfrac{13}{20}$.
34. $\dfrac{5}{x+1} - \dfrac{8}{x+2} = -\dfrac{x}{2x+4}$.
35. $\dfrac{a^2x^2}{b^2} - \dfrac{2ax}{c} + \dfrac{b^2}{c^2} = 0$.
36. $\dfrac{1}{c+x} + \dfrac{1}{d+x} = \dfrac{c+d}{cd}$.
37. $\dfrac{2x+5}{3x-2} - \dfrac{2x+7}{3x-4} + \dfrac{3}{4} = 0$.
38. $\dfrac{x+b}{x+c} + \dfrac{x+c}{x+b} = \dfrac{5}{2}$.
39. $\dfrac{2x}{x-1} + \dfrac{3x-1}{x+2} = \dfrac{5x-11}{x-2}$.
40. $\dfrac{x-3}{x+3} - \dfrac{x+3}{x-3} + 6\tfrac{2}{3} = 0$.
41. $\dfrac{3x+1}{x+8} + \dfrac{x-8}{3x-1} = \dfrac{17}{12}$.
42. $\dfrac{21x^3 - 16}{3x^2 - 4} - 7x = 5$.

288. Solution by Formula. After suitable reduction and transposition every quadratic equation can be written in the form
$$ax^2 + bx + c = 0,$$
where a, b, c, may have *any* numerical values whatever. If therefore we can solve this quadratic, we can solve any.

Transposing, $\quad ax^2 + bx = -c;$ . . . . (1)

dividing by a, $\quad x^2 + \dfrac{b}{a}x = -\dfrac{c}{a}.$

Completing the square by adding to each side $\left(\dfrac{b}{2a}\right)^2$,

$$x^2 + \dfrac{b}{a}x + \left(\dfrac{b}{2a}\right)^2 = \dfrac{b^2}{4a^2} - \dfrac{c}{a};$$

that is, $\quad \left(x + \dfrac{b}{2a}\right)^2 = \dfrac{b^2 - 4ac}{4a^2};$

extracting the square root,

$$x + \dfrac{b}{2a} = \dfrac{\pm \sqrt{(b^2 - 4ac)}}{2a};$$

$$x = \dfrac{-b \pm \sqrt{(b^2 - 4ac)}}{2a}.$$

NOTE. The student will observe that b, the first term of the numerator of the fraction, is the coefficient of x in equation (1) *with its sign changed*, and that $4ac$, under the radical, is *plus* or *minus* according as the signs of a and c in equation (1) are *like* or *unlike*.

289. Instead of going through the process of completing the square in each particular example, we may now make use of this general formula, adapting it to the case in question by substituting the values of a, b, c.

Ex. Solve $\quad 5x^2 + 11x - 12 = 0.$
Here $a = 5$, $b = 11$, $c = -12$.

$$\therefore x = \dfrac{-11 \pm \sqrt{(11)^2 - 4.5(-12)}}{10}$$

$$= \dfrac{-11 \pm \sqrt{361}}{10} = \dfrac{-11 \pm 19}{10} = \dfrac{4}{5}, \text{ or } -3.$$

290. In the result $x = \dfrac{-b \pm \sqrt{(b^2 - 4ac)}}{2a},$

it must be remembered that the expression $\sqrt{(b^2 - 4ac)}$ is the square root of the compound quantity $b^2 - 4ac$, *taken as a whole*. We cannot simplify the solution unless we know the numerical values of a, b, c. It may sometimes happen that these values do not make $b^2 - 4ac$ a perfect square. In such a case the exact numerical solution of the equation cannot be determined.

QUADRATIC EQUATIONS.

Ex. 1. Solve $\quad 5x^2 - 15x + 11 = 0$.

We have $\quad x = \dfrac{15 \pm \sqrt{(-15)^2 - 4 \cdot 5 \cdot 11}}{2 \cdot 5}$

$\qquad\quad = \dfrac{15 \pm \sqrt{5}}{10}$.

Now $\quad \sqrt{5} = 2.236$ approximately.

$\therefore x = \dfrac{15 \pm 2.236}{10} = 1.7236,$ or $1.2764.$

These solutions are correct only to four places of decimals, and neither of them will be found to *exactly* satisfy the equation.

Unless the *numerical* values of the unknown quantity are required it is usual to leave the roots in the form

$$\frac{15 + \sqrt{5}}{10}, \ \frac{15 - \sqrt{5}}{10}.$$

Ex. 2. Solve $\quad x^2 - 3x + 5 = 0$.

We have $\quad x = \dfrac{3 \pm \sqrt{(-3)^2 - 4 \cdot 1 \cdot 5}}{2}$

$\qquad\quad = \dfrac{3 \pm \sqrt{9 - 20}}{2} = \dfrac{3 \pm \sqrt{-11}}{2}$.

But -11 has no square root exact or approximate [Art. 196]; so that no real value of x can be found to satisfy the equation. In such a case the roots are said to be *imaginary* or *impossible* [Art. 266].

291. Solution by Factoring. The following method will sometimes be found shorter than either of those already given.

Consider the equation $x^2 + \tfrac{7}{3}x = 2$.

Clearing of fractions, $3x^2 + 7x - 6 = 0 \ \ . \ . \ . \ . \ (1)$;
by resolving the left-hand side into factors, we have

$$(3x - 2)(x + 3) = 0.$$

Now if *either* of the factors $3x - 2$, $x + 3$, be zero, their product is zero. Hence the quadratic equation is satisfied by either of the suppositions

$$3x - 2 = 0, \text{ or } x + 3 = 0.$$

Thus the roots are $\quad \tfrac{2}{3}, \ -3$.

From this we see that *when a quadratic equation has been simplified and brought to the form of equation* (1), *its solution can be readily obtained if the expression on the left-hand* side can be resolved into factors. Each of these factors equated to zero gives a simple equation, and a corresponding root of the quadratic.

Ex. 1. Solve $\quad 2x^2 - ax + 2bx = ab$.

Transposing, *so as to have all the terms on one side of the equation,* we have
$$2x^2 - ax + 2bx - ab = 0.$$
Now $\quad 2x^2 - ax + 2bx - ab = x(2x - a) + b(2x - a)$
$$= (2x - a)(x + b).$$
Therefore $\quad (2x - a)(x + b) = 0;$
whence $\quad 2x - a = 0, \text{ or } x + b = 0.$
$$\therefore x = \frac{a}{2}, \text{ or } -b.$$

Ex. 2. Solve $\quad 2(x^2 - 6) = 3(x - 4).$
We have $\quad 2x^2 - 12 = 3x - 12;$
that is, $\quad 2x^2 = 3x \quad \ldots \ldots \ldots \ldots$ **(1)**
Transposing, $\quad 2x^2 - 3x = 0.$
$$x(2x - 3) = 0.$$
$$\therefore x = 0, \text{ or } 2x - 3 = 0.$$
Thus the roots are $\quad 0, \frac{3}{2}.$

NOTE. In equation (1) above we might have divided both sides by x and obtained the simple equation $2x = 3$, whence $x = \frac{3}{2}$, which is *one* of the solutions of the given equation. But the student must be particularly careful to notice that **whenever an x is removed by division from every term of an equation** *it must not be neglected, since the equation is satisfied by $x = 0$, which is therefore one of the roots.*

292. Formation of Equations with Given Roots.
It is now easy to form an equation whose roots are known.

Ex. Form the equation whose roots are 3 and $\frac{1}{2}$.
Here $\quad x = 3, \text{ or } x = \frac{1}{2};$
$$\therefore x - 3 = 0, \text{ or } x - \frac{1}{2} = 0;$$
both of these statements are included in
$$(x - 3)(x - \frac{1}{2}) = 0,$$
or $\quad 2x^2 - 7x + 3 = 0.$

From this it also appears that the factors of a trinomial, in the form $ax^2 + bx + c$, can be obtained by placing the expression equal to zero, solving the resulting quadratic equation (Art. 288), and subtracting each root separately from x. We shall return to the subject of this article in Chapter xxx.

QUADRATIC EQUATIONS.

293. Values found for the Unknown Quantity which do not satisfy the Original Equation.

From the following example it will be seen that in solving certain equations values may be obtained which will not satisfy the original equation.

Ex. Solve $\sqrt{x+5} + \sqrt{3x+4} = \sqrt{12x+1}$.

Squaring both sides,

$$x + 5 + 3x + 4 + 2\sqrt{(x+5)(3x+4)} = 12x + 1.$$

Transposing and dividing by 2,

$$\sqrt{(x+5)(3x+4)} = 4x - 4 \quad \ldots \ldots \quad (1).$$

Squaring, $(x+5)(3x+4) = 16x^2 - 32x + 16$,

or $13x^2 - 51x - 4 = 0$,

$(x-4)(13x+1) = 0$;

$\therefore x = 4$, or $-\frac{1}{13}$.

If we proceed to verify the solution by substituting these values in the original equation, it will be found that it is satisfied by $x = 4$, but not by $x = -\frac{1}{13}$. But this latter value will be found on trial to satisfy the given equation if we alter the sign of the second radical; thus,

$$\sqrt{x+5} - \sqrt{3x+4} = \sqrt{12x+1}.$$

On squaring this and reducing, we obtain

$$-\sqrt{(x+5)(3x+4)} = 4x - 4 \quad \ldots \ldots \quad (2);$$

and a comparison of (1) and (2) shows that in the next stage of the work *the same quadratic equation is obtained* in each case, the roots of which are 4 and $-\frac{1}{13}$, as already found.

From this it appears that when the solution of an equation requires that both sides should be squared, we cannot be certain without trial which of the values found for the unknown quantity will satisfy the original equation.

In order that all the values found by the solution of the equation may be applicable, it will be necessary to take into account both signs of the radicals in the given equation.

EXAMPLES XXVI. c.

Solve by the aid of the formula in Art. 288:

1. $3x^2 = 15 - 4x$.
2. $2x^2 + 7x = 15$.
3. $2x^2 + 7 - 9x = 0$.
4. $x^2 = 3x + 5$.
5. $5x^2 + 4 + 21x = 0$.
6. $x^2 + 11 = 7x$.
7. $8x^2 = x + 7$.
8. $5x^2 = 17x - 10$.
9. $35 + 9x - 2x^2 = 0$.
10. $3x^2 = x + 1$.
11. $3x^2 + 5x = 2$.
12. $2x^2 + 5x - 33 = 0$

Solve by resolution into factors:

13. $6x^2 = 7 + x$.
14. $21 + 8x^2 = 26x$.
15. $26x - 21 + 11x^2 = 0$.
16. $5x^2 + 26x + 24 = 0$.
17. $4x^2 = \frac{4}{15}x + 3$.
18. $x^2 - 2 = 2\frac{1}{2}x$.
19. $7x^2 = 28 - 96x$.
20. $96x^2 = 4x + 15$.
21. $25x^2 = 5x + 6$.
22. $35 - 4x = 4x^2$.
23. $12x^2 - 11ax = 36a^2$.
24. $12x^2 + 36a^2 = 43ax$.
25. $35b^2 = 9x^2 + 6bx$.
26. $36x^2 - 35b^2 = 12bx$.
27. $x^2 - 2ax + 4ab = 2bx$.
28. $x^2 - 2ax + 8x = 16a$.
29. $3x^2 - 2ax - bx = 0$.
30. $ax^2 + 2x = bx$.

Solve:

31. $\dfrac{23}{x+4} + \dfrac{3x}{11} = \dfrac{1}{3}(x+5)$.

32. $\sqrt{3x+10} + \sqrt{x+2} = \sqrt{10x+16}$.

33. $\dfrac{3x-4}{x+1} - \dfrac{x-1}{3x+4} + \dfrac{1}{2} = 0$.

34. $bx^2 - \dfrac{6d^2}{b+c} = dx - cx^2$.

35. $x^2 + 2cx - 2dx = 2cd - d^2$.

36. $\sqrt{2x+6} - \sqrt{x+4} = \sqrt{x-4}$.

37. $\dfrac{1}{a+x} + \dfrac{1}{b+x} = \dfrac{a+b}{ab}$.

38. $2cx^2 + 2d^2(x+c) = dx(x+5c)$.

39. $\dfrac{x+m}{x-m} + \dfrac{x-m}{x+m} = \dfrac{x^2+m^2}{x^2-m^2} + \dfrac{x^2-m^2}{x^2+m^2}$.

40. $\dfrac{1}{x+a+b} = \dfrac{1}{b} + \dfrac{1}{a} + \dfrac{1}{x}$.

41. $\sqrt{x+\frac{3}{4}} + \sqrt{3x+\frac{1}{4}} = \sqrt{6x+\frac{1}{4}}$.

42. $\sqrt{x+3} + \sqrt{2x+1} = 2\sqrt{3x-1}$.

43. $\dfrac{x-2}{x-3} + \dfrac{3x-11}{x-4} = \dfrac{4x+13}{x+1}$.

44. $\dfrac{k-n}{2m+x} + \dfrac{m-n}{2k+x} = \dfrac{k+m-2n}{k+m+x}$.

45. $(a-b)x^2 + (b-c)x + c - a = 0$.

46. $a(b-c)x^2 + b(c-a)x + c(a-b) = 0$.

47. $\sqrt{a-x} + \sqrt{b-x} = \sqrt{a+b-2x}$.

48. $\dfrac{1}{a-x} + \dfrac{1}{b-x} = \dfrac{1}{a-c} + \dfrac{1}{b-c}$.

49. $\sqrt{x-p} + \sqrt{x-q} = \dfrac{p}{\sqrt{x-q}} + \dfrac{q}{\sqrt{x-p}}$.

50. $\sqrt{(x-2)(x-3)} + 5\sqrt{\dfrac{x-2}{x-3}} = \sqrt{x^2+6x+8}$.

CHAPTER XXVII.

Equations in Quadratic Form.

294. An equation in the form $ax^{2n} + bx^n = c$, n being a positive or negative integer or fraction, is in **quadratic form**. Thus $x^4 + 4x^2 = 117$, $x^{\frac{4}{3}} + 7x^{\frac{2}{3}} = 44$, and $x^{-\frac{1}{2}} + x^{-\frac{1}{4}} = a$ are equations in quadratic form.

We give a few examples showing that the ordinary rules for quadratic equations are applicable to those in quadratic form.

Ex. 1. Solve $x^4 - 13x^2 = -36$.

By formula [Art. 288]
$$x^2 = \frac{13 \pm \sqrt{(13)^2 - 4(36)}}{2}$$
$$= \frac{13 \pm \sqrt{169 - 144}}{2}$$
$$= \frac{13 \pm 5}{2} = 9 \text{ or } 4;$$
$$\therefore x = \pm 3 \text{ or } \pm 2.$$

Ex. 2. Solve $2x^{\frac{2}{3}} - 3x^{\frac{1}{3}} = 2$.

By formula
$$x^{\frac{1}{3}} = \frac{3 \pm \sqrt{9 + 16}}{4}$$
$$= \frac{3 \pm 5}{4} = 2 \text{ or } -\frac{1}{2}.$$

Raising to the third power, $x = 8$, or $-\frac{1}{8}$.

Ex. 3. Solve $2x^{-\frac{1}{2}} - 9x^{-\frac{1}{4}} = -4$.

By formula, $x^{-\frac{1}{4}} = \dfrac{9 \pm \sqrt{81 - 32}}{4} = \dfrac{9 \pm 7}{4} = 4 \text{ or } \frac{1}{2}.$

Raising to the fourth power,
$$x^{-1} = 256 \text{ or } \tfrac{1}{16};$$
that is,
$$\frac{1}{x} = 256 \text{ or } \tfrac{1}{16};$$
$$\therefore x = \tfrac{1}{256} \text{ or } 16.$$

EXAMPLES XXVII. a.

1. $x^4 - 13x^2 + 36 = 0$.
2. $x^6 + 7x^3 = 8$.
3. $x^6 - 13x^3 = 216$.
4. $8x^6 + 65x^3 + 8 = 0$.
5. $3\sqrt{x} - 3x^{-\frac{1}{2}} = 8$.
6. $27z^{\frac{2}{3}} - 1 = 26z^{\frac{1}{3}}$.
7. $x^4 - 74x^2 = -1225$.
8. $x^{-2} - 2x^{-1} = 8$.
9. $9 + x^{-4} = 10x^{-2}$.
10. $2\sqrt{x} + 2x^{-\frac{1}{2}} = 5$.
11. $6x^{\frac{3}{4}} = 7x^{\frac{1}{2}} - 2x^{-\frac{1}{4}}$.
12. $x^{\frac{2}{3}} + 6 = 5x^{\frac{1}{3}}$.
13. $3z^{\frac{1}{2n}} - x^{\frac{1}{n}} - 2 = 0$.
14. $6\sqrt{x} = 5x^{-\frac{1}{2}} - 13$.
15. $1 + 8x^{\frac{6}{5}} + 9\sqrt[5]{x^3} = 0$.
16. $8x^{\frac{2}{2n}} - 8x^{\frac{3}{2n}} = 63$.

295. Any equation which can be thrown into the form
$$ax^2 + bx + c + p\sqrt{ax^2 + bx + c} = q$$
may be solved as follows. Putting $y = \sqrt{ax^2 + bx + c}$, we obtain
$$y^2 + py - q = 0.$$
Let r_1 and r_2 be the roots of this equation, so that
$$\sqrt{ax^2 + bx + c} = r_1, \quad \sqrt{ax^2 + bx + c} = r_2;$$
from these equations we shall obtain *four* values of x.

When no sign is prefixed to a radical, it is usually understood that it is to be taken as positive; hence, if r_1 and r_2 are both positive, all the four values of x satisfy the *original* equation. If, however, r_1 or r_2 is negative, the roots found from the resulting quadratic will satisfy the equation
$$ax^2 + bx + c - p\sqrt{ax^2 + bx + c} = q,$$
but not the original equation.

Ex. 1. Solve $x^2 - 5x + 2\sqrt{x^2 - 5x + 3} = 12$.
Add 3 to each side; then
$$x^2 - 5x + 3 + 2\sqrt{x^2 - 5x + 3} = 15.$$
Putting $\sqrt{x^2 - 5x + 3} = y$, we obtain $y^2 + 2y - 15 = 0$; whence $y = 3$ or -5.
Thus $\sqrt{x^2 - 5x + 3} = +3$, or $\sqrt{x^2 - 5x + 3} = -5$.

EQUATIONS IN QUADRATIC FORM.

Squaring and solving the resulting quadratics, we obtain from the first $x = 6$ or -1; and from the second $x = \dfrac{5 \pm \sqrt{113}}{2}$. The first pair of values satisfies the given equation, but the second pair satisfies the equation
$$x^2 - 5x - 2\sqrt{x^2 - 5x + 3} = 12.$$

Ex. 2. Solve $3x^2 - 7 + 3\sqrt{3x^2 - 16x + 21} = 16x$.

Transposing, $3x^2 - 16x - 7 + 3\sqrt{3x^2 - 16x + 21} = 0$.

Add 28 to each side; then
$$3x^2 - 16x + 21 + 3\sqrt{3x^2 - 16x + 21} = 28.$$

Proceeding as in Ex. 1, we have
$$y^2 + 3y = 28; \text{ whence } y = 4 \text{ or } -7.$$

Thus $\sqrt{3x^2 - 16x + 21} = 4$ or $\sqrt{3x^2 - 16x + 21} = -7$.

Squaring and solving, we obtain
$$x = 5, \tfrac{1}{3}, \text{ or } \dfrac{8 \pm 2\sqrt{37}}{3}.$$

The values 5 and $\tfrac{1}{3}$ satisfy the original equation. The other values satisfy the equation
$$3x^2 - 7 - 3\sqrt{3x^2 - 16x + 21} = 16x.$$

296. Occasionally equations of the fourth degree may be arranged in expressions that will be in quadratic form.

Ex. Solve $x^4 - 8x^3 + 10x^2 + 24x + 5 = 0$.

This may be written $x^4 - 8x^3 + 16x^2 - 6x^2 + 24x = -5$,

or $(x^2 - 4x)^2 - 6(x^2 - 4x) = -5$;

by formula, $x^2 - 4x = \dfrac{6 \pm \sqrt{36 - 20}}{2} = \dfrac{6 \pm 4}{2} = 5$ or 1;

whence $x = 5, -1,$ or $2 \pm \sqrt{5}$.

The student will notice that in such examples he should divide the term containing x^3 by twice the square root of the first term and then square the result for the third term. In this case a third term of $16x^2$ is required, therefore we write the term $10x^2$ of the original equation in the form $16x^2 - 6x^2$.

297. Equations like the following are of frequent occurrence.

Ex. Solve $\dfrac{x^2-6}{x}+\dfrac{5x}{x^2-6}=6$.

Write y for $\dfrac{x^2-6}{x}$; thus

$$y+\dfrac{5}{y}=6, \text{ or } y^2-6y+5=0;$$

whence $y=5,$ or $1.$

$$\therefore \dfrac{x^2-6}{x}=5, \text{ or } \dfrac{x^2-6}{x}=1;$$

that is, $x^2-5x-6=0$, or $x^2-x-6=0.$

Thus $x=6,\ -1;$ or $x=3,\ -2.$

EXAMPLES XXVII. b.

Solve the following equations:

1. $x^2+x+1=\dfrac{42}{x^2+x}.$

2. $\dfrac{x}{x^2-1}+\dfrac{x^2-1}{x}=2\dfrac{1}{6}.$

3. $\left(x+\dfrac{1}{x}\right)^2-4\left(x+\dfrac{1}{x}\right)=5.$

4. $\dfrac{x^2-3}{x}+\dfrac{3x}{x^2-3}=\dfrac{13}{2}.$

5. $x^2+2\sqrt{x^2+6x}=24-6x.$

6. $\left(x-\dfrac{6}{x}\right)^2+4x-\dfrac{24}{x}=5.$

7. $27x^{\frac{3}{2}}-4=26x^{\frac{3}{4}}.$

8. $x^2+3x-\dfrac{20}{x^2+3x}=8.$

9. $3x^2-4x+\sqrt{3x^2-4x-6}=18.$

10. $2x^2-2x+2\sqrt{2x^2-7x+6}=5x-6.$

11. $x^2+6\sqrt{x^2-2x+5}=11+2x.$

12. $2\sqrt{x^2-6x+2}+4x+1=x^2-2x.$

13. $\sqrt{4x^2+2x+7}=12x^2+6x-119.$

14. $3x(3-x)=11-4\sqrt{x^2-3x+5}.$

15. $x^2-x+3\sqrt{2x^2-3x+2}=\dfrac{x}{2}+7.$

16. $2x^2-2x-17+2\sqrt{2x^2-3x+7}=x.$

17. $2x^2+3x+1=\dfrac{30}{2x^2+3x}.$

18. $x^4-8x^3-12x^2+112x=128.$

19. $x^4+2x^3-3x^2-4x-96=0.$

20. $x^4-10x^3+30x^2-25x+4=0.$

21. $x^4-14x^3+61x^2-84x+20=0.$

CHAPTER XXVIII.

SIMULTANEOUS EQUATIONS, INVOLVING QUADRATICS.

298. We shall now consider some of the most useful methods of solving simultaneous equations, one or more of which may be of a degree higher than the first; but no fixed rules can be laid down which are applicable to all cases.

299. Equations solved by finding the Values of $(x + y)$ and $(x - y)$.

Ex. 1. Solve
$$x + y = 15 \quad \ldots \ldots \quad (1),$$
$$xy = 36 \quad \ldots \ldots \quad (2).$$

From (1) by squaring, $x^2 + 2xy + y^2 = 225$;
from (2), $\quad 4xy = 144$;
by subtraction, $\quad x^2 - 2xy + y^2 = 81$;
by taking the square root, $\quad x - y = \pm 9$.

Combining this with (1) we have to consider the two cases,
$$\left. \begin{array}{l} x + y = 15, \\ x - y = 9. \end{array} \right\} \quad \left. \begin{array}{l} x + y = 15, \\ x - y = -9. \end{array} \right\}$$

from which we find
$$\left. \begin{array}{l} x = 12, \\ y = 3. \end{array} \right\} \quad \left. \begin{array}{l} x = 3, \\ y = 12. \end{array} \right\}$$

Ex. 2. Solve
$$x - y = 12 \quad \ldots \ldots \quad (1),$$
$$xy = 85 \quad \ldots \ldots \quad (2).$$

From (1), $\quad x^2 - 2xy + y^2 = 144$;
from (2), $\quad 4xy = 340$;
by addition, $\quad x^2 + 2xy + y^2 = 484$;
by taking the square root, $\quad x + y = \pm 22$.

Combining this with (1) we have the two cases,
$$\left. \begin{array}{l} x + y = 22, \\ x - y = 12. \end{array} \right\} \quad \left. \begin{array}{l} x + y = -22, \\ x - y = 12. \end{array} \right\}$$

Whence
$$\left. \begin{array}{l} x = 17, \\ y = 5. \end{array} \right\} \quad \left. \begin{array}{l} x = -5, \\ y = -17. \end{array} \right\}$$

300. These are the simplest cases that arise, but they are specially important since the solution in a large number of other cases is dependent upon them.

As a rule our object is to solve the proposed equations *symmetrically*, by finding the values of $x+y$ and $x-y$. From the foregoing examples it will be seen that we can always do this as soon as we have obtained the product of the unknowns, and either their sum or their difference.

Ex. 1. Solve
$$x^2 + y^2 = 74 \quad \ldots \ldots \ldots (1),$$
$$xy = 35 \quad \ldots \ldots \ldots (2).$$

Multiply (2) by 2, then by addition and subtraction we have
$$x^2 + 2xy + y^2 = 144.$$
$$x^2 - 2xy + y^2 = 4.$$
Whence
$$x + y = \pm 12,$$
$$x - y = \pm 2.$$

We have now four cases to consider; namely,

$$\left.\begin{array}{l}x+y=12,\\x-y=2.\end{array}\right\} \quad \left.\begin{array}{l}x+y=12,\\x-y=-2.\end{array}\right\} \quad \left.\begin{array}{l}x+y=-12,\\x-y=2.\end{array}\right\} \quad \left.\begin{array}{l}x+y=-12,\\x-y=-2.\end{array}\right\}$$

From which the values of x are $\quad 7, 5, -5, -7$; and the corresponding values of y are 5, 7, -7, -5.

Ex. 2. Solve
$$x^2 + y^2 = 185 \quad \ldots \ldots \ldots (1),$$
$$x + y = 17 \quad \ldots \ldots \ldots (2).$$

By subtracting (1) from the square of (2) we have
$$2xy = 104;$$
$$\therefore xy = 52 \quad \ldots \ldots \ldots (3).$$

Equations (2) and (3) can now be solved by the method of Art. 299, Ex. 1; and the solution is
$$\left.\begin{array}{l}x = 13, \text{ or } 4,\\y = 4, \text{ or } 13.\end{array}\right\}$$

EXAMPLES XXVIII. a.

Solve the following equations:

1. $x + y = 28,$
$xy = 187.$

2. $x + y = 51,$
$xy = 518.$

3. $x + y = 74,$
$xy = 1113.$

4. $x - y = 5,$
$xy = 126.$

5. $x - y = 8,$
$xy = 513.$

6. $xy = 1075,$
$x - y = 18.$

SIMULTANEOUS EQUATIONS.

7. $xy = 923,$
$x + y = 84.$

8. $x - y = -8,$
$xy = 1353.$

9. $x - y = -22,$
$xy = 3848.$

10. $xy = -2193,$
$x + y = -8.$

11. $x - y = -18,$
$xy = 1363.$

12. $xy = -1914,$
$x + y = -65.$

13. $x^2 + y^2 = 89,$
$xy = 40.$

14. $x^2 + y^2 = 170,$
$xy = 13.$

15. $x^2 + y^2 = 65,$
$xy = 28.$

16. $x^2 + y^2 = 178,$
$x + y = 16.$

17. $x + y = 15,$
$x^2 + y^2 = 125.$

18. $x - y = 4,$
$x^2 + y^2 = 106.$

19. $x^2 + y^2 = 180,$
$x - y = 6.$

20. $x^2 + y^2 = 185,$
$x - y = 3.$

21. $x + y = 13,$
$x^2 + y^2 = 97.$

22. $x + y = 9,$
$x^2 + xy + y^2 = 61.$

23. $x - y = 3,$
$x^2 - 3xy + y^2 = -19.$

24. $x^2 - xy + y^2 = 76,$
$x + y = 14.$

25. $\tfrac{1}{10}(x - y) = 1,$
$x^2 - 4xy + y^2 = 52.$

26. $\dfrac{1}{x} + \dfrac{1}{y} = 2,$
$x + y = 2.$

27. $\dfrac{1}{x} + \dfrac{1}{y} = \dfrac{7}{12},$
$xy = 12.$

28. $ax + by = 2,$
$abxy = 1.$

29. $x^2 + pxy + y^2 = p + 2,$
$qx^2 + xy + qy^2 = 2q + 1.$

301. Equations which can be reduced to One of the Cases already considered. Any pair of equations of the form

$$x^2 \pm pxy + y^2 = a^2 \quad \ldots \ldots \quad (1),$$

$$x \pm y = b \quad \ldots \ldots \quad (2),$$

where p is any numerical quantity, can be reduced to one of the cases already considered; for, by squaring (2) and combining with (1), an equation to find xy is obtained; the solution can then be completed by the aid of equation (2).

Ex. 1. Solve $x^3 - y^3 = 999 \quad \ldots \ldots \quad (1),$
$x - y = 3 \quad \ldots \ldots \quad (2).$

By division, $x^2 + xy + y^2 = 333 \quad \ldots \ldots \quad (3);$
from (2), $x^2 - 2xy + y^2 = 9;$
by subtraction, $3xy = 324,$
$xy = 108 \quad \ldots \ldots \quad (4)$

From (2) and (4), $x = 12, \text{ or } -9,$
$y = 9, \text{ or } -12.$

Ex. 2. Solve $\quad x^4 + x^2y^2 + y^4 = 2613$ . . . . (1),

$\quad\quad\quad\quad\quad\quad\quad x^2 + xy + y^2 = 67$ . . . . (2).

Dividing (1) by (2), $x^2 - xy + y^2 = 39$ . . . . (3).

From (2) and (3), by addition, $x^2 + y^2 = 53$;

by subtraction, $\quad\quad\quad\quad\quad xy = 14$;

whence $\quad\quad\quad\quad\quad\quad\quad x = \pm 7, \pm 2,$
$\quad\quad\quad\quad\quad\quad\quad\quad\quad y = \pm 2, \pm 7.$ } [Art. 300, Ex. 1.]

Ex. 3. Solve $\quad\quad\quad \dfrac{1}{x} - \dfrac{1}{y} = \dfrac{1}{3}$ . . . . (1),

$\quad\quad\quad\quad\quad\quad \dfrac{1}{x^2} + \dfrac{1}{y^2} = \dfrac{5}{9}$ . . . . (2).

From (1), by squaring, $\dfrac{1}{x^2} - \dfrac{2}{xy} + \dfrac{1}{y^2} = \dfrac{1}{9}$;

by subtraction, $\quad\quad\quad\quad \dfrac{2}{xy} = \dfrac{4}{9}$;

adding to (2), $\quad\quad\quad \dfrac{1}{x^2} + \dfrac{2}{xy} + \dfrac{1}{y^2} = 1$;

$\quad\quad\quad\quad \therefore \dfrac{1}{x} + \dfrac{1}{y} = \pm 1.$

Combining with (1), $\quad\quad \dfrac{1}{x} = \dfrac{2}{3}, \text{ or } -\dfrac{1}{3},$

$\quad\quad\quad\quad\quad\quad\quad\quad \dfrac{1}{y} = \dfrac{1}{3}, \text{ or } -\dfrac{2}{3};$

$\quad\quad\quad\quad \therefore x = \tfrac{3}{2}, \text{ or } -3,$
$\quad\quad\quad\quad\quad y = 3, \text{ or } -\tfrac{3}{2}.$ }

EXAMPLES XXVIII. b.

1. $x^3 + y^3 = 407,$
$x + y = 11.$

2. $x^3 + y^3 = 637,$
$x + y = 13.$

3. $x + y = 23,$
$x^3 + y^3 = 3473.$

4. $x^3 - y^3 = 218,$
$x - y = 2.$

5. $x - y = 4,$
$x^3 - y^3 = 988.$

6. $x^3 - y^3 = 2197,$
$x - y = 13.$

7. $x^4 + x^2y^2 + y^4 = 2128,$
$x^2 + xy + y^2 = 76.$

8. $x^4 + x^2y^2 + y^4 = 2923,$
$x^2 - xy + y^2 = 37.$

9. $x^4 + x^2y^2 + y^4 = 9211,$
$x^2 - xy + y^2 = 61.$

10. $x^4 + x^2y^2 + y^4 = 7371,$
$x^2 - xy + y^2 = 63.$

SIMULTANEOUS EQUATIONS.

11. $\dfrac{1}{x^2} + \dfrac{1}{y^2} = \dfrac{481}{576}$,

   $\dfrac{1}{x} + \dfrac{1}{y} = \dfrac{29}{24}$.

12. $\dfrac{1}{x^2} + \dfrac{1}{y^2} = \dfrac{61}{900}$,

   $xy = 30$.

13. $\dfrac{x}{y} + \dfrac{y}{x} = 2\tfrac{1}{2}$,

   $x + y = 6$.

14. $\dfrac{x}{y} + \dfrac{y}{x} = 2\tfrac{16}{21}$,

   $x - y = 4$.

15. $\dfrac{34}{x^2 + y^2} = \dfrac{15}{xy}$,

   $x + y = 8$.

16. $x^3 - y^3 = 56$,

   $x^2 + xy + y^2 = 28$.

17. $4(x^2 + y^2) = 17xy$,

   $x - y = 6$.

18. $x^3 + y^3 = 126$,

   $x^2 - xy + y^2 = 21$.

19. $\dfrac{1}{x^3} + \dfrac{1}{y^3} = 1\tfrac{16}{125}$,

   $\dfrac{1}{x} + \dfrac{1}{y} = 1\tfrac{1}{5}$.

20. $\dfrac{1}{x^3} - \dfrac{1}{y^3} = 91$,

   $\dfrac{1}{x} - \dfrac{1}{y} = 1$.

302. Homogeneous Equations of the Same Degree. The following method of solution may always be used when the equations are *of the same degree and homogeneous.*

Ex. Solve $\qquad x^2 + xy + 2y^2 = 74 \;.\;.\;.\;.\;.\;.\;.\;.$ (1),

$\qquad\qquad 2x^2 + 2xy + y^2 = 73 \;.\;.\;.\;.\;.\;.\;.$ (2).

Put $y = mx$, and substitute in both equations. Thus

$\qquad\qquad x^2(1 + m + 2m^2) = 74 \;.\;.\;.\;.\;.\;.\;.$ (3),

and $\qquad\qquad x^2(2 + 2m + m^2) = 73 \;.\;.\;.\;.\;.\;.\;.$ (4).

By division, $\qquad \dfrac{1 + m + 2m^2}{2 + 2m + m^2} = \dfrac{74}{73}$;

$\therefore\; 73 + 73m + 146m^2 = 148 + 148m + 74m^2$;

$\therefore\; 72m^2 - 75m - 75 = 0$,

or $\qquad 24m^2 - 25m - 25 = 0$;

$\therefore\; (8m + 5)(3m - 5) = 0$;

$\qquad\qquad\therefore\; m = -\tfrac{5}{8}$, or $\tfrac{5}{3}$.

(i.) Take $m = -\tfrac{5}{8}$, and substitute in either (3) or (4).

From (3) $\qquad x^2(1 - \tfrac{5}{8} + \tfrac{50}{64}) = 74$;

$\qquad\qquad\therefore\; x^2 = \dfrac{64 \times 74}{74} = 64$;

$\qquad\qquad\qquad \therefore\; x = \pm 8$;

$\therefore\; y = mx = -\tfrac{5}{8} \times \pm 8 = \mp 5$.

(ii.) Take $m = \tfrac{5}{3}$; then from (3), $x^2(1 + \tfrac{5}{3} + \tfrac{50}{9}) = 74$,

$\qquad\qquad x^2 = \dfrac{74 \times 9}{74} = 9$;

$\therefore\; x = \pm 3$; $\;\therefore\; y = mx = \tfrac{5}{3} \times \pm 3 = \pm 5$.

254   ALGEBRA.

The student will notice that, having found the values of x, we obtained those of y from the equation $y = mx$, using, in each case, the value of m employed in finding those particular values of x.

303. Equations of which One is of the First Degree and the Other of a Higher Degree. We may from the simple equation find the value of one of the unknowns in terms of the other, and substitute in the second equation.

Ex. Solve
$$3x - 4y = 5 \quad \ldots \ldots \ldots (1).$$
$$3x^2 - xy - 3y^2 = 21 \quad \ldots \ldots \ldots (2).$$

From (1) we have
$$x = \frac{5 + 4y}{3};$$

and substituting in (2), $\quad \dfrac{3(5 + 4y)^2}{9} - \dfrac{y(5 + 4y)}{3} - 3y^2 = 21;$

$$\therefore 75 + 120y + 48y^2 - 15y - 12y^2 - 27y^2 = 189;$$
$$9y^2 + 105y - 114 = 0;$$
$$3y^2 + 35y - 38 = 0;$$
$$\therefore (y - 1)(3y + 38) = 0;$$
$$\therefore y = 1, \text{ or } -\tfrac{38}{3};$$

and by substituting in (1), $\quad x = 3$, or $-1\tfrac{37}{9}$.

304. Symmetrical Equations. The following method of solution may *always* be used when the given equations are *symmetrical*, that is, when the unknown quantities in each equation may be interchanged without destroying the equality. The same method may generally be employed with advantage where the given equations are symmetrical except with respect to the *signs* of the terms.

Ex. Solve
$$x^4 + y^4 = 82 \quad \ldots \ldots \ldots (1),$$
$$x - y = 2 \quad \ldots \ldots \ldots (2).$$

Put $\quad x = u + v$, and $y = u - v$;
then from (2) we obtain $\quad v = 1$.

Substituting in (1), $(u + 1)^4 + (u - 1)^4 = 82;$
$$\therefore 2(u^4 + 6u^2 + 1) = 82;$$
$$u^4 + 6u^2 - 40 = 0;$$

SIMULTANEOUS EQUATIONS.

whence $\quad u^2 = 4,\ \text{or} -10;$
and $\quad u = \pm 2,\ \text{or}\ \pm\sqrt{-10}.$
Thus, $\quad x = u + v = 3,\ -1,\ 1 \pm \sqrt{-10};$
$\quad y = u - v = 1,\ -3,\ -1 \pm \sqrt{-10}.$

NOTE. We may assume $x + y = 2u$ and $x - y = 2v$, u and v being *any* unknown quantities, whence we obtain $x = u + v$, and $y = u - v$, the values used in the above.

305. Miscellaneous Cases. The examples we have given will be sufficient as a general explanation of the methods to be employed; but in some cases special artifices are necessary.

Ex. 1. Solve $\quad x^2y^2 - 6x = 34 - 3y\ \ldots\ldots$ (1),
$\quad 3xy + y = 2(9 + x)\ \ldots\ldots$ (2).

From (1), $\quad x^2y^2 - 6x + 3y = 34;$
from (2), $\quad 9xy - 6x + 3y = 54;$
by subtraction, $\quad x^2y^2 - 9xy = -20,$

$$xy = \frac{9 \pm \sqrt{81 - 80}}{2} = \frac{9 \pm 1}{2} = 5\ \text{or}\ 4.$$

(i.) Substituting $xy = 5$ in (2) gives $y - 2x = 3$.
From these equations we obtain $\left.\begin{array}{l}x = 1,\ \text{or}\ -\frac{5}{2},\\ y = 5,\ \text{or}\ -2.\end{array}\right\}$

(ii.) Substituting $xy = 4$ in (2) gives $y - 2x = 6$.
From these equations we obtain $x = \dfrac{-3 \pm \sqrt{17}}{2},$
and $\quad y = 3 \pm \sqrt{17}.$

Ex. 2. Solve $\quad y^2 + yz + z^2 = 49\ \ldots\ldots\ldots$ (1),
$\quad z^2 + zx + x^2 = 19\ \ldots\ldots\ldots$ (2),
$\quad x^2 + xy + y^2 = 39\ \ldots\ldots\ldots$ (3).

Subtracting (2) from (1),
$\quad y^2 - x^2 + z(y - x) = 30;$
that is, $\quad (y - x)(x + y + z) = 30\ \ldots\ldots\ldots$ (4).
Similarly from (1) and (3),
$\quad (z - x)(x + y + z) = 10\ \ldots\ldots\ldots$ (5)

Hence from (4) and (5), by division,

$$\frac{y-x}{z-x} = 3;$$

whence $y = 3z - 2x.$

Substituting in equation (3), we obtain

$$x^2 - 3xz + 3z^2 = 13.$$

From (2), $\quad x^2 + xz + z^2 = 19.$

Solving these homogeneous equations, we obtain

$$x = \pm 2, \; z = \pm 3; \text{ and therefore } y = \pm 5;$$

or $\quad x = \pm \dfrac{11}{\sqrt{7}}, \; z = \pm \dfrac{1}{\sqrt{7}}; \text{ and therefore } y = \mp \dfrac{19}{\sqrt{7}}.$

EXAMPLES XXVIII. a.

1. $5x - y = 17,$
$xy = 12.$

2. $x^2 + xy = 15,$
$y^2 + xy = 10.$

3. $x - y = 10,$
$x^2 - 2xy - 3y^2 = 84.$

4. $3x + 2y = 16,$
$xy = 10.$

5. $3x - y = 11,$
$3x^2 - y^2 = 47.$

6. $x - 3y = 1,$
$x^2 - 2xy + 9y^2 = 17.$

7. $x + 2y = 9,$
$3y^2 - 5x^2 = 43.$

8. $x^2 + y^2 = 5,$
$2xy - y^2 = 3.$

9. $5x + y = 3,$
$2x^2 - 3xy - y^2 = 1.$

10. $3x^2 - 5y^2 = 28,$
$3xy - 4y^2 = 8.$

11. $3x^2 - y^2 = 23,$
$2x^2 - xy = 12.$

12. $x^2 + xy + y^2 = 3\frac{1}{4},$
$2x^2 - 3xy + 2y^2 = 2\frac{3}{4}.$

13. $x^2 - 3xy + y^2 + 1 = 0,$
$3x^2 - xy + 3y^2 = 13.$

14. $7xy - 8x^2 = 10,$
$8y^2 - 9xy = 18.$

15. $x^2 - 2xy = 21,$
$xy + y^2 = 18.$

16. $x^2 + 3xy = 54,$
$xy + 4y^2 = 115.$

17. $x^3 + y^3 = 152,$
$x^2y + xy^2 = 120.$

18. $x^3 - y^3 = 127,$
$x^2y - xy^2 = 42.$

19. $x^3 - y^3 = 208,$
$xy(x - y) = 48.$

20. $x^2y^2 + 5xy = 84,$
$x + y = 8.$

21. $x^2 + 4y^2 + 80 = 15x + 30y,$
$xy = 6.$

22. $9x^2 + y^2 - 63x - 21y + 128 = 0,$
$xy = 4.$

23. $\dfrac{1}{x^2} + \dfrac{1}{y^2} = \dfrac{45}{4},$
$\dfrac{1}{x} - \dfrac{1}{y} = \dfrac{3}{2}.$

24. $\dfrac{1}{x^3} + \dfrac{1}{y^3} = \dfrac{243}{8},$
$\dfrac{1}{x} + \dfrac{1}{y} = \dfrac{9}{2}.$

25. $x^4 + x^2y^2 + y^4 = 931,$
$x^2 - xy + y^2 = 19.$

26. $x^2 + xy + y^2 = 84,$
$x - \sqrt{xy} + y = 6.$

27. $x + \sqrt{xy} + y = 65,$
$x^2 + xy + y^2 = 2275.$

28. $x + y = 7 + \sqrt{xy},$
$x^2 + y^2 = 133 - xy.$

29. $3x^2 - 5y^2 = 7,$
$3xy - 4y^2 = 2.$

30. $5y^2 - 7x^2 = 17,$
$5xy - 6x^2 = 6.$

SIMULTANEOUS EQUATIONS.

31. $3x^2 + 165 = 16xy,$
    $7xy + 3y^2 = 132.$

32. $3x^2 + xy + y^2 = 15,$
    $31xy - 3x^2 - 5y^2 = 45.$

33. $x^2 + y^2 - 3 = 3xy,$
    $2x^2 - 6 + y^2 = 0.$

34. $x^4 + y^4 = 706,$
    $x + y = 8.$

35. $x^4 + y^4 = 272,$
    $x - y = 2.$

36. $x^5 - y^5 = 992,$
    $x - y = 2.$

37. $x^2y^4 - 6xy^2 = -9,$
    $xy - y = 2.$

38. $2x^3 + 2y^3 = 9xy,$
    $x + y = 3.$

39. $x + y = 1072.$
    $x^{\frac{1}{3}} + y^{\frac{1}{3}} = 16.$

40. $xy^{\frac{1}{2}} + yx^{\frac{1}{2}} = 20,$
    $x^{\frac{3}{2}} + y^{\frac{3}{2}} = 65.$

41. $x^{\frac{1}{2}} + y^{\frac{1}{2}} = 5,$
    $6(x^{-\frac{1}{2}} + y^{-\frac{1}{2}}) = 5.$

42. $\sqrt{\frac{x}{y}} + \sqrt{\frac{y}{x}} = \frac{10}{3},$
    $x + y = 10.$

43. $\frac{\sqrt{x} - \sqrt{y}}{\sqrt{x} + \sqrt{y}} + \frac{\sqrt{x} + \sqrt{y}}{\sqrt{x} - \sqrt{y}} = \frac{17}{4},$
    $x^2 + y^2 = 706.$

44. $4x^2 + 5y = 6 + 20xy - 25y^2 + 2x,$
    $7x - 11y = 17.$

45. $x^2y^2 + 400 = 41xy,$
    $y^2 + 4x^2 = 5xy.$

46. $9x^2 + 33x - 12 = 12xy - 4y^2 + 22y,$
    $x^2 - xy = 18.$

47. $xy + ab = 2ax,$
    $x^2y^2 + a^2b^2 = 2b^2y^2.$

48. $(x^2 - y^2)(x - y) = 16xy,$
    $(x^4 - y^4)(x^2 - y^2) = 640 x^2y^2.$

49. $2x^2 - xy + y^2 = 2y,$
    $2x^2 + 4xy = 5y.$

50. $x^2 + y^2 - z^2 = 21,$
    $3xz + 3yz - 2xy = 18,$
    $x + y - z = 5.$

51. $x - y - z = 2,$
    $x^2 + y^2 - z^2 = 22,$
    $xy = 5.$

52. $x^2 + xy + xz = 18,$
    $y^2 + yz + yx = -12,$
    $z^2 + zx + zy = 30.$

CHAPTER XXIX.

Problems leading to Quadratic Equations.

306. We shall now discuss some problems which give rise to quadratic equations.

Ex. 1. A train travels 300 miles at a uniform rate; if the rate had been 5 miles an hour more, the journey would have taken two hours less: find the rate of the train.

Suppose the train travels at the rate of x miles per hour, then the time occupied is $\dfrac{300}{x}$ hours.

On the other supposition the time is $\dfrac{300}{x+5}$ hours;

$$\therefore \frac{300}{x+5} = \frac{300}{x} - 2 \quad \ldots \ldots \quad (1);$$

whence $\quad x^2 + 5x - 750 = 0,$

or $\quad (x+30)(x-25) = 0,$

$$\therefore x = 25, \text{ or } -30.$$

Hence the train travels 25 miles per hour, the negative value being inadmissible.

It will frequently happen that the algebraic statement of the question leads to a result which does not apply to the actual problem we are discussing. But such results can sometimes be explained by a suitable modification of the conditions of the question. In the present case we may explain the negative solution as follows:

Since the values $x = 25$ and -30 satisfy the equation (1), if we write $-x$ for x, the resulting equation,

$$\frac{300}{-x+5} = \frac{300}{-x} - 2 \quad \ldots \ldots \quad (2),$$

will be satisfied by the values $x = -25$ and 30. Now, by changing signs throughout, equation (2) becomes $\dfrac{300}{x-5} = \dfrac{300}{x} + 2$;

and this is the algebraic statement of the following question:

A train travels 300 miles at a uniform rate; if the rate had been 5 miles an hour *less*, the journey would have taken two hours *more*: find the rate of the train. The rate is 30 miles an hour.

PROBLEMS.

Ex. 2. A person, selling a horse for $72, finds that his loss per cent is one-eighth of the number of dollars that he paid for the horse what was the cost price?

Suppose that the cost price of the horse is x dollars; then the loss on $100 is $\frac{x}{8}$.

Hence the loss on x is $x \times \dfrac{x}{800}$, or $\dfrac{x^2}{800}$ dollars;

∴ the selling price is $x - \dfrac{x^2}{800}$ dollars.

Hence
$$x - \frac{x^2}{800} = 72,$$
or
$$x^2 - 800x + 57600 = 0;$$
that is,
$$(x - 80)(x - 720) = 0;$$
$$\therefore x = 80, \text{ or } 720;$$

and each of these values will be found to satisfy the conditions of the problem. Thus the cost is either $80, or $720.

Ex. 3. A cistern can be filled by two pipes in $33\frac{1}{3}$ minutes; if the larger pipe takes 15 minutes less than the smaller to fill the cistern, find in what time it will be filled by each pipe singly.

Suppose that the two pipes running singly would fill the cistern in x and $x - 15$ minutes. When running together they will fill $\left(\dfrac{1}{x} + \dfrac{1}{x-15}\right)$ of the cistern in one minute. But they fill $\dfrac{1}{33\frac{1}{3}}$, or $\dfrac{3}{100}$ of the cistern in one minute; hence

$$\frac{1}{x} + \frac{1}{x-15} = \frac{3}{100},$$
$$100(2x - 15) = 3x(x - 15),$$
$$3x^2 - 245x + 1500 = 0,$$
$$(x - 75)(3x - 20) = 0;$$
$$\therefore x = 75, \text{ or } 6\frac{2}{3}.$$

Thus the smaller pipe takes 75 minutes, the larger 60 minutes. The other solution, $6\frac{2}{3}$, is inadmissible.

Ex. 4. The small wheel of a bicycle makes 135 revolutions more than the large wheel in a distance of 260 yards; if the circumference of each were one foot more, the small wheel would make 27 revolutions more than the large wheel in a distance of 70 yards: find the circumference of each wheel.

Suppose the small wheel to be x feet, and the large wheel y feet in circumference.

In a distance of 260 yards, the two wheels make $\dfrac{780}{x}$ and $\dfrac{780}{y}$ revolutions respectively.

Hence
$$\frac{780}{x} - \frac{780}{y} = 135,$$
or
$$\frac{1}{x} - \frac{1}{y} = \frac{9}{52}. \quad \ldots \ldots \ldots (1).$$

Similarly, from the second condition, we obtain
$$\frac{210}{x+1} - \frac{210}{y+1} = 27,$$
or
$$\frac{1}{x+1} - \frac{1}{y+1} = \frac{9}{70}. \quad \ldots \ldots \ldots (2)$$

From (1),
$$x = \frac{52\,y}{52 + 9\,y};$$
whence
$$x + 1 = \frac{61\,y + 52}{9\,y + 52}.$$

Substituting in (2), $\dfrac{9\,y + 52}{61\,y + 52} - \dfrac{1}{y+1} = \dfrac{9}{70},$

$$70 \times 9\,y^2 = 9(61\,y + 52)(y + 1),$$
$$9\,y^2 - 113\,y - 52 = 0,$$
$$(y - 13)(9\,y + 4) = 0;$$
$$\therefore y = 13, \text{ or } -\tfrac{4}{9}.$$

Putting $y = 13$, we find that $x = 4$. The other value of y is inadmissible; hence the small wheel is 4 feet, the large wheel 13 feet in circumference.

Ex. 5. On a river, there are two towns 24 miles apart. By rowing one half of the distance, and walking the other half, a man performs the journey down stream in 5 hours, and up stream in 7 hours. Had there been no current, each journey would have taken $5\tfrac{3}{4}$ hours. Find the rate of his walking, and rowing, and the rate of the stream.

Suppose that the man walks x miles per hour, rows y miles per hour, and that the stream flows at the rate of z miles per hour.

With the current the man rows $y + z$ miles, and against the current $y - z$ miles per hour.

PROBLEMS. 261

Hence we have the following equations:

$$\frac{12}{x} + \frac{12}{y+z} = 5 \quad \ldots \ldots \ldots (1),$$

$$\frac{12}{x} + \frac{12}{y-z} = 7 \quad \ldots \ldots \ldots (2),$$

$$\frac{12}{x} + \frac{12}{y} = 5\tfrac{2}{3} \quad \ldots \ldots \ldots (3).$$

From (1) and (3), by subtraction, $\dfrac{1}{y} - \dfrac{1}{y+z} = \dfrac{1}{18} \quad \ldots \ldots (4).$

Similarly, from (2) and (3), $\dfrac{1}{y-z} - \dfrac{1}{y} = \dfrac{1}{9} \quad \ldots \ldots (5).$

From (4) $\quad 18z = y(y+z) \quad \ldots \ldots (6);$
and from (5) $\quad 9z = y(y-z) \quad \ldots \ldots (7).$

From (6) and (7), by division, $2 = \dfrac{y+z}{y-z};$

whence $\quad y = 3z;$

∴ from (4) $z = 1\tfrac{1}{2}$; and hence $y = 4\tfrac{1}{2}$, $x = 4$.

Thus the rates of walking and rowing are 4 miles and $4\tfrac{1}{2}$ miles per hour respectively; and the stream flows at the rate of $1\tfrac{1}{2}$ miles per hour.

EXAMPLES XXIX.

1. Find a number whose square diminished by 119 is equal to ten times the excess of the number over 8.

2. A man is five times as old as his son, and the sum of the squares of their ages is equal to 2106: find their ages.

3. The sum of the reciprocals of two consecutive numbers is $\tfrac{13}{42}$: find them.

4. Find a number which when increased by 17 is equal to 60 times the reciprocal of the number.

5. Find two numbers whose sum is 9 times their difference, and the difference of whose squares is 81.

6. The sum of a number and its square is nine times the next higher number: find it.

7. If a train travelled 5 miles an hour faster, it would take one hour less to travel 210 miles: what time does it take?

8. Find two numbers the sum of whose squares is 74, and whose sum is 12.

9. The perimeter of a rectangular field is 500 yards, and its area is 14400 square yards: find the length of the sides.

10. The perimeter of one square exceeds that of another by 100 feet; and the area of the larger square exceeds three times the area of the smaller by 325 square feet: find the length of their sides.

11. A cistern can be filled by two pipes running together in $22\frac{1}{2}$ minutes; the larger pipe would fill the cistern in 24 minutes less than the smaller one: find the time taken by each.

12. A man travels 108 miles, and finds that he could have made the journey in $4\frac{1}{2}$ hours less had he travelled 2 miles an hour faster: at what rate did he travel?

13. I buy a number of foot-balls for $100; had they cost a dollar apiece less, I should have had five more for the money: find the cost of each.

14. A boy was sent for 40 cents' worth of eggs. He broke 4 on his way home, and the cost therefore was at the rate of 3 cents more than the market price for 6. How many did he buy?

15. What are the two parts of 20 whose product is equal to 24 times their difference?

16. A lawn 50 feet long and 34 feet broad has a path of uniform width round it; if the area of the path is 540 square feet, find its width.

17. A hall can be paved with 200 square tiles of a certain size; if each tile were one inch longer each way it would take 128 tiles: find the length of each tile.

18. In the centre of a square garden is a square lawn; outside this is a gravel walk 4 feet wide, and then a flower border 6 feet wide. If the flower border and lawn together contain 721 square feet, find the area of the lawn.

19. By lowering the price of apples and selling them one cent a dozen cheaper, an applewoman finds that she can sell 60 more than she used to do for 60 cents. At what price per dozen did she sell them at first?

20. Two rectangles contain the same area, 480 square yards. The difference of their lengths is 10 yards, and of their breadths 4 yards: find their sides.

21. There is a number between 10 and 100; when multiplied by the digit on the left the product is 280; if the sum of the digits be multiplied by the same digit, the product is 55: find it.

22. A farmer having sold, at $75 each, horses which cost him x dollars apiece, finds that he has realized x per cent profit on his outlay: find x.

23. If a carriage wheel $14\frac{2}{3}$ ft. in circumference takes one second more to revolve, the rate of the carriage per hour will be $2\frac{2}{3}$ miles less: how fast is the carriage travelling?

PROBLEMS. 263

24. A merchant bought a number of yards of cloth for $100; he kept 5 yards and sold the rest at $2 per yard more than he gave, and received $20 more than he originally spent: how many yards did he buy?

25. A broker bought as many shares of stock as cost him $1875; he reserved 15, and sold the remainder for $1740, gaining $4 a share on their cost price. How many shares did he buy?

26. A and B are two stations 300 miles apart. Two trains start simultaneously from A and B, each to the opposite station. The train from A reaches B nine hours, the train from B reaches A four hours after they meet: find the rate at which each train travels.

27. A train A starts to go from P to Q, two stations 240 miles apart, and travels uniformly. An hour later another train B starts from P, and after travelling for 2 hours, comes to a point that A had passed 45 minutes previously. The pace of B is now increased by 5 miles an hour, and it overtakes A just on entering Q. Find the rates at which they started.

28. A cask P is filled with 50 gallons of water, and a cask Q with 40 gallons of brandy; x gallons are drawn from each cask, mixed and replaced; and the same operation is repeated. Find x when there are $8\frac{1}{8}$ gallons of brandy in P after the second replacement.

29. Two farmers A and B have 30 cows between them; they sell at different prices, but each receives the same sum. If A had sold his at B's price, he would have received $320; and if B had sold his at A's price, he would have received $245. How many had each?

30. A man arrives at the railroad station nearest to his house $1\frac{1}{2}$ hours before the time at which he had ordered his carriage to meet him. He sets out at once to walk at the rate of 4 miles an hour, and, meeting his carriage when it had travelled 8 miles, reaches home exactly 1 hour earlier than he had originally expected. How far is his house from the station, and at what rate was his carriage driven?

CHAPTER XXX.

Theory of Quadratic Equations.

MISCELLANEOUS THEOREMS.

307. In Chapter xxvi. it was shown that after suitable reduction every quadratic equation may be written in the form

$$ax^2 + bx + c = 0 \quad \ldots \quad (1),$$

and that the solution of the equation is

$$x = \frac{-b \pm \sqrt{b^2 - 4ac}}{2a} \quad \ldots \quad (2).$$

We shall now prove some important propositions connected with the roots and coefficients of all equations of which (1) is the type.

NUMBER OF THE ROOTS.

308. A quadratic equation cannot have more than two roots.

For, if possible, let the equation $ax^2 + bx + c = 0$ have three *different* roots r_1, r_2, r_3. Then since each of these values must satisfy the equation, we have

$$ar_1^2 + br_1 + c = 0 \quad \ldots \quad (1),$$
$$ar_2^2 + br_2 + c = 0 \quad \ldots \quad (2),$$
$$ar_3^2 + br_3 + c = 0 \quad \ldots \quad (3).$$

From (1) and (2), by subtraction,

$$a(r_1^2 - r_2^2) + b(r_1 - r_2) = 0;$$

divide out by $r_1 - r_2$, which, by hypothesis, is not zero; then

$$a(r_1 + r_2) + b = 0.$$

Similarly from (2) and (3),
$$a(r_2 + r_3) + b = 0;$$
∴ by subtraction, $\quad a(r_1 - r_3) = 0;$

which is impossible, since, by hypothesis, a is not zero, and r_1 is not equal to r_3. Hence there cannot be three different roots.

309. The terms 'unreal,' 'imaginary,' and 'impossible' are all used in the same sense; namely, to denote expressions which involve the square root of a negative quantity, such as
$$\sqrt{-1}, \; \sqrt{-3}, \; \sqrt{-a}.$$
It is important that the student should clearly distinguish between the terms **real** and **rational, imaginary** and **irrational.** Thus $\sqrt{25}$ or 5, $3\tfrac{1}{2}$, $-\tfrac{5}{6}$ are *rational* and *real*; $\sqrt{7}$ is *irrational* but *real*; while $\sqrt{-7}$ is *irrational* and also *imaginary.*

CHARACTER OF THE ROOTS.

310. In Art. 307 denote the two roots in (2) by r_1 and r_2,
$$r_1 = \frac{-b + \sqrt{b^2 - 4ac}}{2a}, \; r_2 = \frac{-b - \sqrt{b^2 - 4ac}}{2a};$$
then we have the following results:

(1) If $b^2 - 4ac$, the quantity under the radical, is *positive*, the roots are **real and unequal.**

(2) If $b^2 - 4ac$ is *zero*, the roots are **real and equal,** each reducing in this case to $-\dfrac{b}{2a}$.

(3) If $b^2 - 4ac$ is *negative*, the roots are **imaginary and unequal.**

(4) If $b^2 - 4ac$ is a *perfect square*, the roots are **rational and unequal.**

By applying these tests the nature of the roots of any quadratic may be determined without solving the equation.

Ex. 1. Show that the equation $2x^2 - 6x + 7 = 0$ cannot be satisfied by any real values of x.

Here $a = 2$, $b = -6$, $c = 7$; so that
$$b^2 - 4ac = (-6)^2 - 4 \cdot 2 \cdot 7 = -20.$$
Therefore the roots are imaginary.

Ex. 2. For what value of k will the equation $3x^2 - 6x + k = 0$ have equal roots?

The condition for equal roots gives
$$(-6)^2 - 4 \cdot 3 \cdot k = 0,$$
whence
$$k = 3.$$

Ex. 3. Show that the roots of the equation
$$x^2 - 2ax + a^2 - b^2 + 2bc - c^2 = 0 \quad \text{are rational.}$$

The roots will be rational provided $(-2a)^2 - 4(a^2 - b^2 + 2bc - c^2)$ is a perfect square. But this expression reduces to $4(b^2 - 2bc + c^2)$ or $4(b-c)^2$. Hence the roots are rational.

RELATIONS OF ROOTS AND COEFFICIENTS.

311. Since $r_1 = \dfrac{-b + \sqrt{b^2 - 4ac}}{2a}$, $r_2 = \dfrac{-b - \sqrt{b^2 - 4ac}}{2a}$,

we have by addition
$$r_1 + r_2 = \frac{-b + \sqrt{b^2 - 4ac} - b - \sqrt{b^2 - 4ac}}{2a} = -\frac{b}{a}. \quad (1),$$

and by multiplication we have
$$r_1 r_2 = \frac{(-b + \sqrt{b^2 - 4ac})(-b - \sqrt{b^2 - 4ac})}{4a^2}$$
$$= \frac{(-b)^2 - (b^2 - 4ac)}{4a^2} = \frac{4ac}{4a^2} = \frac{c}{a} \quad \ldots \quad (2).$$

By writing the equation in the form $x^2 + \dfrac{b}{a}x + \dfrac{c}{a} = 0$, these results may also be expressed as follows:

In a quadratic equation *where the coefficient of the first term is unity*,

(i.) the **sum** of the roots is equal to the coefficient of x with its sign changed;

(ii.) the **product** of the roots is equal to the third term.

NOTE. In any equation the term which does not contain the unknown quantity is frequently called *the absolute term*.

THEORY OF QUADRATIC EQUATIONS.

FORMATION OF EQUATIONS WITH GIVEN ROOTS.

312. Since $-\dfrac{b}{a} = r_1 + r_2$ and $\dfrac{c}{a} = r_1 r_2$,

the equation $x^2 + \dfrac{b}{a}x + \dfrac{c}{a} = 0$ may be written

$$x^2 - (r_1 + r_2)x + r_1 r_2 = 0 \quad \ldots \quad (1).$$

Hence any quadratic may also be expressed in the form

$$x^2 - (\text{sum of roots})\,x + \text{product of roots} = 0 \quad (2).$$

Again, from (1) we have

$$(x - r_1)(x - r_2) = 0 \quad \ldots \quad (3).$$

We may now form an equation with given roots.

Ex. 1. Form the equation whose roots are 3 and -2.

The equation is $\quad (x - 3)(x + 2) = 0,$

or $\qquad\qquad\quad x^2 - x - 6 = 0.$

Ex. 2. Form the equation whose roots are $\tfrac{3}{7}$ and $-\tfrac{4}{5}$.

The equation is $\quad (x - \tfrac{3}{7})(x + \tfrac{4}{5}) = 0;$

that is, $\qquad\qquad (7x - 3)(5x + 4) = 0,$

or $\qquad\qquad\quad 35x^2 + 13x - 12 = 0.$

When the roots are irrational it is easier to use the following method.

Ex. 3. Form the equation whose roots are $2 + \sqrt{3}$ and $2 - \sqrt{3}$.

We have $\qquad$ sum of roots $= 4,$

$\qquad\qquad\quad$ product of roots $= 1;$

$\therefore$ the equation is $\quad x^2 - 4x + 1 = 0,$

by using formula (2) of the present article.

313. The results of Art. 311 are most important, and they are generally sufficient to solve problems connected with the roots of quadratics. In such questions *the roots should never be considered singly*, but use should be made of the relations obtained by writing down the sum of the roots, and their product, in terms of the coefficients of the equation.

Ex. 1. If a and b are the roots of $x^2 - px + q = 0$, find the value of (1) $a^2 + b^2$, (2) $a^3 + b^3$.

We have
$$a + b = p,$$
$$ab = q.$$
$$\therefore a^2 + b^2 = (a+b)^2 - 2ab = p^2 - 2q.$$

Again,
$$a^3 + b^3 = (a+b)(a^2 + b^2 - ab)$$
$$= p\{(a+b)^2 - 3ab\} = p(p^2 - 3q).$$

Ex. 2. If a, b are the roots of the equation $lx^2 + mx + n = 0$, find the equation whose roots are $\dfrac{a}{b}$, $\dfrac{b}{a}$.

We have
$$\text{sum of roots} = \frac{a}{b} + \frac{b}{a} = \frac{a^2 + b^2}{ab},$$
$$\text{product of roots} = \frac{a}{b} \times \frac{b}{a} = 1;$$

$\therefore$ by Art. 312 the required equation is
$$x^2 - \left(\frac{a^2 + b^2}{ab}\right)x + 1 = 0,$$
or $\quad abx^2 - (a^2 + b^2)x + ab = 0.$

As in the last example $a^2 + b^2 = \dfrac{m^2 - 2nl}{l^2}$, and $ab = \dfrac{n}{l}$,

$\therefore$ the equation is $\quad \dfrac{n}{l}x^2 - \dfrac{m^2 - 2nl}{l^2}x + \dfrac{n}{l} = 0,$

or $\quad nlx^2 - (m^2 - 2nl)x + nl = 0.$

Ex. 3. Find the condition that the roots of the equation
$$ax^2 + bx + c = 0$$
should be (1) equal in magnitude and opposite in sign, (2) reciprocals.

The roots will be equal in magnitude and opposite in sign if their sum is zero; therefore $-\dfrac{b}{a} = 0$, or $b = 0$.

Again, the roots will be reciprocals when their product is unity; therefore $\dfrac{c}{a} = 1$, or $c = a$.

Ex. 4. Find the relation which must subsist between the coefficients of the equation $px^2 + qx + r = 0$ when one root is three times the other.

We have $\quad a + b = -\dfrac{q}{p}, \; ab = \dfrac{r}{p};$

but since $a = 3b$, we obtain by substitution
$$4b = -\frac{q}{p}, \; 3b^2 = \frac{r}{p}.$$

THEORY OF QUADRATIC EQUATIONS. 269

From the first of these equations $b^2 = \dfrac{q^2}{16p^2}$, and from the second $b^2 = \dfrac{r}{3p}$.

$$\therefore \dfrac{q^2}{16p^2} = \dfrac{r}{3p},$$

or
$$3q^2 = 16pr,$$

which is the required condition.

314. The following example illustrates a useful application of the results proved in Art. 310.

Ex. If x is a real quantity, prove that the expression $\dfrac{x^2 + 2x - 11}{2(x-3)}$ can have all numerical values except such as lie between 2 and 6.

Let the given expression be represented by y, so that
$$\dfrac{x^2 + 2x - 11}{2(x-3)} = y;$$

then multiplying across and transposing, we have
$$x^2 + 2x(1-y) + 6y - 11 = 0.$$

This is a quadratic equation, and if x is to have real values, $4(1-y)^2 - 4(6y-11)$ must be positive; or simplifying and dividing by 4, $y^2 - 8y + 12$ must be positive; that is, $(y-6)(y-2)$ must be positive. Hence the factors of this product must be both positive or both negative. In the former case y is greater than 6; in the latter y is less than 2. Therefore y cannot lie between 2 and 6, but may have any other value.

In this example it will be noticed that the *expression* $y^2 - 8y + 12$ is positive so long as y does not lie between the roots of the corresponding quadratic equation
$$y^2 - 8y + 12 = 0.$$

This is a particular case of the general proposition investigated in the next article.

315. For all real values of x the expression $ax^2 + bx + c$ has the same sign as a, except when the roots of the equation $ax^2 + bx + c = 0$ are real and unequal, and x lies between them.

Case I. Suppose that the roots of the equation
$$ax^2 + bx + c = 0$$
are real; denote them by r_1 and r_2, and let r_1 be the greater.

Then $ax^2 + bx + c = a\left(x^2 + \dfrac{b}{a}x + \dfrac{c}{a}\right)$

$\qquad = a\{x^2 - (r_1 + r_2)x + r_1 r_2\}$ [Art. 311.]

$\qquad = a(x - r_1)(x - r_2).$

Now if x is greater than r_1 or less than r_2, the factors $x - r_1$, $x - r_2$ are either both positive or both negative; therefore the expression $(x - r_1)(x - r_2)$ is positive, and $ax^2 + bx + c$ has the same sign as a. But if x lies between r_1 and r_2, the expression $(x - r_1)(x - r_2)$ is negative, and the sign of $ax^2 + bx + c$ is opposite to that of a.

CASE II. If r_1 and r_2 are equal, then

$$ax^2 + bx + c = a(x - r_1)^2,$$

and $(x - r_1)^2$ is positive for all real values of x; hence $ax^2 + bx + c$ has the same sign as a.

CASE III. Suppose that the equation $ax^2 + bx + c = 0$ has imaginary roots; then

$$ax^2 + bx + c = a\left\{x^2 + \dfrac{b}{a}x + \dfrac{c}{a}\right\}$$

$$= a\left\{\left(x + \dfrac{b}{2a}\right)^2 + \dfrac{4ac - b^2}{4a^2}\right\};$$

but since $b^2 - 4ac$ is negative [Art. 310], the expression

$$\left(x + \dfrac{b}{2a}\right)^2 + \dfrac{4ac - b^2}{4a^2}$$

is positive for all real values of x; therefore $ax^2 + bx + c$ has the same sign as a.

EXAMPLES XXX. a.

Find (without actual solution) the nature of the roots of the following equations:

1. $x^2 + x - 870 = 0.$
2. $8 + 6x = 5x^2.$
3. $\tfrac{1}{2}x^2 = 14 - 3x^2.$
4. $x^2 + 7 = 4x.$
5. $2x = x^2 + 5.$
6. $(x+2)^2 = 4x + 15.$

Form the equations whose roots are

7. $5, -3.$
8. $-9, -11.$
9. $a + b, \ a - b.$
10. $\tfrac{2}{3}, \tfrac{3}{5}.$
11. $\tfrac{3}{4}a, \ -\tfrac{1}{4}a.$
12. $0, \tfrac{7}{8}.$

THEORY OF QUADRATIC EQUATIONS.

13. If the equation $x^2 + 2(1 + k)x + k^2 = 0$ has equal roots, what is the value of k?

14. Prove that the equation $3mx^2 - (2m + 3n)x + 2n = 0$ has rational roots.

15. Without solving the equation $3x^2 - 4x - 1 = 0$, find the sum, the difference, and the sum of the squares of the roots.

16. Show that the roots of $a(x^2 - 1) = (b - c)x$ are always real.

Form the equations whose roots are

17. $3 + \sqrt{5},\ 3 - \sqrt{5}$. 18. $-2 + \sqrt{3},\ -2 - \sqrt{3}$. 19. $-\dfrac{a}{5},\ \dfrac{b}{6}$.

20. $\tfrac{1}{2}(4 \pm \sqrt{7})$. 21. $\dfrac{a+b}{a-b},\ \dfrac{a-b}{a+b}$. 22. $\dfrac{a}{2b},\ \dfrac{b}{2a}$.

If a, b are the roots of the equation $px^2 + qx + r = 0$, find the values of

23. $a^2 + b^2$.   25. $a^2b + ab^2$.   27. $a^5b^2 + a^2b^5$.

24. $(a - b)^2$.   26. $a^4 + b^4$.   28. $\dfrac{a^2}{b} + \dfrac{b^2}{a}$.

29. If a, b are the roots of $x^2 - px + q = 0$, and a^3, b^3 the roots of $x^2 - Px + Q = 0$, find P and Q in terms of p and q.

30. If c, d are the roots of $x^2 - ax + b = 0$, find the equation whose roots are $\dfrac{c}{d^2},\ \dfrac{d}{c^2}$.

31. Find the condition that one root of the equation $ax^2 + bx + c = 0$ may be double the other.

32. Form an equation whose roots shall be the cubes of the roots of the equation $2x(x - a) = a^2$.

33. Prove that the roots of the equation
$$(a + b)x^2 - (a + b + c)x + \frac{c}{2} = 0$$
are always real.

34. Show that $(a + b + c)x^2 - 2(a + b)x + (a + b - c) = 0$ has rational roots.

35. Show that if x is real the expression $\dfrac{x^2 - 15}{2x - 8}$ cannot lie between 3 and 5.

36. If x is real, prove that $\dfrac{3x^2 + 2}{x^2 - 2x - 1}$ can have all values except such as lie between 2 and $-\tfrac{1}{4}$.

MISCELLANEOUS THEOREMS.

316. The Remainder Theorem. *If any algebraical expre*[ssion]

$$x^n + p_1 x^{n-1} + p_2 x^{n-2} + p_3 x^{n-3} + \cdots + p_{n-1} x + p_n$$

be divided by $x - a$, *the remainder will be*

$$a^n + p_1 a^{n-1} + p_2 a^{n-2} + p_3 a^{n-3} + \cdots + p_{n-1} a + p_n.$$

Divide the given expression by $x - a$ till a remainder is obtained which does not involve x. Let Q be the quotient, and R the remainder; then

$$x^n + p_1 x^{n-1} + p_2 x^{n-2} + \cdots + p_{n-1} x + p_n = Q(x-a) + R.$$

Since R does not contain x, it will remain unaltered whatever value we give to x.

Put $x = a$, then

$$a^n + p_1 a^{n-1} + p_2 a^{n-2} + \cdots + p_{n-1} a + p_n = Q \times 0 + R,$$
$$\therefore R = a^n + p_1 a^{n-1} + p_2 a^{n-2} + \cdots + p_{n-1} a + p_n;$$

which proves the proposition.

From this it appears that when an algebraic expression with integral exponents is divided by $x - a$, the remainder can be obtained at once by writing a in the place of x in the given expression.

Ex. The remainder when $x^4 - 2x^3 + x - 7$ is divided by $x+2$ is
$$(-2)^4 - 2(-2)^3 + (-2) - 7;$$
that is, $\qquad 16 + 16 - 2 - 7$, or 23.

317. In the preceding article the remainder is zero when the given expression is exactly divisible by $x - a$; hence we deduce:

The Factor Theorem. *If any rational and integral expression containing x becomes equal to 0 when a is written for x,* [it is exact]*ly divisible by* $x - a$. (See Art. 105.)

318. To find the condition that $x^2 + px + q$ may be a [perfect] square.

It must be evident that any such general expression cannot be a perfect square unless some particular relation subsists between the coefficients p and q. To find the necessary connection between p and q is the object of the present question.

Using the ordinary rule for square root, we have

$$\begin{array}{r|l} & x^2 + px + q \left(x + \dfrac{p}{2} \right. \\ & x^2 \\ \hline 2x + \dfrac{p}{2} & px + q \\ & px + \dfrac{p^2}{4} \\ \hline & q - \dfrac{p^2}{4} \end{array}$$

If therefore $x^2 + px + q$ be a perfect square, the remainder, $q - \dfrac{p^2}{4}$, must be zero. Hence the condition is determined by placing this remainder equal to zero and solving the resulting equation.

319. Symmetry. An expression is said to be *symmetrical* with respect to the letters it contains when its value is unaltered by the interchange of any pair of them; thus $x + y + z$, $bc + ca + ab$, $x^3 + y^3 + z^3 - xyz$ are symmetrical functions of the first, second, and third degrees respectively.

It is worthy of notice that the only symmetrical expression of the first degree in x, y, z is of the form $M(x+y+z)$, where M is independent of x, y, z.

320. It easily follows from the definition that the sum, difference, product, and quotient of any two symmetrical expressions must also be symmetrical expressions. The recognition of this principle is of great use in checking the accuracy of algebraic work, and in some cases enables us to dispense with much of the labor of calculation. In the following examples we shall assume as true a principle which will be demonstrated in Chap. XLII.

Ex. 1. Find the expansion of $(x + y + z)^3$. We know that the expansion must be a homogeneous expression of three dimensions, and therefore of the form $x^3 + y^3 + z^3 + A(x^2y + xy^2 + y^2z + yz^2 + z^2x + zx^2) + Bxyz$, where A and B are quantities independent of x, y, z.

Put $z = 0$, then A, the coefficient of x^2y, is equal to 3, the coefficient of x^2y in the expansion of $(x + y)^3$.

Put $x = y = z = 1$, and we get $27 = 3 + (3 \times 6) + B$; whence $B = 6$.
Thus $(x + y + z)^3$
$= x^3 + y^3 + z^3 + 3x^2y + 3xy^2 + 3y^2z + 3yz^2 + 3z^2x + 3zx^2 + 6xyz$.

Ex. 2. Find the factors of
$$(b^3 + c^3)(b - c) + (c^3 + a^3)(c - a) + (a^3 + b^3)(a - b).$$

Denote the expression by E; then E is an expression involving a, which vanishes when $a = b$, and therefore contains $a - b$ as a factor [Art. 317]. Similarly it contains the factors $b - c$ and $c - a$; thus E contains $(b - c)(c - a)(a - b)$ as a factor.

Also since E is of the fourth degree, the remaining factor must be of the first degree; and since it is a symmetrical expression involving a, b, c, it must be of the form $m(a + b + c)$. [Art. 319.]

$$\therefore E = m(b - c)(c - a)(a - b)(a + b + c).$$

To obtain m we may give to a, b, c any values that we find most convenient; thus by putting $a = 0$, $b = 1$, $c = 2$, we find $m = 1$, and we have the required result.

NOTE. For further information on the subject of Symmetry, the reader may consult Hall and Knight's Higher Algebra, Chap. XXXIV.

EXAMPLES XXX. b.

Without actual division find the remainder when

1. $x^5 - 5x^2 + 5$ is divided by $x - 5$.
2. $3x^5 + 11x^4 + 90x^2 - 19x + 53$ is divided by $x + 5$.
3. $x^3 - 7x^2a + 8xa^2 + 15a^3$ is divided by $x + 2a$.

Without actual division show that

4. $32x^{10} - 33x^5 + 1$ is divisible by $x - 1$.
5. $3x^4 + 5x^3 - 13x^2 - 20x + 4$ is divisible by $x^2 - 4$.
6. $x^4 + 4x^3 - 5x^2 - 36x - 36$ is divisible by $x^2 - x - 6$.

Resolve into factors:

7. $x^3 - 6x^2 + 11x - 6$.
8. $x^3 - 5x^2 - 2x + 24$.
9. $x^3 + 9x^2 + 26x + 24$.
10. $x^3 - x^2 - 41x + 105$.
11. $x^3 - 39x + 70$.
12. $x^3 - 8x^2 - 31x - 22$.
13. $6x^3 + 7x^2 - x - 2$.
14. $6x^3 + x^2 - 19x + 6$.

MISCELLANEOUS THEOREMS.

Find the values of x which will make each of the following expressions a perfect square:

15. $x^4 + 6x^3 + 13x^2 + 13x - 1.$
16. $x^4 + 6x^3 + 11x^2 + 3x + 31.$

17. $x^4 - 2ax^3 + (a^2 + 2b)x^2 - 3abx + 2b^2.$

18. $4p^2x^4 - 4pqx^3 + (q^2 + 2p^2)x^2 - 5pqx + \dfrac{p^2}{2}.$

19. $\dfrac{a^2x^6}{9} - \dfrac{abx^4}{2} + \dfrac{2acx^3}{3} + \dfrac{9b^2x^2}{16} - \dfrac{5bcx}{2} + 6c^2.$

20. $x^4 + 2ax^3 + 3a^2x^2 + cx + d.$

Find the values of x which will make each of the following expressions a perfect cube:

21. $8x^3 - 36x^2 + 56x - 39.$
22. $\dfrac{x^6}{27} - \dfrac{a^2x^4}{3} + 4a^4x^2 - 28a^6.$

23. $m^3x^6 - 9m^2nx^4 + 39mn^2x^2 - 51n^3.$

24. If n be any positive integer, prove that $5^{2n} - 1$ is always divisible by 24.

Find the factors of

25. $a(b-c)^3 + b(c-a)^3 + c(a-b)^3.$

26. $a(b-c)^2 + b(c-a)^2 + c(a-b)^2 + 8abc.$

CHAPTER XXXI.

Indeterminate Equations of the First Degree.

321. In Art. 167 we saw that if the number of unknown quantities is greater than the number of independent equations, there will be an unlimited number of solutions, and the equations will be *indeterminate*. By introducing conditions, however, we can limit the number of solutions. When *positive integral values* of the unknown quantities are required, the equations are called **simple indeterminate equations**.

The introduction of this restriction enables us to express the solutions in a very simple form.

Ex. 1. Solve $7x + 12y = 220$ in positive integers.

Transpose and divide by the smaller coefficient; thus,

$$x = 31 - y + \frac{3 - 5y}{7};$$

$$\therefore x + y - 31 = \frac{3 - 5y}{7}.$$

Since x and y are to be integers, we must have

$$\frac{3 - 5y}{7} = \text{integer.}$$

Now multiplying the numerator *by such a number that the division of the coefficient of y may give a remainder of unity*, in this case 3, we have

$$\frac{9 - 15y}{7} = \text{integer};$$

that is, $\qquad 1 - 2y + \dfrac{2 - y}{7} = \text{integer};$

and therefore $\qquad \dfrac{2 - y}{7} = \text{integer.}$

INDETERMINATE EQUATIONS.

Let $$\frac{2-y}{7} = m, \text{ an integer};$$

then $$y = 2 - 7m \quad \ldots \ldots \quad (1).$$

Substituting this value in the original equation, we obtain

$$7x + 24 - 84m = 220;$$

$$\therefore x = 28 + 12m \quad \ldots \ldots \quad (2).$$

Equation (1) shows that m may be 0 or have *any negative integral value, but cannot have a positive integral value.*

Equation (2) shows in addition that m may be 0, but cannot have a *negative* integral value greater than 2. Thus the only *positive integral* values of x and y are obtained by placing $m = 0, -1, -2$.

The complete solution may be exhibited as follows:

$$m = 0, -1, -2,$$
$$x = 28, 16, 4,$$
$$y = 2, 9, 16.$$

Ex. 2. Solve $5x - 14y = 11$ in positive integers . . . . (1).
Proceeding as in Example 1, we obtain

$$x = 2 + 2y + \frac{4y+1}{5};$$

$$\therefore x - 2y - 2 = \frac{4y+1}{5} = \text{integer}.$$

Now multiplying the numerator by 4, we obtain

$$\frac{16y+4}{5} = \text{integer};$$

that is, $$3y + \frac{y+4}{5} = \text{integer}.$$

Let $$\frac{y+4}{5} = m, \text{ an integer};$$

$$\therefore y = 5m - 4,$$
and from (1), $$x = 14m - 9.$$

This is called the *general solution* of the equation, and by giving to m any positive integral value, we obtain an unlimited number of values for x and y: thus we have

$$m = 1, 2, 3, 4 \ldots$$
$$y = 1, 6, 11, 13 \ldots$$
$$x = 5, 19, 33, 47 \ldots$$

ALGEBRA.

From Examples 1 and 2 the student will see that there is a further limitation to the number of solutions according as the terms of the original equations are connected by $+$ or $-$. If we have two equations involving three unknown quantities, we can easily combine them so as to eliminate one of the unknown quantities, and can then proceed as above.

Ex. 3. In how many ways can $5 be paid in quarters and dimes?
Let $x =$ the number of quarters, y the number of dimes; then

$$\frac{x}{4} + \frac{y}{10} = 5,$$

or $$5x + 2y = 100;$$

$$\therefore 2x + \frac{x}{2} + y = 50;$$

$$\therefore \frac{x}{2} = p, \text{ an integer};$$

$$\therefore x = 2p,$$

and $$y = 50 - 5p.$$

Solutions are obtained by giving to p the values $1, 2, 3, \ldots, 9$; and therefore the number of ways is 9. If, however, the sum be paid *either* in quarters or dimes, p may also have the values 0 and 10. If $p = 0$, then $x = 0$, and the sum is paid entirely in dimes; if $p = 10$, then $y = 0$, and the sum is paid entirely in quarters. Thus if zero values of x and y are admissible, the number of ways is 11.

EXAMPLES XXXI.

Solve in positive integers:

1. $3x + 8y = 103$. 3. $7x + 12y = 152$. 5. $23x + 25y = 915$.
2. $5x + 2y = 53$.   4. $13x + 11y = 414$. 6. $41x + 47y = 2191$.

Find the general solution in positive integers, and the least values of x and y which satisfy the equations:

7. $5x - 7y = 3$.   9. $8x - 21y = 33$.   11. $19y - 23x = 7$.
8. $6x - 13y = 1$. 10. $17y - 13x = 0$. 12. $77y - 30x = 295$.

13. A farmer spends $752 in buying horses and cows; if each horse costs $37, and each cow $23, how many of each does he buy?

14. In how many ways can $100 be paid in dollars and half-dollars, including zero solutions?

15. Find a number which, being divided by 39, gives a remainder 16, and, by 56, a remainder 27. How many such numbers are there?

CHAPTER XXXII.

INEQUALITIES.

322. Any quantity a is said to be greater than another quantity b when $a-b$ is positive; thus 2 is greater than -3, because $2-(-3)$, or 5, is positive. Also b is said to be less than a when $b-a$ is negative; thus -5 is less than -2, because $-5-(-2)$, or -3, is negative.

In accordance with this definition, *zero must be regarded as greater than any negative quantity.*

323. The statement in algebraic language that one expression is greater or less than another is called an **inequality**.

324. The **sign of inequality** is $>$, the opening being placed towards the greater quantity. Thus, $a > b$ is read "a is greater than b."

325. The **first and second members** are the expressions on the left and right, respectively, of the sign of inequality.

326. Inequalities **subsist in the same sense** when corresponding members in each are the greater or the less. Thus, the inequalities $a > b$ and $7 > 5$ are said to subsist in the same sense.

In the present chapter, we shall suppose (unless the contrary is directly stated) that the letters always denote real and positive quantities.

327. Inequality Unchanged. *An inequality will still hold after each side has been increased, diminished, multiplied, or divided by the same positive quantity.*

For, if $a > b$, then it is evident that
$$a + c > b + c;$$
$$a - c > b - c;$$
$$ac > bc;$$
$$\frac{a}{c} > \frac{b}{c}.$$

328. Term Transposed. *In an inequality any term may be transposed from one side to the other if its sign be changed.*

If $$a - c > b,$$
by adding c to each side,
$$a > b + c.$$

329. Members Transposed. *If the sides of an inequality be transposed, the sign of inequality must be reversed.*

For if $a > b$, then evidently $b < a$.

330. Signs Changed. *If the signs of all the terms of an inequality be changed, the sign of inequality must be reversed.*

When $a > b$, then $a - b$ is positive, and $b - a$ is negative; that is, $-a - (-b)$ is negative, and therefore
$$-a < -b.$$

331. Negative Multiplier. *If the sides of an inequality be multiplied by the same negative quantity, the sign of inequality must be reversed.*

For, if $a > b$, then $-a < -b$, and therefore
$$-ac < -bc.$$

332. Inequalities Combined. *If inequalities, subsisting in the same sense, be either added, or multiplied together, the results will be unequal in the same sense.*

For if $a_1 > b_1$, $a_2 > b_2$, $a_3 > b_3 \cdots a_m > b_m$, it is clear that
$$a_1 + a_2 + a_3 + \cdots + a_m > b_1 + b_2 + b_3 + \cdots + b_m;$$
and
$$a_1 a_2 a_3 \cdots a_m > b_1 b_2 b_3 \cdots b_m.$$

INEQUALITIES.

333. It follows from the preceding article that if $a > b$,
then $$a^n > b^n,$$
and $$a^{-n} < b^{-n},$$
where n is any positive quantity.

334. The subtraction of two inequalities subsisting in the same sense does not *necessarily* give an inequality subsisting in the same sense.

335. The division of an inequality by another subsisting in the same sense does not *necessarily* give an inequality subsisting in the same sense.

The truth of these last statements is readily seen by considering the inequalities
$$5 > 4,$$
$$3 > 2.$$

Subtracting member for member would give $2 > 2$.
Dividing member by member would give $\frac{5}{3} > 2$.

Ex. 1. Find limit of x in the inequality
$$x - \frac{5}{3} > \frac{x}{5} + \frac{11}{15}.$$

Clearing of fractions, we have
$$15x - 25 > 3x + 11.$$
Transposing and combining,
$$12x > 36;$$
$$\therefore x > 3.$$

NOTE. The word "limit" is here used as meaning the range of values that x can have under the given conditions.

Ex. 2. If a, b, c denote positive quantities, prove that
$$a^2 + b^2 + c^2 > bc + ca + ab.$$
For
$$b^2 + c^2 > 2bc,$$
$$c^2 + a^2 > 2ca$$
$$a^2 + b^2 > 2ab.$$
Whence by addition $a^2 + b^2 + c^2 > bc + ca + ab.$

Ex. 3. If x may have any real value, find which is the greater, x^3+1 or x^2+x.

$$x^3+1-(x^2+x)=x^3-x^2-(x-1)=(x^2-1)(x-1)$$
$$=(x-1)^2(x+1).$$

Now $(x-1)^2$ is positive, hence

$$x^3+1 > \text{ or } < x^2+x$$

according as $x+1$ is positive or negative; that is, according as $x >$ or < -1.

If $x = -1$, the inequality becomes an equality.

EXAMPLES XXXII.

Find limit of x in the following three inequalities:

1. $11x - \dfrac{46}{3} < \dfrac{5x}{3} + 3\tfrac{1}{3}$.

2. $(x+2)(x+3) > (x-4)(x-5)$.

3. $x + 5ax - 5ab > b^2$ when $a > b$.

4. Prove that $(ab+xy)(ax+by) > 4abxy$.

5. Prove that $(b+c)(c+a)(a+b) > 8abc$.

6. Show that the sum of any real positive quantity and its reciprocal is never less than 2.

7. If $a^2+b^2 = 1$, and $x^2+y^2 = 1$, show that $ax+by < 1$.

8. If $a^2+b^2+c^2 = 1$, and $x^2+y^2+z^2 = 1$, show that
$$ax+by+cz < 1.$$

9. Which is the greater $\dfrac{a+b}{2}$ or $\dfrac{2ab}{a+b}$?

10. Show that $(x^2y+y^2z+z^2x)(xy^2+yz^2+zx^2) > 9x^2y^2z^2$.

11. Find which is the greater, $3ab^2$ or a^3+2b^3.

12. Prove that $a^3b + ab^3 < a^4 + b^4$.

13. Prove that $6abc < bc(b+c) + ca(c+a) + ab(a+b)$.

14. Show that $b^2c^2 + c^2a^2 + a^2b^2 > abc(a+b+c)$.

15. Show that $2(a^3+b^3+c^3) > bc(b+c) + ca(c+a) + ab(a+b)$.

NOTE. For further information on the subject of Inequalities the reader may consult Hall and Knight's Higher Algebra, Chapter XIX.

MISCELLANEOUS EXAMPLES V.

1. If $a = -1$, $b = 2$, $c = 0$, $d = 1$, $e = -3$, find the value of
$$\frac{a^3(d-c) - \sqrt{3ae} + ab}{d(c-a) - 2ad^2 + \sqrt[3]{4ab}}$$

2. Simplify $[3(a-b+c) - (a-b)(b-c) + \{(a+b-c)(3-b)\}]$.

3. Solve $3x - 4 - \dfrac{4(7x-9)}{15} = \dfrac{4}{5}\left(6 + \dfrac{x-1}{3}\right)$.

4. A man's age is four times the combined ages of his two sons, one of whom is three times as old as the other; in 24 years their combined ages will be 12 years less than their father's age: find their respective ages.

5. Simplify $\left(\dfrac{a^3b}{a^4b^{-3}}\right)^3 \div \left(\dfrac{\sqrt[4]{a^{-\frac{1}{2}}} \times \sqrt[3]{b^{-4}}}{a^3b^2}\right)^4$.

6. Solve (i.) $3\sqrt{x} - 1 = \dfrac{5}{3\sqrt{x} + 7} + 6$.
   (ii.) $\sqrt{8x + 17} - \sqrt{2x} = \sqrt{2x + 9}$.

7. Expand $(2a - 3b^2)^5$.

8. Simplify $\dfrac{1}{2x+1} - \dfrac{1}{3(x+\frac{1}{2})} - \dfrac{1}{6x+3}$.

9. If 3 is added to the numerator a certain fraction is increased by $\frac{1}{4}$; if 3 is taken from the denominator the fraction reduces to $\frac{1}{8}$: find the fraction.

10. Find the value of (i.) $3\sqrt{243} + 2\sqrt{\frac{27}{2}} + 4\sqrt{75} - \sqrt{\frac{5}{4}}$.
    (ii.) $\dfrac{\sqrt{3} + 3\sqrt{2}}{2 + \sqrt{6}}$.

11. Solve (i.) $\dfrac{3}{1-2x} + \dfrac{3}{1+2x} = 16$.
    (ii.) $\frac{4}{3}(x - 2x^2) + \frac{2}{3}(1 - 2x) = 5(\frac{1}{2} - x)$.

12. Find the limit of x in the inequality
$$(x-4)(x-5) > (x-2)(x-1).$$

13. The breadth of a rectangular space is 4 yards less than its length; the area of the space is 252 square yards: find the length of each side.

14. Solve (i.) $x^2 + y^2 = \frac{10}{9}$, $x + y = \frac{4}{3}$.
    (ii.) $2x^2 + xy = 4$, $3xy + 4y^2 = 22$.

15. Find the factors of (i.) $x^3 + 12x^2y - 45xy^2$.
    (ii.) $3x^2 - 31xy + 56y^2$.

16. Simplify $\dfrac{x+1}{2x^3-4x^2}+\dfrac{x-1}{2x^3+4x^2}-\dfrac{1}{x^2-4}$.

17. Solve $\dfrac{x+4}{3}+\dfrac{x+y}{5}=6,\ \dfrac{2y+6}{y}-\dfrac{2x+4}{x}=\dfrac{5}{y}$.

18. Find two numbers whose sum is 22, and the sum of their squares is 250.

19. Simplify $\left[\sqrt[5]{\dfrac{b^2 c^{-\frac{1}{2}}}{b^{-\frac{1}{2}}c^2}}\times\sqrt[3]{\dfrac{b^{-\frac{1}{2}}c}{c^{-\frac{1}{2}}b^1}}\right]^{-4}$.

20. Solve (i.) $\dfrac{x-1}{\sqrt{x}-1}=3+\dfrac{\sqrt{x}+1}{2}$.

   (ii.) $\sqrt{x^2+4x-4}+\sqrt{x^2+4x-10}=6$.

21. For what value of k will the equation $x^2+2(k+2)x+9k=0$ have equal roots?

22. Simplify the fractions:

   (i.) $\dfrac{a-x}{a^2-ax-\dfrac{(a-x)^2}{1-\dfrac{a}{x}}}$.   (ii.) $a-\dfrac{1}{b+\dfrac{1}{a+\dfrac{ab}{a-b}}}$.

23. B pays $28 more rent for a field than A; he has three-fourths of an acre more and pays $1.75 per acre more. C pays $72.50 more than A; he has six and one-fourth acres more, but pays 25 cents per acre less: find the size of the fields.

24. Solve (i.) $\dfrac{x+10}{x-5}-\dfrac{10}{x}=\dfrac{11}{6}$.

   (ii.) $\dfrac{2x}{x-4}+\dfrac{2x-5}{x-3}=\dfrac{25}{3}$.

25. Find the value of $\left(\dfrac{-1+\sqrt{-3}}{2}\right)^n+\left(\dfrac{-1-\sqrt{-3}}{2}\right)^n$ when $n=3$.

26. Rationalize the denominator of $\dfrac{\sqrt{2}}{\sqrt{2}+\sqrt{3}-\sqrt{5}}$ and find a factor which will rationalize $\sqrt[3]{3}-\sqrt{2}$.

27. Find the square root of (i.) $11+4\sqrt{6}$.

   (ii.) $-5+12\sqrt{-1}$.

28. Find the factors of (i.) $a^2-16-6ax+9x^2$.

   (ii.) $343x^6-27y^3$.

29. Solve (i.) $x^3 + y^3 = 18\sqrt{2}$, $x + y = 3\sqrt{2}$.

(ii.) $\dfrac{1}{x^3} + \dfrac{1}{y^3} = \dfrac{9}{8}$, $\dfrac{1}{x} + \dfrac{1}{y} = \dfrac{3}{2}$.

30. A rectangular field is 100 yards wide. If it were reduced to a square field by cutting an oblong piece off one end, the ratio of the piece cut off to the remainder would be less by $\frac{1}{10}$ than the ratio of the remainder to the original field. Find the length of the field.

31. Extract the square root of

(i.) $4x^4 + 12x^3y + 13x^2y^2 + 6xy^3 + y^4$.

(ii.) $\dfrac{x^2}{a^2} - \dfrac{2x}{a} + 3 - \dfrac{2a}{x} + \dfrac{a^2}{x^2}$.

32. Solve (i.) $2x + y + 3z = 13$,
$x + 2y + 4z = 17$,
$4x + 3y + 2z = 16$.

(ii.) $\dfrac{1}{1-x} + \dfrac{1}{\sqrt{x}+1} + \dfrac{1}{\sqrt{x}-1} = 0$.

33. Simplify the fractions

(i.) $\dfrac{1}{1-\dfrac{1}{2x}} \times \dfrac{1}{1-\dfrac{1}{1-x}} + \dfrac{x}{2+\dfrac{1}{x-1}}$.

(ii.) $\dfrac{2x^3 - 7x^2y + 5xy^2 - y^3}{2x^3 + 5x^2y - 5xy^2 + y^3}$.

34. Two places, A and B, are 168 miles apart, and trains leave A for B and B for A simultaneously; they pass each other at the end of one hour and fifty-two minutes, and the first reaches B half an hour before the second reaches A. Find the speed of each train.

35. Solve (i.) $3x^2 + 4x + 2\sqrt{x^2 + x + 3} = 30 - x^2$.

(ii.) $x^4 + y^4 = 706$, $x + y = 8$.

36. Form the equation whose roots are the squares of the sum and of the difference of the roots of

$$2x^2 + 2(m+n)x + m^2 + n^2 = 0.$$

37. Employ the method of Arts. 319, 320 in showing that

$$(a+b)^5 - a^5 - b^5 = 5ab(a+b)(a^2 + ab + b^2).$$

38. Solve $xy(3x+y) = 10$, $27x^3 + y^3 = 35$.

CHAPTER XXXIII.

Ratio, Proportion, and Variation.

336. Definition. Ratio is the relation which one quantity bears to another of the *same* kind, the comparison being made by considering what multiple, part, or parts, one quantity is of the other.

The ratio of A to B is usually written $A : B$. The quantities A and B are called the *terms* of the ratio. The first term is called the **antecedent**, the second term the **consequent**.

337. Ratios are measured by Fractions. To find what multiple or part A is of B, we divide A by B; hence the ratio $A : B$ may be measured by the fraction $\dfrac{A}{B}$, and we shall usually find it convenient to adopt this notation.

In order to compare two quantities, they must be expressed in terms of the same unit. Thus, the ratio of \$2 to 15 cents is measured by the fraction $\dfrac{2 \times 100}{15}$ or $\dfrac{40}{3}$.

NOTE. Since a ratio expresses the *number* of times that one quantity contains another, *every ratio is an abstract quantity.*

338. By Art. 136, $\quad \dfrac{a}{b} = \dfrac{ma}{mb};$

and thus the ratio $a : b$ is equal to the ratio $ma : mb$; that is, *the value of a ratio remains unaltered if the antecedent and the consequent are multiplied or divided by the same quantity.*

339. Comparison of Ratios. Two or more ratios may be compared by reducing their equivalent fractions to a common denominator. Thus, suppose $a : b$ and $x : y$ are two ratios. Now, $\dfrac{a}{b} = \dfrac{ay}{by}$, and $\dfrac{x}{y} = \dfrac{bx}{by}$; hence the ratio $a : b$ is greater than, equal to, or less than the ratio $x : y$ according as ay is greater than, equal to, or less than bx.

340. The ratio of two fractions can be expressed as a ratio of two integers. Thus, the ratio $\dfrac{a}{b} : \dfrac{c}{d}$ is measured by $\dfrac{a}{b} \div \dfrac{c}{d}$ or $\dfrac{ad}{bc}$; and is therefore equivalent to the ratio $ad : bc$.

341. If either, or both, of the terms of a ratio be a surd quantity, then no two integers can be found which will *exactly* measure their ratio. Thus, the ratio $\sqrt{2} : 1$ cannot be exactly expressed by any two integers.

342. If the ratio of any two quantities can be expressed exactly by the ratio of two integers, the quantities are said to be **commensurable**; otherwise, they are said to be **incommensurable**.

Although we cannot find two integers which will exactly measure the ratio of two incommensurable quantities, we can always find two integers whose ratio differs from that required by as small a quantity as we please.

Thus, $\qquad \dfrac{\sqrt{5}}{4} = \dfrac{2.236067\cdots}{4} = .559016 \cdots;$

and, therefore,

$$\dfrac{\sqrt{5}}{4} \text{ is} > \dfrac{559016}{1000000} \text{ and} < \dfrac{559017}{1000000};$$

and it is evident that by carrying the decimals further, any degree of approximation may be arrived at.

343. Ratios are **compounded** by multiplying together the fractions which denote them.

Ex. Find the ratio compounded of the three ratios

$$2a : 3b, \quad 6ab : 5c^2, \quad c : a.$$

The required ratio $= \dfrac{2a}{3b} \times \dfrac{6ab}{5c^2} \times \dfrac{c}{a} = \dfrac{4a}{5c}$.

344. When two identical ratios, $a : b$ and $a : b$, are compounded, the resulting ratio is $a^2 : b^2$, and is called the duplicate ratio of $a : b$. Similarly, $a^3 : b^3$ is called the **triplicate ratio** of $a : b$. Also, $a^{\frac{1}{2}} : b^{\frac{1}{2}}$ is called the **subduplicate ratio** of $a : b$.

EXAMPLES (1) The duplicate ratio of $2a : 3b$ is $4a^2 : 9b^2$.
(2) The subduplicate ratio of $49 : 25$ is $7 : 5$.
(3) The triplicate ratio of $2x : 1$ is $8x^3 : 1$.

345. A ratio is said to be a ratio of **greater inequality**, or of **less inequality**, according as the antecedent is *greater* or *less than* the consequent.

346. If to each term of the ratio $8 : 3$ we add 4, a new ratio $12 : 7$ is obtained, and we see that it is less than the former because $\frac{12}{7}$ is clearly less than $\frac{8}{3}$.

This is a particular case of a more general proposition which we shall now prove.

A ratio of greater inequality is diminished, and a ratio of less inequality is increased, by adding the same quantity to both its terms.

Let $\dfrac{a}{b}$ be the ratio, and let $\dfrac{a+x}{b+x}$ be the new ratio formed by adding x to both its terms.

Now $$\frac{a}{b} - \frac{a+x}{b+x} = \frac{ax - bx}{b(b+x)} = \frac{x(a-b)}{b(b+x)};$$

and $a - b$ is positive or negative according as a is greater or less than b.

Hence, if a is $> b$, $\dfrac{a}{b}$ is $> \dfrac{a+x}{b+x}$;

and if a is $< b$, $\dfrac{a}{b}$ is $< \dfrac{a+x}{b+x}$;

which proves the proposition.

Similarly, it can be proved that *a ratio of greater inequality is increased, and a ratio of less inequality is diminished, by taking the same quantity from both its terms.*

347. When two or more ratios are equal, many useful propositions may be proved by introducing a single symbol to denote each of the equal ratios.

RATIO, PROPORTION, AND VARIATION.

The proof of the following important theorem will illustrate the method of procedure.

If
$$\frac{a}{b} = \frac{c}{d} = \frac{e}{f} = \cdots,$$

each of these ratios $= \left(\dfrac{pa^n + qc^n + re^n + \cdots}{pb^n + qd^n + rf^n + \cdots}\right)^{\frac{1}{n}},$

where p, q, r, n, are any quantities whatever.

Let
$$\frac{a}{b} = \frac{c}{d} = \frac{e}{f} = \cdots = k;$$

then $\quad a = bk, \quad c = dk, \quad e = fk, \cdots;$

whence $\quad pa^n = pb^n k^n, \quad qc^n = qd^n k^n, \quad re^n = rf^n k^n, \cdots;$

$$\therefore \frac{pa^n + qc^n + re^n + \cdots}{pb^n + qd^n + rf^n + \cdots} = \frac{pb^n k^n + qd^n k^n + rf^n k^n + \cdots}{pb^n + qd^n + rf^n + \cdots} = k^n;$$

$$\therefore \left(\frac{pa^n + qc^n + re^n + \cdots}{pb^n + qd^n + rf^n + \cdots}\right)^{\frac{1}{n}} = k = \frac{a}{b} = \frac{c}{d} = \cdots.$$

By giving different values to p, q, r, n many particular cases of this general proposition may be deduced; or they may be proved independently by using the same method. For instance, if

$$\frac{a}{b} = \frac{c}{d} = \frac{e}{f}, \text{ each of these ratios} = \frac{a+c+e}{b+d+f};$$

a result which may be thus enunciated: *When a series of fractions are equal, each of them is equal to the sum of all the numerators divided by the sum of all the denominators.*

Ex. 1. If $\dfrac{x}{y} = \dfrac{3}{4}$ find the value of $\dfrac{5x-3y}{7x+2y}$.

$$\frac{5x-3y}{7x+2y} = \frac{\dfrac{5x}{y}-3}{\dfrac{7x}{y}+2} = \frac{\dfrac{15}{4}-3}{\dfrac{21}{4}+2} = \frac{3}{29}.$$

Ex. 2. Two numbers are in the ratio of $5:8$. If 9 be added to each they are in the ratio of $8:11$. Find the numbers.

Let the numbers be denoted by $5x$ and $8x$.

Then $\quad \dfrac{5x+9}{8x+9} = \dfrac{8}{11}; \quad \therefore x = 3.$

Hence the numbers are 15 and 24.

U

Ex. 3. If $A:B$ be in the duplicate ratio of $A+x:B+x$, prove that $x^2 = AB$.

By the given condition, $\left(\dfrac{A+x}{B+x}\right)^2 = \dfrac{A}{B}$;

$$\therefore B(A+x)^2 = A(B+x)^2,$$
$$A^2B + 2ABx + Bx^2 = AB^2 + 2ABx + Ax^2,$$
$$x^2(A-B) = AB(A-B);$$
$$\therefore x^2 = AB,$$

since $A-B$ is, by supposition, not zero.

EXAMPLES XXXIII. a.

Find the ratio compounded of

1. The duplicate ratio of $4:3$, and the ratio $27:8$.
2. The ratio $32:27$, and the triplicate ratio of $3:4$.
3. The subduplicate ratio of $25:36$, and the ratio $6:25$.
4. The triplicate ratio of $x:y$, and the ratio $2y^2:3x^2$.
5. The ratio $3a:4b$, and the subduplicate ratio of $b^4:a^4$.
6. If $x:y = 5:7$, find the value of $x+y:y-x$.
7. If $\dfrac{x}{y} = 3\tfrac{1}{3}$, find the value of $\dfrac{x-3y}{2x-5y}$.
8. If $b:a = 2:5$, find the value of $2a-3b:3b-a$.
9. If $\dfrac{a}{b} = \dfrac{3}{4}$, and $\dfrac{x}{y} = \dfrac{5}{7}$, find the value of $\dfrac{3ax-by}{4by-7ax}$.
10. If $7x-4y:3x+y = 5:13$, find the ratio $x:y$.
11. If $\dfrac{2a^2-3b^2}{a^2+b^2} = \dfrac{2}{41}$, find the ratio $a:b$.
12. If $2x:3y$ be in the duplicate ratio of $2x-m:3y-m$, prove that $m^2 = 6xy$.
13. If $P:Q$ be the subduplicate ratio of $P-x:Q-x$, prove that $x = \dfrac{PQ}{P+Q}$.
14. If $\dfrac{a}{b} = \dfrac{c}{d} = \dfrac{e}{f}$, prove that each of these ratios is equal to
$$\sqrt[3]{\dfrac{2a^2c + 3c^3e + 4e^2c}{2b^2d + 3d^3e + 4f^2d}}.$$

15. Two numbers are in the ratio of $3:4$, and if 7 be subtracted from each the remainders are in the ratio of $2:3$: find them.

16. What number must be taken from each term of the ratio $27:35$ that it may become $2:3$?

RATIO, PROPORTION, AND VARIATION.

17. What number must be added to each term of the ratio $37:29$ that it may become $8:7$?

18. If $\dfrac{p}{b-c} = \dfrac{q}{c-a} = \dfrac{r}{a-b}$, show that $p + q + r = 0$.

19. If $\dfrac{x}{b+c} = \dfrac{y}{c+a} = \dfrac{z}{a-b}$, show that $x - y + z = 0$.

20. If $\dfrac{a}{b} = \dfrac{c}{d} = \dfrac{e}{f}$, show that the square root of
$$\dfrac{a^6 b - 2\,c^5 e + 3\,a^4 c^3 e^2}{b^7 - 2\,d^5 f + 3\,b^4 c d^2 e^2} \text{ is equal to } \dfrac{ace}{bdf}.$$

21. Prove that the ratio $la + mc + ne : lb + md + nf$ will be equal to each of the ratios $a:b$, $c:d$, $e:f$, if these be all equal; and that it will be intermediate in value between the greatest and least of these ratios if they be not all equal.

22. If $\dfrac{bx - ay}{cy - az} = \dfrac{cx - az}{by - ax} = \dfrac{z + y}{x + z}$, then will each of these fractions be equal to $\dfrac{x}{y}$, unless $b + c = 0$.

23. If $\dfrac{2x - 3y}{3z + y} = \dfrac{z - y}{z - x} = \dfrac{x + 3z}{2y - 3x}$, prove that each of these ratios is equal to $\dfrac{x}{y}$; hence show that either $x = y$, or $z = x + y$.

PROPORTION.

348. Definition. Four quantities are said to be in **proportion** when the ratio of the first to the second is equal to the ratio of the third to the fourth. The four quantities are called **proportionals**, or the **terms** of the proportion. Thus, if $\dfrac{a}{b} = \dfrac{c}{d}$, then a, b, c, d are proportionals. This is expressed by saying that a is to b as c is to d, and the proportion is written

$$a : b :: c : d, \text{ or } a : b = c : d.$$

The terms a and d are called the *extremes*, b and c the *means*.

349. If four quantities are in proportion, the product of the extremes is equal to the product of the means.

Let a, b, c, d be the proportionals.

Then by definition $\dfrac{a}{b} = \dfrac{c}{d}$;

whence $ad = bc$.

Hence if any three terms of a proportion are given, the fourth may be found. Thus if a, c, d are given, then $b = \dfrac{ad}{c}$.

Conversely, if there are any four quantities, a, b, c, d, such that $ad = bc$, then a, b, c, d are proportionals; a and d being the extremes, b and c the means; or *vice versâ*.

350. Continued Proportion. Quantities are said to be in *continued proportion* when the first is to the second, as the second is to the third, as the third to the fourth; and so on. Thus $a, b, c, d, \cdots$ are in continued proportion when

$$\frac{a}{b} = \frac{b}{c} = \frac{c}{d} = \cdots.$$

If three quantities a, b, c are in continued proportion. then

$$a : b = b : c;$$
$$\therefore ac = b^2. \qquad \text{(Art. 349.)}$$

In this case b is said to be a **mean proportional** between a and c; and c is said to be a **third proportional** to a and b.

351. If three quantities are proportionals, the first is to the third in the duplicate ratio of the first to the second.

Let the three quantities be a, b, c; then $\dfrac{a}{b} = \dfrac{b}{c}$.

Now $\dfrac{a}{c} = \dfrac{a}{b} \times \dfrac{b}{c} = \dfrac{a}{b} \times \dfrac{a}{b} = \dfrac{a^2}{b^2}$;

that is, $a : c = a^2 : b^2$.

352. The products of the corresponding terms of two or more proportions form a proportion.

If $a : b = c : d$ and $e : f = g : h$, then will

$$ae : bf = cg : dh.$$

For $\dfrac{a}{b} = \dfrac{c}{d}$ and $\dfrac{e}{f} = \dfrac{g}{h}$; $\therefore \dfrac{ae}{bf} = \dfrac{cg}{dh}$, or $ae : bf = cg : dh$.

RATIO, PROPORTION, AND VARIATION.

Cor. If $\quad a:b=c:d,$
and $\quad b:x=d:y,$
then $\quad a:x=c:y.$

353. Transformations that may be made in a Proportion. If four quantities, a, b, c, d form a proportion, many other proportions may be deduced by the properties of fractions. The results of these operations are very useful, and some of them are often quoted by the annexed names borrowed from Geometry.

(1) If $a:b=c:d$, then $b:a=d:c.$ [Inversion.]

For $\dfrac{a}{b}=\dfrac{c}{d}$; therefore $1 \div \dfrac{a}{b}=1 \div \dfrac{c}{d}$;

that is $\quad\dfrac{b}{a}=\dfrac{d}{c}$;

or $\quad b:a=d:c.$

(2) If $a:b=c:d$, then $a:c=b:d.$ [Alternation.]

For $ad=bc$; therefore $\dfrac{ad}{cd}=\dfrac{bc}{cd}$;

that is, $\quad\dfrac{a}{c}=\dfrac{b}{d}$;

or $\quad a:c=b:d.$

(3) If $a:b=c:d$, then $a+b:b=c+d:d$ [Composition.]

For $\dfrac{a}{b}=\dfrac{c}{d}$; therefore $\dfrac{a}{b}+1=\dfrac{c}{d}+1$;

that is, $\quad\dfrac{a+b}{b}=\dfrac{c+d}{d}$;

or $\quad a+b:b=c+d:d.$

(4) If $a:b=c:d$, then $a-b:b=c-d:d.$ [Division.]

For $\dfrac{a}{b}=\dfrac{c}{d}$; therefore $\dfrac{a}{b}-1=\dfrac{c}{d}-1$;

that is, $\quad\dfrac{a-b}{b}=\dfrac{c-d}{d}$;

or $\quad a-b:b=c-d:d.$

(5) If $a:b=c:d$, then $a+b:a-b=c+d:c-d$.

[Composition and Division.]

For by (3) $\dfrac{a+b}{b}=\dfrac{c+d}{d}$; and by (4) $\dfrac{a-b}{b}=\dfrac{c-d}{d}$;

∴ by division, $\dfrac{a+b}{a-b}=\dfrac{c+d}{c-d}$;

or $a+b:a-b=c+d:c-d.$

Several other proportions may be proved in a similar way.

Ex. 1. If $a:b=c:d=e:f$, show that $2a^2+3c^2-5e^2:2b^2+3d^2-5f^2=ae:bf.$

Let $\dfrac{a}{b}=\dfrac{c}{d}=\dfrac{e}{f}=k$; then $a=bk,\ c=dk,\ e=fk$;

∴ $\dfrac{2a^2+3c^2-5e^2}{2b^2+3d^2-5f^2}=\dfrac{2b^2k^2+3d^2k^2-5f^2k^2}{2b^2+3d^2-5f^2}=k^2=\dfrac{a}{b}\times\dfrac{e}{f}=\dfrac{ae}{bf}$,

or $2a^2+3c^2-5e^2:2b^2+3d^2-5f^2=ae:bf.$

Ex. 2. If
$(3a+6b+c+2d)(3a-6b-c+2d)$
$=(3a-6b+c-2d)(3a+6b-c-2d),$
prove that a, b, c, d are in proportion.

We have $\dfrac{3a+6b+c+2d}{3a-6b+c-2d}=\dfrac{3a+6b-c-2d}{3a-6b-c+2d}.$ [Art. 349.]

Composition and division, $\dfrac{2(3a+c)}{2(6b+2d)}=\dfrac{2(3a-c)}{2(6b-2d)}.$

Alternation, $\dfrac{3a+c}{3a-c}=\dfrac{6b+2d}{6b-2d}.$

Again, composition and division, $\dfrac{6a}{2c}=\dfrac{12b}{4d}$;

whence $a:b=c:d.$

Ex. 3. Solve the equation $\dfrac{x^2+x-2}{x-2}=\dfrac{4x^2+5x-6}{5x-6}$

Division, $\dfrac{x^2}{x-2}=\dfrac{4x^2}{5x-6}$;

whence, dividing by x^2, which gives a solution $x=0$, [Art. 291, note.]

$\dfrac{1}{x-2}=\dfrac{4}{5x-6}$; whence, $x=-2$:

and therefore the roots are $0, -2.$

RATIO, PROPORTION, AND VARIATION.

EXAMPLES XXXIII. b.

Find a fourth proportional to

1. a, ab, c.
2. $a^2, 2ab, 3b^2$.
3. $x^3, xy, 5x^2y$.

Find a third proportional to

4. a^2b, ab.
5. $x^3, 2x^2$.
6. $3x, 6xy$.
7. $1, x$.

Find a mean proportional between

8. a^2, b^2.
9. $2x^3, 8x$.
10. $12ax^2, 3a^3$.
11. $27a^2b^3, 3b$.

If a, b, c be three proportionals, show that

12. $a : a+b = a-b : a-c$.
13. $(b^2 + bc + c^2)(ac - bc + c^2) = b^4 + ac^3 + c^4$.

If $a : b = c : d$, prove that

14. $ab + cd : ab - cd = a^2 + c^2 : a^2 - c^2$.
15. $a^2 + ac + c^2 : a^2 - ac + c^2 = b^2 + bd + d^2 : b^2 - bd + d^2$.
16. $a : b = \sqrt{3a^2 + 5c^2} : \sqrt{3b^2 + 5d^2}$.
17. $\dfrac{a}{p} + \dfrac{b}{q} : a = \dfrac{c}{p} + \dfrac{d}{q} : c$.
18. $\dfrac{b}{a} + \dfrac{a}{b} : \dfrac{ab}{a^2 + b^2} = \dfrac{d}{c} + \dfrac{c}{d} : \dfrac{cd}{c^2 + d^2}$.

Solve the equations:

19. $3x - 1 : 6x - 7 = 7x - 10 : 9x + 10$.
20. $x - 12 : y + 3 = 2x - 19 : 5y - 13 = 5 : 14$.
21. $\dfrac{x^2 - 2x + 3}{2x - 3} = \dfrac{x^2 - 3x + 5}{3x - 5}$.
22. $\dfrac{2x - 1}{x^2 + 2x - 1} = \dfrac{x + 4}{x^2 + x + 4}$.

23. If $(a + b - 3c - 3d)(2a - 2b - c + d)$
$= (2a + 2b - c - d)(a - b - 3c + 3d)$
prove that a, b, c, d are proportionals.

24. If a, b, c, d are in continued proportion, prove that
$$a : d = a^3 + b^3 + c^3 : b^3 + c^3 + d^3.$$

25. If b is a mean proportional between a and c, show that
$4a^2 - 9b^2$ is to $4b^2 - 9c^2$ in the duplicate ratio of a to b.

26. If a, b, c, d are in continued proportion, prove that $b + c$ is a mean proportional between $a + b$ and $c + d$.

27. If $a + b : b + c = c + d : d + a$,
prove that $a = c$, or $a + b + c + d = 0$.

VARIATION.

354. Definition. One quantity A is said to **vary directly** as another B, when the two quantities so depend upon each other that if B is changed, A is changed *in the same ratio*.

Note. The word *directly* is often omitted, and A is said to vary as B.

355. For instance: if a train moving at a uniform rate travels 40 miles in 60 minutes, it will travel 20 miles in 30 minutes, 80 miles in 120 minutes, and so on; the distance in each case being increased or diminished in the same ratio as the time. This is expressed by saying that when the velocity is uniform *the distance is proportional to the time*, or more briefly, *the distance varies as the time*.

356. The Symbol of Variation. The symbol $\propto$ is used to denote variation; so that $A \propto B$ is read "A varies as B."

357. If A varies as B, then A is equal to B multiplied by some constant quantity.

For suppose that $a_1, a_2, a_3 ..., b_1, b_2, b_3 ...$ are corresponding values of A and B.

Then, by definition, $\dfrac{A}{a_1} = \dfrac{B}{b_1}$; $\dfrac{A}{a_2} = \dfrac{B}{b_2}$; $\dfrac{A}{a_3} = \dfrac{B}{b_3}$; and so on;

$\therefore \dfrac{a_1}{b_1} = \dfrac{a_2}{b_2} = \dfrac{a_3}{b_3} = ...$, each being equal to $\dfrac{A}{B}$.

Hence $\dfrac{\text{any value of } A}{\text{the corresponding value of } B}$ is always the same;

that is, $\dfrac{A}{B} = m$, where m is constant.

$\therefore A = mB.$

358. Definition. One quantity A is said to **vary inversely** as another B when A varies *directly* as the reciprocal of B. [See Art. 176.]

Thus if A varies inversely as B, $A = \dfrac{m}{B}$, where m is constant.

The following is an illustration of inverse variation: If 6 men do a certain work in 8 hours, 12 men would do the same work in 4 hours, 2 men in 24 hours; and so on. Thus it appears that when the number of men is increased the time is proportionately decreased; and *vice versâ*.

359. Definition. One quantity is said to **vary jointly** as a number of others when it varies directly as their product.

Thus A varies jointly as B and C when $A = mBC$. For instance, the interest on a sum of money varies jointly as the principal, the time, and the rate per cent.

360. Definition. A is said to **vary directly as B and inversely as C** when A varies as $\dfrac{B}{C}$.

361. Grouping the principles of Arts. 357–360, we have
$A = mB$, if A varies directly as B,
$A = \dfrac{m}{B}$, if A varies inversely as B.
$A = mBC$, if A varies jointly as B and C,
$A = \dfrac{mB}{C}$, if A varies directly as B and inversely as C.

362. If *A* varies as *B* when *C* is constant, and *A* varies as *C* when *B* is constant, then will *A* vary as *BC* when both *B* and *C* vary.

The variation of A depends partly on that of B and partly on that of C. Suppose these latter variations to take place separately, each in its turn producing its own effect on A; also let a, b, c be certain simultaneous values of A, B, C.

1. *Let C be constant* while B changes to b; then A must undergo a partial change and will assume some intermediate value a', where

$$\frac{A}{a'} = \frac{B}{b} \quad \cdot \quad \cdot \quad \cdot \quad \cdot \quad \cdot \quad \cdot \quad (1).$$

13. If $5x - y \propto 10x - 11y$, and when $x = 7$, $y = 5$, find the equation between x and y.

14. If the cube of x varies as the square of y, and if $x = 3$ when $y = 5$, find the equation between x and y.

15. If the square root of a varies as the cube root of b, and if $a = 4$ when $b = 8$, find the equation between a and b.

16. If y varies inversely as the square of x, and if $y = 8$ when $x = 3$, find x when $y = 2$.

17. If $x \propto y + a$, where a is constant, and $x = 15$ when $y = 1$, and $x = 35$ when $y = 5$; find x when $y = 2$.

18. If $a + b \propto a - b$, prove that $a^2 + b^2 \propto ab$; and if $a \propto b$, prove that $a^2 - b^2 \propto ab$.

19. If y be the sum of three quantities which vary as x, x^2, x^3 respectively, and when $x = 1$, $y = 4$, when $x = 2$, $y = 8$, and when $x = 3$, $y = 18$, express y in terms of x.

20. Given that the area of a circle varies as the square of its radius, and that the area of a circle is 154 square feet when the radius is 7 feet: find the area of a circle whose radius is 10 feet 6 inches.

21. The area of a circle varies as the square of its diameter: prove that the area of a circle whose diameter is $2\frac{1}{2}$ inches is equal to the sum of the areas of two circles whose diameters are $1\frac{1}{2}$ and 2 inches respectively.

22. The pressure of wind on a plane surface varies jointly as the area of the surface, and the square of the wind's velocity. The pressure on a square foot is 1 pound when the wind is moving at the rate of 15 miles per hour: find the velocity of the wind when the pressure on a square yard is 16 pounds.

23. The value of a silver coin varies directly as the square of its diameter, while its thickness remains the same; it also varies directly as its thickness while its diameter remains the same. Two silver coins have their diameters in the ratio of 4 : 3. Find the ratio of their thicknesses if the value of the first be four times that of the second.

24. The volume of a circular cylinder varies as the square of the radius of the base when the height is the same, and as the height when the base is the same. The volume is 88 cubic feet when the height is 7 feet, and the radius of the base is 2 feet: what will be the height of a cylinder on a base of radius 9 feet, when the volume is 396 cubic feet?

CHAPTER XXXIV.

Arithmetical, Geometrical, and Harmonical Progressions.

364. A succession of quantities formed according to some fixed law is called a **series**. The separate quantities are called **terms** of the series.

ARITHMETICAL PROGRESSION.

365. DEFINITION. Quantities are said to be in **Arithmetical Progression** when they increase or decrease by a *common difference*.

Thus each of the following series forms an Arithmetical Progression:

$$3, 7, 11, 15, \cdots$$
$$8, 2, -4, -10, \cdots$$
$$a, a+d, a+2d, a+3d, \cdots.$$

The common difference is found by subtracting *any* term of the series from that which *follows* it. In the first of the above examples the common difference is 4; in the second it is -6; in the third it is d.

366. The Last, or nth Term, of an A. P. If we examine the series

$$a, a+d, a+2d, a+3d, \cdots$$

we notice that in any term the coefficient of d is always less by one than the number of the term in the series.

Thus the 3d term is $a+2d$;
6th term is $a+5d$;
20th term is $a+19d$;

and, generally, the pth term is $a+(p-1)d$.

If n be the number of terms, and if l denote the last, or nth term, we have
$$l = a+(n-1)d.$$

367. *The Sum of n Terms in A. P.* Let a denote the first term, d the common difference, and n the number of terms. Also let l denote the last term, and S the required sum; then
$$S = a + (a+d) + (a+2d) + \cdots + (l-2d) + (l-d) + l,$$
and, by writing the series in the reverse order,
$$S = l + (l-d) + (l-2d) + \cdots + (a+2d) + (a+d) + a.$$

Adding together these two series,
$$2S = (a+l) + (a+l) + (a+l) + \cdots \text{to } n \text{ terms} = n(a+l),$$
$$\therefore S = \frac{n}{2}(a+l) \quad \ldots \quad \ldots \quad (1).$$

Since
$$l = a + (n-1)d \quad \ldots \quad \ldots \quad (2);$$
$$\therefore S = \frac{n}{2}\{2a + (n-1)d\} \quad \ldots \quad (3).$$

368. In the last article we have three useful formulæ (1), (2), (3); in each of these any one of the letters may denote the unknown quantity when the three others are known.

Ex. 1. Find the 20th and 35th terms of the series
$$38, 36, 34, \cdots.$$
Here the common difference is $36-38$, or -2.
$\therefore$ the 20th term $= 38 + 19(-2) = 0$;
and the 35th term $= 38 + 34(-2) = -30$.

Ex. 2. Find the sum of the series $5\frac{1}{2}, 6\frac{3}{4}, 8, \cdots$ to 17 terms.
Here the common difference is $1\frac{1}{4}$; hence from (3)

The sum $= \frac{17}{2}\{2 \times \frac{11}{2} + 16 \times 1\frac{1}{4}\}$
$= \frac{17}{2}(11+20) = \frac{17 \times 31}{2} = 263\frac{1}{2}.$

ARITHMETICAL PROGRESSION.

Ex. 3. The first term of a series is 5, the last 45, and the sum 400 find the number of terms, and the common difference.

If n be the number of terms, then from (1),
$$400 = \frac{n}{2}(5 + 45);$$
whence $\qquad n = 16.$

If d be the common difference,
$$45 = \text{the 16th term} = 5 + 15d,$$
whence $\qquad d = 2\frac{2}{3}.$

EXAMPLES XXXIV. a

1. Find the 27th and 41st terms in the series 5, 11, 17, ...
2. Find the 13th and 109th terms in the series 71, 70, 69, ...
3. Find the 17th and 54th terms in the series 10, $11\frac{1}{2}$, 13, ...
4. Find the 20th and 13th terms in the series $-3, -2, -1, ...$
5. Find the 90th and 16th terms in the series $-4, 2.5, 9, ...$
6. Find the 37th and 89th terms in the series $-2.8, 0, 2.8, ...$

Find the last term in the following series:

7. 5, 7, 9, ... to 20 terms.
8. 7, 3, -1, ... to 15 terms.
9. $13\frac{1}{2}$, 9, $4\frac{1}{2}$, ... to 13 terms.
10. .6, 1.2, 1.8, ... to 12 terms.
11. 2.7, 3.4, 4.1, ... to 11 terms.
12. $x, 2x, 3x, $ ... to 25 terms.
13. $a - d, a + d, a + 3d,$ ... to 30 terms.
14. $2a - b, 4a - 3b, 6a - 5b,$ ... to 40 terms.

Find the last term and sum of the following series:

15. 14, 64, 114, ... to 20 terms.
16. 1, 1.2, 1.4, ... to 12 terms.
17. 9, 5, 1, ... to 100 terms.
18. $\frac{1}{4}, -\frac{1}{4}, -\frac{3}{4},$ ... to 21 terms.
19. $3\frac{1}{4}$, 1, $-1\frac{1}{4}$, ... to 19 terms.
20. 64, 96, 128, ... to 16 terms.

Find the sum of the following series:

21. 5, 9, 13, ... to 19 terms.
22. 12, 9, 6, ... to 23 terms.
23. 4, $5\frac{1}{4}$, $6\frac{1}{2}$, ... to 37 terms.
24. $10\frac{1}{2}$, 9, $7\frac{1}{2}$, ... to 94 terms.
25. $-3, 1, 5,$ ... to 17 terms.
26. 10, $9\frac{2}{3}$, $9\frac{1}{3}$, ... to 21 terms.
27. $p, 3p, 5p,$ ... to p terms.
28. $3a, a, -a,$ ... to a terms.
29. $a, 0, -a,$ ... to a terms.
30. $-3q, -q, q,$ ... to p terms.

Find the number of terms and the common difference when

31. The first term is 3, the last term 90, and the sum 1395.
32. The first term is 79, the last term 7, and the sum 1075.
33. The sum is 24, the first term 9, the last term -6.
34. The sum is 714, the first term 1, the last term $58\frac{1}{2}$.
35. The last term is -16, the sum -133, the first term -3.
36. The first term is -75, the sum -740, the last term 1.
37. The first term is a, the last $13\,a$, and the sum $49\,a$.
38. The sum is $-320\,x$, the first term $3\,x$, the last term $-35\,x$.

369. If *any two* terms of an Arithmetical Progression be given, the series can be completely determined; for the data furnish *two* simultaneous equations, the solution of which will give the first term and the common difference.

Ex. Find the series whose 7th and 51st terms are -3 and -355 respectively.

If a be the first term, and d the common difference,

$$-3 = \text{the 7th term} = a + 6\,d;$$
and $\quad\quad -355 = \text{the 51st term} = a + 50\,d;$
whence, by subtraction, $\quad -352 = 44\,d;$
$\therefore d = -8$; and, consequently, $a = 45$.

Hence the series is 45, 37, 29 ....

370. Arithmetic Mean. When three quantities are in Arithmetical Progression, the middle one is said to be the *arithmetic mean* of the other two.

Thus a is the arithmetic mean between $a - d$ and $a + d$.

371. To find the arithmetic mean between two given quantities.

Let a and b be the two quantities; A the arithmetic mean. Then, since a, A, b, are in A.P., we must have

$$b - A = A - a,$$

each being equal to the common difference;

whence $\quad\quad A = \dfrac{a+b}{2}.$

372. Between two given quantities it is always possible to insert any number of terms such that the whole series thus formed shall be in A. P.; and by an extension of the definition in Art. 370, the terms thus inserted are called the *arithmetic means*.

Ex. Insert 20 arithmetic means between 4 and 67.

Including the extremes the number of terms will be 22; so that we have to find a series of 22 terms in A. P., of which 4 is the first and 67 the last.

Let d be the common difference;

then $\qquad 67 =$ the 22d term, $= 4 + 21d$;

whence $d = 3$, and the series is 4, 7, 10, $\cdots$ 61, 64, 67;

and the required means are 7, 10, 13, $\cdots$ 58, 61, 64.

373. To insert a given number of arithmetic means between two given quantities.

Let a and b be the given quantities, m the number of means.

Including the extremes the number of terms will be $m + 2$; so that we have to find a series of $m + 2$ terms in A. P., of which a is the first, and b is the last.

Let d be the common difference;

then $\qquad b =$ the $(m + 2)$th term
$$= a + (m + 1)d;$$

whence $\qquad d = \dfrac{b - a}{m + 1};$

and the required *means* are

$$a + \frac{b-a}{m+1},\ a + \frac{2(b-a)}{m+1},\ \cdots\ a + \frac{m(b-a)}{m+1}$$

Ex. 1. Find the 30th term of an A. P. of which the first term is 17, and the 100th term $- 16$.

Let d be the common difference;

then $\qquad -16 =$ the 100th term
$$= 17 + 99d;$$
$$\therefore d = -\tfrac{1}{3}.$$

The 30th term $\qquad = 17 + 29(-\tfrac{1}{3}) = 7\tfrac{1}{3}.$

Ex. 2. The sum of three numbers in A. P. is 33, and their product is 792: find them.

Let a be the *middle* number, d the common difference; then the three numbers are $a - d, a, a + d$.

Hence $$a - d + a + a + d = 33;$$

whence $a = 11$; and the three numbers are $11 - d, 11, 11 + d$.

$$\therefore 11(11 + d)(11 - d) = 792,$$
$$121 - d^2 = 72,$$
$$d = \pm 7;$$

and the numbers are 4, 11, 18.

Ex. 3. How many terms of the series 24, 20, 16, ⋯ must be taken that the sum may be 72?

Let the number of terms be n; then, since the common difference is $20 - 24$, or -4, we have from (3), Art. 367,

$$72 = \frac{n}{2}\{2 \times 24 + (n - 1)(-4)\}$$
$$= 24n - 2n(n - 1);$$

whence $$n^2 - 13n + 36 = 0,$$
or $$(n - 4)(n - 9) = 0;$$
$$\therefore n = 4 \text{ or } 9.$$

Both of these values satisfy the conditions of the question; for if we write down the first 9 terms, we get 24, 20, 16, 12, 8, 4, 0, -4, -8; and, as the last five terms destroy each other, the sum of 9 terms is the same as that of 4 terms.

Ex. 4. An A. P. consists of 21 terms; the sum of the three terms in the middle is 129, and of the last three is 237; find the series.

Let a be the first term, and d the common difference. Then

$$237 = \text{the sum of the last three terms}$$
$$= a + 20d + a + 19d + a + 18d = 3a + 57d;$$

whence $$a + 19d = 79 \ldots \ldots \ldots (1).$$

Again, the three middle terms are the 10th, 11th, 12th;

hence $$129 = \text{the sum of the three middle terms}$$
$$= a + 9d + a + 10d + a + 11d = 3a + 30d;$$

whence $$a + 10d = 43 \ldots \ldots \ldots (2)$$

From (1) and (2), we obtain $d = 4, a = 3$.

Hence the series is 3, 7, 11, ⋯ 83.

ARITHMETICAL PROGRESSION.

EXAMPLES XXXIV. b.

Find the series in which

1. The 27th term is 186, and the 45th term 312.
2. The 5th term is 1, and the 31st term -77.
3. The 15th term is -25, and the 23rd term -41.
4. The 9th term is -11, and the 102nd term $-150\frac{1}{4}$.
5. The 15th term is 25, and the 29th term 46.
6. The 16th term is 214, and the 51st term 739.
7. The 3rd and 7th terms of an A. P. are 7 and 19; find the 15th term.
8. The 54th and 4th terms are -125 and 0; find the 42nd term.
9. The 31st and 2nd terms are $\frac{1}{2}$ and $7\frac{3}{4}$; find the 59th term.
10. Insert 15 arithmetic means between 71 and 23.
11. Insert 17 arithmetic means between 93 and 69.
12. Insert 14 arithmetic means between $-7\frac{1}{4}$ and $-2\frac{1}{5}$.
13. Insert 16 arithmetic means between 7.2 and -6.4.
14. Insert 36 arithmetic means between $8\frac{1}{2}$ and $2\frac{1}{4}$.

How many terms must be taken of

15. The series 42, 39, 36, ... to make 315?
16. The series $-16, -15, -14, \ldots$ to make -100?
17. The series $15\frac{2}{3}, 15\frac{1}{3}, 15, \ldots$ to make 129?
18. The series 20, $18\frac{3}{4}, 17\frac{1}{2}, \ldots$ to make $162\frac{1}{2}$?
19. The series $-10\frac{1}{2}, -9, -7\frac{1}{2}, \ldots$ to make -42?
20. The series $-6\frac{4}{5}, -6\frac{2}{5}, -6, \ldots$ to make $-52\frac{4}{5}$?
21. The sum of three numbers in A. P. is 39, and their product is 2184: find them.
22. The sum of three numbers in A. P. is 12, and the sum of their squares is 66: find them.
23. The sum of five numbers in A. P. is 75, and the product of the greatest and least is 161: find them.
24. The sum of five numbers in A. P. is 40, and the sum of their squares is 410: find them.
25. The 12th, 85th, and last terms of an A. P. are 38, 257, 395 respectively: find the number of terms.

GEOMETRICAL PROGRESSION.

374. Definition. Quantities are said to be in **Geometrical Progression** when they increase or decrease by a *constant factor*.

Thus each of the following series forms a Geometrical Progression:

$$3, 6, 12, 24, \ldots$$
$$1, -\tfrac{1}{3}, \tfrac{1}{9}, -\tfrac{1}{27}, \ldots$$
$$a, ar, ar^2, ar^3, \ldots$$

The constant factor is also called the *common ratio*, and it is found by dividing *any* term by that which immediately *precedes* it. In the first of the above examples the common ratio is 2; in the second it is $-\tfrac{1}{3}$; in the third it is r.

375. The Last, or nth Term, of a G. P. If we examine the series

$$a, ar, ar^2, ar^3, ar^4, \ldots$$

we notice that *in any term the index of r is always less by one than the number of the term in the series*.

Thus the 3rd term is ar^2;

the 6th term is ar^5;

the 20th term is ar^{19};

and, generally, the pth term is ar^{p-1}.

If n be the number of terms, and if l denote the last, or nth term, we have $l = ar^{n-1}$.

Ex. Find the 8th term of the series $-\tfrac{1}{3}, \tfrac{1}{2}, -\tfrac{3}{4}, \ldots$

The common ratio is $\tfrac{1}{2} \div (-\tfrac{1}{3})$, or $-\tfrac{3}{2}$;

$\therefore$ the 8th term $= -\tfrac{1}{3} \times (-\tfrac{3}{2})^7$

$= -\tfrac{1}{3} \times -\tfrac{2187}{128} = \tfrac{729}{128}$.

376. Geometric Mean. When three quantities are in Geometrical Progression the middle one is called the *geometric mean* between the other two.

377. **To find the geometric mean between two given quantities.**

Let a and b be the two quantities; G the geometric mean. Then since a, G, b are in G. P.,

$$\frac{b}{G} = \frac{G}{a},$$

each being equal to the common ratio;

$$\therefore G^2 = ab;$$

whence $\qquad G = \sqrt{ab}.$

378. **To insert a given number of geometric means between two given quantities.**

Let a and b be the given quantities, m the number of means.

There will be $m+2$ terms; so that we have to find a series of $m+2$ terms in G. P., of which a is the first and b the last.

Let r be the common ratio;

then $\quad b =$ the $(m+2)$th term $= ar^{m+1}$;

$$\therefore r^{m+1} = \frac{b}{a};$$

$$\therefore r = \left(\frac{b}{a}\right)^{\frac{1}{m+1}} \quad \ldots \ldots \quad (1).$$

Hence the required means are ar, ar^2, $\cdots ar^m$, where r has the value found in (1).

Ex. Insert 4 geometric means between 160 and 5.

We have to find 6 terms in G. P. of which 160 is the first, and 5 the sixth.

Let r be the common ratio;

then $\qquad 5 =$ the sixth term $= 160\, r^5$;

$$\therefore r^5 = \tfrac{1}{32};$$

whence, *by trial*, $\qquad r = \tfrac{1}{2};$

and the means are 80, 40, 20, 10.

379. The Sum of n Terms in G. P. Let a be the first term, r the common ratio, n the number of terms, and S the sum required. Then

$$S = a + ar + ar^2 + \cdots + ar^{n-2} + ar^{n-1};$$

multiplying every term by r, we have

$$rS = ar + ar^2 + \cdots + ar^{n-2} + ar^{n-1} + ar^n.$$

Hence by subtraction,

$$rS - S = ar^n - a;$$
$$\therefore (r-1)S = a(r^n - 1);$$
$$\therefore S = \frac{a(r^n - 1)}{r - 1} \quad \ldots \ldots \quad (1).$$

Changing the signs in numerator and denominator

$$S = \frac{a(1 - r^n)}{1 - r} \quad \ldots \ldots \quad (2).$$

NOTE. It will be found convenient to remember both forms given above for S, using (2) in all cases except when r is *positive and greater than* 1.

Since $ar^{n-1} = l$, it follows that $ar^n = rl$, and formula (1) may be written

$$S = \frac{rl - a}{r - 1}.$$

Ex. 1. Sum the series 81, 54, 36, ⋯ to 9 terms.

The common ratio $= \frac{54}{81} = \frac{2}{3}$, which is less than 1;

hence the sum $= \dfrac{81\{1 - (\frac{2}{3})^9\}}{1 - \frac{2}{3}} = 243\{1 - (\frac{2}{3})^9\}$

$= 243 - \frac{512}{81} = 236\frac{56}{81}.$

Ex. 2. Sum the series $\frac{2}{3}, -1, \frac{3}{2}, \cdots$ to 7 terms.

The common ratio $= -\frac{3}{2}$; hence by formula (2)

the sum $= \dfrac{\frac{2}{3}\{1 - (-\frac{3}{2})^7\}}{1 + \frac{3}{2}} = \dfrac{\frac{2}{3}\{1 + \frac{2187}{128}\}}{\frac{5}{2}}$

$= \frac{2}{3} \times \frac{2315}{128} \times \frac{2}{5} = \frac{463}{96}.$

EXAMPLES XXXIV. c.

1. Find the 5th and 8th terms of the series 3, 6, 12, ⋯.
2. Find the 10th and 16th terms of the series 256, 128, 64, ⋯.
3. Find the 7th and 11th terms of the series 64, −32, 16, ⋯.

GEOMETRICAL PROGRESSION.

4. Find the 8th and 12th terms of the series 81, -27, 9, $\cdots$.

5. Find the 14th and 7th terms of the series $\frac{1}{64}, \frac{1}{32}, \frac{1}{16}, \cdots$.

6. Find the 4th and 8th terms of the series .008, .04, .2, $\cdots$.

Find the last term in the following series:

7. 2, 4, 8, $\cdots$ to 9 terms.

8. 2, -6, 18, $\cdots$ to 8 terms.

9. 2, 3, $4\frac{1}{2}$, $\cdots$ to 6 terms.

10. 3, -3^2, 3^3, $\cdots$ to $2n$ terms.

11. $x, x^3, x^5, \cdots$ to p terms.

12. $x, 1, \dfrac{1}{x}, \cdots$ to 30 terms.

13. Insert 3 geometric means between 486 and 6.

14. Insert 4 geometric means between $\frac{1}{4}$ and 128.

15. Insert 6 geometric means between 56 and $-\frac{7}{16}$.

16. Insert 5 geometric means between $\frac{32}{81}$ and $4\frac{1}{2}$.

Find the last term and the sum of the following series:

17. 3, 6, 12, $\cdots$ to 8 terms.

18. 6, -18, 54, $\cdots$ to 6 terms.

19. 64, 32, 16, $\cdots$ to 10 terms.

20. 8.1, 2.7, .9, $\cdots$ to 7 terms.

21. $\frac{1}{72}, \frac{1}{24}, \frac{1}{8}, \cdots$ to 8 terms.

22. $4\frac{1}{2}, 1\frac{1}{2}, \frac{1}{2}, \cdots$ to 9 terms.

Find the sum of the series:

23. 3, -1, $\frac{1}{3}$, $\cdots$ to 6 terms.

24. $\frac{1}{2}, \frac{1}{3}, \frac{2}{9}, \cdots$ to 7 terms.

25. $-\frac{2}{5}, \frac{1}{2}, -\frac{5}{8}, \cdots$ to 6 terms.

26. 1, $-\frac{1}{2}, \frac{1}{4}, \cdots$ to 12 terms.

27. 9, -6, 4, $\cdots$ to 7 terms.

28. $\frac{3}{4}, -\frac{1}{8}, \frac{1}{24}, \cdots$ to 8 terms.

29. 1, 3, 3^2, $\cdots$ to p terms.

30. 2, -4, 8, $\cdots$ to $2p$ terms.

31. $\dfrac{1}{\sqrt{3}}, 1, \dfrac{3}{\sqrt{3}}, \cdots$ to 8 terms.

32. $\sqrt{a}, \sqrt{a^3}, \sqrt{a^5}, \cdots$ to a terms.

33. $\dfrac{1}{\sqrt{2}}, -2, \dfrac{8}{\sqrt{2}}, \cdots$ to 7 terms.

34. $\sqrt{2}, \sqrt{6}, 3\sqrt{2}, \cdots$ to 12 terms.

380. Infinite Geometrical Series. Consider the series

$$1, \frac{1}{2}, \frac{1}{2^2}, \frac{1}{2^3}, \cdots.$$

The sum to n terms $= \dfrac{1-\dfrac{1}{2^n}}{1-\dfrac{1}{2}} = 2\left(1-\dfrac{1}{2^n}\right) = 2-\dfrac{1}{2^{n-1}}$.

From this result it appears that however many terms be taken the sum of the above series is always less than 2. Also we see that, by making n sufficiently large, we can make the fraction $\dfrac{1}{2^{n-1}}$ as small as we please. Thus by taking a sufficient number of terms the sum can be made to differ by as little as we please from 2.

In the next article a more general case is discussed.

381. Sum to Infinity. From Art. 379 we have

$$S = \frac{a(1-r^n)}{1-r} = \frac{a}{1-r} - \frac{ar^n}{1-r}.$$

Suppose r is a proper fraction; then the greater the value of n the smaller is the value of r^n, and consequently of $\dfrac{ar^n}{1-r}$; and therefore by making n sufficiently large, we can make the sum of n terms of the series differ from $\dfrac{a}{1-r}$ by as small a quantity as we please.

This result is usually stated thus: *the sum of an infinite number of terms of a decreasing Geometrical Progression is* $\dfrac{a}{1-r}$; or more briefly, *the sum to infinity is* $\dfrac{a}{1-r}$.

382. Recurring decimals furnish a good illustration of Infinite Geometrical Progressions.

Ex. Find the value of $.4\dot{2}\dot{3}$.

$$.4\dot{2}\dot{3} = .4232323\cdots = \frac{4}{10} + \frac{23}{1000} + \frac{23}{100000} + \cdots = \frac{4}{10} + \frac{23}{10^3} + \frac{23}{10^5} + \cdots$$

$$= \frac{4}{10} + \frac{23}{10^3}\left(1 + \frac{1}{10^2} + \frac{1}{10^4} + \cdots\right) = \frac{4}{10} + \frac{23}{10^3} \cdot \frac{1}{1 - \frac{1}{10^2}}$$

$$= \frac{4}{10} + \frac{23}{10^3} \cdot \frac{100}{99} = \frac{4}{10} + \frac{23}{990} = \frac{419}{990},$$

which agrees with the value found by the usual arithmetical rule.

EXAMPLES XXXIV. d.

Sum to infinity the following series:

1. $9, 6, 4, \cdots$
2. $12, 6, 3, \cdots$
3. $\frac{1}{2}, \frac{1}{4}, \frac{1}{8}, \cdots$
4. $\frac{1}{2}, -\frac{1}{4}, \frac{1}{8}, \cdots$
5. $\frac{1}{3}, \frac{2}{9}, \frac{4}{27}, \cdots$
6. $\frac{3}{5}, -1, \frac{5}{3}, \cdots$
7. $.9, .03, .001, \cdots$
8. $.8, -.4, .2, \cdots$

Find by the method of Art. 382, the value of

9. $.\dot{3}.$ 10. $.1\dot{6}.$ 11. $.\dot{2}\dot{4}.$ 12. $.3\dot{7}\dot{8}.$ 13. $.\dot{0}3\dot{7}.$

HARMONICAL PROGRESSION.

Find the series in which

14. The 10th term is 320 and the 6th term 20.
15. The 5th term is $\frac{27}{16}$ and the 9th term is $\frac{1}{3}$.
16. The 7th term is 625 and the 4th term -5.
17. The 3d term is $\frac{2}{15}$ and the 6th term $-4\frac{1}{2}$.
18. Divide 183 into three parts in G. P. such that the sum of the first and third is $2\frac{1}{10}$ times the second.
19. Show that the product of any odd number of consecutive terms of a G. P. will be equal to the nth power of the middle term, n being the number of terms.
20. The first two terms of an infinite G. P. are together equal to 1, and every term is twice the sum of all the terms which follow. Find the series.

Sum the following series:

21. $y^2 + 2b$, $y^4 + 4b$, $y^6 + 6b$, $\cdots$ to n terms.
22. $\dfrac{3 + 2\sqrt{2}}{3 - 2\sqrt{2}}$, 1, $\dfrac{3 - 2\sqrt{2}}{3 + 2\sqrt{2}}$, $\cdots$ to infinity.
23. $\sqrt{\frac{3}{2}}$, $\frac{1}{3}\sqrt{2}$, $\frac{2}{9}\sqrt{\frac{2}{3}}$, to infinity.
24. $2n - \frac{1}{2}$, $4n + \frac{1}{4}$, $6n - \frac{1}{8}$, $\cdots$ to $2n$ terms.
25. The sum of four numbers in G. P. is equal to the common ratio plus 1, and the first term is $\frac{1}{17}$. Find the numbers.
26. The difference between the first and second of four numbers in G. P. is 96, and the difference between the third and fourth is 6. Find the numbers.
27. The sum of $225 was divided among four persons in such a manner that the shares were in G. P., and the difference between the greatest and least was to the difference between the means as 21 to 6. Find the share of each.
28. The sum of three numbers in G. P. is 13, and the sum of their reciprocals is $\frac{13}{9}$. Find the numbers.

HARMONICAL PROGRESSION.

383. Definition. Three quantities, a, b, c, are said to be in **Harmonical Progression** when $\dfrac{a}{c} = \dfrac{a - b}{b - c}$.

Any number of quantities are said to be in Harmonical Progression when every three consecutive terms are in Harmonical Progression.

384. **The Reciprocals of Quantities in Harmonical Progression are in Arithmetical Progression.**

By definition, if a, b, c are in Harmonical Progression,

$$\frac{a}{c} = \frac{a-b}{b-c};$$

$$\therefore a(b-c) = c(a-b),$$

dividing every term by abc,

$$\frac{1}{c} - \frac{1}{b} = \frac{1}{b} - \frac{1}{a},$$

which proves the proposition. We may therefore define an Harmonical Progression as *a series of quantities the reciprocals of which are in Arithmetical Progression.*

385. Solution of Questions in H. P. Harmonical properties are chiefly interesting because of their importance in Geometry and in the Theory of Sound: in Algebra the proposition just proved is the only one of any importance. There is no general formula for the sum of any number of quantities in Harmonical Progression. Questions in H. P. are generally solved by inverting the terms, and making use of the properties of the corresponding A. P.

Ex. The 12th term of an H. P is $\frac{1}{5}$, and the 19th term is $\frac{3}{22}$: find the series.

Let a be the first term, d the common difference of the corresponding A. P.; then

$$5 = \text{the 12th term} = a + 11d;$$

and $\qquad \frac{22}{3} = \text{the 19th term} = a + 18d;$

whence $\qquad d = \frac{1}{3},\ a = \frac{4}{3}.$

Hence the Arithmetical Progression is $\frac{4}{3},\ \frac{5}{3},\ 2,\ \frac{7}{3},\ \dots$

and the Harmonical Progression is $\frac{3}{4},\ \frac{3}{5},\ \frac{1}{2},\ \frac{3}{7},\ \dots.$

386. Harmonic Mean. When three quantities are in Harmonic Progression the middle one is said to be the *Harmonic Mean* of the other two.

387. To find the harmonic mean between two given quantities.

Let a, b be the two quantities, H their harmonic mean; then $\dfrac{1}{a}, \dfrac{1}{H}, \dfrac{1}{b}$ are in A. P.;

$$\therefore \frac{1}{H} - \frac{1}{a} = \frac{1}{b} - \frac{1}{H},$$

$$\frac{2}{H} = \frac{1}{a} + \frac{1}{b},$$

$$H = \frac{2ab}{a+b}.$$

388. Relation between the Arithmetic, Geometric, and Harmonic Means. If A, G, H be the arithmetic, geometric, and harmonic means between a and b, we have proved

$$A = \frac{a+b}{2} \quad \ldots \ldots \quad (1).$$

$$G = \sqrt{ab}. \quad \ldots \ldots \quad (2).$$

$$H = \frac{2ab}{a+b} \quad \ldots \ldots \quad (3).$$

Therefore
$$AH = \frac{a+b}{2} \cdot \frac{2ab}{a+b}$$
$$= ab = G^2;$$

that is, G is the geometric mean between A and H.

389. Miscellaneous Questions in the Progressions. Miscellaneous questions in the Progressions afford scope for much skill and ingenuity, the solution being often very neatly effected by some special artifice. The student will find the following hints useful.

1. If the same quantity be added to, or subtracted from, all the terms of an A. P., the resulting terms will form an A. P., with the same common difference as before. [Art. 365.]

2. If all the terms of an A. P. be multiplied or divided by the same quantity, the resulting terms form an A. P., but with a new common difference. [Art. 365.]

3. If all the terms of a G. P. be multiplied or divided by the same quantity, the resulting terms form a G. P. with the same common ratio as before. [Art. 374.]

4. If $a, b, c, d \cdots$ be in G. P., they are also in *continued proportion*, since by definition

$$\frac{a}{b} = \frac{b}{c} = \frac{c}{d} = \cdots = \frac{1}{r},$$

Conversely, a series of quantities in continued proportion may be represented by $x, xr, xr^2, \cdots$.

Ex. 1. Find three quantities in G. P. such that their product is 343, and their sum $30\frac{1}{3}$.

Let $\dfrac{a}{r}, a, ar$ be the three quantities;

then we have $\qquad \dfrac{a}{r} \times a \times ar = 343 \ \ldots \ldots \ldots$ (1),

and $\qquad a\left(\dfrac{1}{r} + 1 + r\right) = \dfrac{91}{3} \ \ldots \ldots \ldots$ (2).

From (1) $\qquad a^3 = 343;$

$\qquad \therefore a = 7;$

hence from (2) $\qquad 7(1 + r + r^2) = \tfrac{91}{3} r.$

Whence we obtain $\qquad r = 3, \text{ or } \tfrac{1}{3};$

and the numbers are $\tfrac{7}{3}, 7, 21.$

Ex. 2. If a, b, c be in H. P., prove that $\dfrac{a}{b+c}, \dfrac{b}{c+a}, \dfrac{c}{a+b}$ are also in H. P.

Since $\dfrac{1}{a}, \dfrac{1}{b}, \dfrac{1}{c}$ are in A. P.,

$\dfrac{a+b+c}{a}, \dfrac{a+b+c}{b}, \dfrac{a+b+c}{c}$ are in A. P.;

$\therefore 1 + \dfrac{b+c}{a}, 1 + \dfrac{a+c}{b}, 1 + \dfrac{a+b}{c}$ are in A. P.;

$\therefore \dfrac{b+c}{a}, \dfrac{a+c}{b}, \dfrac{a+b}{c}$ are in A. P.;

$\therefore \dfrac{a}{b+c}, \dfrac{b}{c+a}, \dfrac{c}{a+b}$ are in H. P.

THE PROGRESSIONS.

Ex. 3. The nth term of an A. P. is $\frac{n}{5}+2$: find the sum of 49 terms.

Let a be the first term, and l the last; then by putting $n=1$, and $n=49$ respectively, we obtain

$$a = \tfrac{1}{5} + 2, \quad l = \tfrac{49}{5} + 2;$$

$$\therefore S = \frac{n}{2}(a+l) = \tfrac{49}{2}\left(\tfrac{50}{5} + 4\right)$$

$$= \tfrac{49}{2} \times 14 = 343.$$

Ex. 4. If a, b, c, d, e be in G. P., prove that $b + d$ is the geometric mean between $a + c$ and $c + e$.

Since a, b, c, d, e are in continued proportion,

$$\frac{a}{b} = \frac{b}{c} = \frac{c}{d} = \frac{d}{e};$$

$\therefore$ each ratio $\quad = \dfrac{a+c}{b+d} = \dfrac{b+d}{c+e}.$ [Art. 347.]

Whence $(b+d)^2 = (a+c)(c+e)$.

EXAMPLES XXXIV. e.

1. Find the 6th term of the series $4, 2, 1\tfrac{1}{3}, \ldots$.
2. Find the 21st term of the series $2\tfrac{1}{2}, 1\tfrac{13}{17}, 1\tfrac{9}{13}, \ldots$.
3. Find the 8th term of the series $1\tfrac{1}{3}, 1\tfrac{11}{17}, 2\tfrac{2}{13}, \ldots$.
4. Find the nth term of the series $3, 1\tfrac{1}{2}, 1, \ldots$.

Find the series in which

5. The 15th term is $\tfrac{1}{25}$, and the 23d term is $\tfrac{1}{41}$.
6. The 2d term is 2, and the 31st term is $\tfrac{2}{31}$.
7. The 39th term is $\tfrac{1}{17}$, and the 54th term is $\tfrac{1}{25}$.

Find the harmonic mean between

8. 2 and 4.
9. 1 and 13.
10. $\tfrac{1}{4}$ and $\tfrac{1}{10}$.
11. $\dfrac{1}{a}$ and $\dfrac{1}{b}$.
12. $\dfrac{1}{x+y}$ and $\dfrac{1}{x-y}$.
13. $x+y$ and $x-y$.
14. Insert two harmonic means between 4 and 12.
15. Insert three harmonic means between $2\tfrac{2}{5}$ and 12.
16. Insert four harmonic means between 1 and 6.

17. If G be the geometric mean between two quantities A and B, show that the ratio of the arithmetic and harmonic means of A and G is equal to the ratio of the arithmetic and harmonic means of G and B.

18. To each of three consecutive terms of a G. P., the second of the three is added. Show that the three resulting quantities are in H. P.

Sum the following series:

19. $1 + 1\frac{3}{4} + 3\frac{1}{16} + \cdots$ to 6 terms.

20. $1 + 1\frac{3}{4} + 2\frac{1}{2} + \cdots$ to 6 terms.

21. $(2a + x) + 3a + (4a - x) + \cdots$ to p terms.

22. $1\frac{1}{5} - 1\frac{1}{5} + \frac{4}{5} - \cdots$ to 8 terms.

23. $1\frac{4}{5} + 1\frac{1}{5} + \frac{3}{5} + \cdots$ to 12 terms.

24. If $x - a$, $y - a$, and $z - a$ be in G.P., prove that $2(y - a)$ is the harmonic mean between $y - x$ and $y - z$.

25. If a, b, c, d be in A. P., a, e, f, d in G. P., a, g, h, d in H. P. respectively; prove that $ad = ef = bh = cg$.

26. If a^2, b^2, c^2 be in A. P., prove that $b+c$, $c+a$, $a+b$ are in H. P.

CHAPTER XXXV.

Permutations and Combinations.

390. Each of the *arrangements* which can be made by taking some or all of a number of things is called a **permutation**.

Each of the *groups* or *selections* which can be made by taking some or all of a number of things is called a **combination**.

Thus the *permutations* which can be made by taking the letters a, b, c, d two at a time are twelve in number; namely,

$$ab,\ ac,\ ad,\ bc,\ bd,\ cd,$$
$$ba,\ ca,\ da,\ cb,\ db,\ dc;$$

each of these presenting a different *arrangement* of two letters.

The *combinations* which can be made by taking the letters a, b, c, d two at a time are six in number; namely,

$$ab,\ ac,\ ad,\ bc,\ bd,\ cd;$$

each of these presenting a different *selection* of two letters.

From this it appears that in forming *combinations* we are only concerned with the *number* of things each selection contains; whereas in forming *permutations* we have also to consider the *order* of the things which make up each arrangement; for instance, if from four letters a, b, c, d we make a selection of three, such as abc, this single combination admits of being arranged in the following ways:

$$abc,\ acb,\ bca,\ bac,\ cab,\ cba,$$

and so gives rise to six different permutations.

391. Fundamental Principle. Before discussing the general propositions of this chapter the following important principle should be carefully noticed.

If one operation can be performed in m ways, and (when it has been performed in any one of these ways) a second operation can then be performed in n ways; the number of ways of performing the two operations will be m × n.

If the first operation be performed in *any one* way, we can associate with this any of the n ways of performing the second operation; and thus we shall have n ways of performing the two operations without considering more than *one* way of performing the first; and so, corresponding to *each* of the m ways of performing the first operation, we shall have n ways of performing the two; hence the product $m \times n$ represents the total number of ways in which the two operations can be performed.

Ex. Suppose there are 10 steamers plying between New York and Liverpool: in how many ways can a man go from New York to Liverpool and return by a different steamer?

There are *ten* ways of making the first passage; and with each of these there is a choice of *nine* ways of returning (since the man is not to come back by the same steamer); hence the number of ways of making the two journeys is 10×9, or 90.

This principle may easily be extended to the case in which there are more than two operations each of which can be performed in a given number of ways.

Ex. Three travellers arrive at a town where there are four hotels; in how many ways can they take up their quarters, each at a different hotel?

The first traveller has choice of four hotels, and when he has made his selection in any one way, the second traveller has a choice of three; therefore the first two can make their choice in 4×3 ways; and with any one such choice the third traveller can select his hotel in 2 ways; hence the required number of ways is $4 \times 3 \times 2$, or 24.

392. To find the number of permutations of n dissimilar things taken r at a time.

This is the same thing as finding the number of ways in

which we can fill r places when we have n different things at our disposal.

The first place may be filled in n ways, for any one of the n things may be taken; when it has been filled in any one of these ways, the second place can then be filled in $n-1$ ways; and since each way of filling the first place can be associated with each way of filling the second, the number of ways in which the first two places can be filled is given by the product $n(n-1)$. And when the first two places have been filled in any way, the third place can be filled in $n-2$ ways. And reasoning as before, the number of ways in which three places can be filled is $n(n-1)(n-2)$.

Proceeding thus, and noticing that *a new factor is introduced with each new place filled*, and that at any stage *the number of factors is the same as the number of places filled*, we shall have the number of ways in which r places can be filled equal to

$$n(n-1)(n-2)\cdots \text{to } r \text{ factors.}$$

We here see that each factor is formed by taking from n a number *one less* than that which applies to the place filled by that factor; hence the rth factor is $n-(r-1)$, or $n-r+1$.

Therefore the number of permutations of n things taken r at a time is

$$n(n-1)(n-2)\cdots(n-r+1).$$

COR. The number of permutations of n things taken all at a time is

$$n(n-1)(n-2)\cdots \text{to } n \text{ factors,}$$

or $\qquad n(n-1)(n-2)\cdots 3\cdot 2\cdot 1.$

It is usual to denote this product by the symbol $\lfloor n$, which is read "factorial n." Also $n!$ is sometimes used for $\lfloor n$.

393. We shall in future denote the number of permutations of n things taken r at a time by the symbol ^nP_r, so that

$$^nP_r = n(n-1)(n-2)\cdots(n-r+1);$$

also $\qquad ^nP_n = \lfloor n.$

322 ALGEBRA.

In working numerical examples it is useful to notice that the suffix in the symbol ^nP_r always denotes the number of factors in the formula we are using.

Ex. 1. Four persons enter a carriage in which there are six seats: in how many ways can they take their places?

The first person may seat himself in 6 ways; and then the second person in 5; the third in 4; and the fourth in 3; and since each of these ways may be associated with each of the others, the required answer is $6 \times 5 \times 4 \times 3$, or 360.

Ex. 2. How many different numbers can be formed by using six out of the nine digits 1, 2, 3, ... 9?

Here we have 9 different things, and we have to find the number of permutations of them taken 6 at a time;

$\therefore$ the required result $= {^9P_6}$
$= 9 \times 8 \times 7 \times 6 \times 5 \times 4 = 60480.$

394. To find the number of combinations of n dissimilar things taken r at a time.

Let ^nC_r denote the required number of combinations.

Then each of these combinations consists of a group of r dissimilar things which can be arranged among themselves in $\lfloor r$ ways. [Art. 392, Cor.]

Hence $^nC_r \times \lfloor r$ is equal to the number of *arrangements* of n things taken r at a time; that is,

$$^nC_r \times \lfloor r = {^nP_r} = n(n-1)(n-2)\cdots(n-r+1);$$

$$\therefore {^nC_r} = \frac{n(n-1)(n-2)\cdots(n-r+1)}{\lfloor r} \quad . \quad . \quad (1).$$

Cor. This formula for ^nC_r may also be written in a different form; for if we multiply the numerator and the denominator by $\lfloor n-r$ we obtain

$$\frac{n(n-1)(n-2)\cdots(n-r+1) \times \lfloor n-r}{\lfloor r \lfloor n-r}, \text{ or } \frac{\lfloor n}{\lfloor r \lfloor n-r} \quad . \quad (2);$$

since $n(n-1)(n-2)\cdots(n-r+1) \times \lfloor n-r = \lfloor n$.

It will be convenient to remember both these expressions for ^nC_r, using (1) in all cases where a numerical result is required, and (2) when it is sufficient to leave it in an algebraic shape.

PERMUTATIONS AND COMBINATIONS. 323

Note. If in formula (2) we put $r = n$, we have

$$^nC_n = \frac{\lfloor n}{\lfloor n \lfloor 0} = \frac{1}{\lfloor 0};$$

but $^nC_n = 1$, so that if the formula is to be true for $r = n$, the symbol $\lfloor 0$ must be considered as equivalent to 1.

Ex. From 12 books in how many ways can a selection of 5 be made, (1) when one specified book is always included, (2) when one specified book is always excluded?

(1) Since the specified book is to be included in every selection, we have only to choose 4 out of the remaining 11.

Hence the number of ways $= {}^{11}C_4 = \dfrac{11 \times 10 \times 9 \times 8}{1 \times 2 \times 3 \times 4} = 330.$

(2) Since the specified book is always to be excluded, we have to select the 5 books out of the remaining 11.

Hence the number of ways $= {}^{11}C_5 = \dfrac{11 \times 10 \times 9 \times 8 \times 7}{1 \times 2 \times 3 \times 4 \times 5} = 462.$

395. *The number of combinations of n things r at a time is equal to the number of combinations of n things n − r at a time.*

In making all the possible combinations of n things, to each group of r things we select, there is left a corresponding group of $n - r$ things; that is, the number of combinations of n things r at a time is the same as the number of combinations of n things $n - r$ at a time;

$$\therefore {}^nC_r = {}^nC_{n-r}$$

This result is frequently useful in enabling us to abridge arithmetical work.

Ex. Out of 14 men in how many ways can an eleven be chosen?

The required number $= {}^{14}C_{11} = {}^{14}C_3 = \dfrac{14 \times 13 \times 12}{1 \times 2 \times 3} = 364.$

If we had made use of the formula $^{14}C_{11}$, we should have had to reduce an expression whose numerator and denominator each contained 11 factors.

396. In the examples which follow it is important to notice that the formula for *permutations* should not be used until the suitable *selections* required by the question have been made.

Ex. 1. From 7 Englishmen and 4 Americans a committee of 6 is to be formed: in how many ways can this be done, (1) when the committee contains exactly 2 Americans, (2) at least 2 Americans?

(1) The number of ways in which the Americans can be chosen is $^4C_2$; and the number of ways in which the Englishmen can be chosen is $^7C_4$. Each of the first groups can be associated with each of the second; hence

the required number of ways $= {}^4C_2 \times {}^7C_4$

$$= \frac{\lfloor 4}{\lfloor 2 \lfloor 2} \times \frac{\lfloor 7}{\lfloor 4 \lfloor 3} = \frac{\lfloor 7}{\lfloor 2 \lfloor 2 \lfloor 3} = 210.$$

(2) We exhaust all the suitable combinations by forming all the groups containing 2 Americans and 4 Englishmen; then 3 Americans and 3 Englishmen; and lastly 4 Americans and 2 Englishmen.

The *sum* of the three results gives the answer. Hence the required number of ways $= {}^4C_2 \times {}^7C_4 + {}^4C_3 \times {}^7C_3 + {}^4C_4 \times {}^7C_2$

$$= \frac{\lfloor 4}{\lfloor 2 \lfloor 2} \times \frac{\lfloor 7}{\lfloor 4 \lfloor 3} + \frac{\lfloor 4}{\lfloor 3} \times \frac{\lfloor 7}{\lfloor 3 \lfloor 4} + 1 \times \frac{\lfloor 7}{\lfloor 2 \lfloor 5}.$$

$$= 210 + 140 + 21 = 371.$$

In this example we have only to make use of the suitable formula for *combinations*, for we are not concerned with the possible arrangements of the members of the committee among themselves.

Ex. 2. Out of 7 consonants and 4 vowels, how many words can be made each containing 3 consonants and 2 vowels?

The number of ways of choosing the three consonants is $^7C_3$, and the number of ways of choosing the two vowels is $^4C_2$; and since each of the first groups can be associated with each of the second, the number of combined groups, each containing 3 consonants and 2 vowels, is $^7C_3 \times {}^4C_2$.

Further, each of these groups contains 5 letters, which may be arranged among themselves in $\lfloor 5$ ways. Hence

the required number of words $= \dfrac{\lfloor 7}{\lfloor 3 \lfloor 4} \times \dfrac{\lfloor 4}{\lfloor 2 \lfloor 2} \times \lfloor 5$

$$= 5 \times \lfloor 7 = 25200.$$

EXAMPLES XXXV. a.

1. Find the value of $^5P_4$, $^7P_6$, $^8C_5$, $^{25}C_{23}$.

2. How many different arrangements can be made by taking (1) five, (2) all of the letters of the word *soldier*?

3. If $^nC_8 : {}^{n-1}C_4 = 8 : 5$, find n.

PERMUTATIONS AND COMBINATIONS.

4. How many different selections of four coins can be made from a bag containing a dollar, a half-dollar, a quarter, a florin, a shilling, a franc, a dime, a sixpence, and a penny?

5. How many numbers between 3000 and 4000 can be made with the digits 9, 3, 4, 6?

6. In how many ways can the letters of the word *volume* be arranged if the vowels can only occupy the even places?

7. If the number of permutations of n things four at a time is fourteen times the number of permutations of $n - 2$ things three at a time, find n.

8. From 5 teachers and 10 boys how many committees can be selected containing 3 teachers and 6 boys?

9. If $^{20}C_r = {}^{20}C_{r-10}$, find $^rC_{12}$, $^{18}C_r$.

10. Out of the twenty-six letters of the alphabet in how many ways can a word be made consisting of five different letters two of which must be a and e?

11. How many words can be formed by taking 3 consonants and 2 vowels from an alphabet containing 21 consonants and 5 vowels?

12. A stage will accommodate 5 passengers on each side: in how many ways can 10 persons take their seats when two of them remain always upon one side and a third upon the other?

397. Hitherto, in the formulae we have proved, the things have been regarded as *unlike*. Before considering cases in which some one or more sets of things may be *like*, it is necessary to point out exactly in what sense the words *like* and *unlike* are used. When we speak of things being *dissimilar, different, unlike*, we imply that the things are *visibly unlike*, so as to be easily distinguishable from each other. On the other hand, we shall always use the term *like* things to denote such as are alike to the eye and cannot be distinguished from each other. For instance, in Ex. 2, Art. 396, the consonants and the vowels may be said each to consist of a group of things united by a common characteristic, and thus in a certain sense to be of the same kind; but they cannot be regarded as like things, because there is an individuality existing among the things of each group which makes them easily distinguishable from each other. Hence, in the final stage of the example we considered each group to consist of five *dissimilar* things and therefore capable of ⌊5 arrangements among themselves. [Art. 392, Cor.]

398. **To find the permutations of *n* things, taking them all at a time, when *p* things are of one kind, *q* of another kind, *r* of a third kind, and the rest all different.**

Let there be n letters; suppose p of them to be a, q of them to be b, r of them to be c, and the rest to be unlike.

Let x be the required number of permutations; then if in *any one* of these permutations the p letters a were replaced by p unlike letters different from any of the rest, from this single permutation, without altering the position of any of the remaining letters, we could form ⌊p new permutations. Hence if this change were made in each of the x permutations, we should obtain $x \times$ ⌊p permutations.

Similarly, if the q letters b were replaced by q unlike letters, the number of permutations would be $x \times$ ⌊p $\times$ ⌊q.

In like manner, by replacing the r letters c by r unlike letters, we should finally obtain $x \times$ ⌊p $\times$ ⌊q $\times$ ⌊r permutations.

But the things are now all different, and therefore admit of ⌊n permutations among themselves. Hence

$$x \times \lfloor p \times \lfloor q \times \lfloor r = \lfloor n;$$

that is,
$$x = \frac{\lfloor n}{\lfloor p \lfloor q \lfloor r};$$

which is the required number of permutations.

Any case in which the things are not all different may be treated similarly.

Ex. 1. How many different permutations can be made out of the letters of the word *assassination* taken all together?

We have here 13 letters of which 4 are s, 3 are a, 2 are i, and 2 are n. Hence the number of permutations

$$= \frac{\lfloor 13}{\lfloor 4 \lfloor 3 \lfloor 2 \lfloor 2}$$
$$= 13 \cdot 11 \cdot 10 \cdot 9 \cdot 8 \cdot 7 \cdot 3 \cdot 5$$
$$= 1001 \times 10800 = 10810800.$$

PERMUTATIONS AND COMBINATIONS. 327

Ex. 2. How many numbers can be formed with the digits 1, 2, 3, 4, 3, 2, 1, so that the odd digits always occupy the odd places?

The odd digits 1, 3, 3, 1 can be arranged in their four places in

$$\frac{\lfloor 4}{\lfloor 2 \lfloor 2} \text{ ways} \quad \ldots \ldots \ldots \quad (1).$$

The even digits 2, 4, 2 can be arranged in their three places in

$$\frac{\lfloor 3}{\lfloor 2} \text{ ways} \quad \ldots \ldots \ldots \quad (2).$$

Each of the ways in (1) can be associated with each of the ways in (2).

Hence the required number $= \dfrac{\lfloor 4}{\lfloor 2 \lfloor 2} \times \dfrac{\lfloor 3}{\lfloor 2} = 6 \times 3 = 18$.

399. **To find the number of permutations of n things r at a time, when each thing may be repeated once, twice, ... up to r times in any arrangement.**

Here we have to consider the number of ways in which r places can be filled when we have n different things at our disposal, each of the n things being used as often as we please in any arrangement.

The first place may be filled in n ways, and, when it has been filled in any one way, the second place may also be filled in n ways, since we are not precluded from using the same thing again. Therefore the number of ways in which the first two places can be filled is $n \times n$ or n^2.

The third place can also be filled in n ways, and therefore the first three places in n^3 ways.

Proceeding thus, and noticing that at any stage the index of n is always the same as the number of places filled, we shall have the number of ways in which the r places can be filled equal to n^r.

Ex. In how many ways can 5 prizes be given away to 4 boys, when each boy is eligible for all the prizes?

Any one of the prizes can be given in 4 ways; and then any one of the remaining prizes can also be given in 4 ways, since it may be obtained by the boy who has already received a prize. Thus two prizes can be given away in 4^2 ways, three prizes in 4^3 ways, and so on. Hence the 5 prizes can be given away in 4^5, or 1024 ways.

400. *To find the total number of ways in which it is possible to make a selection by taking some or all of n things.*

Each thing may be dealt with in two ways, for it may either be taken or left; and since either way of dealing with any one thing may be associated with either way of dealing with each one of the others, the number of ways of dealing with the n things is

$$2 \times 2 \times 2 \times 2 \ldots \text{ to } n \text{ factors.}$$

But this includes the case in which all the things are left, therefore, rejecting this case, the total number of ways is $2^n - 1$.

This is often spoken of as "the total number of combinations" of n things.

Ex. A man has 6 friends; in how many ways may he invite one or more of them to dinner?

He has to select some or all of his 6 friends; and therefore the number of ways is $2^6 - 1$, or 63.

This result can be verified in the following manner.

The guests may be invited singly, in twos, threes, ...; therefore the number of selections

$$= {}^6C_1 + {}^6C_2 + {}^6C_3 + {}^6C_4 + {}^6C_5 + {}^6C_6$$
$$= 6 + 15 + 20 + 15 + 6 + 1 = 63.$$

401. *To find for what value of r the number of combinations of n things r at a time is greatest.*

Since $${}^nC_r = \frac{n(n-1)(n-2)\cdots(n-r+2)(n-r+1)}{1 \cdot 2 \cdot 3 \cdots (r-1)r},$$

and $${}^nC_{r-1} = \frac{n(n-1)(n-2)\cdots(n-r+2)}{1 \cdot 2 \cdot 3 \cdots (r-1)};$$

$$\therefore {}^nC_r = {}^nC_{r-1} \times \frac{n-r+1}{r}.$$

The multiplying factor $\frac{n-r+1}{r}$ may be written $\frac{n+1}{r} - 1$, which shows that it decreases as r increases. Hence as r receives the values 1, 2, 3, ... in succession, ${}^nC_r$ is continually increased, until $\frac{n+1}{r} - 1$ becomes equal to 1 or less than 1.

Now $\frac{n+1}{r} - 1 > 1$, so long as $\frac{n+1}{r} > 2$; that is, $\frac{n+1}{2} > r$.

We have to choose the greatest value of r consistent with this inequality.

(1) Let n be even, and equal to $2m$; then
$$\frac{n+1}{2} = \frac{2m+1}{2} = m + \tfrac{1}{2};$$

and for all values of r up to m inclusive this is greater than r. Hence by putting $r = m = \frac{n}{2}$, we find that the greatest number of combinations is ${}^nC_{\frac{n}{2}}$.

(2) Let n be odd, and equal to $2m+1$; then
$$\frac{n+1}{2} = \frac{2m+2}{2} = m + 1;$$

and for all values of r up to m inclusive this is greater than r; but when $r = m+1$, the multiplying factor becomes equal to 1, and
$${}^nC_{m+1} = {}^nC_m; \text{ that is, } {}^nC_{\frac{n+1}{2}} = {}^nC_{\frac{n-1}{2}};$$

and therefore the number of combinations is greatest when the things are taken $\frac{n+1}{2}$, or $\frac{n-1}{2}$ at a time; the result being the same in the two cases.

EXAMPLES XXXV. b.

1. Find the number of permutations which can be made from all the letters of the words,

   (1) *irresistible*, (2) *phenomenon*, (3) *tittle-tattle*.

2. How many different numbers can be formed by using the seven digits 2, 3, 4, 3, 3, 1, 2? How many with the digits 2, 3, 4, 3, 3, 0, 2?

3. How many words can be formed from the letters of the word *Simoom*, so that vowels and consonants occur alternately in each word?

4. A telegraph has 5 arms, and each arm has 4 distinct positions, including the position of rest: find the total number of signals that can be made.

5. In how many ways can n things be given to m persons, when there is no restriction as to the number of things each may receive?

6. How many different arrangements can be made out of the letters of the expression $a^5 b^8 c^6$ when written at full length?

7. There are 4 copies each of 3 different volumes; find the number of ways in which they can be arranged on one shelf.

8. In how many ways can 6 persons form a ring? Find the number of ways in which 4 gentlemen and 4 ladies can sit at a round table so that no two gentlemen sit together.

9. In how many ways can a word of 4 letters be made out of the letters a, b, e, c, d, o, when there is no restriction as to the number of times a letter is repeated in each word?

10. How many arrangements can be made out of the letters of the word *Toulouse*, so that the consonants occupy the first, fourth, and seventh places?

11. A boat's crew consists of eight men of whom one can only row on bow side and one only on stroke side: in how many ways can the crew be arranged?

12. Show that $^{n+1}C_r = {^n}C_r + {^n}C_{r-1}$.

13. If $^{2n}C_3 : {^n}C_2 = 44 : 3$, find n.

14. Out of the letters A, B, C, p, q, r, how many arrangements can be made beginning with a capital?

15. Find the number of combinations of 50 things 46 at a time.

16. If $^{18}C_r = {^{18}}C_{r+2}$, find $^r C_5$.

17. In how many ways is it possible to draw a sum of money from a bag containing a dollar, a half-dollar, a quarter, a dime, a five-cent piece, a two-cent piece, and a penny?

CHAPTER XXXVI.

Probability (Chance).

402. Definition. If an event can happen in a ways and fail in b ways, and each of these ways is equally likely, the **probability**, or the **chance**, of its *happening* is $\dfrac{a}{a+b}$, and of its *failing* is $\dfrac{b}{a+b}$. Hence to find the probability of an event happening, *divide the number of favorable ways by the whole number of ways favorable and unfavorable.*

For instance, if in a lottery there are 7 prizes and 25 blanks, the chance that a person holding 1 ticket will win a prize is $\tfrac{7}{32}$, and his chance of not winning is $\tfrac{25}{32}$.

Instead of saying that the chance of the happening of an event is $\dfrac{a}{a+b}$, it is sometimes stated that *the odds are a to b in favor of the event, or b to a against the event.*

Thus in the above the odds are seven to twenty-five in favor of the drawing of a prize, and twenty-five to seven against success.

403. The reason for the mathematical definition of probability may be made clear by the following considerations:

If an event can happen in a ways and fail to happen in b ways, and all these ways are equally likely, we can assert that the chance of its happening is to the chance of its failing as a to b. Thus if the chance of its happening is represented by ka, where k is an undetermined constant, then the chance of its failing will be represented by kb.

$\therefore$ chance of happening + chance of failing $= k(a+b)$.

Now the event is certain to happen or to fail; therefore the sum of the chances of happening and failing must represent *certainty*. If therefore we agree to take *certainty as our unit*, we have

$$1 = k(a+b), \text{ or } k = \frac{1}{a+b},$$

∴ the chance that the event will happen is $\dfrac{a}{a+b}$,

and the chance that the event will not happen is $\dfrac{b}{a+b}$.

COR. If p is the probability of the happening of an event, the probability of its not happening is $1 - p$.

404. The definition of probability in Art. 402 may be given in a slightly different form which is sometimes useful. If c is the total number of cases, each being equally likely to occur, and of these a are favorable to the event, then the probability that the event will happen is $\dfrac{a}{c}$, and the probability that it will not happen is $1 - \dfrac{a}{c}$.

Ex. 1. (*a*) From a bag containing 4 white and 5 black balls a man draws a single ball at random. What is the chance that it is black?

A black ball can be drawn in 5 ways, since any one of the 5 black balls may be drawn. In the same way any one of the 4 white balls may be drawn.

Hence the chance of drawing a black ball is $\dfrac{5}{4+5}$, or $\dfrac{5}{9}$.

(*b*) Suppose the man draws 3 balls at random. What are the odds against these being all black?

The total number of ways in which 3 balls can be drawn is $^9C_3$, and the total number of ways of drawing 3 black balls is $^5C_3$; therefore the chance of drawing 3 black balls

$$= \frac{^5C_3}{^9C_3} = \frac{5 \cdot 4 \cdot 3}{9 \cdot 8 \cdot 7} = \frac{5}{42}.$$

Thus the odds against the event are 37 to 5.

Ex. 2. From a bag containing 5 red balls, 4 white balls, and 5 black balls, 6 balls are drawn at random. What is the chance that 3 are white, 2 black, and 1 red?

The number of combinations of 4 white balls, taken 3 at a time, is $\frac{4 \cdot 3 \cdot 2}{1 \cdot 2 \cdot 3}$ or 4. In the same manner the number of combinations of 5 black balls, taken 2 at a time, is $\frac{5 \cdot 4}{1 \cdot 2}$ or 10. Since each of the 4 combinations of white balls may be taken with any one of the 10 combinations of black, and with each of the combinations so formed we may take any one of the 5 red balls, the total number of combinations will be $4 \cdot 10 \cdot 5$ or 200. But the number of combinations of the entire number of balls, taken 6 at a time is $\frac{14 \cdot 13 \cdot 12 \cdot 11 \cdot 10 \cdot 9}{1 \cdot 2 \cdot 3 \cdot 4 \cdot 5 \cdot 6}$ or 3003, hence the chance that 3 white, 2 black, and 1 red ball will be drawn at one time is $\frac{200}{3003}$.

Ex. 3. A has 3 shares in a lottery in which there are 3 prizes and 6 blanks; B has 1 share in a lottery in which there is 1 prize and 2 blanks. Show that A's chance of success is to B's as 16 to 7.

A may draw 3 prizes in 1 way; he may draw 2 prizes and 1 blank in $\frac{3 \cdot 2}{1 \cdot 2} \times 6$ ways; he may draw 1 prize and 2 blanks in $3 \times \frac{6 \cdot 5}{1 \cdot 2}$ ways; the sum of these numbers is 64, which is the number of ways in which A can win a prize. Also he can draw 3 tickets in $\frac{9 \cdot 8 \cdot 7}{1 \cdot 2 \cdot 3}$, or 84 ways; therefore A's chance of success $= \frac{64}{84} = \frac{16}{21}$.

B's chance of success is clearly $\frac{1}{3}$; therefore A's chance : B's chance $= \frac{16}{21} : \frac{1}{3} = 16 : 7$.

Or we might have reasoned thus: A will get *all blanks* in $\frac{6 \cdot 5 \cdot 4}{1 \cdot 2 \cdot 3}$, or 20 ways; the chance of which is $\frac{20}{84}$, or $\frac{5}{21}$; therefore A's chance of success $= 1 - \frac{5}{21} = \frac{16}{21}$.

405. From the examples given it will be seen that the solution of the easier kinds of questions in Probability requires nothing more than a knowledge of the definition of Probability, and the application of the laws of Permutations and Combinations.

EXAMPLES XXXVI.

1. A bag contains 5 white, 7 black, and 4 red balls; find the chance of drawing: (*a*) One white ball; (*b*) Two white balls; (*c*) Three white balls; (*d*) One ball of each color; (*e*) One white, two black, and three red balls.

2. If four coins are tossed, find the chance that there should be 2 heads and 2 tails.

3. One of two events must happen: given that the chance of the one is two-thirds that of the other, find the odds in favor of the other.

4. Thirteen persons take their places at a round table. Show that it is 5 to 1 against 2 particular persons sitting together.

5. There are three events A, B, C, one of which must, and only one can, happen; the odds are 8 to 3 against A, 5 to 2 against B. Find the odds against C.

6. A has 3 shares in a lottery containing 3 prizes and 9 blanks; B has 2 shares in a lottery containing 2 prizes and 6 blanks. Compare their chances of success.

7. There are three works, one consisting of 3 volumes, one of 4, and the other of 1 volume. They are placed on a shelf at random. Prove that the chance that volumes of the same works are all together is $\frac{3}{140}$.

8. The letters forming the word *Clifton* are placed at random in a row. What is the chance that the two vowels come together?

9. In a hand at whist what is the chance that the four kings are held by a specified player.

10. There are 4 dollars and 3 half-dollars placed at random in a line. Show that the chance of the extreme coins being both half-dollars is $\frac{1}{7}$.

MISCELLANEOUS EXAMPLES VI.

1. Simplify $\dfrac{b-c}{a^2-(b-c)^2} + \dfrac{c-a}{b^2-(c-a)^2} + \dfrac{a-b}{c^2-(a-b)^2}$.

2. Extract the square root of

(i.) $4x^4 + 6x^3 + \frac{3\cdot 9}{4}x^2 + 15x + 25$.

(ii.) $x^8 - \dfrac{2x^{11}}{a^3} + 2a^4x^4 + \dfrac{x^{14}}{a^6} - 2ax^7 + a^8$.

3. A number of 3 digits exceeds 25 times the sum of the digits by 9; the middle digit increased by 3 is equal to the sum of the other digits, and the unit digit increased by 6 is equal to twice the sum of the other 2 digits: find the number.

4. Find the value of

$2\sqrt{\frac{1}{2}} + 3\sqrt{\frac{2}{3}} - (\frac{2}{5}\sqrt[3]{\frac{3}{5}} + \sqrt[3]{\frac{2\cdot 5}{4}})(\frac{1}{2}\sqrt{6} - \sqrt{24})$.

5. Solve (i.) $2 = \dfrac{\sqrt{2+x} + \sqrt{2-x}}{\sqrt{2+x} - \sqrt{2-x}}$.

(ii.) $\sqrt{3x-11} + \sqrt{3x} = \sqrt{12x-23}$.

MISCELLANEOUS EXAMPLES VI.

6. Solve $\dfrac{2(x+a)}{x+b} + \dfrac{3(x+b)}{x+a} = 5$.

7. The sum of a certain number of terms of an A. P. is 45, and the first and last of these terms are 1 and 17 respectively. Find the number of terms and the common difference of the series.

8. Solve (i.) $\dfrac{2x-3}{x-2} - \dfrac{1}{6} + \dfrac{2x-1}{1-x} = 0$.

(ii.) $\sqrt{12x-5} + \sqrt{3x-1} = \sqrt{27x-2}$.

9. Find the value of the seventh term in the expansion of $(a+x)^n$ when $a = \frac{1}{2}$, $x = \frac{1}{3}$, $n = 9$.

10. A man starting from A at 11 o'clock passed the fourth milestone at 11.30 and met another man (who started from B at 12) at 12.48; the second man passed the fourth milestone from A at 1.40: find the distance between A and B, and the second man's rate.

11. Show that $x^3 + 13 a^2 x > 5 ax^2 + 9 a^3$, if $x > a$.

12. Extract the cube root of
$$44 x^3 + 63 x^2 + x^6 + 27 + 6 x^5 + 21 x^4 + 54 x.$$

13. Solve (i.) $x - y = 3$, (ii.) $2x^2 - 9xy + 9y^2 = 5$,
$x^2 + xy + y^2 = 93$. $4x^2 - 10xy + 11y^2 = 35$.

14. Find a mean proportional between $\dfrac{\sqrt{13 - 8\sqrt{-3}}\,(a^0 + b^0)^{-2}}{ab}$ and the reciprocal of $\dfrac{4 - \sqrt{-3}}{16\,a^3 b}$.

15. Two vessels, one of which sails 2 miles an hour faster than the other, start together upon voyages of 1680 and 1152 miles respectively; the slower vessel reaches its destination one day before the other: how many miles per hour did the faster vessel sail?

16. Solve (i.) $x^6 = 8 + 7 x^3$.
(ii.) $x^{2n} + b^2 = c^2 - 2 bx^n$.

17. Two numbers are in the ratio $2:7$; the numbers obtained by adding 6 to each of the given numbers are in the duplicate ratio of $2:3$. Find the numbers.

18. Solve (i.) $2 bx^2 + 2 b = 4x + b^2 x$.

(ii.) $\dfrac{x+4}{2x+3} + \dfrac{3x+10}{2x} = \dfrac{2x+3}{x-1}$.

(iii.) $\sqrt{x+3} + \sqrt{x+8} = \sqrt{4x+21}$.

(iv.) $x^2 + xy + y = 137$,
$y^2 + xy + x = 205$.

19. Simplify $\dfrac{\left[\sqrt{\dfrac{2+\sqrt{-2}}{2}}-\sqrt{\dfrac{2-\sqrt{-2}}{2}}\right]^2}{2-\sqrt{6}}$.

20. Find the sides of a rectangle the area of which is unaltered if its length be increased by 2 feet while its breadth is diminished by 1 foot, and which loses $\frac{1}{3}$ of its area if its length be diminished by 2 feet and its breadth by 4 feet.

21. The first term of a G. P. exceeds the second term by 1, and the sum to infinity is 81: find the series.

22. Find the number of permutations which can be made from all the letters of the word *Mississippi*.

23. Solve (i.) $\sqrt{x+2}+\sqrt{4x+1}-\sqrt{9x+7}=0$.

(ii.) $\dfrac{2x-3}{\sqrt{x-2}+1}=2\sqrt{x-2}-1$.

(iii.) $\dfrac{2}{x-6+\sqrt{x}}+\dfrac{3}{\sqrt{x}-2}=\dfrac{4}{\sqrt{x}+3}$.

(iv.) $\sqrt[3]{x-a}-\sqrt[3]{x-b}=\sqrt[3]{b-a}$.

24. Find the condition that one root of $ax^2+bx+c=0$ shall be n times the other.

25. Find the value of $x^3-3x^2-8x+15$ when $x=3+i$.

26. Given log 648 = 2.81157, log 864 = 2.93651, find the logarithm of 3 and of 5.

27. Two trains run, without stopping, over the same 36 miles of rail. One of them travels 15 miles an hour faster than the other and accomplishes the distance in 12 minutes less. Find the speeds of the two trains.

28. Extract the square root of
$$9x^4-2x^3y+1\tfrac{63}{81}x^2y^2-2xy^3+9y^4.$$

29. Find, by logarithms, the value of
$$\left\{\dfrac{15(.318)^{\frac{1}{7}}}{16}\right\}^{\frac{11}{17}}.$$

30. Simplify $\dfrac{1+ax^{-1}}{a^{-1}x^{-1}}\times\dfrac{a^{-1}-x^{-1}}{a^{-1}x-ax^{-1}}\div\dfrac{ax^{-1}}{x-a}$.

31. The men in a regiment can be arranged in a column twice as deep as its breadth; if the number be diminished by 206, the men can be arranged in a hollow square three deep having the same number of

men in each outer side of the square as there were in the depth of the column; how many men were there at first in the regiment?

32. Solve (i.) $2x^2 + xy + y^2 = 37,$
$8x^2 + 4xy + y^2 = 73.$

(ii.) $27x^3 + y^3 = 152,$
$3x^2y + xy^2 = 40.$

33. Simplify $8^{\frac{4}{3}} + \sqrt[3]{(2 \times 4^{-5})} - \sqrt[7]{2} \div 4^{-\frac{3}{7}} - (32)^{-\frac{1}{5}}$.

34. A man bought a field the length of which was to its breadth as 8 to 5. The number of dollars that he paid for 1 acre was equal to the number of rods in the length of the field; and 13 times the number of rods round the field equalled the number of dollars that it cost. Find the length and breadth of the field.

35. Solve (i.) $x^2 + xy + 3y^2 = 14 + 2\sqrt{2},$
$2x^2 + xy + 5y^2 = 24 + 2\sqrt{2}.$

(ii.) $2x + 3y = 10,$
$5x^2 + x + y = 4\frac{3}{4}.$

36. Find two numbers whose sum added to their product is 34, and the sum of whose squares diminished by their sum is 42.

37. Find the sixth term in the expansion of each of the following expressions:

(i.) $(a + 3b^{-2})^7$. (ii.) $\left(2a - \dfrac{b^{\frac{1}{2}}}{c^{-2}}\right)^8$. (iii.) $\left(\dfrac{x}{2} - \dfrac{\sqrt[4]{y}}{3}\right)^9$.

38. A varies directly as B and inversely as C; $A = \frac{2}{5}$ when $B = \frac{3}{7}$ and $C = \frac{9}{14}$: find B when $A = \sqrt{48}$ and $C = \sqrt{75}$.

39. Solve (i.) $\sqrt{x+12} + \sqrt[4]{x+12} = 6.$

(ii.) $x^2 + y\sqrt{xy} = 9,$
$y^2 + x\sqrt{xy} = 18.$

40. Form an equation whose roots shall be the arithmetic and harmonic means between the roots of $x^2 - px + q = 0$.

z

CHAPTER XXXVII.

BINOMIAL THEOREM.

406. It may be shown by actual multiplication that
$(a+b)(a+c)(a+d)(a+e)$
$= a^4 + (b+c+d+e)a^3 + (bc+bd+be+cd+ce+de)a^2$
$+ (bcd+bce+bde+cde)a + bcde \quad \ldots \ldots \ldots \quad (1)$

We may, however, write this result by inspection; for the complete product consists of the sum of a number of partial products each of which is formed by multiplying together four letters, *one* being taken from *each* of the four factors. If we examine the way in which the various partial products are formed, we see that

(1) The term a^4 is formed by taking the letter a out of *each* of the factors.

(2) The terms involving a^3 are formed by taking the letter a out of *any three* factors, in every way possible, and *one* of the letters b, c, d, e, out of the remaining factor.

(3) The terms involving a^2 are formed by taking the letter a out of *any two* factors, in every way possible, and *two* of the letters b, c, d, e, out of the remaining factors.

(4) The terms involving a are formed by taking the letter a out of *any one* factor, and *three* of the letters b, c, d, e, out of the remaining factors.

(5) The term independent of a is the product of all the letters b, c, d, e.

Ex. Find the value of $(a-2)(a+3)(a-5)(a+9)$.
The product
$= a^4 + (-2+3-5+9)a^3 + (-6+10-18-15+27-45)a^2$
$\qquad\qquad\qquad\qquad\qquad + (30-54+90-135)a + 270$
$= a^4 + 5a^3 - 47a^2 - 69a + 270.$

BINOMIAL THEOREM.

407. If in equation (1) of the preceding article we suppose $c = d = e = b$, we obtain

$$(a+b)^4 = a^4 + 4a^3b + 6a^2b^2 + 4ab^3 + b^4.$$

We shall now employ the same method to prove a formula known as the **Binomial Theorem**, by which any binomial of the form $a + b$ can be raised to any assigned positive integral power.

408. To find the expansion of $(a+b)^n$ when n is a positive integer.

Consider the expression

$$(a+b)(a+c)(a+d) \cdots (a+k),$$

the number of factors being n.

The expansion of this expression is the continued product of the n factors, $a+b,\ a+c,\ a+d,\ \cdots a+k$, and every term in the expansion is of n dimensions, being a product formed by multiplying together n letters, *one* taken from each of these n factors.

The highest power of a is a^n, and is formed by taking the letter a from *each* of the n factors.

The terms involving a^{n-1} are formed by taking the letter a from *any* $n-1$ of the factors, and *one* of the letters $b,\ c,\ d,\ \cdots k$ from the remaining factor; thus the coefficient of a^{n-1} in the final product is the sum of the letters $b,\ c,\ d,\ \cdots k$; denote it by S_1.

The terms involving a^{n-2} are formed by taking the letter a from *any* $n-2$ of the factors, and *two* of the letters $b,\ c,\ d,\ \cdots k$ from the two remaining factors; thus the coefficient of a^{n-2} in the final product is the sum of the products of the letters $b,\ c,\ d,\ \cdots k$ taken two at a time; denote it by S_2.

And, generally, the terms involving a^{n-r} are formed by taking the letter a from *any* $n-r$ of the factors, and r of the letters $b,\ c,\ d,\ \cdots k$ from the r remaining factors; thus the coefficient of a^{n-r} in the final product is the sum of the products of the letters $b,\ c,\ d,\ \cdots k$ taken r at a time; denote it by S_r.

The last term in the product is $bcd \cdots k$; denote it by S_n.

Hence $\quad (a+b)(a+c)(a+d) \cdots (a+k)$
$= a^n + S_1 a^{n-1} + S_2 a^{n-2} + \cdots + S_r a^{n-r} + \cdots + S_{n-1} a + S_n$.

In S_1 the *number of terms* is n; in S_2 *the number of terms* is the same as the number of combinations of n things two at a time; that is, $^nC_2$; in S_3 *the number of terms* is $^nC_3$; and so on.

Now suppose $c, d, \cdots k$, each equal to b; then S_1 becomes $^nC_1 b$; S_2 becomes $^nC_2 b^2$; S_3 becomes $^nC_3 b^3$; and so on; thus

$(a+b)^n = a^n + {}^nC_1 a^{n-1} b + {}^nC_2 a^{n-2} b^2 + {}^nC_3 a^{n-3} b^3 + \cdots + {}^nC_n b^n$);

substituting for $^nC_1, {}^nC_2, \cdots$ we obtain

$$(a+b)^n = a^n + na^{n-1}b + \frac{n(n-1)}{1 \cdot 2} a^{n-2} b^2$$
$$+ \frac{n(n-1)(n-2)}{1 \cdot 2 \cdot 3} a^{n-3} b^3 + \cdots + b^n$$

the series containing $n+1$ terms.

This is the *Binomial Theorem*, and the expression on the right side is said to be **the expansion** of $(a+b)^n$.

409. The coefficients in the expansion of $(a+b)^n$ are very conveniently expressed by the symbols $^nC_1, {}^nC_2, {}^nC_3 \ldots {}^nC_n$. We shall, however, sometimes further abbreviate them by omitting n, and writing $C_1, C_2, C_3, \ldots C_n$. With this notation we have

$(a+b)^n = a^n + C_1 a^{n-1} b + C_2 a^{n-2} b^2 + C_3 a^{n-3} b^3 + \cdots + C_n b^n$.

If we write $-b$ in the place of b, we obtain
$(a-b)^n = a^n + C_1 a^{n-1}(-b) + C_2 a^{n-2}(-b)^2$
$\qquad + C_3 a^{n-3}(-b)^3 + \cdots + C_n(-b)^n$
$= a^n - C_1 a^{n-1} b + C_2 a^{n-2} b^2 - C_3 a^{n-3} b^3 + \cdots + (-1)^n C_n b^n$.

Thus the terms in the expansion of $(a+b)^n$ and $(a-b)^n$ are *numerically* the same, but in $(a-b)^n$ they are alternately positive and negative, and the last term is positive or negative according as n is even or odd.

BINOMIAL THEOREM.

Ex. 1. Find the expansion of $(a + y)^6$.

By the formula, the expansion

$$= a^6 + {}^6C_1 a^5 y + {}^6C_2 a^4 y^2 + {}^6C_3 a^3 y^3 + {}^6C_4 a^2 y^4 + {}^6C_5 a y^5 + {}^6C_6 y^6$$

$$= a^6 + 6 a^5 y + 15 a^4 y^2 + 20 a^3 y^3 + 15 a^2 y^4 + 6 a y^5 + y^6,$$

on calculating the values of ${}^6C_1$, ${}^6C_2$, ${}^6C_3$, ...

Ex. 2. Find the expansion of $(a - 2x)^7$.

$$(a - 2x)^7 = a^7 - {}^7C_1 a^6 (2x) + {}^7C_2 a^5 (2x)^2 - {}^7C_3 a^4 (2x)^3 + \cdots \text{ to 8 terms.}$$

Now remembering that ${}^nC_r = {}^nC_{n-r}$ after calculating the coefficients up to ${}^7C_3$, the rest may be written down at once; for ${}^7C_4 = {}^7C_3$; ${}^7C_5 = {}^7C_2$; and so on. Hence

$$(a - 2x)^7 = a^7 - 7 a^6 (2x) + \frac{7 \cdot 6}{1 \cdot 2} a^5 (2x)^2 - \frac{7 \cdot 6 \cdot 5}{1 \cdot 2 \cdot 3} a^4 (2x)^3 + \cdots$$

$$= a^7 - 7 a^6 (2x) + 21 a^5 (2x)^2 - 35 a^4 (2x)^3 + 35 a^3 (2x)^4$$
$$- 21 a^2 (2x)^5 + 7 a (2x)^6 - (2x)^7$$

$$= a^7 - 14 a^6 x + 84 a^5 x^2 - 280 a^4 x^3 + 560 a^3 x^4$$
$$- 672 a^2 x^5 + 448 a x^6 - 128 x^7.$$

410. The $(r + 1)$th or General Term. In the expansion of $(a + b)^n$, the coefficient of the second term is ${}^nC_1$; of the third term is ${}^nC_2$; of the fourth term is ${}^nC_3$; and so on; the suffix in each term being one less than the number of the term to which it applies; hence ${}^nC_r$ is the coefficient of the $(r + 1)$th term. This is called the *general term*, because by giving to r different numerical values any of the coefficients may be found from ${}^nC_r$; and by giving to a and b their appropriate indices any assigned term may be obtained. Thus the $(r + 1)$th term may be written

$${}^nC_r a^{n-r} b^r, \text{ or } \frac{n(n-1)(n-2)\cdots(n-r+1)}{\underline{|r}} a^{n-r} b^r.$$

In applying this formula to any particular case, it should be observed that *the index of b is the same as the suffix of C, and that the sum of the indices of a and b is n.*

* See Art. 392, Cor.

Ex. 1. Find the fifth term of $(a + 2x^3)^{17}$.

Here $(r + 1) = 5$, therefore

the required term $= {}^{17}C_4 a^{13}(2x^3)^4$

$= \dfrac{17 \cdot 16 \cdot 15 \cdot 14}{1 \cdot 2 \cdot 3 \cdot 4} \times 16\, a^{13}x^{12}$

$= 38080\, a^{13}x^{12}$.

Ex. 2. Find the fourteenth term of $(3 - a)^{15}$.

Here $r + 1 = 14$, therefore

the required term $= {}^{15}C_{13}(3)^2(-a)^{13}$

$= {}^{15}C_2 \times (-9a^{13})$ [Art. 395.]

$= -945\, a^{13}$.

411. Simplest Form of the Binomial Theorem. The most convenient form of the binomial theorem is the expansion of $(1 + x)^n$. This is obtained from the general formula of Art. 408, by writing 1 in the place of a, and x in the place of b. Thus

$(1 + x)^n = 1 + {}^nC_1 x + {}^nC_2 x^2 + \cdots + {}^nC_r x^r + \cdots + {}^nC_n x^n$

$= 1 + nx + \dfrac{n(n-1)}{1 \cdot 2} x^2 + \cdots + x^n,$

the *general term* being $\dfrac{n(n-1)(n-2)\cdots(n-r+1)}{\underline{|r}} x^r.$

412. The expansion of a binomial may always be made to depend upon the case in which the first term is unity; thus

$(a + b)^n = \left\{ a\left(1 + \dfrac{b}{a}\right) \right\}^n = a^n(1 + c)^n$, where $c = \dfrac{b}{a}$.

Ex. Find the coefficient of x^{16} in the expansion of $(x^2 - 2x)^{10}$.

We have $(x^2 - 2x)^{10} = x^{20}\left(1 - \dfrac{2}{x}\right)^{10}$;

and, since x^{20} multiplies every term in the expansion of $\left(1 - \dfrac{2}{x}\right)^{10}$, we have in this expansion to seek the coefficient of the term which contains $\dfrac{1}{x^4}$.

Hence the required coefficient $= {}^{10}C_4(-2)^4$

$= \dfrac{10 \cdot 9 \cdot 8 \cdot 7}{1 \cdot 2 \cdot 3 \cdot 4} \times 16 = 3360.$

PROOF BY MATHEMATICAL INDUCTION.

413. By actual multiplication we obtain the following identities:

$$(a+b)^2 = a^2 + 2ab + b^2,$$
$$(a+b)^3 = a^3 + 3a^2b + 3ab^2 + b^3,$$
$$(a+b)^4 = a^4 + 4a^3b + 6a^2b^2 + 4ab^3 + b^4.$$

Selecting any one of these, and rewriting so as to exhibit the laws of formation of exponents and coefficients, we have

$$(a+b)^4 = a^4 + \frac{4}{1}a^{4-1}b + \frac{4\cdot 3}{1\cdot 2}a^{4-2}b^2 + \frac{4\cdot 3\cdot 2}{1\cdot 2\cdot 3}a^{4-3}b^3$$
$$+ \frac{4\cdot 3\cdot 2\cdot 1}{1\cdot 2\cdot 3\cdot 4}a^0b^4 \text{ (Art. 216).}$$

If these laws of formation hold for $(a+b)^n$, n being any positive integer, then

$$(a+b)^n = a^n + na^{n-1}b + \frac{n(n-1)}{1\cdot 2}a^{n-2}b^2$$
$$+ \frac{n(n-1)(n-2)}{1\cdot 2\cdot 3}a^{n-3}b^3 + \cdots \quad . \quad . \quad . \quad (1).$$

Multiplying each side of the assumed identity by $(a+b)$ and combining terms, we obtain

$$(a+b)^{n+1} = a^{n+1} + (n+1)a^n b + \frac{n(n+1)}{1\cdot 2}a^{n-1}b^2$$
$$+ \frac{n(n+1)(n-1)}{1\cdot 2\cdot 3}a^{n-2}b^3 + \cdots \quad . \quad . \quad (2).$$

It will be seen that n in (1) is, in every instance, replaced by $(n+1)$ in (2). Hence if the theorem be true for any value of n, it will be true for the next higher value. We have shown by multiplication that the theorem is true when n successively equals 2, 3, and 4; hence it is true when $n = 5$, and so on indefinitely. The theorem is therefore true for *all* positive integral values of n.

414. In the expansion

$$(a + b)^n = a^n + na^{n-1}b + \frac{n(n-1)}{1\cdot 2}a^{n-2}b^2 + \cdots$$

we observe that in *any* term

(1) The exponent of b, the second term of the binomial, is *one less* than the number of the term from the first.

(2) The sum of the exponents is n.

(3) The *last* factor of the denominator of the coefficient is the same as the exponent of the *second term* of the binomial.

(4) The *last* factor of the numerator of the coefficient is the exponent of the *first term* of the binomial increased by 1.

Hence the $(r + 1)$th or **general term** of $(a + b)^n$ is

$$\frac{n(n-1)\cdots(n-r+1)}{1\cdot 2\cdot 3\cdots r}a^{n-r}b^r.$$

Ex. Find the 6th term in the expansion of $(2a + b)^{10}$.
Here $n = 10$, and $r + 1 = 6$.

We have $\dfrac{10\cdot 9\cdot 8\cdot 7\cdot 6}{1\cdot 2\cdot 3\cdot 4\cdot 5}(2a)^5 b^5 = \dfrac{3\cdot 2\cdot 7\cdot 6}{1}(2a)^5 b^5$

$$= 252(2)^5 a^5 b^5 = 8064\, a^5 b^5.$$

Note. The student should observe that the coefficient contains the *same number* of factors in both numerator and denominator.

EXAMPLES XXXVII. a.

Expand the following binomials;

1. $(x + 2)^4$.
2. $(x + 3)^5$.
3. $(a + x)^7$.
4. $(a - x)^5$.
5. $(1 - 2y)^5$.
6. $\left(a - \dfrac{3}{b}\right)^7$.
7. $\left(2 - \dfrac{x}{2}\right)^6$.
8. $\left(2x + \dfrac{y}{2}\right)^4$.
9. $\left(ax + \dfrac{y}{a}\right)^9$.

Write in simplest form:

10. The 4th term of $(1 + x)^{12}$.
11. The 6th term of $(2 - y)^8$.
12. The 5th term of $(a - 5b)^7$.
13. The 15th term of $(2x - 1)^{17}$.
14. The 7th term of $\left(1 - \dfrac{1}{x}\right)^{10}$.
15. The 6th term of $\left(3x + \dfrac{a}{2}\right)^9$.

BINOMIAL THEOREM.

16. Find the value of $(x - \sqrt{3})^4 + (x + \sqrt{3})^4$.
17. Expand $(\sqrt{1 - x^2} + 1)^5 - (\sqrt{1 - x^2} - 1)^5$.
18. Find the coefficient of x^{12} in $(x^2 + 2x)^{10}$.
19. Find the coefficient of x in $\left(x^2 - \dfrac{a}{2x}\right)^{14}$.
20. Find the term independent of x in $\left(2x^2 - \dfrac{1}{x}\right)^{12}$.
21. Find the coefficient of x^{-20} in $\left(\dfrac{x^2}{3} - \dfrac{2}{x^3}\right)^{15}$.

415. Equal Coefficients. *In the expansion of $(1 + x)^n$ the coefficients of terms equidistant from the beginning and end are equal.*

The coefficient of the $(r + 1)$th term from the beginning is ^nC_r.

The $(r + 1)$th term from the end has $n + 1 - (r + 1)$, or $n - r$ terms before it; therefore counting from the beginning it is the $(n - r + 1)$th term, and its coefficient is $^nC_{n-r}$, which has been shown to be equal to ^nC_r [Art. 395]. Hence the proposition follows.

416. Greatest Coefficient. *To find the greatest coefficient in the expansion of $(1 + x)^n$.*

The coefficient of the general term of $(1 + x)^n$ is ^nC_r; and we have only to find for what value of r this is greatest.

By Art. 401, when n is even, the greatest coefficient is $^nC_{\frac{n}{2}}$; when n is odd, it is $^nC_{\frac{n-1}{2}}$ or $^nC_{\frac{n+1}{2}}$; these coefficients being equal.

417. Greatest Term. *To find the greatest term in the expansion of $(a + b)^n$.*

We have $(a + b)^n = a^n\left(1 + \dfrac{b}{a}\right)^n$;

therefore, since a^n multiplies every term in $\left(1 + \dfrac{b}{a}\right)^n$, it will be sufficient to find the greatest term in this latter expansion.

Let the rth and $(r+1)$th be any two consecutive terms. The $(r+1)$th term is obtained by multiplying the rth term by $\dfrac{n-r+1}{r} \cdot \dfrac{b}{a}$; that is, by $\left(\dfrac{n+1}{r}-1\right)\dfrac{b}{a}$. [Art. 410.]

The factor $\dfrac{n+1}{r}-1$ decreases as r increases; hence the $(r+1)$th term is not always greater than the rth term, but only until $\left(\dfrac{n+1}{r}-1\right)\dfrac{b}{a}$ becomes equal to 1, or less than 1.

Now $\left(\dfrac{n+1}{r}-1\right)\dfrac{b}{a} > 1$, so long as $\dfrac{n+1}{r}-1 > \dfrac{a}{b}$;

that is, $\dfrac{n+1}{r} > \dfrac{a}{b}+1$, or $\dfrac{(n+1)b}{a+b} > r$ . . . (1).

If $\dfrac{(n+1)b}{a+b}$ be an integer, denote it by p; then if $r = p$ the multiplying factor becomes 1, and the $(p+1)$th term is equal to the pth; and these are greater than any other term.

If $\dfrac{(n+1)b}{a+b}$ be not an integer, denote its integral part by q; then the greatest value of r consistent with (1) is q; hence the $(q+1)$th term is the greatest.

Since we are only concerned with the *numerically greatest term*, the investigation will be the same for $(a-b)^n$; therefore in any numerical example it is unnecessary to consider the sign of the second term of the binomial. Also it will be found best to work each example independently of the general formula.

Ex. Find the greatest term in the expansion of $(1+4x)^8$, when x has the value $\frac{1}{3}$.

Denote the rth and $(r+1)$th terms by T_r and T_{r+1} respectively; then

$$T_{r+1} = \dfrac{8-r+1}{r} \cdot 4x \times T_r = \dfrac{9-r}{r} \times \dfrac{4}{3} \times T_r;$$

hence $T_{r+1} > T_r$, so long as $\dfrac{9-r}{r} \times \dfrac{4}{3} > 1$;

that is, $36 - 4r > 3r$, or $36 > 7r$.

The greatest value of r consistent with this is 5; hence the greatest term is the sixth, and its value

$$= {}^8C_5 \times (\tfrac{1}{3})^5 = {}^8C_3 \times (\tfrac{1}{3})^5 = \tfrac{5711 \cdot 4}{2 \cdot 1 \cdot 1}.$$

418. Sum of the Coefficients. *To find the sum of the coefficients in the expansion of* $(1+x)^n$.

In the identity

$$(1+x)^n = 1 + C_1 x + C_2 x^2 + C_3 x^3 + \cdots + C_n x^n;$$

put $x = 1$; thus

$$2^n = 1 + C_1 + C_2 + C_3 + \cdots + C_n$$
$$= \text{sum of the coefficients.}$$

COR. $C_1 + C_2 + C_3 + \cdots + C_n = 2^n - 1;$

that is, the total number of combinations of n things *taking some or all of them at a time* is $2^n - 1$. [See Art. 400.]

419. Sums of Coefficients equal. *To prove that in the expansion of* $(1+x)^n$, *the sum of the coefficients of the odd terms is equal to the sum of the coefficients of the even terms.*

In the identity

$$(1+x)^n = 1 + C_1 x + C_2 x^2 + C_3 x^3 + \cdots + C_n x^n,$$

put $x = -1$; thus

$$0 = 1 - C_1 + C_2 - C_3 + C_4 - C_5 + \cdots;$$
$$\therefore 1 + C_2 + C_4 + \cdots = C_1 + C_3 + C_5 + \cdots.$$

420. Expansion of Multinomials. The Binomial Theorem may also be applied to expand expressions which contain more than two terms.

Ex. Find the expansion of $(x^2 + 2x - 1)^3$.

Regarding $2x - 1$ as a single term, the expansion

$$= (x^2)^3 + 3(x^2)^2(2x-1) + 3x^2(2x-1)^2 + (2x-1)^3$$
$$= x^6 + 6x^5 + 9x^4 - 4x^3 - 9x^2 + 6x - 1, \text{ on reduction.}$$

421. Binomial Theorem for Negative or Fractional Index. For a full discussion of the Binomial Theorem when the index is not restricted to positive integral values the student is referred to Chapter XLV. It is there shown that when x is less than unity, the formula

$$(1+x)^n = 1 + nx + \frac{n(n-1)}{1\cdot 2}x^2 + \frac{n(n-1)(n-2)}{1\cdot 2\cdot 3}x^3 + \cdots$$

is true for any value of n.

When n is negative or fractional the number of terms in the expansion is unlimited, but in any particular case we may write down as many terms as we please, or we may find the coefficient of any assigned term.

Ex. 1. Expand $(1+x)^{-3}$ to four terms.

$$(1+x)^{-3} = 1 + (-3)x + \frac{(-3)(-3-1)}{1\cdot 2}x^2 + \frac{(-3)(-3-1)(-3-2)}{1\cdot 2\cdot 3}x^3 + \cdots$$

$$= 1 - 3x + \frac{3\cdot 4}{1\cdot 2}x^2 - \frac{3\cdot 4\cdot 5}{1\cdot 2\cdot 3}x^3 + \cdots$$

$$= 1 - 3x + 6x^2 - 10x^3 + \cdots$$

Ex. 2. Expand $(4+3x)^{\frac{3}{2}}$ to four terms.

$$(4+3x)^{\frac{3}{2}} = 4^{\frac{3}{2}}\left(1 + \frac{3x}{4}\right)^{\frac{3}{2}} = 8\left(1 + \frac{3x}{4}\right)^{\frac{3}{2}}$$

$$= 8\left[1 + \frac{3}{2}\cdot\frac{3x}{4} + \frac{\frac{3}{2}(\frac{3}{2}-1)}{1\cdot 2}\left(\frac{3x}{4}\right)^2 + \frac{\frac{3}{2}(\frac{3}{2}-1)(\frac{3}{2}-2)}{1\cdot 2\cdot 3}\left(\frac{3x}{4}\right)^3 + \cdots\right]$$

$$= 8\left[1 + \frac{3}{2}\cdot\frac{3x}{4} + \frac{3}{8}\cdot\frac{9x^2}{16} - \frac{1}{16}\cdot\frac{27x^3}{64} + \cdots\right]$$

$$= 8 + 9x + \frac{27}{16}x^2 - \frac{27}{128}x^3 + \cdots.$$

422. In finding the **general term** we must now use the formula

$$\frac{n(n-1)(n-2)\cdots(n-r+1)}{\lfloor r}x^r$$

written in full; for the symbol ^nC_r cannot be employed when n is fractional or negative.

Ex. 1. Find the general term in the expansion of $(1+x)^{\frac{1}{2}}$.

$$\text{The } (r+1)\text{th term} = \frac{\frac{1}{2}(\frac{1}{2}-1)(\frac{1}{2}-2)\cdots(\frac{1}{2}-r+1)}{\lfloor r}x^r$$

$$= \frac{1(-1)(-3)(-5)\cdots(-2r+3)}{2^r\lfloor r}x^r.$$

BINOMIAL THEOREM.

The number of factors in the numerator is r, and $r-1$ of these are negative; therefore, by taking -1 out of each of these negative factors, we may write the above expression

$$(-1)^{r-1}\frac{1\cdot 3\cdot 5\cdots(2r-3)}{2^r\lfloor r}x^r.$$

Ex. 2. Find the general term in the expansion of $(1-x)^{-3}$.

$$\text{The } (r+1)\text{th term} = \frac{(-3)(-4)(-5)\cdots(-3-r+1)}{\lfloor r}(-x)^r$$

$$= (-1)^r\frac{3\cdot 4\cdot 5\cdots(r+2)}{\lfloor r}(-1)^r x^r$$

$$= (-1)^{2r}\frac{3\cdot 4\cdot 5\cdots(r+2)}{1\cdot 2\cdot 3\cdots r}x^r$$

$$= \frac{(r+1)(r+2)}{1\cdot 2}x^r,$$

by removing like factors from the numerator and denominator.

423. The following expansions should be remembered:

$(1-x)^{-1} = 1 + x + x^2 + x^3 + \cdots + x^r + \cdots.$

$(1-x)^{-2} = 1 + 2x + 3x^2 + 4x^3 + \cdots + (r+1)x^r + \cdots$

$(1-x)^{-3} = 1 + 3x + 6x^2 + 10x^3 \cdots + \dfrac{(r+1)(r+2)}{1\cdot 2}x^r + \cdots.$

424. The following example illustrates a useful application of the Binomial Theorem.

Ex. Find the cube root of 126 to 5 places of decimals.

$$(126)^{\frac{1}{3}} = (5^3+1)^{\frac{1}{3}} = 5\left(1+\frac{1}{5^3}\right)^{\frac{1}{3}}$$

$$= 5\left(1 + \frac{1}{3}\cdot\frac{1}{5^3} - \frac{1}{9}\cdot\frac{1}{5^6} + \frac{5}{81}\cdot\frac{1}{5^9} - \cdots\right)$$

$$= 5 + \frac{1}{3}\cdot\frac{1}{5^2} - \frac{1}{9}\cdot\frac{1}{5^5} + \frac{1}{81}\cdot\frac{1}{5^7} - \cdots$$

$$= 5 + \frac{1}{3}\cdot\frac{2^2}{10^2} - \frac{1}{9}\cdot\frac{2^5}{10^5} + \frac{1}{81}\cdot\frac{2^7}{10^7} - \cdots$$

$$= 5 + \frac{.04}{3} - \frac{.00032}{9} + \frac{.0000128}{81} - \cdots$$

$$= 5 + .013333\cdots - .000035\cdots + \cdots$$

$$= 5.01329, \text{ to five places of decimals.}$$

EXAMPLES XXXVII. b.

In the following expansions find which is the greatest term:

1. $(x+y)^{17}$ when $x=4, y=3$.
2. $(x-y)^{28}$ when $x=9, y=4$.
3. $(1+x)^4$ when $x=\frac{2}{3}$.
4. $(a-4b)^{15}$ when $a=12, b=2$.
5. $(7x+2y)^{30}$ when $x=8, y=14$.
6. $(2x+3)^n$ when $x=\frac{5}{2}, n=15$.

7. In the expansion of $(1+x)^{25}$ the coefficients of the $(2r+1)$th and $(r+5)$th terms are equal: find r.

8. Find n when the coefficients of the 16th and 26th terms of $(1+x)^n$ are equal.

9. Find the relation between r and n in order that the coefficients of $(r+3)$th and $(2r-3)$th terms of $(1+x)^{3n}$ may be equal.

10. Find the coefficient of x^m in the expansion of $\left(x^2+\dfrac{1}{x}\right)^{2m}$.

11. Find the middle term of $(1+x)^{2n}$ in its simplest form.

12. Find the sum of the coefficients of $(x+y)^{16}$.

13. Find the sum of the coefficients of $(3x+y)^9$.

14. Find the rth term from the beginning and the rth term from the end of $(a+2x)^n$.

15. Expand $(a^2+2a+1)^3$ and $(x^2-4x+2)^3$.

Expand to four terms the following expressions:

16. $(1+x)^{\frac{1}{3}}$.
17. $(1+x)^{\frac{3}{4}}$.
18. $(1+x)^{\frac{2}{5}}$.
19. $(1+3x)^{-2}$.
20. $(1-x^2)^{-3}$.
21. $(1+3x)^{-4}$.
22. $(2+x)^{-3}$.
23. $(1+2x)^{-\frac{1}{2}}$.
24. $(a-2x)^{-\frac{3}{2}}$.

Write in simplest form:

25. The 5th term and the 10th term of $(1+x)^{-\frac{3}{2}}$.

26. The 3d term and the 11th term of $(1+2x)^{\frac{11}{2}}$.

27. The 4th term and the $(r+1)$th term of $(1+x)^{-2}$.

28. The 7th term and the $(r+1)$th term of $(1-x)^{\frac{1}{2}}$.

29. The $(r+1)$th term of $(a-bx)^{-1}$, and of $(1-nx)^{\frac{1}{n}}$.

Find to four places of decimals the value of

30. $\sqrt[3]{122}$.
31. $\sqrt[4]{620}$.
32. $\sqrt[5]{31}$.
33. $1+\sqrt{99}$.

BINOMIAL THEOREM.

Find the value of

34. $(x+\sqrt{2})^4+(x-\sqrt{2})^4$.
35. $(\sqrt{x^2-a^2}+x)^5-(\sqrt{x^2-a^2}-x)^5$.
36. $(\sqrt{2}+1)^6-(\sqrt{2}-1)^6$.
37. $(2-\sqrt{1-x})^6+(2+\sqrt{1-x})^6$.
38. Find the middle term of $\left(\dfrac{a}{x}+\dfrac{x}{a}\right)^{10}$.
39. Find the middle term of $\left(1-\dfrac{x^2}{2}\right)^{14}$.
40. Find the coefficient of x^{18} in $\left(x^2+\dfrac{3a}{x}\right)^{15}$.
41. Find the coefficient of x^{18} in $(ax^4-bx)^9$.
42. Find the coefficients of x^{32} and x^{-17} in $\left(x^4-\dfrac{1}{x^3}\right)^{15}$.
43. Find the two middle terms of $\left(3a-\dfrac{a^3}{6}\right)^9$.

Write in simplest form

44. The 8th term of $(1+2x)^{-\frac{1}{2}}$.
45. The 11th term of $(1-2x^3)^{\frac{11}{2}}$.
46. The 10th term of $(1+3a^2)^{\frac{16}{3}}$.
47. The 5th term of $(3a-2b)^{-1}$.
48. The $(r+1)$th term of $(1-x)^{-2}$.
49. The $(r+1)$th term of $(1-x)^{-4}$.
50. The $(r+1)$th term of $(1+x)^{\frac{1}{2}}$.
51. The $(r+1)$th term of $(1+x)^{\frac{11}{3}}$.
52. The 14th term of $(2^{10}-2^7 x)^{\frac{13}{2}}$.
53. The 7th term of $(3^6+6^4 x)^{\frac{11}{4}}$.

CHAPTER XXXVIII.

LOGARITHMS.

425. DEFINITION. The **logarithm** of any number to a given **base** is the index of the power to which the base must be raised in order to equal the given number. Thus if $a^x = N$, x is called the logarithm of N to the base a.

EXAMPLES. (1) Since $3^4 = 81$, the logarithm of 81 to base 3 **is 4**.

(2) Since $10^1 = 10$, $10^2 = 100$, $10^3 = 1000$, $\cdots$ the natural numbers 1, 2, 3, $\cdots$ are respectively the logarithms of 10, 100, 1000, $\cdots$ to base 10.

426. The logarithm of N to base a is usually written $\log_a N$, so that the same meaning is expressed by the two equations
$$a^x = N; \quad x = \log_a N.$$

Ex. Find the logarithm of $32\sqrt[5]{4}$ to base $2\sqrt{2}$.

Let x be the required logarithm; then, by definition,
$$(2\sqrt{2})^x = 32\sqrt[5]{4};$$
$$\therefore (2 \cdot 2^{\frac{1}{2}})^x = 2^5 \cdot 2^{\frac{2}{5}};$$
$$\therefore 2^{\frac{3}{2}x} = 2^{5+\frac{2}{5}};$$
hence, by equating the indices, $\frac{3}{2}x = \frac{27}{5}$;
$$\therefore x = \frac{18}{5} = 3.6.$$

427. When it is understood that a particular system of logarithms is in use, the suffix denoting the base is omitted. Thus in arithmetical calculations in which 10 is the base, we usually write $\log 2$, $\log 3$, $\cdots$ instead of $\log_{10} 2$, $\log_{10} 3$, $\cdots$.

Logarithms to the base 10 are known as **Common Logarithms**; this system was first introduced in 1615 by Briggs, **a** contemporary of Napier the inventor of Logarithms.

PROPERTIES OF LOGARITHMS.

428. Logarithm of Unity. *The logarithm of 1 is 0.*

For $a^0 = 1$ for all values of a; therefore $\log 1 = 0$, whatever the base may be.

429. Logarithm of the Base. *The logarithm of the base itself is 1.*

For $a^1 = a$; therefore $\log_a a = 1$.

430. Logarithm of Zero. *The logarithm of 0, in any system whose base is greater than unity, is minus infinity.*

For
$$a^{-\infty} = \frac{1}{a^\infty} = 0.$$

Also, since $a^{+\infty} = \infty$, *the logarithm of* $+\infty$ *is* $+\infty$.

431. Logarithm of a Product. *The logarithm of a product is the sum of the logarithms of its factors.*

Let MN be the product; let a be the base of the system, and suppose
$$x = \log_a M, \quad y = \log_a N;$$
so that $\quad a^x = M, \quad a^y = N.$

Thus the product $MN = a^x \times a^y = a^{x+y}$;

whence, by definition, $\log_a MN = x + y = \log_a M + \log_a N.$

Similarly, $\quad \log_a MNP = \log_a M + \log_a N + \log_a P;$
and so on for any number of factors.

Ex. $\quad \log 42 = \log (2 \times 3 \times 7) = \log 2 + \log 3 + \log 7.$

432. Logarithm of a Quotient. *The logarithm of a quotient is the logarithm of the dividend minus the logarithm of the divisor.*

Let $\dfrac{M}{N}$ be the fraction, and suppose
$$x = \log_a M, \quad y = \log_a N;$$
so that $\quad a^x = M, \quad a^y = N.$

Thus the fraction $\dfrac{M}{N} = \dfrac{a^x}{a^y} = a^{x-y}$;

whence, by definition, $\log_a \dfrac{M}{N} = x - y = \log_a M - \log_a N$.

Ex. $\log(2\tfrac{1}{7}) = \log \tfrac{15}{7} = \log 15 - \log 7$
$= \log(3 \times 5) - \log 7 = \log 3 + \log 5 - \log 7$.

433. Logarithm of a Power. *The logarithm of a number raised to any power, integral or fractional, is the logarithm of the number multiplied by the index of the power.*

Let $\log_a(M^p)$ be required, and suppose

$$x = \log_a M, \text{ so that } a^x = M;$$

then $\quad M^p = (a^x)^p = a^{px}$;

whence, by definition, $\log_a(M^p) = px$;

that is, $\quad \log_a(M^p) = p \log_a M$.

Similarly, $\quad \log_a(M^{\frac{1}{r}}) = \dfrac{1}{r} \log^a M$.

Ex. Express the logarithm of $\dfrac{\sqrt{a^3}}{c^5 b^2}$ in terms of $\log a$, $\log b$, and $\log c$.

$\log \dfrac{\sqrt{a^3}}{c^5 b^2} = \log \dfrac{a^{\frac{3}{2}}}{c^5 b^2} = \log a^{\frac{3}{2}} - \log(c^5 b^2)$
$= \tfrac{3}{2} \log a - (\log c^5 + \log b^2) = \tfrac{3}{2} \log a - 5 \log c - 2 \log b$.

434. From the equation $10^x = N$, it is evident that **common logarithms** will not in general be integral, and that they will not always be positive.

For instance, $\quad 3154 > 10^3 \text{ and } < 10^4$;

$\therefore \log 3154 = 3 + \text{a fraction}$.

Again, $\quad .06 > 10^{-2} \text{ and } < 10^{-1}$;

$\therefore \log .06 = -2 + \text{a fraction}$.

Negative numbers have no common logarithms.

435. Definition. The integral part of a logarithm is called the **characteristic**, and the decimal part, when it is so written that it is positive, is called the **mantissa**.

The characteristic of the logarithm of any number to the **base 10** can be written by inspection, as we shall now show.

436. The Characteristic of the Logarithm of Any Number Greater than Unity. It is clear that a number with two digits in its integral part lies between 10^1 and 10^2; a number with three digits in its integral part lies between 10^2 and 10^3; and so on. Hence a number with n digits in its integral part lies between 10^{n-1} and 10^n.

Let N be a number whose integral part contains n digits; then

$$N = 10^{(n-1)+\text{a fraction}};$$

$$\therefore \log N = (n-1) + \text{a fraction.}$$

Hence the characteristic is $n-1$; that is, *the characteristic of the logarithm of a number greater than unity is less by one than the number of digits in its integral part, and is positive.*

437. The Characteristic of the Logarithm of a Decimal Fraction. A decimal with one cipher immediately after the decimal point, such as .0324, being greater than .01 and less than .1, lies between 10^{-2} and 10^{-1}; a number with two ciphers after the decimal point lies between 10^{-3} and 10^{-2}; and so on. Hence a decimal fraction with n ciphers immediately after the decimal point lies between $10^{-(n+1)}$ and 10^{-n}.

Let D be a decimal beginning with n ciphers; then

$$D = 10^{-(n+1)+\text{a fraction}};$$

$$\therefore \log D = -(n+1) + \text{a fraction.}$$

Hence the characteristic is $-(n+1)$; that is, *the characteristic of the logarithm of a decimal fraction is greater by unity than the number of ciphers immediately after the decimal point and is negative.*

438. Advantages of Common Logarithms. Common logarithms, because of the two great advantages of the base 10, are in common use. These two advantages are as follows:

(1) From the results already proved it is evident that the characteristics can be written by inspection, so that only the mantissæ have to be registered in the Tables.

(2) The mantissæ are the same for the logarithms of all numbers which have *the same significant digits;* so that it is sufficient to tabulate the mantissæ of the logarithms of *integers*.

This proposition we proceed to prove.

439. Let N be any number, then since multiplying or dividing by a power of 10 merely alters the position of the decimal point without changing the sequence of figures, it follows that $N \times 10^p$, and $N \div 10^q$, where p and q are any integers, are numbers whose significant digits are the same as those of N.

Now $\log(N \times 10^p) = \log N + p \log 10 = \log N + p$. (1).

Again, $\log(N \div 10^q) = \log N - q \log 10 = \log N - q$. (2).

In (1) an integer is added to $\log N$, and in (2) an integer is subtracted from $\log N$; that is, the *mantissa or decimal portion of the logarithm remains unaltered.*

In this and the three preceding articles the mantissæ have been supposed positive. In order to secure the advantages of Briggs' system, we arrange our work so as *always to keep the mantissa positive*, so that when the mantissa of any logarithm has been taken from the Tables the characteristic is prefixed with its appropriate sign, according to the rules already given.

440. In the case of a negative logarithm the minus sign is written *over the characteristic*, and not before it, to indicate that the characteristic alone is negative, and not the whole expression. Thus $\bar{4}.30103$, the logarithm of .0002, is equivalent to $-4 + .30103$, and must be distinguished from -4.30103, an expression in which both the integer and the decimal are negative. In working with negative logarithms an arithmetical artifice will sometimes be necessary in order to make the mantissa positive. For instance, a result such as -3.69897, in which the whole expression is negative, may be transformed by subtracting 1 from the characteristic and adding 1 to the mantissa. Thus,

$$-3.69897 = -4 + (1 - .69897) = \bar{4}.30103.$$

LOGARITHMS. 357

Ex. 1. Required the logarithm of .0002432.

In Seven-Place Tables we find that 3859636 is the mantissa of log 2432 (the decimal point as well as the characteristic being omitted); and, by Art. 437, the characteristic of the logarithm of the given number is -4;

$$\therefore \log .0002432 = \bar{4}.3859636.$$

This may be written 6.3859636 − 10.

Ex. 2. Find the value of $\sqrt[5]{.00000165}$, given

$$\log 165 = 2.2174839, \ \log 697424 = 5.8434968.$$

Let x denote the value required; then

$$\log x = \log (.00000165)^{\frac{1}{5}} = \tfrac{1}{5} \log (.00000165) = \tfrac{1}{5}(\bar{6}.2174839);$$

the *mantissa* of log .00000165 being the same as that of log 165, and the *characteristic* being prefixed by the rule.

Now $\quad \tfrac{1}{5}(\bar{6}.2174839) = \tfrac{1}{5}(\overline{10} + 4.2174839) = \bar{2}.8434968$

and .8434968 is the mantissa of log 697424; hence x is a number consisting of these same digits, but with one cipher after the decimal point. [Art. 437.]

Thus $\qquad x = .0697424.$

441. Logarithms transformed from Base a to Base b. Suppose that the logarithms of all numbers to base a are known and tabulated.

Let N be any number whose logarithm to base b is required.

Let $y = \log_b N$, so that $b^y = N$;

$$\therefore \log_a (b^y) = \log_a N;$$

that is, $\qquad y \log_a b = \log_a N;$

$$\therefore y = \frac{1}{\log_a b} \times \log_a N,$$

or $\qquad \log_b N = \dfrac{1}{\log_a b} \times \log_a N \ \ . \ \ . \ \ . \ \ . \ \ (1).$

Now since N and b are given, $\log_a N$ and $\log_a b$ are known from the Tables, and thus $\log_b N$ may be found.

Hence *to transform logarithms from base a to base b we multiply them all by* $\dfrac{1}{\log_a b}$; this is a constant quantity, and is given by the Tables; it is known as the *modulus*.

Cor. If in equation (1) we put a for N, we obtain
$$\log_b a = \frac{1}{\log_a b} \times \log_a a = \frac{1}{\log_a b};$$
$$\therefore \log_b a \times \log_a b = 1.$$

442. Logarithms in Arithmetical Calculation. The following examples illustrate the utility of logarithms in facilitating arithmetical calculation.

Ex. 1. Given $\log 3 = .4771213$, find $\log\{(2.7)^3 \times (.81)^{\frac{2}{5}} \div (90)^{\frac{5}{4}}\}$.

The required value $= 3 \log \frac{27}{10} + \frac{2}{5} \log \frac{81}{100} - \frac{5}{4} \log 90$

$$= 3(\log 3^3 - 1) + \frac{2}{5}(\log 3^4 - 2) - \frac{5}{4}(\log 3^2 + 1)$$
$$= (9 + \frac{8}{5} - \frac{5}{2}) \log 3 - (3 + \frac{4}{5} + \frac{5}{4})$$
$$= \frac{81}{10} \log 3 - 5\frac{1}{20} = 4.6280766 - 5.85 = \bar{2}.7780766.$$

The student should notice that the logarithm of 5 and its powers can always be obtained from $\log 2$; thus
$$\log 5 = \log \tfrac{10}{2} = \log 10 - \log 2 = 1 - \log 2.$$

Ex. 2. Find the number of digits in 875^{16}, given
$$\log 2 = .3010300, \log 7 = .8450980.$$
$$\log (875^{16}) = 16 \log (7 \times 125) = 16 (\log 7 + 3 \log 5)$$
$$= 16 (\log 7 + 3 - 3 \log 2)$$
$$= 16 \times 2.9420080 = 47.072128;$$
hence the number of digits is 48. [Art. 436.]

EXAMPLES XXXVIII. a.

1. Find the logarithms of $\sqrt{32}$ and $.03125$ to base $\sqrt[5]{2}$, and 100 and $.00001$ to base $.01$.

2. Find the value of $\log_4 512$, $\log_5 .0016$, $\log_{81} \frac{1}{27}$, $\log_{49} 343$.

3. Write the numbers whose logarithms to bases 25, 3, .02, 1, -4, 1.7, 1000, are $\frac{1}{2}$, -2, -3, 5, -1, 2, $-\frac{2}{3}$ respectively.

Simplify the expressions·

4. $\log \dfrac{(ab^2c^4)^{\frac{1}{6}}}{\sqrt[9]{a^{-3}b^8c^6}}$.

5. $\log \left\{ \left(\dfrac{x^4 y^{-3}}{x^{-1} y^2}\right)^{-3} \div \left(\dfrac{x^{-2} y^3}{xy^{-1}}\right)^5 \right\}$.

6. Find by inspection the characteristics of the logarithms of 3174, 625.7, 3.502, .4, .374, .000135, 23.22065.

LOGARITHMS.

7. The mantissa of log 37203 is .5705780: write the logarithms of 37.203, .000037203, 372030000.

8. The logarithm of 7623 is 3.8821259: write the numbers whose logarithms are .8821259, $\bar{6}$.8821259, 7.8821259.

Given $\log 2 = .3010300$, $\log 3 = .4771213$, $\log 7 = .8450980$, find the value of

9. log 729.　　**10.** log 8400.　　**11.** log .256.
12. log 5.832.　**13.** log $\sqrt[3]{392}$.　**14.** log .3048.

15. Show that $\log \frac{14}{15} + \log \frac{154}{159} - 2\log \frac{7}{9} = \log 2$.

16. Find to six decimal places the value of
$$\log \tfrac{225}{224} - 2\log \tfrac{20}{189} + \log \tfrac{512}{81}.$$

17. Simplify $\log \{(10.8)^{\frac{1}{2}} \times (.24)^{\frac{5}{3}} \div (90)^{-2}\}$, and find its numerical value.

18. Find the value of
$$\log (\sqrt[3]{126} \cdot \sqrt{108} + \sqrt[6]{1008} \cdot \sqrt[3]{162}).$$

19. Find the value of $\log \sqrt[5]{\dfrac{588 \times 768}{686 \times 972}}$.

20. Find the number of digits in 42^{42}.

21. Show that $\left(\dfrac{81}{80}\right)^{1000}$ is greater than 100000.

22. How many ciphers are there between the decimal point and the first significant digit in $\left(\dfrac{2}{3}\right)^{1000}$?

23. Find the value of $\sqrt[5]{.01008}$, having given
$$\log 398742 = 5.6006921.$$

24. Find the seventh root of .00792, having given
$$\log 11 = 1.0413927 \text{ and } \log 500.977 = 2.6998179.$$

25. Find the value of $2\log \frac{7\frac{1}{2}}{9} + \log \frac{135}{32} - 3\log \frac{4\frac{1}{2}}{3}$.

ALGEBRA.

N	0	1	2	3	4	5	6	7	8	9
10	0000	0043	0086	0128	0170	0212	0253	0294	0334	0374
11	0414	0453	0492	0531	0569	0607	0645	0682	0719	0755
12	0792	0828	0864	0899	0934	0969	1004	1038	1072	1106
13	1139	1173	1206	1239	1271	1303	1335	1367	1399	1430
14	1461	1492	1523	1553	1584	1614	1644	1673	1703	1732
15	1761	1790	1818	1847	1875	1903	1931	1959	1987	2014
16	2041	2068	2095	2122	2148	2175	2201	2227	2253	2279
17	2304	2330	2355	2380	2405	2430	2455	2480	2504	2529
18	2553	2577	2601	2625	2648	2672	2695	2718	2742	2765
19	2788	2810	2833	2856	2878	2900	2923	2945	2967	2989
20	3010	3032	3054	3075	3096	3118	3139	3160	3181	3201
21	3222	3243	3263	3284	3304	3324	3345	3365	3385	3404
22	3424	3444	3464	3483	3502	3522	3541	3560	3579	3598
23	3617	3636	3655	3674	3692	3711	3729	3747	3766	3784
24	3802	3820	3838	3856	3874	3892	3909	3927	3945	3962
25	3979	3997	4014	4031	4048	4065	4082	4099	4116	4133
26	4150	4166	4183	4200	4216	4232	4249	4265	4281	4298
27	4314	4330	4346	4362	4378	4393	4409	4425	4440	4456
28	4472	4487	4502	4518	4533	4548	4564	4579	4594	4609
29	4624	4639	4654	4669	4683	4698	4713	4728	4742	4757
30	4771	4786	4800	4814	4829	4843	4857	4871	4886	4900
31	4914	4928	4942	4955	4969	4983	4997	5011	5024	5038
32	5051	5065	5079	5092	5105	5119	5132	5145	5159	5172
33	5185	5198	5211	5224	5237	5250	5263	5276	5289	5302
34	5315	5328	5340	5353	5366	5378	5391	5403	5416	5428
35	5441	5453	5465	5478	5490	5502	5514	5527	5539	5551
36	5563	5575	5587	5599	5611	5623	5635	5647	5658	5670
37	5682	5694	5705	5717	5729	5740	5752	5763	5775	5786
38	5798	5809	5821	5832	5843	5855	5866	5877	5888	5899
39	5911	5922	5933	5944	5955	5966	5977	5988	5999	6010
40	6021	6031	6042	6053	6064	6075	6085	6096	6107	6117
41	6128	6138	6149	6160	6170	6180	6191	6201	6212	6222
42	6232	6243	6253	6263	6274	6284	6294	6304	6314	6325
43	6335	6345	6355	6365	6375	6385	6395	6405	6415	6425
44	6435	6444	6454	6464	6474	6484	6493	6503	6513	6522
45	6532	6542	6551	6561	6571	6580	6590	6599	6609	6618
46	6628	6637	6646	6656	6665	6675	6684	6693	6702	6712
47	6721	6730	6739	6749	6758	6767	6776	6785	6794	6803
48	6812	6821	6830	6839	6848	6857	6866	6875	6884	6893
49	6902	6911	6920	6928	6937	6946	6955	6964	6972	6981
50	6990	6998	7007	7016	7024	7033	7042	7050	7059	7067
51	7076	7084	7093	7101	7110	7118	7126	7135	7143	7152
52	7160	7168	7177	7185	7193	7202	7210	7218	7226	7235
53	7243	7251	7259	7267	7275	7284	7292	7300	7308	7316
54	7324	7332	7340	7348	7356	7364	7372	7380	7388	7396

LOGARITHMS.

N	0	1	2	3	4	5	6	7	8	9
55	7404	7412	7419	7427	7435	7443	7451	7459	7466	7474
56	7482	7490	7497	7505	7513	7520	7528	7536	7543	7551
57	7559	7566	7574	7582	7589	7597	7604	7612	7619	7627
58	7634	7642	7649	7657	7664	7672	7679	7686	7694	7701
59	7709	7716	7723	7731	7738	7745	7752	7760	7767	7774
60	7782	7789	7796	7803	7810	7818	7825	7832	7839	7846
61	7853	7860	7868	7875	7882	7889	7896	7903	7910	7917
62	7924	7931	7938	7945	7952	7959	7966	7973	7980	7987
63	7993	8000	8007	8014	8021	8028	8035	8041	8048	8055
64	8062	8069	8075	8082	8089	8096	8102	8109	8116	8122
65	8129	8136	8142	8149	8156	8162	8169	8176	8182	8189
66	8195	8202	8209	8215	8222	8228	8235	8241	8248	8254
67	8261	8267	8274	8280	8287	8293	8299	8306	8312	8319
68	8325	8331	8338	8344	8351	8357	8363	8370	8376	8382
69	8388	8395	8401	8407	8414	8420	8426	8432	8439	8445
70	8451	8457	8463	8470	8476	8482	8488	8494	8500	8506
71	8513	8519	8525	8531	8537	8543	8549	8555	8561	8567
72	8573	8579	8585	8591	8597	8603	8609	8615	8621	8627
73	8633	8639	8645	8651	8657	8663	8669	8675	8681	8686
74	8692	8698	8704	8710	8716	8722	8727	8733	8739	8745
75	8751	8756	8762	8768	8774	8779	8785	8791	8797	8802
76	8808	8814	8820	8825	8831	8837	8842	8848	8854	8859
77	8865	8871	8876	8882	8887	8893	8899	8904	8910	8915
78	8921	8927	8932	8938	8943	8949	8954	8960	8965	8971
79	8976	8982	8987	8993	8998	9004	9009	9015	9020	9025
80	9031	9036	9042	9047	9053	9058	9063	9069	9074	9079
81	9085	9090	9096	9101	9106	9112	9117	9122	9128	9133
82	9138	9143	9149	9154	9159	9165	9170	9175	9180	9186
83	9191	9196	9201	9206	9212	9217	9222	9227	9232	9238
84	9243	9248	9253	9258	9263	9269	9274	9279	9284	9289
85	9294	9299	9304	9309	9315	9320	9325	9330	9335	9340
86	9345	9350	9355	9360	9365	9370	9375	9380	9385	9390
87	9395	9400	9405	9410	9415	9420	9425	9430	9435	9440
88	9445	9450	9455	9460	9465	9469	9474	9479	9484	9489
89	9494	9499	9504	9509	9513	9518	9523	9528	9533	9538
90	9542	9547	9552	9557	9562	9566	9571	9576	9581	9586
91	9590	9595	9600	9605	9609	9614	9619	9624	9628	9633
92	9638	9643	9647	9652	9657	9661	9666	9671	9675	9680
93	9685	9689	9694	9699	9703	9708	9713	9717	9722	9727
94	9731	9736	9741	9745	9750	9754	9759	9763	9768	9773
95	9777	9782	9786	9791	9795	9800	9805	9809	9814	9818
96	9823	9827	9832	9836	9841	9845	9850	9854	9859	9863
97	9868	9872	9877	9881	9886	9890	9894	9899	9903	9908
98	9912	9917	9921	9926	9930	9934	9939	9943	9948	9952
99	9956	9961	9965	9969	9974	9978	9983	9987	9991	9996

ALGEBRA.

USE OF THE TABLE.

443. On pages 360–361 we give a four-place table containing the mantissæ of the common logarithms of all numbers from 100 to 1000.

444. To find the logarithm of a number.

(a) Suppose the number consists of three figures, as 56.7. In the column headed N find the first two significant figures. On a line with these and in the column having at the top the third figure will be found the mantissa. Thus on a line with 56 and in the column headed 7 we find 7536. To this, which is the decimal part of the logarithm, prefix the characteristic [Art. 436], and we have

$$\log 56.7 = 1.7536.$$

(b) Since in common logarithms the mantissa remains unchanged when the number is multiplied by an integral power of 10, we change one or two-figure numbers into three-figure numbers by addition of ciphers before looking for the mantissæ. The mantissa of log 56 will be that of 560, the only change in the logarithm being in the characteristic.

Thus
$$\log 560 = 2.7482,$$
$$\log \ 56 = 1.7482.$$

In the same manner log 7 has for mantissa that of log 700.

$$\log 700 = 2.8451,$$
$$\log \ \ 7 = 0.8451.$$

(c) Suppose the logarithm of a number of more than three figures, as 62543, is required. Since the number lies between 62500 and 62600, its logarithm lies between their logarithms. In the column headed N we find the first two figures, 62; on a line with these and in the columns headed 5, and 6, we find the mantissæ .7959 and .7966. Prefixing the characteristic [Art. 436], we have

$$\log 62600 = 4.7966,$$
$$\log 62500 = 4.7959.$$

Therefore while the number increases from 62500 to 62600, the logarithm increases .0007. Now our number is $\frac{43}{100}$ of the way from 62500 to 62600; hence if to the logarithm of 62500 we add $\frac{43}{100}$ of .0007, a nearly correct logarithm of 62543 is obtained.

Thus $\qquad$ log 62543 = 4.7959
$$\qquad\qquad\qquad\quad \underline{.0003 \text{ correction}}$$
$$\qquad\qquad\quad = 4.7962$$

(d) Suppose the logarithm of a decimal, as .0005243, is required. The number lies between .0005240 and .0005250. In the column headed N we find the first two significant figures, 52; on a line with these and in the columns headed 4, and 5, we find the mantissæ .7193 and .7202. Prefixing the characteristic [Art. 437], we have

$$\log .0005250 = \overline{4}.7202$$
$$\log .0005240 = \overline{4}.7193$$
$$\text{differences } .0000010 \qquad .0009$$

Now .0005243 is .0000003 greater than .0005240; hence log .0005243 equals log .0005240 plus $\dfrac{.0000003}{.0000010}$ or $\dfrac{3}{10}$ of .0009 (the difference of logarithms);

that is, $\qquad$ log .0005243 = $\overline{4}$.7193
$$\qquad\qquad\qquad\quad \underline{.0003 \text{ (nearly)}}$$
$$\qquad\qquad\quad = \overline{4}.7196$$

In practice *negative characteristics* are usually avoided by adding them to 10 and writing -10 after the logarithm. Thus in the above example $\overline{4}.7196 = 6.7196 - 10$.

445. The increase in the logarithms on the same line, as we pass from column to column, is called the *tabular difference*. In finding the logarithm of 62543, we *assumed* that the differences of logarithms are proportional to the differences of their corresponding numbers, which gives us results that are approximately correct. For greater accuracy we must use tables of more places.

446. To find the number corresponding to a logarithm.

(*a*) Suppose a logarithm, as 1.7466, is given to find the corresponding number.

Look in the table for the mantissa .7466. It is found in the column headed 8 and on the line with 55 in the column headed N. Therefore we take the figures 558, and, as the characteristic is 1, point off two places, obtaining the number 55.8.

(*b*) Suppose a logarithm, as 3.7531, is given to find the corresponding number.

The exact mantissa, .7531, is not found in the table, therefore take out the next larger, .7536, and the next smaller, .7528, and retain the characteristic in arranging the work.

Thus, the number corresponding to 3.7536 is 5670
and the number corresponding to   3.7528 is 5660
                         differences .0008   10

Now the logarithm 3.7531 is .0003 greater than the logarithm 3.7528, and a difference in logarithms of .0008 corresponds to a difference in numbers of 10; therefore we should increase the number corresponding to the logarithm 3.7528 by $\frac{.0003}{.0008}$ or $\frac{3}{8}$ of 10.

Thus the number corresponding to the logarithm

$$3.7531 = 5660$$
$$3.7 \text{ correction}$$
$$ = 5663.7$$

(*c*) Suppose a logarithm, as 8.8225 − 10 or $\bar{2}.8225$, is given to find the corresponding number.

Take out the mantissæ as in the previous example.

The number corresponding to $\bar{2}.8228$ is .0665 [Art. 437.]
The number corresponding to $\bar{2}.8222$ is .0664
                       differences .0006   .0001

Now the logarithm $\bar{2}.8225$ is .0003 greater than the logarithm $\bar{2}.8222$, and a difference in logarithms of .0006 corresponds to a difference in numbers of .0001; therefore we

LOGARITHMS.

should increase the number corresponding to the logarithm $\bar{2}.8222$ by $\dfrac{.0003}{.0006}$ or $\dfrac{3}{6}$ of $.0001$.

Thus

the number corresponding to the logarithm $\bar{2}.8222 = .0664$
the number corresponding to the logarithm $\bar{2}.8225 = .0664$
$$\text{Correction,} \quad .00005$$
$$= .06645$$

EXAMPLES XXXVIII. b.

Find the common logarithms of the following:

1. 50.
2. 203.
3. 6.73.
4. .341.
5. 0.045.
6. 5265.
7. 12345.
8. 0.010203.
9. 354.076.

Find the numbers corresponding to the following common logarithms:

10. 1.8156.
11. 2.1439.
12. 4.0022.
13. $\bar{1}.9131$.
14. $\bar{3}.8441$.
15. $7.4879 - 10$.

447. Cologarithms. The logarithm of the reciprocal of a number is called the *cologarithm* of that number.

Thus $\operatorname{colog} 210 = \log \dfrac{1}{210} = \log 1 - \log 210$.

Since $\log 1 = 0$, we write it in the form $10 - 10$ and then subtract $\log 210$, which gives

$$\operatorname{colog} 210 = (10 - 2.3222) - 10 = 7.6778 - 10.$$

Hence

RULE. *To find the cologarithm of a number, subtract the logarithm of the number from 10 and write -10 after the result.*

448. The advantage gained by the use of cologarithms is the substitution of addition for subtraction

Ex. Find by use of logarithms the value of $\dfrac{4.26}{7.42 \times .058}$.

$$\log \dfrac{4.26}{7.42 \times .058} = \log 4.26 + \log \dfrac{1}{7.42} + \log \dfrac{1}{.058}$$
$$= \log 4.26 + \operatorname{colog} 7.42 + \operatorname{colog} .058$$
$$= .6294 + (9.1296 - 10) + 1.2366$$
$$= 10.9956 - 10.$$

The number corresponding to this logarithm is 9.9.
In finding colog .058 we proceed as follows:

$$\operatorname{colog} .058 = \log \dfrac{1}{.058} = 10 - [\log .058] - 10 \text{ (Art. 447)},$$
$$= 10 - [8.7634 - 10] - 10 \text{ (Art. 437)},$$
$$= 10 - 8.7634 + 10 - 10 = 1.2366.$$

449. Exponential Equations. Equations in which the unknown quantity occurs as an exponent are called *exponential equations*, and are readily solved by the aid of logarithms.

Ex. Find the value of x in $15^x = 28$.
Taking the logarithms of both sides of the equation, we have
$$\log 15^x = \log 28;$$
$$\therefore x \log 15 = \log 28.$$
$$x = \dfrac{\log 28}{\log 15} = \dfrac{1.4472}{1.1761} = 1.2305 +.$$

EXAMPLES XXXVIII. a.

Find by use of logarithms:

1. $\dfrac{24.051 \times .02456}{.006705 \times .0203}$.

2.* $\dfrac{145.206 \times (-7.564)}{448.1 \times (-.2406)(-47.85)}$.

3. $(742.8024)^{\frac{2}{3}}$.

4. $(-.0012045)^{\frac{3}{5}}$.

5. $\dfrac{\sqrt[3]{4.8} \times \sqrt[4]{.002} \times \sqrt[5]{442.6}}{(18)^2 \times .7^3 \times (3.4562)^{\frac{1}{2}}}$.

6. $\dfrac{\sqrt{9.8149} \times 80.80008}{\sqrt[7]{8283} \times (.0006412)^4}$.

7. $845692.1 \times .845856$.

8. $.00010101 \times (7117.1)^6$.

9. $\dfrac{(285.42)^{1.4} \times (5.672)^5}{\sqrt{20} \times \sqrt[3]{.02} \times \sqrt[7]{-124.89}}$.

10. $\sqrt[3]{\dfrac{12.876 \times \sqrt{.068} \times (.005157)^2}{29.029 \times (52.81)^4 \times (.4)^9}}$.

11. $3^{x+2} = 405$.

12. $10^{5-3x} = 27^{-2x}$.

13. $12^{3x-4} \times 18^{7-2x} = 1458$.

14. $2^x \times 6^{x-2} = 5^{2x} \times 7^{1-x}$.

15. $2^{x+y} = 6^y$, $3^x = 3 \times 2^{y+1}$.

16. $3^{1-x-y} = 4^{-y}$, $2^{2x-1} = 3^{3y-x}$.

* Treat negative quantities occurring in logarithmic work as positive. When the numerical result is obtained, determine its sign by the ordinary rules of multiplication and division.

CHAPTER XXXIX.

Interest and Annuities.

450. Questions involving Simple Interest are easily solved by the rules of Arithmetic; but in Compound Interest the calculations are often very laborious. We shall now show how these arithmetical calculations may be simplified by the aid of logarithms. Instead of taking as the rate of interest the interest on $100 for one year, it will be found more convenient to take the interest on $1 for one year. If this be denoted by $$r$, and the amount of $1 for 1 year by $$R$, we have $R = 1 + r$.

451. **To find the interest and amount of a given sum in a given time at compound interest.**

Let P denote the principal, R the amount of $1 in one year, n the number of years, I the interest, and M the amount.

The amount of P at the end of the first year is PR; and, since this is the principal for the second year, the amount at the end of the second year is $PR \times R$ or PR^2. Similarly the amount at the end of the third year is PR^3, and so on; hence the amount in n years is PR^n; that is,

$$M = PR^n;$$

and therefore $\quad I = P(R^n - 1).$

Ex. Find the amount of $100 in a hundred years, allowing compound interest at the rate of 5 per cent, payable quarterly; having given

$\quad \log 2 = .3010300, \ \log 3 = .4771213, \ \log 14.3906 = 1.15808.$

The amount of $1 in a quarter of a year is $(1 + \frac{1}{4} \cdot \frac{5}{100})$ or $\frac{81}{80}$.

The number of payments is 400. If M be the amount, we have
$$M = 100(\tfrac{81}{80})^{400};$$
$$\therefore \log M = \log 100 + 400 (\log 81 - \log 80)$$
$$= 2 + 400 (4 \log 3 - 1 - 3 \log 2)$$
$$= 2 + 400 (.0053952) = 4.15808;$$
whence $M = 14390.6.$

Thus the amount is $\$14390.60$.

NOTE. At simple interest the amount is $\$600$.

452. To find the present value and discount of a given sum due in a given time, allowing compound interest.

Let P be the given sum, V the present value, D the discount, R the amount of $\$1$ for one year, n the number of years.

Since V is the sum which, put out to interest at the present time, will in n years amount to P, we have
$$P = VR^n;$$
$$\therefore V = PR^{-n},$$
and
$$D = P - V = P(1 - R^{-n}).$$

ANNUITIES.

453. An **annuity** is a fixed sum paid periodically under certain stated conditions; the payment may be made either once a year or at more frequent intervals. Unless it is otherwise stated, we shall suppose the payments annual.

454. To find the amount of an annuity left unpaid for a given number of years, allowing compound interest.

Let A be the annuity, R the amount of $\$1$ for one year, n the number of years, M the amount.

At the end of the first year A is due, and the amount of this sum in the remaining $n-1$ years is AR^{n-1}; at the end of the second year another A is due, and the amount of this sum in the remaining $n-2$ years is AR^{n-2}; and so on.

$$\therefore M = AR^{n-1} + AR^{n-2} + \cdots + AR^2 + AR + A$$
$$= A(1 + R + R^2 + \cdots \text{to } n \text{ terms}) = A\frac{R^n - 1}{R - 1}.$$

INTEREST AND ANNUITIES.

455. To find the present value of an annuity to continue for a given number of years, allowing compound interest.

Let A be the annuity, R the amount of \$1 in one year, n the number of years, V the required present value.

The present value of A due in 1 year is AR^{-1};
the present value of A due in 2 years is AR^{-2};
the present value of A due in 3 years is AR^{-3}; and so on.
[Art. 452.]

Now V is the sum of the present values of the different payments;

$$\therefore V = AR^{-1} + AR^{-2} + AR^{-3} + \cdots \text{ to } n \text{ terms}$$
$$= AR^{-1}\frac{1-R^{-n}}{1-R^{-1}} = A\frac{1-R^{-n}}{R-1}.$$

NOTE. This result may also be obtained by dividing the value of M, given in Art. 454, by R^n. [Art. 451.]

COR. If we make n infinite we obtain for the present value a perpetual annuity

$$V = \frac{A}{R-1} = \frac{A}{r}.$$

EXAMPLES XXXIX.

1. If in the year 1600 a sum of \$1000 had been left to accumulate for 300 years, find its amount in the year 1900, reckoning compound interest at 4 per cent per annum. Given

$$\log 104 = 2.0170333 \text{ and } \log 12885.5 = 4.10999.$$

2. Find in how many years a sum of money will amount to one hundred times its value at $5\frac{1}{4}$ per cent per annum compound interest. Given $\log 1055 = 3.023$.

3. Find the present value of \$6000 due in 20 years, allowing compound interest at 8 per cent per annum. Given

$$\log 2 = .30103, \log 3 = .47712, \text{ and } \log 12875 = 4.10975.$$

4. Find the amount of an annuity of \$100 in 15 years, allowing compound interest at 4 per cent per annum. Given

$$\log 1.04 = .01703, \text{ and } \log 180075 = 5.25545.$$

5. What is the present value of an annuity of \$1000 due in 30 years, allowing compound interest at 5 per cent per annum?

ALGEBRA.

N	0	1	2	3	4	5	6	7	8	9
10	0000	0043	0086	0128	0170	0212	0253	0294	0334	0374
11	0414	0453	0492	0531	0569	0607	0645	0682	0719	0755
12	0792	0828	0864	0899	0934	0969	1004	1038	1072	1106
13	1139	1173	1206	1239	1271	1303	1335	1367	1399	1430
14	1461	1492	1523	1553	1584	1614	1644	1673	1703	1732
15	1761	1790	1818	1847	1875	1903	1931	1959	1987	2014
16	2041	2068	2095	2122	2148	2175	2201	2227	2253	2279
17	2304	2330	2355	2380	2405	2430	2455	2480	2504	2529
18	2553	2577	2601	2625	2648	2672	2695	2718	2742	2765
19	2788	2810	2833	2856	2878	2900	2923	2945	2967	2989
20	3010	3032	3054	3075	3096	3118	3139	3160	3181	3201
21	3222	3243	3263	3284	3304	3324	3345	3365	3385	3404
22	3424	3444	3464	3483	3502	3522	3541	3560	3579	3598
23	3617	3636	3655	3674	3692	3711	3729	3747	3766	3784
24	3802	3820	3838	3856	3874	3892	3909	3927	3945	3962
25	3979	3997	4014	4031	4048	4065	4082	4099	4116	4133
26	4150	4166	4183	4200	4216	4232	4249	4265	4281	4298
27	4314	4330	4346	4362	4378	4393	4409	4425	4440	4456
28	4472	4487	4502	4518	4533	4548	4564	4579	4594	4609
29	4624	4639	4654	4669	4683	4698	4713	4728	4742	4757
30	4771	4786	4800	4814	4829	4843	4857	4871	4886	4900
31	4914	4928	4942	4955	4969	4983	4997	5011	5024	5038
32	5051	5065	5079	5092	5105	5119	5132	5145	5159	5172
33	5185	5198	5211	5224	5237	5250	5263	5276	5289	5302
34	5315	5328	5340	5353	5366	5378	5391	5403	5416	5428
35	5441	5453	5465	5478	5490	5502	5514	5527	5539	5551
36	5563	5575	5587	5599	5611	5623	5635	5647	5658	5670
37	5682	5694	5705	5717	5729	5740	5752	5763	5775	5786
38	5798	5809	5821	5832	5843	5855	5866	5877	5888	5899
39	5911	5922	5933	5944	5955	5966	5977	5988	5999	6010
40	6021	6031	6042	6053	6064	6075	6085	6096	6107	6117
41	6128	6138	6149	6160	6170	6180	6191	6201	6212	6222
42	6232	6243	6253	6263	6274	6284	6294	6304	6314	6325
43	6335	6345	6355	6365	6375	6385	6395	6405	6415	6425
44	6435	6444	6454	6464	6474	6484	6493	6503	6513	6522
45	6532	6542	6551	6561	6571	6580	6590	6599	6609	6618
46	6628	6637	6646	6656	6665	6675	6684	6693	6702	6712
47	6721	6730	6739	6749	6758	6767	6776	6785	6794	6803
48	6812	6821	6830	6839	6848	6857	6866	6875	6884	6893
49	6902	6911	6920	6928	6937	6946	6955	6964	6972	6981
50	6990	6998	7007	7016	7024	7033	7042	7050	7059	7067
51	7076	7084	7093	7101	7110	7118	7126	7135	7143	7152
52	7160	7168	7177	7185	7193	7202	7210	7218	7226	7235
53	7243	7251	7259	7267	7275	7284	7292	7300	7308	7316
54	7324	7332	7340	7348	7356	7364	7372	7380	7388	7396

LOGARITHMS.

N	0	1	2	3	4	5	6	7	8	9
55		7404	7412	7419	7427	7435	7443	7451	7459	7466	7474
56		7482	7490	7497	7505	7513	7520	7528	7536	7543	7551
57		7559	7566	7574	7582	7589	7597	7604	7612	7619	7627
58		7634	7642	7649	7657	7664	7672	7679	7686	7694	7701
59		7709	7716	7723	7731	7738	7745	7752	7760	7767	7774
60		7782	7789	7796	7803	7810	7818	7825	7832	7839	7846
61		7853	7860	7868	7875	7882	7889	7896	7903	7910	7917
62		7924	7931	7938	7945	7952	7959	7966	7973	7980	7987
63		7993	8000	8007	8014	8021	8028	8035	8041	8048	8055
64		8062	8069	8075	8082	8089	8096	8102	8109	8116	8122
65		8129	8136	8142	8149	8156	8162	8169	8176	8182	8189
66		8195	8202	8209	8215	8222	8228	8235	8241	8248	8254
67		8261	8267	8274	8280	8287	8293	8299	8306	8312	8319
68		8325	8331	8338	8344	8351	8357	8363	8370	8376	8382
69		8388	8395	8401	8407	8414	8420	8426	8432	8439	8445
70		8451	8457	8463	8470	8476	8482	8488	8494	8500	8506
71		8513	8519	8525	8531	8537	8543	8549	8555	8561	8567
72		8573	8579	8585	8591	8597	8603	8609	8615	8621	8627
73		8633	8639	8645	8651	8657	8663	8669	8675	8681	8686
74		8692	8698	8704	8710	8716	8722	8727	8733	8739	8745
75		8751	8756	8762	8768	8774	8779	8785	8791	8797	8802
76		8808	8814	8820	8825	8831	8837	8842	8848	8854	8859
77		8865	8871	8876	8882	8887	8893	8899	8904	8910	8915
78		8921	8927	8932	8938	8943	8949	8954	8960	8965	8971
79		8976	8982	8987	8993	8998	9004	9009	9015	9020	9025
80		9031	9036	9042	9047	9053	9058	9063	9069	9074	9079
81		9085	9090	9096	9101	9106	9112	9117	9122	9128	9133
82		9138	9143	9149	9154	9159	9165	9170	9175	9180	9186
83		9191	9196	9201	9206	9212	9217	9222	9227	9232	9238
84		9243	9248	9253	9258	9263	9269	9274	9279	9284	9289
85		9294	9299	9304	9309	9315	9320	9325	9330	9335	9340
86		9345	9350	9355	9360	9365	9370	9375	9380	9385	9390
87		9395	9400	9405	9410	9415	9420	9425	9430	9435	9440
88		9445	9450	9455	9460	9465	9469	9474	9479	9484	9489
89		9494	9499	9504	9509	9513	9518	9523	9528	9533	9538
90		9542	9547	9552	9557	9562	9566	9571	9576	9581	9586
91		9590	9595	9600	9605	9609	9614	9619	9624	9628	9633
92		9638	9643	9647	9652	9657	9661	9666	9671	9675	9680
93		9685	9689	9694	9699	9703	9708	9713	9717	9722	9727
94		9731	9736	9741	9745	9750	9754	9759	9763	9768	9773
95		9777	9782	9786	9791	9795	9800	9805	9809	9814	9818
96		9823	9827	9832	9836	9841	9845	9850	9854	9859	9863
97		9868	9872	9877	9881	9886	9890	9894	9899	9903	9908
98		9912	9917	9921	9926	9930	9934	9939	9943	9948	9952
99		9956	9961	9965	9969	9974	9978	9983	9987	9991	9996

461. Value of Any Term. *In the series*

$$a_0 + a_1x + a_2x^2 + a_3x^3 + \cdots,$$

by taking x small enough we may make any term as large as we please compared with the sum of all that follow it; and by taking x large enough we may make any term as large as we please compared with the sum of all that precede it.

(i.) The ratio of any term, as $a_n x^n$, to the sum of all that follow it is

$$\frac{a_n x^n}{a_{n+1}x^{n+1} + a_{n+2}x^{n+2} + \cdots} \text{ or } \frac{a_n}{a_{n+1}x + a_{n+2}x^2 + \cdots}$$

When x is indefinitely small, the denominator can be made as small as we please; that is, the fraction can be made as large as we please.

(ii.) Again, the ratio of the term $a_n x^n$ to the sum of all that precede it is

$$\frac{a_n x^n}{a_{n-1}x^{n-1} + a_{n-2}x^{n-2} + \cdots}, \text{ or } \frac{a_n}{a_{n-1}y + a_{n-2}y^2 + \cdots};$$

where $y = \dfrac{1}{x}$.

When x is indefinitely large, y is indefinitely small; hence, as in the previous case, the fraction can be made as large as we please.

462. The following particular form of the foregoing proposition is very useful.

In the expression

$$a_n x^n + a_{n-1}x^{n-1} + \cdots + a_1 x + a_0,$$

consisting of a finite number of terms in *descending* powers of x, by taking x small enough the last term a_0 can be made as large as we please compared with the sum of all the terms that precede it, and by taking x large enough the first term $a_n x^n$ can be made as large as we please compared with the sum of all that follow it.

Ex. 1. By taking n large enough we can make the first term of $n^4 - 5n^3 - 7n + 9$ as large as we please compared with the sum of all

LIMITING VALUES AND VANISHING FRACTIONS.

the other terms; that is, we may take the first term n^4 as the equivalent of the whole expression, with an error as small as we please provided n be taken large enough.

Ex. 2. Find the limit of $\dfrac{3x^3 - 2x^2 - 4}{5x^3 - 4x + 8}$ when (1) x is infinite; (2) x is zero.

(1) In the numerator and denominator *we may disregard all terms but the first;* hence

$$\lim_{x = \infty} \frac{3x^3 - 2x^2 - 4}{5x^3 - 4x + 8} = \frac{3x^3}{5x^3} = \frac{3}{5}.$$

(2) When x is indefinitely small *we may disregard all terms but the last;* hence the limit is $\dfrac{-4}{8}$, or $-\dfrac{1}{2}$.

VANISHING FRACTIONS.

463. Suppose it is required to find the limit of

$$\frac{x^2 + ax - 2a^2}{x^2 - a^2}$$

when $x = a$.

If we put $x = a + h$, then h will approach the value zero as x approaches the value a.

Substituting $a + h$ for x,

$$\frac{x^2 + ax - 2a^2}{x^2 - a^2} = \frac{3ah + h^2}{2ah + h^2} = \frac{3a + h}{2a + h};$$

and when h is indefinitely small the limit of this expression is $\frac{3}{2}$.

There is, however, another way of regarding the question; for

$$\frac{x^2 + ax - 2a^2}{x^2 - a^2} = \frac{(x - a)(x + 2a)}{(x - a)(x + a)} = \frac{x + 2a}{x + a},$$

and if we *now* put $x = a$ the value of the expression is $\frac{3}{2}$, as before.

If in the given expression $\dfrac{x^2 + ax - 2a^2}{x^2 - a^2}$ we put $x = a$ *before* simplification, it will be found that it assumes the form $\frac{0}{0}$, the value of which is indeterminate [Art. 183]; also we see that it has this form in consequence of the factor

$x - a$ appearing in both numerator and denominator. Now we cannot divide by a *zero factor*, but as long as x is not absolutely equal to a, the factor $x - a$ may be removed, and we then find that the nearer x approaches to the value a, the nearer does the value of the fraction approximate to $\frac{3}{2}$, or in accordance with the definition of Art. 458,

when $x = a$, the limit of $\dfrac{x^2 + ax - 2a^2}{x^2 - a^2}$ is $\dfrac{3}{2}$.

464. Vanishing Fractions. If $f(x)$ and $f'(x)$ are two functions of x, each of which becomes equal to zero for some particular value a of x, the fraction $\dfrac{f(a)}{f'(a)}$ takes the form $\frac{0}{0}$, and is called a *vanishing fraction*.

Ex. 1. If $x = 3$, find the limit of

$$\frac{x^3 - 5x^2 + 7x - 3}{x^3 - x^2 - 5x - 3}.$$

When $x = 3$, the expression reduces to the indeterminate form $\frac{0}{0}$; but by removing the factor $x - 3$ from numerator and denominator, the fraction becomes $\dfrac{x^2 - 2x + 1}{x^2 + 2x + 1}$. When $x = 3$, this reduces to $\frac{1}{4}$, which is therefore the required limit.

Ex. 2. The fraction $\dfrac{\sqrt{3x - a} - \sqrt{x + a}}{x - a}$ becomes $\dfrac{0}{0}$ when $x = a$.

To find its limit, multiply numerator and denominator by the surd conjugate to $\sqrt{3x - a} - \sqrt{x + a}$; the fraction then becomes

$$\frac{(3x - a) - (x + a)}{(x - a)(\sqrt{3x - a} + \sqrt{x + a})}, \text{ or } \frac{2}{\sqrt{3x - a} + \sqrt{x + a}};$$

whence by putting $x = a$ we find that the limit is $\dfrac{1}{\sqrt{2a}}$.

Ex. 3. The fraction $\dfrac{1 - \sqrt[3]{x}}{1 - \sqrt[5]{x}}$ becomes $\dfrac{0}{0}$ when $x = 1$.

To find its limit, put $x = 1 + h$, and expand by the Binomial Theorem. Thus the fraction

$$= \frac{1 - (1 + h)^{\frac{1}{3}}}{1 - (1 + h)^{\frac{1}{5}}} = \frac{1 - (1 + \frac{1}{3}h - \frac{1}{9}h^2 + \cdots)}{1 - (1 + \frac{1}{5}h - \frac{2}{25}h^2 + \cdots)} = \frac{-\frac{1}{3} + \frac{1}{9}h - \cdots}{-\frac{1}{5} + \frac{2}{25}h - \cdots}$$

Now $h = 0$ when $x = 1$; hence the required limit is $\frac{5}{3}$.

LIMITING VALUES AND VANISHING FRACTIONS. 375

465. We shall now discuss some peculiarities which may arise in the solution of a quadratic equation.

Let the equation be
$$ax^2 + bx + c = 0.$$
If $c = 0$, then $ax^2 + bx = 0$;

whence $x = 0$, or $-\dfrac{b}{a}$;

that is, one of the roots is zero and the other is finite.

If $b = 0$, the roots are equal in magnitude and opposite in sign.

If $a = 0$, the equation reduces to $bx + c = 0$; and it appears that in this case the quadratic furnishes only one root, namely, $-\dfrac{c}{b}$. But every quadratic equation has two roots, and in order to discuss the value of the other root we proceed as follows:

Write $\dfrac{1}{y}$ for x in the original equation and clear of fractions; thus, $cy^2 + by + a = 0.$

Now put $a = 0$, and we have
$$cy^2 + by = 0;$$
the solution of which is $y = 0$, or $-\dfrac{b}{c}$; that is, $x = \infty$, or $-\dfrac{c}{b}$

Hence, *in any quadratic equation one root will become infinite if the coefficient of x^2 becomes zero.*

This is the form in which the result will be most frequently met with in other branches of higher Mathematics, but the student should notice that it is merely a convenient abbreviation of the following fuller statement:

In the equation $ax^2 + bx + c = 0$, if a is very small, one root is very large, and as a is indefinitely diminished this root becomes indefinitely great. In this case the finite root approximates to $-\dfrac{c}{b}$ as its limit.

EXAMPLES XL.

Find the limits of the following expressions:

(1) when $x = \infty$. (2) when $x = 0$.

1. $\dfrac{(2x-3)(3-5x)}{7x^2-6x+4}$.

2. $\dfrac{(3x^2-1)^2}{x^4+9}$.

3. $\dfrac{(3+2x^3)(x-5)}{(4x^3-9)(1+x)}$.

4. $\dfrac{(x-3)(2-5x)(3x+1)}{(2x-1)^3}$.

5. $\dfrac{1-x^2}{2x^3-1} \div \dfrac{1-x}{2x^2}$.

6. $\dfrac{(3-x)(x+5)(2-7x)}{(7x-1)(x+1)^3}$.

Find the limits of

7. $\dfrac{x^3+1}{x^2-1}$, when $x = -1$.

8. $\dfrac{\sqrt{x}-\sqrt{2a}+\sqrt{x-2a}}{\sqrt{x^2-4a^2}}$, when $x = 2a$.

9. $\dfrac{(a^2-x^2)^{\frac{1}{2}}+(a-x)^{\frac{3}{2}}}{(a^3-x^3)^{\frac{1}{2}}+(a-x)^{\frac{1}{2}}}$, when $x = a$.

10. $\dfrac{\sqrt{a^2+ax+x^2}-\sqrt{a^2-ax+x^2}}{\sqrt{a+x}-\sqrt{a-x}}$, when $x = 0$.

CHAPTER XLI.

Convergency and Divergency of Series.

466. We have, in Chapter XXXIV., defined a **series** as an expression in which the successive terms are formed by some regular law; if the series terminates at some assigned term, it is called a **finite series**; if the number of terms is unlimited, it is called an **infinite series**.

In the present chapter, we shall usually denote a series by an expression of the form

$$u_1 + u_2 + u_3 + \cdots + u_n + \cdots$$

467. DEFINITIONS. Suppose that we have a series consisting of n terms. The sum of the series will be a function of n; if n increases indefinitely, the sum either tends to become equal to a certain finite *limit*, or else it becomes infinitely great.

An infinite series is said to be **convergent** when the sum of the first n terms cannot numerically exceed some finite quantity, however great n may be.

An infinite series is said to be **divergent** when the sum of the first n terms can be made numerically greater than any finite quantity by taking n sufficiently great.

TESTS FOR CONVERGENCY.

468. When the Sum of the First n Terms of a Given Series is Known. If we can find the sum of the first n terms of a given series, we may ascertain whether it is convergent or divergent by examining whether the series remains finite, or becomes infinite, when n is made indefinitely great

For example, the sum of the first n terms of the series

$$1 + x + x^2 + x^3 + \cdots \text{ is } \frac{1-x^n}{1-x}$$

If x is numerically less than 1, the sum approaches to the finite limit $\frac{1}{1-x}$, and the series is therefore *convergent*.

If x is numerically greater than 1, the sum of the first n terms is $\frac{x^n-1}{x-1}$, and by taking n sufficiently great, this can be made greater than any finite quantity; thus the series is *divergent*.

If $x = 1$, the sum of the first n terms is n, and therefore the series is *divergent*.

If $x = -1$, the series becomes

$$1 - 1 + 1 - 1 + 1 - 1 + \cdots.$$

The sum of an even number of terms is zero, while the sum of an odd number of terms is 1; and thus the sum oscillates between the values 0 and 1. This series belongs to a class which may be called *oscillating* or *periodic convergent series*.

469. When the Sum of the First n Terms of a Given Series is Unknown. There are many cases in which we have no method of finding the sum of the first n terms of a series. We proceed therefore to investigate rules by which we can test the convergency or divergency of a given series without effecting its summation.

470. First Test. *An infinite series in which the terms are alternately positive and negative is convergent if each term is numerically less than the preceding term.*

Let the series be denoted by

$$u_1 - u_2 + u_3 - u_4 + u_5 - u_6 + \cdots$$

where $\qquad u_1 > u_2 > u_3 > u_4 > u_5 \cdots.$

CONVERGENCY AND DIVERGENCY OF SERIES.

The given series may be written in each of the following forms:
$$(u_1 - u_2) + (u_3 - u_4) + (u_5 - u_6) + \ldots \quad (1),$$
$$u_1 - (u_2 - u_3) - (u_4 - u_5) - (u_6 - u_7) - \ldots \quad (2).$$

From (1) we see that the sum of any number of terms is a positive quantity; and from (2) that the sum of any number of terms is less than u_1; hence the series is convergent.

For example, in the series
$$1 - \tfrac{1}{2} + \tfrac{1}{3} - \tfrac{1}{4} + \tfrac{1}{5} - \tfrac{1}{6} + \cdots$$
the terms are alternately positive and negative, and each term is numerically less than the preceding one; hence the series is convergent.

471. Second Test. *An infinite series in which all the terms are of the same sign is divergent if each term is greater than some finite quantity, however small.*

For if each term is greater than some finite quantity a, the sum of the first n terms is greater than na; and this, by taking n sufficiently great, can be made to exceed any finite quantity.

472. Before proceeding to investigate further tests of convergency and divergency, we shall lay down two important principles, which may almost be regarded as axioms.

I. If a series is convergent it will remain convergent, and if divergent it will remain divergent, when we add or remove any *finite* number of its terms; for the sum of these terms is a finite quantity.

II. If a series in which all the terms are positive is convergent, then the series is convergent when some or all of the terms are negative; for the sum is clearly greatest when all the terms have the same sign.

We shall suppose that all the terms are positive unless the contrary is stated.

473. Third Test. *An infinite series is convergent if from and after some fixed term the ratio of each term to the preceding term is numerically less than some quantity which is itself numerically less than unity.*

Let the series beginning from the fixed term be denoted by
$$u_1 + u_2 + u_3 + u_4 + \cdots;$$
and let
$$\frac{u_2}{u_1} < r, \quad \frac{u_3}{u_2} < r, \quad \frac{u_4}{u_3} < r, \cdots,$$
where $r < 1$.

Then
$$u_1 + u_2 + u_3 + u_4 + \cdots$$
$$= u_1 \left(1 + \frac{u_2}{u_1} + \frac{u_3}{u_2} \cdot \frac{u_2}{u_1} + \frac{u_4}{u_3} \cdot \frac{u_3}{u_2} \cdot \frac{u_2}{u_1} + \cdots\right)$$
$$< u_1(1 + r + r^2 + r^3 + \cdots);$$

that is, $< \dfrac{u_1}{1-r}$, since $r < 1$.

Hence the given series is convergent.

474. In the enunciation of the preceding article the student should notice the significance of the words "from and after a fixed term."

Consider the series
$$1 + 2x + 3x^2 + 4x^3 + \cdots + nx^{n-1} + \cdots.$$
Here
$$\frac{u_n}{u_{n-1}} = \frac{nx}{n-1} = \left(1 + \frac{1}{n-1}\right)x;$$

and by taking n sufficiently large we can make this ratio approximate to x as nearly as we please, and the ratio of each term to the preceding term will ultimately be x. Hence if $x < 1$, the series is convergent.

But the ratio $\dfrac{u_n}{u_{n-1}}$ will not be less than 1, until $\dfrac{nx}{n-1} < 1$; that is, until $n > \dfrac{1}{1-x}$.

Here we have a case of a convergent series in which the terms may increase up to a certain point, and then begin to decrease. For example, if $x = \frac{99}{100}$, then $\frac{1}{1-x} = 100$, and the terms do not begin to decrease until after the 100th term.

475. Fourth Test. *An infinite series in which all the terms are of the same sign is divergent if from and after some fixed term the ratio of each term to the preceding term is greater than unity, or equal to unity.*

Let the fixed term be denoted by u_1. If the ratio is equal to unity, each of the succeeding terms is equal to u_1, and the sum of n terms is equal to nu_1; hence the series is divergent.

If the ratio is greater than unity, each of the terms after the fixed term is greater than u_1, and the sum of n terms is greater than nu_1; hence the series is divergent.

476. In the practical application of these tests, to avoid having to ascertain the particular term after which each term is greater or less than the preceding term, it is convenient to find the limit of $\frac{u_n}{u_{n-1}}$ when n is indefinitely increased; let this limit be denoted by l.

If $l < 1$, the series is convergent. [Art. 473.]

If $l > 1$, the series is divergent. [Art. 475.]

If $l = 1$, the series may be either convergent or divergent, and a further test will be required; for it may happen that $\frac{u_n}{u_{n-1}} < 1$, *but continually approaching to* 1 *as its limit when* n *is indefinitely increased*. In this case we cannot name any finite quantity r which is itself less than 1 and yet greater than l. Hence the test of Art. 473 fails. If, however, $\frac{u_n}{u_{n-1}} > 1$, but continually approaching to 1 as its limit, the series is divergent by Art. 475.

We shall use "Lim $\frac{u_n}{u_{n-1}}$" as an abbreviation of the words "the limit of $\frac{u_n}{u_{n-1}}$ when n is infinite."

Ex. 1. Find whether the series whose nth term is $\dfrac{(n+1)x^n}{n^2}$ is convergent or divergent.

Here $\dfrac{u_n}{u_{n-1}} = \dfrac{(n+1)x^n}{n^2} \div \dfrac{nx^{n-1}}{(n-1)^2} = \dfrac{(n+1)(n-1)^2}{n^3} \cdot x;$

$$\therefore \operatorname{Lim} \dfrac{u_n}{u_{n-1}} = x;$$

hence   if $x < 1$ the series is convergent;

if $x > 1$ the series is divergent.

If $x = 1$, then $\operatorname{Lim} \dfrac{u_n}{u_{n-1}} = 1$, and a further test is required.

Ex. 2. Is the series

$$1^2 + 2^2 x + 3^2 x^2 + 4^2 x^3 + \cdots$$

convergent or divergent?

Here $\operatorname{Lim} \dfrac{u_n}{u_{n-1}} = \operatorname{Lim} \dfrac{n^2 x^{n-1}}{(n-1)^2 x^{n-2}} = x.$

Hence   if $x < 1$ the series is convergent;

if $x > 1$ the series is divergent.

If $x = 1$ the series becomes $1^2 + 2^2 + 3^2 + 4^2 + \cdots$, and is obviously divergent.

Ex. 3. In the series

$$a + (a+d)r + (a+2d)r^2 + \cdots + (a+\overline{n-1}\cdot d)r^{n-1} + \cdots,$$

$$\operatorname{Lim} \dfrac{u_n}{u_{n-1}} = \operatorname{Lim} \dfrac{a+(n-1)d}{a+(n-2)d} \cdot r = r;$$

thus if $r < 1$ the series is convergent, and the sum is finite.

477. Fifth Test. *If there are two infinite series in each of which all the terms are positive, and if the ratio of the corresponding terms in the two series is always finite, the two series are both convergent, or both divergent.*

Let the two infinite series be denoted by

$$u_1 + u_2 + u_3 + u_4 + \cdots,$$

and $\qquad v_1 + v_2 + v_3 + v_4 + \cdots.$

The value of the fraction

$$\dfrac{u_1 + u_2 + u_3 + \cdots + u_n}{v_1 + v_2 + v_3 + \cdots + v_n}$$

CONVERGENCY AND DIVERGENCY OF SERIES.

lies between the greatest and least of the fractions
$$\frac{u_1}{v_1}, \frac{u_2}{v_2}, \ldots \frac{u_n}{v_n},$$
and is therefore a *finite* quantity, L say;

$$\therefore u_1 + u_2 + u_3 + \cdots + u_n = L(v_1 + v_2 + v_3 + \cdots + v_n).$$

Hence if one series is finite in value, so is the other; if one series is infinite in value, so is the other; which proves the proposition.

478. Auxiliary Series. The application of the principle of the preceding article is very important, for by means of it we can compare a given series with an *auxiliary series* whose convergency or divergency has been already established. The series discussed in the next article will frequently be found useful as an auxiliary series.

479. The infinite series $\dfrac{1}{1^p} + \dfrac{1}{2^p} + \dfrac{1}{3^p} + \dfrac{1}{4^p} + \cdots$ is always divergent except when p is positive and greater than 1.

CASE I. Let $p > 1$.

The first term is 1; the next two terms together are less than $\dfrac{2}{2^p}$; the following four terms together are less than $\dfrac{4}{4^p}$; the following eight terms together are less than $\dfrac{8}{8^p}$; and so on. Hence the series is less than
$$1 + \frac{2}{2^p} + \frac{4}{4^p} + \frac{8}{8^p} + \cdots;$$
that is, less than a geometrical progression whose common ratio $\dfrac{2}{2^p}$ is less than 1, since $p > 1$; hence the series is convergent.

CASE II. Let $p = 1$.

The series now becomes $1 + \tfrac{1}{2} + \tfrac{1}{3} + \tfrac{1}{4} + \tfrac{1}{5} + \cdots$.

The third and fourth terms together are greater than $\tfrac{2}{4}$ or $\tfrac{1}{2}$; the following four terms together are greater than $\tfrac{4}{8}$ or

$\frac{1}{2}$; the following eight terms together are greater than $\frac{8}{16}$ or $\frac{1}{2}$; and so on. Hence the series is greater than
$$1 + \tfrac{1}{2} + \tfrac{1}{2} + \tfrac{1}{2} + \tfrac{1}{2} + \cdots,$$
and is therefore divergent. [Art. 475.]

CASE III. Let $p < 1$, or negative.

Each term is now greater than the corresponding term in Case II., therefore the series is divergent.

Hence the series is always divergent except in the case when p is positive and greater than unity.

Ex. Prove that the series $\dfrac{2}{1} + \dfrac{3}{4} + \dfrac{4}{9} + \cdots + \dfrac{n+1}{n^2} + \cdots$ is divergent.

Compare the given series with $1 + \dfrac{1}{2} + \dfrac{1}{3} + \cdots + \dfrac{1}{n} + \cdots$.

Thus if u_n and v_n denote the nth terms of the given series and the auxiliary series respectively, we have
$$\frac{u_n}{v_n} = \frac{n+1}{n^2} \div \frac{1}{n} = \frac{n+1}{n};$$
hence $\operatorname{Lim} \dfrac{u_n}{v_n} = 1$, and therefore the two series are both convergent or both divergent. But the auxiliary series is divergent, therefore also the given series is divergent.

This completes the solution of Ex. 1. [Art. 476.]

480. Convergency of the Binomial Series. *To show that the expansion of $(1 + x)^n$ by the Binomial Theorem is convergent when $x < 1$.*

Let u_r, u_{r+1} represent the rth and $(r+1)$th terms of the expansion; then
$$\frac{u_{r+1}}{u_r} = \frac{n-r+1}{r} x.$$

When $r > n + 1$, this ratio is negative; that is, from this point the terms are alternately positive and negative when x is positive, and always of the same sign when x is negative. Now when r is infinite, $\operatorname{Lim} \dfrac{u_{r+1}}{u_r} = x$ numerically; therefore since $x < 1$ the series is convergent if all the terms are of the same sign; and therefore still more is it convergent when some of the terms are positive and some negative. [Art. 472.]

CONVERGENCY AND DIVERGENCY OF SERIES.

EXAMPLES XLI.

Find whether the following series are convergent or divergent:

1. $\dfrac{1}{x} - \dfrac{1}{x+a} + \dfrac{1}{x+2a} - \dfrac{1}{x+3a} + \cdots$,

x and a being positive quantities.

2. $\dfrac{1}{1\cdot 2} + \dfrac{1}{2\cdot 3} + \dfrac{1}{3\cdot 4} + \dfrac{1}{4\cdot 5} + \cdots$.

3. $\dfrac{1}{xy} - \dfrac{1}{(x+1)(y+1)} + \dfrac{1}{(x+2)(y+2)} - \dfrac{1}{(x+3)(y+3)} + \cdots$,

x and y being positive quantities.

4. $\dfrac{x}{1\cdot 2} + \dfrac{x^2}{2\cdot 3} + \dfrac{x^3}{3\cdot 4} + \dfrac{x^4}{4\cdot 5} + \cdots$.

5. $\dfrac{x}{1\cdot 2} + \dfrac{x^2}{3\cdot 4} + \dfrac{x^3}{5\cdot 6} + \dfrac{x^4}{7\cdot 8} + \cdots$.

6. $1 + \dfrac{2^2}{\underline{|2}} + \dfrac{3^2}{\underline{|3}} + \dfrac{4^2}{\underline{|4}} + \cdots$.

7. $\sqrt{\tfrac{1}{2}} + \sqrt{\tfrac{2}{3}} + \sqrt{\tfrac{3}{4}} + \sqrt{\tfrac{4}{5}} + \cdots$.

8. $1 + 3x + 5x^2 + 7x^3 + 9x^4 + \cdots$.

9. $\dfrac{2}{1^p} + \dfrac{3}{2^p} + \dfrac{4}{3^p} + \dfrac{5}{4^p} + \cdots$.

10. $1 + \dfrac{x}{2} + \dfrac{x^2}{5} + \dfrac{x^3}{10} + \cdots + \dfrac{x^n}{n^2+1} + \cdots$.

NOTE. For further information on the subject of Convergency and Divergency of Series the reader may consult Hall & Knight's Higher Algebra, Chapter XXI.

CHAPTER XLII.

UNDETERMINED COEFFICIENTS.

FUNCTIONS OF FINITE DIMENSIONS.

481. In Art. 105 it was proved that if any rational integral function of x vanishes when $x = a$, it is divisible by $x - a$.

Let $$p_0 x^n + p_1 x^{n-1} + p_2 x^{n-2} + \cdots + p_n$$
be a rational integral function of x of n dimensions, which vanishes when x is equal to each of the unequal quantities
$$a_1, \ a_2, \ a_3, \cdots a_n.$$

Denote the function by $f(x)$; then since $f(x)$ is divisible by $x - a_1$, we have
$$f(x) = (x - a_1)(p_0 x^{n-1} + \cdots),$$
the quotient being of $n - 1$ dimensions.

Similarly, since $f(x)$ is divisible by $x - a_2$, we have
$$p_0 x^{n-1} + \cdots = (x - a_2)(p_0 x^{n-2} + \cdots),$$
the quotient being of $n - 2$ dimensions; and
$$p_0 x^{n-2} + \cdots = (x - a_3)(p_0 x^{n-3} + \cdots).$$

Proceeding in this way, we shall finally obtain after n divisions
$$f(x) = p_0(x - a_1)(x - a_2)(x - a_3) \cdots (x - a_n).$$

482. If a rational integral function of n dimensions vanishes for more than n values of the variable, the coefficient of each power of the variable must be zero.

Let the function be denoted by $f(x)$, where
$$f(x) = p_0 x^n + p_1 x^{n-1} + p_2 x^{n-2} + \cdots + p_n;$$

and suppose that $f(x)$ vanishes when x is equal to each of the unequal values $a_1, a_2, a_3, \cdots a_n$; then
$$f(x) = p_0(x - a_1)(x - a_2)(x - a_3) \cdots (x - a_n).$$
Let c be another value of x which makes $f(x)$ vanish; then since $f(c) = 0$, we have
$$p_0(c - a_1)(c - a_2)(c - a_3) \cdots (c - a_n) = 0;$$
and therefore $p_0 = 0$, since, by hypothesis, none of the other factors is equal to zero. Hence $f(x)$ reduces to
$$p_1 x^{n-1} + p_2 x^{n-2} + p_3 x^{n-3} + \cdots + p_n.$$
By hypothesis this expression vanishes for more than n values of x, and therefore $p_1 = 0$.

In a similar manner we may show that each of the coefficients $p_2, p_3, \cdots p_n$ must be equal to zero.

This result may also be enunciated as follows:

If a rational integral function of n dimensions vanishes for more than n values of the variable, it must vanish for every value of the variable.

Cor. If the *function* $f(x)$ vanishes for more than n values of x, the *equation* $f(x) = 0$ has more than n roots.

Hence also, *if an equation of n dimensions has more than n roots it is an identity.*

Ex. Prove that
$$\frac{(x-b)(x-c)}{(a-b)(a-c)} + \frac{(x-c)(x-a)}{(b-c)(b-a)} + \frac{(x-a)(x-b)}{(c-a)(c-b)} = 1.$$

This equation is of *two* dimensions, and it is evidently satisfied by each of the *three* values a, b, c; hence it is an identity.

483. If two rational integral functions of n dimensions are equal for more than n values of the variable, they are equal for every value of the variable.

Suppose that the two functions
$$p_0 x^n + p_1 x^{n-1} + p_2 x^{n-2} + \cdots + p_n,$$
$$q_0 x^n + q_1 x^{n-1} + q_2 x^{n-2} + \cdots + q_n,$$
are equal for more than n values of x; then the expression
$$(p_0 - q_0) x^n + (p_1 - q_1) x^{n-1} + (p_2 - q_2) x^{n-2} + \cdots + (p_n - q_n)$$

vanishes for more than n values of x; and therefore, by the preceding article,

$$p_0 - q_0 = 0,\ p_1 - q_1 = 0,\ p_2 - q_2 = 0, \cdots p_n - q_n = 0;$$

that is, $\quad p_0 = q_0,\ p_1 = q_1,\ p_2 = q_2, \cdots p_n = q_n.$

Hence the two expressions are *identical*, and therefore are equal for every value of the variable. Thus

If two rational integral functions are identically equal, we may equate the coefficients of the like powers of the variable.

Cor. This proposition still holds if one of the functions is of lower dimensions than the other. For instance, if

$$p_0 x^n + p_1 x^{n-1} + p_2 x^{n-2} + p_3 x^{n-3} + \cdots + p_n$$
$$= q_2 x^{n-2} + q_3 x^{n-3} + \cdots + q_n,$$

we have only to suppose that in the above investigation $q_0 = 0,\ q_1 = 0$, and then we obtain

$$p_0 = 0,\ p_1 = 0,\ p_2 = q_2,\ p_3 = q_3, \cdots p_n = q_n.$$

484. The theorem established in the preceding article for functions of finite dimensions is usually referred to as the **Principle of Undetermined Coefficients**. The application of this principle is illustrated in the following examples.

Ex. 1. Find the sum of the series

$$1 \cdot 2 + 2 \cdot 3 + 3 \cdot 4 + \cdots + n(n+1).$$

Assume that

$$1 \cdot 2 + 2 \cdot 3 + 3 \cdot 4 + \cdots + n(n+1) = A + Bn + Cn^2 + Dn^3 + En^4 + \cdots, \quad (1)$$

where $A, B, C, D, E, \cdots$ are quantities independent of n, whose values have to be determined. Change n into $n + 1$; then

$$1 \cdot 2 + 2 \cdot 3 + \cdots + n(n+1) + (n+1)(n+2)$$
$$= A + B(n+1) + C(n+1)^2 + D(n+1)^3 + E(n+1)^4 + \cdots. \quad (2)$$

By subtracting (1) from (2),

$$(n+1)(n+2) = B + C(2n+1) + D(3n^2 + 3n + 1)$$
$$+ E(4n^3 + 6n^2 + 4n + 1) + \cdots.$$

This equation being true for all integral values of n, the coefficients of the respective powers of n on each side must be equal; thus E and all succeeding coefficients must be equal to zero, and

$$3D = 1;\ 3D + 2C = 3;\ D + C + B = 2;$$

whence $\quad D = \tfrac{1}{3},\ C = 1,\ B = \tfrac{2}{3}.$

UNDETERMINED COEFFICIENTS.

Hence the sum $= A + \dfrac{2n}{3} + n^2 + \dfrac{1}{3}n^3$.

To find A, put $n = 1$; the series then reduces to its first term, and

$$2 = A + 2, \text{ or } A = 0.$$

Hence $1 \cdot 2 + 2 \cdot 3 + 3 \cdot 4 + \cdots + n(n+1) = \tfrac{1}{3} n(n+1)(n+2)$.

NOTE. It will be seen from this example that when the nth term is a rational integral function of n, it is sufficient to assume for the sum a function of n which is of one dimension higher than the nth term of the series.

Ex. 2. Find the conditions that $x^3 + px^2 + qx + r$ may be divisible by

$$x^2 + ax + b.$$

The quotient will contain two terms; namely, x and a term independent of x. Hence, we assume

$$x^3 + px^2 + qx + r = (x + k)(x^2 + ax + b).$$

Equating the coefficients of the like powers of x, we have

$$k + a = p, \quad ak + b = q, \quad kb = r.$$

From the last equation $k = \dfrac{r}{b}$; hence by substitution we obtain

$$\dfrac{r}{b} + a = p, \text{ and } \dfrac{ar}{b} + b = q;$$

that is, $\qquad r = b(p - a), \text{ and } ar = b(q - b);$

which are the conditions required.

EXAMPLES XLII. a.

Find by the method of Undetermined Coefficients the sum of

1. $1^2 + 3^2 + 5^2 + 7^2 + \cdots$ to n terms.
2. $1 \cdot 2 \cdot 3 + 2 \cdot 3 \cdot 4 + 3 \cdot 4 \cdot 5 + \cdots$ to n terms.
3. $1 \cdot 2^2 + 2 \cdot 3^2 + 3 \cdot 4^2 + 4 \cdot 5^2 + \cdots$ to n terms.
4. $1^3 + 3^3 + 5^3 + 7^3 + \cdots$ to n terms.
5. $1^4 + 2^4 + 3^4 + 4^4 + \cdots$ to n terms.
6. Find the condition that $x^3 - 3px + 2q$ may be divisible by a factor of the form $x^2 + 2ax + a^2$.
7. Find the conditions that $ax^3 + bx^2 + cx + d$ may be a perfect cube.

8. Find the conditions that $a^2x^4 + bx^3 + cx^2 + dx + f^2$ may be a perfect square.

9. Prove the identity
$$\frac{a^2(x-b)(x-c)}{(a-b)(a-c)} + \frac{b^2(x-c)(x-a)}{(b-c)(b-a)} + \frac{c^2(x-a)(x-b)}{(c-a)(c-b)} = x^2.$$

FUNCTIONS OF INFINITE DIMENSIONS.

485. If the infinite series $a_0 + a_1x + a_2x^2 + a_3x^3 + \cdots$ is equal to zero for every finite value of x for which the series is convergent, then each coefficient must be equal to zero identically.

Let the series be denoted by S, and let S_1 stand for the expression $a_1 + a_2x + a_3x^2 + \cdots$; then $S = a_0 + xS_1$, and therefore, by hypothesis, $a_0 + xS_1 = 0$ for all finite values of x. But since S is convergent, S_1 cannot exceed some finite limit; therefore by taking x small enough, xS_1 may be made as small as we please. In this case the limit of S is a_0; but S is *always* zero, therefore a_0 must be equal to zero identically.

Removing the term a_0, we have $xS_1 = 0$ for all finite values of x; that is, $a_1 + a_2x + a_3x^2 + \cdots$ vanishes for all finite values of x.

Similarly, we may prove in succession that each of the coefficients $a_1, a_2, a_3, \cdots$ is equal to zero identically.

486. If two infinite series are convergent and equal to one another for every finite value of the variable, the coefficients of like powers of the variable in the two series are equal.

Suppose that the two series are denoted by
$$a_0 + a_1x + a_2x^2 + a_3x^3 + \cdots$$
and
$$A_0 + A_1x + A_2x^2 + A_3x^3 + \cdots;$$
then the expression
$$a_0 - A_0 + (a_1 - A_1)x + (a_2 - A_2)x^2 + (a_3 - A_3)x^3 + \cdots$$

UNDETERMINED COEFFICIENTS.

vanishes for all values of x within the assigned limits; therefore by the last article

$$a_0 - A_0 = 0, \; a_1 - A_1 = 0, \; a_2 - A_2 = 0, \; a_3 - A_3 = 0, \; \cdots,$$

that is, $\quad a_0 = A_0, \; a_1 = A_1, \; a_2 = A_2, \; a_3 = A_3, \; \cdots;$

hence the *coefficients of like powers of the variable are equal*, which proves the proposition.

EXPANSION OF FRACTIONS INTO SERIES.

487. Expand $\dfrac{2+x^2}{1+x-x^2}$ in a series of ascending powers of x.

Let $\quad \dfrac{2+x^2}{1+x-x^2} = A + Bx + Cx^2 + Dx^3 + \cdots,$

where $A, B, C, D, \cdots$, are constants whose values are to be determined; then

$$2 + x^2 = A(1+x-x^2) + Bx(1+x-x^2) + Cx^2(1+x-x^2)$$
$$+ Dx^3(1+x-x^2) + \cdots$$

$$= A + \begin{vmatrix} B \\ A \end{vmatrix} x + \begin{vmatrix} C \\ B \\ -A \end{vmatrix} x^2 + \begin{vmatrix} D \\ C \\ -B \end{vmatrix} x^3 + \cdots$$

Equating the coefficients of like powers of x, we have

$A = 2, \quad B + A = 0, \quad C + B - A = 1, \quad D + C - B = 0,$

$\qquad \therefore B = -2; \qquad \therefore C = 5; \qquad \therefore D = -7;$

thus $\quad \dfrac{2+x^2}{1+x-x^2} = 2 - 2x + 5x^2 - 7x^3 + \cdots.$

488. Both numerator and denominator should be arranged with reference to the ascending powers of the same quantity; then dividing the first term of the numerator by the first term of the denominator determines the *form of the expansion*.

Ex. Expand $\dfrac{2}{2x^2 - 3x^3}$ in a series of ascending powers of x.

Dividing x^0, of the first term of the numerator, by x^2, of the first term of the denominator, we obtain x^{-2} for the first term of the expansion; therefore we assume

$$\frac{2}{2x^2 - 3x^3} = Ax^{-2} + Bx^{-1} + C + Dx + \cdots;$$

then $\quad 2 = 2A + \begin{array}{|c}2B \\ -3A\end{array}\Big|\, x + \begin{array}{|c}2C \\ -3B\end{array}\Big|\, x^2 + \begin{array}{|c}2D \\ -3C\end{array}\Big|\, x^3 + \cdots$

Equating the coefficients of like powers of x, we have

$A = 1;\quad 2B - 3A = 0,\quad 2C - 3B = 0,\quad 2D - 3C = 0,$
$\qquad\qquad \therefore B = \tfrac{3}{2};\quad\;\; \therefore C = \tfrac{9}{4};\quad\;\; \therefore D = \tfrac{27}{8};$

thus $\quad \dfrac{2}{2x^2 - 3x^3} = x^{-2} + \tfrac{3}{2}x^{-1} + \tfrac{9}{4} + \tfrac{27}{8}x + \cdots$

$$= \frac{1}{x^2} + \frac{3}{2x} + \frac{9}{4} + \frac{27x}{8} + \cdots$$

EXAMPLES XLII. b.

Expand to four terms in ascending powers of x:

1. $\dfrac{1 + 2x}{1 - x - x^2}$. 2. $\dfrac{1 - 8x}{1 - x - 6x^2}$. 3. $\dfrac{1 + x}{2 + x + x^2}$. 4. $\dfrac{3 + x}{2 - x - x^2}$.

5. $\dfrac{1}{1 + ax - ax^2 - x^3}$. 7. $\dfrac{1}{2x - 3x^2}$. 9. $\dfrac{2 + x}{3x^2 + x^3}$.

6. $\dfrac{2 - 2x + 3x^2}{4 + x + x^2}$. 8. $\dfrac{c}{b - ax}$. 10. $\dfrac{1 + x + x^2}{x + x^3 + x^4}$.

EXPANSION OF SURDS INTO SERIES.

489. Expand $\sqrt{1 + x}$ in ascending powers of x.

Let $\quad \sqrt{1 + x} = A + Bx + Cx^2 + Dx^3 + Ex^4 + \cdots.$

By squaring both sides of the equation, we have

$1 + x = A^2 + \begin{array}{|c}2AB \\ +2AC\end{array}\Big|\, x + \begin{array}{|c}B^2 \\ +2AC\end{array}\Big|\, x^2 + \begin{array}{|c}2AD \\ +2BC\end{array}\Big|\, x^3 + \begin{array}{|c}C^2 \\ +2BD \\ +2AE\end{array}\Big|\, x^4 + \cdots$

Equating the coefficients of like powers of x, we have
$A = 1$; $\quad 2AB = 1$, $\quad B^2 + 2AC = 0$, $\quad 2AD + 2BC = 0$,
$\quad \therefore B = \frac{1}{2}$; $\quad\quad \therefore C = -\frac{1}{8}$; $\quad\quad \therefore D = \frac{1}{16}$:
$\quad\quad C^2 + 2BD + 2AE = 0$;
$\quad\quad\quad \therefore E = -\frac{5}{128}$;

thus $\quad \sqrt{1+x} = 1 + \dfrac{x}{2} - \dfrac{x^2}{8} + \dfrac{x^3}{16} - \dfrac{5x^4}{128} + \cdots$.

NOTE. The expansion can be readily effected by the use of the Binomial Theorem [Art. 421].

EXAMPLES XLII. c.

Expand the following expressions to four terms:

1. $\sqrt{1-x}$.
2. $\sqrt{a-x}$.
3. $\sqrt{a^2 - x^2}$.
4. $\sqrt[3]{2+x}$.
5. $(1+x)^{\frac{2}{3}}$.
6. $(1 \pm x + x^2)^{\frac{1}{2}}$.

REVERSION OF SERIES.

490. To *revert* a series $y = ax + bx^2 + cx^3 + \cdots$ is to express x in a series of ascending powers of y.

Revert the series
$$y = x - 2x^2 + 3x^3 - 4x^4 + \cdots \quad\quad (1).$$
Assume $\quad x = Ay + By^2 + Cy^3 + Dy^4 + \cdots$.

Substituting in this equation the value of y as given in (1), we have

$x = A(x - 2x^2 + 3x^3 - 4x^4 + \cdots) = A(x - 2x^2 + 3x^3 - 4x^4 + \cdots)$
$\quad + B(x - 2x^2 + 3x^3 - 4x^4 + \cdots)^2 = B(x^2 + 4x^4 - 4x^3 + 6x^4 + \cdots)$
$\quad + C(x - 2x^2 + 3x^3 - 4x^4 + \cdots)^3 = C(x^3 - 6x^4 - \cdots \quad\quad)$
$\quad + D(x - 2x^2 + 3x^3 - 4x^4 + \cdots)^4 = D(x^4 + \cdots \quad\quad\quad\quad)$

Equating the coefficients of like powers of x,
$\quad A = 1$; $\quad B - 2A = 0$, $\quad C - 4B + 3A = 0$,
$\quad\quad\quad \therefore B = 2$; $\quad\quad \therefore C = 5$;
$\quad\quad D - 6C + 10B - 4A = 0$,
$\quad\quad\quad\quad \therefore D = 14$.

Hence $\quad x = y + 2y^2 + 5y^3 + 14y^4 + \cdots$.

491. If the series be $y = 1 + 2x + 3x^2 + 4x^3 + \cdots$
put $y - 1 = z$;
then $\qquad z = 2x + 3x^2 + 4x^3 + \cdots$.

Assume $x = Az + Bz^2 + Cz^3 + \cdots$ and complete the work as in Art. 490 after which replace z by its value $y - 1$.

EXAMPLES XLII. d.

Revert each of the following series to four terms:

1. $y = x + x^2 + x^3 + x^4 + \cdots$.
2. $y = x + 3x^2 + 5x^3 + 7x^4 + \cdots$.
3. $y = x - \dfrac{x^2}{2} + \dfrac{x^3}{4} - \dfrac{x^4}{8} + \cdots$.
4. $y = 1 + x + \dfrac{x^2}{2} + \dfrac{x^3}{6} + \dfrac{x^4}{24} + \cdots$.
5. $y = x - \dfrac{x^3}{3} + \dfrac{x^5}{5} - \dfrac{x^7}{7} + \cdots$.
6. $y = ax + bx^2 + cx^3 + dx^4 + \cdots$.

PARTIAL FRACTIONS.

492. A group of fractions connected by the signs of addition and subtraction is reduced to a more simple form by being collected into one single fraction whose denominator is the lowest common denominator of the given fractions. But the converse process of separating a fraction into a group of simpler, or **partial**, fractions is often required. For example, if we wish to expand $\dfrac{3 - 5x}{1 - 4x + 3x^2}$ in a series of ascending powers of x, we might use the method of Art. 487, and so obtain as many terms as we please. But if we wish to find the *general term* of the series, this method is inapplicable, and it is simpler to express the given fraction in the equivalent form $\dfrac{1}{1 - x} + \dfrac{2}{1 - 3x}$. Each of the expressions $(1 - x)^{-1}$ and $(1 - 3x)^{-1}$ can now be expanded by the Binomial Theorem, and the *general term* obtained.

493. We shall now give some examples illustrating the decomposition of a rational fraction into partial fractions. For a fuller discussion of the subject the reader is referred to treatises on Higher Algebra, or the Integral Calculus.

In these works it is proved that any rational fraction may be resolved into a series of partial fractions; and that

(1) To any factor of the first degree, as $x-a$, in the denominator there corresponds a partial fraction of the form $\dfrac{A}{x-a}$.

(2) To any factor of the first degree, as $x-b$, occurring n times in the denominator there corresponds a series of n partial fractions of the form
$$\frac{B}{x-b}+\frac{C}{(x-b)^2}+\cdots+\frac{R}{(x-b)^n}.$$

(3) To any quadratic factors, as x^2+px+q, in the denominator there corresponds a partial fraction of the form $\dfrac{Ax+B}{x^2+px+q}$.

(4) To any quadratic factor, as x^2+px+q, occurring n times in the denominator there corresponds a series of n partial fractions of the form
$$\frac{Ax+B}{(x^2+px+q)}+\frac{Cx+D}{(x^2+px+q)^2}+\cdots+\frac{Rx+S}{(x^2+px+q)^n}.$$

Here the quantities $A, B, C, D, \cdots R, S$, are all independent of x.

We shall make use of these results in the examples that follow.

Ex. 1. Separate $\dfrac{5x-11}{2x^2+x-6}$ into partial fractions.

Since the denominator $2x^2+x-6 = (x+2)(2x-3)$, we assume
$$\frac{5x-11}{2x^2+x-6}=\frac{A}{x+2}+\frac{B}{2x-3},$$
where A and B are quantities independent of x whose values have to be determined.

Clearing of fractions,
$$5x-11 = A(2x-3) + B(x+2).$$

Since this equation is identically true, we may equate coefficients of like powers of x; thus
$$2A+B=5, \quad -3A+2B=-11;$$
whence $\qquad A=3, \; B=-1$.
$$\therefore \frac{5x-11}{2x^2+x-6}=\frac{3}{x+2}-\frac{1}{2x-3}.$$

Ex. 2. Resolve $\dfrac{mx+n}{(x-a)(x+b)}$ into partial fractions.

Assume $\dfrac{mx+n}{(x-a)(x+b)} = \dfrac{A}{x-a} + \dfrac{B}{x+b}$.

$\therefore mx+n = A(x+b) + B(x-a)$ . . . . (1)

We might now equate coefficients and find the values of A and B, but it is simpler to proceed in the following manner:

Since A and B are independent of x, we may give to x any value we please.

In (1) put $x-a=0$, or $x=a$; then

$$A = \frac{ma+n}{a+b};$$

putting $x+b=0$, or $x=-b$, $B = \dfrac{mb-n}{a+b}$.

$$\therefore \frac{mx+n}{(x-a)(x+b)} = \frac{1}{a+b}\left(\frac{ma+n}{x-a} + \frac{mb-n}{x+b}\right).$$

Ex. 3. Resolve $\dfrac{23x - 11x^2}{(2x-1)(9-x^2)}$ into partial fractions.

Assume $\dfrac{23x - 11x^2}{(2x-1)(3+x)(3-x)} = \dfrac{A}{2x-1} + \dfrac{B}{3+x} + \dfrac{C}{3-x}$. (1);

$\therefore 23x - 11x^2 = A(3+x)(3-x) + B(2x-1)(3-x)$
$\qquad\qquad\qquad\qquad + C(2x-1)(3+x).$

By equating the coefficients of like powers of x, or putting in succession $2x-1=0$, $3+x=0$, $3-x=0$, we find that

$$A=1,\ B=4,\ C=-1.$$

$$\therefore \frac{23x-11x^2}{(2x-1)(9-x^2)} = \frac{1}{2x-1} + \frac{4}{3+x} - \frac{1}{3-x}$$

Ex. 4. Resolve $\dfrac{3x^2+x-2}{(x-2)^2(1-2x)}$ into partial fractions.

Assume $\dfrac{3x^2+x-2}{(x-2)^2(1-2x)} = \dfrac{A}{1-2x} + \dfrac{B}{x-2} + \dfrac{C}{(x-2)^2}$;

$\therefore 3x^2+x-2 = A(x-2)^2 + B(1-2x)(x-2) + C(1-2x).$

Let $1-2x=0$, then $A = -\tfrac{1}{3}$;

let $x-2=0$, then $C=-4$.

To find B, equate the coefficients of x^2; thus

$$3 = A - 2B;\ \text{whence}\ B = -\tfrac{5}{3}.$$

$$\therefore \frac{3x^2+x-2}{(x-2)^2(1-2x)} = -\frac{1}{3(1-2x)} - \frac{5}{3(x-2)} - \frac{4}{(x-2)^2}.$$

Ex. 5. Resolve $\dfrac{42-19x}{(x^2+1)(x-4)}$ into partial fractions.

Assume $\dfrac{42-19x}{(x^2+1)(x-4)} = \dfrac{Ax+B}{x^2+1} + \dfrac{C}{x-4}$;

$\therefore 42 - 19x = (Ax+B)(x-4) + C(x^2+1)$.

Let $x = 4$, then $C = -2$;
equating coefficients of x^2, $0 = A + C$, and $A = 2$;
equating the absolute terms, $42 = -4B + C$, and $B = -11$,

$\therefore \dfrac{42-19x}{(x^2+1)(x-4)} = \dfrac{2x-11}{x^2+1} - \dfrac{2}{x-4}$.

494. In all the preceding examples the numerator has been of lower dimensions than the denominator; if this is not the case, we divide the numerator by the denominator until a remainder is obtained which is of lower dimensions than the denominator.

Ex. Resolve $\dfrac{6x^3+5x^2-7}{3x^2-2x-1}$ into partial fractions.

By division,

$$\dfrac{6x^3+5x^2-7}{3x^2-2x-1} = 2x + 3 + \dfrac{8x-4}{3x^2-2x-1};$$

and $\dfrac{8x-4}{3x^2-2x-1} = \dfrac{5}{3x+1} + \dfrac{1}{x-1}$;

$\therefore \dfrac{6x^3+5x^2-7}{3x^2-2x-1} = 2x + 3 + \dfrac{5}{3x+1} + \dfrac{1}{x-1}$.

495. The General Term. We shall now explain how resolution into partial fractions may be used to facilitate the expansion of a rational fraction in ascending powers of x.

Ex. 1. Find the general term of $\dfrac{1+6x}{1-3x+2x^2}$ when expanded in a series of ascending powers of x.

By Ex. 1, Art. 493, we have

$$\dfrac{1+5x}{1-3x+2x^2} = \dfrac{7}{1-2x} - \dfrac{6}{1-x} = 7(1-2x)^{-1} - 6(1-x)^{-1}$$
$$= 7[1 + (2x) + (2x)^2 + \cdots + (2x)^r + \cdots]$$
$$- 6(1 + x + x^2 + \cdots + x^r + \cdots).$$

Hence the $(r+1)$th, or general term of the expansion, is

$$7(2x)^r - 6x^r \text{ or } [7(2)^r - 6]x^r.$$

Ex. 2. Find the general term of $\dfrac{3x^2 + x - 2}{(x-2)^2(1-2x)}$ when expanded in a series of ascending powers of x.

By Ex. 4, Art. 493, we have

$$\dfrac{3x^2 + x - 2}{(x-2)^2(1-2x)} = -\dfrac{1}{3(1-2x)} - \dfrac{5}{3(x-2)} - \dfrac{4}{(x-2)^2}$$

$$= -\dfrac{1}{3(1-2x)} + \dfrac{5}{3(2-x)} - \dfrac{4}{(2-x)^2}$$

$$= -\dfrac{1}{3(1-2x)} + \dfrac{5}{6\left(1-\dfrac{x}{2}\right)} - \dfrac{4}{4\left(1-\dfrac{x}{2}\right)^2}$$

$$= -\dfrac{1}{3}(1-2x)^{-1} + \dfrac{5}{6}\left(1-\dfrac{x}{2}\right)^{-1} - \left(1-\dfrac{x}{2}\right)^{-2}$$

$$= -\tfrac{1}{3}[1 + (2x) + (2x)^2 + \cdots + (2x)^r + \cdots]$$

$$+ \dfrac{5}{6}\left[1 + \left(\dfrac{x}{2}\right) + \left(\dfrac{x}{2}\right)^2 + \cdots + \left(\dfrac{x}{2}\right)^r + \cdots\right]$$

$$- \left[1 + 2\left(\dfrac{x}{2}\right) + 3\left(\dfrac{x}{2}\right)^2 + \cdots + (r+1)\left(\dfrac{x}{2}\right)^r + \cdots\right].$$

Hence the $(r+1)$th or general term of the expansion is

$$\left(-\dfrac{2^r}{3} + \dfrac{5}{6}\cdot\dfrac{1}{2^r} - \dfrac{r+1}{2^r}\right)x^r.$$

496. The following example sufficiently illustrates the method to be pursued when the denominator contains a quadratic factor.

Ex. Expand $\dfrac{7+x}{(1+x)(1+x^2)}$ in ascending powers of x and find the general term.

Assume $\dfrac{7+x}{(1+x)(1+x^2)} = \dfrac{A}{1+x} + \dfrac{Bx+C}{1+x^2};$

$\therefore 7 + x = A(1+x^2) + (Bx+C)(1+x).$

Let $1 + x = 0$, then $A = 3$;

equating the absolute terms, $7 = A + C$, whence $C = 4$;
equating the coefficients of x^2, $0 = A + B$, whence $B = -3$.

$$\therefore \dfrac{7+x}{(1+x)(1+x^2)} = \dfrac{3}{1+x} + \dfrac{4-3x}{1+x^2}$$

$$= 3(1+x)^{-1} + (4-3x)(1+x^2)^{-1}$$

$$= 3\{1 - x + x^2 - \cdots + (-1)^p x^p + \cdots\}$$

$$+ (4-3x)\{1 - x^2 + x^4 - \cdots + (-1)^p x^{2p} + \cdots\}$$

UNDETERMINED COEFFICIENTS.

To find the coefficient of x^r;

(1) If r is even, the coefficient of x^r in the second series is $4(-1)^{\frac{r}{2}}$; therefore in the expansion the coefficient of x^r is $3+4(-1)^{\frac{r}{2}}$.

(2) If r is odd, the coefficient of x^r in the second series is $-3(-1)^{\frac{r-1}{2}}$, and the required coefficient is $3(-1)^{\frac{r+1}{2}}-3$.

EXAMPLES XLII. e.

Resolve into partial fractions:

1. $\dfrac{7x-1}{1-5x+6x^2}$.
2. $\dfrac{46+13x}{12x^2-11x-15}$.
3. $\dfrac{1+3x+2x^2}{(1-2x)(1-x^2)}$.
4. $\dfrac{x^2-10x+13}{(x-1)(x^2-5x+6)}$.
8. $\dfrac{26x^2+208x}{(x^2+1)(x+5)}$.
5. $\dfrac{2x^3+x^2-x-3}{x(x-1)(2x+3)}$.
9. $\dfrac{2x^2-11x+5}{(x-3)(x^2+2x-5)}$.
6. $\dfrac{9}{(x-1)(x+2)^2}$.
10. $\dfrac{3x^3-8x^2+10}{(x-1)^4}$.
7. $\dfrac{x^4-3x^3-3x^2+10}{(x+1)^2(x-3)}$.
11. $\dfrac{5x^3+6x^2+5x}{(x^2-1)(x+1)^3}$.

Find the general term of the following expressions when expanded in ascending powers of x.

12. $\dfrac{1+3x}{1+11x+28x^2}$.
13. $\dfrac{5x+6}{(2+x)(1-x)}$.
14. $\dfrac{x^2+7x+3}{x^2+7x+10}$.
15. $\dfrac{2x-4}{(1-x^2)(1-2x)}$.
19. $\dfrac{2x+1}{(x-1)(x^2+1)}$.
16. $\dfrac{4+3x+2x^2}{(1-x)(1+x-2x^2)}$.
20. $\dfrac{1-x+2x^2}{(1-x)^3}$.
17. $\dfrac{3+2x-x^2}{(1+x)(1-4x)^2}$.
21. $\dfrac{1}{(1-ax)(1-bx)(1-cx)}$.
18. $\dfrac{4+7x}{(2+3x)(1+x)^2}$.
22. $\dfrac{3-2x^2}{(2-3x+x^2)^2}$.

CHAPTER XLIII.

Continued Fractions.

497. An expression of the form $a + \cfrac{b}{c + \cfrac{d}{e + \cdots}}$ is called a *continued fraction*; here the letters a, b, c, $\cdots$ may denote any quantities whatever, but for the present we shall only consider the simpler form $a_1 + \cfrac{1}{a_2 + \cfrac{1}{a_3 + \cdots}}$, where a_1, a_2, a_3, $\cdots$ are positive integers. This will be usually written in the more compact form

$$a_1 + \frac{1}{a_2 +} \frac{1}{a_3 +} \cdots.$$

498. When the number of *quotients* a_1, a_2, a_3, $\cdots$ is finite the continued fraction is said to be *terminating*; if the number of quotients is unlimited the fraction is called an *infinite continued fraction*.

It is possible to reduce every terminating continued fraction to an ordinary fraction by simplifying the fractions in succession beginning from the lowest.

499. To convert a given fraction into a continued fraction.

Let $\dfrac{m}{n}$ be the given fraction; divide m by n; let a_1 be the quotient and p the remainder; thus

$$\frac{m}{n} = a_1 + \frac{p}{n} = a_1 + \frac{1}{\dfrac{n}{p}};$$

divide n by p, let a_2 be the quotient and q the remainder; thus

$$\frac{n}{p} = a_2 + \frac{q}{p} = a_2 + \frac{1}{\dfrac{p}{q}};$$

divide p by q, let a_3 be the quotient and r the remainder; and so on. Thus

$$\frac{m}{n} = a_1 + \cfrac{1}{a_2 + \cfrac{1}{a_3 + \cdots}} = a_1 + \frac{1}{a_2+} \frac{1}{a_3+} \cdots .$$

If m is less than n, the first quotient is zero, and we put

$$\frac{m}{n} = \frac{1}{\dfrac{n}{m}}$$

and proceed as before.

It will be observed that the above process is the same as that of finding the greatest common measure of m and n; hence if m and n are *commensurable*, we shall at length arrive at a stage where the division is exact and the process terminates. Thus every fraction whose numerator and denominator are positive integers can be converted into a terminating continued fraction.

Ex. Reduce $\frac{832}{159}$ to a continued fraction.

Find the greatest common measure of 832 and 159 by the usual process, thus:

```
      159)832(5
          795
          ───
          37)159(4
             148
             ───
             11)37(3
                33
                ──
                4)11(2
                  8
                  ─
                  3)4(1
                    3
                    ─
                    1)3(3
                      3
                      ─
                      0
```

We have the successive quotients 5, 4, 3, 2, 1, 3; hence

$$\frac{832}{159} = 5 + \frac{1}{4+} \frac{1}{3+} \frac{1}{2+} \frac{1}{1+} \frac{1}{3}.$$

500. Convergents. The fractions obtained by stopping at the first, second, third, ⋯ quotients of a continued fraction are called the first, second, third, ⋯ *convergents*, because, as will be shown in Art. 506, each successive convergent is a nearer approximation to the true value of the continued fraction than any of the preceding convergents.

501. To show that the convergents are alternately less and greater than the continued fraction.

Let the continued fraction be $a_1 + \dfrac{1}{a_2+} \dfrac{1}{a_3+} \cdots$.

The first convergent is a_1, and is too small because the part $\dfrac{1}{a_2+} \dfrac{1}{a_3+} \cdots$ is omitted. The second convergent is $a_1 + \dfrac{1}{a_2}$, and is too great because the denominator a_2 is too small. The third convergent is $a_1 + \dfrac{1}{a_2+} \dfrac{1}{a_3}$, and is too small because $a_2 + \dfrac{1}{a_3}$ is too great; and so on.

When the given fraction is a proper fraction, $a_1 = 0$; if in this case we agree to consider zero as the first convergent, we may enunciate the above results as follows:

The convergents of an odd order are all less, and the convergents of an even order are all greater, than the continued fraction.

502. To establish the law of formation of the successive convergents.

Let the continued fraction be denoted by

$$a_1 + \dfrac{1}{a_2+} \dfrac{1}{a_3+} \dfrac{1}{a_4+} \cdots ;$$

then the first three convergents are

$$\dfrac{a_1}{1}, \quad \dfrac{a_1 a_2 + 1}{a_2}, \quad \dfrac{a_3(a_1 a_2 + 1) + a_1}{a_3 \cdot a_2 + 1};$$

and we see that the numerator of the third convergent may be formed by multiplying the numerator of the second convergent by the third quotient, and adding the numerator of the first convergent; also that the denominator may be formed in a similar manner.

Suppose that the successive convergents are formed in a similar way; let the numerators be denoted by $p_1, p_2, p_3, \ldots$, and the denominators by $q_1, q_2, q_3, \ldots$.

Assume that the law of formation holds for the nth convergent; that is, suppose

$$p_n = a_n p_{n-1} + p_{n-2}, \quad q_n = a_n q_{n-1} + q_{n-2}.$$

The $(n+1)$th convergent differs from the nth only in having the quotient $a_n + \dfrac{1}{a_{n+1}}$ in the place of a_n; hence the $(n+1)$th convergent

$$= \frac{\left(a_n + \dfrac{1}{a_{n+1}}\right)p_{n-1} + p_{n-2}}{\left(a_n + \dfrac{1}{a_{n+1}}\right)q_{n-1} + q_{n-2}} = \frac{a_{n+1}(a_n p_{n-1} + p_{n-2}) + p_{n-1}}{a_{n+1}(a_n q_{n-1} + q_{n-2}) + q_{n-1}}$$

$$= \frac{a_{n+1} p_n + p_{n-1}}{a_{n+1} q_n + q_{n-1}}, \text{ by supposition.}$$

If therefore we put

$$p_{n+1} = a_{n+1} p_n + p_{n-1}, \quad q_{n+1} = a_{n+1} q_n + q_{n-1},$$

we see that the numerator and denominator of the $(n+1)$th convergent follow the law which was supposed to hold in the case of the nth. But the law does hold in the case of the third convergent, hence it holds for the fourth, and so on; therefore it holds universally.

Ex. Reduce $\frac{674}{313}$ to a continued fraction and calculate the successive convergents.

By Art. 499, $\dfrac{674}{313} = 2 + \dfrac{1}{6+} \dfrac{1}{1+} \dfrac{1}{1+} \dfrac{1}{11+} \dfrac{1}{2}.$

The successive quotients are 2, 6, 1, 1, 11, 2.

The successive convergents are $\frac{2}{1}, \frac{13}{6}, \frac{15}{7}, \frac{28}{13}, \frac{323}{150}, \frac{674}{313}.$

EXPLANATION. With the first and second quotients take the first and second convergents, which are readily determined. Thus, in this example, 2 is the first convergent, and $2 + \frac{1}{6}$ or $\frac{13}{6}$ the second convergent. The numerator of the third convergent, 15, equals the numerator of the preceding convergent, 13, multiplied by 1, the third quotient, plus 2, the numerator of the convergent next preceding but one. The denominator is formed in a similar manner: thus $7 = 1 \times 6 + 1$.

The fifth convergent $= \dfrac{11(28) + 15}{11(13) + 7} = \dfrac{323}{150}$.

503. If the fraction is a proper fraction, we may consider zero as the first convergent, and proceed as follows:

Reduce $\frac{84}{227}$ to a continued fraction, and calculate the successive convergents.

Proceeding as in Art. 499,

```
227)84(0
    00
    ──
    84)227(2
       168
       ───
       59)84(1
          59
          ──
          25)59(...
```

We obtain $\quad 0 + \dfrac{1}{2+}\dfrac{1}{1+}\dfrac{1}{2+}\dfrac{1}{2+}\dfrac{1}{1+}\dfrac{1}{3+}\dfrac{1}{2}.$

The successive quotients are 0, 2, 1, 2, 2, 1, 3, 2.

Writing $\frac{0}{1}$ for the first convergent and arranging the work as show in the example of the preceding article, we have

Quotients $\qquad$ 0 2 1 2 2 1 3 2.
Convergents $\quad \frac{0}{1}, \frac{1}{2}, \frac{1}{3}, \frac{3}{8}, \frac{7}{19}, \frac{10}{27}, \frac{37}{100}, \frac{84}{227}.$

504. It will be convenient to call a_n the nth *partial* quotient; the *complete* quotient at this stage being

$$a_n + \dfrac{1}{a_{n+1}+}\dfrac{1}{a_{n+2}+}\cdots$$

We shall usually denote the complete quotient at any stage by k.

We have seen that
$$\frac{p_n}{q_n} = \frac{a_n p_{n-1} + p_{n-2}}{a_n q_{n-1} + q_{n-2}}.$$

Let the continued fraction be denoted by x; then x differs from $\frac{p_n}{q_n}$ only in taking the complete quotient k instead of the partial quotient a_n; thus
$$x = \frac{k p_{n-1} + p_{n-2}}{k q_{n-1} + q_{n-2}}.$$

505. To show that if $\frac{p_n}{q_n}$ be the nth convergent to a continued fraction, then
$$p_n q_{n-1} - p_{n-1} q_n = (-1)^n.$$

Let the continued fraction be denoted by
$$a_1 + \frac{1}{a_2+} \; \frac{1}{a_3+} \; \frac{1}{a_4+} \; \cdots;$$
then $p_n q_{n-1} - p_{n-1} q_n = (a_n p_{n-1} + p_{n-2}) q_{n-1} - p_{n-1}(a_n q_{n-1} + q_{n-2})$
$$= (-1)(p_{n-1} q_{n-2} - p_{n-2} q_{n-1})$$
$$= (-1)^2 (p_{n-2} q_{n-3} - p_{n-3} q_{n-2}), \text{ similarly,}$$
$$= \cdot \cdot \cdot \cdot \cdot \cdot \cdot \cdot$$
$$= (-1)^{n-2}(p_2 q_1 - p_1 q_2).$$

But $\quad p_2 q_1 - p_1 q_2 = (a_1 a_2 + 1) - a_1 \cdot a_2 = 1 = (-1)^2;$
hence $\quad p_n q_{n-1} - p_{n-1} q_n = (-1)^n.$

When the continued fraction is *less* than unity, this result will still hold if we suppose that $a_1 = 0$, and that the first convergent is zero.

NOTE. When we are calculating the numerical value of the successive convergents, the above theorem furnishes an easy test of the accuracy of the work.

COR. 1. *Each convergent is in its lowest terms;* for if p_n and q_n had a common divisor it would divide $p_n q_{n-1} - p_{n-1} q_n$ or unity; which is impossible.

COR. 2. *The difference between two successive convergents is a fraction whose numerator is unity, and whose denominator is the product of the denominators of these convergents;* for

$$*\frac{p_n}{q_n} \sim \frac{p_{n-1}}{q_{n-1}} = \frac{p_n q_{n-1} \sim p_{n-1} q_n}{q_n q_{n-1}} = \frac{1}{q_n q_{n-1}}.$$

506. Each convergent is nearer to the continued fraction than any of the preceding convergents.

Let x denote the continued fraction, and $\dfrac{p_n}{q_n}$, $\dfrac{p_{n+1}}{q_{n+1}}$, $\dfrac{p_{n+2}}{q_{n+2}}$ three consecutive convergents; then x differs from $\dfrac{p_{n+2}}{q_{n+2}}$ only in taking the *complete* $(n+2)$th quotient in the place of a_{n+2}; denote this by k; thus

$$x = \frac{k p_{n+1} + p_n}{k q_{n+1} + q_n};$$

$$\therefore\ x \sim \frac{p_n}{q_n} = \frac{k(p_{n+1} q_n \sim p_n q_{n+1})}{q_n(k q_{n+1} + q_n)} = \frac{k}{q_n(k q_{n+1} + q_n)},$$

and $\quad \dfrac{p_{n+1}}{q_{n+1}} \sim x = \dfrac{p_{n+1} q_n \sim p_n q_{n+1}}{q_{n+1}(k q_{n+1} + q_n)} = \dfrac{1}{q_{n+1}(k q_{n+1} + q_n)}.$

Now k is greater than unity, and q_n is less than q_{n+1}; hence on both accounts the difference between $\dfrac{p_{n+1}}{q_{n+1}}$ and x is less than the difference between $\dfrac{p_n}{q_n}$ and x; that is, every convergent is nearer to the continued fraction than the next preceding convergent, and therefore nearer than any preceding convergent.

Combining the result of this article with that of Art. 501, it follows that

The convergents of an odd order continually increase, but are always less than the continued fraction;

The convergents of an even order continually decrease, but are always greater than the continued fraction.

---

* The sign $\sim$ means "difference between."

CONTINUED FRACTIONS. 407

507. To find limits to the error made in taking any convergent for the continued fraction.

Let $\dfrac{p_n}{q_n}, \dfrac{p_{n+1}}{q_{n+1}}, \dfrac{p_{n+2}}{q_{n+2}}$ be three consecutive convergents, and let k denote the complete $(n+2)$th quotient;

then
$$x = \frac{kp_{n+1} + p_n}{kq_{n+1} + q_n};$$

$$\therefore x \sim \frac{p_n}{q_n} = \frac{k}{q_n(kq_{n+1} + q_n)} = \frac{1}{q_n\left(q_{n+1} + \dfrac{q_n}{k}\right)}.$$

Now k is greater than 1, therefore *the difference between the continued fraction x, and any convergent, $\dfrac{p_n}{q_n}$, is less than* $\dfrac{1}{q_n q_{n+1}}$, *and greater than* $\dfrac{1}{q_n(q_{n+1} + q_n)}$.

Again, since $q_{n+1} > q_n$, the error in taking $\dfrac{p_n}{q_n}$ instead of x is less than $\dfrac{1}{q_n^2}$ and greater than $\dfrac{1}{2q_{n+1}^2}$.

508. From the last article it appears that the error in taking $\dfrac{p_n}{q_n}$ instead of the continued fraction is less than $\dfrac{1}{q_n q_{n+1}}$, or $\dfrac{1}{q_n(a_{n+1}q_n + q_{n-1})}$; that is, less than $\dfrac{1}{a_{n+1}q_n^2}$; hence the larger a_{n+1} is, the nearer does $\dfrac{p_n}{q_n}$ approximate to the continued fraction; therefore, *any convergent which immediately precedes a large quotient is a near approximation to the continued fraction.*

Again, since the error is less than $\dfrac{1}{q_n^2}$, it follows that in order to find a convergent which will differ from the continued fraction by less than a given quantity $\dfrac{1}{a}$, we have only to calculate the successive convergents up to $\dfrac{p_n}{q_n}$, where q_n^2 is greater than a.

509. The properties of continued fractions enable us to find two small integers whose ratio closely approximates to that of two incommensurable quantities, or to that of two quantities whose exact ratio can only be expressed by large integers.

Ex. Find a series of fractions approximating to 3.14159.

In the process of finding the greatest common measure of 14159 and 100000, the successive quotients are 7, 15, 1, 25, 1, 7, 4. Thus
$$3.14159 = 3 + \frac{1}{7+}\frac{1}{15+}\frac{1}{1+}\frac{1}{25+}\frac{1}{1+}\frac{1}{7+}\frac{1}{4}.$$

The successive convergents are
$$\frac{3}{1}, \frac{22}{7}, \frac{333}{106}, \frac{355}{113}, \dots.$$

This last convergent which precedes the large quotient 25 is a very near approximation, the error being less than $\dfrac{1}{25 \times (113)^2}$, and therefore less than $\dfrac{1}{25 \times (100)^2}$, or .000004.

510. *Any convergent is nearer to the continued fraction than any other fraction whose denominator is less than that of the convergent.*

Let x be the continued fraction, $\dfrac{p_n}{q_n}$, $\dfrac{p_{n-1}}{q_{n-1}}$ two consecutive convergents, $\dfrac{r}{s}$ a fraction whose denominator s is less than q_n.

If possible, let $\dfrac{r}{s}$ be nearer to x than $\dfrac{p_n}{q_n}$, then $\dfrac{r}{s}$ must be nearer to x than $\dfrac{p_{n-1}}{q_{n-1}}$ [Art. 506]; and since x lies between $\dfrac{p_n}{q_n}$ and $\dfrac{p_{n-1}}{q_{n-1}}$, it follows that $\dfrac{r}{s}$ must lie between $\dfrac{p_n}{q_n}$ and $\dfrac{p_{n-1}}{q_{n-1}}$.

Hence
$$\frac{r}{s} \sim \frac{p_{n-1}}{q_{n-1}} < \frac{p_n}{q_n} \sim \frac{p_{n-1}}{q_{n-1}}, \text{ that is } < \frac{1}{q_n q_{n-1}};$$
$$\therefore rq_{n-1} \sim sp_{n-1} < \frac{s}{q_n};$$

that is, an integer less than a fraction; which is impossible. Therefore $\dfrac{p_n}{q_n}$ must be nearer to the continued fraction than $\dfrac{r}{s}$.

CONTINUED FRACTIONS.

EXAMPLES XLIII. a.

Calculate the successive convergents to

1. $2 + \cfrac{1}{1+} \cfrac{1}{3+} \cfrac{1}{5+} \cfrac{1}{1+} \cfrac{1}{1+} \cfrac{1}{2}.$

2. $\cfrac{1}{2+} \cfrac{1}{2+} \cfrac{1}{3+} \cfrac{1}{1+} \cfrac{1}{4+} \cfrac{1}{2+} \cfrac{1}{6}.$

3. $3 + \cfrac{1}{3+} \cfrac{1}{1+} \cfrac{1}{2+} \cfrac{1}{2+} \cfrac{1}{1+} \cfrac{1}{9}.$

Express the following quantities as continued fractions and find the fourth convergent to each: also determine the limits to the error made by taking the third convergent for the fraction.

4. $\frac{253}{178}$.
5. $\frac{251}{202}$.
6. $\frac{1189}{3927}$.
7. $\frac{729}{2315}$.
8. $.37$.
9. 1.139.
10. $.3029$.
11. 4.316.

12. Find limits to the error in taking $\frac{222}{203}$ yards as equivalent to a metre, given that a metre is equal to 1.0936 yards.

13. Find an approximation to
$$1 + \cfrac{1}{3+} \cfrac{1}{5+} \cfrac{1}{7+} \cfrac{1}{9+} \cfrac{1}{11+} \cdots$$
which differs from the true value by less than .0001.

14. Show by the theory of continued fractions that $\frac{99}{70}$ differs from 1.41421 by a quantity less than $\frac{1}{11830}$.

RECURRING CONTINUED FRACTIONS.

511. We have seen that a *terminating* continued fraction with rational quotients can be reduced to an ordinary fraction with integral numerator and denominator, and therefore cannot be equal to a surd; but we shall prove that a quadratic surd can be expressed as an *infinite* continued fraction whose quotients recur. We shall first consider a numerical example.

Ex. Express $\sqrt{19}$ as a continued fraction, and find a series of fractions approximating to its value.

$$\sqrt{19} = 4 + (\sqrt{19} - 4) = 4 + \frac{3}{\sqrt{19}+4};$$

$$\frac{\sqrt{19}+4}{3} = 2 + \frac{\sqrt{19}-2}{3} = 2 + \frac{5}{\sqrt{19}+2};$$

$$\frac{\sqrt{19}+2}{5} = 1 + \frac{\sqrt{19}-3}{5} = 1 + \frac{2}{\sqrt{19}+3};$$

$$\frac{\sqrt{19}+3}{2} = 3 + \frac{\sqrt{19}-3}{2} = 3 + \frac{5}{\sqrt{19}+3};$$

$$\frac{\sqrt{19}+3}{5} = 1 + \frac{\sqrt{19}-2}{5} = 1 + \frac{3}{\sqrt{19}+2};$$

$$\frac{\sqrt{19}+2}{3} = 2 + \frac{\sqrt{19}-4}{3} = 2 + \frac{1}{\sqrt{19}+4};$$

$$\sqrt{19}+4 = 8 + (\sqrt{19}-4) = 8 + \cdots$$

after this the quotients 2, 1, 3, 1, 2, 8 recur; hence

$$\sqrt{19} = 4 + \frac{1}{2+} \frac{1}{1+} \frac{1}{3+} \frac{1}{1+} \frac{1}{2+} \frac{1}{8+} \cdots.$$

It will be noticed that the quotients recur as soon as we come to a quotient which is double the first.

EXPLANATION. We first find the greatest integer in $\sqrt{19}$; this is 4, and we write $\sqrt{19} = 4 + (\sqrt{19}-4)$. We then express $\sqrt{19}-4$ as an equivalent fraction with a rational *numerator*. Thus

$$\sqrt{19}-4 = \frac{(\sqrt{19}-4)(\sqrt{19}+4)}{\sqrt{19}+4} = \frac{3}{\sqrt{19}+4}.$$

The work now stands

$$\sqrt{19} = 4 + \frac{3}{\sqrt{19}+4} = 4 + \frac{1}{\frac{\sqrt{19}+4}{3}}.$$

We begin the second line with $\dfrac{\sqrt{19}+4}{3}$, the denominator of this complex fraction, which is itself a fraction with a *rational denominator*. The greatest integer in this fraction is 2, and we write

$$\frac{\sqrt{19}+4}{3} = 2 + \frac{\sqrt{19}-2}{3}.$$

We then multiply numerator and denominator by the surd conjugate to $\sqrt{19}-2$, so that after inverting the result $\dfrac{5}{\sqrt{19}+2}$, we again begin a line with a rational denominator. The same series of operations is performed in each of the following lines.

The first seven convergents formed as explained in Art. 502 are

$$\tfrac{4}{1}, \tfrac{9}{2}, \tfrac{13}{3}, \tfrac{48}{11}, \tfrac{61}{14}, \tfrac{170}{39}, \tfrac{1421}{326}.$$

The error in taking the last of these is less than $\frac{1}{(326)^2}$, and is therefore less than $\frac{1}{(320)^2}$ or $\frac{1}{102400}$, and still less than $.00001$. Thus the seventh convergent gives the value to at least four places of decimals.

512. Every periodic continued fraction is equal to one of the roots of a quadratic equation of which the coefficients are rational.

Let x denote the continued fraction, and y the periodic part, and suppose that

$$x = a + \frac{1}{b+}\frac{1}{c+}\cdots\frac{1}{h+}\frac{1}{k+}\frac{1}{y},$$

and

$$y = m + \frac{1}{n+}\cdots\frac{1}{u+}\frac{1}{v+}\frac{1}{y},$$

where $a, b, c, \cdots h, k, m, n, \cdots u, v$ are positive integers.

Let $\frac{p}{q}, \frac{p'}{q'}$ be the convergents to x corresponding to the quotients h, k respectively; then since y is the complete quotient, we have $x = \frac{p'y + p}{q'y + q}$; whence $y = \frac{p - qx}{q'x - p'}$.

Let $\frac{r}{s}, \frac{r'}{s'}$ be the convergents to y corresponding to the quotients u, v respectively; then $y = \frac{r'y + r}{s'y + s}$.

Substituting for y in terms of x and simplifying, we obtain a quadratic of which the coefficients are rational.

The equation $s'y^2 + (s - r')y - r = 0$, which gives the value of y, has its roots real and of opposite signs; if the positive value of y be substituted in $x = \frac{p'y + p}{q'y + q}$, on rationalizing the denominator the value of x is of the form $\frac{A + \sqrt{B}}{C}$, where A, B, C are integers, B being positive since the value of y is real.

Ex. Express $1 + \cfrac{1}{2+} \cfrac{1}{3+} \cfrac{1}{2+} \cfrac{1}{3+} \ldots$ as a surd.

Let x be the value of the continued fraction; then

$$x - 1 = \cfrac{1}{2+} \cfrac{1}{3+(x-1)};$$

whence $2x^2 + 2x - 7 = 0$.

The continued fraction is equal to the positive root of this equation and is therefore equal to $\dfrac{\sqrt{15} - 1}{2}$.

EXAMPLES XLIII. b.

Express the following surds as continued fractions, and find the sixth convergent to each:

1. $\sqrt{3}$.
2. $\sqrt{5}$.
3. $\sqrt{6}$.
4. $\sqrt{8}$.
5. $\sqrt{11}$.
6. $\sqrt{13}$.
7. $\sqrt{14}$.
8. $\sqrt{22}$.
9. $2\sqrt{3}$.
10. $4\sqrt{2}$.
11. $3\sqrt{5}$.
12. $4\sqrt{10}$.
13. $\dfrac{1}{\sqrt{21}}$.
14. $\dfrac{1}{\sqrt{33}}$.
15. $\sqrt{\tfrac{6}{5}}$.
16. $\sqrt{\tfrac{7}{11}}$.

17. Find limits of the error when $\tfrac{268}{65}$ is taken for $\sqrt{17}$.

18. Find limits of the error when $\tfrac{916}{191}$ is taken for $\sqrt{23}$.

19. Find the first convergent to $\sqrt{101}$ that is correct to five places of decimals.

20. Find the first convergent to $\sqrt{15}$ that is correct to five places of decimals.

Express as a continued fraction the positive root of each of the following equations:

21. $x^2 + 2x - 1 = 0$.
22. $x^2 - 4x - 3 = 0$.
23. $7x^2 - 8x - 3 = 0$.

24. Express each root of $x^2 - 5x + 3 = 0$ as a continued fraction.

25. Find the value of $3 + \cfrac{1}{6+} \cfrac{1}{6+} \cfrac{1}{6+} \ldots$.

26. Find the value of $\cfrac{1}{1+} \cfrac{1}{3+} \cfrac{1}{1+} \cfrac{1}{3+} \ldots$.

27. Find the value of $3 + \cfrac{1}{1+} \cfrac{1}{2+} \cfrac{1}{3+} \cfrac{1}{1+} \cfrac{1}{2+} \cfrac{1}{3+} \ldots$.

28. Find the value of $5 + \cfrac{1}{1+} \cfrac{1}{1+} \cfrac{1}{1+} \cfrac{1}{10+} \ldots$.

CHAPTER XLIV.

Summation of Series.

513. Examples of the summation of certain series (Arithmetic and Geometric) have occurred in previous chapters. We will now consider methods for summing other series.

514. Recurring Series. A series $u_0 + u_1 + u_2 + u_3 + \cdots$, in which from and after a certain term each term is equal to the sum of a fixed number of the preceding terms multiplied respectively by certain constants, is called a *recurring series*. A recurring series is of the 1st, 2d, or rth order, according as 1, 2, or r constants are required as multipliers.

515. Scale of Relation. In the series
$$1 + 2x + 3x^2 + 4x^3 + 5x^4 + \cdots,$$
each term after the second is equal to the sum of the two preceding terms multiplied respectively by the *constants* $2x$ and $-x^2$; these quantities being called constants because they are the same for all values of n. Thus
$$5x^4 = 2x \cdot 4x^3 + (-x^2) \cdot 3x^2;$$
that is,
$$u_4 = 2xu_3 - x^2 u_2;$$
and generally, when n is greater than 1, each term is connected with the two that immediately precede it by the equation
$$u_n = 2xu_{n-1} - x^2 u_{n-2}$$
or,
$$u_n - 2xu_{n-1} + x^2 u_{n-2} = 0.$$

In this equation the coefficients of u_n, u_{n-1}, and u_{n-2}, *taken with their proper signs*, form what is called the *scale of relation*.

Thus the series
$$1 + 2x + 3x^2 + 4x^3 + 5x^4 + \cdots$$
is a recurring series in which the scale of relation is
$$1 - 2x + x^2.$$

516. To find any term when the scale of relation is given. If the scale of relation of a recurring series is given, any term can be found when a sufficient number of the preceding terms are known. As the method of procedure is the same, however many terms the scale of relation may consist of, the following illustration will be sufficient:

If $\qquad 1 - px - qx^2 - rx^3$

is the scale of relation of the series
$$a_0 + a_1 x + a_2 x^2 + a_3 x^3 + \cdots$$
we have
$$a_n x^n = px \cdot a_{n-1} x^{n-1} + qx^2 \cdot a_{n-2} x^{n-2} + rx^3 \cdot a_{n-3} x^{n-3},$$
or $\qquad a_n = p a_{n-1} + q a_{n-2} + r a_{n-3};$

thus any coefficient can be found when the coefficients of the three preceding terms are known.

517. To find the scale of relation. If a sufficient number of the terms of a series be given, the scale of relation may be found.

Ex. Find the scale of relation of the recurring series
$$2 + 5x + 13x^2 + 35x^3 + 97x^4 + 275x^5 + 793x^6 + \cdots.$$
This is plainly not a series of the first order. If it be of the second order, to obtain p and q we have the equations
$$13 = 5p + 2q, \text{ and } 35 = 13p + 5q;$$
whence $p = 5$, and $q = -6$. By using these values of p and q, we can obtain the fifth and sixth coefficients; hence they are correct, and the scale of relation is
$$1 - 5x + 6x^2.$$

If we could not have obtained the remaining coefficients with these values of p and q, we would have assumed the series to be of the third order, and formed the equations
$$35 = 13p + 5q + 2r,$$
$$97 = 35p + 13q + 5r,$$
$$275 = 97p + 35q + 13r;$$

whence values for p, q, and r would have been obtained, and trial with the seventh and following coefficients would have shown whether they were correct.

518. If the scale of relation consists of 3 terms it involves 2 constants, p and q; and we must have 2 equations to determine p and q. To obtain the first of these we must know at least 3 terms of the series, and to obtain the second we must have one more term given. Thus to obtain a scale of relation involving two constants we must have at least 4 terms given.

If the scale of relation be $1 - px - qx^2 - rx^3$, to find the 3 constants we must have 3 equations. To obtain the first of these we must know at least 4 terms of the series, and to obtain the other two we must have two more terms given; hence to find a scale of relation involving 3 constants, at least 6 terms of the series must be given.

Generally, to find a scale of relation involving m constants, we must know at least $2m$ consecutive terms.

Conversely, if $2m$ consecutive terms are given, we may assume for the scale of relation

$$1 - p_1 x - p_2 x^2 - p_3 x^3 - \cdots - p_m x^m.$$

519. The Sum of n Terms of a Recurring Series. The method of finding the sum is the same whatever be the scale of relation; for simplicity we shall suppose it to contain only two constants.

Let the series be

$$a_0 + a_1 x + a_2 x^2 + a_3 x^3 + \cdots$$

and let the sum be S; let the scale of relation be $1 - px - qx^2$; so that for every value of n greater than 1, we have

$$a_n - p a_{n-1} - q a_{n-2} = 0.$$

Now $S = a_0 + a_1 x + a_2 x^2 + \cdots + a_{n-1} x^{n-1}$,
$-pxS = -p a_0 x - p a_1 x^2 - \cdots - p a_{n-2} x^{n-1} - p a_{n-1} x^n$,
$-qx^2 S = -q a_0 x^2 - \cdots - q a_{n-3} x^{n-1} - q a_{n-2} x^n - q a_{n-1} x^{n+1}$.

Hence
$$(1-px-qx^2)S = a_0 + (a_1-pa_0)x - (pa_{n-1}+qa_{n-2})x^n - qa_{n-1}x^{n+1},$$
for the coefficient of every other power of x is zero in consequence of the relation
$$a_n - pa_{n-1} - qa_{n-2} = 0.$$
$$\therefore S = \frac{a_0 + (a_1 - pa_0)x}{1 - px - qx^2} - \frac{(pa_{n-1} + qa_{n-2})x^n + qa_{n-1}x^{n+1}}{1 - px - qx^2}.$$

Thus the sum of a recurring series is a fraction whose denominator is the scale of relation.

520. If the second fraction in the result of the last article decreases indefinitely as n increases indefinitely, the formula for the sum of an *infinite* number of terms of a recurring series of the *second order* reduces to
$$S = \frac{a_0 + (a_1 - pa_0)x}{1 - px - qx^2}.$$

If we develop this fraction in ascending powers of x as explained in Art. 487, we shall obtain as many terms of the original series as we please; for this reason the expression
$$\frac{a_0 + (a_1 - pa_0)x}{1 - px - qx^2}$$
is called the *generating function** of the series. The **summation** of the series is the finding of this generating function.

If the series is of the *third order*,
$$S = \frac{a_0 + (a_1 - pa_0)x + (a_2 - pa_1 - qa_0)x^2}{1 - px - qx^2 - rx^3}.$$

521. From the result of Art. 519, we obtain
$$\frac{a_0 + (a_1 - pa_0)x}{1 - px - qx^2} = a_0 + a_1 x + a_2 x^2 + \cdots + a_{n-1} x^{n+1}$$
$$+ \frac{(pa_{n-1} + qa_{n-2})x^n + qa_{n-1}x^{n+1}}{1 - px - qx^2};$$

* Sometimes called the *generating fraction*.

SUMMATION OF SERIES. 417

from which we see that although the generating function
$$\frac{a_0 + (a_1 - pa_0)x}{1 - px - qx^2}$$
may be used to obtain as many terms of the series as we please, it can be regarded as the true equivalent to the infinite series
$$a_0 + a_1 x + a_2 x^2 + \cdots,$$
only if the remainder
$$\frac{(pa_{n-1} + qa_{n-2})x^n + qa_{n-1}x^{n+1}}{1 - px - qx^2}$$
vanishes when n is indefinitely increased; in other words only when the series is convergent.

522. The General Term. When the *generating function* can be expressed as a group of partial fractions the general term of a recurring series may be easily found.

Ex. Find the generating function, and the general term, of the recurring series
$$1 - 7x - x^2 - 43x^3 - \cdots$$
Let the scale of relation be $1 - px - qx^2$; then
$$-1 + 7p - q = 0, \quad -43 + p + 7q = 0;$$
whence $p = 1$, $q = 6$; and the scale of relation is
$$1 - x - 6x^2.$$
Let S denote the sum of the series; then
$$S = 1 - 7x - x^2 - 43x^3 - \cdots$$
$$-xS = \quad -x + 7x^2 + x^3 + \cdots$$
$$-6x^2 S = \quad\quad -6x^2 + 42x^3 + \cdots$$
$$\therefore (1 - x - 6x^2)S = 1 - 8x,$$
$$S = \frac{1 - 8x}{1 - x - 6x^2};$$
which is the generating function.

If we separate $\dfrac{1-8x}{1-x-6x^2}$ into partial fractions, we obtain
$$\frac{2}{1+2x} - \frac{1}{1-3x}.$$

2 K

By actual division, or by the Binomial Theorem.

$$\frac{2}{1+2x} = 2[1 - 2x + (2x)^2 - \cdots + (-1)^r(2x)^r + \cdots]$$

$$-\frac{1}{1-3x} = -[1 + 3x + (3x)^2 + \cdots + (3x)^r + \cdots]$$

Whence the $(r+1)$th, or general term, is

$$[2(2^r)(-1)^r - 3^r]x^r = \{(-1)^r 2^{r+1} - 3^r\}x^r.$$

EXAMPLES XLIV. a.

Find the generating functions of the following series.

1. $1 + 6x + 24x^2 + 84x^3 + \cdots$.
2. $2 + 2x - 2x^2 + 6x^3 - 14x^4 + \cdots$.
3. $3 - 16x + 42x^2 - 94x^3 + \cdots$.
4. $2 - 5x + 4x^2 + 7x^3 - 26x^4 + \cdots$.
5. $4 + 5x + 7x^2 + 11x^3 + \cdots$.
6. $1 + x + 2x^2 + 2x^3 + 3x^4 + 3x^5 + 4x^6 + 4x^7 + \cdots$.
7. $1 + 3x + 7x^2 + 13x^3 + 21x^4 + 31x^5 + \cdots$.
8. $1 - 3x + 5x^2 - 7x^3 + 9x^4 - 11x^5 + \cdots$.

Find the generating function and the general term in each of the following series:

9. $1 + 5x + 9x^2 + 13x^3 + \cdots$.   11. $2 + 3x + 5x^2 + 9x^3 + \cdots$.
10. $2 - x + 5x^2 - 7x^3 + \cdots$.   12. $7 - 6x + 9x^2 + 27x^4 + \cdots$.
13. $3 + 6x + 14x^2 + 36x^3 + 98x^4 + 276x^5 + \cdots$.

THE METHOD OF DIFFERENCES.

523. Let u_n denote some rational integral function of n, and let $u_1, u_2, u_3, u_4, \cdots$ denote the values of u_n when for n the values $1, 2, 3, 4, \cdots$ are written successively.

From the series $u_1, u_2, u_3, u_4, u_5, \cdots$ obtain a second series by subtracting each term from the term which immediately follows it.

The series $u_2 - u_1, u_3 - u_2, u_4 - u_3, u_5 - u_4, \cdots$ thus found is called the *series of the first order of differences*, and may be conveniently denoted by $Du_1, Du_2, Du_3, Du_4, \cdots$.

By subtracting each term of this series from the term that immediately follows it, we have $Du_2 - Du_1, Du_3 - Du_2$

SUMMATION OF SERIES.

$Du_4 - Du_3$ ... which may be called the *series of the second order of differences*, and denoted by D_2u_1, D_2u_2, D_2u_3 ....

From this series we may proceed to form the *series of the third, fourth, fifth*, ··· *orders of differences*, the general terms of these series being $D_3u_r, D_4u_r, D_5u_r,$ ··· respectively.

524. Any Required Term of the Series. From the law of formation of the series

$$u_1, \quad u_2, \quad u_3, \quad u_4, \quad u_5, \quad u_6 \cdots$$
$$Du_1, \quad Du_2, \quad Du_3, \quad Du_4, \quad Du_5, \cdots$$
$$D_2u_1, \quad D_2u_2, \quad D_2u_3, \quad D_2u_4, \cdots$$
$$D_3u_1, \quad D_3u_2, \quad D_3u_3, \cdots$$
$$\cdot \quad \cdot \quad \cdot \quad \cdot \quad \cdot$$

it appears that any term in any series is equal to the term immediately preceding it added to the term below it on the left.

Thus $\quad u_2 = u_1 + Du_1,$ and $Du_2 = Du_1 + D_2u_1.$

By addition, since $u_2 + Du_2 = u_3,$ we have

$$u_3 = u_1 + 2Du_1 + D_2u_1.$$

In an exactly similar manner by using the second, third, and fourth series in place of the first, second, and third, we obtain $Du_3 = Du_1 + 2D_2u_1 + D_3u_1.$

By addition, since $u_3 + Du_3 = u_4,$ we have

$$u_4 = u_1 + 3Du_1 + 3D_2u_1 + D_3u_1.$$

So far as we have proceeded, the numerical coefficients follow the same law as those of the Binomial Theorem. We shall now prove by induction that this will always be the case. For suppose that

$$u_{n+1} = u_1 + nDu_1 + \frac{n(n-1)}{1 \cdot 2}D_2u_1 + \cdots + {}^nC_r D_r u_1 + \cdots + D_n u_1;$$

then by using the second to the $(n+2)$th series in the place of the first to the $(n+1)$th series we have

$$Du_{n+1} = Du_1 + nD_2u_1 + \frac{n(n-1)}{1 \cdot 2}D_3u_1 + \cdots + {}^nC_{r-1}D_r u_1$$
$$+ \cdots + D_{n+1}u_1.$$

By addition, since $u_{n+1} + Du_{n+1} = u_{n+2}$, we obtain
$$u_{n+2} = u_1 + (n+1)Du_1 + \cdots + ({}^nC_r + {}^nC_{r-1})D_r u_1 + \cdots + D_{n+1}u_1.$$
But ${}^nC_r + {}^nC_{r-1} = \left(\dfrac{n-r+1}{r} + 1\right) \times {}^nC_{r-1} = \dfrac{n+1}{r} \times {}^nC_{r-1}$
$$= \frac{(n+1)n(n-1)\cdots(\overline{n+1}-r+1)}{1\cdot 2\cdot 3\cdots(r-1)r} = {}^{n+1}C_r.$$

Hence if the law of formation holds for u_{n+1} it also holds for u_{n+2}, but it is true in the case of u_4, therefore it holds for u_5, and therefore universally. Hence
$$u_n = u_1 + (n-1)Du_1 + \frac{(n-1)(n-2)}{1\cdot 2}D_2 u_1 + \cdots + D_{n-1}u_1.$$

If we take a as the first term of a given series, $d_1, d_2, d_3 \ldots$ as the *first terms* of the successive orders of differences, any term of the given series is obtained from the formula
$$a_n = a + (n-1)d_1 + \frac{(n-1)(n-2)}{\underline{|2}}d_2$$
$$+ \frac{(n-1)(n-2)(n-3)}{\underline{|3}}d_3 + \cdots.$$

525. The Sum of n Terms of the Series. Suppose the series $u_1, u_2, u_3, \ldots$ is the first order of differences of the series
$$v_1, \quad v_2, \quad v_3, \quad v_4, \ldots,$$
then $v_{n+1} = (v_{n+1} - v_n) + (v_n - v_{n-1}) + \cdots + (v_2 - v_1) + v_1$, identically;
$$\therefore\ v_{n+1} = u_n + u_{n-1} + \cdots + u_2 + u_1 + v_1.$$
Hence in the series
$$0, \quad v_2, \quad v_3, \quad v_4, \quad v_5.$$
$$u_1, \quad u_2, \quad u_3, \quad u_4 \cdots$$
$$Du_1, \quad Du_2, \quad Du_3 \cdots$$
the law of formation is the same as in the preceding article;
$$\therefore\ v_{n+1} = 0 + nu_1 + \frac{n(n-1)}{1\cdot 2}Du_1 + \cdots + D_n u_1;$$

that is, $u_1 + u_2 + u_3 + \cdots + u_n$
$$= nu_1 + \frac{n(n-1)}{\lfloor 2} Du_1 + \frac{n(n-1)(n-2)}{\lfloor 3} D_2 u_1 + \cdots + D_n u_1.$$

If, as in the preceding article, a is the first term of a given series, $d_1, d_2, d_3, \cdots$ *the first terms* of the successive orders of differences, the sum of n terms of the given series is obtained from the formula

$$S_n = na + \frac{n(n-1)}{\lfloor 2} d_1 + \frac{n(n-1)(n-2)}{\lfloor 3} d_2$$
$$+ \frac{n(n-1)(n-2)(n-3)}{\lfloor 4} d_3 + \cdots.$$

Ex. 1. Find the 7th term and the sum of the first seven terms of the series 4, 14, 30, 52, 80, ⋯⋯ .

The successive orders of differences are

$$\begin{array}{cccc} 10, & 16, & 22, & 28, \\ & 6, & 6, & 6, \\ & & 0, & 0. \end{array}$$

Here $n = 7$, and $a = 4$.

Hence, using formula, Art. 524, the 7th term

$$= 4 + 6 \cdot 10 + \frac{6 \cdot 5}{1 \cdot 2} \cdot 6 = 154.$$

Using formula, Art. 525, the sum of the first seven terms

$$= 7 \cdot 4 + \frac{7 \cdot 6}{1 \cdot 2} \cdot 10 + \frac{7 \cdot 6 \cdot 5}{1 \cdot 2 \cdot 3} \cdot 6 = 448.$$

Ex. 2. Find the general term and the sum of n terms of the series

12, 40, 90, 168, 280, 432, ⋯.

The successive orders of difference are

$$\begin{array}{ccccc} 28, & 50, & 78, & 112, & 152, \cdots \\ 22, & 28, & 34, & 40, & \cdots \\ 6, & 6, & 6, & \cdots \\ 0, & 0, & \cdots \end{array}$$

Hence the nth term [Art. 524]

$$= 12 + 28(n-1) + \frac{22(n-1)(n-2)}{\lfloor 2} + \frac{6(n-1)(n-2)(n-3)}{\lfloor 3}$$
$$= n^3 + 5n^2 + 6n.$$

Using the formula for the sum of n terms we obtain

$$S_n = 12n + \frac{28n(n-1)}{\underline{2}} + \frac{22n(n-1)(n-2)}{\underline{3}} + \frac{6n(n-1)(n-2)(n-3)}{\underline{4}}$$

$$= \frac{n}{12}(3n^3 + 26n^2 + 69n + 46)$$

$$= \tfrac{1}{12} n(n+1)(3n^2 + 23n + 46).$$

526. It will be seen that this method of summation will only succeed when the series is such that in forming the orders of differences we eventually come to a series in which all the terms are equal. This will always be the case if the nth term of the series is a rational integral function of n.

PILES OF SHOT AND SHELLS.

527. Square Pile. *To find the number of shot arranged in a complete pyramid on a square base.*

The top layer consists of a single shot; the next contains 4; the next 9, and so on to n^2, n being the number of layers: hence the form of the series is

$$1^2,\ 2^2,\ 3^2,\ 4^2, \cdots, n^2.$$

Series   1,   4,   9,   16, $\cdots, n^2$.
1st order of differences   3,   5,   7,
2d order of differences   2,   2,
3d order of differences   0.

Substituting in Art. 525, we obtain

$$S = n + \frac{n(n-1)}{1 \cdot 2} \cdot 3 + \frac{n(n-1)(n-2)}{1 \cdot 2 \cdot 3} \cdot 2 = \frac{n(n+1)(2n+1)}{6}.$$

528. Triangular Pile. *To find the number of shot arranged in a complete pyramid the base of which is an equilateral triangle.*

The top layer consists of a single shot; the next contains 3; the next 6; the next 10, and so on, giving a series of the form

$$1,\ 1+2,\ 1+2+3,\ 1+2+3+4,\ \cdots$$

Series   1,   3,   6,   10,

1st order of differences   2,   3,   4,

2d order of differences   1,   1,

3d order of differences   0.

Hence

$$S = n + \frac{n(n-1)}{1\cdot 2}\cdot 2 + \frac{n(n-1)(n-2)}{1\cdot 2\cdot 3}\cdot 1 = \frac{n(n+1)(n+2)}{6}.$$

529. Rectangular Pile. *To find the number of shot arranged in a complete pile the base of which is a rectangle.*

The top layer consists of a single row of shot. Suppose this row to contain m shot; then the next layer contains $2(m+1)$; the next $3(m+2)$, and so on, giving a series of the form

$$m,\ 2m+2,\ 3m+6,\ 4m+12,\cdots$$

1st order of differences $m+2$, $m+4$, $m+6$,

2d order of differences   2   2,

3d order of differences   0.

Now let l and w be the number of shot in the length and width, respectively, of the base; then $m = l - w + 1$.

Making these substitutions, we have

$$S = \frac{n(n+1)(3l - w + 1)}{6}.$$

EXAMPLES XLIV. b.

1. Find the eighth term and the sum of the first eight terms of the series 1, 8, 27, 64, 125, ….

2. Find the tenth term and the sum of the first ten terms of the series 4, 11, 28, 55, 92, ….

Find the number of shot in:

3. A square pile, having 15 shot in each side of the base.

4. A triangular pile, having 18 shot in each side of the base.

5. A rectangular pile, the length and the breadth of the base containing 50 and 28 shot respectively.

6. An incomplete triangular pile, a side of the base having 25 shot, and a side of the top 14.

7. An incomplete square pile of 27 courses, having 40 shot in each side of the base.

8. Find the ninth term and the sum of the first nine terms of the series $1, 3 + 5, 7 + 9 + 11, \cdots$.

The numbers $1, 2, 3, \cdots$ are often referred to as the *natural numbers*.

9. Find the sum of the squares of the first n natural numbers.

10. Find the sum of the cubes of the first n natural numbers.

11. The number of shot in a complete rectangular pile is 24395; if there are 34 shot in the breadth of the base, how many are there in its length?

12. The number of shot in the top layer of a square pile is 169, and in the lowest layer is 1089; how many shot does the pile contain?

13. Find the number of shot in a complete rectangular pile of 15 courses, having 20 shot in the longer side of its base.

14. Find the number of shot in an incomplete rectangular pile, the number of shot in the sides of its upper course being 11 and 18, and the number in the shorter side of its lowest course being 30.

Find the nth term and the sum of n terms of the series:

15. $4, 14, 30, 52, 80, 114, \cdots$.

16. $8, 26, 54, 92, 140, 198, \cdots$.

17. $2, 12, 36, 80, 150, 252, \cdots$.

18. $8, 16, 0, -64, -200, -432, \cdots$.

19. $30, 144, 420, 960, 1890, 3360, \cdots$.

20. What is the number of shot required to complete a rectangular pile having 15 and 6 shot in the longer and shorter side, respectively, of its upper course?

21. The number of shot in a triangular pile is greater by 150 than half the number of shot in a square pile, the number of layers in each being the same: find the number of shot in the lowest layer of the triangular pile.

SUMMATION OF SERIES. 425

22. Find the number of shot in an incomplete square pile of 16 courses when the number of shot in the upper course is 1005 less than in the lowest course.

23. Show that the number of shot in a square pile is one-fourth the number of shot in a triangular pile of double the number of courses.

INTERPOLATION.

530. The process of introducing between the terms of a series intermediate values conforming to the law of the series is called **interpolation**. An important application is in finding numbers intermediate between those given in logarithmic and other mathematical tables. For this purpose we may employ the formula used in finding the nth term by the Differential Method, giving fractional values to n.

Ex. Given $\log 40 = 1.6021$, $\log 41 = 1.6128$, $\log 42 = 1.6232$, $\log 43 = 1.6335$, ... find $\log 40.7$.

Series   1.6021,   1.6128,   1.6232,   1.6335,
1st order of differences,   .0107,   .0104,   .0103,
2d order of differences, $-$ .0003, $-$ .0001,
3d order of differences, $+$ .0002.

Substituting in formula of Art. 524, we have

$$\log 40.7 = 1.6021 + \frac{7}{10}(.0107) + \frac{7}{10}\left(-\frac{3}{10}\right)\left(\frac{-.0003}{\lfloor 2}\right)$$
$$+ \frac{7}{10}\left(-\frac{3}{10}\right)\left(-\frac{13}{10}\right)\left(\frac{.0002}{\lfloor 3}\right)$$
$$= 1.6021 + .00749 + .000031 + .000009 = 1.6096 +.$$

Here $\log 40$ is the first term ($n = 1$); $\log 41$ is the second term ($n = 2$); hence in introducing the intermediate term $\log 40.7$ we give to n a value 1.7.

EXAMPLES XLIV. c.

1. Given $\log 3 = 0.4771$, $\log 4 = 0.6021$, $\log 5 = 0.6990$, $\log 6 = 0.7782$, ...; find $\log 4.4$.

2. Given $\log 51 = 1.7076$, $\log 52 = 1.7160$, $\log 53 = 1.7243$, $\log 54 = 1.7324$, ...; find $\log 51.9$.

3. Given $\sqrt{5} = 2.236$, $\sqrt{6} = 2.449$, $\sqrt{7} = 2.645$, $\sqrt{8} = 2.828$; find $\sqrt{5.6}$, $\sqrt{7.4}$, and $\sqrt{7.74}$.

4. Given $\sqrt[3]{51} = 3.7084$, $\sqrt[3]{52} = 3.7325$, $\sqrt[3]{53} = 3.7563$, ...; find $\sqrt[3]{51.18}$.

CHAPTER XLV.

BINOMIAL THEOREM. ANY INDEX.

531. In Chapter XXXVII. we investigated the Binomial Theorem when the index was any positive integer; we shall now consider whether the formulæ there obtained hold in the case of negative and fractional values of the index.

Since, by Art. 411, every binomial may be reduced to one common type, it will be sufficient to confine our attention to binomials of the form $(1+x)^n$.

By actual evolution we have

$$(1+x)^{\frac{1}{2}} = \sqrt{1+x} = 1 + \tfrac{1}{2}x - \tfrac{1}{8}x^2 + \tfrac{1}{16}x^3 - \cdots;$$

and by actual division,

$$(1-x)^{-2} = \frac{1}{(1-x)^2} = 1 + 2x + 3x^2 + 4x^3 + \cdots;$$

and in each of these series the number of terms is unlimited.

In these cases we have by independent processes obtained an expansion for each of the expressions $(1+x)^{\frac{1}{2}}$ and $(1+x)^{-2}$. We shall presently prove that they are only particular cases of the general formula for the expansion of $(1+x)^n$, where n is any rational quantity.

This formula was discovered by Newton.

532. Suppose we have two expressions arranged in ascending powers of x, such as

$$1 + mx + \frac{m(m-1)}{1 \cdot 2}x^2 + \frac{m(m-1)(m-2)}{1 \cdot 2 \cdot 3}x^3 + \cdots \quad (1),$$

and $\quad 1 + nx + \dfrac{n(n-1)}{1 \cdot 2}x^2 + \dfrac{n(n-1)(n-2)}{1 \cdot 2 \cdot 3}x^3 + \cdots \quad (2).$

The product of these two expressions will be a series in ascending powers of x; denote it by

$$1 + Ax + Bx^2 + Cx^3 + Dx^4 + \cdots;$$

then it is clear that $A, B, C, \cdots$ are functions of m and n, and therefore the actual values of $A, B, C, \cdots$ in any particular case will depend upon the values of m and n in that case. But the way in which the coefficients of the powers of x in (1) and (2) combine to give $A, B, C, \cdots$ is quite independent of m and n; in other words, *whatever values m and n may have A, B, C, $\cdots$ preserve the same invariable form*. If therefore we can determine the form of $A, B, C, \cdots$ for any value of m and n, we conclude that $A, B, C, \cdots$ will have the same form *for all values* of m and n.

The principle here explained is often referred to as an example of "the permanence of equivalent forms"; in the present case we have only to recognize the fact that *in any algebraic product* the *form* of the result will be the same whether the quantities involved are whole numbers, or fractions; positive, or negative.

We shall make use of this principle in the general proof of the Binomial Theorem for any index. The proof which we give is due to Euler.

533. To prove the Binomial Theorem when the index is a positive fraction.

Whatever be the value of m, positive or negative, integral or fractional, let the symbol $f(m)$ stand for the series

$$1 + mx + \frac{m(m-1)}{1 \cdot 2}x^2 + \frac{m(m-1)(m-2)}{1 \cdot 2 \cdot 3}x^3 + \cdots;$$

then $f(n)$ will stand for the series

$$1 + nx + \frac{n(n-1)}{1 \cdot 2}x^2 + \frac{n(n-1)(n-2)}{1 \cdot 2 \cdot 3}x^3 + \cdots.$$

If we multiply these two series together the product will be another series in ascending powers of x, whose *coefficients will be unaltered in form whatever m and n may be*.

To determine this *invariable form of the product* we may give to m and n any values that are most convenient; for this purpose suppose that m and n are positive integers. In this case $f(m)$ is the expanded form of $(1+x)^m$, and $f(n)$ is the expanded form of $(1+x)^n$; and therefore

$$f(m) \times f(n) = (1+x)^m \times (1+x)^n = (1+x)^{m+n},$$

but when m and n are positive integers, the expansion of $(1+x)^{m+n}$ is

$$1 + (m+n)x + \frac{(m+n)(m+n-1)}{1 \cdot 2} x^2 + \cdots.$$

This then is the *form* of the product of $f(m) \times f(n)$ *in all cases*, whatever the values of m and n may be; and in agreement with our previous notation, it may be denoted by $f(m+n)$; therefore *for all values of m and n*

$$f(m) \times f(n) = f(m+n).$$

Also
$$f(m) \times f(n) \times f(p) = f(m+n) \times f(p)$$
$$= f(m+n+p), \text{ similarly.}$$

Proceeding in this way we may show that

$$f(m) \times f(n) \times f(p) \cdots \text{ to } k \text{ factors} = f(m+n+p+\cdots \text{ to } k \text{ terms}).$$

Let each of these quantities, m, n, p, $\cdots$, be equal to $\frac{h}{k}$, where h and k are positive integers;

$$\therefore \left\{ f\left(\frac{h}{k}\right) \right\}^k = f(h);$$

but since h is a positive integer, $f(h) = (1+x)^h$;

$$\therefore (1+x)^h = \left\{ f\left(\frac{h}{k}\right) \right\}^k;$$

$$\therefore (1+x)^{\frac{h}{k}} = f\left(\frac{h}{k}\right);$$

but $f\left(\frac{h}{k}\right)$ stands for the series

$$1 + \frac{h}{k} x + \frac{\frac{h}{k}\left(\frac{h}{k} - 1\right)}{1 \cdot 2} x^2 + \cdots;$$

BINOMIAL THEOREM. ANY INDEX. 429

$$\therefore (1+x)^{\frac{h}{k}} = 1 + \frac{h}{k}x + \frac{\frac{h}{k}\left(\frac{h}{k}-1\right)}{1\cdot 2}x^2 + \cdots,$$

which proves the Binomial Theorem for any positive fractional index.

534. To prove the Binomial Theorem when the index is any negative quantity.

It has been proved that
$$f(m) \times f(n) = f(m+n)$$
for all values of m and n. Replacing m by $-n$ (where n is positive), we have
$$f(-n) \times f(n) = f(-n+n) = f(0) = 1,$$
since all terms of the series except the first vanish;

$$\therefore \frac{1}{f(n)} = f(-n);$$

but $f(n) = (1+x)^n$ for *any positive* value of n;

$$\therefore \frac{1}{(1+x)^n} = f(-n),$$

or $\qquad (1+x)^{-n} = f(-n).$

But $f(-n)$ stands for the series
$$1 + (-n)x + \frac{(-n)(-n-1)}{1\cdot 2}x^2 + \cdots;$$

$$\therefore (1+x)^{-n} = 1 + (-n)x + \frac{(-n)(-n-1)}{1\cdot 2}x^2 + \cdots;$$

which proves the Binomial Theorem for any negative index.

535. It should be noticed that when $x < 1$, each of the series $f(m)$, $f(n)$, $f(m+n)$ is *convergent*, and $f(m+n)$ is the true arithmetical equivalent of $f(m) \times f(n)$. But when $x > 1$, all these series are *divergent*, and we can only assert that if we multiply the series denoted by $f(m)$, by the series denoted by $f(n)$, the first r terms of the product will agree with the first r terms of $f(m+n)$, whatever finite value r may have.

CHAPTER XLVI.

Exponential and Logarithmic Series.

536. The advantages of common logarithms have been explained in Art. 438, and in practice no other system is used. But in the first place these logarithms are calculated to another base and then transformed to base 10.

In the present chapter we shall prove certain formulæ, known as the **Exponential and Logarithmic Series**, and give a brief explanation of the way in which they are used in constructing a table of logarithms.

537. To expand a^x in ascending powers of x.

By the Binomial Theorem, if $n > 1$.

$$\left(1+\frac{1}{n}\right)^{nx}$$

$$=1+nx\cdot\frac{1}{n}+\frac{nx(nx-1)}{\lfloor 2}\cdot\frac{1}{n^2}+\frac{nx(nx-1)(nx-2)}{\lfloor 3}\cdot\frac{1}{n^3}+\cdots$$

$$=1+x+\frac{x\left(x-\dfrac{1}{n}\right)}{\lfloor 2}+\frac{x\left(x-\dfrac{1}{n}\right)\left(x-\dfrac{2}{n}\right)}{\lfloor 3}+\cdots \quad (1).$$

By putting $x=1$, we obtain

$$\left(1+\frac{1}{n}\right)^{n}=1+1+\frac{1-\dfrac{1}{n}}{\lfloor 2}+\frac{\left(1-\dfrac{1}{n}\right)\left(1-\dfrac{2}{n}\right)}{\lfloor 3}+\cdots \quad (2).$$

But $\qquad \left(1+\dfrac{1}{n}\right)^{nx}=\left\{\left(1+\dfrac{1}{n}\right)^{n}\right\}^{x};$

hence the series (1) is the xth power of the series (2); that is,

$$1 + x + \frac{x\left(x - \frac{1}{n}\right)}{\lfloor 2} + \frac{x\left(x - \frac{1}{n}\right)\left(x - \frac{2}{n}\right)}{\lfloor 3} + \cdots$$

$$= \left\{1 + 1 + \frac{1 - \frac{1}{n}}{\lfloor 2} + \frac{\left(1 - \frac{1}{n}\right)\left(1 - \frac{2}{n}\right)}{\lfloor 3} + \cdots \right\}^x;$$

and this is true however great n may be. If, therefore, n be indefinitely increased, we have

$$1 + x + \frac{x^2}{\lfloor 2} + \frac{x^3}{\lfloor 3} + \cdots = \left(1 + 1 + \frac{1}{\lfloor 2} + \frac{1}{\lfloor 3} + \cdots\right)^x.$$

The series $\quad 1 + 1 + \dfrac{1}{\lfloor 2} + \dfrac{1}{\lfloor 3} + \dfrac{1}{\lfloor 4} + \cdots$

is usually denoted by e; hence

$$e^x = 1 + x + \frac{x^2}{\lfloor 2} + \frac{x^3}{\lfloor 3} + \frac{x^4}{\lfloor 4} + \cdots.$$

Write cx for x, then

$$e^{cx} = 1 + cx + \frac{c^2 x^2}{\lfloor 2} + \frac{c^3 x^3}{\lfloor 3} + \cdots.$$

Now let $e^c = a$, so that $c = \log_e a$; by substituting for c we obtain

$$a^x = 1 + x \log_e a + \frac{x^2 (\log_e a)^2}{\lfloor 2} + \frac{x^3 (\log_e a)^3}{\lfloor 3} + \cdots.$$

This is the **Exponential Theorem**.

538. The series

$$1 + 1 + \frac{1}{\lfloor 2} + \frac{1}{\lfloor 3} + \frac{1}{\lfloor 4} + \cdots,$$

which we have denoted by e, is very important, as it is the base to which logarithms are first calculated. Logarithms to this base are known as the Napierian system, so named after Napier, the inventor of logarithms. They are also called *natural* logarithms from the fact that they are the first logarithms which naturally come into consideration in algebraic investigations.

When logarithms are used in theoretical work it is to be remembered that the base e is always understood, just as in arithmetical work the base 10 is invariably employed.

From the series the approximate value of e can be determined to any required degree of accuracy; to 10 places of decimals it is found to be 2.7182818284.

Ex. 1. Find the sum of the infinite series
$$1 + \frac{1}{\lfloor 2} + \frac{1}{\lfloor 4} + \frac{1}{\lfloor 6} + \cdots.$$

We have $\quad e = 1 + 1 + \dfrac{1}{\lfloor 2} + \dfrac{1}{\lfloor 3} + \dfrac{1}{\lfloor 4} + \cdots;$

and by putting $x = -1$ in the series for e^x, we obtain
$$e^{-1} = 1 - 1 + \frac{1}{\lfloor 2} - \frac{1}{\lfloor 3} + \frac{1}{\lfloor 4} - \cdots.$$

$$\therefore e + e^{-1} = 2\left(1 + \frac{1}{\lfloor 2} + \frac{1}{\lfloor 4} + \frac{1}{\lfloor 6} + \cdots\right);$$

hence the sum of the series is $\frac{1}{2}(e + e^{-1})$.

Ex. 2. Find the coefficient of x^r in the expansion of $\dfrac{a - bx}{e^x}$.

$$\frac{a - bx}{e^x} = (a - bx)e^{-x}$$

$$= (a - bx)\left\{1 - x + \frac{x^2}{\lfloor 2} - \frac{x^3}{\lfloor 3} + \cdots + \frac{(-1)^r x^r}{\lfloor r} + \cdots\right\}.$$

The coefficient required $= \dfrac{(-1)^r}{\lfloor r} \cdot a - \dfrac{(-1)^{r-1}}{\lfloor r-1} \cdot b$

$$= \frac{(-1)^r}{\lfloor r}(a + rb).$$

539. To expand $\log_e(1 + x)$ in ascending powers of x.

From Art. 537,
$$a^y = 1 + y \log_e a + \frac{y^2(\log_e a)^2}{\lfloor 2} + \frac{y^3(\log_e a)^3}{\lfloor 3} + \cdots.$$

In this series write $1+x$ for a; thus $(1+x)^y$

$$=1+y\log_e(1+x)+\frac{y^2}{\underline{|2}}\{\log_e(1+x)\}^2+\frac{y^3}{\underline{|3}}\{\log_e(1+x)\}^3+\cdots(1).$$

Also by the Binomial Theorem, when $x<1$ we have

$$(1+x)^y=1+yx+\frac{y(y-1)}{\underline{|2}}x^2+\frac{y(y-1)(y-2)}{\underline{|3}}x^3+\cdots\quad(2).$$

Now in (2) the coefficient of y is

$$x+\frac{(-1)}{1\cdot 2}x^2+\frac{(-1)(-2)}{1\cdot 2\cdot 3}x^3+\frac{(-1)(-2)(-3)}{1\cdot 2\cdot 3\cdot 4}x^4+\cdots;$$

that is, $\quad x-\dfrac{x^2}{2}+\dfrac{x^3}{3}-\dfrac{x^4}{4}+\cdots.$

Equate this to the coefficient of y in (1); thus we have

$$\log_e(1+x)=x-\frac{x^2}{2}+\frac{x^3}{3}-\frac{x^4}{4}+\cdots.$$

This is known as the **Logarithmic Series**.

540. Except when x is very small the series for $\log_e(1+x)$ is of little use for numerical calculations. We can, however, deduce from it other series by the aid of which Tables of Logarithms may be constructed.

541. In Art. 539 we have proved that

$$\log_e(1+x)=x-\frac{x^2}{2}+\frac{x^3}{3}-\cdots;$$

changing x into $-x$, we have

$$\log_e(1-x)=-x-\frac{x^2}{2}-\frac{x^3}{3}-\cdots.$$

By subtraction,

$$\log_e\frac{1+x}{1-x}=2\left(x+\frac{x^3}{3}+\frac{x^5}{5}+\cdots\right).$$

Put $\dfrac{1+x}{1-x}=\dfrac{n+1}{n}$, so that $x=\dfrac{1}{2n+1}$; we thus obtain

$$\log_e(n+1)-\log_e n=2\left\{\frac{1}{2n+1}+\frac{1}{3(2n+1)^3}+\frac{1}{5(2n+1)^5}+\cdots\right\}.$$

From this formula by putting $n = 1$ we can obtain $\log_e 2$. Again by putting $n = 2$ we obtain $\log_e 3 - \log_e 2$; whence $\log_e 3$ is found, and therefore also $\log_e 9$ is known.

Now by putting $n = 9$ we obtain $\log_e 10 - \log_e 9$; thus the value of $\log_e 10$ is found to be $2.30258509\cdots$.

To convert Napierian logarithms into logarithms to base 10 we multiply by $\dfrac{1}{\log_e 10}$, which is the *modulus* [Art. 441] of the common system, and its value is $\dfrac{1}{2.30258509\cdots}$, or $.43429448\cdots$; we shall denote this modulus by M.

By multiplying the last series throughout by M we obtain a formula adapted to the calculation of common logarithms. Thus

$M \log_e(n+1) - M \log_e n =$
$$2 M \left\{ \frac{1}{2n+1} + \frac{1}{3(2n+1)^3} + \frac{1}{5(2n+1)^5} + \cdots \right\};$$

that is, $\log_{10}(n+1) - \log_{10} n =$
$$2 \left\{ \frac{M}{2n+1} + \frac{M}{3(2n+1)^3} + \frac{M}{5(2n+1)^5} + \cdots \right\}.$$

Hence if the logarithm of one of two consecutive numbers be known, the logarithm of the other may be found, and thus a table of logarithms can be constructed.

EXAMPLES XLVI.

1. Show that

    (1) $e^{-2} = 1 - \dfrac{2^3}{\lfloor 3} + \dfrac{2^4}{\lfloor 4} - \dfrac{2^5}{\lfloor 5} + \cdots$;

    (2) $\dfrac{e^2 - 1}{2e} = 1 + \dfrac{1}{\lfloor 3} + \dfrac{1}{\lfloor 5} + \dfrac{1}{\lfloor 7} + \cdots$.

2. Expand $\log \sqrt{1+x}$ in ascending powers of x.

3. Prove that $\log_e 2 = \frac{1}{2} + \frac{1}{12} + \frac{1}{30} + \frac{1}{56} + \cdots$.

4. Show that $\log_{10}\left(\dfrac{1}{1-x}\right) = \dfrac{1}{\log_e 10}\left(x + \dfrac{x^2}{2} + \dfrac{x^3}{3} + \cdots\right)$.

5. Prove that $\log\dfrac{1+x}{1-3x} = 4x + 4x^2 + \dfrac{28}{3}x^3 + 20x^4 + \cdots$.

6. Show that if $x > 1$, $\log\sqrt{x^2 - 1} = \log x - \dfrac{1}{2x^2} - \dfrac{1}{4x^4} - \dfrac{1}{6x^6} - \cdots$.

CHAPTER XLVII.

DETERMINANTS.

542. Consider two homogeneous linear equations
$$a_1 x + b_1 y = 0,$$
$$a_2 x + b_2 y = 0;$$
multiplying the first equation by b_2, the second by b_1, subtracting and dividing by x, we obtain
$$a_1 b_2 - a_2 b_1 = 0 \quad \ldots \ldots \quad (1).$$
This result is sometimes written
$$\begin{vmatrix} a_1 & b_1 \\ a_2 & b_2 \end{vmatrix} = 0,$$
and the expression on the left is called a **determinant**. It consists of two *rows* and two *columns*, and in its expanded form or *development*, as seen in the first member of (1), each term is the product of two quantities; it is therefore said to be of the *second order*. The line $a_1 b_2$ is called the *principal diagonal*, and the line $b_1 a_2$, the *secondary diagonal*.

The letters a_1, b_1, a_2, b_2 are called the *constituents* of the determinant, and the terms $a_1 b_2$, $a_2 b_1$ are called the *elements*.

THE VALUE OF THE DETERMINANT AFTER CERTAIN CHANGES.

543. Since $\begin{vmatrix} a_1 & b_1 \\ a_2 & b_2 \end{vmatrix} = a_1 b_2 - a_2 b_1 = \begin{vmatrix} a_1 & a_2 \\ b_1 & b_2 \end{vmatrix}$,

it follows that *the value of the determinant is not altered by changing the rows into columns, and the columns into rows.*

Again, it is easily seen that

$$\begin{vmatrix} a_1 & b_1 \\ a_2 & b_2 \end{vmatrix} = - \begin{vmatrix} b_1 & a_1 \\ b_2 & a_2 \end{vmatrix}, \text{ and } \begin{vmatrix} a_1 & b_1 \\ a_2 & b_2 \end{vmatrix} = - \begin{vmatrix} a_2 & b_2 \\ a_1 & b_1 \end{vmatrix};$$

that is, *if we interchange two rows or two columns of the determinant, we obtain a determinant which differs from it only in sign.*

544. Let us now consider the homogeneous linear equations

$$a_1 x + b_1 y + c_1 z = 0,$$
$$a_2 x + b_2 y + c_2 z = 0,$$
$$a_3 x + b_3 y + c_3 z = 0.$$

By eliminating x, y, z, we obtain

$$a_1(b_2 c_3 - b_3 c_2) + b_1(c_2 a_3 - c_3 a_2) + c_1(a_2 b_3 - a_3 b_2) = 0,$$

or
$$a_1 \begin{vmatrix} b_2 & c_2 \\ b_3 & c_3 \end{vmatrix} + b_1 \begin{vmatrix} c_2 & a_2 \\ c_3 & a_3 \end{vmatrix} + c_1 \begin{vmatrix} a_2 & b_2 \\ a_3 & b_3 \end{vmatrix} = 0.$$

This is usually written

$$\begin{vmatrix} a_1 & b_1 & c_1 \\ a_2 & b_2 & c_2 \\ a_3 & b_3 & c_3 \end{vmatrix} = 0,$$

and the expression on the left being a determinant which consists of three rows and three columns is called a determinant of *the third order*.

545. By a rearrangement of terms, the expanded form of the above determinant may be written

$$a_1(b_2 c_3 - b_3 c_2) + a_2(b_3 c_1 - b_1 c_3) + a_3(b_1 c_2 - b_2 c_1),$$

or
$$a_1 \begin{vmatrix} b_2 & b_3 \\ c_2 & c_3 \end{vmatrix} + a_2 \begin{vmatrix} b_3 & b_1 \\ c_3 & c_1 \end{vmatrix} + a_3 \begin{vmatrix} b_1 & b_2 \\ c_1 & c_2 \end{vmatrix};$$

hence
$$\begin{vmatrix} a_1 & b_1 & c_1 \\ a_2 & b_2 & c_2 \\ a_3 & b_3 & c_3 \end{vmatrix} = \begin{vmatrix} a_1 & a_2 & a_3 \\ b_1 & b_2 & b_3 \\ c_1 & c_2 & c_3 \end{vmatrix};$$

that is, *the value of the determinant is not altered by changing the rows into columns, and the columns into rows.*

DETERMINANTS.

546. Minors. From the preceding article,

$$\begin{vmatrix} a_1 & b_1 & c_1 \\ a_2 & b_2 & c_2 \\ a_3 & b_3 & c_3 \end{vmatrix} = a_1 \begin{vmatrix} b_2 & c_2 \\ b_3 & c_3 \end{vmatrix} + a_2 \begin{vmatrix} b_3 & c_3 \\ b_1 & c_1 \end{vmatrix} + a_3 \begin{vmatrix} b_1 & c_1 \\ b_2 & c_2 \end{vmatrix}$$

$$= a_1 \begin{vmatrix} b_2 & c_2 \\ b_3 & c_3 \end{vmatrix} - a_2 \begin{vmatrix} b_1 & c_1 \\ b_3 & c_3 \end{vmatrix} + a_3 \begin{vmatrix} b_1 & c_1 \\ b_2 & c_2 \end{vmatrix} \quad . \quad (1).$$

Also from Art. 544,

$$\begin{vmatrix} a_1 & b_1 & c_1 \\ a_2 & b_2 & c_2 \\ a_3 & b_3 & c_3 \end{vmatrix} = a_1 \begin{vmatrix} b_2 & c_2 \\ b_3 & c_3 \end{vmatrix} - b_1 \begin{vmatrix} a_2 & c_2 \\ a_3 & c_3 \end{vmatrix} + c_1 \begin{vmatrix} a_2 & b_2 \\ a_3 & b_3 \end{vmatrix} \quad . \quad . \quad (2).$$

We shall now explain a simple method of writing down the expansion of a determinant of the third order, and it should be noticed that it is immaterial whether we develop it from the first row or the first column.

From equation (1) we see that the coefficient of any one of the constituents a_1, a_2, a_3 is that determinant of the second order which is obtained by *omitting* the row and column in which it occurs. These determinants are called the *minors* of the original determinant, and the left-hand side of equation (1) may be written

$$a_1 A_1 - a_2 A_2 + a_3 A_3,$$

where A_1, A_2, A_3 are the minors of a_1, a_2, a_3 respectively.

Again, from equation (2), the determinant is equal to

$$a_1 A_1 - b_1 B_1 + c_1 C_1,$$

where A_1, B_1, C_1 are the minors of a_1, b_1, c_1 respectively.

547. The determinant $\begin{vmatrix} a_1 & b_1 & c_1 \\ a_2 & b_2 & c_2 \\ a_3 & b_3 & c_3 \end{vmatrix}$

$$= a_1(b_2 c_3 - b_3 c_2) + b_1(c_2 a_3 - c_3 a_2) + c_1(a_2 b_3 - a_3 b_2)$$
$$= -b_1(a_2 c_3 - a_3 c_2) - a_1(c_2 b_3 - c_3 b_2) - c_1(b_2 a_3 - b_3 a_2);$$

hence $\begin{vmatrix} a_1 & b_1 & c_1 \\ a_2 & b_2 & c_2 \\ a_3 & b_3 & c_3 \end{vmatrix} = - \begin{vmatrix} b_1 & a_1 & c_1 \\ b_2 & a_2 & c_2 \\ b_3 & a_3 & c_3 \end{vmatrix}.$

Thus it appears that *if two adjacent columns, or rows, of the determinant are interchanged, the sign of the determinant is changed, but its value remains unaltered.*

If for the sake of brevity we denote the determinant

$$\begin{vmatrix} a_1 & b_1 & c_1 \\ a_2 & b_2 & c_2 \\ a_3 & b_3 & c_3 \end{vmatrix}$$

by $(a_1 b_2 c_3)$, then the result we have just obtained may be written

$$(b_1 a_2 c_3) = -(a_1 b_2 c_3).$$

Similarly we may show that

$$(c_1 a_2 b_3) = -(a_1 c_2 b_3) = +(a_1 b_2 c_3).$$

548. Vanishing of a Determinant. *If two rows or two columns of the determinant are identical the determinant vanishes.*

For let D be the value of the determinant, then by interchanging two rows or two columns we obtain a determinant whose value is $-D$; but the determinant is unaltered; hence $D = -D$, that is $D = 0$. Thus we have the following equations,

$$a_1 A_1 - a_2 A_2 + a_3 A_3 = D,$$
$$b_1 A_1 - b_2 A_2 + b_3 A_3 = 0,$$
$$c_1 A_1 - c_2 A_2 + c_3 A_3 = 0.$$

549. Multiplication of a Determinant. *If each constituent in any row, or in any column, is multiplied by the same factor, then the determinant is multiplied by that factor.*

For
$$\begin{vmatrix} ma_1 & b_1 & c_1 \\ ma_2 & b_2 & c_2 \\ ma_3 & b_3 & c_3 \end{vmatrix}$$

$= ma_1 \cdot A_1 - ma_2 \cdot A_2 + ma_3 \cdot A_3 = m(a_1 A_1 - a_2 A_2 + a_3 A_3);$

which proves the proposition.

Cor. If each constituent of one row, or column, is the same multiple of the corresponding constituent of another row, or column, the determinant vanishes.

DETERMINANTS.

550. A Determinant expressed as the Sum of Two Other Determinants. *If each constituent in any row, or column, consists of two terms, then the determinant can be expressed as the sum of two other determinants.*

Thus we have

$$\begin{vmatrix} a_1+d_1 & b_1 & c_1 \\ a_2+d_2 & b_2 & c_2 \\ a_3+d_3 & b_3 & c_3 \end{vmatrix} = \begin{vmatrix} a_1 & b_1 & c_1 \\ a_2 & b_2 & c_2 \\ a_3 & b_3 & c_3 \end{vmatrix} + \begin{vmatrix} d_1 & b_1 & c_1 \\ d_2 & b_2 & c_2 \\ d_3 & b_3 & c_3 \end{vmatrix};$$

for the expression on the left,

$$= (a_1+d_1)A_1 - (a_2+d_2)A_2 + (a_3+d_3)A_3$$
$$= (a_1 A_1 - a_2 A_2 + a_3 A_3) + (d_1 A_1 - d_2 A_2 + d_3 A_3);$$

which proves the proposition.

In like manner if each constituent in any one row, or column, consists of m terms, the determinant can be expressed as the sum of m other determinants.

Similarly, we may show that

$$\begin{vmatrix} a_1+d_1 & b_1+e_1 & c_1 \\ a_2+d_2 & b_2+e_2 & c_2 \\ a_3+d_3 & b_3+e_3 & c_3 \end{vmatrix}$$

$$= \begin{vmatrix} a_1 & b_1 & c_1 \\ a_2 & b_2 & c_2 \\ a_3 & b_3 & c_3 \end{vmatrix} + \begin{vmatrix} a_1 & e_1 & c_1 \\ a_2 & e_2 & c_2 \\ a_3 & e_3 & c_3 \end{vmatrix} + \begin{vmatrix} d_1 & b_1 & c_1 \\ d_2 & b_2 & c_2 \\ d_3 & b_3 & c_3 \end{vmatrix} + \begin{vmatrix} d_1 & e_1 & c_1 \\ d_2 & e_2 & c_2 \\ d_3 & e_3 & c_3 \end{vmatrix}.$$

In general if the constituents of the three columns consist of m, n, p terms, respectively, the determinant can be expressed as the sum of mnp determinants.

Ex. 1. Show that $\begin{vmatrix} b+c & a-b & a \\ c+a & b-c & b \\ a+b & c-a & c \end{vmatrix} = 3abc - a^3 - b^3 - c^3.$

The given determinant

$$= \begin{vmatrix} b & a & a \\ c & b & b \\ a & c & c \end{vmatrix} - \begin{vmatrix} b & b & a \\ c & c & b \\ a & a & c \end{vmatrix} + \begin{vmatrix} c & a & a \\ a & b & b \\ b & c & c \end{vmatrix} - \begin{vmatrix} c & b & a \\ a & c & b \\ b & a & c \end{vmatrix}.$$

440   ALGEBRA.

Of these four determinants the first three vanish, Art. 548; thus the expression reduces to the last of the four determinants; hence its value

$$= -\{c(c^2 - ab) - b(ac - b^2) + a(a^2 - bc)\}$$
$$= 3abc - a^3 - b^3 - c^3.$$

Ex. 2. Find the value of $\begin{vmatrix} 67 & 19 & 21 \\ 39 & 13 & 14 \\ 81 & 24 & 26 \end{vmatrix}$.

We have

$$\begin{vmatrix} 67 & 19 & 21 \\ 39 & 13 & 14 \\ 81 & 24 & 26 \end{vmatrix} = \begin{vmatrix} 10+57 & 19 & 21 \\ 0+39 & 13 & 14 \\ 9+72 & 24 & 26 \end{vmatrix} = \begin{vmatrix} 10 & 19 & 21 \\ 0 & 13 & 14 \\ 9 & 24 & 26 \end{vmatrix} + \begin{vmatrix} 57 & 19 & 21 \\ 39 & 13 & 14 \\ 72 & 24 & 26 \end{vmatrix}$$

$$= \begin{vmatrix} 10 & 19 & 21 \\ 0 & 13 & 14 \\ 9 & 24 & 26 \end{vmatrix} = \begin{vmatrix} 10 & 19 & 19+2 \\ 0 & 13 & 13+1 \\ 9 & 24 & 24+2 \end{vmatrix} = \begin{vmatrix} 10 & 19 & 2 \\ 0 & 13 & 1 \\ 9 & 24 & 2 \end{vmatrix}$$

$$= 10 \begin{vmatrix} 13 & 1 \\ 24 & 2 \end{vmatrix} + 9 \begin{vmatrix} 19 & 2 \\ 13 & 1 \end{vmatrix} = 20 - 63 = -43.$$

551. Simplification of Determinants. Consider the determinant

$$\begin{vmatrix} a_1 + pb_1 + qc_1 & b_1 & c_1 \\ a_2 + pb_2 + qc_2 & b_2 & c_2 \\ a_3 + pb_3 + qc_3 & b_3 & c_3 \end{vmatrix};$$

as in the last article we can show that it is equal to

$$\begin{vmatrix} a_1 & b_1 & c_1 \\ a_2 & b_2 & c_2 \\ a_3 & b_3 & c_3 \end{vmatrix} + \begin{vmatrix} pb_1 & b_1 & c_1 \\ pb_2 & b_2 & c_2 \\ pb_3 & b_3 & c_3 \end{vmatrix} + \begin{vmatrix} qc_1 & b_1 & c_1 \\ qc_2 & b_2 & c_2 \\ qc_3 & b_3 & c_3 \end{vmatrix};$$

and the last two of these determinants vanish [Art. 549, Cor.]. Thus we see that the given determinant is equal to a new one whose first column is obtained by subtracting from the constituents of the first column of the original determinant equimultiples of the corresponding constituents of the other columns, while the second and third columns remain unaltered.

Conversely,

$$\begin{vmatrix} a_1 & b_1 & c_1 \\ a_2 & b_2 & c_2 \\ a_3 & b_3 & c_3 \end{vmatrix} = \begin{vmatrix} a_1 + pb_1 + qc_1 & b_1 & c_1 \\ a_2 + pb_2 + qc_2 & b_2 & c_2 \\ a_3 + pb_3 + qc_3 & b_3 & c_3 \end{vmatrix}$$

and what has been here proved with reference to the first column is equally true for any of the columns or rows; hence it appears that in reducing a determinant we may replace any one of the rows or columns by a new row or column formed in the following way:

Take the constituents of the row or column to be replaced, and increase or diminish them by any equimultiples of the corresponding constituents of one or more of the other rows or columns.

After a little practice it will be found that determinants may often be quickly simplified by replacing two or more rows or columns simultaneously: for example, it is easy to see that

$$\begin{vmatrix} a_1 + pb_1 & b_1 - qc_1 & c_1 \\ a_2 + pb_2 & b_2 - qc_2 & c_2 \\ a_3 + pb_3 & b_3 - qc_3 & c_3 \end{vmatrix} = \begin{vmatrix} a_1 & b_1 & c_1 \\ a_2 & b_2 & c_2 \\ a_3 & b_3 & c_3 \end{vmatrix};$$

but in any modification of the rule as above enunciated, care must be taken to leave one row or column unaltered.

Thus, if on the left-hand side of the last identity the constituents of the third column were replaced by $c_1 + ra_1$, $c_2 + ra_2$, $c_3 + ra_3$, respectively, we should have the former value increased by

$$\begin{vmatrix} a_1 + pb_1 & b_1 - qc_1 & ra_1 \\ a_2 + pb_2 & b_2 - qc_2 & ra_2 \\ a_3 + pb_3 & b_3 - qc_3 & ra_3 \end{vmatrix},$$

and of the four determinants into which this may be resolved there is one which does not vanish, namely

$$\begin{vmatrix} pb_1 & -qc_1 & ra_1 \\ pb_2 & -qc_2 & ra_2 \\ pb_3 & -qc_3 & ra_3 \end{vmatrix}.$$

Ex. 1. Find the value of $\begin{vmatrix} 29 & 26 & 22 \\ 25 & 31 & 27 \\ 63 & 54 & 46 \end{vmatrix}$.

The given determinant

$$= \begin{vmatrix} 3 & 26 & -4 \\ -6 & 31 & -4 \\ 9 & 54 & -8 \end{vmatrix} = -3 \times 4 \times \begin{vmatrix} 1 & 26 & 1 \\ -2 & 31 & 1 \\ 3 & 54 & 2 \end{vmatrix} = -12 \times \begin{vmatrix} 1 & 26 & 1 \\ -3 & 5 & 0 \\ 1 & 2 & 0 \end{vmatrix}$$

$$= -12 \begin{vmatrix} 1 & 1 & 26 \\ 0 & -3 & 5 \\ 0 & 1 & 2 \end{vmatrix} = -12 \begin{vmatrix} -3 & 5 \\ 1 & 2 \end{vmatrix} = 132.$$

EXPLANATION. In the first step of the reduction keep the second column unaltered; for the first new column diminish each constituent of the first column by the corresponding constituent of the second; for the third new column diminish each constituent of the third column by the corresponding constituent of the second. In the second step take out the factors 3 and -4. In the third step keep the first row unaltered; for the second new row diminish the constituents of the second by the corresponding ones of the first; for the third new row diminish the constituents of the third by twice the corresponding constituents of the first. The remaining steps will be easily seen.

Ex. 2. Show that $\begin{vmatrix} a-b-c & 2a & 2a \\ 2b & b-c-a & 2b \\ 2c & 2c & c-a-b \end{vmatrix} = (a+b+c)^3.$

The given determinant

$$= \begin{vmatrix} a+b+c & a+b+c & a+b+c \\ 2b & b-c-a & 2b \\ 2c & 2c & c-a-b \end{vmatrix} = (a+b+c) \times \begin{vmatrix} 1 & 1 & 1 \\ 2b & b-c-a & 2b \\ 2c & 2c & c-a-b \end{vmatrix}$$

$$= (a+b+c) \times \begin{vmatrix} 1 & 0 & 0 \\ 2b & -b-c-a & 0 \\ 2c & 0 & -c-a-b \end{vmatrix}$$

$$= (a+b+c) \times \begin{vmatrix} -b-c-a & 0 \\ 0 & -c-a-b \end{vmatrix} = (a+b+c)^3.$$

EXPLANATION. In the first new determinant the first row is the sum of the constituents of the three rows of the original determinant, the second and third rows being unaltered. In the third of the new determinants the first column remains unaltered, while the second and third columns are obtained by subtracting the constituents of the first column from those of the second and third respectively. The remaining transformations are sufficiently obvious.

EXAMPLES XLVII. a.

Calculate the values of the determinants:

1. $\begin{vmatrix} 1 & 1 & 1 \\ 35 & 37 & 34 \\ 23 & 26 & 25 \end{vmatrix}.$

2. $\begin{vmatrix} 13 & 16 & 19 \\ 14 & 17 & 20 \\ 15 & 18 & 21 \end{vmatrix}.$

3. $\begin{vmatrix} 13 & 3 & 23 \\ 30 & 7 & 53 \\ 39 & 9 & 70 \end{vmatrix}.$

4. $\begin{vmatrix} a & h & g \\ h & b & f \\ g & f & c \end{vmatrix}.$

5. $\begin{vmatrix} 1 & z & -y \\ -z & 1 & x \\ y & -x & 1 \end{vmatrix}.$

6. $\begin{vmatrix} 1 & 1 & 1 \\ 1 & 1+x & 1 \\ 1 & 1 & 1+y \end{vmatrix}.$

7. $\begin{vmatrix} a-b & b-c & c-a \\ b-c & c-a & a-b \\ c-a & a-b & b-c \end{vmatrix}.$

8. $\begin{vmatrix} b+c & a & a \\ b & c+a & b \\ c & c & a+b \end{vmatrix}.$

9. Without expanding the determinants, prove that

$$\begin{vmatrix} a & b & c \\ x & y & z \\ p & q & r \end{vmatrix} = \begin{vmatrix} y & b & q \\ x & a & p \\ z & c & r \end{vmatrix} = \begin{vmatrix} x & y & z \\ p & q & r \\ a & b & c \end{vmatrix}.$$

Solve the equations:

10. $\begin{vmatrix} a & a & x \\ m & m & m \\ b & x & b \end{vmatrix} = 0.$

11. $\begin{vmatrix} 15-2x & 11 & 10 \\ 11-3x & 17 & 16 \\ 7-x & 14 & 13 \end{vmatrix} = 0.$

Prove the following identities:

12. $\begin{vmatrix} b+c & c+a & a+b \\ q+r & r+p & p+q \\ y+z & z+x & x+y \end{vmatrix} = 2 \begin{vmatrix} a & b & c \\ p & q & r \\ x & y & z \end{vmatrix}.$

13. $\begin{vmatrix} 1 & a & a^2 \\ 1 & b & b^2 \\ 1 & c & c^2 \end{vmatrix} = (b-c)(c-a)(a-b).$

14. $\begin{vmatrix} 1 & 1 & 1 \\ a & b & c \\ a^3 & b^3 & c^3 \end{vmatrix} = (b-c)(c-a)(a-b)(a+b+c).$

Calculate the value of the determinants:

15. $\begin{vmatrix} 3 & 6 & 9 \\ 4 & 7 & 10 \\ 5 & 8 & 11 \end{vmatrix}.$

16. $\begin{vmatrix} 1 & 1 & 1 \\ x & y & z \\ x^2 & y^2 & z^2 \end{vmatrix}.$

APPLICATION TO THE SOLUTION OF SIMULTANEOUS EQUATIONS OF THE FIRST DEGREE.

552. The properties of determinants may be usefully employed in solving simultaneous linear equations.

Let the equations be

$$a_1 x + b_1 y + c_1 z + d_1 = 0,$$
$$a_2 x + b_2 y + c_2 z + d_2 = 0,$$
$$a_3 x + b_3 y + c_3 z + d_3 = 0;$$

multiply them by A_1, $-A_2$, A_3 respectively and add the results, A_1, A_2, A_3 being minors of a_1, a_2, a_3 in the determinant

$$D = \begin{vmatrix} a_1 & b_1 & c_1 \\ a_2 & b_2 & c_2 \\ a_3 & b_3 & c_3 \end{vmatrix}.$$

The coefficients of y and z vanish in virtue of the relations proved in Art. 548, and we obtain

$$(a_1 A_1 - a_2 A_2 + a_3 A_3)x + (d_1 A_1 - d_2 A_2 + d_3 A_3) = 0.$$

Similarly we may show that

$$(b_1 B_1 - b_2 B_2 + b_3 B_3)y + (d_1 B_1 - d_2 B_2 + d_3 B_3) = 0,$$

and $(c_1 C_1 - c_2 C_2 + c_3 C_3)z + (d_1 C_1 - d_2 C_2 + d_3 C_3) = 0.$

Now $a_1 A_1 - a_2 A_2 + a_3 A_3 = -(b_1 B_1 - b_2 B_2 + b_3 B_3)$
$$= c_1 C_1 - c_2 C_2 + c_3 C_3 = D;$$

hence the solution may be written

$$\frac{x}{\begin{vmatrix} d_1 & b_1 & c_1 \\ d_2 & b_2 & c_2 \\ d_3 & b_3 & c_3 \end{vmatrix}} = \frac{-y}{\begin{vmatrix} d_1 & a_1 & c_1 \\ d_2 & a_2 & c_2 \\ d_3 & a_3 & c_3 \end{vmatrix}} = \frac{z}{\begin{vmatrix} d_1 & a_1 & b_1 \\ d_2 & a_2 & b_2 \\ d_3 & a_3 & b_3 \end{vmatrix}} = \frac{-1}{\begin{vmatrix} a_1 & b_1 & c_1 \\ a_2 & b_2 & c_2 \\ a_3 & b_3 & c_3 \end{vmatrix}}$$

or more symmetrically

$$\frac{x}{\begin{vmatrix} b_1 & c_1 & d_1 \\ b_2 & c_2 & d_2 \\ b_3 & c_3 & d_3 \end{vmatrix}} = \frac{-y}{\begin{vmatrix} a_1 & c_1 & d_1 \\ a_2 & c_2 & d_2 \\ a_3 & c_3 & d_3 \end{vmatrix}} = \frac{z}{\begin{vmatrix} a_1 & b_1 & d_1 \\ a_2 & b_2 & d_2 \\ a_3 & b_3 & d_3 \end{vmatrix}} = \frac{-1}{\begin{vmatrix} a_1 & b_1 & c_1 \\ a_2 & b_2 & c_2 \\ a_3 & b_3 & c_3 \end{vmatrix}}.$$

DETERMINANTS.

Ex. Solve
$$x + 2y + 3z - 13 = 0,$$
$$2x + y + z - 7 = 0,$$
$$3x + 4y + 3z - 21 = 0.$$

We have

$$\frac{x}{\begin{vmatrix} 2 & 3 & -13 \\ 1 & 1 & -7 \\ 4 & 3 & -21 \end{vmatrix}} = \frac{-y}{\begin{vmatrix} 1 & 3 & -13 \\ 2 & 1 & -7 \\ 3 & 3 & -21 \end{vmatrix}} = \frac{z}{\begin{vmatrix} 1 & 2 & -13 \\ 2 & 1 & -7 \\ 3 & 4 & -21 \end{vmatrix}} = \frac{-1}{\begin{vmatrix} 1 & 2 & 3 \\ 2 & 1 & 1 \\ 3 & 4 & 3 \end{vmatrix}}$$

or
$$\frac{x}{-8} = \frac{-y}{24} = \frac{z}{-16} = \frac{-1}{8};$$

whence $x = 1$, $y = 3$, and $z = 2$.

EXPLANATION. The denominator of x is a determinant formed by taking the coefficients in each column *except that of* x. In the same manner for the denominators of y and z we omit the columns of coefficients of y and z. The last determinant is formed by taking the three columns of coefficients of x, y, and z.

553. Suppose we have the system of four homogeneous linear equations

$$a_1 x + b_1 y + c_1 z + d_1 u = 0,$$
$$a_2 x + b_2 y + c_2 z + d_2 u = 0,$$
$$a_3 x + b_3 y + c_3 z + d_3 u = 0,$$
$$a_4 x + b_4 y + c_4 z + d_4 u = 0.$$

From the last three of these, we have, as in the preceding article,

$$\frac{x}{\begin{vmatrix} b_2 & c_2 & d_2 \\ b_3 & c_3 & d_3 \\ b_4 & c_4 & d_4 \end{vmatrix}} = \frac{-y}{\begin{vmatrix} a_2 & c_2 & d_2 \\ a_3 & c_3 & d_3 \\ a_4 & c_4 & d_4 \end{vmatrix}} = \frac{z}{\begin{vmatrix} a_2 & b_2 & d_2 \\ a_3 & b_3 & d_3 \\ a_4 & b_4 & d_4 \end{vmatrix}} = \frac{-u}{\begin{vmatrix} a_2 & b_2 & c_2 \\ a_3 & b_3 & c_3 \\ a_4 & b_4 & c_4 \end{vmatrix}}.$$

Substituting in the first equation, the eliminant is

$$a_1 \begin{vmatrix} b_2 & c_2 & d_2 \\ b_3 & c_3 & d_3 \\ b_4 & c_4 & d_4 \end{vmatrix} - b_1 \begin{vmatrix} a_2 & c_2 & d_2 \\ a_3 & c_3 & d_3 \\ a_4 & c_4 & d_4 \end{vmatrix} + c_1 \begin{vmatrix} a_2 & b_2 & d_2 \\ a_3 & b_3 & d_3 \\ a_4 & b_4 & d_4 \end{vmatrix} - d_1 \begin{vmatrix} a_2 & b_2 & c_2 \\ a_3 & b_3 & c_3 \\ a_4 & b_4 & c_4 \end{vmatrix} = 0.$$

This may be more concisely written in the form

$$\begin{vmatrix} a_1 & b_1 & c_1 & d_1 \\ a_2 & b_2 & c_2 & d_2 \\ a_3 & b_3 & c_3 & d_3 \\ a_4 & b_4 & c_4 & d_4 \end{vmatrix} = 0;$$

the expression on the left being a determinant of the fourth order.

Also we see that the coefficients of a_1, b_1, c_1, d_1 taken with their proper signs are the *minors* obtained by omitting the row and column which respectively contain these constituents.

554. More generally, if we have n homogeneous linear equations

$$a_1 x_1 + b_1 x_2 + c_1 x_3 + \cdots + k_1 x_n = 0,$$
$$a_2 x_1 + b_2 x_2 + c_2 x_3 + \cdots + k_2 x_n = 0,$$
$$\cdots \cdots \cdots \cdots \cdots$$
$$a_n x_1 + b_n x_2 + c_n x_3 + \cdots + k_n x_n = 0,$$

involving n unknown quantities $x_1, x_2, x_3, \cdots x_n$, these quantities can be eliminated and the result expressed in the form

$$\begin{vmatrix} a_1 & b_1 & c_1 & \cdots & k_1 \\ a_2 & b_2 & c_2 & \cdots & k_2 \\ \cdot & \cdot & \cdot & & \cdot \\ a_n & b_n & c_n & \cdots & k_n \end{vmatrix} = 0.$$

The left-hand member of this equation is a determinant which consists of n rows and n columns, and is called a determinant of the nth order.

The discussion of this more general form of determinant is beyond the scope of the present work; it will be sufficient here to remark that the properties which have been established in the case of determinants of the second and third orders are quite general, and are capable of being extended to determinants of any order.

555. Signs of the Terms. Although we may develop a determinant by means of the process described above, it is not always the simplest method, especially when our object is not so much to find the value of the whole determinant, as to find the signs of its several elements.

556. The expanded form of the determinant

$$\begin{vmatrix} a_1 & b_1 & c_1 \\ a_2 & b_2 & c_2 \\ a_3 & b_3 & c_3 \end{vmatrix}$$

$$= a_1b_2c_3 - a_1b_3c_2 + a_2b_3c_1 - a_2b_1c_3 + a_3b_1c_2 - a_3b_2c_1;$$

and it appears that each element is the product of three factors, one taken from each row, and one from each column; also the signs of half the terms are $+$ and of the other half $-$. When written as above the signs of the several elements may be obtained as follows. The first element $a_1b_2c_3$, in which the suffixes follow the arithmetical order, is positive; we shall call this the leading element; every other element may be obtained from it by suitably interchanging the suffixes. The sign $+$ or $-$ is to be prefixed to any element according as the number of *inversions* of order in the line of suffixes is even or odd; for instance in the element $a_3b_2c_1$, 2 and 1 are out of their natural order, or inverted with respect to 3; 1 is inverted with respect to 2; hence there are three *inversions* and the sign of the element is negative; in the element $a_3b_1c_2$ there are two inversions, hence the sign is positive.

557. The determinant whose leading element is $a_1b_2c_3d_4\cdots$ may thus be expressed by the notation

$$* \Sigma \pm a_1b_2c_3d_4\cdots,$$

the $\Sigma \pm$ placed before the leading element indicating the aggregate of all the elements which can be obtained from it by suitable interchanges of suffixes and adjustment of signs.

Sometimes the determinant is still more simply expressed by enclosing the leading element within brackets; thus $(a_1b_2c_3d_4\cdots)$ is used as an abbreviation of $\Sigma \pm a_1b_2c_3d_4\cdots$.

* The Greek letter Sigma.

Ex. In the determinant $(a_1b_2c_3d_4e_5)$ what sign is to be prefixed to the element $a_4b_3c_1d_5e_2$?

Here 3, 1, and 2 are inverted with respect to 4; 1 and 2 are inverted with respect to 3, and 2 is inverted with respect to 5; hence there are six inversions and the sign of the element is positive.

558. Determinant of Lower Order. If in Art. 554, each of the constituents $b_1, c_1, \cdots k_1$ is equal to zero, the determinant reduces to a_1A_1; in other words it is equal to the product of a_1 and a determinant of the $(n-1)$th order, and we easily infer the following general theorem:

If each of the constituents of the first row or column of a determinant is zero except the first, and if this constituent is equal to m, the determinant is equal to m times that determinant of lower order which is obtained by omitting the first column and first row.

Also since by suitable interchange of rows and columns any constituent can be brought into the first place, it follows that if *any* row or column has all its constituents except one equal to zero, the determinant can be immediately expressed as a determinant of lower order.

This is sometimes useful in the reduction and simplification of determinants.

Ex. Find the value of

$$\begin{vmatrix} 30 & 11 & 20 & 38 \\ 6 & 3 & 0 & 9 \\ 11 & -2 & 36 & 8 \\ 19 & 6 & 17 & 22 \end{vmatrix}.$$

Diminish each constituent of the first column by twice the corresponding constituent in the second column, and each constituent of the fourth column by three times the corresponding constituent in the second column, and we obtain

$$\begin{vmatrix} 8 & 11 & 20 & 5 \\ 0 & 3 & 0 & 0 \\ 15 & -2 & 36 & 9 \\ 7 & 6 & 17 & 4 \end{vmatrix},$$

and since the second row has three zero constituents, this determinant

DETERMINANTS. 449

$$= 3 \begin{vmatrix} 8 & 20 & 5 \\ 15 & 36 & 9 \\ 7 & 17 & 4 \end{vmatrix} = 3 \begin{vmatrix} 8 & 20 & 5 \\ 8 & 19 & 5 \\ 7 & 17 & 4 \end{vmatrix} = 3 \begin{vmatrix} 0 & 1 & 0 \\ 8 & 19 & 5 \\ 7 & 17 & 4 \end{vmatrix} = -3 \begin{vmatrix} 8 & 5 \\ 7 & 4 \end{vmatrix} = 9.$$

EXAMPLES XLVII. b.

Calculate the values of the determinants:

1. $\begin{vmatrix} 1 & 1 & 1 & 1 \\ 1 & 2 & 3 & 4 \\ 1 & 3 & 6 & 10 \\ 1 & 4 & 10 & 20 \end{vmatrix}$.

2. $\begin{vmatrix} 7 & 13 & 10 & 6 \\ 5 & 9 & 7 & 4 \\ 8 & 12 & 11 & 7 \\ 4 & 10 & 6 & 3 \end{vmatrix}$.

3. $\begin{vmatrix} a & 1 & 1 & 1 \\ 1 & a & 1 & 1 \\ 1 & 1 & a & 1 \\ 1 & 1 & 1 & a \end{vmatrix}$.

4. $\begin{vmatrix} 0 & 1 & 1 & 1 \\ 1 & b+c & a & a \\ 1 & b & c+a & b \\ 1 & c & c & a+b \end{vmatrix}$.

5. $\begin{vmatrix} 3 & 2 & 1 & 4 \\ 15 & 29 & 2 & 14 \\ 16 & 19 & 3 & 17 \\ 33 & 39 & 8 & 38 \end{vmatrix}$.

6. $\begin{vmatrix} 1+a & 1 & 1 & 1 \\ 1 & 1+b & 1 & 1 \\ 1 & 1 & 1+c & 1 \\ 1 & 1 & 1 & 1+d \end{vmatrix}$.

7. $\begin{vmatrix} 0 & x & y & z \\ x & 0 & z & y \\ y & z & 0 & x \\ z & y & x & 0 \end{vmatrix}$.

8. $\begin{vmatrix} 0 & x & y & z \\ -x & 0 & c & b \\ -y & -c & 0 & a \\ -z & -b & -a & 0 \end{vmatrix}$.

Solve the equations:

9. $4x - 5y + 2z = 11$,
$2x + 3y - z = 20$,
$7x - 4y + 3z = 33$.

10. $\dfrac{x}{2} + \dfrac{y}{3} + \dfrac{z}{4} = 7$,
$x + 2y + 3z = 48$,
$\dfrac{x}{3} - \dfrac{2y}{3} + \dfrac{z}{3} = 4$.

11. $2x - y + 3z - 2u = 14$,
$x + 7y + z - u = 13$,
$3x + 5y - 5z + 3u = 11$,
$4x - 3y + 2z - u = 21$.

12. $x + y + z = 1$,
$ax + by + cz = k$,
$a^2x + b^2y + c^2z = k^2$.

13. $ax + by + cz = k$,
$a^2x + b^2y + c^2z = k^2$,
$a^3x + b^3y + c^3z = k^3$.

14. $x + y + z + u = 1$,
$ax + by + cz + du = k$,
$a^2x + b^2y + c^2z + d^2u = k^2$,
$a^3x + b^3y + c^3z + d^3u = k^3$.

2 G

CHAPTER XLVIII.

THEORY OF EQUATIONS.

559. General Form of an Equation of the nth Degree. Let $p_0 x^n + p_1 x^{n-1} + p_2 x^{n-2} + \cdots + p_{n-1} x + p_n$ be a rational integral function of x of n dimensions, and let us denote it by $f(x)$; then $f(x) = 0$ is the general type of a *rational integral equation* of the nth degree. Dividing throughout by p_0, we see that without any loss of generality we may take

$$x^n + p_1 x^{n-1} + p_2 x^{n-2} + \cdots + p_{n-1} x + p_n = 0$$

as the *general form* of a rational integral equation of any degree.

Unless otherwise stated the coefficients $p_1, p_2 \cdots p_n$ will always be supposed rational.

If any of the coefficients $p_1, p_2, p_3, \cdots p_n$ are zero, the equation is said to be *incomplete*, otherwise it is called *complete*.

560. Any value of x which makes $f(x)$ vanish is called a root of the equation $f(x) = 0$.

561. We shall assume that every equation of the form $f(x) = 0$ has a root, real or imaginary. The proof of this proposition will be found in treatises on the *Theory of Equations;* it is beyond the range of the present work.

562. Divisibility of Equations. *If a is a root of the equation $f(x) = 0$, then is $f(x)$ exactly divisible by $x - a$.*

Divide the first member by $x - a$ until the remainder no longer contains x. Denote the quotient by Q, and the remainder, if there be one, by R. Then we have

$$f(x) = Q(x - a) + R = 0.$$

THEORY OF EQUATIONS. 451

Now since a is a root of the equation $x = a$, therefore
$$Q(a-a) + R = 0,$$
hence $\qquad R = 0;$

that is, the first member of the given equation is exactly divisible by $x - a$.

563. Conversely, *if the first member of $f(x) = 0$ is exactly divisible by $x - a$, then a is a root of the equation.*

For, the division being exact,
$$Q(x-a) = 0,$$
and the substitution of a for x satisfies the equation; hence a is a root.

DIVISION BY DETACHED COEFFICIENTS.

564. The work of dividing one multinomial by another may be abridged by writing only the coefficients of the terms. The following is an illustration.

Ex. Divide $3x^5 - 8x^4 - 5x^3 + 26x^2 - 33x + 26$ by $x^3 - 2x^2 - 4x + 8$.

```
1 + 2 + 4 − 8) 3 − 8 −  5 + 26 − 33 + 26 (3 − 2 + 3
              3 + 6 + 12 − 24
              ─────────────────
                 − 2 +  7 +  2 − 33
                 − 2 −  4 −  8 + 16
                 ────────────────────
                        3 −  6 − 17 + 26
                        3 +  6 + 12 − 24
                        ─────────────────
                                − 5 +  2
```

Thus the quotient is $3x^2 - 2x + 3$ and the remainder is $-5x + 2$.

It should be noticed that in writing the divisor, the sign of every term *except the first* has been changed; this enables us *to replace the process of subtraction by that of addition* at each successive stage of the work.

HORNER'S METHOD OF SYNTHETIC DIVISION.

565. For convenience we again give an explanation of **Horner's Method of Synthetic Division**, which has already been considered in Art. 63.

Let us take the example of the preceding article. The arrangement of the work is as follows:

```
 1 | 3 − 8 −  5 + 26 − 33 + 26
 2 |     6 + 12 − 24
 4 |        − 4 −  8 + 16
−8 |               6 + 12 − 24
   ─────────────────────────────
     3 − 2 +  3 +  0 −  5 +  2
```

EXPLANATION. The column of figures to the left of the vertical line consists of the coefficients of the divisor, the sign of each after the first being changed; the second horizontal line is obtained by multiplying 2, 4, − 8 by 3, the first term of the quotient. We then add the terms in the second column to the right of the vertical line; this gives − 2, which is the coefficient of the second term of the quotient. With the coefficient thus obtained we form the next horizontal line, and add the terms in the third column; this gives 3, which is the coefficient of the third term of the quotient.

By adding up the other columns we get the coefficients of the terms in the remainder.

566. In employing this method in the following articles our divisor will be of the form $x \pm a$, which enables us to still further simplify the work, as the following example shows:

Ex. Find the quotient and remainder when $3x^7 - x^6 + 31x^4 + 21x + 5$ is divided by $x + 2$.

```
3 −1   0   31   0    0   21   5 | −2
   −6  14  −28  −6   12  −24   6
  ───────────────────────────────────
3 −7  14    3  −6   12  − 3  11
```

Thus the quotient is $3x^6 - 7x^5 + 14x^4 + 3x^3 - 6x^2 + 12x - 3$, and the remainder is 11.

EXPLANATION. The first horizontal line contains the coefficients of the dividend, *zero coefficients being used to represent terms corresponding to powers of x which are absent*. The divisor is written at the right of this line *with its sign changed* (Art. 564) and 1, the coefficient of x, omitted. The first term of the third horizontal line, which contains the quotient, is the result of dividing 3, the coefficient of x^7 in the dividend, by 1, the coefficient of x in the divisor. This is then *multiplied* by the divisor − 2, and the result − 6, the first term of the second horizontal line; the sum of − 1 and − 6 gives − 7, the second term of the quotient, which multiplied by -2 gives 14 for the second term of the second horizontal line; the addition of 14 and 0 gives 14 for the third term of the quotient, which multiplied by -2 gives -28 for the third term of the second line, and so on.

567. Number of Roots. *Every equation of the nth degree has n roots, and no more.*

Denote the given equation by $f(x) = 0$, where
$$f(x) = x^n + p_1 x^{n-1} + p_2 x^{n-2} + \cdots + p_n.$$
The equation $f(x) = 0$ has a root, real or imaginary; let this be denoted by a_1; then $f(x)$ is divisible by $x - a_1$, so that
$$f(x) = (x - a_1) f_1(x),$$
where $f_1(x)$ is a rational integral function of $n-1$ dimensions. Again, the equation $f_1(x) = 0$ has a root, real or imaginary; let this be denoted by a_2; then $f_1(x)$ is divisible by $x - a_2$, so that
$$f_1(x) = (x - a_2) f_2(x),$$
where $f_2(x)$ is a rational integral function of $n-2$ dimensions.

Thus $\quad f(x) = (x - a_1)(x - a_2) f_2(x).$

Proceeding in this way, we obtain
$$f(x) = (x - a_1)(x - a_2) \cdots (x - a_n).$$
Hence the equation $f(x) = 0$ has n roots, since $f(x)$ vanishes when x has any of the values $a_1, a_2, a_3, \cdots a_n$.

Also the equation cannot have more than n roots; for if x has any value different from any of the quantities $a_1, a_2, a_3, \cdots a_n$, all the factors on the right are different from zero, and therefore $f(x)$ cannot vanish for that value of x.

In the above investigation some of the quantities $a_1, a_2, a_3, \cdots a_n$ may be equal; in this case, however, we shall suppose that the equation has still n roots, although these are not all different.

568. Depression of Equations. If one root of an equation is known it is evident from the preceding paragraph that we may by division reduce or *depress* the equation to one of the next lower degree containing the remaining roots. So if k

454   ALGEBRA.

roots are known we may depress the equation to one of the $(n-k)$th degree. All the roots but two being known, the depressed equation is a quadratic from which the remaining roots are readily obtained.

569. Formation of Equations. Since $f(x)=(x-a_1)(x-a_2)\cdots(x-a_n)$ [Art. 567], we see that an equation may be formed by *subtracting each root from the unknown quantity and placing the continued product of the binomial factors thus formed equal to* 0.

Ex. Form the equation whose roots are 1, -2, and $\frac{1}{2}$.
$$(x-1)(x+2)(x-\tfrac{1}{2})=0;$$
$$\therefore 2x^3+x^2-5x+2=0.$$

EXAMPLES XLVIII. a.

1. Show that 4 is a root of $x^3-5x^2-2x+24=0$.
2. Show that $+3$ is a root of $x^3-7x^2+7x+15=0$.
3. Show that $-\frac{1}{3}$ is a root of $6x^3+17x^2-4x-3=0$.
4. Show that $\frac{2}{5}$ is a root of $10x^3-3x^2-9x+4=0$.
5. One root of $x^3+6x^2-6x-63=0$ is 3; find the others.
6. One root of $x^3-23x^2+166x-378=0$ is 7; find the others.
7. One root of $x^3-2x^2+6x-9\frac{5}{27}=0$ is $\frac{2}{3}$; what are the others?
8. Two roots of $x^4-15x^2+10x+24=0$ are 2 and 3; find the others.
9. Two roots of $x^4-3x^3-21x^2+43x+60=0$ are 3 and 5; find the others.
10. One root of $x^3+2ax^2+5a^2x+4a^3=0$ is $-a$; what are the others?
11. Form the equation whose roots are -1, -2, and -5.
12. Form the equation whose roots are -2, -3, $+\frac{1}{2}$, and $-\frac{1}{3}$.

570. Relations between the Roots and the Coefficients. Let us denote the equation by
$$x^n+p_1x^{n-1}+p_2x^{n-2}+\cdots+p_{n-1}x+p_n=0,$$
and the roots by $a, b, c, \cdots k$; then we have identically
$$x^n+p_1x^{n-1}+p_2x^{n-2}+\cdots+p_{n-1}x+p_n$$
$$=(x-a)(x-b)(x-c)\cdots(x-k);$$

THEORY OF EQUATIONS.

hence, by multiplication, we have

$x^n + p_1 x^{n-1} + p_2 x^{n-2} + \cdots + p_{n-1} x + p_n$
$= x^n - S_1 x^{n-1} + S_2 x^{n-2} - \cdots + (-1)^{n-1} S_{n-1} x + (-1)^n S_n.$

Equating the coefficients of like powers of x in this identity, we have

$$-p_1 = S_1,$$
$$p_2 = S_2,$$
$$-p_3 = S_3,$$
$$(-1)^n p_n = S_n,$$

in which S_1 stands for the sum of the roots $a, b, c \cdots k$; S_2 stands for the sum of the products of the roots taken two at a time, and so on to S_n, which equals the continued product of all the roots. That is:

(1) The coefficient of the second term *with its sign changed* equals the sum of the roots.

(2) The coefficient of the third term equals the sum of all the products of the roots taken two at a time.

(3) The coefficient of the fourth term *with its sign changed* equals the sum of all the products of the roots taken three at a time, and so on.

(4) The last term equals the continued product of all the roots, the sign being + or − according as n is even or odd.

571. It follows that if the equation is in the general form:

(1) The sum of the roots is zero if the second term is wanting.

(2) One root, at least, is zero if the last term is wanting.

572. The student might suppose that the relations established in the preceding article would enable him to solve any proposed equation; for the number of the relations is equal to the number of the roots. A little reflection will show that this is not the case; for suppose we eliminate any $n-1$ of the quantities $a, b, c, \cdots k$, and so obtain an equation to determine the remaining one; then since these quantities are involved symmetrically in each of the equations, it is clear that we shall always obtain an equation having the same coefficients; this equation is therefore the original equation with some one of the roots $a, b, c, \cdots k$ substituted for x.

Let us take for example the equation
$$x^3 + p_1 x^2 + p_2 x + p_3 = 0;$$
and let a, b, c be the roots; then
$$a + b + c = -p_1,$$
$$ab + ac + bc = +p_2,$$
$$abc = -p_3.$$

Multiply these equations by $a^2, -a, 1$ respectively and add; thus $\quad a^3 = -p_1 a^2 - p_2 a - p_3,$
that is, $\quad a^3 + p_1 a^2 + p_2 a + p_3 = 0,$
which is the original equation with a in the place of x.

The above process of elimination is quite general, and is applicable to equations of any degree.

573. If two or more of the roots of an equation are connected by an assigned relation, the properties proved in Art. 570 will sometimes enable us to obtain the complete solution.

Ex. 1. Solve the equation $4x^3 - 24x^2 + 23x + 18 = 0$, having given that the roots are in arithmetical progression.

Denote the roots by $a - b, a, a + b$; then the sum of the roots is $3a$; the sum of the products of the roots two at a time is $3a^2 - b^2$; and the product of the roots is $a(a^2 - b^2)$; hence we have the equations
$$3a = 6, \quad 3a^2 - b^2 = \tfrac{23}{4}, \quad a(a^2 - b^2) = -\tfrac{9}{2};$$
from the first equation we find $a = 2$, and from the second $b = \pm \tfrac{5}{2}$, and since these values satisfy the third, the three equations are consistent. Thus the roots are $-\tfrac{1}{2}, 2, \tfrac{9}{2}$.

Ex. 2. Solve the equation $24x^3 - 14x^2 - 63x + 45 = 0$, one root being double another.

Denote the roots by $a, 2a, b$; then we have
$$3a + b = \tfrac{7}{12}, \quad 2a^2 + 3ab = -\tfrac{21}{8}, \quad 2a^2 b = -\tfrac{15}{8}.$$
From the first two equations, we obtain
$$8a^2 - 2a - 3 = 0;$$
$$\therefore a = \tfrac{3}{4} \text{ or } -\tfrac{1}{2}, \text{ and } b = -\tfrac{5}{3} \text{ or } \tfrac{25}{12}.$$

It will be found on trial that the values $a = -\frac{1}{2}$, $b = \frac{23}{12}$ do not satisfy the third equation $2a^2b = -\frac{15}{8}$; hence we are restricted to the values $a = \frac{1}{4}$, $b = -\frac{3}{8}$.

Thus the roots are $\frac{3}{4}, \frac{1}{2}, -\frac{1}{3}$.

574. Although we may not be able to find the roots of an equation, we can make use of the relations proved in Art. 570 to determine the values of symmetrical * functions of the roots.

Ex. Find the sum of the squares and of the cubes of the roots of the equation $x^3 - px^2 + qx - r = 0$.

Denote the roots by a, b, c; then $a + b + c = p$, $bc + ca + ab = q$.

Now $a^2 + b^2 + c^2 = (a + b + c)^2 - 2(bc + ca + ab) = p^2 - 2q$.

Again, substitute a, b, c for x in the given equation and add; thus

$$a^3 + b^3 + c^3 - p(a^2 + b^2 + c^2) + q(a + b + c) - 3r = 0;$$
$$\therefore a^3 + b^3 + c^3 = p(p^2 - 2q) - pq + 3r = p^3 - 3pq + 3r.$$

EXAMPLES XLVIII. b.

Form the equation whose roots are:

1. $\frac{2}{3}, \frac{1}{2}, \pm\sqrt{3}$.
2. $0, 0, 2, 2, -3, -3$.
3. $2, 2, -2, -2, 0, 5$.
4. $a + b, a - b, -a + b, -a - b$.

Solve the equations:

5. $x^4 - 16x^3 + 86x^2 - 176x + 105 = 0$, two roots being 1 and 7.

6. $4x^3 + 16x^2 - 9x - 36 = 0$, the sum of two of the roots being zero.

7. $4x^3 + 20x^2 - 23x + 6 = 0$, two of the roots being equal.

8. $3x^3 - 26x^2 + 52x - 24 = 0$, the roots being in geometrical progression.

9. $2x^3 - x^2 - 22x - 24 = 0$, two of the roots being in the ratio of 3 : 4.

10. $24x^3 + 46x^2 + 9x - 9 = 0$, one root being double another of the roots.

11. $8x^4 - 2x^3 - 27x^2 + 6x + 9 = 0$, two of the roots being equal but opposite in sign.

* A function is said to be *symmetrical* with respect to its variables when its value is unaltered by the interchange of any pair of them; thus $x + y + z$, $bc + ca + ab$, $x^3 + y^3 + z^3 - xyz$ are symmetrical functions of the first, second, and third degrees respectively. [See Art. 319.]

12. $54x^3 - 39x^2 - 26x + 16 = 0$, the roots being in geometrical progression.

13. $32x^3 - 48x^2 + 22x - 3 = 0$, the roots being in arithmetical progression.

14. $6x^4 - 29x^3 + 40x^2 - 7x - 12 = 0$, the product of two of the roots being 2.

15. $x^4 - 2x^3 - 21x^2 + 22x + 40 = 0$, the roots being in arithmetical progression.

16. $27x^4 - 195x^3 + 494x^2 - 520x + 192 = 0$, the roots being in geometrical progression.

17. $18x^3 + 81x^2 + 121x + 60 = 0$, one root being half the sum of the other two.

18. Find the sum of the squares and of the cubes of the roots of $x^4 + qx^2 + rx + s = 0$.

575. Fractional Roots. *An equation whose coefficients are integers, that of the first term being unity, cannot have a rational fraction as a root.*

If possible suppose the equation

$$x^n + p_1 x^{n-1} + p_2 x^{n-2} + \cdots + p_{n-2} x^2 + p_{n-1} x + p_n = 0$$

has for a root a rational fraction in its lowest terms, represented by $\dfrac{a}{b}$. Substituting this value for x and multiplying through by b^{n-1}, we have

$$\frac{a^n}{b} + p_1 a^{n-1} + p_2 a^{n-2} b + \cdots + p_{n-1} a b^{n-2} + p_n b^{n-1} = 0.$$

Transposing,

$$-\frac{a^n}{b} = p_1 a^{n-1} + p_2 a^{n-2} b + \cdots + p_{n-1} a b^{n-2} + p_n b^{n-1}.$$

This result is impossible, since it makes a fraction in its lowest terms equal to an integer. Hence a rational fraction cannot be a root of the given equation.

576. Imaginary Roots. *In an equation with real coefficients imaginary roots occur in pairs.*

Suppose that $f(x) = 0$ is an equation with real coefficients, and suppose that it has an imaginary root $a + ib$; we shall show that $a - ib$ is also a root.

THEORY OF EQUATIONS.

The factor of $f(x)$ corresponding to these two roots is

$$(x-a-ib)(x-a+ib), \text{ or } (x-a)^2 + b^2.$$

Let $f(x)$ be divided by $(x-a)^2 + b^2$; denote the quotient by Q, and the remainder, if any, by $Rx + R'$; then

$$f(x) = Q\{(x-a)^2 + b^2\} + Rx + R'.$$

In this identity put $x = a + ib$, then $f(x) = 0$ by hypothesis; also $(x-a)^2 + b^2 = 0$; hence $R(a+ib) + R' = 0$.

Equating to zero the real and imaginary parts,

$$Ra + R' = 0, \quad Rb = 0;$$

and b by hypothesis is not zero,

$$\therefore R = 0 \text{ and } R' = 0.$$

Hence $f(x)$ is exactly divisible by $(x-a)^2 + b^2$, that is, by

$$(x-a-ib)(x-a+ib);$$

hence $x = a - ib$ is also a root.

577. In the preceding article we have seen that if the equation $f(x) = 0$ has a pair of imaginary roots $a \pm ib$, then $(x-a)^2 + b^2$ is a factor of the expression $f(x)$.

Suppose that $a \pm ib$, $c \pm id$, $e \pm ig$, ⋯ are the imaginary roots of the equation $f(x) = 0$, and that *$\phi(x)$ is the product of the quadratic factors corresponding to these imaginary roots; then

$$\phi(x) = \{(x-a)^2 + b^2\}\{(x-c)^2 + d^2\}\{(x-e)^2 + g^2\} \cdots.$$

Now each of these factors is positive for every real value of x; hence $\phi(x)$ is always positive for real values of x.

578. As in Art. 576 we may show that in an equation with *rational* coefficients, surd roots enter in pairs; that is, if $a + \sqrt{b}$ is a root then $a - \sqrt{b}$ is also a root.

Ex. 1. Solve the equation $6x^4 - 13x^3 - 35x^2 - x + 3 = 0$, having given that one root is $2 - \sqrt{3}$.

* The Greek letter Phi.

Since $2-\sqrt{3}$ is a root, we know that $2+\sqrt{3}$ is also a root, and corresponding to this pair of roots we have the quadratic factor x^2-4x+1.

Also
$$6x^4 - 13x^3 - 35x^2 - x + 3 = (x^2 - 4x + 1)(6x^2 + 11x + 3);$$

hence the other roots are obtained from
$$6x^2 + 11x + 3 = 0, \text{ or } (3x+1)(2x+3) = 0;$$

thus the roots are $\quad -\frac{1}{3}, \ -\frac{3}{2}, \ 2+\sqrt{3}, \ 2-\sqrt{3}$.

Ex. 2. Form the equation of the fourth degree with rational coefficients, one of whose roots is $\sqrt{2}+\sqrt{-3}$.

Here we must have $\sqrt{2}+\sqrt{-3}$, $\sqrt{2}-\sqrt{-3}$ as one pair of roots, and $-\sqrt{2}+\sqrt{-3}$, $-\sqrt{2}-\sqrt{-3}$ as another pair.

Corresponding to the first pair we have the quadratic factor $x^2 - 2\sqrt{2}\,x + 5$, and corresponding to the second pair we have the quadratic factor
$$x^2 + 2\sqrt{2}\,x + 5.$$

Thus the required equation is
$$(x^2 + 2\sqrt{2}\,x + 5)(x^2 - 2\sqrt{2}\,x + 5) = 0,$$
or $\qquad\qquad\qquad (x^2+5)^2 - 8x^2 = 0,$
or $\qquad\qquad\qquad x^4 + 2x^2 + 25 = 0.$

EXAMPLES XLVIII. c.

Solve the equations:

1. $3x^4 - 10x^3 + 4x^2 - x - 6 = 0$, one root being $\dfrac{1+\sqrt{-3}}{2}$.

2. $x^4 - 36x^2 + 72x - 36 = 0$, one root being $3-\sqrt{3}$.

3. $x^4 + 4x^3 + 5x^2 + 2x - 2 = 0$, one root being $-1+\sqrt{-1}$.

4. $x^4 + 4x^3 + 6x^2 + 4x + 5 = 0$, one root being $\sqrt{-1}$.

TRANSFORMATION OF EQUATIONS.

579. The discussion of an equation is sometimes simplified by transforming it into another equation whose roots bear some assigned relation to those of the one proposed. Such transformations are especially useful in the solution of cubic equations.

580. To transform an equation into another whose roots are those of the original equation with their signs changed.

Let $f(x) = 0$ be the equation.

Put $-y$ for x; then the equation $f(-y) = 0$ is satisfied by every root of $f(x) = 0$ with its sign changed; thus the required equation is $f(-y) = 0$.

If the given equation is

$$x^n + p_1 x^{n-1} + p_2 x^{n-2} + \cdots + p_{n-1} x + p_n = 0,$$

then it is evident that the required equation will be

$$y^n - p_1 y^{n-1} + p_2 y^{n-2} - \cdots + (-1)^{n-1} p_{n-1} y + (-1)^n p_n = 0;$$

therefore the transformed equation is obtained from the original equation by *changing the sign of every alternate term beginning with the second*.

NOTE. If any term of the given equation is missing it must be supplied with zero as a coefficient.

Ex. Transform the equation $x^4 - 17 x^2 - 20 x - 6 = 0$ into another which shall have the same roots numerically with contrary signs. We may write the equation thus:

$$x^4 + 0 x^3 - 17 x^2 - 20 x - 6 = 0.$$

By the rule, we have

$$x^4 - 0 x^3 - 17 x^2 + 20 x - 6 = 0,$$

or $\qquad x^4 - 17 x^2 + 20 x - 6 = 0.$

581. To transform an equation into another whose roots are equal to those of the original equation multiplied by a given factor.

Let $f(x) = 0$ be the equation, and let q denote the given quantity. Put $y = qx$, so that when x has any particular value, y is q times as large; then $x = \dfrac{y}{q}$, and the required equation is

$$\left(\frac{y}{q}\right)^n + p_1 \left(\frac{y}{q}\right)^{n-1} + p_2 \left(\frac{y}{q}\right)^{n-2} + \cdots + p_{n-1}\left(\frac{y}{q}\right) + p_n = 0.$$

Multiplying by q^n, we have

$$y^n + p_1 q y^{n-1} + p_2 q^2 y^{n-2} + \cdots + p_{n-1} q^{n-1} y + p_n q^n = 0.$$

Therefore the transformed equation is obtained from the original equation by *multiplying the second term by the given factor, the third term by the square of this factor, and so on.*

582. The chief use of this transformation is *to clear an equation of fractional coefficients.*

Ex. Remove fractional coefficients from the equation
$$2x^3 - \tfrac{2}{3}x^2 - \tfrac{1}{4}x + \tfrac{3}{16} = 0.$$
Put $x = \dfrac{y}{q}$ and multiply each term by q^3; thus
$$2y^3 - \tfrac{2}{3}qy^2 - \tfrac{1}{4}q^2y + \tfrac{3}{16}q^3 = 0.$$
By putting $q = 4$ all the terms become integral, and on dividing by 2, we obtain
$$y^3 - 3y^2 - y + 6 = 0.$$

583. To transform an equation into another whose roots exceed those of the original equation by a given quantity.

Let $f(x) = 0$ be the equation, and let h be the given quantity. Assume $y = x + h$, so that for any particular value of x, the value of y is greater by h; thus $x = y - h$, and the required equation is $f(y - h) = 0$.

Similarly if the roots are to be *less* by h, we assume $y = x - h$, from which we obtain $x = y + h$, and the required equation is $f(y + h) = 0$.

584. If n is small, this method of transformation is effected with but little trouble. For equations of a higher degree the following method is to be preferred:

Let $\quad f(x) = p_0 x^n + p_1 x^{n-1} + p_2 x^{n-2} + \cdots + p_{n-1} x + p_n;$
put $x = y + h$, and suppose that $f(x)$ then becomes
$$q_0 y^n + q_1 y^{n-1} + q_2 y^{n-2} + \cdots + q_{n-1} y + q_n.$$
Now $y = x - h$; hence we have the identity
$$p_0 x^n + p_1 x^{n-1} + p_2 x^{n-2} + \cdots + p_{n-1} x + p_n$$
$$= q_0 (x-h)^n + q_1 (x-h)^{n-1} + \cdots + q_{n-1}(x-h) + q_n;$$
therefore q_n is the remainder found by dividing $f(x)$ by $x - h$; also the quotient arising from the division is
$$q_0 (x-h)^{n-1} + q_1 (x-h)^{n-2} + \cdots + q_{n-1}.$$

THEORY OF EQUATIONS.

Similarly q_{n-1} is the remainder found by dividing the last expression by $x - h$, and the quotient arising from the division is

$$q_0(x - h)^{n-2} + q_1(x - h)^{n-3} + \cdots + q_{n-2};$$

and so on. Thus $q_n, q_{n-1}, q_{n-2}, \cdots$ may be readily found by Synthetic Division. The last quotient is q_0, and is obviously equal to p_0.

Hence to obtain the transformed equation,

Divide $f(x)$ by $x \pm h$ according as the roots are to be greater or less by h than those of the original equation, and the remainder will be the last term of the required equation. Divide the quotient thus found by $x \pm h$, and the remainder will be the coefficient of the last term but one of the required equation; and so on.

Ex. Find the equation whose roots exceed by 2 the roots of the equation

$$4x^4 + 32x^3 + 83x^2 + 76x + 21 = 0.$$

The required equation will be obtained by substituting $x - 2$ for x in the proposed equation; hence in Horner's process we employ $x + 2$ as divisor, and the calculation is performed as follows:

```
4   32   83   76   21  |+2
4   24   35    6   | 9
4   16    3   | 0
4    8   |−13
4   | 0
4
```

Thus the transformed equation is

$$4x^4 - 13x^2 + 9 = 0, \text{ or } (4x^2 - 9)(x^2 - 1) = 0.$$

The roots of this equation are $+\frac{3}{2}, -\frac{3}{2}, +1, -1$; hence the roots of the given equation are

$$-\tfrac{1}{2}, -\tfrac{7}{2}, -1, -3.$$

585. To transform a complete equation into another which wants an assigned term.

The chief use of the substitution in the preceding article is to remove some assigned term from an equation.

Let the given equation be
$$p_0x^n + p_1x^{n-1} + p_2x^{n-2} + \cdots + p_{n-1}x + p_n = 0;$$
then if $y = x - h$, we obtain the new equation
$$p_0(y+h)^n + p_1(y+h)^{n-1} + p_2(y+h)^{n-2} + \cdots + p_n = 0,$$
which, when arranged in descending powers of y, becomes
$$p_0y^n + (np_0h + p_1)y^{n-1}$$
$$+ \left\{ \frac{n(n-1)}{\lfloor 2} p_0h^2 + (n-1)p_1h + p_2 \right\} y^{n-2} + \cdots = 0.$$

If the term to be removed is the second, we put $np_0h + p_1 = 0$, so that $h = -\dfrac{p_1}{np_0}$; if the term to be removed is the third, we put
$$\frac{n(n-1)}{\lfloor 2} p_0h^2 + (n-1)p_1h + p_2 = 0,$$

and so obtain a quadratic to find h; and, similarly, we may remove any other assigned term.

Sometimes it will be more convenient to proceed as in the following example.

Ex. Remove the second term from the equation
$$px^3 + qx^2 + rx + s = 0.$$

Let a, b, c be the roots, so that $a + b + c = -\dfrac{q}{p}$. Then if we increase each of the roots by $\dfrac{q}{3p}$, in the transformed equation the sum of the roots will be equal to $-\dfrac{q}{p} + \dfrac{q}{p}$; that is, the coefficient of the second term will be zero.

Hence the required transformation will be effected by substituting $x - \dfrac{q}{3p}$ for x in the given equation.

As the *general type* of a cubic equation can be reduced to a more simple form by removing the second term, the student should carefully notice that the transformation is effected by substituting x minus the coefficient of the second term divided by the degree of the equation, for x in the given equation.

586. To transform an equation into another whose roots are the reciprocals of the roots of the proposed equation.

Let $f(x) = 0$ be the proposed equation; put $y = \dfrac{1}{x}$, so that $x = \dfrac{1}{y}$; then the required equation is $f\left(\dfrac{1}{y}\right) = 0$.

One of the chief uses of this transformation is to obtain the values of expressions which involve symmetrical functions of negative powers of the roots.

Ex. If a, b, c are the roots of the equation
$$x^3 - px^2 + qx - r = 0,$$
find the value of
$$\frac{1}{a^2} + \frac{1}{b^2} + \frac{1}{c^2}.$$

Write $\dfrac{1}{y}$ for x, multiply by y^3, and change all the signs; then the resulting equation
$$ry^3 - qy^2 + py - 1 = 0,$$
has for its roots
$$\frac{1}{a}, \frac{1}{b}, \frac{1}{c};$$
hence
$$*\Sigma\frac{1}{a} = \frac{q}{r}, \quad \Sigma\frac{1}{ab} = \frac{p}{r};$$
$$\therefore \Sigma\frac{1}{a^2} = \frac{q^2 - 2pr}{r^2}.$$

587. Reciprocal Equations. If an equation is unaltered by changing x into $\dfrac{1}{x}$, it is called a *reciprocal equation*.

If the given equation is
$$x^n + p_1 x^{n-1} + p_2 x^{n-2} + \cdots + p_{n-2} x^2 + p_{n-1} x + p_n = 0,$$
the equation obtained by writing $\dfrac{1}{x}$ for x, and clearing of fractions, is
$$p_n x^n + p_{n-1} x^{n-1} + p_{n-2} x^{n-2} + \cdots + p_2 x^2 + p_1 x + 1 = 0.$$
If these two equations are the same, we must have
$$p_1 = \frac{p_{n-1}}{p_n}, \; p_2 = \frac{p_{n-2}}{p_n}, \; \cdots, \; p_{n-2} = \frac{p_2}{p_n}, \; p_{n-1} = \frac{p_1}{p_n}, \; p_n = \frac{1}{p_n};$$

* $\Sigma\dfrac{1}{a}$ stands for the sum of all the terms of which $\dfrac{1}{a}$ is the type.

from the last result we have $p_n = \pm 1$, and thus we have two classes of reciprocal equations.

(i.) If $p_n = 1$, then
$$p_1 = p_{n-1}, \; p_2 = p_{n-2}, \; p_3 = p_{n-3}, \cdots;$$
that is, the coefficients of terms equidistant from the beginning and end are equal.

(ii.) If $p_n = -1$, then
$$p_1 = -p_{n-1}, \; p_2 = -p_{n-2}, \; p_3 = -p_{n-3}, \cdots;$$
hence if the equation is of $2m$ dimensions $p_m = -p_m$, or $p_m = 0$. In this case the coefficients of terms equidistant from the beginning and end are equal in magnitude and opposite in sign, and if the equation is of an even degree the middle term is wanting.

588. Standard Form of Reciprocal Equations. Suppose that $f(x) = 0$ is a reciprocal equation.

If $f(x) = 0$ is of the first class and of an odd degree it has a root -1; so that $f(x)$ is divisible by $x + 1$. If $\phi(x)$ is the quotient, then $\phi(x) = 0$ is a reciprocal equation of the first class and of an even degree.

If $f(x) = 0$ is of the second class and of an odd degree, it has a root $+1$; in this case $f(x)$ is divisible by $x - 1$, and as before $\phi(x) = 0$ is the reciprocal equation of the first class and of an even degree.

If $f(x) = 0$ is of the second class and of an even degree, it has a root $+1$ and a root -1; in this case $f(x)$ is divisible by $x^2 - 1$, and as before $\phi(x) = 0$ is a reciprocal equation of the first class of an even degree.

Hence *any reciprocal equation is of an even degree with its last term positive, or can be reduced to this form;* which may therefore be considered as the standard form of reciprocal equations.

589. A reciprocal equation of the standard form can be reduced to an equation of half its dimensions.

Let the equation be
$$ax^{2m} + bx^{2m-1} + cx^{2m-2} + \cdots + kx^m + \cdots + cx^2 + bx + a = 0;$$

dividing by x^m and rearranging the terms, we have

$$a\left(x^m + \frac{1}{x^m}\right) + b\left(x^{m-1} + \frac{1}{x^{m-1}}\right) + c\left(x^{m-2} + \frac{1}{x^{m-2}}\right) + \cdots + k = 0.$$

Now $\quad x^{p+1} + \dfrac{1}{x^{p+1}} = \left(x^p + \dfrac{1}{x^p}\right)\left(x + \dfrac{1}{x}\right) - \left(x^{p-1} + \dfrac{1}{x^{p-1}}\right);$

hence writing z for $x + \dfrac{1}{x}$, and giving to p in succession the values $1, 2, 3 \cdots$ we obtain

$$x^2 + \frac{1}{x^2} = z^2 - 2;$$

$$x^3 + \frac{1}{x^3} = z(z^2 - 2) - z = z^3 - 3z;$$

$$x^4 + \frac{1}{x^4} = z(z^3 - 3z) - (z^2 - 2) = z^4 - 4z^2 + 2;$$

and so on; and generally $x^m + \dfrac{1}{x^m}$ is of m dimensions in z, and therefore the equation in z is of m dimensions.

590. **To find the equation whose roots are the squares of those of a proposed equation.**

Let $f(x) = 0$ be the given equation; by putting $y = x^2$, we have $x = \sqrt{y}$, and therefore the required equation is $f(\sqrt{y}) = 0$.

Ex. Find the equation whose roots are the squares of those of the equation

$$x^3 + p_1 x^2 + p_2 x + p_3 = 0.$$

Putting $x = \sqrt{y}$, and transposing, we have

$$(y + p_2)\sqrt{y} = -(p_1 y + p_3);$$

whence $\quad (y^2 + 2p_2 y + p_2^2)\, y = p_1^2 y^2 + 2 p_1 p_3 y + p_3^2,$

or $\quad y^3 + (2p_2 - p_1^2) y^2 + (p_2^2 - 2 p_1 p_3) y - p_3^2 = 0.$

EXAMPLES XLVIII. d.

1. Transform the equation $x^5 - 5x^4 + 9x^3 - 9x^2 + 5x - 1 = 0$ into another which shall have the same roots with contrary signs.

2. Transform the equation $2x^3 - 4x^2 + 7x - 3 = 0$ into another whose roots shall be those of the first multiplied by 3.

3. Transform the equation $x^3 - 7x - 6 = 0$ into another whose roots shall be those of the first multiplied by $-\frac{1}{2}$.

4. Transform the equation $x^3 - 4x^2 + \frac{1}{4}x - \frac{1}{8} = 0$ into another with integral coefficients, and unity for the coefficient of the first term.

5. Transform the equation $3x^4 - 5x^3 + x^2 - x + 1 = 0$ into another the coefficient of whose first term is unity.

6. Transform the equation $x^4 + 10x^3 + 39x^2 + 76x + 65 = 0$ into another whose roots shall be greater by 4.

7. Transform the equation $x^4 - 12x^3 + 17x^2 - 9x + 7 = 0$ into another whose roots shall be less by 3.

8. Diminish by 1 the roots of the equation
$$2x^4 - 13x^2 + 10x - 19 = 0.$$

9. Find the equation whose roots are greater by 4 than the corresponding roots of $x^4 + 16x^3 + 72x^2 + 64x - 129 = 0$.

10. Solve the equation $3x^3 - 22x^2 + 48x - 32 = 0$, the roots of which are in harmonical progression.

11. The roots of $x^3 - 11x^2 + 36x - 36 = 0$ are in harmonical progression; find them.

Remove the second term from the equations:

12. $x^3 - 6x^2 + 10x - 3 = 0.$

13. $x^4 + 4x^3 + 2x^2 - 4x - 2 = 0.$

14. Transform the equation $x^3 - \dfrac{x}{4} - \dfrac{3}{4} = 0$ into one whose roots exceed by $\frac{1}{2}$ the corresponding roots of the given equation.

15. Diminish by 3 the roots of the equation
$$x^5 - 4x^4 + 3x^2 - 4x + 6 = 0.$$

16. Find the equation each of whose roots is greater by unity than a root of the equation $x^3 - 5x^2 + 6x - 3 = 0$.

17. Find the equation whose roots are the squares of the roots of
$$x^4 + x^3 + 2x^2 + x + 1 = 0.$$

18. Form the equation whose roots are the cubes of the roots of
$$x^3 + 3x^2 + 2 = 0.$$

THEORY OF EQUATIONS.

If a, b, c are the roots of $x^3 + qx + r = 0$, form the equation whose roots are

19. $ka^{-1}, kb^{-1}, kc^{-1}$.

20. b^2c^2, c^2a^2, a^2b^2.

21. $\dfrac{b+c}{a^2}, \dfrac{c+a}{b^2}, \dfrac{a+b}{c^2}$.

22. $bc + \dfrac{1}{a}, ca + \dfrac{1}{b}, ab + \dfrac{1}{c}$.

Solve the equations:

23. $2x^4 + x^3 - 6x^2 + x + 2 = 0$.
24. $x^4 - 10x^3 + 26x^2 - 10x + 1 = 0$.
25. $x^5 - 5x^4 + 9x^3 - 9x^2 + 5x - 1 = 0$.
26. $4x^6 - 24x^5 + 57x^4 - 73x^3 + 57x^2 - 24x + 4 = 0$.

DESCARTES' RULE OF SIGNS.

591. When each term of a series has one of the signs $+$ and $-$ before it, a *continuation* or *permanence* occurs when the signs of two successive terms are the *same:* and a *change* or *variation* occurs when the signs of two successive terms are *opposite*.

592. Descartes' Rule. *In any equation, the number of positive roots cannot exceed the number of variations of sign, and in any complete equation the number of negative roots cannot exceed the number of permanences of sign.*

Suppose that the signs of the terms in a multinomial are $+ + - - + - - - + - + -$; we shall show that if this multinomial is multiplied by a binomial whose signs are $+ -$, there will be at least one more change of sign in the product than in the original multinomial.

Writing only the signs of the terms in the multiplication, we have

$$
\begin{array}{c}
+ + - - + - - - + - + - \\
+ - \\
\hline
+ + - - + - - - + - + - \\
- - + + - + + + - + - + \\
\hline
+ \pm - \mp + - \mp \mp + - + - +
\end{array}
$$

a double sign, spoken of as an *ambiguity,* being placed wherever there is a doubt as to whether the sign of a term is positive or negative.

Examining the product we see that

(i.) An ambiguity replaces each continuation of sign in the original multinomial;

(ii.) The signs before and after an ambiguity or set of ambiguities are unlike;

(iii.) A change of sign is introduced at the end.

Let us take the most unfavorable case and suppose that all the ambiguities are replaced by continuations; from (ii.) we see that the number of changes of sign will be the same whether we take the upper or the lower signs; let us take the upper; thus the number of changes of sign cannot be less than in

$$++--+----+-+-+,$$

and this series of signs is the same as in the original multinomial with an additional change of sign at the end.

If then we suppose the factors corresponding to the negative and imaginary roots to be already multiplied together, each factor $x-a$ corresponding to a positive root introduces at least one change of sign; therefore no equation can have more positive roots than it has changes of sign.

To prove the second part of Descartes' Rule, let us suppose the equation complete and substitute $-y$ for x; then the *permanences* of sign in the original equation become *variations* of sign in the transformed equation. Now the transformed equation cannot have more *positive* roots than it has *variations* of sign, hence the original equation cannot have more *negative* roots than it has *permanences* of sign.

Whether the equation $f(x)=0$ be *complete* or *incomplete* its roots are equal to those of $f(-x)$ but opposite to them in sign; therefore the negative roots of $f(x)=0$ are the positive roots of $f(-x)=0$; but the number of these positive roots cannot exceed the number of *variations* of sign in $f(-x)$; that is, the number of negative roots of $f(x)=0$ cannot exceed the number of *variations* of sign in $f(-x)$.

We may therefore enunciate *Descartes' Rule* as follows:

An equation $f(x) = 0$ cannot have more positive roots than there are variations of sign in $f(x)$, and cannot have more negative roots than there are variations of sign in $f(-x)$.

Ex. Consider the equation $x^9 + 5x^8 - x^3 + 7x + 2 = 0$.

Here there are two changes of sign, therefore there are at most two positive roots.

Again $f(-x) = -x^9 + 5x^8 + x^3 - 7x + 2$, and here there are three changes of sign, therefore the given equation has at most three negative roots, and therefore it must have at least four imaginary roots.

593. It is very evident that the following results are included in the preceding article.

(i.) If the coefficients are all positive, the equation has no positive root; thus the equation $x^5 + x^3 + 2x + 1 = 0$ cannot have a positive root.

(ii.) If the coefficients of the even powers of x are all of one sign, and the coefficients of the odd powers are all of the contrary sign, the equation has no negative root; thus the equation

$$x^7 + x^5 - 2x^4 + x^3 - 3x^2 + 7x - 5 = 0$$

cannot have a negative root.

EXAMPLES XLVIII. e.

Find the nature of the roots of the following equations:

1. $x^4 + 2x^3 - 13x^2 - 14x + 24 = 0$.

2. $x^4 - 10x^3 + 35x^2 - 50x + 24 = 0$.

3. $3x^4 + 12x^2 + 5x - 4 = 0$.

4. Show that the equation $2x^7 - x^4 + 4x^3 - 5 = 0$ has at least four imaginary roots.

5. What may be inferred respecting the roots of the equation $x^{10} - 4x^6 + x^4 - 2x - 3 = 0$?

6. Find the least possible number of imaginary roots of the equation $x^9 - x^5 + x^4 + x^2 + 1 = 0$.

594. Derived Functions. *To find the value of $f(x+h)$, when $f(x)$ is a rational integral function of x.*

Let $f(x) = p_0 x^n + p_1 x^{n-1} + p_2 x^{n-2} + \cdots + p_{n-1} x + p_n$; then
$$f(x+h) = p_0(x+h)^n + p_1(x+h)^{n-1} + p_2(x+h)^{n-2} + \cdots$$
$$+ p_{n-1}(x+h) + p_n.$$

Expanding each term and arranging the result in ascending powers of h, we have

$p_0 x^n + p_1 x^{n-1} + p_2 x^{n-2} + \cdots + p_{n-1} x + p_n$
$+ h\{np_0 x^{n-1} + (n-1)p_1 x^{n-2} + (n-2)p_2 x^{n-3} + \cdots + p_{n-1}\}$
$+ \dfrac{h^2}{\lfloor 2}\{n(n-1)p_0 x^{n-2} + (n-1)(n-2)p_1 x^{n-3} + \cdots + 2p_{n-2}\}$
$+ \ldots \ldots \ldots \ldots \ldots \ldots$
$+ \dfrac{h^n}{\lfloor n}\{n(n-1)(n-2)\cdots 2 \cdot 1\, p_0\}.$

This result is usually written in the form
$$f(x+h) = f(x) + hf'(x) + \frac{h^2}{\lfloor 2} f''(x) + \frac{h^3}{\lfloor 3} f'''(x) + \cdots + \frac{h^n}{\lfloor n} f^n(x),$$

and the functions $f'(x)$, $f''(x)$, $f'''(x)$, $\cdots$ are called the *first, second, third, $\cdots$ derived functions* of $f(x)$.

Examining the coefficients of h, $\dfrac{h^2}{\lfloor 2}\cdots$, we see that *to obtain $f'(x)$ from $f(x)$ we multiply each term in $f(x)$ by the index of x in that term, and then diminish the index by unity.*

Similarly we obtain $f''(x)$, $f'''(x)$, $\cdots$.

595. Equal Roots. *If the equation $f(x) = 0$ has r roots equal to a, then the equation $f'(x) = 0$ will have $r-1$ roots equal to a.*

Let $\phi(x)$ be the quotient when $f(x)$ is divided by $(x-a)^r$; then $f(x) = (x-a)^r \phi(x)$.

Write $x + h$ in the place of x; thus
$$f(x+h) = (x-a+h)^r \phi(x+h);$$

$$\therefore f(x) + hf'(x) + \frac{h^2}{\underline{|2}} f''(x) + \cdots$$

$$= \{(x-a)^r + r(x-a)^{r-1}h + \cdots\}\{\phi(x) + h\phi'(x) + \frac{h^2}{\underline{|2}}\phi''(x) + \cdots\}.$$

In this identity, by equating the coefficients of h, we have

$$f'(x) = r(x-a)^{r-1}\phi(x) + (x-a)^r\phi'(x).$$

Thus $f'(x)$ contains the factor $x-a$ repeated $r-1$ times; that is, the equation $f'(x) = 0$ has $r-1$ roots equal to a.

Similarly we may show that if the equation $f(x) = 0$ has s roots equal to b, the equation $f'(x) = 0$ has $s-1$ roots equal to b; and so on.

From the foregoing proof we see that if $f(x)$ contains a factor $(x-a)^r$, then $f'(x)$ contains a factor $(x-a)^{r-1}$; and thus $f(x)$ and $f'(x)$ have a common factor $(x-a)^{r-1}$. Therefore if $f(x)$ and $f'(x)$ have no common factor, no factor in $f(x)$ will be repeated; hence *the equation $f(x) = 0$ has or has not equal roots, according as $f(x)$ and $f'(x)$ have or have not a common factor involving x.*

596. It follows that in order to obtain the equal roots of the equation $f(x) = 0$, *we must first find the highest common factor of $f(x)$ and $f'(x)$, and then placing it equal to zero, solve the resulting equation.*

Ex. Solve the equation $x^4 - 11x^3 + 44x^2 - 76x + 48 = 0$, which has equal roots.

Here $\quad f(x) = x^4 - 11x^3 + 44x^2 - 76x + 48,$

$$f'(x) = 4x^3 - 33x^2 + 88x - 76;$$

and by the ordinary rule we find that the highest common factor of $f(x)$ and $f'(x)$ is $x-2$; hence $(x-2)^2$ is a factor of $f(x)$; and

$$f(x) = (x-2)^2(x^2 - 7x + 12)$$

$$= (x-2)^2(x-3)(x-4);$$

thus the roots are 2, 2, 3, 4.

LOCATION OF THE ROOTS.

597. *If the variable x changes continuously from a to b the function $f(x)$ will change continuously from $f(a)$ to $f(b)$.*

Let c and $c+h$ be any two values of x lying between a and b. We have

$$f(c+h)-f(c) = hf'(c) + \frac{h^2}{\underline{|2}}f''(c) + \cdots + \frac{h^n}{\underline{|n}}f^n(c);$$

and by taking h small enough, the difference between $f(c+h)$ and $f(c)$ can be made as small as we please; hence to a small change in the variable x there corresponds a small change in the function $f(x)$, and therefore as x changes gradually from a to b, the function $f(x)$ changes gradually from $f(a)$ to $f(b)$.

598. It is important to notice that we have not proved that $f(x)$ always increases from $f(a)$ to $f(b)$, or decreases from $f(a)$ to $f(b)$, but that it passes from one value to the other without any sudden change; sometimes it may be increasing and at other times it may be decreasing.

599. *If $f(a)$ and $f(b)$ are of contrary signs then one root of the equation $f(x) = 0$ must lie between a and b.*

As x changes gradually from a to b, the function $f(x)$ changes gradually from $f(a)$ to $f(b)$, and therefore must pass through all intermediate values; but since $f(a)$ and $f(b)$ have contrary signs the value zero must lie between them; that is, $f(x) = 0$ for some value of x between a and b.

It does not follow that $f(x) = 0$ has *only one* root between a and b; neither does it follow that if $f(a)$ and $f(b)$ have the *same* sign $f(x) = 0$ has no root between a and b.

600. *Every equation of an odd degree has at least one real root whose sign is opposite to that of its last term.*

In the function $f(x)$ substitute for x the values $+\infty$, 0, $-\infty$, successively, then

$$f(+\infty) = +\infty, \quad f(0) = p_n, \quad f(-\infty) = -\infty.$$

If p_n is positive, then $f(x) = 0$ has a root lying between 0 and $-\infty$, and if p_n is negative $f(x) = 0$ has a root lying between 0 and $+\infty$.

601. Every equation which is of an even degree and has its last term negative has at least two real roots, one positive and one negative.

For in this case
$$f(+\infty) = +\infty, \quad f(0) = p_n, \quad f(-\infty) = +\infty;$$
but p_n is negative; hence $f(x) = 0$ has a root lying between 0 and $+\infty$, and a root lying between 0 and $-\infty$.

602. If the expressions $f(a)$ and $f(b)$ have contrary signs, an odd number of roots of $f(x) = 0$ will lie between a and b; and if $f(a)$ and $f(b)$ have the same sign, either no root or an even number of roots will lie between a and b.

Suppose that a is greater than b, and that $c, d, e, \cdots k$ represent all the roots of $f(x) = 0$, which lie between a and b. Let $\phi(x)$ be the quotient when $f(x)$ is divided by the product $(x-c)(x-d)(x-e)\cdots(x-k)$; then
$$f(x) = (x-c)(x-d)(x-e)\cdots(x-k)\phi(x).$$
Hence $f(a) = (a-c)(a-d)(a-e)\cdots(a-k)\phi(a)$.
$$f(b) = (b-c)(b-d)(b-e)\cdots(b-k)\phi(b).$$

Now $\phi(a)$ and $\phi(b)$ must be of the same sign, for otherwise a root of the equation $\phi(x) = 0$, and therefore of $f(x) = 0$, would lie between a and b [Art. 599], which is contrary to the hypothesis. Hence if $f(a)$ and $f(b)$ have contrary signs, the expressions
$$(a-c)(a-d)(a-e)\cdots(a-k),$$
$$(b-c)(b-d)(b-e)\cdots(b-k)$$
must have contrary signs. Also the factors in the first expressions are all positive, and the factors in the second are all negative; hence the number of factors must be odd, that is, the number of roots $c, d, e, \cdots k$ must be odd.

Similarly if $f(a)$ and $f(b)$ have the same sign the number of factors must be even. In this case the given condition is satisfied if $c, d, e, \ldots k$ are all greater than a, or less than b; thus it does not necessarily follow that $f(x)=0$ has a root between a and b.

EXAMPLES XLVIII. f.

1. Find the successive derived functions of $2x^4 - x^3 - 2x^2 + 5x - 1$.

Solve the following equations which have equal roots:

2. $x^4 - 9x^2 + 4x + 12 = 0$.   3. $x^4 - 6x^3 + 12x^2 - 10x + 3 = 0$.
4. $x^5 - 13x^4 + 67x^3 - 171x^2 + 216x - 108 = 0$.
5. $x^5 - x^3 + 4x^2 - 3x + 2 = 0$.
6. $8x^4 + 4x^3 - 18x^2 + 11x - 2 = 0$.

7. Show that the equation $10x^3 - 17x^2 + x + 6 = 0$ has a root between 0 and -1.

8. Show that the equation $x^4 - 5x^3 + 3x^2 + 35x - 70 = 0$ has a root between 2 and 3, and one between -2 and -3.

9. Show that the equation $x^4 - 12x^2 + 12x - 3 = 0$ has a root between -3 and -4, and another between 2 and 3.

10. Show that $x^5 + 5x^4 - 20x^2 - 19x - 2 = 0$ has a root between 2 and 3, and a root between -4 and -5.

STURM'S THEOREM AND METHOD.

603. In 1829, Sturm, a Swiss mathematician, discovered a method of determining completely the number and situation of the real roots of an equation.

604. Let $f(x)$ be an equation from which the equal roots have been removed, and let $f_1(x)$ be the first derived function. Now divide $f(x)$ by $f_1(x)$, and denote the remainder *with its signs changed* by $f_2(x)$. Divide $f_1(x)$ by $f_2(x)$ and continue the operation, which is that of finding the H.C.F. of $f(x)$ and $f_1(x)$, except that the signs in every remainder are changed before it is used as a divisor, until a remainder is obtained independent of x; the signs in this remainder must also be changed. No other changes of sign are allowed.

THEORY OF EQUATIONS. 477

The expressions $f(x)$, $f_1(x)$, $f_2(x), \cdots f_n(x)$ are called *Sturm's Functions*.

Let $Q_1, Q_2, \cdots Q_{n-1}$ denote the successive quotients obtained; then the steps in the operation may be represented as follows:

$$f(x) = Q_1 f_1(x) - f_2(x),$$
$$f_1(x) = Q_2 f_2(x) - f_3(x),$$
$$f_2(x) = Q_3 f_3(x) - f_4(x),$$
$$\cdots \cdots \cdots \cdots$$
$$f_{n-2}(x) = Q_{n-1} f_{n-1}(x) - f_n(x).$$

From these equalities we obtain the following:

(1) **Two consecutive functions cannot vanish for the same value of x.**

For if they could, all the succeeding functions would vanish, including $f_n(x)$, which is impossible, as it is independent of x.

(2) **When any function except the first vanishes for a particular value of x, the two adjacent functions have opposite signs.**

Thus in $f_2(x) = Q f_3(x) - f_4(x)$ if $f_3(x) = 0$, we have

$$f_2(x) = -f_4(x).$$

We may now state **Sturm's Theorem.**

If in Sturm's Functions we substitute for x any particular value a and note the number of variations of sign; then assign to x a greater value b, and again note the number of variations of sign; the number of variations lost is equal to the number of real roots of $f(x)$ which lie between a and b.

(1) Let c be a value of x which makes some function *except the first* vanish; for example, $f_r(x)$, so that $f_r(c) = 0$. Now when $x = c$, $f_{r-1}(x)$, and $f_{r+1}(x)$ have contrary signs, and thus just before $x = c$ and also just after $x = c$, the three functions $f_{r-1}(x)$, $f_r(x)$, $f_{r+1}(x)$ have one permanence of sign and one variation of sign, hence no change occurs in the

number of variations when x passes through a value which makes a function except $f(x)$ vanish.

(2) Let c be a root of the equation $f(x)=0$ so that $f(c)=0$. Let h be any positive quantity.

Now $\quad f(c+h)=f(c)+hf'(c)+\dfrac{h^2}{\lfloor 2}f''(c)+\cdots,\quad$ [Art. 594.]

and as c is a root of the equation $f(x) = 0$, $f(c) = 0$, hence

$$f(c+h) = hf'(c) + \dfrac{h^2}{\lfloor 2}f''(c) + \cdots.$$

If h be taken very small, we may disregard the terms containing its higher powers and obtain

$$f(c+h) = hf'(c),$$

and as h is a positive quantity, $f(c+h)$ and $f'(c)$ have the same sign. That is, the function just after x passes a root has the same sign as $f'(x)$ *at a root.*

In a like manner we may show that $f(c-h) = -hf'(c)$, or that the function just before x passes a root has a sign opposite to $f'(x)$ *at a root.* Thus as x increases, *Sturm's Functions* lose one variation of sign only when x passes through a root of the equation $f(x)=0$.

There is at no time a gain in the number of variations of sign, hence the theorem is established.

605. In determining the whole number of real roots of an equation $f(x) = 0$ we first substitute $-\infty$ and then $+\infty$ for x in Sturm's Functions: the difference in the number of variations of sign in the two cases gives the whole number of real roots.

By substituting $-\infty$ and 0 for x we may determine the number of negative real roots, and the substitution of $+\infty$ and 0 for x gives the number of positive real roots.

606. When $+\infty$ or $-\infty$ is substituted for x, the sign of any function will be that of the highest power of x in that function.

607. Let us determine the number and situation of the real roots of $x^3 + 3x^2 - 9x - 4 = 0$.

Here $f_1(x) = 3x^2 + 6x - 9$.

Now any *positive* factor may be introduced or removed in finding $f_2(x), f_3(x)$, etc., for the *sign* of the result is not affected by so doing; hence multiplying the original equation by 3, we have

$$3x^2 + 6x - 9 \overline{)3x^3 + 9x^2 - 27x - 12}(x+1$$
$$\underline{3x^3 + 6x^2 - 9x}$$
$$3x^2 - 18x - 12$$
$$\underline{3x^2 + 6x - 9}$$
$$3)-24x - 3$$
$$\overline{-8x - 1} \quad \therefore f_2(x) = 8x + 1.$$

$$8x + 1\overline{)24x^2 + 48x - 72}(3x + 5$$
$$\underline{24x^2 + 3x}$$
$$9)45x - 72$$
$$\overline{5x - 8}$$
$$8$$
$$\overline{40x - 64}$$
$$\underline{40x + 5}$$
$$-69 \quad \therefore f_3(x) = 69.$$

We therefore have

$$f(x) = x^3 + 3x^2 - 9x - 4,$$
$$f_1(x) = 3x^2 + 6x - 9,$$
$$f_2(x) = 8x + 1,$$
$$f_3(x) = 69.$$

	$f(x)$	$f_1(x)$	$f_2(x)$	$f_3(x)$	
When $x = -\infty$ we have	$-$	$+$	$-$	$+$	3 variations.
When $x = +\infty$ we have	$+$	$+$	$+$	$+$	no variations.
When $x = 0$ we have	$-$	$-$	$+$	$+$	1 variation.

Hence the number of real roots is 3, of which one is positive and two are negative.

To determine the situation of these roots we substitute different numbers, commencing at 0 and working in each direction, thus:

480 ALGEBRA.

	$f(x)$	$f_1(x)$	$f_2(x)$	$f_3(x)$	
$x=-\infty$	−	+	−	+	3 variations.
$x=-5$	−	+	−	+	3 variations.
$x=-4$	+	+	−	+	2 variations.
$x=-3$	+	±	−	+	2 variations.
$x=-2$	+	−	−	+	2 variations.
$x=-1$	+	−	−	+	2 variations.
$x=0$	−	−	+	+	1 variation.
$x=1$	−	±	+	+	1 variation.
$x=2$	−	+	+	+	1 variation.
$x=3$	+	+	+	+	no variation.
$x=\infty$	+	+	+	+	no variation.

Thus one root lies between -4 and -5; a second lies between 0 and -1, and the third lies between 2 and 3.

EXAMPLES XLVIII. g.

Determine the number and situation of the real roots of:

1. $x^3 - 4x^2 - 6x + 8 = 0.$
2. $2x^4 - 11x^2 + 8x - 16 = 0.$
3. $x^3 - 7x + 7 = 0.$
4. $x^4 - 4x^3 + 6x^2 - 12x + 2 = 0.$
5. $x^4 - 4x^3 + x^2 + 6x + 2 = 0.$
6. $x^4 - x^3 + x - 1 = 0.$
7. $x^3 - 9x^2 + 23x - 16 = 0.$
8. $x^5 + x^3 - 2x^2 + 2x - 1 = 0.$

GRAPHICAL REPRESENTATION OF FUNCTIONS.

COÖRDINATES.

608. Two lines drawn at right angles to each other as in Fig. 1 form a simple system of lines of reference. Their intersection, O, is called the *origin*. Distances from O along XX' are called *abscissas*; distances from XX' on a line parallel to YY' are called *ordinates*.

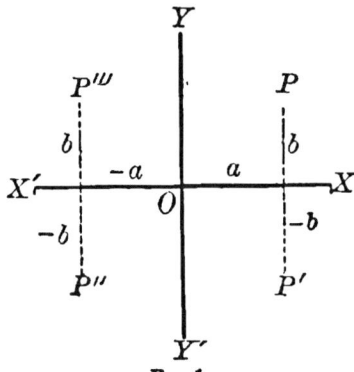

Fig. 1.

609. Abscissas measured to the *right* of the origin are considered *positive*, and to the *left*, *negative*. Ordinates measured above XX' are considered *positive*, and when taken *below* XX' are *negative*.

THEORY OF EQUATIONS.

610. The abscissa and ordinate of a point are called the *co-ordinates* of that point, and the lines XX' and YY' are called Co-ordinate Axes, Axis of X, and Axis of Y, or Axis of Abscissas, and Axis of Ordinates.

611. *Any* point in the plane can be given by means of these co-ordinates: thus the point P of Fig. 1 is located by measuring the distance a to the *right* of O on the axis of abscissas, and then taking a distance b vertically upwards.

Since a and b can be either positive or negative, a point P' is found by taking a positive and b negative; P'' is found by taking a negative and b negative; and P''' is found by taking a negative and b positive.

Abscissas and ordinates are generally represented by x and y respectively. Thus for the point P, $x = a$, and $y = b$; for P', $x = a$, and $y = -b$, etc.

612. Instead of writing "the point whose co-ordinates are 5 and 3," a more concise form is used: thus the point (5, 3) means that the point will be found by taking an abscissa of 5 units and an ordinate of 3.

Locate the points $(3, -2)$; $(5, 8)$; $(-4, 4)$; $(-8, -3)$.

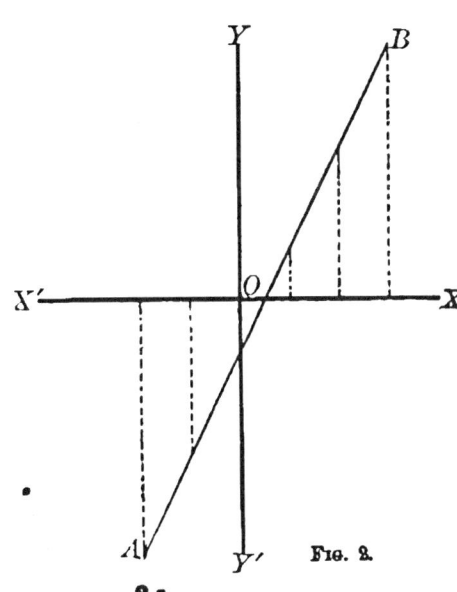

Fig. 2.

GRAPH OF A FUNCTION.

613. Let $f(x)$ be any rational integral function of x, and let us place it equal to y. If we give a series of numerical values to x we can obtain corresponding values for y. Now laying off the values of x as abscissas, and the corresponding values of y as ordinates, we have a series of points which lie upon a line called the *graph* of the given function.

Ex. 1. Construct the graph of $2x - 1$.

Let $2x - 1 = y$. Giving to x successive values, we obtain the corresponding values of y as follows:

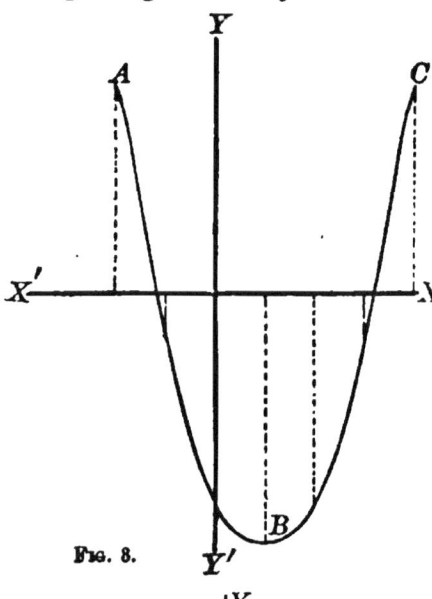

Fig. 8.

$x = -2, \ y = -5.$
$x = -1, \ y = -3.$
$x = 0, \ \ y = -1.$
$x = 1, \ \ y = 1.$
$x = 2, \ \ y = 3.$
$x = 3, \ \ y = 5.$

Locating these points as explained in Art. 611 and drawing a line through them, we have in this case the straight line AB, Fig. 2, as the *graph* required.

Ex. 2. Plot the equation $x^2 - 2x - 4$.

Putting $y = x^2 - 2x - 4$, we obtain the following values:

$x = -2, \ y = 4.$
$x = -1, \ y = -1.$
$x = 0, \ \ y = -4.$
$x = 1, \ \ y = -5.$
$x = 2, \ \ y = -4.$
$x = 3, \ \ y = -1.$
$x = 4, \ \ y = 4.$

The points lie on the line ABC, Fig. 3, which is the *graph* of the given equation.

Ex. 3. Plot the *graph* of $x^3 - 2x$.

Assuming $y = x^3 - 2x$, we have

$x = -2, \ y = -4.$
$x = -1, \ y = 1.$
$x = 0, \ \ y = 0.$
$x = 1, \ \ y = -1.$
$x = 2, \ \ y = 4.$

Fig. 4.

The line $ABCD$, Fig. 4, is the required *graph*.

By taking other values between those assumed, we may locate the curve with greater precision.

THEORY OF EQUATIONS.

614. In giving values to x it is evident that the substitution of a root gives $y=0$, that is, the ordinate, or distance from the Axis of Abscissas, is 0; hence where the graph cuts the Axis of X we have the location of a real root, and the graph will cross the Axis of X as many times as the equation has real and unequal roots. If the roots of the equation be imaginary, the curve will not touch the Axis of X.

EXAMPLES XLVIII. h.

Construct the graphs of the following functions:

1. $2x-3$.
2. x^2+2x+1.
3. x^2-5.
4. x^3+x-1.
5. x^3-2.
6. x^3-5x+3.
7. x^4-3x^2+3.
8. $x^3+3x^2+5x-12$.

SOLUTION OF HIGHER NUMERICAL EQUATIONS.

COMMENSURABLE ROOTS.

615. A real root which is either an integer or a fraction is said to be **commensurable**.

By Art. 582 we can transform an equation with fractional coefficients into another which has all of its coefficients integers, that of the first term being unity: hence we need consider only equations of this form. Such equations cannot have for a root a rational fraction in its lowest terms [Art. 575], therefore we have only to find the integral roots. By Art. 570 the last term of $f(x)$ is divisible by every integral root, therefore to find the commensurable roots of $f(x)$ it is only necessary *to find the integral divisors of the last term and determine by trial which of them are roots.*

616. Newton's Method. If the divisors are small numbers we may readily ascertain by actual substitution whether they are roots. In other cases we may use the method of Arts. 562 and 566 or the *Method of Divisors*, sometimes called *Newton's Method*.

Suppose a to be an integral root of the equation

$$x^n + p_1 x^{n-1} + p_2 x^{n-2} + \cdots + p_{n-1} x + p_n = 0.$$

By substitution we have
$$a^n + p_1 a^{n-1} + p_2 a^{n-2} + \cdots + p_{n-1} a + p_n = 0.$$
Transposing and dividing throughout by a, we obtain
$$\frac{p_n}{a} = -p_{n-1} - \cdots - p_2 a^{n-3} - p_1 a^{n-2} - a^{n-1},$$
in which it is evident that $\frac{p_n}{a}$ must be an integer. Denoting $\frac{p_n}{a}$ by Q and transposing $-p_{n-1}$,
$$Q + p_{n-1} = -\cdots - p_2 a^{n-3} - p_1 a^{n-2} - a^{n-1}.$$
Dividing again by a gives
$$\frac{Q + p_{n-1}}{a} = -\cdots - p_2 a^{n-4} - p_1 a^{n-3} - a^{n-2}.$$

Again, as before, the first member of the equation must be an integer. Denoting it by Q_2 and proceeding as before, we must after n divisions obtain a result
$$\frac{Q_{n-1} + p_1}{a} = -1.$$

Hence if a represents one of the integral divisors of the last term we have the following rule:

Divide the last term by a and add the coefficient of x to the quotient.

Divide this sum by a, and if the quotient is an integer add to it the coefficient of x^2.

Proceed in this manner, and if a is a root of the equation each quotient will be an integer and the last quotient will be -1.

The advantage of Newton's method is that the obtaining of a fractional quotient at any point of the division shows at once that the divisor is not a root of the equation.

Ex. Find the integral roots of $x^4 + 4x^3 - x^2 - 16x - 12 = 0$. By Descartes' Rule the equation cannot have more than one positive root, nor more than three negative roots.

The integral divisors of -12 are $\pm 1, \pm 2, \pm 3, \pm 4, \pm 6$. Substitution shows that -1 is a root, and that $+1$ is not a root.

THEORY OF EQUATIONS.

To ascertain if 2 is a root, arrange the work as follows:

$$\begin{array}{r|l} 1 + 4 - 1 - 16 - 12 & \underline{2} \\ -1 - 6 - 11 - 6 & \\ \hline -2 - 12 - 22 & \end{array}$$

Hence 2 is a root.

EXPLANATION. The first line contains the coefficients of the original equation, and the divisor 2. Dividing the *last* term, -12, by 2 gives a quotient -6; adding -16, the coefficient of x, gives -22. Dividing -22 by 2 gives -11; adding -1, the coefficient of x^2, gives -12. Dividing -12 by 2 gives -6; adding $+4$, the coefficient of x^3, gives -2, which divided by 2 gives a final quotient of -1, hence 2 is a root.

Since the equation can have no more than one positive root, we will only make trial of the remaining negative divisors, thus:

$$\begin{array}{r|l} 1 + 4 - 1 - 16 - 12 & \underline{-6} \\ + 2 & \\ \hline -14 & \end{array} \qquad \begin{array}{r|l} 1 + 4 - 1 - 16 - 12 & \underline{-4} \\ + 3 & \\ \hline -13 & \end{array}$$

Hence -6 is not a root.   Hence -4 is not a root.

$$\begin{array}{r|l} 1 + 4 - 1 - 16 - 12 & \underline{-3} \\ -1 - 1 + 4 + 4 & \\ \hline +3 + 3 - 12 & \end{array} \qquad \begin{array}{r|l} 1 + 4 - 1 - 16 - 12 & \underline{-2} \\ -1 - 2 + 5 + 6 & \\ \hline +2 + 4 - 10 & \end{array}$$

Hence -3 is a root.   Hence -2 is a root.

EXAMPLES XLVIII. 1.

Solve the following equations, which have one or more integral roots:

1. $x^3 - 9x^2 + 26x - 24 = 0$.
2. $x^3 - x - 2x^2 + 2 = 0$.
3. $2x^3 + 5x^2 - 11x + 4 = 0$.
4. $4x^3 - 20x^2 + 31x - 14 = 0$.
5. $x^3 - 2x^2 - 29x + 30 = 0$.
6. $x^3 - 8x^2 + 5x + 14 = 0$.
7. $x^4 - 2x^3 - 7x^2 + 8x + 12 = 0$.
8. $x^4 - 4x^3 - 14x^2 + 36x + 45 = 0$.
9. $x^4 - 3x^2 - 42x - 40 = 0$.
10. $x^4 - 10x^2 - 20x - 16 = 0$.
11. $x^4 + 8x^3 + 9x^2 - 8x - 10 = 0$.
12. $x^4 + 2x^3 - 7x^2 - 8x + 12 = 0$.
13. $x^4 - 3x^2 - 6x - 2 = 0$.
14. $x^4 - 2x^3 - 12x^2 + 10x + 3 = 0$.
15. $6x^4 - x^3 - 17x^2 + 16x - 4 = 0$.
16. $x^4 - 2x^3 - 13x^2 + 14x + 24 = 0$.
17. $x^4 + 4x^3 - 22x^2 - 4x + 21 = 0$.
18. $x^4 + 2x^3 - 7x^2 - 8x + 12 = 0$.
19. $x^4 - 6x^2 - 16x + 21 = 0$.
20. $x^4 + 4x^3 - x^2 - 16x - 12 = 0$.
21. $2x^4 - x^3 - 29x^2 + 34x + 24 = 0$.
22. $x^5 - 3x^4 - 5x^3 + 15x^2 + 4x - 12 = 0$.

617. The Cube Roots of Unity.

Suppose $x = \sqrt[3]{1}$; then $x^3 = 1$, or $x^3 - 1 = 0$;

that is $(x-1)(x^2 + x + 1) = 0$.

∴ either $x - 1 = 0$, or $x^2 + x + 1 = 0$;

whence $x = 1$, or $x = \dfrac{-1 \pm \sqrt{-3}}{2}$.

It may be shown by actual involution that each of these values when cubed is equal to unity. Thus unity has three cube roots,

$$1, \quad \frac{-1 + \sqrt{-3}}{2}, \quad \frac{-1 - \sqrt{-3}}{2};$$

two of which are imaginary expressions.

Let us denote these by a and b; then since they are the roots of the equation

$$x^2 + x + 1 = 0,$$

their product is equal to unity;

that is, $ab = 1$;

∴ $a^3 b = a^2$;

that is, $b = a^2$, since $a^3 = 1$.

Similarly we may show that $a = b^2$.

618. Since *each of the imaginary roots is the square of the other*, it is usual to denote the three cube roots of unity by $1, \omega, \omega^2$.*

Also ω satisfies the equation $x^2 + x + 1 = 0$;

∴ $1 + \omega + \omega^2 = 0$;

that is, *the sum of the three cube roots of unity is zero*.

Again $\omega \cdot \omega^2 = \omega^3 = 1$;

therefore (1) *the product of the two imaginary roots is unity*;

(2) *every integral power of ω^3 is unity*.

* The Greek letter Omega.

CARDAN'S METHOD FOR THE SOLUTION OF CUBIC EQUATIONS.

619. The general type of a cubic equation is
$$x^3 + Px^2 + Qx + R = 0,$$
but as explained in Art. 585 this equation can be reduced to the simpler form
$$x^3 + qx + r = 0,$$
which we shall take as the *standard form* of a cubic equation.

620. We proceed to solve the equation $x^3 + qx + r = 0$.
Let $x = y + z$; then
$$x^3 = y^3 + z^3 + 3yz(y+z) = y^3 + z^3 + 3yzx,$$
and the given equation becomes
$$y^3 + z^3 + (3yz + q)x + r = 0.$$

At present y, z are any two quantities subject to the condition that their sum is equal to one of the roots of the given equation; if we further suppose that they satisfy the equation $3yz + q = 0$, they are completely determinate. We thus obtain

$$y^3 + z^3 = -r \quad \cdots \cdots \quad (1),$$
$$z^3 = -\frac{q^3}{27 y^3} \quad \cdots \cdots \quad (2);$$

hence $\quad y^3 - \dfrac{q^3}{27 y^3} = -r,\ \text{or}\ y^6 + ry^3 = \dfrac{q^3}{27}.$

Solving this equation,
$$y^3 = -\frac{r}{2} + \sqrt{\frac{r^2}{4} + \frac{q^3}{27}} \quad \cdots \cdots \quad (3).$$

Substituting in (1), $\quad z^3 = -\dfrac{r}{2} - \sqrt{\dfrac{r^2}{4} + \dfrac{q^3}{27}} \quad \cdots \cdots \quad (4).$

We obtain the value of x from the relation $x = y + z$; thus

$$x = \left\{-\frac{r}{2} + \sqrt{\frac{r^2}{4} + \frac{q^3}{27}}\right\}^{\frac{1}{3}} + \left\{-\frac{r}{2} - \sqrt{\frac{r^2}{4} + \frac{q^3}{27}}\right\}^{\frac{1}{3}} \quad . \quad (5)$$

The above solution is generally known as *Cardan's Solution*, as it was first published by him in the *Ars Magna*, in 1545. Cardan obtained the solution from Tartaglia; but the solution of the cubic seems to have been due originally to Scipio Ferreo, about 1505.

In this solution we assume $x = y + z$, and from (2) find $z = -\dfrac{q}{3y}$, hence *to solve a cubic equation of the form*

$$x^3 + qx + r = 0$$

we substitute $y - \dfrac{q}{3y}$ *for* x.

Ex. Solve the equation $x^3 - 15x = 126$.

Put $y - \left(\dfrac{-15}{3y}\right)$ or $y + \dfrac{5}{y}$ for x, then

$$y^3 + 15y + \frac{75}{y} + \frac{125}{y^3} - 15y - \frac{75}{y} = 126,$$

or
$$y^3 + \frac{125}{y^3} = 126,$$

whence
$$y^6 - 126 y^3 = -125.$$
$$\therefore y^3 = 125,$$
$$\therefore y = 5.$$

But $x = y + \dfrac{5}{y} = 6.$

Dividing the given equation $x^3 - 15x - 126 = 0$ by $x - 6$, we obtain the depressed equation

$$x^2 + 6x + 21 = 0,$$

the roots of which are $-3 + 2\sqrt{-3}$, and $-3 - 2\sqrt{-3}$.

Thus the roots of $x^3 - 15x = 126$ are 6, $-3 + 2\sqrt{-3}$, and $-3 - 2\sqrt{-3}$.

BIQUADRATIC EQUATIONS.

621. We shall now give a brief discussion of some of the methods which are employed to obtain the general solution of a biquadratic equation. It will be found that in each of the methods we have first to solve an auxiliary cubic equation; and thus it will be seen that as in the case of the cubic, the general solution is not adapted for writing down the solution of a given numerical equation.

THEORY OF EQUATIONS.

622. The solution of a biquadratic equation was first obtained by Ferrari, a pupil of Cardan, as follows:

Denote the equation by
$$x^4 + 2px^3 + qx^2 + 2rx + s = 0;$$
add to each side $(ax + b)^2$, the quantities a and b being determined so as to make the left side a perfect square; then
$$x^4 + 2px^3 + (q + a^2)x^2 + 2(r + ab)x + s + b^2 = (ax + b)^2.$$
Suppose that the left side of the equation is equal to $(x^2 + px + k)^2$; then by comparing the coefficients, we have
$$p^2 + 2k = q + a^2, \ pk = r + ab, \ k^2 = s + b^2;$$
by eliminating a and b from these equations, we obtain
$$(pk - r)^2 = (2k + p^2 - q)(k^2 - s),$$
or $\quad 2k^3 - qk^2 + 2(pr - s)k + p^2s - qs - r^2 = 0.$

From this cubic equation one real value of k can always be found [Art. 600]; thus a and b are known. Also
$$(x^2 + px + k)^2 = (ax + b)^2;$$
$$\therefore x^2 + px + k = \pm (ax + b);$$
and the values of x are to be obtained from the two quadratics
$$x^2 + (p - a)x + (k - b) = 0,$$
and $\quad x^2 + (p + a)x + (k + b) = 0.$

Ex. Solve the equation
$$x^4 - 2x^3 - 5x^2 + 10x - 3 = 0.$$
Add $a^2x^2 + 2abx + b^2$ to each side of the equation, and assume
$$x^4 - 2x^3 + (a^2 - 5)x^2 + 2(ab + 5)x + b^2 - 3 = (x^2 - x + k)^2;$$
then by equating coefficients, we have
$$a^2 = 2k + 6, \ ab = -k - 5, \ b^2 = k^2 + 3;$$
$$\therefore (2k + 6)(k^2 + 3) = (k + 5)^2;$$
$$\therefore 2k^3 + 5k^2 - 4k - 7 = 0.$$
By trial, we find that $k = -1$; hence $a^2 = 4, \ b^2 = 4, \ ab = -4.$
But from the assumption, it follows that
$$(x^2 - x + k)^2 = (ax + b)^2.$$

Substituting the values of k, a and b, we have the two equations
$$x^2 - x - 1 = \pm (2x - 2);$$
that is $\quad x^2 - 3x + 1 = 0$, and $x^2 + x - 3 = 0$;

whence the roots are $\quad \dfrac{3 \pm \sqrt{5}}{2}, \dfrac{-1 \pm \sqrt{13}}{2}.$

623. The following solution was given by Descartes in 1637.

Suppose that the biquadratic equation is reduced to the form
$$x^4 + qx^2 + rx + s = 0;$$
assume $x^4 + qx^2 + rx + s = (x^2 + kx + l)(x^2 - kx + m)$;
then by equating coefficients, we have
$$l + m - k^2 = q, \quad k(m - l) = r, \quad lm = s.$$
From the first two of these equations, we obtain
$$2m = k^2 + q + \frac{r}{k}, \quad 2l = k^2 + q - \frac{r}{k};$$
hence substituting in the third equation,
$$(k^3 + qk + r)(k^3 + qk - r) = 4sk^2,$$
or $\quad k^6 + 2qk^4 + (q^2 - 4s)k^2 - r^2 = 0.$

This is a cubic in k^2 which always has one real positive solution [Art. 600]; thus when k^2 is known the values of l and m are determined, and the solution of the biquadratic is obtained by solving the two quadratics
$$x^2 + kx + l = 0, \text{ and } x^2 - kx + m = 0.$$

Ex. Solve the equation
$$x^4 - 2x^2 + 8x - 3 = 0.$$
Assume $\quad x^4 - 2x^2 + 8x - 3 = (x^2 + kx + l)(x^2 - kx + m);$
then by equating coefficients, we have
$$l + m - k^2 = -2, \quad k(m - l) = 8, \quad lm = -3;$$
whence we obtain $\quad (k^3 - 2k + 8)(k^3 - 2k - 8) = -12k^2,$
or $\quad k^6 - 4k^4 + 16k^2 - 64 = 0.$

THEORY OF EQUATIONS. 491

This equation is clearly satisfied when $k^2 - 4 = 0$, or $k = \pm 2$. It will be sufficient to consider one of the values of k; putting $k = 2$, we have

$$m + l = 2, \ m - l = 4; \text{ that is, } l = -1, \ m = 3.$$

Thus $x^4 - 2x^3 + 8x - 3 = (x^2 + 2x - 1)(x^2 - 2x + 3);$

hence $x^2 + 2x - 1 = 0$, and $x^2 - 2x + 3 = 0;$

and therefore the roots are $-1 \pm \sqrt{2}, 1 \pm \sqrt{-2}$.

624. The general algebraic solution of equations of a degree higher than the fourth has not been obtained, and Abel's demonstration of the impossibility of such a solution is generally accepted by mathematicians. If, however, the coefficients of an equation are numerical, the value of any real root may be found to any required degree of accuracy by the method of Art. 626.

EXAMPLES XLVIII. k.

Solve the following equations:

1. $x^3 - 18x = 35$.
2. $x^3 + 72x - 1720 = 0$.
3. $x^3 + 63x - 316 = 0$.
4. $x^3 + 21x + 342 = 0$.
5. $28x^3 - 9x^2 + 1 = 0$.
6. $x^3 - 15x^2 - 33x + 847 = 0$.
7. $2x^3 + 3x^2 + 3x + 1 = 0$.
8. $x^3 - 6x^2 + 3x - 18 = 0$.
9. $8x^3 - 36x + 27 = 0$.
10. $x^3 - 15x - 4 = 0$.
11. $x^4 + 8x^3 + 9x^2 - 8x - 10 = 0$.
12. $x^4 + 2x^3 - 7x^2 - 8x + 12 = 0$.
13. $x^4 - 3x^2 - 6x - 2 = 0$.
14. $x^4 - 2x^3 - 12x^2 + 10x + 3 = 0$.

INCOMMENSURABLE ROOTS.

625. The incommensurable roots of an equation cannot be found exactly. If, however, a sufficient number of the initial figures of the root have been found to distinguish it from the other roots we may carry the approximation to the exact value to any required degree of accuracy by a method first published in 1819 by W. G. Horner.

HORNER'S METHOD OF APPROXIMATION.

626. Let it be required to solve the equation
$$x^3 - 3x^2 - 2x + 5 = 0 \quad \ldots \quad (1).$$
By Sturm's Theorem there are 3 real roots and one of them lies between 1 and 2; we will find its value to four places of decimals, which will sufficiently illustrate the method.

Diminishing the roots of the equation by 1 [Arts. 583, 584], we have

$$
\begin{array}{rrrr|l}
1 & -3 & -2 & +5 & \underline{|1} \\
  & 1 & -2 & -4 & \\ \cline{2-4}
  & -2 & -4 & 1 & \\
  & 1 & -1 & & \\ \cline{2-3}
  & -1 & -5 & & \\
  & 1 & & & \\ \cline{2-2}
  & 0 & & &
\end{array}
$$

The transformed equation is
$$y^3 - 5y + 1 = 0 \quad \ldots \quad (2).$$
Equation (1) has a root between 1 and 2. The roots of equation (2) are each less by 1 than those of equation (1); hence equation (2) has a root between 0 and 1. This root being less than unity the higher powers of y are each less than y. Neglecting them, we obtain an approximate value of y from $-5y + 1 = 0$, or $y = .2$.

Diminishing the roots of (2), the first transformed equation, by .2, we have

$$
\begin{array}{rrrr|l}
1 & \pm 0 & -5 & +1 & \underline{|.2} \\
  & .2 & .04 & .992 & \\ \cline{2-4}
  & .2 & -4.96 & .008 & \\
  & .2 & .08 & & \\ \cline{2-3}
  & .4 & -4.88 & & \\
  & .2 & & & \\ \cline{2-2}
  & .6 & & &
\end{array}
$$

THEORY OF EQUATIONS.

The transformed equation is

$$z^3 + .6 z^2 - 4.88 z + .008 \quad \ldots \quad (3).$$

Equation (2) has a root between .2 and .3; the roots of equation (3) are less by .2 than those of equation (2); hence equation (3) has a root between 0 and .1. Neglecting in equation (3) the terms involving the higher powers, as was done in the case of the first transformed equation, we have

$$-4.88 z + .008 = 0, \text{ or } z = .001.$$

Diminishing the roots of (3), the second transformed equation, by .001, we have

```
1    +.6         -4.88          +.008        |.001
      .001        .000601       -.004879399
      ----        --------       ----------
      .601       -4.879399       .003120601
      .001        .000602
      ----        --------
      .602       -4.878797
      .001
      ----
      .603
```

The transformed equation is

$$v^3 + .603 v^2 - 4.878797 v + .003120601 \ldots (4).$$

Equation (3) has a root between .001 and .002; the roots of equation (4) are less than those of equation (3) by .001; therefore equation (4) has a root between 0 and .001. Neglecting the terms involving v^3 and v^2, and solving

$$-4.878797 v + .003120601 = 0,$$

we have $v = .0006$. Diminishing the roots of (4), the third transformed equation, by .0006, we find this to be the correct figure for the fourth decimal place; hence 1.2016 is the value, to the fourth decimal place, of the root which lies between 1 and 2.

Denoting the coefficients of the successive transformed equations by (A), (B), (C), etc., the work is more compactly arranged thus:

```
   1      − 3           − 2              + 5        [1.2016
          1             − 2             − 4
         ─────         ─────        (A) ─────
         − 2           − 4              1
          1           − 1             − .992
         ─────  (A)   ─────       (B)  ─────
         − 1          − 5              .008
          1             .04           − .004879399
    (A)  ─────         ─────      (C)  ─────────
          0           − 4.96           .003120601
          .2            .08
         ─────    (B) ─────
          .2          − 4.88
          .2            .000601
         ─────         ─────
          .4          − 4.879399
          .2            .000602
    (B)  ─────    (C) ─────
          .6          − 4.878797
          .001
         ─────
          .601
          .001
         ─────
          .602
          .001
         ─────
    (C)  .603
```

We may now state the rule for finding the approximate value of a positive incommensurable root by Horner's Method.

Rule. *Find the integral part of the root by Sturm's Theorem or method of Art. 602.*

Transform the equation into another, each of whose roots shall be less by the integral part of the root.

If in this transformed equation the coefficient of the first power of the unknown quantity and the last term have the same sign, another figure of the root should be found by the method used to find the integral part of the root. If, however, the signs of these terms are unlike, divide the latter by the former, and the first figure of the quotient will be, approximately, the next figure of the root.

Transform the last equation into another whose roots shall be less by this approximate figure of the root found by division, and proceed as before to find another figure of the root.

THEORY OF EQUATIONS.

627. It sometimes happens that the division of the last term of the first transformed equation by the coefficient of x in that equation gives a quotient greater than unity. In that case, as where the signs of these terms are alike, we obtain another figure of the root by the method used to obtain the integral part of the root.

628. If in any transformed equation *after the first* the signs of the last two terms are *the same*, the figure of the root used in making the transformation is too large and must be diminished until these terms have unlike signs.

629. If in any transformed equation the coefficient of the first power of the unknown quantity is zero, we may obtain the next figure of the root by using the *coefficient of the second power of the unknown quantity as a divisor and taking the square root of the result*.

630. *Negative incommensurable roots* may be found by transforming the equation into one whose roots shall be positive [Art. 580], and finding the corresponding root. This result with its sign changed will be the root required.

631. Any Root of Any Number. By Horner's Method we can find approximately any root of any number; for placing $\sqrt[n]{a}$ equal to x we have for solution the equation $x^n = a$, or $x^n - a = 0$.

EXAMPLES XLVIII. 1.

Compute the root which is situated between the given limits in the following equations:

1. $x^3 + 10 x^2 + 6 x - 120 = 0$; root between 2 and 3.
2. $x^3 - 2 x - 5 = 0$; root between 2 and 3.
3. $x^4 - 2 x^3 + 21 x - 23 = 0$; root between 1 and 2.
4. $x^3 + x - 1000 = 0$; root between 9 and 10.
5. $x^3 + x^2 + x - 100 = 0$; root between 4 and 5.
6. $2 x^3 + 3 x^2 - 4 x - 10 = 0$; root between 1 and 2.
7. $x^3 - 46 x^2 - 36 x + 18 = 0$; root between 0 and 1.

8. $x^3 + x - 3 = 0$; root between 1 and 2.

9. $x^3 + 2x - 20 = 0$; root between 2 and 3.

10. $x^3 + 10x^2 + 8x - 120 = 0$; root between 2 and 3.

11. $3x^3 + 5x - 40 = 0$; root between 2 and 3.

12. $x^4 - 12x^2 + 12x - 3 = 0$; root between -3 and -4.

13. $x^5 - 4x^4 + 7x^3 - 863 = 0$; root between 4 and 5.

Find the real roots of the following equations:

14. $x^3 - 3x - 1 = 0$.
16. $x^4 - 8x^3 + 12x^2 + 4x - 8 = 0$.

15. $x^3 - 22x - 24 = 0$.
17. $x^4 + x^3 + x^2 + 3x - 100 = 0$.

Find to four decimals, by Horner's Method, the value of the following:

18. $\sqrt[3]{11}$. 19. $\sqrt[3]{13}$. 20. $\sqrt[3]{5}$. 21. $\sqrt[3]{7}$.

MISCELLANEOUS EXAMPLES VII.

1. Simplify $b - \{b - (a+b) - [b - (b - \overline{a-b})] + 2a\}$.

2. Find the sum of
$a + b - 2(c+d)$, $b + c - 3(d+a)$ and $c + d - 4(a+b)$.

3. Multiply $\frac{1}{2}x + \frac{2}{3}y$ by $x - \frac{1}{3}y$.

4. If $x = 6$, $y = 4$, $z = 3$, find the value of $\sqrt[3]{2x + 3y + z}$.

5. Find the square of $2 - 3x + x^2$.

6. Solve $\dfrac{x+3}{x-1} + \dfrac{x-4}{x-6} = 2$.

7. Find the H.C.F. of $a^3 - 2a - 4$ and $a^3 - a^2 - 4$.

8. Simplify $\dfrac{2a}{a+b} + \dfrac{2b}{a-b} - \dfrac{a^2+b^2}{a^2-b^2}$.

9. Solve $\left.\begin{array}{l}\dfrac{3}{5}x + \dfrac{y}{4} = 13 \\ \dfrac{1}{3}x - \dfrac{y}{8} = 3\end{array}\right\}$.

10. Two digits, which form a number, change places when 18 is added to the number, and the sum of the two numbers thus formed is 44: find the digits.

11. If $a = 1$, $b = -2$, $c = 3$, $d = -4$, find the value of
$$\dfrac{a^2b^2 + b^2c + d(a-b)}{10a - (c+b)^2}.$$

MISCELLANEOUS EXAMPLES VII. 497

12. Subtract $-x^2 + y^2 - z^2$ from the sum of
$\frac{1}{3}x^2 + \frac{1}{4}y^2$, $\frac{1}{5}y^2 + \frac{1}{3}z^2$, and $\frac{1}{3}z^2 - \frac{1}{4}x^2$.

13. Write the cube of $x + 8y$.

14. Simplify $\dfrac{x^2 + xy}{x^2 + y^2} \times \dfrac{x^4 - y^4}{xy + y^2} \times \dfrac{y}{x}$.

15. Solve $\frac{3}{5}(2x - 7) - \frac{2}{3}(x - 8) = \dfrac{4x + 1}{15} + 4$.

16. Find the H.C.F. and L.C.M. of
$x^4 + x^3 + 2x - 4$ and $x^3 + 3x^2 - 4$.

17. Find the square root of $4a^4 + 9(1 - 2a) + 3a^2(7 - 4a)$.

18. Solve $\left.\begin{array}{l} y = \dfrac{x + a}{2} + \dfrac{b}{3} \\ x = \dfrac{y + b}{2} + \dfrac{a}{3} \end{array}\right\}$.

19. Simplify $\left(\dfrac{a}{x + a} - \dfrac{x}{x - a}\right) \div \dfrac{x^2 + a^2}{x^2 + ax}$.

20. When 1 is added to the numerator and denominator of a certain fraction the result is equal to $\frac{3}{2}$; and when 1 is subtracted from its numerator and denominator, the result is equal to 2: find the fraction.

21. Show that the sum of $12a + 6b - c$, $-7a - b + c$ and $a + b + 6c$, is six times the sum of $25a + 13b - 8c$, $-13a - 13b - c$, and $-11a + b + 10c$.

22. Divide $x^2 - xy + \frac{3}{16}y^2$ by $x - \frac{1}{4}y$.

23. Add together $18\left\{\dfrac{2x}{9} - \dfrac{1}{6}\left(\dfrac{2y}{3} + z\right)\right\}$,

$24\left(\dfrac{3x}{8} - \dfrac{2y - 3z}{12}\right)$, and $30\left\{\dfrac{7z}{15} - \dfrac{4}{5}(2x - y)\right\}$.

24. Find the factors of (i.) $10x^2 + 79x - 8$. (ii.) $729x^6 - y^6$.

25. Solve $\dfrac{2x - 1}{5} + \dfrac{5x + 3}{17} = 3 - \dfrac{4x - 118}{11}$.

26. Find the value of
$(5a - 3b)(a - b) - b\{3a - c(4a - b) - b^2(a + c)\}$,
when $a = 0$, $b = -1$, $c = \frac{1}{2}$.

27. Find the H.C.F. of $7x^3 - 10x^2 - 7x + 10$ and $2x^3 - x^2 - 2x + 1$.

28. Simplify $\dfrac{x^2 - 7xy + 12y^2}{x^2 + 5xy + 6y^2} \div \dfrac{x^2 - 5xy + 4y^2}{x^2 + xy - 2y^2}$.

2 K

29. Solve $\begin{aligned} 3abx + y &= 9b \\ 4abx + 3y &= 17b \end{aligned}$.

30. Find the two times between 7 and 8 o'clock when the hands of a watch are separated by 15 minutes.

31. If $a = 1$, $b = -2$, $c = 3$, $d = -4$, find the value of
$$\sqrt{d^2 - 4b} + a^2 - \sqrt{c^3 + b^3 + a + d}.$$

32. Multiply the product of $\frac{1}{4}x^2 - \frac{1}{2}xy + y^2$ and $\frac{1}{2}x + y$ by $x^3 - 8y^3$.

33. Simplify by removing brackets $a^4 - \{4a^3 - (6a^2 - 4a + 1)\}$
$- [-2 - \{a^4 - (-4a^3 - 6a^2 - 4a)\} - (8a - 1)]$.

34. Find the remainder when $5x^4 - 7x^3 + 3x^2 - x + 8$ is divided by $x - 4$.

35. Simplify $\dfrac{x^2 + y^2}{x^2 - xy} \times \dfrac{xy - y^2}{x^4 - y^4} \times \dfrac{x}{y}$.

36. Solve $\begin{aligned} \dfrac{x-11}{3} + y &= 18 \\ 2x + \dfrac{y-13}{4} &= 29 \end{aligned}$.

37. Find the square root of $4x^6 - 12x^4 + 28x^3 + 9x^2 - 42x + 49$.

38. Solve $.006x - .401 + .723x = -.005$.

39. Find the L.C.M. of $x^3 + y^3$, $3x^2 + 2xy - y^2$, and $x^3 - x^2y + xy^2$.

40. A bill of $12.50 is paid with quarters and half-dollars, and twice the number of half-dollars exceeds three times that of the quarters by 10: how many of each are used?

41. Simplify $(a+b+c)^2 - (a-b+c)^2 + (a+b-c)^2 - (-a+b+c)^2$.

42. Find the remainder when $a^4 - 3a^3b + 2a^2b^2 - b^4$ is divided by $a^2 - ab + 2b^2$.

43. If $a = 0$, $b = 1$, $c = -2$, $d = 3$, find the value of
$$(3abc - 2bcd)\sqrt[3]{abc - c^3bd + 3}.$$

44. Find an expression which will divide both $4x^2 + 3x - 10$ and $4x^3 + 7x^2 - 3x - 15$ without remainder.

45. Simplify $\dfrac{a + \dfrac{ab}{a-b}}{a^2 - \dfrac{2a^2b^2}{a^2+b^2}} \times \dfrac{\dfrac{1}{a^2} - \dfrac{1}{b^2}}{\dfrac{1}{a} - \dfrac{1}{b}}$.

46. Find the cube root of $8x^3 - 2x^2y + \dfrac{xy^2}{6} - \dfrac{y^3}{216}$.

47. Solve $\begin{aligned} 9x + 8y &= 43xy \\ 8x + 9y &= 42xy \end{aligned}$.

48. Simplify $\dfrac{3}{x-4} - \dfrac{2}{x-5} - \dfrac{x-7}{(x-2)(x-3)}$.

49. Find the L. C. M. of
$8x^3 + 38x^2 + 59x + 30$ and $6x^3 - 13x^2 - 13x + 30$.

50. A boy spent half of his money in one shop, one-third of the remainder in a second, and one-fifth of what he had left in a third. He had 20 cents at last: how much had he at first?

51. Find the remainder when $x^7 - 10x^6 + 8x^5 - 7x^3 + 3x - 11$ is divided by $x^2 - 5x + 4$.

52. Simplify $4\left\{a - \dfrac{3}{2}\left(b - \dfrac{4c}{3}\right)\right\}\left\{\dfrac{1}{2}(2a-b) + 2(b-c)\right\}$.

53. If $a = \frac{25}{16}$, $b = 1$, $c = \frac{3}{4}$, prove that
$$(a - \sqrt{b})(\sqrt{a} + b)\sqrt{a - b} = \dfrac{3c^4}{\sqrt{a - c^2}}.$$

54. Find the L. C. M. of $x^2 - 7x + 12$, $3x^2 - 6x - 9$, and $2x^2 - 6x - 8$.

55. Find the sum of the squares of $ax + by$, $bx - ay$, $ay + bx$, $by - ax$; and express the result in factors.

56. Solve $\dfrac{x}{6} + \dfrac{y}{4} = \dfrac{3x - 5z}{4} = \dfrac{z}{8} + \dfrac{7y}{16} = 1$.

57. Simplify $\dfrac{a^3 + b^3}{a^4 - b^4} - \dfrac{a+b}{a^2 - b^2} - \dfrac{1}{2}\left\{\dfrac{a-b}{a^2 + b^2} - \dfrac{1}{a-b}\right\}$.

58. Solve $x - \left(3x - \dfrac{2x+5}{10}\right) = \dfrac{1}{6}(2x + 67) + \dfrac{5}{3}\left(1 + \dfrac{x}{5}\right)$.

59. Add together the following fractions:
$$\dfrac{2}{x^2 + xy + y^2},\ \dfrac{-4x}{x^3 - y^3},\ \dfrac{x^2}{y^2(x-y)^2},\ \dfrac{-x^2}{x^3 y - y^4}.$$

60. A man agreed to work for 30 days, on condition that for every day's work he should receive $2.50, and that for every day's absence from work he should forfeit $1.50; at the end of the time he received $51: how many days did he work?

61. Divide $\dfrac{3x^5}{4} + 27 - \dfrac{43x^2}{4} - 4x^4 + \dfrac{77x^3}{8} - \dfrac{33x}{4}$ by $\dfrac{x^2}{2} + 3 - x$.

62. Find the value of
$$\dfrac{4y}{5}(y - x) - 35\left[\dfrac{3x - 4y}{5} - \dfrac{1}{10}\left\{3x - \dfrac{5}{7}(7x - 4y)\right\}\right]$$
when $x = -\frac{1}{2}$ and $y = 2$.

63. Simplify $\dfrac{10x-11}{3(x^2-1)} - \dfrac{10x-1}{3(x^2+x+1)} + \dfrac{x^2-2x+5}{(x^3-1)(x+1)}$.

64. Find the cube root of $\dfrac{a^3c^3}{b^3}x^6 - \dfrac{3a^2c}{b}x^5 + \dfrac{3ab}{c}x^4 - \dfrac{b^3}{c^3}x^3$.

65. Solve $\dfrac{4x-17}{x-4} + \dfrac{10x-13}{2x-3} = \dfrac{8x-30}{2x-7} + \dfrac{5x-4}{x-1}$.

66. Find the factors of (i.) x^3+5x^2+x+5. (ii.) $x^2-2xy-323y^2$.

67. Solve $\left. \begin{array}{l} \frac{1}{3}(x+y)+2z=21 \\ 3x-\frac{1}{2}(y+z)=65 \\ x+\frac{1}{2}(x+y-z)=38 \end{array} \right\}$.

68. Simplify $\dfrac{x+2y}{\frac{2}{7}x-y} \cdot \dfrac{3x^2+63xy+70y^2}{2x^2+3xy-35y^2}$.

69. Find the square root of $-(3b-2c-2a)^3\{2(a+c)-3b\}$.

70. The united ages of a man and his wife are six times the united ages of their children. Two years ago their united ages were ten times the united ages of their children, and six years hence their united ages will be three times the united ages of the children: how many children have they?

71. Find the sum of
$x^2-3xy-\tfrac{2}{3}y^2$, $2y^2-\tfrac{2}{3}y^3+z^2$, $xy-\tfrac{1}{3}y^2+y^3$, and $2xy-\tfrac{1}{3}y^3$.

72. From $\{(a+b)(a-x)-(a-b)(b-x)\}$ subtract $(a+b)^2-2bx$.

73. If $a=5$, $b=4$, $c=3$, find the value of
$\sqrt[3]{6abc+(b+c)^3+(c+a)^3+(a+b)^3-(a+b+c)^3}$.

74. Find the factors of
(i.) $3x^3+6x^2-189x$. (ii.) $a^2+2ab+b^2+a+b$.

75. Solve $\left. \begin{array}{l} px=qy \\ (p+q)x-(q-p)y=r \end{array} \right\}$.

76. Simplify $\dfrac{x+\frac{y}{2}}{2x^2+xy+\frac{y^2}{2}} - \dfrac{x^2-\frac{y^2}{2}}{4\left(x^3-\frac{y^3}{8}\right)}$.

77. Solve $\dfrac{x-7}{x+7} + \dfrac{1}{2(x+7)} = \dfrac{2x-15}{2x-6}$.

78. Reduce $\dfrac{x^4-x^2-2x+2}{2x^3-x-1}$ to its lowest terms.

MISCELLANEOUS EXAMPLES VII.

79. Add together the fractions:
$$\frac{1}{2x^2 - 4x + 2}, \quad \frac{1}{2x^2 + 4x + 2}, \quad \text{and} \quad \frac{1}{1 - x^2}.$$

80. A number consists of three digits, the right-hand one being zero. If the left-hand and middle digits be interchanged, the number is diminished by 180; if the left-hand digit be halved, and the middle and right-hand digit be interchanged, the number is diminished by 336: find the number.

81. Divide $1 - 5x + \frac{152}{15}x^3 - \frac{108}{225}x^4 - \frac{28}{9}x^5$ by $1 - x - \frac{14}{15}x^2$.

82. If $p = 1$, $q = \frac{1}{2}$, find the value of
$$\frac{(p^2 + q^2) - (p - q)\sqrt{p^2 + 2pq + q^2}}{2p + q - \{p - (q - p)\}}.$$

83. Multiply $\dfrac{3x^3}{2} - 5x^2 + \dfrac{x}{4} + 9$ by $\dfrac{x^2}{2} - x + 3$.

84. Find the L. C. M. of
$$(a^2b - 2ab^2)^2, \quad 2a^2 - 3ab - 2b^2, \quad \text{and} \quad 2(2a^2 + ab)^2.$$

85. Solve $\dfrac{2x + 3}{x + 1} = \dfrac{4x + 5}{4x + 4} + \dfrac{3x + 3}{3x + 1}$.

86. Reduce $\dfrac{5x^3 - 14x^2 + 16}{3x^3 - 2x^2 + 16x - 48}$ to its lowest terms.

87. Find the square root of
$$4a^4 + 9\left(a^2 + \frac{1}{a^2}\right) + 12a(a^2 + 1) + 18.$$

88. Solve $\left.\begin{array}{l}\dfrac{x}{2a} + \dfrac{y}{3b} = a + b \\ \dfrac{3x}{a} - \dfrac{2y}{b} = 6(b - a)\end{array}\right\}.$

89. Multiply
$$3x + 4y + \frac{11xy}{x - \frac{3}{4}y} \quad \text{by} \quad 10x - 3y - \frac{11xy}{\frac{x}{4} + y}.$$

90. A bag contained ten dollars in dimes and quarters; after 17 dimes and 6 quarters were taken out, three times as many quarters as dimes were left: find the number of each coin.

91. Find the value of
$$5(a - b) - 2\{3a - (a + b)\} + 7\{(a - 2b) - (5a - 2b)\},$$
when $a = -\frac{1}{9}b$.

92. Divide $3x^4 - 5x^3 + 7x^2 - 11x - 13$ by $3x - 2$.

93. Find the L. C. M. of

$15(p^3 + q^3)$, $5(p^2 - pq + q^2)$, $4(p^2 + pq + q^2)$, and $6(p^2 - q^2)$.

94. Resolve into factors:

   (i.) $a^3 - 8b^{15}$ (ii.) $-x^2 + 2x - 1 + x^4$.

95. Solve $\dfrac{x+a}{x+b} = \dfrac{x+3a}{x+a+b}$

96. Simplify

   (i.) $\dfrac{35 a^2b^2c^2 - 49 b^3c^3}{65 a^5bc - 91 a^3b^2c^2}$.   (ii.) $\dfrac{y^4 - 7y^3 + 8y^2 - 12y}{2y^2 - 2y - 60}$.

97. Solve $\left.\begin{array}{l} 7x - 9y + 4z = 16 \\ \dfrac{x+y}{3} = \dfrac{x+y+z}{2} \\ 2x - 3y + 4z - 5 = 0 \end{array}\right\}$.

98. Simplify $\dfrac{y^2 - \dfrac{2y}{y-1}}{y^2 - \dfrac{2y}{y+1}} \div \left(\dfrac{y^2 - 5y - 6}{y^2 - 6y + 5} \times \dfrac{y-2}{y+2}\right)$.

99. Find the square root of

$$\dfrac{4a^2 - 12ab - 6bc + 4ac + 9b^2 + c^2}{4a^2 + 9c^2 - 12ac}$$

100. An express leaves New York at 3 P.M. and reaches Albany at 6; the ordinary train leaves Albany at 1.30 P.M. and arrives at New York at 6. If both trains travel uniformly, find the time when they will meet.

101. Solve (i.) $.6x + .75x - .1\dot{6} = x - .58\dot{3}x + 5$.

   (ii.) $\dfrac{37}{x^2 - 5x + 6} + \dfrac{4}{x-2} = \dfrac{7}{3-x}$.

102. Simplify (i.) $\dfrac{a+x}{a^2 + x + ax^2} + \dfrac{a-x}{a^2 - ax + x^2} + \dfrac{2x^3}{a^4 + a^2x^2 + x^4}$.

   (ii.) $(1+x)^2 \div \left\{1 + \dfrac{x}{1 - x + \dfrac{x}{1 + x + x^2}}\right\}$.

103. Find the square root of

$$a^6 + \dfrac{1}{a^6} - 6\left(a^4 + \dfrac{1}{a^4}\right) + 15\left(a^2 + \dfrac{1}{a^2}\right) - 20;$$

also the cube root of the result.

104. Divide $1 - 2x$ by $1 + 3x$ to 4 terms.

MISCELLANEOUS EXAMPLES VII.

105. I bought a horse and carriage for $450; I sold the horse at a gain of 5 per cent, and the carriage at a gain of 20 per cent, making on the whole a gain of 10 per cent: find the original cost of the horse.

106. Find the divisor when $(4a^2 + 7ab + 5b^2)^2$ is the dividend, $8(a + 2b)^2$ the quotient, and $b^2(9a + 11b)^2$ the remainder.

107. Solve (i.) $5x(x - 3) = 2(x - 7)$.

(ii.) $\dfrac{1}{(x-1)(x-2)} + 6 = \dfrac{3}{x-2} + \dfrac{2}{x-1}$.

108. If $x = a + b + \dfrac{(a-b)^2}{4(a+b)}$, and $y = \dfrac{a+b}{4} + \dfrac{ab}{a+b}$,

prove that $(x - a)^2 - (y - b)^2 = b^2$.

109. Find the square root of

$$49x^4 + \dfrac{1051 x^2}{25} - \dfrac{14 x^3}{5} - \dfrac{6x}{5} + 9.$$

110. Solve $\dfrac{a+x}{a^2 + ax + x^2} + \dfrac{a-x}{a^2 - ax + x^2} = \dfrac{3a}{x(a^4 + a^2 x^2 + x^4)}$.

111. Subtract $\dfrac{x+3}{x^2 + x - 12}$ from $\dfrac{x+4}{x^2 - x - 12}$,

and divide the difference by $1 + \dfrac{2(x^2 - 12)}{x^2 + 7x + 12}$.

112. Find the H. C. F. and L. C. M. of

$2x^2 + (6a - 10b)x - 30ab$ and $3x^2 - (9a + 15b)x + 45ab$.

113. Solve (i.) $2cx^2 - abx + 2abd = 4cdx$.

(ii.) $\dfrac{x}{2(x+3)} - 2\dfrac{5}{24} = \dfrac{x^2}{x^2 - 9} - \dfrac{8x - 1}{4(x-3)}$.

114. If $a = 1$, $b = 2$, $c = 3$, $d = 4$, find the value of

$\dfrac{a^b + b^c + c^d}{b^a + c^b + d^c + (a+b)(b+c)} + 3(a^a + b^b + c^c)\left(\dfrac{1}{a} + \dfrac{1}{b} + \dfrac{1}{c}\right)$.

115. I rode one-third of a journey at 10 miles an hour, one-third more at 9, and the rest at 8 miles an hour; if I had ridden half the journey at 10, and the other half at 8 miles per hour, I should have been half a minute longer on the way: what distance did I ride?

116. The product of two factors is $(3x + 2y)^3 - (2x + 3y)^3$, and one of the factors is $x - y$: find the other factor.

117. If $a + b = 1$, prove that $(a^2 - b^2)^2 = a^3 + b^3 - ab$.

118. Resolve into factors:

(i.) $x^3 + y^3 + 3xy(x+y)$. (ii.) $m^3 - n^3 - m(m^2 - n^2) + n(m-n)^2$.

ALGEBRA.

119. Solve (i.) $\left.\begin{array}{l}x^3 - y^3 = 28 \\ x^2 + xy + y^2 = 7\end{array}\right\}.$ (ii.) $\left.\begin{array}{l}x^2 - 6xy + 11y^2 = 9 \\ x - 3y = 1\end{array}\right\}.$

120. Find the square root of
$$(a-b)^4 - 2(a^2 + b^2)(a-b)^2 + 2(a^4 + b^4).$$

121. Simplify the fractions

(i.) $\dfrac{1}{a^2 - \dfrac{a^3 - 1}{a + \dfrac{1}{a+1}}}.$ (ii.) $\dfrac{\left(1 + \dfrac{1}{x}\right) \times \left(1 - \dfrac{1}{x}\right)^2}{x - \dfrac{1}{x}}.$

122. Find the H. C. F. of
$$a^2b + b^2c - abc - ab^2 \text{ and } ax^2 + ab - a^2 - bx^2.$$

123. A village had two-thirds of its voters Republicans: in an election 25 refused to vote, and 60 went over to the Democrats; the voters were now equal. How many voters were there altogether?

124. Solve (i.) $\dfrac{x^2}{a+b} + (a-b) = \dfrac{2ax}{a+b}.$

(ii.) $\dfrac{3}{x} + \dfrac{2}{y} = 6\left(\dfrac{1}{y} - \dfrac{1}{2x}\right) = 2.$

125. Simplify (i.) $\left(1 + \dfrac{y^2 + z^2 - x^2}{2yz}\right) \div \left(1 - \dfrac{x^2 + y^2 - z^2}{2xy}\right).$

(ii.) $\dfrac{(x+1)^3 - (x-1)^3}{(x+1)^4 - (x-1)^4}.$

126. Divide
$$x^4 + (a-1)x^3 - (2a+1)x^2 + (a^2 + 4a - 5)x + 3a + 6$$
by $x^2 - 3x + a + 2.$

127. Resolve into factors:

(i.) $x^2 + 5xy - 24y^2 + x - 3y.$ (ii.) $x^3 - \dfrac{4}{x}.$

128. Find the square root of $p^2 - 3q$ to three terms.

129. Solve (i.) $\dfrac{x-5}{x-6} - \dfrac{x-6}{x-7} = \dfrac{x-1}{x-2} - \dfrac{x-2}{x-3}.$

(ii.) $ax + 1 = by + 1 = ay + bx.$

130. Find the H. C. F. of
$$3x^2 + (4a - 2b)x - 2ab + a^2 \text{ and } x^3 + (2a - b)x^2 - (2ab - a^2)x - a^2b.$$

131. Simplify

(i.) $\dfrac{(x^a)^3}{x^{b+c}} \times \dfrac{(x^b)^3}{x^{c+a}} \times \dfrac{(x^c)^3}{x^{a+b}}.$ (ii.) $x^{\frac{1}{2}} y^{\frac{1}{3}} \left(\dfrac{y^{\frac{1}{4}}}{x^{\frac{1}{5}}}\right)^2 \div \dfrac{y^{-\frac{1}{4}}}{x^{\frac{1}{4}}}.$

MISCELLANEOUS EXAMPLES VII.

132. At a cricket match the contractor provided dinner for 27 persons, and fixed the price so as to gain $12\frac{1}{2}$ per cent upon his outlay. Six of the cricketers being absent, the remaining 21 paid the fixed price for their dinner, and the contractor lost $\$3$: what was the charge for the dinner?

133. Prove that $x(y+2) + \dfrac{x}{y} + \dfrac{y}{x}$ is equal to a, if
$$x = \frac{y}{y+1} \text{ and } y = \frac{a-2}{2}.$$

134. Find the cube root of
$$x^3 - 12x^2 + 54x - 112 + \frac{108}{x} - \frac{48}{x^2} + \frac{8}{x^3}.$$

135. Find the H.C.F. and L.C.M. of
$$x^3 + 2ax^2 + a^2x + 2a^3 \text{ and } x^3 - 2ax^2 + a^2x - 2a^3.$$

136. Simplify

(i.) $42\left\{\dfrac{4x-3y}{6} - \dfrac{3x-4y}{7}\right\} - 56\left\{\dfrac{3x-2y}{7} - \dfrac{2x-3y}{8}\right\}.$

(ii.) $\dfrac{4b+a}{3b+a} + \dfrac{a-4b}{a-3b} + \dfrac{a^2-3b^2}{a^2-9b^2}.$

137. Resolve $4a^2(x^3 + 18ab^2) - (32a^6 + 9b^2x^3)$ into four factors.

138. Solve (i.) $5\sqrt{3x-1} = \sqrt{75x-29}.$

(ii.) $\dfrac{xy}{x+y} = 70, \quad \dfrac{xz}{x+z} = 84, \quad \dfrac{yz}{y+z} = 140.$

139. Show that the difference between
$$\frac{x}{x-a} + \frac{x}{x-b} + \frac{x}{x-c} \text{ and } \frac{a}{x-a} + \frac{b}{x-b} + \frac{c}{x-c}$$
is the same whatever value x may have.

140. Multiply $x^{\frac{3}{2}} + 2y^{\frac{3}{2}} + 3z^{\frac{3}{2}}$ by $x^{\frac{3}{2}} - 2y^{\frac{3}{2}} - 3z^{\frac{3}{2}}.$

141. Walking $4\frac{1}{4}$ miles an hour, I start $1\frac{1}{2}$ hours after a friend whose pace is 3 miles an hour; how long shall I be in overtaking him?

142. Express in the simplest form

(i.) $(8^{\frac{2}{3}} + 4^{\frac{3}{2}}) \times 16^{-\frac{3}{4}}.$

(ii.) $\dfrac{\left\{9^n \cdot 3^2 \times \dfrac{1}{3^{-n}}\right\} - 27^n}{3^{3n} \times 9}.$

143. Find the square root of
$$\frac{x}{y} + \frac{y}{x} + 3 - 2\sqrt{\frac{x}{y}} - 2\sqrt{\frac{y}{x}}.$$

144. Simplify

(i.) $\left(\dfrac{x}{x-1} - \dfrac{1}{x+1}\right) \cdot \dfrac{x^3-1}{x^6+1} \cdot \dfrac{(x-1)^2(x+1)^2 + x^2}{x^4+x^2+1}$

(ii.) $\left\{\dfrac{a^4-y^4}{a^2-2ay+y^2} + \dfrac{a^2+ay}{a-y}\right\} \times \left\{\dfrac{a^5-a^3y^2}{a^3+y^3} + \dfrac{a^4-2a^3y+a^2y^2}{a^2-ay+y^2}\right\}.$

145. Find the value of

(i.) $\sqrt{8} + \sqrt{50} - \sqrt{18} + \sqrt{48}.$ (ii.) $\sqrt{35 + 14\sqrt{6}}.$

146. Solve (i.) $\dfrac{x-b}{x-a} - \dfrac{x-a}{x-b} = \dfrac{2(a-b)}{x-(a+b)}.$

(ii.) $\begin{rcases} 2x + 3y = 1\frac{1}{2} \\ 4x^2 + 9xy + 9y^2 = 11 \end{rcases}$

147. Show that

$$\dfrac{(a+b)^3 - c^3}{(a+b) - c} + \dfrac{(b+c)^3 - a^3}{b+c-a} + \dfrac{(c+a)^3 - b^3}{c+a-b}$$

is equal to $2(a+b+c)^2 + a^2 + b^2 + c^2.$

148. Divide $a - x + 4a^{\frac{1}{4}}x^{\frac{3}{4}} - 4a^{\frac{3}{4}}x^{\frac{1}{4}}$

by $a^{\frac{1}{2}} + 2a^{\frac{1}{4}}x^{\frac{1}{4}} - x^{\frac{1}{2}}.$

149. Find the square root of

$(a-1)^4 + 2(a^4+1) - 2(a^2+1)(a-1)^2.$

150. How much are pears a gross when 12 more for a dollar lowers the price five cents a dozen?

151. Show that if a number of two digits is six times the sum of its digits, the number formed by interchanging the digits is five times their sum.

152. Find the value of

$$\dfrac{1}{(a-b)(b-c)} - \dfrac{1}{(b-c)(a-c)} - \dfrac{1}{(c-a)(b-a)}.$$

153. Multiply

$3 + 5x - \dfrac{12 + 41x + 36x^2}{4+7x}$ by $5 - 2x + \dfrac{26x - 8x^2 - 14}{3-4x}.$

154. If $x - \dfrac{1}{x} = 1$, prove that $x^2 + \dfrac{1}{x^2} = 3$, and $x^3 - \dfrac{1}{x^3} = 4.$

155. Solve (i.) $\dfrac{3x}{11} + \dfrac{23}{x+4} = \dfrac{1}{3}(x+5).$

(ii.) $\begin{rcases} 2x^2 - 3y^2 = 23 \\ 2xy - 3y^2 = 3 \end{rcases}.$

MISCELLANEOUS EXAMPLES VII.

156. Simplify (i.) $1\frac{1}{3}\sqrt{20} - 3\sqrt{5} - \sqrt{\frac{1}{5}}$. (ii.) $\dfrac{\sqrt{x}}{y^{-\frac{1}{3}}}\left(\dfrac{\sqrt[4]{y}}{x^{\frac{1}{6}}}\right) \div \dfrac{y^{-\frac{1}{4}}}{x^{\frac{1}{4}}}$.

157. Find the H.C.F. of $(p^2 - 1)x^2 + (3p - 1)x - p(p - 1)$ and
$p(p + 1)x^2 - (p^2 - 2p - 1)x - (p - 1)$.

158. Reduce to its simplest form

$$\dfrac{ax + \dfrac{a}{y}}{x - \dfrac{1}{y}} \times \dfrac{x^2 + \dfrac{1}{y^2}}{bx^2 - \dfrac{b}{y^2}} \times \dfrac{\frac{1}{3}(xy - 1)^2}{\frac{1}{3}(x^4y^4 - 1)}.$$

159. Find the square root of
(i.) $1 - 2^{2n+1} + 4^{2n}$.   (ii.) $9^n - 2 \cdot 6^n + 4^n$.

160. A clock gains 4 minutes a day. What time should it indicate at 6 o'clock in the morning in order that it may be right at 7.15 P.M. on the same day?

161. If $x = 2 + \sqrt{2}$, find the value of $x^2 + \dfrac{4}{x^2}$.

162. Solve (i.) $\dfrac{\sqrt{x} + a}{\sqrt{x} - b} = \dfrac{\sqrt{x} - a}{\sqrt{x}}$.   (ii.) $\dfrac{\sqrt{1+x} + \sqrt{1-x}}{\sqrt{1+x} - \sqrt{1-x}} = 3$.

163. Simplify $\dfrac{a^2}{(b-a)(c-a)} + \dfrac{b^2}{(c-b)(a-b)} + \dfrac{c^2}{(a-c)(b-c)}$.

164. Find the product of $\frac{1}{2}\sqrt{5}$, $\frac{1}{2}\sqrt[3]{2}$, $\sqrt[6]{80}$, $\sqrt[3]{5}$, and divide

$\dfrac{8 - 4\sqrt{5}}{\sqrt{5} + 1}$ by $\dfrac{3\sqrt{5} - 7}{5 + \sqrt{7}}$.

165. Resolve $9x^6y^2 - 576y^2 - 4x^8 + 256x^2$ into six factors.

166. Simplify (i.) $\dfrac{1 - \dfrac{a^2}{(x+a)^2}}{(x+a)(x-a)} \div \dfrac{x(x+2a)}{(x^2 - a^2)(x+a)^2}$.

(ii.) $\dfrac{6x^2y^2}{m+n} \div \left[\dfrac{3(m-n)x}{7(r+s)} \div \left\{\dfrac{4(r-s)}{21xy^2} + \dfrac{r^2 - s^2}{4(m^2 - n^2)}\right\}\right]$.

167. Simplify (i.) $(a^{1+\frac{q}{p}})^{\frac{p}{p+q}} \div \sqrt[p]{\dfrac{a^{2p}}{(a^{-1})^{-p}}}$.

(ii.) $\sqrt{14 - \sqrt{132}}$.

168. Find the H.C.F. and L.C.M. of
$20x^4 + x^2 - 1$, $25x^4 + 5x^3 - x - 1$, $25x^4 - 10x^2 + 1$.

169. Solve (i.) $a + x + \sqrt{2ax + x^2} = b$.

(ii.) $x + 9\frac{1}{4} + \dfrac{1}{\dfrac{x}{7} + \dfrac{11}{8}} = 8$.

170. The price of photographs is raised $3 per dozen, and customers consequently receive ten less than before for $5: what were the prices charged?

171. If $\left(a + \dfrac{1}{a}\right)^2 = 3$, prove that $a^3 + \dfrac{1}{a^3} = 0$.

172. Find the value of

$$\frac{x+2a}{2b-x} + \frac{x-2a}{2b+x} + \frac{4ab}{x^2-4b^2} \quad \text{when} \quad x = \frac{ab}{a+b}.$$

173. Reduce to fractions in their lowest terms

(i.) $\left(\dfrac{1}{x} + \dfrac{1}{y} + \dfrac{1}{z}\right) \div \left(\dfrac{x+y+z}{x^2+y^2+z^2-xy-yz-zx} - \dfrac{1}{x+y+z}\right) + 1$.

(ii.) $\left(1 - \dfrac{56}{x+4} + \dfrac{42}{x+3}\right)\left(1 + \dfrac{56}{x-4} - \dfrac{42}{x-3}\right)$.

174. Express as a whole number

$$(27)^{\frac{2}{3}} + (16)^{\frac{3}{4}} - \frac{2}{(8)^{-\frac{2}{3}}} + \frac{\sqrt[4]{2}}{(4)^{-\frac{7}{8}}}.$$

175. Simplify

(i.) $\dfrac{n}{1-x^n} + \dfrac{n}{1-x^{-n}}$.   (ii.) $\sqrt[4]{97 - 56\sqrt{3}}$.

176. Solve (i.) $\dfrac{x-4a}{x-3a} + \dfrac{x-5a}{x-4a} = \dfrac{x+6a}{x-4a} + \dfrac{x+5a}{x-3a}$.

(ii.) $\left.\begin{array}{l} 3x^2 + xy + 3y^2 = 8\frac{1}{4} \\ 8x^2 - 3xy + 8y^2 = 17\frac{3}{4} \end{array}\right\}$.

177. Find the square root of $\dfrac{a^2x^2 + 2ab^2x^3 + b^4x^4}{a^{2m} + 2a^m x^n + x^{2n}}$.

178. Simplify

(i.) $\dfrac{b}{\sqrt{a}} \times \sqrt[3]{ac} \times \dfrac{\sqrt[4]{c^3}}{\sqrt{b}} \times \dfrac{\sqrt{b^{-1}}}{a^{-\frac{1}{6}}}$.   (ii.) $\left\{\dfrac{(9^{n+\frac{1}{4}}) \times \sqrt{3 \times 3^n}}{3\sqrt{3^{-n}}}\right\}^{\frac{1}{n}}$.

179. A boat's crew can row 8 miles an hour in still water: what is the speed of a river's current if it take them 2 hours and 40 minutes to row 8 miles up and 8 miles down?

MISCELLANEOUS EXAMPLES VII.

180. If $a = x^2 - yz$, $b = y^2 - zx$, $c = z^2 - xy$, prove that
$$a^2 - bc = x(ax + by + cz).$$

181. Find a quantity such that when it is subtracted from each of the quantities a, b, c, the remainders are in continued proportion.

182. Simplify (i.) $\left(x + y - \dfrac{1}{x + y - \frac{xy}{x+y}}\right) \times \dfrac{x^3 - y^3}{x^2 - y^2}$.

(ii.) $\dfrac{2(7x - 4)}{6x^2 - 7x + 2} + \dfrac{x - 10}{6x^2 - x - 2} - \dfrac{2(4x - 1)}{4x^2 - 1}$.

183. Find the sixth root of
$$729 - 2916 x^2 + 4860 x^4 - 4320 x^6 + 2160 x^8 - 576 x^{10} + 64 x^{12}.$$

184. Simplify

(i.) $\dfrac{1}{x + \sqrt{x^2 - 1}} + \dfrac{1}{x - \sqrt{x^2 - 1}}$.

(ii.) $\sqrt[4]{16} + \sqrt[3]{81} - \sqrt[3]{-512} + \sqrt[5]{192} - 7\sqrt[5]{9}$.

185. Solve (i.) $\dfrac{5}{6 - \dfrac{5}{6 - \dfrac{5}{6 - x}}} = x.$

(ii.) $\left. \begin{array}{l} x^2 y^2 + 192 = 28\, xy \\ x + y = 8 \end{array} \right\}.$

186. Simplify
$$\dfrac{b - c}{a^2 - (b - c)^2} + \dfrac{c - a}{b^2 - (c - a)^2} + \dfrac{a - b}{c^2 - (a - b)^2}.$$

187. Solve (i.) $x - 15\tfrac{3}{4} + \dfrac{5}{x - 15\tfrac{3}{4}} = 6.$

(ii.) $2(x + y^{-1}) = 3(x^{-1} - y) = 4.$

188. If $xy = ab(a + b)$ and $x^2 - xy + y^2 = a^3 + b^3$, prove that
$$\left(\dfrac{x}{a} - \dfrac{y}{b}\right)\left(\dfrac{x}{b} - \dfrac{y}{a}\right) = 0.$$

189. Find the H. C. F. of
$$(2a^2 - 3a - 2)x^2 + (a^2 + 7a + 2)x - a^2 - 2a$$
and $(4a^2 + 4a + 1)x^2 - (4a^2 + 2a)x + a^2.$

190. Multiply $\sqrt{2x} + \sqrt{2(2x - 1)} - \dfrac{1}{\sqrt{2x}}$

by $\dfrac{1}{\sqrt{2x}} + \sqrt{2(2x - 1)} - \sqrt{2x}.$

191. Divide $a^4b^2 + b^4c^2 + c^4a^2 - a^2b^4 - b^2c^4 - c^2a^4$
by $a^2b + b^2c + c^2a - ab^2 - bc^2 - ca^2$.

192. Simplify

(i.) $\dfrac{7}{2(x+1)} - \dfrac{1}{6(x-1)} - \dfrac{10x-1}{3(x^2+x+1)}$.

(ii.) $\left\{ \dfrac{\sqrt{x+a}}{\sqrt{x-a}} - \dfrac{\sqrt{x-a}}{\sqrt{x+a}} \right\} \times \dfrac{\sqrt{x^3-a^3}}{\sqrt{(x+a)^2 - ax}}$.

193. If p be the difference between any quantity and its reciprocal, q the difference between the square of the same quantity and the square of its reciprocal, show that
$$p^2(p^2 + 4) = q^2.$$

194. A man started for a walk when the hands of his watch were coincident between three and four o'clock. When he finished, the hands were again coincident between five and six o'clock. What was the time when he started, and how long did he walk?

195. If n be an integer, show that $7^{2n+1} + 1$ is always divisible by 8.

196. Simplify $\dfrac{\left(p + \dfrac{1}{q}\right)^p \left(p - \dfrac{1}{q}\right)^q}{\left(q + \dfrac{1}{p}\right)^p \left(q - \dfrac{1}{p}\right)^q}$.

197. Find the value of

(i.) $\dfrac{7 + 3\sqrt{5}}{7 - 3\sqrt{5}} + \dfrac{7 - 3\sqrt{5}}{7 + 3\sqrt{5}}$.

(ii.) $\dfrac{\sqrt{1+x} + \sqrt{1-x}}{\sqrt{1+x} - \sqrt{1-x}}$ when $x = \dfrac{2b}{b^2+1}$.

198. If $a + b + c + d = 2s$, prove that
$$4(ab+cd)^2 - (a^2+b^2-c^2-d^2)^2 = 16(s-a)(s-b)(s-c)(s-d).$$

199. A man buys a number of articles for $5, and sells for $5.40 all but two at 5 cents apiece more than they cost; how many did he buy?

200. Find the square root of
$$2(81x^4 + y^4) - 2(9x^2 + y^2)(3x - y)^2 + (3x - y)^4.$$

201. If $x:a :: y:b :: z:c$, prove that
$$(bc + ca + ab)^2(x^2 + y^2 + z^2) = (bz + cx + ay)^2(a^2 + b^2 + c^2).$$

202. If a man save $10 more than he did the previous year, and if he saved $20 the first year, in how many years will his savings amount to $1700?

MISCELLANEOUS EXAMPLES VII.

203. Given that 4 is a root of the quadratic $x^2 - 5x + q = 0$, find the value of q and the other root.

204. A person having 7 miles to walk increases his speed one mile an hour after the first mile, and finds that he is half an hour less on the road than he would have been had he not altered his rate. How long did he take?

205. If $(a+b+c)x = (-a+b+c)y = (a-b+c)z = (a+b-c)w$,

show that $\quad \dfrac{1}{y} + \dfrac{1}{z} + \dfrac{1}{w} = \dfrac{1}{x}$.

206. Find a Geometrical Progression of which the sum of the first two terms is $2\frac{2}{3}$, and the sum to infinity $4\frac{1}{5}$.

207. Simplify $\quad \dfrac{\left(1+\dfrac{x}{y}\right)^m \left(1-\dfrac{y}{x}\right)^n}{\left(1+\dfrac{y}{x}\right)^n \left(1-\dfrac{x}{y}\right)^m}$.

208. A man has a stable containing 10 stalls; in how many ways could he stable 5 horses?

209. In boring a well 400 feet deep the cost is 27 cents for the first foot and an additional cent for each subsequent foot; what is the cost of boring the last foot, and also of boring the entire well?

210. If a, b are the roots of $x^2 + px + q = 0$, show that p, q are the roots of the equation
$$x^2 + (a+b-ab)x - ab(a+b) = 0.$$

211. Extract the square root of $7 - 30\sqrt{-2}$.

212. If $\dfrac{x+z}{y} = \dfrac{z}{x} = \dfrac{x}{z-y}$, determine the ratios $x : y : z$

213. If a, b, c are in H. P., show that
$$\left(\dfrac{3}{a} + \dfrac{3}{b} - \dfrac{2}{c}\right)\left(\dfrac{3}{c} + \dfrac{3}{b} - \dfrac{2}{a}\right) + \dfrac{9}{b^2} = \dfrac{25}{ac}.$$

214. Find the number of permutations which can be made from all the letters of the words

(i.) *Consequences*, (ii.) *Acarnania*.

215. Expand by the Binomial Theorem $(2a - 3x)^5$; and find the numerically greatest term in the expansion of $(1+x)^n$, if $x = \frac{3}{5}$, and $n = 7$.

216. When $x = \dfrac{\sqrt{3}}{4}$, find the value of
$$\dfrac{1+2x}{1+\sqrt{1+2x}} + \dfrac{1-2x}{1-\sqrt{1-2x}}.$$

217. Simplify $\dfrac{x^2 - bc}{(a-b)(a-c)} + \dfrac{x^2 - ca}{(b-c)(b-a)} + \dfrac{x^2 - ab}{(c-a)(c-b)}$

218. Solve the equations
  (i.) $(x^2 - 5x + 2)^2 = x^2 - 5x + 22.$
  (ii.) $\left(x^2 + \dfrac{1}{x^2}\right)^2 + 4\left(x^2 + \dfrac{1}{x^2}\right) = 12.$

219. Prove that
$$(y-z)^3 + (x-y)^3 + 3(x-y)(x-z)(y-z) = (x-z)^3.$$

220. Out of 16 consonants and 5 vowels, how many words can be formed each containing 4 consonants and 2 vowels?

221. If $b - a$ is a harmonic mean between $c - a$ and $d - a$, show that $d - c$ is a harmonic mean between $a - c$ and $b - c$.

222. In how many ways may 2 red balls, 3 black, 1 white, 2 blue be selected from 4 red, 6 black, 2 white, and 5 blue; and in how many ways may they be arranged?

223. The sum of a certain number of terms of an arithmetical series is 36, and the first and last of these terms are 1 and 11 respectively: find the number of terms, and the common difference of the series.

224. Expand by the Binomial Theorem
  (i.) $\left(2 - \dfrac{3a}{4}\right)^5.$ (ii.) $(1 - \tfrac{2}{3}x)^{\frac{3}{2}}$ to five terms.

225. Solve
$$x^2 - xy + x = 35.$$
$$xy - y^2 + y = 15.$$

226. Simplify $\dfrac{2\sqrt{10}}{3\sqrt{27}} \times \dfrac{15\sqrt{21}}{4\sqrt{15}} \div \dfrac{5\sqrt{14}}{7\sqrt{48}}$ and find the value of $\dfrac{1}{3\sqrt{5} - 6}$, given that $\sqrt{5} = 2.236.$

227. By the Binomial Theorem find the cube root of 128 to six places of decimals.

228. There are 9 books, of which 4 are Greek, 3 are Latin, and 2 are English; in how many ways could a selection be made so as to include at least one of each language?

229. Simplify
  (i.) $\dfrac{\sqrt{45x^3} - \sqrt{80x^3} + \sqrt{5a^2x}}{a - x}.$
  (ii.) $\left\{\dfrac{x^{\frac{1}{2}} + x^{-\frac{1}{2}}}{x^2 - x + 1} - \dfrac{x^{\frac{1}{2}} - x^{-\frac{1}{2}}}{x^2 + x + 1}\right\} \div \left\{\dfrac{x^{\frac{1}{2}} + 2x^{-\frac{1}{2}}}{x^3 - 1} - \dfrac{x^{\frac{1}{2}} - 2x^{-\frac{1}{2}}}{x^3 + 1}\right\}$

230. (i.) Form the quadratic equation whose roots are $5 \pm \sqrt{6}$.

(ii.) If the roots of $x^2 - px + q = 0$ are two consecutive integers, prove that $p^2 - 4q - 1 = 0$.

231. Solve $x^3 + 1 = 81(y^2 + y)$; $x^2 + x = 9(y^3 + 1)$.

232. Find $\log_{16} 128$, $\log_4 \sqrt{128}$, $\log_2 \tfrac{1}{4}$; and having given
$$\log 2 = .3010300 \text{ and } \log 3 = .4771213,$$
find the logarithm of .00001728.

233. A and B start from the same point, B five days after A; A travels 1 mile the first day, 2 miles the second, 3 miles the third, and so on; B travels 12 miles a day. When will they be together? Explain the double answer.

234. Solve the equations:

(i.) $2^x = 8^{y+1}$, $9^y = 3^{x-9}$.

(ii.) $z^x = y^{2x}$, $2^x = 2 \times 4^z$, $x + y + z = 16$.

235. The sum of the first 10 terms of an arithmetical series is to the sum of the first 5 terms as 13 is to 4; find the ratio of the first term to the common difference.

236. Find the greatest term in the expansion of $(1-x)^{-\frac{4}{3}}$ when $x = \tfrac{12}{13}$.

237. Five gentlemen and one lady wish to enter an omnibus in which there are only three vacant places; in how many ways can these places be occupied (1) when there is no restriction, (2) when one of the places is to be occupied by the lady?

238. (i.) Given $\log 2 = .301030$, $\log 3 = .477121$, and $\log 7 = .845098$, find the logarithms of .005, 6.3, and $(\tfrac{49}{216})^{\frac{1}{3}}$.

(ii.) Find x from the equation $18^{3-4x} = (54\sqrt{2})^{3x-2}$.

239. If P and Q vary respectively as $y^{\frac{1}{2}}$ and $y^{\frac{1}{3}}$ when z is constant, and as $z^{\frac{1}{2}}$ and $z^{\frac{1}{3}}$ when y is constant, and if $x = P + Q$, find the equation between x, y, z; it being known that when $y = z = 64$, $x = 12$; and that when $y = 4z = 16$, $x = 2$.

240. Simplify
$$\log \tfrac{138}{85} + 2 \log \tfrac{12}{7} - \log \tfrac{148}{90} + \log \tfrac{77}{171}.$$

241. If the number of permutations of n things 4 at a time is to the number of combinations of $2n$ things 3 at a time as 22 to 3, find n.

242. If $\dfrac{1}{a} + \dfrac{1}{c} = \dfrac{1}{2b-a} + \dfrac{1}{2b-c}$, prove that $2b$ is either the arithmetic mean between $2a$ and $2c$, or the harmonic mean between a and c.

243. If ^nC_r denote the number of combinations of n things taken r together, prove that

$$^{n+2}C_{r+1} = {^nC_{r+1}} + {^nC_{r-1}} + (2 \times {^nC_r}).$$

244. Find (i.) the characteristic of log 54 to base 3.

(ii.) $\log_{10}(.0125)^{\frac{1}{3}}$. (iii.) the number of digits in 3^{45}.
Given $\log_{10} 2 = .30103$, $\log_{10} 3 = .47712$.

245. Write the $(r+1)$th term of $(2ax^2 - x^3)^{\frac{1}{3}}$, and express it in its simplest form.

246. At a meeting of a debating society there were 9 speakers; 5 spoke for the affirmative, and 4 for the negative. In how many ways could the speeches have been made, if a member of the affirmative always spoke first, and the speeches were alternately for the affirmative and the negative?

247. Form the quadratic equation whose roots are

$$a + b + \sqrt{a^2 + b^2} \text{ and } \frac{2ab}{a + b + \sqrt{a^2 + b^2}}.$$

248. A point moves with a speed which is different in different miles, but invariable in the same mile, and its speed in any mile varies inversely as the number of miles travelled before it commences this mile. If the second mile be described in 2 hours, find the time taken to describe the nth mile.

249. Solve the equations:

(i.) $x^2(b-c) + ax(c-a) + a^2(a-b) = 0$.
(ii.) $(x^2 - px + p^2)(qx + pq + p^2) = qx^3 + p^2q^2 + p^4$.

250. Prove by the Binomial Theorem that $\sqrt{8}$ is the value, to infinity, of

$$1 + \frac{3}{4} + \frac{3 \cdot 5}{4 \cdot 8} + \frac{3 \cdot 5 \cdot 7}{4 \cdot 8 \cdot 12} + \cdots.$$

251. A and B run a mile race. In the first heat A gives B a start of 11 yards and beats him by 57 seconds; in the second heat A gives B a start of 81 seconds and is beaten by 88 yards: in what time could each run a mile?

252. A train, an hour after starting, meets with an accident which detains it an hour, after which it proceeds at three-fifths of its former rate and arrives 3 hours after time; but had the accident happened 50 miles farther on the line, it would have arrived $1\frac{1}{2}$ hours sooner: find the length of the journey.

MISCELLANEOUS EXAMPLES VII.

253. Expand for 4 terms by the method of Undetermined Coefficients $\dfrac{2}{3x^2 - 2x^3}$.

254. A body of men were formed into a hollow square, three deep, when it was observed that with the addition of 25 to their number a solid square might be formed, of which the number of men in each side would be greater by 22 than the square root of the number of men in each side of the hollow square: required the number of men.

255. Expand into a series $\sqrt{a^2 + b^2}$.

256. Solve the equation $\sqrt{2x-1} + \sqrt{3x-2} = \sqrt{4x-3} + \sqrt{5x-4}$.

257. Separate $\dfrac{7x^2 + 22x + 5}{(x+3)(x^2-1)}$ into partial fractions.

258. Solve the equation $x^4 - 5x^2 - 6x - 5 = 0$.

259. Find the generating function of
$$1 + 5x + 7x^2 + 17x^3 + 31x^4 + \cdots.$$

260. Separate $\dfrac{3x - x^2 - 4}{(x^2+1)(x^2-x-2)}$ into partial fractions.

261. Solve the equation $x^4 + 3x^2 = 16x + 60$.

262. Express $\tfrac{733}{555}$ as a continued fraction and find the fourth convergent.

263. What is the sum of n terms of the series $1, 8, 27, 64, \ldots$?

264. The sum of 6 terms of the series $1 - x\sqrt{-1} - x^2 + \cdots$ is equal to 65 times the sum to infinity; find x.

265. Convert $2\sqrt{5}$ into a continued fraction.

266. Find limits of the error when $\tfrac{919}{191}$ is taken for $\sqrt{23}$.

267. Sum to infinity the series
$$3 - x - 2x^2 - 16x^3 - 28x^4 - 676x^5 + \cdots.$$

268. Find value of $\dfrac{1}{3+}\dfrac{1}{2+}\dfrac{1}{1+}\dfrac{1}{3+}\dfrac{1}{2+}\dfrac{1}{1+}\cdots$.

269. Solve, by Cardan's Method, the equation
$$x^3 - 30x + 133 = 0.$$

270. Solve the equation $x^3 - 13x^2 + 15x + 189 = 0$, having given that one root exceeds another root by 2.

271. Solve the equation $x^4 - 4x^2 + 8x + 35 = 0$, having given that one root is $2 + \sqrt{-3}$.

272. Sum to infinity the series
$$4 - 9x + 16x^2 - 25x^3 + 36x^4 - 49x^5 + \ldots.$$

273. Solve the equation $x^4 - 12x^3 + 47x^2 - 72x + 36 = 0$.

274. Solve the equation $\begin{vmatrix} 4x & 6x+2 & 8x+1 \\ 6x+2 & 9x+3 & 12x \\ 8x+1 & 12x & 16x+2 \end{vmatrix} = 0.$

275. Solve the equation $2x^5 + x^4 + x + 2 = 12x^3 + 12x^2$.

276. Given $\log 2 = .30103$, and $\log 3 = .47712$, solve the equations:

(i.) $6^x = 1^y \div 6^{-x}$. (ii.) $\sqrt{5^x} + \sqrt{5^{-x}} = \frac{26}{15}$.

277. Find the value of $1 + \cfrac{1}{3+} \cfrac{1}{2+} \cfrac{1}{3+} \cfrac{1}{2+} \cdots$ in the form of a quadratic surd.

278. Separate $\dfrac{x^3 + 7x^2 - x - 8}{(x^2 + x + 1)(x^2 - 3x - 1)}$ into partial fractions.

279. Find the general term when $\dfrac{3x-8}{x^2-4x-4}$ is expanded in ascending powers of x.

280. Solve the equations:

(i.) $\dfrac{\sqrt[3]{x+y} - \sqrt[3]{x-y}}{\sqrt[3]{x+y} + \sqrt[3]{x-y}} = 3, \ x^2 + y^2 = 65$.

(ii.) $\sqrt{2x^2+1} + \sqrt{2x^2-1} = \dfrac{2}{\sqrt{3-2x^2}}$.

(iii.) $x^5 - 4x^4 - 10x^3 + 40x^2 + 9x - 36 = 0$.

CHAPTER XLIX.

Graphical Representation of Functions.

632. Definition. Any expression which involves a variable quantity x, and whose value is dependent on that of x, is called a **function of x**.

Thus, $3x+8$, $2x^2+6x-7$, $x^4-3x^3+x^2-9$ are functions of x of the first, second, and fourth degree respectively.

633. The symbol $f(x)$ is often used to denote briefly a function of x. If $y=f(x)$, by substituting a succession of numerical values for x, we can obtain a corresponding succession of values for y which stands for the value of the function. Hence, in this connection it is sometimes convenient to call x the **independent variable**, and y the **dependent variable**.

634. Consider the function $x(9-x^2)$, and let its value be represented by y.

Then, when $\quad x=0, \quad y=0\times 9 = 0,$
when $\quad x=1, \quad y=1\times 8 = 8,$
when $\quad x=2, \quad y=2\times 5 = 10,$
when $\quad x=3, \quad y=3\times 0 = 0,$
when $\quad x=4, \quad y=4\times(-7) = -28,$
and so on.

By proceeding in this way we can find as many values of the function as we please. But we are often not so much concerned with the actual values which a function assumes for different values of the variable as with *the way in which the value of the function changes*. These variations can be very conveniently represented by a **graphical** method which we shall now explain.

635. Two straight lines XOX', YOY' are taken intersecting at right angles in O, thus dividing the plane of the paper into four spaces XOY, YOX', $X'OY'$, $Y'OX$, which are known as the first, second, third, and fourth quadrants respectively.

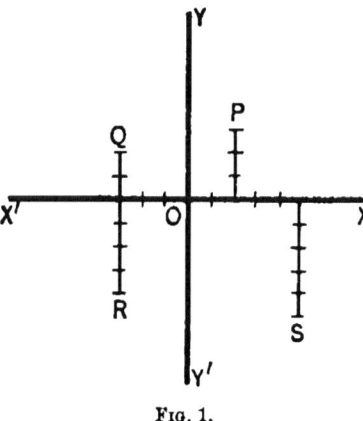

Fig. 1.

The lines XOX', YOY' are usually drawn horizontally and vertically; they are taken as lines of reference and are known as the **axis of x and the axis of y** respectively. The point O is called the **origin**. Values of x are measured from O along the axis of x, according to some convenient scale of measurement, and are called **abscissas**, *positive* values being drawn to the *right* of O along OX, and *negative* values to the *left* of O along OX'.

Values of y are drawn (on the same scale) parallel to the axis of y, from the ends of the corresponding abscissas, and are called **ordinates**. These are *positive* when drawn *above* XX', *negative* when drawn *below* XX'.

636. The abscissa and ordinate of a point taken together are known as its **coördinates**. A point whose coördinates are x and y is briefly spoken of as "the point (x, y)."

The coördinates of a point completely determine its position in the plane. Thus, if we wish to mark the point $(2, 3)$, we take $x = 2$ units measured to the right of O, $y = 3$ units measured perpendicular to the x-axis and above it. The resulting point P is in the first quadrant. The point $(-3, 2)$ is found by taking $x = 3$ units to the left of O, and $y = 2$ units above the x-axis. The resulting point Q is in the second quadrant. Similarly the points $(-3, -4)$, $(5, -5)$ are represented by R and S in Fig. 1, in the third and fourth quadrants respectively.

GRAPHICAL REPRESENTATION OF FUNCTIONS.

This process of marking the position of a point in reference to the coördinate axes is known as **plotting the point**.

637. In practice it is convenient to use **squared paper**; that is, paper ruled into small squares by two sets of equidistant parallel straight lines, the one set being horizontal and the other vertical. After selecting two of the intersecting lines as axes (and slightly thickening them to aid the eye), one or more of the divisions may be chosen as our unit, and points may be readily plotted when their coördinates are known. Conversely, if the position of a point in any of the quadrants is marked, its coördinates can be measured by the divisions on the paper.

In the following pages we have used paper ruled to tenths of an inch, but a larger scale will sometimes be more convenient. See Art. 657.

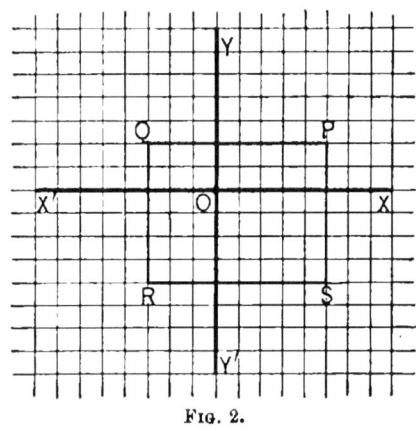

FIG. 2.

Ex. Plot the points $(5, 2)$, $(-3, 2)$, $(-3, -4)$, $(5, -4)$ on squared paper. Find the area of the figure determined by these points, assuming the divisions on the paper to be tenths of an inch.

Taking the points in the order given, it is easily seen that they are represented by P, Q, R, S in Fig. 2, and that they form a rectangle which contains 48 squares. Each of these is *one-hundredth* part of a *square* inch. Thus, the area of the rectangle is .48 of a square inch.

EXAMPLES XLIX. a.

[*The following examples are intended to be done mainly by actual measurement on squared paper; where possible, they should also be verified by calculation.*]

Plot the following pairs of points and draw the line which joins them:

1. $(3, 0), (0, 6)$.
2. $(-2, 0), (0, -8)$.
3. $(3, -8), (-2, 6)$.
4. $(5, 5), (-2, -2)$.
5. $(-2, 6), (1, -3)$.
6. $(4, 5), (-1, 5)$.

7. Plot the points (3, 3), (− 3, 3), (− 3, − 3), (3, − 3), and find the number of squares contained by the figure determined by these points.

8. Plot the points (4, 0), (0, 4), (− 4, 0), (0, − 4), and find the number of units of area in the resulting figure.

9. Plot the points (0, 0), (0, 10), (5, 5), and find the number of units of area in the triangle.

10. Show that the triangle whose vertices are (0, 0), (0, 6), (4, 3) contains 12 units of area. Show also that the points (0, 0), (0, 6), (4, 8) determine a triangle of the same area.

11. Plot the points (5, 6), (− 5, 6), (5, − 6), (− 5, − 6). If one millimeter is taken as unit, find the area of the figure in square centimeters.

12. Plot the points (1, 3), (− 3, − 9), and show that they lie on a line passing through the origin. Name the coördinates of other points on this line.

13. Plot the eight points (0, 5), (3, 4), (5, 0), (4, − 3), (− 5, 0), (0, − 5), (− 4, 3), (− 4, − 3), and show that they are all equidistant from the origin.

14. Plot the two following series of points:

    (i.) (5, 0), (5, 2), (5, 5), (5, − 1), (5, − 4);

    (ii.) (− 4, 8), (− 1, 8), (0, 8), (3, 8), (6, 8).

Show that they lie on two lines respectively parallel to the axis of y, and the axis of x. Find the coördinates of the point in which they intersect.

15. Plot the points (13, 0), (0, − 13), (12, 5), (− 12, 5), (− 13, 0), (− 5, − 12), (5, − 12). Find their locus, (i.) by measurement, (ii.) by calculation

16. Plot the points (2, 2), (− 3, − 3), (4, 4), (− 5, − 5,) showing that they all lie on a certain line through the origin. Conversely, show that for *every* point on this line the abscissa and ordinate are equal.

GRAPH OF A FUNCTION.

638. Let $f(x)$ represent a function of x, and let its value be denoted by y. If we give to x a series of numerical values, we get a corresponding series of values for y. If these are set off as abscissas and ordinates respectively, we plot a succession of points. If *all* such points were plotted,

GRAPHICAL REPRESENTATION OF FUNCTIONS. 521

we should arrive at a line, straight or curved, which is known as the **graph** of the *function* $f(x)$, or the **graph** of the *equation* $y = f(x)$. The variation of the function for different values of the variable x is exhibited by the variation of the ordinates as we pass from point to point.

In practice, a few points carefully plotted will usually enable us to draw the graph with sufficient accuracy.

639. The student who has worked intelligently through the preceding examples will have acquired for himself some useful preliminary notions which will be of service in the examples on simple graphs which we are about to give. In particular, before proceeding farther he should satisfy himself with regard to the following statements:

(i.) The coördinates of the origin are (0, 0).
(ii.) The abscissa of every point on the axis of y is 0.
(iii.) The ordinate of every point on the axis of x is 0.
(iv.) The graph of all points which have the same abscissa is a line parallel to the axis of y. (*e.g.* $x = 2$.)
(v.) The graph of all points which have the same ordinate is a line parallel to the axis of x. (*e.g.* $y = 5$.)
(vi.) The distance of any point $P(x, y)$ from the origin is given by $OP^2 = x^2 + y^2$.

Ex. 1. Plot the graph of $y = x$.

When $x = 0$, $y = 0$; thus the origin is one point on the graph.

Also, when
$$x = 1, 2, 3, \cdots -1,$$
$$-2, -3, \cdots,$$
$$y = 1, 2, 3, \cdots -1,$$
$$-2, -3, \cdots.$$

Thus the graph passes through O, and represents a series of points each of which has its ordinate equal to its abscissa, and is clearly represented by POP' in Fig. 3.

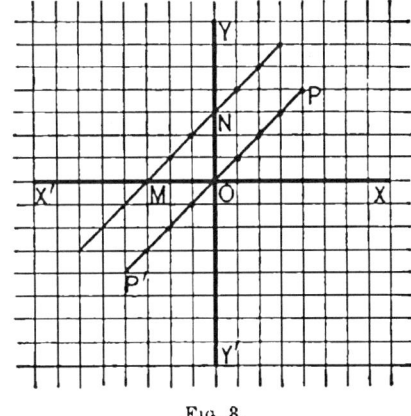

Fig. 8.

522   ALGEBRA.

Ex. 2. Plot the graph of $y = x + 3$.

Arrange the values of x and y as follows:

x	3	2	1	**0**	−1	−2	**−3**	...
y	6	5	4	**3**	2	1	**0**	...

By joining these points we obtain a line MN parallel to that in Example 1.

The results printed in heavier type should be specially noted and compared with the graph. They show that the distances ON, OM (usually called the *intercepts on the axes*) are obtained by separately putting $x = 0$, $y = 0$ in the equation of the graph.

NOTE. By observing that in Example 2 each ordinate is 3 units greater than the corresponding ordinate in Example 1, the graph of $y = x + 3$ may be obtained from that of $y = x$ by simply producing each ordinate 3 units in the positive direction.

In like manner the equations

$$y = x + 5, \quad y = x - 5,$$

represent two parallel lines on opposite sides of $y = x$ and equidistant from it, as the student may easily verify for himself.

Ex. 3. Plot the graphs represented by the following equations:

(i.) $y = 2x$;
(ii.) $y = 2x + 4$;
(iii.) $y = 2x - 5$.

Here we only give the diagram, which the student should verify in detail for himself, following the method explained in the two preceding examples.

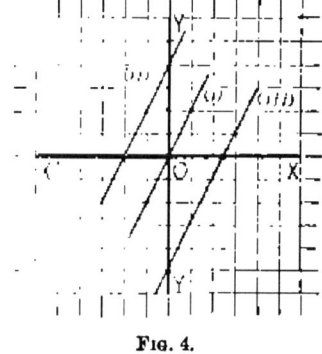

FIG. 4.

EXAMPLES XLIX. b.

[*In the following examples Nos. 1–18 are arranged in groups of three; each group should be represented on the same diagram so as to exhibit clearly the position of the three graphs relatively to each other.*]

Plot the graphs represented by the following equations:

1. $y = 5x$.
2. $y = 5x - 4$.
3. $y = 5x + 6$.
4. $y = -3x$.
5. $y = -3x + 3$.
6. $y = -3x - 2$.

GRAPHICAL REPRESENTATION OF FUNCTIONS. 523

7. $y + x = 0$.   8. $y + x = 8$.   9. $y + 4 = x$.
10. $4x = 3y$.   11. $3y = 4x + 6$.   12. $4y + 3x = 8$.
13. $x - 5 = 0$.   14. $y - 6 = 0$.   15. $5y = 6x$.
16. $3x + 4y = 10$.   17. $4x + y = 9$.   18. $5x - 2y = 8$.

19. Show by careful drawing that the last three graphs have a common point whose coördinates are 2, 1.

20. Show by careful drawing that the equations
$$x + y = 10, \quad y = x - 4$$
represent two straight lines at right angles.

21. Draw on the same axes the graphs of $x = 5$, $x = 9$, $y = 8$, $y = 11$. Find the number of units of area enclosed by these lines.

22. Taking one tenth of an inch as the unit of length, find the area included between the graphs of $x = 7$, $x = -3$, $y = -2$, $y = 8$.

23. Find the area included by the graphs of
$$y = x + 6, \quad y = x - 6, \quad y = -x + 6, \quad y = -x - 6.$$

24. With one millimeter as linear unit, find in square centimeters the area of the figure enclosed by the graphs of
$$y = 2x + 8, \quad y = 2x - 8, \quad y = -2x + 8, \quad y = -2x - 8.$$

640. The student should now be prepared for the following statements:

(i.) For all numerical values of a the equation $y = ax$ represents a straight line through the origin.

(ii.) For all numerical values of a and b the equation $y = ax + b$ represents a line parallel to $y = ax$, and cutting off an intercept b from the axis of y.

641. Conversely, since every equation involving x and y only in the first degree can be reduced to one of the forms $y = ax$, $y = ax + b$, it follows that *every simple equation connecting two variables represents a straight line*. For this reason an expression of the form $ax + b$ is said to be a **linear function** of x, and an equation such as $y = ax + b$, or $ax + by + c = 0$, is said to be a **linear equation**.

Ex. Show that the points $(3, -4)$, $(9, 4)$, $(12, 8)$ lie on a straight line, and find its equation.

Assume $y = ax + b$ as the equation of the line. If it passes through the first two points given, their coördinates must satisfy the above equation. Hence
$$-4 = 3a + b, \quad 4 = 9a + b.$$
These equations give $\quad a = \tfrac{4}{3}, \quad b = -8.$

Hence $\quad y = \tfrac{4}{3}x - 8, \quad$ or $4x - 3y = 24$,

is the equation of the line passing through the first two points. Since $x = 12$, $y = 8$ satisfies this equation, the line also passes through (12, 8). This example may be verified graphically by plotting the line which joins *any two* of the points and showing that it passes through the third.

APPLICATION TO SIMULTANEOUS EQUATIONS.

642. It was shown in Art. 167 that in the case of a simple equation between x and y, it is possible to find as many pairs of values of x and y as we please which satisfy the given equation. We now see that this is equivalent to saying that we may find as many points as we please on any given straight line. If, however, we have two simultaneous equations between x and y, there can be only one pair of values which will satisfy both equations. This is equivalent to saying that two straight lines can have only one common point.

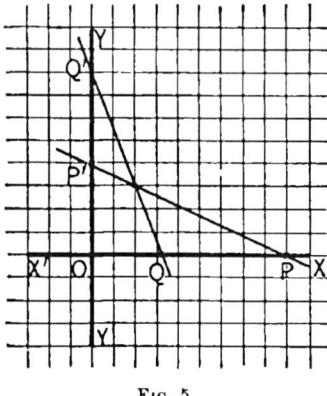

Fig. 5.

Ex. Solve graphically the equations:
$$3x + 7y = 27, \quad 5x + 2y = 16.$$

If carefully plotted these two equations will be found to represent the lines in the diagram. On measuring the coördinates of the point at which they intersect it will be found that $x = 2$, $y = 3$, verifying a solution by method of Art. 171.

643. It will now be seen that the process of solving two simultaneous equations is equivalent to finding the coördinates of the point (or points) at which their graphs meet.

GRAPHICAL REPRESENTATION OF FUNCTIONS.

644. Since a straight line can always be drawn by joining *any* two of its points, in solving *linear* simultaneous equations graphically, it is only necessary to plot two points of each line. The points where the lines meet the axes will usually be the most convenient to select.

645. Two simultaneous equations lead to no finite solution if they are inconsistent with each other. For example, the equations
$$x + 3y = 2, \quad 3x + 9y = 8$$
are inconsistent, for the second equation can be written $x + 3y = 2\frac{2}{3}$, which is clearly inconsistent with $x + 3y = 2$. The graphs of these two equations will be found to be two parallel straight lines which have no finite point of intersection.

Again, two simultaneous equations must be independent. The equations
$$4x + 3y = 1, \quad 16x + 12y = 4$$
are not independent, for the second can be deduced from the first by multiplying throughout by 4. Thus *any pair of values* which will satisfy one equation will satisfy the other. Graphically these two equations represent two coincident straight lines which of course have an unlimited number of common points.

EXAMPLES XLIX. c.

Solve the following equations, in each case verifying the solution graphically:

1. $y = 2x + 3$,
   $y + x = 6$.

2. $y = 3x + 4$,
   $y = x + 8$.

3. $y = 4x$,
   $2x + y = 18$.

4. $2x - y = 8$,
   $4x + 3y = 6$.

5. $3x + 2y = 16$,
   $5x - 3y = 14$.

6. $6y - 5x = 18$,
   $4x = 3y$.

7. $2x + y = 0$,
   $y = \frac{1}{3}(x + 5)$.

8. $2x - y = 3$,
   $3x - 5y = 15$.

9. $2y = 5x + 15$,
   $3y - 4x = 12$.

10. Prove by graphical representation that the three points (3, 0), (2, 7), (4, −7) lie on a straight line. Where does this line cut the axis of y?

11. Prove that the three points (1, 1), (− 3, 4), (5, − 2) lie on a straight line. Find its equation. Draw the graph of this equation, showing that it passes through the given points.

12. Show that the three points (3, 2), (8, 8), (− 2, − 4) lie on a straight line. Prove algebraically and graphically that it cuts the axis of x at a distance $1\frac{1}{3}$ from the origin.

646. We shall now give some graphs of functions of higher degree than the first.

Ex. 1. Plot the graph of $2y = x^2$.

Corresponding values of x and y may be tabulated as follows:

x	...	3	2.5	2	1.5	1	0	− 1	− 2	− 3	...
y	...	4.5	3.125	2	1.125	.5	0	.5	2	4.5	...

Here, in order to obtain a figure on a sufficiently large scale, it will be found convenient to take two divisions on the paper for our unit.

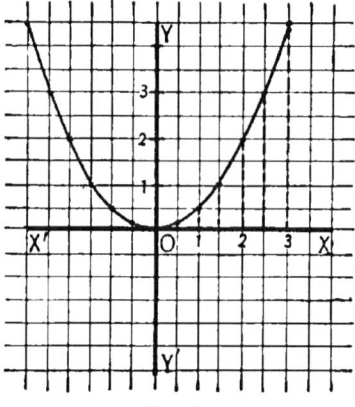

Fig. 6.

If the above points are plotted and connected by a line drawn freehand, we shall obtain the curve shown in Fig. 6. This curve is called a **parabola**.

There are two facts to be specially noted in this example.

(i.) Since from the equation we have $x = \pm \sqrt{2y}$, it follows that for every value of the ordinate we have two values of the abscissa, *equal in magnitude and opposite in sign*. Hence the graph is symmetrical with respect to the axis of y; so that after plotting with care enough points to determine the form of the graph in the first quadrant, its form in the second quadrant can be inferred without actually plotting any points in this quadrant. At the same time, in this and similar cases beginners are recommended to plot a few points in each quadrant through which the graph passes.

(ii.) We observe that all the plotted points lie above the axis of x. This is evident from the equation; for since x^2 must be positive for all values of x, every ordinate obtained from the equation $y = \dfrac{x^2}{2}$ must be positive.

In like manner the student may show that the graph of $2y = -x^2$ is a curve similar in every respect to that in Fig. 6, but lying entirely below the axis of x.

NOTE. Some further remarks on the graph of this and the next example will be found in Art. 651.

Ex. 2. Find the graph of $y = 2x + \dfrac{x^2}{4}$.

Here the following arrangement will be found convenient:

x	3	2	1	0	-1	-2	-3	-4	-5	-6	-7	-8
$2x$	6	4	2	0	-2	-4	-6	-8	-10	-12	-14	-16
$\dfrac{x^2}{4}$	2.25	1	.25	0	.25	1	2.25	4	6.25	9	12.25	16
y	8.25	5	2.25	0	-1.75	-3	-3.75	-4	-3.75	-3	-1.75	0

From the form of the equation it is evident that every positive value of x will yield a positive value of y, and as x increases y also increases. Hence the portion of the curve in the first quadrant lies as in Fig. 7, and can be extended indefinitely in this quadrant. In the present case only two or three positive values of x and y need be plotted, but more attention must be paid to the results arising out of negative values of x.

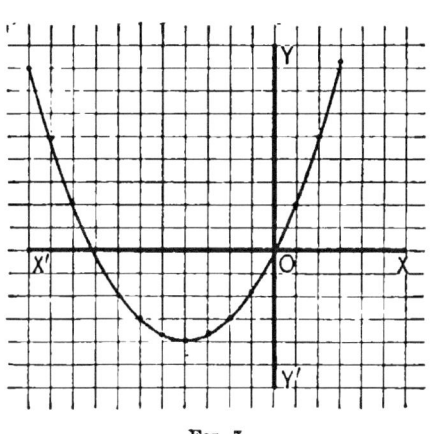

FIG. 7.

When $y = 0$, we have $\dfrac{x^2}{4} + 2x = 0$; thus the two values of x in the graph which correspond to $y = 0$ furnish the roots of the equation $\dfrac{x^2}{4} + 2x = 0$.

647. If $f(x)$ represents a function of x, an approximate solution of the equation $f(x) = 0$ may be obtained by plotting the graph of $y = f(x)$, and then measuring the intercepts made on the axis of x. These intercepts are values of x which make y equal to zero, and are therefore roots of $f(x) = 0$.

648. If $f(x)$ gradually increases till it reaches a value a, which is algebraically greater than neighboring values on either side, a is said to be a **maximum value** of $f(x)$.

If $f(x)$ gradually decreases till it reaches a value b, which is algebraically less than neighboring values on either side, b is said to be a **minimum** value of $f(x)$.

When $y = f(x)$ is treated graphically, it is now evident that maximum and minimum values of $f(x)$ occur at points where the ordinates are algebraically greatest and least in the immediate vicinity of such points.

Ex. Solve the equation $x^2 - 7x + 11 = 0$ graphically, and find the minimum value of the function $x^2 - 7x + 11$.

Put $y = x^2 - 7x + 11$, and find the graph of this equation.

x	0	1	2	3	3.5	4	5	6	7
y	11	5	1	-1	-1.25	-1	1	5	11

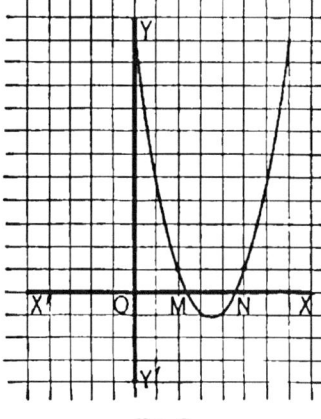

Fig. 8.

The values of x which make the function $x^2 - 7x + 11$ vanish are those which correspond to $y = 0$. By careful measurement it will be found that the intercepts OM and ON are approximately equal to 2.38 and 4.62.

The algebraical solution of
$$x^2 - 7x + 11 = 0$$
gives $\quad x = \tfrac{1}{2}(\pm 7\sqrt{5}).$

If we take 2.236 as the approximate value of $\sqrt{5}$, the values of x will be found to agree with those obtained from the graph.

GRAPHICAL REPRESENTATION OF FUNCTIONS.

Again, $x^2 - 7x + 11 = (x - \tfrac{7}{2})^2 - \tfrac{5}{4}$. Now $(x - \tfrac{7}{2})^2$ must be positive for all real values of x except $x = \tfrac{7}{2}$, in which case it vanishes, and the value of the function reduces to $-\tfrac{5}{4}$, which is the least value it can have.

The graph shows that when $x = 3.5$, $y = -1.25$, and that this is the algebraically least ordinate in the plotted curve.

649. The following example shows that points selected for graphical representation must sometimes be restricted within certain limits.

Ex. Find the graph of $x^2 + y^2 = 36$.
The equation may be written in either of the following forms:

$$\text{(i.) } y = \pm\sqrt{36 - x^2}; \quad \text{(ii.) } x = \pm\sqrt{36 - y^2}.$$

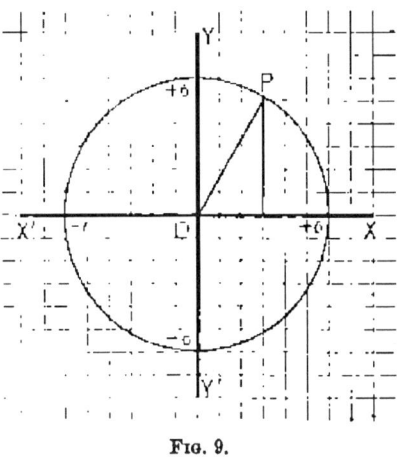

Fig. 9.

In order that y may be a real quantity we see from (i.) that $36 - x^2$ must be positive. Thus x can only have values between -6 and $+6$. Similarly from (ii.) it is evident that y must also lie between -6 and $+6$. Between these limits it will be found that all plotted points will lie at a distance 6 from the origin. Hence the graph is a circle whose centre is O and whose radius is 6.

This is otherwise evident, for the distance of any point $P(x, y)$ from the origin is given by $OP = \sqrt{x^2 + y^2}$. [Art. 639.]
Hence the equation $x^2 + y^2 = 36$ asserts that the graph consists of a series of points all of which are at a distance 6 from the origin.

NOTE. To plot the curve from equation (ii.), we should select a succession of values for y and then find corresponding values of x. In other words we make y the *independent* and x the *dependent* variable. The student should be prepared to do this in some of the examples which follow.

2 M

EXAMPLES XLIX. d.

1. Draw the graphs of $y = x^2$, and $x = y^2$, and show that they have only one common chord. Find its equation.

2. From the graphs, and also by calculation, show that $y = \dfrac{x^2}{8}$ cuts $x = -y^2$ in only two points, and find their coördinates.

3. Draw the graphs of

   (i.) $y^2 = -4x$; (ii.) $y = 2x - \dfrac{x^2}{4}$; (iii.) $y = \dfrac{x^2}{4} + x - 2$.

4. Draw the graph of $y = x + x^2$. Show also that it may be deduced from that of $y = x^2$, obtained in Example 1.

5. Show (i.) graphically, (ii.) algebraically, that the line $y = 2x - 3$ meets the curve $y = \dfrac{x^2}{4} + x - 2$ in one point only. Find its coördinates.

6. Find graphically the roots of the following equations to 2 places of decimals:

   (i.) $\dfrac{x^2}{4} + x - 2 = 0$; (ii.) $x^2 - 2x = 4$; (iii.) $4x^2 - 16x + 9 = 0$;

   and verify the solutions algebraically.

7. Find the minimum value of $x^2 - 2x - 4$, and the maximum value of $5 + 4x - 2x^2$.

8. Draw the graph of $y = (x-1)(x-2)$ and find the minimum value of $(x-1)(x-2)$. Measure, as accurately as you can, the values of x for which $(x-1)(x-2)$ is equal to 5 and 9 respectively. Verify algebraically.

9. Solve the simultaneous equations.

$$x^2 + y^2 = 100, \quad x + y = 14;$$

and verify the solution by plotting the graphs of the equations and measuring the coördinates of their common points.

10. Plot the graphs of $x^2 + y^2 = 25$, $3x + 4y = 25$, and examine their relation to each other where they intersect. Verify the result algebraically.

650. It should be observed that when the symbols for zero and infinity are used in the sense explained in Arts. 181, 182, they are subject to the rules of signs which affect other algebraical symbols. Thus we shall find it convenient to use a concise statement such as "when $x = +0$, $y = +\infty$"

GRAPHICAL REPRESENTATION OF FUNCTIONS. 531

to indicate that when a *very small and positive* value is given to x, the corresponding value of y is *very large and positive*.

651. If we now return to the examples worked out in Art. 646, in Example 1, we see that when $x = \pm \infty$, $y = +\infty$; hence the curve extends upwards to infinity in both the first and second quadrants. In Example 2, when $x = +\infty$, $y = +\infty$. Again y is negative between the values 0 and -8 of x. For all negative values of x numerically greater than 8, y is positive, and when $x = -\infty$, $y = +\infty$. Hence the curve extends to infinity in both the first and second quadrants.

The student should now examine the nature of the graphs in Examples XLIX. d. when x and y are infinite.

Ex. Find the graph of $xy = 4$.
The equation may be written in the form
$$y = \frac{4}{x},$$
from which it appears that when $x = 0$, $y = \infty$ and when $x = \infty$, $y = 0$. Also y is positive when x is positive, and negative when x is negative. Hence the graph must lie entirely in the first and third quadrants.

It will be convenient in this case to take the positive and negative values of the variables separately.

(1) *Positive values:*

x	0	1	2	3	4	5	6	...	∞
y	∞	4	2	$1\frac{1}{3}$	1	.8	$\frac{2}{3}$	...	0

Graphically these values show that as we recede farther and farther from the origin on the x-axis in the positive direction, the values of y are positive and become smaller and smaller. That is, the graph is continually approaching the x-axis in such a way that by taking a sufficiently great positive value of x we obtain a point on the graph as near as we please to the x-axis, but never actually reaching it until $x = \infty$. Similarly, as x becomes smaller and smaller the graph approaches more and more nearly to the positive end of the y-axis, never actually reaching it as long as x has any finite positive value, however small.

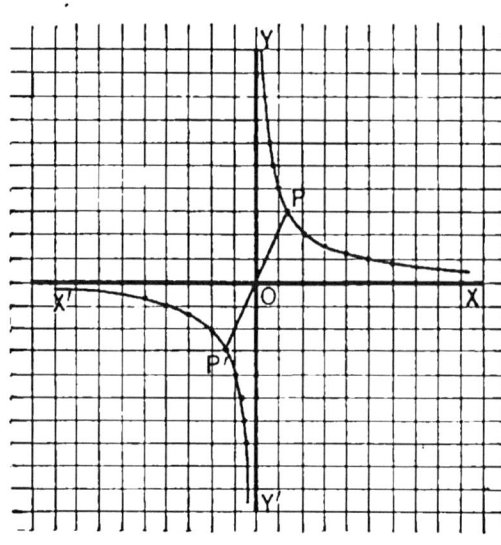

Fig. 10.

(2) *Negative values:*

x	-0	-1	-2	-3	-4	-5	...	$-\infty$
y	$-\infty$	-4	-2	$-1\frac{1}{3}$	-1	$-.8$	...	-0

The portion of the graph obtained from these values is in the third quadrant as shown in Fig. 10, and exactly similar to the portion already traced in the first quadrant. It should be noticed that as x passes from $+0$ to -0 the value of y changes from $+\infty$ to $-\infty$. Thus the graph, which in the first quadrant has run away to an infinite distance on the positive side of the y-axis, reappears in the third quadrant coming from an infinite distance on the negative side of that axis. Similar remarks apply to the graph in its relation to the x-axis.

652. When a curve continually approaches more and more nearly to a line without actually meeting it until an infinite distance is reached, such a line is said to be an **asymptote** to the curve. In the above case each of the axes is an asymptote.

653. Every equation of the form $y = \dfrac{c}{x}$, or $xy = c$, where c is constant, will give a graph similar to that exhibited in the example of Art. 651. The resulting curve is known as a **rectangular hyperbola**, and has many interesting properties. In particular we may mention that from the form of the equation it is evident that for every point (x, y) on the curve there is a corresponding point $(-x, -y)$ which satisfies the equation. Graphically this amounts to saying that any line through the origin meeting the two branches of the curve in P and P' is bisected at O.

654. In the simpler cases of graphs, sufficient accuracy can be obtained usually by plotting a few points, and there is little difficulty in selecting points with suitable coördinates. But in other cases, and especially when the graph has infinite branches, more care is needed. The most important things to observe are (1) the values for which the function $f(x)$ becomes zero or infinite; and (2) the values which the function assumes for zero and infinite values of x. In other words, we determine the *general character* of the curve in the neighborhood of the origin, the axes, and infinity. Greater accuracy of detail can then be secured by plotting points at discretion. The selection of such points will usually be suggested by the earlier stages of our work.

The existence of symmetry about either of the axes should also be noted. When an equation contains no *odd* powers of x, the graph is symmetrical with regard to the axis of y. Similarly the absence of odd powers of y indicates symmetry about the axis of x. Compare Art. 646, Ex. 1.

Ex. Draw the graph of $y = \dfrac{2x+7}{x-4}$. [See fig. on next page.]

We have $y = \dfrac{2x+7}{x-4} = \dfrac{2+\dfrac{7}{x}}{1-\dfrac{4}{x}}$, the latter form being convenient for infinite values of x.

(i.) When $\quad\quad\quad y = 0, \quad x = -\tfrac{7}{2},$
  When $\quad\quad\quad y = \infty, \quad x = 4;$

∴ the curve cuts the axis of x at a distance -3.5 from the origin, and meets the line $x = 4$ at an infinite distance.

If x is positive and very little greater than 4, y is very great and positive. If x is positive and very little less than 4, y is very great and negative. Thus the infinite points on the graph near to the line

$x = 4$ have positive ordinates to the right, and negative ordinates to the left of this line.

(ii.) When $\qquad x = 0, \quad y = -1.75,$
When $\qquad x = \infty, \quad y = 2;$

∴ the curve cuts the axis of y at a distance -1.75 from the origin, and meets the line $y = 2$ at an infinite distance.

By taking positive values of y very little greater and very little less than 2, it appears that the curve lies above the line $y = 2$ when $x = +\infty$, and below this line when $x = -\infty$.

The general character of the curve is now determined: the lines $PO'P'$ $(x = 4)$ and $QO'Q'$ $(y = 2)$ are asymptotes; the two branches of the curve lie in the compartments $PO'Q$, $P'O'Q'$, and the lower branch cuts the axes at distances -3.5 and -1.75 from the origin.

To examine the lower branch in detail, values of x may be selected between $-\infty$ and -3.5 and between -3.5 and 4.

x	$-\infty$	...	-16	-8	-6	-3.5	-1	0	2	3	...	4
y	2	...	1.25	.75	.5	0	-1	-1.75	-5.5	-13	...	$-\infty$

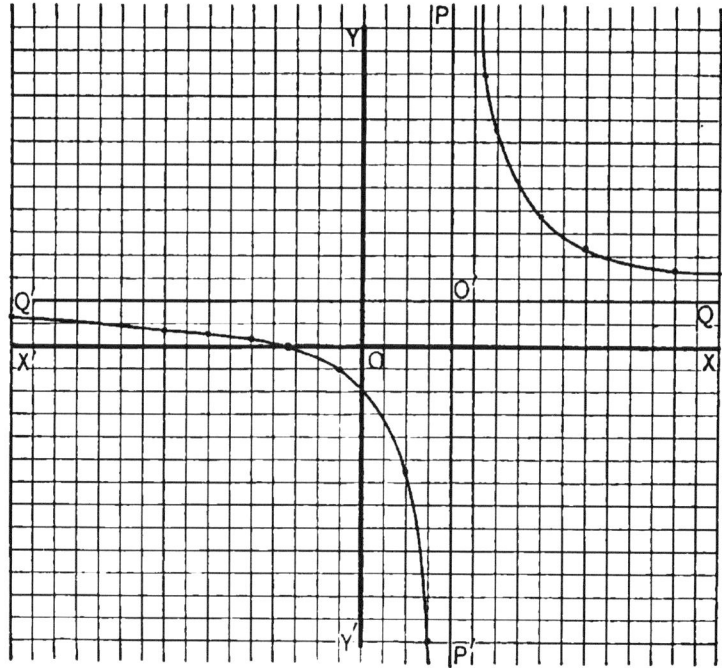

Fig. 11.

GRAPHICAL REPRESENTATION OF FUNCTIONS. 535

The upper branch may now be dealt with in the same way, selecting values of x between 4 and ∞. The graph will be found to be as represented in Fig. 11.

655. When the equation of a curve contains the square or higher power of y, the calculation of the values of y corresponding to selected values of x will have to be obtained by evolution, or else by the aid of logarithms. We give one example to illustrate the way in which a table of four-figure logarithms may be employed in such cases.

Ex. Draw the graph of $y^3 = x(9 - x^2)$.

For the sake of brevity we shall confine our attention to that part of the curve which lies to the right of the axis of y, leaving the other half to be traced in like manner by the student.

When $x = 0$, $y = 0$; therefore the curve passes through the origin. Again, y is positive for all values of x between 0 and 3, and vanishes when $x = 3$; for values of x greater than 3, y is negative and continually increases numerically.

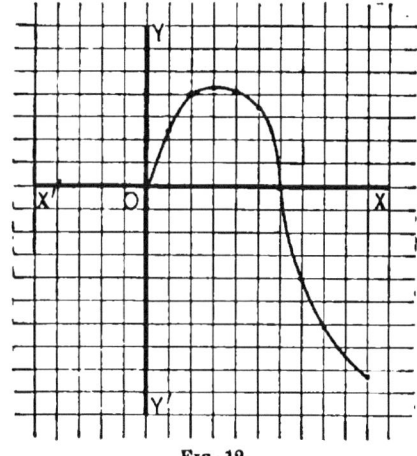

FIG. 12.

x	0	1	2	3	4	5	6	...
x^2	0	1	4	9	16	25	36	...
$9 - x^2$	9	8	5	0	-7	-16	-27	...
y^3	0	8	10	0	-28	-80	-162	...
$\log y^3$			1		1.4472*	1.9031*	2.2095*	...
$\log y$			.3333		.4824	.6344	.7365	...
y	0	2	2.15	0	-3.04	-4.31	-5.45	...

* In taking logarithms of the successive values of y^3, the negative sign is disregarded, but care must be taken to insert the proper signs in the last line which gives the successive values of y.

These points will be sufficient to give a rough approximation to the curve. For greater accuracy a few intermediate values such as $x = 1.5, 2.5, 3.5 \cdots$ should be taken, and the resulting curve will be as in Fig. 12, in which we have taken *two tenths of an inch as our linear unit*.

MEASUREMENT ON DIFFERENT SCALES.

656. For convenience on the printed page we have supposed the paper to be ruled to tenths of an inch, generally using one of the divisions as our linear unit. In practice, however, it will often be advisable to choose a unit much larger than this in order to get a satisfactory graph. For the sake of simplicity we have hitherto measured abscissas and ordinates on the same scale, but there is no necessity for so doing, and it will often be found convenient to measure the variables on different scales suggested by the particular conditions of the question.

As an illustration let us take the graph of $y = \dfrac{x^2}{2}$, given in Art. 646. If with the same unit as before we plot the graph of $y = x^2$, it will be found to be a curve similar to that there shown, but elongated in the direction of the axis of y. In fact, it will be the same as if the former graph were stretched to twice its length in the direction of the y-axis.

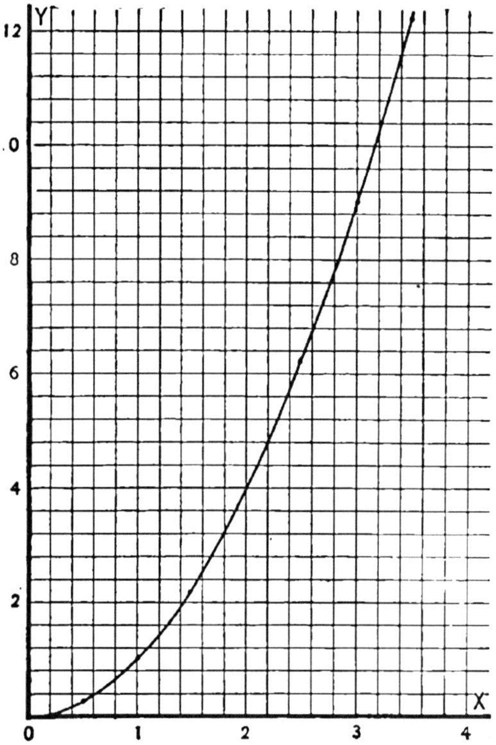

FIG. 13.

GRAPHICAL REPRESENTATION OF FUNCTIONS. 537

657. Any equation of the form $y = ax^2$, where a is constant, will represent a parabola elongated more or less according to the value of a; and the larger the value of a the more rapidly will y increase in comparison with x. We might have very large ordinates corresponding to very small abscissas, and the graph might prove quite unsuitable for practical applications. In such a case the inconvenience is obviated by measuring the values of y on a considerably smaller scale than those of x.

Speaking generally, whenever one variable increases much more rapidly than the other, a small unit should be chosen for the rapidly increasing variable and a large one for the other. Further modifications will be suggested in the examples which follow.

658. On pages 536 and 537 we give for comparison the graphs of

$y = x^2$ (Fig. 13),

and

$y = 8x^2$ (Fig. 14).

In Fig. 13 the unit for x is twice as great as that for y.

In Fig. 14 the x-unit is ten times the y-unit.

It will be useful practice for the student to plot other similar graphs on the same or a larger scale. For example, in Fig. 14 the graphs of $y = 16 x^2$

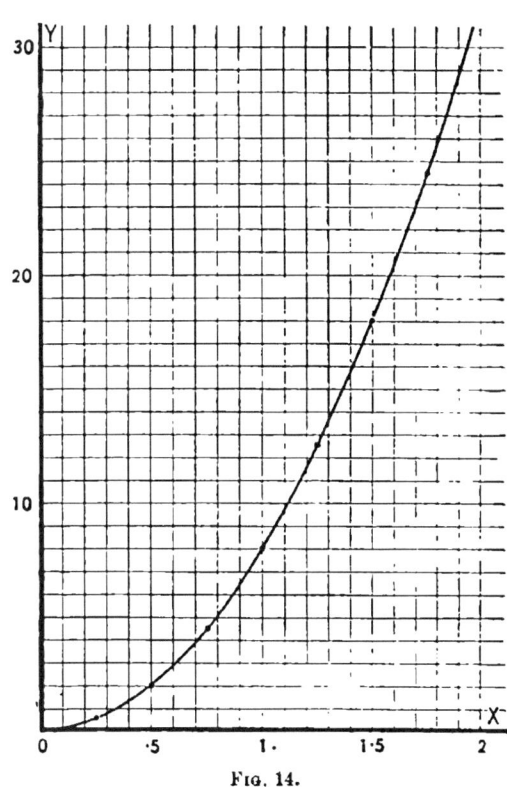

Fig. 14.

and $y = 2x^2$ may be drawn and compared with that of $y = 8x^2$.

EXAMPLES XLIX. e.

1. Plot the graph of $y = x^3$. Show that it consists of a continuous curve lying in the first and third quadrants, crossing the axis of x at the origin. Deduce the graphs of

(i.) $y = -x^3$; (ii.) $y = \tfrac{1}{2} x^3$.

2. Plot the graph of $y = x - x^3$. Verify it from the graphs of $y = x$, and $y = x^3$.

3. Plot the graph of $y = \dfrac{1}{x^2}$, showing that it consists of two branches lying entirely in the first and second quadrants. Examine and compare the nature and position of the graph as it approaches the axes.

4. Discuss the general character of the graph of $y = \dfrac{a}{x^2}$ where a has some constant integral value. Distinguish between two cases in which a has numerical values, equal in magnitude but opposite in sign.

5. Plot the graphs of

(i.) $y = 1 + \dfrac{1}{x}$; (ii.) $y = 2 + \dfrac{10}{x^2}$.

Verify by deducing them from the graphs of $y = \dfrac{1}{x}$, and $y = \dfrac{10}{x^2}$.

6. Plot the graph of $y = x^3 - 3x$. Examine the character of the curve at the points $(1, -2)$, $(-1, 2)$, and show graphically that the roots of the equation $x^3 - 3x = 0$ are approximately -1.732, 0, and 1.732.

7. Solve the equations:
$$3x + 2y = 16, \quad xy = 10,$$
and verify the solution by finding the coördinates of the points where their graphs intersect.

8. Plot the graphs of

(i.) $y = \dfrac{15 - x^2}{x}$; (ii.) $x = \dfrac{10 - y^2}{y}$,

and thus verify the algebraical solution of the equations $x^2 + xy = 15$, $y^2 + xy = 10$.

9. Trace the curve whose equation is $y = \dfrac{x}{2 - x}$, showing that it has two branches, one lying in the first and third quadrants, and the other entirely in the fourth. Find the equations of its asymptotes.

GRAPHICAL REPRESENTATION OF FUNCTIONS. 539

Plot the graphs of

10. $y = \dfrac{1+x}{1-x}.$
11. $y = \dfrac{1+x^2}{1-x}.$

12. $y = \dfrac{x^2-15}{x-4}.$
13. $y = \dfrac{(x-1)(x-2)}{x-3}.$

14. $y = \dfrac{x^2+x+1}{x^2-x+1}.$
15. $y = \dfrac{x^2+5x+6}{x^2+1}.$

16. $y = x^3 - 6x^2 + 11x - 6.$
17. $10y = x^3 - 5x^2 + x - 5.$

18. $y = \dfrac{20}{x^2+2}.$
19. $y = \dfrac{40x}{x^2+10}.$
20. $y = \dfrac{x(8-x)}{x+5}.$

21. $y = \dfrac{(x-2)(x-3)}{x-5}.$
22. $y = \dfrac{(x-1)(x-2)(x+1)}{4}.$

23. $y^2 = x^2 - 5x + 4.$
24. $4y^2 = x^2(5-x).$

25. $y^2 = \dfrac{x(3-x)(x-8)}{x^2+5}.$
26. $y^2 = \dfrac{(x+7)(x-4)(x-10)}{x^2+5}.$

27. $y^2 = \dfrac{x^2(49-x^2)}{50}.$
28. $y^2 = \dfrac{(81-x^2)(x^2-4)}{100}.$

29. $5y^3 = x(x^2-64).$
30. $5y^3 = x^2(36-x^2).$

31. Plot the graphs of $y = x^3$, and of $y = 2x^2 + x - 2$. Hence find the roots of the equation $x^3 - 2x^2 - x + 2 = 0$.

32. Find graphically the roots of the equation
$$x^3 - 4x^2 - 5x + 14 = 0$$
to three significant figures.

659. Besides the instances already given there are several of the ordinary processes of arithmetic and algebra which lend themselves readily to graphical illustration.

For example, the graph of $y = x^2$ may be used to furnish numerical square roots. For since $x = \sqrt{y}$, each ordinate and corresponding abscissa give a number and its square root. Similarly cube roots may be found from the graph of $y = x^3$.

Ex. 1. Find graphically the cube root of 10 to 3 places of decimals.
The required root is clearly a little greater than 2. Hence it will be enough to plot the graph of $y = x^3$ taking $x = 2.1, 2.2, \ldots$. The corresponding ordinates are 9.26, 10.65, ….

540 ALGEBRA.

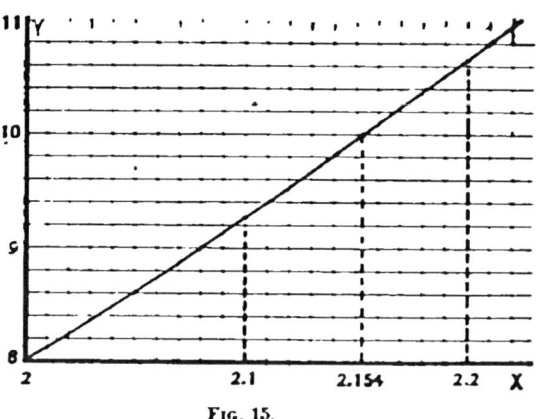

Fig. 15.

When

$x = 2$, $y = 8$.

Take the axes through this point and let the units for x and y be 10 inches and .5 inch respectively. On this scale the portion of the graph differs but little from a straight line, and yields results to a high degree of accuracy.

When $y = 10$, the measured value of x will be found to be 2.154.

Ex. 2. Show graphically that the expression $4x^2 + 4x - 3$ is negative for all real values of x between .5 and -1.5, and positive for all real values of x outside these limits. [Fig. 16.]

Put $y = 4x^2 + 4x - 3$, and proceed as in the example given in Art. 648, taking the unit for x four times as great as that for y. It will be found that the graph cuts the axis of x at points whose abscissas are .5 and -1.5; and that it lies below the axis of x between these points. That is, the value of y is negative so long as x lies between .5 and -1.5, and positive for all other values of x.

Or we may proceed as follows:

Put $y_1 + 4x^2$, and $y_2 = -4x + 3$, and plot the graphs of these two equations. At their points of intersection $y_1 = y_2$, and the values of x at these points are found to be .5 and -1.5. Hence for these values of x we have

$$4x^2 = 4x + 3,$$
or $4x^2 + 4x - 3 = 0.$

Thus the roots of the equation

$$4x^2 + 4x - 3 = 0$$

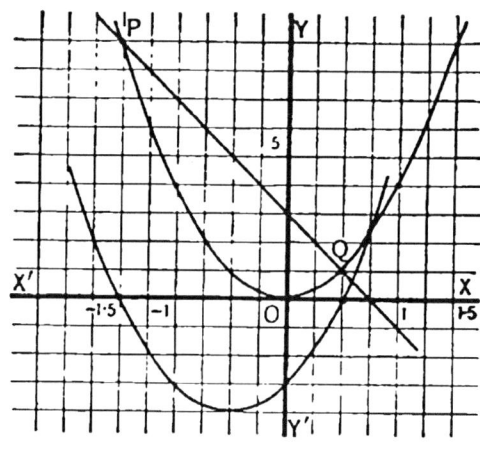

Fig. 16.

GRAPHICAL REPRESENTATION OF FUNCTIONS. 541

are furnished by the abscissas of the common points of the graphs of $4x^2$ and $-4x+3$.

Again, between the values .5 and -1.5 for x it will be found graphically that y_1 is less than y_2, hence $y_1 - y_2$, or $4x^2 + 4x - 3$ is negative.

Both solutions are here exhibited.

The upper curve is the graph of $y = 4x^2$; PQ is the graph of $y = -4x + 3$; and the lower curve is the graph of $y = 4x^2 + 4x - 3$.

660. Of the two methods in the last example the first is the more direct and instructive; but the second has this advantage:

If a number of equations of the form $x^2 = px + q$ have to be solved graphically, $y = x^2$ can be plotted once for all on a convenient scale, and $y = px + q$ can then be readily drawn for different values of p and q.

Equations of higher degree may be treated similarly.

For example, the solution of such equations as

$$x^3 = px + q, \quad \text{or} \quad x^3 = ax^2 + bx + c$$

can be made to depend on the intersection of $y = x^3$ with other graphs.

Ex. Find the real roots of the equations

(i.) $x^3 - 2.5x - 3 = 0$; (ii.) $x^3 - 3x + 2 = 0$.

Here we have to find the points of intersection of

(i.) $y = x^3$, (ii.) $y = x^3$,
$y = 2.5x + 3$; $y = 3x - 2$.

Plot the graphs of these equations, choosing the unit for x five times as great as that for y.

It will be seen that $y = 2.5x + 3$ meets $y = x^3$ only at the point for which $x = 2$. Thus 2 is the only real root of equation (i.).

Again $y = 3x - 2$ *touches* $y = x^3$ at the point for which $x = 1$, and cuts it where $x = -2$.

Corresponding to the former point the equation $x^3 - 3x + 2 = 0$ has two equal roots. Thus the roots of (ii.) are $1, 1, -2$.

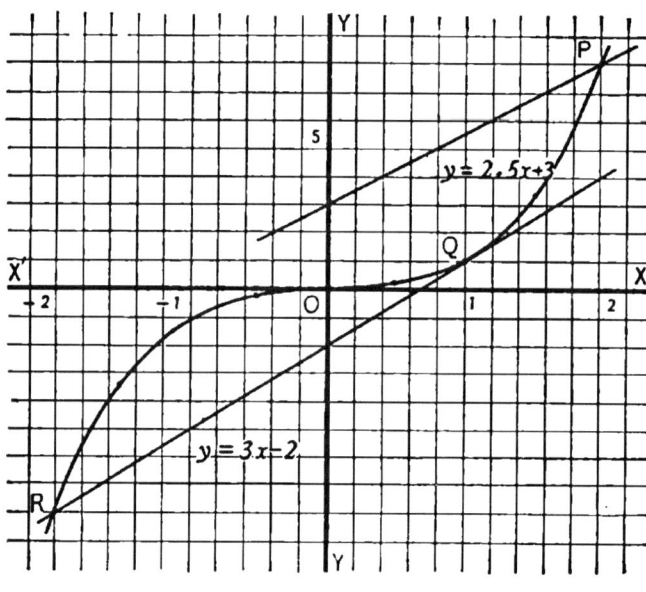

Fig. 17.

661. In Art. 642 we have given the graphical solution of two *linear* simultaneous equations. As the principle is the same for equations of any degree, the few examples of this kind on pages 531, 540 have been given without special explanation. It may, however, be instructive here to show the graphical solution of some of the equations discussed in Chap. xxviii.

Ex. Solve the following equations graphically:

(i.) $\left. \begin{array}{l} x - y = 2 \\ xy = 35 \end{array} \right\}$. (ii.) $\left. \begin{array}{l} x^2 + y^2 = 74 \\ xy = 35 \end{array} \right\}$.

(Compare Art. 300, Ex. 1.)

Here $xy = 35$ is represented by a rectangular hyperbola [Art. 651]; $x - y = 2$ is the line QS, and $x^2 + y^2 = 74$ is represented by the circle. The roots of (i.) are the coördinates of Q and S; that is,

$$x = 7, \ y = 5; \ \text{or} \ x = -5, \ y = -7.$$

The roots of (ii.) are the coördinates of P, Q, R, and S; that is,

$$x = 5, \ y = 7; \ x = 7, \ y = 5; \ x = -7, \ y = -5; \ x = -5, \ y = -7.$$

GRAPHICAL REPRESENTATION OF FUNCTIONS.

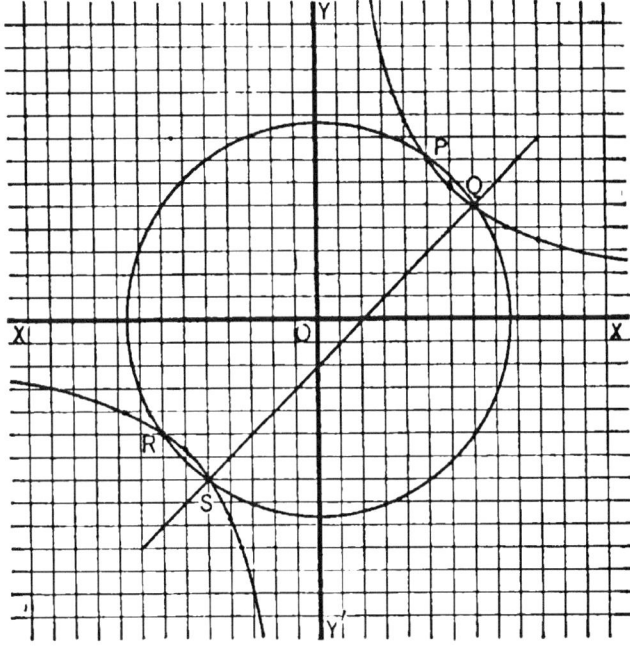

Fig. 18.

EXAMPLES XLIX. f.

1. Draw the graph of $y = x^2$ on a scale twice as large as that in Fig. 13, and employ it to find the squares of .72, 1.7, 3.4; and the square roots of 7.56, 5.29, 9.61.

2. Draw the graph of $y = \sqrt{x}$ taking the unit for y five times as great as that for x.

By means of this curve check the values of the square roots found in Example 1.

3. From the graph of $y = x^3$ (on the scale of the diagram of Art. 659) find the value of $\sqrt[3]{9}$ and $\sqrt[3]{9.8}$ to 4 significant figures.

4. A student who was ignorant of the rule for cube root required the value of $\sqrt[3]{14.71}$. He plotted the graph of $y = x^3$, using for x the values 2.2, 2.3, 2.4, 2.5, and found 2.45 as the value of the cube root. Verify this process in detail. From the same graph find the value of $\sqrt[3]{13.8}$.

5. Find graphically the values of x for which the expression $x^2 - 2x - 8$ vanishes. Show that for values of x between these limits the expression is negative and for all other values positive. Find the least value of the expression.

6. From the graph in the preceding example show that for any value of a greater than 1 the equation $x^2 - 2x + a = 0$ cannot have real roots.

7. Show graphically that the expression $x^2 - 4x + 7$ is positive for all real values of x.

8. On the same axes draw the graphs of
$$y = x^2, \ y = x + 6, \ y = x - 6, \ y = -x + 6, \ y = -x - 6.$$
Hence discuss the roots of the four equations
$$x^2 - x - 6 = 0, \ x^2 - x + 6 = 0, \ x^2 + x - 6 = 0, \ x^2 + x + 6 = 0.$$

9. If x is real, prove graphically that $5 - 4x - x^2$ is not greater than 9; and that $4x^2 - 4x + 3$ is not less than 2. Between what values of x is the first expression positive?

10. Solve the equation $x^3 = 3x^2 + 6x - 8$ graphically, and show that the function $x^3 - 3x^2 - 6x + 8$ is positive for all values of x between -2 and 1, and negative for all values of x between 1 and 4.

11. Show graphically that the equation $x^3 + px + q = 0$ has only one real root when p is positive.

12. Trace the curve whose equation is $y = 2^x$. Find the approximate values of $2^{4 \cdot 75}$ and $2^{5 \cdot 25}$. Express 12 as a power of 2 approximately.
Prove also that $\log_2 26.9 + \log_2 38 = 10$.

13. By repeated evolution find the values of $10^{\frac{1}{2}}$, $10^{\frac{1}{4}}$, $10^{\frac{1}{8}}$, $10^{\frac{1}{16}}$. By multiplication find the values of $10^{\frac{3}{16}}$, $10^{\frac{5}{16}}$, $10^{\frac{6}{16}}$, $10^{\frac{7}{16}}$, $10^{\frac{9}{16}}$. Use these values to plot a portion of the curve $y = 10^x$ on a large scale. Find correct to three places of decimals the values of log 3, log 1.68, log 2.24, log 34.3. Also by choosing numerical values for a and b, verify the laws
$$\log ab = \log a + \log b; \quad \log \frac{a}{b} = \log a - \log b.$$

[*By using paper ruled to tenths of an inch, if 10 in. and 1 in. be taken as units for x and y respectively, a diagonal scale will give values of x correct to three decimal places and values of y correct to two.*]

14. Calculate the values of $x(9 - x)^2$ for the values 0, 1, 2, 3, ... 9 of x. Draw the graph of $x(9 - x)^2$ from $x = 0$ to $x = 9$.
If a very thin elastic rod, 9 inches in length, fixed at one end, swings like a pendulum, the expression $x(9 - x)^2$ measures the tendency of the rod to break at a place x inches from the point of suspension. From the graph find where the rod is most likely to break.

15. The reciprocal of a number is multiplied by 2.25 and the product is added to the number. Find graphically what the number must be if the resulting expression has the least possible value.

16. Show graphically that the expression $4x^2 + 2x - 8.75$ is positive for all real values of x except such as lie between 1.25 and -1.75. For what value of x is the expression a minimum?

17. Find graphically the real roots of the equations:

(i.) $x^3 + x - 2 = 0$.   (ii.) $x^3 - 7x + 6 = 0$.

18. Draw the graphs of

$$x + y = 9\tfrac{1}{2}, \quad xy = 12, \quad x^2 - y^2 = 32,$$

on the same axes. Hence find the solutions of the following pairs of simultaneous equations:

(i.) $\left.\begin{array}{c} x + y = 9\tfrac{1}{2} \\ xy = 12 \end{array}\right\}.$ (ii.) $\left.\begin{array}{c} x^2 - y^2 = 32 \\ x + y = 9\tfrac{1}{2} \end{array}\right\}.$ (iii.) $\left.\begin{array}{c} x^2 - y^2 = 32 \\ xy = 12 \end{array}\right\}.$

19. Draw the graphs of $y = x^3$ and $y = 3x^2 - 4$ on the same axes, and find the roots of the equation $x^3 - 3x^2 + 4 = 0$.

Show that the expression $x^3 - 3x^2 + 4$ is negative for values of x less than -1, and positive for all other values of x.

20. From a graphical consideration of the following pairs of simultaneous equations:

(i.) $x^2 + y^2 = a,$ (ii.) $x + y = a,$
$xy = b,$ $xy = b,$

explain why (i.) has either *four* solutions or none, while (ii.) has *two* solutions or none.

21. Draw the graphs of $y = x^3$ and $y = x^2 + 3x - 3$ on the same axes.

Hence find the roots of the equation $x^3 - x^2 - 3x + 3 = 0$ to three places of decimals, and discuss the sign of the expression $x^3 - x^2 - 3x + 3$ for different values of x.

PRACTICAL APPLICATIONS.

662. In all the cases hitherto considered the equation of the curve has been given, and its graph has been drawn by first selecting values of x and y which satisfy the equation, and then drawing a line so as to pass through the plotted points. We thus determine accurately the position of as many points as we please, and the process employed assures us that they all lie on the graph we are seeking. We could obtain the same result without knowing the equation of the curve provided that we were furnished with a sufficient number of corresponding values of the variables *accurately calculated*.

Sometimes from the nature of the case the form of the equation which connects two variables is known. For example, if a quantity y is directly proportional to another quantity x it is evident that we may put $y = ax$, where a is some constant quantity. Hence in all cases of direct proportionality between two quantities the graph which exhibits their variations is a straight line through the origin. Also, since two points are sufficient to determine a straight line, it follows that in the cases under consideration, we only require to know the position of one point besides the origin, and this will be furnished by any pair of simultaneous values of the variables.

Ex. 1. Given that 5.5 kilograms are roughly equal to 12.125 pounds, show graphically how to express any number of pounds in kilograms. Express $7\frac{1}{2}$ pounds in kilograms, and $4\frac{1}{4}$ kilograms in pounds.

Here measuring pounds horizontally and kilograms vertically, the required graph is obtained at once by joining the origin to the point whose coördinates are 12.125 and 5.5.

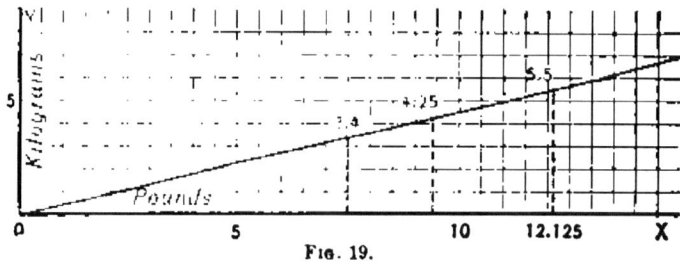

Fig. 19.

By measurement it will be found that $7\frac{1}{2}$ pounds = 3.4 kilograms, and $4\frac{1}{4}$ kilograms = 9.37 pounds.

Ex. 2. The expenses of a school are partly constant and partly proportional to the number of boys. The expenses were \$3250 for 105 boys, and \$3710 for 128. Draw a graph to represent the expenses for any number of boys; find the expenses for 115 boys, and the number of boys that can be maintained at a cost of $3550.

If the expenses for x boys are represented by $\$ y$, it is evident that x and y satisfy a linear equation $y = ax + b$, where a and b are constants. Hence the graph is a straight line.

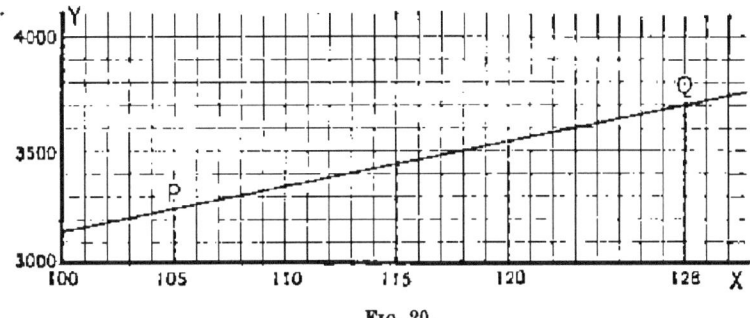

Fig. 20.

As the numbers are large, it will be convenient if we begin measuring ordinates at 3000, and abscissas at 100. This enables us to bring the requisite portion of the graph into a smaller compass. The points P and Q are determined by the data of the question, and the line PQ is the graph required.

By measurement we find that when $x = 115$, $y = 3450$; and that when $y = 3550$, $x = 120$. Thus the required answers are $3450, and 120 boys.

663. Sometimes corresponding values of two variables are obtained by observation or experiment. In such cases the data cannot be regarded as free from error; the position of the plotted points cannot be absolutely relied on; and we cannot correct irregularities in the graph by plotting other points selected at discretion. All we can do is to draw a curve to lie as evenly as possible among the plotted points, passing through some perhaps, and with the rest fairly distributed on either side of the curve. As an aid to drawing an even continuous curve a thin piece of wood or other flexible material may be bent into the requisite curve, and held in position while the line is drawn. When the plotted points lie approximately on a straight line, the simplest plan is to use a piece of tracing paper or celluloid on which a straight line has been drawn. When this has been placed in the right position the extremities can be marked on the squared paper, and by joining these points the approximate graph is obtained.

Ex. 1. The following table gives statistics of the population of a certain country, where P is the number of millions at the beginning of each of the years specified.

Year	1830	1835	1840	1850	1860	1865	1870	1880
P	20	22.1	23.5	29.0	34.2	38.2	41.0	49.4

Let t be the time in years from 1830. Plot the values of P vertically and those of t horizontally and exhibit the relation between P and t by a simple curve passing fairly evenly among the plotted points. Find what the population was at the beginning of the years 1848 and 1875.

The graph is given in Fig. 21 on the opposite page. The populations in 1848 and 1875, at the points A and B respectively, will be found to be 27.8 millions and 45.3 millions.

Ex. 2. Corresponding values of x and y are given in the following table:

x	1	4	6.8	8	9.5	12	14.4
y	4	8	12.2	13	15.3	20	24.8

Supposing these values to involve errors of observation, draw the graph approximately and determine the most probable equation between x and y. [See Fig. 22.]

After carefully plotting the given points we see that a straight line can be drawn passing through three of them and lying evenly among the others. This is the required graph.

Assuming $y = ax + b$ for its equation, we find the values of a and b by selecting two pairs of simultaneous values of x and y.

Thus substituting $x = 4$, $y = 8$, and $x = 12$, $y = 20$ in the equation, we obtain $a = 1.5$, $b = 2$. Thus the equation of the graph is $y = 1.5x + 2$.

664. In the last example as the graph is linear it can be produced to any extent within the limits of the paper, and so any value of one of the variables being determined, the

GRAPHICAL REPRESENTATION OF FUNCTIONS.

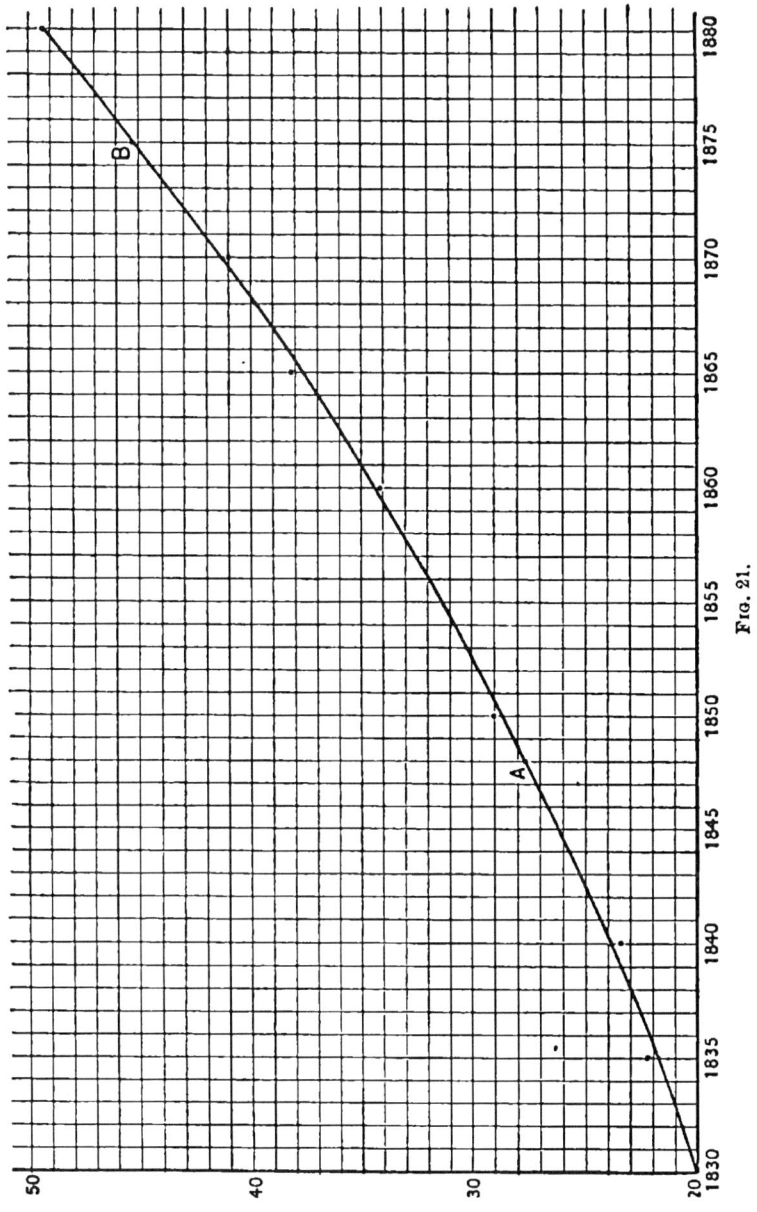

Fig. 21.

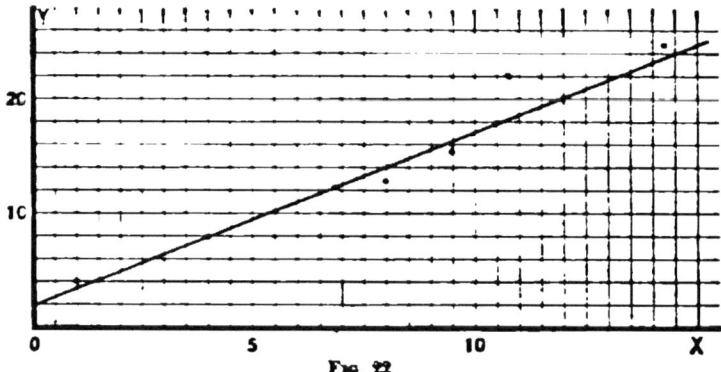
Fig. 22.

corresponding value of the other can be read off. When large values are in question this method is not only inconvenient but unsafe, owing to the fact that any divergence from accuracy in the portion of the graph drawn is increased when the curve is produced beyond the limits of the plotted points. The following example illustrates the method of procedure in such cases.

Ex. In a certain machine P is the force in pounds required to raise a weight of W pounds. The following corresponding values of P and W were obtained experimentally:

P	3.08*	3.9	6.8	8.8	9.2	11*	13.3
W	21	36.25	66.2	87.5	103.75	120	152.5

By plotting these values on squared paper, draw the graph connecting P and W, and read off the value of P when $W = 70$. Also determine a linear law connecting P and W; find the force necessary to raise a weight of 310 pounds, and also the weight which could be raised by a force of 180.6 pounds.

As the page is too small to exhibit the graphical work on a convenient scale, we shall merely indicate the steps of the solution, which is similar in detail to that of the last example.

Plot the values of P vertically and the values of W horizontally. It will be found that a straight line can be drawn through the points corresponding to the results marked with an asterisk, and lying evenly among the other points. From this graph we find that when $W = 70$, $P = 7$.

Assume $P = aW + b$, and substitute for P and W from the values corresponding to the two points through which the line passes. By solving the resulting equations we obtain $a = .08$, $b = 1.4$. Thus the linear equation connecting P and W is $P = .08\,W + 1.4$.

This is called the **Law of the Machine**.

From this equation, when $W = 310$, $P = 26.2$, and when $P = 180.6$, $W = 2240$.

Thus a force of 26.2 pounds will raise a weight of 310 pounds; and when a force of 180.6 pounds is applied the weight raised is 2240 pounds.

NOTE. The equation of the graph is not only useful for determining results difficult to obtain graphically, but it can always be used to check results found by measurement.

665. The example in the last article is a simple illustration of a method of procedure which is common in the laboratory or workshop, the object being to determine the law connecting two variables when a certain number of simultaneous values have been determined by experiment or observation.

Though we can always draw a graph to lie fairly among the plotted points corresponding to the observed values, unless the graph is a straight line it may be difficult to find its equation except by some indirect method.

For example, suppose x and y are quantities which satisfy an equation of the form $xy = ax + by$, and that this law has to be discovered.

By writing the equation in the form

$$\frac{a}{y} + \frac{b}{x} = 1, \text{ or } au + bv = 1;$$

where $u = \dfrac{1}{y}$, $v = \dfrac{1}{x}$, it is clear that u, v satisfy the equation of a straight line. In other words, if we were to plot the points corresponding to the reciprocals of the given values, their linear connection would be at once apparent. Hence the values of a and b could be found as in previous examples, and the required law in the form $xy = ax + by$ could be determined.

Again, suppose x and y satisfy an equation of the form $x^n y = c$, where n and c are constants.

By taking logarithms, we have

$$n \log x + \log y = \log c.$$

The form of this equation shows that $\log x$ and $\log y$ satisfy the equation to a straight line. If, therefore, the values of $\log x$ and $\log y$ are plotted, a linear graph can be drawn, and the constants n and c can be found as before.

Ex. The weight, y grams, necessary to produce a given deflection in the middle of a beam supported at two points, x centimeters apart, is determined experimentally for a number of values of x with results given in the following table:

x	50	60	70	80	90	100
y	270	150	100	60	47	32

Assuming that x and y are connected by the equation $x^n y = c$, find n and c.

$\log x$	$\log y$
1.699	2.431
1.778	2.176
1.845	2.000
1.903	1.778
1.954	1.672
2.000	1.519

From pages 360, 361 we obtain the values of $\log x$ and $\log y$ given here corresponding to the observed values of x and y. By plotting these we obtain the graph given in Fig. 23, and its equation is of the form

$$n \log x + \log y = \log c.$$

To obtain n and c, choose *two extreme points through which the line passes*. It will be found that when

$$\log x = 1.642, \ \log y = 2.6,$$

and when

$$\log x = 2.1, \quad \log y = 1.21.$$

Substituting these values, we have

$$2.6 + n \times 1.642 = \log c \ \ldots \ldots \ldots \ldots \text{(i.)},$$
$$1.21 + n \times 2.1 \ = \log c \ \ldots \ldots \ldots \ldots \text{(ii.)};$$
$$\therefore 1.39 - 0.458\, n = 0;$$

whence $\quad\quad\quad\quad n = 3.04.$

$\therefore$ from (ii.) $\log c = 6.38 + 1.21$
$\quad\quad\quad\quad\quad\quad\quad = 7.59;$
$\therefore c = 39 \times 10^6$, from the tables.

Thus the required equation is $x^3 y = 39 \times 10^6$.

The student should work through this example in detail on a larger scale. The figure below was drawn on paper ruled to tenths of an inch and then reduced to half the original scale.

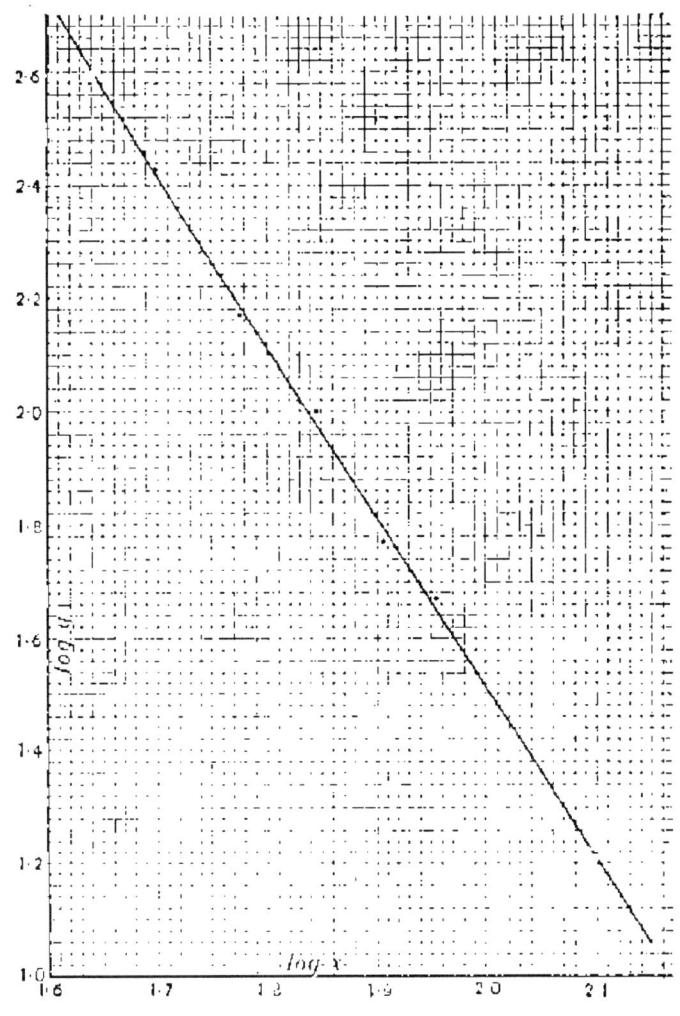

FIG. 23.

EXAMPLES XLIX. g.

1. Given that 6.01 yards = 5.5 meters, draw the graph showing the equivalent of any number of yards when expressed in meters.

Show that 22.2 yards = 20.3 meters approximately.

2. Draw a graph showing the relation between equal weights in grains and grams, having given that 18.1 grains = 1.17 grams.

Express (i.) 3.5 grams in grains.
(ii.) 3.09 grains as a decimal of gram.

3. If 3.26 inches are equivalent to 8.28 centimeters, show how to determine graphically the number of inches corresponding to a given number of centimeters. Obtain the number of inches in a meter, and the number of centimeters in a yard. What is the equation of the graph?

4. The following table gives approximately the circumferences of circles corresponding to different radii:

C	15.7	20.1	31.4	44	52.2
r	2.5	3.2	5	7	8.3

Plot the values on squared paper, and from the graph determine the diameter of a circle whose circumference is 12.1 inches and the circumference of a circle whose radius is 2.8 inches.

5. For a given temperature, C degrees on a Centigrade thermometer are equal to F degrees on a Fahrenheit thermometer. The following table gives a series of corresponding values of F and C:

C	-10	-5	0	5	10	15	25	40
F	14	23	32	41	50	59	77	104

Draw a graph to show the Fahrenheit reading corresponding to a given Centigrade temperature, and find the Fahrenheit readings corresponding to 12.5° C. and 31° C.

By observing the form of the graph find the algebraical relation between F and C.

6. At different ages the mean after-lifetime ("expectation of life") of males, calculated on the death rates of certain years, was given by the following table:

Age	6	10	14	18	22	26	27
Expectation	50.38	47.60	44.26	40.96	37.89	34.96	34.24

Draw a graph to show the expectation of life of any male between the ages of 6 and 27, and from it determine that of persons aged 12 and 20.

7. If W is the weight in ounces required to stretch an elastic string till its length is l inches, plot the following values of W and l:

W	2.5	3.75	6.25	7.5	10	11.25
l	8.5	8.7	9.1	9.3	9.7	9.9

From the graph determine the unstretched length of the string, and the weight the string will support when its length is 1 foot.

8. The highest and lowest marks gained in an examination are 297 and 132 respectively. These have to be reduced in such a way that the maximum for the paper (200) shall be given to the first candidate, and that there shall be a range of 150 marks between the first and last. Find the equation between x, the actual marks gained, and y, the corresponding marks when reduced.

Draw the graph of this equation, and read off the marks which should be given to candidates who gained 200, 262, 163 marks in the examination.

9. A body starting with an initial velocity, and subject to an acceleration in the direction of motion, has a velocity of v feet per second after t seconds. If corresponding values of v and t are given by the annexed table,

v	9	13	17	21	25	29	33	37	41	45
t	1	2	3	4	5	6	7	8	9	10

plot the graph exhibiting the velocity at any given time. Find from it (i.) the initial velocity, (ii.) the time which has elapsed when velocity is 28 feet per second. Also find the equation between v and t.

10. The connection between the areas of equilateral triangles and their bases (in corresponding units) is given by the following table:

Area	.43	1.73	3.90	6.93	10.82	15.59
Base	1	2	3	4	5	6

Illustrate these results graphically, and determine the area of an equilateral triangle on a base of 2.4 feet.

11. A body falling freely under gravity drops s feet in t seconds from the time of starting. If corresponding values of s and t at intervals of half a second are as follows:

t	.5	1	1.5	2	2.5	3	3.5	4
s	4	16	36	64	100	144	196	256

draw the curve connecting s and t, and find from it

(i.) the distance through which the body has fallen after 1·8″;
(ii.) the depth of a well if a stone takes 3·16″ to reach the bottom.

12. A body is projected with a given velocity at a given angle to the horizon, and the height in feet reached after t seconds is given by the equation $h = 64t - 16t^2$. Find the values of h at intervals of ¼th of a second and draw the path described by the body. Find the maximum value of h, and the time after projection before the body reaches the ground.

13. The following table gives the sun's position at 7 A.M. on different dates:

Mar. 23	Apr. 3	Apr. 20	May 8	May 27	June 22	July 18	Aug. 5	Aug. 25
80° E.	82° E.	85° E.	89° E.	92° E.	95 E.	94° E.	91° E.	85° E.

Show these results graphically, and estimate approximately the sun's position at the same hour on June 8.

14. At a given temperature p pounds per square inch represents the pressure of a gas which occupies a volume of v cubic inches. Draw a curve connecting p and v from the following table of corresponding values:

p	36	30	25.7	22.5	20	18	16.4	15
v	5	6	7	8	9	10	11	12

15. Plot on squared paper the following measured values of x and y, and determine the most probable equation between x and y:

x	3	5	8.3	11	13	15.5	18.6	23	28
y	2	2.2	3.4	3.8	4	4.6	5.4	6.2	7.25

16. Corresponding values of x and y are given in the following table:

x	1	3.1	6	9.5	12.5	16	19	23
y	2	2.8	4.2	5.3	6.6	8.3	9	10.8

Supposing these values to involve errors of observation, draw the graph approximately, and determine the most probable equation between x and y. Find the correct value of y when $x = 19$, and the correct value of x when $y = 2.8$.

17. The following corresponding values of x and y were obtained experimentally:

x	0.5	1.7	3.0	4.7	5.7	7.1	8.7	9.9	10.6	11.8
y	148	186	265	326	388	436	529	562	611	652

It is known that they are connected by an equation of the form $y = ax + b$, but the values of x and y involve errors of measurement. Find the most probable values of a and b, and estimate the error in the measured value of y when $x = 9.9$.

18. In a certain machine, P is the force in pounds required to raise a weight of W pounds. The following corresponding values of P and W were obtained experimentally:

P	2.8	3.7	4.8	5.5	6.5	7.3	8	9.5	10.4	11.75
W	20	25	31.7	35.6	45	52.4	57.5	65	71	82.5

Draw the graph connecting P and W, and read off the value of P when $W = 60$. Also determine the law of the machine, and find from it the weight which could be raised by a force of 31.7 pounds.

19. The following values of x and y, some of which are slightly inaccurate, are connected by an equation of the form $y = ax^2 + b$.

x	1	1.6	3	3.7	4	5	5.7	6	6.3	7
y	3.25	4	5	6.5	7.4	9.25	10.5	11.6	14	15.25

By plotting these values, draw the graph, and find the most probable values of a and b.

Find the true value of x when $y = 4$, and the true value of y when $x = 6$.

20. The following table gives corresponding values of two variables, x and y:

x	2.75	3	3.2	3.5	4.3	4.5	5.3	6	7	8	10
y	11	9.8	8	6.5	6.1	5.4	5	4.3	4.1	4	3.9

These values involve errors of observation, but the true values are known to satisfy an equation of the form $xy = ax + by$. Draw the graph by plotting the points determined by the above table, and find the most probable values of a and b. Find the correct values of y corresponding to $x = 3.5$, and $x = 7$.

21. Observed values of x and y are given as follows:

x	100	90	70	60	50	40
y	30	31.08	33.5	35.56	37.8	40.7

GRAPHICAL REPRESENTATION OF FUNCTIONS.

Assuming that x and y are connected by an equation of the form $xy^n = c$, find n and c.

22. The following values of x and y involve errors of observation:

x	66.83	63.10	58.88	51.52	48.53	44.16	40.36
y	144.5	158.5	177.8	208.9	236.0	264.9	309.0

If x and y satisfy an equation of the form $x^n y = c$, find n and c.

MISCELLANEOUS APPLICATIONS OF LINEAR GRAPHS.

666. When two quantities x and y are so related that a change in one produces a proportional change in the other, their variations can always be expressed by an equation of the form $y = ax$, where a is some constant quantity. Hence in all such cases, the graph which exhibits their variations is *a straight line through the origin,* so that in order to draw the graph it is only necessary to know the position of one other point on it. Such examples as deal with work and time, distance and time (when the speed is uniform), quantity and cost of material, principal and simple interest at a given rate per cent, may all be illustrated by linear graphs through the origin.

Ex. 1. *At 8 A.M. A starts from P to ride to Q, which is 48 miles distant. At the same time B sets out from Q to meet A. If A rides at 8 miles an hour, and rests half an hour at the end of every hour, while B walks uniformly at 4 miles an hour, find graphically*

    (i.) *the time and place of meeting;*
    (ii.) *the distance between A and B at 11 A.M.;*
    (iii.) *at what time they are 14 miles apart.*

In Fig. 24, on the following page, let the position of P be chosen as origin; let time be measured horizontally from 8 A.M. (1 inch to 1 hour), and let distance be measured vertically (1 inch to 20 miles).

In 1 hour A rides 8 miles; therefore the point D (1, 8) marks his position at 9 A.M. In the next half hour he makes no advance towards Q; therefore, the corresponding portion of the graph is DE. The details of A's motion may now be completed by the broken line PDEFGHKX.

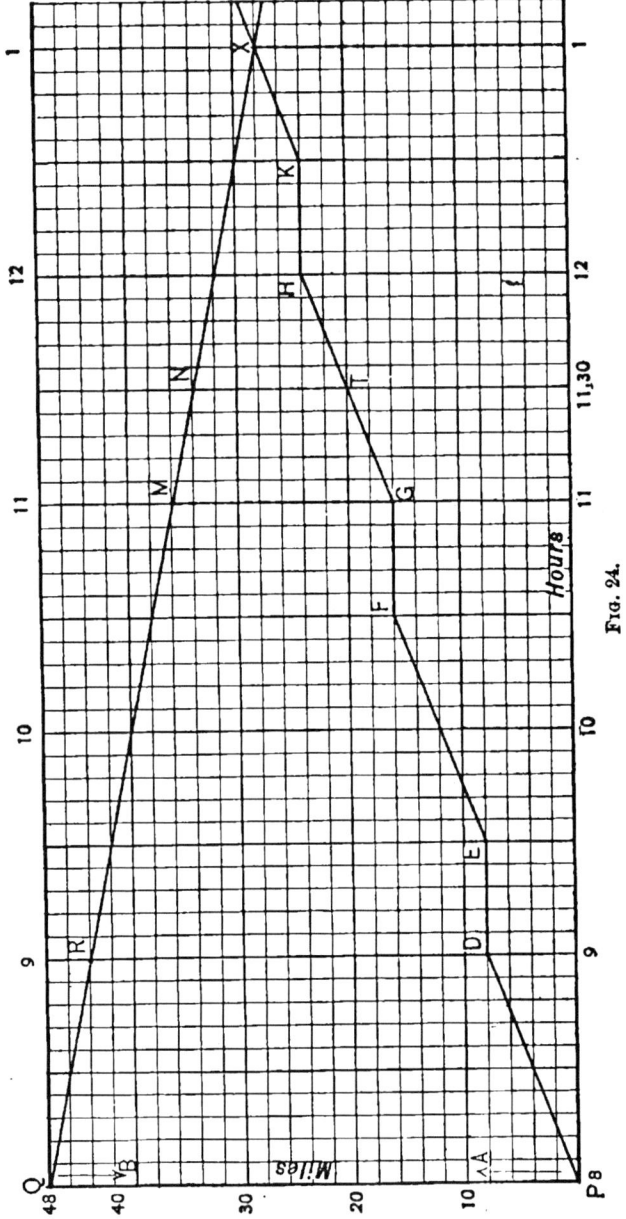

Fig. 24.

GRAPHICAL REPRESENTATION OF FUNCTIONS.

On the vertical axis, mark PQ to represent 48 miles and mark the hours on the horizontal line through Q. At 9 A.M. B has walked 4 miles towards P. Measuring a distance to represent 4 miles *downwards* we get the point R, and QR produced is the graph of B's motion. It cuts A's graph at X. Hence the point of meeting is X, which is 28 miles from P, and the time is 1 P.M.

The distance between A and B at any time is shown by the difference of the ordinates. Thus at 11 A.M. their distance apart is MG, which represents 20 miles.

Lastly, NT represents 14 miles; thus A and B are 14 miles apart at 11.30 A.M.

Ex. 2. *A, B, and C run a race of 300 yards. A and C start from scratch, and A covers the distance in 40 seconds, beating C by 60 yards. B, with 12 yards start, beats A by 4 seconds. Supposing the rates of running in each case to be uniform, find graphically the relative positions of the runners when B passes the winning post. Find also by how many yards B is ahead of A when the latter has run three fourths of the course.*

In Fig. 25 let time be measured horizontally (0.5 inch to 10 seconds), and distance vertically (1 inch to 60 yards). O is the starting point for A and C; take OP equal to 0.2 inch, representing 12 yards, on the vertical axis: then P is B's starting point.

A's graph is drawn by joining O to the point which marks 40 seconds. From this point measure a vertical distance of 1 inch downwards to Q. Then since 1 inch represents 60 yards, Q is C's position when A is at the winning post, and OQ is C's graph.

Along the time-axis take 1.8 inch to R, representing 36 seconds; then PR is B's graph.

Through R draw a vertical line to meet the graphs of A and C in S and T respectively. Then S and T mark the positions of A and C when B passes the winning post.

By inspection RS and ST represent 30 and 54 yards respectively.

Thus B is 30 yards ahead of A, and A is 54 yards ahead of C.

Again, since A runs three fourths of the course in 30 seconds, the difference of the corresponding ordinates of A's and B's graphs after 30 seconds will give the distance between A and B. By measurement we find VW = .0.45 inch, which represents 27 yards.

It is recommended that the student draw a figure for himself on a scale twice as large as that given in Fig. 25.

667. When a variable quantity y is partly constant and partly proportional to a variable quantity x, the algebraical relation between x and y is of the form $y = ax + b$, where a and b are constant. The corresponding graph will therefore

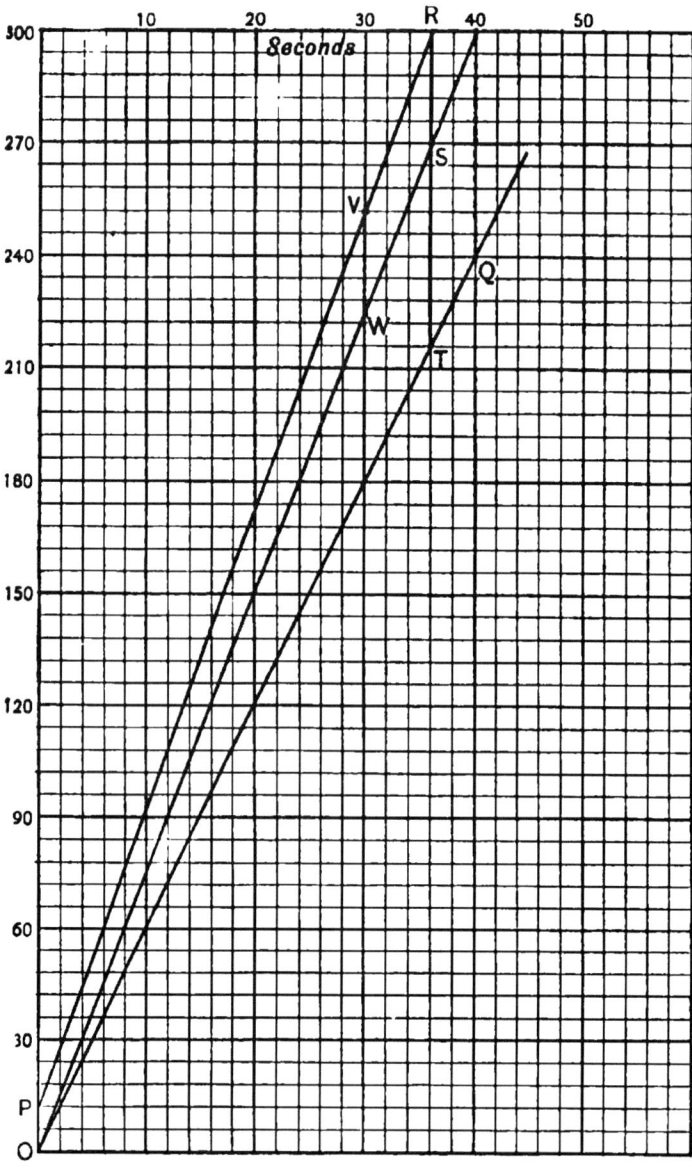

Fig. 25.

be a straight line; and since a straight line is completely determined when the positions of two points are known, it follows that, in all problems which can be illustrated by linear graphs, it is sufficient if the data furnish for each graph two independent pairs of simultaneous values of the variable quantities.

Some easy examples of this kind have already been given on page 546 and in Examples XLIX. g. We shall now work out two more examples.

Ex. 1. In a certain establishment the clerks are paid an initial salary for the first year, and this is annually increased by a fixed bonus, the initial salary and the bonus being different in different departments. A receives $1000 in his 10th year, and $1450 in his 19th. B, in another department, receives $1050 in his 5th year and $1250 in his 13th. Draw graphs to show their salaries in different years. In what year do they receive equal salaries? Also find in what year A earns the same salary as that received by B for his 21st year.

In Fig. 26 let each horizontal division represent 1 year; and let the salaries be measured vertically, beginning at 1000, with 1 division to represent $10.

If the salary at the end of x years is denoted by $\$y$, it is evident that in each case we have a relation of the form $y = ax + b$, where a and b are constant. Thus the variations of time and salary may be represented by linear graphs.

Since no bonus is received for the first year, $x = 9$, when $y = 1000$, and $x = 18$, when $y = 1450$. Thus the points P and Q are determined, and by joining them we have the graph for A's salary. Similarly, the graph for B's salary is found by joining P' (4, 1050) and Q' (12, 1250).

These lines have the same ordinate and abscissa at L, where $x = 16$, $y = 1350$. Thus A and B have the same salary when each has served 16 years, that is in their 17th year. Again B's salary at the end of 20 years is given by the ordinate of M, which is the same as that of Q which represents A's salary after 18 years.

Thus A's salary for his 19th year is equal to B's salary for his 21st year.

Ex. 2. Two sums of money are put out at simple interest at different rates per cent. In the first case the amounts at the end of 6 years and 15 years are $1300 and $1750 respectively. In the second case the amounts for 5 years and 20 years are $1650 and $2100. Draw graphs from which the amounts may be read off for any year, and find the year in which the principal with accrued interest will

564 ALGEBRA.

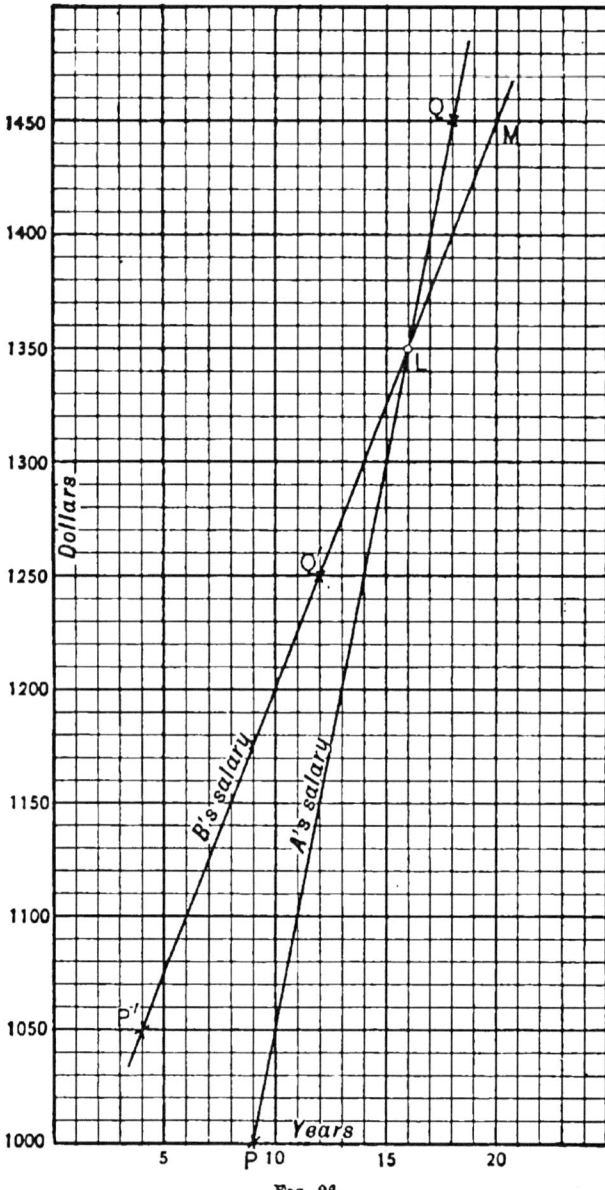

Fig. 26.

amount to the same in the two cases. Also from the graphs read off the value of each principal.

When a sum of money is at simple interest for any number of years, we have

Amount = Principal + Interest,

where principal is constant, and interest varies with the number of years. Hence the variations of amount and time may be represented by a linear graph in which x is taken to denote the number of years, and y the number of dollars in the corresponding amount.

Here, as the diagram is inconveniently large, we shall merely indicate the steps of the solution which is similar in detail to that of the last example. The student should draw his own diagram.

Measure time horizontally (1 inch to 10 years), and amount vertically (1 inch to $200) beginning at $1300.

The first graph is the line joining L (6, 1300) and M (15, 1750). The second graph is the line joining L' (5, 1650) and M' (20, 2100). In each of these lines the ordinate of any point gives the Amount for the number of years given by the corresponding abscissa.

Again LM, and L'M' intersect at a point P where $x = 25$, $y = 450$. Thus each principal with its interest amounts to $2250 in 25 years.

When $x = 0$ there is no interest; thus the principals will be obtained by reading off the values of the intercepts made by the two graphs on the y-axis. These are $1000 and $1500 respectively.

NOTE. To obtain the result $y = 200$ it will be necessary to continue the y-axis downwards sufficiently far to show this ordinate.

EXAMPLES XLIX. h.

1. At noon A starts to walk at 6 miles an hour, and at 1.30 P.M. B follows on horseback at 8 miles an hour. When will B overtake A? Also find
   (i.) when A is 5 miles ahead of B;
   (ii.) when A is 3 miles behind B.

[Take 1 inch horizontally to represent 1 hour, and 1 inch vertically to represent 10 miles.]

2. By measuring time along OX (1 inch for 1 hour) and distance along OY (1 inch for 10 miles) show how to draw lines
   (i.) from O to indicate distance travelled towards Y at 12 miles an hour;
   (ii.) from Y to indicate distance travelled towards O at 9 miles an hour.

If these are the rates of two men who ride towards each other from two places 60 miles apart, starting at noon, find from the graphs when they are first 18 miles from each other. Also find (to the nearest minute) their time of meeting.

3. Two bicyclists ride to meet each other from two places 95 miles apart. A starts at 8 A.M. at 10 miles an hour, and B starts at 9.30 A.M. at 15 miles an hour. Find graphically when and where they meet, and at what times they are 37½ miles apart.

4. A and B start at the same time to go from New York to Fairview, A walking 4 miles an hour, B riding 9 miles an hour. B reaches Fairview in 4 hours, and immediately rides back to New York. After 2 hours' rest he starts again for Fairview at the same rate. How far from New York will he overtake A, who has in the meantime rested 6¼ hours?

5. At what distance from New York, and at what time, will a train which leaves New York for Hyde Park at 2.33 P.M., and goes at the rate of 35 miles an hour, meet a train which leaves Hyde Park at 1.45 P.M. and goes at the rate of 25 miles an hour, the distance between New York and Hyde Park being 80 miles?
Also find at what times the trains are 24 miles apart.

6. A, B, and C set out to walk from Chicago to Aurora at 5, 6, and 4 miles an hour respectively. C starts 3 minutes before and B 7 minutes after A. Draw graphs to show (i.) when and where A overtakes C; (ii.) when and where B overtakes A; (iii.) C's position relative to the others after he has walked 45 minutes.
[Take 1 inch horizontally to represent 10 minutes, and 1 inch to the mile vertically.]

7. X and Y are two towns 35 miles apart. At 8.30 P.M. A starts to walk from X to Y at 4 miles an hour; after walking 8 miles he rests for half an hour and then completes his journey on horseback at 10 miles an hour. At 9.48 A.M. B starts to walk from Y to X at 3 miles an hour; find when and where A and B meet. Also find at what times they are 6¼ miles apart.

8. A can beat B by 20 yards in 120, and B can beat C by 10 yards in 50. Supposing their rates of running to be uniform, find graphically how much start A can give C in 120 yards so as to run a dead heat with him. If A, B, and C start together, where are A and C when B has run 80 yards?

9. A, B, and C run a race of 200 yards. A gives B a start of 8 yards, and C starts some seconds after A. A runs the distance in 25 seconds and beats C by 40 yards. B beats A by 1 second, and when he has been running 15 seconds he is 48 yards ahead of C. Find graphically how many seconds C starts after A. Show also

GRAPHICAL REPRESENTATION OF FUNCTIONS. 567

from the graphs that if the three runners started even they would run a dead heat.

[Take 1 inch to 40 yards, and 1 inch to 10 seconds.]

10. A cyclist has to ride 75 miles. He rides for a time at 9 miles an hour and then alters his speed to 15 miles an hour covering the distance in 7 hours. At what time did he change his speed?

11. A and B ride to meet each other from two towns X, and Y, which are 60 miles apart. A starts at 1 P.M., and B starts 36 minutes later. If they meet at 4 P.M., and A gets to Y at 6 P.M., find the time when B gets to X. Also find the times when they are 22 miles apart. When A is halfway between X and Y, where is B?

12. The distance between two towns X and Y is 119 miles; if I were to set out at noon to cycle from X, riding 23 miles the first hour and decreasing my pace by 3 miles each successive hour, find graphically how long it would take me to reach Y. Also find approximately the time at which I should reach a town 48 miles from Y.

13. At 8 A.M. A begins a ride on a motor car at 20 miles an hour, and an hour and a half later B, starting from the same point, follows on his bicycle at 10 miles an hour. After riding 36 miles, A rests for 1 hour 24 minutes, then rides back at 9 miles an hour. Find graphically when and where he meets B. Also find (i.) at what time the riders were 21 miles apart, (ii.) how far B will have ridden by the time A gets back to his starting point.

14. I row against a stream flowing $1\frac{1}{4}$ miles an hour to a certain point, and then turn back, stopping two miles short of the place whence I originally started. If the whole time occupied in rowing is 2 hours 10 minutes, and my uniform speed in still water is $4\frac{1}{2}$ miles an hour, find graphically how far upstream I went.

[Take 1.2 of an inch horizontally to represent 1 hour, and 1 inch to 2 miles vertically.]

15. One train leaves Albany at 3 P.M. and reaches New York at 6 P.M.; a second train leaves New York at 1.30 P.M. and arrives at Albany at 6 P.M.; if both trains are supposed to travel uniformly, at what time will they meet? Show from a graph that the time does not depend upon the distance between New York and Albany.

16. At 7.40 A.M. the accommodation train starts from Hudson and reaches New York at 11.40 A.M.; the express starting from New York at 9 A.M. arrives at Hudson at 11.40 A.M.: if both trains travel uniformly, find when they meet. Show, as in Ex. 15, that the time is independent of the distance between New York and Hudson, and verify this conclusion by solving an algebraical equation.

17. A boy starts from home and walks to school at the rate of 10 yards in 3 seconds, and is 20 seconds too soon. The next day he walks at the rate of 40 yards in 17 seconds, and is half a minute late. Find graphically the distance to the school, and show that he would have been just in time if he had walked at the rate of 20 yards in 7 seconds.

18. A body is moving in a straight line with varying velocity. The velocity at any instant is made up of the constant velocity with which it was projected (measured in feet per second) diminished by a retardation of a constant number of feet per second in every second. After 4 seconds the velocity was 320, and after 13 seconds it was 140. Draw a graph to show the velocity at any time while the body is in motion.

A second body projected at the same time under similar conditions has a velocity of 450 after 5 seconds, and a velocity of 150 after 15 seconds. Show graphically that they will both come to rest at the same time. Also find at what time the second body is moving 100 feet per second faster than the first, and determine from the graphs the velocity of projection in each case.

19. In a certain examination the highest and lowest marks gained in a Latin paper were 153 and 51. These have to be reduced so that the maximum (120) is given to the first candidate, and the minimum (30) to the lowest. This is done by reducing all the marks in a certain ratio, and then increasing or diminishing them all by the same number. In a Greek paper the highest and lowest marks were 161 and 56; after a similar adjustment these become 100 and 40 respectively. Draw graphs from which all the reduced marks may be read off, and find the marks which should be finally given to a candidate who scored 102 in Latin and 126 in Greek.

Show also that it is possible in one case for a candidate to receive equal marks in the two subjects both before and after reduction. What are the original and reduced marks in this case?

MISCELLANEOUS GRAPHS.

1. Plot the graphs of
$$2y = 3(x-4), \ 3y = 1 - 5x,$$
obtaining at least five points on each graph. Find the coördinates of the point where they meet.

2. Draw the graphs represented by
$$y = 5 - 3x, \ y = \tfrac{1}{3}(x+5);$$
and find the coördinates of their point of intersection.

GRAPHICAL REPRESENTATION OF FUNCTIONS. 569

3. By finding the intercepts on the axes draw the graphs of

(i.) $15x + 20y = 6$; (ii.) $12x + 21y = 14$.

In (i.) take 1 inch for unit, and in (ii.) take six tenths of an inch as unit. In each case explain why the unit is convenient.

4. Solve $y = 10x + 8$, $7x + y = 25$ graphically.

[Unit for x, one inch; for y, one tenth of an inch.]

5. From the graph of the expression $11x + 6$, find its value when $x = 1.8$. Also find the value of x which will make the expression equal to 20.

6. With the same units as in Ex. 4 draw the graph of the function $\dfrac{36 - 5x}{3}$. From the graph find the value of the function when $x = 1.8$; also find for what value of x the function becomes equal to 8.

7. Show that the straight lines given by the equations

$$9y = 5x + 65,\ 5x + 2y + 10 = 0,\ x + 3y = 11,$$

meet in a point. Find its coördinates.

8. Draw the triangle whose sides are given by the equations:

$$3y - x = 9,\ x + 7y = 11,\ 3x + y = 13;$$

and find the coördinates of its vertices.

9. Show graphically that the values of x and y which satisfy the equations
$$5x = 2y - 18,\ 5y = 6 - 7x,$$
also satisfy the equation $x + y = 2$.

10. Draw the graphs of (i.) $y = x^2$, (ii.) $y = 8x^2$.
In (i.) take $0.4''$ as unit for x, $0.2''$ as unit for y.
In (ii.) take $1''$ as unit for x, $0.1''$ as unit for y.

11. On the same scale as in Ex. 10 (ii.) draw the graph of $y = 16x^2$. Show that it may also be simply deduced from the graph of Ex. 10 (ii.).

12. Plot the graph of $y = x^2$, taking 1 inch as unit on both axes, and using the following values of x:

$$-0.4,\ -0.3,\ -0.2,\ -0.1,\ 0,\ 0.1,\ 0.2,\ 0.3,\ 0.4.$$

13. Draw the graph of $x = y^2$, from $y = 0$ to $y = 5$, and thence find the square roots of 7 and 3.6.

[Take $0.2''$ as unit for x, $1''$ as unit for y.]

14. Draw the graph of $y = 5 + x - x^2$ for values of x from -2 to $+3$, and from the figure obtain approximate values for the roots of the equation $5 + x - x^2 = 0$.

[Take $1''$ as unit for x, $0.2''$ as unit for y.]

15. Draw the graphs of

(i.) $5x + 6y = 60$, (ii.) $6y - x = 24$, (iii.) $2x - y = 7$;

and show that they represent three lines which meet in a point.

16. Solve the following equations graphically:

(i.) $x^2 + y^2 = 53$, (ii.) $x^2 + y^2 = 100$,
$y - x = 5$; $x + y = 14$;
(iii.) $x^2 + y^2 = 34$, (iv.) $x^2 + y^2 = 36$,
$2x + y = 11$; $4x + 3y = 12$.

[Approximate roots to be given to one place of decimals.]

17. Solve the equation $3 + 6x = x^2$ graphically, and find the maximum value of the expression $3 + 6x - x^2$.

18. Draw the graphs of x^2 and $3x + 1$. By means of them find approximate values for the roots of $x^2 - 3x - 1 = 0$.

19. If 24 men can reap a field of 29 acres in a given time, find roughly by means of a graph the number of acres which could be reaped in the same time by 15, 33, and 42 men respectively.

20. The highest marks gained in an examination were 136, and these are to be raised so that the maximum is 200. Show how this may be done by means of a graph, and read off, to the nearest integer, the final marks of candidates who scored 61 and 49 respectively.

21. Draw a graph which will give the square roots of all numbers between 25 and 36, to three places of decimals.

[Plot the graph of $y = x^2$, beginning at the point (5, 25), with $10''$ and $0.5''$ as units for x and y respectively.]

22. I want a ready way of finding approximately 0.866 of any number up to 10. Justify the following construction. Join the origin to a point P whose coördinates are 10 and 8.66 (1 inch being taken as unit); then the ordinate of any point on OP is 0.866 of the corresponding abscissa. Read off from the diagram,

0.866 of 3, 0.866 of 6.5, 0.866 of 4.8, and $\dfrac{1}{0.866}$ of 5.

23. A starts from New York at noon at 8 miles an hour; two hours later B starts, riding at 12 miles an hour. Find graphically at what time and at what distance from New York B overtakes A. At what times will A and B be 8 miles apart? If C rides after B,

starting at 3 P.M. at 15 miles an hour, find from the graphs
(i.) the distances between A, B, and C at 5 P.M.;
(ii.) the time when C is 8 miles behind B.

24. If O and Y represent two towns 45 miles apart, and if A walks from Y to O at 6 miles an hour while B walks from O to Y at 4 miles an hour, both starting at noon, find graphically their time and place of meeting.

Also read off from the graphs
(i.) the times when they are 15 miles apart;
(ii.) B's distance from Y at 6.15 P.M.

25. At 8 A.M. A starts from P to ride to Q which is 48 miles distant. At the same time B sets out from Q to meet A. If A rides at 8 miles an hour, and rests half an hour at the end of every hour, while B walks uniformly at 4 miles an hour, find graphically
(i.) the time and place of meeting;
(ii.) the distance between A and B at 11 A.M.;
(iii.) at what time they are 14 miles apart.

26. The following table gives statistics of the population of a certain country, where P is the number of millions at the beginning of each of the years specified.

Year	1830	1835	1840	1845	1850	1855	1860
P	20	22	24.5	28	31	36	41

Let t be the time in years from 1830. Plot the values of P vertically and those of t horizontally and show the relation between P and t by a simple curve passing fairly evenly among the plotted points. Find what the population was at the beginning of the years 1847 and 1858.

27. The salary of a clerk is increased each year by a fixed sum. After 6 years' service his salary is raised to $1280 and after 15 years to $2000. Draw a graph from which his salary may be read off for any year, and determine from it (i.) his initial salary, (ii.) the salary he should receive for his 21st year.

28. Draw the graphs of $y = x^2$ and $2y = x + 3$ on the same diagram. Deduce the roots of the equation $2x^2 - x - 3 = 0$.

29. Taking 1 inch as unit, plot the graph of $y = x^3 - 3x$, taking the following values of x:

0, ±.2, ±.4, ±.6, ±.8, ±1, ±1.2, ±1.4, ±1.6, ±1.8, ±2.

Find the turning points, and the value of the maximum or minimum ordinates between the limits given.

30. From the graph in **Ex.** 29 find to two places of decimals the roots of $x^3 - 3x = 0$.

31. Solve the following pairs of equations graphically:

(i.) $x + y = 15$,   (ii.) $x = y = 3$,   (iii.) $x^2 + y^2 = 13$,
    $xy = 36$; $xy = 18$; $xy = 6$.

32. An india-rubber cord was loaded with weights, and a measurement of its length was taken for each load as tabulated. Plot a graph to show the relation between the length of the cord and the loads.

Load in pounds	10	12	17	21	23	25
Length in centimeters	36.4	37.7	40.5	43.0	44.3	45.4

What was the length of the cord unloaded?

33. The mean temperature on the first day of each month, on an average of 50 years, had the following values:

Jan. 1, 37°;   May 1, 50°;   Sept. 1, 59°;
Feb. 1, 38°;   June 1, 57°;   Oct. 1, 54°;
Mar. 1, 40°;   July 1, 62°;   Nov. 1, 46°;
April 1, 45°;   Aug. 1, 62°;   Dec. 1, 41°.

Represent these variations by means of a smooth curve.

[The difference of length of different months may be neglected.]

34. A manufacturer wishes to stock a certain article in many sizes; at present he has five sizes made at the prices given below:

Length in inches	20	27	33	45	54
Price in dollars	11	14.5	20	35	48.5

Draw a graph to show suitable prices for intermediate sizes, and find what the prices should be when the lengths are 30 inches and 46 inches.

35. Several tourists set out for a station 3 miles distant and go at the rate of 3 miles an hour. After going half a mile one of them has to return to the starting point; at what rate must he now walk in order to reach the station at the same time as the others?

36. A motor car on its way to Bristol overtakes a cyclist at 9 A.M.; the car reaches Bristol at 10.30 and after waiting 1 hour returns, meeting the cyclist at noon. Supposing the speeds of car and cyclist to be uniform, find when the cyclist will reach Bristol. Also compare the speeds of the car and cyclist.

THE following pages contain advertisements of a few of the Macmillan books on kindred subjects

The Teaching of Mathematics in Secondary Schools

BY

ARTHUR SCHULTZE

Formerly Head of the Department of Mathematics in the High School of Commerce, New York City, and Assistant Professor of Mathematics in New York University

Cloth, 12mo, 370 pages, $1.25

The author's long and successful experience as a teacher of mathematics in secondary schools and his careful study of the subject from the pedagogical point of view, enable him to speak with unusual authority. "The chief object of the book,' he says in the preface, "is to contribute towards making mathematical teaching less informational and more disciplinary. Most teachers admit that mathematical instruction derives its importance from the mental training that it affords, and not from the information that it imparts. But in spite of these theoretical views, a great deal of mathematical teaching is still informational. Students still learn demonstrations instead of learning how to demonstrate."

The treatment is concrete and practical. Typical topics treated are: the value and the aims of mathematical teaching; causes of the inefficiency of mathematical teaching; methods of teaching mathematics; the first propositions in geometry; the original exercise; parallel lines; methods of attacking problems; the circle; impossible constructions; applied problems; typical parts of algebra.

THE MACMILLAN COMPANY

64-66 Fifth Avenue, New York

CHICAGO   BOSTON   SAN FRANCISCO   DALLAS   ATLANTA

Geometry, Revised Edition

BY

ARTHUR SCHULTZE

Formerly Head of the Department of Mathematics in the High School of
Commerce of New York City, and Assistant Professor of
Mathematics in New York University

AND

F. L. SEVENOAK

Principal of the Stevens School, Hoboken, N.J.

Plane Geometry $0.80
Plane and Solid Geometry . . . 1.10

In the revised edition, prepared by Dr. Schultze, the familiar merits of the earlier edition have been preserved and some additional features have been added. The student is introduced gradually and systematically to the solution of geometrical exercises. A new collection of practical exercises is given, and there are improvements in the typographical form of demonstrations. Modern symbols and phraseology are used throughout.

THE MACMILLAN COMPANY

64–66 Fifth Avenue, New York

CHICAGO   BOSTON   SAN FRANCISCO   DALLAS   ATLANTA

Algebra for Beginners

BY

H. S. HALL AND S. R. KNIGHT

Authors of "Algebra for Colleges and Schools," etc. Revised and adapted to American Schools by F. L. Sevenoak, Principal of the Stevens School, Hoboken, N.J.

Cloth, 12mo, 188 pages, $.60

This book contains the essential elements of the subject without the more complex and difficult parts. It will be found to meet the wants of all who do not require a knowledge of algebra beyond quadratic equations — that portion of the subject usually covered in the examination for admission to American colleges.

Elements of Algebra

BY

H. S. HALL AND S. R. KNIGHT

Authors of "Algebra for Colleges and Schools," etc. Revised and adapted to American Schools by F. L. Sevenoak, Principal of the Stevens School, Hoboken, N.J.

Cloth, 12mo, 366 pages, $.90

This book contains the first thirty-eight chapters of the authors' "Algebra for Colleges and Schools." It is designed for use in classes in which the more advanced phases of the subject are not studied or in which the use of an elementary and an advanced book is preferred.

THE MACMILLAN COMPANY

64-66 Fifth Avenue, New York

CHICAGO   BOSTON   SAN FRANCISCO   DALLAS   ATLANTA

PRACTICAL PHYSICS FOR SECONDARY SCHOOLS

By N. HENRY BLACK, of the Roxbury Latin School, Boston, and
Prof. HARVEY N. DAVIS, of Harvard University

Cloth, 12mo., illustrated, 488 pages, list price, $1.25

"In preparing this book," say the authors in the Preface, "we have tried to select only those topics which are of vital interest to young people, whether or not they intend to continue the study of physics in a college course.

"In particular, we believe that the chief value of the informational side of such a course lies in its applications to the machinery of daily life. Everybody needs to know something about the working of electrical machinery, optical instruments, ships, automobiles, and all those labor-saving devices, such as vacuum cleaners, fireless cookers, pressure cookers, and electric irons, which are found in many American homes. We have, therefore, drawn as much of our illustrative material as possible from the common devices in modern life. We see no reason why this should detract in the least from the educational value of the study of physics, for one can learn to think straight just as well by thinking about an electrical generator, as by thinking about a Geissler tube. . . . .

"To understand any machine clearly, the student must have clearly in mind the fundamental principles involved. Therefore, although we have tried to begin each new topic, however short, with some concrete illustration familiar to young people, we have proceeded, as rapidly as seemed wise, to a deduction of the general principle. Then, to show how to make use of this principle, we have discussed other practical applications. We have tried to emphasize still further the value of principles, that is, generalizations, in science, by summarizing at the end of each chapter the principles discussed in that chapter. In these summaries we have aimed to make the phrasing brief and vivid so that it may be easily remembered and easily used."

The new and noteworthy features of the book are the admirable selection of familiar material used to develop and apply the principles of physical science, the exceptionally clear and forceful exposition, showing the hand of the master teacher, the practical, interesting, thought-provoking problems and the superior illustrations.

THE MACMILLAN COMPANY
64-66 Fifth Avenue, NEW YORK CITY

BOSTON		ATLANTA		DALLAS
	CHICAGO		SAN FRANCISCO	

To avoid fine, this book should be returned on
or before the date last stamped below

OCT 25 1938
DEC 6 1950
JUL 29 1954

Richmondshire And The Vale Of Mowbray

Edmund Bogg

Nabu Public Domain Reprints:

You are holding a reproduction of an original work published before 1923 that is in the public domain in the United States of America, and possibly other countries. You may freely copy and distribute this work as no entity (individual or corporate) has a copyright on the body of the work. This book may contain prior copyright references, and library stamps (as most of these works were scanned from library copies). These have been scanned and retained as part of the historical artifact.

This book may have occasional imperfections such as missing or blurred pages, poor pictures, errant marks, etc. that were either part of the original artifact, or were introduced by the scanning process. We believe this work is culturally important, and despite the imperfections, have elected to bring it back into print as part of our continuing commitment to the preservation of printed works worldwide. We appreciate your understanding of the imperfections in the preservation process, and hope you enjoy this valuable book.

To mike

This is a great Book too and William Grainge gets a mention too the author of your 1st book I sent you

Enjoy

Christine

Stay House

THE LOWER VALLEY OF THE YORE

AND

THE VALE OF MOWBRAY.

Richmondshire

AND THE

Vale of Mowbray.

BY

EDMUND BOGG,

AUTHOR OF

"TWO THOUSAND MILES IN WHARFEDALE."
"THE BORDER COUNTRY."   "EDEN VALE."
AND
"THE OLD KINGDOM OF ELMETE."
Etc., Etc.

IN TWO VOLUMES.

VOL. I.

THE VALE OF MOWBRAY.

158 ILLUSTRATIONS AND 4 MAPS.

LONDON: ELLIOT STOCK.
LEEDS: JAMES MILES.

1906.

Br 5228.24.5

Gift of
William Endicott, Jr.
(I)

PREFACE.

If any excuse be needed for a Preface, it must be found in the Writer's desire to draw attention to the compelling motive for this work—that love of the Beautiful and the Fugitive in Nature and Man's handiwork which he would have others enjoy. Scenery remains, and the glories of Earth and Sky repeat themselves with the pageant of the Seasons; but much of ancient monument, and more of Local Custom and Tradition pass away. A Chronicler's labour, before it is too late, is never all "Love's Labour Lost," and having tried—successfully or not rests with others to say—to perpetuate something of the features (past and present) of the Ancient Kingdom of Elmete, of Wharfeland, of Nidderdale, and of Yore Vale in former works, it seems to the author an unwritten command to round off his labours with a final account of the golden Vale (of Mowbray) and that historic territory of Richmondshire (told in the Second Volume to follow) through which runs that artery of a river—the Swale. The apology for the task lies in the dominant character and position of this central part of that which may not inaptly be termed the Heart of York's Shire!

Thanks are due and here given to the Rev. F. Addison, Rev. J. C. Fowler, Wm. Foggitt, J.P., Dr. Arnold Lees and Robert Rodwell for their contributions on Geology, Botany, and Animated Nature; and I also thank the Rev. J. C. Fowler, Robert Rodwell, John Pennington, Walter Pattison, George Parker, Tom Fox, J. H. Barker, and G. Thompson, for the loan of blocks and drawings.

EDMUND BOGG.

LEEDS,
    October, 1906.

Index to Illustrations.

PAGE.
6	The Devil's Arrows	P. Robinson
10	The Middle Arrow	Edmund Bogg
12	The Southern Arrow	Edmund Bogg
13	Tesselated Pavement, Aldborough	
16	Lovers' Walk, Aldborough	P. Robinson
20	Cross and Manor House, Aldborough	A. Haselgrave
22	Aldborough Church	Edmund Bogg
24	Saxon Relics, Boroughbridge	
27	Old House, Boroughbridge	A. Haselgrave
29	Boroughbridge Hall	A. Haselgrave
30	Staveley Village	A. Haselgrave
32	Grafton Village	W. Brooke
33	Old Punch Bowl, Marton	Edmund Bogg
34	Little Ouseburn	P. Robinson
36	Low Dunsforth	
38	Great Ouseburn	Gilbert Foster
43	Old Cottage, Kirby Hill	Edmund Bogg
44	Old Well, Kirby Hill	A. Haselgrave
46	Sobieski Statue, Newby	
48	Tapestry Room, Newby	Watson
50	A Bend of the River	Gilbert Foster
51	Sharrow Village	Gilbert Foster
54	Bishop Monckton	Edmund Bogg
56	Markenfield Hall	P. Robinson
60	The Monks' First Shelter	Gilbert Foster
62	The Tower of Fountains'	Edmund Bogg
65	Fountains from the South	P. Robinson

viii.

PAGE.

67	Fountains Abbey	P. Robinson
69	Nine Altars' Chapel	Richardson
71	Fountains Hall	G. Parker
73	Cellarium, Fountains'	G. Parker
76	The Old Yew, Fountains	G. Parker
79	The Skell and Laver Country (Map)	
81	Azerley	Edmund Bogg
83	Laverton	Edmund Bogg
87	The Laver at Winksley	Gilbert Foster
90	Ripon Minster	G. Parker
95	Chapel of St. Mary Magdalene	
101	The Horn Blower	G. Parker
103	Ripon Minster	G. Parker
105	Ripon Market-Place	G. Parker
107	The Markenfield's Tomb	W. Brook
108	On the Yore, Ripon	G. Parker
112	Yoredale (Map)	
113	Norton Conyers	P. Robinson
114	Aumbry at Wath	
117	Well Village	Owen Bowen
120	Street Scene, Well	Edmund Bogg
121	Tanfield	Edmund Bogg
126	Tanfield from the Bridge	Gilbert Foster
129	The Marmion Tombs	P. Robinson
132	Mickley	Edmund Bogg
135	Hackfall	G. Watson
137	Kirby Malzeard	Edmund Bogg
139	Ancient Cross, Masham	Edmund Bogg
141	The Square, Masham	P. Robinson
144	The Wyville Chapel	Edmund Bogg
145	Grave Covers, Masham	
147	Fearby	Edmund Bogg
149	Colsterdale	Owen Bowen
150	Moor-Farm, Fearby	Owen Bowen
154	Yore Banks, Tanfield	

PAGE.		
160	Thirsk (Vignette)	
161	Thirsk, Birds-eye view	T. Fox
165	Timber-frame Cottage	Edmund Bogg
167	Thirsk Market-Place	Edmund Bogg
170	Finkle Street, Thirsk	Edmund Bogg
173	William Hall	
175	The Holms, Thirsk	Edmund Bogg
177	Kirkgate, Thirsk	Edmund Bogg
179	Going to Market, Sutton Road	Gilbert Foster
181	T. G. Baker (about 1870)	J. Pennington
183	George Gill (Bellman)	J Pennington
184	Willy Flintoff	J Pennington
186	Worlds' End Brig	Walter Pattison
188	Rev. F. Addison	E. Forbes
191	South Kilvington Church	J. Pennington
195	Rev. W. T. Kingsley	E. Forbes
197	Cribbie Dodgshon	J Pennington
199	Reach of Cold-beck	Gilbert Foster
201	Old Manor, Thornton	J. Pennington
203	Cross, Sandhutton	R Rodwell
205	Carlton Miniott	T Fox
210	Runic Cross, Cundall	A. Vivian
214	Topcliffe (Vignette)	
215	Topcliffe Church, from the Swale	A. Vivian
217	Home of the Percies	F. Dean
220	The Percy Pennont	
223	Tournament	F. Dean
225	Maiden Bower (Plan)	
227	Where Swale and Cod meet	A. Vivian
229	Topcliffe from Swale Bridge	R. Rodwell
231	Rev. H. Hawkins, M.A.	Clarke
233	Market Cross, Topcliffe	Basker
236	Swale at Topcliffe	R. Rodwell
239	Old Church, Carlton	R. Rodwell
242	Ford at Balk	Owen Bowen
244	Balk Grange	R. Rodwell
246	The Beck at Thirkleby	R. Rodwell

X.

PAGE.		
249	Old Font, Birdforth Church	E. Forbes
251	Timber-framed House, Husthwaite	Edmund Bogg
252	Great Husthwaite	Gilbert Foster
256	Coxwold	W. G. Foster
258	Fauconberg Arms, Coxwold	W. Wright
261	Fauconberg Monument	W. Wright
263	Shandy Hall, Coxwold	Edmund Bogg
269	Byland Abbey	W. Wright
171	Thirsk and Coxwold District (Map)	
274	Byland Antiquary	Kester
276	Job Skelton	J. R. Clarke
278	West-Front, Byland	Edmund Bogg
284	High Kilburn	Owen Bowen
287	The Two Kilburns	Owen Bowen
289	Kilburn and White Horse	Owen Bowen
291	Baynes' Arms	
293	A Kilburnite	E. Forbes
295	Osgodby Hall	R. Rodwell
298	White Horse from West	T. Fox
302	Old Crab Mill, Sutton	Edmund Bogg
306	Roulston Scar and Hode Hill	Edmund Bogg
309	Gormire	Edmund Bogg
313	Legend of the Cliff	Gilbert Foster
316	Wissoncliff	Edmund Bogg
318	Felixkirk	R. Rodwell
321	Interior, Feliskirk Church	R. Rodwell
324	Feliskirk Church, S.E.	R. Rodwell
329	The Hambletons (Map)	R. Rodwell
336	Naton and Crab Mill	R. Rodwell
338	Dick Megginson	E. Forbes
340	James Barnett	E. Forbes
342	Leake Church	R. Rodwell
344	Leake, West End	R. Rodwell
350	Upper Silton Church	Gilbert Foster
355	Boltby Scar	Owen Bowen
358	Thomas Sunley	E. Forbes
362	A Fox (from Life)	J. Pennington

PAGE.		
365	Vale of Mowbray	Owen Bowen
367	Black Hambleton Country (Map)	R. Rodwell
369	Moor Scene, Hambleton	Owen Bowen
370	The Road to Slapestones	Edmund Bogg
371	The Chequers Inn Sign	J. C. Fowler
372	Chequers Inn (Interior)	Owen Bowen
374	Inn from the Slapestones	J. C. Fowler
376	Thimbleby Bank	Owen Bowen
378	Osmotherley from S.E.	Owen Bowen
386	Osmotherley (from Back Lane)	Thompson
380	Osmotherley Cross	Thompson
386	Middlestee Valley	Thompson
387	Old Bob Abbott	Kester
390	Mount Grace Priory	Owen Bowen
393	Cell at Mount Grace	R. Rodwell
394	Remains of Church, Mount Grace	J. H. Barker
398	Robert Rodwell	E. Forbes
399	An Otter (from Life)	J. Pennington
400	Robert Lee	E. Forbes
403	The Buzzard	J. Pennington
413	William Foggitt, J.P., F.L.S.	E. Forbes
428	Middlestee Valley, from White House Farm	Thompson

The Valley of the Yore.

CHAPTER I.

Introductory Sketch.

Of the Isuer of the Brigantes and Isurium of the Roman Boroughbridge and Aldborough what shall I write?

From the great number of Roman relics discovered, Aldborough has been not inaptly termed the Yorkshire Pompeii.

From the second to the fifth century a city existed here adorned with all the art and luxury which the refinement of the Latins of that age could bestow. But long before the Roman invaders had reached these shores, in fact, before even the Wolf-suckled twins, Romulus and Remus had founded the City of Rome—the "Devil's Arrows" (the wonder of travellers) had been reared, and in greater numbers than we find them to day. The remains of these go far to prove the existence of a Celtic City, standing in pre-Roman days between the little river Tut and the Yore.

Historic light faintly gleams on the district during the first century of the Christian Era, and reveals the infamous queen of the Brigantes, Cartismandua, holding her court at these places, followed by her base alliance with the Romans, and her betrayal to the latter of the heroic Caractacus who, after having defied the Legions of Rome among the fastnesses of Wales for many a year, had fled to her as a forlorn hope. This great Celtic leader shines forth like a brilliant star on the horizon, from out the deep shadows of our early history. All along the Welsh border line, and also deep in the heart of its hills, one may still trace this hero's work.

The deeply entrenched hills guard every approach whence as from an Eagle's eyrie, he so long kept the invaders at bay. Thus few places have witnessed the light and shadows of history, the transformations, the strange scenes, romantic, pathetic and tragic, as the two places under survey, during the last 2000 years. It has heard the musical voices of the Celt mingling with those of the Latin Invaders. It has listened to the wild shout of the incoming war bands of the Saxons, half savage hordes from Northern Germany and the shores of the Baltic, when Aldborough, the Isurium of the Romans, was strewn with debris and ashes and left a wreck; and the luxury and refinement of the Latins was swept away in the lust and plunder of that second invasion.

The Devil's Arrows, Boroughbridge.　　　　*P. Robinson.*

It has witnessed the flappings of that dread Raven Standard of the land-ravager, and heard the strange half musical, half savage, chant of the uncouth Sea Kings from Jutland, Danesland, and Scandinavia, ascending the Yore in their War Keels. It has heard the march of the steel-clad Norman, and witnessed the almost insatiable fury of the Conqueror, who swore by the splendour of God the punishment which should befall those who withstood him. It has seen strange men from the wilds of Galloway, with others from the Borders, and heard the jargon of their base mingled speech, at the time these men were led by Randolph and the Black Douglas to battle and victory at Myton Meadows, when the women of York were praying for their husbands, sons, and sweethearts who had gone forth to fight, fated never to return.

Around the old wooden bridge which here in mediæval days spanned the Yore, the trumpet of war sounded and a terrible struggle ensued, which ended in the defeat of the great Earls of Lancaster and Hereford.

In later centuries the turmoil of war has happily not been brought to its doors. Yet it has often witnessed (being on the great North road) the marchings to and fro of armies.

In the eighteenth and early nineteenth centuries it was a noted coaching centre, the busiest between Ferrybridge and Carlisle. Coaches have rolled into the shadowland of the past, so have the old-time drovers, who brought the huge droves of sheep and cattle from the North through the town. Even Barnaby Fair, once so notable, is fast dwindling down.

The thoughtful man will find these places for rest and meditation, and will probably, like the writer, think how strange that these rude monoliths, reared by the Celts, and on which doubtless the Roman soldier gazed upon during his first entry into the British City. should still remain, though shrunk and deeply furrowed by the storm, rain and snow of two thousand winters. Their use and origin the historian and antiquary may muse and wrangle over, but the secret of their real meaning will doubtless never be unfolded. Nevertheless they will remain to us as a Monument and Memorial of a people, the Celts, who were thrust aside from their homeland here into the wilds of the West, by a nation of conquerors who brought their up-to date civilisation, and planted in their stead Temple and Palace and luxurious Homes and Baths, which centuries ago fell beneath the soil and upgrowth of vegetation, until the very site was almost forgotten.

CHAPTER II.

The Devil's Arrows—The Ancient Isuer of the Briton—and Aldborough the Isurium of the Romans.

Exactly where the British City stood, cannot be determined, but it probably extended from the precincts of the River Tut, along the fringe of the river and the higher ground eastwards to Aldborough. Probably the walls of the Roman City did not include any of the British Capital. That a numerous population existed here for thousands of years the huge monoliths of stone bear witness. Only one name stands forth prominently from amongst the Kings and Queens who have held their court at Isuer, and that one is Cartismandua (of infamous memory), and—says Phillips—the Gaelic meaning of her name would read Cathair-ys-maen-ddu, "The Queen of the City of Great Stones."

Before the first century of the Christian era had nearly run its course, the rule of the Brigantes (the name given to the Britons who resided between the Humber and the Tyne) at Isuer had passed into the hands of the Romans, and Cartismandua had quarrelled with her husband Venutius. Story runs that during the Prince's Campaign in Wales, fighting in the cause of Caractacus, she had taken to herself a Roman lover. Be this as it may, the outcome of the trouble was a split, and civil war amongst the Brigantes. With the assistance of other tribes, and the disaffected Brigantes, Venutius made war on Cartismandua. The battle going against her, she craved assistance of the Romans for help to prop up her tottering power.

Just previously, Caractacus—so long the glory of his nation and the terror of the enemy—had fought his last fight and then fled north, across the Severn and through the Cannock Forest and over the Pennines to the court of Cartismandua, doubtless, longing to have another opportunity of smiting the invaders of his country. His hopes were cruelly dispelled; for the stipulation made between the Queen and the Romans for the assistance of the latter, was the treacherous betrayal of her kinsman—the prince was a relation of hers—into the hands of the enemy, to enhance the triumph and glory of the victorious army on their return and parade through the streets of Rome.

This took place about the year A.D. 51; but the gallant deeds of this brave soldier prince, and his undaunted Reply when before the tribunal of Cæsar, shine out with a brilliant lustre across the gulf of eighteen centuries.† For has he not been the model of the historian, the poet, the artist, and the com-

---

† His descendants (The Cradocks) have still emblazoned on their shield the motto: "Betrayed, Not Conquered."

poser, whilst the name of the false-hearted Queen has been branded with infamy?* Her further history can be told in a few words.

Unable to hold her own against Venutius, even with the assistance she invoked, she fled south with the cohorts of Didius about the year 54, and so passed into obscurity for ever.

Venutius, a great leader and a worthy representative of Caractacus, became King of the Brigantes, and successfully maintained his own against the efforts of the enemy, keeping the kingdom intact for a period of sixteen years, until A.D. 70, when the strength of the nation gradually waned before the superior power of Rome.

The Middle Arrow. [*E. Bogg.*

---

* How like her prototype, Cleopatra of the Nile, was the queen. The three attributes of feminine distinctiveness were lacking in each; that which marks the woman, the

THE DEVIL'S ARROWS.

Were the Devil's Arrows so named by the Saxons on their arrival fourteen centuries ago? To them the mystery which surrounded the huge monoliths, would appear so strange, that their presence could only be accounted for by the subtle dealings of his Satanic Majesty. Hence we may arrive at the name.

But again, their present name may be derived from "dool stones," set up to mark a boundary or the limit of the city in prehistoric ages. The transition of the word "dool" to "devil stones" would easily come about, as the old spelling was "deuil."

The Arrows are situated a few hundred paces to the west of Boroughbridge. To-day they are three in number, and stand almost due north and south; their height varying from 18 feet to $22\frac{1}{2}$ feet, and the weight estimated at from 20 to 36 tons. The depth of the shafts below the surface varies from $4\frac{1}{2}$ to $6\frac{1}{2}$ feet. The Arrows are of Millstone Grit and have been roughly dressed, as the chisel marks on the base of the stones below ground show. Formerly they were higher, but the effect of rains during untold centuries has ground them considerably less. The stones were probably quarried at Plumpton, being similar in character to the Grit rock of that place.

Now Peter Franck, a fisherman who travelled much about the world to enjoy his sport, came to Boroughbridge in 1694, and says he saw seven of these standing stones, Dr. Stukley mentions five, and John Leyland, in his travels, saw "four great stones wrought by man's hands," but no inscription upon them. Camden, in 1592, saw four, but one of them at

---

wife, the mother, were cast aside. Spurred on by a sordid, selfish ambition, each could walk complacently over the troubles and ravages of their bleeding country into the arms of the strong one—the conqueror—whoever he might be.

One of the Devil's Arrows.   [E. Bogg.

the time was thrown down, "for," says he, "the accursed love of gain." Part of this one is still to be seen, built into the Peggy bridge which crosses the Tut* on the entrance to the town, the top portion being preserved in the grounds of Aldborough Manor and this goes far to prove—and I have very carefully considered the question, and examined the ground —that the original number of stones was far greater, and reached from the Yore, in equal distances to the Tudlad of Leyland's time, or the Staveley Beck of to-day. If this argument is correct, 2,000 years ago there would be a line of at least 12 standing monoliths, guarding the western approach to Isur Brigantium, the 'water-city' of the Brigantes.

* Tut supposed to be a contraction of "Tutelina, the Roman Goddess."

Thousands of times the questions have been asked, What are these stones? Whence came they? and how moved hither? and for what purpose were they reared on this spot?

Since Leyland's time, nearly four centuries ago, historians have been continuously trying to answer the questions. Leyland, Camden, Drake, Hearne, Gale, Lister, and several other historians

Tesselated Pavement from Aldborough, depicting the Capitoline Wolf, Romulus and Remus.

ascribe their presence to the Romans. Hargrove tells a pretty traditional story of how these four great stones were set up after the death of the Emperor Severus by his Empress, to perpetuate the memory of a reconciliation effected after a great feud between their two sons, Caracalla and Geta.

All these guesses are wide of the truth. Roman work indeed! The stones were standing in their present position but in far greater numbers before ever its founders had been suckled, or the very name of Rome was heard of in Celt-land, or a stone of that afterwards famous city had been placed upon another. Besides, whoever on contrasting these rude monoliths with the skilled work of the Latins at Isurium adjoining, would ever dream of ascribing them to the Romans?

Many of the religious customs of the Celtic people were identical with those of the Phœnicians, such, for instance, as the use of rude war chariots, the worship of fire or Sun-worship, Baal (Bel, or Beal, Celtic), the erection of huge pillars of stone, both as symbols, and objects of veneration, and also of large circles of rock, formed for places of worship, and altars of unhewn stone, for sacrificial purposes,—those enumerated, and many others, resembled those of the Easterns. The three stones, the work of a race who preceded the Brigantes, are doubtless the sole relics of a great monument somewhat similar to those stupendous works of prehistoric man found in different parts of the world, many of which point to the earliest form of religion—worship of the Sun, the author of life, light and warmth. Here one fair summer's eve, some years ago, the writer was musing before one of the rude monoliths, trying in vain to unravel the unfathomable mystery which surrounds them. Suddenly, the mist of thousands of years was dispelled by a voice breaking in on the stillness. "Ah sae, mister, dean't ya knaw what them steans are, and hoo they gat theer?" Acknowledging my lack of information on the subject, he replied that "they were t' devil's arrows," and that a "lang time syne," Aldborough had excited the wrath of his Satanic Majesty, so away to Howe Hill he flew, and there planting his tremendous bow, at the same time repeating the following:

> "Borolrigg keep out o' the way,
> For Audboro' Town
> I will ding down"—

sent forth his giant arrows of stone; but that they all fell short of the mark, will be seen from those left standing! So much for legend.

In a field adjoining the stones, and known as Arrow Close, a large quantity of shaped flints were found when digging foundations in 1879. All but one were thrown away through the lack of knowledge of the workmen on the subject of Archeology The one preserved is an imperfect spear head of the Palæolithic period, and from the large number found, it is thought by Dr. Leadman that here there had been a manufactory of flints.

Aldborough (so named in contrast to Newburgh by the Brigg) the site of the Roman Isurium, is rather over half-a-mile east of Boroughbridge, and is reached by a very pleasant way, shaded by fine trees.

Aldborough Manor, the seat of A. S. Lawson, Esq., stands partly on the western wall of the Roman city, and the road enters the precincts of the city by the Manor. The line of the walls can still be distinctly traced running from the north through the pasture, thence across the line of road by the Manor, and through the gardens to the southern extremity. On the east, the bulwark which encloses all the present Aldborough, can also be traced. The place is mentioned in the fourth Iter as 17 miles from Eboracum (York), and 24 miles from Cattaractone (Catterick) to the north. And the seventh Iter gives it as 17 miles from Olicana (Ilkley). Ptolemy describes the sixth legion as occupying the city; this legion afterwards became incorporated with the ninth, and the latter is also supposed to have garrisoned this city, and a title bearing their legionary mark found here and still preserved confirms this.

Lovers' Walk, Aldborough.

The circuit of the walls measures about 2,500 yards, and the included area incloses about 60 acres, the walls varying from 9 to 15 feet in thickness. Relics of the wall and other interesting fragments, portion of pillars, altars, &c., are still to be seen in the grounds of Aldborough Manor. We may here mention that it is due to the care and interest in such matters of Andrew Sherlock Lawson, Esq., that the full extent of the city wall can still be traced.

The City was walled like that at Eboracum, but without the angle towers. Near the south-east angle is an artificial hill, called Studforth. Leyland gives us the following quaint notice of this camp: "Adelburge is about a quarter of a mile from Boroughbridge. This was, in the Romanes' tyme, a great city on Watheling Streate, called Isuria Brigantum, and was walled, whereof I saw '*Vestigia sed quædam tenuia.*' It stode by south west on We (Ure) river. The compace of it hath been by estimation a mile. There be now large felds fruitful of corn in the very place whereof the town was; and in these felds yerely be found in ploughing many coynes of sylver and brasse, of the Roman stampe. There hath been found also sepulchres, aquæductus, tesselata pavimenta, &c. There is a hill on the side of the feld where the old town was, caullid Stothart, as if it had been the kepe of a castle." Evidences of Roman occupation are most numerous—altars, statues, pottery, querns, armour, coins, roads, &c., whilst mosaic and tesselated pavements are in fine preservation, and still retain a freshness of colour simply wonderful, considering 1,800 years have passed since they were fashioned.

On the departure of the Romans, the incoming Saxons made it a settlement, and probably made addition to the city, and thus the Roman Isurium was named by the Saxon, Aldborough. In the general havoc and ruin caused by the Danish invasion of the ninth century, this city was sacked and burnt, and nearly every vestige of British, Roman, and Saxon occupation lay buried beneath the surface for several centuries, and this has no doubt been the cause of preserving what in most instances might have perished. In the Domesday survey, it was returned as waste. Soon after the conquest, the old Roman road, which ran through Isurium, and crossed the Yore at Milby, was diverted, being carried some few hundred yards higher up the river, where a bridge was afterwards erected, and a new town sprang into existence, significantly named Newburgh, or the Burgh by the bridge, afterwards gradually changing to Boroughbridge. Aldburgh and its surroundings are very lovely. The Church with its battlemented tower, almost framed in trees, forms a delightful picture, and is supposed to have been erected about 1360, and stands within the old walled inclosure. In the east end of the north aisle there is a fine old brass memorial to William de Aldburgh, the founder of the edifice (its patron saint being St. Andrew), which represents the Knight in complete armour with shield and sword, the first bearing the Aldburgh Arms, a fesse between three cross crosslets. The Chancel is 15th century work, and curiously is ascribed to another William Aldborough. There is also a slab of James Brooke, twice Lord Mayor of York, who died December 6th, 1675, aged 82.*

The register reached back to 1538, in which there was a record of the burial of a Chantry Priest named Thomas Smythe in 1544, who, no doubt, ministered in the Chapel of the north aisle. The officiating of Chantry Priests finally came to an end in England in 1547. The register also mentions a plague which took place at Boroughbridge in 1604 very briefly, "wherein died 80 at least," and also a foundling whom nobody seems to have claimed, " Elizabeth Nobody, daughter of Nobody, baptized in 1578." One vicar in the past has made use of

---

* The Museum stands at the top of the village, and the Roman pottery, glass, iron, and bronze work, coins, busts, altars, armour, &c., is one of the best in the country.

the register to stigmatize Cromwell as "An impious arch Rebel." Had that vicar lived in our time, and read the story of that great man as written by Carlyle and others, he would probably never have penned the above words.

There has evidently been a Norman, or perhaps Saxon, Church on this site, for the first vicar mentioned here is of the early date 1316, nearly half a century before the building of the present church.

The Roman Temple dedicated to Mercury is generally supposed to have stood on this site, and the old image of Mercury in bas-relief, which was dug up in the churchyard, is now built into the east wall of the vestry. Against the west wall of the nave there is also a Roman altar.

The village green, with its row of ancient property, wears a pretty rural aspect. Here are the old stocks, said to have been brought from Boroughbridge. Parts of Aldborough Hall, to the south-east of the church, are of considerable age, and in the past, this was the seat of the De Aldburghs.

All the village characters here swear by the Romans, "we are all Roomans here, and if ye come to Rome ye mun do as Roomans do," and so, at the village inn we listened to a character sing "Tar a Rinkle," and another native sing "Home Sweet Home," with many variations, and Tommy Parker, the newsagent, better known as "t'owd Rooman," hold forth in song with his rasping voice.

The town of Boroughbridge gradually sprang into existence as the Normans became masters in England, 1066, when the revival of trade and cultivation of the land took place after the ruin, havoc, and desolation of the Conqueror's ravaging hand.

There seems to have been no attempt to make Aldborough a stronghold, or even to re-build the city Roman fashioning. The ancient home of the Celts and the Romans was to be only a record of the past, despised and almost forgotten, for, the Roman road which up to that time had passed through Aldborough and crossed the river by ford near Milby, was diverted more to the west and a fording place made at Boroughbridge. Thus Aldborough became almost depopulated, and a new town grew up along the line of the road leading to the ford, which received the name Newborough to distinguish it from the Old

Cross and Old Manor House, Aldborough.

Burgh (Aldborough). A century or so later a strong rude wooden bridge was built, and the town growing apace, received its present name.

MEDIÆVAL HISTORY.—Like Tadcaster, built round its bridge and standing on the highway to York, Boroughbridge has been the scene of many notable events. As at Tadcaster, a battle was fought at the bridge. Soon after the Conquest, a Norman church was built, and part of a Norman door with beakhead moulding was found when pulling down the chapel, which, previous to 1850, stood in the centre of the market place. Judging from the Norman doorway preserved, the original church must have been exceedingly rich in sculpture. It contained two Chantries, those of St. Saviour and St. Agatha. Standing as the town does, at the N.W. limit of a navigable river, and at the intersection of so many roads all radiating from the bridge, the wonder is that the town had not seen more of War. However, this place is associated for all time with a most important event in English History—the Battle of Boroughbridge. There are few darker pages in our history than those which relate to the incapable Rule of Edward II., when England lost the prestige she had attained during the strong iron rule of that glorious soldier, King Edward I. Disastrous and dark indeed, were those 25 years which followed his death. This was the time when the Scots reived the whole north of England with impunity, none to withstand them, even penetrating to the very walls of York, burning town, village, and church at will, whilst famine and disease followed closely on their footsteps.

"Oh day of revenge and of misfortune," says the Monk of Malmesbury, "day of destruction and of disgrace, evil and cursed day, not fit to be reckoned in the circle of the year." Days of humiliation, sorrow and disastrous failure, when the glory

Aldborough Church. [*Edmund Bogg.*

of English arms was tarnished by defeat at Bannockburn, Byland Abbey, and Myton Meadows,—such was the state of the country through the incapacity and misgovernment of Edward II. that led the Barons to rise in revolt against him and his favourites. These circumstances led up to the battle of Boroughbridge. The Earls of Lancaster and Hereford were in command of the rebel army and were rapidly retreating before a much superior force of the King. They came to Boroughbridge, intending to reach the northern counties. Here, unknown to them, they were confronted at the bridge and ford by a superior army in the King's cause led by Sir Andrew de Harcla. A terrible fight for the the possession of the bridge took place, across which, to the insurgents, lay their only hope of escape and safety. 'Tis said a Welshman, armed with a long spear, hid somewhere beneath the bridge, and as Humphrey de Bohun (the Earl of Hereford) with a body of soldiers was attempting to storm the bridge, he thrust his spear through an opening in the timbers, and gashed the Earl's bowels so that he fell forward mortally wounded, thus died the most renowned Knight in Christendom. Still struggling, Lancaster made a final effort to cross the river, but being again repulsed, his troops lost heart and fled. Lancaster took refuge in the old chapel, which formerly stood in the Market place, relics of which can be seen in the new church (see sketch), but no sanctuary was to protect the defeated baron; he was dragged from the church, stripped of his armour and carried to York, where he was hooted with the derisive cries of " Hail, King Arthur!" From York he was conveyed to his own castle at Pontefract, and lowered into a deep, gloomy dungeon, and soon afterwards condemned to death by the revengeful Edward, who had never forgotten or forgiven the Earl's share in the death of his favourite, Piers Gaveston. Mounted on a miserable hack, amidst the gibes and insults of the populace, he was led to the block. Thus perished one of the mightiest Earls in Christendom.

Nowadays, Boroughbridge presents the appearance of a decaying town, and wears a far different aspect as regards trade and prosperity to what it did three quarters of a century ago. At that period it was, for its size, the briskest and most well-to-do town in the Kingdom. The navigation of the Aire and Calder, which the men of North Yorkshire in the 17th century were afraid of, injured its trade only very slightly. The great change in its destiny came about between 1840 and 1850, when the railway between York and Newcastle was opened, and the other lines in the immediate neighbourhood a few years later diverting the trade it formerly enjoyed into other channels,

24 THE VALLEY OF THE YORE.

Remains of Saxon Work removed from the old Church at Boroughbridge and rebuilt into the new structure.

From 1553 to the passing of the Reform Bill in 1832, Boroughbridge and Aldborough were represented at Westminster by two members, but at the latter period both places were disfranchised. During the Civil War in 1644, part of Prince Rupert's forces were quartered in the town just previous to the fight at Marston, and the story goes that the old church was used by the troops as barracks. In this instance at least, it was the gallant Rupert and not Cromwell who committed sacrilege. In 1745, during the rising on behalf of the Pretender, a contingent, marching north to join General Wade's forces, passed through the town and encamped in Langthorpe field. But the town, standing as it does on the great north road, has witnessed the passing to and fro of many august personages, and anxious scenes, dramatic and pathetic, have occurred in the accidental meeting of people so varied in tastes and often with interests so antagonistic. Apart from the numerous coaches running through and changing horses at the "Crown" or the "Three Greyhounds," there was also a number of stage waggons continually on the road. Added to which, Boroughbridge was a busy and lively port, having a regular service of vessels for carrying all kinds of material and produce between that place and the port of Hull. It was also noted for ship —or we should say keel—building, and this trade, along with repairing, employed a large amount of labour. We are told that as late as 1840 two sea-going schooners were launched from the stocks here, opposite the mouth of the little river Tut, the vessels could only be floated down the river when at flood. Keels bringing all kinds of goods were continually arriving, which many carts, stage waggons, great lumbering vehicles drawn by six, eight, and sometimes ten horses, and carriers' carts distributed over the country for 30 miles around, and returning, brought to the vessels goods for export, such as farm produce, timber, lead, stones, and linen the latter being largely manufactured at Knaresborough.

We have some proof of its trade as a port of shipment as far back as 1697. In that year a petition from the ancient borough of Northallerton was presented to the House setting forth "that large quantities of lead, butter, linen, and other commodities and produce for export are daily carried to Burrough-Briggs, and thence sent by water upon the river Ouse to be distributed to many parts of the Kingdom and also beyond the seas, and should the river Ayre and Calder be made navigable it will drain the river Ouse and ruin their trade, they therefore, pray that the above river shall not be made navigable"

It is said that the canal was often so thronged with boats, that it was quite an easy matter to cross on the boats from one side of the canal to the other. We have already said that the town was the busiest stage centre between Ferrybridge and Carlisle, and consequently there was always a lot of strangers in the town. Added to the bustle and activity at the river side, the passing through of coach and stage waggons, and a heterogeneous mixture of all kinds of vehicles, horsemen of all grades, immense droves of half wild cattle and sheep, in charge of drovers as shaggy, unkempt, and wild as the cattle under their care, who were generally on the move from the north towards the south, and who mostly came this way. At times a few of the herd would become footsore and could not keep pace with the rest, such had to be shod, after the manner of horses, and one smith at Langthorpe, we are told, has made as much as six pounds in a day and a night by shoeing these footsore cattle. Thirty thousand peculiar nails for shoeing bullocks were made in this shop at Langthorpe in one year. Then again, who has not heard of the great Barnaby Fair in the forties and fifties of last century; it was the most celebrated carnival in all the country side. At that time it was noted for the horses, cattle and sheep brought there for sale, besides every kind of implement for agricultural and domestic uses, hardware, jewellery, and cutlery and every kind of gewgaw then in use. About that time, the fair used to last from ten to fifteen days, and was the occasion of a general holiday for miles around. The town owned or hired several specially swift boats known as Barnaby Boats which, for weeks prior to the fair, were continually bringing in cargoes from London, Hull, and other large centres, a great variety of articles needed for sale at the fair. All available space within the precincts

Old House, Boroughbridge.

of the town was filled with booths and stalls. Tinkers, hawkers, and gypsies with every description of caravan and vehicle, etc., were allotted to the wayside and waste land in the immediate district, and these made a large motley army in themselves. On special days the goodly array of public houses was quite unable to satisfy the needs of such a thirsty crew of craving humanity as usually assembled in the town at Barnaby. But here as well as elsewhere, the curious old Charter came in useful. It ordained that anyone could sell ale or beer without a license on Great and Little Fair days for 48 hours, on the 22nd and 23rd June, on one condition only—that of hanging out a bush in front of their homes. Such were known as Bush Houses, and many of the inhabitants availed themselves of this easy means of adding to their income by hanging out a bush and placing an ale bench in front of their house. There are still to be seen several staples driven into the walls to hold the bush for the above object. Ah well! all this was in the good old days, even Barnaby is prosaic enough now, and life only drags on slowly in the old town.

Since 1840, when the line from York to Newcastle was opened, and later that from Knaresbro,' the road and river traffic has gradually dwindled down, and is now almost a thing of the past. No rattling of mail coach, or the sounding horn of the post-boy is heard, or the panting of weary steeds, or the running hither and thither of grooms and postillions, or the bellowing of immense droves of half wild cattle and horses, in many instances numbering from one to two thousand, mingled with the shouts and curses of the still more wild drovers.

To the antiquary and historian the district is full of interest. The stocks, which stood on Chapel Hill where the Fountain now stands, like the Cross erected to commemorate the battle of Boroughbridge, have been removed to Aldborough. The stocks were in great request at Barnaby fair, and men and women were often placed in them side by side, to pay the penalty of their short-comings. About the middle of last century an old Waterloo veteran, whose proper name was Richard Fryer, often found himself accommodated in the stocks, to the amusement of the younger generation. Fryer was better known by his nick-name, "Bung-hole Dick." Story said, that during the above battle he was found hiding in a barrel and peeping through the bung hole.

The Hall, Boroughbridge.

The town is comprised practically in four streets,—The Horsefair, Fishergate, High Street, and St. James's Square. The men of Aldborough, from their connection with a great historic people of the past (the Romans), claim precedence over their neighbours at Boroughbridge, never dreaming that in point of antiquity the latter may have a longer record than their own. In our opinion the city over which Cartismandua ruled when the Romans appeared on the scene 1800 years ago, stood between the Tut on the west, St. James's Square on the north, and stretching east towards Aldborough. There is many a pitched battle between the lads of the two towns representing on the one part "The Romans of Aldborough," and on the other, "The English" of Boroughbridge. I have often been in company with Aldborough men of whom everyone swears by the Roomans. "We are all Roomans," they say, though judging by their features, not the least resemblance or strain of Roman blood remains in Aldborough. One prominent Aldboroughite remarked "We've gott'nt cross and stocks frae Borobridge an' we'll ev't Devil's Arrows yit; wead a' hed em afore noo, only the'll tak sae mich shifting here."

Staveley.

Roccliffe stands a short distance to the west of the Devil's Arrows. It has a large green and a few antique homesteads and a pretty church approached through an avenue of yews.

Two miles beyond is the village of Staveley, where the church, which has been entirely rebuilt, is on a commanding eminence, the spire forming a prominent landmark. Within the graveyard is part of a Norse cross. John Wesley preached from an altar tomb here, which is still pointed out, as is also another stone, said to cover the body of "Tit Poole," celebrated as a witch, who dwelt in this village. A lane, still called Tit Poole's Lane, preserves her memory.

Crossing the little river Tut, half a mile brings us to Copgrove, a delightful spot, meaning the cop, or top of the grove, a most appropriate name, for the spot is a perfect labyrinth of groves, miniature vales, and hills and dells, and delightful belts of woodland, through which the Stainley Beck in serpentine course and frantic haste is ever leaping and bounding. Copgrove Church is an interesting, quaint, little structure, with nave, chancel, small gallery, and bell gable. There was a Church at this place in Saxon times; of the early structure the chancel arch remains, and is unique. Here is a spring of water, known as St. Mungo's Well. In olden times, the healing virtues of its water were of great repute. The river Tut rises just beyond Brearton, passes the moated site of Walkingham Hall on the left, and Farnham on the right, and, after about a six and a half miles course, enters the river at Boroughbridge.

Miniskip, a plain red-bricked village, lying a little over a mile south of Boroughbridge, contains evidences of antiquity. Two miles further on the higher ridge of the Yore watershed are the picturesque villages of Marton and Grafton; from the latter can be seen beautiful far reaching landscapes. York Minster looms out of the distance to the south-east, and all the delightsome varying phases of the Vale Country landscape across the Ouse to the Hambleton Hills north and east. It was in this district where the following incident occurred. A preacher was taking duty at a church, where a sermon once in a fortnight or three weeks was deemed sufficient, and on entering the pulpit, the good man was surprised to find inside "a sitting goose," which caused

Grafton.

the preacher both anxiety and amusement, although on the the whole, she (the goose) behaved very well during the sermon. The man who had charge of the edifice had "set" her there as being a most quiet place. The village of Marton stands on slightly higher ground a few hundred yards to the south. Its character is distinctly rurality. The Punch Bowl Inn, with its yellow washed exterior, and the circular pound with its wall of rubble are interesting features. The church has been entirely re-built. The old structure stood about one hundred and fifty yards to the south of the present one. When the Scots harried these parts in the 14th century, the sanctuary was nearly destroyed, the marks of fire being very apparent still. The old church was in a most ruinous condition long before its demolition, and the same remark would apply to this church as was said of another equally ruinous and ancient, of which Sir Gilbert Scott when requested to give his opinion regarding its condition, remarked: "Well, gentlemen, the only reason I can assign for it being standing to-day is that it did not fall yesterday." Several portions of shafts, caps, and 12th century tombstones, and an ancient piscina are preserved in the new church.

The late Parson Lunn was quite a notable man in his way, a passionate lover of music, and his well-known figure, driving about the district in his donkey-trap will long dwell in the memory of the natives, who relate many droll stories of him. Twenty minutes' walk across the fields, we reach the pretty villages of Great and Little Ouseburn, but as their name indicates, lying in the watershed of the Ouse. Both places are full of interesting features however, and will repay a visit. The principal objects are the Churches, beautifully situated amongst trees, the Lake, and Moat Hall. Here some twenty-four years ago the government set up a road telegraph line through the village of Great Ouseburn, and an old man, who had watched the operations with great interest, meeting the postman shortly afterwards, exclaimed against the great expense, "all aboot nowt, for nowt ivver cam." "Yes," said the official, "they're always coming, and I'm taking one out now." "Weel, weel," said the old man, "that beeats all; ah taake me chair ootside t' deer on Monday morning an ah've sat all t' week, an ah've nivver seen nowt come yet."

The Old Punch Bowl, Marton   [E. Bogg.

But we must hasten on to the meeting place of the two rivers, the Yore and the Swale.

We pass on our way High Dunsforth, like the two last villages, purely agricultural and rural, situated far from the busy haunts of men. How pleasant it is to remember the little cottages, the gardens and orchards, abundantly laden with fine fruit, filling the air with faint balsamic perfume on our visit. It was at this place that a worthy couple lived, man and wife, for 76 years; they were married at 19, and both died at the age of 95, within a few weeks of each other.

It was in this district when drilling wheat came into fashion that it became possible to use the horse-hoe, the teeth being so arranged that they passed between the rows of wheat without injuring them. The operation required a little care, and became known in the parish as "wakkening 't wheat," from the following circumstances:—A farm lad, who had been sent to his work, returned home at night, saying, "Ma word, I hev wakkened that wheat up," and it was found next day that he had hoed up nearly the whole field, and thought himself clever.

Yonder, over the river, is the ancient village of Aldwark, which had an existence in Roman days, as forging forward we soon reach Low Dunsforth, a quaint lowland village; on our last visit, there were still some thickly thatched roofs and other primitive relics of bygone generations. The old church, of Saxon origin, was pulled down in 1860, and the present structure built; portions of early Norman work are preserved in the vestry, also an ancient font in the graveyard. In 1860 the old Saxon church was pulled down, and about thirty Saxon coins, mostly silver pennies, were discovered among the *debris* as well as a clay ring, probably used as a weight for a fishing net. They are still in existence and, as they give approximately the date of the old church, it is to be hoped that at some time they may find a final resting place in some permanent museum.

The road leading from Low Dunsforth southwards, is called Old Marygate, perhaps from a gate which barred the way where it joined the York road near Grafton. The natives say there was something very uncanny about this gate, as always after dusk, it would open and shut mysteriously to travellers without any apparent cause.

Crossing over the Ouse by the Ferryboat (there was one when the writer was last this way) we soon reach Myton, the scene of the great battle between the English and Scotch— The White Battle, or Chapter of Myton—which ended so disastrously to the Southrons. The story of events which made it possible for the Scots to nearly capture the English Queen, then resting at Brotherton, and raid the country even around the walls of York, and led up to the White battle, is indeed a sorry one in English History. It took place at Myton October 12th, 1319. Robert Bruce was then King of Scotland, and few better Monarchs ever ruled. Edward, the second of that name, was King in England and, in his capacity as ruler, was the

Low Dunsforth.

very antithesis of Bruce. Sir James Douglas (The Black Douglas) in his great raid through Yorkshire having gained intelligence that the Queen Isabel had taken up her abode with only a small retinue, somewhere outside the walls of York, determined to capture her. But he does not appear to have been certain of the exact place of her abode. It was this lack of knowledge which led to his failure to seize the Queen. One of his spies was taken in York, and in fear, disclosed the scheme of his leader, and only just in the nick of time, for the bold raiders were only a short distance from Brotherton when the object of their swift secrecy march became known. The Queen fled swiftly and gained safety and shelter within the old City walls. So narrow had been her escape, that almost before the gates of the Capital were shut, the bulk of the Scottish army appeared before the walls, demanding admittance into the city. Instead, the aged Archbishop Melton, honour to his name (although disaster attended his bold fight), had the bulwarks properly manned, which, added to the strength of the fortifications, were impregnable to any assault the Scots could bring to bear upon it. So disappointed, baffled and angry were they that so rich a city was not to be their prize, nor the Queen their captive, that the Scots rode round the walls throwing out all manner of gibe and insulting epithets on the clerics and citizen soldiers sheltered behind the ramparts. One hot tempered Celt more daring than his fellows, rode boldly up to Micklegate Bar and accused the Queen of all manner of immoralities, and at the same time thundered forth a challenge to any man to come forth and clear her fame. This was more than the defenders could bear, for very shame they scarcely dared to look each other in the face. The venerable Archbishop (he was a De Melton) forgot the sacredness of his calling in his burning desire to wipe out the vile insults which had been heaped upon the defenders and their Queen. His indignation was thoroughly aroused, his aged frame shook with the impetuosity and fire which had long lain dormant beneath his priestly garb. In a stirring speech he called upon the citizens and clergy to arm and punish the invaders for their insolence. His eloquence appears to have been irresistible, for there was not a man or youth — no matter what their calling, churchman or citizen — able to bear arms who did not respond to that heart-burning appeal, that strange yearning call for vengeance.

York at that time might aptly be termed a City of Churches. There were the Friaries, the Monastery of St Mary's, the Cathedral, and numerous others, and from all the churchmen, monks and friars, came forth (an army in themselves) at the call of the Archbishop to do battle and uphold the honour and ancient glory of their city. We are told, that at the time there were not fifty trained soldiers in York. Perhaps never

GREAT OUSEBURN. [Gilbert Foster.

before in the history of the world did such a motley army set forth on such a venture.

In addition to the clergy, the army was made up of beadsmen, traders, citizen apprentices, and even beggars helped to swell this strange army of avengers, none too old and none too young who were able to bear arms. The Scots, realizing the imprudence of delay and the impossibility of storming the city, departed in a northerly direction, raiding and plundering on their march. They had not proceeded far over the plains in the direction of Myton, when the Archbishop with his "army," utterly unskilled in the art of war, issued from the city in pursuit. The Bishop of Ely (Lord High Chancellor of England) rode by the side of the aged prelate, but like him, knew little of the tactics of war. Behind them rode Sir Nicholas Fleming (the Lord Mayor), and Sir John de Wareham, followed in queue by the multitude of clergy in white surplices, and monks, canons, friars and other ecclesiastics, all dressed in the full panoply of their particular order; and then came the remainder of this strange force armed with whatever came first to hand, all kinds of antique weapons. Such was the mob that went forth from York on that fatal day to battle with sixteen thousand of Robert Bruce's best trained soldiers, inured to all the hardships of war, men before whom Froissart says: "The most renowned Knight of Christendom had fallen as wheat before the reaper." The Scots, perceiving that they were followed, and not knowing the character of the foe, continued to retreat rapidly until they reached Myton. Here, crossing the Swale near to where it meets the Yore, they took up their positions in Myton Meadows to the rear of a number of haystacks, to which they set fire, so the wind blowing from the north wafted the blinding smoke into the faces of the Archbishop's army. Nothing daunted by this clever ruse, the pursuers pressed forward across the Swale, not yet perceiving exactly where their enemy had made a stand. The Scots, who had formed into the shape of a shield, with tremendous shouts now charged furiously on the English, and, separating into two divisions, one gained the rear between the bridge and the enemy, thus by a prompt flank movement as effectual then as now, closing the main avenue of escape. Nevertheless, this citizen and priestly crowd fought with all the courage of heroes for a time, and many a Scotchman fell under the terrible blows from the heavy maces swung by monks or friars, whilst the prentice lads and citizens hacked, hewed and thrust with axe, sword, pike, and fork. But to no ultimate avail, they were no match for the Scotchmen. In less than an hour four thousand men and youths, churchmen with their white robes stained crimson, strewed the field of battle. Many were drowned in trying to cross the river, here by Myton flowing sullen and treacherous. Few, if any, would have escaped from the death-trap into which the Scots had lured them, had not the Earl of Murray taken pity on the confused helpless mass of struggling clerics and laymen, and given orders for the slaughter to cease. Then, when the fierce thirst for blood was satiated, and the demon passions raised by hand to hand death-struggle quelled, that awful sight of so many surpliced churchmen dead and dying, sent a fearsome thrill of horror into the minds of the victors, and such a superstitious awe as of some impending disaster for that day's work took possession of their minds, that, instead of pursuing the remnant of the defeated army, they also fled hurriedly from the fateful field. All that day and through the long hours of night, the womenfolk and children gazed anxiously from the city walls of York, watching and waiting for those who would never return,—the wife for her husband, the children for their fathers, the young women for their sweethearts. And when the tidings of the sad disaster reached them, they hurried forth to the battlefield to succour the wounded and seek out their dead. Amongst the heaps of slain was found the body of Sir Nicholas Fleming, the Lord Mayor, besides other civic dignitaries. For many a year the stalls in the Cathedral were only half occupied, and it was quite as long before the gaps made in the choir were filled. A quarter of a century later the monks and priors were wont to mourn over the vacancies, as they told the sad story of Myton Meadows,—the one set conflict in English History betwixt the "Church Militant" and trained soldiers, and perhaps the most unequal battle on record.

An aged monk of the period writing of this battle, says "The Archbishop and all other prelates fled, and God pitying them, they so escaped; and also the triumphal standard of the Archbishop, the pike of which was of silver, and on the top of which was fixed the gilded image of our Lord Jesus Christ. The cross-bearer, on a swift horse, plunged into the river, and by swimming to the other bank is carried off; and then skirting a willow-garth he left his horse, and hid the cross of the præsul in a very dense thicket, and in the twilight he thus escaped. In the place where the cross was hidden a poor man had for a short time been lurking, and coming up after the retreat of the clerk he took the cross, and twisting around it some bands of hay he kept it in his cottage until after the search, when he returned it to the Bishop."

From Myton the Scots spread over the country as far as the bridge at Castleford, and then, turning west by Ayerdale and Wherfdale, about the feast of the Exaltation of the Holy Cross (14th September), they scarcely spared a town. They burned and ravaged, and led away many captives. They re-entered their own country by the Cheviots with great booty.

Connected with Myton are two other strange scenes. Roger de Mowbray, that famous warrior, the founder of Byland

Abbey, to which he retired when wearied with the war and and turmoil of the world, and having assumed the monastic garb, he spent peacefully the remaining fifteen years of his life, and was interred within the Abbey, in an arch on the south side of the chapter-house, and over his tomb was a carving of the sword he had wielded so ably whilst living. After having slept there in peace for 600 years, all that was left of his mortal body was again to pass over the fertile vale, whose name of Mowbray will ever remain a memorial to his memory. In 1819 the Squire of Myton, Martin Stapylton, for some reason, caused the body to be disinterred and removed from Byland to the church yard of Myton-on-Swale. It was widely felt in later times that an act of desecration had been committed; and therefore, when a vacancy occurred in the living of Myton, about thirty years ago, the bones of the old warrior-monk were disinterred by night, and consigned to their original resting place at Byland, and, as it was in accordance with public opinion, no one interfered.

The following is an interesting item :—" Thomas Clyderhow, of the parish of Mytton, bequeaths his sowle to Almighty God, our Lady St. Marie, and all the holie companie in heaven; and his body to be buryed in the Parish Church of All Hallows, of Mytton; his best beast for a Mortuarie, and a cow to Richard Denby, Priest thereof, to say a trentall of masses for my sowle. Also my will is to have a Dirge at my place, and to have 12 Priestes to say a Masse for my Sowle upon the day that I shall be buryed. I give unto the window in the lofte in Mytton Church, 2d."

We must now hurry along the banks of the Yore, west from the junction of the two rivers past Ellingborough and Milby. It was at the latter place where the old ford of the Romans crossed the Yore and proceeded north to Cataractonium

Old Cottage, Kirby Hill. [*Edmund Bogg.*

(Catterick). This length of the river reaching up to the bridge is a popular resort of the anglers from Leeds and other large centres of industry, as here have been many captures of large fish, particularly pike and chubb. Yonder, on the skyline to the north stands Kirby Hill, its place-name indicating that it was founded by Danes, although a watch tower, on the line of the old road, probably stood near this spot in Roman times. Here are two draw-wells of great depth and antiquity.

The church was restored in 1870; it contains a Norman font, and in the walls of the tower is part of a Roman altar, and in the burial ground part of a Norse cross. An inscription on a stone to the memory of Margaret Hindley reads :

"Whence I came it matters not,
To whom related, or by whom begot;
A heap of dust is all that remains of me,
'Tis all I am, and all the proud shall be.

Kirkby stands on a fine elevation, adjoining Leeming Lane, famed in annals of trotting and racing matches. A short distance west of the "Blue Bell," and on the Ripon road, is Skelton Windmill, from whence fine views of the surrounding country are to be obtained.*

Old Well, Kirkby Hill.

The river at Boroughbridge is the dividing line between the North and West Ridings of Yorkshire, Langthorpe to the north of the river, although a suburb of Boroughbridge, being in the North Riding. It was formerly notable for its nail making industry, and in the coaching times the smiths here were in constant request, for the shoeing of horses, and bullocks too, when the latter became footsore from their long tramp over the hard roads from the Border. About two miles from

---

* Many years ago, the body of an unknown man was found at this spot. The expense of the interment fell to the parish where the corpse was found. As the parishioners of Kirkby were remiss in complying with the above custom, the people of Skelton removed the body to a place of burial in their churchyard, and, by an old law, claimed this land for their parish.

Langthorpe we reach Skelton, a place possessing no striking characteristic. The Lych Gate and old church, partly ivy-clad with its quaint bell gable are interesting. A stone in the churchyard records the death by drowning, in the hunting accident referred to later, of the boatman and his son, James:—

> "He shall return no more
> To his house, neither shall
> His place know him any more."

In summer time the path by the river side from Langthorpe is very pretty indeed. By this route we pass Brampton Hall, now only an ordinary farmhouse. In olden times it was a seat of the Tancreds. There are numbers of shapely dressed stones which have belonged to a former and more important house, scattered about the farm, and the moat which cut off access from the north as the river did on the south, and the deep ditch on the west prove its original importance. Across the latter there still remains an ancient bridge, on which consummate skill and care has been exercised. As a specimen of good work, and a relic of the past, it is worthy of care and preservation. Nevertheless, from wilful neglect, lack of interest and a little labour and plaster, it will soon fall to ruins.

Proceeding, we soon reach Newby Park, and entering the spacious demesne, we come to the exquisite Memorial church, erected by Lady Mary Vyner to the Glory of God, and to the memory of her son, Frederick Vyner, who was assassinated by Greek Brigands, May, 1870. The architect was Mr. Burgess, Grantham. The church is without exception, the most beautiful and elaborate of any memorial church erected in recent times. Everything is of the best character, the woodwork of the pews is of cedar (the font and cover were the gift of the Most Noble The Marquis of Ripon, K.G.), the frontal of the altar table and the initial capitals of the church service book were executed by Lady Mary Vyner (as a labour of love). The church is in the decorated Gothic, akin to the types met with in Normandy.

Leaving the church for the Hall and crossing the undulating sward, the paths wind through delightful glades, handsomely adorned with oak, ash, cedar, and purple beech: through such charming vistas we approach the Hall, whose red front, tipped with white, forms a pretty contrast to the surrounding trees and leafage. Opposite the main entrance stands the famous equestrian statue of John Sobieski, King of Poland, in the act of trampling on a Turk. This statue was bought at Leghorn by Sir R. Vyner in 1675, and was altered to represent Charles II. trampling on Oliver Cromwell —only a feeble retaliation on the old warrior, for making kings tremble, and the name of England respected.

Statue of John Sobieski.

What strange scenes and incidents in Poland's history spring to the mind whilst gazing on this imposing sculpture! Strange, that this nation has not been able to keep intact, when her armies led by Sobieski (the most able and valiant leader of his time) the Champion of Protestant Europe, could achieve such phenomenal successes. He delivered the western world from what appeared to be an irresistible and overwhelming invasion of the Turks, who invested Vienna with an immense army. All Europe stood aghast and trembled at the appearance of this huge advancing wave bursting over the Continent. And not a nation to deliver the old city from its peril. None did we say? Yes, there was Poland. Led by John Sobieski, the Polish troops burst and fell like an overwhelming avalanche on the Turks besieging Vienna. That city, and with it Europe, was delivered from this terrible infidel peril, for the man sent from God (whose name was John) Sobieski so utterly defeated and demoralized the Turkman foe, that it fled hurriedly to its own land as one man. And yet this nation of Poland, who were able under the leadership of Sobieski, to deliver the continent from such a catastrophe, were unable to save themselves. The old Aristocracy caused its ruin. The nation became divided and fell a prey to the greedy maws of Russia, Prussia, and Austria.*

---

* This famous equestrian statue of John Sobieski, King of Poland, was seen by Sir Robert Vyner in a sculptor's yard at Leghorn, and having purchased it, altered the name of the Polish Monarch to Charles II. whilst the fallen Turk was named Oliver Cromwell; thus re-christened, it was placed in the Stocks Market, in honour of Charles II., from there it was removed to Gantlery, and later, to its present position. Sir Robert Vyner was Lord Mayor of London in 1675. On one occasion, when he was honoured with the company of Charles II., His Majesty was for retiring early. "But Sir Robert, filled with good liquor and loyalty, laid hold of the King, and swore: 'Sir, you shall take t' other bottle.'" The merry monarch looked kindly at him, and, with a smile and graceful air repeated a line of an old song, "He that's drunk is as great as a king," and so, turning back, made merry with Sir Robert.

48 THE VALLEY OF THE YORE.

The Tapestry Room, Newby. [*Watson.*

Here at Newby Park Ferry, in February, 1869, there happened one of the most lamentable hunting accidents on record, and one which cast a gloom over the whole county. The author of "Saddle and Sirloin," when speaking of this melancholy accident, says: "Death is more fearful when it is in direct contrast with pleasure, and the little ferry on the Ure will be remembered so long as that dark river rolls its dark waters from the moors to the Ouse, as the scene of the most fearful tragedy in hunting history." A fox was found at Stainley, which crossed the river at Newby Park. Sir Charles Slingsby was crossing, with other gentlemen, in the ferry boat, when there was a scrimmage among the horses. Old Saltfish, belonging to Sir Charles, became restive, and jumping out, he became entangled in the chains, and upset the boat, bringing about the sad catastrophe.

From the Park a mile or so, Givendale, standing on the east bank of the Yore, is reached. This is an ancient site, which evidences around it testify. Here, early in the fourteenth century, dwelt Simon-de-Ward, high Sheriff of Yorkshire; it was he who led 400 yeomen to the assistance of Sir Andrew-de-Harcla, at the Boroughbridge fight.

Passing up the river, we next reach Bridge Hewick, a mile and a half east of Ripon. This spot is most interesting. "Here," says Leland, "was a faire chapel of free stone on the farther ripe of the Ure, at the very end of Hewick Bridge, made by a hermit, who was a mason, and it was not fully finished." A portion of the walls of this chapel were standing until a few years ago.

Less than a mile east is Copt, or Top Hewick, situated just on the edge of the rising and gently undulating land stretching east to Marton-le-Moors. The one distinctive

A Bend of the River,

feature at Copt Hewick is the large and beautiful green, at the east end of the village. Finely situated on the brow of the hill, just beyond, is Copt Hewick Hall. Here was found a Roman tombstone, and other relics, proving the site ancient. At the foot of the green just mentioned are the outlines of a moat, which, in olden times, probably encircled the manor of Sir Roger de Hewick.

To the north of this village, and two and a half miles from Ripon, is " Blois Hall," and near to this spot are the remains of what has once been a large circular entrenchment; the place is still known as Battle Ground. This is one of the many entrenched sites and encampments, circular and otherwise, which are to be traced here and there, from hence right across the Vale country, a dozen miles or more north, to Bedale.

Returning Ripon-wards, we pass along beautiful lanes bordered with sweet-smelling hedgerows, over meadows, and past orchards and gardens, with the noble towers and high roof of the cathedral ever growing clearer to the vision, and the purple landscape stretching far away beyond. Here is

Sharrow Village. [W. G. Foster.

Sharrow village, a place of shady nooks, overhanging trees and trim lawns. The church is a well-built structure, with a commanding tower. There is a story told anent the building of this church, by R. Blakeborough, of one Willie Dobbin, of Hutton Conyers, a character in his way:

For eleven months and a fortnight of the year he was an abstainer, but the remaining fortnight he was an equally good example of the besotting effect of drink. The funny, or sad part of the business was, from the time he became sober he commenced to look forward to his fortnight's spree, with a zest worthy of a better cause. "Ther's nobbut three months ti gan noo afoor t' races, an' then ah'll mak things spin," he was wont to say. On one occasion, when doing some repai s to Sharrow Church, Bishop Longfellow, who had called upon the Vicar, accosted Willie whilst at work, and endeavoured to point out to him the evil of his periodical outbursts. Willie listened very attentively to all the Bishop had to say, and then argued his own case as follows:—"Neea doot all 'at ya've sed's reet ez owt 'at sike ez yow c'u'd saay, bud ho'd on a bit. Noo, ah ken wha ya be hard eneeaf, bud ah knaw 'at ya tak a glass yersen. Ah deeant meean 'at ya mak a beast o' yersen ur owt o' that mak, bud noo ah's sayin' nowt but what's trew, when ah saay 'at ya'll tak a glass o' summat ti yer dinner, ur mebbe tweea; noo deeant ya?" To this the Bishop assented. "An' ya'll tak anuther afoor ya gan ti bed, noo deeant ya?" Again the Bishop assented. "An' noos an' agaan yan atween tahams; noo ah's reet, isn't ah?" To this also the Bishop had to agree. "Wha, then," continued Willie, "if you add up all 'at yoe tak i' twelve month an' add up all 'at ah tak i' t' race week, an' t' week efter ti taper off, ya'll finnd oot wheea's t' gertest drinker o' t' tween on uz; noy think it ower" Suffice it to say, argument was lost on Willie.

At Sharrow there are still to be seen the remains of one of the old Sanctuary crosses, that stood at all the principal approaches to the city. In olden times, there were eight in all, and they were known as "mile crosses," the limits of the sanctuary being a radius of one mile from the church. A person fleeing from his pursuers was not always considered safe, after passing inside the limits of the mile radius, but once within the walls of the sanctuary, the person who arrested the criminal committed a most heinous offence.

Before entering the city of Ripon we must turn to the

west bank of the Ure, to describe the Skell country and the district traversed by the stream.

The stream which enters the Ure at Newby Park from where it rises, drains the lands between Brimham Rocks and the Skell country, flowing through Sawley Park and forward to Markington and Wormald Green, then bends south for three or four miles, passing Stainley, leaving the pretty village of Burton Leonard half-a-mile to the north, then twisting and turning through groves and woods and under rustic bridges and through the most beautiful undulating scenery at Copgrove, bends to the north and enters the river Ure opposite Newby Park. We have not space to mention more than briefly the interesting places in the river basin of this stream, but the most beautiful part of its course is around Copgrove, which means "capping or overtopping grove"; this name is most appropriate, for the spot is a perfect labyrinth of mound and ridge grove, and belts of woodland, through which flows, in serpentine course, the noisy beck, in eager haste to join the "brimming river."

A mile and a half west of the Yore, and nearly opposite to Newby, lies the village of Bishop Monkton, a charming old settlement composed chiefly of one long winding street, down which a clear and limpid stream flows. One of the main characteristics of the place are the numerous bridges thrown over this stream. The "Mason's Arms," with its old windows, is an interesting structure, reminiscent of bygone times. The church, although of commanding architecture, is modern. Nearly every object the eye rests upon here, wears a rural aspect. The children at play, the ducks and geese in the stream sending forth showers of spray, the farm lads returning from the fields with their teams of horses, or the cattle wending homewards from the pasture at milking time; all add charm to the vista in our memories.

54   THE VALLEY OF THE YORE.

Bishop Monkton.   [*Edmund Bogg.*

Half an hour's saunter across the rising land we reach Burton Leonard, partly situated in a slight hollow and on the slope of the hill. This district, like Copgrove on the ridge of the lowland limestone wold, is beautifully undulating with dell and knoll. In the centre of the village is a hillside green, which commands fine views across the house roofs to the landscape beyond. The church is modern, but the impress of old time is deeply stamped in long disused quarries and other features, on the surface of the land about the village.

Markington, nearly two and a half miles due west from the latter place, consists of one long narrow street. It is only ordinary in type and wears no distinctive feature. Stainley Beck bubbles through a miniature vale west of the street, and invests the scene with some charm and interest. At the entrance to the village is Markington Hall, its mullions and gables, with the mill adjoining lends a touch of antique dignity, relieving the place from mediocrity. Amongst the inhabitants are a few very notable characters, bearing such cognomens as "Lord Salisbury," "Kruger," "The Squire," etc. The latter, according to village gossips, has had a most remarkable career, and a life with many side-lights and incidents. His name (The Squire) bespeaks his former position, that of a gentleman of the old school, which his manners and bearing betray. It was pitiful to watch the thin pathetic figure convulsed and visibly worn with a distressing cough, from which he was then suffering. "Jos," the son of Robin, a draper or tailor, and jack-of-all-trades by profession, is known as the village fool, and it would, without doubt, be impossible to find a greater one than he. But above all others, the most original character is Charlie Oddyman. No artist of ability would pass him by without transferring his unique personality to paper or canvas. A rare face and figure to sketch either with pen or pencil is that of Oddyman when engaged playing dominoes at the old village hostel. A big, dark hued, unkempt, swarthy, slouching "mak" of humanity, yet withal handy about a farm. And at cricket, with ball or bat, in rural districts he has few rivals. Watching him to-night, deeply engrossed in a game of dominoes, gulping down glass after glass of beer as the play proceeds, we listen to his peculiar drawling speech and quaint sayings, his dark luminous eyes glowing with excitement; his scarf unfolded, hangs loosely and half tied at the side of his neck, like an old rag. His powerful frame heaves with deep suppressed excitement, his big feet shuffles and swings about, his ungainly figure betokening great strength like that of some wild animal. Even the cap he wears is characteristic of the man, with its neb hanging, flapping over his right ear. The stem of his dark clay, which is only an inch long, is thrust into the extreme corner of his mouth, right up to the head, which is turned sideways and rests within a hair's breadth of his cheek. Every portion of his garments seems to hang on his figure awry, as though it had no wish to be beholden to another. Such is a rough sketch of a character, quite unique.

Leaving Markington for Markenfield Hall and Fountains, we follow the Stainley Beck, coursing its way through a wooded dell. Crossing this stream, we turn west and pass the small hamlet of Inglethorpe, and a little further on, the Grange of the same name, evidently an ancient site judging from old foundations, gnarled old trees, and other evidences of bygone

Markenfield Hall (formerly the home of the Markenfields).

occupancy. Half a mile further and we reach Markenfield Hall, hidden away as it were amongst fields, peaceably resting in its old age out of the track of the hurrying world; for the place lies some distance away from any main road.

It was a winter's eve when we made our first visit, many years ago; the sun was just drooping behind a bank of ashy grey-purple clouds, whose edges were faintly tinged with a rosy glow, and the serried line of the hill tops, fringed with trees, stood dark and clear in outline against the fading light. We had often anticipated the pleasure a visit to the old moated hall of Markenfield would afford, but had never imagined treading our way thither over ground covered with snow in the gloom of a winter's night. After floundering and stumbling over several fields we came to a farm, where by candle-light the farmer men were foddering the horses in the stable. On enquiry, we found we were still nearly a mile away. One of the men pointing over the fields, said:—"Can ya see yon poplar tree? Mak straight as a rush for it." So we did, to the best of our knowledge, make a rush, but it only landed us into a turnip field among some sheepfolds, and then over two more fields we groped. At length we reached the venerable structure, secluded from the busy world, a perfect realization of a moated grange. Crossing the bridge which spans the moat, and through the gateway, we found ourselves in a spacious courtyard. All was silent, not a sight or sound of life until our footsteps aroused the watch-dog. Crossing the courtyard we approached the door and raised the knocker, letting it fall with a bang, loud enough to awaken the echoes and shadowy figures who had departed hence centuries ago, and who now live in imagination before us. Passing through the lower stories of the grand old house, picturesque and rich with old associations, we ascend the massive oak staircase to the banqueting hall and private chapel. Musing in these rooms with only the light of a tallow candle, casting ghostly shadows on the old carvings, we fully realized the description of Tennyson's "Moated Grange," where

> "Old faces glimmered through the doors,
> Old footsteps trod the upper floors."

Then out into the night, we look on to the dark silent waters of the moat which surrounds the house,

> "About a stone-cast from the house,
> A sluice with blacken'd waters slept;
> And o'er it many round and small,
> The cluster'd marish mosses crept."

In the time of the Markenfields, there may have been a suitable approach in keeping with such a house; but if there is one now, I have never seen it during my visits. Outside the moat, on the east and south sides, are the barns, sheds, stables, and byres. The house and buildings form an enclosed quadrangle. A stone bridge on the site of the former draw bridge, gives access through the gateway into the large square courtyard. This bridge is the only alteration to the complete mediæval residence as it stood three or four centuries ago. The architecture is of various periods. The two late Norman, or rather transition, arches on the right hand as we enter possibly date from the latter years of the thirteenth century; and the foundations and lower parts of the walls of the hall proper from about the same date. But the house has undergone great structural alterations during the fifteenth and sixteenth centuries. The moat filled with water is from fourteen to eighteen feet wide, and varies in depth, encompassing the four sides of the quadrangle. It was in the large courtyard here that Sir Ninian Markenfield mustered his tenantry previous to marching to battle on Flodden Field, and for many a long year after we can imagine the story of that famous march and fight being told round the ingle, on a winter's night. But evil days were in store for the old family. They were staunch Catholics, and can one wonder, considering they had all been reared within sound and sight of Fountains and Ripon? and the religious associations of their home were closely bound up with the old faith.

Sir Thomas—grandson of Sir Ninian, of Flodden fame—dwelt many years abroad, so that, unrestrained, he might observe freely the same creed as his ancestors had done. But when the rebellion was brewing and came to a head in the North, to favour the cause of Mary Stuart, Sir Thomas Markenfield returned and joined in that forlorn hope, the north country gentlemen, amongst whom was Sir Richard Norton and his eight good sons, who dwelt at Norton Conyers and Rilston: their fateful story, Wordsworth has told in imperishable verse.

History relates the futility of the Rising, and tells how Sir Thomas, with other north country gentry, fled over the sea, and wandered abroad fugitives and landless exiles. Even his young brother, John, was attainted and the estates forfeited to the Crown, and the Markenfields knew their old home no more. Yet their spirits seem to hover about the old hall, which still remains a monument to their name, being the most perfect moated house in the north. Effigies and tombs to their memory are also in the north transept of Ripon Minster. And so, musing on the history and traditions of this family, we follow the footpath across the meadows to Fountains, a most beautiful walk in summer time. On the rise, we see the fair city of Ripon and its Minster, showing forth plainly in the warm morning sunlight. We have now reached the Hill Border, and woods, dell, vale and moorland stretch and rise alternately to the west. High above towers Howe Hill, from whence the devil shot from his immense bow, those huge arrows, intending to smash the old city of Aldborough; but they all fell short of the mark. And those who are in any way incredulous about this matter, may still see the arrows standing bolt upright where they fell, by Borobridge town.

The First Shelter.

All along the high ridge from Howe Hill to the banks of the Skell, one may look across a magnificent vista spreading out between the Ouse and Tees, from the field of Marston to Standard Hill, with the blue dim shadows of the Hambleton Hills for the background, whilst deep down in the bosom of the Skell, lies the fair ruins of Fountains, and immediately beyond, the park and woods of Studley Royal, where herds of dun and fallow deer roam, and the Skell meanders through sylvan shades and scenes of forest grandeur. Beyond, over the tree tops, rises the beautiful spire of Studley Church, and further still, the city of Ripon, its grey Minster tower looming in the picture, giving dignity and grandeur to a scene teeming with history, romance and legend.

Delightfully situated is the Abbey of Fountains. If the stranger should approach the place by the road leading from the Park to Alfield, turning aside to the left by a footpath before reaching the latter place, he will be suddenly arrested by a massive square tower rising above the trees, and fancy at once conjures it to be the huge tower of some hoary castle keep. Approaching nearer, this illusion is suddenly dispelled. We are on the high bank of the river Skell and find the huge tower rises from the ruins, occupying the whole width of the bosom of the valley. To adequately describe this scene, beautiful even to-day in midwinter, is almost beyond the power of pen, the harmony of this monastic wreck being so perfect and lovely. The antique silver hue of the ruin, the dark sombre yews rooted so deeply into the walls of rock, which overlook it to the north, forms a striking contrast to the grey walls and the stately tower of the church, soaring so forcefully upwards from the green turf into the blue skies as if to be in constant touch with heaven. The Skell winds and chatters its way beneath the foundations of the great abbey. In front, and blending sweetly with

The Tower, Fountains Abbey. [*E. Bogg.*

the smooth closely clipped turf, is the cloister (or Domus Conversorium—a most interesting feature of this abbey) which stretches nearly across the little valley. Above it are the walls of the dormitory, and dark green yews rise out of the cloister court in the centre of the ruin, and through the high graceful arches we see the blue sky, and the clouds sailing across, and swaying branches of trees; beside it, to the left, are the abbot's house, whilst the waters of the rivulet lave its walls; and just beyond, near the old bridge by the thicket of yew and beech trees stands the patriarch of Skelldale, an ancient yew, older than the abbey but from its wasting limbs its life's sap is fast ebbing; and near by are two others, the remains of the few which were fully grown when the thirteen monks were transplanted here from St. Mary's, York, to begin their life's work anew. Again we look on this monastic gem set in its natural ring of green turf and meadow, and hanging woods and hillsides, from whence stately trees rise and throw forth arching branches, bowering antique bits of silver grey and ivy-clad ruin, the whole combining to form a very paradise of loveliness.

The glory of Fountains is its magnificent position, and its history is in its name, the key to which lies in that of its river, the Skell, from the Norse 'keld,' a spring or fountain. Long before the monks of St. Mary's came this way, the district around the upper banks of the Skell, was inhabited by Celts. Robin Hood was a frequenter of Fountains dale, and wherever Robin's footsteps are found, they are besides those of the Celt. The Celtic ownership is apparent enough in the early charters. As in the case of Byland, for which a Kuldee priest was disturbed at Hode (Hood), so at Fountains there was dispute and overturning before the monks could firmly establish themselves and commence the erection of their permanent church and monastery. It will be well to relate the story of the founding of this monastery.

The first chapter of the story is told by the aged monk of Kirkstall, nearly a century after the event, when in his hundredth year. It opens with the rebellion of the Prior and twelve Benedictine monks of St. Mary's, York, who had set their minds on dreams of higher holiness and a sterner discipline in monastic life, such as was enjoined by the Cistercians, whose piety and strictness of rule had spread at this period throughout

Christendom. When the old abbot learnt their story he threatened, and tried by all means to turn them from the error of their way—to no purpose ; at length the disappointed monks told their trouble to good Archbishop Thurstan, "one who loved all religion," says a historian, and he promised to intercede on their behalf with the abbot. On the morning of Thurstan's visit, he and his attendants were met at the door of the chapter-house, where a great crowd of angry monks from St. Mary's and other monasteries had gathered together expressly to defy the superior authority of the Archbishop. They clamoured and hooted and would have none of his advice and counsel, and the thirteen monks for some time were in great fear of bodily harm. Thurstan, pained and shocked by such an undignified exhibition on the part of God-fearing men, tried his utmost to pacify them, but at length growing impatient said, "Since ye try to strip my office of its authority, I now strip you for the time being of your functions—your church is closed." At this came other shouts and an uproar of voices breathing defiance, and amid the turmoil the dissatisfied brothers who yearned for a holier and nobler life were borne away by the Archbishop. From this incident and the holy impulse of those thirteen monks of St. Mary's who were transplanted to the valley of the Skell, arose the beautiful Cistercian abbey of Fountains', where by day, says an old chronicler, "they laboured ceaselessly and by night rose for vigils, there were none who ate the bread of idleness, or took rest until wearied out by toil." Such was the origin of the storied pile of Fountains'.

It was in the depth of winter when the thirteen monks migrated to Fountain dale, and there was no house ready to shelter them. Apart from which,—an old chronicle tells us—the spot had an evil reputation. In this we can see the presence and resistance of the Celt or the Anglic (to the invader) who had been ousted from his patrimony. "It was a spot," says one, "left uninhabited in all ages of the past, a mere jungle of brambles, and so placed in the hollow of the hills and overhanging rocks, that it seemed more fit for the den of wild

Fountains from the South.

animals than for human use." It was surely a noble sight to see men girded with such faith and fervour that they were not turned aside by the bitterness of winter, nor the terrors of loneliness, nor yet by the lack of every kind of goods; their purses held no money, and their barns no corn; and stories tell how, in the centre of the valley there stood a large elm tree, leafy after the manner of its kind, which used aforetime to shelter harts in winter and in summer, and to this these Holy men came for refuge, among its branches making a sort of roof for the beds formed with straw and stubble upon the ground. Here they dwelt some time, until the snow and rain penetrated through the rude shelter. The story is very fervidly graphic, but those who have seen the place may well wonder why the monks took shelter under trees at all, when the high rocky bank on the north side of the valley is so well adapted for shelter,—where a rude lean-to structure might easily have been erected by a body of men in a few hours, particularly in a spot where wood and branches of trees abounded, when a safe and warm shelter might have been erected proof against the fiercest storm. Anyhow, the chronicler states that they left the shelter of the large elm tree for a more rainproof one around seven stately evergreen yews which were of colossal size, the trunk of one being mentioned as having been 27 feet in girth. Thus they passed their first months of privation, and as their piety became noised abroad other poor brethren joined them.

So passed two years of hardship and toil, which, we should imagine, was not so great as the old chronicler relates, for the woods abounded with game, and the streams with fish; yet, we are told, they had decided to abandon the spot which up to then had barely yielded sufficient subsistence for an existence. Amidst all their poverty they were ever charitable,

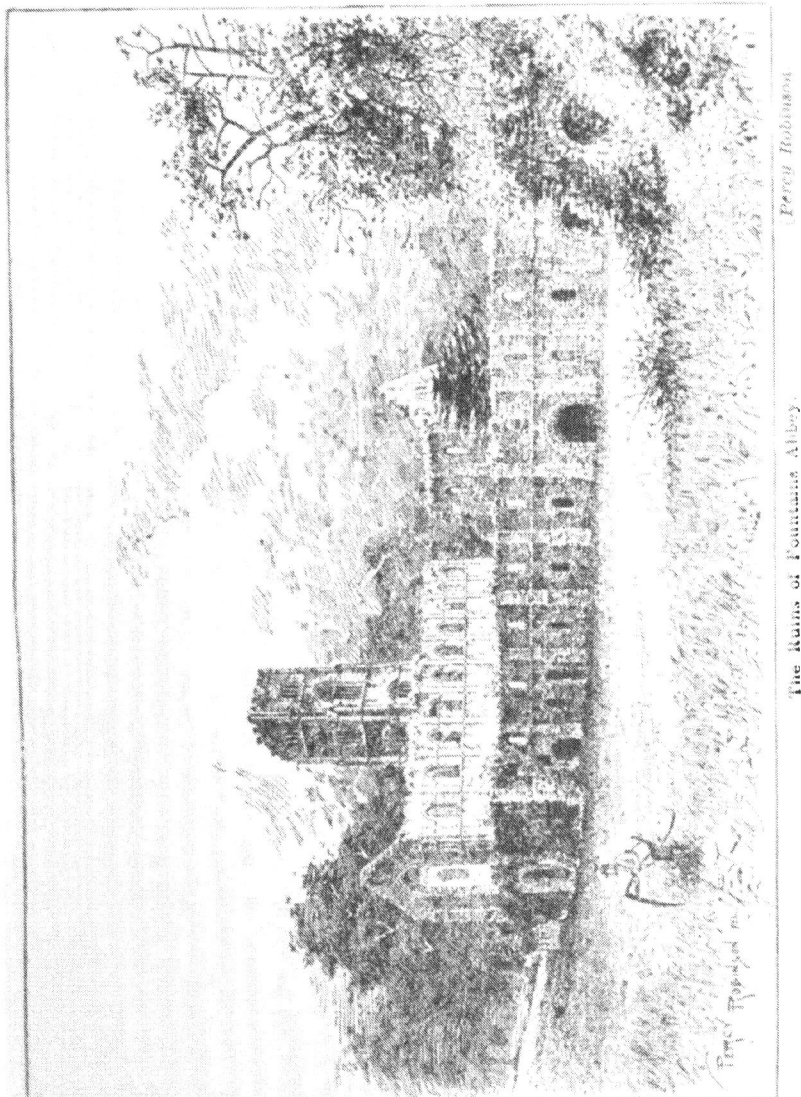

The Ruins of Fountains Abbey. Percy Robinson

for which the following anecdote will suffice. One day a traveller, hungry and weary, begged for a morsel of bread, but before complying with the stranger's request, the almoner consulted the Abbot, who enquired the amount of bread there was in the possession of the house. "Only two loaves and a half," replied the almoner. "Then give him a loaf," said the Abbot; "the Lord will provide." This hope and trust was soon fulfilled, for just after, a cart filled with loaves was seen coming down the hill side, a present from the Lord of Knaresboro', who had heard of their distress. Gradually their hardships became less, for about this time one of the monks writes:—"We have bread and cheese, butter and ale, and we shall soon have beef and mutton."

A few years later their trials and privations became a thing of the past, for Hugh, Dean of York, became seriously ill, was conveyed hither, and, dying soon after, left them much property, and benefactions now came in from other quarters. Lords, barons, and knights vied with each other in gifts of lands and goods; the great Percy family were munificent in their donations. And so there gradually arose in this sequestered vale a magnificent fane, such as the monks in the days of their privations could never have pictured, the ruins of which, pilgrims and strangers from all parts of the globe still come to view. We have not space to give even a brief history of the Abbey. If the visitor will but muse among the stately ruins, sufficient food for thought and imagination will be found. For there will rise up before the mental gaze such a host of monks, priests, and churchmen, attendants, domestics, husbandmen, and gallant cavalcades of the great and powerful, passing to and fro to worship, some of which, in after years, when satiated with the pomp and vanities and turmoil of the world, gave largely of money and land to be allowed to spend their closing days

The Chapel of the Nine Altars.

amidst the beautiful scenes of Fountains. Rest, says one, they had not found on earth, amidst the waves of crime and human care; and so they wished to slumber beneath or near the Abbey walls, where the bells might toll and prayers be said for them beside the limpid waters of the purling Skell. Hither the corpse of many a noble warrior has been borne to the tomb; here rest members of the famous house of the Percys. Here, too, was borne by his retainers, Lord Henry de Percy; he had withstood the deathful career of storm and siege, and performed daring deeds of arms on many a hard-fought field, and had followed the banner of the martial Edward into the wilds of Scotland; and he prayed that his body might find a resting-place within the Abbey walls. A host of others, equally great in church and camp, found a resting place here. Where are now the tombs and monuments of this army of abbots, monks, churchmen, lords, barons, knights, and squires, for few traces remain, except, perchance, a mound, a few tomb covers and fragments of richly sculptured marble? Yet, why look for monuments? Is not the exquisite ruin, although but a shell of its former grandeur, a sufficient monument and magnificent memorial for all who sleep within or near its walls? Leaving the shadow of the aged yew, we pass through the ruins. Delicious and beautiful bits of green scenery painted by nature, are to be seen, framed by men's handiwork, in the most graceful of arches. The church is nearly 400 feet long, with a magnificent tower 167 feet in height, and, when complete, must have been one of the noblest sanctuaries in England.

Like most Cistercian Monasteries in Yorkshire, there was a hermit and a well (we might instance Kirkstall and Byland in further proof). The displacement of Sir Robert of Knaresborough from his Halikeld was also attempted by the Cistercians,

Fountain's Hall.

but failed. Robert had been one of the brethren of Fountains before he retired to the hermitage below Knaresborough. The monastery spoken of in the later life of St. Robert by the monk Stonelai, is called the "novum monasterium," which means the new monastery, that is, Fountains, and not Newminster in Northumberland, nor even the monastery in Ripon. Aaliz de Gant's donation was but a little later than 1176, the year she gave Brimham to the Convent.

That the church was much damaged by fire in 1146, underwent restoration, on apparently a small scale, has really to be proven as a fact. There are parts of the present church which agree with the Charters, but not with the church " damaged by fire." The Chapter House, Galilee porch, and lower part of the nave are transition Norman, which may be dated as of the year quoted. The shafts of the nave pillars are of this period, but the arches above them are pointed, and must be referred to the early English period. When, therefore, it is stated John of York " refounded the church on a grand plan in 1203," it must be understood that he changed the character of the work in part executed, and developed an original plan in the new style. The same thing occurred at Kirkstall, where the shafts of the nave pillars are also transition Norman, and the arches pointed precisely like those at Fountains.

As to the magnificence of the completed structure no doubt has ever been raised; nor is there room to dispute the dates assigned to their construction. By the time these works were constructed, monasticism had consolidated its sway, which was complete in its young manhood, and early fell in the decay and disorders of age. As a monastic institution, Fountains became one of the most important in England, though it never had the National status of the great Benedictine foundations hereabouts,—St. Mary's of York and Selby, whose abbots were

The Cellarium, Fountains Abbey.

mitred and Lords of Parliament. As a scholarly institution, it was on a par with the rest—"fat bellies made lean pates." It is a fact, however, that not a few of its monks were good wood-rangers and determined poachers; the court rolls of Knaresborough prove that. Two of the most daring of these adventurers were Thomas and William Cleseby—trained possibly on Chaucer's maxim, then newly current:—

> "He gaf nat of that text a pulled hen,
> That seith, that hunters been noon holy men."

but on the contrary:—

> "Therefore he was a pricasous aright;
> Greyhoundes he hadde as swifte as fowel in flight,
> Of prikyng and of huntyng for the hare
> Was at his best, for no cost wolde he spare."

Romance, story and tradition of Robin Hood cluster thickly around Fountains. There is the well that some Kuldee priest, and likely enough before him some Druid, had held in sanctity—Robin Hood's well,—sculptures commemorative of him are in a buttress of the Lady Chapel. A famous tradition respecting him says, that a monk of the abbey encountered and overcame him, threw him into the Skell, and, for a time held both him and a strong body of his archers at bay, but was at length overset by them and induced to throw in his lot with theirs of "the merrie men." A metrical version of the tradition tells about Robin's boast of his prowess:—

> That caused Will Scarlett to laugh,
> He laughed full heartily,
> "There lives a curtail Friar in Fountains Abbey,
> Will beat both him and thee."

> This curtail Friar had kept Fountains Dale
> Seven long years and more;
> There was neither Knight, Lord nor Earl,
> Could make him yield before.*

When analysed, these verses will be found to contain the history of the foundation of Fountains. The curtail Friar was of the order of St. Austin, the favourites of the people, whilst the strict Cistercians were their abhorrence.

Again we are wandering by the banks of the Skell above where the stream passes under the Abbey walls, and, turning to look on the ruins, the noble temple rises in its magnificence, perfect before our gaze—a marvellous monument and record to the untiring zeal and religious devotion of the first monks, who not only earnestly prayed from their hearts, but also toiled unceasingly with their hands. Many who afterwards reaped the fruits of their labours, were not actuated by the same spirit. William Thirsk, the thirty-seventh Abbot, furnished a remarkable instance of degeneration. What a beautiful and peaceful retreat this has been to those weary of the pomp and vanity of the world, or the storm of siege and battle, and a strange story interwoven with the romance, pathos and tragedy, this place could unfold. Fountains Hall, adjoining, was built from the material obtained from the Abbot's house, soon after the dissolution of the monasteries.

The Hall is a most picturesque structure, with round arched gateway of Jacobean type, a charming herb garden per-

---

* It was on the banks of the Skell the bold outlaw encountered the curtail Friar. The pair fought a dreadful fight, and in the combat Robin was worsted and thrown into the Skell, which caused him to put his horn to his mouth "and to blow blastes three, whereupon his merry men came tripping o'er the green; thereupon the friar set his fist to his mouth to whistle whutes three, when half a hundred good band dogs came running o'er the lea." This fight ended in the outlaw requesting the Friar to join his company, which, tradition says, he accepted, and was afterwards known as "Friar Tuck," of outlaw fame. Legend says Robin Hood's bow and arrows were hung up inside the Abbey for centuries.

fumed with the aroma of old English flowers and spicy simples, rosemary and lavender, hyssop and rue. It is a rare jewel in a delightful setting, subdued in colouring and in perfect harmony with its surroundings. "It is a place which the fingers of time

The Old Yew Trees at Fountains.

have so lovingly touched since old Stephen, the Procter, quarried from the Abbot's house close by, and wrought out in stone, this fancy so beautiful as to deserve forgiveness, even for the vandalism in that which he destroyed." Before departing, we take another look eastward through the branches of large intervening trees. Birds are warbling their vespers, the Skell murmurs as it ripples along past the ancient mill, harmonizing sweetly and blending in fitness with the ageing bridge and the aged yews. The monk's wall stretching beyond, on the hill side, and the grey ruins resting so beautifully in an arcadian bower in the bosom of the Skell, whose sweet musical cadences make concords in one's mind with the solemn chantings of the Cistercian brethren across the gulf of time.

* * * *

Dr. Arnold Lees contributes the following note on the Botany of this Arcadian region:

"How shall one, briefly, do justice to the vegetation of Studley Royal? In its luxuriance, due in part to the warm nature of the lime-soil on which it stands, and in part to the fostering skill of far-back foresters, it is Royal indeed.

"At Fountains especially Old and New meet, and harmonize wonderfully: there are the Yews older than the pearly-grey Abbey walls or the silver and bronze lichens which dapple and protect the very stones of which they were built. On the cornices of the ruined chapels the pale-rosy Feather Pink, quite a rare flower, crowns the slowly-decaying monument of monkish art and soul with a crest whose motto might be "Resurgam," for like all nature's handiwork, it lives again each Spring, to the anthems of innumerable nesting daws and doves. Older, too, than the ruins is the Dwale or deadly Night-shade, which each year in proximity to the walls, springs up in broken places; its companion, the yellow Mullein or "High-Taper," that when in bloom looks not unlike the lighted wax candle long ago illuminating the Lady-chapel and altar at the celebrations of the dim dark past. About the crumbling masonry of Fountains Hall grows the gay yellow Fumitory, aflame like a summer sunset seen through the lattices of its emerald foliage. Both the Bee and the Fly Orchis, the single blooms of which are like the one insect or the other respectively crawling up a scaly and nigh leafless blade, are to be found in this sinuous vale of the river Skell. The Bee grows in open turf and bays of the lime cliff where stone has been quarried, and the Fly in the banks of the bluebelled glades of the woodland paths.

"The pale-blue perennial Flax is likewise a native of certain dry limey fields in the Fountains' demesne, with the Montane St. John's Wort, the Felwort gentian, and the Wood Barley; whilst in contrast—as long-ago introduced flowers, perhaps brought by some "simpler" of a monk—in spring certain meads are full of Lent-Lily and purple Spring Crocus, and the moist banks and stony bed of the little river Skell itself are in July over-run with pleasing patches of the monkey-flower Mimulus, whose blossoms hang funnel-like each side the top of its sappy stem, yellow with spotted gaping mouth. This plant was only introduced into England from North America in 1812, so is the latest in time of all the flora here; and though there are other interesting wild flowers to be gathered at Fountains, with this 19th century item I must make an end."

* * * * * *

The village of Aldfield lies to the north of Fountains, the Church being a seventeenth century structure. An inscription on a tombstone records: "Here lieth Anthony Robinson, late of Fountains, who died May 1st, 1756, Aged 81.

> My hammer and stiddy lies decline,
>   My bellows too, has lost its wind,
> My fire extinguist—my forge is done.
>   And in the dust my voice is laid.
> My coals is spent, my iron gone,
>   My last nail driven, my work is done."

Aldfield and its surroundings bear tokens of an anciently inhabited district. Several evidences of early occupation have been found in the shape of Kelts, beads, and fragments of coarse pottery. The most interesting object, however, is a fine gold torque, found in 1818, near Studley Hall, concealed between two large stones. Within a little distance of this place, was also found a large bronze sword, which the discoverer immediately threw away, lest as he sagely averred, he might be bewitched by its possession. The lapse of a century, and the consequent stride of education, has certainly enlarged the minds of the labourer; where is the fellow to-day who, in fear, would fling such a find from him?

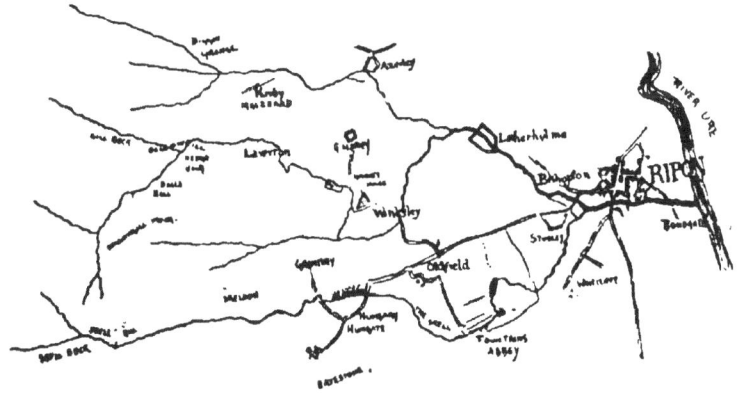

CHAPTER III.

STRETCHING between the moors of Malzeard on the north, Brimham on the south, and Pateley on the west, is a tract of land some eight miles in width, the greater part of which has never been brought under cultivation.

This highland is cleft with numerous glens and gorges, beautiful with intricate woodland; spreading over large boulders are immense trees, branches from which, levelled by the storms of many winters, still lie half hidden by rich green moss and rank vegetation; now and again a leaping cataract lends a silver beauty to the scene. Two or three miles onward the waters of these glens join and form the Skell on the south, and the Laver and the Azerley beck on the north. After flowing several miles the Laver and Skell meet near Ripon, and join the Ure half a mile south of the old city. The first rivulet on the north rises on Kex Moor, near to Foulgate Nook commonly called by the natives "Faud yat neak," and thence runs over Grewelthorpe and Malzeard Moors, where the dale assumes a fine sweeping character, and two or three streams meet just to the west of Kirkby Malzeard, and then pass the outskirts of this village.

Two miles onward by the stream Azerley, a picturesque spot, is reached. Here is an old mill, a small lake, and a pretty rivulet, murmuring under fine trees, old railing and bridges, and stepping stones over the beck; in fact, all manner of curves and corners, which make up beautiful pictures. Onward, by copse and hedgerow, the stream flows into the river Laver, midway between Azerley and Bishopton. Standing midway

Azerley.—Winter Scene.   [Edmund Bogg

between the two streams is Galphey (locally Gawpeh), which we reach by following the old pack-horse track. Passing this pleasant rural hamlet, we come to the pretty river Laver, which rises on Dallowgill Moor, adjoining Ramsgill and Kirky Malzeard Moors. The deep glen through which the stream flows for several miles is known by the name of Dallowgill. At the very source of the stream ridge rises over ridge, a vast expanse of billowy heather, over which a pack-horse track passes to Ramsgill. A mile down the dale the stream silvers through an oak wood, here the glen being of great depth and beauty. Perched on the summit of the cliff above are huge rocks worn by, but left from the glacial period, assuming the shape of some rude fortress (resembling those at Almas Cliff); and others at some far-distant date have been hurled by gigantic force into the bed of the stream—here roofed over with vegetation, a region of rich moss and fern, and delightful with the melody of the gurgling streams, sparkling rills foaming, leaping, and singing onwards. A mile lower two becks meet, and just beyond is the church, which stands on the high bank above; here and there dotted in various positions are the homes of the dales'-people. About half a mile north of the church is the hamlet of Greygarth. For many years there dwelt in Dallowgill a curious character known as "Awd Neddy," who maintained an existence by doing odd jobs, carrying firewood to the homesteads, etc., for which he always obtained some refreshment and a few pence; he also acted as a carrier to and from Pateley Bridge. The writer once met him on his return journey from the above place, and he was completely surrounded by various articles, each fastened separately to a thick cord around his body; his appearance on this occasion was most comical. He has on many occasions tramped to Masham for a bucket of lime, carrying the same the whole distance of nine miles. During his many tramps over the moors he had, from exposure and falls, some very marvellous escapes.

Situated on a lofty plateau on the southern bank of the Laver, and near to a farm on the edge of the moor called Castiles, are the remains of large British earthworks. The main work, or citadel, is about 80 yards in diameter; the whole at some period has been surrounded by a wall of immense thickness. The camp has been used as a quarry for generations by the farmers; there are also several barrows and remains of pit dwellings, pointing alike to a very remote period of occupation.

Still passing downwards with the stream by woodland and meadow and over picturesque bridges we come to Laverton,

Laverton. [*Edmund Bogg.*

the most peaceful of villages, the ivy-clad cots red tiled and blending sweetly with the blossoming orchards. Two miles and a half further the Laver winds its devious course, and then in half-circle sweeps round the village of Winksley. This village stands on the high bank above the beck, and, seen from the valley, forms a fine subject for a picture. The church is not at all picturesque, having a barn-like appearance, with an ugly tower added, of no architectural beauty, and it does not at all harmonise with the surroundings. The village inn is reached by an ascent of several steps, which must often prove a dangerous exit to those who imbibe too freely. The day is fast closing, the shadows are lengthening, so we wander around the old farmstead; the toilers are coming in from the fields, and the fowls are going to roost. We hear the distant lowing of oxen; and here, by the old cartshed, the calves are feeding. Thus sauntering and musing on these commonplace things, we are suddenly seized by the trousers from behind; it is only the hissing jealous old gander who thus keeps watch and ward over the yard! Now we are indoors, seated by the old mullioned window of the farm kitchen, watching the sun gradually slant behind the woods, through which sweetly filters the beautiful Laver. We can just catch the faint sound of its murmuring, and here and there a gleam of its waters tipped with a light golden hue. We are still looking through the window, as the expiring rays are fanning out through the woodland, forming a screen of gold between our vision and the west; the light gently grows fainter, and night takes possession of the vale, only the far-away hills which meet the horizon are margined with deep vermilion. After passing Winksley the Laver sweeps through a lovely vale in a south-western course, then bending round flows east, forming three parts of a circle, and so passes on to meet the Skell, just below the High Cleugh.

A character in Winksley was Long Tommy Brown, known as "Long Tommy," to distinguish him from another Tommy Brown, who was known as "Short Tommy." Long Tommy was sexton at Winksley, and for over 40 years had said "Amen." He stated that he had buried over 400 people, and although he could neither read nor write, he had a most remarkable memory, and a faculty for making intricate calculations. Many of the farmers in the district used to send him problems, which he would solve while thrashing his oats or smoking his pipe. William Hawksworth, who with his brother was joint tenant of Markenfield Hall, once sent him the following: "If a cubic foot of brass was drawn out into wire ⅛ of an inch in diameter, how far would it reach?" This difficult question Long Tommy answered correctly without putting down a single figure. Long Tommy once assisted in a curious proceeding. A widow, named Clark, died at the age of 97, and before dying requested that the bones of her husband, buried 54 years before, should be dug up and put into her coffin, and, strange to say, this curious request was complied with by her relatives. She was buried in a large coffin, and after the people had left the churchyard the coffin was brought up again, the lid unscrewed, and Long Tommy produced a bag full of bones, which he had hid in the church after opening out the grave the previous day; these were put in the coffin with the corpse, and again replaced in the grave. The son of this couple was present at the proceedings, and handled the skull of his father, who had died 54 years before. This took place in 1841. Long Tommy died in 1856.

The Skell Country.

The tiny river Skell, which wanders under the ruins of Fountains has its birth on Pateley Moors, a mile and a half above, and east of, the little village of Wath. Its first course is through desolate regions, after which, the entire distance to Ripon, the valley is full of charms; pleasant old lanes which twist and turn, bordered by hedgerows, where the woodbine and wild rose mingle their perfume. Easton beck murmurs through a charming woodland gorge; here the branches curve gracefully, forming cool and shady bowers, and the woodland path leads through an immense rock of sandstone, split in two, and some sixty feet in height. Further onward this stream filters into the lake at Grantley Hall, standing in a finely timbered park, presenting many picturesque bits of scenery. On the higher ground, at the head of the glen, is a rural farm with yellow washed sides, forming a charming picture. Between this glen and the Grantleys the land is intersected with pleasant little vales, and the Skell passes through coppice and hazel groves overlooked by ridgy upland. In such a spot rests the old-time hamlet of Hungate, and past the cottage doors the beck winds in many a curve, and old railings and hedges twist along its devious banks. On the brow of the hill above Hungate is the village of High Grantley, and just off the village street is the old Hall or Manor House, now doing duty as a farm-house. It is an interesting structure with fine mullion windows, suggesting to us mystery and tradition; the antique oak panelling has been removed to Grantley Hall. From the barn we hear the sound of threshing with the old primitive flail; in the paddock is a goose in charge of a brood of goslings, over which the old gander keeps watch and ward, and follows us with jealous eyes and outstretched neck, fiercely hissing meanwhile. Passing through High Grantley, whose inn bears the curious sign of a Blackamoor, the crest of the Grantleys, we met an aged inhabitant, who thus addressed us:—"Noo, whativer are ye deeing; takin' likenesses?" "Yes, will you have yours taken?" "Nay, nivver; av allus said me and oor Nanny ell niver ev oore's tean, and wen we get put et grund we leave nowt beoynt us, then we sa'ant ivver be seen ony mair."

A narrow road leads us down into Low Grantley. The situation is exceedingly beautiful, facing a valley intersected by other vales, and the outlook across the country delightful. Following the hill and vale, with the beautiful rivulets and clustering hedgerows winding on either side, until we come to the quiet little village of Aldfield.

THE VALLEY OF THE YORE.

The Laver at Winksley. *(Gilbert Foster.)*

A little distance from the Ripon and Pateley Bridge road midway between Winksley and Bishopston, a fine view of the Cathedrel City can be obtained; to the south are the dark blue woods massing on the high ridges; from this standpoint the billowy land falls sharply down to the Yore and the great plain, dotted with innumerable villages and farms, tower and spire, and old-time windmills, spreads far away to the ancient City of York, making a magnificent landscape. Ripon Cathedral, with its massive towers looms forth grand and impressive above the town,—the scene being beautiful beyond pen to describe. From Aldfield let us wander to Ripon by the road leading through the grounds of Studley Royal. Ere having reached the entrance gates, we are arrested by the beautifully finished architecture of the church, which is situated on the most elevated portion of the park on the west. The edifice is of the thirteenth century decorated style, and in its construction, no expense having been spared, it stands, a rare example of highly finished work. In design and richness of ornamentation, it is considered one of the most perfect churches in the kingdom. The foundation stone was laid in 1871 by the Most Honourable the Marchioness of Ripon. The inscription upon the stone, which is placed at the north-east angle of the building is as follows:—" ✠ IN : HONOREM : BEATÆ : MARIÆ : VIRGINIS : HANC : PETRAM : POSUIT : HENRIETTA : COMITESSA : DE : GREY : ET : RIPON : DIE : ANNUNCIATIONIS : A. : D. MDCCCLXXI."

A little distance to the north of the church stands the Hall, the home of the Marquis of Ripon, on or near the site of the ancient manorial hall of the seventeenth century. Following the drive through the Park, Riponwards, with its picturesque undulations, its dells and dingle, and enriched by the varied grouping of noble trees, we see far away, in the valley, at the extremity of the long avenue of green leafage, the Cathedral of Ripon, its two square towers showing forth almost hidden in the grey shadows rising over the city. And looking backwards, to the western extremity of the Park, from whence we have come, we see the beautiful new church of St. Mary, standing forth conspicuously from its fine situation, its elegant spire soaring divinely into the skies, as if seeking commune with things celestial. Of the other objects and well-known beauty spots in the Park lying about the meandering Skell, The Octagon Tower, The Rotunda, The Pleasaunce, The Temple of Piety and Fame, Anne Boleyn's Seat, or the Surprise View of Fountains, we have nothing to add, the Guide Books sufficiently indicating their charms.* We hasten along past a herd of stately red deer and the white dappled coats of fallow deer, and reaching Studley, we pass from the sombre shady avenues in the Park, stroll over the open meadows and very soon reach the precincts of the city of old-time memories and customs some lingering from that younger world we customarily call the "old."

Ripon.

The part that Ripon has played in the affairs of the North is of surpassing interest. The foundation of the city is doubtless due to the energy and religious zeal of St. Wilfrid. The existence of Killinghall, and the occupation of the south bank of the Nidd by an unrelenting Kuldee Priesthood bespeaks the religious strife between the two Orders of Monasticism of that early period.‡ The ancient form of the name is Hreppum. The Angle word "Hrepp" signifies a territorial division, having its modern equivalent in "Raper" of the southern portions of

---

* See Parker's Guides to Fountains.

‡ In the year 1695, there was found in Ripon a considerable number of Saxon coins, viz., of their brass Sticcas, of which there were eight to a penny. They were of the late race of the Kings of Deira, or rather the Sub-Kings, after Egbert had subdued it to a part of his monarchy.

of England, as the "Wapentakes" are in the north. The latter word is Norse, as in the main the people who use it are Norse also,—therein lies the difference. There are several places in England whose names begin with Hrepp; like Ripon, they all have the peculiarity of very ancient importance. Repton in Derbyshire, may be taken as a leading case in point; it "was a seat of the Mercian Kings," where a Nunnery was founded before 660, and a 'Black Priory' in 1172. Combining

The Minster, Ripon.

Fountains with Ripon, and substituting an Archbishop for a King, that is the history of the ancient Cathedral City. Wilfrid, a zealous, unyielding churchman, who had been a missionary among the northern Germans when tribesmen were occupying England, became a great patron of Monastic Orders, like the Cistercians, whose mission was to 'reform the Benedictine rule.'

Wilfrid's mission was to supplant the Kuldee clergy of this district, established by Eata, Abbot of Melrose in 661, by Monks of orthodox caste. He obtained the Royal permission to do so, re-building the Monastery in 690, on a much grander scale, and peopling it by a fraternity of less primitive character. The Archbishop's move in this direction, fashioned by his territory being designated the 'Lega Sancti Wilfridi,' was a factor leading to the Synod of Nidd, held in the open fields in 705. This Synod is not well reported, but enough is known of it to attribute it to a struggle between the Archbishop and Monasticism, and the Kuldee clergy of Killinghall—the hall of the Chapeldon, as that word means, the prefix 'Kil' exposing its Celtic origin. This Synod, held on the banks of the above river, did not by any means end as fully in favour of Monasticism, as the Archbishop desired. On the west bank of the Nidd it did not take effect until generations later. East and north of it the rule of Wilfrid was triumphant. He was a staunch adherent of the Romish Church in all its usages. His love and good taste for the beautiful in architecture was of a superior order, whilst his example greatly improved and cultivated the minds of the Anglian people in church building. He erected the noble Abbey of Hexham, and beautified the Cathedral Church of York, and, for that period, built a magnificent Abbey at his See of Ripon. Remains of Wilfrid's Churches, both at Hexham and Ripon, are to be seen in the Crypts; at the latter place it is a most interesting relic of the early church.

Wilfrid's chief fault was his jealous and unrelenting bitterness against the members of the old, yet true, British church, and its customs and usages. Legend tells that he was born at Ripon, and how at that eventful time a strange super-natural light shone over the house. And when he died, those who were in the death-chamber could hear the rustling of the angel's wings who had come to bear away the good man's spirit. He was buried on the south side of the altar of his own church at Ripon, and his gorgeous shrine covered with gold, silver and precious stones, was carried round the church on Festival days. A strong-willed human Saint, full of ambition, fiery energy, and love of Architectural Art, he planted here the splendour of Roman ritual. He has been strongly associated with the fortunes and history of Ripon these twelve hundred years.

There are several strange miraculous stories told concerning the ancient Monastery, around which the city of Ripon grew. It was here that Saint Cuthbert dwelt for a short period, when a young man; and being guest-master for the monks one night, he entertained an angel unawares. The legend tells that on going out of the Hospice early one winter's morning, he found a young man sitting there, who from his appearance had travelled all night through the snow, and had turned aside in search of shelter, rest and food. 'Yat alle nighte had travilde hongyr colde it seemed him weary and aylde (ailed).' St. Cuthbert washed the stranger's feet and chafed his hands, and placed them on his bosom for warmth; and requested him to stay till the third hour of the day so that he might take food and be rested and refreshed for travel. The stranger answered that he could not linger, for he was journeying to his home very far away. At which Cuthbert hastened to prepare hot bread from the oven, and at his urgent request the guest stayed awhile, till the prayer of the hour of tierce was over, and the meal was nigh at hand. But lo! when Cuthbert brought in the loaves from the oven, he found the guest had gone. Hurrying to the door, to see whither he had departed, he found no footprints in the snow to mark the way he had taken, at which he marvelled greatly. Returning into the guest-room he found it full of a strange sweet odour, the three loaves which he had brought were fairer, whiter, and sweeter than common bread—

"Hade he sa faire nane sene
In whiteness lily, rose in odour,
It passes honey in sweet savour."

and he knew that his visitor had been an angel, coming there to feed, and not to be fed. Such is the story handed down by the monks from the far off past.

During the earliest incursions of the Danes, the monastery was burnt and the community scattered or slaughtered. About 886 King Alfred restored the monastery, and the city, appointing a "wakeman" to blow periodically as a warning against thieves; the custom and the office continuing to the present day—to this we shall again refer.

King Athelston, by his victory of Brunanburgh, advanced the destinies of Ripon; among other things affecting the city, he gave the monastery the right of frithstool and sanctuary, the same as to Hexham and Beverley. One of the several stones which formerly marked the precincts of the monastery, still stands in the Sharrow township—the Scire-ed or Shire-water, taking name from the beck. There is evidence of another of those Sanctuary Crosses having stood at Hutton Conyers. The moral tone of the community at this period must have been good, for in Athelston's Charter it is laid down that the men of Ripon may be believed by their yea and by their nay in all disputes; the administration of an oath being superfluous.

The monastery and city whilst under the control of the Danes, were destroyed again in 940 by Edred, brother of Edmund, "the apostle of the English," whose name was associated with the church of Knaresburgh, and this probably affords the key to the dedication of that church, for it is certain the later attributions have no proof in evidence. The chieftain Anlaff, whose memorial cross is supposed to stand in Leeds Parish Church, had stirred the turbulent into the revolt which Edred suppressed, and desolating their kingdom of Northumbria with fire and sword, "divested it for ever of the name of a kingdom." The monastic power was again revived by St. Dunstan, until he "was banished from the kingdom, and the Benedictine monks expelled from several monasteries to be restored to the secular canons, their original owners."

The Norman Conquest furnished a dread day to Ripon, crushed by the Conqueror in the wrath engendered by the revolt of Earl Edwin therein in 1069. Archil, the thane of Ripley, was one of the chief leaders of this outbreak, which was suppressed by the fiercest vengeance, Archil, among many others hereabouts, being deprived of his lands. The family of Trusbut rose upon their ruins to high distinction, of which fact the churches of Goldsborough, Ribston, and Kirk Deighton bear strong evidence.

The revival of Ecclesiastical prominence in Ripon is due to Archbishop Roger, 1154-1181. The north transept and other parts of the cathedral are attributed to him, somewhat doubtfully. Among the late Norman work of those parts, contemporary Early English appears, rendering it probable that the structure must not be dated earlier than 1200, and be due to a change in the plans actually prepared under the supervision of Archbishop Roger, the new style being inserted after his death. From this time the vicissitudes of the city have been pronounced. One incident occurred on 21st October, 1221, when Gasfrid de Neville had to provide for Walter, Archbishop of York, ten 'breimas' (the fish, bream) from the King's vivarium of the Fosse, to stock that of Ripon. This start in park-keeping indicates the time when the Norman Cathedral had reached some completeness, and the Archbishop's residence was again fitted to receive its occupants. Matters had settled into canonical form before 1372, when the Archbishop appointed John of Carlton keeper of his park and beasts of chase at Ripon, for 16 years. The cathedral was likewise sharing in the good things. In 1407 a patent was granted to the Chantrey for the exaltation of the Holy Cross in the Collegiate Church of Ripon. Moreover, the spirit of traffic was making itself felt to the con-

venience of friends. In 1488, the Archbishop granted to John Arthington, for 800 years, a parcel of land in Rypon for a yearly rent of 20s. As to the judgment of felons, the execution of them, their goods, chattels and lands, his officers may be Justices of the Peace within the liberties of Beverley and Ripon. In pre-norman times Ripon had many Royal visits. In the Scottish Wars of Edward III., when the King was moving from York, Knaresborough, and hereabouts to Newcastle, the city had sundry passing visits. It was inhabited for some time in 1405 by Henry IV. and his full court; it was again visited in 1617 by James, on his way to Scotland; in 1638 and 1644 by Charles. In matters political, it has also had distinction, having been twice the scene of treaty arrangements with the Scots. Its last military experience was in 1643, when it was held by the Parliamentary troops, who were driven out of it by a Royalist force under Sir John Malone. The ancient Collegiate Church was promoted to the dignity of a Cathedral in 1826, when the See of Ripon was created and filled by Dr. C. T. Longley, the headmaster of Harrow. The ancient Archdeaconry of Richmond, one almost as powerful as a Bishopric, is still an office of great patronage and dignity.

There is no actual proof that Ripon has ever been walled in with stone as at York. Situated between the Yore and the Skell—natural bulwarks on the south-east and north, it would only require a deep ditch and high earthen rampart, running across the north-west side from river to river, to be placed in a fairly defensible position. But of whatever character the defences of the town partook they were evidently not strong enough to resist the Scots, who on two occasions, in 1319 and the following year, visited Ripon. On their first visit they extorted from the inhabitants £1,000 in lieu of destroying the town. In the following year they returned and carried out their former threat, pillaging and firing the place. From the the above sad disaster it is evident that the city has never been sufficiently protected by ramparts to withstand the rude shock of arms. Ripon is full of old-time memories, ancient customs, and antique bits of architecture; the oldest portion of masonry, the crypt, dates back over 1200 years. Ripon was granted a frid, " frith or peace stool,"and the privilege of sanctuary by King Athelstone in 924. The Rhyming Charter of these privileges conferred by the King is said to have been written by a monk in later centuries. Exactly where all the mile crosses stood (there were eight in number), no one knows. Supposing there were eight approaches to the city, each would be guarded by its cross, within which limits the evil-doer fleeing from his pursuers would find refuge. The base of one cross alone remains, the one at Sharrow known as Sharrow (Scire) Cross, and points to this ancient custom and privilege of sanctuary. The following strange scene took place in the church of Ripon on the morrow of St. Lawrence's Day, 1452, vividly pourtraying the lawlessness of the time, and also proving the strong power of judgment and the certain power of punishment possessed by the church at this period. John Slingsby, of North Studley, with seventeen others who had invaded the Liberty of Ripon by force of arms, and in a manner of war, making assaults upon the household of Sir Randulf Pigott, submitted to the authority of the Chapter of Ripon, and did penance, walking in procession to the church, heads and feet bare, each man bearing in one hand a burning wax candle half-a-pound in weight, and in the other a naked sword held upright in form of a cross, marched to the shrine of St. Wilfrid, and deposited there the arms and the candles as oblations, and then received absolution.

The Old Market place was formerly on the site known as Black Bull Square, and it was here at the Market Cross that Sir Richard Norton and Sir Ninian Markenfield and other gentry of the North in 1569 unfurled their great standard. They attended high mass in the Cathedral Church before they marched on their mission of rebellion, the sequels of which were confiscated estates, death, or outlawry. The Market Place is a fine spacious square, the obelisk in the centre known as the Cross, is some ninety feet high, its finial consists of the arms of Ripon—a bugle horn and spur rowell. What has become of the old Market Cross, which must have been a picturesque object, more in keeping with the History of Ripon than the present obelisk? Leland tells us that "The very place where the market stood and heart of the town is, was formerly called Holly Hill, by reason of the Holly trees there growing." Kirkgate is a characteristic winding thoroughfare, leading to the church, and, although much modernised, it still retains a charm of bygone times. Allhallowgate, as its name implies, is very ancient, and wears a primitive look. The precincts of this street are doubtless the most anciently occupied in Ripon. It was the northern fringe of the city far into the middle ages. St. Wilfrid is said to have built a church in this street, and dedicated it to All Hallows, hence the name of the street. Middle Row, a "narrow way," is another relic of old time, which like other ancient landmarks, is doomed soon to disappear. Westgate and Blossomgate point to a boundary and entry by a "bar" or gate into the town. In the prefix of Skellgate, situated on the south side of the minster, we have a Norse naming, Skell meaning a spring or fountain. Here one Zacharias Jepson (a native of Ripon) founded and endowed in 1672 a hospital for twenty orphan boys. Bondgate is, as its name implies, another old street, in which are situated the chapel and almshouses of St. John the Baptist, and for centuries the men of Bondgate were famed for the making of saddletrees, which readily found customers from far and near. Here in this street Eugene Aram spent some years of his boyhood. In High and Low St. Agnesgate, wending deviously on the south side of the minster, are still seen quaint bits of distinctive architecture. Here is also the Hospital of St. Anne, now roofless, neglected and desolate. The arch of the chancel and its lower walls alone remain, and a few relics in shape of a piscina and holy water stoup and brackets. St. Marygate is named from a chapel dedicated to St. Mary, the Blessed Virgin. Not a trace of the structure now remains. John Leland says, "The old abbey stood where is now a chapel of Our Lady, in a bottom one close distant from the new minster." Apart from the Cathedral, the old chapel of St. Mary Magdalene is perhaps the most interesting architectural feature in Ripon. Attached to the chapel was an hospital for the relief of the poor and also for those afflicted with the dread scourge of leprosy; and in after centuries a hospice to the many strangers, mendicant clergy and wayfaring men attracted to Ripon during the middle ages by the fame of the shrine of St. Wilfrid and the sanctuary rights of the city. The pious humanity of St. Anne and St. Mary Magdalene are now perpetuated in charities. Previous to 1889 the Bell gable held a sham wooden bell, on which hangs an oft told story, written by Barney Coult, that if true (which we should very much doubt), is not very creditable to the memory of the person concerned: this story we need not repeat. The wood bell, I believe, is still to be seen in the churchwarden's chest, within the church. Although neglected in its old age, rusty and cobwebbed, there is a rare charm and fascination about this sacred edifice tempting one to linger.*

---

* The chief thing deserving notice in this venerable chapel is the old stone altar, which is approached by two steps, seven inches high and sixteen inches broad. The surface before the altar is adorned with tesselations of coloured marble, stone and brick, white, grey and black, one circle immediately in the centre being of a more elaborate pattern than the rest. The altar has four crosses of dedication very plainly indented at the four corners, the centre one obliterated; it is six feet seven inches long, three feet broad, and two feet eight inches high. There is a small piscina under a three cusped arch, with the orifice at the back. There is a bracket on each side of the altar, and one on the north wall, all plain; also an old altar stone, with the five crosses plainly to be distinguished, on the floor under the south chancel wall. Whence could this have been brought? Perhaps the piety of someone, shocked by the irreverent use of altars by the Puritans, brought it hither from some neighbouring church. If so, it has escaped destruction indeed, but not neglect.

The Horn-blowing at Ripon.

This old custom of Horn-blowing, a survival of pre-conquest times, still lingers at two places on the banks of the Yore, viz.: Ripon and Bainbridge. It has been the writer's pleasure to hear the horn blown at both the above places. At Bainbridge the horn is blown at ten o'clock, at Ripon, every night at nine. The origin of this curious custom dates from Saxon times, when its chief magistrate was called the "Wakeman." Doubtless it was the first Wakeman after the town was incorporated in the reign of King Alfred, 886, who instituted the ceremony of Horn-blowing. As to "Wakeman," it is a Norse proper name. A John le Wake was a soldier in the army of William the Conqueror, and he married the heiress of Malcolm Desberic, a Saxon thane, and settled at Ripon. Whether he gave the name of wakeman to the chief magistrate, or his servant who carried out his task, does not appear certain. Why this person came in William's army is another question. For Herwaldus le Wake, or Wakeman ("Hereward the Wake" of Charles Kingsley's novel), held the Normans at bay in the fen country for a long time, and was one of the last of the Saxon chieftains to submit to the Conqueror, and he was of the same family. The Wakeman crest was an embattled tower, and on the summit a watchman holding a club. It was the duty of the Wakeman to order that a horn should be blown every night a it nine o'clock. It may have anciently implied two things—a Curfew, and also the setting of the watch, or night guard. At its sounding in former times the people put out their fires, for in those days the houses were chiefly of wood, and floors were covered with rushes, and beds, etc., were of straw, so the putting out of fires was a wise precaution. The law in Saxon times was, "If anybody after Horn-blowing was robbed on the gateside within the towne, the Wakeman was bound to make the loss

Horn-blowing at Ripon.

good if it was proved that he and his servants did not do his duties at night time." To maintain this watch he received from every householder that had but one door, the annual tax of twopence, and from the owner of a gate, door, and back door fourpence by the year of dutie. Although the ancient custom is still retained, the benefits arising from it have long since lapsed. In 1604, King James I., granted a new charter to the city, whereby it became a borough governed by a mayor, recorder, and twelve alderman, with twenty-four common council men and a town clerk. This charter was obtained chiefly by the efforts of Hugh Ripley, a "merchant and mercer" of the town, who was wakeman at that time, and was nominated by the crown as the first mayor. Near one of the pillars of the great tower of Ripon Cathedral a bust is placed to his memory, bearing the following inscription:—

"Here lies entombed the body of Hugh Ripley, late of this town, Merchant, who was the last wakeman, and thrice Major (Mayor), by whose good endeavours this town first became a Majoraltie; and lived to the age of 84 years, and died in the year of our Lord, 1637."

At nine by the clock every night three long wierd-sounding blasts, as if welling up from the echoes of old time, are blown before the Mayor's door and one immediately afterwards at the cross while the seventh bell of the Cathedral is ringing. The ancient and possibly the original horn is not used now. It is shaped similarly to the Horn of Ulphas, which is still preserved in the vestry of York Minster.

Apart from Saddletrees, Ripon in the past was also famed for the manufacture of cross-bows and spurs—Ripon Rowels. It is Ben Jonson who says, "As true as Ripon Rowels, there is an angel if my spurs be not right Ripon," and again, "Whip me with wire-

Ripon Cathedral—South East. [G. Parker.

headed rowels of sharp Ripon spurs." The rowel was so ingeniously placed, says Frank Buckland, that the sharp point of the star of which it is composed would not show unless pressed against something. Another interesting object at Ripon is Ailsa, Illshaw, or Ailcey Hill, shaped like a huge tumulus. It is situated a bow shot from the east end of the Minster, and to all appearances it is artificially reared. Wallcott says Ailsi Hill is a barrow raised over Elsi, or Ella, and his brave Northumbrians, slain in battle with the Norsemen in 867. Another old writer says it is "Composed of human skeletons" laid in regular order, greatly decayed, and discernible from top to bottom. Certain it is that human remains have been found intermixed with the gravel, pointing it as a place of sepulchre. In 1695, the Archbishop of York presented Ralph Thoresby of Leeds, with several brass coins of Osbright and Ella, two Northumbrian Princes, who both of them fell in the year 867, warring against the Danes. These coins were taken out of a remarkable tumulus, at the north-east end of Ripon, and at a short distance from the Minster. The tumulus, locally called Alice Hill, is nearly of a conical form, the circumference at the base being about 900 feet, and the height of the slope 72 yards from the base to the summit. It is composed of sand, gravel, and human bones.

1796.—On October 16th, at about 6 o'clock in the morning the inhabitants of Ripon were greatly alarmed by an earthquake, which shook almost every house in the town: a mile from which, near Littlethorp, about three roods of ground sunk 19 fathoms, and a large ash tree, growing on the spot, entirely disappeared. For some time the gulph continued to increase and an immense body of water issued from it, which filled the inhabitants with fear, for as there were no coalpits in the neighbourhood, it was evidently a great internal convulsion.

Ripon Market Place. [G. Parker.

1830.—January 4th, died at Bishopton, near Ripon, in his 105th year, Francis Wilkinson, after having spent a laborious but not most temperate life. Of all the eccentric looking characters, the one known as 'The Old Boots of Ripon' was the most remarkable. Travellers who passed through this town knew him well as Tom Crudd, the Boots, and he rarely missed an opportunity of exhibiting himself, especially to those who were likely to "tip" him well. His nose and chin were of such an extraordinary length that he could easily hold a coin between them, and all coins that were put to this test he, of course, naturally kept. As silver coins were always preferred, he eventually amassed, it is said, a comfortable fortune. The many other interesting themes and objects in the city of Ripon space will not allow us to mention.

The west front of the Minster is of austere simplicity and a fine example of early English work. The interior is most interesting. A high wide light nave, timber-roofed; a fine transept of Transition-Norman; a beautiful choir, with a grand eastern window, and richly carved tabernacle over the stalls, and a groined roof of wood. In the dark crypt, the original work of the first church, situated under the central tower, is a hole in the wall, known by the name of St. Wilfrid's Needle. For generations, and even to this day, females squeeze through this needle, and woe be to the unlucky one who is unable to pass, as the safe passage is a proof of moral purity, and speedy marriage. A writer says, "A camel could not pass through the eye of a needle, but through this needle there is an ample eye for almost any person to thread with ease." How suggestive to ponder for an instant on the vital continuity of ideas; enshrined in this dark cell, the home of holy abstraction, of agonised aspiration in prayer, and feel the link which still holds the chain of the past to the present. In the chapel of St. Andrew will be seen the tombs and effigies of the Markenfields and the Blackets, of Newby-on-Ure. The first-named, with the Nortons, attended high mass in the Cathedral on joining in the rebellion which ended so disastrously for them.

With regret we leave Ripon with the strange memories, traditions and incidents in its long historic life, a wonderfully continuous story, stretching over thirteen centuries, which if its tale could be properly written, would sound more stirring and marvellous than any conjured-up old romance. As we wend down the hill to the old bridge with its numerous arches, and mount the opposite hill leading to Hutton Conyers, we turn to look again from this elevation, over the city which has so long a record of civil and ecclesiastical dignity, its historic tradition and antiquated customs. The evening light is mellowing down in the west, blending a softening glow over the solemn grey old Cathedral, even as its life through the centuries casts the fascinating spell of glamour, peculiar to these quaint cobwebbed cities of the past. On the brow of the hill where the lanes diverge, are the remains of the hoary Sharrow Cross. Down below the river is visible,—to the ear a song without words; from the river the land swells in gentle undulations, on one of which rises the sanctuary towers of the Minster fane, to which troubled and fearsome souls fled to for rest from their pursuers; beyond can be seen the well-wooded domain of Fountains, and dimly indicated, the eminence of How Hill—a picture in three panels of the present peace of things in a settled land, the early age turmoil of endeavour after the attainment of ideals, and the still earlier struggles and fierce foray of which we know so little in the days when this vale was a forest of wild nature.

On the Ure, Ripon, below the Bridge.   [G. Parker

Leaving the Thirsk road a quarter of a mile east of the river, we turn up the by-lane, and soon reach Hutton Conyers. A century or so ago there was a large unenclosed moor lying between this place and the villages of Marton Dishforth and Rainton, known as Hutton Conyers Moor. The lord of the manor at the period mentioned, was William Aislabie, of Studley Royal, and appertaining to this moor there was a singular custom :—

"The occupiers of messuages and cottages within the several towns of Hutton Conyers, Baldersby, Rainton, Dishforth, and Hewick, have a right of estray for their sheep to certain limited boundaries on the common, and each township has a shepherd. The lord's shepherd has a pre-eminence of tending his sheep on every part of the common, and wherever he herds the lord's sheep, the several other shepherds are to give way to him, and give up their *hoofing-place* so long as he pleases to de-pasture the lord's sheep thereon.

"The lord holds his court the first day in the year, to entitle those several townships to such right of estray; the shepherd of each town attends the court, and does fealty, by bringing up to the court a large *apple-pie* and a twopenny *sweet-cake* (except the shepherd of Hewick, who compounds by paying sixteenpence for ale, which is drank as after mentioned) and a *wooden spoon*; each pie is cut in two by the bailiff, one half is divided between the steward, bailiff, and the tenant of the coney warren before mentioned, and the other half in six parts, and divided among the six shepherds of the above mentioned six townships. In the pie brought by the shepherds an inner one is made, filled with prunes. The cakes are divided in the same manner. The bailiff of the manor provides *furmety* and *mustard*, and delivers to each shepherd a *slice of cheese* and a *penny roll*. The furmety well mixed with mustard is put in an earthen pot, and placed in a hole in the ground in a garth belonging to the bailiff's house, to which place the steward of the court with the bailiff's tenant of the warren, and six shepherds adjourn with their respective wooden spoons. The bailiff provides spoons for the stewards, the tenant of the warren, and himself. The steward first pays respect to the furmety by taking a large spoonful; the bailiff has the next honour; the tenant of the warren next, then the shepherd of Hutton Conyers, and afterwards the other shepherds by regular turns. Then each person is served with a glass of ale (paid by the sixteen pence brought by the Hewick shepherd) and the health of the lord of the manor is drunk; then they adjourn to the bailiff's house, and the further business of the court is proceeded with.

"Each pie contains about a peck of flour, is about sixteen or eighteen inches diameter, and as large as will go into the mouth of an ordinary oven. The bailiff of the manor measures them with a rule, and takes the diameter, and if they are not of a sufficient capacity he threatens to return them and fine the town. If they are large enough he divides them with rule and compasses into four equal parts, of which the steward claims one, the warrener another, and the remainder is divided amongst the shepherds. In respect to the *furmety* the top of the dish in which it is put is placed level with the surface of the ground; all persons present are invited to eat of it, and those who do not are not deemed loyal to the lord

"Every shepherd is obliged to eat of it, and for that purpose is to take a spoon in his pocket to the court, for if any of them neglect to carry a spoon with them he is to lay him down on his belly, and sup the furmety with his face to the pot, or dish, at which times it is usual by way of sport to some of the bystanders to dip his face into the furmety, and sometimes a shepherd for the sake of diversion will purposely leave his spoon at home."

Here was a Manor Hall of some note as vestiges still show, and here also stood one of the sanctuary crosses known as Athelstone Cross.

Between Hutton Conyers and Marton le-moors there are to be seen sites of camps and entrenchments; and vestiges of primitive dwellings have been discovered in the vicinity. To the north-east of Blois Hall are the remains of a remarkable circular entrenchment and several tumuli of great interest.*
Wandering along pleasant country lanes, over rich pastures, and past fields of waving corn with the Yore flowing broadly onward

---

* At Little Nunwick, a mile north of Hutton Conyers, there was formerly some sort of female religious establishment, as its name denotes, and the ordnance map shews a system of landers, or fish-ponds named "Hall Garth," but of the building hardly a trace remains. Here grows the "Roast-Beef Iris," a purple flag or flower-deluce with a disagreeable smell. Singularly, and scarcely a coincidence, on the opposite (or S.W.) bank of the Yore, with which a ford across the here shallow bed of the stream communicates, is another string of pools, one of which, as the map shews, has long borne the name of "Queen Mary's Dubb." Why, tradition is silent regarding it. But all this district was a stronghold of Catholicism in the old days, and even the survival of on-lingering pot-herbs and physic-garden plants marks in many a spot the site of long vanished occupation. Such are the sweet Flag, *Acorus*, and the Strict Sedge by the Dub; Wild Liquorice on the bank above; the great yellow Leopard's Bane in the eyots of the river near North Stainley.

to the west, we reach Norton Conyers, the home in Tudor times of old Richard Norton, that fierce Squire, who clung so tenaciously to the old faith, that the wonder is he did not lose his head as well as his estates. His name still survives here as at Bolton and Rylstone. The muse of Wordsworth has linked the memory of the Nortons to this place and those above-mentioned for all time. We pass through the park gates to look at the fine old Elizabethan mansion, with its many gables and chimneys, interesting both to the antiquary and the historian; it stands in a beautifully timbered park extending west to the Yore. Such names as the Nortons and the Greames recall great deeds of chivalry, romantic associations, tragic and pathetic episodes to our memory. We cannot stay now to tell the story of the hapless Nortons; it has been told and re-told times out of number. In the name of the house (Norton Conyers) the remembrance of this family will long survive. But there is one story which still lingers strongly in the minds of the country people, well worth recording. The Nortons had long lost their patrimony and had become scattered and wanderers, and during the Civil Wars the estates had passed into the keeping of Sir Richard Graham, who being a staunch Royalist and Master of the Horse to Charles the First, took part in the great fight at Marston Moor, and, we are told, when the day was lost and himself wounded, and faint and weary with smiting, he turned his horse's head homewards, towards Norton Conyers, so that he might die in peace under his own roof. But having been seen to leave the field of battle, he was so closely pursued that he galloped his steed into the large hall and up the broad stairway

Another version of the story says that it was Cromwell who watched Sir Richard ride off the field, and it was he who gave chase to him in the gloaming of that battle-night. Across the

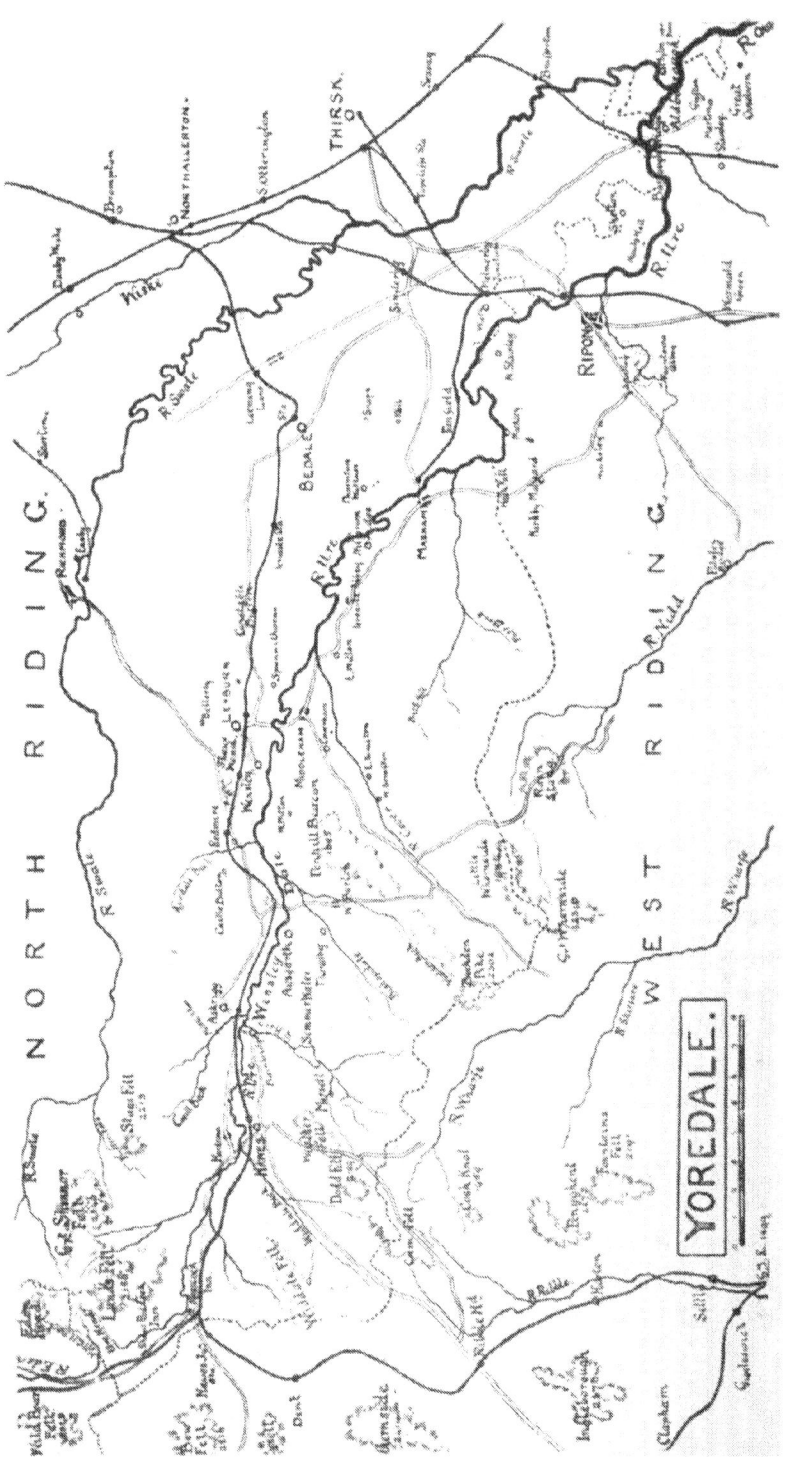

Norton Conyers.   *Percy Robinson.*

fields and highways, through the two Hammertons and Borobridge past Kirkby Hill the chase continued to Norton Conyers, Sir Richard was far in advance of his great foeman, and had already been placed in his bed when Cromwell thundered into the hall, and urged his war steed up the staircase, and dismounting, so shook his old adversary in arms, that he died forthwith. Such are the traditions told by the local people, who, if you are at all incredulous, will tell you of the impressions of footprints left by Cromwell's charger still to be seen at the top of the grand staircase unto this day.*

---

* In the early years of the Stuart Kings, Norton Conyers passed into the possession of the Grahams, who trace their descent from the renowned Greame, who commanded the Scotch army in the year 420 A.D., and stormed the defences which the Emperor Severus had erected between the Forth and the Clyde. From this furious onslaught, that place has ever since borne the name of "Greame's Dyke." The Grahams were staunch Royalists—a member of this family particularly distinguished himself at the battle of Edge Hill, was dreadfully wounded, and left for dead amongst the slain all the night following the battle. "The ancient and powerful family of Graham," says Sir Walter Scott, in the "Lady of the Lake," "held extensive possessions in the counties of Dumbarton and Stirling." Few families can boast of more historical renown, having claim to three of the most remarkable characters in the Scottish annals. Sir John Greame, the faithful and undaunted partaker of the labours and patriotic warfare of Wallace, fell in the unfortunate field at Falkirk, in 1298. The celebrated Marquess of Montrose, in whom De Retz saw realised his abstract ideal of the heroes of antiquity, was the second of these worthies.

Sir Richard Graham was certainly very severely wounded at Marston fight, but his death did not occur until some years later. King James and his son, Charles, were both guests here, and the room in which they slept is still known as the "King's Chamber."

The old village of Wath (meaning a ford) is only a short distance from the Hall, consisting of a wide street of well-built cottages, with the church of St. Mary at the east end. In the centre of the village is the Police Station with Court room, where Petty Sessions are held on the last Saturday in each month.

The ancient church is a monument of judicious restoration (a labour of love), the work of the late rector, the Rev. W. C. Lukis, a very eminent archæologist, antiquary, botanist, and also an artist of ability.

Aumbry, Wath Church.

The old-time relics have been preserved at the time of the restoration with such care and reverence, that, even to the most casual and indifferent observer, these remains of the ancient church must possess some amount of interest. To an antiquary, this place is a veritable mine of treasure. The sacristy is very curious, and contains an ancient and finely carved Flemish oak chest, and an oblique niche, or "squint," commands the altar table. In pre-Reformation days there has been a room over the sacristy; the priest's chamber, the stone steps leading to this upper room, and the half-circular landing at the top, leading to the sleeping apartment of the priest or sacristan in charge of the sacred vessels, etc., have been carefully preserved; he could sit and watch through the "squint" the high altar and the lights burning. Hung in the vestry is a sketch of the old church in water colour, taken just previous to the restoration by the late W. C. Lukis, showing the old timbered roof and the high-boxed pews. Built in the north wall are several fragments of stone Saxon work, heads of crosses, etc., and the chancel contains a sedilia and double piscina. In the south transept are many brasses, shields, and other mementoes and memorials of the Nortons and Grahams; and explains that here was the burial place for centuries of the Nortons and Grahams, of Norton Conyers. Here is a brass to the memory of Richard Norton, Chief Justice of the Queen's Bench, and Katherine, his wife, A.D. 1420. And another, adorned with shield and other symbols of earthly greatness, tells of Sir John Norton, who died 1520, and of Margaret, his wife, daughter of Sir Roger-le-Ward, of Guiseley and Givendale. One inscription reads:—

Nobled virtue lyes within this tomb,
Whose life and death inferiour was to none;
Her soules in Heaven, this tomb is but a tent,
Her endless worth is her own monument.

In the south wall is a canopied recess containing the tomb of John de Apulby, founder of the Chapel of St. John the Baptist, A.D. 1333; in the same recess is a coffin-lid with a floreated cross of the thirteenth century. The transept on this side also contains several recesses, all having some special use in the olden days. And in the graveyard by the porch stands the early English font.

Near to Wath is Melmerby (said to mean the dwelling-place of Melmor, the Dane). The village is of no special interest except for its new-looking Manor House and buildings—the older features of the place having disappeared.

Just on the precints of Wath is Howgrave (a fine field of study for the archæologist) and Middleton Quernhow, with its pretty green and fine old tree. Here, at the picturesque old hall with ivy-mantled front, though now desolate and fast falling to ruins, formerly dwelt the Herberts. The remains of a large fishpond are still to be traced at the back of the house. The Herberts sided with the Roundheads during the great civil war. Afterwards when Thomas Herbert was chosen to attend on the fallen monarch, he became greatly attached to him and served him faithfully to the end. On the morning of the execution he told Herbert to take the watch with him that hung by the bed. In passing through the park the king inquired the hour, at the same time taking the watch in his hand and looking, then handing it again to his faithful servant with these words: "Keep this in memory of me." In the following reign this Thomas Herbert was made a baronet.

About two and a half miles north-west of Wath, across the corn country and near to Nosterfield and Thornborough (both names suggestive of old time occupation), are three large well marked entrenchments. The largest and most perfect is near "Camp House," and is in form circular, and encloses an area of 540 feet. The rampart of earth is from 35 to 40 feet in width and varies in height, at the present time, from 10 feet to 16 feet. Besides the two earthworks, there are other entrenchments now hid by a wood, midway between Nosterfield and Camp House; these trenches are in some places still full

Well, and the Vale of Mowbray.   [Owen Bowen.

15 feet deep. Here, we are told, was a cell or chapel, for the use of a priest praying for the souls of the slain. Centuries have rolled by since those earthworks were raised, and there is not the slightest proof by what tribe or people they were formed, Celt, Anglian, or Dane; but this much may be safely said, they tell of some dire struggle between rival races for supremacy over this broad vale of Mowbray.

Nosterfield, a small village standing on the edge of the great plain, possesses few features to attract the tourist. The old inn, with antique interior, was formerly the resort of lime burners from the kilns, which lie midway between this place and Well. The quarries here have not been worked for a number of years and have now been re-beautified by nature into a wild garden; in summer time when flowers are in bloom, the spot is a perfect arcady, whilst from one's feet, eastwards, stretches the magnificent panorama of the vale of Mowbray, skyscape and landscape varying with the days and months, but ever an auburn plain to the artist's eye. Here also on summer evenings the glow-worms are wont to hang out their fieldstar lamps, illuminating almost super naturally hedgerow and bank, as if lit by the hands of fairy folk. Before turning aside to the west bank of the Yore, let us make a brief visit to Well, which village physiographically stands in the valley of the Swale, although the attractions and the sympathies of its inhabitants lie to the west chiefly, in the Yore valley, and naturally so, seeing that Tanfield is only two miles away and Ripon the chief market and capital of the district is of easy approach by road or rail. Although geographically speaking Swale may claim its infant tributary flowing down the whole length of Well street, the inhabitants swear by Wensleydale. "In what valley is your village situated?" I enquired of a wiseacre on my first entering the place many years ago. "In Wensleydil," he replied sharply to my enquiry; and when I pointed out that the stream of the village found its bourne in the Swale, and therefore he must consider himself of Swaledale, "Ah! well that may be," he replied, "but we still belang t' Wensleydil."

A most charming village is Well, although the people of Snape and Bedale affect to ignore this statement, each thinking their own town far its superior in picturesque and physical attractions.

Just on the west approach to the village a little stream bursts out of the limestone rock and filters through the beautiful wood of the Hermitage and thence down the steep hill road, and through the village street. It was this little stream which led the incoming Saxon to name the place Welle, the welling up of water, and so the name has remained through the centuries, beautiful in its derivative simplicity. A very brief description of the place must suffice. Let us stand under the trees yonder on the brow of the hill, near to where the Romans of old had their villas and baths, remains of which can still be seen; first we note (if it be springtime) the richness of the greensward and the numerous wild flowers, primroses, cowslips, etc., abounding there, then we notice how gracefully the trees, in their early prime, hang bower-like and add to the beauty and composition of the surroundings, and our eyes wander down the slope to the red-tiled roofs of dwellings, framed in the foreground by orchards, now whitely decked in the bridal attire of Spring. Now we follow the street twisting with the stream into all manner of curves and irregularities of outline, whilst rising high over all is the massive grey tower of the village church. Down the street with its fifty bridges, the beck wanders, gurgling a sweet simple melody; here and there the ducks disport in its waters or rest by its margin, as if oblivious of all around. A few geese, in charge of an old gander with outstretched neck and dignified demeanour, march and gabble along the street; or should it be milking time on our visit, the cotter's cows passing to and from the pastures add to the rare picturesqueness.

The Village Street, Well [Edmund Bogg.

Yet even here change and signs of the times are very apparent, the new gradually displacing the old, breaking in upon the harmony and effect of the whole. And, as with the inanimate, so with the human life, a great change has come about the place, the young people we knew of old have become men and women, and disappeared about the world. The happy, homely, contented faces of the old ladies—Hannah Parnaby and Jane Smith—who so hated new-fangled things and "clip claps," etc., who worked and toiled far into four score year and ten, with many other friends who always greeted us so kindly and made us so much at home on our visits here; have now been gathered to the great harvest of the dead in the old churchyard yonder, where the dark gaunt firs hang their funeral plumes over the scene. As we shall have to refer to Well

Tanfield Church and the Tower of the Marmions. [*Edmund Bogg*

again in our chapter on the Vale of Mowbray, we say Adieu, and turn our footsteps towards the west bank of the Yore. How delightfully the road rises and dips. We can follow it with the eye nearly all the way to Tanfield. It was here in the valley, where the bye-road turns sharply to Masham, that an ancestor of Lord Latimer slew the great dragon which infested and terrorised the district in days long since gone by. Our thoughts wander from the dragon and its slayer, to the far reaching and beautiful vistas stretching across Mowbray Vale to the Hambletons. We can follow the various prominences and headlands, and the ravines penetrating the moors, as the sun shoots its searching light across hill and dale. The White Horse of Kilburn and the Grey Mare of Wisson Cliff stand forth prominently. And then the eye wanders farther afield over Coxwold, Easingwold and Crake, to the dim grey towers of York looming in the distance, and the filmy haze of background, away over the walls and towers of the ancient city, proclaiming the Wold hills, the eastern ribs of the Derwent valley; it is truly a scene to call forth wonder. Surely the plains of Heaven could not be more soul entrancing and lovely.

We are fast approaching Tanfield and can already see the two towers, that of the gateway and of the church, adding dignity and a touch of romance to the view. The mediæval tombs of the Marmions and the tower of their castle still remaining, shed a spell of glamour over this place.

CHAPTER IV.

Tanfield, Hackfall, and Masham.

Returning to the west bank of the Yore, and commencing our pilgrimage anew from the old Cathedral City, we follow the road leading through the billowy landscape, or loiter away a pleasant hour by the river bank. In three miles and a half we reach Castle Dykes, a place—before the discovery of foundations of walls and remains of pavements and dwellings, half a a century ago—actually without any history or traditions concerning it. Now the local people connect the spot with murder, war, bloodshed and pillage, which they relate with circumstantial detail. The camp is doubtless of Roman construction, and situated on its north side by the edge of what was formerly a swamp, which was a sufficient defence when the camp was formed. And the ford or path across the swamp has evidently been at that early period greatly used, as tho' needing a fortress here to guard it and the fords over the river in this vicinity. It was thoroughly explored in 1874 by the late Rev. W. C. Lukis, rector of Wath, when remains and vestiges of military occupation were found, all pointing to the invasion of the Latins.

We pass North Stainley, surrounded by natural charms and interesting features of bygone days. Now the road skirts the wide and beautiful domain of Slemingford, with its ancient hawthorns and other trees, adding picturesqueness to a scene of loveliness. Soon we reach the precincts of Tanfield.

Tanfield is notable both for its natural charms and historic significance. At no other place in the valley does the river appear so important, so lovely, so broadly flowing. At no other place probably does the dignity of the past appear so strikingly evident. Considered from a romantic, a scenic, or antiquarian view, few districts will better repay a visit than the one between Tanfield and Masham, by way of Mickley and Hackfall. Seen from the fine bridge over the river looking up or down the dale, are a series of beautiful pictures, and at no other place do the gentle undulations break up and diversify the landscape more charmingly. The village, skirting the north-east bank of the Yore is widely straggling; and its chief interest, both pictorial and antiquarian, is centered between the bridge and the church and the Gateway Tower. Looking up the Yore, here so wide and grand, the range of ancient buildings with old walls and gardens, artistic through irregularity of outline and rising sheer above the water, adding interest, dignity and importance, are the towers of the church and the Gateway of the redoubtable Marmions. And where is the one who has read Sir Walter Scott's Chronicle, and is not interested in that sounding name? The very mention of Marmion brings to our mind a host of memories. We hear the pawing and prancing of the spirited war steed, the jingle of military accoutrements, the rattle of chain and clank of mail, the travail and turmoil of war. The old grey weather-beaten tower, with its rich oriel light, seems eloquent of high associations and hallowed by the "derring-do" of a chivalrous family.

West Tanfield is interesting mostly in the fact that for 200 years it was the residence and burial place of the Marmion family, heroes who had in many a battle been, well worthy of the poem. Grand, however, as they were in annals military, they were not the only magnates of Tanfield. In much earlier times, the Marmions, lords of Fontenay in Normandy, were however, highly distinguished. Robert de Marmion followed the Conqueror, receiving from him a grant of "Tamworth's town and tower," as well as of Scrivelesby, in Lincolnshire. One or both of these possessions was held by the service of being the royal champion, as the ancestors of Marmion had formerly been of the Dukes of Normandy. But after, Tamworth passed from the Marmions when that branch of the family became extinct in Philip de Marmion, who died without male issue in 1292. Ultimately Scrivelesby descended by another of the co-heiresses to Sir John Dymoke, and remains in that family, whose representative is Hereditary Champion of England to the present day.

At the Domesday period Torchill was Lord of Tanfield, when the manor passed to Alan, Lord of Richmond, and second cousin of the Conqueror, who held it in a species of trust. There can be little doubt that the first actual grantee was either Bodin, who also possessed Melsonby and Brampton, or his brother Bardulph; either of whom was most probably the founder of the parish church. At a very early period Tanfield was the property of the Fitz Hughes; and by the latter was carried in marriage, early in the thirteenth century, to the equally honourable family of the Marmions. Robert Marmion in 1215 married

Amice, daughter and heiress of Jernagan Fitz Hugh. Their son, William, married Dora de Dover, whose son, John, in 1314-15 had a license to castellats and embattle the hermitage in Tanfield wood, "which seems to be that romantic and secluded spot in sight of the beauties of Hackfall, where the lords of Aylesbury have long had a hunting seat." This site was probably abandoned by the Marmions for the one contiguous to the church, when they began to build their castle. (This spot known as the Hermitage in Tanfield Wood, was probably the abode of some Kuldee priest from the very earliest days of Christianity in Northumbria. The abode of a solitary priest sent forth southward by St. Columba from Iona, to preach the gospel to the heathen.

Unfortunate as to male issue, the second John Marmion was succeeded by the children of his son-in-law, Sir John Gray, who took the name of Marmion, yet in the next generation the name again became extinct and the estate went by Elizabeth Grey's grand-daughter back to the Fitz Hughes, from whom it had come 200 years before. This lapse might have led to the abandonment of the castle of Tanfield, for the Fitz Hughes would not require a residence there.

Whether it was one of these Tanfield Marmions who, *temp.* Edward II., performed the chivalrous feat before Norham Castle, woven by Bishop Percy into his ballad "The Hermit of Warkworth" is not known but Leland says he was a Marmion, the story running thus:—"About this tyme there was a greate feste made yn Lincolnshire, to which came many gentlemen and ladies, and amonge them one lady brought a heaulme for a man of warre, with a very riche creste of gold to William Marmion, Knight, with a letter of commandement of her lady that he should go into the dangerest place in England, and then to let the heaulme be seene and known as famous So he went to Norham; whither within four days of cumming cam Philip Mowbray, guardian of Berwicke having yn his hande 40 men of armes, the very flower of men of the Scottish marches. Thomas Gray, capitayne of Norham, seynge this brought his garrison afore the barriers of the castel, behind whom cam William richly arrayed as alglittering in gold, and wearing the heaulme, his lady's present. Then said Thomas Gray to Marmion 'Sir Knight ye be cum hither to fame your helmet, mount upon your horse and ryde like a valiant man to your foes ever here at hand, and I forsake God if I rescue not thy bodye deade or alyve as I myself wyl dye for it.' Whereupon he toke his cursere and rode among the throng of enemyes, the which laid sore stripes on him and pulled him at the last out of his sadel to the grounde. Then Thomas Gray, with all the whole garrison lette ryde yn among the Scottes and so wounded them and their horses, that they were overthrown, and Marmion, sore beten was horsed agayn and with Gray persewed the Scottes yn chase."

The Marmion Tower and Tanfield Church from the Bridge.

Marmion tower is a rectangular building with a battlemented turret. The above-mentioned oriel window is in the chamber over the gateway, a fine apartment, and was probably added about 1880 to 1400, whilst in the west wall of the same chamber, is an early English window of two lights, and a massive stone fireplace. From the summit of the angle tower, splendid views are obtained over the surrounding country. A fine well of water was some time ago discovered just within the castle grounds,—a necessity during a state of siege. We may gain some idea from the present gateway of the magnificence and feudal power of the Marmions in the heydey of their pride and glory. Although we have used the word "Castle," it is very doubtful if such a fortress ever existed here. A Manor Hall would be a more appropriate term, for the intended castle was never completed. Yet the place is not all imaginary, for passing into the church we see there the effigies of this martial race resting on finely sculptured tombs, emblazoned and embellished with the armorial bearings of this family, peacefully reposing, as it were, from century to century, with hands clasped and upraised, pointing towards heaven, breathing out their souls in the attitude of prayer and supplication. The sight of these effigies fill us with deep solemnity, the very ground should be held sacred where they rest, for surely, though slowly, by time, exposure, and the rude hand of the despoiler, they too are crumbling to decay. They appear to us like faithful and silent sentinels, who, having performed great deeds of valour and wisdom, have thus fallen to slumber, and are now waiting until they shall be called forth on the great day of resurrection. The church was originally a Norman structure, but the restoration having been carried out in such bad taste, much of the earlier building has been obliterated. It consists of nave and chancel, with north aisle, the latter being very wide. Between the two, and at the junction of nave and chancel, in one of the piers of the arch, is a curious chamber or cell, similar to a confessional; it is 5½ feet by 4 feet, with transverse openings and squint. Antiquarians have differed greatly about the use of this little cell, and in its way it is quite unique in church architecture. Some have named it the invalid's pew, others say it was used by the head of the Marmions, another, it was the place from whence the Sacristan tolled the Sanctus bell at the elevation of the host. Up to the last restoration the small belfry containing the Anglus Bell was immediately over the roof above the recess. The most plausible idea is that of a chantry from whence the priest could watch the high altar and also the tomb of Robert Marmion and his wife Laura, where on festival days, candles were kept burning.

The most beautiful tomb is the one standing in the centre of the north aisle at the east end. The two alabaster figures represent Sir Robert de Marmion and his wife, Laura St. Quintin.

"And here beneath the northern aisle,
A tomb with Gothic sculpture fair,
Does still Sir Marmion's image bear."

He is attired in mail armour, with a camlet of chain and pointed helmet, his head resting on an empty casque, his feet on a lion couchant. Lady Marmion is attired in a semi-religious dress adorned with the arms of St. Quentin, her head rests on pillows supported by angels, her feet are on a lioness. These figures are protected by a perfect iron hearse of hand wrought iron, with prickets for lights. Two mutilated figures of a Knight and a lady rest in the north wall, under a canopy which is a splendid example of 14th century work, adorned with fine mouldings, cuspings, and crocketings. The next figures, cut out of friable stone, are much defaced and mutilated; another effigy is attired in a loose robe, her feet resting on a dog, typical of fidelity. The last figure at the east end is cross-legged and of small stature, and covered with chain armour, over which a robe is loosely thrown, the feet rest on a lion passant. This one is said to represent the sickly Lord Robert,

The Tombs of the Marmions.

third Baron Marmion.* A strange impressive air of mortality and antiquity pervades this aisle, the ancient burial place of the Marmions, whose chivalry and prowess have been so deeply interwoven with the historic chronicles of the past.

A tombstone in the graveyard records:—" Here lyeth the body of Francis Thompson, of Binso, who died A.D. 1746, in the 112th year of his age." Another epitaph reads:—

> "Why all this toil for triumphs of an hour?
> What tho' we wade in wealth or soar in fame.
> Earth's highest station ends, here too he lies,
> And dust to dust concludes the noblest song."

John Leland says, "The townlet of West Tanfelde standeth on a ground hard by Ure, a ryver of a colour for the most part of soden water by reson of the colour and the morish nature of the soile of Wencedale, from whense it cometh. There be two faire parks at Tanfelde, and mostely plenty of wood. The castelle of Tanfelde, or rather as it is now a meane (middling) manor-place, longing to the Lord Parr, standeth hard on a ripe (bank) of Ure, wher I saw no notable building but a faire tour de gate-house and a haulle of quarrid stone."

The place still remains very much as the old antiquary described it, and his account proves that it had been forsaken long before the Civil War—the period at which some writers assert it was dismantled. The lower storeys of the Marmion Chantry, adjoining the churchyard, are still intact. These rooms

---

* "In the church of West Tanfield be divers tumbes in a chapelle on the north side of the church of Marmions, whereof one (with the sculptures of a knight and a lady) is in the arch of the walle, and that seemeth most aunoient. There lyeth thare alone a lady with the apparaill of vowes, and another lady with a crownet on her head. Then is there an high tumbe of alabaster (with two very fair figures of a warrior and his dame) in the middle of the chapel wher, as I heard say, lyeth one Lord John Marmion, and in the south side of the chapelle is another tumbe of the Marmions buried alone."

are below the roadway, and are most interesting features. This chantry was restored in 1668 by Matthew Beckwith, son of Roger Beckwith, of Aldborough, and on a stone built in over the doorway, he wrote in Latin the following :—*

> "If religion flourish, then I live."
> M. B. 1668.

A Mr. Littleton was then rector of Tanfield, and dwelt near. It is said there was a feud between the two, and so by way of retort he put over his door :—

> "I do not heed the man the more,
> That hangs religion at his door."

The first inscription remained over the door of the chantry house until a few years ago, and was given by a late occupant to an antiquary. The walls of the lower rooms, comprising store warehouse and cellar, are those of the original foundations, and date from the 14th century. The mullions and the doorway at the back have been inserted at the restoration, when the chantry was altered into dwellings at the above date, 1668. The row of houses clustering near the river,

---

* The silvestral Horse-Mint, the tuberous-rooted Comfrey, and the Virgin-Mary Milk Thistle, all grow either in Magdalen banks opposite Hagfall, or in the old camp site known as the "Barrows," at Mickley. In 1887 the dwarf Danes-blood Elder grew in the latter spot, supposed to mark the burial place of those colonising invaders who succumbed to the common fate but not necessarily at the hand of the foeman. The "barrows" are merely rough and irregular mounds, mostly now overgrown with vegetation, adjacent to which, on the level above the slope to the river, the rectangular trench-lines of an ancient "camp" or enclosure may be made out. This and the camp half a mile west of Hagfall are so unlike in scheme the string of horseshoe or wheel camps at Nosterfield and Thornborough, as to suggest that the former were those of the invaders and the latter of the Kelt or aboriginal defenders. At any rate, it is noticeable that all the camp sites from Thornborough to Hutton Moor and Copt Hewick, where there is a very fine one, are circular and with an adit and exit like a circus.

between the bridge and the church, are the most ancient in Tanfield, the foundations of which were laid five or six centuries ago. About a mile west of Tanfield, and on the north bank of the river, are ancient foundations of pre-conquest date, pointing to a monastic settlement, doubtless of Celtic or Iona priesthood training (the hermitage in Tanfield wood, previously mentioned), the history of which has passed into oblivion.

Edmund Bogg.] A February Day, Mickley.

The scenery during the 2½ miles walk from Tanfield to Mickley is fine; now along the banks of the river and across strips of charming mead, and anon, over steep banks of delightful woodland. The path winds under huge old trees, beech, sycamore and oak, and over rustic stiles we pass into fields of furze and patches of heather, where bramble bush and hazel thrive, and wild flowers bloom luxuriantly from February to November. I remember in passing this way through the moorland meadows in the autumn, such a marvellous vision of golden yellow, as leads the memory to still retain it vividly. The land for several hundred yards was one mass of golden ragwort; the time was about sunset, which added to the intensity of the gorgeous skyscape, and by way of strong contrast, the patch was shut in by the dark solemn depths of woodland. Last time the writer was in this vicinity, the track along the banks of the river was in a disgraceful condition of dis-repair, in fact, it was absolutely dangerous for a native, let alone a stranger, to walk that way after sunset.

Past old Slenningford, finely situated high above the river and sheltered by wood, we reach Mickley, a pretty, secluded, and rural village, resting in the dip of surrounding hills, and on by the deep bend of the Yore. Here was formerly a flax mill which found employment for about 150 hands. Another industry was that of chair-making, but both these industries are now of the past, and the population having dwindled, several of the houses have become tenantless and fallen into a state of semi-ruin.

Both approaches to Mickley are fine, the one from the north being particularly charming. Green meadows and woodland, of large limbed trees, and on the other, glimpses of the river. A winding down-hill road, leading into the picture, where the yellow walls of ancient property, forms a pleasant and striking contrast to the landscape. For those who love peace and seclusion, this district is a perfect paradise in summer time. The restful murmur of music is ever sounding from the river, lulling to repose the minds of the weary.

Half a mile east of the river is Tanfield Hall; a mile and a half west is antique Grewelthorpe, long famed for its production of delicious cream cheeses. But here we are at the eastern entrance to Hackfall, one of the most delightful spots in the vale of the Yore.*

Every lover of the sublime and picturesque will be delighted with the shady solitude of the solemn woods, hanging high o'er the river, through every opening of which delightful peeps are to be obtained; here and there are dark avenues which the light can scarcely pierce; now the path winds up some steep incline where a brook is gurgling out a song of wild delight, as it flashes and plunges down the shady dells, between banks of fern and bramble; now the path leads through beautiful arches composed of huge trees and dense foliage, the glittering sunshine casting the shadows of the leaves and branches on the path, like the images of saints on some old cathedral aisle; or a huge rock stands boldly forth from the precipice above, bathed in the full glow of sunlight, its riven form and weathered flanks "adding to the outlook over the river a sense of age and immobility." Rustic seats and grottoes are so placed that the tired traveller can rest, and at the same time feast his eyes on the luxuries in nature; or where lovers can breathe of constancy and bliss, and tell the old, old story under a noble canopy of natural construction. And so we wander; and the lovely, the majestic, the beautiful, the fascinating, still continue to increase until we reach Mowbray Point, just before sunset, and look over the thousands of green-robed trees on to the winding river below, majestically flowing through a

---

* George Cuitt, a local artist of great repute, says, when speaking of Hackfall:— "it is situated in Hags', or Witches' Vale, whence its name of 'Hags' Vale' has, by corruption, assumed its present orthography. There is no situation, indeed, which could be more appropriately peopled, through superstitious fancy of the olden time with witches, demons, and fairies, than this deep, sequestered, gloomy vale; nor indeed, even in the beautiful country in which it is situated, in which nature and art are so exquisitely blended, that the eye cannot discern the line which separates them, can a spot be found more delightful to the lover of romantic scenery."

wondrous gorge, and hear the noise of rippling waters, commingling with the music of birds and other sounds in wild life. The enchanting views obtained from this standpoint are indeed marvellous. The vale of Mowbray and York opens out and stretches far away into the distant horizon sweetly dotted with towns and villages, York Minster on one hand, and northward

Hackfall. [C Watson.

over the vale of Mowbray to the Tees on the other. Between these points of vision rest the towns of Bedale, Northallerton, the Cleveland country, the wall-like front of Hambledon Hills, and the town of Thirsk resting under the latter.

The gorge bears ample evidence of the ravages of water during the cycle of ages, vast rocks are strewn in the woodland washed by water when the bed of the river was much higher, whilst in some places, deep curves of great depth have been scooped out of the overhanging woods by the mad fury of whirling currents, and giant trees and debris have been borne seaward by the resistless strength of rushing waters; ever and again the river murmurs and meanders, then dashes along with a sullen roar, until, reaching the deeper channel, it becomes more tranquil.

Summer visitors do not realize the beauty of these woods in the leafless stage of winter. At this time you are alone with nature in her sternest mood, and only the call and chatter of birds, the sighing of breezes amongst the rank grass, the soughing and plashing of the river can be heard. Mowbray Point looms high over above the treetops, half hidden in mist curling up from the valley below like some phantom fiend. Under this aspect it looks like the outer-work or barbican of some old-world gigantic keep. Huge rocks—which are hidden during summer in vegetation—uprear, and monstre trees fling forth their skeleton arms across the path, adding strength and character to the scene. The mist suddenly unfolds its winding sheet, discovering beautiful woodland aisles, the russet bracken and long grasses bend their forms earthwards, and only the holly bushes are green. The miniature glens; the visionary walls of grey castles appear, as if haunted by gnomes or giant folk of the old world; such are the impressions one receives in this forest of Hackfall when attired in the snowy vest of winter.

Grewelthorpe, where one can obtain the famous cream cheese, is just on the western fringe of Hackfall, and a public footpath leads from Mickley through the woods to the above place. The north end of the village is the prettiest part, but it is a straggling place, with a few old homesteads, a new church of some architectural dignity, a wide street and green.

Kirkby Malzeard. [*Edmund Bogg.*

The great blot, from an architectural and pictorial standpoint, is the ugly Wesleyan Chapel with its deep sloping roof, bulking on to the street. The lack of architectural features is, however, amply compensated by the beauty of the surrounding magnificent scenes and charming vistas across woods, moorland and river can be obtained a short distance from the village street. The distance by field path and road from Grewelthorpe to Kirkby Malzeard is about a mile and a half. The prospect is very commanding, and the appearance bespeaks the former dwelling-place of a powerful Baron. A strong castle was raised here by Robert de Mowbray, whose son, Roger de Mowbray was a renowned soldier, and fought at the battle of the Standard, being at that period only a youth *

---

* The castle stood on an eminence near the church. In the mansion grounds adjoining many vestiges of this fortress have been unearthed from time to time, and also portions of armour and several ancient spear heads. In the early years of Edward I., a Roger de Mowbray was summoned by him to answer by what right or warrant he claimed to have free chase at Kirby Malzeard, where he had a gallows for the punishment of poachers, and other offenders; and also, why he had free warren in Nidderdale and the adjoining lands. His answer was, that he and all his ancestors from the time of the Conquest had had free warren in his manor of Kirby Malzeard, which is within the forest of Nidderdale, etc. As to Galgah, Gruelthorpe, Atherlhagh, Mikeihagh, Winkerslegh, and Aldefelde, he claimed no warren therein. The jury of great men who met to decide, do say that Roger only claimed what his ancestors had always used, and he had not, contrary to report, enlarged his hunting domain, so he was left in undisturbed possession of same.

For rebellion against Henry II. (1118), his castles at Kirkby Malzeard and Thirsk were besieged and afterwards dismantled by the order of the monarch. In 1307 Edward I. granted a market to John de Mowbray for this place. It was formerly one of the largest parishes in England.

The Church is a most commanding structure, backed on the north and east by fine trees, the beautiful grounds of Colonel Cathcart adjoining; looking westward the massive tower stands out finely against the dark billowy moors. The erection of the tower probably dates from the close of the 14th century, and the fine Norman doorway the middle of the 12th century. Over the porch is a sundial, dated 1671; the east end of the south side was the chantry chapel of the De Mowbrays. In this chapel is a mural stone of the Saxon period, very closely allied to runic work, the chancel contains a good example of a sedelia. There is a leper's window, outside of which the lepers were wont to stand and hear the service, they not being permitted to enter the church. A tombstone near the porch records the burial of the three wives of Christopher Walker, whose ages range from 63 the first wife, the second wife 33, and the third 23. [This needs no comment.] At the east end of the churchyard is a slight mound on which stands the shaft and base of an ancient cross. The mound is still known as 'Mot,' or 'Moot' hill, a name traceable to Danish occupation, the Folkesmot, where the people of the district assembled in pre-Conquest days to discuss and settle local questions affecting the general welfare of the district. An ancient pathway, embowered with trees, runs from the churchyard, and is known as the "Lover's Walk." The original foundation of the old yellow-walled inn, with its antique domestic fittings, dates back over several centuries. In the 17th century there were several so-called wise men and wise women, who used strange charms, etc., to cure heartache, earache, and certain other manner of diseases. Amongst many others summoned before a court held in Kirkby Malzeard Church, December 16th, 1639, was Janet Burniston, of this parish, her offence being the carrying a dead man's skull out of the churchyard and laying it under Christopher Head, thinking therewith to charm him asleep. The judge, in dismissing her, admonished her to bring the said skull into the churchyard again.

Here, some two hundred years ago, lived Christopher Pinkney, a member of the Quakers. He was very superstitious, and used frequently to entertain his more sceptical neighbours with accounts of divine revelations of which he had been the channel. One cold winter's night, as he and his wife were sitting warming themselves by the fireside, a loud blow was

heard on the window shutter, and a deep voice addressed him thus:
"Christopher Pinkney, take down thy staff from behind thy door, and go
forth and smash the windows of the wicked steeple house at Kirkby
Malzeard." Christopher, doubting perhaps his own perception, said to
his wife, "Dost thou hear the voice of the Lord?" She, full of faith,
replied, "Yea, verily! and thou must go and do even as it has been
commanded thee." So Christopher took his stick, and sallying forth to
the church, broke such of the windows as were within reach. The
voice he had heard was that of the village glazier, whose name was Green.
He had watched the poor fanatic's proceedings, and lost no time in laying an information before the authorities, thus securing half the penalty;
the grateful churchwardens also gave him the job of repairing the shattered
panes.

From Grewelthorpe, the farmery of delicious cheeses, we push
on to Masham; the first half mile is over rising ground, and
the scenery around of a fine and charming character. From
the edge of the common is a magnificent prospect, the valleys
of the Burn and the Yore, the woods of Swinton and the moorland spreading away north and west. Down in the valley, and
yet raised on a plateau, is the town of Masham, the beautiful spire of its church cutting the skyline, a pleasant feature to rest the eye and gladden the mind. Across the river is Ald-borough Hall, where there are ancient entrenchments. A Roman road passed this way into Wensleydale, and here-abouts is an ancient fording place and earthwork. On the brow of the land, a few hun-dred yards east of Aldborough, is the ancient village of Binso, possibly from the Welsh Bryn—the brow or ridge of a hill,

Remains of Saxon Cross, Masham Churchyard.
E. Bogg.

Formerly the place was of more importance, as the sites of several houses manifest; right in the centre of the green is a conical-shaped hill, evidently a tumulus, and on the crest of the mound stands a very ancient tree, known to the natives as " Binso Church."* A mile and a half further along the east bank of the river are High and Low Burton, the latter an ancient residence around which are indications of moat and earthwork. In Anglian days "a tun or ton was a place surrounded by a hedge, or rudely protected by a palisade, inside of which was a dwelling, and the "bur" was the produce or bearing of the land belonging thereto—the bear, crop —hence we get Barton, the Bear-ton," Burton. In the north, solitary farmsteads are still called "tons"; from a number of such enclosures, or "tono," we derived the word "toun" (town). Formerly a Catholic chapel and burial ground were attached to this house.

Now let us cross the meadow by the footpath, and over the bridge into Masham, pausing on the bridge for few moments to take note of the beauty of the situation and the surrounding landscape, the broad, shoaly river overhung on the east bank with trees, cattle drinking at the brink, or a camp of travelling tinkers in picturesque grouping on the green, over which the town, with its beautiful church and tapering spire, so finely presides.

Masham.

The name of this town is derived from Mass, *i.e.*, the Holy Feast of the Lord's Supper, in later times the Holy Communion; and the Anglo-Saxon Ham, an enclosure, that which

---

* This is a curiously suggestive name to have been given to a very old tree. Bearing in mind that in pre-Christian days, trees—oak or elm—were held sacred and worship conducted at their foot, may we not have in this survived name a glimpse of the Celtic rite carried out on elevated "bryns" such as this one?

binds in,—the home of a family or tribe. Here, in the reign of King Edwin (7th century), a church was reared, and the the place was known as the Mass-Ham, *i.e.*, the Mass town or home. Masham is the only town of that name mentioned in the Gazetteer; and as the syllable Mas, or Maes indicates water and swamp, the site may represent a "lake-dwelling" of the very earliest times. We need not be startled by this wild hypothesis, for the name of the river Wiske is a Celtic survival, equal to

The Square, Masham.

proving that the "ancient Britons" had settlements hereabouts. In the neighbouring Swinton we have another trace of these primitive folk—the Swein or peasants of the Norseman, whose residence is well described in the Danby. However, Masham is the country town of "an ancienté territorie called Massam-skyre"; remoteness, sparseness, seclusion, and all such things as mere lake-dwellers were desirous of. That this place had been a settlement of the Brigantes, previous to the Anglian invasion, evidences around fully support, and its naturally strong, commanding position on the west bank of the river, or we might say in the angle formed by rivers, would make it a difficult place to subjugate; and all along the river way in this district, judging from vestiges of camp, vallum, and earthwork, there was some very severe fighting before the Northmen ousted the Celtic people, and afterwards built their Ham. At the Conquest this manor came into the hands of Alan, Earl of Richmond, next to Roger de Mowbray, and from him to Walter de Buhere; afterwards to Sir John Walton, and later to the Scropes of Bolton, and from them the Manor passed by marriage to the Danbys, and now belongs to Lord Masham (Sam Lister), of silk manufacturing fame.

The visible antiquity of Masham centres in its church, a structure having a fine Norman west doorway; early English as to the rest, with a lofty tower and spire figuring conspicuously in the landscape from far about. It contains several monuments, including a brass of 1689 and a monument to Sir Marmaduke Nyville, Bart. In the Norman features of the church, so rapidly changed to early English, we have characteristics often observed in this district. The living is a vicarage united with that of Kirkby Malzeard. The Mowbrays granted the free forest of Masham to Sir John de Walton, whose grand-daughter Joan, carried it by marriage to Sir Geoffrey le Scrope. The church was given to York Cathedral by Roger de Mowbray, and appropriated to the prebend of Masham, the richest stall in the Cathedral until dissolved by Archbishop Holgate in 1546, and there is a verification in Leland's description of this "quick" market town. The church contains tombs of the Danbys of Swinton, but none of the Scropes of Masham. Sir Christopher Danby, a simple patriotic Knight, fought at Flodden; Henry le Scrope, Lord Masham and friend of Henry V., was executed for treason, "intending to kill Henry of Lancaster, the usurper," in 1415, and Shakespeare has given him immortality. He had married Joan, widow of Edward, Duke of York. The plot was very obscure, perhaps contemptible, but it cost Scrope and his co-conspirator, Sir Thomas Grey, their lives. Sir Henry Fitz Hugh obtained the lands hereabouts for life.

The first charter was obtained by Sir John de Walton in the year 1250, to hold a market at his manor at Masham on Fridays. A second charter was granted to Geoffrey le Scrope some eighty years later, to hold a market at the manor of Masham on Wednesdays, "and one fair of four days, to wit, on the eve of the day of St. Barnabas the Apostle, and for the two days following." Leland, in his description of the town, says :—" Masseham' has a praty quik market town, and a fair Chirch, an a bridge of tymbre, a little bynethe Masseham on the other side of Yore ryver lye the Aldebury village. At the end of Masseham townlet, I passed over a fair ryver called Bourne, it goeth into the Ure thereby a little bynethe the bridge." The market is now of small importance, but the cattle and sheep fair, held on the 17th and 18th of September, is said to be one of the largest in the kingdom, from thirty-five to forty thousand eep being brought annually to this fair. Wool combing was at one time the staple trade of Masham, but through the introduction of machinery for the combing and dressing of wool, etc., the industry left the town. Open house is kept during the fair, and all householders are expected to provide a plentiful supply of roast beef and pickled cabbage, drink and other necessaries, for the well-being of travellers, and all are made welcome, be they rich or poor.* Clean streets at

* We missed old Adams, the barber (a singular and original character), on our last visit. We were sor y to find he had gone the appointed way of all flesh. Probably his ability to drain unnumbered glasses had not lengthened his days, although he was wont to boast "He ah'd gotten seasoned to, an fowks wor nobbut killed 'et t'seasoning." Nevertheless he was a rare chip of the old school, and never so happy as when following the hounds on foot, or telling stories of the old coaching days, etc., etc.

the two entrances of the town lead to a spacious market place. In the centre stands the shaft of the old cross. Should you visit Masham at any time except market or fair days it is quite possible you may have the large old-world square all alone to roam in, or you may gaze from the windows of the old King's Head whilst resting, without any bustling sounds of men or business to disturb your reverie. The houses adjoining three sides of the market are picturesquely irregular. The church, with its noble tower and spire, and Norman doorway to the east, renders the perspective pleasing and impressive.

The Wyville Chapel and Monument.   [*Edmund Bogg*.

The church is dedicated to St. Mary, and is of ancient date, and although the fabric has undergone several restorations, there are fragments of original Norman masonry, and even relics of the Anglo-Danish period, notably the lower portion of a most curious and ancient churchyard cross, now standing opposite the south porch; considering their early date the figures are finely carved, those round the top representing the twelve apostles, and those around the lower portion the adoration of the Magi. The interior of the church is interesting; the east end of the north aisle was the chapel and burial-place of the Wyvilles, of Little Burton. Here is a beautiful monument to Sir Marmaduke Wyville and his wife; beneath it are the figures of his six sons, clad in armour, and also figures of his two daughters, all kneeling with hands clasped in the attitude of prayer. The front of the tomb is guarded by a fine example of old ironwork.

The east end of the south aisle was the chapel and burial place of the Danbys of Swinton, who inherited the lands of Mashamshire from the Scropes. There is a large mural monument and several tablets to their memory. In this aisle are fragments of early tombs and portions of Danish scroll work, etc. The epitaph on brass to the memory of Christopher Kay and Jane Nicholson, is curious. The initial letters of the text of the memorial lines accompanying the Arms form the name of Christopher.

Another epitaph in the churchyard says:—

> "Here lies an old ringer, beneath the cold clay,
> Who has rung many peals both to serious and gay;
> Thro' grandsires and triplets with ease he could range,
> Till death called his Bob, and brought round his last change."

On the north side of the burial ground is a stone in memory of "Julius Cæsar Ibbetson, an artist, eminent for his taste and skill in painting rustic figures, cattle, and rural scenery. He died October 13th, 1817, aged 58. This humble memorial was erected by the affection of his widow. Here also rest the remains of John Batley Ibbetson, youngest son of Julius Cæsar Ibbetson, who died November 21st, 1821, aged 6 years." Not far away is another gravestone, in memory of a brother artist, " George Cuitt, who died 15th July, 1854, aged 74. His memory lives in his works and the hearts of his friends." The churchyard contains an early Norman font, with the old staples remaining, on which was affixed the cover to save the water from pollution. This ancient relic of the Norman church was lost for some considerable time, and was only discovered a few years ago in a cowhouse, having been sacrilegiously used as an urinal.

The River Burn

This important tributary enters the Yore half a mile south of Masham, and drains an extensive range of moorland to the west of the town. The main stream has numerous feeders in its twelve-mile course, all of which rise within the boundaries of Mashamshire. The Burn has its fountain at the foot of the great Haw, opposite to where the Nidd Valley bends round due west. Of the many vales and glens which pierce these moors, the most beautiful is the vale of the Burn. Huge masses of limestone are thrown down in the most grotesque and conceivable shapes along the side of the glen; aged oaks and other trees are abundant, and in its lower reaches the Burn silvers delightfully through the woods and park of Swinton. Swinton of old the property of the Danbys, now the estate of Samuel Cunliffe Lister (Lord Masham), is one of the most beautiful domains in England. It owes much of its beauty to the Mr. Danby who occupied it a century and a half ago—"who has surrounded his house with a most beautiful park, finely wooded and well watered; and has shown great taste and propriety in his plantations and pleasure grounds. With much ex-

Fearby. [Edmund Bogg.

pense he has brought several miles a small moorland stream through his park and gardens, where it in some places breaks into fine lakes, and in others contracts itself to the size of a little rill, which winds and plashes through the woods, here falling in cascades, and there withdrawing from the eye, hides itself in the tufted groves." To the same gentleman it is owing that "the roads which branch every way round Swinton are admirable; formed in so excellent a manner as to be superior to most turnpikes." In these days the house was "a convenient structure, elegantly furnished." It is now far beyond that, for Lord Masham has made it one of the foremost county mansions, to which the Corporations of Leeds and Harrogate, in the valleys beyond, are adding most extensive lakes in the nature of reservoirs.

Three miles west of Masham, situated on the hill side near the Burn, is the village of Healey. A church was built at this place in 1848 by Admiral Vernon Harcourt, and the parish was formed out of those of Masham and Kirkby Malzeard. Beyond Healey, the moors north and west from the foot of Colsterdale to near Lofthouse, are under our survey—a scene of wild and sweeping breadth and magnitude. In this grand panorama of moorland the Leeds and Harrogate reservoirs are now being formed. A little nearer Masham is Fearby; a cottage on the green is known as the chapel house, and the altar belonging to this chapel is still to be seen embedded in the floor. This was endowed with an annuity of £5, for praying at Fearby for the souls of James Cooper and his parents for ever, and was payable out of the revenues of Coverham Abbey, at the time of its dissolution. Near to Healey aforementioned, there were formerly circles of upright stones and other relics suggestive of Druidical origin. The name Healey, says John Fisher, is derived from "Heil," holy or sacred, and "ley," pasture or meadow; and Healey Bales, near to, means the land sacred to Baal. There are many places in this neighbourhood with names that conjure up visions of Pagan times, such as "Baal Hill," "Baal Bank," "Beldon Gill," etc.

Kirk Gill cuts deep into the hills; here coal mines have existed for centuries, and here the winter's fuel is still obtained. The monks of Jervaulx owned an extensive tract of land in

Old Farm, Colsterdale. [Owen Bowen.

Colsterdale, in the 12th century; there appears to have been coal and iron mines there, for in the year 1250, Sir John de Walton bound himself by deed to the monks of Jervaulx, "never to raise a forge in Colsterdale, nor give nor sell any iron mines therein." The sides of the glen are strewn with huge masses of rock which ages ago have been dislodged from the crags above. Further up the Gill the scene is most beautiful; the oak trees, whose growth and decay have marked by a thousand years, have ceased to vegetate, and are coated by masses of beautiful moss. Birk Gill glistens in the sunlight on this bright October morning. The moorland is profusely covered with cranberry plant, loaded with clustering fruit. Here, in this nature's garden, the moor birds feed, and wild animals—the fox, badger, and polecat still roam, and even the marten (or wild cat) until very recently haunted this solitude. Grimes Gill and Pott Becks have their rise to the west, and a mile or so east of Goyden Pot, and, after joining into one stream unite with the Burn near to Healey. Pott Hall lies midway between these becks. Ilton, a hamlet standing about

A Moorland Farm near Fearby. [*Owen Bowen*

3 miles west of Masham, contains several old steads; it is a characteristic, venerable, moorland hamlet. Let us wander with the Burn riverwards; how sweetly the stream glitters as it swishes and gurgles its merry way under huge trees, by fine woodland and wide spreading moor, interspersed with furze and bracken; and a few old cottages with roofs of thatch, contribute charm and character to the picture, linking the past to the present. Passing beneath the bridge, the Burn empties into the Yore, half a mile below Masham.

The Botany of Lower Yore-Vale

FROM MASHAM TO BOROBRIDGE.

BY

WILLIAM FOGGITT (J.P., F.L.S.).

There is no Flora richer or more luxuriant than a riparian one; no walk more attractive or enjoyable to a botanist than that by a river side, and such a tract we purpose briefly to review by following the course of the Yore from Masham to Borobridge, which, with the adjacent fields, is a very Paradise to the lover of wild flowers. Within easy distance of our starting point grow many noteworthy species: Actæa spicata—Bane-berry, very poisonous as its name imports, but happily rare, for it is confined to the counties of York and Westmoreland; Ranunculus Lingua—the greater Spearwort, the giant of the Buttercup family; Drosera rotundifolia—the round-leaved Sundew, a truly carnivorous creature, the long, bright-red, gland-tipped tentacles of its leaves being exceeding sensitive to the slightest insect touch, proving an abundant fly-trap. The sparkling diamond-like drops call up Scott's beautiful lines:

> "That pearly dew, so soft, so clear,
> It rivals all but beauty's tear."

Geranium phæum, the dusky Crane's-bill; Parnassia palustris—Grass of Parnassus, as beautiful of blossom as classic in name:

> "Parnassian grass, with chaliced bloom,
> And globes nectareous, like the Earl's
> Rich coronet beset with pearls."

Jasione montana—Sheep's Scabious with its delicate lilac-blue balls of bloom; Artemisia Absinthium—Wormwood, intensely bitter, the chief ingredient in that highly esteemed but exceedingly seductive French liquor Absinthe; Menyanthes trifoliata—Buckbean, one of the prettiest of our wild flowers and virtuous as well as beautiful, for the leaves are an excellent stomachic and tonic, and as such are held in great repute, reminiscent of lines which as a boy I used frequently to read upon a window pane in the front street of a quaint old Yorkshire town:

> "If beauty and virtue in one woman be,
> And if she want a husband, pray send her to me,"

to which the poetical engraver's name was subscribed. He became shortly after a successful medical practitioner, and whether the result of the unique advertisement or not, married a lady both virtuous and beautiful, the daughter of an eminent clergyman, the Rev. Henry Greaves, historian of Cleveland.

Doronicum Pardalianches—Leopard's Bane, with its showy yellow bloom ; Pinguicula vulgaris—the Butterwort, with its spurred violet flowers and viscid leaves like the Sundews carnivorous, entrapping and then digesting and assimilating insects; Verbascum pulverulentum—the hoary Mullein, a representative of a singular genus, all the species of which appear suddenly without human agency, and then after a year or two as mysteriously disappear ; the following Orchids : Gymnadenia conopsea, the fragrant Orchis with long spikes of purple flowers the delicious aromatic smell of which so strongly resembles our garden Clove-pink ; Ophrys apifera—the Bee Orchis, which insect each flower strikingly resembles:

> "Perchance the fragrant load may bind
> Its limbs, I'll set the captive free ;
> I sought the living bee to find,
> And found the picture of a bee."

Neottia nidus-avis—the Bird's-nest Orchis, a brown leafless saprophyte, often overlooked from its similarity in colour to the dead umber beech leaves among which in shade it grows ; Epipactis latifolia—the broad-leaved Helleborine, the tallest of our Orchids ; Epipactis palustris, the marshi Helleborine, with pale pinkish flowers, and Ophrys muscifera—the Fly Orchis, another instance of mimicry ; and the graceful and much prized Oak and Beech Ferns, remarkable for the circumstance that in most instances where one is found, the other is not far away.

Pursuing the river we cannot go far without seeing the three species of Ribes—the well-nigh ubiquitous Gooseberry, Ribes Grossularia, and the Red and Black Currant—Ribes rubrum and nigrum. Though all truly wild, it is tolerably certain that none of the three is indigenous, but probably all bird-sown from garden trees. The writer has seen all three epiphytal, upon pollarded willows within a few yards of each other.

The two Cherries are also in evidence, Prunus Padus - the Bird Cherry, only fit for birds, and Prunus Avium, the wild Cherry or Gean, the supposed parent of our much esteemed garden Cherry. We are sure to notice the familiar Oxlip, a hybrid between the Primrose and Cowslip, and like most hybrids, much more robust than either parent, a fact observed by our late Laureate as testified in the lines :

> "As Cowslip unto Oxlip is,
> So seemed she to the boy";

Trifolium medium—the Zig-zag Clover, the beautiful purple flowers of which are so showy in upland regions ; Myosotis sylvatica—the Wood Forget-me-not, the clear blue flowers of which are very attractive in our mountain woods, where it occasionally occurs with pure white corollas; Tanacetum vulgare—Tansy, the aromatic leaves of which strongly suggest Tansy pudding, formerly in great repute during Lent ; and Rosa arvensis, with its wealth of ivory white flowers and almost round naked scarlet fruit.

When we reach Hackfall we enter a rich botanical district and soon espy the three species of Cardamine—C. amara, the large flowered Bitter-cress, so bonny with its cream-white petals and purple anthers—C. sylvatica, the sylvan Lady's Smock with its flexuous stem ; and C. Pratensis, the "milk maids" of village children, all true heart-strengtheners as the generic name declares. Growing amongst them, or hard by, you will find the two Golden Saxifrages—Chrysosplenium alternifolium and C. oppositifolium—the alternate and opposite leaved Golden Saxifrages; *Euonymus europæus*—the Spindle-tree known also as Prick-wood, the brilliant food of which from its peculiar shape has gained for itself in France the name "Bonnet du Pretre," Priest's-cap; Viburnum Opulus—the Guelder-rose, probably a corruption of Elder-rose, the outer and showier strap-shaped flowers of the clusters being barren, whilst the small unattractive inner ones are fertile and produce the transparent rich red berries so often seen as added charms on the breasts of village maidens. Under cultivation these inner flowers become barren also and form the well known Snowball of our shrubberies, conferring additional beauty at the expense of fertility:

"Silver globes, light as the foamy surf,
That the wind severs from the broken wave."

Epilobium angustifolium—the wild French or narrow-leaved Willow Herb—the abundant rich magenta flowers of which are highly attractive and often found where there has been a clearing of timber. In Canada they call it Fire-weed from its habit of springing up after a prairie fire. In some parts of Yorkshire I have seen whole acres covered with it after trees have been felled. Solidago virgaurea—golden rod, a showy species, happily named; Eupatorium cannabinum—hemp agrimony, from its hemp-like leaves; Paris quadrifolia, Herb of equal parts, True-love or One-berry; Pyrola minor, the lesser winter-green so-called from its ever-green leaves, very pretty with its onesided racemes of pink-tinged-white waxy flowers; Geum intermedium—a hybrid between the wood and water Avens, and like the Oxlip stronger than either of its parents; Hieracium prenanthoides—the clasping hawkweed, a rare species of this puzzling genus, ninety seven of which are described in the ninth edition of Babington's Manual, abundant on rocks high above the river; Hieracium murorum, the wall or golden hawkweed plentiful on a steep bank near the Grewelthorp entrance; and Campanula latifolia, the giant bell-flower, "the throat wort with its azure bells," of Scott, very showy: Hackfall's flower-glories all of these.

Verbascum Thapsus—the great Mullein, high taper or flannel flower, is attractive. The wood abounds in sedges, notable among which is Carex pendula, the great drooping sedge, the female spikes of which are so large and heavy that the plants bend beneath their load. Sedges are a large family, very grass like in appearance, but, with a few exceptions, have their male and female inflorescence on different spikes of the same plant, being included in the great Linnean order Monœcia or one housed. Their leaf sheaths are entire, whilst those of grasses are split. Rare grasses occur in these woods; Hordeum sylvaticum—the Wood Barley, whilst on the opposite side of the river, upon Maudlin (Magdalene) banks, is Festuca sylvatica—the Wood Fescue, its first-known North Yorkshire locality; Equisetum maximum—the horsetail is strongly in evidence, the fertile leafless plant appearing in April, whilst the graceful luxuriant, verdant, leafy barren stems are at their best during midsummer. The elegant Chantarelle, Cantharellus cibarius, with its rich yellow colour and luscious apricot smell is an edible fungus which occurs chiefly under the beech trees. In the South of England these fungi were dressed, on state occasions, for the banquets of the Freemasons, by whom they were highly esteemed. Between Hackfall and Tanfield the yellow star of Bethlehem—Gagea lutea occurs in several spots, the pretty blossoms of which some birds are so passionately fond of that occasionally it is very difficult to find a flower intact.

Banks of the Yore, Tanfield. [*Walter Pattison.*

At Tanfield upon the Castle and other old walls grow Saxifraga tridactylites, the rue leaved Saxifrage ; Sedum dasyphyllum, the bonny thick leaved stone crop ; Sedum reflexum, the showy great yellow stone-crop ; Lactuca muralis, the wall lettuce ; Lactuca virosa, the strong scented lettuce the smell of which is very similar to that of opium, It has long been esteemed as soporific, which possibly explains its presence on the walls of most Castles and Abbeys ; Linaria Cymbalaria, the ivy leaved Snapdragon, popularly known as "Mother of thousands," and certainly a very prolific species ; Parietaria officinalis, the pellitory of the wall, much esteemed for its medicinal properties, and found upon nearly all Abbey and Castle walls, the only exception I know being those of Rievaulx. The many jointed and rigid Poas, Poa compressa and Schlerochloa rigida, also occur.

In fields and upon the railway embankment adjacent to Tanfield on the north side of the river the botanist will have a splendid harvest, for here he will find Helleborus viridis, the green Hellebore ; Aquilegia vulgaris, the Columbine, with flowers both white and blue ; Helianthemum vulgare, the rock rose ; Viola hirta, the hairy violet ; Cochlearia officinalis the medicinal scurvy grass, formerly held in high repute as an antiscorbutic ; Silene inflata, the Bladder campion ; Stellaria nemorum, the Wood Stitchwort ; Hypericum dubium, and H. humifusum, the square stalked and trailing St. John's Worts; Spiræa Filipendula, the beautiful "Dropwort" so called from the pea-like tubers which hang by slender threads from its roots; Rosa spinosissima, the Burnet rose ; Rosa tomentosa, the Downy dog rose ; and Rosa arvensis, the trailing field rose are all very distinct and beautiful; Poterium muricatum, the Muricated Salad Burnet, a very rare species ; Medicago sativa, the purple Lucerne ; Trifolium procumbens. the Hop trefoil ; Galium ochroleucum, a luxuriant hybrid between the white and yellow Bedstraws, the only Yorkshire record ; Scabiosa columbaria, the small or limestone Scabious; Myrrhis odorata, the sweet Cicely, the whole plant redolent of Anise, formerly much used as a cattle condiment ; Malva moschata, the Musk mallow; Trollius europæus, Globe flower, locally known as "dumplings"; Salvia verbenaca, Wild clary ; Calamintha Clinopodium, Basil thyme; Calamintha officinalis, Medicinal calamint ; Centaurea Scabiosa, the great knapweed ; Filago minima, the least cudweed ; Campanula glomerata, the clustered bell-flower; Gentiana Amarella, the autumnal Gentian or Felwort ; Erythræa Centaurium, the red centaury so much prized by herbalists ; Chlora perfoliata, the yellow Centaury; the last three all belong to the gentian family and are intensely bitter ; Samolus Valerandi, Brookweed ; Atropa Belladonna, deadly nightshade ; Ophrys muscifera and Ophrys apifera, the bee and fly orchids ; Orchis ustulata, dwarf Orchis ; Orchis pyramidalis, pyramidal Orchis with its dense rose-red spikes ; Colchicum autumnale, Meadow saffron, long esteemed a specific for gout, the leafless flowers of which called "naked ladies" appear in the autumn, and the deep green leaves and seed capsules in the following spring.

> "Sir William sat in his old arm chair,
> Nursing his gouty knee ;
> And the Lady Dorothy tall and fair,
> Was mixing his colchicum tea ;
> And Beatrice with her bright blue eyes,
> Was teaching her kitten to catch the flies."

Bromus erectus, the upright Brome grass, a true lime-loving species Ophioglossum vulgatum, Adder's tongue and Botrychium Lunaria, Moonwort or Grape Fern, are some of the rarer and more interesting plants of this very floriferous region.

Between Tanfield and Ripon the following occur—Helleborus fœtidus, the Bear's foot or stinking Hellebore, which flowers in early March ; Anemone Pulsatilla, the Pasque flower ; Thlaspi arvense, Penny cress, so called from the resemblance of the pods to the silver pennies of our Tudor Kings ; Barbarea præcox, Winter or American cress, an esteemed early salad ; Lychnis Githago. corn cockle, a pretty colonist, less frequent than formerly ; Cerastium arvense, a chickweed with large white flowers and honeyed fragrance ; Saxifraga granulata, the white meadow Saxifrage, interesting for the numerous small pink bulbils or grains borne upon the roots, by which the plant is propagated ; Rosa Sabini, Sabine's Rose, a beautiful species but densely prickly ; Petasites vulgaris, Butter-bur, with female flowers. In many districts, notably around the well-worked Thirsk, the female flowers are entirely absent, but in Wensleydale, from Semmer water to below Ripon, they are very abundant in many places ; Hyoscyamus niger—Henbane, probably Hen Bean, for domestic fowl seem somewhat partial to it, a weird and forbidding looking plant with greenish-yellow flowers and clammy and sticky leaves, but very highly esteemed medicinally ; Verbascum virgatum—the large-flow red Mullein; Echium vulgare—the Viper's Bugloss, a very showy creature with rough tubercled stems, and abundant handsome flowers which in bud are bright red, as they open changing to purple, and when fully expanded of a brilliant blue. This change of colour may be noticed in many others of the Borage family.

Salix triandra and Salix rubra are both in evidence, the latter, so attractive with its red stamens, grows al ng the whole length of the river-banks; several other willows also occur. Allium oleraceum—the field Garlic and Allium vineale—the crow Garlic, so remarkable for their bulbiferous umbels, which drop off and produce new plants; Ornithogalum umbellatum—the white star of Bethlehem, the bulbs of which are supposed to have been the dove's dung of the Bible. The flowers only open at mid-day and in bright weather, so that probably they are frequently overlooked. Daphne Laureola—Spurge Laurel, an evergeeen with greenish-yellow flowers, blossoming in January and February. Near Tanfield Mill from time to time a number of casuals have occurred, of which we will mention but a few. Sisymbrium Sophia, Flixweed, a Crucifer, with deeply divided leaves and graceful pods, which make a beautiful table decoration; Erysimum orientale—the Hare's ear Cabbage; Alyssum incanum—the Hoary Madwort; Saponaria Vaccaria—the pink Soapwort, a charming plant; Malva parviflora and M. verticillata—the small-flowered and whorled Mallows; Salvia verticillata—the whorled Clary; Solanum rostratum, a densely prickly Nightshade, with yellow flowers; Amsinckia lycopsioides—the yellow Bugloss. These are but a few of the visitors to Tanfield Mill, which has long been a happy hunting ground to the writer.

Upon the "Batts," a sandy tract near the Mill, Morchella esculenta (the Morel), a much prized esculent fungus; and Peziza venosa—locally known as "Jew's Ear" (but not the Jew's Ear of Mycologists), another edible species, occur in fair plenty in the early Springtime. Two men, whom the writer on one occasion met with collecting Morels, said they had a ready market in Ripon for them at two shillings per pound.

Near Melmerby Station, Rhamnus catharticus—Buckthorn, and Arenaria tenuifolia—the slender-leaved Sandwort, an infrequent species, occur; in an adjacent pond, Hottonia palustris - the rare Water Violet, and Lythrum Salicaria—the Purple Loosestrife, flourish; whilst in neighbouring fields may be gathered that most beautiful plant Primula farinosa—Bird's Eye Primrose, with its attractive pink flowers and mealy leaves—the "Bird's-een" of the village children. This true floral gem is confined to our six Northern Counties, and an accomplished veteran botanist is said to have screamed with delight when he first saw it. In a garden on the south side of the station is a fine bush of the Red Mezereon, with pure white flowers; and in another on the south side a marvellous bed of Aubrietia purpurea, a handsome crucifer, both worthy a visit.

In the Vicarage shrubbery at Wath are many thousands of Winter Aconite—Eranthis hyemalis—a veritable "field of the cloth of gold." This golden display in the early spring-time is most delightful. These are especially noteworthy, for the wait at Melmerby Station is often long and wearisome.

Within easy distance of Ripon the following interesting plants have been observed:—Adonis autumnalis—Pheasant's Eye; Ranunculus hirsutus—Hairy Buttercup; Lepidium Draba—Whitlow Pepperwort; Lepidium ruderale—Narrow-leaved Pepperwort; Silene anglica—English Catch-fly; Hypericum montanum—Mountain St. John's Wort; Melilotus officinalis— Tall Melilot; M. alba—White Melilot; M parviflora—Small-flowered Melilot; Medicago denticulata—Toothed Medick; Lathyrus Aphaca—Yellow Vetchling; Epilobium roseum—Rose Willow Herb; E. obscurum—Square-stalked Willow Herb; Bryonia Dioca—White Bryony; Œnanthe Phellandrium Fine-leaved Water Dropwort; Caucalis latifolia—Broad-leaved Hedge Parsley; Galium tricorne—Corn Bed-straw; Centaurea Solstitialis—St. Barnaby's Thistle; Crepis setosa—Bristly Hawk's-beard; Chrysanthemum segetum—Yellow Corn Marigold; Cichorium Intybus—Chicory or Succory, with beautiful cerulean blue, but very ephemeral, flowers; Spiranthes autumnalis—Autumnal Lady's Tresses; Rumex Hydrolapathum—Great Water Dock; Lamium Galeobdolon—Yellow Dead Nettle; Erigeron acris—Blue Fleabane; Gentiana campestris—Field Gentian; Silene noctiflora—Night-flowering Campion; and many others. All the foregoing are more or less rare. On the walls of Fountain's Abbey, Dianthus plumarius—Common Pink, and Linaria Cymbalaria—Ivy-leaved Snapdragon, both very abundant and decorative, the latter so much as to have gained for itself the name of "Studley Ivy"; and in the woods, Impatiens Noli-me-tangere—Yellow Balsam, or Touch-me-not; Dipsacus pilosus—Shepherd's Rod, or Small Teasel; Dipsacus sylvestris—Large Teasel; Mimulus luteus—Monkey Flower; Monotropa hypopitys—Yellow Bird's Nest, a curious leafless parasite, with many other varieties, occur. In the woods of Mackershaw grow the scarce Epipactis ovalis—the oval-leaved Helleborine, and the almost equally rare Carex digitata—Fingered Sedge. Between Ripon and Boroughbridge, by the banks of, or in, the river, grow the following:—Ranunculus fluitans—the long floating Crowfoot; Stachys palustris—Marsh Woundwort; Mentha piperita—Peppermint; Hippuris vulgaris—Mare's tail; Lithospermum officinale—Officinal Gromwell; Lysimachia Nummularia—Moneywort or Creeping Jenny; Atriplex deltoidea—Triangular Orache; Potamogeton perfoliatus—Perfoliate Pondweed; P densus—opposite-leaved Pondweed; Scirpus sylvaticus—Wood Club-rush; Scirpus lacustris—the true Bulrush; Allium Scorodoprasum—Sand Leek; Colchicum autumnale—Meadow Saffron; Blysmus compressus—Broad-leaved Blysmus; and a host of others.

We have cursorily reviewed the plants of the Yore from Masham to Boroughbridge, and little more than a tithe has been told. Each time we revisit the much-loved spot we see new beauties and gain new treasures; and it is a mine far from being exhausted. We can commend it safely to all lovers of wild flowers.

"Ye wildings of Nature I dote upon you."

WILLIAM FOGGITT.

The Vale of Mowbray.

CHAPTER I.

The Vale of Mowbray. Around the name of this far-reaching and fertile valley, permeated throughout with the footprints of a forgotten race, there is interwoven a spell of glamour and an old-world sound, telling of Baronial rule, and the Knightly deeds and storied charm of princely grandeur, as it were the echo of a vibrating cadence of never dying music, welling from the fount of distant time. For around this plangent name here is linked the pomp and circumstance of military pride, glory, and renown peculiar to the Norman crusading era. The numerous throng and the flitting to and fro of blazoned cavalcades, the glitter of harness, the jingle of chain, and clank of mail accoutrements, has passed into shadow-land for ever. Yet, in this name of Mowbray, there is en-chronicled a story of great resolve, high endeavour, doughty deed and chivalrous enterprise. A name which cannot die or be tarnished with the rust of ages, for the magic of that word is impressed so indissolubly on every yard of this plain, also in the history of the English

Nation, as to render it imperishable. The several castles and numerous monastic institutions which arose in feudal glory and architectural magnificence, by the will-power and religious zeal of the owners of that magic name, have fallen or will fall into ruin and decay, until perchance, not a fragment remains, and only turf covered mounds on the surface survive to tell of the work of the great chiefs of old. But the name of the men (The Mowbrays) at whose bidding they arose, will not perish as long as the story of the English people survives. The potent name stamped by the Mowbrays on this great plain of Thirsk, covering upwards of 400 square miles, and extending over 20 miles or more from east to west and the same distance from north to south, has for its boundary on the east the Hambletons and the Howardian range of hills, and on the west those of Richmondshire, from the spurs of Teesdale to the bluffs of Mashamshire and Ripon.

A good heritage is this great valley, having within it numerous small hill spurs and lateral vales, as for instance, those of the Codbeck and the Wiske, which are amongst the larger water courses, with numerous smaller streams, beautifying and intersecting the valley in all directions in their journey to the Swale. The plain and its limiting bulwarks are visibly scarred with tumuli, camps, entrenchments, earthworks of castles, and moated sites, all proclaiming the story of foray and strife through centuries of fighting (before the valley found rest) between Celt and Roman, and the Anglian, Norsemen and Scot of later times. In its ancient kirks, we have remains of monastic houses and cells, pointing to the religious zeal of the Kuldee priests who carried forth the gospel of Christ from the decay of Druidism; and those of the later Norman church are also manifest.

The Mowbrays.

Like many other noble names in English history, the Mowbrays came from Normandie at the Conquest. A Roger de Mowbraie or Mowbray, came in William's army of adventurers in quest of land and fortune, and rewards of land plunder far beyond their dreams or expectations fell to their share. The names of the pre-Conquest owner of Thirsk, the Anglian Thane and Danish Earl (Orm and Thor) sink into oblivion, and pale before that one word—Mowbray, which family dominated this district for centuries, and have left behind for all time the impression of their footsteps. The seed plot and nursery place of this potent race of warriors, whose deeds of chivalry have become enshrined in the annals of fame, was of Normandie. Moubrai was a Commune in the Canton of Percie in the above state. The Percies and Mowbrays in their Normandy homeland, were neighbours and comrades in arms as they afterwards also became in England, for their territories joined, and in history we often find their names united in one common cause. Amongst the twenty-five steel-clad Barons assembled at Runnymede, June 15th, 1215, met to enforce King John to sign the great Magna Charter, are four distinguished names: William and Robert de Mowbray, and Richard and Robert de Percie—and who shall say that this great Seal and Charter was not planned and worked out in the halls of these chieftains, for none were greater than the Mowbrays and Percies, and, although they have left the impress of their names and deeds deeply engraven on history, the signing of the Magna Charta will stand as their best memorial through time. Thus we find the houses had much in common, and both bear the lion on their escutcheon.

One of the great fighting clerics in William's army, Geoffrey, Bishop of Constances, rendered signal service at the

Bird's-eye View of Thirsk, from the Church Tower.

[T. Foe, Thirsk.

battle of Senlac, for which he received by grant from the Conqueror 280 Vills, or Manors, which at his death in 1093, he left to his nephew, Robert de Mowbray. It was at this period that the Castle of Thirsk arose in all the feudal dignity and magnificence of the period. There was a fortified house here prior to the Conquest, which is supposed to have been built about 950. It is questionable if it occupied the same site as the one afterwards reared by the Mowbrays. There are vestiges pointing to this first stronghold having stood on the land on the east of the church between the beck and the mill, where a mound and traces of moat are still visible. This spot would be very easily surrounded by water, thus cutting off access and adding to the defences. The earthworks of the Norman castle built by the Mowbrays are still strongly in evidence, a wide deep ditch and high earthen rampart and a mound showing the position of the castle keep. A great portion of the moat has become obliterated, the present town of Thirsk having been built over it. From appearances, it extended south-east to border of the present Market Place. Its ramifications plainly bespeak a goodly structure, capable of housing a large following of knights and men-at-arms, and of withstanding assault and seige. Yet investigation and scrutiny of the deeply-moated site tells us nothing of a stone-built castle having stood here, and with the exception of the church there is no building of high antiquity where the materials could have again been used.

A hundred paces north-west of the church, there is a low wall built of large shapely dressed stones, but even this material may have been spared when the church was re-built. From observation we conclude that with the exception of a few courses of stones above ground, this castle of the Mowbrays was built of wood, hence no durable remains. Yet all visitors who pass over the Croft containing the earthworks, will be convinced this castle of Thirsk has been no mean thing, and here in the almost regal splendour of that rude period dwelt the Mowbrays, all of which name were notable warriors and equally distinguished for their generosity to the church.

Robert de Mowbray, whose deeds are deeply imprinted in English History, twice rebelled against King William (The Red). On the last occasion he was captured and imprisoned, and his lands confiiscated and given to Nigel de Albina, whose mother was of Mowbray lineage. Robert spent 30 years of his life a prisoner in the King's castle at Windsor, and when aged and blind he was restored to liberty by Henry the First. The defier of Kings in his old age sought admission into the Abbey of Saint Albans, which he had enriched so generously in the days of his glory. And so this noble baron "assumed the monastic garb and devoted to religion the serene evening of a life whose noon had been spent amid the turmoil of strife."

The glamour of pathetic story and romantic incident is strongly in evidence of Gundreda de Gourney, widow of the above Nigel de Albina, during the rule at her castle of Thirsk. The spell of romance which was weaving itself at this period in the family, runs as follows :—Nigel de Albina, as a youth, greatly favoured by Henry I., was made the king's bow bearer, and was of good natural towardliness, and great hope. He took Robert Carthose prisoner at the battle of Tenchebrai (1106), when English axes retaliated on Norman spears, conquering Normandie in revenge for Hastings. By acquisition of lands bestowed on him (the Mowbrays) by the king, he became one of the most potent of the Anglo-Norman Nobility. He took to wife Gundreda de Gourney, and by her he had an only son, whom the king surnamed Mowbray. And so it came about the exchange of lands and name from Albina to that of Mowbray, and their son became in due course the illustrious Roger, who took part in the Standard Fight and went to the Holy Land, where he gained further renown and glory, fought and slew a giant Pagan in single combat. Amongst other great gifts to the church, he was the founder of Byland Abbey and Newburgh Priory. Nigel died at, or near, Rouen, where he was buried, and the boy Roger became a Ward of the Crown, and the widow Gundreda retired to her castle of Thirsk to devote herself to dolour and divinity, and to the upbringing of her son, whom the church afterwards found such a magnificent patron. One scene in the life of this great Lady of Thirsk opens out thus: A company of monks had fled from Calder Abbey before the depredations of the Scots, and having been refused admission into their parent home at Furness, had wandered abroad homeless, so story runs, not scarcely knowing whither all their belongings and books, etc., were in a wagon drawn by eight oxen, and during their journeying came by chance upon the town of Thirsk. And doubtless having often heard of Gundreda the Bountiful, they timidly approached the castle, and on the Seneschal learning their story, they were admitted. And here their wants were supplied and they were entertained as the guests of Lady Gundreda for some short period. From Thirsk she found them a dwelling at Hode (of which place we shall speak later). Here she supplied them with all necessaries till her son Roger came of age. Hode was not fully to the liking of the monks, and the sending of provisions from Thirsk was at times very inconvenient. So at his mother's request young Mowbray gave them in 1140 his vaccary, or cow—pasture of Combe, and all the land of Wilden and Scakilden and Erghum, for their support.

Timber-framed Cottage, Thirsk. [E. Bogg.

The story of the founding of Byland belongs to the history of the Vale of Mowbray. Its existence only came to pass by the generous donors from their castle of Thirsk, so let us continue the tale.

Gerald, the first abbot, died at Hode in 1143, when Roger, the sub-cellarer was appointed, who again applied to the Lady Bountiful to induce her son to give them a larger space of ground, as the situation at Hode was too confined, whereupon he readily assigned them the Church and old town of Byland or Bella-landa, upon the moor and near the river Rie, part of Gundreda's dower. But this, being so near the Abbey of Rieval, each could hear the sound of the bells of the other. This was unseemly and could not long be borne, and being in many accounts inconvenient and in rather a bleak position,— the monks had ever an eye for rich pasturage and beauty of situation—so in 1147 this community of monks removed to

Stocking, near Cukeswald under Blakhow Hill, where Roger de Mowbray gave them two carucates of waste land, upon which they built their monastery. The town of Byland being reduced to a grange the preceding year, the monks had built a chapel at Scalton. To this new place they repaired and built a small stone church, a cloister, and other houses, where they remained 30 years, having many donations made to them. After having cleared a large tract of moorland and drained the marshes, the monks again removed on the Eve of All Saints, 1177, a little more to the eastward, near to Burtoft and Beresclive, between Whitaker and the foot of Cambe Hill, when the abbey dedicated to the B.V.M. at length was settled in a noble church and monastery.

The great revolt of the Mowbrays, 1173 and 1174, is a chapter in National History too important to relate here except to state that this revolt led to the destruction of the castle of Thirsk, "For having his castles of Oxholme and Mallizard besieged and taken by the bpp. of Lincoln (the king's base son), he hastened to ye King, then at Northampton, and surrendered his castle at Thirsk, and thereupon had his pardon granted, which said castlees of Thirsk and Kirkby Mallizard ye King soone after caused to be demolished."

The castle, we are told, was destroyed by fire, being completely overwhelmed and reduced to ashes; and the power of the Mowbrays, for the time being, was subverted. The easy destruction of the castle by fire leads us to the conclusion that it was built entirely of wood. In due time Thirsk rose from its ashes and continued to furnish a residence of the Mowbrays, who held the manor of Woodhall at Thirsk. And here for the present we leave the history of the castle and its noble owners.

The Market Place, Thirsk. [Edmund Bogg

CHAPTER II.

Thirsk.

A small settlement, but of no striking significance, existed here in Celtic times. A few lowly wattle and clay huts dotted here and there amongst the willows and brushwood along the east bank of the Codbeck—the Coed, ancient British for a wood, which the little river in that bygone period hereabouts wandered through. Thirsk, as the chief place in the fascinating vale of Mowbray, remains comparatively new ground both to the antiquary and tourist. Of Celtic founding as its name, Tre-ussig—the settlement by the water, plainly indicates. The name of the stream (The Coed) is also another survival of old British nomenclature; and a hundred other evidences of its antiquity, reaching back to British times, can be found within a short radius of the famous old town.

The Domesday form of the name is "Tresche," the vulgar pronunciation Thrusk, both conclusive evidence of its ancient etymology. Domesday account tells that in Tresche, Orm held eight Carucates to be taxed, land to four ploughs taxable value 20 shillings. A second manor was held by Tor, who had twelve Carucates of land to be taxed; and one Hugh had here ten villanes, having two ploughs and eight acres of meadow. Value in the Confessor's reign, four pounds, now at the Domesday survey, ten shillings. So we find that after the fierce vengeance of the Conqueror had swept over the town, its taxable value had been reduced to an eighth of its pre-Norman prosperity. The name Thirsk, written variously Tresche, Tresch, Thrysk, Tresussig, or Uisge—its terminal one with

Usk, Esk, Wisk—meaning the spot by the water, is unique, for no other place in England bears it, and few places have such a history. The town is divided into two parts, designated Old and New Thirsk. The Old Town stands along the east bank of the Codbeck. Adjoining the west bank is a fortified site known as the Moat, of pre-Norman construction, in which we find further proof of its great antiquity and also conclusive evidence of the position the town occupied from the British to the Norman period. The condition of the town began to change when the Mowbrays appeared upon the scene towards the close of the XIth century, and their great stronghold of timber, typical of feudalism, arose to the south west of the river, and some three hundred paces from the older settlement.

Artificially, it was rendered as impregnable as its low situation would permit, this being strikingly evident from the depth of the moat and height of the banks. New Thirsk owes its existence to the Norman Castle. During its erection a throng of craftsmen would congregate, merchants naturally anxious to create a trade were attracted hither, a population of serfs and retainers of the potent Mowbray settled within or near the castle, a market became a necessity: this came about early in the twelfth century, and during the following two or three centuries the Square and the Streets leading to it gradually developed.

Thirsk was summoned to send Burgesses to Parliament in the reign of Edward the First. But from the above period and until 1553, there appears to have been no representatives sent. After that year, and until 1832, Thirsk was represented at Westminster by two members. And so strong were the Franklands of Thirkleby centred in Thirsk, that the return of members was practically in their hands. At the Redistribution

170   THE VALE OF MOWBRAY

Bill of 1835, the town was erased from the list of Parliamentary boroughs. The following are the main arteries of the town:—The Market Place, a fine spacious square broken by two

Finckle Street, Thirsk.   Edmund Bogg.

intrusive blocks of property; the most ancient way on the north side is known as the middle' (where the Penningtons have dwelt, father and sons, for generations), and lends to the square the picturesque charm of antiquity. Hutton, who visited the town in 1808, thinks differently about the middle row—he says, "It is a handsome town eleven miles from the 'Tontine,' but is disgraced by a shabby range of buildings in the centre of the Market Place—rubbish surrounded by beauty." He further adds, "It is situated on the Great Road from London to the North, yet it contains but one Inn for the reception of travellers; but it is an excellent one, though kept by a woman, Mrs. Cass."

We beg to differ with Hutton on this picturesque corner of Thirsk. Unsightly, indeed! and spoiling the symmetry of the Square. Exactly opposite is the effect it has to the eye of an artist and to all who find pleasure in the antiquated features of our ancient burghs. The Old Shambles, which stood nearly in the centre of the area, were demolished in 1857. The ancient Market Cross, with broken shaft (a venerable relic of antiquity) has given place to a new Clock Tower. The Tolbooth, an antique feature in the Square, past which the coaches rattled in pre-railway days, was accidentally burnt down in 1834. The circle which was formerly allotted to bull-baitings is still pointed out. The ring to which the beast was fastened was taken up about 50 years ago, previous to which Grainge says, a custom prevailed among the young men of Thirsk on the completion of their apprenticeship to meet together in a carouse at midnight at the Bull ring, and drink to each other with the arm holding the glass passed through the ring. Not long ago the writer (a guest of the Penningtons), whose house was in the centre of the ancient middle, was aroused from slumber by a roystering crew of revellers, which kept on into the small hours of the morning. "Surely," thought he, "'tis the 'prentices keeping up at the

Bull ring the old-time custom of our forefathers." No butcher was allowed to kill a bull and expose its flesh for sale in the market without having first baited him. Many people were heavily fined for not adhering to this now obsolete practice. In this instance happily, the time-honoured custom has passed, let us hope, for ever.

There are a goodly array of shops on the south of the Market Square. On this side are also the two principal inns, "The Three Tuns," and "The Golden Fleece"; now-a-days quite enough, only being aroused from slumber when the bustle and activity of country-side life is centred on Monday's Market in the large square. At these times and also on Fair days and at the Race Meetings, the old inns seem to come to life again and partake of the palmy days of the past. What a din, medley, and confused mixture of humanity the square holds on these days, presenting curious phases and startling characteristics of human life. George Blythe and John and William Hall, the latter two father and son, built up the reputation of the "Fleece" until it became the most notable coaching house between York and Darlington. Mr. William Hall, born in 1818, passed his youth and early manhood when the good old coaching was in the height of its glory. In his middle life he saw the coaches gradually withdrawn into vistas of the bygones. Living to a good old age, he became a well-known local figure, a link, as it were, connecting the gay stirring scenes of travelling by coach to the prosaic days of railway travel. Mr. Hall generally kept upwards of fifty horses in his possession for coaching purposes. How silent is this old inn yard to-day compared with the activity displayed in the past; the hurry and scurry and running hither and thither of groom and stableman; the rattling of wheels and clattering of hoofs and fiery sparks flying from the cobbled pavement; hark to the sounding horn and crack of the coachman's whip; how merrily the coach rolls onward, the dogs bark and chase the flying wheel, and the children scamper as the gaily coloured vehicle swings round the corner of the market and speeds along the highway north.

Another Thirsk character, also connected with coaching was old Billy Baines, postboy in the town for upwards of 50 years.

Mr. William Hall.

He was father of Billy Baines junior, equally well-known and the most diminutive figure on the north road as "Wee Bainie," and long employed as postboy at the New Inn, Easingwold.

The Three Tuns Inn, a commodious hostel with fine entrance hall, was originally built as a "Dowager House" for the family of Bell. And a substantial one too, with its range of antique out-buildings, columbary and large gardens, typical of the Stuart and early Jacobean period. Some of the rooms still contain the oak pannelling, and on the wall of an upstair apartment is a coat of arms, probably of the Bell Family.

Fincle Street leads east from the Market Place to the bridge spanning the Codbeck. It is supposed to receive its name from Vincle, Danish for a corner. According to the Rev. Addison the name Finkle or Fincle, found in many of our old towns, is supposed to have been given by the Flemings who settled during the mediæval period in England in great numbers, Vincle in their language signifies a booth or waggon containing merchandise. And to-day in South Africa, booths outside the towns are called winkles. Seen from the bridge the street, with its cluster of old roofs, is very picturesque. In it is situated an ancient hostelry (The Old Three Tuns). Ingramgate runs east from the bridge to the junction of four roads. The one leading north, from its great length, is named Long Street; on the east of it is the Poor Man's Corn-mill. The street leading south is named Barbeck, not, as some people suppose, from Barbican, a fortified entrance, for apart from the castle the town had no fortifications. At this entrance there was probably a Bar House, and near by is a beck, dividing Thirsk from the parish of Bagby, hence Barbeck. This street contains two or three ancient timber framed and thatched roofed cottages. In pre-Reformation times at the end of this street there stood a small chapel dedicated to St. Giles. The first mention of this chapel is in 1345, and is named "The Chapel of St. Giles, in Brynkellhow Gate, in the town of Thirsk." Not a stone or mound remains to mark its site, yet in the name of the Croft, Chapel Close Hill is the sure indication of its former site.

The Inn here at the Cross Roads bears for its sign a White Mare depicted in the act of leaping with its affrighted rider over the cliff into the waters of Gormire.

From the north-east corner of the Market, runs Millgate (here the large corn mills are situated), and joining on to Bridge Street which runs north to St. James' Green, and into Old Thirsk. Here are some very ancient houses. The name St. James, given to the Green, is from a chapel which once stood here dedicated to the above Saint. It was evidently demolished centuries ago, for not a stone or even a mark to denote its site remains. It is several times mentioned in early records, and human bones have been found when digging, doubtless pointing to the site of a graveyard, and two paved causeways, broken up many years ago, led from opposite angles to the supposed site of the chapel. Piper Lane and Stammergate extends from the Green east to the Long Street. The field adjoining the latter is called Stoneybrough, from the great number of stones formerly found on the surface. Stane is the local pronunciation of stone, hence Stammergate may derive from Stane-moor-gate.

The Holms. [*Edmund Bogg*

From this street we cross the Codbeck and past the old moated site of pre-Norman date, and by the Lady's Well (a favourite shrine in the old days for the sweethearting folk), into the Holms. This picturesque willow grove extends from Norby, a small outlying settlement of Thirsk (and as its name tells us, of Danish naming), to the Mills. This grove, with the walk along the banks of the mill stream, is perhaps the most charming part of Thirsk. Quaint bits of old treed roofs and antique gables show forth from the intervening willowy foreground. Above us are overhanging branches, and below they are reflected in the water mirror. The web-footed fowls disport in the water, and the birds carol delightsome melody. Seen through the trees of the 'Marage' forming the rook colony, is the ivy-covered front of the Hall and the Church—the Cathedral of the Vale, its stately tower looming majestically forth beautiful in its proportions and ecclesiastical symbolism. Turn to the grove and the wooing and union of streams, where old railings twist and curve by bank and stream in this old-world antique garden corner, all suggesting to the mind harmony of form and colour. Across the 'Marage,'* where the rooks are clamouring during nesting operations, we obtain a glimpse of

---

* An unique place-name survival at Thirsk is the shady fish-pond, ringed round with trees, situated between the old Manor Hall and Church bank and the artificial mill-cut. It is known locally as the 'Marage.' The word is a very curious one, being a conjoint of *mar* (in the Northumberland and Norse dialect meaning a small piece of water, not necessarily sea-water tho' its root is *mare* Latin, the sea), and the old French suffix *age*, which always had the force of expressing the word to which it is added in some new modified relation. In this case, the "marage" is "the fish and fowl water" or preserve; and no doubt in far back times it was as common a term for a tenanted fish or duck preserve as *messuage* is to this day for a dwelling place with its offices. Nowhere else in Britain is there a similiar "marage," and the name has been overlooked in our dialect dictionaries; though there is a mar-pool near Whitby, and two or three meres styled *mars* on the Border. Now, the "marage" is supplied from the mill cut by a trapped sluice, as its water level is much lower than the artificial race which cut it off from the Cod beck and its remarkable willow-garth. The marage itself must have existed as long as the river. This grand old willow-garth is an unique picture; a track of marshy land on the west side of Codbeck is covered with a veritable grove of ancient willows—both the white and the crack willow—in all stages of growth, some in their prime, others young and vigorous, ready to take the place in course of time of the decaying and decrepit giants whose stumps alone attest their age to-day. A finer and more picturesque natural ripe-wood does not exist in Yorkshire.

another interesting feature, the stately tower of the Parish Church rising so solidly into space, with its finials and its artistically pierced battlements which give dignity and further charm to this old corner of Thirsk.

Kirkgate.   [Edmund Bogg.

The Parish Church alone, the chief architectural feature in the town, contains sufficient interest for a journey hither. The edifice is dedicated to St. Mary Magdalene. At the suppression of Monasteries it passed to the Archbishop of York, and is now the central church in his archdeaconry. Few churches can equal it in size, stateliness, and correctness of architectural detail and finish. Style perpendicular or florid, the tower is 80 feet high finished with an embrasured battlement, and pierced. The Parvise over the south porch was formerly inhabited by a Priest or Anchorite. Old John Leland speaking of a Parvise, says they were Studying Chambers and in his time were called "Paradise." Another says that the word Parvise is simply a corruption of Paradise. The Parvise at Thirsk still contains some of its original features. John Foxe, in his "Acts and Monuments," gives a long and curious account of a recluse named Thomas Parkinson, who at about that period inhabited this chamber. The story is too long for insertion. The interior of the church is strikingly impressive, with nothing unsightly to mar the fine effect, the nave being separated from the aisles by lofty piers; the moulding of piers and arches are of exceed-fine character and finish. At the east end of both aisles there were formerly two chantry chapels. The one in the south aisle, dedicated to St. Ann, still remains. The roof of the nave of open woodwork is strikingly bold, the effect of the whole cannot be better described than in the following:— "Surely some part of the effect of a Gothic Cathedral resides in that excess of length over breadth, affording a long perspective, directing the eye towards the altar through an avenue of oft repeated parts, and creating, as it were, an artificial infinite. The roof as well as the walls and arches being so composed as to enhance this effect. Groin beyond groin, boss beyond boss is seen, first of all distinct and clear, then by degrees approaching and touching each other on the perspective, and at last, lost in the complexity of the whole." The chancel contains piscinæ and three fedilia. These seats were formerly used by the officiating priests, the deacon and the sub-deacon, who retired there during the chanting of the hymn, "Gloria in Excelsis." On the North side of the chancel a door gives entrance to a staircase leading down to the crypt. The Communion table is a supposed relic from Byland Abbey. There is a North or "Devil's" door still in use. Of old, through this door the fiends were wont to fly with dismal howl on the baptism and admittance of a child into the church. In these days of high culture the devil seems to have changed his tactics. The door, however, for his exit in to the sunless regions of the north, still remains. How suggestive of the ancient superstitions and beliefs are the situations of these north doorways. The one on the south, the proper entrance, illumined with the sun's rays penetrating the interior and gilding the walls with a subdued halo, whilst the doorway to the north is the exit to the cold cheerless sunless region of darkness and night.

Many striking pictures of the church tower can be obtained, perhaps the most commanding is the one seen from the Park, near the front of the Hall.

The Sutton Road, nearing Thirsk. [*Gilbert Foster*,

Kirkgate, as its name denotes, the street between the church and Market Place, contains interesting bits of architecture, and the curve of the street with the church makes a charming picture. The King's Head at the south end of the street is an ancient hostelry, where old-world things fashioned in the days of our grandmothers are cherished with due reverence, rare prints after Moreland and Reynolds, and antique curios. In a way the interior is a small museum, jealously guarded by Mrs. Wain, the primly kind landlady, who exhibits all the quaint charm of manner and person peculiar to the Fifties of the last century, which Charles Dickens was so apt a master at portraying. The late Mr. B. Smith, a clever local artist, has left behind in his pictures a few glimpses of the old life and notable characters residing in Thirsk during the forties and fifties of the last century. Doubtless manners and customs have vastly changed since then, yet here are still residing several notable men of marked characteristics and superior intelligence, who will leave their mark on the footprints of time, and the old town will be none the poorer for their strenuous lives. For example, there is the Rev. F. Addison, a man of deep knowledge, who, after assiduously labouring in varied fields of thought and research, still adds to the scholarly literature of the district at the age of four score and four, and is as interesting and youth-like in his illuminative conversation as a man just on the threshold of fame with all the glamour and romance of the world still glittering before him.

John Gilbert Baker, the *doyen* of British field-botanists, and a Fellow of the Royal Society, is a Native of the Vale, —he was born at Osmotherley. It was from Thirsk, however, that in 1863 he issued that scarce book (many copies having been destroyed by fire), entitled "North Yorkshire:

J. G. Baker at the Kew Herbarium.

Studies of its Geology, Botany, Climate and Physical Geography," a classic companion to Professor Phillips' "Rivers and Mountains of Yorkshire," of eight years previously. In 1859, Mr. Baker had worthily won his spurs in the literary lists by contributing a masterly summary of the Physical Geology and Botany of Thirsk and its environs, to Grainge's "Vale of Mowbray." This condensed account of the eternal rocks and the mutable forms which grow upon them, and change and pass like men and manners with the years, will not easily be superseded, and as time goes become more and more valuable as a local picture of the past.

Thirsk now suffers commercially for having kept the railway away from its streets—over a mile, but formerly a very pleasant summer walk, through fields and by the site of Thirsk's ancient castle of which neither stick nor stone remains, though no dispute can arise on the point of its existence. Latterly the old footpath through the fields to the station has been tampered with; the hedgerow and trees have been stubbed up; and instead of hedgerow, trees, and flowers, a long row of dark monotonous railings has been substituted, marring the rural beauty of this approach.

Crossing by the footpath, a promenade for the Thirsk folk, we reach Sowerby. Sowerby, a large well-built pleasant village separated from Thirsk only by a few hundred yards, forms an interesting and pretty suburb. The name Sowerby is doubtless a corruption of the word Southby, as distinctive to Norby—the hamlets to the north and south. Yet the Doomsday spelling of the word seems opposed to this derivation: "In Sorebi Orm had two carucates to be taxed land to one plough." In its domestic architecture the village shows several interesting examples, and in the part known as the City there is quite a large town-like aspect about, with pleasant looking villas and old fashioned cottages with large walled-in gardens scented with old English flowers. The church, a very ancient foundation, has been thoroughly restored and greatly altered, and the interior is a peculiar jumble of architecture. The south entrance contains a very fine example of a Norman doorway. The old church was a quaint cob-webbed-looking structure of Norman architecture. The environment specially picturesque,—huge wide-branching elms wave benediction over the churchyard where the grass grows luxuriously above the tombs of mortality—and the wild flowers flourish abundantly and blend in harmonious colours with a scene of loveliness.

The ancient family of Lasscells were Lords of this village for at least five hundred years. In the Frank province of Touraine there is a village named Lassele, from which it is supposed

George Gill, the old Bell man of Thirsk—a well-known local character.
[Drawn by J. Pennington.

this family received their name. One Picot-de-Lascells, a Norman knight from Lassele, took part in the invasion of England by the Conqueror, and fought in the contingent of Alan, Earl of Richmond, for his valor afterwards receiving the Manor of Scruton. Several members of this ancient family are buried in their own chapel of St. Oswald of Sowerby. "In 1446

William Lascells is buried in the chappell of St. Oswald's of Sowerby in the tomb of his ancestors, as others of their family were." On the south corner of the churchyard stands a farm-

WILLIE FLINTOP, Preacher and Fiddler. etc.
[*Drawn by J. Pennington*

house still known as the Manor House. It is an old structure yet not the original one, for there are abundant signs of an important place having stood here, doubtless the ancient Manorial Hall of the Lascells. But this district has yielded much earlier proofs of its occupation than ancient names, manor halls, and church. "Saxty Way" points to a very early road, probably Roman, which crossed west by north from the old ford towards Carlton Miniott, prior to the ordnance survey in 1850. Sufficient of the old rig or raised way had been laid bare for it to be entered on the Ordnance Map, quite three-quarters of a mile. It was doubtless a branch road from the Malton Street leading north-west to Thornton-le-Street and Romanby.

A curious ancient Pack-horse Bridge (World's End Bridge) crosses the Codbeck (very picturesque hereabouts), and from hence the path leads to a tumulus on the east bank of the stream, known as "Pudding Pie Hill," perhaps from its resemblance to a pie or pudding. The hill was opened about fifty years ago, and was found to be a funeral mound and contained skeletons, some in crouched postures. There were funeral urns and other relics found, which were presented by Lady Frankland Russell to the York Museum. For generations the popular legend with children had been, that the hill had been raised by, and was the dwelling-place of, fairy folk; and story ran, that if any person should run nine times round the barrow and then stick a knife into the centre at the top and place their ear there and listen, he or she would hear the fairies conversing in their underground chamber. Until the mound was opened its origin had been a source of conjecture. Even Jefferson, the historian of Thirsk, says it was originally raised on which to build a watch tower for the Mowbray Castle of Thirsk. A most strange and foolish guess when we consider the height of the land immediately behind it. All speculation was set at rest by the excavation under the command of Lady Frankland Russell in 1855. The mound has probably been the burial place of a small band of the first Anglian settlers in this district, say about early in the 6th century. In the centre of the barrow, and 16 feet from the surface, lay the skeleton of a warrior of more than ordinary size. His legs and arms were crossed, his shield had rested on his breast, but the central boss of it only remained with the rivets which had held it to the wood. By his right side lay the handle of a sword, so that he had probably been buried in full dress, with all his arms and accoutrements.

World's End Bridge [*Walter Pattison*]

On the evidence, this warrior and leader of the band who had followed him hither from their homeland beyond the sea, had been first buried and then the huge mound raised over him, and afterwards the members of his clan had been laid to rest on either side and above, and further soil heaped over their bodies. The circumference of the mound at the base being upwards of 160 yards, and the height about 17 feet. The Barrow bears a close resemblance to the one (Howe Hill) at Duggleby on the Wolds, opened some years ago by Mr. Mortimer, and which yielded such a great quantity of relics and human remains.

CHAPTER III.

Notes on the Geology of the Vale of Mowbray, by Rev. F. Addison, M.A. (Dur.)

Geological Secretary of the Thirsk Naturalists' Society.

EACH division of England may have its advantages in some respects, but this vale lays claim to natural scenery and climate. The rocks are chiefly of the later strata and include the various Oolitic series, so called from the Greek word *oon*, an egg. The series is sometimes called the Jurassic, from similar deposits and fossil shells in a French range of hills.

Below the oolitic are the Liassic strata, reaching from the foot of the Hambleton range past Thirsk and occurring again near the river Swale by Topcliffe.

Next is the new red sandstone, showing itself by great deposits of red sand at Sandhutton, and reaching to the Swale.

Although great numbers of flint implements have been found on the surface of the moor above the cliffs, yet no stratum of the chalk formation containing flints has yet been found. Probably they would be purchased from other Celtic tribes in the chalk districts.

Blocks of granite have often been found, chiefly in the district once flooded by the sea. But one large block, about four feet in diameter, and the same in height, is on a hill

The Rev. F. ADDISON. [*Ernest Forbes.*

near the Hambleton rocks; and since it is about four hundred feet above the level of Thirsk, probably it has been drifted to its present locality during one of the ice age periods. The same alteration of the level of the earth shows us that the well known alterations of the sea in periods of vast cycles of time have caused the topmost and other strata of the Hambleton range to be filled with fossil shells and millepores and other remains of former animal life.

It is rather interesting that the most common fossil in these rocks, the Ammonite, though furnished internally with a minute syphon running throughout all its folds, and thus able to escape its enemies by diving at will, should have altogether disappeared in a living form from the earth. But a mollusk (the Belemnite) having its shell internally, and being the precursor of the present formidable Octopus, may have waged continual conflict with the Ammonite, and have caused its extinction.

The small lake, Gormire, has, apparently, been formed by subsidence,—an ancient landslip. The higher land around it is basin shaped, and thus the surplus water from the lake can can only find an outlet in one place where the earth forms a swallow hole. The water traverses beneath White Mare Cliffs and finds an exit in a neighbouring ravine This evidence of passage under the hill reminds one of another passage under the same cliffs, called the Devil's parlour, because of the danger of examining it. These caverns furnish the reason why in an earthquake the sound of the grinding together of the underground rocks is so great.

In reference to the mineral resources of the district it may be said that for building purposes most of the stone is of excellent quality, there is also a good supply of lime and also of bricks from a number of kilns in the lower levels of the district. For the origin of this plentiful supply of clay we must go back to that remote period when the volcanic hills poured out their comminuted ashes and fine dust to be afterwards by rain washed from the moors into the valleys and forming beds of clay. Thus we cannot claim it as indigenous to the district. In like manner the basaltic lava or blue metal (as it is called) has flowed over the river Tees into Cleveland, and from thence is brought to be (on account of its hardness) the sole repairer of our highways. There is often found in it circular nodules of great hardness and having the appearance of shells. These may remind visitors to Hambleton near the top of the Sutton descent, of the same phenomenon in these rocks, and which appear as if cannon balls; they were formed by the action of the aggregation of iron particles.

But the chief interest at the present period is in the presence (in almost all the Hambleton rocks) of ironstone. In the oolitic strata exposed in the cliffs above Gormire and Roulston Scar the evidence is insufficient to prove it rich enough for smelting purposes on the spot, more especially as coal occurs only sparingly in the vale. But for more than one hundred years Thirsk has been known for its medicinal springs, thus affording the evidence that oxide of iron must lie at their source in the hills. At a small stream near the town, called Whitlas Beck the spring causes the stones to be quite red, with deposit of rust oxide of iron. Other springs occur from there to Thornton-le-street. It is probable that a stratum in the Lias formation (which joins the Oolite) may cause these springs and also may have coloured the sand and gravel of the neighbouring fields of a reddish brown. As the Lias is (of course) under the Oolite, the ravines and small valleys at the northern side of the Hambleton Moors may furnish the same ironstone which is there smelted so profitably.

CHAPTER IV.

Interesting Places in the Vale of Mowbray around Thirsk.

'Tis a pleasant walk on leaving Thirsk by the Holms and crossing the fields by the Codbeck side to the pretty rural village of Kilvington, with its quaint cottages and pleasant garden plots, perfumed with the aroma of flowers.

The Church of St Wilfrid, with its high yew-clipped hedge-border standing by the little green at the junction of the roads, is venerable. In fact, everything at this place has an aspect of time-worship. The Church is hoar with many signs of antiquity, and affixed to the vicarage walls so that all who run may read is a notice in large characters, warning those who are liable to walk in their sleep that "Man Traps and Spring Guns are set in these grounds at night."

South Kilvington Church. [*John Pennington.*

Now, as we have already observed, everything the eye rests upon is venerable, but the venerable Rector in spite of his 90 years, is a bit of a wag. The paint on the board threatening man traps is fifty years old, and so the warning is not there now to terrorise trespassers, but simply to show the sign-writers of to-day the quality of the pigment used fifty years ago! The exterior of the church does not show any striking features of architecture. It is a lowly unpretentious fane, appealing to the senses more from its antique hue than any stately splendour. The old weather-worn gravestones lean beneath overhanging branches; and on the walls of the church, standing out against the mould of age, is a brilliant golden creeper and others of more sombre hues, all blending into the delightful harmony and unison of the true rococo. The lovely porch and weatherbeaten belfry complete an unassuming though reverently-impressive scheme.

The flickering rays of sunlight dancing on the sombre hued walls, endue the ancient casket, as it were, with the spirit of life, and express the poetical chequer of shadow and of gleam which marks the Pilgrim's road from the font to the tomb. The interior has undergone complete restoration, yet the charm of age and dignity of the past still delightfully lingers. There is a beautiful and primitive simplicity in complete accord with its surroundings. Its very walls and ancient vessels seem to breathe out messages of history: stored with undying thought, they are witnesses to habits and customs long since passed. Previous to the restoration the access between Nave and Chancel was through a very narrow aperture, yet the abutments and springings were of great bulk and strength, and the ornaments on the arch were very similar in character to those at Kirkdale, indications which go far to prove that this part of the structure was of pre-Norman date.

The Font of black limestone or Purbeck Marble, octagon in shape, is large and unique in character, the nearest approach to it being those of Bolton, Catterick and Kirbymoorside. From the size of the bowl it has evidently been fashioned for baptisms by immersion. On the compartments of the Octagon are sculptured eight shields of arms and quarterings of the Scropes of Upsall, Masham, and Bolton. It is a goodly object of mediæval art work, being right nobly fashioned with moulded stem, and the inscription on the base, in bold characters, reads—

"Dns. Thomas le Scrop et Elizabeth, uxor eius."

From this it appears that the donors were a Lord Thomas Scroop, of Upsall, during the latter half of the 16th century, and his wife. It was first placed in his chapel at Upsall, and afterwards removed to Kilvington. During the Seventies of the last century the church underwent a judicious restoration under the supervision of present venerable rector, The Rev. W. T. Kingsley, who removed much of the incongruous and unsightly. The old stalls on the north side were replaced with those of more artistic work, and the flooring of the church, which was originally of primitive mud (into which the dust of bodies laid beneath ages ago penetrated, and human bones at times protruded), was put into a proper condition of repair. The carving of the organ and the stalls on the north side of chancel are chiefly, if not wholly, the work of the rector himself, whose artistic bent shews forth in wood carving as well as in painting and music. There are two Holy Water receptacles, the one by the south entrance being a fine specimen. Fragments of ancient stained glass still remain in the windows to represent the skill attained in this branch of art centuries ago. The north, or Devil's door, is still intact, and the Bell Gable containing two bells, one inscribed "'Jesus be our speed.' 1695. E.C. C.W."

Inscribed on a memorial slab in the chancel floor are the following:—

MARGARET HEBER	1780.
MARY HEBER	1788.
EDWARD HEBER, M.A.	1795.

Whether the above Edward was a descendant of the Hebers, of which Bishop Heber was a member, we cannot say, but we should imagine there will be some connection.

The village stands on light loamy soil and in a very healthy situation, several instances of longevity being on record here. For instance, "1666, Matthew Carter-de-Thornbrough, Nov. 8th, in the 112th year of his age." Grainge speaks of a person named Bosomworth living in this village with whom he had conversation, then nearly ninety, and who informed him that there was formerly in the parish four houses known as Light Houses, two of which stood on the village green, one in Thornbrough, and one in Upsall, which had to provide lights for the church on festivals, etc. The same person also remembered a woman doing penance during service for calling her neighbour ill names. Perhaps there are few parallels to the scene witnessed here in this quaint churchyard in the spring of 1905, where the person who was being interred was aged 96 and the clergyman who conducted the service had reached his 90th year.

The Rectory, the home of the Rev. W. T. Kingsley (who by the way is a cousin of that celebrated writer, Charles Kingsley), is approached through an intricate bower or arched pathway of greenery. With the exception of one infirmity, that of deafness, the frost of ninety winters has not fallen heavily upon the rector. His figure is still robust and his appearance hale and hearty. His fine dark expressive eyes gleam 'neath a forehead marked with great intelligence, features denoting

The Rev. W. T. Kingsley, Rector of Kilvington. [*Ernest Forbes.*

strength and capability, surrounded by locks hoar with years, a beard as white and silvery as his hair: a venerable patriarch, typifying all the charm of old-world courtliness, as we observed him pass one beautiful Sabbath morning, robed in white surplice, through the chancel door to Service. He was a friend and contemporary of such men as Turner and Ruskin, and his association with such genius must be deeply treasured.

The village is bounded on three sides by the streams Codbeck, Spittlebeck on the north, and Whitlasbeck on the south.

The name of the latter stream is said to be derived from the ghost of a girl (who had been basely murdered by her lover), haunting its precincts,—hence White-lass-beck! This is altogether too fanciful, however. Lass (laddess contracted) is a late middle-English word for girl, and the old map-name for the beck is "Whitlas," just as we have "Yowlas" for a dale in the Howardian tract. Whit meant White doubtless; but the "lass" or "as" as in Yordas is merely the possessive termination, indicative of quality. Why this should be specially the White Beck, unless often whitened with foam or scum-like water below a weir, we do not know; but another little tributary of the Coed-beck to the north is "Spittle-beck," and the next beyond, "Broad-beck"—all of them with the affix indicative of a quality or character, viz.: wooded, narrow, shallow, etc.

In bygone times the highways in this vicinity were often the scene of robberies by violence and the arena of many a brutal fight. Fish hawkers, huxters, and drivers of stage waggons were often waylaid, sorely maltreated, and then robbed of their goods. More than one person has been done to death, and many a cracked crown and broken limb has been received on this length of road. But this is a matter of the past—the road is now as safe for travellers as any highway in the Kingdom.

Game-keepers are well known to be the modern ogres of trespassers, tho' the points of Law in that matter are well known to be (1) being in pursuit of game, and (2) the doers of assessable damage. As illustrating the way in which your simple herbalist may turn the sharp corner of a keeper's wrath, a good story is told of Mr. Kingsley worth repeating here. He was one day, soon after his acceptance of the living of Kilvington, botanizing in some preserved woodland, and was tracked down and surprised by an angry keeper just as he was in the act of sampling a tiny growth. The rector, even at this period,

CRIBBIE DODGSON, an old Thirsk character, Ratcatcher and Sheep Washer, etc.
(*Drawn by John Pennington.*)

was afflicted with a slight deafness which has grown more acute with increasing years. "What are yo' doing here?" shouted the keeper, "don't you know you're trespassing?" "Prunus Avium," replied the rector, placing his hand to his ear—using the latin equivalent of the wilding he had gathered. "What d' ye say?" shouted the keeper again repeating his charge of trespass. "Wild Cherry," replied the rector, now using the common English name of the plant. "What?" again vociferated the infuriated warden of the woodland, "you're trespassing, I say." "I'm going to graft it on a stock in my garden," rejoined the rector, and suiting the action to the word he slung the cutting over his shoulder and departed in peace! The keeper was for once thoroughly taken aback and sorely puzzled. The trespasser had neither dog nor gun and so he was permitted to get away "scot-free." Probably a light was dawning on his mind, yet the story has its moral—"Answer not a fool according to his folly,"—the gentle answer does at times turn away the wrath even of the man of velveteen.

North Kilvington, a scattered township, lies between Spittlebeck and the Codbeck. It lies in the Wapontake of Allertonshire. To the left of the highway after crossing the Spittlebeck, will be seen a moated site of considerable extent. Here within this enclosure formerly stood one of the Halls of the Meynells, an influential family of great antiquity, who came in with the Conqueror, fought at Hastings, and having their name inscribed amongst the great warriors on the scroll of Battle Abbey. They were staunch Catholics generation after generation and kept up an unswerving devotion in the old faith, consequently the family suffered for their religion. During the Act of the disarming of the Papists, we find stated that Roger Meynell, Esq., of Kilvington Hall had his "Bay Stone Horse" seized and adjudged to be forfeited to their Majesties use, the horse to be delivered up to the High Sheriff to be disposed of according to law. Verily, what injustice has been done in the name of religion.

The disused chapel (locally known as the Catholic Mass) still remains, but the Old Hall has long been demolished, and the stones carted away and used again in other buildings. Still the place breathes of antiquity, and those who run can plainly read history here. Spittlebeck, which runs past, is said to take its name from a lazar-house which formerly stood near the site of the Old Hall, where it joins the Cod, but the word "Spittle" in old English speech likewise meant anything narrow and tonguelike, a prong, a spade's depth, twelve inches, as well as saliva.

A Meadow Scene, with a reach of the Codbeck, at South Kilvington.
{*Gilbert Foster.*

In the early years of the Victorian Reign, a ghost haunted the precincts of Barrowby Bridge, and the nerves of the people became so shattered by its nocturnal wanderings that a gentleman named Consett left by will two pounds yearly to be paid out of Brawith Park estate to the priest of North Kilvington for the laying of the restless spirit. Once annually the good man repaired to the bridge and "exorcised" the unhappy spirit by laying it low for the forthcoming year, and so for the small sum of two pounds, the "Will-o'-the-Wisp" spirit was bottled up in the earth. Regularly the money was paid until 1866, when the North Kilvington Roman Catholic Chapel was closed and the priest removed. What became of the ghost and the sterling article since that date local gossip does not state.

The modern Hall built by Thomas Meynell in 1815, possesses no striking features—but the landscape around it, embracing the whole range of the Hambleton and the far-reaching Vale of Mowbray, affords delightful vistas for the eye to roam over.

About a mile and a quarter west from North Kilvington as the crow flies, stands the village of Thornton-le-Street, half-circled by the truant windings of the Codbeck. The full name of the village is very significant of its history and early owners. The prefix Tor, or Thor, denotes its Saxon occupier in pre-Norman days, and Ton, or Toune, the hedged-in enclosure of the settlement by the road or street where the Romans of old, with measured and stately tramp, continually passed north and south. Portions of this line of street can still be traced in the vicinity. The Old Manor Hall, with quaint gables and old chimneys, standing in the meadow between Codbeck and the road, add pleasing features to the landscape. Connected with the Old Hall, known as "Wood End," is the sad story of the betrayal and arrest (A.D. 1641) of that good man the old missionary priest, John Lockwood, by a base hound, one Cuthbert Langda'e, of Thirsk, who heaped all manner of hardships and indignities on the aged prisoner during their journey from here to York. To his inhuman captor when he had delivered him safely into the hands of the jailor at York, Lockwood spoke as follows: "Hark you, Cuthbert, I have given you a great deal of trouble in bringing me to this happy place, here, take this angel for your pains, and the Lord be with you." Sad to relate the old missionray was executed, and his head and quarters were exposed on the bars of the old city. Such inhuman deeds were perpetrated in the name of religion in the "good old days" of which we are wont to to sing without reflecting.

Old Manor House, Thornton le-Street.   [*J. Pennington.*

The present Hall stands in the centre of a large and well cultivated park, where nature and art combine to form scenes of exceeding loveliness. The Hall, one of the seats of the Earl of Cathcart, is modern, and contains very choice paintings. The Church, dedicated to St. Leonard (anciently a separate parish held with North Otterington, under the patronage of the Bishops of Durham) contains the nave and chancel, and dates from the 12th Century, which the circular font and north doorway proclaim. There is an ancient stoup in the south wall of chancel; the floor is also below the level of the ground, and other features denote its early foundation. The structure has now undergone thorough and judicious restoration There are two other Thorntons (Thornton-le-Moor and Le-Beans) in this district, but these will come in with the account of Northallerton in a later chapter.

Returning Thirskwards, and about two miles north from that place, situated in a dark wood between the two roads leading to Thornton and Kirby Wiske on the lands known as "Dowlands," is a moated site. Here in pre-Reformation times stood Arden Nunnery. Little is known respecting its history; it is said to have been demolished during the suppression of monasteries in the reign of Henry VIII. In 1150 Peter de Hoton gave three carucates of land to this priory, along with the site on which it was built; and a Roger de Hoton gave to this priory two bovates of land near Thirsk, A.D.1251 The Hotons, or Huttons, dwelt at Sand Hutton, and appear to have been great benefactors to this nunnery. In the 13th century a William de Carlton was a benefactor. Half-a-mile further south, near to Dowland's cottage, and not far from the lane formerly known as Gallows Lane, there is a series of mounds about thirty in number having the appearance of graves and locally known as such. Tradition says the inmates of the adjoining nunnery were interred here, but the graves, if they be such, are of more recent date. Besides, how can we suppose that the nuns would be interred so far beyond the pale of the nunnery without any sign to mark their resting place. The Gallows of Thirsk stood not far from this spot, and the more credible supposition is that they are the graves of malefactors from the gallows-tree adjoining.

Sandhutton Cross [*R. Rolwell.*

From here we strike the ancient footpath which runs over the fields and past hedgerow from Thirsk to Sandhutton, a very pleasant path which crosses the railway just to the north of Thirsk Station, and thence over the red-sandstone sub-soil to Hutton. In the hedgerow corner of a field, where the path crosses a deep dyke, is an ancient stone pillar, and let into a larger stone at its base is a morticed socket. Locally this stone is known as Sandhutton Cross, doubtless so placed in olden times to mark boundaries, for here the townships of Thirsk, Carlton Miniott, and Sandhutton meet. Grainge says

"The busy tongue of tradition, however, reports that at some unknown period the town of Thirsk was ravaged by the plague, and the Market was held in the open fields here, and this cross was erected at that date."

Less than a mile from hence we reach Sandhutton. Its prefix Sand, which distinguishes it from the many other Huttons, also denotes that it stands on the bed of new red sandstone strata, which reaches from hence to the Swale. The De Hotons, a family of considerable note were the sub-lords of the Mowbrays at this manor in mediæval times. The village is cleanly, well built, and pleasantly situated amid healthy surroundings, which, added to the quiet and even tenor of their lives, greatly conduces to the longevity of the inhabitants. Grainge records the burial of six inhabitants whose ages range from 90 to 100 years—a sure proof of healthy and agreeable environment. There was a very curious bye-law relating to the keeping of geese at this village, "That every husbandman shall only keep two geese, and every Girseman (goose-cotter) one, upon paine to forfeit 5/-." The new Church was built in 1878 on the site of a small antique structure which was remarkable for the primitive simplicity of its form and the extreme rudeness of its masonry, consisting only of nave, chancel, and a small turret containing one bell.

A mile north of Sandhutton is Breckenbrough Hall. The Castle, which formerly stood here, was long a seat of the Lascelles of Sowerby, etc. Camden says of this place, "Brekenbak, belonging to the truly ancient and famous family of Lascelles."

Carlton Miniott is a small pleasant-looking red brick and tiled village, situated in fat corn land on the highway leading from Thirsk to Ripon, and some two miles from the former. A Walter de Carleton held three carucates of land here during

Carlton Miniott. (Tom Fox.

the reign of Edward the First, and his descendents continued to reside about the district for generations later. The appellation Miniott given to this Carlton to distinguish it from others, was bestowed upon it by a family of that name, one John Miniott, a person of note, who was a property-owner here in the 14th century. The antique and primitive-looking ivy-covered Church, of simple and rude construction, has now given place to a neat well-built structure.

About a mile from Carlton we reach the crossing of roads, where stands the inn called "Busby Stoop." The origin of the name is as follows:—Ten minutes' walk west of Kirby Wiske stands a farmhouse bearing the name of Dannoty Hall, purchased late in the 17th century by one Daniel Auty, who had formerly been a Leeds Clothier, and who, waxing rich very rapidly, was generally suspected of illegal doings. He is said to have been an expert coiner, having secret rooms fitted up at the lonely house for that purpose In due course it came about that a man named Busby courted and married his daughter, and at length was admitted a trusted partner in the illegal business. A quarrel arose between the two men both greedy for ill-gotten wealth. Busby murdered Auty, his father-in-law, for which crime he was tried, convicted, executed and hung in chains on the gibbet at the Cross Roads. His bones were rattling in the chains just over two hundred years ago. Not a relic of the chains, gibbet, or stoop remains, yet the memory of the crime and the name of the evil doer (Busby) will doubtless live on through the centuries, a warning to those criminally disposed.

Ralph Thoresby, the antiquary of Leeds, in passing this way, May 17th, 1703, says:—

"Along the banks of the Swale are the very pleasant gardens of Sir William Robinson, lately Lord Mayor of York, but a few miles after, a more doleful object of Mr. Busby hanging in chains for the murder of his father in-law, Daniel Auty, formerly a Leeds Clothier, who having too little honesty to balance his skill in engraving, etc., was generally suspected for coining and other indirect ways of attaining that estate which was the occasion of his death, even within sight of his own house."

A short tramp west is Skipton-on-Swale, a resort of fishermen from the busy centres. Here the Swale rolls sluggishly onward through meadows and rich arable land we wander over fields and along lanes perfumed with clover, and past hedgerows laden with honeysuckle and flecked with wild roses and other flowers. At Skipton we cross the river and turn towards Baldersby. One notable picture of this river now flowing through the lowlands, is to be seen from a curve of the banks near Catton, with the fine steeple of St. James, Baldersby, in the middle distance We pass through this village, extremely rural like its neighbours.

"By side of the Sons of Odin thow shalt fashion a tale to be told
In the Hall of the happy Baldur, nor there shall the tale grow old."

Baldersby bespeaks a Danish founding, Baldur, the great War God of the Norse. Midway between Baldersby and Rainton, we pass St James' Green. Here stands the beautiful Church of St. James, its spire seeking communion with the clouds, thus being a notable landmark for miles around. Adjoining the Church are several neat cottages of old English style of architecture, and with the magnificent Church form a striking feature of this district. Here during the fifties of the last century dwelt a vicar's churchwarden, who, when angry, was much given to profane swearing. One day the reverend vicar called to reprove and excommunicate him. On being accused of the offence, he exclaimed:—"Me swear; me swear; now't o't sort, sir! Whoever could mak up sik a tale? I knaw! Why it's that auld Willy Robinson, damn him!"

A good mile further, by hedgerowed footpath and over fields of waving corn brings us to the pleasant village of Rainton. Here was a Chapel in 1280, then in the patronage of Thomas, son of Allan de Arches. It afterwards became attached to the Abbey of Fountains. It long ago fell to ruin, but its memory is still retained in a field called Chapel Flatts. The foundations of the mediæval hall adjoining it, can still be traced. A spear head, stone battle axe and flint arrows and other relics of far-past occupation have been found near this village.

There is a pretty little green where the geese march with stately mien to hold gooselike conclave, and where the children romp and shout; further down the street is a butcher's cart, from which the owner is showing to best advantage a small joint of meat to a thrifty cottager; the postman is on his daily round and the village shopkeeper is discussing in his mind the business of a stranger who has just entered the village. Such were the figures which lent life and animation to Rainton on our visit. Some fifty-five years ago, there was an old road-mender living in Rainton named Fawcett; he was a crusty, mendacious old person, much addicted to stealing hedgestakes. There was a farmer in this village who kept his hedges in beautiful order, and was often annoyed at finding gaps in them by the roadsides, so two of his sons devised a plan to detect and punish the offender. Having first bored a hole in a tempting stake and filled it up with gunpowder, they plugged the hole, and replanted the stake loosely in the hedgerow. Next evening it was gone, and the boys hid themselves near old Fawcett's cottage to see and hear the result, probably peeping through the keyhole. The fire was lit, the kettle put on to boil, and the solitary man sat down to warm himself until tea should be ready. Suddenly there was a loud explosion, a startled cry, and darkness. The boys ran away, and were much surprised to hear nothing about the matter next day. The curious part of the story is, that the facts only came to light about thirty-five years later. A sister of the boys, talking over village stories with a lady who left Rainton thirty years ago, told of her brothers' pranks. "Ah," said the lady "that explains the mystery! Fawcett did speak of the explosion, but with bated breath; he thought it was the work of fairies, who came down the chimney, blew 't'kettle clean oop, and steeaked t'door.' He was very much alarmed, and no doubt conscience reproved him. He never suspected a gunpowder plot, and we never guessed anything either. I wonder you never heard about old Fawcett and the fairies," added the lady, "for all the village heard of it at the time." The fairies taught old Fawcett such a lesson that it completely cured his purloining propensities.

The old Methodist Chapel, built in 1811, gave place to a new one in 1869. It is now, or was lately, the residence of the village shoe-maker, a man of might and a worthy son of St. Crispin. Many a motley assembly has been gathered together within those walls, and many eccentric characters, yet faithful preachers, have poured forth an earnest appeal from that little pulpit. There was the old man who drove the miller's cart from Boroughbridge and delivered sacks of flour to the surrounding villages. He was preaching one Sabbath of the rich man who pulled down his barns to build greater. Now the family pew of Mr. Stevinson before alluded to, was on one side of the pulpit, so, pointing to this gentleman by way of giving greater force to his argument, he said, "And what would ye say of Mr. Stevinson if he was to do sike a thing? Wouldn't ye say he was a big feeal?" There was a gallery in that little chapel, and in the front pew in the gallery used to sit a farmer, Anthony Blanchard by name.

When he thought the preacher too long-winded, and dinner time approached, he would draw his large watch out of his "fob" and hook the chain upon a nail fixed inside the pew for the purpose. Thus the watch hung on the edge of the gallery, and the preacher's attention was drawn to the fact that it was time to "wind up." On our last visit we missed good old Richard Wray; he had departed to his long rest. For fifty years he had been a faithful shepherd to the Stevinsons.

Ruined Cross, Cundall. [*A. Vivian.*

Seen from the rise just out of the village on the Dishforth road, Rainton forms a very interesting picture. The group of old farm buildings on the left, with mullions and quaint-gabled roofs and antique columnary, are not the work of to-day but of generations gone by. The tall spire of St. James' shews forth finely in the middle distance above fields of ripening corn, and the Hambleton Range in the background looms faintly in the blue grey atmosphere.

Dishforth, a mile and a half south, is a village possessing some very well-built Jacobean homesteads, an Old Manor House, and two curiously-gabled Inns. The Church, which has been thoroughly restored, rests on an ancient foundation. An old sepulchral slab and holy water stoup speak of bygone days. The roads at the opposite ends of the village lead to Borobridge and Ripon. Leaving these dusty highways we take green lane and field path, and in three miles we reach the quiet pretty village of Cundall, an interesting spot with humble cottages perfumed with old English plants, a new Mansion and Hall, and a new Church, resting in the lap of pleasant woodland. The church stands on a slight eminence, and the graveyard contains one hoary relic pointing to the early days of Christianity at this place—a Runic or Saxon cross, with carving of interlaced work on all sides, and grotesque figures. It was found built into the church-wall at the Restoration; it is now in the church-yard. It is a relic left from the days of our earliest history, and greater care should be taken in its preservation.

Between Cundall and Topcliffe the country is pleasantly diversified, undulating, and intersected with wave-like hill crests rising from the banks of the Swale. It was a winter's afternoon when the writer last walked this way; the sky was all aglow with a golden and crimson flush, and old Swale caught up the colour and shone with crimson brilliance amid white snow fields, a picture of strange contrast. Looking westwards towards Ripon, receded a far-reaching landscape, robed in a mantle of white; heavy purple clouds (whose outer edges were fringed with burnished gold), overhanging the middle distance. The trees stood forth weird and skeleton-like (revealing at one moment the beautiful symmetry of proportion, the next shadowy and unreal) between the white shroud of snowfields and the deep vermilion and golden hue of the sky background, whose upper edges gradually changed into rich pearl and silver grey. Except for the familiar objects, trees and hedgerows, the scene was truly oriental in its strange charm and rich phantasy of colour.

To the right, between Cundall and Aisenby, is a series of Leckby's—Leckby Farm, Leckby Pallace, and Leckby Grange,

Like Aisenby and Baldersby, standing on the west bank of the Swale, their origin in a Danish settlement is bespoken in the "by." The Swale in this part of its course—"The Lakeby Country"—flows in a rather deeply troughed serpentine bed, with few fords or syrtes, by reason of the ridged reef-like barriers of "red-sand" rock which hereabouts cross the Vale obliquely, and on the west bank at Leckby (that is, lake-by, a place of water) we have a good example of a steep bluff, eroded by water in past ages, and of a red colour, which contrasts finely with the green vegetation around it. Between Cundall and Aisenby are a number of "by's," all in association with water, Lakeby (as it used to be spelt—though housewives "leck" clothes now, i.e., sprinkle water on them before ironing) Leckby "Villa," Leckby "Pallace" (a storehouse, a paled-in place, not a bishop's mansion), and Lakeby "Car" (car, a watery place, a marsh). These spots are of no great interest from the historic outlook, but the unusual conformation of the land into slacks, and very barrow-like knolls and reefs, tree-crowned, can hardly fail to strike the observer with a subtle suggestion of old-world comings and goings, campings and buryings, altho' I believe none of the barrow-like mounds have been dug into. Leckby Car is a dreary "pocket" of wet peaty boggy land, and watery thicket, contracting in its area year by year from reclamatory afforestation, but has for a century been the botanist's paradise—perhaps the richest spot in Yorkshire for rare and singular wild flowers. Here grows, or grew (according to Henry Baines and Arnold Lees, the floralists) the fly-catching and 'eating' Long-leaved Sundew, the pore-leaved Swamp Arrow-rush, the deadly Cowbane *Cicuta*, the Bog-pimpernal, and the tassel-crowned Loristripe (*Lysimachia thyrsiflora*); whilst near the "pallace," now a farmstead, in the hedge, the Dane's-Elder yet flourishes for a silent witness to the truth of the place-name story of the Northmen's early usurpation of the soil.

Aisenby, is a picturesque village situated on the high bank of the Swale half a mile from Topcliffe. Dr. Carter Mitchell tells of a curious character living at this place during the first half of the last century. A clever strong-willed woman, well versed in necromancy—the dead magic art—crafty and subtle withal. She was of tall commanding prescence, a sort of enchantress in appearance except for a fearsome squint, which to some extent marred her staid majesty, although it added to her visage that darksome spell of awe as a priestess of forbidden spells. By her neighbours she was looked upon as a witch, for it was the period when witches and hags, etc., were wont to ride on dark dree nights through the air on broomsticks, and so the people were ever careful not to give her any cause for offence. Some there were who had unwittingly angered her and felt the influence of her evil eye and invisible power. A baleful glance from her was a sure portent of calamity in some form or another. Cattle alive and hearty in the morning were in the evening struck with sudden disease or even dead. Even the blight on the potato crop was ascribed to her evil influence of overlooking the field. Such, we are told, was Pegg Lumley, of Aisenby.

CHAPTER V.

Topcliffe

Topcliffe.

SOME four miles (and long ones) out of Thirsk, S.W., standing forth conspicuously on the high commanding banks of the Swale is Topcliffe, for centuries a famous seat of the Percies, and a resting place of the Kings of England, and even their destiny has been worked out here on more than one occasion. Time was when Topcliffe was a place of even more regal grandeur. Far away back into the dawning of our history, it has evidently been a dwelling-place of Kings and Princes, and even the High Priest of Druidism has performed his rites here. Footsteps of the old British race are strongly engraven in the soil hereabouts, even in the dedication of the church to the good apostle of Iona (St. Columba) we obtain further proof of it. A mile down the river is Maiden Bower, from "Mai" great, and "don" a fortified hill. Two bowshots further down the Swale is Elmire, whose ancient name was Elmet-mere—the origin of the first word being like that of the British Kingdom of Elmet—Elmtree (or Sacred, for the elm was a witch tree), Holyland. Near by the latter spot is Crakehill; the prefix Crake (Crag) is British for Rock. Aisenby, a suburb of Topcliffe, is said to mean the residence of the Gods. Half a mile up stream, and within the old park of the Percies, is Kibber Hill, the Kil-baer of the Celt—a chapel farmstead—the first hallowed spot where the hermit missionary established his lonely cell, and from whence spread abroad the blessings of Christianity. Just across the river is Baldersby, where in the days of the Sea-kings, the Norse God Balder was enthroned.

Topcliffe Church from the Small. [*4. Vivian*

To closely study the antique mould of Mowbray Vale, the folk lore and the curious temper traits of its inhabitants, the student should begin at Topcliffe, for the place has a paramount place in Yorkshire history and a veritable plethora of Celtic and Celto-Norse associations. One of the great and earliest feats of Conversion was here or hereabouts performed. About 620, and after the marriage of Edwin, King of Northumbria to Ethelburgha, a Christian Princess and daughter of Ethelbert,

King of Kent, St. Paulinus, who usually followed the Court preaching and baptising converts, surpassed himself and brought about the foundation of a Bishop's See at York. His crowd of converts became so great that in one day Paulinus is said to have baptized no fewer than twelve thousand in the river Swale. To reward these great services, Edwin erected the See of York, and is even said to have obtained from Pope Honorius an archbishop's pall for the zealous Paulinus. Be that, however, as it may, and without selecting Topcliffe as the actual scene of the baptisms, we maintain that no more likely place has been discovered.

If Topcliffe were notable for housing the Percies only, that alone would be sufficient to render it for ever famous. For eight hundred years at least and so on until our time, a Percy held land " in right of descent " from a Percy who obtained it by right of conquest from King William in 1066. Whether or not it may be difficult to prove the unbroken descent and extraction of the Percies from Rollo (the " devil-dare " sea-king of the ninth century, who ravaged the English coast and finally settled in Normandy) we know not, and perhaps no one can tell from whence they sprang—Goth, Teuton, or Scandinavian. Still it is generally understood that the first known scion of the family was a sea-king named Manifred, who ravaged Neustria; this was about 866, and this old ravager's son, Geoffrey, was a daring warrior in the army of Rollo during the Conquest and settling down of the Vikings in Normandy towards the end of the ninth century. The village of Percie (which still exists) seems to have fallen to his share of spoil, and from that circumstance the great house of Percies have received their name. With the exception perhaps of the Royal Family, no house can show a direct extraction from Saxon Royalty. The nearest approach

Alnwick, the Princely seat of the Percies. [*F. Dean.*

in this proud line of descent is that of the great house of the Percies. Coming to the real facts of history, the Percies trace their lineage from a Knight of that name who followed the banner of William of Normandie to the Conquest and spoilation of England in 1066—a trusty and valiant soldier, William de Percie by name, whose daring prowess and doughty deeds were fully recognised by the Conqueror, otherwise he would never have rewarded him so munificently, since William the Norman was not the man to requite a laggard in arms. In Lincolnshire the Percies obtained 32 Lordships, and 86 fell to his share in Yorkshire, amongst which, Topcliffe and Spofforth were their chief seats for centuries.

For other services, which history does not state, Hugh Lupus, the fierce Earl of Chester, the Conqueror's nephew, gave the Percies the Lordship of Whitby and a goodly stretch of adjacent territory, and to banish the uneasy qualms of conscience (which often come to those who suddenly grow rich on the burdens and misery of others) he rebuilt the Abbey of Whitby which had been destroyed by a Pagan sea-king, an ancestor of his, during one of the Danish invasions; and further to ease his conscience he married the Lady Emma de Port, of Saxon lineage, a daughter and heiress of Gospatrick the Earl. As an old writer quaintly puts it:—"Having lieged her possessions, he wedded hyr that was verye heire to them." He bore the cognomen of "Algernon William the Whiskered." After having gained a plentitude of this world's goods he followed the banner of Peter the Hermit to the Holy Land, where he died. His heart was enclosed in a casket according to the custom of the times, and eventually found a resting place under the high altar in Whitby Abbey. This man was the true founder of the great house of Percie, and stamped the impress of this name so deeply in the English soil that it has lasted all through the centuries. What a magnificent history the house can point to! Strange vicissitudes of fortune, and scenic episodes of startling grandeur; probably no other family has offered such a stout resistance to regal tyranny, or stood so valiantly always in the breach to stem the tide of invasion. They were ever in the front ranks of Freedom, and the name of Richard de Percy is amongst the illustrious twenty-five steel-clad barons who assembled at Runnymede and demanded from King John the granting and signing of the "Magna Charter"— the great charter and foundation of English Liberty.

Having briefly reviewed the opening chapter and rise of the Percies, the greatest uncrowned family in Europe, let us wander down the old green lane to view the site of their former stronghold below Topcliffe, where tyrants have been made to tremble and Kings "weighed in the balance and found wanting." The lane, a little over half a mile in length, ends at the great moat, the long line of entrenchment surrounding this Percy stronghold. There are no ruins or the slightest sign of stone-work, and in this way the site bears a close resemblance to the Mowbray Castle at Thirsk. Doubtless the structure was of wood with a few courses of rubble or stone as a base. On the north the site is doubly moated, whilst on the other two sides the rivers Codbeck and Swale converge until their waters unite, which circumstance, added to the entrenchment running along the edge of the Scarp facing the rivers, forms a natural barrier to this place. The Plan fully demonstrates the natural and artificial defences of the site. A conical mound on the extreme west of the quadrangular enclosure bears the name of Manor Hill, and here within the inner moated area stood Cock Lodge, the home of the Percies, to which the broken surface of the ground bears witness.

It has been said that this house of the Percies stood on the site of a Roman camp. It may have been so, but on that question we may reasonably have our doubts. Certainly this apex of land where the two rivers meet is the most advantageous spot for a camp or castle in the district, and has evidently been used successively as such by different people since the time of the Brigantes. Between the two trenches stretching from the Swale to Codbeck and which cut off communication on the north, was the Home Park, a stretch of several acres; outside of this boundary was the Old Park of the Percies, spreading over hundreds of acres, which Leland says "was six or seven miles in cumpace and well woodid."

Pennon of Sir Henry Percy, captured by Douglas in single combat with Hotspur before the walls of Newcastle.

What strange and stirring scenes this (now lonely) situation has witnessed since the Percies took possession eight centuries ago. Here in the old days was to be heard the jingle of steel-linked armour and the clang and rattle of mail; the champing and pawing of restive war steeds, all gaily caparisoned for war or pleasure. And down the dim distance of the past one can discern gorgeous pageants and tilts and tournaments, Knights and Ladies coming forth to grace the court of the Percies. Other sounds borne to us on the wings of time is the harsh grating of the drawbridge, the sound of horns, the rattle of pikes and twang of the bow and noise accompanying the march of a multitude of horsemen and footmen to the many battlefields for where there was fighting, sure enough a Percy was to be found. Fearful scenes have been enacted here. Time was when this spot resounded with hoarse cries of a frenzied mob on murder bent, and ruthless deeds were done to be mourned over in the days which followed.

To-day the place is a sanctuary of peace; the turbulence attending the court of a powerful Baron of olden times has passed from the place for ever. Fleecy clouds sail across the sky, flinging their shadows over the greensward. The undulating landscape around, though not far reaching, is one to be admired. The Swale wends past deep banks of sandstone, and woodland brake on one side and on the other bright green meadows, and in the distance the church tower can be seen rising above the village roofs and trees. The sounds borne to our reverie to-day are those of moving water, the warbling of birds, the wail of pewits, the flight of a startled partridge, and the browsing of cattle besides us. Yet, as we have already observed, this spot was a resting place of kings, and the abode of men at the sound of whose name kings have trembled.

In the campaigns against Scotland the Edwards frequently rested here, and the splendour of life at Topcliffe was revived during that war. In Edward the Second's peregrinations in Yorkshire after the execution of Gaveston and the death of Henry de Percy at Bannockburn, Topcliffe bore its share in the vicissitudes of the time. In 1315 Topclive and Spofford with their parks were placed under the supervision of one Robert Dammony a piece of gross and pernicious favouritism. The downfall of the Dammony's occurred within a few years, when Topcliffe was returned to the young Henry Percy, and again became a place where the history of England was made. Perhaps the glory of Topcliffe rose to its greatest height during the lifetime of the celebrated Harry Hotspur, who was often at Topcliffe when not in battle harness pricking against the Scots. Hotspur, so named from his frequent "pricking,"—one who was never at rest if there was any fighting to be done. The above appellation was bestowed by the Scots:—"Bloody with spurring, fiery red with speed." His most celebrated encounters were those against Douglas before the walls of Newcastle, and at Otterburn and at Hambledon. At the latter battle he captured the doughty Douglas. He was slain at the battle of Shrewsbury in conflict with the King. It was the gallant Sir Philip Sydney who said:— "I never heard the old song of Percy and Douglas that I found not my heart moved more than with a trumpet."

Leland thus describes Topcliffe:—"It is an uplandish town whose pretty manor-place stands on a hill (the Maiden Bower) about half a mile from the town, almost on the ripe of Swale." This was "the mansion of their very ancient and noble family," in ruins for many years, but how long we do not know. We are, however, assured that in 1538 it was "a pretty manor-place." In 949 the states of Northumberland assembled here and took the oath of allegiance to Edred, the West Saxon, the first monarch styled King of Britain. Soon after the Norman Conquest, William de Percy had the manor wherein were 26 carucates of land at geld, 35 villanes and 14 borders—a state of agricultural development and population belonging to importance and great antiquity. The whole manor was three miles long and two broad, and taxed at £5. The domain of Knaresbrough, forest and liberty, was at the same time taxed at £6, though of ten times the extent—thus proving the ancient value of Topcliffe.

Maiden Bower.

Wedged into the apex of land, as it were, between the meet of rivers and site of the Percy stronghold, are the remains of a much earlier encampment, circular in shape and evidently of British construction. Adjoining this position is a high circular mound of artificial construction with a series of seven terraces

Tournaments. [Drawn by Frank Dean.

running spirally around it. The hill does not appear to have been subjected to any excavating-antiquary attempting to set at rest the secret of its origin. Yet its size and shape does not coincide with the ordinary sepulchral tumuli. Around it, and even on the mound are a number of very old wych (elm) trees, the successors of a more ancient grove, in its old age when the first Percy rode on to the scene. Again, are the present trees the offspring and remnant of a deep shady grove or bower of huge trees, amid whose shady recesses the Druids worshipped, and has this relic of pre-historic days been constructed for purposes of fire worship? The God of Fire—Bel or Baal, the Beltiane Fire, the cult of fire worship—lingered in this country far into the days of Christianity. Fire worship was introduced into this island from the East by the Phœnicians, and the word Baal still linger in many of our old Yorkshire place-names, a survival in the word only of the ancient Canaanitish worship. Baal-Bec, Isaac Taylor says, was the chief seat of the worship of Baal, the ruins of whose temple, with its substructure of colossal stones, is still one of the wonders of the world. The artificial hill is known by the name of Maiden (or Maidon) Bower. There are several pre-historic sites bearing the name Maiden Bower or Castle, three being within the watershed of the Swale. The question arises, what is the proper explanation of the word Maiden and Bower? The antiquity of the mound is in its name, but for what special object the hill was constructed —a temple for fire or sun worship, or the deeper subtleties of Druidism, a place of assembly where the laws were discussed, the moot or meeting place—is only guess work. The place is a mystery. The Celtic word Merddin seems to have some connection with one of the earliest names of this island, "Clás Merdin," the Garden of Merdin. The word Bower is said to be from the Celtic "Bwr," an enclosure. Again, Maiden Bower is a combination of the Celtic "Meol" (a round-tipped hill), and

THE VALE OF MOWBRAY.

the Norse "Baer" or "Bear" (a farmstead). Doubtless the name means a great fortified hill from the Celtic "Mai" (great), and "dun" or "don" (a hill)—hence Maidon. Although the hill itself is not fortified strongly, in the old days a ditch has certainly run round it, and on the north and west it is defended by the Celtic stronghold, whilst within the apex of the rivers where it stands it could only be approached by crossing the water. Its situation can easily be understood by the annexed plan.

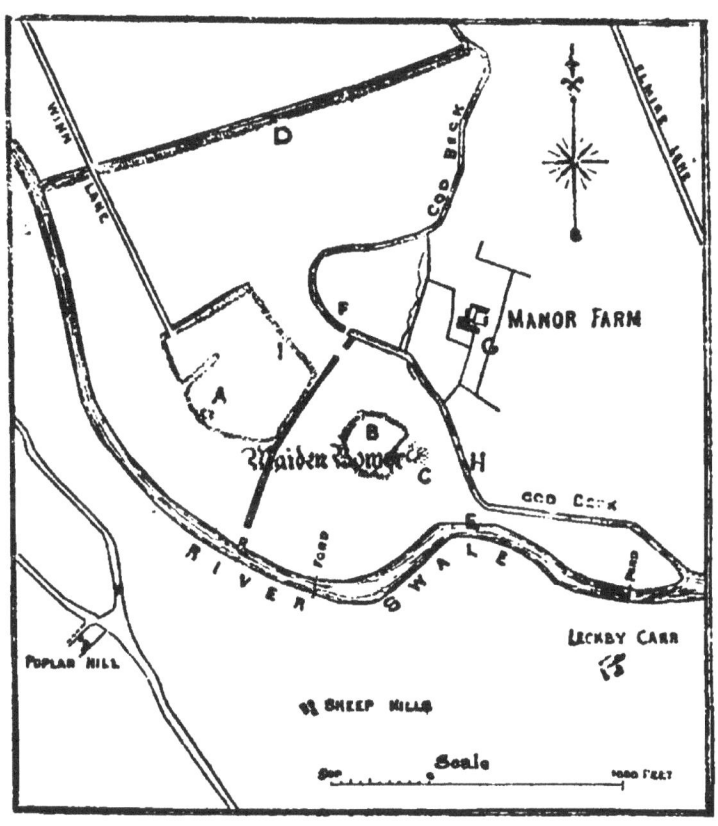

(*Barker Topcliffe*)
A—Site of Cock Lodge (supposed Roman Camp). B—British Camp. C—Maiden Bower. D—Outer Ditch. E—British Remains found. F—Bridge. G—Farm. H—Remains of Old Bridge.

A quantity of flint flakes were discovered by Dr. Carter Mitchell near the Swale, shewing that the manufacture of flint (brought here from distant parts) had been carried on at this place.

Immediately over the Codbeck and on the high opposite bank stands the Manor Farm, the ancient Manor of the Percies. The old manor farmhouse which stood here in the time of the later Percies has long ago given place to a new house, in turn showing signs of age. Within its walls are to be seen relics of the earlier structure, and in the orchard, a little nearer the river, the site of the old manor house is very distinct. Even this house was formerly protected by a trench, cutting off its connection on the north.

The village of Topcliffe is pleasantly situated on the high east bank of the Swale which curves so picturesquely past. It is a place of great antiquity—vestiges of tumulus and other evidences of very early occupation explain this. The church stands forth conspicuously on the highest point of land, and near it in pre-Norman times a fortress has stood. In Mr. Barker's garden there is a moated site,—tradition says, that within it formerly was the Moot Hall, the meeting place for discussing the town business, or where matters of importance were mooted. The old Tolbooth still remains, its upper rooms being reached by a flight of stone steps from the outside; and the natives still point to a table in this room, on which they aver a king's ransom was paid, doubtless referring to the transaction the payment of a stipulated sum by the English Commissioner to the Scottish army who lay in the vicinity, and were holding the King a prisoner, and who on receiving half of the sum agreed upon they should hand over the hapless monarch (King Charles) into the keeping of the English and return to their own country. From the above occurrence it has been facetiously observed "That Topcliffe seems to have been the only market in England for the sale of Kings."

THE VALE OF MOWBRAY.

Where the Swale and Codbeck nearly meet. Maiden Bower on the right, Cock Lodge immediately beyond.
[A. Vivian.

An old mansion, which in later days became the George and Dragon (now demolished), and said to have been the largest hotel between York and Edinburgh, was originally the residence of the Topcliffe family, who were of some standing and antiquity, and by intermarriage, akin to the Percies.

In the days of our fathers, Topcliffe Fair (locally called "Topley"), 17th and 18th July, was one of the most important in the North of England, both for horses, sheep, and nearly all manner of merchandise; and on the days of the fair any person could procure a license for selling beer by displaying a green bush or branch at his door. And so drinking booths were erected at every lane end leading toward Topcliffe for three miles around, so that folks travelling to the fair were able to quench their thirst, not only at the fair, but in their coming and returning also. For instance, a booth was erected at Norton le Clay, one at Dishforth, one at Rainton and Aisenby, etc., and every village around reared its refreshment saloon on this auspicious occasion. The fields on the edge of the town Thirskwards, were filled with encampments, the tents, waggons, vans, and carts of potters, tinkers and gipsies, and the riff-raff and scum of the countryside. Another site where all the roughs, thimble-riggers, and horse-lifters of the kingdom congregated, was on the land lying between the village and the mill. These characters were a perfect terror to the law-abiding folk, and special constables had to be duly sworn to keep order. They carried a long stout rod, shod with a metal point. During the fair free fights were continually in progress down Mill Lane, and it was very generally understood that every quarrel which occurred during the year, no matter how trivial, had to be settled off with a stand-up fight at Topley Fair. It was a long standing custom and died hard. Even the women folk, in those good old days, had also their "arena," or place of tournament for fisticuffs; the latter was a plot of land, to the left across the bridge.

Topcliffe from the Bridge. [*R. Rodwell.*

Most of the Topcliffites of middle life will remember old Bessie Wood—quite a character in her way, and a hard working one too. We of to-day grumble about the number of hours we have to work and small remuneration we receive for same. Betty Wood's livelihood was earned by going out a washing clothes (or "charing" to speak more locally correct). It was Betty's duty to begin her long day's task just after midnight, and keep on toiling until 8 o'clock in the evening, and all for the pittance of *one shilling per day*. "Old Stooley," a cripple from Kilburn, who having lost the use of both his legs from above the knee, managed to work his way about the world by a kind of stool arrangement, hence his cognomen, "Stooley." Nevertheless with this serious infirmity he put many a big idle hulking fellow to shame. By his primitive means of locomotion he worked the feast and fairs in and around the Vale of Mowbray selling nuts, etc.

But by far the best known local character, a remarkable man in his line, was Bobby Johnson. He kept the "Shoulder of Mutton Inn," at Aisenby Smiddy. By great industry and shrewdness as innkeeper, butcher, and small farmer, he had amassed some £20,000 to £30,000, and, as he had no children, but several nephews and nieces, he was an object of some interest. One of his nieces lived with him, and one day was called out by a man on horse-back to supply him with drink. As he was drinking it, he bent down to the young woman and said, "ah've cum to put love to thee." The reply was prompt, "Whar ef it's me ye want, ahse heer; bud ef it's brass ye want, it's all settled on Barker's (a nephew) bairns." Our friend, with other young people, was once taken to see Bobby, and when one of the party asked him for some advice on matrimony for the young men, he began : "They mus hav a sweet peer an' not a crab whativer ye deea, an' thou mun hev a woman who knows oo ta keep 'od a munny whativer tha dees." He had bought land at various times, but one field purchased during the French War he always described a "bowt i' Bonnyparte." Bobby on one occasion was driving home from Ripon Market (he was always the first into the market and first to return), when he learnt that the Prince of Wales (our present King) with the shooting party from Studley was actually then (at his passing) having lunch on the lawn at Hutton Moor House. Without more ado he drew up his horse and went up to the shooters and enquired for the Prince. Being a well-known character, he was introduced, and the Prince shook hands with him. Bobby remarked, "Hoo are ye? Ah's pleased te see ye. Hoo's yer muther? Ye mun tell her ye hev shakken hand wi' oade Bobby Johnson, ef Aisenby."

During the early years of the Rev. Hawkins' ministry at Top-cliffe, two old people, man and woman, who each occupied an alms-house adjoining at Dishforth, and who in due course became intimate, so much so, that they concluded that one of the almshouses

Rev. Henry Hawkins, M.A. [Clarke

would be sufficient for both. So they applied to the Rev. H. Hawkins to make them man and wife, and he, good man that he was, saw no legal bar to their matrimony. The aged Wooster was, however, very deaf, and in answer to the clergyman's "Wilt thou take this woman to thy wedded wife, etc.," he turned to his intended spouse "What dis eh say, Nanny?" She explained in a loud voice, "He wants tha to tell him if tha'll hev ma for thee wedded wife." The old man warmly replied, "Wha of coarse ah will, why thoo knaws that's just what ave com heer for ta hev tha." In the vestry the minister put the usual question of age, and she again turned to prompt him. "He wants to knaw hoo oade (old) thoo is." "Wha thoo knaws ah'm just seme age as oade Bobby Johnson, we wur boathe born et seame day."

The above Rev. Henry Hawkins, M.A., was 53 years vicar of Topcliffe, and was a liberal churchman, a large-hearted Christian, and benevolent to the poor—a man respected by all, whose memory will be long and lovingly cherished. He died October, 1891, aged 78. A marble cross in the churchyard marks his resting place.

As we have observed, during the Scottish campaigns of the Edwards, Topcliffe was a frequent meeting place of the Kings. In his first campaign, 1327, Edward III. journeying from York halted at Topcliffe. In 1333 returning from Newcastle he was at Topcliffe, 9th August, and Knaresborough on the 15th. So he thus spent a week between the two places, hunting as was his wont, probably with the Percies. In the next year, 1334, he varied his journey, being at Helmsley on the 31st May, and North-allerton on 2nd June. In this fashion his goings and comings were repeated during the war.

The later political associations of Topcliffe have been of a more dismal character. In 1489 Parliament granted Henry VII. a subsidy for carrying on the French War; it was found so heavy that the whole North Country burst into a flame of opposition—"the people upon a sudaine grew into great mutinie and said openly they had endured of late yeares a thousand miseries, and neither could nor would pay the subsidie." Henry Percy, the fourth Earl of Northumberland, then Lord Lieutenant for Yorkshire, wrote to inform the King of the discontent, and praying an abatement; the King replied that the tax should be paid to the utmost, and no mitigation allowed. This message being incautiously delivered by the Earl, the populace rose, and supposing him to be the promoter of the calamity, broke into the Manor House at Topcliffe, and, despite stout resistance, "assayling the Earl in his house, slew him and divers of his attendants." The Earl Percy could never have been captured in this fortress of manor wood by a rustic population, if the place had been at that period in a proper state of defence, goes without saying. The Percy shrine in Beverley Minster was erected to the memory of this Earl and his wife, a daughter of William Herbert, Earl of Pembroke. The funeral obsequies of the Earl were carried out in the most lavish scale on record. The tradition in the locality is, that a fellow named Gibson slew the Earl.

Remains of Market Cross, Topcliffe. [*Barker.*

Thomas Percy, Earl of Northumberland, who in 1569 raised the rebellion against Elizabeth ("The Rising in the North") narrowly escaped being taken prisoner in his house here, in 1588. His co-conspirators thought he was wavering in the Cause, so they sent a servant with orders to bustle in and knock loudly at his chamber door, telling him hastily to shift for himself for the enemy was nigh, whereupon he hurried to his keeper's house. At the same instant other of the leaders caused the bells of the town to be rung backward and thus succeeded in gaining a goodly number to join in the Rebellion.

> "Now was the North in arms:
> They shine in warlike trim from Tweed to Tyne,
> At Percy's voice; and Neville sees
> His followers gathering in from Tees:
> Seven hundred Knights, retainers all
> Of Neville, at their master's call
> Had sate together in Raby Hall,"

In the mournful career of King Charles I., Topcliffe played its part. In 1646 the Scots army lay in this neighbourhood; when it was agreed between the English Parliament and the Scots Commissioners that on £100,000 being paid by the former and received by the latter at Topcliffe, the Scots army should quit all their garrisons south of the Tyne within ten days. When the Scots in their march from Newark to Newcastle passed through this village, 16th May, 1646, the King, a prisoner, dined here and took leave of Sir Henry Slingsby, "one of his most faithful servants."

The Church, dedicated to St. Columba, was granted by William de Percy in 1226 to the Cathedral of York; the Dean and Chapter being patrons of the living. The most remarkable monuments being that to Thomas de Topclyff and his lady, whose full length effigies on a gravestone, inlaid with brass, are in the north aisle. Whether mere retainers of the Percys, or originally a branch of the family, the Topclyffes were an ancient house; their arms were PAR PALE AND SABLE, THREE CRESCENTS COUNTERCHANGED"—the crescents being of the Percy coat. John Toppeclyve was rector of St. Mary's, Castlegate, York, in 1302, presented by Sir Henry Percy, that church being in their presentation. Another branch of this family resided at Topcliffe Hall in the parish of West Ardsley. The tomb of a Sir John Topcliffe is in the middle of the chancel floor at Woodkirk Church. This Sir John was a notable man, was Chief Justice of Ireland, and Master of the Hunt, etc. The old mansion of the Topcliffes, a grand type of a Tudor Hall, has been partly demolished, and now serves as a farm house; the family appears to have become extinct. Another John Topcliffe was rector of All Saints in the above city, in 1466, and a Richard Topcliffe was M.P. for Beverley in 1572.

At Baldersby park in the Forties dwelt George Hudson, the railway king, at that time in the zenith of his fame. His square pew in Topcliffe Church was upholstered in rich crimson, in which he had a reading desk, where he used to stand up with his portly back turned on the vicar, and if the sun shone on the occupants of the pew, Mrs. Hudson would put up her fine parasol. In those days wind and string instruments sent forth their music from the east end of the gallery. On all matters connected with railways, Hudson was looked up to as the greatest authority. The entertainments at his mansion in the city were patronised by the greatest nobility in the land—none were too great to do him homage. His round of visits among the Peerage was like that of a Prince. But the railway mania of the Forties was followed by a reaction, and when the crash came and the railway bubble burst, George Hudson was speedily dethroned, and those who had been the most servile during his brief reign hissed the loudest at his fall.

In the early years of the last century, a person named John Meek was miller at Topcliffe Mill. He was a miserly old fellow, and is known in Baring Gould's "Yorkshire Oddities" as "Old Mealy Face." He was so parsimonious that he was wont on going from home to press his face into the flour in the bin, leaving its impression, so that on his return he might discover if any meal had been taken, and severely reprimand his wife for her extravagance. The poor woman (his third wife) was an industrious, kind-hearted, hard-working person, and the chief sufferer from her husband's pinching. It was "Mealy Face" who made the following remarks to the clergyman at Topcliffe, who had received a call to labour in a new vineyard, " that had not the call added another hundred a year to his stipend, the Lord might have kept on calling till the day of judgment, and ye would not have heard," said John. The writer was told several other characteristic stories of the miller by Mr Barker, an aged man, who, in his youth, was in the employ of "Old Mealy Face."

Regarding the place name Topcliffe, there is not the slightest doubt that it refers to its fine position ("the top of the cliffs") the best and most prominent on the banks of the Swale hereabouts. Some writers say that the name is derived from "tad," a fox, as in Tadencliffe, which signifies "Foxes' cliff." The fine bluff of red sand stone of which the cliff consists is a favourite place for foxes to earth in. It is very easy of excavation, soft and friable when first bored, hence the resort of foxes.

The Swale, Topcliffe. [*R. Rodwell.*

The most notable house of the old class is that of the Angel Inn, large and roomy, with long passages, and furniture reminiscent of coaching days. It is in such a house where one might expect to still hear the echo of the coachman's horn. Just on the outskirts of Topcliffe and where the road branches off to Dalton and Sessay, formerly stood the gallows, where the criminals suffered the extreme penalty of the law. Following the above road we soon pass over the Codbeck, deviously wending its way to its bourne with the Swale at Maiden Bower. Half-a-mile to the south are the Elmires

Elmire Grove and Elmire House and Crakehill Farm and Cottage. ("Crake") Celtic "craig"—a rock. Some years ago several daggers were found here by a labourer when draining. The natives connecting the Elmires with the Maiden Bower earthworks tell mythical stories of a great battle in this part, but who the combatants were they seem to have only a very hazy notion, one local worthy remarking to our questioning, "all at ah knaw aboot it, it wor a varry big war between th' English and French"; and it may be that the man was not so far out—for the tradition handed down may point to the great struggle of the conquest era between the Anglians and the Norman French. It is a beautiful district, meadow, grove, and delightful undulating cornland, with a succession of ridges and rounded hills; in lush pasture the sleek cattle graze, the farm lads whistle in the field, and the birds add their praise in song. Through this posy land of variegated colour, the old Swale, with its load of water, rolls slowly onwards to its bourne, never to return, or only, it may be, in the form of cloud-dropped rain over the heights of Kisdon and Birkdale in the far north-west.

On our right hand in crossing the fields by footpath to Dalton, is the isolated hill called Barf, which is a phonetic Saxon way of spelling *bargh* or *barugh*, which in its turn represents the old Norse *bjarg*, and means a low ridge of elevated land. There is a similar barf near Selby. The village of Dalton is only of ordinary type, pretty enough in summer time, with numerous flower gardens, fruitful orchards, and curiously hedged-in crofts, yet possessing no object of striking significance. The chief features are sinuous windings of the street and the beck which wanders alongside it. This little stream at times becomes an unruly torrent, flooding the roadway, and the crossing at the ford is then a rather adventurous undertaking. Sergeant Franks, a Crimean veteran, now in his 88th year and a man much esteemed, lives in this village, for nearly fifty years a soldier, and one of the few now living who witnessed the famous Balaclava Charge. Story says that once upon a time giants dwelt at Dalton. And yonder some little distance from the town formerly stood an old corn mill, now demolished. In front of the miller's house was a long mound, which from time out of memory had borne the name of the Giant's Grave. Some forty years ago the mound was opened, and my informant (then a boy) who watched the operation with eager interest— said the skeleton which was then laid bare was of abnormal size, and in the debris was found a weapon somewhat shaped like the blade of a scythe. This relic, the giant's sword, was long preserved at the mill. Story also tells that this giant in his lifetime ground men's bones to make his bread of—that one day out foraging on Pilmoor caught in his huge net a youth named Jack, whom the giant brought to the mill, and caused him to do all the menial work. Jack served the giant a long time, but at length grew weary of bondage, and determined to be free. Topley fair was nigh at hand, but to all Jack's entreaty the giant angrily refused to let him attend the famous yearly gathering. On the day of the fair the man of might ate enormously at dinner, and afterwards fell into a deep slumber. Jack saw his opportunity. He boldly grasped the giant's sword and slew him, and also the huge hound which zealously guarded the entrance; forth he then fled to Topcliffe and joined in the feasting and revelry. The mill, now re-built, is nearer Sessay than Dalton, and another version connects the Dawnays and Darrells, of Sessay, with the giant's death, and names one young Sir Guy Dawnay as the bold knight who adventured his life in slaying the Giant of Dalton Mill.

In passing through Dalton 'tis well to guard against the Headless Woman, who haunts the precincts of a lonely old barn. A toil-worn wayfarer once sought shelter in this building for the night. At midnight he awoke in a fright, and before him stood the apparition of a female, holding in her hands her head, from whence issued a strange unnatural light. The fear of the man was so great, that he sprang with such force at the wall as to break a large hole in it; this hole was long shown to strangers as vouching the truth of the story.

The Ancient Church, Carlton Miniott, before the Restoration. [R. Rodwell.
See page 206.

To the ordinary tourist there is nothing in the landscape around Dalton to cause them to linger. To the student of Natural History, the district is full of interest. Just to the north of the village, the Codbeck, the "bonny" Codbeck, as Drayton calls the stream, and the Willow Beck meet. The latter stream bears many names in its coursing from its rise on Boltby Moors to its junction with the Codbeck. It is named "Gurtop Beck" at Boltby, "Thirkleby Beck," "Isles Beck," and "Willow Beck." The scenery all the way along this watercourse, particularly between Thirkleby and its spring-head, are of the most beautiful and varied character. Passing on to Bagby, we cross the straight track of the N.E.R. from York to Darlington, the product of the Railway King. Just to the south is Sessay station, and near to is the stable and carriage-house built for George Hudson's benefit. It was here that he alighted from or boarded the train when living in almost regal splendour at Baldersby Park. The now-a-days almost deserted roads were then alive with glittering equipages passing to and from Baldersby.

Now, past dark belts of woodland where the famous duck decoys are situated, with the woods of Thirkleby and its beautiful avenue of limes to the south, we reach the Thirsk and York highway. The Thirkleby vicinage presents a fine "show" to that natural open-air scientist, the "bird-man"; for hereabouts, ponds and the serpentine windings of the Vale becks, like snakes in the grass, between narrow reed-deckt banks, have afforded that local magnate. Sir Ralph Payne-Gallwey, M.B.O.U., the means of constructing a famous "Decoy" for wild-fowl, and resuscitating an old and profitable sport and pursuit combined. Sir Ralph has also revived that grand old lure of the born hunter, Falconry—the most picturesque of chases conducted by means of trained Peregrines, a sight that seen in act is an exhibition of the apotheiosis of birdly courage and pluck. That now almost extinct bird of the wilderness, the swamp-loving Bittern or Butterbump, has been occasionally heard in a damp valley near Hood Hill. Sir Ralph is, however, not only an ornithologist and a "shot," he is a bow-man too! The most erroneous notions prevail as to how far an arrow can be sent by hand from long or cross-bow. With Robin Hood tradition in mind, some have said a mile—some a thousand yards; both absurdly exaggerated distances. Not long ago, however, taking up the practice of archery, it is, we believe we are correct in saying, Sir Ralph's proud distinction to have shot an arrow from a Turkish bow nearly 367 yards—the farthest flight of which exact and indisputable record has been made. Archery, with other legacies of prowess and deeds of "daren doe" from the "good old days," have been left behind so much in the hurry-scurry of "muddied oaf," that this feat of arms is surely worth preservation.

Here by the road side is a farm house, which in coaching days was the Old Griffin Inn. Nearly opposite is an immense sycamore, a notable tree always pointed out by the driver of the mail coach as the largest on the road between London and Edinburgh. Half a mile nearer Thirsk, and a field's-length from the road, situated as its name implies on a slight rise of land, is Spittle Hill, denoting the site of, or otherwise the land belonging to, the middle-age leper Hospital of Bagby.

Bagby village, with its one twining and irregular street, contains several picturesque features. Antique houses are found in some instances stretching backward to the Tudor period. In the crofts on either side of the street, are extensive foundations and one or two vestiges of moated sites, but whether pointing to an ancient hall or manor house, or to the foundations of the hospital which existed here in the middle ages, we cannot say. Be that as it may, Bagby is hoar with antiquity, as its Danish place-name testifies. Its pre-domesday value was eight pounds which fell to forty shillings when the "Mailed Fist" of the Conqueror had battered it. Bagby had a priest to look after the spiritual welfare of its inhabitants, when the surrounding villages (not even Thirsk) were possessed of one, and Kirkby Knowle, six miles distant (now its head) was formerly one of its dependencies. Doubtless it has been a place of considerable importance in the past, but its early history is in oblivion. Its situation on the rising billowy ground, which by gentle gradations recedes to the plain, suggests to the eye pleasant retiring bowers. The Church of Bagby, unique in its style of architecture and its peculiar interior arrangement, stands on the north side of the village. Although this church is not mentioned in Domesday, it is of very ancient date and has undergone several restorations. Antiquated customs of Eld and a charm of rural simplicity appear to linger around this lowly fane. As one watches the worshippers gather or disperse, it all looks like some pictured story rather than a scene in the 20th century. Tradition says that during the reign of Henry the Second, three hundred soldiers were stationed here to guard the district from outlaws and robbers, whose lairage was in the inacces-

The Ford, Balk. [Owen Bowen.

sible ground about Whitestonecliffe. After several skirmishes and some severe fighting, they were at length ousted from their natural stronghold. These outlaws, who made the Hambletons their place of refuge, and swooped down on the Norman who dwealt in the plain, were the original Anglo-Danish inhabitants who had been despoiled of their lands, and from being owners of the soil had in many instances become serfs to the oppressor. Only little more than half a century had elapsed since they had been relieved of their birthright, and no wonder they fled to the hill fastnesses. They were not mere robbers, but the best type of Anglian or Norse manhood who would not submit to the yoke of the invader, and so, like Robin Hood, for years kept up an incessant warfare against the "Constituted Authority" for the time.

To the student of history, a walk along the serried edge of the Hambletons not only reveals the story of this particular strife between the Anglian and Norman, but also that of other rival races through earlier centuries. But during the reign of the second Henry, the outlaws seem to have found a master and to have been dispersed, and Bagby, at that period evidently of some consequence, was the place where the troops were quartered during the struggle.

In almost every direction from Thirsk there are charming walks by field path and green lanes. The one which we are now following runs some distance by the Codbeck side from Ingramgate and thence over Duckett Ings and by the deep hollow of Barbeck, where the fruitage of orchard and garden shew luxuriantly, over the York Road and again across fields, until we reach Woodcock Farm standing on the first outspur of the Hambletons. It is a beautiful autumn morning, hedgerow and trees tinged with the colour-change of the season. Turning, we look Thirskwards, and see the antique tower over the roofs of the town piercing the soft pearly-grey atmosphere. October! yet so warm and enervating that a skylark, probably deceived by the unwonted clemency of nature, has mounted into the heavens and is pouring forth an ode of high praise. Then comes over the fields on the wings of the breeze the sweet subdued music of pealing bells from the grey church tower of Thirsk. Now we pass into a wide lane. How beautiful this lane is to-day; the green road and the rich vegetation which borders it, a bosky dell teeming with loveliness; the tall thick hedgerows draped and brocaded with ripening haw and bramble and many another berry. In such a lane sweethearts love to linger, and here amongst nature's charms one could dream through a long Summer's day. Another delightful walk, and of even more varied character, is that from Sutton village to Balk and Thirkleby. This walk is so charming that words cannot adequately describe it. The road runs over curiously hedged-in meadow crofts thickly carpeted with field flowers—yellow of buttercup, blue of geranium, and white of parsley rex. through dimpling dells and thickets, by the sinuous turnings of the beck, a typical trout stream and the haunt of the kingfisher, which in its swift flight, shimmers past like a living jewel; and as we press onward, from every copse, tree and hedgerow we hear the bird-folk jubilantly warbling their joy of living. Through such delightful phases of Nature we reach Balk.

Balk Grange. [R. Rodwell

Balk, a Rurality! charming in colour and composition, dark green orchards, deep red roofs, a stream rippling over the roadway, willowy hedgerows, antique homesteads, quaint wooden bridges and a shimmering mill race, where flocks of ducks and geese disport—all these things go to make up a picture right restful to the eye. Here by the side of the beck, Balk is one of those slumberous places with some dignity and the antiquity of the past presiding over it. The large mill was formerly used for the manufacture of linen. The beck at times floods the roadway to such a depth as to make the crossing a perilous undertaking. Men and their teams have been swept down by the irresistible force of the torrent; at such times, vehicles are hauled over the wooden footbridge. From here we have a fine view of the Hambletons, with Hood Hill in the middle distance and the foreground road winding up the picture. Following along the east bank of the stream we reach Balk Grange, an antique-timbered and thatched structure, standing by the beck—here a perfect Tennyson's "Brook," gurgling onward, beautiful in its many turnings 'neath o'erarching tree and hedgerow. And so, wandering by this most delightful of field paths, we reach Thirkleby Mill, the surroundings of which are delightful in the charm with which Nature has clothed them. We have now reached Thirkleby itself.

Thirkleby was for two centuries the home of the Franklands, baronets, a family which sprang from Fewston in the Forest of Knaresborough, where in the remote centuries their ancestor was a Free-man holding free-land, as the Castle rolls still show. Of late, the Payne-Galways have occupied it, Sir William Payne-Galway being M.P. for Thirsk during a considerable period. The mansion is situated on an eminence to the west of the village, and is not of very imposing architecture, but the surroundings are beautiful; the gardens, and the many tall graceful trees lend a peaceful, yet stately, dignity to the place. The park is luxuriantly clothed with very fine timber, and some good conifers have been judiciously introduced. There is a pretty view of Thirkleby Church—of All Hallows - once a chapel to Coxwold by some now void arrangement, for the dedication proves the church to have been of the oldest Teutonic foundation, the terminal " by " denoting the Danish origin. Oliver de Buscy held the land under Roger de Mowbray.

Near Thirkleby Mill. [R. Rodwell.

The patronage then belonged to Roger de Mowbray, who gave it to the Prior and Convent of Newburgh, the vicarage being ordained in 1269. A few particulars of the ancient state of the church can be gathered. In 1558, vicar Bryan Barker wills to be buried in the churchyard, hard against the church-porch door. In 1563, William Askwith, in the churchyard as nigh the Cross as maybe. Other Askwiths are buried in the chancel.

Passing the park we reach Great Thirkleby, as the maps call it, High Thirkleby according to the inhabitants—a peaceful rural village, standing on a slope with well-preserved houses and trim gardens—evidently a prosperous village. A clear stream divides High and Low Thirkleby, conveyances having to cross by a primitive ford running along the stream for a distance, and then up the steep Hill. Foot passengers are provided with a narrow wooden bridge, close to which is a splendid apple tree. From this point a sweet picture meets the eye; the foreground is a luxuriant meadow, with hedgerows and trees comprising a diversified middle distance; while a picturesque broken outline is given to a high background by the village itself, beyond which again, is a vista of distant hills—a typical English landscape. To-day, early June, the Thirklebys are still perfumed with the may and other flowers; the hedgerows and widely-spreading orchards are rapidly being covered with a mantle of leafy green.

Roger de Thirkelby, of whose lineage and early life history is silent, was one of the four justice itinerants appointed in 1240, and "second to none in his knowledge of the laws." With a fair degree of certainty we may guess that he was one of the younger Mowbrays.

Little Thirkleby is indeed a beautiful spot, standing on high ground with fine views and charming surroundings—woods, pasture, stream, orchard, and gardens; the air breathing of pleasant flowers, and the district full of the song of happy birds, to-day busy nesting and love making. From Thirkleby the road leads to Birdforth, two miles, and long ones too.

In our walk we leave Hutton Sessay, a quiet rural village, on our right, whilst a mile and a half further west is Sessay, a straggling place, the home of old of the historic family of Darrel, retainers of the Percies. The scions of this house were noteable men, and have left their mark in history. They were laid to rest in their own church of St. Cuthberts. The old hall is now called Church Farm, and it is supposed the original church stood here. The new church, built by Lady Downes, with lych gate and schools adjoining, makes a very charming architectural group, and seen from the meadows over the beck, forms a very fine picture.

Camden says " Sezay, formerly the estate of the Darells, and after that, of the Dawnies, who flourished long under the title of Knights till Sir John Dawnie was by King Charles the Second advanced to the dignity of Viscount Dawne, in the Kingdom of Ireland."

BIRDFORTH.

Birdforth, the head of the Wapentake of that name, now a small obscure hamlet with about 40 inhabitants, was in Anglian days a place of sufficient importance as to give its name to the Wapentake, and at that period doubtless the seat of a numerous population. It certainly is not a very central spot for the head of the division, for about three hundred yards south and just over the stream, stands the boundary post of the Bulmer West division.

A WAPENTAK. The old Norse word " vapna," means a weapon, and " taka," to grasp or touch : hence the Norse " vapnatak," meaning the touching of weapons. Tacitus says that in the assemblies of Teutonic warriors, when they wished to express their assent to any proposal, the armed warriors struck their spears together. The laws of Edward the Confessor also state that when a new chief of the Wapentake was appointed, the other chiefs or freemen met him at the usual place of assembly. Here the chief dismounted from his horse, and held his spear erect while the other chiefs touched his spear with theirs, in token of fealty to the King, whom the chief represented. Most of us, when children, have taken part in the game known as " tiggy, tiggy," or more correctly—" tiggery, tiggery, touch wood,"—this child's game is a survival of the touching of weapons at the wapentake, the magic touch or contact.

Norman Font, Birdforth Church [*Ernest Forbes.*

Birdforth Church, like Husthwaite and Old Byland, bespeaks a very ancient foundation, repaired and restored from time to time as folks thought necessary. There are no windows in the north wall. This was a wise plan of our forefathers, for it certainly kept the cold north wind out of the church when glass was a luxury. The only connection with the north was that afforded by the Devil's door, "old Nick's favourite line of retreat (like that of the Russians in in the late war) to the North." It is a small plain structure of few interesting features, with a curious brick bell chamber on the west. The interior is small and aisleless, thick walls, fine Norman font, the entrance door and chancel arch is devoid of ornament and and are evidently pre-Norman. Several important finds of ancient coins of the reign of Ethelred and Edgar have been discovered here from time to time. Elphin and Birdforth Beck divides the latter place from Thormanby.

A long mile away, on the slope of the opposite rise, is the village of Thormanby, standing on the southern verge of Mowbray

Vale and on the western spur of the Howardian Range. The church of St. Mary's (or All Saints) is very interesting, and well worthy of a visit. It was given to the Nuns of Molesby, to which it was appropriated. The first recorded rector is Henry de Sunilinton, 1235. The present rector, like Mr. Kingsley, of Kilvington, is a craftsman as well as preacher. The reading desk, made from the sound parts of old oak pews, is the work of his hands (a good thing, says one, if all doctrines was as sound). The pulpit is simplicity itself, formed from the door posts of ancient pews, with their turned knobs forming a Venetian battlement, with sermon stand resting above as a central feature. The church has been lately restored, and many of its ancient features have been swept away. The brick tower is naturally beautified with a green mantle of ivy. The name of the village bespeaks its Danish origin. Thor was a common Scandinavian name. Gamel Arkle and Orm were land-owners here in pre-Norman days. The Old Hall, now a farm house, still presents some distinctive features of antiquity.

In our journey to Coxwold we pass the Husthwaite villages, situated a little on either side of the Thirsk and Malton line. Carlton Husthwaite stands on the northern slope of the valley, and about 6 miles from Thirsk. In the middle of the green stands the church, a small, plain, oblong structure, with a dwarf tower projecting on the west. On the north side the edifice is windowless. Built early in the 17th century, it is entirely open to the green, with neither fence or graveyard. Carlton Husthwaite is unique for large houses, the Hall, the Old Hall, and Manor House. The first-named is pleasantly situated in the middle of the village, with leafy surroundings. The Old Hall and Manor House (of Jacobean architecture) stands at the west end of the village and lend dignity to the approach. But by far the most interesting picture is the large black and white timber-framed house with stone plinth and hipped thatched roof still in good condition. A further charm is given to this antique structure by a gigantic horse-chestnut, whose immense branches cast fitful gleam and shadow over the house.

A little over a mile from Carlton, Husthwaite is reached by road and footpath crossing the N.E.R. at Husthwaite gate station and the beck flowing past from Byland. The village stands on the western slope of the Howardian range looking south from Coxwold. It stands on a plateau, its ancient fane blending a touch of architectural dignity and symbol of antiquity to the scene. The

Timber framed House, Carlton Housthwaite. *Edmund Bogg.*

etymology of the name is very apparent—the "hus" (a house) and "thwaite" (a forest-clearing). Anciently it stood on the western verge of the great forest of Galtres, and its origin, like most of the villages in the district, is due to Scandinavian settlers.

The village contains quite a number of large well-built houses. There is a small triangular Green, on which stands a quaint brick-built house. Adjoining the green is the old-time "Black Bull," with its timber and plaster black and white upper storey, and a silhouette sign, forming a very picturesque feature of the past. The church is of pre-Norman foundation, signs of this early age still remain to be seen in the chancel arch. All the main features point to the 12th century, or Norman period. Without going into details we might say to the archeologists this venerable relic of antiquity is well worthy of inspection. Amongst the memorials there is one to the Rev. John Winter, vicar of Birdforth, and for 65 years curate of this parish.

Husthwaite.

Around this village are many signs of antiquity. Two Roman roads or streets crossed in this vicinity. Fragments of these ways are still to be traced; one of these roads crossed the Derwent, near Stamford Bridge, and ran in a north-west direction to Thirsk and Thornton-le-Street. The other, known as the Malton Street, connected Aldborough and Malton. The ancient Manor Hall, where of old the Lords of the place dwelt in stately dignity, has been replaced by one of smaller dimensions. A mile east by the road side leading to Malton, is an entrenchment, and from Beacon Bank (whence the signal by flame was sent forth) is another entrenchment, running for a quarter of a mile along the edge of the steep Scarp in a north-easterly direction.

Two miles north from Husthwaite, with the vale between the Howardian and the Hambleton Hills stretching east towards Hemsley, we approach Coxwold.

Antiquarian Notes on and around the Hambletons.

In reference to the antiquities of the district, it may be observed that it was inhabited at a very early period. The traces of these occur not only on the hills, but also on the lower elevations. The traces of some of those on the edge of Hambleton are given in the one inch Ordnance Map. Besides tumuli (enclosing urn burials) there are Cassen Dikes (cast up ramparts or ridges), also numerous little dwellings, partly made with soil, and which would doubtless be covered with branches and skins. In an extent of 3 or 4 miles probably there would be several hundreds of the natives and their families. By means of flint spear and arrow-heads they would chase the deer and hares, and the rabbits on the hills and in the valley beneath. There was also a colony of them adjoining Norby, Thirsk. The river there would be convenient for fishing (by banking the several streams). Where their funeral urns were found is at a safe height from floods. There is also an interesting settlement of the early natives near Byland Abbey. It is about a mile from the Abbey, and situated at the top of a nearly precipitous position. The separate dwellings are larger than those before spoken of. Many tumuli are near. These early settlers were not the first inhabitants of England; Stonehenge in the south, and in Yorkshire the monolith at Rudston and the lofty stones near Borobridge, called the "Devil's Arrows," probably point to an earlier race.*

Several large tumuli occur, but they are probably early Anglo-Saxon. One is at Feliskirk, opposite the vicarage, but has not been opened; but more will be told when we come to deal with their particular localities.

CHAPTER VI.

Round about Coxwold, Byland, and Kilburn.

The very name of Coxwold suggest pleasant scenes and old-world associations. The prefix Cok, Cox, or Cocks, through Caulx (according to Streatfield and Taylor) is connected with Calli or Kalli, a spring or fountain, such as often wells up in the chalk (or calc) beds of rock. Coxwold is *not* on the wold of chalk rock, but springs are a feature of the land hereabouts. We might instance the name of Coxey Hills near Louth. We have in the name the nomenclature of the Celt, and in the suffix (wald) the tongue of the Anglian is revealed. Thus in the first glimmerings of its history we find here a settlement of Celts, supported by Wildon, the Celts hill and Kilburn, where a Celtic Kil or Chapel remains, speaking to us of the very earliest conversion of the Celt from the cult of

---

* Addison.

Druidism to Christianity. Still standing there by the Burn, under the lee of the hills, a hoary sentinel, a link in the long chain of evidence reminding us of the old story of Kuldeeism and of the earliest seeds of Christianity planted in these parts.

Coxwold is not of the ordinary village type. It is interesting and delightfully picturesque, both in form and colour, and in its main features distinctively unique. Look at it from whichever point one may, a wonderful charm prevails, compelling the stranger to linger and refresh his soul on a beautiful picture, imbued as it were, with romance, poetry, and bygone things and people, which mere words fail to portray. The surroundings of Coxwold are delightfully romantic—diversified with undulating wave-like land, hill, moor, wood, stream, rich arable, and meadow. The one long street comprising the village, rises from the valley by a gentle ascent to the brow of the hill at the head of the town. Here are the Church and the two Halls (Colville Hall and Shandy Hall), and the ancient Grammar School, antique and crumbling with the mould of years, charming in form and colour, with sweet old-world gardens perfumed with the aroma of flowers around them.

The street forms a fine old English picture, with its ancient gables, old fashioned windows, stone mullions and high-raised cobbled causeways. The dark brown and green hue of its roofs, and the creamy white and grey of its walls, all overgrown by a clinging filigree creeper (the fire thorn), to-day, late Autumn, covered with a wealth of scarlet berries. A delightful glamour of subtle tints pervades the old street. The mystic shades of green, grey, silver, russet and brown, old gold, and the brilliant hue of scarlet berries glittering from the walls the whole length of the street, beautified with the transient flickerings of light and shadow, and softened and shaded into almost every conceivable hue—make up a scene to be felt rather than described. At the upper end of the village, and standing almost in the middle of the street, is a

256 THE VALE OF MOWBRAY.

Street Scene, Coxwold. [W. G. Foster.

huge old Wych Elm, with its gaunt far-reaching arms presiding over the road and causeway—a memorial of the past, it seems verily to be bound up with the life of the place. Coxwold shorn of its immemorial elm would indeed appear lonesome.

If this majestic elm could speak, it could tell of many scenes of mirth or sorrow, and gallant deeds and courtesies. It might recount the sayings of Laurence Sterne, the incomparable jester, novelist and wit, who for seven years dwelt at the old hall yonder. It might tell of the comings and goings of mail-clad knights who dwelt here in Tudor times, or it might have heard the clattering hoofs of Edward the Second's charger during that monarch's flight before the victorious Scots at the fight of Byland. It might tell of the gallant Cavaliers of the Stuart period, or whisper softly of that great secret—the passing of the great Oliver's body to the wall-like tomb at Newburgh. Times out of number it has heard the story lustily vociferated from thirty throats at the Fauconberg Arms adjoining, of how the gallant Sir George rode in that famous charge made by the "Six Hundred" at Balaclava, and if its branches might break silence, they would tell how gallantly he rode out again, one of the lucky survivors.

"Honour the brave and bold,
Long shall the tale be told."

Stately stands the hoary tree beloved of all, a mute witness as it may appear, but if your imagination and hearing be sufficiently acute you can hear when the autumn wind moans and whispers fitfully among its branches many a story more strange than told of in old romance. Adjoining the old Wych elm stands the "Fauconberg Arms," a typical hostel of olden times. It has lately been restored, and the ancient roof of thatch has given place to one of tiles. Yet the effect of the interior has not been visibly marred. There still remains all the quaintness and flavour to an inn of olden times.

Among the finest of churches of this most interesting ecclesiastical district, that of St. Michael's, of Coxwold, stands foremost. It is a magnificent structure, style chiefly perpendicular, but with unique octagonal tower. Not only is the lantern octagonal but that form prevails from the foundations to the summit. Round the walls runs a pierced battlement, similar to the one at Thirsk, and the crocketed and flying buttresses add to the stately beauty of this interesting church. The architecture is that of the late 14th or early 15th century.

The Fauconberg Arms, Coxwold. [*William Wright.*

Entering the church we behold fine monuments—its pride and glory. The Belasyse family (Lords Fauconberg) especially are well represented; Coxwold having furnished them with a dower house. The oldest of the tombs in the chancel is an altar supporting the effigies of Sir William Belasyse and that of his wife.

On the dado panels of the tomb are the figures of their children. This stone is also a memorial to the artist who designed and built it, for along the plinth is carved in bold characters:—"JOHN BROWN DID CARVE THIS TOMBE ALONE OF HASLEWOOD STONE." Dame Ursula Belasyse of Cockswold, widow, late wife unto Sir Henry Belasyse of Newburgh, knight and baronet, was buried there in 1623; Grace Belasyse in 1659. The Wildons of Wildon Grange and the Darrells of Angram Grange were buried there before the Dissolution of Monasteries. The Deyvills, originally of Thornton-in-the-Hill, which they held of the Lords Mowbray by the rent of 3s., were people of distinction. In September, 1498, Elig. Vavasour, of Thornton-le-Hill, juxta Newburgh, willed to be buried in the church of Cockwold, and bequeathed to the altar of St. Mary in that church one chalice of silver with a paten, one corporall and two best candlesticks to stand upon her sepulchre.

The ancient family of Colville, tenants of Roger de Mowbray and usually styled "of Cukeswald," had their residence at Yeresley or Eversley. In 1361, the King conferred to Thomas de Maulay, as granted to him by Peter de Maulay, the Manor of Cokewald and other lands. In 1316-17, the King confirmed to Norman de Colville in fee the Manors of Cukesvalte, Overton and Everley held of the heirs of Roger de Mowbray by the service of a knight's fee; market and fair at Cukesvalte as in the Charter of 21, Edward I., 1292-3; his park of Buldendike of Everle and the liberty of Sac, Soc, etc. The glories of market and fair have long passed out of human ken.

The old late-Tudor Hall of the Colvilles adjoins the west side of the graveyard, and is a remarkably fine example of that age, with heavy mullions, quaint gables, ponderous chimneys, and leaded windows. On either side of the entrance gate are recesses or seats for men guarding the entrance. Its thick walls, crumbled and cob-webbed with age, antique doors and oak pannelling, all belong to an age long since passed. The charming Elizabethian garden and orchard, combined with its ancient paths and borders fragrant with flowers and fruit, all belong to an old world. The Colvilles, Lords of Coxwold, formerly resident at this hall, were tenants of the Mowbrays and great benefactors to the Monks of Byland and the Canons of Newburgh.

Just without the village is Shandy Hall, a picturesque, antique gabled house, notable from having for seven years been the home of Laurence Sterne, who during that period, was incumbent of Coxwold. He also held the livings of Sutton and Stillington. According to his own testimony he seems to have enjoyed his life at Coxwold. In answer to a letter from a friend congratulating him on his appointment, he writes as follows:—

"I return to my new habitation fully determined to write as hard as can be, and thank you most cordially for your letter of congratulation upon my Lord Fauconberg having presented me with the living of this place; though your congratulation comes somewhat of the latest, as I have been possessed of it (the living) some time. I hope I have been of some service to his Lordship, and he has sufficiently requited me. 'Tis seventy guineas a year in my pocket, though worth a hundred, but obliges me to have a curate to officiate at Sutton and Stillington. 'Tis within a mile of his Lordship's seat and park. 'Tis a very agreeable ride out in the chaise I purchased for my wife. Lyd has a pony which she delights in. Whilst they take these diversions I am scribbling away at my "Tristram." These two volumes are, I think, the best. I shall write as long as I live; 'tis, in fact, my hobby-horse; and so much am I delighted with my Uncle Toby's imaginary character that I am become an enthusiast. My Lydia helps to copy for me, and my wife knits and listens as I read her chapters."

To another friend he afterwards wrote:—

"I am as happy as a prince at Coxwold, and I wish you could see in how princely a manner I live. 'Tis a land of plenty; I sit alone down to venison, fish, and wild fowl, or a couple of fowls or ducks, with curds, strawberries and cream, and all the simple plenty which a rich valley (under Hambleton Hills) can produce, with a clean cloth on my table, and a bottle of wine on my right hand to drink your health. I have a hundred hens and chickens about my yard, and not a parishioner catches a hare, or a rabbit, or a trout, but he brings it as an offering to me. I am in high spirits. Care never enters this cottage. I take the air every day in my post-chaise with the two long-tailed horses."

Under the conditions described in the above letters, one cannot understand how Sterne could be otherwise than happy at Coxwold.

Monument to the First and Second Lords Fauconberg. [*W. Wright*

Newburgh Park, a short mile from Coxwold, resting in the lap of beautiful surroundings between the Hambleton and Howardian Hills, is the seat of the Wombwells, Baronets. Sir George Wombwell (the present Baronet) was one who rode with the gallant

"Six Hundred" in that famous Charge of the Light Brigade at Balaclava. He had two horses killed under him and was taken prisoner, but escaped by boldly leaping upon the back of a passing riderless steed belonging to the enemy, which bore him safely into the English lines.

About Newburgh there is a twofold charm—the historical glamour which is always associated with monkish settlements and ancient sites; and secondly, the loveliness of its situation. Environing woods and glades, with magnificent vistas over the Vale of Mowbray and the moors to the north and east, spread almost away from its doors. As at Bolton and Fountaine and many other religious sites, the stately sylvan surroundings of the house are due to the Kings license in 1382 that the Prior might impark his wood of Newburgh, where the deer could be preserved, and the foot of the poacher marked a crime. One of the famous country houses of Yorkshire, it is the survival of a priory of Augustinian Canons founded in 1145 by Roger de Mowbray, one of the witnesses being Roger de Daivilla, "my seneschal." Many churches were granted to this priory—an institution founded as a counterpoise to Byland. The strength of the Kuldee priesthood and the loyalty of their congregations were nowhere more effectual in barring the Cistercians than here. The career of the house was in nowise distinguished beyond the moral and mental characteristics of such places, save that in its early period it produced a chronicler of scholarly repute, known in history as William of Newburgh. An impression of the Common Seal of Newburgh represents the B.V. crowned and bearing in her hand a lily. She is seated in a plain and antique seat, having in her lap the Divine Infant. The legend runs thus:—"SIGILLUM : SANCTE : MARIE : DE : NEVBVRGO."

The Canons had a house at Thirsk which they used with some freedom. In 1275, "the cellarer traffics in horses and has a rough Tongue." When the house was surrendered it had become rich, its revenue amounting in clear receipts to £367 8s. 3d. The site was granted 38 Hen. VIII. to Anthony Belasyse, chaplain to Henry VIII. The family of Belasyse rose to fame by the tact and skill of the devout chaplain. His nephew, Sir William Belasyse succeeded him in the ownership, whose grandson, "for his great merits," was

Shandy Hall, Coxwold [*Edmund Bogg.*

created Lord Fauconberg, but must not be confused with the old baron of that name. Thomas, the eldest grandson of that peer, succeeded his grandfather, and married as his second wife Mary, third daughter of Oliver Cromwell, Lord Protector. The estates came to Sir George Wombwell, Bart., of Wombwell, by marriage in 1825. The present Baronet is Sir George Orby Wombwell, one of the heroes of the immortal Charge. The silly story runs that

Cromwell insisted upon the decapitation of all the splendid oaks in Newburgh Park before he would consent to his daughter's marriage with a Royalist. Although Newburgh has been much altered and added to, the old portions remain practically as they were seven centuries ago. The local people believe that Cromwell's remains are safely housed in the tower, saved from desecration by Lady Belasyse, a wise and worthy woman, more fitted to maintain the post of "Lord High Protector" than her brothers.

It is quite natural that a woman of her strong character and filial affection would be anxious to secure and hide the body of her father from the vile vengeance of his enemies, and would leave no stone unturned to accomplish that object. Terrible old Noll, terrible to his enemies even in death! Kings and Princes trembled at the very sound of his name, and even after his spirit had fled they were fearful lest the grim warrior and smiter of kings was not quite dead. So they set about to make sure, and wreaked a despicable vengeance on this great man's corpse. The body was dragged from the coffin and ousted from Westminster Abbey, "the proper burial place of this, the greatest of men." On Monday, the 28th of January, 1660-1, it was dragged in a cart from the Abbey to the Red Lion Inn in Holborn. And on Wednesday, the 30th of January, it was carried upon a sledge from Holborn to Tyburn; there it was taken out of its coffin and hanged on the gallows until sunset; at sunset it was cut down and beheaded; the trunk was buried in a deep pit beneath the gallows, and the head stuck on a pole upon the top of Westminster Hall. No reason is assigned why the body of Cromwell should have laid in the Red Lion Inn, Holborn, from Monday the 28th of January, until Wednesday the 30th, before the base tools of his enemies should have wreaked their hatred by hanging the corpse on the gallows and decapitation and mutilation. Is it not possible that during that interval Cromwell's retainers, by bribe or otherwise, may have effected an exchange of bodies, and thus the man who made kings and tyrants tremble, have been borne Northwards and secretly immured within the walls of Newburgh Priory, where so many relics of Cromwell are to be seen.

The supposed tomb of Cromwell occupies the end of a narrow chamber at the head of a flight of steep stairs, and it is a huge mass of stonework built and cemented into the walls, apparently with the object of making it impenetrable. Why should we doubt the truth of this story of the burial here, handed down by the Belasyses for generations, and fully believed in by the local people. Certainly no more suitable place could have been chosen for its hiding than the home of his daughter. The present owner, Sir George, could doubtless soon set matters at rest by opening the supposed tomb. The secret is in their hands and probably will ever remain so. It matters little where his body rests : the greatness of the man shines forth more clearly as the generations succeed, and the name of Oliver Cromwell will survive, and his collossal figure stand forth as a signal denial of the divine right of kings when his slanderers, those who dragged him from his tomb and heaped all manner of obloquy on his body, will have long been forgotten.

Resting under the south end of the Hambletons, and about 1½ miles north from Coxwold, are the ruins of Byland Abbey.

BYLAND.

THERE is to be found a singular mixture of romance and truth interwoven in the story of the founding of most Monasteries. Take, for instance, that told of the thirteen monks who were driven forth from the Abbey of St. Mary's, York, and who, after many tribulations, found a resting place in Skelldale, a wild romantic glen ; and wishing to imitate the sanctity of their brethren at the Cistercian Abbey of Rievaulx, there gradually arose from this small beginning that magnificent Abbey of Fountains, whose ruins strangers from all parts of the world come to view. And so we might tell of Jervaulx in Yoredale, and Kirkstall in Airedale. But none of the above can point to a more interesting chapter, than the founding of Byland. The harrying of the monks by the Scots; driven from the Calder in Cumberland; their varied wanderings; many attempts to found a permanent home; and their final settlement here at Byland, is a story of trial, hope, and sorrow, ending in final triumph as strange as any tale told us in old romance.

Before describing the Abbey, it would be well to give a brief outline of the story of the monks' wanderings, and their attempts to found a monastery at different spots, and the causes and incidents which led up to the building of Byland Abbey. The story opens out in the early years of the 12th century. The Cistercian Abbey of Furness had been erected and colonized by monks from that of Savigny, in Normandy, in 1127, and the valley of the Night-shade had been changed from a wilderness of solitude and woods to an arcadian bower of peace and plenty. Seven years later, in 1134, a few monks went forth from the mother monastery of Furness to found an establishment of the same order at Calder, in Cumberland. Here they toiled unceasingly for four years, until the peace of the North was broken, and Picts and Scots burst across the border, burning and plundering in their march. Calder, lying near the border, Gerald, the Abbot, with twelve of his brethren wisely fled southward to the protection of their parent home at Furness. Yet strange as it may seem, those whose right it was to protect and comfort them in this hour of their need, denied them admittance into the monastery, closing the gates and casting them adrift again into the world. So with a rude waggon drawn by oxen, containing all their moveable property, books and vestments, they journeyed over the hills to Thirsk. Doubtless they had heard of the generosity of Lady Gundreda de Mowbray, mother of the famous Roger. Story says that she watched the approach of the monks, all travelled-stained and weary, from the turrets of the castle, and was so moved by pity and compassion that she burst into tears. In her the monks found a life-long friend. After being housed for some time at Thirsk they were sent to Hode (now Hood Grange), where Lady Gundreda's relative, Robert de Alneto, a monk from Whitby, was living the life of an anchorite. Roger de Mowbray had a small castle at Hode, and the foundations of the keep and the impress of the monk's occupation are still visible.

At Hode they only remained a few years when their benefactress bestowed upon them the church and town of Old Byland on the moor (or Bella-launda), not far from the Abbey of Rievalx, and in this vicinity they also remained some years; but the site was not a desirable one for the building of an abbey. The estates of Wildon and Stocking, near Kilburn, were also given to the brethren. Both the latter are still in evidence to attest the former presence of the monks. Their traces are also visible in a secluded valley known as Cockerdale, running right up into the jaws of the Hambletons under Cam Hill, and at Oldstead nearer Byland, they built a stone church and cloister, and from evidences of this place it seems to have been their intention of erecting a durable monastery. It is a lovely situation, though the place for building purposes is a trifle too confined, otherwise the place is not unlike that of Fountains. However, after nearly 40 years perambulation in search of a spot to found a permanent home, meanwhile waxing rich in foods and land, their period of probation came to an end. Roger de Mowbray gave them a desirable site in the delightful curvature or bay in the Hambletons, at the foot of Cambe Hill. Here the erection of the beautiful Abbey of Byland was commenced in 1177. By the year 1203 it must have been fairly complete, for at that time the monks begged of King John the lead to roof their church with.

How silent and deserted the place seems as we wander past ruined arch and column in the twilight of this November evening. No sound but our own footsteps amongst dead vegetation and withered leaves, and that of the wind sighing through the deserted building, speaking to us so eloquently of the past. Where are now the men who reared this magnificent fane—the abbot who presided in almost regal state; the brethren who formerly habited in cowl and gown flitted like spectral shadows so silently to and fro; the copier of manuscripts and the illuminator who worked and studied so diligently in their quiet cells; and those who cultivated the fields and attended to the cattle or performed the heavier labours of the establishment? They are all gone—not even a shadow or trace of them remains. The abbey is roofless and in utter ruin (and was in the last century even used as a quarry), and perchance a broken stone may be a record of a burial, or a nameless mound mark where they lay at rest.

In his old age, after years of turmoil and strife, weary of the world and fighting, the old warrior and the founder of the abbey — Roger de Mowbray—laid aside helm and pennon, ungirded his steel armour and sheathed his sword for ever, and, robing himself in monastic garb, spent peaceably the last fifteen years of his life; and when he died, the monks laid him to rest near his mother in an arch on the south side of the Chapter house, and over his tomb was carved the sword he had so ably wielded whilst living. Here his body rested for 600 years but in 1819, the Squire of Myton (Martin Stapylton) opened the tomb and removed the bones of the old warrior during a fearful storm in the night-time to the churchyard of Myton-on-Swale. This act of desecration was keenly felt, and therefore, about twenty-four years ago when a vacancy occurred in the living of Myton the remains of the old Crusader were once more disinterred by night and consigned to their original resting place at Byland.

Byland Abbey.   [William Wright.

Closely connected with this abbey, and equally as romantic as the career of Roger de Mowbray, is the story of that remarkable man, Wymund the Saxon, as told by the old chronicler, William of Newburgh. Wymund, as his name hints, was of Anglian parentage with no particular status in the society of that rude age. Why he became a monk at Furness history does not state, but by close diligence and study he attained great fame as a transcriber and illuminator of missals and manuscripts. He was of tall stature and commanding personality. One may well speculate if any of his after enterprises formulated in his fertile brain whilst artistically employed in his quiet cell at Furness. It came about that Olane the Dane (King of Man), became a benefactor to the Abbey of Furness, and so it came to pass Wymond and others were despatched by the Abbot to the Island to promote the interest of the monks. His talents, strong characteristics and commanding figure impressed the Manxmen forcibly. He was made Bishop of the Island, and thus the name Weymund heads the list of Bishops of Sodar and Man.

Singular as it may appear, after having gained the respect and full confidence of the Manxmen, he laid claim to the crown of Scotland, describing himself in this venture to be the son of Angus, Earl of Moray, who had been slain whilst prosecuting his right of heirship to the crown as a descendent of Macbeth. Gathering together a fleet of boats manned by Manxmen and Adventurers who flocked to his standard, he not only harried the coast with fire and sword, but marched swiftly on to the mainland and met with singular success. "Somerled," Lord of the Isles, gave him his daughter in marriage, and the first-born of this union he named Donald Macbeth. The best and bravest knights and men-at-arms were sent against him, but all to little purpose. He seems to have had a charmed life. If the force arrayed against him were greatly superior he retired to his ships, only to renew his depredations later. During one of these skirmishes he was felled to the earth by a blow from an axe, but even in this instance, though he suffered defeat he managed to escape with the bulk of his army, and soon reappeared with another body of Manxmen. After a long spell of fighting and adventure, whose very truth is as interesting as any fictitious story, Earls and Bishops paying him tribute, and King David of Scotland even granting him possessions and privi-

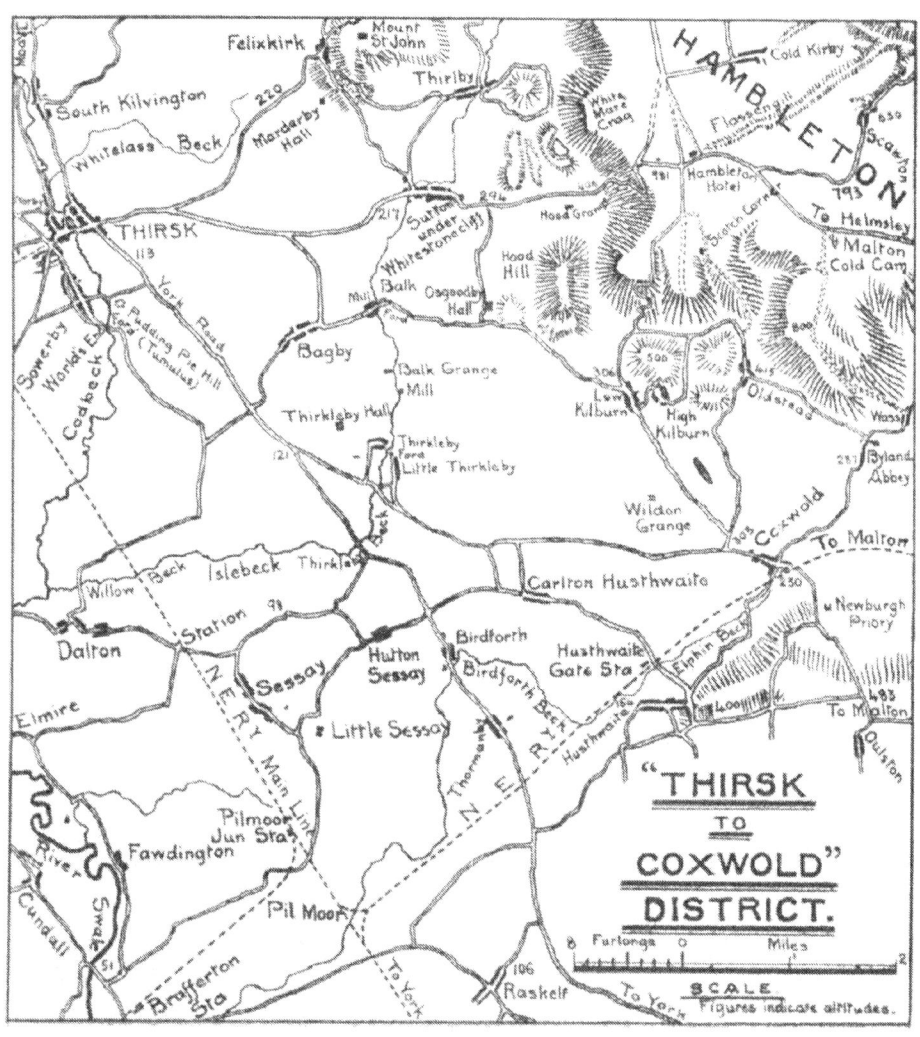

leges so that the west land of his country might rest from the harrying of war.

Nothing, however, seems to have curbed the wild spirit of this fighting prelate; he yet once more unfurled his standard, but his usual good fortune forsook him. He was captured and "deprived of sight and virility," and handed over to the custody of King David, who for many years held the blind warrior bishop a prisoner in his castle keep at Roxburgh, which stood in the apex between the Teviot and Tweed, the Marchmond of a remote antiquity—an abode of Kings. His captors seem to have regarded him with some amount of pity and compassion, yet his misdeeds were many, and the great wonder is that he was not put to death. In his old age he was set free and sent to his Cistercian brethren at Byland. We should imagine the even tenor of the monkish life would be a trifle perturbed by the intrusion into their fold of this grim old fighting bishop. Poor old Wymund, he was by nature a true Berserker, and had it been his fortune to have lived a century or so earlier he might have captured a kingdom and founded a dynasty.

What a singular scene is that at Byland when the old maimed warrior, with the monks crowding about him, told the story of his forays and fights for a kingdom; or again, after vespers in winter time, when the huge logs blazed merrily on the hearth casting fitful lights and shadows alternately on the visages of eager listeners, and the storm swept down from the hills, and the winds moaned or howled round the abbey. We can see the monks gathered round the old blind hero of many a fight, hearkening with a strange glow lighting up their sombre faces to his many tales of adventure by land and sea, and fascinated by the strange light and fierce thirst for vengeance which tortured his strong nature; for he was wont to exclaim "that he was never overcome in battle, save by the faith of a silly bishop, and had they left him but the eye of a sparrow his enemies would have little cause to boast of what they had done to him." The old warrior is sleeping beneath the green sward, and resting soundly enough now under the shadow of broken arch and column, and the story of his sinister career invests the old ruin with an halo of even greater interest.

Battle of Byland Abbey.

Nearly six centuries have rolled past since this quiet nook of Byland resounded with the turmoil and alarm of war. It came about as follows:—King Edward II., thinking to emulate the greatness of his father, invaded Scotland, but lacking both the courage and skill in war possessed by his sire, the invasion was a disastrous failure. The march of the English was bloodless; one lame bull (so story says) was the only spoil captured between the English border and Edinburgh, which caused the Earl of Warenne to sarcastically remark "By my faith I never saw dearer beef." Unable to obtain provisions the English army was obliged to retire, famine and sickness followed in their wake; 16,000 soldiers are said to have perished in a few days. Hurrying South, the remnant of the army with the king encamped in the hollow at the foot of the hills near Byland, the king taking up his quarters within the abbey. But the tables were suddenly turned; the Scots from being invaded now becoming the invaders. Half-wild highlanders from the hills of Galloway, mounted on hardy ponies, swept across the border on the heels of the enemy down the Tees valley and along the old road to the southern edge of the range, they struck the old track by way of Slapestones and over the western edge of Black Hambleton. They had almost reached the top of the bank (still known as "Scotch Corner") before the English were aware of their presence. It was here at the head of the pass that the English force, led by the Earl of Richmond, met one portion of the Scots. Another chosen body, led by Robert Bruce, made their way down the cliff—(known as "The Thief's Highway"; it starts to descend at the west end of the deep trench and bank between Sutton Bank top and Roulston Scar, skirts the bottom of the Scar, and so down difficult ground to the low country. But the Roulston Scar corner of Hambleton would screen the movement.)—and got to the rear of the English, who were soon vanquished, and the Scotch, with loud war cries, burst like a thunder-spate down on the abbey.

The Old Antiquary of Byland Abbey. {*Kester*

Edward hearing the wild shouting and the din of fight creeping nearer, leapt into the saddle, set spurs to his charger and never drew reign until safely sheltered within the portcullis of Bootham Bar, York. All the Royal treasure, baggage, and warlike stores were captured, and the king himself was within an ace of being taken prisoner, for Walter Stewart, the bold leader, with a chosen body of 500 horse chased the king up to the very walls of York. It was an exciting chase for the Scots, but a dangerous and stern one for the feckless king, nevertheless, he won sanctuary within the walled city. It was a sorry time for Byland and the country around, and for many a long day there was mourning among the people and the monks of Byland, and for generations later was told around the ingle fire on winter's nights the story of that fearful visitation of war, and the humiliation brought upon them by the inglorious rule of the Second Edward.

In its old age and period of desolation and ruined grandeur, Byland still contains men of note and marked characteristics. For example there is the old Antiquary with his venerable appearance, white locks, and fine expressive face (not unlike the portraits of Tolstoi). The Antiquary is one of Robert Burns' type of manhood, no fawning or servility in his nature, not even to the Baronet to whom his little cottage standing by the abbey belongs, will he lower the flag of his lofty ideal. Our friend is a man of child-like simplicity, upright and equally courteous to all, yet of unbending principle where the dignity of his manhood is concerned.

"The gowd is but the guinea stamp,
A man's a man for 'a that."

But the strong characteristic of the Antiquary is the love he bears to the ruins. He never wearies of showing one the entrance to the underground passages, which in reality are only the vaults of the outer buildings to the establishment. But the Antiquary assures one this is the entrance portal to a subterranean region more wonderful than Aladdin's cave. He leads one to another part of the monastery and proudly points to the several recesses in the lower story, which are only inside widenings of windows to the basement. These, he explains, were the ovens of the establishment, and here all the joints of venison and beef were made savoury to a turn. He tells one of the punishment inflicted on the monks for their misdeeds; how many times they were wont to walk round the triforium, etc. And so the old man gossips on the different features of the monastic buildings, not always correctly, but what matter! his is a very interesting originality.

Job Skelton, of Byland and Wass. [*J. R. Clarke*

Old Job Skelton, of Byland and Wass, was another striking type of humanity. Job lived to a good old age and was of weird and striking countenance. His hoary locks, wintry with years, fell in tangled profusion below his shoulders, added to which, his long frosted beard and grizzly moustache gave to him a venerable and seer-like aspect. Job eked out his existence in varied employments consonant with a man of his tpye in a country district. Independent by nature, yet in a great manner dependent on the charity of the wealthy class. The Squire, Major Stapleton, was probably one of

Job's best and truest friends. Their greeting was always a hearty "Good morning, Major," and a hand shake. Job's wardrobe was generally stocked from the Major's cast-off suits, etc. Job's time on earth spun out far beyond the allotted time of three score years and ten, in fact, if there was an atom of truth in his statements, his years must have run into centuries, for he was wont to aver " Ah noa moor aboot 'tAbbey than onybody." His usual phrase to strangers being, " Wha ah owt ta knaw aboot 't oade Abbey, fer ah sarved 't measons when they built it." Of course this was in the 12th century, so further comment is unnecessary.

Mary Robson was another remarkable personality and reached the great age of 96. She was looked up to by the local people as a genius, having worked out in silk during her long lease of life a picture of the Abbey. In the old days, no one in these parts was better known than Sarah Richardson, the aged landlady of "Byland Abbey Inn."

Poor Thomas Rymer, he has lately passed to his long home. We can see the figure of the old man before us as we write, returning homeward from his daily labour bearing on his shoulders a large branch wherewithal to replenish his winter's fire. His name is a notable one, and the question arises: was he a descendant of the famous "Thomas the Rhymer" of Earlston by the Tweed, who for seven years disappeared into Elfin-land with his fairy lover. It is a rather singular coincidence that the beck which takes Byland water down Husthwaite way is called " Elphin beck " (Elfin).

And so we might continue gossiping on local worthies, but let us return to the Abbey, now only a roofless shell. Standing by the west front, even now magnificent in its ruin, our thoughts glance backward to the time when it stood complete in all its monastic stateliness and grandeur—a former resting place of Kings. Through its superb west portals all the chivalry of the North, aye, and even of the South, have passed and re-passed.

Robert the Bruce, and Randolph and the Black Douglas, with their knights and retainers, have worshipped here, and have also taken tribute from the monks so that they might have peace. How strangely alluring is this storied ruin even in this, the hour of its sad desolation. The noble west front presents a varied and striking picture. The central porch, terminating in a trefoil arch, invites

West Front, Byland Abbey. [*Edmund Bogg.*
The figure in foreground is that of Thomas Rymer.

one to enter a realm in which the "spirit of the beautiful" appears even to-day to hold regal sway; the one on the south is semi-circular, and that on the north pointed. Above the central doorway are nine lancet-headed arches, the whole surmounted by the splendid cusp of what has been a magnificent circular window.

From its broken side on the south sweeping in a fine curve to the north (which on this side is complete from base to fine-less pinnacle, rising upwards, as it were, to the throne of Mercy). Fragments of walls, arch, and bases of columns, etc., peer out on every side from under a screen of ivy leaf and spray, or a covering of turf and rank vegetation. The disappearance of the high central parts of the church is a great loss to its impressiveness.

The ordinary sightseer who drives or walks along the road past the Abbey sees the well-known west front with broken wheel-like window and its one remaining pinnacle ; and along the north a great length of ivy-clad wall. But to the unimaginative the interior is even more disappointing. The storied pillars and their arches have all disappeared, and left but fragments of their bases, particularly those of the massive columns that supported the great central tower. The picturesque grouping, and mingling of ruin and foliage are seen to the best on the south and east—grey fragments of wall rising among the trees and underwood well repay wanderings backward and forward, for they bring to view every few yards a picture more entrancing than the last ; ever new compositions, ivy-clothed ruined wall, column and arch, seen through the leafless intricate branches of trees in late Autumn. That beautiful bit of Clerestory standing forth so conspicuously at the angle of the chancel with the south transept, mourning all its brethren who have vanished! Irregular mounds and ridges conceal all that remains of the foundation of extensive buildings, little left but the church, and only enough of that to excite the keenest regrets. Change ! change everywhere ! trees, grass, lichen, moss and ivy, now beautifying those deserted walls where formerly the dim figures of monks glided, and the organ pealed forth its solemn music. Its mission now has been strangely altered. The magnificance of the structure, the elegance, the sublimity and substantial grandeur have gone like its music ;

but a new life creeps over and clings to its ancient walls, and new thoughts stir the minds of modern worshippers at the sight of these old records of past life and of what will follow on.

Wass.

Wass, or to be more correct, Byland-with-Wass—either a proper name (Anglo-Saxon Wassa and Wassan) or another form of the British Wysg—a form of uisg, water (Taylor); according to Streatfield the Norse "veisa" and Saxon "vase," alike connoted still or stagnant water or marshy ground, which would be the case before the monks took possession—is a charmful village situated at the foot of the Hambletons, at the "Carfax" or junction of four cross roads in a combe or bay, whence three ravines debouch on the plain. This hamlet, half encircled by tree-clothed declivities, through which two of the ways climb under shadowy boughs making a sun-flecked twilight at midsummer; to the Hambleton plateau, is indeed a cameo of Nature's and man's fashioning combined; truly a beautiful arcadian village,

"The world forgetting, by the world forgot."

and most delightfully situated in its hill and wood environage. Grey, white and yellow time and lichen-stained cottage walls of varied tones, stand charmingly each in its own little garden plot gay with old fashioned gilly flowers and sweet-scented bush foliage, orcharded with fruit trees, and made still sweeter to the ear by the feathered choristers that warble the livelong day, and sometimes far into the night, for the blackcap, and even the nightingale some years, spend the summer as far north as these secluded glens of the Vale's eastern border, among the dim-lit greenery of which they pair, nest and rear their young.

Then beyond are the dark firs silhouetted against the sky in picturesque irregularity of outline, or less sharply shewn out against the aerial tones of colour of the masses of foliage covering the higher slopes of the hillsides, make a picture that once viewed the mind cannot readily forget. At a later season of year when last visited, the features of the scene were somewhat changed, although in their way equally beautiful. The summit ridge half shrouded in a grey canopy of raincloud appeared to have dropped down, curtain-like, as if to mark the new act in Nature's Play of the Seasons, and so invest with a strange blend of mystery and sublimity, the ground-works of hill and dale under ordinary conditions of no such very striking character. Now Nature weaves the dun or sere colours from shed foliage into a carpet of the richest mosaic, such as man's handiwork cannot rival. The sycamore leaves turn to wine-stained sienna, the chestnut to rich ochre, the elm to pale yellow, and then flutter singly or in flocks down in the autumn gusts; the old-gold of the larch needles and pallid green of the ashtree's sparse leaves, with a few of the ruddy brown scalloped leaves from the oaktrees, intermingle upon the roadways or lie lightly heaped upon the turf; one and all exquisite in their individual delicacy of character and purity of shade. The blue spirals of smoke from the cottages (antique in their hue of age), filters through the branches of "neighbourly" trees like the sycamore, and is pleasant to view as light wisps of curling smoke ever is. The lindens, with their amber foliage soon to fall,—nay, some has already fallen and carpets the streets,—begin to shew bare spars to the sky. Showers of crisp brown, lavender-grey or ashen-hued leaves float lightly earthwards and work a transformation on the ground or turf, more magical than any carpet from an Eastern loom. Overhead we hear the cawing of rooks flying homewards, the chatter of starlings as they collect in flocks for their autumn migration, whilst from the gardens come the pensive notes of the robin and trill of the wren, and these, with the rustling of sere falling leaves, are sounds harmonizing with the scene. In the background rises the bossy wooded declivity, fading almost imperceptibly into the universal grey sky above. To the south, still looking over the roofs of the picturesque village, is the open side of the "bay," with Byland Abbey in the "offing,"—as one may surely put it—and the undulating landscape, enchantingly varied, recedes and melts into far-away distance.

The "Wombwell Arms," yellow-walled, trailed over with flowering or berried creepers, the steep wooded slopes rising tier above tier behind, form a picture with quite a Norwegian aspect.

Let us now climb up the twining hill-road to the bank top, in the deep shadow of woods, and past rocky chasmed ravines scooped deeply into the edge of the moor. Reaching the rim of the rise the tumultuous mass of waving branches lies at our feet like a green sea, over the crests of which we gaze across to the Howardians hills and the plain of Mowbray. Turning eastwards we view the valley of the Rye, beloved of fishermen for its well-stocked water. Choosing our path we cross the first breadth of waste heatherland, the woods fringing the edge of the Hambletons receding to the south and west. Crossing the Thirsk to Helmsley highway, and on past the keeper's cottage, we invade the precincts of another large moor, locally known as the deer park, which gradually inclines down into the unsurpassed dale of the Rye at Rievaulx. Two miles N.W. planted on the moor plateau itself is the village of Scawton, reminiscent of monkish hands; and over the wooded gills falling down from Scawton and Cold Kirkby, finely situated for receiving the salubrious breezes that play over these high levels most days in the year, is Old Byland, or Byland-on-the-Moor. The track through the almost primæval heather is deeply scored by the feet of countless generations; cave-men, Celt, Saxon, Dane and Northman, and Scot have all crossed the moory waste by this footroad. It was, also, the monk's way between the two Abbeys (Rievaulx and Byland) during the four centuries of their sojourn in this district; and many a procession of cowled figures must have been seen wending their way solemnly from one House of God to the other. Strangely silent and weird to-day is this wilderness of heath and cottongrass. We feel as though suddenly translated backwards to those days of Peace and Strife, Prayer and Passion, in which the monks held such sway. In imagination we hear the pealing of Abbey bells, or the sound of chant or festival chorus is borne to our ears on the invisible wafts of air. Ah! it is only a reverie. Troops of dun red-deer sniff the air, uneasily throwing up their antlers, in the distance, and scenting our approach gaze suspiciously in our direction. Then packing round their great antlered chieftain, retreat not precipitously as if in fear, but with measured leisurely pace and some renewed looking back, further into the lonelier recesses of the moor. Through such scenes we pass from Byland and drop down into the charming Paradise of the Rye at Rievaulx; but as this particular dale is not comprised in Mowbray-land we must hark back, unwillingly it may be, to our proper province, and recommence our peregrination.

Leaving Byland by the still intact old abbey gateway, with the fragments of monastic buildings cropping up here from the grassy turf, we can still trace for a little further the ancient boundary wall of the abbey. The road to Oldstead passes at the foot of the Abbey Bank Wood which clothes the hillside Northward from Wass, and farther on, on the same steep slope are Elm Hag and Snever Wood. Behind, on the moor's edge, overlooking this wood is Mount Snever Observatory, a prominent landmark projecting above the woodland which thickly clothes the slope of the Hambletons here as elsewhere, and shews forth like some hoar tower or castle keep, stretching yet further north, and bounding in Byland Moor is Great Cockerdale Wood, Cold Cam, and Cam Hill, both undoubted Celtic names. On the high moor a scene of wild forlorn grandeur prevails. Gorse bushes, dwarfed and twisty thorntrees and masses of dark pines alike stand forth grotesquely against a background of stormy sky.

High Kilburn. [Owen Bowen

Oldstead Hall rests in a beautiful secluded valley, penned in by fine woods, a veritable Rosamond's bower, only not of roses alone, by a stream than which the Eastern one of Bendemeer could not have been more bewitching. The house is not very pretentious. The old mill adjoining is probably the successor of the ancient Monks' Mill. Those shrewd judges of sites brought not only education but industry there, and doubtless quite meant to stay, had it not been for the grant of Byland by Roger de Mowbray. In the dark days of winter, shut in by deep barriers of forest, this spot assumes a sombre and secluded aspect indeed. In Spring and

Summer it is an Eden, its ground enamelled with wild flowers, and is not only enringed but half hidden in luxuriant verdure: it is then a true Arcadian retreat. Here in this lovely-lone dell, at the foot of Cockerdale, the monks after many varied wanderings and vicissitudes built their first stone church and cloister, also the mill, and trained the waters of Cockerdale to flow thereunto. Traces of the artizan-priests' works are still apparent. It was from the high moor, at "Scots' Corner" less than a mile away, that the wild Scotch rushed down from the hills by way of Oldstead, swept aside or captured an English force (under the Earl of Richmond) and great booty in and around Byland.

The road from Oldstead to Kilburn sweeps round between Scawling Wood and the serried edge of the Hambletons, here called High Town Brow. And just across Hell Hole Ravine, is a place known as "Fairies' Table." We will follow the path leading through Oldstead village, a quiet reposeful place. Down the lane into the valley leading to Coxwold a small stream wimples over the road, in wet seasons flooding widely out on either side. From here two paths on the high and lower bank cross to the Kilburns, each leading one through lovely dells and glades, where in Spring primroses and bluebells are enshrined in every nook with equally beautiful wildings in the fuller hours of Summer-time, and, later, as the Bard might have put it with truth.

"I know a bank where the wild thyme grows."

Nor do the three months from May to August show all the beautiful colour contrasts of this district. In Autumn the foliage around varies from a delicate lemon yellow through all the scale to the deepest blue-green shades of the dense masses of evergreen hollies, &c., and the richest orange-russet and crimson. The wan yellow of the hazel hedges, flushed with the wine-red of the bramble leaves, and graceful sprays of the wild briar, with their plentiful supply of scarlet hips, and the bronze of the heart-leaved

T

bryony, almost rival the floral beauties of June. The madder-purple of the mature hawthorn leaves, with its dark velvety-crimson fruit—the bird's winter dessert—the half stripped beech branches alternating between orange-brown and red under the light, with a thick carpet of leaves beneath to match, woven into a magical pattern with the pale gold leaves wafted hither from the branches of a neighbouring ash.

The deep crimson flush on the towering larches, and the rich splendour of the masses of oak, make vivid contrasts, intensifying as they fade away mile after mile in the pearly grey of the atmosphere. Through such unforgettable landscape pictures we reach High Kilburn. This old-world hamlet stands on the hill plateau overlooking the village and vale of Low Kilburn. The houses are ranged around a large green, or were so originally; now many of them are in the last stages of crumbling decay. Nevertheless it is one of those charming rustic abodes in which one is tempted to linger, and having left, re-visit—a spot to dream away a long summer's day "far from the madding crowd." Old thatched cots breathe sentiment, pathos and story. The beautiful green has a large pond in it, on and over which geese and ducks hold noisy conclave. High Kilburn is a characteristic goose village, and we are impressed by this fact on our very entrance. The gabbling flocks lend it a certain individuality of its own: dignity and domesticity combined. Is it not somewhere said that Rome was once saved from the invader by the cackling of geese?

Down the steeply-descending path, and through the Kirk gates, we enter Low Kilburn. This as a settlement is, perhaps, one of the most ancient in the district. Its name comes from "Kil," a Celtic word for a cell of a religious house, or a hermitage, and "burn" the Anglian term for a stream. It is worthy of mention that with this one exception, all the lesser watercourses in the Vale of Mowbray, east of the Swale at anyrate, are styled Becks (Bach), a

The Two Kilburns from the West. [Owen Bowen.

name of Scandinavian origin. In its passage from the Hambletons this burn flows through the entire length of the township, in fact, the roadway and stream together fill up the bottom of the little vale. The houses, with their pretty garden plots, are of necessity situated on the gentle slopes. It is this unique disposition which gives to the village its singular charm. The best point to view Kilburn is about a quarter of a mile away on the Thirsk road. From here the scene spread before us is most picturesque and alluring, as well in composition as colour and general effect. From here the church tower, in reality only low, appears much loftier than it does from any other point of view. The mingling of hues, the slumberous peace which prevails, the romance, as it were, of the whole; the village reposing in its sleepy hollow in the sunlight sparkles radiantly like some rare jewel in a setting of hills. In truth, pen cannot depict its manifold beauties.

One writer ventures the remark that Kilburn presents a rather dilapidated appearance! To some it may be a difficult matter to say in what its great charm and beauty consists. Its indescribable loveliness lies in its simply perfect rural simplicity and its abandonment to the spirit of Nature. In Spring and early Summer it is a poem in colour; the air laden with sweetness, the drowsy perfume of May-blossom, the faint aroma of the first honeysuckle, the forest of fruit trees in flower, and the scent of innumerable other blooms combine to from a symphony of the senses with the hum of bees, the undertone of bird voices, aye, and even that most delicate of sounds — the faint rustle of butterflies on the wing — a thing which can be heard by who " have ears to hear."

Another good standpoint for viewing the two Kilburns and their boundary hills, is from the high ground in the fields at the south end of the village. From here the whole place with its medley of houses, garden and orchard crofts, and the burn with its numerous bridges (almost thirty, I think) comes into sight;

THE VALE OF MOWBRAY. 289

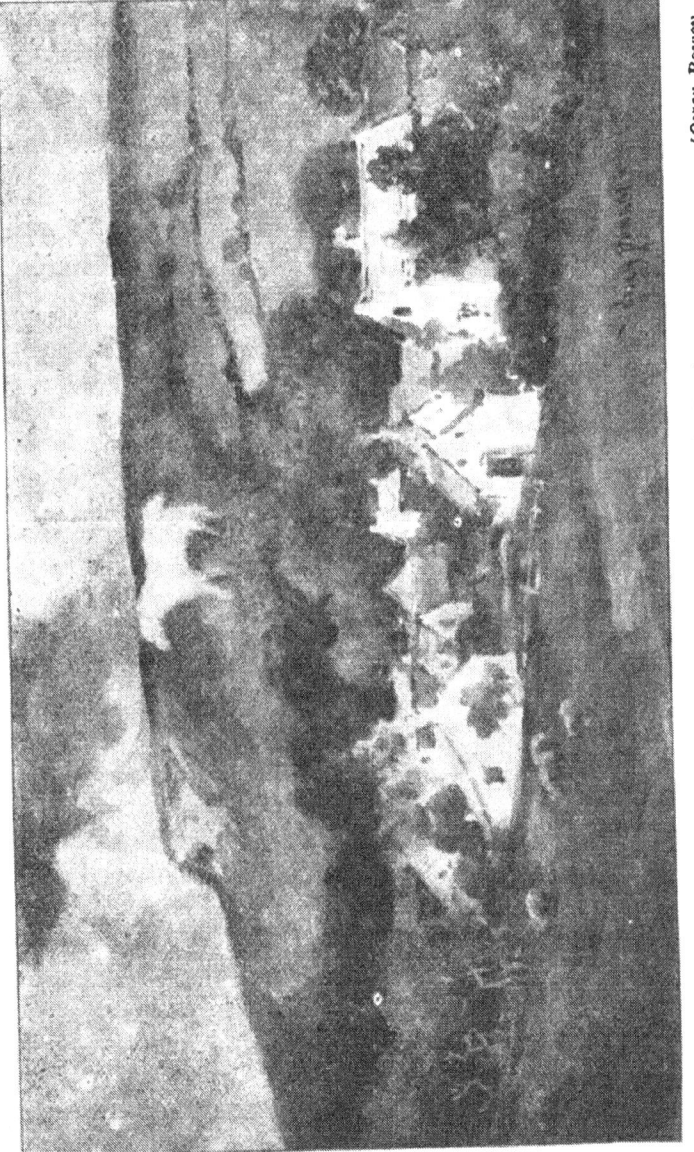

Kilburn and the White Horse, from the South.   [Owen Bowen.

the nearly half-circle of hills holds it as in an embrace. Even in late Autumn, when the austere gloom of approaching Winter broods over Roulston Scar and the cowled Hood Hill stands sternly forth with its crowning fringe of trees—at such a time the "White Horse of Kilburn," half shrouded in grey mist, looks veritably a gigantic beast guarding the frontier of some ancient world. This simile is not inappropriate, for, on the hills immediately above, reposing in the turf-covered barrows, remain all that is left of a long vanished race. Every object eye rests upon is singularly beautiful in the transient phases of light and shadow, illumination or colour. The incrusted greys of old flag roofs, and the dark mossed green or madder-brown tiles of others, rambling old houses with rough-hewn beams and heavy mullioned windows, moss-clad or fern-tufted wall, are shaded into every tint conceivable; no two homesteads are alike, all are individual in character as it were, and as irregular as the ground on which they rest and rust with time. The contour lines of the street, the turnings of the stream, the interposition of garden or orchard bypaths and old lanes teeming with blossom amid the foliage in the summer, or bedraggled with the dead and fungus specked vegetation in winter, give the whole scene that half wild beauty and the indefinable witchery which characterises it.

The old Manor Hall of Kilburn is a charming picture of antiquity, with its heavy mullioned windows, quaint gables, all overtrailed with creepers, a happy haunt of birds which nest in its recesses and fly in and out unmolested. The house, still strong and durable, with its surroundings repeats the same story of olden time—Tudor or early Jacobean. This hall was originally the property and residence of the Baynes' family, and was reared by one Christopher Baynes, in the reign of James I. A shield in front of the house bears the coat of this family: two shin-bones crossed, and above is the crest, a hand grasping a jawbone. The ancient Church, picturesque and dignified, resting in fine surroundings on the east of the village street, is dedicated to Saint Mary. Its architectural features bespeak an early twelfth century erection, with the addition of a North aisle in the following one. During the Sixties of last century it underwent thorough renovation, but its old features have been carefully handled, and where possible retained intact. The entrance portal and likewise

The Coat of Arms of the Baynes Family.

the chancel arch are Norman,—the latter with its clustered shafts, on the Capitals of which are the carved figures of lions (the Mowbray coat)—are of fine type. In the vestry are two ancient grave covers: we should surmise the present structure is the one raised on the site of the Kil or Kul-dee chapel. The village is chiefly in the hands of the Ecclesiastical Commissioners, and possesses certain privileges, such as exemption from toll in Thirsk market, etc.

The old hostel abutting the churchyard wall, deserves mention for its quaint interior, various levels, sanded floors, and in front of which every Plot day the never-missed bon-fire blazes and crackles merrily.

For tourist and Summer visitor Kilburn is a good centre from which to see the pleasant surroundings by gorse-margined byway and field path. To those interested, the antiquarian and folk-lorist, the edge of the Hambletons between Kilburn and the Boltby Scar, is a stretch of moor deeply scored and indelibly marked with the "vestigia" of an old-world race. The moorland is visibly graven with rampart and trench, evidencing the dour and dire struggles of rival races, expulsion, or victory and extermination! These vestiges do not refer to one period only, but probably to many, the results of centuries of feud and fray, from the days of the Brigantes to the settling down of the Normans—an era of over a thousand years. Mr. Sanders, of Cold Kirkby, has spent much time in investigating this area of land dotted over with barrow and tumulus, and his explorations have been rewarded from time to time by gathering together perhaps one of the finest private collections of flints, weapons of warfare, and implement tools in the county.

CHAPTER VII.

Leaving Low Kilburn we follow the hilly Thirsk Road past Stocking House, in olden times a possession of the monks of Byland. To the right of us the White Horse stands out palely outlined against the green and brown of the Hambleton slope. To the South, demarked by Snapehill and its woods, the vale opens a misty vista of beauty for quite a score of miles. A little further and we arrive

A well-known Kilburnite.

at Osgodby Hall. Its name, without much doubt tells its tale of a Danish origin. The site of the homestead is a fine one, on an elevation cut off to the east and south by a deep ravine, and formerly to the north-west was effectively guarded by a treacherous swamp, a quagmire that like a quicksand could engulph horse and man of an invading force. The gateway and front of the hall is Jacobean, whilst other parts reveal Tudor or even an earlier period. The interior has been modernised, yet still retains its old pannelling in parts. A building at the back, weather-stained and time-toned, with belfry and bell, appears to indicate that it was at some period used as a chapel. Allowing for the admixture of architectural styles, the result is artistic, a picturesque grouping, and has certainly, seen better days. It is peculiarly one of those places the varied features of which whisper the secrets of a bygone world of culture, custom and convention. Could it speak what a tale it would unfold ! the hopes unattained, the fears realised of its former occupants, stern men and gentle women, episodes of gallant courtesy, passing scenes of mirth, bouts of revelry and interludes of solemn sorrow, tearful eyes and knees bent in prayerful silence, in the far back days of "auld lang syne." Adjoining the old garden (with its terrace and fine gateway), once doubtless sweet with old-fashioned herbs, is an extensive orchard, a tangled thicket-like wilderness now sloping down to the deep ravine—a happy haunt of birds, thrush and finch and wren, that remembering with the swallows' instinct a suitable sanctuary, return here year after year to pair and build their nests and rear their young unmolested ; in Spring sheltered and full of primrose promise, in Summertime an Arcadia of the feathered race with a myriad of flowers, and in Autumn the twisty moss-hung boughs laden with their distinctive crops of rosy-cheeked or lemon-tinted pippins. Over against this secluded nature-garden, to the north-east is Hood Hill, whither we are bound. It was in this then primaeval wilderness that Osgod the Dane settled in the 9th or 10th century, to be followed two hundred years later by Norman Knight and learned Monk (the only scholar of the time), at Hode (Hood-grange) adjoining.

The hood-shaped hill with its huge cowl of rock, on which legend says the "Dowl," or devil, left his footmark, stands up sombre and solitary—a huge deposit left over with the debris from the Titanic earth-forge of an ancient epoch before Man appeared on the scene. The brushwood clad slopes are in their prime, for the virid sameness of Summer leafage has mellowed into mystic shades of sage-grey and burnt umber under the chemic force of coming frost. The flame-red hips of the briar may be picked out among

Osgodby Hall. JR. Rodwell.

the purple bronzed leaves of the hawthorn and bramble, and one may plainly catch the sad whispers of falling leaves, whilst the few russet oak leaves that still cling to their twigs rustle audibly against one another and tremble with a shimmer in the cold morning sunlight. Here in this almost aboriginal forest scarce birds and shy animals still linger; magpies and flocks of wild pigeon are common, while "felfers" (field-fares) from the far North come

here in Autumn and chatter noisily through the Winter to wing
their way back to the Arctic Circle for their annual Summer visit.
Sometimes the feather-legged eagle-like buzzard may be seen
wheeling and gyrating in the air high over the slopes. Foxes,
badgers and stoats have here their haunts. Let us climb up
through the breast-high bracken to the pine cope or crown of Hood
Hill. The monk's-hood like configuration of the crest is said to have
originated its name. The busy tongue of tradition, however, says
that the name commemorated Robin Hood who, with his "Merry
Men" affected the hill-fastnesses hereabouts; but the hill was
named Hode long, long before the famous Robin came this way at
all. It might be that Robin of Hood received his patronymic from
the hill itself. There are not lacking some facts to suggest that
this bold isolated eminence has been artificially made more impregnable and commanding than it was naturally. On its very crest a
deep trench and a scarp of bush-clad rock in front of the defenders
has made the more accessible part almost unapproachable. Here-
about along the wall-like front of the Hambletons the outlawed and
those who would not yield to the Invader, found a secure refuge.
So late as the time of Henry II. a desperate battle was fought on
Hood Hill between the King's troops and the outlaws, in which
the latter were worsted and driven from their retreat. On the
south side of the hill rests a huge conglomerated rock (ice borne
and stranded here), said to weigh twenty tons, on which the
"keensighted" can see a depression like a gigantic footprint.
Legend, too, has it that the "happy valley" just North of
Hood Hill and Roulston Scar was a secluded and sacred retreat of
the Druids, and at the introduction of Christianity into these parts,
a great assembly gathered to consider which of the two religions
should in future be adopted. The Devil, in the garb of a Druidical
priest, came with the worshippers of Baal. Being foiled in argument he flapped his brazen wings in anger and flew across the
happy valley carrying the stone, which he dropped on Hood Hill!

There it remains to witness! But there is clearly some link in the chain of events missing. Another legendary story, and an old one, connected with this stone is, that when the dinner-bell rang at Osgodby Hall the stone rolled down for its repast, and regularly returned to the crest after the meal—an old woman's legend "signifying nothing" because opposed to all natural law, but sufficiently out-of-the-way to be mentioned here.

But now let us wander down to Hood Grange by the eastern slope and the "happy valley"—a primæval waste of moor and forest land, yet teeming with the natural beauty of an infinitely varied wild life. Here, one chances to-day to see trees flockful of stock-doves of pearly blue-grey with iridescent glossy plumage, and as a foil to their quakerly charm the strongly-contrasted white and black magpies, with coveys or flights of redwings and felfers by the hundred; a hawk wheels through the clear air or a kestrel hovers and poises above a stretch of furze-clad common, eye on the alert to fall like a stone on some luckless fieldmouse or small bird the moment it leaves cover. A buzzard circles and sweeps athwart the sheer steep of Roulston Scar, whilst ever and anon a hoarse croaking cry directs our attention to a corbie crow resting on the edge of the cliff, almost hoar-white as his mate of Lapland's snows spoken of by the poet:

"Where the wild hare and crow whiten in surrounding snow."

A bold and striking scene displays itself to our gaze. At a lower level is a large tangled wood, the myriad leaf-clad branches of which from our point of view stand out in Summer like the tossing manes of a host of wild coursers against the broken background of Roulston, with its crannied ledges whereon feathered life finds a shelter and a nesting place. The age-grey hue of the curving scarp, the orange-russet of the sunlit bracken on the hill slopes the gradations from purple to grey and the rich blue-green of the pines, one buttress of Roulston brilliant in light, whilst a strong shadow is cast far along the slope, make up a picture strongly engraven on our memory. The bay-like basin of the hillside, stretching from Roulston to White Mare's Crags, the zig-zag white of the Sutton bank road stepping up to the Hambleton plateau, bits of silvery crag protruding here and there, the feathery fern, green turf, purple wood, gorse-clothed bank—are features of loveliness we might descant on for ever. A change comes, however, as we look: between the beauty at our feet and the sky overhead clouds, like phantoms, sweep and sail across the scene. They

The White Horse of Kilburn. [*T. Fox.*

presage change if not storm, and we too must hurry on. Through such crowding impressions of beauty we reach Hood Grange, a place brimful of memories filling up the time-cup of a thousand years! The Grange stands in a most secluded position in a beautiful curvature of the Hambleton's bluff face, which in its bay-like line is typical of having been slowly carved and scooped out by the age-long wave wash of that inland sea which once filled the Vale of Mowbray. The moorlands, and curved-in oval sweeps from Roulston's stark headland to the frowning cliff of the White Mare. In the centre of this Eden-like bower, known as the Happy Valley, rests Hode (or Hood) Grange, the history of which reaches back to the early days of the Conquest. Yet generations, even centuries, prior to the founding of Byland there dwelt here a regular succession of hermits or priests ministering to the people sparsely settled around.

Soon after the era of Norman invasion, Hode seems to have been added to the fee of Whitby Abbey, for we find that when Robert de Alneto, a monk of Whitby, comes on the scene to take up the life of a hermit, he did not find this Hode a barren wilderness but a lowly hermit's cell with its stripe of cultivated land and a pasturage for cattle, which a long line of Kuldee priests, by the labour of their hands (all the while sowing the seed of Christianity) had made habitable. So Robert of Whitby began his rule at Hode by rooting out the last of the hermits! This Robert de Alneto was a native of Normandy, and a near relation of the widow Gundreda de Mowbray; it might even be that he came to Hode at her invitation. Be this as it may, Robert had not been long settled at Hode when the monks who had fled from Calder before the incursing Scots, and who were refused shelter by their brethren of Furness, appeared on the scene. They had heard of the kindness of the great lady of Thirsk. With all their belongings, in a wain drawn by oxen, they made their way, slowly, across the country to her Castle. Philip, 3rd Abbot of Byland, who tells the story, says that when Gundreda saw the miserable plight the monks were in she was so moved as to burst into tears. After providing for their immediate wants, and keeping them some weeks in her own Castle, she sent them at the wish of her kinsman, Robert the hermit, to Hode (Hood), granting them for their maintainance several good plots of land thereabout. The monks came to Hode in 1138 and stayed until 1143—five years only—increasing in numbers and landed possessions meanwhile. Possibly the site was not in every respect to their liking; anyway, in 1143, the Lady Bountiful gave them her vill at Byland-on-the-Moor, to which place they "trekked," Robert de Alneto continuing at Hode until his death. Such is an outline of the history of Hode as a hermitage and monastery. The poet Spenser tells in verse :—

> "A little lowly hermitage it was,
> Down in a dale, hard by a forest's side;
> Far from resort of people that did pass
> In travail to and fro; a little wyde
> There was an holy chappel edifyde,
> Wherein the hermite dewly wont to say
> His holy things each morne and eventyde.
> Thereby a christall streame did gentley play,
> Which from a sacred fountain welled forth alway."

Yes! the hermitage here answers full enough to the Elizabethan poet's lines. The old track, sinuously trending down the steep slope of the Hambletons, passes within a bowshot of Hood, and we imagine many a lone benighted wanderer lost on the wild heath, with the wind whistling in his ears like the pipes of fiends, would rejoice to catch the sound of bells from the hermitage telling the angelus, or hour of evening prayer, and with it succour for the weary wanderer. Or, peradventure, when crossing over the wold in the deepening twilight, some came unconsciously upon the rim of the steep Hambleton scarp and were arrested in time by the friendly warning and welcome of the bells. A romantic region this, indeed, with its echoing rocks and caverns, the prominent characteristics of which are wildness and loneliness, and who could fail to say *Ave Maria* on seeing—after dark terrorised steps—the beauteous light flashing forth from the sanctuary, the hermitage walls?

History reports that Roger de Mowbray had a Castle at Hode, doubtless one reared to guard the frontier of the Hambletons, and make watchful outlook on the outlawed, disaffected Anglo-Danish men who inhabited the natural fastnesses of morass and moor-ravine in this district of nature-made strongholds. Roger was a true warrior, and fought valorously in the Crusading ranks in the Holy Land. Dugdale asserts that on his return from Palestine he fought "with dragons and lions in the valley of Sarranell, afterwards returning to his Castle at Hode." Our Crusader seems to have much affected the society of monks, perhaps because of their more cultured and intellectual qualities ; and becoming weary of strife and ambition became a monk himself, attached to Byland whose generous benefactor he had been, and there at length he died. Of the Mowbray's Castle at Hode not a scrap or coign remains above ground, but the foundations of the boundary walls are still traceable in a croft just to the west of the present house, with two portions of the moat and vallum.

The Grange Farmstead probably dates from the early 17th century, with fragments of the ancient monastic structure still visible, old perpendicular tracery, a stone coffin inserted in a wall, and a gothic window cut down to form a doorway. Bits of ancient moulded window jambs show forth here and there among the farm buildings, stabling for horses and sheds for cattle where formerly hermit and then monk knelt in prayer! The occupations of Eld are replaced by the garnering of harvests and the rearing of cattle, nevertheless, the place breathes its story of the past, the always moving tale of slow but inevitable change. Yes! Hood Grange is a secluded spot,

"The world forgetting, by the world forgot."

Set in a happy valley reminiscent of the Eastern one of Rasselas, and guarded by the natural fortifications of Roulston and White Mare's Scars. From many points the house makes a pretty picture, a limpid alder-shaded beck winding near by, pleasant to the ear is its unending song. The roof of the old Grange is of grey flagstone and dark red tiles, the gables a yellowish pearl with the lichen of a hundred years at least clinging to its slowly mouldering stone : a charming object, the handiwork of Nature in Age. For a background to the South the precipitous Scar of Roulston is upreared, and on the right are the fir-green slopes of

Hood Hill. The pass betwixt is still a "forest" ravine (known as the Devil's stride), appearing, as it were, to lead through an enchanted portal to some ancient but mysterious unexplored world.

Old Crab Mill, Sutton. [*Edmund Bogg*.
The figure on the right of the picture is that of Sam Worley.

Sutton, or Sutton-under-Whitestonecliffe from its location under the lee of that wall of rock, and also to distinguish it from all the other Suttons, lies by the main highway leading from Thirsk to the Hambletons. It is about a mile from Hood Grange, and short of four from Thirsk, and is a settlement of extreme antiquity, like Kilburn probably of British foundation, albeit the place-name bears the stamp of Anglo-Saxon coinage. King William's Survey mentions a "Priest" and a "Mill" as existing here at that period.

The mill still remains, but neither priest nor chapel in which he could officiate, continues the succession from the establishment of Domesday. The Chapel of Ease was demolished early in the 17th century, for which the Vicar of Felixkirk had to provide a chaplain for mass celebration thrice a week. The greater part of the parish was in the possession of the Knights Hospitallers residing at Mount St. John. Soon after the dissolution of Monasteries it was absorbed in the estates of the Archbishop of York for a fee simple of £13 12s. 4d. In olden times a family named Sutton were resident at the Hall here, and they were probably connected by marriage with the Walkinghames of Ravensthorpe. Sutton is unique in its own way, its environage a paradise of ever-changing beauty as we write: a memory of one visit recalls the banks carpeted with the white stars of the windstars, anemone, hedgerow and wayside strewn with pale yellow clusters of primroses, the sheen of azure bluebells adorning the woodland and coppice glades. The fresh green of the fields where the lambs were skipping, the glancing lights of the swift moving brook, the quaint homesteads, the golden patches of early flowering gorse, the frowning buttresses of the Hambleton Hills which the sunlight gilds the purple distance, changing momently as the orb of light sets with a kaleidoscopic effect; all these passing impressions are phases of a scene that must live in memory while life lasts. This charmful up and down village, set in a frame of rustic simplicity, consists chiefly of one long street from the east end of which uptowers the White Mare's Cliff. In an old-world recess, about the centre of the village, is set and still remains an old "crab" mill (see annexed picture), where was made from crab apples the vinegar known as verjuice, an obsolete industry. Under the shade of o'er-stretching boughs the street winds easterly to that ancient hostelry "The Seven Stars," with the zig-zag skyline rim of the Hambletons forming a magnificent background to the landscape.

In this connection, and not without reference to the very steep highway from the Hambleton Hotel down Sutton bank, it may not be thought too trivial to relate—as told by a Skald of Thirsk, one Robert Rodwell—the "legend" (as he dubs it, tho' it was all fact) of Sam Worley and his Dead Cow! There was undoubted farce in the affair, if no tragedy.

SAM WORLEY'S COW.

Sam Worley at Scawton had bought a dead cow,
    And drove it away in his cart;
The same night I listened to Sam telling how
    Horse and cart, cow and he, came to part.

'Twas a cold drive o'er Hambleton plain from the farm,
    And the hostel was tempting, and cosy and warm;
So Sam had one whiskey, then went to the door,
    Saw the horse was still there, so went back for one more;
'Twas beyond a fair joke, so, at length, right away
    Broke the steed grown impatient, to Sammy's dismay:
        And to warm his chilled bones,
        Rattled down o'er the stones—
        Would have broken his neck
        If he'd not got a check
From the brake, and the cow shaken out "crop and neck."

But the beast undetached was still held by a rope,
    So that all the way down that most terrible slope
Went the cart with its trailer, until at the foot,
    The harness or drag-rope gave way, and the brute—
The live stock and dead stock stopped dead.
    For a gent. uppassing it was a grim find
In the dark; all this property gone astray:
    All this damaged gear, with the horse standing near,
And the faithful dog still holding the rein,
    And the carcase behind; a "get up" very queer:
But where was the driver? 'Twas not very plain,
    Was he living, or dead, or betwixt and between?

The search was exciting and anxious and keen,
    Until Sam cut it short with his Yorkshire broad:
You may make very sure he had something to say,
    Before taking his lonely homeward road.

> And then at the "Seven Stars" on his way,
> Thought the horse needed fast'ning, if he was to stay,
> So he tied him with care, in the proper place there,
> Ere he told by the ingle all about the affair.

A footpath runs over the fields from here by way of Cleaves Farm to Butterdale and Gormire. 'Tis a lovely day, and the mantle of early Summer has been cast green with a sheen of silver over the scene. Cleaves Farmhouse rests under the shelter of the three wooded hill flanks, set sentinel-like over the large pool Gormire or mere, on the west. North-west a magnificent panorama spreads out—right over the Kirby Knowle and Mount St. John, the hill buttresses about Upsall and Borrowby block the view, but further to the west, across the undulating plain, we see in dim lines the moor and hill barriers of the Pennine 'backbone' of Northern England. Turning our gaze back again to a point of the compass more to the east, through the delightful woods of the second bank we look on a secluded dell called Butterdale, an alluring spot indeed, a "sleepy hollow away from the madding crowd" and the rack of the world struggle, a true Rip Van Winkle's land, a place of perfect peace. Here is a miniature Gormire—a pool with its water hidden under a coppery film of Pond Weed, disturbed only by diving moorhens. The dark tint of the serried Spruces seen beyond the copper hue of the weed-covered mere, the whisper of the reed stems fringing it with the intrusive cry of the waterfowl and the croon of doves from the leafy covert; such are some of the dominant notes of lorn but lovely Butterdale. The surrounding banks bloom with wild hyacinth and stitchwort, herb Robert and ground ivy, with the aroma of hawthorn scenting the air, and the rougher banks barricaded with thorny furze ablaze with the yellow bloom of Spring. In the Summer and on into August their place is taken by the wild briar-roses, white and pink; and the orange of the autumn flowering furze, which is a different kind from that which blooms in Spring.

Roulston Scar and Hood Hill, from the top of Sutton Bank Road.—A Winter Scene.
[*Edmund Bogg*.

From here we climb the steep gradient of the east bank and through a natural gateway or well-nigh leaf covered porch, we get a fine prospect of the gaunt and furrowed precipice of White Mare Crag with the variegated wooded hill spurs trending step-like down to the rippled sands of Gormire, a blue or grey jewel according as its waters mirror an azure or a clouded sky, set in green and in outline quite that of the moon in its second quarter. Passing over the crown of the ridge, the shimmering surface of the lakelet (the largest next to Semerwater in Yorkshire) laughs up at us like a face dimpled with smiles. On a bright day such as this, in its circlet of hills, the half-moon lake, rather over a mile in circuit, is a beautiful Nature-set Gem indeed! The mere level is just over 500 feet above mean tide height, and the land rises more or less abruptly on every side, steepest to the east, and geologists say that it had its origin in a great slip of the high land on the east, for no watercourse above ground feeds it, its supply, like that of a dew-pond, coming mainly from the rain and such surface drainage as the immediate slopes down to it occasion. The overflow in very wet weather escapes into the hillside to the east, through a natural crack in the strata; and popular story has it that it emerges again to light in the vicinity of Cold Kirkby. This seems to sound like water running up-hill. A tradition too says that a goose was once upon a time turned into the overflow hole at Gormire, and following the subterranean channel emerged from darkness denuded of all its feathers at Kirbymoorside! The greatest depth of this little lake is only some forty feet. That it has been formed by some titanic convulsion is apparent from the three wave-like ground swells holding in its waters on the west. Glacial action too, has been rife hereabouts in that long past Æon known to geologists as the Ice age. The mere has been very erroneously described as bottomless, but if so, it could contain no water. It is traditionally and contradictorily too supposed that it can never be dried up—a rhyme has it that

"When Gormire riggs shall be clothed with hay,
White Mare of Wissoncliff 'll bear it away."

Very old women, too, will gabble of a submerged city, whose roofs below its waters can still be descried, and even of gold and silver dishes to be glimpsed under certain conditions of the air and the gazer's mind!

Yet another myth is, that once upon a time where the rippled waters of Gormire now rest, stood the Castle and park owned by a doughty Knight and his fair lady; but a fiend in the shape of Jealousy stalked around, and under its baleful influence the Knight slew his lady and concealed her body. Nemesis swiftly overtook him, however; a huge volume of water burst from the hill side, overwhelming the Castle and with it the unknightly wrongdoer, and so the picturesque "tarn" was formed.

> "There is a magnet-like attraction in
> These waters to the imaginative mien,
> That links the viewless with the visible,
> And pictures things unseen."

This loadstone influence is felt by those who essay the feat of swimming across the lake, but the why or wherefore of the strange sensation they cannot explain. A strange weird sense of loneliness pervades this Vale edge tarn, broken it may be in Summer by casual visitors, pic-nickers, sportsmen, or naturalists intent upon probing its living mysteries; whilst in times of hard frost the keen ring of the steel skate will make shrill music above the silent locked-up water, and gay girl voices mingle with the busy bee-like hum of many feet upon the ice. To-day, it is early Summer, and the warm brown below and green above of the reeds clustering on its northern margin, afford a fine contrast to the bridal lace-veiled attire of the blossoming hawthorns crowded in thickets under the cliff. The sheen of the water, the rich yellow of the whinblossom, the gentle sighing of the zephyr through brake and branch, the jackdaws busily a'nest in the cliff, the mocking echo of the cuckoo's double call, and the minor chords of many bird throats,

> "Happy voices softly singing
> Songs of love that still are ringing—
> Still are ringing in our ears."

Gormire is veritably "a haunt of coot and hern," a retreat of the mallard whose "marigold ducklings" may be espied threading the reeds buoyantly in early May, whilst in the dead and drear time of late November the fluting song of a wild swan may be heard winging its way hither. In late Autumn Gormire assumes a more stern-like aspect; a half moon of water coldly glitters at the foot of a ghostly white cliff, imprisoned in its triple barriers; a cold blast shivers through the pines and bracken; to the east a bare-branched thicket seems to cling with difficulty to the

Gormire from the Pine Wood. [*Edmund Bogg*.

slope rising steep and more steeply to the knife-like edge of Whitestonecliffe, now viewed through a shroud of rain-cloud, the declivity strewn with blocks of rock of all sizes perched fearsomely at all angles; the north end of the lake is a dank bed of dying weeds; and even the wild fowl do not seem festive to-day— a heron stalks disconsolately on the margin of the mere, and perhaps a few waterhens or coot glide soberly above on the surface of the water, but the prevailing feeling is one of Desertion and Dearth: Winter, the cruel time for wild life, is at hand, and only the well fur-clothed denizens of the wild—(this is a great resort of Badgers)—remain here all the year round. This shyest of wild creatures has had "an earth" here for years. A farmer living near told the writer that he had "killed four in 1904"—a thing much to be deprecated, for the badger harms not the farmer.

WHITESTONECLIFFE.

The face of the overhanging rock is roughly 120 feet from the top to the green slope below, composed chiefly of huge conglomerate particles of what is called oolitic limestone, showing traces of a brecciated structure of late formation. The huge blocks piled one upon another in utter confusion at the cliff foot—

"Confusedly hurled
   Like fragments from an early world"

—are almost devoid of fossils, but in the lower stratum spherical balls of iron ore concretion are not uncommon. The origin of the name Whitestonecliffe, or White Mare Crag, may be found in the fact that after a great slip or fall of boulders, the cliff from a distance assumed a white colour, until in time, through the action of the oxygen in the air and rain-water (which is acid and acts on the minerals in the soil), its face became permeated and stained with the tinge of iron. At the great tumble in 1755, described by John Wesley (at that time preaching in the vicinity), thousands upon thousands of tons fell, leaving the whole face of the cliff white, and as seen from a view-point, say near the Swale some miles off, it appears to take the shape of a horse. I have more than once noticed this resemblance; so the title is obvious enough—white the hue, and mare for this particular outline, the other and later one cut in the turf being known as the "White Horse.". And indeed there exists a legend of a White Mare on Hambleton which "ran away," and leapt with her rider from the cliff into the waters of Gormire.

A bridle path winds along near the eastern fringe and climbs aloft through the "hanging wood"; here in Spring is Nature's floral symphony, a wealth of blazing golden gorse, with rich undertone of other blooms lending additional beauty to the scene, for here and there overpowering the verdure of the turf, in the open or in shade, are masses of pale primroses, the azure wild hyacinth, and the turquoise-edged forget-me-not! Among them, studding this true wild Queen Mab's Garden, are huge masses of mossy and weather-stained blocks of stone, fallen from the cliffs above. While here, musing on the wondrous open-air spectacle, a large rough-legged buzzard circled aloft for some time the wild wood doves (its natural prey) fly away in terror. All down the hill slope from the cliff to the low lands near Thirlby beck is a serried mass of whins and old hawthorns, all flecked and tinted to a kind of oxydised silver hue from the growth upon them of lichens, the crowns of the thorn trees like a rich crimson velvet with their crop of ripening haws. An uncountable flock of speckle-breasted felfers bespangle this royal purple like unto pearls upon some oriental fabric; all the while Gormire is a ripple of smiles among its reeds, and ever with a low laugh laves the sandy beach below.

Concerning White Mare's Cliff the tradition following is told by Rev. Richard Abbey in "The Castle of Knaresbro'." We are told there once lived an Abbot of Rievaulx more devoted to secular than to sacred service. Among his belongings he was the proud possessor of a white Arab mare of great beauty and speed.

> "And the joyful life of her earlier days
> Shone in her eyes at the Abbot's praise, . . .
> But gentle and mild
> As a little child,
> Tho' full of old love for the desert wild."

At a neighbouring castle resided a Knight, Sir Harry de Scriven, who, too, owned a favourite barb "Nightwind," ever carrying its master "well up" in the chase. Betwixt these two, cleric and lay, was abiding jealousy, by reason of which each was ever ready to play some practical joke upon the other. Sir Harry, on "Nightwind" one eventide in autumn had his opportunity, and took it. Seeing the Abbot "drinking and blinking" in the well-known hostelry on Black Hambleton, the Knight joined him, with an April Fool's errand or a wild goose chase on which to send him. "My lord Abbot," he cried out, "a yeoman is sick, on Hambleton Moor, and he prays you be quick, and shrive him, poor sinner, and get him to heaven . . . his wife bye the bye has the beauty of Seven!" That was the bait and "Nightwind" was offered as a loan, himself as guide. The Abbot craftily offered his white mare—the Knight should ride—they were equals, and so to stirrups both, and the wild frolic commenced. Over and over the darkening plain, ever nearer the cliff's dizzy steep, did the Abbot on the Knight's horse beckon and decoy the Knight on his tricky Arab mare. The Knight onlured, but ever a hand's breadth behind, became distraught with choler

> "So the Knight never knew,
> As nearer they drew
> To that terrible spot on the Hambleton Heath,
> Where it falls in sheer wall to the valley beneath."

The end came quickly, and with a transformation most devilish—for "Too late! They are over! They gallop in air!" Before he met his death on the jagged bed of fallen rocks at the foot of the cliff, he saw the Abbot on his black barb suspent in air over him in the very act of changing into the Evil One himself!

> "Two horns on the head of the Abbot were growing,
> And his feet cloven-hoof'd in the stirrups were showing,"

and a voice derisively called out:

> "If you must play a trick,
> Try it not on Old Nick;
> I'll see you, Below, when I visit the sick."

A gruesome legend; but, nevertheless, admissible here in this sporting land and interesting as a variation on a very, very old theme indeed.

[*W. G. Foster.*

Leaving 'fancy' we come to an incident that might easily have ended differently and worse.

A Foxhunter's Narrow Escape.

There was a sensational hunting at the final run of the Bilsdale Hounds. A fox was found at South Woods Cover, and ran by Lake Gormire round the bottom of the White Mare of Whitestonecliffe. Several horsemen crossed over the wall which fences off the edge of this precipitous cliff, and seeing hounds turned and jumped the wall back again on to the moor. One horseman, riding a young horse, was awaiting his turn to jump, when the animal became impatient and ran back. The rider had the presence of mind to throw himself from the saddle, though not before the mare was on the very edge of the cliff, from which there is a sheer drop of 120 feet on to the crags below. The action of the rider caused the horse, which was losing its balance, to dart forward in the very nick of time.

At the very foot of the crag a split or fracture is called "The Fairies' Parlour"—a better sounding name than the one at Roulston connected with His Sable Highness the King of Evil. The three prominent Scars of this Hambleton Ridge are Roulston, 950 feet, Whitestonecliffe, 1056 feet, and Boltby, 1075 feet, the rise being to the North. This eastern scarp is not unlike the seacliffs of the coast in its bay-like indentations and contours, and indeed, incalculable ages ago, when an inland sea covered the Vale plain, its waves dashed wildly at times up against these bastion western-facing Scars, and huge leviathans of the deep sported and bellowed where now stand village and town. The scene looking west from the Scarp is panoramic indeed—a wide bewildering vale, dotted with clustering hamlet dwellings, a few canopies of reek above the towns, many a tree clump, silver strip of river, thatched rick, and hedge-bounded meadows or arable land—the varied hues all blent in the distance into a purple haze like the pictures of Claude Lorraine. Now through whins and erratic blocks we scramble down, by way of Skipton Hill to Thirlby.

Thirlby is a real bit of Scania in Yorkland—a really pretty little hamlet nestling under the lee of the Hambletons, with the pale face of Wisson-cliff looking down into the village street. A double ford at the junction of two roads gives passage way over the, at times, rushing torrent-like beck, bordered by neat farmsteads and rural cottages. There is a road up Thirlby bank to the Hambleton Plain, one of the rudest and roughest imaginable, and now seldom used, altho' there were wheelmarks in the Fall of 1905, probably the first made for some length of time. Here, too, was an Inn, having a paradoxical sign—

"What sign this is, no man can tell,
Yet 'tis a sign there's ale to sell!"

Less than a mile up the romantic beck is Ravensthorpe Mill and the site of the ancient Manor House of Ravensthorpe, where an extensive and deep moat tells of the bygone territorial dignity of its owners. In Norman days it belonged to that noble fighting family the De Roos. In the early Fourteenth century it became the property of the Walkynghames of Walkyngham Park, near Knaresborough. Sir John of that name, served Edward III. right loyally in the Scot's Wars, and lies buried at Feliskirk, likewise his wife, the Lady Joan, whose will, dated 30th Jan., 1346, orders that she be buried in the church "against the sepulchre of Sir John Walkyngham, her husband." The two effigies doubtless indicate Sir John and his Lady.

Up stream is the village of Boltby, in the parish of Feliskirk and is situated in a triangular hollow of the Hambletons and under Boltby Scar, the scene about being wild, lonely, and yet attractive. We are here right in the heart of Scandinavian Yorkshire; one proof of this is to be found in the names of the great bulk of the places we are about to visit. The Domesday Survey describes the spot as belonging to Hugh, son of Baldric. In early Norman times it fell to one Odo de Boltby, whose Castle is supposed to have stood near the road leading over the Hambletons. Very pleasant indeed is the bijou ville of Boltby, filling the mouth of the pleasant Gurtof valley down which and across the highway courses the beck of many names—Gurtof beck, next Thirlby beck, again Sutton beck, Balk beck, Thirkleby beck, Isle beck (where it divides and joins again enclosing a ridge of land), and finally Willow beck, under which alias it empties itself into the Cold (Wooded) beck above Dalton. And during its course at the many fords at flood times it is the occasion of many a mishap, ending even in drowning — such being its unruly violence at times of flood.

Wisson-Cliff from Thirlby Bank. [*Edmund Bogg.*

At Boltby there is a chapel of ease built in 1855, with a burial ground, but there wasn't one to the old church. Linen-weaving was an industry formerly carried on here to some considerable extent. Old customs and traditions linger yet in these retired parts. The dead were originally borne from Boltby to the mother church for burial at Feliskirk, in very primitive fashion, on a bier and swathed in linen and uncoffined, and placed in the earth with only a slab laid over the corpse. Record says that the last occasion of this being done was on a hot summer's day, less than a century back, when the long black hair of the head becoming loose hung in strands below the bier, productive of awe — and no wonder — among the simple but superstitious bearers. The practice was, in consequence, soon afterwards discontinued.

Two miles of winding undulating road, with heather, fern, and woods on our right, and to the south a maze of dells and low hills, the Vale spreading away to the plain, we reach the entrance gates to Mount Saint John. But before describing this let us drop down the sinuous road leading past the characteristic church of St. Felix*, and enter into Feliskirk. This typical village viewed from any point (like Kilburn) appears a rare gem in a delightful setting, lying mainly in a sort of diminutive dell, among the outer spurs of the brooding hill range, with the rich green masses of woodland of Mount Saint John rising from its doors. It answers to the description of that rare Elysium situated in the land of the Blest. In Spring and Summer the place is aglow with blossom and colour, and through the lattice of one's bedroom window ever in wafts their delightsome fragrance, steeped as it were with the rapturous sound of feathered warblers, and the undertone of a myriad humming insects. More than this even, the dignity of a vast antiquity seems to hang a spell over it. It is approached, says one, by lanes so deep and narrow that (on occasion) the drifting snow renders the place almost unapproachable, but in Summertide these same lanes are flanked with hedges and flowery banks, flushed with the bouquet of odoriferous wild flowers, and the entrances of the village are overarched by fine trees throwing a mosaic-like shadow of quivering leopard-like spots on the road beneath. The church, with its grey time-toned walls and tower, ancient doorway, and its large sloping hillside graveyard, forms another fitting illustration to Gray's "Elegy," besides the one which the God's acre of Stoke Pogis

---

* Felixkirk, or the Church of St. Felix, now usually spelt Feliskirk.

inspired. Adjoined to the gardens is a surrounding band of flower-specked lush green pastureland. To the west the ground declines gently into the grandly spacious Vale of Mowbray. Apart from this bay-like expansion, to the west it is snugly ensconced in the lap of surrounding high land. A lengthy and important history is attached to the district of which Feliskirk is the head-centre, and to which the earliest name of this village gives the key.

The Village of Felixkirk. [Robert Rodwell

The Domesday name of the place is Fridebi (Frid meant peace—as Felix means happy). It may be that this name was given it by the primal Teutonic invaders to mark some cessation of strife between them and the Celts. In course of years the Scandinavians, more turbulent than the Teutons, swept aside the Anglo-Saxon settlers and added his "by"—the vill terminal—to the Fride (peace settlement) of the original founders of the place. So may have come Frideby. The dedication of the Kirk to St. Felix (the happy Saint) is, as it were, the responding chord which makes for harmony. St. Felix, a disciple of St. Paulinus, was the first Bishop of East Anglia in the early 7th century. At King William's Survey, like Boltby, it was in the hold of a Skane-Hugh, son of Baldric. It certainly seems strange that its older name should have fallen into disuse. But in early Norman times many strangers settled hereabouts, and when the church was erected and dedicated to St. Felix (early 12th century), and the terminal "Kirk" was tacked on to it, the older "by," as denoting a place, ceased to be among the spoken current terms, and gradually it became forgotten.

At the entrance of the village from Thirsk, there is a large spherical howe, in part of Nature's formation, but the upper portion is artificial so formed in the early ages to serve as a tumulus where the Chiefs of the old Race, and perhaps their successors, were laid to rest. In the field on the opposite bank of the road, another mound of artificial semblance attracts attention. Soon these mounds may perhaps yield up their dead treasure, and so reward the spade of some enterprising antiquary.

At the foot of the howe is the village inn, where tourists or others can obtain food and drink, always found satisfactory and not unreasonably charged for. Such inns, are indeed a boon to travellers, and for this reason should not be left without mention. The vicarage, with its yellow-washed walls, stands close to the top of the knowle, a most commanding position overlooking the village and many a mile of broken hill country, a magnificently delightful vista for the eye to roam over ; hanging woods, dimly stretching moor, golden furze on purple heather ; while to the west spreads, as one writer declares, the most beautiful panoramic view in the world, that of the Vale of Normandy excepted. During the first half of last century, one Peggy Allison kept the inn, at that time situated at the east side of the top, not the foot, of the howe. The old house has long disappeared, but Peggy's orchard is still known by her name! The old landlady was wont to retire betimes to bed, and her usual custom was actually (it is said) to leave her customers to draw their own beer and chalk up the reckoning behind the door, to be settled for at some future day. At that date Public houses were open all night. In these degenerate days, one is afraid that Peggy Allison's custom would not conduce to either prosperity or sobriety.

Let us now pass to the Church—the main link in the chain of historic evidence hereabouts. In the early months of the year countless snowdrops and daffodils wave a mute blessing over the grave mounds, and the birds, never seeming to weary (for it is their love-time), pour out their music from swelling throats all the livelong day. The church, which has undergone several renovations, and one judicious restoration, (almost a re-building), dates from the opening years of the 12th century; and there are indications that the present structure superseded one of Anglo-Danish origin, although Domesday makes no mention of one at that period, yet we need not be surprised when we consider that the Pre-Conquest value of the place was thirty-five shillings, and this had dropt to five only at King William's Survey. Herein we have fully illustrated the calamity and depreciation which had fallen on the district. The interior consists of nave, two aisles, chancel, and tower. A Norman doorway and other fragments of round arched work remain. The most interesting part is the chancel, which during the last restoration was re-built with the apse on the original lines and finished off with an interlacing arcade according to the design of the early church. Doubtless the builder of the circular east end, had in mind the work of the Knights of the Temple, as the London Temple Church, the finest of the four round churches still in existence in this country. And it is well to remember that the proud martial figures of the Knights of St. John passed in and out of this church through the old Norman doorway in the chancel six or seven centuries ago. The semi-

Interior of Felixkirk Church, showing the Apse
[R. Rodwell.

circular apse was very common in Norman churches; an inheritance from the earliest Christian Basilicas. The German builders of that period were often not content with an apse at the chancel end, but put one at the opposite extremity too. Are the circular churches an expression of the same feeling which prompted the ancient Druids to form huge circles of stones for their temples?

Under a canopied and crocketted recess within the sacrarium, reposes restful and silent the effigy of a Knight in chain armour, his legs crossed and his arms resting on his breast as if in prayer; with sword and shield and spurs, as when in life he was ready for action, and a lion couchant is at his feet. Opposite, on the floor, is the effigy of a lady, her hands also joined in supplication, and two angels support her head. It has long been an open question to whom these two figures refer. There are no marks or heraldic devices to guide one to any solution. Most writers assign them to members of the once great and powerful race of the De Roos, who at an early period held the Manor of Ravensthorpe. To our minds, the effigies are more likely those of Sir John Walkyngham of Walkyngham, and the Lady Joan, his wife. Ravensthorpe Manor in this parish, has been previously referred to as their property at that date, and he was buried in Felixkirk Church, and in 1346, Joan his wife, willed to be buried in this church against the sepulchre of her husband, so that there is really every reason to believe that these effigies represent the latter-named persons. There is indeed a strange spell thrown upon the observer on entering in this unique Kirk. The solidity of the structure, the massive pillars and capitals, and the sturdy span of the pointed arches, the architectural elaboration of the two semi-circular ones, the apse ending of the chancel, the deep splay of the windows, the stern and solitary figure of mailed Knight and his Consort: all these features contribute to give an impression of mediæval glamour to the place.*

NEVISON'S HOUSE, MARDERBY HALL, AND MOUNT ST. JOHN.

A few hundred yards over the fields N.W. from Feliskirk, on land known as Upsal Park, is a farmhouse designated 'Nevison's' —the tongue of gossip, rarely wagging without some slight foundation for its tales, says this was the resort of the notorious highwayman described by Charles II. as "Swift Nick," and a cottage a bit further south of the farm is called "Nick's House." To all appearance the farmhouse may have been built 250 years ago, and at some period has evidently been in the occupation of a person named Nevison, for on the walls are the initials I. N. in iron corroded with age and exposure. On another wall-face are pieces of

---

* The family of Conyers of Heskett,‡ was both worthy and ancient. Thomas Conyers of Heskett, gent., in 1579, wills to be buried in the churchyard, near unto his wife and children He left a widow, Elizabeth, who in 1588, wills to be "buried in the chancell of Phillisk Church." Other members of this family were buried here. Torre records that the church of St. Felix in Clyveland was given to the Prior and Brethren of the Hospital of St. John of Jerusalem in England, to whom it was appointed by Walter Giffard, Archbishop of York, who, on 16th April, 1279, ordained "that this church, whereof the Hospitallers are patrons, be appropriated to them, saving to the Archdeacon his archdeaconal rights; and that the said house do, out of this church, by the hands of John de Cracecombe, who possessed this church, at their presentation receive yearly at Michaelmas 40s. as long as he shall live, which John shall have the residue obventions, fruits and profits of the church in the name of a Temple benefice without cure, during his life; also shall have the houses and area annexed to the church. And that all ordinary and extraordinary burdens of the church when they happen shall be divided between the said Master John and Thomas de Cawood, their vicar of the church. The collation to the vicarage shall totally belong to the Archbishop and his successors, which said ordination was confirmed by the Chapter of York, under their Common Seal 1st May, 1279." On 9th November, 1314, an Inquisition was taken touching the portion of this vicarage of Felicekirk, finding the possessions of the vicarage, and the value of the temporalities; all of which are enumerated in a long list by Torre "The sum of the rents and profits of this vicaridge do extend to £20 3s. 2d.; out of which the vicars are bound to find one parochial priest in the church of St Felix and one chappelaine in the chapell of Boltesby, and a third chappelaine to celebrate three days in the week in the chappell of Sutton-super-Whitsoncliff. The Master and Brethren have to cover the chancell at their own cost, and the vicar to find books, vestments, and other ornaments of the chancell."

‡ Hesketh Hall and Hesketh Grange, once the home of the Conyers, lies near the road leading from Boltby to Hawnby.

curved iron, and story has it these were the shoes of his steed, which, once in a snowstorm he *reversed*, so that pursuers might be baffled and led to suppose the shoe marks were coming away from instead of going in the direction they really took. In the church

Felixkirk Church, S.E. View. [*R. Rodwell.*

register of South Kilvington - the house being in that parish—are several entries of baptism and burial of Nevisons. The Nevison was King of the " high-toby men " of the great North Road ; and facts assist in connecting this farm with one of the places he at times made his abode, perhaps to hide in and rest, at peace with all men, for a brief space. Even to-day the place is lonesome and little visited, hid away from the bustling haunts of men. Still, it is well to reflect for a moment, that with all his compensating qualities of courtliness, adroit wit, and gallantry, "Swift Nick" paid the penalty of his high-handed deeds on the gallow's-tree at York Castle in 1685. Sentiment may be wasted on such a man, easily enough, but there are endless stories—from sympthisers, it would seem—of how, Robin Hood-like, he bestowed upon the poor what he took, willy-nilly, at pistol's mouth, from the rich. He is said to have levied a quarterly tribute on the Northern drovers and carriers, in return for which tax, he safeguarded them from the other lesser Knights of the Road!

But we must be brief—neither time nor space for outlawry's anecdotes are ours. Half a mile south of Feliskirk, set by a stream at the foot of the hill, with wooded slopes rising steeply to Mount St. John, is the ancient site of Marderby. This name is most instructive from the place-name standpoint. In Domesday it is written Mar-tre-bi, and as belonging to Hugh, son of Baldric. In its prefix *Mar* and its central *tre* we find, with most probability, the boundary dwellings of the Celt, *mar* as in *March* denoting a border of delimitation; whilst, without any doubt, in the final *bi*, the Dane is revealed. Marderby Hall is now only a farmstead, but round about it are significant indications both of its ancientry and former importance.

We will now climb up through the fern-sweet undergrowth of the woodland upsloping, flower bedecked, and aglow with sunlight, a scene which our artist friend, Walter Pattison, loves so well to pourtray in his pictures. The woods around Mount St. John are even more luxuriantly bewitching: rich beyond comparison in their bridal veil of beauty at that sweetest time of the year when Spring weds Summer. The history of Mount St. John is too long to be fully related in this book, but briefly, the facts are these. William de Perci, the founder of the great house, gave to the Knights

Hospitallers land about here to the amount of "Five Knights' fees," upon which a "Preceptory" was established dedicated to St. Mary. The De Roos gave them the Manor on which the community settled, and yet other lands were bestowed by Roger de Mowbray, Adam Fossard, Sir William Cautlow, Alice Gaunt, Oda de Boltbi, and Baldwin de Wake. One of the duties of these knights was to provide refreshment and shelter for pilgrims at their "hospices," protecting them if need be from injury or insult during their sojournings in the Holy Land.

This order of Knights of St. John of Jerusalem, or Knights Hospicers as they were most commonly styled, took its rise and name from an inn (or Hospitium) built at Jerusalem for the use of pilgrims visiting the Holy Land, dedicated to St. John the Baptist. After loss of their possessions in Palestine, the Knights settled in the island of Rhodes in consequence. When the Turks took possession of that island in Greek seas, the Knights migrated to Malta, their pennon or flag bearing the peculiarly formed cross with floriated segments, now universally known as the Maltesian Cross. But this is a digression. Only a fragment of the original house remains, but the place still bears the stamp of sanctity and reverend age.

While excavating some years ago near the house, foundations of the original building and a quantity of human remains were unearthed. The present house is situated near the summit of the highest ground hereabouts, and enclosed in a grove of fine grown trees. The imagination can without effort mentally figure the transits, in and out, of knights habited in bright chain armour, with armorial emblems blazoned on the surcoat; and in fancy, too, hear the jingling mail and the proud impatient pawing of their war-steeds. Here to Mount St. John came, during its hey-day of prosperity and fame, nearly all the great Barons and the flower of the chivalry of the North. Father Campion, the Jesuit, is said to have been secreted here at a time when his holy person was much "wanted" by his enemies.

It has been truthfully said that one of the most lovely walks in Yorkshire is that between the Evangelist's Mount and Kirkby Knowle by the Boltby road. Past barren heathland, precipitous woodland slopes, bosky dells and ravines, we descend into a pleasant bower-like retreat under the "Knoll"—whence Kirkby Knowle, another form of the word, derived its appellation. It is hemmed in on three sides by hills, its only outway being to the west. The present Kirk is modern enough, but the vestiges of two pre-Norman crosses, and the bowl of a Norman font reveal an Anglo-Danish foundation. The whole place furnishes evidence of hoar antiquity. In its remoteness from the hives of industry, its charm of rustic simplicity and pastoral beauty can better be felt than put into words. Marks of ancient enclosure and defensible positions are apparent—indeed everything the eye, to-day rests upon, is attractive and interesting, alike in colour or contour, be it the hue and line of moor, wood, or lowland vale. At Domesday, Kirkby Knowle was comprised in the extensive Manor of Bagby, a place quite six miles away. To-day the order is reversed: Bagby is a Chapelry in the parish of Kirkby Knowle.

When the first great Survey was made, its overlord was Hugh, son of Baldric, the best endowed landowner in these parts. Wm. Grainge says that the name of Ella was extremely common formerly in this and other villages around, commemorative of descendents of Ella, son of Ida, the Anglian King of Northumberland. Of this numerous clan was John Ella, the well-known musician, founder and director of the London Musical Union, and for 25 years a member of the Italian Opera orchestral band. A writer in the *Falcon* tells us that the old church contained a perfect specimen of the old Squire's family pew, filling the entire west end of the church, with chairs, footstools, etc., and high curtains affixed to brass rod work so that the occupants might, at their will and pleasure, be screened off from both preacher and congregation! Further, the service could not be commenced before the arrival of the Squire's party! And it was usual for the ringers to only begin to call the congregation together when the Squire's equipage was seen coming down the hill almost a mile away! An important man, the Squire, truly, in those days, when even Worship must wait for squirearchical countenance! Over this capacious pew was the gallery from which the musicians and vocalists sent forth their weird and solemn music from a variety of instruments now never seen in "quires and places" where anthems are sung.*

In the graveyard is a stone to the memory of Elizabeth Farding, who died April 2nd, 1821, aged 98 years, for 70 years a servant in the employ of Francis Smith of New Buildings. On the east of the village is the Grange Farm, a picturesque example of an old-time residence. Above its roof the tree-clad Knowle shews finely in the morning light. Yet a little further N.E., situated in a wood on the moorland slope, is a miniature Gormire, formed as the larger water itself was—by a landslip which took place in 1799. Past this lakelet an old, now almost disused, cart track mounts the face of the hill and joins the old road over the Hambletons near Lime-kiln House. A mile N.W. and situate on a steep declivity, is a goodly mansion known as the New Building, a title bestowed upon it by James Danby who purchased the ruinous Kirby Knowle Castle (standing in the middle of the 17th century), and after re-building, conferred on it the present name. Bygone generations, however, always and for long called it the New biggin. In days when knights rode forth to war in suits of glittering steel

---

* It was at such a church where the parson always waited in a kind of awe and suspense the coming of the Squire that the following incident took place. A "relief" parson, not knowing the custom, began "When the wicked man ——' when the clerk suddenly chimed in "Please, Sir, he hasn't come yet."

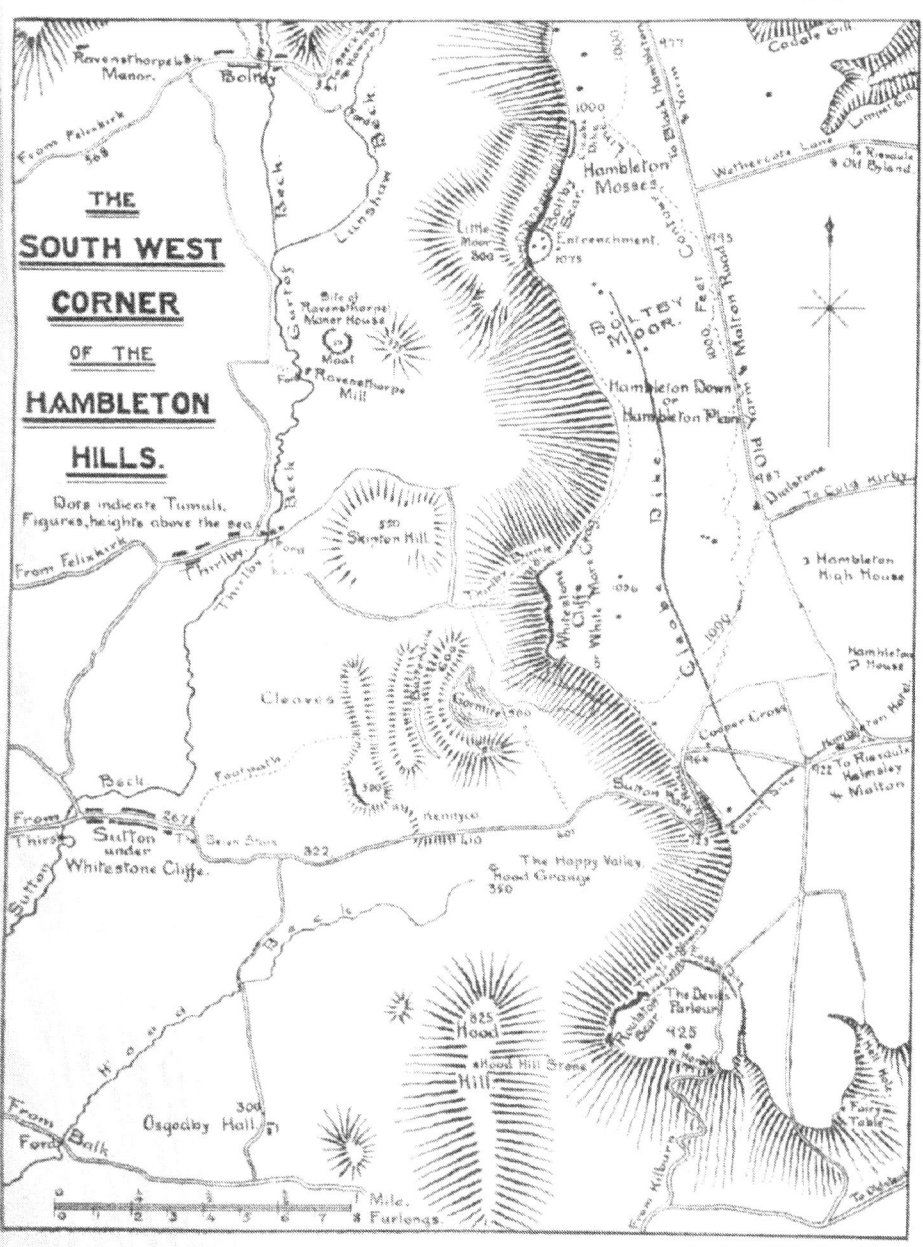

[Drawn by Robert Rodwell

mail, it had the prouder title of Kirby Knowle Castle. In early Norman times it had come into the hands of the Lascelles, a knight called Picot de Laselle, who sprang from a ville named Laselle in the French province of Touraine. He came to England in the train of Alan, Earl of Richmond, and fought at Hastings, receiving as his share of land-spoil the Lordship of Scruton, it is supposed. At first sight the description "New" seems to be misapplied, for in the distance it looks like an early castellated Tudor stronghold, but bearing in mind the various alterations of the 17th century, the name "New" must be taken relatively. It is fit enough, and the commanding situation this battlemented structure occupies is indeed Ideal, brooding in its eyrie in the woods near the top of the moor and sheltered from the cold blasts of "rude Boreas" by the round detached brae of Knayton Moor, and from the eastern keen dry winds of Spring by the Boltby and Kirkby highlands. It nestles in the lap of tangled woodland, its very lawn battlemented; and in "February fill-dike" on the slope below, thousands of snowdrops deck the ground like living snowflakes, superseded later by a wealth of other wild flowers, red campion, blue forget-me-not, and white stitchworts. From the garden the ground declines steeply through the park, till losing itself in the great plain of Mowbray's Vale, which stretches out south and west for thirty miles or more. The view-scape is one of loveliness and luxuriance combined, perhaps without equal in the land. When the air is clear, the white puffs of steam from the iron horse can be seen as the train leaves the station at York, and its course can be followed till it enters Darlington. Through this expanse of champaign the two rivers, Swale and Yore, wind ribbon-like, and numerous tributary becks tumble tortuously from both eastern and western boundary to swell the growing tribute which Ouse makes to the Humber, and Humber to the Sea.

The hall demesne appears to-day a network of gardens, retrieved by the effort of man from the lone savagery of a primitive wilderness—so high is the pitch of cultivation it has reached. Gilpin, in his "Picturesque Tour," says of this scene:—"Here Nature hath wrought with her broadest pencil; the parts are ample, the composition perfectly correct. I scarcely remember anywhere an extensive view so full of beauties and so free from fault." The Cathedrals of both York and Ripon can be distinctly made out, and the hill contours, and dim blue-grey stretches of the western uplands, the vista extending almost to the confines of Westmoreland.

During the 14th to 16th centuries, this Old Biggin, or Knowle Castle, belonged to the Constables- a notable family from the East Riding. In spite of the "Reformation" they appear to have remained staunch Catholics, for the name of Constable is found in the list of Recusants in the reign of Queen Bess. In corroboration of this, in the most ancient part of the present house is a secret chamber, only 3 feet 6 inch square, by 6 feet in height. Most of the older halls were thus provided with a hidden refuge whereto fugitives or Catholic suspects might "lie low," *perdu* they called it, when and while the spies of Royalty or the Law were abroad. There were private chapels in most of the houses of the Nobility, and here the priest who had been driven out of their benefices found a safe asylum. Such men as Father Campion, Robert Parsons and Henry Garnett were continually and secretly officiating according to the Roman Catholic ritual, saying Mass upon portable tables in upper chambers and secret places. There was no great risk to these men between the years 1559 and 1569, for the Squirearchy were nearly all their friends. But after the unfortunate outbreak (the Rising of the North) any Catholic priest continuing to exercise his priestly office, did so at the risk of his life, and anyone receiving absolution from such a person were likewise subject to severe punishment.

In a couple of bow shots (if the bow was in the hands of the famous archer of Thirkelby) we should arrive at Upsal, where stood in former days, a stronghold of the Mowbrays, and later the the far-famed Scroopes. The Scroopes of Masham and this place held court here in all the feudal, almost royal, splendour of the Baronial period. Yet hardly a fragment of their castle exists to-day, —truly

"Time, time his withering hand hath laid
 On battlement and tower;
And where rich banners were displayed,
 Now only waves a flower."

The village itself stands on the slope of the Hambletons, with a magnificent overlook of its own over the Vale-land, which is both the dominant and most beautiful feature in this part of Yorkshire; and from its situation half way up the south-western shoulder of Knayton Moor, or Woolamoor is, from a distance, the most conspicuous of all the villages in the Vale. Its name, Upsal, is distinctively Scandinavian; and in baptising it the first settler of that Viking race may have had in mind Upsala, his birthplace between the North Sea and the Baltic Sea. "Up" means elevated, high, upp, a hill, and "sal," old Norse "Salr" (a large house, "gaard," a hall), or place of high state; so its name was very possibly—plausibly at anyrate—given to it to distinguish it from a residential place on the plain, such for instance as the Hall at North Kilvington; seen from hence the name "Up" is very apparent. Anyhow the name is Swedish, "Upsalir"— the high hall. The New Hall, a commanding structure, stands in a fine park, in the angle of the roads, adjoining the street, and viewed from the S.E. and from below, in contrast with the New Biggin which appears like some medieval Knight's abode, the scene appeals forcibly to the imagination.

Savouring of some old-word Border scene, attainted of Mythology or Romance, it is a place from whence the Knights on errands of battle or, it might be, of tourney only, or to decide some disputed question of heraldic bearing of arms—the Bend Or dispute was a notable example—rode forth. Superstition was ever most rife among the Scandinavian peoples--it is even to-day—and the belief then was that dragons and monster beasts infested these districts. It is supposed to have been a spot set apart for religious assembly in the days of Druidism, and the old names and Scanian tales dating far back in the centuries, give to the place a character of uncanny remoteness. Grainge mentions such names "Brown Mordikes" and "Ulnes-mote," now corrupted into Woolmoor. These are derived from the Scandinavian "Ullo," wool, and "mote," a place of meeting, which again may have reference to the yearly assembly for the shearing of sheep (a great festival held by all early pastoral races) rather than to the spot of Law meet, the *ge-mote* with which in other parts of Yorkshire we are familiar.

Of the right noble family of Scropes we have here no space to speak of at length. A representative of this illustrious family still lives at Danby Hall, on the Yore. Their actions are indelibly engraved on the scrolls of history, and can never die. If the full story of their Castle at Upsal could be written the strangest and most dramatic scenes would be set forth. The present edifice (modern Gothic) is raised in part on the site of the one built by Geoffrey and Henry Scrope in or about Edward the Third's reign. This, in its turn, had doubtless been placed on the ruins of the original Danish stronghold which was in existence at the time of the Conquest. Some remains of the old Castle of the Scropes still exist, but the old walls were long used as a quarry, and their massive grouted rubble cores offered a stern resistance to the pick.

The village holds several examples of the taste in architecture of the late Captain Turton. One old farmhouse is conspicuous by its plain exterior and absence of all decoration, but the storms of many a winter have made it a study "in the grace of the years that are dead," in colour and soft crumbling lines. Most of the

W

houses shew much individuality in design. The main entry to the Forge has appropriately the form of a large horseshoe fully furnished with nails and caulkings; and the smaller flanking doorway of the carpenters' and blacksmiths' shops have symbolic carvings in marble inlaid in their masonry. Many relics in the shape of armour, jewellery, and coins have been found from time to time about the Castle precincts.

The Crock of Gold.

William Grainge tells the following legend regarding a Dream and Buried Treasure. Generations ago there resided in the village of Upsal a man who dreamt, three successive nights, that if he went to London Bridge he would hear of something greatly to his advantage. He went; travelling the whole distance, Upsal to London Town, "his fortune for to find" as the ballad has it, on "shank's galloway," *i.e.*, on foot. Arrived at London he took his station on the bridge, and at length was accosted by a strange-looking man, who enquired "What are you waiting here so long for?" After some hesitation, he told his thrice-repeated dream. The man laughed at his simplicity, and remarked that he had that night dreamed a very curious dream too: which was, that if he went and dug under a bourtree (Bottery) bush in Upsal Castle in Yorkshire he would find a pot of gold, but he did not know where Upsal was, and he asked if the countryman could tell him. Seeing some "advantage" in secrecy, our pilgrim from the very place pleaded ignorance of the locality, returned home hot-foot, digged beneath the bourtree (the elder) and lo! did there find a crock filled with gold; and on the cover an inscription in a language he did not understand. The pot and lid were, however, preserved. One day a Jew-like bearded stranger made his appearance, saw the pot, and deciphered the inscription, which read

"Look lower—where this stood
Is another twice as good."

On hearing this, the man of Upsal repaired to the bush, resumed his spade, dug deeper, and found of a verity another crock by far bigger and more valuable than the first, heartened by which, he dug deeper still, and lo! found yet another more valuable than Numbers 1 and 2!

This digger and discoverer is said to have been Henry Lord Scrope, the builder of the castle. The same tradition, the similar finding of three (sacred number) crocks of gold, in consequence of a dream three nights repeated, has been assigned to other places. Upsal, however, appears to have as good a claim to this yielding of secreted coin as the very best of them. Prove it of course no one can, but the constant tradition of the inhabitants, preserved unimpaired through all the years that have passed; and, moreover the identical bottery bush 'neath which the treasure was found by digging—an elder near the N.W. corner of the ruins—alike attest a faith in Effort, and perhaps contain the kernal of a prophecy symbolising the value of deep drainage in agriculture—of "digging deeper" at anyrate!

The Lost Corpse.

Another story connected with this district is that of the missing corpse. The aged man who told the story in the Sixties to the late Revd. A. T. Atwood, of Knayton, was a youth of some eighteen summers when the incident took place, and one of the bearers. The mourners were conveying the body to Kirkby Knowle for burial, and taking the short cut by the old green lane locally known as the Beech Path, and through or by Beck-stead Wood, when—in the very words of the teller—"Just as we arrived at that spot, we set down the body for a rest. 'Twas a hot autumn day, the nuts were enticing—'twas 'tbest nut year I remember,—and so we all went off to gather 'em, and when we came back the corpse was gone!" "Washed away by the burn, I suppose?" "No, sir,

I wish it had been, for there, we should then have got it back. The coffin was there, untouched by mortal man. We lifted it up—it felt light, as an empty coffin would be. We ran with it to Kirkby Knowle, and the parson did the burying, but the corpse was gone—was lost. It was all along of our nutting."

Concerning "Chophead Loaning," an old lane between South Kilvington and Upsal, is the following tradition. After the battle of Boroughbridge (so disastrous to the Earl of Lancaster and his followers) John de Mowbray in his attempt to reach his Manor House of Upsal, was captured here in this lane and immediately beheaded, and his armour and dismembered limbs were suspended from the branches of a large oak; and for generations later only those of stout heart dare pass the spot after dark, for there was heard a sound of strange voices and whisperings, like a subdued dirge or requiem for the dead.

Knayton from the Lane Ends, showing the base of Crab Mill. [R. Rodwell.

There is nothing to call for notice between Upsal and Knayton, which place is about a mile and a half—as crows fly—W. N.W., and four miles north of Thirsk, but has no special feature or point of great interest. Its steeply pitched red roofs are picturesque enough, as seen through the encircling trees crowning a rounded ridge, a field's length east of the North Road leading from Thirsk to red-roofed Yarm. The old road formerly ran right through the village. The tourist would do well to wend his way up Swan Lane, and view the gardens and orchards which border the village street, then by another back to the main road at the four lane end. Here by the wayside are the remains of an old crab mill, with the broken upper stone lying on the broader lower one, the oblique furrows of which are now to some extent worn down where the edge of the upper stone travelled round on the pulped fruit. Opposite are the "horsing steps" of the Three Tuns Inn, of use in pillion times. The origin of the word Knayton is to be found in the Saxon "Knape" or "Knap,"—the back or spine of a ridge. Grainge ventures on the statement that the name derives from "Knave"—a servant; but this seems to me very questionable.

Between the villages, is the Knayton and Borrowby School, built on the site of the old Tithebarn; from here we dip down to Borrowby Bridge over the windings of Broad beck, one of the main tributaries of Cod-beck. In the year 1589, a bridge across this beck "was builded at the charge of the Countie." A water-mill stands a little way up the stream, gaining its power from the weir at the "Hell Kettle," higher up. Borrowby Mill stands in a sweet little dell, and "Aude" Dick Megginson, the Miller, is quite a quaint character. A chat with Dick opens up in the mind vivid vistas into bygone times and places: he would equally fit the description of Chaucer's "Miller," where he tells the tale of the carpenter, and the carpenter returns the compliment by telling the tale of a miller; and that other "Jolly Miller" of the Dee, whose troll was ever—

"I care for nobody, no—not I,
And nobody cares for me."

Dick Megginson. [*Ernest Forbes*.

Truly, old folk-speech remains with Megginson; his eyes glisten like live coals when "talking as is my way" of "moutering," and grinding grist, fish tickling or shooting, or bemoaning and bewailing the "beck bein't robbed o' its watter" to feed the local reservoirs for drinking purposes. The modern sanitary view of the question does not appeal to his mind of course. He is wont to say "They saant hev t' watter frae t' mill as lang as ahm alaave (alive)." Of a verity Dick is a real old-fashioned standard of Middle-age rural

England, and rightly so, for his ancestors were millers at Arden Mill in Ryedale in days of the Tudor Kings, and son has succeeded father as Miller of Arden since that period.

North of the bridge the new turnpike, made for stage coaches, turns to the right along the lower ground and past Leake. The old road kept to dryer ground, and went straight up the hill behind the main street of Borrowby and along the top of the ridge beyond. Borrowby is mentioned in Domesday Book as Bergebi, a duplication in place-names, "Burg"— a borough, and "by"—a town or "ton," hedged in for mutual protection, conferred first by Angles and added to by the Danes; and it belongs to Allertonshire. The prefix "berg" denotes a place of importance, doubtless a stronghold of some note occupied its site in pre-Domesday times, whilst "by" shews indubitably that the Scandinavian once held possession. This is fully borne out by the fact that in the 11th century one Canute, a Dane, held here eight carucates of land under William de Percy. It may be that the place marks a frontier post, located as it is on the extreme southern march or limit of Allertonshire. The ground around the Cross proves conclusively that a stronghold, doubtless built of timber, once stood here. A market was held here formerly, and the place was far more populous than now. On the west side of the main street on the ridge is an open space; in the centre of this stands the Market Cross, little the worse for wear from the tooth of time. The upper stone (the crossed portion) partakes of a Maltese character. Both market and fair are now traditions merely —long, long gone. Like its sister village, Borrowby is surrounded by orchard-close and garden, and the red-tiled roofs (over the browns and greys of the old stone houses) rising terrace-like one above another up the spur end of the hill, forms a rural and artistic, nay, a joyous picture to the eye open to quaint charm in architecture, and one conspicuous from afar. Its salubrity is apparent to all, but if one needs a witness to this it is to be found in James Barnett, an old man of 97, who is still hale and hearty, and not only fetches water from the well but does odd jobs in the gardens round about also. He was a hand-loom weaver when the weaving of linen from blue-flowering flax flourished here—upwards of 200 of the inhabitants having been at one time occupied in the industry.

James Barnett.

James Barnett first saw light in Ebenezer Street, Leeds, in 1809—so he nears his century; and the spot was near that on which now stands that busy hive of competition and commerce— the Leeds Public Market. This was in Barnett's boyhood a meadow. Think of it! a mead in which buttercups and daisies grew! and into which with other lads he often enough trespassed after grass-larks' nests may be, and the apples in the orchards, much to the annoyance of the old Vicar of Leeds. It was then in all reality the "Vicar's Croft," suggestive enough for us who know that the name still remains, though the Croft is now one of bricks and mortar, flagstones, and the "fruits of the earth," animal and vegetable, oranges, bananas, tomatoes, plovers eggs in Spring, and mistletoe at Christmas, brought literally from every quarter of the globe! The green fields are far to seek to-day, indeed, and yet, we reflect, Progress is a fine thing—the good of the Many is better than the perquisite of a solitary cleric. It is nearly 80 years since Barnett last set foot in Leeds, and one may vividly imagine how strangely changed, how awesomely unfamiliar the place about

Vicar Lane and Kirkgate would appear to the old man who, we are told, over 90 years ago hearkened to the great "Rejoicings" over the English-Prussian Victory on the field of Waterloo. A few years later only, he watched the 44th Regiment leave the Barracks (then in Woodhouse Lane) to guard the sea-girt rock Prison in which Napoleon was kept fretting his heart out as he paced the terrace at Longwood, his head on his chest, his eyes gazing out North to the continent he would never disturb again. However, before the corps reached St. Helena, the "Man of Blood," the disturber of the World's peace, had passed to a rest the world could not give him, and lay buried

"With a green willow for all pyramid,
Which stirred a little if the low wind did"

in the bare rock-hewn cemetery of "the island off Africa."

The old town of Leeds (City now) has grown five-fold since Barnett left it "by the York road," in the rumbling old stage-waggon eighty-three years ago. His parents sleep, peaceably enough, in St. John's churchyard. A relic of the old street in which Jamie was born remains, and the old chapel of Ebenezer in the street of that name is now a warehouse, while he, himself, in the Borrowby district, home of his manhood and old age, he is almost universally known as "the Last of the Weavers."

LEAKE.

From Borrowby we follow the old lane and field-path, and in less than a mile reach the ancient Manor Hall and Church of Leake. It is Sunday afternoon, the congregation now dispersing in all directions, some to a great distance. The largest group (among them the clergyman), follow the highway to Knayton. Others are to be seen wending their steps by field, road and footpath, one of which leads through the graveyard and across the fields to Silton. Leake is the mother-church to Knayton-cum-Brawith, Borrowby, Landmoth-with-Catto, Gueldable, Crosby, Nether-Silton, and one portion of Kepwick. Leake is thus seen to be the hub or nave of the spiritual wheel of this extensive parish; and the bells from Leake's

Leake Church from the S.W.   [R. Rodwell

hoary tower gather the flock to their shepherd from every point of the compass. Grainge says the word Leake is doubtless derived from "Lech," British for a stone, or "Crom-lech," a stone table. But it appears to us that the word is far more likely to come from the Norse "Lœkr," a lake, mere, or tarn. The place lies in a kind of hollow in the hills, with the land north and east shelving to a still lower level, which has formerly been marshland more or less retentive of water, or dotted with pools in a rainy season. Now, only a diminished streamlet bickers its way east to join the Borrowby beck.

Strange tales indeed are chronicled of Leake. Old men prate to us stories of this place, which were handed down to them by their grandsires, these, in their turn receiving them orally from their forelders. The very ground seems impregnated with past associations, these in a measure vouching for the truth of the old-world traditions. Leake proper consists of only a Church and Manor House adjacent. The former rises in the centre of a well-stocked God's acre, and it has a fine tho' low Norman tower with an ornate upper storey. The two round columns of the North aisle, with their carved capitals and arches are likewise Norman. The rest of this church must be referred to the late Perpendicular period. The columns of the South aisle are octagonal, with incised capitals. The clerestory walls and roof generally present indications of decay, the beams bent and the walls out of plumb. We understand the church is soon to be thoroughly restored. The pews in the nave show a considerable display of Jacobean carved work. At the entrance to the choir are two stall ends with elaborately carved finials, outstanding from the face of which are carved figures, as if to guard the entrance one a reptilian monster, the other a kind of a winged dragon. On the north of the altar, which is a very plain one, is an aumbry. There is a piscina in the wall of the south aisle, indicative that here has been a chapel, doubtless belonging to the Danbys, who, in the Tudor and early Jacobean period, resided at the Hall. Built into the exterior south wall are two very ancient carven stones, evidently parts of an earlier structure, relating to the Danish period (Tenth century). On one stone is graven the figure of the pascal lamb, much defaced. The church roof is of low pitch, with a valuable old lead covering.

Leake Church. [R. Rodwell.

Leake Hall, now a farmhouse, almost joins on to the church, and is a Tudor-time erection, in part modernised. Yet with its remaining gables, quaint chimneys, time-toned roof and old mullioned windows, it is still picturesque in the extreme and a fine example of a Squire's abode in middle English time. The interior still shrines much that is curious and antique, a fine oaken staircase with massive steps dark with age, and wainscotted upper rooms adorned with panels of crests and shields.

But let us relate some of the traditions of Leake. The first has reference to the church, and, as the story runs, states that it was originally intended to erect it half a mile west of its present position on the top of Borrowby Bank (from whence there is a magnificent outlook over the coast-like front of the Hambletons) where it would have been a conspicuous object for miles around. But strange to say, all material brought to this spot during the day was mysteriously removed unseen of any eye during the night to the site whereon the church now stands. Rumour has it that Leake was once a populous village of some 1,500 souls, and the place was erased from the earth, or razed to the ground during a great foray of the ever-marauding Scots. Whatever may be the truth as to this, one thing is certain, viz., that the foundations of buildings extend to some distance in the fields around the church, and numerous ridges are still perceivable; and old men who have worked on the Hall Farm here from their very childhood, say that whenever digging or draining operations caused the ground to be delved, foundations and paved ways are continually struck, and even human bones and stone coffins unearthed. One old paved hollow-way, running north and south, can still be traced to the west of the Hall and close to the east end of the churchyard wall, is still known as the Danes' Lane; from which many cartloads of stones have been taken to mend local highways.

The story concerning a great massacre of Danes, and which may be the one which was general all over Eastern England on the festival of St. Brice, 13th November, 1002, shews it to have been of a gruesome character here at any rate. The folk-tale says, that during one of the Danish invasions the Skanes (being without wives) swooped down on Leake, slew or evicted all the Anglian males, and seized and held their wives and womenfolk by sheer force, and apart from making them do service, compelled them to great manual labour. This double bondage at length became unbearable, and a secret compact and understanding was come to among the women who, each having armed herself with some weapon, slew her particular captor in the night-time! The story of Jael and Sisera over again with only a slight difference. Those Danes who escaped are said to have been chased by the women of Leake down Dane's Lane; and from that circumstance it has ever since borne that name. According to oral tradition more than 500 men perished in this secret and sudden revolt of the women of Leake from their condition of bondage and wifehood "by capture." Their revenge struck such terror to the hearts of the other Danes in contiguous territories, that they at once fled the district. For long afterwards the women of Leake were treated by their menfolk with increased honour. As we have already remarked, this tradition doubtless has reference to the date when the great Massacre of the Danes took effect all over the country. All these facts and rumours point to some great calamity, fire, sword, or pestilence, overwhelming Leake.

Even poor "Old Noll" is blamed for these mishaps by some of the natives. One fellow told us that "toune o' Leek" was "blawn doon by aude Oliver Crumwell." Grainge states that when the churchyard was drained in 1852, a great heap of human bones was found, these appearing to have been thrown indiscriminately into a pit after a sanguinary strife. Nearly a century ago a writer records a discovery of stone coffins and other relics of man here. It is quite evident that some chapter in the history of Leake has never found a first-hand chronicler. It may have been raided by the Danes, or swept off the earth by the fearsome vengeance of William the Norman, or, in after centuries, destroyed by the incursion of the Scots. Some say it was ruined at the Standard Fight; this is erroneous; the Scots did not penetrate so far south in that disastrous raid. Sure it is, that some swift visitation fell upon this place.

During the early years of the bygone century, a master tailor and his two apprentices from Silton, had been working at Leake Hall, as was the custom in the "good old days." In the dark they were returning home by the churchyard path already mentioned, when at the foot of the stone stee in the north wall of the graveyard, several black Scotch bullocks were laid, one of them close against the bottom step. The master led the way as befitted his dignity and rank, and in passing over the steps fell astride the beast. In sudden fright it leapt to its feet and frantically plunged around the field, half maddened by shouts and the heart-rending shrieks of the master tailor. The two terrified lads, doubtless conscience-stricken, rushed back to the Hall, explaining with gasping breath "Here are the trimmings, and here the buttons and linings, but the dowl (devil) has run away with the master and the piece of broadcloth."

We have lingered too long at Leake, so let us take field-path and byroad by the very way probably the Danes fled from their pursuers, noting, as we go, the spot where at one time a substantial bridge spanned the brook or beck, now called "Leake Stell." Stell is the Norse word for a still or stagnant dike, and is a common term for water cuts here and further North.

Nether, or Lower Silton, is finely placed on the slope of the upland overlooking the country to the Hambletons and the South. The name is possibly without parallel, and its derivation calls for at least two alternative explanations. Both Siltons stand on a 'sill' or flat ledge of land from which water, whether spring or rainfall, would drain fastly off. *Sila* in Norse means to drain quickly, and both in past times, and even to-day in country districts, farmer's wives and milkmen are wont to "sile" the cow's milk. The other alternative etymology is that Sil is a form of *Sal* (as with Up-sal) a Hall, an important place; in Germany *Saals* are halls to this day. The final *ton* is of course Anglian—a place, a town, from *tynan*—

to hedge in or enclose. Tuns were first fenced round, dwellings being built within, and afterwards the words meant a collection of huts around the tun of the chieftain. Nether Silton is a township and chapelry in the parish of Leake. The situation is a fine one, and the environment delightfully picturesque, comprising hill, valley, knoll, moor and pleasant groves of trees. The chapel-of-ease is a plain structure, and was rebuilt in 1812. The altar-rails, presented by the late R. M. Jaques, Esq., formerly belonged to the old *Dreadnought*, training-ship of the Navy. The ancient Hall is by far the most interesting building at Silton, and dates from the end of the 16th century. In a field west of the house is a rough block of stone with a singular inscription in Capitals, each letter being the initial of a word:—

"Here The Good Old Manor House Stood,
 The Back Beams Were Oak The Great Walls Were Good"

and so runs the ditty:—

```
        H T G O M H S
       T B B W O T G W W G
        T W A T E W A H H
        A T C L A B W H E Y
            A.D. 1765.
        A W P S A Y A A.
```

It was an idea of the old Squire Hickes (whose forbears dwelt here) to place this unintelligible inscription on this stone to mark the spot where the old middle-age Manor Hall stood, and a link in the long chain of evidence, beginning with Bern, the Northumbrian chieftain, resident at the Siltons in the 8th century.

A mile North, and peacefully resting in its old age in a secluded hollow of the hills, is Over Silton Church. It stands quite half a mile from the village. It was a late April day that of our visit to this place, and the daffodils in thousands were swinging and nodding their bi-coloured yellow trumpets in benediction over the mounds of the dead in this God's acre; and over the church itself storm-blighted pines were waving their plumes like sprays, as it were, in sympathy with the solemn spirit of the scene. As the harvest of daffodils fade, a change of colour and contrast spreads over the place, a wealth of hyacinth carpets the graveyard in azure blue. The exterior of the church is much more striking than the interior. The entrance is through a Norman arch, ornamented with Chevron work. The roof of the nave is of very low pitch and covered with lead, with square-headed perpendicular windows, and the arms of the Nevill & Scrope, Archbishops during the 14th century, are inset into the roof of the nave. The base of ancient cross is in the churchyard, the shaft, if I mistake not, was brought hither from a field near the village. There are several very curious grave-covers here; one near the porch is very much like an effigy, and also others that call for comment, but space will not permit of their separate enumeration.

The village itself stands half a mile west, on much higher ground, and about it the land shows signs of very ancient occupation. The venerable Bede in his Saxon chronicle states, that here, in the year 780, at Silton, "the high-reeves of the Northumbrians burned Bern the Eldorman, on the 8th day before the Kalends of January." What Bern's offence was is not stated, but one thing is plain enough: a stirring deed of history was done here upwards of eleven hundred years ago. The village presents no remarkable features, unless its invigorating air and far-reaching prospects be such; but, without exaggeration, perhaps the finest view in the county may be had from the high ground north of the village. A little to the west is Caer-how hill, again in its terms a duplication of syllables having one meaning—"Caer," a hill fortress, and "how," a hill. Gnipe Hill, from the Danish "Gnypa," a promontory or point of land, which here, truly, runs between the two Siltons and precisely describes the word. To the N.W. of the

Upper Silton Church. (Gilbert Foster

village in the "Scarrs," is a cavern formerly known by the name Hobthrush Hall. Of old this antre was the home of a fairy or goblin, who (according to tradition—not always to be sworn by) was in the habit of leaping, at one spring, from the moor above his den to the top of Carlhow hill! The distance is fully half a mile. This goblin or gnome appears to have been kindly by nature, and particularly so to the farmer on whose land his "hall" was situated. For this man it was Hob's custom to churn cream in the nighttime whilst the family slept, his only recompense being a huge shive of bread and butter. One night the cream in the churn was set as usual, but the bread and butter was by an oversight forgotten. The apparent negligence so preyed upon Hob that, from the very occasion he forsook "butter bringing," and removed himself to another part of the countryside where his midnight and magical labours were better appreciated. Still, his abode is locally known as Hobby's hall.

A footpath leads from Silton to Thimbleby, and the views all the way are exceedingly fine, stretching westwards to Ingleborough hill, and northward far into the County of Durham. To the south the prospect opens out over the expanse of the Mowbray plain and far down into the Vale of York. Lower down, in the valley bed, at a spot called Nun House, lies a buried treasure. This is nought less than a bull's skin choke-full of gold. The number of coins such a full-sized belt would hold is almost incredible.

But leaving this treasure-trove to be searched for by who will, we descend by the two Siltons and along old lanes and bits of moorland; the springtime species of gorse showing its gold on every hand; the becks gurgling forth their melody, and birds warbling their refrain. On every side through such charming surroundings as the mind loves to dwell upon, we reach Kepwick, erswthile noted for its stone and lime industry. Sorrow beck has its rise under Black Hambleton, and with its numerous tributaries drains all the wild desolate sweep of Kepwick moor. It flows into Codbeck, some mile and a half below Borrowby. About a mile south of Kepwick, and just over the hill brow, is the village of Cowesby. In King William's Survey this name is written Cahosbi. Possibly the designation is supposably derived from "Cow," and the Danish "bi," a farm-holding, where milch-kine were kept. But there are other less obvious and perhaps less misleading etymologies. To "cower low" is to squat down, and has a connection with cove, cover, covert, and the Icelandic spelling is "Kowra," to lie quiet, hidden or covered in. Now the place is environed on three sides by the Hambletons, standing in a veritable cove, and lies secluded, cowering down in a covert-like hollow of the land, and we almost think it most likely it got its name from that circumstance. The alternative derivation is possibly less likely, viz.: that "cow" came (like "by") from the Danish "Kue,"—subdued or coerced. In this view, Cowesby would mean the place last subdued, acquired by conquest by the Danes. The lonely character of the village, its little importance, are, however, against this supposed explanation. The hill which separates Cowesby from Kepwick is named Penhill. The prefix "Pen" is certainly Celtic, and here again we have duplication of a place-name of one meaning.

The Cowesby 'hospital,' a low quaintly interesting building, is devised for the Poor of the Manor of Cowesby. The Church, dedicated to St. Michael and the Holy Angels, was only erected in 1846. The early Norman font from the old church is still in use. The Revd. John Oxlee was lately rector of Cowesby, and here the valuable Library of his father, also the Revd. John Oxlee, and one of the most proficient linguists of his time, was preserved.

The scenery about the Old Mill is especially charming. Its name now would seem a misnomer, for its machinery is gone and the stream course diverted. The springs here are highly mineralised, impregnated with iron, and for that reason tonic in debility. Cowesby Hall, built from the designs of Salvin, the eminent architect, is surpassingly well set in an amphitheatre of the Hambleton spurs, and embosomed in mead, wood, and heathery swells. The late Squire, Thomas W. Lloyd, was a man of great sympathies. 'Tis a more than pleasant walk from Cowesby to Kepwick, which latter place rests on the northern slope of Penhill, a bold buttress of the Hambletons, that range again making a fine and bold background for another delightfully rural place. The Vale of Mowbray, lovely as it is, owes much to the massive buttresses of the Hambletons along it eastern border. The higher moors recede away in a firm yet gentle undulating line—a scroll of earth unrolled, and profusely engraven with natural runes of rock and vegetation.

Kepwick and Nether Silton confront each other from opposite slopes of ths spurs, guarding one of the three main passes over Hambleton, the road to Arden Hawnby and Helmsley which trends up along the steep rise of heathland from which the magnificent views of Mowbray Vale—above praise in the scenic sense—are obtainable.

CHAPTER VIII.

A WALK ON THE HAMBLETONS.

By way of a change and a detour, we leave the moor-top at Kepwick Bank. Starting from Thirsk by way of Finkle Street, and the Sutton Road, in an hour's sharp walking we arrive at the picturesquely wooded village of Felixkirk, and beyond, on the hill, we leave the tree-clad summit of Mount Saint John to the right. From the road to Boltby (with its sharp turns and sudden ups and downs), we get charming peeps through the trees over the Vale, and glimpses into romantic ravines and up to heather-clad bluffs of hill. A little way on and the full panorama of the Hambletons comes in sight, with the three great Scars which have for uncountable ages kept grim watch and ward over the Vale. Now we descend into Boltby, nestling like a brooding fowl in the Gurtof valley, with the beck fresh from its moorland cradle, babbling and birling across the very village street—a phase of Nature full of attraction from its simple rurality. Crossing at the ford-way of Lunshaw Beck we soon gain the terrace of the lower moor, and then by a stiffish climb attain the rock-strewn base of the jackdaw-beloved Boltby Scar. Gaining the summit, fringed by gaunt, weird and gale-swept larches, that have stood sentinel over village, vale and the stern hill-land, day in and out, for many a year, we survey the scene from an eminence of 1,070 feet. This is the height above sea-level of Boltby Scar, but its imposing character is due to the fact of its rising so suddenly from the undulating plain below.

The surface of the moor from Roulston Scar to the base of Black Hambleton is noticeably graven with trench and rampart, and dotted here and there with the barrows and tumuli of an ancient race of men. Towards the southern end of Boltby Scar is a semicircular entrenchment with its steep cliff-defended rear, and three tumuli within, one outside and a short distance to the south-east are five other tumuli. Our first sight of these was in the deepening twilight of a stormy New Year's day, when the wind whistled and shrieked across the lonely haunted heath, and the curlew sent forth its melancholy wail-like dirge, as of some lost soul, and the moor beneath the canopy of gloom overhead grew to be a veritable land of mystery. Under the spell of Fancy's loom, the scene became impregnated with the shadowy forms of an old-world race. The tumuli seemed to our impressed mind as if imbued again with life, and stood out, huge and dim and lone,

THE VALE OF MOWBRAY. 355

Looking across Boltby from the Scar-   [Owen Bowen,

surrounded by giant shapes moving to and fro, guarding the graves from the hostile or curious foot of the intruder!

Near these tumuli is the northern terminal of Eston Cleave Dike, or Cleabe Dike, the longest of the many trenches (such as Casten Dike) which Pre-historic and even men of Historic times have strongly fortified. In this S.W. corner of the Hambletons the remains of several British dwellings have been unearthed here in the quadrangle above Sutton Bank. Mr. Sanders, of Cold Kirkby (apart from flint weapons) has found many objects of interest. Among these is a pale blue glass bead, on which in white is an ornament resembling the chevron of heraldry. This bead dates back to the Bronze Age and days of sun-worship, when the Brigantes—a branch of the Celts—traded with the Phœnicians, from whom they obtained such things. All the tumuli and barrows have been delved in by the treasure-hunting antiquary; and several were examined by Canon Greenwell, nearly 50 years ago now.

Looking eastward from the two tumuli there is a magnificent view of the Hambleton plateau, sloping down towards Rievaulx, with its 'Terrace' and 'Harriet Air.' The undulating moors north and east far as the eye can see, stretch out in mysterious prospect. A little further on the old Malton and Yarm road, or 'Hambleton Street,' is reached; and on it is the 'Dialstone' farm, now a lonely homestead, but in coaching times a hotel, where the road-borne traveller found 'creature comforts' in days of storm. The sundial stone, dated 1705, is still here in the wall by the gate, but the metal plate has long vanished. Less than a mile south is the Hambleton Hotel, where one may still obtain the refreshment man everywhere desires. The moor plateau here is still used as a training ground for racehorses, fine air and springy turf with plenty of verge, and many have been the celebrated cup-winners that the turf has reared and trained here. Endless stories might also be told anent the sport, for the whole place seems saturated with incidents connected with racers and jockeys since the days of the celebrated Duke of Buckingham (who hunted the district) onwards. The gills hereabouts are very lovely, deep and narrow; Flassengill, leading down to Rievaulx, is of indescribable beauty, especially in its trees' bridal attire of Spring.

Cold Kirkby.

This village stands fully exposed to the fury of the biting blasts, on the shelving moorland, but in the water-basin of the Rye. Nor does it belie its naming by the Danes—"Caud,"—for it both looks and is "cold," with its grey limestone walls and grey Church in cold keeping, standing exposed on a promontory formed by the forking head of a gill or ravine. The church is only a plain affair, but the font is ancient, and probably the only relic of the ancient thatched fane.

Among local traditions there is a story of Willie Moffitt, and an unexplained memorial to his wife. She, a faithful woman, died, and was laid to rest. During the burial service Willie was missed, but at its conclusion was observed struggling up the gill (which is immediately below) with a large flat stone on his shoulder. This he placed at the head of the open grave, remarking "There noo, that'll dea varry weel." Clearly he had 'spotted' the slab in the gill beck sometime previously, but, however that be, the stone is still there.

There is another tale of a local wiseacre who gravely informed us that the old pre-historic trenches, already alluded to, were dug at the battle of Waterloo to keep out "owd Bonyparty."

At the end of the village leading to Old Byland, on our visit dwelt in old age, Thomas Sunley, a cobbler. His cot was a sort of farmer's boys' club-house. They were all very kind to the old man in their rough way, bringing many a meal to him. Poor Sunley has now, alas! migrated after the fate of his kind, to the

'House' at Helmsley, after many an up and a down in the course of a long life. For several winters he worked in the woods at Pilmoor, bark-stripping, walking the 25 miles distance daily, out and home again. His woodcraft testimony was naively curious: "'Ave snickled a hare or two in ma time, besides gam at runs a'

Interior of Thomas Sunley's Cottage. [*Ernest Forbes*.

two legs, and a' knaw ivory in an' oot o't moor, an' a' only yance seed a ghost. 'A was cummin' over't moor fra' Hemsley i't dark, an' a ugly thing clicked me by't leg, an a' run and lost him,

Appen it war only a badger—there were lots aboot i' them days." One thing he remembered distinctly—the "Stocks" on Stocks Hill: why, we cannot say.

Since writing the above we have learnt that Sunley has passed to his long home.

From Cold Kirkby a footway with many a rise and dip and curve brings us to Old Byland, situated at the edge of a deep gill. There are fine prospects looking down the valley with the 'Terrace' of Rievaulx for a background, and at one place the Abbey's hoary ruins can be seen framed in greenery, laid in the deep lap of lovely Ryedale. Times have changed strangely, woefully some will say, happily others—since the cowled Brothers dwelt here. They have left scarcely any traces of their sojourn except the irregular ridged surface of the turf which now covers up the foundations of monastic domiciles just west of the village. These monks met a great want in their day and place—perhaps the need for their self-denying seclusion is no less now, but, as we say, times have changed to a life more strenuous and faster pace. The Norman sculptured stones built into the squat church tower, which scarcely reaches to the height of the main roof (and where the bell-ropes swing in the open porch under the tower when the southern wind blows in) complete the visible memorials of the long-dead standard bearers of a church, militant even to-day. The entrance arch is a half circle, moulded on the face, and the chancel arch somewhat on similar lines and very heavy, with a large plain Norman font. The sculptured stones and earlier features of the church are doubtless the work of the monks, and in many respects they are a copy of those in the church of St. Bees, Cumberland, the district from which the monks of Byland came in their migration. There is a fine and large village green here, on which flourishes an ancient and umbrageous wide-armed wych (or sacred) elm. Here, too, at the south end are the Stocks, and at the other extremity the bowl of a big Norman font turned upside down. There is every reason to believe this font to be the original one used by the monks in their church at Byland-on-the-Moor. It is a pretty and truly rural old English village, yet for the monks it lay far too exposed—and they yearned for a cosy pastoral corner like that in which their co-worshippers of Rievaulx were ensconced; and when the clear toned ringing melody of their bells came, now faint now clear and louder on the breeze, floating Bylandwards, their hearts were stirred with unrest; until finally their uttered discontent reached the ears of their generous patron and benefactor, and he, despite many previous donations, gave them that beautiful situation among meadow cornland at the foot of the Hambletons, where at last they consummated their highest aspirations and erected the permanent Monastery of Byland.

Reluctantly leaving this lovely spot, a short walk carries us to the edge of Cadale Gill winding east and west, with the white walls of the grist-mill shewing out in strong contrast to the black-green funereal firs and spruces grouped picturesquely around it. 'Tis a beautiful and unusual picture the road-way pearly-grey in the light winding downhill, the irregularity of every outline, the unexpected turn or tone of this or that, the mingled brown, green and purple of the gill's side, the varied hues of the flower-heralds of Spring in thicket and on bank; all these features combine to form a scene of exquisite charm. Down into the gill-trough and over its stream we climb through the wood on the sunny side, and again stand on the high tableland. From the brim of the bank we can look straight down into the nests of the rooks in the topmost branches of the trees towering up from the bottom! Soon we can see Hawnby Hill and Easterside rising up as the north-east guards of Ryedale, like huge long-backed leviathans of the deep, black and frowning, away to the north and north-east. After passing Morton Grange, where many fragments of masonry point backward into the long sped lives of bygone generations, we, a little further on, reach the summit of Morton Bank, and from here look down into quite half-a-dozen dales. 'Tis a wonderful bit of stream-carving, the resistless work of Nature through the ages that have passed since the Ice-grip relaxed its mighty tomb-like seal from the earth. To attempt a description of these Hambleton dales, or gills or gorges, cut deep down into the land, would be futile indeed without the genius for word-painting of a Ruskin.

In the centre of the picture rises Hawnby Hill and Easterside, rearing their hog-backed line of bulk proudly among the jutting promontories of the moors and ramifying gills around. To the east lies Bilsdale, and almost at our feet is Ryedale extending away to the north. From the deep hollow the red roofs of Hawnby rise tier on tier up the steep village street. A wonderful sight is this expanse of hills and dales, over which sunlight and shadow alternately sweep. This is certainly the Arcadia of the Hambletons. Old farms and cottages, with their environing sheen of primroses and bluebells, nestle here and there in the lee of the woodland from whence the blue reek of turf fires ascend in a slow spiral; and around the farms cattle pasture, and geese wander sedately and foolishly gabble. Few districts show more varied beauties of form and colour than the one viewed from Morton Bank. The old guide post at the junction of roads at the bank top, has certainly seen better days: its arms have gone, and, as a substitute, some wag in mockery has thrust into the socket a rude stake, the gaunt arms pointing tauntingly up into the sky, like the banner inscribed "Excelsior."

Down the steep slope of Morton Bank, in the shade of birk and hazel, we reach Hawnby Bridge, and passing a lovely intricately foliaged bend of the Rye, arrive at the foot of the village street.

But Hawnby, the most delightful of mountain villages, does not come within the limits of our pages, so we go by the end of the uphill street and its comfortable and home-like hotel, and take the path by the mill-race and through the lonely churchyard by the river, standing aloof from the abode of the living. Following the dale upward, we obtain rest and food at a very ancient farm, yet curiously enough named the 'New' Hall. Now, under the shadow

The Fox. [*John Pennington.*

of Coom Hill, we enter Thorodale, which almost cuts Hambleton in two, and separates Black Hambleton from the southern and major part of the range. Here in a most secluded situation, surrounded by ancient woods, is Arden Hall, once a nunnery, still retaining its old-time Nun's well, hidden in trees, to the rear of the house. A lonely nook, this of Arden! A lovely wooded gill, an old water-mill, and the Arden wild flowers, whose beauties are proverbial. The winding of the stream, the green of the uplands with ranges of woodland showing tier above tier, the lavender turf-reek filtering through the branches of the trees, mingle antique hues with richer colouring. Grainge says " the situation of Arden is one of loveliness and complete seclusion," it stands nearly in the centre of the little valley on the southern brink of Arden beck. To the south the hills rise abruptly, thickly clad with wood; eastwards the valley bends in such a manner that the hills of Hawnby and Easterside seem to close it in completely.

Of the Priory, the only relic existent now is an ancient chimney which still retains its antique character. Story, responsible for so much, says, that so long as this chimney stands it serves as a Title-Deed through which the Lord of the Manor receives an annual payment of £40 from the owner of the Park Lands of Upsal. A spring of limpid water is known a the Nun's Well. The herb-garden was formerly the Nuns' burial place,—a pretty thought: the sweet lives ended, to lie at rest beneath the sweet sage, marjoram and basil; lavender and rosemary too, perchance, for all time. Human bones in evidence of the fact have frequently been dug up here. After the Dissolution of the Monasteries, it came into the hands of the famous family of the Tancreds of Boroughbridge and Whixley.

We have already told that Arden Mill was the home of Dick Megginson, now the Miller of Borrowby, and the Megginsons have been millers at Arden, and listened to the groaning and creaking, the rumbling and splashing of the mill wheel since the days of Chaucer.

We now take the path up the devious edge of Thorodale, a wild and eerie moorland walk, a " haunt of ancient peace " (except when the winds howl and shriek over the Hambletons), and so too of scarce birds and wild animals. It was here that a fox, absorbed in thoughts of supper, trotting leisurely over the uneven ground making doubtless for the woods of Arden, almost ran into our very hands. For an instant he stood amazed, but only for an instant, ere he darted off at an angle and quickly put distance between us. It was an introduction of the briefest, and such un-Reynard-like lack of craft must be very unusual if not an unique occurrence.

We have now climbed to the western edge of the Hambletons, and the wondrous Vale of Mowbray is spread panorama-like before us. Limekiln House, once an inn of the Hambleton 'street,' deserted now, is on our right, and Kepwick village in front, but far below: a wonderful scene, rich in variety of colour and tone, subtly blent in harmony. The seemingly interminable stretch of country, shading off in the far-away air until earth and sky are blended into one, with the setting sun raying out golden spokes of light, in half circle, from a bed of stormy clouds; the grey-blue line of mystic hills, with a diffusion of hazy gold over Bedale, the view carrying even into Swaledale, ridge beyond ridge, a grey cloud or faint wisps of smoke suspent over and marking the whereabouts of Northallerton and Richmond; these are some of the details of the marvellous prospect, to which, however, a pen-picture can hardly do justice. The sight of the moving trains, curls of travelling cloud that die away there to rise into view yonder, accentuate the sense of distance. The Mashamshire hills, low green or heathery moors, are steeped also in the opulent light of the All Light-giving Orb. Strange contrast when we turn north, south, or east—there the Hambletons are massed dark and threatening, the silence broken only by the wailing cry of the plover.

Folk-lore states that once upon a time there dwelt in a cave in the adjacent lonesome tract of Black Hambleton, a Witch, one Abigail Craister by name. In former days, as is well known, the poor creatures accounted possessed of evil powers of charm and evil-eye, were not only severely persecuted at the hands of their fellow beings, but were even at times wickedly hunted by hounds. The recital goes on to tell how "once Abigail being hard pressed

THE VALE OF MOWBRAY.

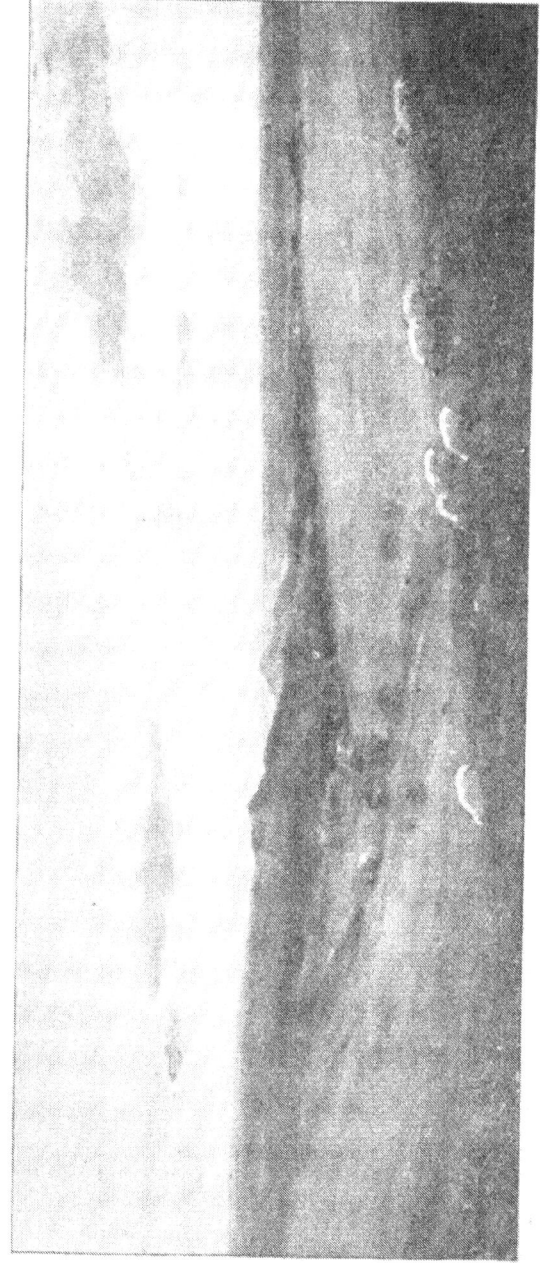

Looking Southward across the Vale of Mowbray, from Windy Gill Ridge. [Owen Bowen.

by the hounds, did from ye cliffs fling herself bodily into Gormire Lake, and there sinking came not forth from that place but from a Keld or spring ower nine good miles from the lake." On another occasion she was observed " of several trusty folk " to " rise from white steam astride her besom, and take for ower Kilburn towards Coxwold."

We are again in the land of "Barrows" and grave mounds, marking where some old British or Anglian Chieftain sleeps his last long sleep. Peace to their souls, their deeds were great in battle. A mile or so south, where an old track from Arden to Kirkby Knowle crosses the old 'green road' of the Hambleton Street, the shaft of Steeping Cross still stands among the 'besom ling.' Further down the track, by the head of Windy Gill, remains the base of Friar's Cross; and further along Windy Gill Ridge there are barrows and mounds. Down the old cart-track across Windy Gill Ridge we can look right down into quiet Cowesby—old-world and seclusive—and over a vast expanse south by west, York towers; and far away, north-west beyond Richmond to the Tees country, this wide outlook extends.

Kirkby Knowle Moor, with its uneven edge of serried trees, may be well seen from here, and more to the south is Cinquecliffe Woods and the wide demesne of Thirkleby, and far beyond, the rising ground about Ripon and Harrogate. Around us is an ocean of heather, gorse and bracken, and a defile curving down to the level of the Vale, with mile on mile of wood, pasture and arable, beautiful contours and curves harmonising to make a magnificent landscape, its pearly and green fields all one rippling silvery green sea of colour. The old moorland track now slants down athwart the head of Gurtopp valley, now barred to wheels by blocks of fallen stone and trees, and unremoved a hundred years or more; and so gently descending, we at last reach Kirkby Knowle,

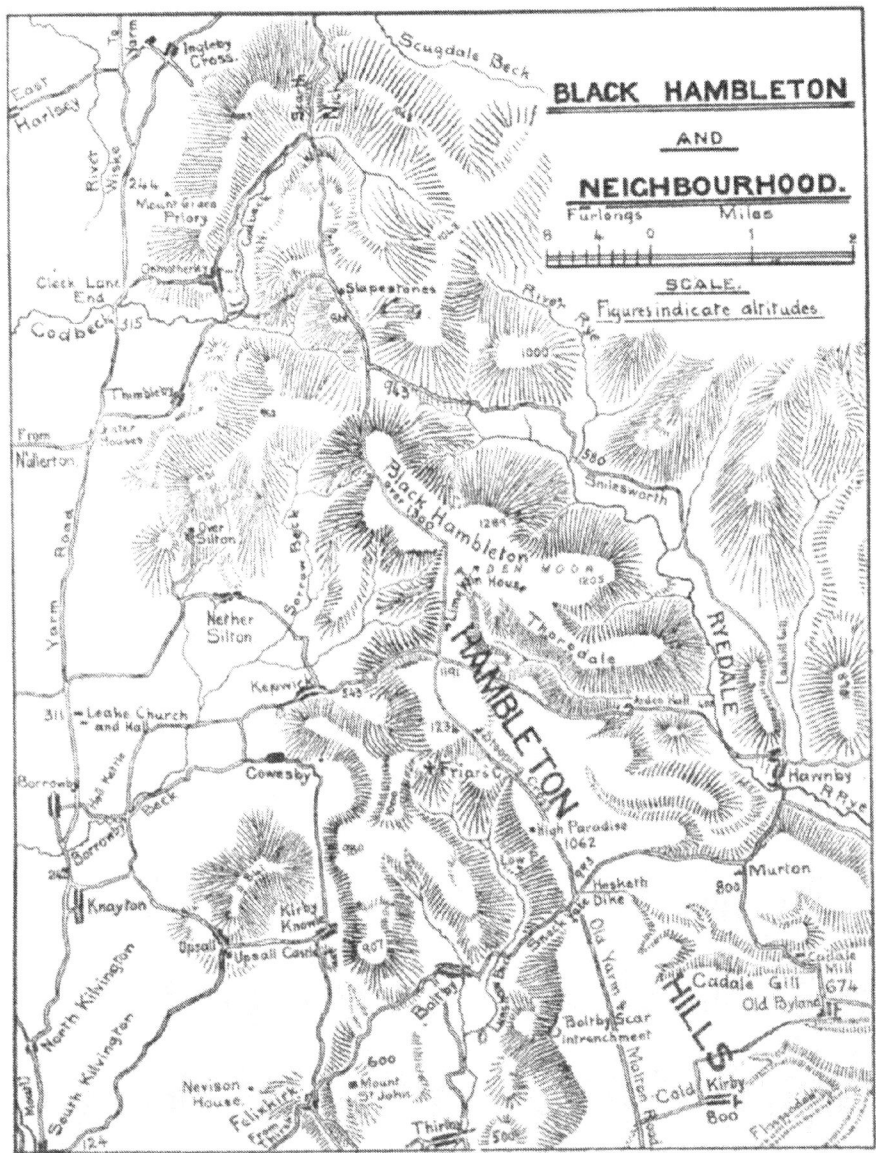

CHAPTER IX.

ROUND ABOUT OSMOTHERLY.

WE start our peregrinations again from Limekiln house and follow the old 'street' (here almost hid by heather), over the edge of Black Hambleton. When last this way we descried two buzzards circling and swooping down at times for nearer view of their furry or feathered prey over the crest of this lonesome hill. Across the eastern section of Thimbley Moor, and past the roadside farm, we reach the Chequers Inn at Slapestones. To those who prefer secluded paths and wild moorland scenery to the hard and dust-clouded motor-blighted highways, a fine walk from Thirsk may be taken, via Barrowby and Leake. From the latter the footpath leads over the fields to Low Silton—the scene of Bern's punishment (according to Bede's Chronicle) at the hands of the High Reeves of Northumbria, in 780. No doubt the old Manor Hall here is the 3rd or 4th in succession to the one dwelt in by Bern the Elderman at that period. Apart from its historic link, it is a prettily situated, clean, stone-built village. Under Hunter's Hill, beautiful with golden gorse, spring and autumn, the lane wends through a retired tree-clothed valley past Swinestone Cliff, and gently rises thence to Thimbley Moor. Here it is well to pause and take a look back on the way we have come. The fine lines of hill and valley, slope and trend, with many a broken curve down to the plain of Mowbray stretching out dimly and maplike to the south.

After passing the N.W. end of Black Hambleton, a fine view opens out in an opposite direction. There is the Moor House and Chequers Inn at Slapestones, and behind are the ruins of Solomon's Temple; below us and to the left, Osmotherly, sunlit and charmingly placed on the spur of the hills, is to be seen above the upper reach of the Codbeck valley (where the curlews shriek to the listening waste), circling round from the head of Ryedale by Scarth Nick, S.W. to the end of Rueberry nearest Osmotherly. We get just a glimpse of the champaign to the north-east through the frowning jaws of the "Nick" itself, away over village and grange to the mouth of the Tees. Opposite, over Thimbley, the scene recedes across Mowbray Vale, over the town of Northallerton and across Richmondshire to the western hills, faintly demarking the frontier (as it were) of another world.

It is, truly, a charming up-and-down hill-road that leads to the Chequers Inn at Slapestones. The way from the south cuts across a picturesque boulder-strewn ravine near the inn, and there can be little doubt that it is from the steep slippery gradient down

Moorland Scene near Black Hambleton. [*Owen Bowen.*

to the brook ('slape' in Yorkshire dialect) that its name is derived. Here on the bare smooth-worn living rock, which in winter was often 'slape' or slippery enough to make a lasting impression on the memories of wayfarers when coaches came and went. The hostelry, yclept "Ye Chequers" of old, is mostly known by the title of "Slapestones." It is a truly rural moorland

The Road leading down to Slapestones. [*Edmund Bogg.*

homestead, and from its [front a fine prospect unfolds. Away over wild heathland and sterile waste, and across the beautiful country to the west, the scene unrolls itself; spacious and inspiriting from its beauteous breadth. The swinging inn sign projects from the wall, and represents a chessboard, and on this is inscribed the admonition—

> "Be not in haste,
> Step in and taste,
> Ale to-morrow for Nothing."

But alas! to-morrow never comes: it is always 'to-day' (and we pay) when the traveller calls! However, it is told of a man who ardently desired to avail himself of a goodly fill of ardent liquor that he stayed the whole of one day and night in hope of being served free. When morning came, much to his disappointment and surprise, the next day brought the "free ale of to-morrow" not one instant nearer his parched lips and thirsty throat. This inn has been 'kept,'—and it must therefore have kept them—by the Flintoffs for quite a hundred years. John, the late landlord, died some years back now, at a great age. The interior bears every sign of antiquity, and is furnished in keeping. Among its features we must mention the Delf rack, with its goodly array of shining pewter ware. On the open hearthstone a turf fire smoulders and glows by turns, emitting a grateful warmth and with it the pleasant aroma of the moors, which offends not the most delicate nostril. A poem might be written about the peat reek —Nature sacrificed to man's need, in kinship with the incense of worship. It is averred that the 'vital spark' of Slapestone inn-fire has never

The Sign of The Chequers Inn Slapestones

Rev. J. C. Fowler

been extinguished, or failed to ignite the added fuel every morning for these hundred and fifty years! at least, during the Flintoff tenancy this fire has been kept alight, as was the sacred flame in the Temples of Vesta   A most toothsome hot cake is provided here.   The lid of the big frying pan is hung over the fire until hot, then the pan is heated too, the bottom covered with the dainty cakes ; the lid is covered with red-hot turves, and with fire above and below in this way a palatable cake, browned on both sides, is produced to the hungry wayfarers' profound satisfaction.

Interior of the Chequers Inn.   [*Owen Bowen*.

The roads from here either to Stokesley by way of Scarth Nick, or to Osmotherly, are varied and interesting at every bend. Or, one may take the moor-path, with the ruddy tiled roofs of Osmotherly in front and in view all the way.

From the moor we take the field-path and drop down into a delightful glen, then again up the steep side of the wooded hill and so gain Osmotherly. This approach can be varied by those who have the necessary leisure, with a visit to Scarth Nick. This is a remarkable nick or passage in the hill border between the Codbeck basin and the flat country stretching towards the Tees. A few hundred yards from Slapestones inn stands a gaunt unfinished building, known locally as Solomon's Temple. It now fast falls into utter ruin. It is said to have been built by one intent on retirement—"the world forgetting, by the world forgot"—but he either changed his mind or had ill calculated the cost beforehand. The funds at his disposal failed, and so it remains to this day a rebuke to his folly, a mockery of his 'wisdom.' An old hermit, one Matt. Walker, long held undisputed 'squatter's right' possession of the place, but he died some time ago at the great age of ninety years.

Pursuing the road north, along the shelf of the moor, past two or three hill farms, at the coming-home time of the kye (milking hour), down below us on the left being Wild Goose Nest, we reach a very steep descent which falls down precipitously to the infant Codbeck. Beyond the Sheepwash, we enter the portal of Scarth Nick, a term synonomous with the Boer term 'Nek.' This nick is a pass or gap in the Cleveland Hills between the Codbeck valley and the Swainby country, the waterparting betwixt Tees and Swale. From the moor, half a mile south, a most grandiose view of the Cleveland Hills is to be got, with the deep ravine or canyon of Scugdale, and Whorlton and Swainby villages (the latter in foreground), and the wave-like hill crests of moorland with the conical mount of Roseberry 'Topping' rising in their background like the cone of an ancient volcano.

Turning our gaze we see the villages of the rolling plain right to the flame and smoke vomiting iron furnaces around Teesmouth;

and west, along the rising country, till vision is blocked by the distant moors of the upper Tees Valley. Back through the 'pass' we once more reach the Codbeck at Sheepwash, and for some distance follow the sinuosities of the valley, up a gently rising road whence fine 'bits' are to be noticed, to Osmotherly once more. We drop down the steep hill street of the T-shapen town, to the old market cross in the centre.

The Chequers, Slapestones   [*Rev. J. C. Fowler*

As a place-name, Osmotherley is perhaps unique. Doubtless it has an origin in "Osmond," a personal name, and "ley," a meadow or field; another example of like conjunction being Osmondthorpe near Leeds. The name has been altered through a babel of tongues and in the course of the centuries to its present form. Story adds that it means the place where "Os, by his mother, lie" is altogether too bookish a fancy. Setting aside this, the old legend asserts it came about through the death of young Prince Oswald by drowning, and so intense was the Queen-mother's temperament that she, too, died of grief a few days later, and found a narrow bed by her beloved.

"When King Oswald's son was born, who was called Oswald, the wise men and magicians were sent for to Court to predict and foretell the life and fortunes of the new-born prince. They all agreed that he would be drowned. The indulgent maternal Queen would have carried him to Cheviot, a remarkable hill in their own country, but for the troubles then existing in the North. She, therefore, brought him to a lofty hill in Cleveland called Roseberry, and caused a cell or cave to be made near the top thereof, in order to prevent his foretold unhappy death; but, alas! in vain; for the fates, who spare nobody, dissolved the rugged rocks into a flowing stream; and by drowning the son put a period to all the mother's cares, though not to her sorrows, for, ordering him to be interred in Tiviotdale Church, she mourned with such inconsolable grief that she soon followed him, and was, according to her fervent desire, laid by her tender beloved child. The heads of the mother and son cut in stone may be seen at the east end of Tiviotdale church, and from the saying of the people, 'Os by his mother lay,' the place at length got the name of Osmotherley."

The legend is given here for what it is worth; there is some plausible ground in calamity to render this idea acceptable to those who like derivations made to order. Some tragic occurence may have overtaken the royal house at this place, yet even so, it has no bearing on the name of this straggling town.

Osmotherley is in the old division of Allertonshire, distant about 11 miles from Thirsk, and 7 from Northallerton. It rests on

The Ravine and Thimbleby Bank from near Slapestones.   [*Owen Bowen*

a high tableland half way up the southern end of a hooked spur of the Cleveland Hills, which slopes down steeply east and south from the town to the romantic valley along which the Codbeck winds its upper hill country course between the Cleveland spurs and those of Hambleton.

The town is made up of two wide streets, one at right angles to the other, T shape, and is built of stone. It finds mention in King William's Survey as a "Manor in Osmundrelac, Ligulf and Eilaf had 5 carucates to be taxed land to two plows." The church, dedicated to St. Peter, was once in the patronage of the See of Durham, now under Ripon. It stands on the south side of the street leading west. Rebuilt practically during the last century, it has undergone restorations at different periods, so that little of interest remains to us except the runic fragments in the porch, remnants of the early pre-Norman church. The fine south doorway with four shafts and the two orders of arch mouldings, Chevron and Bird's beak, remains. The bowl of the great font, with its carved cable decoration, is existing, and also Norman. The chancel-arch and part of a sedilia in the wall south of the altar are examples of early 14th century work, the whole consisting of nave, chancel, south aisle, and a western tower. The interior is fine and well lighted, the rough masonry being in strong contrast with the delicately worked mouldings. A great harvest of the dead, brought here for burial since St. Aidan's time, lie around the walls outside. Without much doubt this monument to God was due to St. Aidan, or a disciple of the Iona school who traversed the lonely Cheviots and the wild Border marches, southwards and eastwards to here, spreading the glad tidings of Christ's gospel of patient faith and renunciation in their path as they went like the sower casts his seed. From the field south of the church is a good view over the bleach grounds, and the woods about Thimbleby Hall, and down along Thimbleby Moor to the Hanging Stone. From this point the stone seems in a perilous position, yet, we suppose it must have weathered the wind-forces of many a thousand years, and it will probably hang there thousands more.

About the centre of Osmotherley is the Market Cross, put up only in 1874, on the site of a much older one. Near it lies an ancient-looking stone slab, much worn. Osmotherley is the 'Capital' of the district, and was once a chartered market town. Very old men can recollect fish being sold there on Sabbath mornings regularly upon the slabstone. To-day itinerant fish hawkers still use it. In old days the Feast here lasted a whole week and the Cross was a rendezvous of all the gay spirits of the place. Old Bob Douthwaite a violinist from Northalverton, was always requisitioned for this and other rural saturnalie around. He is said to have fiddled at

378　　THE VALE OF MOWBRAY.

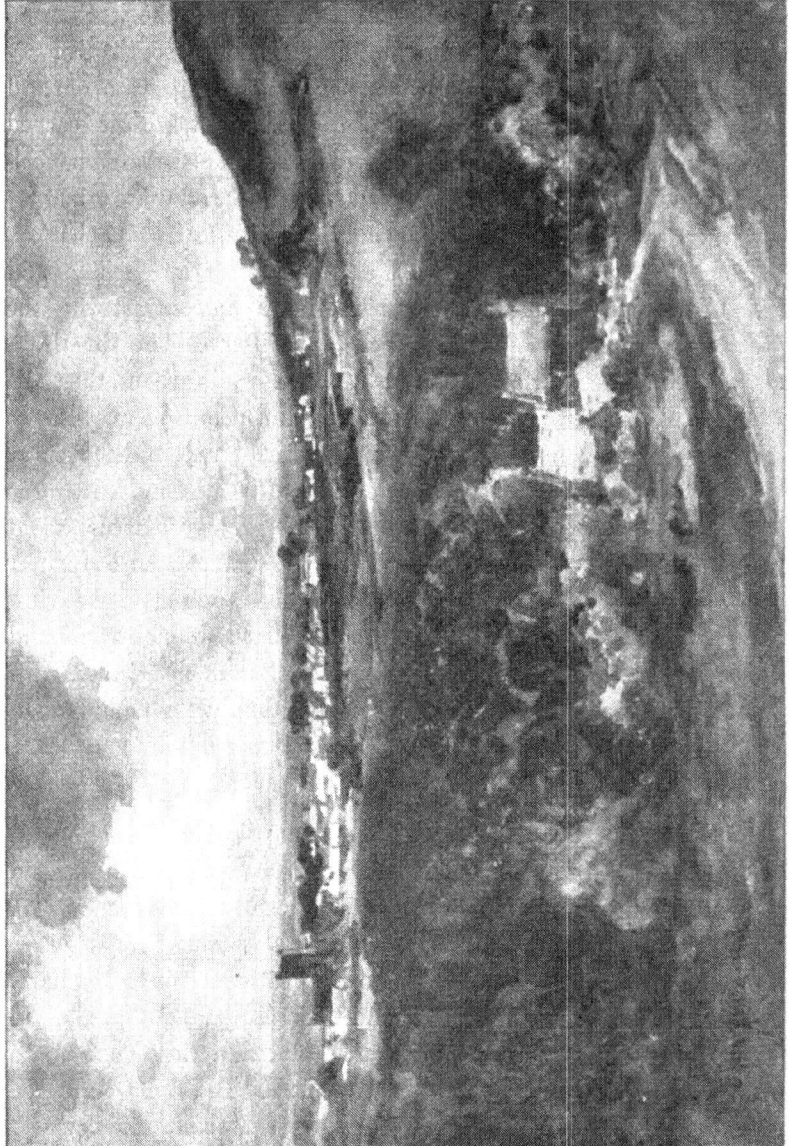

Osmotherley from South East.　　[Owen Bowen]

Osmotherly Feast for 50 years without once missing. The inns never closed their doors during feast-week, and mirth (and more) ran riot. The dancing around the Cross was kept up the whole night, and Old Bob never faltered in his music-making exertion, except possibly to drain a tankard himself. Story says that he used to fall asleep, and yet play on in a dream! During the Thirties and Forties of last century the town is described by a writer as one of the most primitive and lawless he had ever been in. In the Fifties, the Rev. Henry Jones, the vicar, was wont to go the round of the Public Houses to insist upon their closure at the proper hour. And it was no unusual spectacle at weddings to have a stand-up fight in the church for the possession of the bell ropes; for, of course, who rang the bells got the fee for doing so! It was during some such drunken brawl that one bell, originally from Mount Grace, was broken. This vicar, by his determined and resolute stand, gradually changed the old state of things for one much better.

Years ago the moors around Osmotherley were the haunt of Smugglers, and whiskey stills were worked in lonesome out-of-the-way places. One Denison by name, for years carried on a roaring business in the inebriating fluid, and most of the villagers were in one way or another interested in harbouring and keeping the traffic 'quiet.' For a long time the officers of the Customs were kept in the dark, but, at last the ringleaders were caught napping, or were betrayed. Arrested, they were sent to York Castle, there to do long and lonely penance for their 'spiritual' misdeeds. Yet still the secret distillation continued—one still raided, another was erected, although after the wholesale arrests mentioned, the trade seems to have received its death blow and gradually dwindled away.

Another event of the town was the bursting of the drill or linen mill's dam. On the 8th of August, 1857, a waterspout burst

Osmotherley from Back Lane. (Thompson)

over the moors to the east of the town; the beck swelled and caused the dam to give way; a deluge of pent-up water swept in fell fury down the valley. It was in the early morning, as luck had it. A working man saw the reservoir at the instant of giving way, and was just in the nick of time to rush to the mill and warn the weavers, who fled to the high ground not a moment too soon to save their lives. Like Borrowby and Brompton, Osmotherley was a generation or two ago noted for hand-loom weaving. This industry is now almost obsolete. Only four hand-loom weavers remains now in the three towns, viz., at Brompton.

There were some notable characters amongst these old weavers. The names which follow are a few out of many jotted down from the reminiscences of an aged weaver. Their very sound savours of the charm of bygone dialect. "Why, I remember Dick Pollitt, Willy Dummy, Bob Russell, and Lukey and Matt Bulmer. Then there was oade Jack and George Healey, oade Tommy Bargett, Jack Miller, and Tommy and Mike Smith; but, stop a bit," said the ancient of days, tapping afresh his memory, "there was also oade Willy and Jack Saddler, Ossy Thompson, Georgie Moore, and Willy Scaife." These were all well-known figures, moving about the village during the generations that have fled, engaged in hand-loom weaving, heckling and flax dressing. The two last women of the old race of knitters here, were Becky Reed and Betty Marley. For several weeks before the 5th of November, most memorable of Plot Days, the lads of Osmotherley get together gradually a huge pile of timber and sticks by the old Cross at the junction of the streets; and many a quaint village picture, typical of rural custom, is to be obtained when the lads, yoked team-like, drag on to the scene of later action a big load of thorns, to commemorate that greatest of fizzles associated for ever, one almost thinks—for bonfires shed a lurid and smoky glare yet in the quieter corners of even our big towns—with the name of Yorkshire Guy.

z

In 1745, a severe distemper raged among the horned cattle around Osmotherley, a great number dying; and the loss fell heavily on both the farmer and those smaller owners who kept one or two cows. It was this visitation that caused the Parish Clerk to compose that surely unique psalm, sung by the whole congregation save five farmers, who wept, so moved were they by sorrow. The early part of the psalm tells of the cattle that perished and the names of the owners! Three of the verses ran as follows:—

> No Christian's bull nor cow, they say,
>   But takes it out of hand;
> And we shall have no cows at all
>   I doubt within the land.
>
> The Doctors, though they all have spoke
>   Like learned gentlemen,
> And told us how the entrails look
>   Of cattle, dead and gren.
>
> Yet they do nothing do at all,
>   With all their learning stare,
> So, Heaven drive out this plague away,
>   And vex us not, no mare.

The singing of this "sacred ballad" so satisfied the congregation at the first singing, that it was demanded a second time at the end of the service. The clergyman was not, it appears, in the old clerk's confidence, for at the conclusion he said, "Why John, what psalm was that we have had to-day? Surely it was not one of David's?" "Nea, nea," replied the old fellow, proud of the dignity suddenly attained to, "David nivver meade sik a psalm sin he were born. It's yen o' me oane makkin'."

John Wesley several times visited Osmotherley. The first occasion was probably in 1745, and he was here preaching again ten years later. When the great Convulsion occurred at Whitemare's Crag, Wesley, in his journal, says "that the explosion resembled the sound of many cannon, and the oscillation of the ground was distinctly felt as far away as Northallerton." A day or two later Wesley rode over to examine the cliff, and among other remarks says that that part of the cliff from which the torn mass came "was so bright in colour, and so high, that it is plainly visible to all the country around."

The scenery about Osmotherley is very fine, and the air exhilarating. The view from Rueberry is exceedingly beautiful and far reaching. The walk up the here diminutive brook of Codbeck, past Yeoman's Mill and Wild-Goose Nest, through gorse and heather to Scarth Nick, is truly delightful. Another stroll is by the path through the chapel yard on the east side of the main street—here is the old chapel where John Wesley preached—and from here the way trends across the pasture land until we unexpectedly strike the brink of a deep and sequestered ravine. Here a steep dip leads into the sinuous channel of the Codbeck. The scene strikingly picturesque, romantic even. Deep down is the stream, snake-like and glittering. From the high steps we look down the winding footpath and the curves of the profusely wooded scarp, and note rich flower-gemmed pastures, the gaunt edge of Thimbleby Moor, the semi-wild luxuriance of vegetation in wood and ravine, here and there a farmstead marking the site of an old settlement; the waving plumes of the fir-trees and the bold dark mass of Black Hambleton filling in the background.

About a mile full south is the little rural village of Thimbleby in Osmotherley parish. At Domesday it was in the Soke of the Manor of Alverton, and the name is written Timbel-bi, which either means the place whence timber was obtained, or the place built entirely of wood logs. The Scandinavian word for timber is "timner," and "timmor" which the Norman-French scribes at the Survey would soften to Timbel and so we arrive at the Danish designation, Timbelby. The origin of the name is the same as Thimble Great and Thimble Little, in the parish of Fewston, in the Washburn Valley. The village is situated along the foot of

Osmotherley Cross. [Thompson.

the steep western slope of Thimbleby Moor, a spur of Black Hambleton, amid delightful scenic surroundings. Of old, Thimbleby Manor belonged to the great Yorkshire family of Wandefords, of Kirklington and (later) Castlecomer, Ireland. Thimbleby Lodge sits retired in a beautiful nook at the foot of an external angle of the hills, a little distance from the village, environed in fine timber and scenery. The village inn bears the sign of the "Fighting Cocks" (reminiscent of the popular 'sport,' now discredited because of its one-time associations with cruelty), and its landlord to-day, "Oade Bob Abbott," is a notable fox-hunter. It is his proud boast to have followed the hounds for over 70 years. Both according to his own and Blakeborough's testimony, he is 94 years of age—the oldest huntsman in the saddle still 'up' when Reynard breaks away. This is a little questionable, however; one fears Bob Abbot dwells too much in the land of Fancy where are the "Castles of Spain." Notwithstanding his assertion as to his hoary age, and his "Wha, I remember Waterloo weal eneaf," his years may more safely set down as not much over 76. Nevertheless, he is an 'Original,' both out and in the hunting field. He is a cousin, so he states, of the late Bobby Dawson, the deservedly celebrated Bilsdale huntsman, and rode after 'ye foxe' for two score years with him. For many seasons Bobby Dawson attended meets mounted on an aged dark-brown mare, and—as my informant put it—was "one of the most marvellous men in History!" "Aboot foxes," during his long experience he had acquired a knowledge that seemed second nature. He knew by instinct, as it were, which line the fox would take in the chase, and he was invariably 'in' at 'the Kill.' He was wont to talk to his steed, 'tis said, "Noo then, oade meer, thoo mun sluther on, wilt tha?" And she knew as well as Bobby, apparently, which line the fox would take and the hounds follow. In his time the Bilsdale meets were summoned by sound of horn. On hearing it each farmer who kept a hound would set off to the rendezvous by

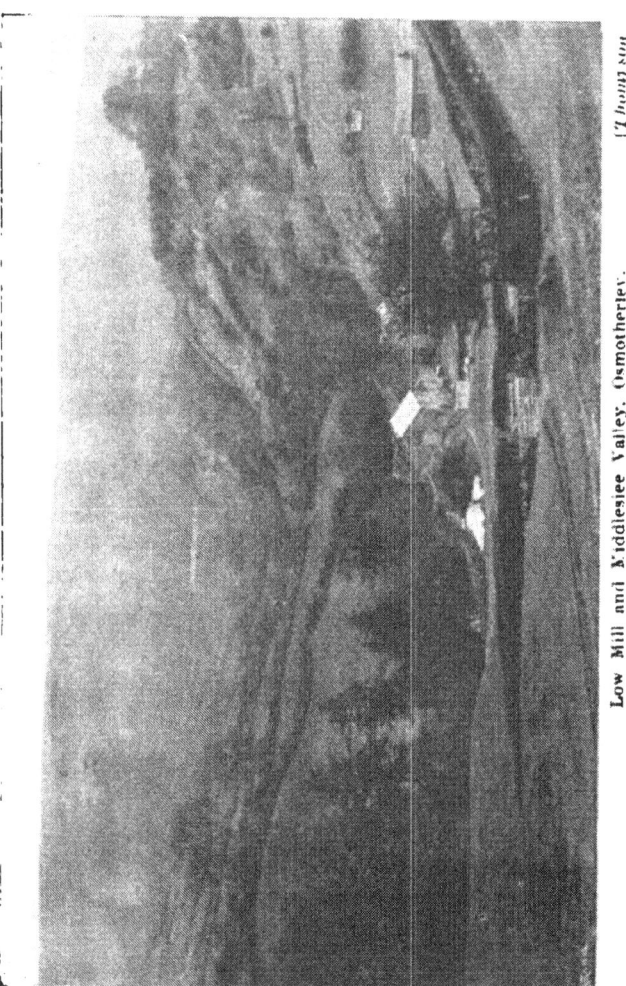

Low Mill and Kiddiesjee Valley, Osmotherley. [Thompson

sound, and were presently to be seen coming from every point of the compass, as it were attracted by that loadstone, to the horn-blower. Once on a time the York and Ainsty, and the Bilsdale hunts had a joint field-day on their respective borders. The York men were magnificently mounted and chaffed the hill-men about their under-sized and rough-coated galloways. Later in the day, the chance of the chase led into difficult hill country. Now it was the turn of the Bilsdalesmen, who turned easily in their pigskin and sarcastically inquired "Where are the York and Ainsty men now?" and other questions not so mildly put.

A little south, on Thimbleby bank, is the Hanging Stone. It is finely balanced on slender supports, and viewed from below the wonder is it doesn't instantly topple down. Below, in the valley, is Nun's House, now a farm, said to be the site of a nunnery, and foundations of ancient date have been discovered from time to time. Little is known about it however, save that in Norman times, one Philip de Colville, Lord of Thimbleby, was the founder of a Thimbleby Priory, and this was doubtless identical with the farm known as Nun's House. It is here that the hoard of gold, which is said to fill a bull's hide, is hidden.

Bob Abbott. [*Kester.*]

Upwards of another mile, south-west from Thimbleby, where three roads meet, are the Jeater houses—a place a generation or two back inhabited by Jet workers, which the appellation denotes. This trade is a fluctuating and erratic one, entirely dependent on Fashion—that most fickle of jades. Both jet-working and stone-quarrying were formerly an important industry hereabouts; but to-day, the cutters and polishers of jet are conspicuous by their absence. Westwards, not a mile from Jeater houses, is the tiny hamlet of Sigston Smithy, and further west still, at a bend of the road, is Kirkby Sigston. The Church (of St. Lawrence) here, although altered at different times and thoroughly restored, still contains fragments of the 12th century Norman structure. The portion of a Runic cross bears testimony to the antiquity of the place, and its name bespeaks its Danish founding. Bits of ancient glass, on which are displayed the arms of Wassand, Colville, and Sigston, shew the armigerial dignity of its former lords. A castle formerly stood here; its site can still be made out. In mediæval days this was the home of the De Sigstons; but several members of the Lascelles family are also buried in this church. Their residence at Stanks Hall is less than a mile away.

From Sigston Smithy we follow the old road to Foxton, a village scarcely worthy of the name, and following the turns of the road reach Ellerbeck, charmingly situated on the banks of the Codbeck. It has a most rural aspect, each cot with its garden plot, and the beck winding by the side of the village street has many pretty bits which linger in the memory. It has a mention in Domesday as "Elre-bec." The terminal "bec," the Norse "bac," bespeaks its Norse paternity. Its pre-Conquest lord was a Norseman, Hugh, son of Baldric, a name we have several times come across before. A mile north-west of Ellerbeck and west of Osmotherly, is the township of West Harlsey, composed of a few farms and scattered cottages. A castle formerly stood here, too, and slight vestiges of it may be observed. Old gossipy John Leland mentions this place in his usual quaint manner. He tells us that here "Strangwais, the Judge, builded a pratty Castelle." Sir James was, clearly, a notable personage, for in 1541, after the Dissolution of Monasteries, Mount Grace Priory, with property adjacent, was granted to Sir James Strangeways, Knt., to hold *in capite* for military service. More to the north, on the ridge dividing the basins of the Wiske and Codbeck, is the village of East Harlsey. The church dedicated to St. Oswald, is of great age, reaching back as far as the 9th century. Among the relics of mediæval times is the effigy of a knight, an ancient broken grave-cover, and memorial to the Lascelles. The village has a distinctly rural character, and the prospect from its commanding situation is one to be admired. Under two miles by field-path, crossing the Yarm turnpike by the Tontine Inn—a busy place in the past, when the public moved about the world in coaches, and the jingling of harness and the rattle of of wheels gave liveliness to the highways—we at length arrive at the beautiful and romantic ruins of Mount Grace Priory.

Mount Grace Priory.

The ruins of this monastery are situated at the foot of a steep hill clothed with magnificent woods, and in Spring with luxuriant herbage, a mosaic of primroses and the stars of the windflower anemone, with rose campion and the summer blooms which follow after the sylvan air perfumed with the aroma of honeysuckle, and in decay with the delicate pungency of the woodruffe, sweet as hay, even in death. An ocean of trees wave plumed crests over the Priory, crowned with sombre masses of Scot's fir.

The greystone tower of the church stands out against the sea of woodland, the broken walls, the roofless cells, with here and there a note of tender green or a splash of deep red where the

390 THE VALE OF MOWBRAY

Mount Grace Priory from the East.
(Owen Bowen.)

Manor Hall roof is seen through the lacing of the intervening trees, making an unforgettable picture. Ever and anon a sunbeam irradiates the woods with a flood of gold, and sparkles in iridescent illumination on the old grey weather-stained tower of the church that still soars skyward above the ruined monastic fragments, a legacy for the generations that succeed one another to muse upon. The Priory site is romantic and secluded in the extreme, lying under its sheltering hills, thicket-clad, as if to hide away its walls from the peering eyes of a busy world, and the sacred ground itself from the tread of the trespassing crowd. Yea, Mount Grace is truly a delightful spot from the scenic aspect, for the Nature lover, and last of all, that student of the Old, the Antiquary, who may investigate and ponder upon its habitations within a habitation, solemn, silent, a haunt of ancient peace and mute memories! The position well fits it for a Carthusian Monastery— Nature aiding Man. The Carthusian Order was founded about 1084 by Bruno, of Cologne. At Chartreuse, near Grenoble, S.E. France, and wherever we find the letters C.H.A.R.T.E., as in Charterhouse Street, London, etc., the spelling is traceable to this Order, or has connection with it. Previous to the founding of the Carthusians, monks were not solitaries, did not dwell alone in a cell severed from their fellows. Apart from religious services, prayers, etc., their lives were social, their hours of recreation spent in pursuing their several common avocations, dining, or conversing as they paced the arcaded cloister or the abbey garden enclosure. If a person really desired the life of a hermit or anchorite he removed to some solitary place and hewed himself a cell out of the rock; or built himself a shelter of logs in some lonesome sylvan glade; retiring there, his days were those of a recluse. But, until Henry the Second founded the Carthusian Abbey of Whitham in 1178, no such isolation from co-religionists had become the rule in any of the monastic orders in this country. When this system solitariness was established by the Carthusians, it was regarded a startling innovation, a strict proof of greater sanctity. Thus it came to pass that the Carthusian rule never found great favour in this country, as is shown by the number of such establishments never exceeding nine. The discipline was too stern, the code too severe, the prison-like life too lonely and exacting to take a deep root in the freer minds of men in our austere northern climate. Apart from their hermit-like existence, they were enjoined not to eat flesh-meat, to fast every Friday (bread and water only allowed), and, further, always to eat alone in their cells except on certain occasions of high festival. To all this they were to observe an almost perpetual silence. Neither were they permitted to leave their apartments except to go to church, without express leave from their superior. So it is that we find to our ideas their lives were spent both unsocially and unnaturally.

The cells where the monks dwelt were two storeyed, and ran round three sides of the large quadrangular enclosure. The fourth side was bounded by the church. There was a small bedroom, a workshop and other offices, behind which lay a little plot of garden ground, an allotment which each monk tended by himself as compensation for solitude. At the side of the doorway to each cell, is an opening in the wall about a foot square, which has a sharp angle in it, so that food or any other requisite could be passed into the cell without the servant-almoner being seen. In doctrine, the Carthusians differ very slightly from their brethren of the other Orders of monasticism obedient to Rome. But in their ritual and ceremony of High Mass there is a considerable departure from the common usage. The Carthusian rite is still the same all over the world as that laid down at Grenoble, nearly a thousand years back, and which shews a distinct affinity to the Oriental as distinguished from the Roman usage. The Order boasts that it has never changed, for the simple reason that it has never stood in need of reform. "SEMPER EADEM" is its motto—"ever the same"—all through its life of ten centuries! The supreme pontiff has always upheld and approved the simplicity and ritual, its old plain song or chant, and all its ancient ceremonies; while otherwise the Roman Catholic Church has modified or added variations to its observances. At the grand workshop of the Carthusian Order of Montreuil, there has recently been produced a facsimile of their ancient service-books, perhaps the most beautifully printed book the world has ever seen.

Entrance to a Cell. [*B. Bodwell*

This monastery was founded by Thomas Holland, Lord Wake and Earl of Kent. In the foundation deed he states why he chose the Carthusian Order. It was the admiration and the love he had

had from his early youth for their holy and peculiar rules, and for the persons living under them, as also for the affection of the Assumption of the Glorious Virgin and Saint Nicholas. It would only occupy too much space to describe adequately the ruins even of Mount Grace. The spell is there, but the spirit that imbued it has fled! 'Tis a place of ancient memories, a theme for archæologists to dilate upon; and more! In fancy we can rebuild and rehabitate it with the cowled forms of Eld; watch them enter or emerge from their quiet cells, to join in matins or even-song. To the unimpressionable the place is dead—to them the ruins tell no tale. The breeze whispering eerily among the leaves of the overhanging trees reveals to them no secrets relating to the former life

Remains of Church, Mount Grace.

of the place. The little cells, where in profound silence the solitary monk knelt in prayer, or diligently studied, illuminated missals or transcribed texts, or when in need of relaxation worked among the herbs in the garden plot, tells no story of sorrow, trial, or of the moulding of their nature in submission to the Divine Will. The far-away echo of sweetly chiming bells, swelling up from the very throat of Old Time, fails to catch their ears! The tolling of the Angelus (hour of prayer, when every head must bend), arouses not their attention. To such, the place is only a ruin, beauteous in its phases of season and colour—grey, green, golden—that is all! But to those who love to associate ancient ruins with the spirit of the past, this Mount of Grace appeals eloquently. The pulses of the past vibrate again, and the roofless fane breathes out its life as in the hey-day of its glory! In imagination we mark again the silent community, figures of monks gliding to and fro; one hears the chimes and responding echoes of the fervent Amens, and the choral strains rising and floating and dying away down the recesses of the long-drawn aisles, even though the words may be unintelligible to our ears and the figures belonging to a byegone world. Thus the Priory stands erect again before us, repeopled not only in the flesh but in the spirit: a thing of the past—present still!

Just within the wood, east of the ruins, is the necessary Well, which is said to have supplied the Priory with the draught of Life. It is known by the name of St. John's Well, also the Wishing Well, whereunto (of course) lovers, sweetheart and swain, are wont to adjourn to breathe their fond heart's desires. The local custom is to stick pins through ivy leaves, throw them into the water, and then give utterance to their most secret and ardent desires, which story adds is sure to come to pass.

Nearly on the summit of the moor, east of the Priory, are the ruins of Our Lady's Chapel, founded 1515. In days of yore, numerous miracles by the aid of Our Lady were said to have been performed here. The path leading from the Priory was formerly known as Our Lady's Steps. It is also thought to have been the burying place of the monastery. Tombstones were there 60 or 70 years ago; all have now gone. During the reign of Elizabeth and that of James, this spot became a place of pilgrimage of those who adhered to the doctrines of the Old Faith. A little way north are the several disused quarry holes, whence the stone for the monastic buildings has been obtained.

Animated Nature in Thirskland.

By R. RODWELL.

I.

The Red, Fallow, and Roe Deer cannot be described as wild now in the Vale of Mowbray, though they occasionally break bounds and "get shot" as such.

The Badger, our English bear, loves the lonely hillsides, where there is no one to disturb his nightly rambles. The family at the base of White Mare Crag must have had a spacious establishment, judging by the debris deposited outside.

It is usually a short-lived sensation to see the head of an Otter emerge from the waters of the Codbeck when twilight is fading into the night; they are shy and wary, but now and then the word goes round among the Thirsk anglers that he has left his footprints along the water-side within the town;—and they make remarks.

The Fox receives his share of notice here. One pack of foxhounds meet at Thirsk, two others at the next stations north and south, another at the Hambleton Hotel, and the Bilsdale Hounds claim Upsal not far away. The moorland foxes have given them many a long run, sometimes well into the night.

The Hedgehog, Stoat, and Weasel are of a retiring disposition, and the old English Black-Rat is rare.

The brown Water Vole is fairly abundant along the streams, and there is the Shrew Mouse, the Long-Tailed Field Mouse and his short-tailed brother the Vole.

It is some years ago now since the last Marten was killed near Thirsk, but formerly that rare woodland sweetmart was indubitably in evidence; stuffed specimens are extant: yet still that bushy-tailed nutcracker, the Squirrel, makes his lightning dart along the boughs, and daring leaps from tree to tree.

Robert Rodwell.   *Ernest Forbes*

Thirsk people praise the old brown Trout of the Codbeck and there are Grayling also ; and Lampreys find their way up the beck. There are Crayfish in Gormire and the innumerable toads there at pairing time, on shore and in the water, make an extraordinary sight.

The Common Snake or Haggworm is found in the lowlands. I have seen the little Blindworm or Slowworm at Boltby, and Mr. Lee has had many a Viper hunt along the sunny slopes of the Hambletons, ending in a "kill."

I made my first acquaintance with the Glowworm's indescribable illumination in the grass in going up Sutton Bank to the big bonfire on Roulston Scar at the Jubilee in 1897. Many were the fires scattered over the Vale and the hills beyond—visible from our unrivalled coign of vantage ; and many the attempts at their location. Many, many too the miniature beacon-lights or fairy lamps of the Noctiluca or "Night-light" beetle, not inappropriately supplementing the wilder flambeaux of the Sixty Years Celebration. After all was over on the hills, Walter Pattison and I enjoyed a free morning concert most of the way back to Thirsk

Otter. [*J. Pennington*

II.

THE BIRDS OF THE VALE OF MOWBRAY.

Though there is not much that is specially remarkable in the bird life of this district, Mr. Robert Lee, the vertebrate Secretary of the Thirsk Naturalists' Society, has kindly furnished a list of one hundred and eighty-six feathered residents, migrants or casual visitors, which have been brought to his knowledge during his forty years experience in Thirsk; with other information regarding them, and the wild animals still left.

Many of these birds are rare here, and they range in size from the white-tailed Eagle and the Wild Swans, down to that smallest of British birds, the Golden Crested Wren; and in abundance from the ubiquitous Sparrow to the Nightingale, which years ago lured Thirsk people to make evening pilgrimages to Thirkleby.

There is a strange fascination about birds, though dulled to most of us by familiarity. The variety and beauty of their plumage, the grace of their movements on the wing; which no doubt has suggested the symbolic gift of wings to the angels; their perfect power over an element in which man has had little success as yet; the mystery of the instinctive perfection of their nest-building; and the kinship of feeling we recognise in their song.

Robert Lee. [*Ernest Forbes*.

ANIMATED NATURE IN THIRSKLAND.

Rosalind's saying that "Beauty provokes thieves sooner than gold," has a sad significance to the feathered creation. In contradistinction to the scientific desire to record such truth of Nature as may be practicable, can we consider that the primitive animal instinct to kill for food has been at all ennobled by the human developments of unnecessary slaughter, merely for its own sake, for the sordid joys of unintelligent possession, or the despicable vanity which leads to the display in dress, &c., of such character-indicating trophies?

Bird life, unlike that of the furry fauna, is on every hand, and at all times; from the songsters' joyous greeting of the earliest dawn, to the chattering wonder of invisible night travellers at the lighted street lamps far below, as instinctively they wing their way to some far distant goal. Birds overhead in nights of storm, may well have given rise to the "Gabriel's Hounds" and other eerie superstitions, in the first instance.

The Gyr Falcon and the Peregrine Falcon are very rare visitors. Times have changed for the Falcons since they were so jealously preserved for the sport of hawking; but even then they had not always the victory: the sword-

Common Buzzard. [*J. Pennington.*

beak of the heron would tell its tale sometimes. The Hobby, the Lesser Kestrel and the Kite are also very rare ; the Kestrel or Windhover is decreasing in numbers, and the Merlin, the smallest of our falcons, is not very often met with. The Sparrow Hawk is the most common of the hawk tribe ; the Common Buzzard and the Rough-Legged Buzzard are not often seen, but the year before last several were shot on Hambleton—the wing-spread reaching to as much as 45 to 48 inches. The Honey Buzzard and the Hen Harrier are very rare.

As the street lamps of Thirsk are not lighted in the summer, we may see the Owl winging its silent flight in the more open spaces of the town ; or hear its hoot in the woods about the country-side as it follows its quest of "rats and mice and such small deer"; a paying form of sport which should induce more gratitude than it does from the farmer and gamekeeper.

The Crested Pewit or Lapwing consumes legions of the enemies of the farmer, still it has need of all its artfulness to hold its own. The young chicks, even from the shell, can lie low and counterfeit irregular grey green patches of moss to perfection. A graceful creature, alike on the ground and in its singularly varied flight—at a distance, singly or in flocks, in a moment visible or invisible according to the angle of its wing planes in the air : and on the whole it lends perhaps more life and interest to country walks than any other bird.

The Thrushes are common, the Throstle's frequent song, the rich flute-notes from the Blackbird's yellow bill, and the Fieldfare's announcement of the approach of winter are familiar to most, yet none the less delightful. The Ring Ousel on the dry walls of the moorlands appears like a blackbird with a sore throat that has to wear a white chest protector up there.

The three Shrikes or Butcher Birds are rare, the Pied and Grey Wagtails are common, but the Yellow one, so canary-like, is scarce; there are six Tits and four Buntings about ; the Waxwing as a rare winter visitant brings its delicate and beautiful red sealing-wax-tipped plumage from Lapland ; and the Crossbill is another infrequent visitor from the Continental pine woods.

The Starling is not afraid of showing the metallic sheen of his feathers near the haunts of men, and is the most like a four-pointed star of any bird we see o'erhead.

The Raven is rare ; but not so the Rook, which attracts a considerable amount of attention from its frequent presence, its ill-understood changes of roosting places, and the summary judicial proceedings, which are taken under rook-law against offending members of the community. The Magpie may be sometimes seen in small flocks in secluded spots; but the "chattering" Jay, the only gaily coloured member of the crow tribe, like the three Woodpeckers, hides itself among the trees: while the Cuckoo is just as much at home amid the leafy sprays of the lowlands as on the grey walls up among the ling.

Rough-Legged Buzzard [J. *Pennington.*

The Roller is only known to have indulged in its antics once hereabouts; whereas the Kingfisher not infrequently shows his flash of blue splendour as he wings his wavy flight under the boughs which shade the becks. He knows his way under Thirsk Bridges; this Spring, one passed the writer between the green and the church, alighted on the hedge on the opposite bank; not many yards away, showed its red breast while scrutinizing the still figure near, then concluding it was safe to attend to business, made a swoop into the water, perched and swooped again and again until it was lost among the pollard willows of the "Holmes,"

The Black Swift, with its sabre blade-like wings, seems as fond of Thirsk town as the little Sandmartin is of the rippling reaches down the beck.

The Night Jar is not often noticed, for it is shy of the light, and its flight very quick and noiseless; but the scythe-billed Curlew can be seen and heard from afar upon the moors, where the Grouse feed on the heather.

The Heron occasionally visits Gormire and the becks, but being somewhat shy and rather a night bird, its wide flapping wings are not so often seen. The Bittern and the Ruff are very rare, and the Spotted Crake is scarce, but the voice of the Corncrake or Landrail is well known, far better than its form; it may be approached very closely and startled into flight, if you "Tread softly, that the blind mole may not hear a foot fall."

The Dipper or Water Ousel is often seen by the becks; the Water Hen is found on many quiet waters, and there are generally some bald-headed Coots rippling the waters of Gormire.

The Whooper Swan and Bewick's Swan are very rare, but the Mute Swan is less so: and all of the seven kinds of Wild Geese which have been noticed in the district are only accidental visitors; of the thirteen Wild Ducks enumerated, some are much more frequent visitors than the Geese, and know Gormire and other waters, besides Sir Ralph Payne-Gallwey's decoy near Thirkleby.

There are four kinds of Grebes, the Great Northern Diver, the Black-Throated and Red-Throated Divers, three Terns, six Gulls, three Skuas, and the Fork-Tailed and Stormy Petrels.

Also there is the Puffin or Sea Parrot, the Razorbill, the Little Auk, Guillemot and Gannet.

It may not be a far cry from the Vale of Mowbray to the usual haunts of sea or shore birds, but the casual visitors or regular migrants from Africa, the Russian Empire and the Arctic Circle must be regarded as no mean travellers. From time to time many put in an appearance for a season, but their sojourn is merely that of a storm-bound guest. It would serve no useful purpose to enumerate their several names as catalogued by Mr. Lee, but the scarce Scoter, the Grey Phalarope, the Collared Pratincole, and Manx Shearwater were amongst them.

The Flower Chronicle of the Vale of Mowbray.

By WILLIAM FOGGITT, j.p., f.l.s.

THE beautiful Vale of Mowbray, with its "mountain, meadow, moss, and moor," is one of the richest and most exhaustively explored in the kingdom. Here John Gilbert Baker, F.R.S., F.L.S., a distinguished scientist of whom our county may well be proud, for seventeen years strenuously laboured and botanically reigned supreme, at the end of which, he was appointed Sub-Curator and subsequently Curator of the Royal Herbarium at Kew, which positions he honourably and efficiently held for 35 years.

We purpose introducing you to its splendid and well-nigh unrivalled flora in reviewing two or three of its chief botanical localities, and then taking a cursory glance at the remainder noticing only the less frequent and more remarkable plants. Let us visit the mountain first, for mountains our hills may be designated, and such the poet has sung them. Six miles east north-east of Thirsk is situate Boltby, a picturesque village immediately to the north of which is a lovely and secluded valley called Gurtoft, known also as Boltby Glen, which, for many years, was one of the most frequented and happiest hunting grounds of the Thirsk Natural History Society in its earliest and palmiest days—very literally palmiest, because the willows, locally palms, in which the neighbourhood abounds were, at that time, an especially fascinating and diligently pursued study. This dell, full of romance, of which I could tell if space would allow, was immensely rich in Mosses, for

> " . . . . here steeped,
> And striped, and starred in colours manifold,
> Mosses that 'twould be sin to tread upon,"

and we had amongst us then, and happily he liveth still, as enthusiastic as fully half a century ago, an indefatigable bryologist who now resides in the North of

Ireland, and has there done, and is even now doing, much to add to its already rich muscological flora. I refer to John Henry Davies, who like Mr. Baker, is a much loved and life-long friend.

We will approach Gurtoft by way of Kirkby Knowle. As we near the village we shall find on the banks of the road-side stream the two Golden Saxifrages—*Chrysosplenium oppositifolium* and *alternifolium*, which, in the days of primitive physic were held in high repute as stone-expellers; Hemp Agrimony, a showy composite with pinkish flowers, so called from its hemp-like leaves; and Cardamine sylvatica, the flexuous-stemmed Lady's Smock, a true heart-strengthener, as its name imports. On walls in the village the rue-leaved Saxifrage grows, and in climbing the hill-side pasture at the east end we are almost sure to see the Moonwort or Grape Fern—*Botrychium Lunaria*—the "seeds" or spores of which were supposed to render the possessor invisible. Entering the wood by the bridle road we shall notice in an adjacent bog the elegant *Equisetum sylvaticum*, which both in its fertile and barren fronds, is the loveliest of the Horsetails, growing under the shade of a grove of *Salix Helix*, the Rose Willow, probably so called from the rich, rose-coloured red-currant-like galls which frequently abound upon its leaves. The same swamp is gay with Marsh Marigolds, the Virgin Mary's golden flower, known in some parts of Yorkshire as "publicans," for their fondness for drink; but "teetotallers" would be a more appropriate name. Immediately above is a secluded tarn, said to have been caused about a century ago by a land-slip, on the margin of which is abundance of *Acorus Calamus*—the sweet Flag—the sword-shaped leaves of which give out, especially when bruised, an agreeable aromatic odour, and were formerly much used for strewing the floors of churches. The abundant underground stems (rhizomes) were once highly valued as a stomachic and sold under the name of *Calamus Aromaticus*, the market, according to Syme's English Botany, being chiefly supplied from Norfolk, where an acre of river-side land abounding in this plant would let for an annual rental of £40.

The wood below is now known as "Shoot Wood." Leaving this secluded tarn and following the bridle path which leads diagonally up the hill, we pass a number of self-sown trees of *Pinus sylvestris*—the Scotch Fir—the "evergreen Pine" of Sir Walter Scott, interspersed with the graceful Mountain Ash, the "rowan" of that "wizard of the North," locally known as "Witch Wood," the branches of which were up to quite recently hung in cowsheds to ward off the "Evil Eye."

"Rowan Tree and red thread,
Put the witches at their speed."

As you near the summit in oozy ground you will be greeted with the violet-like flowers of *Pinguicula vulgaris*—the Butter-wort—so called from the greasiness of its radical rosettes of yellowish-green leaves which, covered with minute viscid glands, detain tiny insects until they are gradually enfolded and finally absorbed. Having attained the summit, and crossing over a short heathery moor, you pass through an abundance of Cotton grass, the large silvery heads of which, when in fruit, are singularly beautiful, intermingled with patches of the scaly-stemmed Clubrush, *Scirpus cæspitosus*, and interspersed with the graceful nodding spikes of the green-ribbed Sedge (*Carex binervis*). In the sphagnous bog where the stream rises, we are gladdened with the charming flowers and delicious fragrance of the Lancashire bog *Asphodel*, and hard by, the round-leaved Sundew, *Drosera rotundifolia*, another insectivorous plant, the pretty red gland-tipped hairs which fringe the leaves, call them tentacles, if you will, although unaffected by heavy raindrops, are exceedingly sensitive to the slightest animal touch, enfolding, absorbing, and assimilating the tiny insects that alight thereon. A high authority has calculated that "a portion of woman's hair weighing the 80,000th part of a grain is sufficient to provoke movement."

We soon reach the Glen, and near the entrance "close couched upon the heathery moor," or "'neath dwarfish shrubs of birch and oak" is abundance of that rare and lovely floral gem, *Trientalis europæa*, the Chickweed Wintergreen, which, in England, is confined to five of our northernmost counties, attaining its southern limit in Yorkshire. Entering the valley's gorge we shall find the steep banks adorned with the glossy evergreen box-like leaves and flesh-coloured flowers of the red Whortleberry intermingled with its more abundant and better-known relative the Bilberry. The pale-pink wax-like corollas of the former split at their ends into four reflexed segments, and shaped somewhat like those of the Lily of the Valley are strikingly beautiful, to be followed, as summer advances, by the delicious and decidedly wholesome fruit which is largely imported into this country from Sweden and other parts of the Baltic as Cranberries. The writer discovered this many years ago through a keg of so-called Cranberries he had purchased of a ocal confectioner in which were the tell-tale leaves and clustered fruit of the Whortleberry. There is, happily, no harm in the misnomer for the berries are fully equal, if not superior, both in deliciousness and wholesomeness to the genuine article.

On one occasion during a long mountain ramble, on a hot summer's day, upon the East Moors north of Helmsley, the writer and a botanical companion were fully persuaded that each ate a quart of this luscious fruit not only without hurt but with full satisfaction; and on their return in the afternoon overtook a Helmsley gentleman with a large can-full which he called, and said were constantly sold in their town under the name of Cranberries. The more abundant Whortleberry, with its bluish-black stainful fruit, is largely used locally as a conserve and makes an excellent and enjoyable tart. It is familiarly known in Yorkshire as "Blaeberry," and in Lancashire as "Whimberry," in both which counties it is in much request. During frequent rambles in the English Lake district blaeberry jam was in constant evidence upon the hotel tables.

Lower down, where the valley widens and is more wooded, grow the much prized Oak and Beech Ferns, surrounded by the Hard-fern or Rough Spleenwort, doubly noticeable from its biformed fronds, the linear erect rigid fertile, and the sub-prostrate broader barren ones springing rosette-like from the same rootstock. Here too we shall see the hay-scented mountain fern *Lastrea Oreopteris*, intermingled with its better known congeners *dilatata*, *spinulosa*, and *Filix-mas*. Hard by too is the Lady-fern, *Filix-fœmina*, happily named, for it is the most graceful of our native species, and

> "Where the copse-wood is the greenest,
> Where the fountain is the sheenest,
> Where the morning dew lies longest,
> There the lady-fern grows strongest."

Many moss-laden tree trunks are richly adorned with the common Polypody, and the crumbly banks enlivened with Brittle-fern, *Cystopteris fragilis*. A little lower down, where the valley widens and the natural wood ceases, in a swampy spot that rare floral beauty, *Primula farinosa*—the mealy Primrose, the "Birds'-een" of rustics—formerly grew in abundance, but owing to drainage and the planting of trees it is well-nigh extinct; however, fortunately, it still grows in fair plenty by an adjacent hill-side stream. This rarity is confined to the six northernmost English counties and one Scotch locality. Here also, in swampy ground, flourish the Marsh Violet;

Anagallis tenella, the bonny bog pimpernel; the buckbean, *Menyanthes trifoliata*; the Marsh Valerian with its two sorts of flowers, and the creeping Willow, whilst the hill-sides are splendid with the stately Foxglove.

Cultivated land is now reached, and here last year a field of Vetches yielded abundance of the beautiful Corn Cockle—*Agrostemma Githago*, a decreasing colonist; and a showy purple vetch, *Vicia varia*. Hereabouts in the pastures flourishes the Sweet Cicely, *Myrrhis odorata*, known to village children as "Cough-drops," a large umbellifer with milk-white flowers, redolent of Anise, and formerly in high repute as a cattle condiment. The village walls and roofs yield the Whitlow grass and the great yellow stonecrop *Sedum reflexum*, closely adjacent fields *Polygonum Bistorta*, the snakeweed with its twice twisted root; and in an adjoining hedgerow, *Galium Mollugo*, the great white bed-straw. The last name conveys a wrong impression, for it is a corruption of bead-straw, the many jointed stems of some species being formerly used by the Irish peasantry for telling their beads.

On the banks of the stream, below the village, may be seen *Trollius europæus*, Globe-flower, the "dumplings" of children; *Helleborus viridis*, Green-hellebore; *Cardamine amara*, Bittercress, with its showy purple extruding stamens; *Rosa villosa*, the downy rose, with its bright-red flowers, to be succeeded by abundant scarlet pome-shaped fruit; *Gagea lutea*, the yellow Star-of-Bethlehem, the flowers of which, in some seasons, are so much cropped by birds, presumably pheasants, that it is exceedingly difficult to find them; *Narcissus pseudo-narcissus*, the Lent-Lily, in popular phrase "daffadown-dilly," probably a corruption of Saffron Lily; *Salix pentandra*, the bay-leaved willow, the showiest of the genus, the large polished glandular leaves of which, on a warm day, diffuse their odour to a considerable distance; *Berberis vulgaris*, the Barberry, the intensely yellow bark of which was formerly held, on the doctrine of signs, in high esteem as a remedy for jaundice, and the orange to red fruit makes an agreeable and wholesome "preserve." Some years ago a much-respected Thirsk tradesman and his wife, used to spend an annual day's holiday in collecting the berries for conserve, and probably they enjoyed the outing even more than the resulting jam.

Near the Mill, a few years ago, a considerable quantity of that mysterious plant, Henbane, Hyoscyamus niger sprang up: a species not so black as painted, for it is a splendid sedative, probably as effectual, and certainly not nearly so seductive, as Opium. Henbane, possibly Hen-bean, for I have, more than once, seen domestic fowl feeding amongst it, and, to all appearance, picking its scattered seeds, is a weird-looking creature with forbidding smell and unpleasant clammy viscid leaves; it has the habit of springing up on newly-disturbed ground, frequently in churchyards, flourishing for a few years in diminishing quantity, and finally disappearing.

> "Folding its tents like the Arabs,
> And as silently stealing away."

The banks of a small tributary stream are adorned with the much admired *Paris quadrifolia*—"True-love" or "One-berry"—which is often found with 3, 5, and even 6 leaves; *Carex paniculata*, with its stout hassocks, one of the largest of our many sedges, of which the Vale of Mowbray boasts 34 species. *Equisetum maximum*, the giant Horsetail, the fertile stems of which are produced sparingly in spring, and the very showy barren ones abundantly during the summer months.

Leaving the village and climbing the hill to "Sneck Yat," we are sure to see *Helianthemum vulgare*, the rock rose, a true sun-worshipper; *Gentiana Amarella var præcox*; *Habenaria chlorantha*, the greater butterfly Orchis; and very probably *Ophrys muscifera*, the fly Orchis, the flowers of which so strikingly resemble a fly that the writer has more than once been deceived.

Attaining the summit, and crossing the moor, we shall notice the abundant evergreen foliage of *Empetrum nigrum*, the Crow-berry, locally Ling-berry, remarkable for bearing black fruit in Britain, purple in North, and red in South America! Grouse are said to be partial to its berries, which, to human-kind, are edible but not commendable; and trailing mid heather and heath, the bright green foliage and long rope-like stems of *Lycopodium clavatum*, the stag's horn Club moss, popularly Traveller's Joy, and such it proves, for on several occasions I have seen it wreathed around the hats of tourists and even of well-known botanists.

The great High-priest of Nature beautifully sang of the idle shepherd boys—

> "On pipes of sycamore they play
> The fragments of a Christmas hymn,
> Or with that plant, which in our dale,
> We call Wolf's claws or Fox's tail,
> Their rustic hats they trim."

These Lycopods are highly interesting, being diminutive representatives of the oldest terrestrial plants on our globe, for during the Coal period they grew to the size of giant forest trees, attaining a height of sixty and more feet, and with proportionately strong and stout trunks. The plants of this genus have learnt, by long experience, how to rough it, and are generally found on wind swept moors. In sandy tracts *Sagina nodosa*, the knotted Spurrey, is very attractive on bright days; and here and there, close shrouded under the ling, the lesser Twayblade, *Listera cordata*, with its heart shaped foliage, one of the tiniest and frailest of our Orchids, is sure to reward a diligent search.

A short walk brings us to the head of Yowlass, a secluded quadrifurcate limestone valley, the northernmost fork of which is a perfect paradise of wild flowers, for here, on the limestone rocks, occurs plentifully the rare Spring Cinque-foil (Potentilla verna), whilst the steep grassy banks are gay with the purple Columbine; Cerastium arvense, with its pretty white flowers and honied fragrance; *Geranium sanguineum*, the blood-red Cranesbill; Hypericum montanum, the mountain St. John's-wort; Spiræa Filipendula, the Dropwort, the pea-like tubers of which hang by slender threads; Anthyllis vulneraria, Kidney Vetch, or "Lamb-toe sweet creeping o'er the banks in sunny-time"; Geum intermedium, a robust hybrid between the wood and water Avens; Agrimonia odorata, the leaves and stem of which are covered with fragrant glands, a much taller and stronger plant than its well-known congener; Rubus saxatilis, the stone-bramble, a low growing species, somewhat resembling the Strawberry, and yielding choice red fruit; Rosa spinosissima, the Burnet or Scotch Rose, frequently cultivated in gardens; Rosa Sabini, another densely prickly species, both of which are low growing; Poterium Sanguisorba, the Salad-Burnet; Scabiosa Columbaria, the small Scabious, with its sky blue flowers; Euonymus europæus, the spindle tree, with its deeply lobed quadrangular rose-coloured fruit, splitting at the top in a cruciform manner, and known in France as "bonet d' Pretre"—Priest's cap; Picris hieraciodes the bristly ox-tongue; Carduus eriophorus, the truly majestic woolly headed Thistle, the lower leaves of which are often two feet in length; Campanula glomerata, the clustered Bell-flower; Cynoglossum officinale, the Hound's tongue, with strong mice-like smell; Lithospermum officinale, the medicinal Gromwell, the polished marble-like seeds of which, as its generic name indicates, are exceedingly hard; Pyrola minor, the lesser Wintergreen, with its rose-coloured bloom; the two Gentians Amarella and campestris; Verbascum Thapsus, the great yellow Mullein or Flannel-flower, so called from its very woolly leaves, and which, in the late Autumn, with its tall rigid stems, and sessile persistent bud-like capsules, is strongly suggestive of ' Aaron's rod that budded," indeed in some parts it is known by that name; Carlina vulgaris, the Carline thistle, in allusion to imperial Charlemagne, and a beautiful legend; Calamintha Acinos, Basil Thyme; Calamintha Clinopodium, Wild Basil; and Origanum vulgare, Wild Marjoram, with both red and white flowers, a fragrant group; the Lily of the Valley, Convallaria majalis, with its lovely flowers and delicious smell; Epipactis ensifolia, the sword-leaved Helleborine; Neottia nidus-avis, the Bird's-nest Orchis, with fawn-coloured flowers and intertwined roots; and Ophrys apifera, the Bee-Orchis, which greatly resembles the smaller wild humble bee; Carex digitata, the fingered Sedge; Melica nutans, the nodding Melic; Avena pratensis, the mountain Oat-grass, and Hordeum sylvaticum, the wood-barley.

Where the hill-side is more wooded, Actæa spicata, the Bane-berries, a very poisonous species confined to the Counties of York and Westmoreland, flourishes, and abundance of Deadly Nightshade, Atropa Belladonna, worthy its lethal name, for some seventy years ago its purple luscious-looking fruit lured two children of a neighbouring farmer to their death. On the other hand it is very potent and useful in medicine.

A neighbouring wood yields Monotropa hypopitys, the Yellow Bird's-nest, a strange-looking dingy yellow leafless saprophyte, destitute of chlorophyll, somewhat resembling parasitical Toothwort and the Broomrapes, and supposed to feed upon decaying vegetable matter.

In a subjacent bog, where a perennial full flowing spring issues from the limestone, and by an open aqueduct, which seems to run up-hill, and supplies the elevated village of Old Byland with water, are a number of interesting species, for here grow the beautiful grass of Parnassus; Galium uliginosum, the marsh Bedstraw; Montia fontana, Blinks, with flowers gleaming in the sunlight; Crepis paludosa, the marsh Hawkweed, with its attractive yellow bloom; Epipactis palustris, the marsh Helleborine, an infrequent Orchid; Schœnus nigricaxs, the black bog-rush; and Blysmus compressus, the broad-leaved Blysmus. Crumbling rocks close at hand are decorated with the black and green Spleenworts and Cystopteris fragilis, the brittle Fern. In a moorland pasture, at no great distance, is a bright patch of Carduus acaulis, with its rich dark-crimson flowers, apparently stemless, its northernmost home in Britain, and still nearer well-nigh a rood of copsy hill-side is radiant with the deep-blue petals and showy yellow anthers of Jacobs-ladder, Polemonium cœruleum, and hard by abundance of Inula Conyza, the Ploughman's Spikenard, which, with many other rural names, such as Shepherd's Clock, Shepherd's Needle, Shepherd's Purse, Shepherd's Weather-glass, is strongly remindful of the simpler life; whilst hillside pastures hard by afford the much-coveted Ophrys apifera, the bee Orchis, and of which the poet sings—

> "Perchance the fragrant load may bind
> Its limbs, I'll set the captive free;
> I sought the living bee to find,
> And found the picture of a bee."

William Foggitt, J.P., F.L.S.　　[*Ernest Forbes*

Even whilst I write two of the Misses Gallwey have discovered a new and abundant locality for this splendid mimic of the plant world.

The transition from the hills, with their interesting valleys, to the low-lying heaths is easy, and to two typical ones readily accessible by railway, Pilmoor and Leckby Carr, we briefly introduce you, the first named of which, with its sphagnous bogs, and extensive ponds, yields many rare and interesting species. A pool at the south-west of the moor, is resplendent with the showy purple flowers of numerous Carduus pratensis, the meadow Thistle, not happily called for its home is usually in bogs, and here you have, almost always, to wade for it. It is very much like, but less robust than, its upland congener Carduus heterophyllus, the melancholy Thistle, the flowering heads of which are locally known as shaving-brushes. Intermingled, but you must wade to secure it, is Utricularia minor, the lesser Bladder wort, the least in size of an interesting genus, the vesicles of which have suggested both the scientific and popular names. These bladders, which give buoyancy to the plant, and float it upon the water, are metamorphosed leaves, formed like little oblong bags, with lids, which open inward, and prove an abundant fly-trap. "All hope abandon ye who enter here," might appropriately be inscribed upon these doors, which go back readily to admit tiny animalcules, but close immediately the creature has entered, when the victim soon dies in its prison-house, and is shortly decomposed and assimilated. How truly "one half the world does not know how the other half lives."

On the margin of this and other of the ponds is an abundance of Hypericum elodes, the marsh Saint John's wort, which, with its pronounced aromatic foenugreek-like smell, strongly suggestive of cattle-spice, and its soft shaggy stem and leaves, differs widely from the other members of that much admired genus.

Other waters and their margins yield Comarum palustre, the strawberry-headed Trefoil; Lythrum Salicaria, the showy purple loose-strife with its polymorphic flowers; Helosciadum inundatum, the least Water-parsnip, the tiniest of our umbellifers; Menyanthes trifoliata, the bog-bean, so lovely with its sweet fringed flowers; Stellaria glauca, the marsh stitchwort; Epilobium palustre, the marsh willow weed; Scutellaria galericulata, the skull cap; Veronica scutellata, the marsh speedwell; Rumex Hydrolapathum, the great water-dock; the three Duckweeds, Lemna minor, trisulca, and polyrhiza; Alisma ranunculoides, the lesser water plantain, with its sweet buttercup-like flowers; Scirpus fluitans, the floating club-rush; Scirpus lacustris, the true bull-rush, which gracefully bows to every breeze, although the name, possibly a corruption of pool-rush, is more generally given to the Typhæ—the reed-maces, which are stiff as pokers; several interesting sedges; Aira uliginosa, the bog hair-grass, a rare, or much overlooked species—Molinia cœrulea, the blue Melic, and Pilularia globulifera, the Pill-wort, a species allied to and generally included among our ferns,—remarkably singular with its slender rhizomes and filiform leaves plentifully covered with hairy globular pill-like capsules, which suggested the name.

Scattered over the moor among abundance of ling, and the two beautiful heaths—Erica cinerea and tetralix, are many choice plants of which we can mention but a few—Genista anglica, the needle furze or petty whin, with its bonny pea-green leaves, beautiful yellow flowers and attractive bright red fruit pods; the tiny Radiola millegrana, the thyme-leaved All-seed or Flax-seed, rarely more than an inch high although closely related to our stately and showy Linseed; the very beautiful Gentiana Pneumonanthe, or marsh Gentian, with its deep blue flowers, the largest of its genus in this country; Salix repens, the creeping willow, a variable species, often with shining silvery foliage; Narthecium ossifragum, the Lancashire bog-asphodel, the specific name of bone breaker being in allusion to a strange and quite erroneous superstition, formerly held by farmers, that bones of sheep partaking of this plant would gradually rot; Gymnadenia conopsea, a very pretty Orchid, with delicious clove-like fragrance; Habenaria albida, the lesser butterfly Orchis, another fragrant gem; Orchis latifolia, the marsh Orchis; and abundance of Listera ovata, the greater Tavay-blade; Osmunda regalis, the stately Royal Fern grew sparingly many years ago, but has long been extinct—the last two plants of it were cherished and shown in a cottage upon the moor until a comparatively recent date. Luzula multiflora, and its variety congesta, the many headed wood-rush, partial to heaths; Equisetum hyemale, the winter horse-tail, which *blooms in Summer*, the rough naked stems of which so abound in flint that it used to be largely imported into this country for polishing purposes, from Holland, under the name of Dutch rushes; Lycopodium inundatum, a rare small prostrate Lycopod, occasionally found upon boggy heaths.

Sandy fields closely adjacent, and enclosed somewhat recently from the moor, yield Lepidium campestre, the Mithridate Pepperwort; Teesdalia nudicaulis, a pretty little crucifer, named in honour of Mr. Teesdale, one of the pioneers of Yorkshire Botany, who wrote the first Flora of York, and was for many years gardener to the then Earl of Carlisle, during which time he introduced the charming Villarsia nymphæoides, the yellow fringed Buckbean, into the Lake at Castle Howard, where it still abundantly and increasingly flourishes, and is well worthy a special visit; Ornithopus perpusillus, the least Birds-foot Trefoil, the pods of which so strongly suggest the name; Silene anglica, the English Catchfly, one of a genus the viscid calyces of which entrap, but do not devour insects; Trifolium medium, the zig-zag clover, a very attractive species, truly native, which several of the clovers are not; Epilobium angustifolium, the French Willow-weed, with its abundant and splendid magenta flowers, known as the "fire weed" in Canada, because it springs up abundantly after the great prairie conflagrations; Filago minima, an infrequent and very hoary species of Cudweed; Senecio viscosus, the stinking Groundsel, with fleshy very viscid foliage; Rhinanthus major, the greater yellow rattle, with its elegant yellow blue tipped flowers; Galeopsis versicolor, the large Hemp nettle, with spacious variegated corollas; Myosotis versicolor, the yellow and blue forget-me-not, which like so many of the Borage order has colour-changing flowers; Lepidium campestre, the Mithridate Pepperwort; and Erythræa Centauruim, the red Centaury, with its rich pink flowers, intensely bitter like others of the Gentian family, and much esteemed and largely sold by herbalists as an appetising stomachic—the bordering copse yields Rhamnus Frangula, the berry bearing Alder, and in less quantity Rhamnus catharticus, the purging Buckthorn, two species of a genus, the fruit of which yields a rich yellow die, and is sold commercially under the name of "French Berries," and those of the Buckthorn, expressed and made into Syrup, are largely used as a powerful cathartic for, *and fit only for*, dogs, being too griping for human-kind—The canine tribe have to "grin and bear it." The dried juice of the Rhamni, under the name of sap-green, is much esteemed by water colour painters.

In an adjacent wood, the Spindle-tree, the Lily of the Valley, and Epipactis latifolia, the broad-leaved Helleborine, the tallest of our Orchids, flourish; neighbouring fields supply Viper's bugloss, Echium vulgare, Chicory, with its heavenly blue, but very ephemeral, flowers; and abundance of a rare crucifer, Barbarea stricta, the small flowered yellow Rocket, with its long slender dense racemes and erect adpressed fruit pods. It is here worthy of mention that all the numerous species of the cruciferous order are innocent, wholesome, and antiscorbutic. In a bordering lane is a very large tree— self-sown—of Pyrus scandica, the lobed leaved "White Beam."

At no great distance from Pilmoor, for the two were included in one of the excursions of the Yorkshire Naturalists' Union, is another ericetal sphagnous bog called Leckby Carr. Carr is a mossy tract more or less under water, and often, from its low situation, difficult to drain, and such on the west side of the Kingdom are better known as "Mosses." The one now under observation was, fifty years ago, typical, the accumulated accretions of sphagnum having made it a tremulous and treacherous morass, covered over with the long trailing wiry stems, tiny bonny leaves, and dainty rich red crane-necked flowers of Vaccinium oxyococcos, the true Cranberry, the fruit of which was at one time a source of revenue to the bordering farmers. Fully half a century ago this was a noted and much visited botanical locality, for here in the writer's experience : The rare, much sought, and greatly prized Scheuchzeria palustris grew in abundance, and at that time a local gentleman used to collect annually hundreds of specimens for the Edinburgh Botanical Exchange Club and other distributors. "Ah lack a day those times are fled!" The once famous Scheuchzeria is a thing of the past, and now nearly, probably quite extinct *in all its British localities.* Even more abundant were the two Sundews, Drosera rotundifolia and Anglica, the former previously described, the latter the largest and the rarest of the family. On a bright day these fly traps, with their fringed leaves, tipped with diamond like drops, glistening in the sun, made the Carr resplendent, and no spot supplies more animalcule food than a marsh in Summer time. Here, still grows plentifully, Lysimachia thyrsiflora, the tufted Loosestrife, a variety of the Primrose order, confined in England, and that locally, to four or five English counties.

Other noteworthy residents are Œnanthe Phellandrium, the fine leaved Water Dropwort, a poisonous umbellifer; the berry bearing Alder; the white beak-sedge, with its silvery, changing to chestnut, spikelets; Carex curta, the white Sedge; and Calamagrostis stricta, a tall and somewhat rare Reed-grass.

In bordering hedgerows and fields grow Malva moschata, the Musk-mallow, the prettiest among its native congeners; Sambucus Ebulus, the dwarf Elder or Danewort, so called from an old superstition that it sprang up wherever Danish blood had been spilt. Carduus Marianus, the Virgin Mary's Milk-Thistle, another legendary name given in superstitious times, its milky veins reputed to be caused by the Virgin's fallen milk as she nursed the infant Christ; Erigeron acris, the blue Flea-bane, a composite plant, with purplish florets; Marrubium vulgare, the white Horehound, with hoary, intensely bitter, medicinally famous, leaves; and Colchicum autumnale, the meadow Saffron, the "autumnal Crocus" of Wordsworth, even more therapeutically famous, and very noteworthy because its attractive flesh-coloured flowers, popularly "naked ladies," decorate low lying meadows in the autumn, whilst the large deeply lobed seed-capsules, with their deep-green coriaceous enveloping leaves are produced in the following Spring.

A smaller Carr, within easy distance, supplies (Enanthe Lachenalii, the Parsley Water Dropwort. A few miles to the north there was, a few years ago, a marsh similar to the one at Leckby, known as Newsham Carr, now unhappily lost by drainage, where the rare and very poisonous Water Hemlock Cicuta virosa grew in abundance. Here also flourished Ranunculus Lingua, the greater Spearwort, the giant of the Buttercup family, differing from the great majority of its order in having tongue-shaped undivided leaves; *Carex teretiuscula* and *Carex stricta*, the lesser parnicled and tufted Sedges, both infrequent species, but the former the rarer of the two; in a swampy spot by the Wiske, near to Newsham, is plenty of Hippuris vulgaris, the Mare's tail, a neat aquatic, which much more resembles a horse's tail than the Equisetum popularly so called, and very shortly distant Newby Carr, with its broad intersecting ditches, is amply decorated by the lovely flowering rush, *Butomus umbellatus*, which, with its symmetrically round stem, and showy umbels of conspicuous bright red flowers, is one of the most charming of our native species. Here, also, grow Sagittaria sagittifolia, the water Arrowhead, another remarkably beautiful plant; Utricularia valgaris, the Bladder wort, the largest of a curious genus; and Hydrocharis-morsus-ranæ—the frail white (three petalled) flowering Pondweed, in some parts appropriately called "Pride of the Water"; Samolus Valerandi, a modest looking plant of the Primrose order; Lysomachia Nummularia, Moneywort or Creeping Jenny; Lysomachia vulgaris, common yellow Loosestrife, happily named, for how can jarring passions prevail in the presence of such beautiful colours and contours? Here, too, are Marsh Stitchwort, with its starry flowers; Hypericum Androsœmum, Tutsan, a rare species of St. John's Wort bearing abundance of purplish-black pulpy berries which, on pressure, yield a copious deep-red juice, and have suggested the specific title, literally *man's blood;* Polygonum minus, the lesser Snakeweed; *Sparganium simplex* and *minimum*, two Bur-reeds, prim monœcious aquatics with globular heads of flowers, the latter much the rarer.

We will conclude with a glance at our lacustrine flora for the Vale of Mowbray boasts a good sized lakelet called Gormire, below Whitestonecliffe, the bold bare oolitic limestone rocks of which are a far visible landmark. Beneath its waters are myriads of *Littorella lacustris* which only flowers when true to its popular name—Shoreweed—and I have, in this locality, only once seen it in bloom, and that, fortunately on the occasion of the visit of the Yorkshire Naturalists' Union, nineteen years ago, when upwards of 100 of its members were sumptuously entertained by the then President, Sir Ralph Payne Gallwey and his excellent Lady—her Ladyship honouring the guests by her personal attendance at that never-to-be-forgotten banquet. At that time the lake was singularly low and a broad margin of sandy shore exposed. After tempestuous weather the surface of the water is covered with innumerable tufts of the semi-cylindrical fleshy leaves of this plant, which, intermingled with countless disjointed stems of Marsh Horsetail, calls up Milton's lines

" . . . . Or scattered sedge afloat,
When, with fierce winds Orion armed
Hath vexed the Red Sea coast."

Here also, but hugging the shore is abundance of that singular fern-ally, the Pillwort. Other noteworthy submerged species are two Pondweeds, *heterophyllus* and *lucens*, the former readily known by its two shapes of leaves, the latter the largest of the genus in this country, attaining a length of several yards, its shining diaphanous leaves several inches long; and Myrophyltum alterniflorum a species of Milfoil closely allied to the Mare's-tail, the myriad comb-like leaves of which are very beautiful. The male flowers with their yellow anthers rise out of the water until they have shed their pollen. The water is covered in many places with aquatic Ranunculi, which with their pure white petals, abundant yellow stamens and roundish floating leaves are very noticeable. The rare tufted Loosestrife, well-nigh in England confined to Yorkshire, occurs plentifully on the lake, but chiefly in the north-east corner, where it is mingled with Buckbean, always charming with its bearded pinkish flowers. The banks afford many interesting species, including Marsh Stitchwort, Water Purslane, Whorled Mint, Marsh Speedwell; and a form of Epilobium palustre, to which Mr. Baker, from its strap-shaped leaves, gave the name of *ligulatum*, whilst hard by is abundance of a small-leaved Rubus known to Botanists as Baker's bramble, first so-named by Dr. F. A. Lees; the adjacent wood yields Wood Stitchwort, and a neighbouring tract of boggy land is gay with the white flowers of the ivy-leaved Buttercup, Marsh Violet, Butterwort, Marsh Pennywort, the bonny Bog Pimpenel, intermingled with Lousewort and Arrow-grass, *Trigloclim palustre* with its linear semi-cylindrical leaves and long racemes of greenish flowers. A pond at a little distance abounds in the sweetly beautiful Water Violet, *Hottonia palustris*; and the little-known *Veronica parmularia*, a form of Marsh Speedwell, densely clothed with jointed hairs. The steep banks, as you ascend the hill, are adorned with Viper's Bugloss, Blood-red Cranesbill, Lily of the Valley, and Upright Cudweed, *Gnaphalium sylvaticum*, with its pinkish heads of flowers.

On the summit are several Club-mosses, the *L. clavatum* mentioned previously, the Cypress-leaved *L. alpinum*; the Fir Club-moss, *L. selago*; and *L. selaginoides*, the least and most frequent of the four, and hard by, the Mountain Everlasting, the English Edelweiss with both white and pink florets, the male and female blooms growing upon distinct plants. Other wet spots abounds in botanical attractions, viz: those two veritable naiads *Nymphæa alba* and *Nuphar luteum*, the white and yellow Water Lilies—the latter from its vinous smell popularly known as Brandy bottles. The flowers of these two, at the close of day, sink beneath the water to emerge again with the rising sun! The poet has sung them—

"Those virgin lilies all the night,
Bathing their beauties in the lake,
That they may rise more fresh and bright
When their beloved sun's awake."

or Sir Walter Scott in a morning picture—

"The water-lily to the light,
Her chalice rears of silver bright."

Both ripen their fruit under water. Here, too, are the Great Water Plantain, with its spreading sprays of pink-tinged flowers and polymorphic leaves according as they are submerged, floating or aerial. Two Reed-maces, popularly bulrushes (pool-rushes?), Typha latifolia and T. angustifolia, the latter much the rarer of the two; Yellow Flag Iris, Pseudacorus, the heraldic Lily of France, with its showy flowers; Water Persicaria, truly amphibious, and whether on land or in water, truly beautiful; Hemlock Water Dropwort, a very poisonous "Kex," and its ally *Ænanthe fistulosa*; Great Yellow Cress, *Armoracia amphibia*, closely allied to the well-known Horse-radish; these are found as well:—several species of Potamogeton including *crispus, densus, pectinatus, perfoliatus* and *pusillus*; three Water milfoils, *alterniflorum, spicatum*, and *verticillatum*; *Zannichellia palustris,* horn-fruited pond-weed with translucent leaves, minute flowers and beaked fruit; Water Speedwell, Marsh Red rattle, and last but not least that foreign invader, not of our shores, but of our waters, the Canadian Water-weed or Water-Thyme, which, first noticed in 1842, soon spread with frightful rapidity along our canals and streams, much impeding navigation. Happily the plague is stayed, and its rapid increase by natural causes arrested. The boatmen on the Cam very wrongly gave their mosty worthy Professor the credit of its introduction, and put up to it by some wag dubbed it "*Babingtonia diabolica*," but, probably, there is more of good than of evil in it, for it rapidly oxygenates and purifies stagnant water.

On spongy pond margins grow two typical Ranunculi, *scelaratus* and *flammula*, both as evil as their names, for they are probably the most virulent of that very acrid genus; the former has been used by vagrants to blister their legs, and thus excite compassion. Marsh Yellow Cress, *Nasturtum terrestre*, another amphibious plant; square-stalked St. John's wort, *Hypericum tetragœrum*; the wildly luxuriant Willow-herb, the "Apple-pie" of our boyhood; *Sium angustofolium*, Marsh Bedstraw gay, Flea-bane (a clay lover), *Pulicaria dysenterica*, strongly suggestive of cats; Tansy, reminding us of Tansy pudding; two Bur-marigolds, *Bidens cernua* and *tripartita*; the Butterbur Petasites, the umbrageous leaves of which are known as "Umbrellas" and "Wild Rhubarb"; two Figworts; the tufted water Forget-me-not; Gipsywort, *Lycopus*, with the juice of which would-be gipsies are said to stain their skins; Water Pepper, *Polygonum Hydropiper* (very pungent to taste), *Polygonum mite*, much less frequent, and Orchis latifolia, Marsh Orchis, and in one spot only, abundance of a luxuriant and beautiful hybrid, between *latifolia* and *maculata* (both parents being present); these make up a full list indeed!

Our rivers are gay with the long floating tassels and attractive yellowish-white flowers of *Ranunculus fluitans*, whilst their banks are abundantly decorated with the yellow meadow Rue, Yellow Cress Rocket, two species of Cabbage, both showy; Dame's Violet, *Hesperis matronalis*; Creeping Yellow Cress; Scurry Grass, long held in high repute as an antiscorbutic; *Lepidium Draba*, Pepperwort, in one spot only for many years; Soapwort, with its abundant pale pink flowers, the leaves of which are an excellent substitute for soap; rosy small-flowered Willow-herb; two currants, black and red, and their more frequent associate, the Gooseberry—all abundant (bird sown) and frequent epiphytal upon pollarded trees; Hemlock, with its red-speckled stem and mice-like smell, supposed to have supplied the poison-cup of Socrates; Wild Angelica, *Angelica sylvestris*, with double-winged fruit and bloomy purple stems, the stateliest of our native Kexes; the universally loved Forget-me-not, the legendary history of which has surrounded it with such a charming halo of romance; Spearmint and Peppermint, a colony of the former abundantly and constantly supplying the table of one of our best farmers; some sixteen kinds of Willow, including Lambert's; Scirpus sylvaticus, a large handsome Club-rush with spreading branches; and the great Reed, Arundo Phragmites, which supplies an abundant and enduring table decoration, deserve mention: brevity, however, cries "Hold!"

If we glance at our pastures and meadows, what an embarassment of riches a grass field yields! In one place over 160 distinct species have been counted. As summer advances many fields are gay with the white flowers of Sneezewort, Achillea Ptarmea, and its cousin the thousand-leaved Yarrow, A. Millefolium, so widely popular as an excellent and innocent stomachic; Yellow with Agrimony, Agrimonia Eupatoria, equally prized by herbalists; Dyer's green-weed, Genista tinctoria, a Plantaganet flower; and Dandelion (dent d'lion, from its sharp toothed leaves) a true Chrysanthemum, the white plumed globes of seeds of which are so universally manipulated by youngsters to tell the time of day—

> "Dandelion with globe of down,
> The schoolboy's clock in every town,
> At which the truant puffs amain,
> To conjure lost hours back again."

red with Betony, Betonica officinalis, also medicinal, and the black Knapweed, Centaurea nigra; and blue with the round heads of Devil's bit, Scabiosa succisa, the roots of which are reputed to have been bitten off by the Evil One through jealousy of its virtues. One of the earliest meadow flowers is Goldenlocks, Ranunculus auricomus, on which it is difficult to find a perfect corolla, the petals, for the most part, being abortive or deformed. It is an unique creature, destitute of the acidity possessed by all the other plants of this large order, and thus sometimes called the "Sweet Buttercup." The "wee crimson-tipped flower," the Daisy—Bellis perennis—perennial beauty, is ubiquitous and omnipresent

> "From Spring through all seasons still blossoming bright,
> Emblem of constant unshaken endurance,
> Striving perpetual to sunshine and light."

Celandine, Wordsworth's favourite flower, Ranunculus Ficaria,—"stars which on earth's firmament do shine"; Lady's Smock, Cardamine pratensis, a true heart strengthener, as its name imparts, the "milk maids" of children, so neat in its sober attire; Milkwort, Polygala, literally much milk, credited with increasing the secretion in cows, occurs with red, white, blue, and lavender petals, called also Rogation flower from the time of its opening; two species of Lychnis, the red Campion, and ragged Robin, Lychnis diurna, and floscu-culi; blue meadow Geranium, G. pratense; Birdsfoot Trefoil, Lady's fingers of youngsters, from the shape of its seed pods; Yellow meadow Vetchling, Lathyrus pratensis; various Clovers and Vetches; Lady's Mantle, Alchemilla vulgaris, the vandyked margin of the leaf having suggested the name; Meadow Sweet, Spiræa Ulmaria, rightly called Queen of the Meadows; Shepherd's Clock or Goat's beard, Tragopogon pratensis, which closes its flowers at midday; Red Burnet, Sanguisorba officinalis; Sawwort, Serratula tinctoria, with its beautifully serrate leaves; Silaus pratensis, Sulphur-wort, from the brimstone smell of its roots; four species of Crepis Hawk's beard, Crepis taraxcifolia, virens, nicæensis and biennis, all but virens being rare: the writer knows one meadow which rejoices in thousands of them; Eyebright, Euphrasia, the virtues of which Milton sang when the angel transported our first parent to the specular mount:

> "Then purged with euphrasy and rue
> The visual nerve, for he had much to see."

Several Orchids, green winged, dwarf, and spotted, Orchis morio, ustulata and maculata; Fragrant Orchis, odorous of clove, Gymnadenia conopsea; green or frog Orchis, Habenaria viridis; the white and the drooping Star of Bethlehem, Ornithogalum umbellatum and nutans; one meadow has for fully seventy years gloried in four Narcissi, Narcissus pseudo Narcissus, biflorus, incomparabilis, and poeticus, the last the Pheasants-eye or Poets' Narcissus; another field yields three species of Garlic, Allum vineale, oleraceum and Scorodoprasum, all bearing bulbiferous flowers.

We have pictured a goodly number of pascual and pratal plants, and barely a tithe have been named, not even "the rath primrose that decks the mead," nor the favourite cowslip that calls up visions of cowslip wine and cowslip tea, both innocent beverages; or of romping childhood throwing its cowslip balls, the flowers being collected together in a globular form and called "Tosties"; nor that pearl, the Marguerite, so full of romantic story; nor the poet-loved flower, the Hare-bell, Campanula rotundifolia—the writer inclines to Hair-bell, the thread-like stems so long frail and delicate being moved by the slightest zephyr,

> "'Een the slight hare-bell raised its head,
> Elastic from her airy tread";

nor those two singular ferns the Adder's tongue, Ophioglossum, and Grape-fruit, Botrychium, the localities of which are legion; but a sharp eye is needed to detect them.

Our woods and copses, especially in spring-time, are gay with flowers among the earliest is the wood anemone, "that ne'er uncloses her leaves until they are blown on by the wind," varied with the sky-blue of the wood Forget-me-not, dubbed rare in our Manuals but very plentiful in some of the woods of our beauteous Vale, intermixed with the less showy Woodruff Asperula odorata, which, when dried, yields to book or drawer a delightful and enduring fragrance. A book in which a few leaves were placed and which were taken out when the volume was bound fully 25 years ago is still odorous although constantly used; Wood Sorrel, Oxalis acetosella, Wood Sorrel, the delicately streaked pinkish-white flowers of which are locally known as "fairy-bells," and the pleasant acidulated foliage much enjoyed by children, whilst the three lobed leaf is by many deemed the Shamrock of St. Patrick—the triune leaf; although the Irish favour one or more species of clover; Cow-wheat Melampyrum pratense with its yellow-lipped flowers and corn-shaped fruit; Lysimachia nemorum, the yellow Pimpernel; Hairy Violet, Viola hirta, with conspicuous flowers, partial to limestone; Wood Sanicle, Sanicula europœa, much esteemed for its healing virtues; Enchanter's Nightshade, Circæa lutetiana, so full of innocent charms; Wood Sage, Teucrium Scorodonia, and many other sweet dryads.

Our lanes and hedge-banks are abundantly decorated, but we can only point out a few. The smooth Tower-Mustard, Turritis glabra; Greater Celandine, Chelidoninm majus, the plentiful orange juice of which is esteemed a specific for corneal specks; bladder Campion Silene inflata, so noticeable with its inflated calyox; Stitchwort Stellaria Holostea, the 'Stars' of children, remindful that this and many other of the scientific names of the great Linnæus were adopted from our popular ones, as "flos-cuculi," Cuckoo-flower, "Bursa pastoris," Shepherd's purse, "Pecten Veneris," Venus' comb, "Hippuris," Mare's tail, "Hippocrepis," Horse-shoe, "Ornithopus," Bird's-foot, and many others. The Sweet Violet, Viola odorata, with white, lavender and blue flowers, but which rarely, if ever, produce fruit, the abundant capsules produced later in the summer resulting from inconspicuous, inodorous, greenish, apetalous flowers; long-stalked Cranesbill, Geranium columbinum, with bonny rose-coloured corollas; Rest Harrows, Ononis compestris and arvense, with their beautiful rose-pink petals, the latter from its sweet root locally known as Wild Liquorice; Potentilla anserina and reptans, with their bright yellow buttercup-like flowers, the former with silver-haired leaves, the latter a true Cinque-foil; Strawberry-headed Clover, Trifolium fragiferum; Gloryless or Moschatel, a modest retiring creature to my mind most glorious; Gout-weed Egopodium Podagraria, highly esteemed as a remedy for that painful and stubborn disease, known as Bishop-weed in Scotland because the Scotch say "as difficult to get rid of as the Bishops"; Greater Burnet Saxifrage Pimpinella magna, with its showy umbels of pure white flowers; Galium Aparine, Cleavers called by children "Sweethearts" because they stick; Vervain, Verbena officinalis, highly venerated by the ancients, and still as one of its popular names "Simpler's joy" imports, Repute by herbalists; strong-scented Lettuce, Lactuca virosa, the juice of which under the name of Lactuarium was formerly used in medicine as a substitute for opium; Burdock, Arctium majus, the roots of which are collected by herbalists, and the flower heads called burs covered with hooked phyllaries attaching themselves readily to clothes, to which Shakespeare in speaking of poor relations alludes when he says "they are burs, they stick where they are thrown." Other bank plants are Greater Periwinkle, Vinca major; red Bartsea, Bartsia Odontites; yellow Figwort, Scrophularia veræa; Giant Bell-flower, Campanula latifolia; Wild Marjoram, Origanum vulgare, a plant much esteemed by the Greeks; Basil Thyme Calamintha Clinopodium; Calamint, Calamintha officinalis; Catmint, Nepeta Cataria, which like Valerian has a strange attraction for cats; Stachys ambigua, a hybrid Wound-wort, a cross between palustris and sylvatica; Greater Plantain, Plantago major, popularly Bird-seed, called also Way-bread (should it not be Way-bred?) for it is known to the natives in North America as "white man's foot" because it sprang up wherever the Colonists made a path, and its wayside habit in this country is the same; and last but not least, Germander Speedwell, Veronica Chamædrys, the Bird's eyes of children and the "Eyebright" of some poets, for one sings—

> "Blue Eye-bright! loveliest flower of all that blow
> In flower-loved England! Flower whose hedge-side gaze
> Is like an infants."

Garlanding the hedges are many good things, among which are the tufted Vetch, Vicia Cracca, with its showy purplish-blue flowers; Woodbine; great Convolvulus; Bitter-sweet, the pellucid red fruit of which is known to children as "poison berries"; White Bryony, Bryonica dioica, often from its leaves and general habit called the "Wild Vine"; Black Bryony Tamus communis, the thick fleshy roots of which are popularly known as "Mandrakes"—the writer has seen specimens much resembling the human thigh; these bryonies, which Science puts far asunder, have both bright-red berries, and are both climbing clinging bines. The Hop, the tender branches of which used to be cooked and eaten like Asparagus, and esteemed very wholesome, likewise adorns the hedges.

Noticeable among our hedge-row trees are the two Cherries, the Bird Cherry and the Gean, the former with racemes, the latter with umbels of pure white flowers; the sloe and bullace, the black fruit of which is harsh, only edible by the omnivorous schoolboy, and of which the poet sings—

> "Black were her eyes as the berry that grows on the thorn by
> the way-side,
> Black, yet how brightly they gleamed through the shade of
> her tresses."

The English field Maple in many lanes enters largely into the composition of our hedges, and is popularly known as "dog-oak," being in late seasons a frequent substitute on Royal Oak Day for the genuine article not yet in leaf; the Sycamore or false Plane-tree, the winged seeds of which float far and wide sowing themselves everywhere so that, although not a true nature, it is fast becoming one of our most abundant trees. It is certainly one of the most umbrageous and safest of shelters, for it has a comparative immunity from the lightning's stroke. Guelder Rose, which under cultivation becomes the Snow-ball of our gardens, to the loss of fertility, its less showy inner flower producing abundant glassy bright-red fruit which may often be seen adorning the bosoms of village maidens; the Elder, so widely and abundantly bird-sown, the dense white umbels of which were once mistaken by an inexperienced Cockney who reported he had seen "cauliflowers growing upon trees!" The Dogwood, the wood of which is as hard and horny as its name; but supreme among our septal beauties are the lovely Roses which makes our lanes fragrant and adorn our hedgerows all through July.

> "How fair is the rose, what a beautiful flower,
>   The glory of April and May"

was not written by any High Priest of Nature. The writer has seen roses in December, ice in June, but roses in April, never. We would especially mention *Rosa villosa, tomentosa, Robertsoni, spinossima* and *arvensis* as inhabitants of the Vale-hedges around Thirsk.

We will close with a glance at a few of the plants of cultivated land, call them *weeds* if you will. The Corn Buttercup, the prickly fruit of which known to farmers as "Stavesacre," is very poisonous and used for killing vermin in cattle; *Myosurus minimus*, Mousetail, named from the shape of its prolonged spike of fruit; three species of Poppy, the scarlet flowers of which set the cornfields all ablaze; next of field colonisers comes Cichorium with its attractive cærulean blue but very ephemeral flowers; the Corn Blue-bottle, the late Emperor William's favourite flower, equally beautiful and not nearly so perishable; *Carduus nutans* and *acanthoides*, the Musk and Welted Thistles and occasionally *Carduus setosus* a rare and almost glabrons variety of the common Corn Thistle; two Chamomiles *Anthemis arvensis* and *Cotula*, this strong-smelling and blistering to the human skin; Scentless Mayweed; the beautiful yellow Toadflax, locally the "Butter and eggs" of children; Hemp or Bee Nettles, the last—the Bee—a very showy species with variegated flowers; Corn Woundwort, and *Stachys ambigua*, already mentioned; Corn Groomwell, Corn Bugloss, Corn Sow Thistle; Corn Marigold, a terrible plague on some farms; two species of Venus' Looking Glass, with bonny lilac-blue flowers, *Specularia hybrida* and *Speculum*; Corn Bindweeds, lovely striped trumpets; Clover Dodder or Hellweed, a parasite upon Clover which quite strangles its host, and sometimes occurs in such large quantity as to impede and even arrest the reaper. The writer once witnessed such a case where the reaper was stayed and had to be cleared at least every fifty yards. Broomrape, Orobanche minor, also parasitical upon clover and occasionally in alarming abundance, but in such cases the rotation of crops usually extirpates the unwelcome guest; Scarlet and Blue Pimpernels, the former sometimes occurring with flesh-coloured flowers; Darnel, a reputed poisonous grass, but happily rare in our dale fields. An especial reference to two Rarities must conclude our list of the plants of cultivated land: the sharp-leaved Fluellin, *Linaria Elatine*, which has occurred annually whatever the crop in an arable field near Wood End, since it was first noticed fully thirty years ago; and *Anthoxanthum Puelii*, first cousin to the hay-scented vernal grass which scents our hay and is an irritating factor in causing summer catarrh or "hay fever." This last has come up for ten years in corn-land a mile south-east of Thirsk, sometimes in great abundance.

Such is a fairly full sketch of the flora of the Vale of Mowbray. This so-called Chronicle pretends not to be a scientific paper, but aims to be a popular one, and the writer craves indulgence for the too frequent use of scientific names.

END OF VOLUME I.

Middlestee Valley, Osmotherley, from White House Farm. [Thompson

INDEX.

A

	PAGE
Abbeys	61, 277
Addison, Rev.	188
Aisenby	211, 213
Aldborough	13, 17
Aldwark	35
Aldfield	78, 88
Animals	150, 397
Antiquities	98, 115, 119, 178, 226, 237, 253, 292, 356
Antiquary of Byland	274
Arden-Hawnby	353, 363
Arden	362
Autumn Tints	281
Azerley	80

B

	PAGE
Bagby	241
Baker, J. G.	180
Baldersby	207, 234
Balk	242, 245
Barnaby Fair	7
Baynes (fam.)	290
Belasyse (fam.)	258
Birdforth	248
Birds	240, 244, 296, 308, 397
Black Hambleton	369
Blois Hall	50

	PAGE
Boltby	315, 354
Boroughbridge	21
Botany of Fountains	77
,, Yorevale	110, 119, 131, 151
,, Mowbray Vale	212, 239, 311, 330, 405
Bower—the Maiden	222
Brampton Hall	45
Breckenbrough	204
Burn (river)	146
Burton Leonard	54
Butterdale	305
Byland	265, 279
Byland Abbey, Battle of	273

C

	PAGE
Carlton Miniott	204
Carlton-Husthwait	251
Castiles Farm	82
Caydale Gill	360
Characters	29, 33, 55, 84, 120, 143, 183, 188, 192, 195, 197, 208, 213, 229, 230, 235, 276, 338, 340, 381, 385, 387
Chophead-Loaning	336
Cockerdale	267
Codbeck	159, 352, 383

Cold-Kirby	357
Colsterdale	149
Colville (fam.)	259
Conyers (fam.)	323
Copgrove	31
Copt-Hewick	50
Cowesby	352
Coxwold	254
Crock of Gold	334, 351
Cromwell's Corpse	264, 346
Crosses	139, 203, 210, 233
Cundall	211
Customs (old)	109, 199, 351

D

Dalton	237
Danby (fam.)	145
Devil's Arrows	6, 11
Devil's Doors	178-9
Devilstone, The	296
Devil's-stride	302
Dialstone, The	356
Dishforth	109, 210
Dowlands	202
Duggleby	186
Dunsforth	34, 36

E

Earthquakes	104
Earthworks	83, 116, 131, 202, 222, 315, 356
Easterside	361
Ellerbeck	388
Elmires	237
Etymologies	158, 174, 176, 196, 199, 215, 224, 235, 318, 325, 337

F

Fairs	228
Fearby	147
Felixkirk	317
Flassengill	357
Flower Chronicle	405
Fonts	249
Fountains Abbey	59 et seq.
Fountains Hall	75

G

Gallwey (fam.)	240
Galphey	81
Geology of Vale	187, 190
Ghost-Laying	199, 248
Givendale	49
Gnipe Hill	349
Gormire Lake	189
Gormire-the-less	305, 328
Grantley, Low	86
Great Ouseburn	38
Grewelthorpe	136
Gurtopp Gill	366

H

Hackfall	134
Hall (fam.)	172
Hambleton Hill	369
Hanging-stone, The	377
Hawkins (fam.)	231
Hawnby Hill	361
Hawnby	362
Healey	148
Hewick	49
Hobthrush Cave	351
Hode	267, 299

Hood Hill	290, 294
Horn-Blowing	100
Husthwaite	250
Hutton Conyers	109

I—J

Inns	32, 44, 172, 174, 206, 241, 282, 292, 368, 370
Ironstone	190
Jeatter-houses	388
John Wesley	382

K

Kepwick	351
Kibber Hill	215
Kilburn	284
Kilvington	191, 198
Kingsley, Rev	195
Kirby Hill	43
Kirkby-Malzeard	137
Kirkby-Knowle	327
Kirk Gill	146
Knights of St John	326
Knowle Castle	331

L

Lascelles (fam.)	182, 284
Laverton	83
Laws of Trespass	195
Leake	339, 341, 345
Leckbys (the three)	211
Little Nunwick	110
Lost Corpse	335
Low Kilburn	286

M

Maps	79, 11, 225, 271, 329
Marage, The	176
Marderbi Hall	323
Markenfield (fam.)	58
Markenfield	56
Markington	54
Marmion (fam.)	124
Marmion's Tower	127
Masham	140
Melmerby	116
Mickley	133
Minskip	31
Mount St. John	317, 323, 325
Mount Grace	389
Mowbray fam.)	160, 267, 300
Myton	35, 40

N

Nether Silton	347
Newburgh Park	261
Newby Park	45, 49
Norton Conyers	113
Nosterfield	118
Nuns'-wick	110

O

Old Biggin	331
Old Byland	359
Oldstead	284
Ornithology	240, 397
Osgodby Hall	295
Osmotherley	373, 375
Over-Silton	348

P

Pack-horse Bridges	185
Pennington (fam.)	170
Percy (fam.)	218, 233
Play of the Seasons	281, 285

Q

	PAGE
Quernhow	116

R

	PAGE
Rainton	208
Ravensthorpe	315
Ripon	159
Roccliffe	30
Rodwell (fam.)	304
Roger de Mowbray	268
Roman Roads	185, 253
Roulston Scar	290, 306, 354

S

	PAGE
Sandhutton	203, 204
Saxty-way	185
Scarth-Nick	373
Scrope (fam.)	193, 333
Shandy Hall	260
Sharrow	51
Sigston Smithy	388
Skipton-on-Swale	207
Slapestones	368
Sleningford	123
Sorrow Beck	351
Sowerby	182
Spittle-beck	199
St. Cuthbert	92
Sterne (Lawrence)	257
Sutton	302
Swale (river)	211, 239

T

	PAGE
Tanfield	122
Thimbleby	351, 377
Thirkleby	240, 245, 247
Thirlby	314
Thirsk Castle	166
Thirsk	168
Thormanby	249
Thornborough	116
Thornton-le-Street	200
Thorowdale	363
Topcliffe	214
Top-Hewick	49
Tumuli	185, 254, 319, 354, 366

U

	PAGE
Upsal	332
Ure (river)	49, 53

V

	PAGE
Vale of Mowbray	158, 364
,, Yore	5
Vyner (fam.)	45, 47

W

	PAGE
Wass	280
Wath	114
Well Village	118
Wensleydale	118
Whitemare Cliff	189, 311
White Horse of Kilburn	289, 298
Whitelas (beck)	195
Whitstone Cliff	242, 310, 316
Witch Abigail	364
World's End	186
Wymund the Saxon	269

Y

	PAGE
Yew Trees	76
Yore (river)	49 et seg.
Yore Vale	5

Z

	PAGE
Zoology	150, 358, 362, 397

ERRATA.

VALLEY OF THE YORE.

Page 99, line 16, for "Barney Coult" read "Baring Gould."

VALE OF MOWBRAY.

Page 168, line last, for "its terminal one" read "the terminal with."

Page 174, line 77, for "Winkles" read "Vincles or Vinkles."

Page 210, title of Cross, for "ruined" read "Runic."

Page 215, title of illustration, for "Small" read "Swale."

Page 237, line 20, for "Saxon" read "Saxty."

Page 251, title of illustration, for "Housthwaite" read "Husthwaite."

Page 270, line 5, for "Olane" read "Olave."